P9-AFB-683

Problems and Materials in
FEDERAL INCOME TAXATION

EDITORIAL ADVISORS

Vicki Been
Elihu Root Professor of Law
New York University School of Law

Erwin Chemerinsky
Dean and Distinguished Professor of Law
University of California, Irvine, School of Law

Richard A. Epstein
Laurence A. Tisch Professor of Law
New York University School of Law
Peter and Kirsten Bedford Senior Fellow
The Hoover Institution
Senior Lecturer in Law
The University of Chicago

Ronald J. Gilson
Charles J. Meyers Professor of Law and Business
Stanford University
Marc and Eva Stern Professor of Law and Business
Columbia Law School

James E. Krier
Earl Warren DeLano Professor of Law
The University of Michigan Law School

Richard K. Neumann, Jr.
Professor of Law
Hofstra University School of Law

Robert H. Sitkoff
John L. Gray Professor of Law
Harvard Law School

David Alan Sklansky
Yosef Osheawich Professor of Law
University of California at Berkeley School of Law

Kent D. Syverud
Dean and Ethan A. H. Shepley University Professor
Washington University School of Law

Elizabeth Warren
Leo Gottlieb Professor of Law
Harvard Law School

ASPEN CASEBOOK SERIES

Problems and Materials in
FEDERAL INCOME TAXATION
Eighth Edition

SANFORD M. GUERIN
Professor of Law
Sandra Day O'Connor College of Law
Arizona State University

PHILIP F. POSTLEWAITE
Harry R. Horrow Professor of Law and
Director of the Tax Program
Northwestern University School of Law

ADAM H. ROSENZWEIG
Professor of Law
Washington University School of Law

Wolters Kluwer
Law & Business

Copyright © 2013 Sanford M. Guerin; Jennifer Joan Postlewaite and
Jessalyn Chase Postlewaite; and Adam Rosenzweig.

Published by Wolters Kluwer Law & Business in New York.

Wolters Kluwer Law & Business serves customers worldwide with CCH,
Aspen Publishers, and Kluwer Law International products. (www.wol-
terskluwerlb.com)

No part of this publication may be reproduced or transmitted in any
form or by any means, electronic or mechanical, including photocopy,
recording, or utilized by any information storage or retrieval system,
without written permission from the publisher. For information
about permissions or to request permissions online, visit us at www.
wolterskluwerlb.com, or a written request may be faxed to our
permissions department at 212-771-0803.

To contact Customer Service, e-mail customer.service@wolterskluwer.com,
call 1-800-234-1660, fax 1-800-901-9075, or mail correspondence to:

    Wolters Kluwer Law & Business
    Attn: Order Department
    PO Box 990
    Frederick, MD 21705

Printed in the United States of America.

1 2 3 4 5 6 7 8 9 0

ISBN 978-1-4548-1066-7

Library of Congress Cataloging-in-Publication Data

Guerin, Sanford M.
  Problems and materials in federal income taxation / Sanford M. Guerin,
Philip F. Postlewaite, Adam H. Rosenzweig. — 8th ed.
    p. cm. — (Aspen casebook series)
  ISBN 978-1-4548-1066-7
  1. Income tax — Law and legislation — United States — Cases.
I. Postlewaite, Philip F., 1945- II. Rosenzweig, Adam. III. Title.

  KF6369.G78 2012
  343.7305'2 — dc23

                2012033269

SUSTAINABLE FORESTRY INITIATIVE

Certified Sourcing
www.sfiprogram.org
SFI-01234

SFI label applies to the text stock

About Wolters Kluwer Law & Business

Wolters Kluwer Law & Business is a leading global provider of intelligent information and digital solutions for legal and business professionals in key specialty areas, and respected educational resources for professors and law students. Wolters Kluwer Law & Business connects legal and business professionals as well as those in the education market with timely, specialized authoritative content and information-enabled solutions to support success through productivity, accuracy and mobility.

Serving customers worldwide, Wolters Kluwer Law & Business products include those under the Aspen Publishers, CCH, Kluwer Law International, Loislaw, Best Case, ftwilliam.com and MediRegs family of products.

CCH products have been a trusted resource since 1913, and are highly regarded resources for legal, securities, antitrust and trade regulation, government contracting, banking, pension, payroll, employment and labor, and healthcare reimbursement and compliance professionals.

Aspen Publishers products provide essential information to attorneys, business professionals and law students. Written by preeminent authorities, the product line offers analytical and practical information in a range of specialty practice areas from securities law and intellectual property to mergers and acquisitions and pension/benefits. Aspen's trusted legal education resources provide professors and students with high-quality, up-to-date and effective resources for successful instruction and study in all areas of the law.

Kluwer Law International products provide the global business community with reliable international legal information in English. Legal practitioners, corporate counsel and business executives around the world rely on Kluwer Law journals, looseleafs, books, and electronic products for comprehensive information in many areas of international legal practice.

Loislaw is a comprehensive online legal research product providing legal content to law firm practitioners of various specializations. Loislaw provides attorneys with the ability to quickly and efficiently find the necessary legal information they need, when and where they need it, by facilitating access to primary law as well as state-specific law, records, forms and treatises.

Best Case Solutions is the leading bankruptcy software product to the bankruptcy industry. It provides software and workflow tools to flawlessly streamline petition preparation and the electronic filing process, while timely incorporating ever-changing court requirements.

ftwilliam.com offers employee benefits professionals the highest quality plan documents (retirement, welfare and non-qualified) and government forms (5500/PBGC, 1099 and IRS) software at highly competitive prices.

MediRegs products provide integrated health care compliance content and software solutions for professionals in healthcare, higher education and life sciences, including professionals in accounting, law and consulting.

Wolters Kluwer Law & Business, a division of Wolters Kluwer, is headquartered in New York. Wolters Kluwer is a market-leading global information services company focused on professionals.

The Importance of Honor and Integrity*

by Taylor Leigh Guerin

I regard integrity to be a consciousness constituting and illuminating a sense of worth. It is who we are when no one is looking, what we live to represent, what we fight for, and how we ultimately perceive ourselves. The notion of honor is like a precious piece of a puzzle, completing the foundation for my system of values. Contrary to popular belief, honor is not an image assigned to us by our peers. Honor is a feeling that we invest in ourselves, an awareness we work to achieve, and a treasure we defend by our integrity. Unfortunately, many believe that we must sacrifice pleasure to be honorable. I argue just the opposite, for within the attempts to be honorable lies the realization of happiness. I do not think we can separate our actions and choices from the person we become. Our fate lies in the quality of our choices and the heart we display to the world.

I find that people today perceive honor merely as a fashionable social code, often failing to value themselves and others by a worthwhile standard, such as character. A general trend has occurred in which we have become preoccupied by other attractions (such as pecuniary wealth or social standing) and do not hold ourselves responsible for our surroundings. Compassionate and empathetic human beings must extend their responsibilities to their communities. For example, the atrocities of war should not be separated from the quiet and comfort of our lives, for to ignore such atrocities enables them to be repeated. Although we may not be provided the occasion to prove ourselves in large scale acts of violence and injustice, we have similar obligations in smaller scaled, yet equally significant moments. Participating as audience to a person being slandered without acknowledging that the words being spoken are false or unfair, tests us and challenges us to be more than passive witnesses. I believe that we must stand up for what we believe, despite the threats posed to personal comfort or security. After all, none are safe when no one will defend truth or justice.

Honor is a creed that transcends social, economic, and racial boundaries; it is something we can define for ourselves, but it does not necessarily categorize us. Honor unites me with people and allows me to find security in the promise that interactions I have with others will be worthwhile, honest and true. Building upon the foundations of intellectual vitality and a pluralistic perception of the world, I have extended the importance of the enlightened mind to the values of a strengthened character. In summary, honor is a unique, intangible signature, created by the coalescing of ones heart, mind, and soul.

---

* From a senior speech written and delivered by graduating senior Taylor Leigh Guerin to the Phoenix Country Day School.

And next is Ruth Muyskens and her lovely (one-and-a-half-year-old) son, Matthew Postlewaite. Reminds me of a story. Bishop Sheen one Sunday was preaching to a packed audience when a young child began to cry. His mother attempted to calm the child, without success, and then stood and started to exit. Bishop Sheen stopped his sermon and said: "Madam, the child is not disturbing the congregation, the child is not disturbing me, and certainly the child is not disturbing God." To which the mother said, "Bishop Sheen, you don't understand, *you* are disturbing the child."

> Justice Anthony Kennedy
> On his introduction of guests
> at a dinner celebrating his 60th birthday
> July 23, 1996 at Salzburg, Austria

> To our children and grandchildren
> Jennifer,
> Jessalyn,
> Matthew,
> Madison,
> Reid, and
> Peyton

No matter where life takes you, may you always show such humility, grace, and humanity. We love you!

PFP

"Success comes from knowing that you did your best to become the best that you are capable of becoming."

"If you're not making mistakes, then you're not doing anything."

"It's what you learn after you know it all that counts."

—John Wooden

For my family, and especially my wife, who helped teach me the true meaning of success and how to overcome the mistakes.

AHR

SUMMARY OF CONTENTS

CONTENTS

CHAPTER 2
THE CONCEPT OF GROSS INCOME

CHAPTER 4
CHOOSING THE PROPER TAXPAYER   191

C H A P T E R 5
TIMING OF GROSS INCOME

241

CHAPTER 6
DEUCTIONS FOR TRADE OR BUSINESS EXPENSES   351

CHAPTER 7
CAPITAL GAINS AND LOSSES   463

CHAPTER 8
INVESTMENT AND PERSONAL DEDUCTIONS   547

C H A P T E R 9
TIMING OF DEDUCTIONS AND TAX SHELTERS 641

C H A P T E R 10
COMPUTING TAX LIABILITY

PREFACE

This text differs from most current income tax casebooks in a number of respects. Many tax texts, with their particularized analysis of the law's subtle twists, are more akin to treatises than casebooks. Unfortunately, when inundated by detail on entering the complex world of income taxation, readers often become confused and frustrated. This text seeks to mitigate that problem by focusing on major concepts and their underlying policies.

The text stresses a problem-solving approach through the use of numerous, short problems interspersed among the relevant materials. This problem-solving approach parallels a "real world" experience and thus helps to develop legal and analytic skills. Moreover, the text and problems focus on property transactions and their attendant tax consequences. Because federal income taxation is a prerequisite to other tax courses, such as corporate or partnership taxation, the taxation of property transactions—an essential building block for the advanced tax courses—has been emphasized.

Although much of the study of federal income taxation focuses on acquiring a technical knowledge of the tax system, one should also be able to integrate this information and its intended policy into a broader social context. Toward that goal, Chapter 1 presents a broad introductory overview of the federal income tax system. It does so by offering a collection of readings that highlight the components of the taxing system. Thus, the major considerations of the tax system are confronted—constitutionality, economic impact, revenue generation, administration, and illegality and ethical concerns. It should also be noted that the selections of Chapter 1 reflect the various "sources" of the tax law—case law (Tax Court and circuit court decisions), governmental studies, legislative histories, and law review articles.

Starting with Chapter 2, the text follows the taxing formula, beginning with gross income and then moving through tax deductions and credits to tax rates and tax returns. The statutory taxing formula begins with gross income, a concept encompassing the "accessions to wealth" on which an individual is taxed. This is discussed in Chapter 2. Although "gross income" is a broad concept, Congress has narrowed its scope by excluding various specific items on policy grounds. These exclusions are discussed in Chapter 3. Additional gross income issues, including to whom gross income is attributed and when a particular item of gross income is includable, are presented in Chapters 4 and 5 respectively.

After determining gross income, taxable income is calculated by subtracting statutorily prescribed deductions. Issues involving deductions are discussed in Chapters 6 through 9. The permissible deductions fall into four classes: (1) those associated with the conduct of the taxpayer's trade or business; (2) those associated with an activity that, while not a trade or business, is engaged in for the production of income; (3) those not within the first two categories (i.e., personal expenses that typically would be denied deductibility) but that, for specific policy reasons, Congress has authorized as deductions; and (4) artificial deductions — those for which the taxpayer did not expend funds but that are allowed in support of various other policies (for example, the personal exemption).

Issues involving the calculation of taxable income and the different tax rates, including the alternative minimum tax (AMT), are discussed in Chapter 10. In addition, the Code authorizes various credits that may be subtracted and, in limited cases, mandates additional taxes that must be added to the regular tax liability. These issues are also presented in Chapter 10.

The material in this text, and its accompanying teacher's manual, is current through July 1, 2007. These materials reflect the valuable assistance of a variety of people to whom the authors express their thanks. Initially, the authors wish to thank the fine staffs of their respective institutions, Arizona State University College of Law, Northwestern University School of Law, and Washington University School of Law, as well as our publisher, Aspen Publishers. Without their assistance, the project would still be in its embryonic stage. We further wish to thank the members of our federal income taxation classes at Arizona State, Northwestern, and Washington University, on whom we inflicted various drafts of this text, as well as Tracey Guerin for her invaluable research assistance. That usage, accompanied by student comments and reactions to the materials, permitted a far better refinement of the product than we would have attained operating in a vacuum.

In order to ease the reading of the cases, some citations have been omitted without the use of ellipses, and in some instances footnotes in cases and other quoted material have been eliminated without indication. Any footnotes that were not edited retain their original numbers, while footnotes of the editors are indicated by an asterisk or other symbol.

In this text, the word "section" or a section symbol (§) refers to sections of the Internal Revenue Code and the Regulations promulgated thereunder; Regulation or Reg., or Proposed Regulation or Prop. Reg. refers to Treasury Department Regulations; Revenue Ruling or Rev. Rul. refers to Rulings published by the Internal Revenue Service; Revenue Procedure or Rev. Proc. refers to Service published Procedures; and Private Letter Ruling or Priv. Let. Rul. refers to Private Rulings (without precedential value) issued by the Service.

Sanford M. Guerin
Philip F. Postlewaite
Adam H. Rosenzweig

September 2012

ACKNOWLEDGMENTS

We would like to thank the following authors and copyright holders for permission to use their works.

Association of the Bar of New York, The Lawyer's Role in Tax Practice, 36 Tax Law. 865 (1983). The article was prepared by the Special Committee on the Lawyer's Role in Tax Practice, the members of which were John H. Alexander, David E. Watts, M. Bernard Aidinoff, Renato Beghe, D. Bret Carlson, M. Carr Ferguson, Jr., Marjorie E. Gross, Gordon D. Henderson, Boris Kostelanetz, Jerome Kurtz, James B. Lewis, Mitchell E.Menaker, John C. Richardson, Sidney I. Roberts, James R. Rowen, David Sacks, and George G. Tyler, Copyright # American Bar Association.

Augustyn, Research in Federal Income Taxation, 38 U. Fla. L. Rev. 767 (1986). Copyright © 1986 by the University of Florida Law Review. Reprinted with permission.

Bittker, A "Comprehensive Tax Base" as a Goal of Income Tax Reform, 80 Harv. L. Rev. 925 (1967). Copyright © 1967 by the Harvard Law Review.

Bittker, Effective Tax Rates: Fact or Fancy?, 122 U. Pa. L. Rev. 780 (1974). Copyright © 1974 by Boris I. Bittker.

Note, Realizing Appreciation without Sale: Accrual Taxation of Capital Gains on Marketable Securities, 34 Stan. L. Rev. 857 (1982).

Pine, Everyone's a Critic of U.S. Tax System, Washington Post, Mar. 31, 1978 at 8, col. 1.

Surrey, Tax Incentives as a Device for Implementing Government Policy: A Comparison with Direct Government Expenditures, 83 Harv. L. Rev. 705 (1970). Copyright © 1970 by the Harvard Law Review.

Will, Morality and the "Martini Lunch," Newsweek, Oct. 17, 1977. Copyright © 1977 by Newsweek, Inc. All rights reserved. Reprinted by permission.

Problems and Materials in
FEDERAL INCOME TAXATION

INTRODUCTION

A. DEVELOPMENT OF THE INCOME TAX

"[T]axes are the lifeblood of government, and their prompt and certain availability an imperious need." *Bull v. United States*, 295 U.S. 247, 259 (1935).

"Taxes are what we pay for civilized society. . . ." *Compania General de Tabacos de Filipinas v. Collector*, 275 US 87, 100 (1927) (Holmes, J. dissenting).

"Any one may so arrange his affairs that his taxes shall be as low as possible; he is not bound to choose that pattern which will best pay the Treasury; there is not even a patriotic duty to increase one's taxes." *Helvering v. Gregory*, 69 F.2d 809, 810 (2nd Cir. 1934) (L. Hand, J.).

1. Introduction

Every society, whatever its form of government, must establish some means of supporting itself. However attractive the notion of a voluntary system of funding the government may be, the idea invariably falls short when it comes to actually separating individuals from their wealth. Taxes provide the government with a means to extract wealth from its society to support itself.

For this reason, the power to impose taxes has been (and continues to be) one of the most controversial aspects of government and the law. Of course, taxes played a central role in the formation of the United States, with the common refrain "no taxation without representation" serving as a rallying cry for the colonists opposing British rule. For some, the phrase still resonates; opposition to taxes, even with representation, drives much of the modern tax policy debate.

The difficulty with analyzing any system of taxation is that taxes are meaningless in and of themselves; if the government merely burned all the money it collected, no tax would seem defensible. Rather, what must be taken into account is what taxes provide, who should pay to provide that benefit, and whether the tax burden justifies the governmental benefits.

In modern times, the primary means of the United States federal government to fund itself is through income taxes. Although traditionally one tends to focus on income taxes when thinking of taxation, governments can and do raise revenue in many other ways. For example, the early United States federal government funded itself primarily through import tariffs. Some other familiar forms of taxes are imposed at the state and local level, such as property taxes and sales taxes. The modern federal government also employs more than just income taxes as well. For example, one supplement to the United States "ordinary" income tax is a hybrid form of income tax — the "excess profits" tax. Congress previously imposed the excess profits tax to prevent war profiteering, but the tax has reappeared on occasion as a "windfall profits" tax on oil producers. The federal government imposes a variety of excise taxes — or taxes on the privilege of the manufacture, sale, or consumption of a good or product — on certain commodities such as alcohol, tobacco, and gasoline, as well as a gift and estate tax on the value of wealth transferred from a grantor or decedent to a beneficiary. Each of these is wholly separate and independent from the income tax.

The income tax has many supporters. But theoretically, there are a number of alternatives to the taxation of income, many of which have proponents who contend they are superior to taxing income. In recent years many commentators have advocated use of a *consumption* tax to replace and/or supplement the income tax at the federal level. Such a tax would tax only personal consumption and not income. The arguments supporting a consumption tax are based on the belief that the tax laws should not unduly burden socially preferred behavior by influencing the decision between consuming and saving. Consumption tax advocates argue that it is more efficient to tax only income that is consumed, thereby exempting from taxation income that is saved, because savings are merely a form of deferred consumption and the tax should not be imposed until such savings are consumed.

Consumption taxes come in many forms. The most familiar is the retail sales tax, or a tax on the purchase of goods or services imposed at the point of sale (most cash register receipts list such taxes paid). Another form of consumption tax — the value-added tax (VAT) — has found increasing favor in many countries and in some academic circles over more traditional notions of income taxation. For instance, several European countries have adopted some form of VAT, and Canada has adopted a goods and services tax substantially similar to a VAT. Loosely defined, the VAT is a tax on all the elements of gross national product — that is, a tax on the market value of all goods and services produced in a country during a given period. Thus, a company's VAT is based on its total sales to customers *less* the value of any purchases that it made from others already subject to the tax. In short, the company pays a tax on the value it "added on" to the materials that passed through its hands — for example, the difference between the value of the peanuts it bought and the peanut butter it sold. The VAT is effectively built into the price of the good as it passes through the supply chain, with the final consumer ultimately paying the entire cost of the VAT through this increased price. It is for this reason a VAT is considered a consumption tax notwithstanding that it is not charged to the consumer at the point of sale like a retail sales tax.

Similarly, the United States has imposed some form of wealth *transfer* tax, in the form of the gift and estate tax, for a long time. The federal government has generally not relied on imposing taxes on wealth itself, however. A wealth tax is a tax not on the *increase* in a person's wealth (that is, income) but on the *aggregate* amount of an individual's wealth. For example, a real property tax is imposed on an annual basis by most state and local governments on the total assessed value (as opposed to any increase in value) of the property on an annual basis. The real property tax is the most significant wealth tax employed in the United States.

There are also many forms of taxation that, while rarely encountered by most taxpayers, are important in specialized areas of the law. For example, among others: (1) those who work in an international context may encounter import and export taxes; (2) employers must pay an employment tax on wages paid to employees; and (3) franchise taxes are imposed on the exercise of rights granted by the government (the most common franchise taxes are those that states impose on the privilege of carrying on business as a corporation). One venerable form of franchise tax, the poll tax, was struck down by the enactment of the Twenty-fourth Amendment in 1964 with respect to federal elections, and declared unconstitutional with regard to state elections in Harper v. Virginia Board of Elections, 383 U.S. 663 (1966).

As quickly becomes apparent, that taxes are necessary to support the functioning of government and society does not inform what type of taxes should be imposed or how the burdens of a tax should be allocated. Although the United States currently relies primarily on an income tax, that was not always the case, nor is it clear that it necessarily should be. A brief history of the U.S. income tax can assist in determining why an income tax might be preferable and inform how to read and interpret the income tax itself.

2. Constitutionality of the Income Tax

Immediately following the War for Independence, the colonies considered how to govern and interact as free and independent states. The mechanism they adopted was embodied in the Articles of Confederation, which established a loose confederation of the thirteen newly sovereign states. Under the Articles of Confederation, the central government had very limited power. In particular, the Articles expressly denied the central government the power to directly impose taxes on the people. Rather, to fund the central government the Articles called for voluntary payments to be made from the states as needed to fund operations. As would be expected, this did not go well, with several states often refusing to contribute anything to the central government.

This flaw in the operation of the Articles of Confederation led to the call for a new convention to amend the Articles and make them more effective. This has since come to be known as the Constitutional Convention. At the Constitutional Convention, rather than amend the Articles the framers chose to abandon the Articles and write a new constitution based on the premise of a strong but limited federal government with the power to fund itself directly through the imposition of taxes. This taxing power was enumerated in Article I, Section 8 of the Constitution, which provides that Congress shall have the power to lay and collect taxes, duties, imposts, and excises. On its face, this is an expansive provision, especially in light of the rejection of the Articles of Confederation, in that it grants broad and direct powers to impose and collect taxes on individuals to the federal government. Afraid of the potential overreach and tyranny of a federal government with such strong direct powers to impose tax, however, two limitations on this authority were enumerated in Article I. Article I, Section 8 provides that all duties, imposts, and excises be uniform throughout the United States (the "uniformity" requirement). Article I, Section 9 provides that no capitation or other direct tax may be imposed unless it is done in proportion to the census or enumeration (the "apportionment" requirement).

Pursuant to this new power Congress adopted various measures, including import tariffs, taxes on businesses, and taxes on land, to finance the operations of the nascent federal government. Not surprisingly, these new direct taxes were not popular, at least with a subset of Americans. One of the most notorious instances involved the Whiskey Excise Tax of 1791, enacted under the taxing power of Article I, Section 8 of the newly ratified Constitution. Some small farmers and distillers protested paying the tax, eventually leading to marches, rallies, and even violence committed toward tax collectors. This has generally come to be known as the Whiskey Rebellion. By 1794 President Washington ordered federal military intervention to stop the insurrection and collect the taxes, which he did by conscripting an armed militia. Thus, the first militia raised under the banner of the United States, including conscripts, and the first use of military force by the United States under the Constitution occurred not to repel invaders or to defend liberty or democracy, but to ensure the proper collection of taxes duly enacted under the new taxing power of Article I, Section 8.

Washington's forceful response to the Whiskey Rebellion, along with similar responses to other smaller anti-tax rebellions, eventually led to the general acceptance of the legitimacy of the taxing power of the federal government under the new Constitution. Protestors eventually changed tactics, from violent insurrections to legal challenges, claiming that certain federal taxes violated the two restrictions to the taxing power under the Constitution. The primary challenges to the early tax laws involved claims that such taxes were "direct" taxes that were not apportioned among the states, thus violating Article I, Section 9. Taxpayers met with varying degrees of success. For example, the Supreme Court held that a federal tax on carriages was a valid "excise" tax rather than an unconstitutional direct tax (Hylton v. United States, 3 U.S. (3 Dall.) 171 (1796)). The challenge to the tax had been that it disproportionately affected wealthy, urban states such as New York compared to poorer and more rural states, thus violating the requirement that taxes be apportioned in accordance with population under Article I, Section 9. The Supreme Court rejected this challenge on the grounds that an excise tax is not a "direct" tax, and thus the apportionment requirement did not apply. Since Congress clearly had the power to impose the tax under Article I, Section 8 and the tax clearly was uniform throughout the United States (in that it did not exempt some states), the Court upheld its constitutionality.

Cases like *Hylton* did not deter taxpayers from continuing to challenge other taxes on similar grounds, however. Finally, one broke through. In Pollock v. Farmers' Loan & Trust Co., 157 U.S. 429 (1895), the Supreme Court held that a tax on rents from real estate was a "direct" tax on the real estate itself and thus was unconstitutional as violating the apportionment clause because it was not allocated among the states based on population but rather was allocated based on the location of the most valuable property. At first, *Pollock* appeared to kill the ability of the federal government to impose any form of income tax, since wealth and population never completely matched. Rather than sound the death knell of the federal taxing power, however, the Supreme Court quickly discovered myriad exceptions to the rule announced in *Pollock*. For example, shortly thereafter the Supreme Court held that a tax on the income of corporations was a valid excise tax on the privilege of incorporation rather than an invalid income tax under *Pollock* notwithstanding that it was a tax measured on income (Flint v. Stone Tracy, 220 U.S. 107 (1911)), and that an inheritance tax was a valid excise tax on the *transfer* of wealth rather than an invalid direct tax on the wealth itself (Knowlton v. Moore, 178 U.S. 41 (1900)).

Notwithstanding these victories, Congress ultimately responded to the uncertainty arising from the *Pollock* decision by passing the Sixteenth Amendment to the Constitution, authorizing taxes on *income* without regard to the apportionment clause. Note the phraseology of the Sixteenth Amendment; it does not grant a new taxing power to the federal government, rather it only lifts the apportionment requirement from taxes imposed on incomes. In this manner, Congress could impose an income tax without worrying about violating the *Pollock* doctrine or relying on some disingenuous excise tax hook. The amendment was ratified by the states and became effective on February 25, 1913. The Supreme Court upheld the amendment's constitutionality in Brushaber v. Union Pacific Railroad, 240 U.S. 1 (1916) against challenges that it violated, among other things, the Fifth Amendment, stating that "the Constitution does not conflict with itself by conferring, on the one hand, a taxing power, and taking the same power away, on the other, by the limitations of the due process clause." Thus, notwithstanding criticism that the Sixteenth Amendment "legalized theft," the foundation of the present income tax system was established by the early twentieth century. The amendment has spawned voluminous legislation, most recently codified into the Internal Revenue Code of 1986.*

While the Internal Revenue Code thereby generally enjoys constitutional sanction, aggressive taxpayers continue to raise constitutional objections to provisions of it, at least as applied to them. As the following discussion and cases illustrate, those objections usually fail, perhaps because when it comes to avoiding such certainties as death or taxes, there is nothing new under the sun. Courts usually treat "constitutional" objections as frivolous, and as evidenced by the *Morelli* and *Autenrieth* cases discussed below, the brevity and tone of many of these decisions reveal the courts' impatience with the claims and general unwillingness to entertain seriously taxpayers' constitutional objections to the payment of income tax.

Morelli v. Commissioner, T.C. Memo 1981-293, is a primer of unsuccessful arguments that purport to justify a taxpayer's failure to pay his income tax and is also an example of the rather offhand treatment of constitutional claims by the courts. In *Morelli*, the taxpayer claimed protection under the Fourth Amendment, but a lack of supportive reasoning left the court unconvinced. Nor was the court

---

*The Tax Reform Act of 1986 amended the Internal Revenue Code of 1954 and redesignated it as the Internal Revenue Code of 1986. Because some of the material in this casebook arose prior to 1986, references to the Internal Revenue Code of 1954 should be interpreted accordingly. While there have been numerous changes to the tax laws since 1986, there has not been a fundamental reenactment of the entire Internal Revenue Code since 1986, hence the name.

persuaded by the taxpayer's claim that the Fifth Amendment privilege against incrimination provided the right to refuse to complete a tax return. The taxpayer also argued that paper money had "no intrinsic value" and therefore its receipt did not constitute income; that only self-assessed taxes could be collected and he had assessed no taxes against himself; and that he had realized no income because he had furnished an equivalent value in services. The court remained unconvinced and entered a decision for the Commissioner.

A more thoughtful treatment of constitutional claims appears in Autenrieth v. Cullen, 418 F.2d 586 (9th Cir. 1969), in which plaintiffs sought a tax refund based on the First and Fourteenth Amendments. Claiming conscientious objection to the Vietnam War, 124 plaintiffs argued that they could not be compelled to finance the war and that they were therefore entitled to a refund of the percentage of their taxes spent in support of military activities. Some claimed a 17-percent refund, and others claimed a 67-percent refund. The 17-percent figure represented the percentage of total federal income tax revenue that had been spent in 1965 and 1966 to support the Vietnam War, while the 67-percent figure represented the amount to support all past, present, and possible wars. Plaintiffs based their case on theories of equal protection and free exercise of religion. Holding that "nothing in the Constitution prohibits the Congress from levying a tax upon all persons, regardless of religion, *for support of the general government*," the court made it clear that prorating income tax revenues to specific government activities is not an acceptable basis for a tax refund. Id. at 588 (emphasis added). The court noted the Code's neutrality toward religious matters, and expressed concern about the government's ability to function should the taxpayers' approach be permitted.

As evidenced by the disposition of constitutional issues in cases such as *Brushaber*, *Morelli*, and *Autenrieth*, most constitutional challenges to the income tax fail. This fact generally reflects the tendency of courts to consider tax laws an issue of property rights rather than one of "fundamental personal rights or liberties." The one substantive constitutional debate in the field of taxation that continues to rear its head, however, is the scope of the definition of "income" in the Sixteenth Amendment. As discussed above, this can be crucial because if tax is not a tax on income, then it must either not be a direct tax, such as under *Stone Tracy*, or be struck down under *Pollock*. The Supreme Court confronted this issue in 1929 in Taft v. Bowers, 278 U.S. 470 (1929). *Taft* involved a taxpayer who received appreciated property as a gift. Under the law at the time (and currently) upon sale of the property the recipient would owe tax on the entire amount of the gain, even gain attributable to appreciation accrued prior to time of the gift. The taxpayer in *Taft* argued that Congress could not tax gain that had accrued prior to the taxpayer's receipt of the property, notwithstanding clear statutory language to this effect, because such gain was not properly "income" to the recipient but rather was income to the donor of the gift. In rejecting this claim, the Court stated: "To accept the view urged in behalf of petitioner undoubtedly would defeat, to some extent, the purpose of Congress to take part of all gain derived from capital investments. To prevent that result and insure enforcement of its proper policy, Congress had power to require that for purposes of taxation the donee should accept the position of the donor in respect of the thing received. And in so doing, it acted neither unreasonably nor arbitrarily." Id. at 482-483. In effect, once the Court determined that the tax as a whole was properly on income for purposes of the

Sixteenth Amendment, it deferred to Congress as to the specific scope and means of taxing that income, at least to the extent that Congress did not act unreasonably or arbitrarily.

Notwithstanding the ruling in *Taft*, throughout the over eighty years since taxpayers have continued to contend that different receipts fall outside the definition of "income" for purposes of the Sixteenth Amendment. Of course, the taxing power continues to prove controversial, most recently in the case of National Federation of Independent Business v. Sebelius, 567 U.S. ____ (2012), more commonly known as the Obamacare decision, which is discussed in more detail in other chapters. Consider the following cases, twenty-five years apart, in which the courts refused to accept the contention of taxpayers that certain items fell outside of the constitutional definition of income. While reading these cases, consider the relevance, if any, of Article I, Section 8 in addition to the Sixteenth Amendment.

HELLERMANN v. COMMISSIONER
77 T.C. 1361 (1981)

EKMAN, J. . . .

. . . The sole issue for our decision is whether that portion of gain from the sale of property, which is attributable solely to inflation, is income within the meaning of the 16th Amendment. . . .

Petitioners purchased four buildings in 1964 for $93,312. They sold the buildings in 1976 for $264,000, and reported a . . . gain of $170,688 on their 1976 return. . . .

Petitioners claim that much of their reported gain on the sale of the four buildings was due to inflation. They point out that the Consumer Price Index (CPI) had approximately doubled between 1964 and 1976. Thus, even though they received more dollars on the sale than they had paid to purchase the buildings, each 1976 dollar they received was worth less than each 1964 dollar they paid. . . .

Petitioners assert that they should not be taxed on their nominal gain, but only on their economic gain. They argue that the portion of their nominal gain which is attributable solely to inflation does not constitute taxable income within the meaning of the 16th Amendment. Instead, they contend that, economically speaking, such gain is a return of capital. As they correctly observe, tax on a return of capital is a direct tax, subject to apportionment. They maintain that to the extent the Internal Revenue Code permits that portion of nominal gain which is attributable to inflation to be taxed, it is an unconstitutional exercise of the Congress' power. They conclude that the Code must be interpreted in a manner which does not permit such gain to be taxed as income. As an appropriate means to that end, petitioners suggest that we adjust nominal gain to reflect the effects of inflation. . . .

We note at the outset that we have several times denied taxpayers deductions for losses due to inflation, on grounds that the tax law is not written to account for inflation. These cases do not control the decision in this case because they deal with deductions, not income. Deductions are a matter of legislative grace, and the Congress has absolute discretion to refrain from taxing what would otherwise be taxable income. In contrast, Congress may not constitutionally tax as income, without apportionment, receipts which represent a return of capital.

We reject petitioners' contention that nominal gain is not taxable income within the meaning of the 16th Amendment on two grounds. First, we rely on the well-established doctrine that Congress has the power and authority to establish the dollar as a unit of legal value with respect to the determination of taxable income, independent of any value the dollar might also have as a commodity. Legal Tender Cases, 79 U.S. (12 Wall.) 457 (1870). In the Legal Tender Cases, supra, the Supreme Court held that Congress had the power to declare treasury notes ("greenbacks"), which were backed by gold, to be legal tender. The Court held that paper money could be on a par with gold coins because both had the same legal value. The Court recognized that the statutory value of the nation's currency might not correspond to the market value of the bullion which backed the paper or from which the gold coins were made. It termed this discrepancy the difference between legal and intrinsic value. However, it did not doubt that Congress had the power to legislate such a difference. . . .

Petitioners concede that Congress has the power to require that the income tax be paid in dollars as legal tender, but argue that it does not have the power to measure gain in terms of dollars, because such dollars do not have a constant value. Given the reasoning behind the holding of the Legal Tender Cases, we must disagree. Dollars have constant legal value under the uniform monetary system created by Congress. When petitioners sold the buildings in 1976, they realized a gain in legal value. The 16th Amendment does not prevent the Congress from taxing such gain as income if it chooses to do so.

As our second ground for rejecting petitioners' arguments, we rely upon the doctrine of common interpretation. As was stated by Judge Learned Hand, "[the] meaning [of income] is . . . to be gathered from the implicit assumptions of its use in common speech." Thus the meaning of income is not to be construed as an economist might, but as a layperson might. Petitioners received many more dollars for the buildings than they had paid for them. The extra dollars they received are well within the common perception of income, even though each 1976 dollar received represents less purchasing power than each 1964 dollar paid. Petitioners' nominal gain may or may not equal their real gain in an economic sense. Nonetheless, neither the Constitution nor tax laws "embody perfect economic theory."

Based on the foregoing, we find that petitioners' nominal gain represented a change in legal value. Thus, petitioners' nominal gain is taxable income within the meaning of the 16th Amendment. Accordingly, we hold that petitioners are liable for the . . . tax as determined by respondent. . . .

PERRY v. COMMISSIONER
T.C. Memo 2006-77

CHABOT, J.
. . . In 2001, petitioners realized and recognized a [net] long-term capital loss in the amount of $9,256.63, as they claimed on their 2001 tax return. In 2003, petitioners realized and recognized a net long-term capital loss of $60,641.96, as they claimed on their 2003 tax return. . . .

In the notice of deficiency for each year, respondent disallowed the claimed capital loss deduction for that year to the extent the loss exceeded $3,000, and also made consequential adjustments to itemized deductions and (for 2003) personal exemption deductions. . . . Petitioners do not contest the mathematical correctness of respondent's computations. . . .

By disallowing that part of the loss that exceeds $3,000, petitioners contend, respondent is taxing petitioners on "income that does not exist. Petitioners believe that section 1211(b) violates the power granted Congress in the Sixteenth Amendment, and if the Court agrees, it should rule accordingly." . . .

Article I, section 8, of the U.S. Constitution gives to the Congress the "Power To lay and collect Taxes." Under sections 2 (cl. 3) and 9 (cl. 4) of article I, "direct" taxes must be apportioned among the States in proportion to census populations. The Sixteenth Amendment has the effect of overriding the direct-tax-apportionment requirement with respect to "taxes on incomes, from whatever source derived."

. . . Petitioners contend they should be allowed to deduct the entire amounts of their realized and recognized capital losses, in accordance with their tax returns. For petitioners to prevail, they might have to persuade us of all the following: (1) The limitation of section 1211(b) causes the sections 1 and 55 taxes to not be income taxes under the Sixteenth Amendment; (2) the sections 1 and 55 taxes as limited by section 1211(b) constitute direct taxes that must be apportioned; and (3) full deductibility of capital losses is the preferred way to save the entire income tax from invalidation. . . .

Petitioners claim that the effect of the $3,000 loss limitation is to tax them on "income that does not exist." They are mistaken. Petitioners are being taxed under section 1 only on the aggregate of the other categories of income that they in fact realized, recognized, and reported — their income that does exist.

The tax treatment of capital losses has varied over the years. As discussed in Davis v. United States, 87 F.2d 323 (2d Cir. 1937), section 23(r) of the Revenue Act of 1932 . . . allowed losses from the sale or exchange of stocks and bonds held for less than two years only to the extent of gains from the sale of such securities. The taxpayer in *Davis* had $13,285 of what we now would call short-term capital losses, which was greater than the amount of his net taxable income. The taxpayer contended that, as a result, he did not have net income for the taxable year, so that his "net taxable income" was not income, and thus the tax on his net taxable income was not a Sixteenth Amendment permitted income tax.

The Circuit Court of Appeals analyzed the situation as follows:

> While the computation of income is made with due and necessary regard to periods of time, which are established years either calendar or fiscal, it cuts altogether too fine to say that true, and therefore taxable, income can only be ascertained by putting together all the profit and loss transactions of the period and determining net income accordingly regardless of the fact that they may in whole or in part be quite unrelated except for the time element and the fact that they were those of the same taxpayer. If, for instance, a separate and distinct transaction during the year results in a net realized gain to the taxpayer in and of itself, income which is taxed has been received, but Congress may, or may not, have allowed deductions which as a matter of computation will relieve that income in whole or in part from the taxation to which otherwise it would be subject. . . .

Accordingly, the Circuit Court of Appeals upheld the constitutionality of the section 23(r) limitation.

To the same effect is White v. Commissioner, 37 B.T.A. 1106 (1938). The taxpayer sustained a net loss in his securities trading. After discussing *Davis*, we stated in *White* as follows:

> This petitioner, however, asserts that the deduction he seeks is not a statutory deduction, but falls within the first classification of deductions made by the court in the *Davis* case, wherein the court speaks of taking from all receipts "certain necessary items like cost of property sold," and contends that the respondent's action denies him the right to deduct from gross receipts the cost of all items purchased by him in the conduct of his business. In other words petitioner denies that he can have income in any amount until he has recovered his aggregate cost, and his entire argument is based upon the proposition that the denial of the right to reduce gross receipts by aggregate cost creates income where none in fact exists and, therefore, makes the application of 23(r) unconstitutional as to his business.
>
> That portion of petitioner's argument relative to the denial of his right to use cost is answered in part by the court in the *Davis* case, wherein it states that a net gain realized by a taxpayer from a separate and distinct transaction constitutes income that may, or may not, be subject to tax depending upon whether the Congress has allowed deductions which as a matter of computation will relieve that income in whole or in part from taxation, and by the further statement that "net income for any taxable period need not necessarily be the same as net taxable income for that period, and the variation may be to the extent that Congress has seen fit either to allow, to limit, or to deny deductions within its control as a matter of grace." The facts in this proceeding illustrate the truth of the court's observations. This petitioner as a matter of fact lost money upon the basis of his operations over the entire year, and if all his losses were deductible he could have no statutory net income. However, in the absence of a statutory right to reduce other income by losses from stock speculations, and in view of the specific limitation of 23(r), petitioner's computation must show a statutory net income subject to tax. . . .

The foregoing disposes of all of petitioners' contentions, including the asserted constitutional distinction between a "capital loss" and "a deductible expense item."

This debate over what is "income" and whether that question is dispositive of whether a tax is constitutional has proven tricky, even to the most sophisticated lawyers. For example, in Murphy v. United States, 460 F.3d 79 (D.C. Cir. 2006) a panel of the Court of Appeals for the District of Columbia found that a provision of the Internal Revenue Code which effectively taxed damages for mental anguish was unconstitutional on the theory that pain and suffering type damages were not income for purposes of the Sixteenth Amendment but rather simply made the plaintiff whole. This holding was controversial, to say the least. Regardless of the substantive merits of the holding—whether damages for pain and suffering are income or merely make the person whole—the court fell into the same analytical trap as many taxpayers—equating whether something is an income tax for purposes of the Sixteenth Amendment with whether Congress has the power to impose the tax at all. The power to tax arises under Article I, Section 8, not the Sixteenth Amendment. Consequently, so long as the taxes are not "direct" as in *Pollock* they may be imposed without regard to the apportionment requirement even if they are not income taxes within the meaning of the Sixteenth Amendment. In such cases, the Sixteenth Amendment proves irrelevant—if apportionment does not apply, for example with respect to an excise tax on carriages under *Hylton*, the "income" question proves moot. The panel must have recognized this, as it subsequently reconsidered the case *sua sponte* and, upon reconsideration, withdrew its initial opinion and issued a new opinion holding upholding the tax. In the new opinion, the court held that it need not rule on whether damages for pain and suffering were income for purposes of the Sixteenth Amendment because Congress could constitutionally tax such damages as a type of excise tax, much like *Knowlton* and *Stone Tracy*. As a result, the Internal Revenue Code lives to fight another day.

There has recently been a resurgence of the debate over the scope and breadth of the taxing power under the Constitution, apparently raising many deeply held beliefs about the proper role and scope of the federal government. In particular, the federal government's ability to use its taxing power to regulate, encourage or require certain behavior has received renewed scrutiny. For example, if the government can impose a tax on individuals if they do not buy health insurance, the thinking goes, what prevents it from taxing those who don't eat broccoli or exercise enough? The problem with most of these arguments, notwithstanding any intuitive appeal they may have, is that they do not take into account the actual Constitutional framework and history of the taxing power. As seen in cases such as *Hylton*, *Stone Tracy*, *Taft*, *Knowlton*, *Autenrieth*, and even *Murphy*, Congress can pass any tax it wishes under Article I, Section 8 so long as it is uniform among the states and, if it is a direct tax, it is apportioned among the states based on population. If it is not a direct tax (such as an excise tax) or it is an income tax, then even the apportionment requirement does not apply. Without violating an independent restriction of the Constitution, such as imposing a poll tax or a tax on certain speech based on its content, the power to tax proves quite broad indeed. In fact, this was precisely the point of including it in the Constitution and scrapping the failed approach of the Articles of Confederation in the first place. As deeply as some may feel about taxation in the modern debate, we have yet to see a repeat of the Whiskey Rebellion (at least so far). There is little doubt that there would be an unprecedented uproar if any modern President ordered the National Guard to forcibly collect federal taxes at the point of a rifle, yet that is precisely what President Washington did, and the framers, many of whom were in the executive or legislative branches at the time, seemed to have little problem with it. To the extent the intent and actions of the framers in the nascent republic has any relevance to interpreting the Constitution it would seem to lead in one direction . . . that of an extremely broad and deep taxing power.

B. THE STRUCTURE OF THE TAX LAW

1. Tax Policy: Equity and Efficiency Goals

Given the broad Congressional power to tax, the next question becomes not *whether* Congress can impose a particular tax, but rather what type of tax *should* be used to fund the federal government. At first glance, the tax laws appear to be an overwhelming maze of rules enacted solely with the intent to confuse law students encountering them for the first time, with little thought put into what an ideal tax system would look like. Notwithstanding the initial appeal of this conclusion, however, the tax laws are — at least nominally — enacted for specific policy reasons. At times, however, these policies can conflict, leading to difficult choices and balancing of relative preferences.

In the past, tax policy theorists have concentrated primarily on whether the federal income tax is equitable, that is, does the income tax fairly apportion the costs and benefits of society among the people? To this end, theorists have used two measures of the fairness of the income tax: does the income tax treat taxpayers with equal incomes similarly (horizontal equity), and does it differentiate appropriately among taxpayers with unequal incomes (vertical equity)? Applying the notion that pretax income furnishes the basis of comparison for determining whether taxpayers are equals, most equity theorists conclude that the Code fails in this regard because there is often significant disparity in the tax liability of those with equal pretax income.

A second group of tax theorists argues that efficiency ought to be the primary goal of economic policy. These efficiency theorists focus on whether the tax allowances built into the present system allocate resources efficiently while raising the revenue necessary to fund the government. The two views do not necessarily diverge on specific issues, however. For example, while equity theorists criticize tax allowances for imposing disparate tax burdens on taxpayers in the same economic position, efficiency theorists charge that many of these same allowances misallocate resources.

Professor Bittker, one of the leading tax scholars of all time, emphasizes that equity and efficiency, as normative standards, rest on different assumptions about taxpayer behavior. Equity theorists contend that tax allowances will not change taxpayer behavior or that, if changes do occur, they will not appreciably alter pre-tax income. By contrast, efficiency theorists predict that tax-favored behavior will increase with a corresponding decrease in alternatives not favored by a tax allowance. Bittker, Equity, Efficiency, and Income Tax Theory: Do Misallocations Drive Out Inequities?, 16 San Diego L. Rev. 735 (1979). In assessing these competing theories, Professor Bittker concludes:

> It is hard to see how the normative standards favored by either equity or efficiency theorists can be applied with confidence to existing law while the behavioral consequences of most tax allowances remain *terra incognita*. Only when they are mapped will we be able to say with assurance whether particular tax allowances generate inequities, misallocations, or some of each. Until then, intuition and political preferences must be the basis for analysis because scholars, alas, can legitimately claim little more authority than the average citizen.

Id. at 748.

Although use of the federal tax system to regulate the economy has acquired increasing legitimacy over the past two decades, policymakers have been less than perfect in achieving the desired results; indeed, predicting the population's response to any given measure is often difficult. Thus, many critics question the efficacy of attempts to achieve substantial economic objectives through the tax system.

The following excerpt from the Joint Committee on Taxation explains one approach to balancing these disparate policies when drafting or designing tax laws.

JOINT COMMITTEE ON TAXATION, DESCRIPTION AND ANALYSIS OF PROPOSALS TO REPLACE THE FEDERAL INCOME TAX
58-59 (1995)

C. CRITERIA FOR ANALYSIS OF TAX SYSTEMS

1. IN GENERAL

Analysts generally judge tax systems in terms of how well the tax system answers four different questions.

- First, does the tax system promote or hinder economic efficiency[?] That is, to what extent does the tax system distort taxpayer behavior? Does the tax system create a bias against the domestic production of goods and services? To what extent does it promote economic growth?
- Second, is the tax system fair? Does the tax system treat similarly situated individuals similarly? Does the tax system account for individuals' different capacities to bear the burden of taxation?
- Third, is the tax system simple? Is it costly for taxpayers to determine their tax liability and file their taxes?
- Fourth, can the tax system be easily administered by the government and can it induce compliance by all individuals? Is enforcement costly? Can some individuals successfully avoid their legal liabilities?

The design of a tax system involves tradeoffs between these different goals. Measures designed to ensure compliance may increase the complexity of taxation for individual filers. Measures designed to promote simplicity may create distortions in individual choice of investments. Measures designed to promote growth may alter the distribution of the tax burden.

In 2005, the President's Advisory Panel on Federal Tax Reform issued a report analyzing how to balance the competing factors of equity, efficiency, and simplicity in undertaking fundamental reform of the federal income tax system. In reading the following excerpt, ask yourself why the task of crafting a simple, fair, and efficient tax regime can prove so difficult.

REPORT OF THE PRESIDENT'S ADVISORY PANEL ON FEDERAL TAX REFORM, SIMPLE, FAIR AND PRO-GROWTH: PROPOSALS TO FIX AMERICA'S TAX SYSTEM
(2005)

AN ARBITRARY AND UNEQUAL SYSTEM

A tax code, like any law, should rest squarely on the notion that it will remain largely the same, from year to year, from person to person. In a court of law, there is an expectation by the judge, jury, and all other parties that the law will be equally and fairly applied based on well-established and consistent judicial principles. Yet our tax code shares few, if any, of these features.

Taxpayers cannot plan ahead: The tax system is a kaleidoscope of shifting credits, rates, and benefits because many of the tax code's most prominent features — the tax rate for ordinary income, the child tax credit, the lower tax on dividends and capital gains — may shift wildly from one year to the next, and in some cases simply expire. . . .

This uncertainty has clear effects. If you own a small business and are contemplating an investment in new equipment, the tax provision that quadruples the portion of that investment that can be written-off immediately is an incentive to go forward with the investment. Yet because of the scheduled expiration . . . of this provision, your decision to invest may be rushed. Such an investment — timed as it is to a provision in the tax code rather than to economic fundamentals — may turn out to be ill-advised and waste economic resources. In any case, the tax code's constant phase-ins and phase-outs are a nuisance at best, and a negative force at worst, in the daily economic lives of American families and businesses.

The tax code treats similar taxpayers in different ways: Taxpayers with the same income, family situation, and other key characteristics often face different tax burdens. Such differing treatment creates a perception of unfairness in our tax code. For example, taxpayers in states with high state and local income and property taxes receive higher deductions than taxpayers who live in lower-tax states with fewer state-provided services. Taxpayers with substantial employer-provided health insurance benefits receive in-kind compensation that is not taxed, while taxpayers who buy the same health insurance on their own usually pay tax on the income used to purchase the insurance. . . . How much or little taxpayers pay in tax is sometimes dependent on where they happen to live, the choices made by their employers, and whether they are married.

The differences in treatment are not always set by design. Rather, the different amounts similarly situated taxpayers often pay is sometimes a reflection of the tax code's complexity. While some taxpayers may take advantage of special provisions that are available to them, others do not. Someone who claims legal credits and deductions has done nothing wrong, yet unequal outcomes suggest that our tax code unfairly benefits those with the time and resources to make sense of it. This situation conflicts with basic principles of equity and erodes public confidence in the system.

The tax code treats similar income differently: As part of our system of progressive taxation, income is taxed at increasing rates as a taxpayer's annual income increases. This creates a tax rate called the "marginal rate." The marginal tax rate is the rate paid on the last dollar of income earned — it measures how much tax you pay on additional, or marginal, income. . . . The effective marginal tax rate can differ substantially from the schedule of basic tax rates described above. This element is complicated by various exclusions, deductions, and credits, and the web of accompanying phase-ins and phase-outs. Some credits and deductions are available to people only when they earn more or less than a certain amount of income. The idea behind setting a limitation on the income one can earn before claiming certain deductions and credits is to target the benefits to those perceived to have the greatest need. But that creates a set of counterintuitive and counterproductive economic consequences that may keep many families from trying to earn more than they currently do.

... Low-income taxpayers face very high marginal tax rates, even higher than those with substantially larger incomes. Moreover, even small changes in income can cause large changes in marginal tax rates. For example, our single mother with two children enjoys a negative tax rate on each extra dollar of earnings up to $11,000 because she receives a $40 tax credit for every $100 earned through the [Earned Income Tax Credit]. As she earns more, however, her tax rate rises sharply. At an income level of $25,000, she pays $31 of tax on each additional $100 earned. So instead of receiving $140 in total wages and tax benefits for each extra $100 earned, she now receives only $69 on every extra $100 of earnings [because the credit is slowly disallowed as income increases].

... It could be that some well-meaning lawmaker wanted to avoid handing out federal tax credits to high-earning families. But even the best intentions cannot guard against the law of unintended consequences. One such consequence is handing a tax credit to a family that didn't really need it and would have sent their child to college anyway. In this case, the government spent money on a tax benefit that did not change the behavior that it was designed to affect—and thus provided a windfall to the family. Another unintended consequence is that these credits may lead to a higher cost of education for those who do not receive the credits. There is some evidence, for instance, that the credit may encourage colleges and universities to increase tuition, thereby capturing some of the benefit of the credit. A third consequence is that everyone else's taxes are higher.

THE TAX CODE IN OUR LIVES

The tax code reaches into daily events, and by multiplication of rules and conditions, makes itself into an economic hazard. Yet there are examples of the tax code's failure to account for economic progress when it does occur. In the case of our technology industries, we have a sector of the economy larger in size than health care, and crucial to future job growth and living standards. These technology-based industries depend heavily on how our tax code defines the useful life of all technology. These definitions, laid out in depreciation schedules, permit purchasers of computers and other high-technology equipment to take a deduction against their income for the cost of that equipment over a period of time. The depreciation schedules for technology have always been a source of some controversy; companies routinely discard new computers and other technological equipment after only three years while the depreciation schedules call for a five-year lifespan. Why? Congress based the current depreciation schedule for computers on studies of the useful lives of surplus government typewriters from the late 1970s. Only in our tax code can a late-1970s typewriter be viewed as the same as a high-end, multimedia laptop. ...

THREE BURDENS OF THE TAX SYSTEM

... Taxes create administrative costs for the government, compliance costs for taxpayers, and efficiency costs for the national economy.

What are administrative costs? Administrative costs are perhaps the easiest costs to understand because they represent the direct costs incurred by the government to manage and administer the income tax system. These costs include the budget of the Internal Revenue Service and other parts of the Treasury Department that help maintain the income tax system, as well as relevant expenses incurred by other government agencies. These costs total more than $10 billion per year.

What are compliance costs? Compliance costs represent the time and resources expended by taxpayers to interact with the income tax system. These costs include the value of individuals' time spent learning about the tax law, maintaining records for tax purposes, completing and filing tax forms, and responding to any correspondence from the IRS or to an IRS audit. Compliance costs also include amounts paid to others to conduct any of these tasks on behalf of an individual or a business.

Individuals are estimated to spend a total of 3.5 billion hours each year complying with the income tax system. On average, individuals spend 26 hours annually on their taxes, and $166 per return on out-of-pocket costs for the services of tax professionals, filing fees, and software purchases. Total yearly compliance costs are difficult to estimate, in part because estimating the value of the time people spend on their tax returns is difficult. Nevertheless, the Treasury Department estimates that total costs for complying with the individual income tax amount to almost $100 billion per year. In addition, businesses are estimated to spend over three billion hours complying with the tax system, at a total yearly cost of $40 billion. This total cost of approximately $140 billion means that one dollar is spent on compliance costs for every seven dollars collected in federal income taxes. Other estimates of total compliance costs are somewhere between $100 billion to $200 billion.

What are efficiency costs? Finally, the income tax imposes efficiency costs on the economy. These costs arise when high tax rates discourage work, savings, and investment; distort economic decisions of individuals and businesses; and divert resources from productive uses in our economy. Our tax code contains all kinds of incentives for taxpayers to favor activities or goods that are taxed less than others. Provisions for the taxation of wages, of gains on the sale of securities and homes, or of other economic activities influence how much people work and save. As one small business owner explained to the Panel, the tax code affects almost every business decision he makes: where to invest, when to invest, how much to invest, what kinds of machines and equipment to use in production, how to finance investment, etc.

When taxpayers change their behavior to minimize their tax liability, they often make inefficient choices that they would not make in the absence of tax considerations. These tax-motivated behaviors divert resources from their most productive use and reduce the productive capacity of our economy. Economic growth suffers as taxpayers respond to the tax laws rather than to underlying economic fundamentals. These distortions waste economic resources, reduce productivity, and, ultimately lower living standards for all.

These effects are profound. . . . Economists call this the "excess burden" of taxation. Its very name indicates that the true cost of a tax exceeds the tax bill people pay or the revenue that is collected.

. . . [T]he excess burden, or cost, of the tax code grows more than proportionately as tax rates increase. In fact, economic theory suggests that if you double the tax rate, you quadruple the excess burden. This means that high tax rates have disproportionately high economic costs associated with them.

. . . It would be difficult, however, to imagine a tax system that has no excess burden. Excess burden arises from people adopting less efficient behavior. A tax that does not induce people to alter their behavior would be one that does not depend on behavior at all. For example, a tax imposed on anyone with green eyes would be impossible to avoid for someone with green eyes. A real-life example of this was the poll tax, or flat charge on all adults living in a jurisdiction, which was highly efficient in collecting revenue, but perceived as extremely unfair because it applied equally to all people, regardless of wealth. As a result, these types of taxes have been rejected as revenue raising devices.

For this reason, it is clear that raising revenue through taxation requires some distortions in the economy. One goal of good tax policy is to minimize these distortions within a "fair" tax structure. The trade-off between fairness and efficiency in raising revenue is one of the central challenges of designing a tax system. Economic analysis can describe the efficiency cost of different taxes, but fairness is much more difficult to define and different policymakers may have different views of what constitutes tax fairness. . . .

2.   *The Progressive Rate Structure*

A fundamental feature of the United States system of income taxation is its progressive, or graduated, nature; taxpayers with more taxable income pay a greater percentage rate of tax than taxpayers with less taxable income. This is accomplished by subjecting additional increments of income to increasingly higher rates of tax. By way of example, for a taxpayer with taxable income of $20,000, assume that the final increment of income is taxed in the 10-percent tax bracket (the marginal rate), while a taxpayer with taxable income of $100,000 has the final increment of income taxed in the 30-percent tax bracket. Viewing the overall percentage tax liability (effective rate) of each of these two taxpayers and not merely the final increment, the taxpayer with $20,000 of taxable income might have a total tax liability of $1,000, resulting in an effective tax rate of only 5 percent, while the taxpayer with $100,000 of taxable income might have a total tax liability of $20,000, resulting in an effective rate of 20 percent. It is important to understand that as taxable income increases, the higher tax rate applied to the upper increments does not affect the lower increments. Thus, taxpayers do not retain less after-tax income when an additional amount of income is earned and taxed in a higher tax bracket.

Progressivity is premised on two concepts: ability to pay and marginal utility of taxpayers' income. Ability to pay refers to the idea that everyone should contribute to the common good based on what they can afford. Thus, under ability to pay, wealthier people should pay higher taxes simply because they can afford to. Ability to pay theory presumes there is a fixed dollar amount that needs to be raised and the only question is how to share the cost.

Decreasing marginal utility of money differs from ability to pay in that it focuses on the actual value of money to individuals. Under decreasing marginal utility theory, each dollar becomes less valuable as people have more money — one dollar is worth more to a starving person who can use it to survive than one dollar is to a person with $1 billion in the bank who may use it to light their cigar. If this is true, it is obviously preferable to tax the wealthier person before the starving person if the government needs to raise one dollar of revenue.

Although they differ significantly in the details, both ability to pay and declining marginal utility theory support some form of a progressive tax structure. What that means in application can vary widely, however. Typically, a tax is considered *progressive* if the tax rate increases as the value of the tax base increases, while a tax is *proportional* if the tax rate remains constant for all values of the tax base (in the common vernacular, such a tax is often called a flat tax), and a tax is *regressive* if the tax rate decreases as the value of the tax base increases. Frequently, however, the terms "progressive" and "regressive" are used to refer to the relation between the tax rate and the ability to pay, not the tax rate and the tax base. It is in this sense that sales taxes are often referred to as regressive. A 5 percent sales tax is technically proportional because the same flat tax rate applies to $2 items and to $2,000 items. But a sales tax is regressive in effect because the 5 percent of any given item represents a larger proportion of the income of a person who earns $2,000 than a person who earns $20,000. Progressivity here is defined in terms of "ability to pay."

At this point it is helpful to focus on progressivity as a concept. The concept of progressivity has fostered heated debate among professionals and non-professionals alike. Is the present income tax truly progressive? What are the jurisprudential and economic underpinnings of the federal income tax? Have congressional amendments, which lowered the maximum rates from 70 percent to 35 percent, eroded its progressivity? To what extent should one take account of government benefits and services in assessing progressivity?

In the following article, Art Pine of the Washington Post offers a glimpse into the complexity of the United States tax system and into the interests that the system serves. Pine contends that when all taxes are taken into account, "the nation's overall tax system becomes 'proportional.'" Although Pine's article is dated, his discussion and conclusions sound eerily reminiscent of modern public policy debates.

PINE, EVERYONE'S A CRITIC OF U.S. TAX SYSTEM
Washington Post, March 31, 1978, at 8, col. 1

Start talking about who gets hit hardest under the American tax system, and you're headed for a certain argument. Everyone has his own idea of how the tax system is biased. And there are enough seemingly conflicting statistics around so no one has to come out a liar.

To liberals, the big shortcoming in the tax system is that so many of the tax breaks go to the rich. To conservatives, the problem is that wealthy persons have to shoulder so much of the total tax burden. To some, the system is far too progressive. To others, it's not.

The problem has come to the fore in recent weeks in the face of new studies from the Treasury Department and the congressional Joint Committee on Taxation that highlight specific aspects of the overall U.S. tax structure — and not always in ways that please everyone.

The surveys . . . show these major findings:

Just as conservatives have been contending, higher-income taxpayers do indeed pay the bulk of all federal income taxes.

Statistics show the richest one-fourth of American taxpayers . . . took home half the reportable income in 1977 and paid 70 percent of all federal personal income taxes — an astonishing figure by any measure.

By contrast, those in the poorest one-fourth . . . received less than 5 percent of reportable income in the nation and paid a minuscule 0.1 percent or less of the total federal income tax tab.

But, just as the liberals have been complaining, the richer taxpayers receive the lion's share of the special tax breaks — deductions, credits and other kinds of write-offs — that the income tax system has to offer.

Of an estimated $84 billion in special tax breaks last year, almost half went to the [top] five percent of all taxpayers. . . .

Despite the "progressive" structure of the federal income tax system — which taxes the rich more heavily than the poor — the federal income tax isn't the great income leveler it's commonly thought to be.

While the income tax does hit wealthier persons proportionally harder than less-affluent ones, on average it has relatively little effect in redistributing income in this country, as some liberals would like to see.

For example, the richest one-fourth of American taxpayers took home 55.5 percent of the reportable income last year before federal income taxes were taken out. But after taxes, they still had 53.2 percent. The income tax had relatively little impact.

When federal Social Security taxes and state and local taxes of all kinds are included, the nation's overall tax system becomes "proportional" — that is, it taxes both richer and poorer taxpayers at about the same rate — 31 to 33 percent of their total income.

It's only when government "transfer payments" are taken into account — welfare and Social Security benefits and other major programs — that the system actually shifts significant amounts of income from rich to poor.

How can all these findings be correct? And what does it all mean?

Well, confusing as some of these conclusions may seem at first blush, tax experts say they aren't contradictory at all.

It shouldn't surprise anyone, for example, that the wealthier segment of society pays the bulk of the total federal income tax tab. After all, that's the way it's supposed to work: The system taxes only those persons with income. Those who have larger incomes theoretically are taxed more heavily than the rest. The only surprise is the extent to which richer taxpayers bear the burden.

Nor is it any great wonder that the more affluent taxpayers claim the bulk of the special tax breaks. The bigger your income, the more every deduction is worth in dollars. And many big tax breaks are skewed toward investments, which are made mostly by persons with money.

The reason the federal income tax isn't much of an income redistributor is that except for the few extremely rich and extremely poor, the tax rates paid by most income groups aren't that dramatically different from one another.

The high tax rates listed for those in the upper income brackets rarely are the ones actually paid. In the first place, wealthier taxpayers can reduce their taxable income by deductions. And the highest rates apply only to the upper portions of a taxpayer's income.

Finally, the impact of Social Security taxes and state and local taxes — to convert the overall tax system from a progressive one to a proportional one in which all taxpayers pay roughly the same percentage — isn't much of a surprise, either.

Both the Social Security tax and state and local taxes are extremely "regressive" — hitting the poor harder than the rich. As a result, their effect is to offset — or at least nullify — the mild progressivity of the federal income tax. And so it goes on.

As might be expected, each segment of the taxpaying public takes umbrage at the notion that the other fellow may be getting hit harder, and ballyhoos those statistics that conform most to what it wants to hear. Conservatives emphasize that richer taxpayers pay most of the taxes. Liberals stress that the burden isn't skewed enough.

The fact is, however, that each of these findings is a valid one, and illustrates some point about the structure of our tax system.

What these studies show, collectively, is that the tax system that's evolved is a complex patchwork of compromises that doesn't really please any segment of the population completely.

On the other hand, neither does the system go overboard in fulfilling the social goals of any one group or segment. Its main impact seems simply as a conduit for collecting taxes — shortcomings and all. . . .

3.   *Macroeconomic Growth and Income Taxation*

Recall that, as discussed in the President's Advisory Panel on Federal Tax Reform Report, considerations of efficiency, equity, and redistribution undergird the Internal Revenue Code and its numerous amendments. Among these, Congress at times has prioritized macroeconomic policy considerations in the Code. In other words, rather than looking to the impact of taxes on an individual basis looking to the impact on the economy as a whole. One need look no further than the descriptive title of the Economic Recovery Tax Act of 1981 to grasp the perceived importance of these considerations. Indeed, economic policy cannot be separated from taxation. For example, to motivate taxpayers to purchase certain assets, Congress has at various times enacted an investment tax credit and provided accelerated rates for depreciation, while at other times it has enacted hiring tax credits to combat unemployment. The following reading affords an insight into the use of the Code for these purposes.

TAX INCENTIVE ACT OF 1981
H.R. Rep. No. 201, 97th Cong., 1st Sess. 16-18 (1981)

GENERAL REASONS FOR THE BILL

The committee believes that extensive tax reductions are needed to relieve excessive tax burdens and to promote economic growth.

The economy has deteriorated over several years, and the tax laws have contributed to this trend by putting successively greater tax burdens on the income from productive activities. Whether from work, investment or savings, income has been subjected to effectively higher tax rates year after year since 1977. Meanwhile, unemployment has risen and worker productivity has declined. Neither investment nor savings have been adequate for necessary adjustments to higher energy costs, international competition and technological advances. For the third consecutive year, the rate of economic growth is likely to be below its postwar average.

The committee believes that a major tax cut is essential to a solid economic recovery. In structuring the tax reduction program, the committee has attempted to design measures which equitably increase incentives for individuals and businesses, whatever their circumstances, to earn, produce, save and invest. In fixing the size of the tax cut, the committee has attempted to provide the appropriate amount of stimulus for a broad and orderly economic expansion, instead of a smaller amount that would be ineffectual or a larger amount that would be inflationary.

INDIVIDUAL INCOME TAX REDUCTIONS

The committee believes that the tax burden on individuals has become excessive. The proportion of household income that is paid in individual income and social security taxes is now greater than at any other time in the last two decades, and sizable increases in these taxes are occurring in 1981. . . . The committee believes that an equitable tax reduction is needed, sufficient in every income class, insofar as it is feasible, to offset these tax increases, so that the proportion of household income that is paid in individual income and employee social security taxes is no higher than it was in 1980.

The second reason for the personal tax reduction is to stimulate economic recovery. High tax rates on additional dollars of income received not only discourage additional work and savings but also encourage tax avoidance schemes that tie up capital and inventiveness in unproductive uses. The committee believes that these marginal tax rates should be lowered in every tax bracket and that the greatest reduction should be made in the top bracket. However, the committee believes that rate reductions below the top bracket should be targeted to middle-income people. . . .

CAPITAL FORMATION AND PRODUCTIVITY TAX REDUCTIONS

The committee believes that the key to substantial economic growth is a revitalized and efficient business sector which produces at the lowest possible costs. The ordinary need for new investment to modernize plant and equipment has been made even more urgent by rapid technological advances, aggressive international competition, environmental and safety goals, and high energy costs. However, investment spending net of what is required merely to replace retired assets has been too small for several years, and productivity has fallen. . . .

The committee believes that the modernization of plant and equipment in the nation's basic heavy industries is essential for a well-grounded economic recovery. However, some of these industries, now economically distressed, are expected to be too little affected in the short run by other provisions of the committee bill that are intended to promote investment. Therefore, the committee has concluded that a tax cut should be structured that will encourage the immediate rebuilding of these distressed industries.

The committee believes that a new tax incentive for research and development is needed to maintain American preeminence in an activity that has contributed heavily to increased productivity.

The committee believes that a reduction is required in taxes on income from savings. Greater savings are needed to fund increased levels of investment for economic expansion. In addition, participation in individual retirement plans should be encouraged, for these plans are an important part of the retirement system. The bill, therefore, provides incentives for individuals to make greater contributions to private retirement accounts and to a new type of savings certificate. It also extends tax incentives for individual retirement accounts to many more taxpayers.

The committee is concerned that, after years of inflation, more transfers of property are being subjected to these taxes. The impact has been especially great on farms and small businesses, traditional and important areas of high productivity. The committee believes that substantial reductions in these taxes are needed. The committee also believes that windfall profit tax reductions are needed to encourage oil production and improve the equity of this tax.

The intent of the committee has been to structure tax reductions for stimulating saving, investment and productivity that are appropriate in the different circumstances under which different businesses operate. Long-term economic growth requires the effort of all persons and all businesses, and the benefits of growth should be equitably shared by all.

C.   ILLEGALITY AND ETHICAL CONSIDERATIONS

In studying the federal income tax system at the individual level, one should consider the legal and ethical constraints imposed on taxpayers and their advisers. Counseling a client about a potential tax liability inevitably presents delicate professional and moral questions. Moreover, while the adversarial system finds ample support in the tax law, counselors must temper their zeal; taxpayers cannot refuse to pay taxes. If there is taxable income, one must file a return and pay the appropriate tax liability. It should be noted, however, that the existence of an underground economy documents that this governing principle is not universally accepted.

The role of the lawyer in enforcing and administering the tax laws is a complicated one, involving the intersection of legal obligations under the Code, legal and ethical obligations to the client, and ethical obligations to the bar. Practicing tax law demands more than just technical wizardry. For example, tax lawyers must decide when not to give advice regarding activities that they consider to be unethical or illegal. Should the attorney inform a client of a dubious, but financially advantageous, tax planning device? Should a client be advised of ways to hide a questionable transaction from the Service? Should a client be encouraged to play the audit lottery game?

The following case provides an example of how these considerations can conflict, and how illegal activity can occur under the tax law even when relatively minimal amounts of revenue are at stake. These issues are discussed in more detail in Chapter 9.

UNITED STATES v. GREENBERG
735 F.2d 29 (2d Cir. 1984)

KEARSE, J.

Defendant Jack Greenberg appeals from a judgment entered in the United States District Court for the Eastern District of New York after a jury trial before Jacob Mishler, Judge, convicting him on one count of filing a materially false corporate income tax return, in violation §7206(1); two counts of filing materially false personal income tax returns, in violation of §7206(1); and one count of willfully failing to file a federal income tax return, in violation of §7203. . . .

BACKGROUND

. . . With respect to the charges that Greenberg filed, jointly with his wife, false personal income tax returns for the years 1976 and 1977, in violation of §7206(1), the evidence was that for each of those years, Greenberg overreported his wife's income and underreported his own. For 1976, Mrs. Greenberg was reported to have had a gross income of some $32,000, when in fact she had none; Greenberg was reported to have had earnings of some $4,400, when in fact his earnings were approximately $25,000. For 1977, Mrs. Greenberg was reported to have had gross income of some $35,000, when in fact she had none; Greenberg was reported to have had gross receipts of some $66,000, when in fact his gross receipts were more than $100,000. Greenberg testified that the purpose of these false allocations was to present a picture that would enable Mrs. Greenberg to obtain credit in her own name despite having no occupation. Notwithstanding these misallocations, the variance between the taxes paid by the Greenbergs and the taxes actually owing under a proper allocation was $48. . . .

DISCUSSION

. . . Where a false statement is made to a public body or its representative, materiality refers to the impact that the statement may reasonably have on the ability of that agency to perform the functions assigned to it by law. The question is not what effect the statement actually had; its actual effect would plainly present an issue of fact. The question is rather whether the statement had the potential for an obstructive or inhibitive effect. A consideration of this potential requires an analysis of the responsibilities of the public agency — responsibilities that are assigned by law — and analysis of the relevance of the statement to those responsibilities. Both relevance and the nature of a duty are traditionally questions of law to be decided by the court. Perforce the interrelationship of these two legal questions is a question of law. . . .

The purpose of §7206(1) is not simply to ensure that the taxpayer pay the proper amount of taxes — though that is surely one of its goals. Rather, that section is intended to ensure also that the taxpayer not make misstatements that could hinder the Internal Revenue Service ("IRS") in carrying out such functions as the verification of the accuracy of that return or a related tax return. . . .

Greenberg's argument that the misstatements were not material because they resulted in, at most, minimal underpayments of taxes ignores the potential of the misstatements for impeding the IRS's performance of its responsibilities. The fraudulent description . . . presented a distorted picture of . . . the owners' income. The fraudulent allocation of income to Mrs. Greenberg on the joint personal returns, with the corresponding underreporting of Greenberg's own income, gave a similar distorted view. All of these distortions had the potential for hindering the IRS's efforts to monitor and verify the tax liability of PRP and the Greenbergs.

In short, the district court correctly determined that the false statements made and assisted by Greenberg were material.

D.   THE TAXING FORMULA

Notwithstanding the constitutional, policy, administrative, and ethical considerations that underlie the federal income tax laws, at their most fundamental the tax laws are enacted to calculate the tax liability owed to the government for each taxpayer in a taxable year. Since every provision of the Internal Revenue Code and its Regulations, rulings, and interpretations relates directly or indirectly to this issue, it is logical to frame the study of the tax laws around the formula that the Code implicitly adopts as the means for taxpayers to calculate their tax liability. We refer to this framework as the "taxing formula." The taxing formula will not be found in any particular provision of the Code or the Regulations, but rather, upon close inspection of the mechanics and application of the tax laws as a whole, its presence becomes readily apparent.

Although tax reform proponents have advocated simple and concise methods for taxing income, for various policy reasons, discussed above, the formula currently employed by Congress is neither simple nor concise. The taxing formula, in equation form, is summarized as follows:

$$
\begin{array}{l}
\text{Gross income} \\
-\ \text{\S62 deductions} \\
\hline
\text{Adjusted gross income} \\
-\ \text{Standard deduction or itemized deductions} \\
-\ \text{Personal exemptions} \\
\hline
\text{Taxable income} \\
\times\ \text{Tax rate} \\
\hline
\text{Tax liability} \\
-\ \text{Credits} \\
+\ \text{Additional taxes} \\
\hline
\text{Final liability}
\end{array}
$$

The statutory taxing formula begins with gross income, a concept that encompasses the "accessions to wealth" on which an individual is taxed. This is discussed in Chapters 2 through 5. Although "gross income" is a broad concept, Congress has narrowed its scope by excluding various specific items on policy grounds. These exclusions are discussed in Chapter 3. Additional gross income issues, including *to whom* gross income is attributed and *when* a particular item of gross income is includable, are presented in Chapters 4 and 5, respectively.

After determining gross income, taxable income is calculated by subtracting statutorily prescribed deductions. Issues involving deductions are discussed in Chapters 6 through 9. The permissible deductions fall into four classes: (1) those associated with the conduct of the taxpayer's trade or business; (2) those associated with an activity that, while not a trade or business, is geared to the production of income; (3) those not within class (1) or (2) (such as personal expenses that typically would be denied deductibility) but that Congress has specifically authorized as deductions; and (4) artificial deductions (those for which the taxpayer did not expend funds but that are allowed on policy grounds, such as the personal exemption).

Subtracting deductions from gross income to arrive at taxable income involves two steps. First, adjusted gross income is calculated by subtracting the deductions allowed by §62 of the Code. Then, personal exemptions plus the greater of the standard deduction or itemized deductions are subtracted from adjusted gross income to arrive at taxable income.

Taxable income is then multiplied by the tax rate specified in the Code to yield the taxpayer's tax liability. Issues involving taxable income and the different tax rates are discussed in Chapter 10. In addition, the Code authorizes various credits that may be subtracted from the above-determined tax liability. These issues are also presented in Chapter 10. Ultimately, the taxpayer determines the final tax liability, the amount that must be remitted to the federal government, typically on or before that mystical date—April 15.

The following is an example using the above described approach in order to study a hypothetical taxpayer's tax setting and to determine his or her tax liability using the statutory rates in effect in 2007 (some numbers may be different in different years due to inflation adjustments). Taxpayer *A* and his spouse, *B*, have two young children. During the year, both are associate attorneys at mid-size law firms, with *A* earning $43,000 and *B* earning $60,000. *A*'s firm provides health insurance coverage for its employees, and the premiums for the year attributable to *A* and his family's coverage total $4,000. Additionally, *A* sold stock, sustaining a loss of $3,000. Given their working schedule, *A* and *B* hire a babysitter to care for their children in their home and pay him $13,000 for his services. For the year, *A* and *B* have the following itemized deductions: home mortgage interest expense, $18,000; home property taxes, $6,000; and state income taxes, $5,000. *A* and *B* file a joint return for the taxable year. Their tax liability for the year is $8,243, determined as follows:

$103,000 Gross income (the $4,000 of insurance coverage
                  is excluded under §106)
−   3,000 §62 deductions (loss from the sale of property,
                  §165; §62(a)(3))
_____
$100,000 Adjusted gross income
− 29,000 Standard deduction ($5,000, §63(c)(2)) or itemized
                  deductions ($18,000 mortgage interest, §163, and
                  $11,000 state and local taxes, §164)
−   8,000 Personal exemptions (§151)
_____
$63,000 Taxable income

$12,843 Tax liability (§1(a) — $5,535 plus 28% of excess over
                  $36,900)
−4,600 Credits (child care credit, §21; child tax credit, §24)
_____0 Additional taxes
$8,243 Final tax liability

The remainder of this book is organized around the taxing formula — that is, the statutory formula adopted by Congress to calculate taxable income and final tax liability. For those not previously inclined to take a course in federal income tax, the combination of the words "tax" and "formula" in the same sentence, let alone the same book, may be cause for fear and panic. There is no need to fear! The taxing formula is merely the structure through which Congress has imposed its taxing power — there are no differential equations or other advanced calculus involved. Following this formula provides a useful framework, or roadmap, upon which to build an overall understanding of the rules, structures, and policies of the United States federal income tax law, and how such rules, structures, and policies relate and interconnect.

CHAPTER 2

THE CONCEPT OF
GROSS INCOME

A. INTRODUCTION

Once it is determined that an income tax is the preferred means of society to fund its operations, it becomes necessary to figure out what "income" means. Unfortunately, this can prove much more difficult than would appear. Some contend that gross income broadly includes *any* improvement in an individual's economic well-being — such as the annual increase in the value of one's home — while others support a narrower meaning, limited only to *cash* receipts. The tax law concept of gross income, however, appears to rest on an imprecisely defined, sliding scale somewhere between these two views.

Section 61(a), the definitional provision of the Internal Revenue Code, describes gross income as "all income from whatever source derived" — a catch-all description that was borrowed from the text of the Sixteenth Amendment. Although Congress has, for varying policy reasons, excluded specific forms of "accessions to wealth" from gross income, neither the Sixteenth Amendment nor the Code provides a useful comprehensive definition of income or even specific guidelines for determining whether a given item falls within the meaning of the term. In fact, illustrative items were intentionally omitted from the first income tax bill because the term *income* was deemed complete. It became the task of the courts to interpret the sweeping language of the Code.

In Eisner v. Macomber, 252 U.S. 189 (1920), one of the first cases to interpret income, the Supreme Court stated that "income may be defined as the gain derived from labor, from capital, or from both combined." Id. at 207. Unfortunately, this definition created more uncertainty than it dispelled. According to this definition, items such as prizes, awards, scholarships, punitive damage awards, and discovered wealth might not constitute income, notwithstanding that they clearly represent an increase in wealth, because they are not the products of either personal services or capital investments. Of course, this led to clever taxpayers making precisely these arguments before the courts, that is, that particular receipts, though clearly accessions to wealth, should not be treated as income under *Eisner*.

Eventually, in the face of overwhelming confusion, uncertainty, and litigation generated by *Eisner*, the Supreme Court discarded the *Eisner* labor-capital formula in Commissioner v. Glenshaw Glass Co., 348 U.S. 426 (1955). The taxpayers in *Glenshaw Glass* argued that the receipt of a punitive damages award in a private antitrust action was not income under *Eisner*. The Supreme Court disagreed and stated that income includes any "undeniable accessions to wealth, clearly realized, and over which the taxpayers have complete dominion." Id. at 431. Although the *Glenshaw Glass* definition of income has become the accepted formulation, and it has resolved many of the *Eisner* problems, it does not necessarily provide an answer to many modern income inclusion questions because it cannot be applied precisely to the multifarious circumstances that generate tax consequences. In the wake of *Glenshaw Glass*, however, what is clear is that the definition of gross income can no longer be limited only to returns on labor or capital but encompasses any accession to wealth. Thus, one is left to look to other definitions of income to provide some semblance of definitional scope.

Most theoretical economists rely on some version of the so-called "Haig-Simons" formulation of income, named after two prominent economists who promoted it, which provides that "personal income may be defined as the algebraic sum of (1) the market value of rights exercised in consumption and (2) the change in the value of the store of property rights between the beginning and the end of the period. . . ." H. C. Simons, Personal Income Taxation 50 (1938). "Under this concept income is equal to the algebraic sum of consumption plus the change in the individual's net worth during the year or other accounting period. . . . It asks simply, how much could this individual have spent for consumption during the year while remaining as well off in terms of net worth at the end of the year as he was at the beginning of the year." Brazer, The Economics of Tax Reform, Proceedings of the Fifty-Sixth Annual Conference of the National Tax Association 47 (1963).

The economist's definition of income, however, is not suitable for determining tax liability. To begin with, not all "rights exercised in consumption" have market values. What is the market value of the music "consumed" at a free concert by a music lover? Moreover, the Haig-Simons definition includes as income all increases in the value of an individual's "store of property rights." For example, if a house increases in value during a year, the owner's net worth has increased. Even though there is a market, and thus a market value, insuperable practical problems would arise were Congress to tax the annual increase in the value of every taxpayer's home, absent a sale.

For the accountant, on the other hand, income encompasses only realized amounts — that is, assets that have been converted into money or other property by economic transactions, such as sales or exchanges. The mere increase in the value of property is not income to the accountant unless the appreciation in value has been "realized." The accounting concept of income and its realization requirement are more analogous to the tax law concept of income than the economist's definition. The tax law concept, however, goes beyond the accountant's definition because the tax law incorporates policy considerations in determining whether to tax an accession to wealth or whether to exclude it from gross income.

One conceptual difficulty in distilling an all-encompassing definition of income for purposes of tax law stems from the attempt by the law to steer a middle course between an economist's broad definition of income and an accountant's narrow definition of income, primarily for policy reasons. The student of tax law must therefore keep in mind that defining gross income for purposes of §61 requires a uniquely legal analysis, synthesizing the economic and accounting definitions with statutory interpretative tools and policy implications.

In analyzing gross income, four critical issues must be addressed: (1) *What* items are included in gross income? (2) What is the *amount* of such inclusions? (3) To *whom* are these accessions gross income? (4) *When* must an accession to wealth be included in gross income? Each of these questions is discussed separately in the following chapters.

B. FORMS OF GROSS INCOME

1. Compensation for Services and Sale of Appreciated Property

Code: §§61(a), 1001(a) to (c)
Regulations: §§1.61-1, 1.61-2(a)

The receipt of compensation for services is probably the most familiar source of gross income. Compensation for services takes many forms. Under §61(a)(1), gross income includes "[c]ompensation for services, including fees, commissions, fringe benefits, and similar items." These accessions to wealth arise from a compensatory relationship and are attributable to the rendition of labor. Consequently, the Service will closely scrutinize a transaction between an employer and employee that is not characterized as compensation, to determine if it is, in fact, disguised compensation.

Section 61(a)(3) includes "[g]ains derived from dealings in property," another broad category of gross income. Gain from a property transaction, which is statutorily defined in §1001(a), is computed by subtracting the adjusted basis of the property sold from the amount realized by the taxpayer on the disposition. Adjusted basis generally represents the taxpayer's cost of acquiring the property, while the amount realized represents the total economic benefit received in exchange for the property. Section 1001(b) defines the amount realized as the sum of any money received plus the fair market value of any property or other economic benefit received in the transaction. For example, if a taxpayer acquires property for $5,000 (the adjusted basis) and subsequently sells it for $15,000 (the amount realized), the gain is $10,000. Property transactions are discussed in greater detail in section E.

Problems

2-1.   Isaac Jackson's salary for the year, pursuant to his contract with his employer, was $35,000. He received monthly paychecks, which totaled $29,000 for the year — the differential attributable to withheld federal and state taxes. Ruth Jackson, his wife, received a salary that totaled $46,000, but her take-home pay was only $32,000 — the differential also attributable to withheld federal and state taxes.

a. What is the amount of the Jacksons' gross income?

b. What result if Ruth Jackson were offered a $10,000 bonus by her employer in recognition of her superior services, but she declined the offer? Does she have gross income?

2-2. Harold Jones purchased an automobile for $9,000. One year later, he sold the car for $10,000 and ten shares of publicly traded stock worth $1,000.

a. What is Jones's adjusted basis for the automobile?

b. What is the amount realized by Jones on the sale?

c. What is the amount included in Jones's gross income?

2. *Income without Receipt of Cash*

Code: §§61, 83(a)(1)

Regulations: §§1.61-2(d)(1) to (3); 1.61-21(a)(1) to (2); 1.61-21(b)(1) to (2); 1.83-1(a)(1)

Gross income questions frequently arise when a taxpayer receives something that, though clearly an economic benefit, is not money. Under the Haig-Simons definition of income, as well as that of *Glenshaw Glass*, such in-kind payments should be included in gross income because the recipient has enjoyed a "clear accession to wealth." Further, if gross income did not include in-kind receipts, taxpayers could avoid tax liability simply by negotiating to be paid in the form of food, free rent, and other necessities of life instead of cash. Consequently, the receipt of an in-kind benefit, whether property, services, or some other form of economic benefit, gives rise to two important issues: (1) does the in-kind receipt constitute gross income; and (2) if so, how is the value of such receipt measured in computing gross income?

Section 61 explicitly includes noncash receipts in gross income. Thus, a taxpayer who receives a parcel of land as compensation for services rendered has gross income. In effect, the recipient of compensation in the form of land or other in-kind benefit is treated the same as one who receives cash as compensation and uses the cash to purchase the land or other benefits.

Two important questions must be considered when determining which in-kind receipts are included in gross income. First, should the characterization of an in-kind receipt as gross income depend on the type of relationship that exists between the parties, such as employer/employee, neighbor/neighbor, parent/child? The type of relationship may be important because the more interpersonal and less business-based the relationship, the less likely it is that the receipt is compensatory in nature. Second, what effect does inclusion of noncash receipts in gross income have on the taxpayer's ability to pay the resulting tax liability? Of course, an in-kind receipt, unless reduced to cash, cannot be used to satisfy a tax liability.

In addition to determining which noncash receipts are included in gross income, the receipt of in-kind income often raises difficult valuation issues. Indeed, different valuation methods often dictate radically different tax results. The tax law generally adopts the purely objective standard of fair market value — that is, the price that would be reached in a transaction between a willing buyer and a willing seller. See, e.g., Reg. §20.2031-1(b).

In some limited instances, however, the tax law may use the taxpayer's subjective value of a particular item, or some other value between the objective and subjective values. The use of the subjective valuation method is based on the notion that in-kind receipts often do not provide the same freedom of choice as the receipt of cash, and therefore it would be unfair to tax the recipient on the market value of the receipt. For example, consider a taxpayer who receives a blue Ford Escort as compensation for services rendered. Although similar cars sell on the open market at a particular price (an objective standard), the taxpayer's subjective preference for a red Subaru may mean the taxpayer values the blue Ford Escort much lower than the market value (subjective standard). Therefore, it may be unfair to include the higher market price of the car in gross income since the taxpayer did not enjoy that much in consumption value. On the other hand, one can question the validity of this assumption because the taxpayer chose to accept the car, which indicates (at least in part) that the taxpayer acquiesced to receipt of the car in lieu of (an equal amount of) cash. Further, presumably little would stop the taxpayer from selling the blue Ford Escort to someone who did value it at the full fair market value, in which case the taxpayer would have received the full benefit of the value of the car. Thus, the fairness rationale might not always justify the use of a subjective standard of valuation.

For example, in Rooney v. Commissioner, 88 T.C. 523 (1987), the taxpayers, who had previously rendered services to clients in a precarious financial condition, agreed to accept goods and services as payment. The Tax Court held that the retail price of such items was the appropriate standard for determining the amount includable in gross income. The transactions did not constitute "forced purchases," which might permit an alternative, subjective valuation.

In reading the following case, consider whether it might be appropriate to use a valuation method other than the retail or "arm's-length" price. Does it make sense to apply the arm's-length price at all times unless the transaction was "forced" on the taxpayer? Should liquidity concerns or other considerations play a role in this determination?

McCANN v. UNITED STATES
81-2 U.S.T.C. ¶9689 (Ct. Cl. Tr. Div. 1981), aff'd,
696 F.2d 1386 (Fed. Cir. 1983)

WHITE, J.

. . . Elvia R. McCann and Mrs. Leone A. McCann, who are husband and wife and residents of Shreveport, Louisiana, made a round trip between Shreveport and Las Vegas, Nevada, in 1973 for the purpose of attending a seminar (the term used by the witnesses) that was conducted in Las Vegas by Mrs. McCann's employer, Security Industrial Insurance Company (Security). All the traveling and other expenses of Mr. and Mrs. McCann in connection with attendance at the Las Vegas seminar were paid by Security.

In filing their joint income tax return for 1973, the McCanns did not include in their gross income any amount reflecting the cost to Security of paying the McCanns' expenses on the Las Vegas trip.

The Internal Revenue Service, upon auditing the McCanns' 1973 income tax return, decided that the fair market value of the Las Vegas trip should have been included in the McCanns' gross income, determined the amount of the fair market value of the trip, and issued a deficiency notice.

Mr. and Mrs. McCann paid the deficiency, amounting to $199.16, plus accrued interest of $64.97. . . .

Security is engaged in the sale of life, burial, and accident insurance. . . .

An agent qualifies to attend a seminar if he or she achieved a specified net increase in sales during the preceding calendar year. . . .

Each agent . . . who qualifies to attend a seminar is entitled to take along his or her spouse, or another family member. . . . All travel and other expenses of employees and their guests attending seminars are paid by Security.

However, agents who qualify for seminars are not required to attend; and their promotional opportunities are not adversely affected if they fail to attend.

Security emphasizes the pleasure aspects of seminars. The company schedules sightseeing tours; furnishes participants with lists of tennis courts and golf courses at, and descriptive travel brochures concerning, seminar sites; and chooses locations which (in the opinion of the company) will have "excitement" and "charisma" for qualifying employees. . . .

The total cost to Security of the Las Vegas seminar amounted to $68,116.96. This amount included all the expenses (airfare, lodging, meals, cocktail parties, sightseeing tours, shows, local transportation, and gratuities) of each individual who attended the seminar. . . .

The first question to be decided . . . is whether, as determined by the Internal Revenue Service, the McCanns should have included in their 1973 income tax returns, as part of their gross income, an amount based upon the cost to Security of defraying their travel and other expenses on the trip to Las Vegas.

In this connection, the Code defines gross income as meaning "all income from whatever source derived. . . ." The Supreme Court has said that Congress intended by this statutory provision to tax *all* gains, except those specifically exempted (Commissioner v. Glenshaw Glass Co., 348 U.S. 426, 430 (1955)) and that the term income includes any economic or financial benefit conferred as compensation, however accomplished (Commissioner v. Smith, 324 U.S. 177, 181 (1945)).

An implementing regulation declares that gross income may include money, property, services, meals, accommodations, or stock, or may be in any other form. Treas. Reg. §1.61-1(a).

Thus, in a situation where an employer pays an employee's expenses on a trip that is a reward for services rendered by the employee, the value of the reward must be regarded as income to the employee.

The all-expenses trip to Las Vegas — with its airfare, lodging, meals, cocktails, sightseeing tours, shows, local transportation, and gratuities — which Mr. and Mrs. McCann received from Security was obviously an economic benefit to them. Moreover, they received this benefit as a reward for Mrs. McCann's good work in increasing her net sales by a specified amount during the preceding calendar year (1972). Only 47 agents, out of 400 agents employed by Security, qualified for the 1973 seminar in Las Vegas by achieving the required net increase in sales during 1972. The 47 agents (or so many of them as wished to make the trip) were rewarded by receiving from Security the all-expenses trip to Las Vegas for themselves and their spouses, or other family members. The 353 agents who failed to achieve the specified net increase in sales during 1972 did not receive the reward.

Therefore, the reward to Mrs. McCann, although not in the form of money, was clearly compensation to her for the services that she had rendered to Security during 1972, and was within the meaning of income, as that term is used in §61(a). . . .

When services are paid for in a form other than in money, it is necessary to determine the fair market value of the thing received. Treas. Reg. §1.61-2(d)(1).

In the present case, the Internal Revenue Service decided that the fair market value of the Las Vegas trip which Mr. and Mrs. McCann received from Security was equivalent to the cost of the trip to Security. At the trial, the plaintiff did not introduce any evidence challenging the correctness of the administrative determination on this point. Accordingly, in view of the presumption of legality which supports official administrative actions the determination of the Internal Revenue Service concerning the fair market value of the Las Vegas trip which Mr. and Mrs. McCann received from Security will be accepted by the court as correct. . . .

Note on United States v. Gotcher

Although the court in *McCann* found that the value of the trip to Las Vegas was included in gross income, cases with similar facts have given rise to opposite results. One such case is United States v. Gotcher, 401 F.2d 118 (5th Cir. 1968). The taxpayer in *Gotcher* was a car dealer who received an all-expenses-paid trip to Germany to tour a Volkswagen automobile manufacturing facility. The taxpayer had been offered a Volkswagen dealership in the United States, and Volkswagen paid for the trip to Germany in an effort to convince him that the dealership was a sound investment. The Commissioner asserted a tax deficiency based on the taxpayer's failure to include the value of the trip in his gross income.

In holding that the value of the trip was not includable in income, the court recognized two prerequisites to gross income: (1) "there must be an economic gain" and (2) "this gain must primarily benefit the taxpayer personally." Id. at 121. The court concluded that the trip was predominantly business-related and that the taxpayer did not benefit personally from it.

The court cited two reasons in support of its conclusion. First, the taxpayer spent most of his time in Germany touring manufacturing facilities and dealerships. Second, Volkswagen planned both the schedule and the facilities to be toured. Recalling the Supreme Court's definition of income articulated in *Glenshaw Glass*, the court found that the taxpayer's lack of control over the trip (the potential economic gain) weighed heavily in the taxpayer's favor. The court found that the personal benefit received was clearly subordinate to the business purpose of the trip. "When this indirect economic gain is subordinate to an overall business purpose, the recipient is not taxed." Id. at 124.

A comparison of the facts in *McCann* and *Gotcher* helps explain their differing results. The most significant difference was that McCann's trip was organized primarily for the personal benefit of the agents while Gotcher's trip was organized primarily for the benefit of Volkswagen. In addition, in *McCann*, the taxpayer was an employee of the company providing the benefit, while in *Gotcher* the taxpayer was not. In *McCann*, the agents were not required to attend the seminars, while in *Gotcher* the court found that the taxpayer had no choice but to go to Germany due to the "reality of the business world." Finally, in *McCann*, the taxpayer received significant amounts of time for personal diversions in Las Vegas, while in *Gotcher* the taxpayer's trip was preplanned and controlled.

Notwithstanding the intuitive appeal of *Gotcher* (and the self-interested preference of taxpayers to avoid income from employer paid trips), unsurprisingly the Internal Revenue Service has been less than enthusiastic about adopting a broad reading of *Gotcher*. Further, as discussed in more detail in Chapter 3, Treasury Regulations provide a more explicit way to avoid income to employees for employer-mandated business trips under so-called "accountable plan" rules.

Problems

2-3. In December, Matilda Smith received an automobile as a sales bonus from her employer. At the time, the list price of the car was $12,000.
   a. Does she have gross income? If so, how much?
   b. What result if she sold the car one year later for $14,000?

2-4. Geraldine Sikes worked for Raton Corporation, which owned a house in which it allowed Sikes to live rent-free. The rental value of the house was $20,000 per year, partly because the property included a private tennis court. Without the tennis court, the house would have had a rental value of $18,500 per year. Sikes not only hated tennis and never used the court but actually felt that it constituted an eyesore.
   a. Does Sikes have gross income and, if so, in what amount?
   b. What result in *a* if Sikes paid the corporation $9,000 per year to rent the house?
   c. What result in *a* if Sikes agreed to make the house available, once a week, for company cocktail parties? Once a month? Once a year?

2-5. Terrence Moots, a law firm associate, is sent on a five-day trip at his employer's expense to see a client in Paris, France, a city that he wanted to visit. What result if:
   a. Each evening, after concluding business discussions, Moots spends five hours sightseeing with a group of vacationing tourists?
   b. Moots remains in Paris, at his own expense, for a one-week vacation at the end of the business trip?
   c. In *a* and *b*, Moots's spouse accompanies him, and the law firm pays her expenses for the first five days?

2-6. Professor Albert Johnson received free copies of recently published casebooks from publishers who hoped he would use their books in his courses. The retail sales price of the textbooks received by Johnson during the year was $400.
   a. Are there any gross income consequences on receipt of the books?
   b. What result in *a* if Johnson received only one book with a retail sales price of $17?
   c. What result to Johnson if he sells the books to students for $300?

3. *Barter Transactions*

Code: §§61, 1001
Regulations: §§1.61-1(a), 1.61-2(d)(1)

As demonstrated by the *McCann* decision, gross income may arise from unconventional in-kind receipts. The Regulations confirm and broaden this concept by stipulating that income may be realized "in the form of services, meals, accommodations, stock, or other property, as well as in cash." Reg. §1.61-1(a).

For example, an attorney who wishes to have work done in her garden has three options: (1) render legal services to others for cash and use the funds derived from such efforts to pay a gardener; (2) render legal services to the gardener in exchange for the gardening; or (3) do the gardening herself. In the first situation, both the attorney and the gardener clearly have gross income to the extent of their cash receipts because the cash represents compensation for services. In the third situation, the attorney would have no gross income, even though she realized an economic benefit (this is an example of imputed income, which is not included in gross income and is discussed in section D3.) The second situation represents a "barter transaction." Barter transactions present difficulties because they partially resemble both the first and third alternatives, but are not identical to either.

In Revenue Ruling 79-24, which follows, the Service considered barter transactions in which services were exchanged for services and rent-free use of property. If the parties in these barter cases had dealt with each other on a cash payment basis and structured the transactions independently of each other (for example, the lawyer hires the housepainter and pays cash for his services, and, thereafter, the housepainter hires the lawyer and does the same), is there any doubt as to the proper result? How, if at all, should a barter transaction differ for tax purposes? Should it be the substance or the form of these transactions that governs the tax results? If there is no difference in the substance of barter and cash transactions, why would taxpayers enter into barter exchanges?

REV. RUL. 79-24
1979-1 C.B. 60

Facts

Situation 1. In return for personal legal services performed by a lawyer for a housepainter, the housepainter painted the lawyer's personal residence. Both the lawyer and the housepainter are members of a barter club, an organization that annually furnishes its members a directory of members and the services they provide. All the members of the club are professional or trades persons. Members contact other members directly and negotiate the value of the services to be performed.

Situation 2. An individual who owned an apartment building received a work of art created by a professional artist in return for the rent-free use of an apartment for six months by the artist.

LAW

The applicable sections of the Internal Revenue Code . . . and the Income Tax Regulations thereunder are 61(a) and 1.61-2, relating to compensation for services.

Section 1.61-2(d)(1) of the regulations provides that if services are paid for other than in money, the fair market value of the property or services taken in payment must be included in income. If the services were rendered at a stipulated price, such price will be presumed to be the fair market value of the compensation received in the absence of evidence to the contrary.

HOLDINGS

Situation 1. The fair market value of the services received by the lawyer and the housepainter are includible in their gross incomes under section 61 of the Code.

Situation 2. The fair market value of the work of art and the six months fair rental value of the apartment are includible in the gross incomes of the apartment-owner and the artist under section 61 of the Code.

Problem

2-7.   William Presser, a former newspaper editor, agreed to edit the law review article of his friend, John Gibson, in exchange for the use of Gibson's beach house. Presser spent several evenings working on the article. He and his family then spent the Thanksgiving weekend at Gibson's cottage.

a. Does Presser have any gross income, and, if so, how is the amount determined?

b. Does Gibson have any gross income, and, if so, how is the amount determined?

c. How would the answers to *a* and *b* change if, in addition, Presser was required to pay Gibson $1 per night for the use of the beach house?

d. What result if instead of editing Gibson's article, Presser promised to have a wooden deck constructed in the rear of Gibson's cottage in return for use of the cottage for two months? Assume Presser spent $200 for materials and paid a contractor $800 for labor. The increased value of the house was $1,000.

e. What result in *d* if Presser spends $200 for materials, but instead of hiring a contractor he performs the labor himself?

4.   Unanticipated Gains

Code: §61(a)
Regulations: §1.61-14

As noted earlier, in *Glenshaw Glass* the Supreme Court abandoned "the gain from labor or capital" standard for defining gross income and held that punitive damages awarded in a private antitrust suit were gross income. The new standard of "undeniable accessions to wealth" announced in *Glenshaw Glass* appeared on its face to be all-encompassing; upon closer inpsection, however, an examination of the facts in *Glenshaw Glass* demonstrates a nexus between the income-earning activities (business activities hampered by antitrust violations) and the resulting receipt (the punitive damages), thus leaving open the question of whether receipts without such a nexus are included in the definition of gross income.

After *Glenshaw Glass*, lower courts and Treasury Regulations addressed this gap, further refining and expanding the boundaries of the gross income concept to include receipts without a compensatory nexus. For example, could receipts for such minimal activities as the finding money in the street constitute gross income? *See* Cesarini v. United States, reproduced below.

Further, should it matter if unanticipated gains are in the form of cash as opposed to property or other noncash items? Should the taxpayer who finds $100 on the street be treated the same as the taxpayer who finds a gold brooch in the backyard? If so, then, as with income arising from noncash compensation, the proper method of valuation of unanticipated noncash gains arises as an issue. Should the conceptual difficulty inherent in requiring inclusion of unanticipated gains in gross income militate in favor of a more lenient valuation standard? Moreover, to what extent should the lack of transferability affect whether an item constitutes gross income, or instead should it affect the valuation issue? These issues will be considered in more detail in section B5 of this chapter.

CESARINI v. UNITED STATES
296 F. Supp. 3 (N.D. Ohio 1969), aff'd per curiam,
428 F.2d 812 (6th Cir. 1970)

YOUNG, J.

. . . In 1957, the plaintiffs purchased a used piano at an auction sale for approximately $15.00. . . . In 1964, while cleaning the piano, plaintiffs discovered the sum of $4,467.00 in old currency. . . . Being unable to ascertain who put the money there, plaintiffs exchanged the old currency for new at a bank, and reported the sum of $4,467.00 on their 1964 joint income tax return as ordinary income from other sources. On October 18, 1965, plaintiffs filed an amended return . . . requesting a refund in the amount of $836.51, the amount allegedly overpaid as a result of the former inclusion of $4,467.00 in the original return for the calendar year of 1964. . . .

Plaintiffs make [two] alternative contentions in support of their claim that the sum of $836.51 should be refunded to them. First, that the $4,467.00 found in the piano is not includable in gross income under Section 61. Secondly, even if the retention of the cash constitutes a realization of ordinary income under Section 61, it was due and owing in the year the piano was purchased, 1957, and by 1964, the statute of limitations had elapsed. . . .

. . . Subsections (1) through (15) of Section 61(a) . . . list fifteen items specifically included in the computation of the taxpayer's gross income, and Part II of Subchapter B of the 1954 Code (Sections 71 et seq.) deals with other items expressly included in gross income. While neither of these listings expressly includes the type of income which is at issue in the case at bar, Part III of Subchapter B (Sections 101 et seq.) deals with items specifically *excluded* from gross income, and found money is not listed in those sections either. This absence of express mention in any of the code sections necessitates a return to the "all income from whatever source" language of Section 61(a) of the code, and the express statement there that gross income is "not limited to" the following fifteen examples. Section 1.61-1(a) of the Treasury Regulations, the corresponding section to Section 61(a) in the 1954 Code, reiterates this broad construction of gross income, providing in part:

> Gross income means all income from whatever source derived, unless excluded by law. *Gross income includes income realized in any form*, whether in money, property, or services. (Emphasis added.)

The decisions of the United States Supreme Court have frequently stated that this broad all-inclusive language was used by Congress to exert the full measure of its taxing power under the Sixteenth Amendment to the United States Constitution.

In addition, the Government in the instant case cites and relies upon an I.R.S. Revenue Ruling which is undeniably on point:

> The finder of treasure-trove is in receipt of taxable income, for Federal income tax purposes, to the extent of its value in United States currency, for the taxable year in which it is reduced to undisputed possession.

Not only have the taxpayers failed to list a specific exclusion in the instant case, but also the Government *has* pointed to express language covering the found money, even though it would not be required to do so under the broad language of Section 61(a) and the . . . Supreme Court decisions interpreting it. . . .

Although not cited by either party, and noticeably absent from the Government's brief, the following Treasury Regulation appears in the 1964 Regulations, the year of the return in dispute:

§1.61-14. Miscellaneous Items of Gross Income

> (a) In general. In addition to the items enumerated in section 61(a), there are many other kinds of gross income. . . . *Treasure trove, to the extent of its value in United States currency, constitutes gross income for the taxable year in which it is reduced to undisputed possession*. (Emphasis added.)

. . . This Court is of the opinion that Treas. Reg. §1.61-14(a) is dispositive of the major issue in this case if the $4,467.00 found in the piano was "reduced to undisputed possession" in the year petitioners reported it, for this Regulation was applicable to returns filed in the calendar year of 1964.

This brings the Court to the second contention of the plaintiffs: that if any tax was due, it was in 1957 when the piano was purchased, and by 1964 the Government was blocked from collecting it by reason of the statute of limitations. Without reaching the question of whether the voluntary payment in 1964 constituted a *waiver* on the part of the taxpayers, this Court finds that the $4,467.00

sum was properly included in gross income for the calendar year of 1964. Problems of when title vests, or when possession is complete in the field of federal taxation, in the absence of definitive federal legislation on the subject, are ordinarily determined by reference to the law of the state in which the taxpayer resides, or where the property around which the dispute centers is located. Since both the taxpayers and the property in question are found within the State of Ohio, Ohio law must govern as to when the found money was "reduced to undisputed possession" within the meaning of Treas. Reg. §1.61-14 and Rev. Rul. 61-53-1, Cum. Bull. 17.

In Ohio, there is no statute specifically dealing with the rights of owners and finders of treasure trove, and in the absence of such a statute the common-law rule of England applies, so that "title belongs to the finder as against all the world except the true owner." Niederlehner v. Weatherly, 78 Ohio App. 263, 69 N.E.2d 787 (1946), appeal dismissed, 146 Ohio St. 697, 67 N.E.2d 713 (1946). The *Niederlehner* case held, inter alia, that the owner of real estate upon which money is found does not have title as against the finder. Therefore, in the instant case if plaintiffs had resold the piano in 1958, not knowing of the money within it, they later would not be able to succeed in an action against the purchaser who *did* discover it. Under Ohio law, the plaintiffs must have actually *found* the money to have superior title over all but the true owner, and they did not discover the old currency until 1964. Unless there is present a specific state statute to the contrary, the majority of jurisdictions are in accord with the Ohio rule. Therefore, this Court finds that the $4,467.00 in old currency was not "reduced to undisputed possession" until its actual discovery in 1964, and thus the United States was not barred by the statute of limitations from collecting the $836.51 in tax during that year. . . .

. . . [T]his taxpayer's suit for a refund . . . must be dismissed.

Problems

2-8. Lucinda Paskin was digging in her backyard when she found a gold brooch. A reputable appraiser estimated the value of the find to be $16,000. Two weeks later, at an auction, Paskin sold the brooch for $14,000. Does Paskin have gross income and, if so, how much?

2-9. Professor Harold Levi liked to browse through various bookstores in the cities that he visited. In one old bookstore in Paris he paid $850 for a rare first edition of Joyce's *Ulysses*, which he knew was worth at least $2,000. When Levi returned to the United States, he sold the book to a friend for $1,800.

    a.   Does Levi have gross income when he buys the book? If so, how much?

    b.   Does he have gross income when he sells the book? If so, how much?

    c.   What result in *a* if Levi had purchased the rare book for $850 from his employer at a time when both parties knew it was worth $2,000?

    d.   What result in *a* if instead of purchasing the book, Levi had found it in a trash bin?

    e.   What result if Levi's friend found the book and later, not knowing the value of the book, sold it to Levi for $5?

5. *Prizes and Awards*

Code: §74

Much like treasure trove, prizes and awards present an interesting challenge to the tax law conception of gross income. Like other gross income, prizes and awards on their face clearly represent an accession to wealth. After all, who wouldn't want to win the lottery? But this is not as clear as it first appears. All players in the lottery paid the same full fair market value for their tickets, but it just so happened that one was worth a lot of money while the others became worthless. So why isn't this the same as a house appreciating in value? Further, in most cases, the taxpayer has undertaken some effort to win the prize or award, such as buying a lottery ticket or entering a contest, making it seem like the prize is some type of reward to effort. But what if the award was unsolicited, such as a Nobel Prize? Does that change the analysis? Should it?

Much to the dismay of gameshow, sweepstakes, and lottery winners, Congress enacted §74 to provide the answer. Section 74(a) provides that prizes and awards are generally included in gross income. Regulation §1.74-1(a) states that "[p]rizes and awards which are includable in gross income include (but are not limited to) amounts received from radio and television giveaway shows, door prizes, and awards in contests of all types."

Prior to its amendment in 1986, §74(b) provided a limited exception to the broad sweep of §74(a) in certain cases. The §74(b) exclusion was designed to reward activities that primarily benefit society rather than the individual who received the award. That did not mean, however, that the prize could not benefit the recipient. Prior to 1986, awards such as Nobel and Pulitzer prizes, notwithstanding their sizable amounts, qualified for the exclusion even if the recipients kept the cash prizes for their own consumption. Under the prior version of §74(b), "prizes and awards made primarily in recognition of religious, charitable, scientific, educational, artistic, literary, or civic achievement" were excludable only if the recipient (1) took no action to compete for the award and (2) was not required as a condition of the award to perform substantial future services.

By 1986, this was considered too generous, at least with respect to those taxpayers who kept the cash prizes, leading Congress to reverse its longstanding legislative approach to such meritorious efforts. The current version of §74(b) now only excludes prizes or awards from gross income if they are made primarily in recognition of religious, charitable, scientific, educational, artistic, literary, or civic achievement, and (1) the recipient was selected without any action on his part to enter the contest or proceeding, (2) the recipient is not required to render substantial future services as a condition to receiving the prize or award, and (3) the prize or award is transferred to a governmental unit or certain charitable organizations. In justifying its expansion of the scope of §74, Congress emphasized the economic enhancement that arises on the receipt of prizes and awards and the definitional difficulties that arose under §74(b).

Prizes and awards generally increase an individual's net wealth in the same manner as any other receipt of an equivalent amount that adds to the individual's economic well-being. For example, the receipt of an award for scientific or artistic achievement in the amount of $10,000 increases the recipient's net wealth and ability to pay taxes to the same extent as the receipt of $10,000 in wages, dividends, or prizes and awards that are taxable under current law. Accordingly, the committee believes that prizes and awards should generally be includable in income even if received due to achievement in fields such as the arts and sciences.

In addition, the committee is concerned about problems of complexity that have arisen as a result of the present-law exclusion under section 74(b). The questions of what constitutes a qualifying form of achievement, whether an individual took action to enter a contest or proceeding, and whether or not the conditions of receiving a prize or award involve rendering "substantial" services, have all caused some difficulty in this regard. Finally, the present-law exclusion may in some circumstances serve as a possible vehicle for the payment of disguised compensation.

H.R. Rep. No. 426, 99th Cong., 1st Sess. 104 (1985).

Prizes and awards present particularly difficult valuation issues, precisely because they are not a product of negotiated exchanges. In a barter transaction, by contrast, the taxpayers agree to an even exchange of value in the form of rent, services, or both. Of course, most people would accept an unsolicited in-kind prize even if it is not exactly of the type they would have chosen absent the prize. If a game show offered you a free Toyota Prius but you really wanted a Dodge pickup truck, would you turn down the free Prius? Does that mean the Prius is worth the same to you as someone who really wants one? Should it matter?

TURNER v. COMMISSIONER
T.C. Memo 1954-38

MURDOCK, J.

FINDINGS OF FACT

The petitioners are husband and wife who filed a joint return for 1948 with the collector of internal revenue for the District of North Carolina. They reported salary of $4,535.16 for 1948.

Reginald, whose name had been selected by chance from a telephone book, was called on the telephone on April 18, 1948 and was asked to name a song that was being played on a radio program. He gave the correct name of the song and then was given the opportunity to identify a second song and thus to compete for a grand prize. He correctly identified the second song and in consideration of his efforts was awarded a number of prizes, including two round trip first-class steamship tickets for a cruise between New York City and Buenos Aires. The prize was to be one ticket if the winner was unmarried, but, if he was married, his wife was to receive a ticket also. The tickets were not transferable and were good only within one year on a sailing date approved by the agent of the steamship company.

The petitioners reported income on their return of $520, representing income from the award of the two tickets. The Commissioner, in determining the deficiency, increased the income from this source to $2,220, the retail price of such tickets.

Marie was born in Brazil. The petitioners had two sons. Reginald negotiated with the agent of the steamship company, as a result of which he surrendered his rights to the two first-class tickets, and upon payment of $12.50 received four round trip tourist steamship tickets between New York City and Rio de Janeiro. The petitioners and their two sons used those tickets in making a trip from New York City to Rio de Janeiro and return during 1948.

The award of the tickets to Reginald represented income to him in the amount of $1,400.

OPINION

Persons desiring to buy round trip first-class tickets between New York and Buenos Aires in April 1948, similar to those to which the petitioners were entitled, would have had to pay $2,220 for them. The petitioners, however, were not such persons. The winning of the tickets did not provide them with something which they needed in the ordinary course of their lives and for which they would have made an expenditure in any event, but merely gave them an opportunity to enjoy a luxury otherwise beyond their means. Their value to the petitioners was not equal to their retail cost. They were not transferable and not salable and there were other restrictions on their use. But even had the petitioner been permitted to sell them, his experience with other more salable articles indicates that he would have had to accept substantially less than the cost of similar tickets purchased from the steamship company and would have had selling expenses. Probably the petitioners could have refused the tickets and avoided the tax problem. Nevertheless, in order to obtain such benefits as they could from winning the tickets, they actually took a cruise accompanied by their two sons, thus obtaining free board, some savings in living expenses, and the pleasure of the trip. It seems proper that a substantial amount should be included in their income for 1948 on account of the winning of the tickets. The problem of arriving at a proper fair figure for this purpose is difficult. The evidence to assist is meager, perhaps unavoidably so. The Court, under such circumstances, must arrive at some figure and has done so.

Problems

2-10. Roberta Jacobson, a law professor specializing in the integration of the fields of anthropology and the law, was awarded the MacArthur Foundation "creative genius" award of $50,000 a year for five years. Does Jacobson have gross income?

2-11. In the Olympic Games, Jennifer Heiden wins five three-ounce gold medals.
   a. Does Heiden have gross income?
   b. If so, what method of valuation should be used to determine the amount of gross income?

C. THE ROLE OF DEBT IN GROSS INCOME

The treatment of debt plays a vital role in the United States federal income tax laws. An understanding of many complexities in the tax laws, including virtually all tax shelter transactions, requires an understanding of the tax, legal, and economic characteristics of debt.

1. What Is Debt?

Debt in its most basic form is the transfer of money in exchange for the transferee's promise to repay in the future. The lender is generally referred to as the "creditor," and the borrower is generally referred to as the "debtor." Upon making a loan, the creditor transfers money to the debtor in exchange for the debtor's obligation to repay the amount of money loaned, plus interest. The obligation to repay, which generally stipulates that the debtor repay a fixed amount at a specified time in the future, is an asset of the creditor, and a liability to the debtor, regardless of the form it takes — that is, whether it is reflected in a contract, in a negotiable instrument such as a bond, or otherwise.

From a balance sheet perspective, because the debtor receives money from the creditor in return for the obligation to repay the creditor a corresponding amount, the debtor is no better or worse off immediately after a loan than immediately before such loan. From a cash-flow perspective, however, the debtor is better off, since there is now cash available for investment or consumption that was not available prior to receiving the loan. In fact, that is the entire point of incurring the debt in the first place.

All debt issued at arm's length between unrelated third parties will bear interest, regardless whether it is paid regularly or at maturity. Interest is commonly defined as "compensation for the use or forbearance of money." Deputy v. DuPont, 308 U.S. 488, 498 (1940). In essence, the creditor is charging the debtor for the cash-flow privilege of immediately using money that the creditor could have consumed immediately rather than making the loan.

From a legal perspective, interest is often stated as a single rate on the principal amount of the loan. For example, a $1,000 loan may bear 10 percent simple interest annually, meaning that the debtor will owe the creditor $100 interest at the end of each year. Interest is not a single economic concept, however; generally, interest consists of three components:

1. Inflation: Inflation is the increase in the costs of goods and services over time (the Consumer Price Index is one measure of inflation). As a result of inflation, goods generally cost more in the future than they cost currently. Thus, it will require more cash to acquire the identical amount of goods or services in the future than it does today.
2. Time value of money: People generally prefer to have the choice to consume currently rather than have to wait to consume in the future. As a result, money has an inherent time value — that is, money today is worth more than money tomorrow. To induce a creditor to lend money in exchange for

a promise to repay, a creditor will require compensation for the creditor's deferral of consumption.

3. Credit risk: Whenever a creditor lends money to a debtor, the creditor assumes a risk that the debtor will not repay the loan, notwithstanding the debtor's promise to pay. As a result, a creditor will charge the debtor for the assumed risk that the loan may not be repaid.

Taking these factors into consideration, the amount of interest charged on any particular loan will differ depending on its terms. For example, due to time value of money, the longer amount of time before a loan must be repaid (or "matures"), generally the higher the interest rate that will be charged. Similarly, the higher the inflation rate at the time a loan is made, or the higher it is expected to be during the life of the loan, the higher the interest rate.

Interest generally is calculated in one of two methods: (1) simple, and (2) compound. Simple interest for any period is the product of the stated interest rate and the stated principal amount of the loan, regardless whether interest is paid. Thus, as noted above, a $1,000 loan bearing simple interest of 10 percent per year will result in a $100 interest obligation each year (that is, 10 percent of $10,000).

Compound interest is more complicated. Compound interest is calculated by adding accrued but unpaid interest for a period back into the principal before calculating the next period's interest. For example, if a $1,000 loan bears 10-percent interest per year compounded semiannually, and the debtor is only required to make payments annually, then at the end of the first six months $50 of interest (that is, 5 percent of $1,000) would compound (or be added to the principal), resulting in a total principal of $1,050. At the end of the second six months, interest of $52.50 (that is, 5 percent of $1,050) would compound. Thus, at the end of the year, total interest would be $102.50 ($50 plus $52.50), as opposed to $100 in the case of simple interest.

Compound interest represents the "re-investment" potential of deferred payments of interest. If interest did not compound, every creditor would require that all interest be paid as it accrued. Returning to the previous example, if the debtor paid the creditor $50 interest at the end of the first six months, the creditor could make a new $50 loan to a third party at 10-percent interest. At the end of the second six-month period, the creditor would receive another $50 from the initial debtor, plus an additional $2.50 (that is, 5 percent of $50) from the second debtor. A creditor will therefore only permit a debtor to defer payment of interest if the creditor is made whole for this opportunity cost (that is, not being able to make this second loan) by charging compound interest.

As the examples demonstrate, compound interest grows faster than simple interest, even if they are accruing at the same nominal rate, and the difference grows exponentially the longer interest continues to compound.

2. *Receipts Subject to Claims*

In determining whether receipts constitute accessions to wealth, it is important to consider whether cash or other property received is subject to the claims of third parties. Borrowed funds are a common example of a receipt of this type. As discussed above, if a taxpayer borrows $1,000 from a bank, although the taxpayer has received $1,000 to use and spend as he or she pleases, the acknowledged obligation to repay $1,000 makes it clear that no net accession to wealth has arisen. As a result, few would categorize the $1,000 cash received by the borrower as an undeniable accession to wealth. The tax law has reached the same conclusion. See United States v. Rochelle, 384 F.2d 748, 751 (5th Cir. 1967) ("A loan does not in itself constitute income to the borrower, because whatever temporary economic benefit he derives from the use of the funds is offset by the corresponding obligation to repay").

In some instances, the obligation to repay may be disputed, however. For example, when a debtor pays a disputed debt, the creditor takes the payment under a "claim of right," which is subject to the debtor's claim. In other words, the creditor is claiming the ownership right over the money, notwithstanding that the creditor may be required to refund all or part of the payment if the dispute is subsequently settled in the debtor's favor. The Supreme Court, in North America Oil Consolidated v. Burnet, 286 U.S. 417 (1932), held that an accession to wealth held under such a "claim of right" is sufficient for income inclusion, notwithstanding a competing claim.

The claim of right doctrine, enunciated by the court in *North American Oil* (*NAO*), provides that when a taxpayer receives funds with (1) a contingent obligation to repay, because the sum is either disputed or mistakenly paid, and (2) no limitation on the use of the funds exists, those funds are included in the taxpayer's income in the year they are received. In *NAO*, the taxpayer corporation received funds in 1917 that were the subject of ongoing litigation. The dispute continued until 1922, when the suit was resolved in favor of North American Oil, which as a result did not have to repay the sum. The issue was in what year the funds held contingently from 1917 until 1922 should be reported as income by North American Oil. Unlike traditional debt, although North American Oil arguably had an obligation to repay the funds, the obligation was contingent on the outcome of the litigation; thus, the initial receipt of the funds was without restriction as to their use or disposition. The Supreme Court held that because North American Oil became entitled to the funds, subject to a claim of right, in 1917, that was the proper year for their inclusion in income. The Supreme Court reasoned that such a rule gave substance to the annual accounting period, giving finality to the tax year by not holding it open until the eventual resolution of the dispute, stating:

> The net profits earned by the property in 1916 were not income of the year 1922 — the year in which the litigation with the government was finally terminated. They became income of the company in 1917, when it first became entitled to them and when it actually received them. If a taxpayer receives earnings under a claim of right and without restriction as to its disposition, he has received income which he is required to return, even though it may still be claimed that he is not entitled to retain the money, and even though he may still be adjudged liable to restore its equivalent. . . . If in 1922 the Government had prevailed, and the company had been obliged to refund the profits received in 1917, it would have been entitled to a deduction from the profits of 1922, not from those of any earlier year.

Id. at 424.

As demonstrated by the cases that follow, the fundamental proposition — borrowed funds are not included in income, but funds subject to a claim of right are — is tested if the borrower does not acknowledge an obligation to repay. In attempting to develop the contours of the doctrine, courts have focused on several factors: (1) the recipient's legal obligation to repay; (2) the recipient's recognition of an obligation to repay; and (3) an intention by the recipient to satisfy that obligation. In reading the following cases, consider what weight these three factors should be given in making this determination.

INDUCTOTHERM INDUSTRIES, INC. v. UNITED STATES
351 F.3d 120 (3rd Cir. 2003)

Ambro, Circuit Judge.

This appeal involves a dispute between a taxpayer and the Internal Revenue Service about the proper time to recognize income and losses. The taxpayer maintains that it was not required to recognize the proceeds from the sale of goods as income in the year it received those proceeds because the funds were subject to a governmental blocking order and, under the Claim of Right Doctrine, it did not have unfettered discretion as to the funds. . . . The District Court held in favor of the Government. . . . We affirm.

Background

In 1989, taxpayer Inductotherm Industries, Inc. ("Inductotherm") . . . contracted with Iraq to manufacture three vacuum furnaces. One furnace ("Furnace A") is an Induction Skull Melting Furnace. The other two ("Furnaces B and C") are Electron Beam Furnaces — a technology that later became disfavored and apparently is no longer in widespread use today. Iraq represented that the furnaces would be used to manufacture prosthetics for veterans of the Iran-Iraq war. It later came to light that Iraq instead intended to use the furnaces in its nuclear weapons program. Inductotherm was unaware of Iraq's true intentions.

As the three furnaces were about to be exported to Iraq, it invaded Kuwait. In response, on August 2, 1990, President George H.W. Bush entered an Executive Order — the Iraqi Sanctions Regulation — blocking all property in which Iraq had an interest. As applied to Inductotherm, the Executive Order precluded the sale or transfer of the three furnaces without the permission of the Office of Foreign Assets Control ("OFAC"). Moreover, all funds in which Inductotherm had an interest due to the Iraqi contract were blocked pursuant to the Executive Order unless OFAC issued a license unblocking them. At the time, those funds in which Iraq potentially had an interest included a $6.4 million letter of credit ("LC") and Iraq's $1.1 million deposit for the three furnaces. Moreover, because Inductotherm had received this $1.1 million deposit, OFAC took the position that Iraq had a property interest in all three furnaces and thus they were blocked property.

To mitigate its losses, Inductotherm attempted to find new buyers for the furnaces. It sold Furnace A to Mitsubishi in its 1991 tax year for approximately

$1.8 million. Rather than place the sale proceeds in a blocked account, Inductotherm commingled them with other corporate funds . . .

When the Government learned of the Mitsubishi sale, it directed Inductotherm to block the sale proceeds. . . . Inductotherm disputed, inter alia, the applicability of the Executive Order to the sale proceeds, and protracted litigation ensued. . . . Ultimately, the D.C. Circuit held that the furnaces, and the proceeds therefrom, were blocked property but could be released if Inductotherm placed the $1.1 million deposit in a blocked account . . .

Meanwhile, when filing its tax returns, Inductotherm did not record the 1991 Furnace A sale proceeds as taxable income in 1991, reasoning that . . . it did not have unfettered discretion to dispose of the proceeds. It urges that, under the Claim of Right Doctrine . . . if a taxpayer does not have unfettered discretion with respect to funds, those funds need not be recognized as income. . . .

DISCUSSION

A. FURNACE A

Inductotherm argues that it was not required to treat the sale proceeds for Furnace A as income in 1991 under the Claim of Right Doctrine. That Doctrine, set out in North American Oil Consolidated v. Burnet, 286 U.S. 417 (1932), holds that funds received by a taxpayer will be considered income if (1) "a taxpayer receives earnings under a claim of right" and (2) "without restriction as to its disposition," "even though it may still be claimed that [the taxpayer] is not entitled to retain the money, and even though [the taxpayer] may still be adjudged liable to restore its equivalent." Id. at 424.

Here, Inductotherm has conceded that it received the Furnace A proceeds under a "claim of right," i.e., it acknowledged its entitlement to the proceeds. However, it disputes that it held the Furnace A proceeds without restriction as to disposition in 1991. Inductotherm reasons that the Executive Order, issued during its 1991 tax year, required it to place the funds in a blocked account (which, however, it did not do) and thus restricted its discretion as to those funds in 1991. Inductotherm relies principally on a line of cases holding that public utilities were not required to recognize as income customers' deposits . . . which those utilities clearly were obligated to return, despite the fact that the utilities commingled the funds (as Inductotherm did). See, e.g., Commissioner v. Indianapolis Power & Light Co., 493 U.S. 203 (1990) . . .

The Government argues that these utility cases are not analogous because the first prong of the Claim of Right Doctrine was not satisfied: the utilities did not claim that they were entitled to the funds for their own benefit. Rather, they conceded at all times that they held the funds in a fiduciary capacity or, at least, with a clear obligation to return the funds. Moreover, as to the second prong, the utilities' discretion with respect to the funds was at all times limited by extensive regulatory oversight by state administrative agencies. The Government directs our attention instead to James v. United States, 366 U.S. 213 (1961), which held that money embezzled must be included in income, even though it likely would have to be disgorged in the future. . . . In James, it was clear that the embezzler had no right to the funds at issue. Nonetheless, because the embezzler treated the funds as his own during the relevant tax year, he was required to recognize those funds as income.

We agree with the Government. As already noted, Inductotherm's concession (no doubt correct) that it asserted title to the proceeds of Furnace A's sale in 1991 answers the first prong of the Claim of Right Doctrine.

As to the Doctrine's second prong (no disposition restriction on the sale proceeds), Inductotherm, having commingled the funds instead of blocking them, placed itself in a position of complete dominion over those funds (at least during the 1991 tax year). In this context, the Executive Order was "a potential or dormant restriction . . . which depends on the future application of rules of law to present facts [and therefore was] not a 'restriction on use' within the meaning of North American Oil v. Burnet." Healy v. Commissioner, 345 U.S. 278 (1953). . . . [A]s with any regulation or criminal law, the Government had the discretion not to pursue Inductotherm's Executive Order violation. Thus, Inductotherm's control over the Furnace A proceeds was analogous to that of the embezzler in James . . .

That Inductotherm was required after the conclusion of the 1991 tax year to block the Furnace A proceeds is in no way relevant to the analysis. There are numerous cases in which a taxpayer treated funds as its own in one year, only to find that it was required to disgorge them in a later year. In all these cases, courts required the taxpayer to recognize the funds as income in the year received, notwithstanding the later disgorgement . . .

In this context, the Claim of Right Doctrine does not shield the Furnace A proceeds from being income in 1991. . . .

Under the Claim of Right Doctrine, Inductotherm was required to recognize proceeds from the sale of Furnace A in the year it received those proceeds, 1991. . . . We therefore affirm the District Court's grant of summary judgment in favor of the Government.

KREIMER v. COMMISSIONER
T.C. Memo 1983-672

DRENNEN, J. . . .

[The issue is] whether various amounts obtained by petitioners in the form of loans are includible in gross income. . . .

FINDINGS OF FACT . . .

Petitioners were interested in forming their own insurance surety company. In 1969, petitioners, along with a group of investors from St. Louis, formed Mount Vernon Investment Company (Investment), Mt. Vernon Surety Company (Surety), and Mt. Vernon Insurance Agency (Agency). . . .

Shortly after Surety was organized, petitioners sought to obtain reinsurance, that is, insurance to insure the surety bonds which Surety wrote. In this regard, they contacted Interstate Fire Insurance Company (Interstate) of Chattanooga, Tennessee. Initially, Interstate agreed to reinsure Surety for 50 percent of the losses incurred on surety bonds written in Surety's name. In addition, Agency was permitted to write surety (financial guarantee bonds) bonds in Interstate's name for up to $100,000 for each insured or risk. The purpose of this latter agreement was to allow Agency to write surety bonds on Surety's behalf in states other than Georgia, which was the only state in which Surety was licensed to engage in business. Surety agreed to reinsure Interstate 50 percent on surety bonds written by Agency in Interstate's name.

On September 29, 1969 Agency entered into an agreement with Old Reliable Fire Insurance Company (Old Reliable), which allowed Agency to write surety bonds in Old Reliable's name in Missouri up to a maximum limit on one insured or risk of $100,000. Surety agreed to reinsure Old Reliable for 50 percent of the surety bonds written to reinsure Old Reliable for the other 50 percent. . . .

In late 1970 and early 1971, friction developed between petitioners and the St. Louis investors. On March 10, 1971 petitioners entered into an agreement with the other shareholders of Investment to purchase all of the Surety and Agency stock owned by Investment and in return to sell all of their stock in Investment to Investment. Petitioners agreed to pay $675,000 cash for the Surety and Agency stock with the balance of the purchase price being paid for with the stock of Investment transferred by petitioners to Investment. . . .

OPINION

In order to finance their purchase of the majority stock of Surety and Agency from Investment for $675,000 cash plus other considerations, petitioners employed a scheme to borrow the necessary cash from banks or other lending agencies by using Interstate financial guarantee bonds which they were authorized to issue. Having doubts whether it was lawful for them to issue these surety bonds to secure loans made directly to themselves, and whether Interstate and/or the lending agencies would approve the issuance and use of such bonds as security for such loans, petitioners engaged the services of Lewis and others to disguise the true identity of themselves as the actual borrowers. The scheme was to have Lewis or another party chosen by Lewis apply to the financial institutions for loans to corporate entities which they controlled, have the original loans made in the name of those entities, and then have those entities transfer the funds to petitioners' wholly owned corporation, Guaranty Management Co., Inc. . . .

[I]t seems clear from the evidence that petitioners used this scheme to prevent either the lenders or Interstate from discovering that they were the ultimate borrowers on the loans collateralized with these bonds.

. . . Respondent argues that petitioners' misrepresentation of the loan transactions and the use of the proceeds for their own benefit resulted in the receipt of "gross income" under section 61 of the Code. Petitioners argue that these were bona fide loans which they at all times intended to repay and, in fact, did repay.

It is well established that gains from fraudulent or illegal activity can constitute gross income, even though the taxpayer procures his gain under no rightful claim and may have a legal obligation to repay the ill-gotten gain. As the Supreme Court stated in holding that funds obtained by extortion constituted taxable income:

> An unlawful gain, as well as a lawful one, constitutes taxable income when its recipient has such control over it that, as a practical matter, he derives readily realizable

economic value from it. That occurs when cash, as here, is delivered by its owner to the taxpayer in a manner which allows the recipient freedom to dispose of it at will, even though it may have been obtained by fraud and his freedom to use it may be assailable by someone with a better title to it.

Rutkin v. United States, 343 U.S. 130, 137 (1952) (citations omitted). Since *Rutkin* . . . the courts have found various embezzlers and swindlers to be taxable on the proceeds of their illegal schemes.

However, it is equally well established that gross income does not include loans. United States v. Rochelle, 384 F.2d 748, 751 (5th Cir. 1967). As one court stated: "A loan does not in itself constitute income to the borrower, because whatever temporary economic benefit he derives from the use of the funds is offset by the corresponding obligation to repay them."

That a loan does not constitute income, however, does not mean that a taxpayer will be permitted to escape taxation by cloaking an unlawful or fraudulent scheme in the guise of a loan. Whether a transaction constitutes a loan for income tax purposes depends primarily on whether the parties entered into the transaction with the intention that the money advanced be repaid.

In James v. United States, [366 U.S. 213 (1961),] the Supreme Court clarified the income tax treatment of illegal gains, and articulated a test for distinguishing between taxable income and loans. In holding that embezzled funds constituted gross income, the Court stated:

> When a taxpayer acquires earnings, lawfully or unlawfully, without the consensual recognition, express or implied, of an obligation to repay and without restriction as to their disposition, "he has received income which he is required to return, even though it may still be claimed that he is not entitled to retain the money, and even though he may still be adjudged liable to restore its equivalent." . . . This standard brings wrongful appropriations within the broad sweep of "gross income;" it excludes loans.

. . . Although the Court in *James* was concerned with the treatment of embezzled funds, the test has been applied by lower courts to render taxable various illegal or fraudulent schemes purporting to be loans. . . .

In this case, there is no question that petitioners misrepresented the transactions in order to obtain funds to finance their acquisition of Surety and Agency. . . . However, the basic issue in this case is not whether petitioners are guilty of misrepresentation, but whether the proceeds of the loans constitute gross income, and this depends on whether the parties intended that the money be repaid. . . .

In *Rochelle*, the taxpayer induced numerous people to "invest" in various bogus ventures. He represented himself as a promoter of many highly profitable businesses, none of which existed. His "almost magnetic powers in presenting his promotion schemes" persuaded many investors to "loan" him money with an expectation that they would acquire a part interest in the enterprise and realize substantial profits. The taxpayer used the funds for his personal benefit without restriction; in fact, they constituted the sole source of income to support his lavish life-style. He ultimately became bankrupt. In holding that the funds constituted gross income, the court stated: "Where the loans are obtained by fraud, and where it is apparent that the recipient recognizes no obligation to repay, the transaction becomes a 'wrongful appropriation [and comes] within the broad sweep of gross income.'" . . .

[W]here fraudulent conduct evinces the absence of a bona fide intent to repay, no loan exists and the perpetrator is taxed accordingly on his ill-gotten gain. Respondent argues that [this requires] a finding of gross income in this case. However, other than outlining in detail the specifics of petitioners' complicated loan transactions, respondent offers few facts in support of his contention that petitioner did not intend to repay the loans. As we stated above, a finding of fraudulent conduct does not in itself establish a lack of intent to repay. We are convinced, viewing the record as a whole, that petitioners intended at all times to repay these loans, did in fact repay them, and cannot be held to have received income from these transactions.

. . . While petitioners misrepresented the nature of the loans in order to avoid scrutiny by either the lenders or Interstate, in every respect they treated the obligations as bona fide debt. The loans were assumed by Guaranty pursuant to written agreements, and in addition, indemnification agreements were prepared. Petitioners paid interest on the loans. It also appears that petitioners had a sufficient net worth and cash flow from their business to repay the loans. In addition, the testimony of all witnesses indicates that petitioners at all times intended to repay the loans.

Respondent concedes that the factual patterns in *Rochelle* . . . differ from the factual pattern in this case. Indeed, petitioners' conduct bears little similarity to the fraudulent schemes in those cases. . . . In this case, petitioners, who enjoyed a good reputation in their field, misrepresented the identity of the ultimate borrower on the loans in order to finance their acquisition of the Surety and Agency stock and thereby develop their own business. Despite the impropriety of their conduct, we think that petitioners intended to repay these loans; their business depended on it. The cases cited by respondent are simply inapposite to the underlying business purpose of the loans in this case. . . .

In summary, we think that the respondent in this case has relied too much on the fact of petitioners' improper conduct and too little on the effect of that conduct. The picture that emerges from the record is not one of swindlers or embezzlers of the type found in *James* or its progeny; rather, it is one of a legitimate (albeit highly risky) enterprise whose owners, for reasons not entirely clear, felt compelled to resort to misrepresentations in order to obtain necessary financing. Petitioners apparently assumed that, by paying off the loans, the impropriety of their use of Interstate's bonds would never surface. Unfortunately, Interstate's growing concern about the highly risky financial guarantee bond business resulted in an examination that revealed the scheme. The petitioners have "paid the price" of their indiscretion in the form of criminal convictions, repayment of the funds, and, presumably, the loss of their business. We think that respondent's effort to add an income tax deficiency on top of these misfortunes must fail. . . .

Problems

2-12. Jack Hemingway played weekly racquetball games with some of his colleagues. One day, at the end of the year, he wagered and won three bottles of fine wine valued at $90.
  a.   Does Hemingway have gross income? If so, how much?
  b.   What result if gambling was illegal in Hemingway's state of residence?
  c.   What result if he resided in a state in which the possession of alcohol was illegal?

2-13. Janet Wysoki borrowed $6,000 from Jeff Billingham in August.
  a.   What result if Wysoki intends to repay the loan and does so in the next year? Does she have gross income? If so, how much and when?
  b.   What result in *a* if Wysoki intended to repay the loan but is unable to do so in the next year because of financial difficulties?
  c.   What result if Wysoki does not intend to repay the loan? Does she have gross income? If so, how much and when?
  d.   What result in *a* if Wysoki intended to repay the loan but changes her mind in the next year and decides not to repay the loan?

2-14. John Townsend received $35,000 in sales commissions.
  a.   In January of the next year, before Townsend filed his tax return, Townsend's employer successfully sued Townsend and recovered $20,000 in commissions that had been wrongfully paid to him. What amount of income should Townsend report?
  b.   What result in *a* if Townsend's employer sued for the wrongfully paid commissions and recovered $20,000 in the next year?
  c.   What result in *b* if the $20,000 recovery was in the current year?
  d.   Assume that Townsend returned the contested $20,000 portion of the commissions to the employer on December 15, and thereafter sued to recover that amount. The parties settled for $10,000 in the next year. What result?

3.   Discharge of Indebtedness

Code: §61(a)(12)
Regulations: §1.61-12(a)

Since the receipt of borrowed funds is not treated as income when received due to the *presence* of an offsetting obligation to repay, it follows that a taxpayer could have gross income if and when that obligation is *removed* without payment, such as if it is discharged or forgiven. In effect, the tax law recognizes that the discharge of an obligation to repay is economically the same as permitting the taxpayer to keep the borrowed cash forever — much like it had been the taxpayer's money all along. Stated another way, the removal of a liability can be as much of an income event to a taxpayer as the receipt of cash, if as a result the taxpayer now has more cash or assets over which to exercise "dominion and control" — that is, available to use for their personal consumption.

Consequently, without providing for income from the discharge of indebtedness, taxpayers could easily avoid including traditional income items, such as compensation, in gross income. For example, consider a lawyer whose work for a client entitles her to a $5,000 fee and to whom the lawyer owes $7,000 from a previous loan. Rather than collecting the fee in cash, the lawyer requests that the client cancel $5,000 of the lawyer's $7,000 preexisting obligation to the client. In such a case, the lawyer has not received cash or property, but she does have a net economic gain, as well as an increase in net worth, of $5,000, since the lawyer no longer owes the client $5,000. Section 61(a)(1), therefore, requires that the $5,000 be included in her gross income as compensation for services.

The preceding discussion considers debts discharged in exchange for other consideration, such as for services rendered. The discharge of indebtedness doctrine of §61(a)(12) is not applicable to these situations, however. Rather, it contemplates some reduction in the obligation to repay other than due to repayment in the form of cash or through providing goods or services. For example, what is the result if a debt is discharged for less than its face amount, not in return for services rendered but because of the debtor's unstable financial condition? Consider a taxpayer who borrows $5,000 from a bank and, six months later, before making any principal payments on the loan, informs the bank that he cannot repay the entire $5,000 and will likely have to file for bankruptcy. In anticipation of the borrower's potential bankruptcy, the bank accepts $4,000 in full satisfaction of the $5,000 loan. Clearly the bank did not intend to compensate the borrower for his inability to repay the bank. Instead, the bank was willing to accept less than the full amount of the loan rather than risk the chance of receiving even less in bankruptcy proceedings. Does the lack of a compensatory motive permit the discharged debt to bypass inclusion in gross income? If so, how does that reconcile with the fact that the borrower received a total of $5,000 and only repaid $4,000, realizing a net economic gain of $1,000?

The Supreme Court faced this issue in United States v. Kirby Lumber Co., 284 U.S. 1 (1931), holding that the taxpayer was required to include in income the difference between the face amount of a debt instrument and the amount paid to satisfy the debt instrument, to wit: "As a result of its dealings it made available . . . assets previously offset by the obligation of bonds now extinct. . . . The defendant . . . has realized within the year an accession to income, if we take words in their plain popular meaning, as they should be taken here." Id. at 3. Although *Kirby Lumber* seemingly settled the issue of discharge of indebtedness as gross income, the reasoning used by the Court has been subject to a substantial amount of criticism. Does *Kirby Lumber* apply only if the taxpayer has the assets that are no longer burdened by a debt? If so, what about the bankrupt taxpayer described above? The taxpayer has no assets left after paying $4,000 to the bank, but yet still realized a net $1,000 gain because the taxpayer no longer needs to repay $1,000 of the original $5,000 loan. Would it matter if the amount of the original loan was disputed and the $4,000 was a negotiated settlement?

Section 61(a)(12) and Regulation §1.61-12, enacted to address discharge of indebtedness, provide that gross income includes income from the discharge of indebtedness. These provisions appear to settle the question of whether a taxpayer has income from the discharge of an obligation to repay, in particular in circumstances where there is a payment or purchase of the taxpayer's obligation at less than its face amount. However, the issues raised in *Kirby Lumber* continue to arise in litigation, with disagreement regarding the appropriate standard to apply to determine as to when a discharge of indebtedness has arisen. When reading the following cases, consider the issue of the appropriate balance to determine when gross income has arisen upon the discharge of indebtedness.

ZARIN v. COMMISSIONER
916 F.2d 110 (3rd Cir. 1990)

Cowen, J.

David Zarin ("Zarin") appeals from a decision of the Tax Court holding that he recognized $2,935,000 of income from discharge of indebtedness resulting from his gambling activities, and that he should be taxed on the income. . . . After considering the issues raised by this appeal, we will reverse.

Zarin was a professional engineer who participated in the development, construction, and management of various housing projects. A resident of Atlantic City, New Jersey, Zarin occasionally gambled, both in his hometown and in other places where gambling was legalized. To facilitate his gaming activities in Atlantic City, Zarin applied to Resorts International Hotel ("Resorts") for a credit line in June, 1978. Following a credit check, Resorts granted Zarin $10,000 of credit. Pursuant to this credit arrangement with Resorts, Zarin could write a check, called a marker, and in return receive chips, which could then be used to gamble at the casino's tables.

Before long, Zarin developed a reputation as an extravagant "high roller" who routinely bet the house maximum while playing craps, his game of choice. Considered a "valued gaming patron" by Resorts, Zarin had his credit limit increased at regular intervals without any further credit checks, and was provided a number of complimentary services and privileges. By November, 1979, Zarin's permanent line of credit had been raised to $200,000. Between June, 1978, and December, 1979, Zarin lost $2,500,000 at the craps table, losses he paid in full.

Responding to allegations of credit abuses, the New Jersey Division of Gaming Enforcement filed with the New Jersey Casino Control Commission a complaint against Resorts. Among the 809 violations of casino regulations alleged in the complaint of October, 1979, were 100 pertaining to Zarin. Subsequently, a Casino Control Commissioner issued an Emergency Order, the effect of which was to make further extensions of credit to Zarin illegal.

Nevertheless, Resorts continued to extend Zarin's credit limit through the use of two different practices: "considered cleared" credit and "this trip only" credit. Both methods effectively ignored the Emergency Order and were later found to be illegal. By January, 1980, Zarin was gambling compulsively and uncontrollably at Resorts, spending at many as sixteen hours a day at the craps table. During April, 1980, Resorts again increased Zarin's credit line without further inquiries. That same month, Zarin delivered personal checks and counter checks to Resorts which were returned as having been drawn against insufficient funds. Those dishonored checks totaled $3,435,000. In late April, Resorts cut off Zarin's credit.

Although Zarin indicated that he would repay those obligations, Resorts filed a New Jersey state court action against Zarin in November, 1980, to collect the $3,435,000. Zarin denied liability on grounds that Resort's claim was unenforceable under New Jersey regulations intended to protect compulsive gamblers. Ten months later, in September, 1981, Resorts and Zarin settled their dispute for a total of $500,000. . . . The sole issue before this Court is whether the Tax Court correctly held that Zarin had income from discharge of indebtedness. Section 108 and section 61(a)(12) of the Code set forth "the general rule that gross income includes income from the discharge of indebtedness." . . .

Under the Commissioner's logic, Resorts advanced Zarin $3,435,000 worth of chips, chips being the functional equivalent of cash. At that time, the chips were not treated as income, since Zarin recognized an obligation of repayment. In other words, Resorts made Zarin a tax-free loan. However, a taxpayer does recognize income if a loan owed to another party is cancelled, in whole or in part. The settlement between Zarin and Resorts, claims the Commissioner, fits neatly into the cancellation of indebtedness provisions in the Code. Zarin owed $3,435,000, paid $500,000 with the difference constituting income. Although initially persuasive, the Commissioner's position is nonetheless flawed. . . .

Instead of analyzing the transaction at issue as cancelled debt, we believe the proper approach is to view it as disputed debt or contested liability. Under the contested liability doctrine, if a taxpayer, in good faith, disputed the amount of a debt, a subsequent settlement of the dispute would be treated as the amount of debt cognizable for tax purposes. The excess of the original debt over the amount determined to have been due is disregarded for both loss and debt accounting purposes. Thus, if a taxpayer took out a loan for $10,000, refused in good faith to pay the full $10,000 back, and then reached an agreement with the lendor that he would pay back only $7,000 in full satisfaction of the debt, the transaction would be treated as if the initial loan was $7,000. When the taxpayer tenders the $7,000 payment, he will have been deemed to have paid the full amount of the initially disputed debt. Accordingly, there is no tax consequence to the taxpayer upon payment.

The seminal "contested liability" case is N. Sobel, Inc. v. Commissioner. In Sobel, the taxpayer exchanged a $21,700 note for 100 shares of stock from a bank. In the following year, the taxpayer sued the bank for recision, arguing that the bank loan was violative of state law, and moreover, that the bank had failed to perform certain promises. The parties eventually settled the case in 1935, with the taxpayer agreeing to pay half of the face amount of the note. In the year of the settlement, the taxpayer claimed the amount paid as a loss. The Commissioner denied the loss because it had been sustained five years earlier, and further asserted that the taxpayer recognized income from the discharge of half of his indebtedness.

The Board of Tax Appeals held that since the loss was not fixed until the dispute was settled, the loss was recognized in 1935, the year of the settlement, and the deduction was appropriately taken in that year. Additionally, the Board held that the portion of the note forgiven by the bank "was not the occasion for a freeing of assets and that there was no gain. . . ." Therefore, the taxpayer did not have any income from cancellation of indebtedness.

There is little difference between the present case and Sobel. Zarin incurred a $3,435,000 debt while gambling at Resorts, but in court, disputed liability on the basis of unenforceability. A settlement of $500,000 was eventually agreed upon. It follows from Sobel that the settlement served only to fix the amount of debt. No income was realized or recognized. When Zarin paid the $500,000, any tax consequence dissolved. The Commissioner argues that Sobel and the contested liability doctrine only apply when there is an unliquidated debt; that is, a debt for which the amount cannot be determined. Since Zarin contested his liability based on the unenforceability of the entire debt, and did not dispute the amount of the debt, the Commissioner would have us adopt the reasoning of the Tax Court, which found that Zarin's debt was liquidated, therefore barring the application of *Sobel* and the contested liability doctrine.

We reject the Tax Court's rationale. When a debt is unenforceable, it follows that the amount of the debt, and not just the liability thereon, is in dispute. Although a debt may be unenforceable, there still could be some value attached to its worth. This is especially so with regards to gambling debts. In most states, gambling debts are unenforceable, and have "but slight potential. . . ." Nevertheless, they are often collected, at least in part. For example, Resorts is not a charity; it would not have extended illegal credit to Zarin and others if it did not have some hope of collecting debts incurred pursuant to the grant of credit.

Moreover, the debt is frequently incurred to acquire gambling chips, and not money. Although casinos attach a dollar value to each chip, that value, unlike money's, is not beyond dispute, particularly given the illegality of gambling debts in the first place. This proposition is supported by the facts of the present case. Resorts gave Zarin $3.4 million dollars of chips in exchange for markers evidencing Zarin's debt. If indeed the only issue was the enforceability of the entire debt, there would have been no settlement. Zarin would have owed all or nothing. Instead, the parties attached a value to the debt considerably lower than its face value. In other words, the parties agreed that given the circumstances surrounding Zarin's gambling spree, the chips he acquired might not have been worth $3.4 million dollars, but were worth something. Such a debt cannot be called liquidated, since its exact amount was not fixed until settlement.

To summarize, the transaction between Zarin and Resorts can best be characterized as a disputed debt, or contested liability. Zarin owed an unenforceable debt of $3,435,000 to Resorts. After Zarin in good faith disputed his obligation to repay the debt, the parties settled for $500,000, which Zarin paid. That $500,000 settlement fixed the amount of loss and the amount of debt cognizable for tax purposes. Since Zarin was deemed to have owed $500,000, and since he paid Resorts $500,000, no adverse tax consequences attached to Zarin as a result.

ROOD v. COMMISSIONER
T.C. Memo 1996-248, affd. without published opinion 122 F.3d 1078
(11th Cir.1997)

Wells, Judge:

. . . The only issue presented in the instant case is whether petitioner realized income from the cancellation of an allegedly disputed gambling debt written off by a casino.

Findings of Fact

. . . Petitioner is an attorney who was recognized in 1991 for 50 years of membership in the Florida Bar. He is a former president of the Association of Trial

Lawyers of America, the Tampa and Hillsborough County Bar Associations, the Florida Academy of Trial Lawyers, and the Junior Bar of the State of Florida. Prior to 1985, petitioner maintained a line of credit at Caesar's Palace ("Caesar's" or "the casino"), a casino in Las Vegas, Nevada, where he gambled.

. . . Petitioner incurred gambling debts at Caesar's. On November 23, 1984, Caesar's extended $110,000 of credit to petitioner. Caesar's generally expected payment of the outstanding balance of petitioner's account at the end of one trip to the casino at the time of his next trip, holding the account up to 60 days.

. . . By March 1988, [petitioner had] a balance of $355,000, according to the casino's records. A letter . . . from Caesar's general counsel to petitioner stated that the casino required petitioner to pay his account in full immediately and that, if he did not contact Caesar's account representative within 15 days, the casino would turn petitioner's account over to a law firm or a collection agency to institute legal proceedings against him if necessary. The letter further stated that (1) any suit commenced against petitioner would be filed in Nevada and (2) once judgment was obtained against petitioner, Caesar's would then have the judgment enforced against him by the courts of his home state. It was Caesar's usual practice to proceed in this manner in the event a lawsuit was instituted against a debtor.

. . . Petitioner and the casino continued to negotiate a settlement. . . . Petitioner subsequently signed an allowance receipt that was received by Caesar's . . . that requested $255,000 be written off his account balance to induce him to make payment on the account. In accordance with an agreement between Caesar's and petitioner, petitioner paid Caesar's $100,000 by check dated June 29, 1988, that was received by the casino on September 2, 1988.

. . . Caesar's wrote off the $255,000 balance of petitioner's account in September 1988 and noted in its records that (1) no attempt should be made to collect that amount should petitioner return to the casino to gamble and (2) no credit would be extended to petitioner in the future due to the settlement.

. . . Petitioner did not report the $255,000 written off by Caesar's as income from the cancellation of indebtedness on his 1988 Federal income tax return.

OPINION

Section 61(a)(12) provides the general rule that gross income includes income from the cancellation of indebtedness. The amount of the income includable generally is the difference between the face value of the debt and the amount paid in satisfaction of the debt. The income is recognized in the year cancellation occurs. A frequently cited rationale for the rule is that the cancellation results in an accession to income by effecting a freeing of assets previously offset by the liability arising from the indebtedness. United States v. Kirby Lumber Co., 284 U.S. 1, 3 (1931). If, however, the cancellation of all or part of a debt is made in settlement of a dispute concerning the debt, no income from cancellation of indebtedness arises. N. Sobel, Inc. v. Commissioner, 40 B.T.A. 1263, 1265 (1939). Settlement in such circumstances does not occasion a freeing of assets and accession to income.

Petitioner, relying on Zarin v. Commissioner, 916 F.2d 110 (3d Cir. 1990), revg. 92 T.C. 1084 (1989), claims that he disputed his debt to Caesar's, that his payments to Caesar's were in settlement of the dispute, and that therefore he realized no income upon the cancellation of the $255,000 that Caesar's claimed it was owed by petitioner.

. . . Petitioner contends that the casino's efforts to settle the debt were the result of its realization that a cage employee had mishandled chips and the difficulty of winning a suit against petitioner for collection of the amount it claimed he owed. . . . [T]he casino's assistant collection manager . . . offered the following considerations that would have induced Caesar's to settle petitioner's account for less than the outstanding balance: (1) the age of and minimal payments that had been received on petitioner's account; (2) the cost of collecting the remaining balance of his account were a suit instituted against petitioner; and (3) the benefit to the casino of receiving a lump sum in the amount of the settlement versus payments over a long period of time. Such considerations are not the result of concerns on the part of Caesar's as to the enforceability of petitioner's debt. Petitioner argues that the fact that the casino settled petitioner's debt indicates that the debt was disputed. We do not agree. As to petitioner's contention, we find useful the analysis in Exchange Sec. Bank v. United States, which involved a cancellation of indebtedness resulting from the settlement of litigation to collect a debt. The District Court offered the following analysis of the effect of a settlement that has been made for some of the reasons advanced by Caesar's in the instant case:

> On the other hand . . . [the debtor] may actually owe the debt; and yet . . . [the creditor], confronted with a denial of liability, may be willing to settle, saving the time and expense of litigation, by accepting a much smaller payment than that actually owing. Where there are serious problems of proof or of collectibility, or when . . . [the creditor] is confronted with unusual policy considerations, he may even be willing to dismiss the suit without any payment. In such situations it seems clear that . . . [the debtor] would thereby realize cancellation of indebtedness income subject to the "insolvency" and "gift" exceptions.

. . . Consequently, although, given the fact that Caesar's settled with petitioner, one might infer the existence of a dispute concerning the debt, and the amount of the settlement might be an indicator of the relative merits of their respective positions, such circumstances are not conclusive of whether a debt is disputed in good faith for purposes of deciding whether or not a debtor has realized income from the cancellation of indebtedness as a result of the settlement. If a settlement alone were sufficient to establish the disputed nature of a debt, a taxpayer whose liability for the full amount of a settled debt was not in question would reap a windfall in the form of an untaxed freeing of the assets previously offset by the liability represented by the debt. In contrast, in the case of a settlement of a truly disputed debt, the settlement does not give rise to an accession to income due to the freeing of the debtor's assets because the amount of the assets that were offset by the debt is not clear.

. . . Accordingly, we hold that petitioner . . . realized income from the cancellation of indebtedness in the amount of the balance of that account written off by Caesar's.

Problem

2-15. To reduce the number of its low-interest mortgages, City Bank offered a 10-percent discount to each borrower with an existing low-interest mortgage who would prepay the balance. John Johnson, who had borrowed money from the financial institution in order to purchase a residence from a third party, paid the financial institution $180,000 cash in full payment of his $200,000 note and mortgage.

    a. Does Johnson have gross income? If so, how much?

    b. Does Johnson have gross income if he prepaid $100,000 of the $200,000 debt with a $90,000 cash payment? If so, how much?

    c. Does Johnson have gross income if he extinguishes $100,000 of the debt by paying $75,000 in cash and performing $15,000 of services for the bank? If so, how much?

    d. What result in *c* if instead of performing $15,000 of services for the bank, Johnson transfers $75,000 cash plus an asset worth $15,000, which he had purchased earlier in the year for $8,000?

D. LIMITATIONS ON GROSS INCOME

Notwithstanding the breadth of the gross income concept as formulated in *Glenshaw Glass*, it is not *all*-encompassing. Numerous limitations circumscribe the scope of the *Glenshaw Glass* concept so that not every receipt or economic benefit is includable in gross income.

1. *Recovery of Capital*

Code: §§1001, 1012

The §61 definition of gross income requires an economic gain. Therefore, the Code's definition of gross income — "all income from whatever source derived" — is not as expansive as it may seem. To be includable as income under the *Glenshaw Glass* formula, there must be "an accession to wealth," not merely the recovery of one's original capital investment. Thus, the lender's receipt of a $100 loan repayment is a return of capital, not income. Although the lender received cash, that cash represents a return of the cash that the lender originally gave the borrower, and thus there is no profit, economic gain, or overall increase in net worth. Similarly, when one receives a rebate on the purchase of an asset, the rebate is classified as a reduction in purchase price (return of capital) and does not give rise to gross income.

In general, when a taxpayer sells an asset for more than its cost, the difference between the sales price and the asset's cost is gain. For example, if an asset is purchased for $100 and is subsequently sold for $1,000, the gain is $900 (gross income) and $100 is a recovery of invested capital. The recovery of capital rationale is also the basis for the distinction between compensatory damages (excluded from gross income) and damages representing lost profit (included in gross income), topics that are discussed further in Chapter 3.

Although the Supreme Court has not specifically addressed whether recovery of capital is constitutionally guaranteed, early cases implied that, when computing taxable gain, a taxpayer had a constitutional right to subtract the cost of the property sold from the sales proceeds. In Stanton v. Baltic Mining Co., 240 U.S. 103 (1916), however, the Supreme Court suggested that a taxpayer may not be entitled to tax-free recovery of the cost of property. In *Stanton*, a stockholder of a coal mining company sued to recover taxes paid by the company. A special clause in the tax law limited the company's deduction for the depletion of ore deposits to 5 percent of its annual gross receipts. Unable to deduct the entire cost of the depletion of ore deposits, the stockholder argued that the clause placed an unconstitutional tax on the mine property. The Supreme Court held that Congress's specific limitation on the deduction for the depletion of ore deposits was allowable, thereby implying that the recovery of a capital investment is founded upon legislative prerogative rather than constitutional right.

Courts have seldom been compelled to resolve the issue of the recovery of capital because Congress has provided for the tax-free recovery of capital in most situations. For instance, in computing gain or loss arising on the sale of property, §1001(a) of the Code expressly provides that taxpayers are to offset the costs incurred in acquiring the property against the proceeds of the sale.

Although the distinction between return of capital and receipt of income may seem clear in theory, it often becomes muddied in practice. One frequently encountered issue is the allocation of the amount realized between return of capital and taxable gain. Another issue is related to the timing of the capital recovery. Returns from annuities, insurance proceeds, sales of partial interests, or installment sales, all of which often involve a taxpayer's original capital outlay, raise the issue of which cost recovery system to employ. For example, if property is purchased for $100 and sold for $1,000, payable at the rate of $100 per year for ten years, only $900 of income should arise after taking the taxpayer's $100 capital investment into account. Determining *when* that $100 capital investment is to be taken into account is an issue on which Congress and the courts have a variety of options — the initial investment could offset the first or the last year's receipt, or any one of the other eight years, or it could be prorated at $10 per year over the life of the ten-year payment period. The Code's solution to these issues is discussed in Chapter 5.

REV. RUL. 81-277
1981-2 C.B. 14

ISSUE

Does payment by a contractor of a sum of money to a buyer in exchange for a release of the buyer's claims against the contractor for failure to fulfill a contract result in income to the buyer or a return of capital?

FACTS

In 1969 corporation M agreed to construct a nuclear generating plant for corporation P at a price of $250x$ dollars. The construction contract specified that M would provide, at no additional cost to P, any additional items that later were determined to be necessary to deliver a complete, safe, licensable, fully operational plant. During the construction period regulatory agencies imposed stricter environmental safeguards on nuclear generating plants than were in effect at the time the contract was signed. Disputes arose between M and P over M's obligation to provide for stricter safeguards and to include them as part of the delivered plant at the original contract price. To the date of the dispute, P has paid M $230x$ dollars of the contract price of $250x$ dollars.

The parties eventually settled their dispute by agreeing that the terms of the 1969 contract must be met by both parties. They also agreed that M was responsible to deliver a plant that met the stricter environmental safeguards and that it would cost an additional $40x$ dollars. P was required to forward $20x$ dollars to M to complete P's payment obligation under the contract.

In light of these agreements, P paid M $20x$ dollars, the value of the work performed under the contract but unpaid at the time of the settlement agreement. M paid P $40x$ dollars representing the estimated cost to satisfy the stricter environmental standards rather than completing the plant's construction. Both parties then executed general releases to each other and M ceased its construction activities.

P then contracted with a third party to finish construction of the nuclear generating plant. P eventually had to pay the third party $50x$ dollars to obtain a plant that satisfied the regulatory agencies standards.

LAW AND ANALYSIS

Section 61 of the Internal Revenue Code provides that gross income means all income from whatever source derived, including income realized in any form.

Section 1012 of the Code provides that the basis of property is usually its cost. Section 1.1012-1(a) of the Income Tax Regulations provides that cost is the amount paid for property in cash or other property. Section 1016(a) provides that adjustments are made to the basis of property for expenditures, receipts, losses, or other items properly chargeable to the capital account.

Inherent in section 61 of the Code is the concept of economic gain. For a taxpayer to have income under section 61, there must be an economic gain that benefits the taxpayer personally. United States v. Gotcher, 401 F.2d 118 (5th Cir. 1968).

The determination of whether the proceeds received in a lawsuit or received in settlement of a lawsuit constitute income under section 61 of the Code depends on the nature of the claim and the actual basis for recovery. If the recovery represents damages for lost profits, it is taxed as ordinary income. If, however, the recovery is treated as a replacement of capital, the damages received from the lawsuit are treated as a return of capital and are not taxable as income. Payments by the one causing a loss that do no more than restore a taxpayer to the position he or she was in before the loss was incurred are not includible in gross income because there is no economic gain.

In the present situation, the effect of the settlement agreement was that M would compensate P for M's failure to provide a fully operational and licensable plant for $250x$ dollars as agreed upon under the contract. The payment from M to P of $40x$ dollars represents the estimated present damages P has incurred because of the breach of contract, determined under the settlement agreement as the estimated additional costs needed to satisfy new regulatory standards that were necessary to deliver a complete, safe, licensable, fully operational plant as required under the contract. P has received no economic gain as a result of the $40x$ dollars payment and is merely being made whole under the contract. P is being restored to the position that it would have been in if M had fulfilled the terms of the contract.

HOLDING

The $40x$ dollars payment from M to P represents a return of capital and is not income to P. The basis of the plant in P's hands should be adjusted downward to $210x$ dollars from its cost basis of $250x$ dollars ($230x$ dollars plus the $20x$ dollars payment from P to M) to reflect the $40x$ dollars payment, and adjusted upward to $260x$ dollars when P incurs expenses of $50x$ dollars to finish construction of the plant.

Note on Return of Human Capital

The traditional analysis involving the return of capital exception from gross income, as reflected in Revenue Ruling 81-277, has involved returns of invested capital—that is, money. However, some taxpayers have also argued that certain proceeds should not be included in gross income if they represent a return of "human capital," or the inherent value that taxpayers have in their body, skills, efforts, and so forth.

The return of human capital theory has been controversial, and understandably so. Taken to an extreme, many payments thought of as clearly constituting gross income could be thought of as return of human capital. For example, one could argue that salary for services rendered is really compensation for exploiting the human capital of an employee, meaning that salary and wages would not be gross income! Few taxpayers have raised this extreme version of the human capital argument, and no courts have accepted it. See, for example, The Florida Bar v. Behm, 41 So.3d 136 (Fla. 2010) (rejecting claim that failure to pay tax should not result in disbarment because fees for legal services were not income but rather replacement for human capital); Chamberlain ex rel. Chamberlain v. United States, 401 F.3d 335 (5th Cir. 2005) (prejudgment interest not a return of human capital). However, one particular application of this theory did meet with some limited (and temporary) success. See Murphy v. Internal Revenue Service, 460 F.3d 79 (D.C. Cir. 2006) (damages for emotional distress are a return of human capital), vacated 2007-1 USTC ¶ 50, 228, rev'd on reh'g 493 F.3d 170 (2007). As discussed in Chapter 1, this ruling was eventually vacated because the court concluded Congress had the power to impose tax even if the receipts at issue did not constitute gross income.

Another interesting facet of the return of capital doctrine arose in a case involving the sale of blood plasma. See United States v. Garber, 607 F.2d 92 (5th Cir. 1979). *Garber* involved an appeal by the taxpayer who had been convicted of willfully and knowingly attempting to evade income tax liability on income earned from the sale of her blood plasma. The prosecution argued that, if the exchange were treated as the sale of a product, the entire sales price would be income because the defendant had incurred no expense to procure the product. Moreover, even if the sale were characterized as a sale of services, all gain would be income. The defense argued, however, that the human body is a kind of capital asset and therefore the exchange of a part of one's body for cash does not produce income.

The District Court agreed with the prosecution and ruled, as a matter of law, that the sale of blood plasma, whether a personal service or product, generated gross income. The jury returned a guilty verdict. The Fifth Circuit, reviewing the verdict, admitted that "[t]he tax treatment of earnings from the sale of blood plasma or other parts of the human body is an uncharted area in tax law." Id. at 99. The court ruled that evidence concerning the unsettled question of the correct tax treatment for exchanges of blood plasma should have been presented to the jury because it touched on the issue of willfulness. However, the court did not specifically decide whether the exchange was taxable, stating that a criminal proceeding was an inappropriate forum for the interpretation of tax law. The dissent argued that the sale was taxable.

Had the Circuit Court held that such a transaction involved the sale of a product rather than a service, would Garber's tax liability have been affected? In a subsequent case, Green v. Commissioner, 74 T.C. 1229 (1980), the Tax Court compared the sale of blood to "the usual sale of a product by a manufacturer to a distributor or of raw materials by a producer to a processor." Id. at 1234. If the dissent in *Garber* was correct in arguing that the taxpayer's "basis in the plasma is the cost of its constituent parts, which in this case is zero," is the debate over whether to characterize the sale of plasma as a service or a product relevant?

The only other court to directly consider the issue also avoided taking a definitive position, stating that "our resolution of this case leaves open the question whether the sale or contribution of blood is the performance of a service or the sale or contribution of a product, as did the former Fifth Circuit in United States v. Garber." Lary v. United States, 787 F.2d 1538, 1540 (11th Cir. 1986). Why have courts struggled with the issue of whether the sale of blood plasma should be treated as a service or as the sale of a product? What about the sale of other products related to the body? For example, in recent years a number of advocacy groups have arisen to encourage the sale or trade of mother's milk for use by infants who cannot otherwise nurse. Should this activity be treated similarly to the sale of blood plasma? See Internal Revenue Service General Counsel Memorandum 36418 (1975) ("Milk is a commodity, whether from a human being or a cow. The donee receives bottles of frozen mother's milk just as it might get bottles of cow's milk from a dairy or store. . . . It would be unrealistic and out-dated to say that in this case the taxpayer is performing services as a wet nurse for the recipient baby. The taxpayer merely gave away property she possessed"). Should it matter whether the property is replenishable, such as blood, or whether it may be given or sold only once, such as an eye or a kidney? See *Garber*, 589 F.2d at 850 (Clark, J., dissenting) ("[Garber] was selling tangible property in the form of a constituent part of her blood. This was as much a product as if Mrs. Garber had sold an eye or one of her kidneys.").

In light of this debate, what tax advice should be given to a taxpayer interested in selling or donating body parts?

Problems

2-16.   Jane Till paid $400,000 for her house. Subsequently, on discovering that the roof was defective, she sued the builder and recovered $20,000.
   a.   Does she have gross income? If so, how much? What is her basis for the house?
   b.   What result in *a* if the roof was repaired at a total cost of $15,000? Does she have gross income? If so, how much? What is her basis for the house?

2-17.   While parked in a parking lot, Brigette Monette's car was destroyed by a drunk driver. She brought suit to recover the $10,000 that she had paid for the car but ultimately settled for $4,000.
   a.   Does she have gross income? If so, how much?
   b.   What result in *a* if she sued for $20,000 and settled for $12,000?

2-18.   Tom Jacobs purchased an automobile for the advertised price of $8,000, with a $1,000 cash rebate to follow from the factory.
   a.   Does he have gross income when he receives the rebate? If so, how much?
   b.   What is his basis in the car after he receives the rebate?

2.   Unrealized Gains

Code: §1001
Regulations: §§1.61-6(a), 1.1001-1(a)

Assume you buy a ticket to a concert for $100 and the show quickly sells out. Suddenly, tickets are being sold on eBay for $500. You even had friends post on Facebook that they are looking for tickets and will pay any price. You have no plans to sell because you really want to attend the concert, but the ticket you own is now worth substantially more than you paid for it. Do you have an accession to wealth and thus gross income?

This hypothetical presents an example of unrealized appreciation. Although property goes up in value, the gain is not realized. On the other hand, there is no doubt that you are wealthier than you were before. Do you have gross income? The realization doctrine answers this question in the negative — there is no gross income from appreciation in property until that gain is realized.

Realization is a fundamental concept that has a pervasive influence on tax law. The realization requirement generally ensures that the inherent gains or losses in investment are not taxed until they have been severed from the capital that created them. Severance occurs on a sale, exchange, or other disposition of the property. Consequently, the annual appreciation in the value of an asset is not included in gross income until the year in which that appreciation is realized through a taxable disposition. At the time of disposition, the total appreciation in value — not merely the appreciation occurring in the year of sale — is included in gross income. For example, assume that a taxpayer purchased a rental home in year 1 for $100,000, the house increased in value by $10,000 per year from year 1 through year 6, and the taxpayer sold it on January 1, year 7 for $160,000. Although the taxpayer had an increase in net worth of $10,000 per year, gross income from the appreciation was not realized until year 7, at which time the gross income from the sale of the house was $60,000.

At one time it appeared that the Supreme Court considered realization to be constitutionally required. The Court held in Eisner v. Macomber, 252 U.S. 189 (1920), that if the increase in value of a taxpayer's investment were taxed prior to the severance of such gain from the capital asset, it would constitute a direct tax requiring an apportionment among the states by population. In *Glenshaw Glass* the Court retreated from *Eisner*, characterizing realization as an administrative rule rather than a constitutional requirement. In its formulation of gross income in *Glenshaw Glass*, however, the Court referred to realization as a prerequisite. Regardless, Congress addressed the problem by enacting §1001(a) of the Code, which employs similar terminology for sales or exchanges of property. Therefore, regardless whether as a matter of Constitutional directive or statutory mandate, unrealized appreciation is, for the most part, not included in gross income.

But should Congress consider including unrealized gains in gross income if it could? The article that follows analyzes arguments supporting and opposing the realization requirement. It should be noted, however, that two problems would arise if there were no realization requirement: first, the *valuation problem*, or the administrative burden associated with valuing all property at year's end, and second, the *liquidity problem*, or the burden on a taxpayer who must pay an income tax based on economic gains (appreciation in value) when the taxpayer has not received sufficient cash from the investment with which to pay the resulting tax liability.

NOTE, REALIZING APPRECIATION WITHOUT SALE: ACCRUAL TAXATION OF CAPITAL GAINS ON MARKETABLE SECURITIES
34 Stan. L. Rev. 857 (1982)

Since the Supreme Court's landmark decision in Eisner v. Macomber, capital gains income has not been subject to taxation until the taxpayer sells the underlying capital asset. Although *Macomber*'s treatment of capital gains income does not reflect economic reality, the courts and the Internal Revenue Code generally require realization — i.e., sale of the appreciated asset — before income will be recognized and taxed. This "realization" requirement enables high-income taxpayers to defer the payment of taxes on large amounts of unrealized capital gains income.[4] . . .

THE ADVANTAGES AND DISADVANTAGES OF TAXING APPRECIATION WITHOUT REALIZATION

The realization requirement is a significant administrative rule in any income tax system; it determines what increments of wealth will be presently taxed and what increments will be taxed in the future. The realization requirement enables taxpayers to strategically target gains and losses for particular tax years. . . .

A. THE ADVANTAGES OF ANNUALLY TAXING APPRECIATION

The federal tax system relies primarily on the personal income tax to generate governmental revenues, and generally favors taxing the appreciation of capital assets in the year the appreciation occurs. Taxing without regard to realization has three principal advantages: It broadens the tax base, it improves the equity of the tax system, and it encourages efficient asset sales.

1. *Broadening the Income Tax Base*

Under an income tax, income is taxed unless substantial policy reasons justify excluding it from the tax base. The annual appreciation in the value of capital assets is part of the tax base and should be taxed unless doing so can be shown to be substantially disadvantageous. Eliminating the realization requirement for capital assets would result in unrealized capital gains being included in the tax base; exclusion reduces the size of the tax base and forces the remaining items to bear a higher tax rate.

2. *Improving the Equity of the Income Tax*

A second advantage of eliminating the realization requirement is that it would improve the equity of the tax system. Wealth in the United States is generally more concentrated than income. Because of the realization requirement, the wealthiest members of society can defer the payment of taxes on substantial amounts of unrealized capital gains income. This ability to defer taxes amounts to an interest-free loan from the government to the taxpayer; consequently, the realization requirement allows the wealthy to keep more funds invested, increases the return on their initial investment, and allows them to defer even more taxes. Furthermore, when they eventually sell their capital assets, the deferral means that fewer real dollars are paid in taxes. The result is that the effective rate of tax on the appreciation of capital assets is much lower than the nominal rate.

The principle of vertical equity requires that individuals be taxed according to their ability to pay. Well-to-do taxpayers have a greater ability to pay than low-income taxpayers, and therefore should bear relatively larger tax burdens. The

---

4. Deferral is one of the principal elements of a capital gain and, indeed, of any tax shelter. By deferring recognition of income for tax purposes, a taxpayer is able to delay paying taxes and effectively obtains an interest-free loan from the government.

realization requirement allows well-to-do taxpayers to defer payment of taxes on unrealized capital gains income and, in some cases, to escape payment of taxes entirely through section 1014's stepped-up basis at death. Section 1014 increases the basis of a capital asset to its fair market value at the date of the owner's death; appreciation that has accrued on the asset is never taxed. High-income taxpayers with substantial amounts of capital gains income are thereby able to pay taxes on a smaller percentage of their income than lower-income taxpayers. Eliminating the realization requirement would improve the general equity of the income tax by increasing its progressivity.

3. The "Lock-in" Phenomenon

The realization requirement and the stepped-up basis at death combine to lock investors into their investment portfolios. Because taxpayers do not have to pay taxes on the increase in value of an asset until they sell or exchange it, taxpayers will resist selling appreciated property even though they may have better available investments, or are in need of cash. The investors are said to be "locked in" because of the tax penalty that they would incur if they were to sell their property and realize the gains. If the investor is well-to-do and elderly, the lock-in problem becomes even more acute: The incentives to hold an asset until death so that the basis can be increased to market value—allowing the unrealized gain to escape taxation entirely—become even greater.

The lock-in problem not only inconveniences investors who would prefer to sell their appreciated assets, but also impedes the flow of capital from one investment to another. Older investments that are no longer as profitable as newer ones tend to be kept longer, and new investments have more difficulty attracting capital than would be optimal. Eliminating the realization requirement would mean that capital gains income would be taxed regardless of whether the asset had been sold. Taxpayers would therefore have no incentive to retain less profitable investments to avoid paying taxes, and the lock-in phenomenon would be eliminated.

B. PROBLEMS WITH TAXING APPRECIATION

Although eliminating the realization requirement will increase the theoretical accuracy of the tax system, in application it could encounter significant problems. These problems relate to the valuation of capital assets, the "paper" nature of unrealized capital gains, the effect on the capital markets, and the economic responses of private parties to the change in the tax rules.

1. Valuation and Liquidity

One argument against taxing unrealized capital appreciation is that capital assets cannot be accurately valued until they are sold. Some assets are easier to value than others. Closing stock prices appear in the financial sections of major newspapers and are accurate indicators of value. Valuing real estate or partnership interests, on the other hand, requires an appraisal and involves significant administrative costs. Silver and art collections are still harder to value, the results even more uncertain, and the attempt to value even more expensive. . . .

2.   *Paper Gains and Cash Flow Problems*

Even if valuation could be performed accurately, the gain is only a "paper gain" — one that accrues even though the taxpayer receives no cash. This paper gain can be lost at any time until the taxpayer sells the underlying asset. Shareholders with substantial paper gains in one year are at risk until they liquidate their investment; they can easily lose the profit if the market falls in subsequent years. If the asset is illiquid and the investor is unable easily to convert the asset to cash, or if he can do so only at a substantial cost, taxing the unrealized capital gains income may create inequity.

Because a paper gain does not generate cash, taxing such a gain can create cash squeezes. Taxpayers may have tax liabilities, but not the cash necessary to pay them. To pay their taxes, they will be forced to sell some of their assets. If the taxpayers cannot borrow against their unrealized gains, they will have to sell assets they otherwise would have retained.

3.   *Effect on Equity Markets*

Annually taxing stock appreciation would drive down stock prices, or at least cause them to increase less rapidly, because it would reduce a stockholder's after-tax return. Corporations that raise capital in the equity markets would therefore find equity capital to be relatively more expensive; they would have to sell more shares at a lower price to raise the same amount of capital. . . .

An appreciations tax also seems likely to increase the pressures for higher dividend payments, further reducing a corporation's available cash. Under current law, dividends are taxed twice, while retained earnings are taxed only at the corporate level. With an appreciations tax, both retained earnings and dividends would be taxed twice, and the bias against paying dividends would be reduced. In addition, shareholders, especially those with substantial holdings, could be expected to demand higher dividends to provide cash to pay the appreciations tax. If the corporation did not pay higher dividends, some shareholders could be expected to choose to sell some of their holdings so that they could pay their taxes, thereby depressing the stock's price. And this, in turn, would make the cost of equity capital even greater to the corporation.

4.   *Private Responses to Changed Rule*

Since some assets are more liquid and more easily valued than others, most proposals to eliminate the realization requirement target specific groups of assets. To avoid thorny valuation and liquidity problems, these proposals would tax only the appreciation of those capital assets that are easily valued and relatively liquid. Other capital assets would continue to be taxed as they are under the current tax law. Unfortunately, the decision to tax only some assets' capital appreciation probably would cause private investors to shift their funds from assets subject to the appreciations tax into assets not subject to the tax, thereby distorting optimal investment behavior.

In tax law, the problem of drawing lines between taxed and untaxed behavior is troublesome because there are powerful financial incentives to be on the untaxed side of the line, and large amounts of capital tend to flow from more heavily taxed investments into those less heavily taxed. If only stocks traded on major exchanges were taxed, there would be a tremendous incentive not to be listed on the exchanges. If shares of all publicly held corporations were taxed, there would be a drive to "go private" or stay private. If commercial real estate is taxed and residential real estate is not, capital will flee the commercial real estate market into the residential market. Arbitrary line-drawing in the tax area creates substantial economic distortion; any division between those assets made subject to the appreciations tax and those assets not made so should seek to minimize this distortion. . . .

3. Imputed Income

Imputed income is generated in two situations: (1) when taxpayers derive an economic benefit from the ownership and use of their own property (such as the rental value of one's own home) and (2) when taxpayers derive an economic benefit from performing services for themselves (such as mowing one's own lawn). Imputed income is excluded from the income tax base. This exclusion originated in, and has been perpetuated through, the administrative practice of the Internal Revenue Service and is not embodied in a specific Code provision. Two primary reasons for not taxing imputed income are valuation difficulties and early misgivings about the constitutionality of taxing imputed income.

The concept of imputed income can be best understood by analyzing examples of situations in which it most frequently arises. First, imputed income can arise from the use or consumption of one's own personal assets. For example, taxpayer A, who buys a $200,000 home (having an annual rental value of $20,000), should be compared with taxpayer B, who invests $200,000 in interest-bearing securities with a 10-percent rate of return (yielding $20,000 in interest income, all of which is includable in gross income). For her lodging needs, B rents the home next door to A's, which is identical to A's, for $20,000 per year. Ignoring the costs of home ownership, the economic positions of A and B appear identical, yet the tax positions of A and B differ strikingly. B's interest income must be included in gross income, whereas A's imputed income — the rental value of his home — is not. Yet the economic positions of A and B are similar. Each has a $200,000 investment, from which each is deriving an annual $20,000 economic benefit. However, only B is taxed.

Obviously, the decision to rent or buy a home is a matter of personal choice, assuming that both taxpayers are financially able to purchase a home if they so desired. Are the costs of home ownership sufficiently burdensome to warrant distinguishing between taxpayers who purchase rather than rent their homes? Is the difference merely an acknowledgment of the administrative burden that would result from an attempt to tax imputed rental income?

The definition of income encompassed by §61 and *Glenshaw Glass* may be sufficiently broad to include imputed income. Moreover, despite valuation difficulties, local governments impose property taxes. The property tax valuation could be multiplied by an appropriate interest rate in order to arrive at the economic return from the investment, with the attendant expenses subtracted to determine gross income.

Does the failure to tax imputed income from property encourage consumption, and is it counterproductive to the government's efforts to halt inflation? If imputed income is not taxed, should there be a deduction for tenants, in order to place them on an equal footing with homeowners? If imputed income from property were taxed, what would be the tax consequences on a sale of the asset? Should a distinction between large items (such as homes and cars) and small items (such as vacuum cleaners and can openers) be drawn?

Imputed income also arises from the performance of services. If a taxpayer prepares a meal, he does not incur gross income equal to the amount it would have cost to have the same meal prepared at a restaurant. Nor will a taxpayer who chooses to mow his lawn himself, instead of paying a neighborhood child $350 for the summer, have $350 of gross income. Is the economic benefit in such a situation offset by the effort expended?

Different concerns may arise in the area of more substantial services, such as those of a spouse who remains at home to perform domestic chores, care for children, or both. To hire someone to perform such services might cost $20,000 or more per year. Assuming the spouse could work outside the house for $30,000, what decision should the domestic spouse make absent taxes? By contrast, what decision would the domestic spouse make if the tax system did not treat the activities similarly? That compensation for work outside the home is taxed, while imputed income from the performance of domestic chores is not, could be a disincentive to outside work. Assuming a tax of $12,000 (given a marginal rate of 40 percent and a joint return) on wages, it is economically better after-tax for the spouse to stay home. (See discussion in Chapter 10.) Is this efficient? Further, if one assumes that women generally have been second earners in households, does this effectively discriminate against women from joining the market workforce? If so, how could this be remedied? For example, could there be some value for domestic services (based on the number of family members, the size of the house, and so forth) that would be included in gross income for tax purposes? While this would treat domestic and market work the same for tax purposes, thereby removing the disincentive to market work, it would also end up with a tax bill due for the domestic worker who has earned no cash with which to pay the tax.

Although taxing the value of domestic services may be permissible under the statutory formula, the economic benefits derived from the performance of services for one's self or for family members are generally exempt from tax. The primary problems in taxing imputed income from services, which have led to its exclusion, are administrative and valuation difficulties and the potential burden on the poor, the industrious, and the creative.

The most complex imputed income issues generally arise in the context of a bargain-purchase, where the taxpayer through some skill negotiates a lower than market price for a transaction. In cases like Commissioner v. Daehler, which follows, the courts have attempted to ferret out the boundaries among imputed income transactions (taxpayer services for himself), commercial sales transactions (independent buyers and sellers exchanging identical items at different prices due to their particular negotiating skills or specific factual circumstances), and employment transactions (compensation for services rendered to another). The decisions appear to focus on the employment relationship. If this relationship exists, gross income will be found unless the taxpayer can document that an identical transaction would have taken place with an independent third party.

COMMISSIONER v. DAEHLER
281 F.2d 823 (5th Cir. 1960)

WISDOM, J. . . .

. . . Kenneth Daehler, the taxpayer, is a real estate salesman in Fort Lauderdale, Florida, employed by Anaconda Properties, Inc. Anaconda is a registered real estate broker. Daehler's commissions are on a sliding scale of 50 to 75 percent, depending on the volume of sales transacted. The established commission for selling vacant property in the Fort Lauderdale area is 10 percent of the selling price.

For some time Daehler had been looking for ocean front property for himself. Early in July 1952 he made a written offer of $52,500 for ten lots at Willingham Beach, outside of Fort Lauderdale. After conferring with Anaconda's sales manager as to procedure, Daehler made his offer to purchase on an Anaconda form reciting that he offered $52,500 for the property. He signed as "purchaser" and executed a check, payable to Anaconda, in the amount of $5,250, as earnest money, for submission with the offer.

Anaconda's sales manager, at Daehler's request, went to the office of the real estate broker representing the seller and stated that he had a customer who would pay $52,500 in cash. No previous offer had been made for the property, and if the owner had been released from the obligation of paying the 10 percent brokerage commission, he would have sold the property to anyone for the sum of $47,250, the net amount, exclusive of certain taxes and costs, he did receive. Later, the taxpayer substituted a check for $5,250 in favor of the seller's agent.

After the sale was consummated the two real estate brokers divided the commission. Anaconda then paid the taxpayer $1,837.50, representing 70 percent of its check for $2,625.

A majority of the Tax Court, five judges dissenting, held that since Daehler was buying for himself he was not acting as a salesman; the $1,837.50 was not income to the taxpayer but a reduction in the purchase price. 31 T.C. 722. Similarly, in the *Minzer* case the Tax Court held for the taxpayer on the ground that he was a broker and not an employee. 31 T.C. 1130.

Judge Jones, speaking for the Court in Commissioner v. Minzer denied the validity of these distinctions [279 F.2d 338, 340 (5th Cir. 1960)].

> It does not seem to us that the tax incidence is dependent upon the tag with which the parties label the connection between them. The agent or broker, or by whatever name he be called, is to receive or retain a percentage of the premiums on policies procured by him, called commissions, as compensation for his service to the company in obtaining the particular business for it. The service rendered to the company, for which it was required to compensate him, was no different in kind or degree where the taxpayer submitted his own application than where he submitted the application of another. In each situation there was the same obligation of the company, the obligation to pay a commission for the production of business measured by a percentage of the premiums. In each situation the result was the same to the taxpayer.

These principles are controlling in the instant case. . . . Daehler's commission was a compensatory payment for services.

Daehler performed a service for his employer in regard to [the] real estate purchase identical with the services performed in other transactions. The services were worth 30 percent of $2,625 to the employer. They were worth 70 percent of $2,625 to the employee. We see no escape from the conclusion that the amount he received from his employer was compensation for the actions he performed growing out of the employer-employee relationship. Compensation for such services is taxable income of whatever kind and in whatever form it is received, short of a specific exception to the broad statutory definition of gross income.

Problems

2-19.   Phillip Granville, a lawyer, normally charges $1,400 for drafting a will.
    a.   If he drafts his own will, does he have gross income of $1,400?
    b.   If Granville has his will drafted by another lawyer, Judith Thorndale, while he does Thorndale's will in return, do Granville or Thorndale have gross income? If so, how much?

2-20.   Karen Small, a real estate broker, wished to purchase a home for her family.
    a.   Assume that she takes one week off work in order to find and purchase a $100,000 home at a distressed price of $90,000. The home was not listed for sale with any realtor. Does she have gross income? If so, how much?
    b.   What if she buys the home in *a* for $90,000 because the seller is not required to pay anyone the customary $10,000 sales commission. Does she have gross income? If so, how much?
    c.   What result if she buys a home for $100,000 and receives a commission of $10,000 on the sale? Does she have gross income? If so, how much?
    d.   What result in *c* if the $10,000 commission is credited against the purchase price (thus reducing the price to $90,000) instead of being paid to Small in cash?

4.   Administrative Exceptions to Gross Income

At times, Congress, the Treasury Department, or the Internal Revenue Service has determined that, as a matter of administrative convenience, certain receipts that could be treated as gross income under both the Haig-Simons definition of income and under *Glenshaw Glass* should nonetheless not be considered gross income. There are a number of conceptual reasons why such receipts, technically includable in gross income, are not so included, but perhaps the most appealing is that the transaction costs of collecting the tax on such items would exceed the tax revenue collected. In such circumstances, does it make sense for the government to insist on a "pure" definition of gross income? If not, at what point should the government draw this line? Further, would excepting certain types of receipts from gross income encourage taxpayers to seek out these types of income rather than more traditional types of income, such as compensation for services? Would that be problematic from a tax policy standpoint? Is it more useful to think of such administrative exceptions as more in the nature of traditional exceptions from gross income such as return of basis, realization, or imputed income?

Consider the following situations in which the government has announced that certain receipts will not be includable in gross income. In particular, consider the government's reasons for excluding these types of receipts, and whether including some types of receipts but not others may raise issues of "fairness" in not treating all taxpayers the same depending solely on the type of income they receive (this concept is commonly referred to as "horizontal equity"). Perhaps certain types of receipts, such as disaster relief, should not be taxed precisely out of concerns of fairness? If so, is it appropriate for such receipts not to be included in gross income *administratively* rather than pursuant to a specific *statutory* exclusion from gross income, such as those discussed in Chapter 3?

a. Frequent Flier Miles

Assume an employer requires an employee travel to China twice a year to attend a trade conference. The company pays for business class seats nonstop to China for these trips. After three years, the employee has accumulated enough frequent flier miles to earn one free roundtrip first-class ticket to Hawaii, and goes on a personal vacation. Is the trip to Hawaii gross income? While this looks similar to *McCann* (in which the trip to Las Vegas was included in gross income), it also looks like a rebate or discount which would not be included in gross income. Does it matter that the employer paid for the airline tickets? Would it matter if the miles were earned not through flights to China but rather by using a company credit card?

ANNOUNCEMENT 2002-18
2002-1 C.B. 621

The IRS will not assert that any taxpayer has understated his federal tax liability by reason of the receipt or personal use of frequent flyer miles or other in-kind promotional benefits attributable to the taxpayer's business or official travel. Any future guidance on the taxability of these benefits will be applied prospectively. The relief provided by this announcement does not apply to travel or other promotional benefits that are converted to cash, to compensation that is paid in the form of travel or other promotional benefits, or in other circumstances where these benefits are used for tax avoidance purposes.

Most major airlines offer frequent flyer programs under which passengers accumulate miles for each flight. Individuals may also earn frequent flyer miles or other promotional benefits, for example, through rental cars or hotels. These promotional benefits may generally be exchanged for upgraded seating, free travel, discounted travel, travel-related services, or other services or benefits.

Questions have been raised concerning the taxability of frequent flyer miles or other promotional items that are received as the result of business travel and used for personal purposes. There are numerous technical and administrative issues relating to these benefits on which no official guidance has been provided, including issues relating to the timing and valuation of income inclusions and the basis for identifying personal use benefits attributable to business (or official) expenditures versus those attributable to personal expenditures. Because of these unresolved issues, the IRS has not pursued a tax enforcement program with respect to promotional benefits such as frequent flyer miles.

Consistent with prior practice, the IRS will not assert that any taxpayer has understated his federal tax liability by reason of the receipt or personal use of frequent flyer miles or other in-kind promotional benefits attributable to the taxpayer's business or official travel. Any future guidance on the taxability of these benefits will be applied prospectively.

b.   General Welfare Programs

Congress has often decided to provide cash payments to certain classes of people, such as victims of natural disasters and disabled veterans. Are these cash payments gross income? On one hand, they are clearly accessions to wealth in the form of cash. On the other hand, Congress presumably authorized these payments not to enrich the recipients for services or in the nature of a prize, but to make a community whole which unexpectedly lost everything in a tornado. Does this make it a nontaxable return of capital, or not an accession to wealth at all? Should the Internal Revenue Service consider the intent of Congress in other unrelated statutes to interpret the Internal Revenue Code?

REV. RUL. 98-19
1998-1 C.B. 840

ISSUE

Is a relocation payment authorized pursuant to Title I of the Housing and Community Development Act of 1974 (the "Act"), funded under the 1997 Emergency Supplemental Appropriations Act for Recovery From Natural Disasters (the "Supplemental Act"), and made by a local jurisdiction to an individual moving from a flood-damaged residence to another residence, includible in the individual's gross income under §61 of the Internal Revenue Code?

FACTS

Pursuant to the Act and the Supplemental Act, a resident of a local jurisdiction, within a Presidentially-declared disaster area in the upper Midwest, received a relocation payment from the local jurisdiction to help defray the expenses of moving from the resident's flood-damaged residence to another residence. . . .

LAW AND ANALYSIS

Section 61 and the Regulations thereunder provide that, except as otherwise provided by law, gross income means all income from whatever source derived.

The Service has held that payments made under legislatively provided social benefit programs for the promotion of general welfare are not includible in a recipient's gross income. See Rev. Rul. 76-373, 1976-2 C.B. 16, which holds that relocation payments received by individuals pursuant to §105(a)(11) of the Act are in the nature of general welfare and are not includable in the gross incomes of recipients.

HOLDING

A relocation payment authorized pursuant to the Act, funded under the Supplemental Act, and made by a local jurisdiction to an individual moving from a flood-damaged residence to another residence, is in the nature of general welfare and is not includible in the individual's gross income under §61.

c. Caught Baseballs

"The one constant through all the years, Ray, has been baseball. America has rolled by like an army of steamrollers. It has been erased like a blackboard, rebuilt and erased again. But baseball has marked the time. This field, this game: it's a part of our past, Ray. It reminds of us of all that once was good and it could be again."[1]

"Baseball's status in the life of the nation is so pervasive that it would not strain credulity to say the Court can take judicial notice that baseball is everybody's business. To put it mildly and with restraint, it would be unfortunate indeed if a fine sport and profession, which brings surcease from daily travail and an escape from the ordinary to most inhabitants of this land, were to suffer in the least because of undue concentration by any one or any group on commercial and profit considerations. The game is on higher ground; it behooves every one to keep it there."[2]

On October 27, 2011 a then little-known third baseman for the Saint Louis Cardinals had one of the most memorable hits in baseball history — a game winning home run in the bottom of the eleventh inning of Game Six of the World Series. One lucky fan jumped out of the stands and retrieved the ball. Later, the fan chose to return the ball as a memento of the historic home run. Does the fan have gross income? Is the baseball treasure trove, like in *Cesarini*? Is it a §74 prize like a lottery or game show? Although the fan must have bought a ticket to the game — much in the same way a person buys a lottery ticket — was it really the effort of the fan catching the ball that led to the accession to wealth, much like the person who mows their own lawn? Is the ball imputed income? Does the third baseman have income when the ball is returned?

These difficult issues were first squarely presented when the single season home run record was shattered by two people in the same year — Mark McGwire and Sammy Sosa — leading to several valuable baseballs being caught by fans, some of which were sold and some of which were returned. Does it matter if the person sells the ball on eBay rather than keeping it? Should there be a different rule if the person returns the ball? Is there a difference between a record-breaking home run ball and a run-of-the-mill foul ball caught by a spectator in the stands? Is there something about baseball that makes it different from other sports like football,

---

1. Field of Dreams. Directed by Phil Alden Robinson, 1989.
2. Flood v. Kuhn, 309 F.Supp. 793, 797 (S.D.N.Y.1970).

hockey, or tennis? Do fans have to return footballs, or hockey pucks or tennis balls that go into the stands?

IR-98-56
Internal Revenue Service (I.R.S.) News Release

In response to press speculation resulting from events in major league baseball, the Internal Revenue Service today provided a brief explanation of the basic income and gift tax principles that would apply to a baseball fan who catches a home run ball and immediately returns it.

In general, the fan in these circumstances would not have taxable income. This conclusion is based on an analogy to principles of tax law that apply when someone immediately declines a prize or returns unsolicited merchandise. There would likewise be no gift tax in these circumstances. The tax results may be different if the fan decided to sell the ball.

Commenting on this situation, IRS Commissioner Charles O. Rossotti said, "Sometimes pieces of the tax code can be as hard to understand as the infield fly rule. All I know is that the fan who gives back the home run ball deserves a round of applause, not a big tax bill."

Problems

2-21. Over the course of a two-year period, Kathryn Masse flew regularly on United Airlines for personal trips. Having joined United's frequent flyer program, Masse had sufficient mileage to entitle her to a round-trip ticket to Australia at no additional cost. United's regular coach class round-trip fare to Australia is $1,700.
   a. What result if Masse flies to Australia?
   b. What result if, instead of using the tickets, she sells her rights to Paul Lichner for $1,100?
   c. Under the facts in *b*, are there any tax consequences to Lichner when he uses the tickets?
   d. What result to Lichner if he sells the tickets for $1,500?
   e. What result in *a* if the mileage flown had been on business and her employer had paid for the tickets?

E.   DISPOSITION OF PROPERTY

Code: §§1001(a) to (c), 1012, 1016(a)(1) to (2)
Regulations: §§1.1001-2(a) to (c), examples (1), (2), (6), (7), (8); 1.1012-1(a); 1.1016-2(a), (b)

1. Gains on the Disposition of Property

Section 61(a)(3) provides that gains from dealings in property are included in gross income. Unlike other forms of income, however, gains from dealings in property require multiple considerations at the same time. While gains from property are included in gross income, such gains are also subject to two of the four exceptions to gross income: (1) gain from property is not gross income until the gain is realized, and (2) gain from property does not include amounts received as a return of the initial capital investment in the property. In effect, "gains from property" refers to *net* gains realized on the sale or exchange of property.

On the sale or exchange of appreciated property, gain is determined by comparing the *adjusted basis* of the property transferred and the *amount realized* by the taxpayer on the disposition. A gain is realized to the extent the amount realized exceeds the adjusted basis. Thus, to calculate gross income arising on the sale of property, the transferor must determine both the amount realized on the disposition and the adjusted basis of the property transferred.

Section 1001(b) defines the amount realized as the sum of money received, plus the fair market value of any property received. Whether the transferor receives cash, property, or services, a benefit has been realized, and this benefit is measured by the value of any cash, property, or services received. Thus, the amount realized represents the total economic benefit received in exchange for the property transferred.

Similarly, as previously explained in section C3 of this chapter, because an economic benefit accrues whenever the transferee cancels or assumes the transferor's indebtedness or acquires the property subject to a debt, the amount realized includes the amount of the debt cancelled or assumed. In general, it makes no difference whether the debt is related to the property or whether the seller is personally liable for the debt. The seller is relieved of an obligation, and the amount of debt relief is therefore included as an amount realized. In effect, the seller is treated as receiving cash and using it to settle the preexisting obligation.

After computing the amount realized on the disposition, the taxpayer's next step in computing the gain (or loss) realized is determining the adjusted basis of the transferred property. The concept of adjusted basis is therefore of paramount importance in the computation of gross income arising from property dispositions. Conversely, adjusted basis is not relevant in determining gross income earned from the rendition of services. The reason for the difference is logical—any amount realized in exchange for services rendered creates an economic gain, whereas an amount realized on the transfer of property creates economic gain only to the extent that amount exceeds the transferor's cost for the property sold. In effect, adjusted basis serves as an account to track the amount of a taxpayer's tax-free return of capital.

Adjusted basis is a term of art specifically defined in the Code. Notwithstanding the general concept that basis represents a taxpayer's investment in property, adjusted basis can mean only what is defined in the Code—no more, no less. Section 1012 provides the general rule applicable to most purchases of property: basis equals the taxpayer's cost of acquiring the property. On the purchase of property, cost includes not only cash paid by the taxpayer but also the fair market value of other property transferred or services rendered in exchange for the property received. In addition, a cost basis includes certain acquisition expenses, such as broker's and attorney's fees.

If the purchaser acquires two or more properties in one transaction, the total cost basis must be allocated among the individual properties. In the absence of an arm's-length allocation by the purchaser and the seller, the allocation will be based on the relative fair market values of the acquired properties at the time of purchase.

As will be seen in Chapter 3, however, the taxpayer's basis depends on the manner in which the property was acquired. Different rules determine the basis of property acquired by purchase, gift, inheritance, or exchange. Moreover, although these rules determine the initial or unadjusted basis of property, that basis must be adjusted for certain subsequent events. For instance, as discussed at Chapter 6, depreciation deductions decrease basis (see §1016(a)(2)), whereas capital improvements to the property increase basis (see §1016(a)(1)). It is easy to understand why capital improvements increase basis. Assume, for example, that Smith purchases a home for $100,000 cash and subsequently pays a builder $20,000 to add a two-room addition. It is clear that if Smith later sells the house for $150,000, she has an overall economic gain of $30,000; but what is the tax result? At the time she purchased the house, Smith had a $100,000 cost basis, and when she sold it she had a $150,000 amount realized. Without adjusting the cost basis for the $20,000 improvement, a $50,000 gain is realized, obviously an incorrect result. Thus, to derive the proper result, the $100,000 cost basis is increased by the $20,000 capital improvement, resulting in a $120,000 adjusted basis and a $30,000 gain.

2. The Realization Requirement

As discussed above, the realization requirement is embodied in §1001(a), which defines gain only as the amount realized over the adjusted basis. Curiously, however, neither §1001 nor any other provision of the Code explicitly defines a realization event. Section 1001(b) provides that "amount realized" arises from a "sale or other disposition" but gives no context on what an "other disposition" entails. Must it be substantially similar to a sale? Does it require an exchange of one type of property for another? Can economically identical properties be exchanged for each other and be a disposition? The Supreme Court addressed precisely that issue below.

COTTAGE SAVINGS ASSOCIATION v. COMMISSIONER
499 U.S. 554 (1991)

JUSTICE MARSHALL delivered the opinion of the Court: The issue in this case is whether a financial institution realizes tax-deductible losses when it exchanges its interests in one group of residential mortgage loans for another lender's interests in a different group of residential mortgage loans. We hold that such a transaction does give rise to realized losses.

I

Petitioner Cottage Savings Association (Cottage Savings) is a savings and loan association (S&L) formerly regulated by the Federal Home Loan Bank Board (FHLBB). Like many S&L's, Cottage Savings held numerous long-term, low-interest mortgages that declined in value when interest rates surged in the late 1970s. These institutions would have benefited from selling their devalued mortgages in order to realize tax-deductible losses. However, they were deterred from doing so by FHLBB accounting regulations, which required them to record the losses on their books. Reporting these losses consistent with the then-effective FHLBB accounting regulations would have placed many S&L's at risk of closure by the FHLBB.

The FHLBB responded to this situation by relaxing its requirements for the reporting of losses. In a regulatory directive known as "Memorandum R-49," dated June 27, 1980, the FHLBB determined that S&L's need not report losses associated with mortgages that are exchanged for "substantially identical" mortgages held by other lenders.[2] The FHLBB's acknowledged purpose for Memorandum R-49 was to facilitate transactions that would generate tax losses but that would not substantially affect the economic position of the transacting S&L's.

This case involves a typical Memorandum R-49 transaction. On December 31, 1980, Cottage Savings sold "90% participation interests" in 252 mortgages to four S&L's. It simultaneously purchased "90% participation interests" in 305 mortgages held by these S&L's.[3] All of the loans involved in the transaction were secured by single-family homes, most in the Cincinnati area. The fair market value of the package of participation interests exchanged by each side was approximately $4.5 million. The face value of the participation interests Cottage Savings relinquished in the transaction was approximately $6.9 million.

On its 1980 federal income tax return, Cottage Savings claimed a deduction for $2,447,091, which represented the adjusted difference between the face value of the participation interests that it traded and the fair market value of the participation interests that it received. As permitted by Memorandum R-49, Cottage Savings did not report these losses to the FHLBB. . . .

---

2. Memorandum R-49 listed 10 criteria for classifying mortgages as substantially identical.

The loans involved must:
1. involve single-family residential mortgages,
2. be of similar type (e.g., conventionals for conventionals),
3. have the same stated terms to maturity (e.g., 30 years),
4. have identical stated interest rates,
5. have similar seasoning (i.e., remaining terms to maturity),
6. have aggregate principal amounts within the lesser of 2 1/2% or $100,000 (plus or minus) on both sides of the transaction, with any additional consideration being paid in cash,
7. be sold without recourse,
8. have similar fair market values,
9. have similar loan-to-value ratios at the time of the reciprocal sale, and
10. have all security properties for both sides of the transaction in the same state.

Record, Exh. 72-BT.

3. By exchanging merely participation interests rather than the loans themselves, each party retained its relationship with the individual obligors. Consequently, each S&L continued to service the loans on which it had transferred the participation interests and made monthly payments to the participation-interest holders.

Because of the importance of this issue to the S&L industry and the conflict among the Circuits over whether Memorandum R-49 exchanges produce deductible tax losses, we granted certiorari. We now reverse.

II

Rather than assessing tax liability on the basis of annual fluctuations in the value of a taxpayer's property, the Internal Revenue Code defers the tax consequences of a gain or loss in property value until the taxpayer "realizes" the gain or loss. . . . As this Court has recognized, the concept of realization is "founded on administrative convenience." Under an appreciation-based system of taxation, taxpayers and the Commissioner would have to undertake the "cumbersome, abrasive, and unpredictable administrative task" of valuing assets on an annual basis to determine whether the assets had appreciated or depreciated in value. . . .

Section 1001(a)'s language provides a straightforward test for realization: to realize a gain or loss in the value of property, the taxpayer must engage in a "sale or other disposition of [the] property." The parties agree that the exchange of participation interests in this case cannot be characterized as a "sale" under §1001(a); the issue before us is whether the transaction constitutes a "disposition of property." The Commissioner argues that an exchange of property can be treated as a "disposition" under §1001(a) only if the properties exchanged are materially different. The Commissioner further submits that, because the underlying mortgages were essentially economic substitutes, the participation interests exchanged by Cottage Savings were not materially different from those received from the other S&L's. Cottage Savings, on the other hand, maintains that *any* exchange of property is a "disposition of property" under §1001(a), regardless of whether the property exchanged is materially different. Alternatively, Cottage Savings contends that the participation interests exchanged were materially different because the underlying loans were secured by different properties.

We must therefore determine whether the realization principle in §1001(a) incorporates a "material difference" requirement. If it does, we must further decide what that requirement amounts to and how it applies in this case. We consider these questions in turn.

A

Neither the language nor the history of the Code indicates whether and to what extent property exchanged must differ to count as a "disposition of property" under §1001(a). Nonetheless, we readily agree with the Commissioner that an exchange of property gives rise to a realization event under §1001(a) only if the properties exchanged are "materially different." The Commissioner himself has by regulation construed §1001(a) to embody a material difference requirement:

> Except as otherwise provided . . . the gain or loss realized from the conversion of property into cash, *or from the exchange of property for other property differing materially either in kind or in extent*, is treated as income or as loss sustained." Treas. Reg. §1.1001-1. . . .

We conclude that Treasury Regulation §1.1001-1 *is* a reasonable interpretation of §1001(a). . . .

Treasury Regulation §1001-1 is also consistent with our landmark precedents on realization. In a series of early decisions involving the tax effects of property exchanges, this Court made clear that a taxpayer realizes taxable income only if the properties exchanged are "materially" or "essentially" different. . . . The Commissioner's construction of the statutory language to incorporate these principles certainly was reasonable.

B

Precisely what constitutes a "material difference" for purposes of §1001(a) of the Code is a more complicated question. The Commissioner argues that properties are "materially different" only if they differ in economic substance. To determine whether the participation interests exchanged in this case were "materially different" in this sense, the Commissioner argues, we should look to the attitudes of the parties, the evaluation of the interests by the secondary mortgage market, and the views of the FHLBB. We conclude that §1001(a) embodies a much less demanding and less complex test.

Unlike the question *whether* §1001(a) contains a material difference requirement, the question of *what constitutes* a material difference is not one on which we can defer to the Commissioner. For the Commissioner has not issued an authoritative, prelitigation interpretation of what property exchanges satisfy this requirement. Thus, to give meaning to the material difference test, we must look to the case law from which the test derives and which we believe Congress intended to codify in enacting and reenacting the language that now comprises §1001(a).

We start with the classic treatment of realization in Eisner v. Macomber. In *Macomber*, a taxpayer who owned 2,200 shares of stock in a company received another 1,100 shares from the company as part of a pro rata stock dividend meant to reflect the company's growth in value. At issue was whether the stock dividend constituted taxable income. We held that it did not because no gain was realized. We reasoned that the stock dividend merely reflected the increased worth of the taxpayer's stock, and that a taxpayer realizes increased worth of property only by receiving "something of exchangeable value *proceeding from* the property."

In three subsequent decisions — United States v. Phellis, Weiss v. Stearn, and Marr v. United States — we refined *Macomber*'s conception of realization in the context of property exchanges. In each case, the taxpayer owned stock that had appreciated in value since its acquisition. And in each case, the corporation in which the taxpayer held stock had reorganized into a new corporation, with the new corporation assuming the business of the old corporation. While the corporations in *Phellis* and *Marr* both changed from New Jersey to Delaware corporations, the original and successor corporations in *Weiss* both were incorporated in Ohio. In each case, following the reorganization, the stockholders of the old corporation received shares in the new corporation equal to their proportional interest in the old corporation.

The question in these cases was whether the taxpayers realized the accumulated gain in their shares in the old corporation when they received in return for those shares stock representing an equivalent proportional interest in the new corporations. In *Phellis* and *Marr*, we held that the transactions were realization events. We reasoned that because a company incorporated in one state has "different rights and powers" from one incorporated in a different state, the taxpayers in *Phellis* and *Marr* acquired through the transactions property that was "materially different" from what they previously had. In contrast, we held that no realization occurred in *Weiss*. By exchanging stock in the predecessor corporation for stock in the newly reorganized corporation, the taxpayer did not receive "a thing really different from what he theretofore had." As we explained in *Marr*, our determination that the reorganized company in *Weiss* was not "really different" from its predecessor turned on the fact that both companies were incorporated in the same State.

Obviously, the distinction in *Phellis* and *Marr* that made the stock in the successor corporations materially different from the stock in the predecessors was minimal. Taken together, *Phellis*, *Marr*, and *Weiss* stand for the principle that properties are "different" in the sense that is "material" to the Internal Revenue Code so long as their respective possessors enjoy legal entitlements that are different in kind or extent. Thus, separate groups of stock are not materially different if they confer "the same proportional interest of the same character in the same corporation." However, they *are* materially different if they are issued by different corporations or if they confer "differen[t] rights and powers" in the same corporation. No more demanding a standard than this is necessary in order to satisfy the administrative purposes underlying the realization requirement in §1001(a). For, as long as the property entitlements are not identical, their exchange will allow both the Commissioner and the transacting taxpayer easily to fix the appreciated or depreciated values of the property relative to their tax bases.

In contrast, we find no support for the Commissioner's "economic substitute" conception of material difference. According to the Commissioner, differences between properties are material for purposes of the Code only when it can be said that the parties, the relevant market (in this case the secondary mortgage market), and the relevant regulatory body (in this case the FHLBB) would consider them material. Nothing in *Phellis*, *Weiss*, and *Marr* suggests that exchanges of properties must satisfy such a subjective test to trigger realization of a gain or loss.

Moreover, the complexity of the Commissioner's approach ill serves the goal of administrative convenience that underlies the realization requirement. In order to apply the Commissioner's test in a principled fashion, the Commissioner and the taxpayer must identify the relevant market, establish whether there is a regulatory agency whose views should be taken into account, and then assess how the relevant market participants and the agency would view the transaction. The Commissioner's failure to explain how these inquiries should be conducted further calls into question the workability of his test.

Finally, the Commissioner's test is incompatible with the structure of the Code. Section 1001(c) of Title 26 provides that a gain or loss realized under §1001(a) "shall be recognized" unless one of the Code's nonrecognition provisions applies. One such nonrecognition provision withholds recognition of a gain or loss realized from an exchange of properties that would appear to be economic substitutes under the Commissioner's material difference test. This provision, commonly known as the "like-kind" exception, withholds recognition of a gain or loss realized "on the exchange of property held for productive use in a trade or business or for investment . . . for property of like kind which is to be held either for productive use in a trade or business or for investment." If Congress had expected that exchanges of similar properties would *not* count as realization events under §1001(a), it would have had no reason to bar recognition of a gain or loss realized from these transactions.

C

Under our interpretation of §1001(a), an exchange of property gives rise to a realization event so long as the exchanged properties are "materially different"— that is, so long as they embody legally distinct entitlements. Cottage Savings' transactions at issue here easily satisfy this test. Because the participation interests exchanged by Cottage Savings and the other S&L's derived from loans that were made to different obligors and secured by different homes, the exchanged interests did embody legally distinct entitlements. Consequently, we conclude that Cottage Savings realized its losses at the point of the exchange.

The Commissioner contends that it is anomalous to treat mortgages deemed to be "substantially identical" by the FHLBB as "materially different." The anomaly, however, is merely semantic; mortgages can be substantially identical for Memorandum R-49 purposes and still exhibit "differences" that are "material" for purposes of the Internal Revenue Code. Because Cottage Savings received entitlements different from those it gave up, the exchange put both Cottage Savings and the Commissioner in a position to determine the change in the value of Cottage Savings' mortgages relative to their tax bases. Thus, there is no reason not to treat the exchange of these interests as a realization event, regardless of the status of the mortgages under the criteria of Memorandum R-49. . . .

IV

For the reasons set forth above, the judgment of the Court of Appeals is reversed, and the case is remanded for further proceedings consistent with this opinion.

So ordered.

Note

Regulation §1.1001-1 provides that a taxpayer realizes income when properties exchanged are "materially different." In *Cottage Savings*, the Court found no guidance from either the Code or the Regulation through which to define a material difference. The Court fashioned its own test and held that properties are materially different if the legal entitlements associated with the property are different in kind or extent. While *Cottage Savings* involved an exchange of properties, there is no reason to believe that the Court's "different legal entitlements" test could not also apply to a *single* property if its legal entitlements were sufficiently altered or modified. For example, assume a bank made a mortgage loan to a family which fell on hard times, and offered to help by extending the period to repay the mortgage—has there been a realization event? Without further guidance, the *Cottage Savings* test could have the harsh result of deemed exchanges arising from such minor modifications to debt instruments.

In response to this concern, Regulation §1.1001-3 was promulgated to determine when modifications to debt instruments result in realization events. To result in a deemed exchange under this regulation, a modification to the debt instrument must be "significant." Reg. §1.1001-3(e). Bright line tests are provided for specific types of modifications of debt instruments that are automatically considered "significant." If a modification is not specifically addressed in one of the bright line tests, then under the "general significance rule," the modifications to the property's legal rights and obligations must be "economically significant" under all of the facts and circumstances in order to result in a deemed exchange. This "economically significant" test generally will require a more significant change than does the *Cottage Savings'* "different legal entitlements" test.

Problem

2-22. On May 30, Mary Jorgensen purchased fifty shares of Abbottsford Laboratory stock for $5,000. On December 31, the closing market quotations showed that the stock was worth $15,000. On that day, Tom Ford offered to purchase the stock for $15,000; however, Jorgensen rejected the offer, preferring to retain the stock. Later in the evening, Jorgensen borrowed $10,000 from Ford, payable on July 4 of the next year, and accruing interest at a rate of 13 percent. As collateral for the loan, Jorgensen pledged her shares of Abbottsford stock.

    a.   Has Jorgensen realized a gain as a result of the documented worth of the shares?

    b.   Did she realize a gain through Ford's offer?

    c.   Did she realize a gain by borrowing $10,000 and using the stock as collateral?

3.   Special Issues in Determining Adjusted Basis

a.   Taxable Exchanges of Property

When property is purchased for cash, the adjusted basis is relatively easy to determine. Under §1012, the basis of property is its cost; thus, the basis of property purchased for cash is the amount of cash paid. More difficult questions arise when noncash properties are exchanged for each other.

Why should this be the case? Should not these two always be the same amount? Not necessarily. Consider the following hypothetical. Assume a taxpayer owns a vintage model car which originally cost $20,000 and maintained a fair market value of $20,000. The taxpayer decides to sell that car and a buyer who is an avid collector of vintage cars asks to buy it, but does not have any cash. Rather, the buyer proposes to trade a new car worth $30,000 in exchange. Although this appears to be a bad deal for the buyer, maybe the buyer does not like new cars, or has always been searching for this type of vintage car to finish the collection, or for some other reason values the vintage car as much as the new car. For the taxpayer, this is a great deal because the new car is worth $10,000 more than the vintage car could be sold for to anyone else. So the taxpayer trades the vintage car to the buyer in exchange for the new car worth $30,000. The question that arises is what is the taxpayer's basis in the new car? Was the taxpayer's "cost" $20,000 — the value of the vintage car given up — or $30,000 — the value of the new car received? What does "cost" mean in this context?

At one time there were two views regarding this question. The minority view held that the fair market value of the "old" property the taxpayer transferred in the exchange was the amount paid and thus was the "cost" basis of the property the taxpayer received. Budd International Corp. v. Commissioner, 143 F.2d 784 (3d Cir. 1944). Unfortunately, on exchanges of property of unequal value, application of the minority view resulted in taxpayers realizing an incorrect amount of gain or loss on a subsequent disposition of the acquired property. For example, assume the above taxpayer immediately turned around and sold the new car for $30,000. What would be the result? The taxpayer would have realized a $10,000 taxable gain on the exchange of the old car (an amount realized of $30,000 — the value of the new car received — less the basis of $20,000) and then again realized another $10,000 of taxable gain on the sale of the new car for cash. Under this rule, the taxpayer effectively would be taxed twice on a single $10,000 economic benefit.

Recognizing this problem, the majority rule, relied on by the court in Philadelphia Park Amusement v. United States, 126 F. Supp. 184 (Ct. Cl. 1954), provided that property acquired in a taxable exchange of properties takes a cost basis equal to *its* fair market value. The rationale for this rule appears logical only after one considers that it is based on an analysis of tax, not actual economic, cost.

> The succinct statement that "the basis of property shall be the cost of such property" although clear in principle, is frequently difficult in application. One view is that the cost basis of property received in a taxable exchange is the fair market value of the property *given* in the exchange. The other view is that the cost basis of property received in a taxable exchange is the fair market value of the property *received* in the exchange. The view that "cost" is the fair market value of the property given is predicated on the theory that the cost to the taxpayer is the economic value relinquished. The view that "cost" is the fair market value of the property received is based upon the theory that the term "cost" is a tax concept and must be considered in the light of the designed interrelationship of sections [of the Code] . . . and the prime role that the basis of property plays in determining tax liability. We believe that when the question is considered in the latter context that the cost basis of the property received in a taxable exchange is the fair market value of the property *received* in the exchange.
>
> When property is exchanged for property in a taxable exchange the taxpayer is taxed on the difference between the adjusted basis of the property given in exchange and the fair market value of the property received in exchange. For purposes of determining gain or loss the fair market value of the property received is treated as cash and taxed accordingly. To maintain harmony with the fundamental purpose of these sections, it is necessary to consider the fair market value of the property received as the cost basis to the taxpayer. The failure to do so would result in allowing the taxpayer a stepped-up basis, without paying a tax therefor, if the fair market value of the property received is less than the fair market value of the property given, and the

taxpayer would be subjected to a double tax if the fair market value of the property received is more than the fair market value of the property given. By holding that the fair market value of the property received in a taxable exchange is the cost basis, the above discrepancy is avoided and the basis of the property received will equal the adjusted basis of the property given plus any gain recognized, or that should have been recognized, or minus any loss recognized, or that should have been recognized.

Id. at 188 (underline emphasis added).

Interestingly, although *Philadelphia Park Amusement* relied on the majority rule, the court actually held that where the value of property received cannot be ascertained, the fair market value of the property transferred should be used to determine the basis of the property received. The court reasoned that in arm's-length negotiations the fair market values of the properties exchanged should be equal. Regardless, *Philadelphia Park* has come to stand for the proposition that cost basis equals the fair market value of property received, not paid, when those two are not equal.

Problems

2-23. On February 7, Delores Resnik purchased ten shares of IBM stock for $100 per share. She sold the shares for $120 per share on August 1. Resnik incurred a $7.50 per share broker's fee both in acquiring and selling the stock.
  a. What is her basis in the IBM stock?
  b. What is her amount realized on the sale of the IBM stock?
  c. What is her gain realized on the sale of the IBM stock?

2-24. On January 1, Sanford Smith acquired 100 shares of Xerox stock at a total cost of $60 per share. On December 1, when the Xerox stock reached a market value of $100 per share, Smith exchanged the 100 shares of stock for a parcel of undeveloped land with an appraised value of $10,000.
  a. What is Smith's gain realized on the Xerox stock disposition?
  b. What is Smith's basis in the land?

2-25. Arthur Wyatt, taking advantage of Tim Jones's inexperience, exchanged CBS stock, having an adjusted basis of $10,000 and a fair market value of $15,000, in return for Jones's General Motors stock, having an adjusted basis of $20,000 and a fair market value of $16,000.
  a. What is each party's gain or loss?
  b. What is each party's basis in the property acquired?

b. Debt Incurred in the Acquisition of Property

As discussed in section C3 of this chapter, debt often raises challenging tax law issues, particularly with regard to debt incurred to acquire property. One reason debt can cause complications is because multiple types of debt exist, each raising different tax considerations.

Different types of debt are treated differently for tax purposes in part because of the varying amount of risk a lender may be willing to accept in making a loan.

One of the primary factors a creditor considers in making a loan and determining the appropriate interest rate is the debtor's credit risk—that is, the risk that the debtor will not repay the loan. To protect against credit risk, a creditor may seek security for the loan. A debt is secured if the creditor requires specific property as security or collateral for the repayment of the debt. In general, if a debtor fails to repay (or "defaults on") a secured debt, the creditor has the right to foreclose upon the collateral or secured property. A home mortgage is a common example of a secured loan. In a home mortgage, a debtor borrows money from a creditor to purchase a house, and in exchange the debtor gives the creditor a note and mortgage pledging the house as security for the loan.

An unsecured loan is one in which no specific property is supplied as collateral for repayment. Instead, the creditor relies solely on the debtor's general ability to repay the loan. As a result, if the debtor defaults on an unsecured loan, the creditor has no special rights to, or interests in, any specific property of the debtor. Credit card debt is an example of unsecured debt. When using a credit card to purchase goods or services, the credit card company in effect loans money to the cardholder on an unsecured basis.

Debt is "recourse" if the debtor is personally liable for repayment of the full amount of the loan. Assume a debtor borrows $1,000 on a recourse basis to purchase a piano, which secures the debt. After two years, the debtor defaults on the loan and surrenders the piano to the creditor. At that time, the piano is worth $750. Because the debt is recourse, the debtor remains liable to the creditor for the remaining $250. Debt is "nonrecourse" if the debtor is not personally liable for repayment of the debt in excess of the value of the property securing the debt. In the previous example, if the debt had been nonrecourse instead of recourse, the debtor would not be required to pay the remaining $250 to the creditor. Rather, the surrender of the piano to the creditor would extinguish the debt, notwithstanding that the creditor received only $750 of value toward the original $1,000 obligation.

In Crane v. Commissioner, 331 U.S. 1 (1947), the Supreme Court propounded one of the most important and controversial principles of tax law—the entire amount of *any* debt incurred in the acquisition of property is included in the purchaser's cost basis at the time the property is acquired, not at a later date when the debt is paid. For example, if the taxpayer purchases property worth $100,000 in exchange for $20,000 cash plus an $80,000 note and first mortgage to the seller, the taxpayer-purchaser has a $100,000 cost basis at the time of acquisition. Moreover, the taxpayer's subsequent mortgage payments to the bank will have no impact on basis.

The *Crane* rule is premised on the assumption that the purchaser will satisfy the debt over time; thus, regardless when the purchaser pays the $80,000, the long-term consequences are the same as if the property had been purchased for cash. If, however, the obligation is not discharged by the time the purchaser disposes of the property, the unsatisfied amount of the obligation is debt relief and, as discussed in section C3 of this chapter, is included in the amount realized on the disposition. Therefore, on acquisition and disposition, debt incurred and debt relief are treated as equivalent to cash paid and received, respectively.

The *Crane* rule is defensible on economic grounds because depreciation deductions should be allowed without producing negative basis. Moreover, the *Crane* rule is justified not only by economic reality but also by its practical consequences because it enables the purchaser to determine the cost basis of property as of the date of acquisition. Without the *Crane* rule, basis would fluctuate, increasing with each principal payment of the debt.

Some commentators have argued that nonrecourse debt should *not* be included in the cost basis of property because the debtor can abandon the property and lose only his rights in the encumbered asset. Other commentators contend that as long as the fair market value of the encumbered property exceeds the amount of the outstanding nonrecourse debt, the obligor has equity in the property and generally will continue to service the debt to protect this interest. Based on this latter view and the economic reality it reflects, courts have held that a nonrecourse purchase money debt is included in the purchaser's cost of acquiring property. See, e.g., Mayerson v. Commissioner, 47 T.C. 340 (1966).

CRANE v. COMMISSIONER
331 U.S. 1 (1947)

Mr. Chief Justice Vinson delivered the opinion of the Court.

The question here is how a taxpayer who acquires depreciable property subject to an unassumed mortgage, holds it for a period, and finally sells it still so encumbered, must compute her taxable gain.

Petitioner was the sole beneficiary and the executrix of the will of her husband, who died January 11, 1932. He then owned an apartment building and lot subject to a mortgage,[1] which secured a principal debt of $255,000.00 and interest in default of $7,042.50. As of that date, the property was appraised for federal estate tax purposes at a value exactly equal to the total amount of this encumbrance. Shortly after her husband's death, petitioner entered into an agreement with the mortgagee whereby she was to continue to operate the property — collecting the rents, paying for necessary repairs, labor, and other operating expenses, and reserving $200.00 monthly for taxes — and was to remit the net rentals to the mortgagee. This plan was followed for nearly seven years, during which period petitioner reported the gross rentals as income, and claimed and was allowed deductions for taxes and operating expenses paid on the property, for interest paid on the mortgage, and for the physical exhaustion of the building. Meanwhile, the arrearage of interest increased to $15,857.71. On November 29, 1938, with the mortgagee threatening foreclosure, petitioner sold to a third party for $3,000.00 cash, subject to the mortgage, and paid $500.00 expenses of sale.

Petitioner reported a taxable gain of $1,250.00. Her theory was that the "property" which she had acquired in 1932 and sold in 1938 was only the equity, or the excess in the value of the apartment building and lot over the amount of the mortgage. This equity was of zero value when she acquired it. No depreciation could be taken on a zero value.[2] Neither she nor her vendee ever assumed the mortgage, so, when she sold the equity, the amount she realized on the sale was the

---

1. The record does not show whether he was personally liable for the debt.

2. This position is, of course, inconsistent with her practice in claiming such deductions in each of the years the property was held. The deductions so claimed and allowed by the Commissioner were in the total amount of $25,500.00.

net cash received, or $2,500.00. This sum less the zero basis constituted her gain. . . .

The Commissioner, however, determined that petitioner realized a net taxable gain of $23,767.03. His theory was that the "property" acquired and sold was not the equity, as petitioner claimed, but rather the physical property itself, or the owner's rights to possess, use, and dispose of it, undiminished by the mortgage. The original basis thereof was $262,042.50, its appraised value in 1932. Of this value $55,000.00 was allocable to land and $207,042.50 to building. During the period that petitioner held the property, there was an allowable depreciation of $28,045.10 on the building, so that the adjusted basis of the building at the time of sale was $178,997.40. The amount realized on the sale was said to include not only the $2,500.00 net cash receipts, but also the principal amount of the mortgage subject to which the property was sold, both totaling $257,500.00. The selling price was allocable in the proportion, $54,471.15 to the land and $203,028.85 to the building. . . .

Logically, the first step under this scheme is to determine the unadjusted basis of the property, and the dispute in this case is as to the construction to be given the term "property." If "property," as used in that provision, means the same thing as "equity," it would necessarily follow that the basis of petitioner's property was zero, as she contends. If, on the contrary, it means the land and building themselves, or the owner's legal rights in them, undiminished by the mortgage, the basis was $262,042.50.

We think that the reasons for favoring one of the latter constructions are of overwhelming weight. In the first place, the words of statutes — including revenue acts — should be interpreted where possible in their ordinary, everyday senses. The only relevant definitions of "property" to be found in the principal standard dictionaries are the two favored by the Commissioner, i.e., either that "property" is the physical thing which is a subject of ownership, or that it is the aggregate of the owner's rights to control and dispose of that thing. "Equity" is not given as a synonym, nor do either of the foregoing definitions suggest that it could be correctly so used. Indeed, "equity" is defined as "the value of a property . . . above the total of the liens. . . ." The contradistinction could hardly be more pointed. Strong countervailing considerations would be required to support a contention that Congress in using the word "property," meant "equity." . . .

A further reason why the word "property" should not be construed to mean "equity" is the bearing such construction would have on the allowance of deductions for depreciation and on the collateral adjustments of basis.

Section 23(1) permits deduction from gross income of "a reasonable allowance for the exhaustion, wear and tear of property. . . ." Section 23(n) declare[s] that the "basis upon which exhaustion, wear and tear . . . are to be allowed" is the basis "for the purpose of determining the gain upon the sale" of the property, which is the basis "adjusted . . . for exhaustion, wear and tear . . . to the extent allowed (but not less than the amount allowable). . . ."

Under these provisions, if the mortgagor's equity were the basis, it would also be the original basis from which depreciation allowances are deducted. If it is, and if the amount of the annual allowances were to be computed on that value, as would then seem to be required, they will represent only a fraction of the cost of the corresponding physical exhaustion, and any recoupment by the mortgagor of the remainder of that cost can be effected only by the reduction of his taxable gain in the year of sale. If, however, the amount of the annual allowances were to be computed on the value of the property, and then deducted from an equity basis, we would in some instances have to accept deductions from a minus basis or deny deductions altogether. The Commissioner also argues that taking the mortgagor's equity as the basis would require the basis to be changed with each payment on the mortgage, and that the attendant problem of repeatedly recomputing basis and annual allowances would be a tremendous accounting burden on both the Commissioner and the taxpayer. Moreover, the mortgagor would acquire control over the timing of his depreciation allowances.

. . . It may be added that the Treasury has never furnished a guide through the maze of problems that arise in connection with depreciating an equity basis, but, on the contrary, has consistently permitted the amount of depreciation allowances to be computed on the full value of the property, and subtracted from it as a basis. Surely, Congress' long-continued acceptance of this situation gives it full legislative endorsement.

We conclude that the proper basis is the value of the property, undiminished by mortgages thereon, and that the correct basis here was $262,042.50. The next step is to ascertain what adjustments are required . . . in making any depreciation adjustments whatsoever.

. . . The Tax Court found on adequate evidence that the apartment house was property of a kind subject to physical exhaustion, that it was used in taxpayer's trade or business, and consequently that the taxpayer would have been entitled to a depreciation allowance, except that, in the opinion of that Court, the basis of the property was zero, and it was thought that depreciation could not be taken on a zero basis. As we have just decided that the correct basis of the property was not zero, but $262,042.50, we avoid this difficulty, and conclude that an adjustment should be made as the Commissioner determined.

Petitioner urges to the contrary that she was not entitled to depreciation deductions, whatever the basis of the property, because the law allows them only to one who actually bears the capital loss, and here the loss was not hers but the mortgagee's. We do not see, however, that she has established her factual premise. There was no finding of the Tax Court to that effect, nor to the effect that the value of the property was ever less than the amount of the lien. Nor was there evidence in the record, or any indication that petitioner could produce evidence, that this was so. . . .

. . . At last we come to the problem of determining the "amount realized" on the 1938 sale. . . . If the "property" to be valued on the date of acquisition is the property free of liens, the "property" to be priced on a subsequent sale must be the same thing.

Starting from this point, we could not accept petitioner's contention that the $2,500.00 net cash was all she realized on the sale except on the absurdity that she sold a quarter-of-a-million dollar property for roughly 1 percent of its value, and took a 99 percent loss. Actually, petitioner does not urge this. She argues, conversely, that because only $2,500.00 was realized on the sale, the "property" sold must have been the equity only, and that consequently we are forced to accept her contention as to the meaning of "property." We adhere, however, to what we have already said on the meaning of "property," and we find that the absurdity is avoided by our conclusion that the amount of the mortgage is properly included in the "amount realized" on the sale.

Petitioner concedes that if she had been personally liable on the mortgage and the purchaser had either paid or assumed it, the amount so paid or assumed would be considered a part of the "amount realized." The cases so deciding have already repudiated the notion that there must be an actual receipt by the seller himself of "money" or "other property," in their narrowest senses. It was thought to be decisive that one section of the Act must be construed so as not to defeat the intention of another or to frustrate the Act as a whole, and that the taxpayer was the "beneficiary" of the payment in "as real and substantial [a sense] as if the money had been paid it and then paid over by it to its creditors."

Both these points apply to this case. The first has been mentioned already. As for the second, we think that a mortgagor, not personally liable on the debt, who sells the property subject to the mortgage and for additional consideration, realizes a benefit in the amount of the mortgage as well as the boot.[37] If a purchaser pays boot, it is immaterial as to our problem whether the mortgagor is also to receive money from the purchaser to discharge the mortgage prior to sale, or whether he is merely to transfer subject to the mortgage — it may make a difference to the purchaser and to the mortgagee, but not to the mortgagor. Or put in another way, we are no more concerned with whether the mortgagor is, strictly speaking, a debtor on the mortgage, than we are with whether the benefit to him is, strictly speaking, a receipt of money or property. We are rather concerned with the reality that an owner of property, mortgaged at a figure less than that at which the property will sell, must and will treat the conditions of the mortgage exactly as if they were his personal obligations. If he transfers subject to the mortgage, the benefit to him is as real and substantial as if the mortgage were discharged, or as if a personal debt in an equal amount had been assumed by another.

Therefore we conclude that the Commissioner was right in determining that petitioner realized $257,500.00 on the sale of this property.

Petitioner contends that the result we have reached taxes her on what is not income within the meaning of the Sixteenth Amendment. If this is because only the direct receipt of cash is thought to be income in the constitutional sense, her contention is wholly without merit. If it is because the entire transaction is thought to have been "by all dictates of common sense . . . a ruinous disaster," as it was termed in her brief, we disagree with her premise. She was entitled to depreciation deductions for a period of nearly seven years, and she actually took them in almost the allowable amount. The crux of this case, really, is whether the law permits her to exclude allowable deductions from consideration in computing gain. We have already showed that, if it does, the taxpayer can enjoy a double deduction, in effect, on the same loss of assets. The Sixteenth Amendment does not require that result any more than does the Act itself.

Affirmed.

---

37. Obviously, if the value of the property is less than the amount of the mortgage, a mortgagor who is not personally liable cannot realize a benefit equal to the mortgage. Consequently, a different problem might be encountered where a mortgagor abandoned the property or transferred it subject to the mortgage without receiving boot. That is not this case.

Problem

2-26.   What was Isolde Francis's cost basis, in each of the following examples, if she purchased a home worth $100,000 from Stephanie Smith for the stipulated consideration?

   a.   Francis paid Smith $100,000 cash, which she borrowed minutes earlier from the First National Bank.

   b.   Francis agreed to personally assume a $100,000 debt secured by the acquired property.

   c.   Francis gave a $100,000 nonrecourse note to Smith.

   d.   Francis assumed an $80,000 obligation encumbering the acquired property and gave Smith a nonrecourse note for $20,000.

   e.   Francis did not assume the $80,000 obligation in *d* above but agreed to acquire the property "subject to" the debt. In addition, she paid $12,000 cash, which she borrowed from the First National Bank on a nonrecourse basis, and gave Smith a nonrecourse note for $8,000.

c.   Debt Incurred after Property Acquisition

As *Crane* illustrates, the basis of property acquired by purchase generally equals the purchase price—that is, cash plus liabilities incurred in acquiring the property. Although the *Crane* case decided the issue for debt incurred in the acquisition of property, it did not provide any guidance concerning debt incurred after the date of acquisition. For example, what is the tax result when a taxpayer purchases property for $100,000 cash and, two years later, after the property has appreciated in value to $200,000, borrows $140,000 from the bank by executing a first mortgage on the property? This example raises two important issues: (1) Does the taxpayer increase basis by the $140,000 postacquisition debt incurred; and (2) does the postacquisition loan transaction (which results in the taxpayer's receiving $140,000 cash) constitute a realization event, resulting in a $40,000 gain at the time the loan proceeds are received? With regard to the first issue, the question is whether the postacquisition loan is considered a "cost" of acquiring the property pursuant to §1012. With regard to the second issue, the question is whether the fact that cash was received in excess of the taxpayer's basis mandates realization of a $40,000 ($140,000 minus $100,000) gain at that time or, alternatively, whether there is no gain *realized* because the receipt of the $140,000 cash was accompanied by a $140,000 obligation to repay. Another aspect of the second issue is whether a postacquisition nonrecourse loan, secured only by the property, constitutes a realization event because there is no personal liability for repayment, or whether it has no current tax effect, as is the case with an unsecured loan with personal liability.

Woodsam Associates v. Commissioner, 198 F.2d 357 (2d Cir. 1952), illustrates the principle that when property is mortgaged as security for a loan for a purpose other than the property's acquisition, no current tax consequences arise because there has been no sale, exchange, or other disposition. The same result occurs if the liability is a nonrecourse debt in excess of the basis of the encumbered property. Moreover, such debt does not represent the *cost* of the property; thus, it is not included in basis.

In *Woodsam*, the taxpayer refinanced real property by giving the lender a nonrecourse mortgage in excess of the property's basis. Arguing that refinancing constituted a taxable disposition, the taxpayer urged the court to find taxable gain on the transaction, with a concomitant increase in basis to the extent of that gain. The court disagreed with the taxpayer's theory and held that the refinancing was not a taxable event. Because the taxpayer had not disposed of the property but remained its owner after the refinancing, the court concluded that no gain was realized and the basis of the property was unaffected.

The *Woodsam* court provided the following rationale for its holdings:

> The contention of the petitioner may now be stated quite simply. It is that, when the borrowings subsequent to her acquisition of the property became charges solely upon the property itself, the cash she received for the repayment of which she was not personally liable was a gain then taxable to her as income to the extent that the mortgage indebtedness exceeded her adjusted basis in the property. That being so, it is argued that her tax basis was, under familiar principles of tax law, increased by the amount of such taxable gain. . . .
>
> While this conclusion would be sound if the premise on which it is based were correct, we cannot accept the premise. It is that the petitioner's transfer made a taxable disposition of the property . . . when the second consolidated mortgage was executed, because she had, by then, dealt with it in such a way that she had received cash, in excess of her basis, which, at that time, she was freed from any personal obligation to repay. Nevertheless, whether or not personally liable on the mortgage, "The mortgagee is a creditor, even though the mortgagor is not liable for the debt. He is not the less a creditor because he has recourse only to the land, unless we are to deny the term to one who may levy upon only a part of his debtor's assets." C.I.R. v. Crane, 2 Cir., 153 F.2d 504, 506. Mrs. Wood merely augmented the existing mortgage indebtedness when she borrowed each time and, far from closing the venture, remained in a position to borrow more if and when circumstances permitted and she so desired. And so, she never "disposed" of the property to create a taxable event which is a condition precedent to the taxation of gain. "Disposition" . . . is the "getting rid, or making over, of anything; relinquishment." . . . Nothing of that nature was done here by the mere execution of the second consolidated mortgage; Mrs. Wood was the owner of this property in the same sense after the execution of this mortgage that she was before. As was pointed out in our decision in the *Crane* case, ". . . the lien of a mortgage does not make the mortgagee cotenant; the mortgagor is the owner for all purposes. . . . He has all the income from the property; he manages it; he may sell it; any increase in its value goes to him; any decrease falls on him, until the value goes below the amount of the lien. Realization of gain was therefore, postponed for taxation until there was a final disposition of the property. . . ."

Id. at 359.

4. *Amount Realized from Debt Relief*

As discussed in section C3 of this chapter, the relief from the discharge of a debt obligation may result in an increase in the net wealth of a taxpayer. Thus, under §61(a)(12), discharge of indebtedness can result in gross income. Similarly, a taxpayer may be relieved of his or her obligation on indebtedness in connection with the sale or exchange of property. This could occur when the purchaser acquires the taxpayer's property subject to a preexisting debt or otherwise assumes the taxpayer's obligation. In this case, the taxpayer no longer has the obligation to repay the indebtedness but also no longer holds the property that was the subject of the debt. Should such "debt relief" be treated as discharge of indebtedness income under §61(a)(12)? If not, should this economic benefit be income at all, and if so, how should it be treated? Should the answer differ if the debt is nonrecourse (where the taxpayer is indifferent as to the whether the property is sufficient to satisfy the debt) as opposed to recourse (where the taxpayer would remain liable for any shortfall)? Does it matter whether the debt was incurred in connection with the purchase of the property or was incurred subsequently? These questions have been confronted by Congress, the IRS, and the courts (including the Supreme Court) for many years, and yet have never been fully resolved.

The following section discusses the development and evolution of the law addressing these debt relief and property issues. In reading the cases, rulings, and discussions, consider what the proper role of debt in developing the concepts of gross income discussed earlier in this chapter should be, and whether the developing law approaches this standard.

a. Nonrecourse Indebtedness

Regulation §1.1001-2 provides the general rule that the amount realized on the disposition of encumbered property includes the full amount of any debt relief. The rule applies without regard to whether the discharged liability was incurred in conjunction with the purchase or after the date of the property's acquisition.

The reason for including debt relief from a purchase money obligation as an amount realized was addressed by the Supreme Court in *Crane*. The Court reasoned that because the debt had been included in the seller's basis, thereby increasing the amount of depreciation deductions and the measure for determining gain, it was essential to equalize this tax and economic benefit by including the amount of debt relief as an amount realized by the seller. Without this adjustment to the amount realized, the true amount of economic gain or loss would not be taxed.

For example, assume that X purchases property worth $100,000 in exchange for $20,000 cash plus the assumption of an $80,000 mortgage. X's basis is $100,000. If X subsequently sells that property for $110,000, with the purchaser paying $30,000 and assuming the $80,000 mortgage, X realizes a real economic gain of $10,000. If, however, the amount realized for tax purposes only included the $30,000 cash received, X would realize a $70,000 tax *loss*. To correct this potential loophole, case law treats the $80,000 debt relief as part of the amount realized, resulting in a total amount realized of $110,000 and a $10,000 taxable gain, matching the economic gain.

Although §1.1001-2 of the Regulations reflects the *Crane* holding, as well as the above policies, it does not incorporate footnote 37 of the *Crane* opinion. In footnote 37, the Court indicated that if a nonrecourse liability exceeds the value of the property on the date of disposition, the excess amount might not be included as an amount realized. The footnote implies that because the transferor would receive an economic benefit only to the extent of the value of the property, the amount realized might be limited to that amount.

The Fifth Circuit in Tufts v. Commissioner, 651 F.2d 1058 (5th Cir. 1981), adopted the reasoning of the *Crane* footnote by limiting the amount realized from nonrecourse debt relief to the fair market value of the taxpayer's encumbered property. The *Tufts* court relied on the economic benefit theory implicit in footnote 37. When a taxpayer is at risk only to the extent of the value of the encumbered property, the economic benefit on disposition of the encumbered property can equal only the value of the property. The *Tufts* court reasoned that a debtor has no economic incentive to pay an amount in excess of the value of the property that would be lost on default. Thus, when the property is transferred subject to a nonrecourse obligation, the debtor-transferor's economic benefit is limited to the elimination of a possible claim against the value of the property transferred. Because no further benefit has been received, the amount realized should also be limited to this extent.

The following examples illustrate the tax benefits available if the Fifth Circuit's approach in *Tufts* is controlling. Assume that *A* purchases a $100,000 building in return for a $100,000 nonrecourse note payable to the seller. Further assume that *A* pays no principal on the note. The next year, at a time when the property's value has declined to $60,000, *A* abandons the property subject to the $100,000 obligation. The analysis employed by the Fifth Circuit in *Tufts* would allow *A* to recognize a $40,000 tax loss on the transaction ($60,000 value less adjusted basis of $100,000). Thus, *A* would have a $40,000 deductible loss at no tax or economic cost.

The deduction version of this theory, relied on in Millar v. Commissioner, 577 F.2d 212 (3d Cir. 1978), is in direct opposition to the Fifth Circuit's economic benefit analysis in *Tufts*. In *Millar*, the Third Circuit held that a taxpayer should have included the full amount of a nonrecourse loan in the amount realized on surrender of the property despite the fact that the obligation exceeded the property's value. The court noted that the taxpayer had benefited by including the liability in the adjusted basis and had taken sizable deductions against that basis. To exclude the amount of the liability from the amount realized would be tantamount to giving the taxpayer a double deduction.

In its review of *Tufts*, which follows, the United States Supreme Court reversed the Fifth Circuit, adopting an analysis similar to that of *Millar*.

COMMISSIONER v. TUFTS
461 U.S. 300 (1983)

Justice Blackmun delivered the opinion of the Court.

Over 35 years ago in Crane v. Commissioner, 331 U.S. 1 (1947), this Court ruled that a taxpayer, who sold property encumbered by a nonrecourse mortgage (the amount of the mortgage being less than the property's value), must include the unpaid balance of the mortgage in the computation of the amount the taxpayer realized on the sale. The case now before us presents the question whether the same rule applies when the unpaid amount of the nonrecourse mortgage exceeds the fair market value of the property sold.

I

On August 1, 1970, respondent Clark Pelt, a builder, and his wholly owned corporation, respondent Clark, Inc., formed a general partnership. The purpose of the partnership was to construct a 120-unit apartment complex in Duncanville, Tex., a Dallas suburb. Neither Pelt nor Clark, Inc., made any capital contribution to the partnership. Six days later, the partnership entered into a mortgage loan agreement with the Farm & Home Savings Association (F&H). Under the agreement, F&H was committed for a $1,851,500 loan for the complex. In return, the partnership executed a note and a deed of trust in favor of F&H. The partnership obtained the loan on a nonrecourse basis: neither the partnership nor its partners assumed any personal liability for repayment of the loan. Pelt later admitted four friends and relatives, respondents Tufts, Steger, Stephens, and Austin, as general partners. None of them contributed capital upon entering the partnership.

The construction of the complex was completed in August 1971. During 1971, each partner made small capital contributions to the partnership; in 1972, however, only Pelt made a contribution. The total of the partners' capital contributions was $44,212. In each tax year, all partners claimed as income tax deductions their allocable shares of ordinary losses and depreciation. The deductions taken by the partners in 1971 and 1972 totalled $439,972. Due to these contributions and deductions, the partnership's adjusted basis in the property in August 1972 was $1,455,740.

In 1971 and 1972, major employers in the Duncanville area laid off significant numbers of workers. As a result, the partnership's rental income was less than expected, and it was unable to make the payments due on the mortgage. Each partner, on August 28, 1972, sold his partnership interest to an unrelated third party, Fred Bayles. As consideration, Bayles agreed to reimburse each partner's sale expenses up to $250; he also assumed the nonrecourse mortgage.

On the date of transfer, the fair market value of the property did not exceed $1,400,000. Each partner reported the sale on his federal income tax return and indicated that a partnership loss of $55,740 had been sustained. The Commissioner . . . , on audit, determined that the sale resulted in a partnership capital gain of approximately $400,000. His theory was that the partnership had realized the full amount of the nonrecourse obligation. . . .

II

. . . At issue is the application of [§1001(b)] to the disposition of property encumbered by a nonrecourse mortgage of an amount in excess of the property's fair market value.

A

In Crane v. Commissioner, this Court took the first and controlling step toward the resolution of this issue. Beulah B. Crane was the sole beneficiary under the will of her deceased husband. At his death in January 1932, he owned an apartment building that was then mortgaged for an amount which proved to be equal to its fair market value, as determined for federal estate tax purposes. The widow, of course, was not personally liable on the mortgage. She operated the building for nearly seven years, hoping to turn it into a profitable venture; during that period, she claimed income tax deductions for depreciation, property taxes, interest, and operating expenses, but did not make payments upon the mortgage principal. In computing her basis for the depreciation deductions, she included the full amount of the mortgage debt. In November 1938, with her hopes unfulfilled and the mortgagee threatening foreclosure, Mrs. Crane sold the building. The purchaser took the property subject to the mortgage and paid Crane $3,000; of that amount, $500 went for the expenses of the sale.

Crane reported a gain of $2,500 on the transaction. She reasoned that her basis in the property was zero (despite her earlier depreciation deductions based on including the amount of the mortgage) and that the amount she realized from the sale was simply the cash she received. The Commissioner disputed this claim. He asserted that Crane's basis in the property [under §1014] was the property's fair market value at the time of her husband's death, adjusted for depreciation in the interim, and that the amount realized was the net cash received plus the amount of the outstanding mortgage assumed by the purchaser.

In upholding the Commissioner's interpretation, the Court observed that to regard merely the taxpayer's equity in the property as her basis would lead to depreciation deductions less than the actual physical deterioration of the property, and would require the basis to be recomputed with each payment on the mortgage. The Court rejected Crane's claim that any loss due to depreciation belonged to the mortgagee. The effect of the Court's ruling was that the taxpayer's basis was the value of the property undiminished by the mortgage.

The Court next proceeded to determine the amount realized [under §1001(b)]. In order to avoid the "absurdity" of Crane's realizing only $2,500 on the sale of property worth over a quarter of a million dollars, the Court treated the amount realized as it had treated basis, that is, by including the outstanding value of the mortgage. To do otherwise would have permitted Crane to recognize a tax loss unconnected with any actual economic loss. The Court refused to construe one section of the Revenue Act so as "to frustrate the Act as a whole."

Crane, however, insisted that the nonrecourse nature of the mortgage required different treatment. The Court, for two reasons, disagreed. First, excluding the nonrecourse debt from the amount realized would result in the same absurdity and frustration of the Code. Second, the Court concluded that Crane obtained an economic benefit from the purchaser's assumption of the mortgage identical to the benefit conferred by the cancellation of personal debt. Because the value of the property in that case exceeded the amount of the mortgage, it was in Crane's economic interest to treat the mortgage as a personal obligation; only by so doing could she realize upon sale the appreciation in her equity represented by the $2,500 boot. The purchaser's assumption of the liability thus resulted in a taxable economic benefit to her, just as if she had been given, in addition to the boot, a sum of cash sufficient to satisfy the mortgage.

In a footnote, pertinent to the present case, the Court observed:

> Obviously, if the value of the property is less than the amount of the mortgage, a mortgagor who is not personally liable cannot realize a benefit equal to the mortgage.

Consequently, a different problem might be encountered where a mortgagor abandoned the property or transferred it subject to the mortgage without receiving boot. That is not this case. Id. at 14, n.37.

B

This case presents that unresolved issue. We are disinclined to overrule *Crane*, and we conclude that the same rule applies when the unpaid amount of the non-recourse mortgage exceeds the value of the property transferred. *Crane* ultimately does not rest on its limited theory of economic benefit; instead, we read *Crane* to have approved the Commissioner's decision to treat a nonrecourse mortgage in this context as a true loan. This approval underlies *Crane*'s holdings that the amount of the nonrecourse liability is to be included in calculating both the basis and the amount realized on disposition. That the amount of the loan exceeds the fair market value of the property thus becomes irrelevant.

When a taxpayer receives a loan, he incurs an obligation to repay that loan at some future date. Because of this obligation, the loan proceeds do not qualify as income to the taxpayer. When he fulfills the obligation, the repayment of the loan likewise has no effect on his tax liability.

Another consequence to the taxpayer from this obligation occurs when the taxpayer applies the loan proceeds to the purchase price of property used to secure the loan. Because of the obligation to repay, the taxpayer is entitled to include the amount of the loan in computing his basis in the property; the loan, under §1012, is part of the taxpayer's cost of the property. Although a different approach might have been taken with respect to a nonrecourse mortgage loan,[5] the Commissioner has chosen to accord it the same treatment he gives to a recourse mortgage loan. The Court approved that choice in *Crane*, and the respondents do not challenge it here. The choice and its resultant benefits to the taxpayer are predicated on the assumption that the mortgage will be repaid in full.

When encumbered property is sold or otherwise disposed of and the purchaser assumes the mortgage, the associated extinguishment of the mortgagor's obligation to repay is accounted for in the computation of the amount realized. Because no difference between recourse and nonrecourse obligations is recognized in calculating basis,[7] *Crane* teaches that the Commissioner may ignore the nonrecourse nature of the obligation in determining the amount realized upon disposition of

---

5. The Commissioner might have adopted the theory, implicit in *Crane*'s contentions, that a nonrecourse mortgage is not true debt, but, instead, is a form of joint investment by the mortgagor and the mortgagee. On this approach, nonrecourse debt would be considered a contingent liability, under which the mortgagor's payments on the debt gradually increase his interest in the property while decreasing that of the mortgagee. Because the taxpayer's investment in the property would not include the non-recourse debt, the taxpayer would not be permitted to include that debt in basis.

We express no view as to whether such an approach would be consistent with the statutory structure and, if so, and *Crane* were not on the books, whether that approach would be preferred over *Crane*'s analysis. We note only that the *Crane* Court's resolution of the basis issue presumed that when property is purchased with proceeds from a nonrecourse mortgage, the purchaser becomes the sole owner of the property. Under the *Crane* approach, the mortgagee is entitled to no portion of the basis. The nonrecourse mortgage is part of the mortgagor's investment in the property, and does not constitute a coinvestment by the mortgagee.

7. The Commissioner's choice in *Crane* "laid the foundation stone of most tax shelters," by permitting taxpayers who bear no risk to take deductions on depreciable property. Congress recently has acted to curb this avoidance device by forbidding a taxpayer to take depreciation deductions in excess of amounts he has at risk in the investment. Real estate investments, however, are exempt from this

the encumbered property. He thus may include in the amount realized the amount of the nonrecourse mortgage assumed by the purchaser. The rationale for this treatment is that the original inclusion of the amount of the mortgage in basis rested on the assumption that the mortgagor incurred an obligation to repay. Moreover, this treatment balances the fact that the mortgagor originally received the proceeds of the nonrecourse loan tax-free on the same assumption. Unless the outstanding amount of the mortgage is deemed to be realized, the mortgagor effectively will have received untaxed income at the time the loan was extended and will have received an unwarranted increase in the basis of his property. The Commissioner's interpretation of §1001(b) in this fashion cannot be said to be unreasonable.

C

The Commissioner in fact has applied this rule even when the fair market value of the property falls below the amount of the nonrecourse obligation. Because the theory on which the rule is based applies equally in this situation, we have no reason, after *Crane*, to question this treatment.[11]

Respondents received a mortgage loan with the concomitant obligation to repay by the year 2012. The only difference between that mortgage and one on which the borrower is personally liable is that the mortgagee's remedy is limited to

---

prohibition. Although this congressional action may foreshadow a day when nonrecourse and recourse debts will be treated differently, neither Congress nor the Commissioner has sought to alter *Crane*'s rule of including nonrecourse liability in both basis and the amount realized.

11. Professor Wayne G. Barnett, as amicus in the present case, argues that the liability and property portions of the transaction should be accounted for separately. Under his view, there was a transfer of the property for $1.4 million, and there was a cancellation of the $1.85 million obligation for a payment of $1.4 million. The former resulted in a capital loss of $50,000, and the latter in the realization of $450,000 of ordinary income. Taxation of the ordinary income might be deferred under §108 by a reduction of respondents' bases in their partnership interests.

Although this indeed could be a justifiable mode of analysis, it has not been adopted by the Commissioner. Nor is there anything to indicate that the Code requires the Commissioner to adopt it. We note that Professor Barnett's approach does assume that recourse and nonrecourse debt may be treated identically.

The Commissioner also has chosen not to characterize the transaction as cancellation of indebtedness. We are not presented with and do not decide the contours of the cancellation-of-indebtedness doctrine. We note only that our approach does not fall within certain prior interpretations of that doctrine. In one view, the doctrine rests on the same initial premise as our analysis here — an obligation to repay — but the doctrine relies on a freeing- of-assets theory to attribute ordinary income to the debtor upon cancellation. See United States v. Kirby Lumber Co., 284 U.S. 1, 3 (1931). According to that view, when nonrecourse debt is forgiven, the debtor's basis in the securing property is reduced by the amount of debt canceled, and realization of income is deferred until the sale of the property. Because that interpretation attributes income only when assets are freed, however, an insolvent debtor realizes income just to the extent his assets exceed his liabilities after the cancellation. Lakeland Grocery Co. v. Commissioner, 36 B.T.A. 289, 292 (1937). Similarly, if the nonrecourse indebtedness exceeds the value of the securing property, the taxpayer never realizes the full amount of the obligation canceled because the tax law has not recognized negative basis.

Although the economic benefit prong of *Crane* also relies on a freeing-of-assets theory, that theory is irrelevant to our broader approach. In the context of a sale or disposition of property under §1001, the extinguishment of the obligation to repay is not ordinary income; instead, the amount of the canceled debt is included in the amount realized, and enters into the computation of gain or loss on the disposition of property. According to *Crane*, this treatment is no different when the obligation is nonrecourse: the basis is not reduced as in the cancellation-of-indebtedness context, and the full value of the outstanding liability is included in the amount realized. Thus, the problem of negative basis is avoided.

foreclosing on the securing property. This difference does not alter the nature of the obligation; its only effect is to shift from the borrower to the lender any potential loss caused by devaluation of the property. If the fair market value of the property falls below the amount of the outstanding obligation, the mortgagee's ability to protect its interests is impaired, for the mortgagor is free to abandon the property to the mortgagee and be relieved of his obligation.

This, however, does not erase the fact that the mortgagor received the loan proceeds tax-free and included them in his basis on the understanding that he had an obligation to repay the full amount. When the obligation is canceled, the mortgagor is relieved of his responsibility to repay the sum he originally received and thus realizes value to that extent within the meaning of §1001(b). From the mortgagor's point of view, when his obligation is assumed by a third party who purchases the encumbered property, it is as if the mortgagor first had been paid with cash borrowed by the third party from the mortgagee on a nonrecourse basis, and then had used the cash to satisfy his obligation to the mortgagee.

Moreover, this approach avoids the absurdity the Court recognized in *Crane*. Because of the remedy accompanying the mortgage in the nonrecourse situation, the depreciation in the fair market value of the property is relevant economically only to the mortgagee, who by lending on a nonrecourse basis remains at risk. To permit the taxpayer to limit his realization to the fair market value of the property would be to recognize a tax loss for which he has suffered no corresponding economic loss. Such a result would be to construe "one section of the Act . . . so as . . . to defeat the intention of another or to frustrate the Act as a whole."

In the specific circumstances of *Crane*, the economic benefit theory did support the Commissioner's treatment of the nonrecourse mortgage as a personal obligation. The footnote in *Crane* acknowledged the limitations of that theory when applied to a different set of facts. *Crane* also stands for the broader proposition, however, that a nonrecourse loan should be treated as a true loan. We therefore hold that a taxpayer must account for the proceeds of obligations he has received tax-free and included in basis. Nothing in either §1001(b) or in the Court's prior decisions requires the Commissioner to permit a taxpayer to treat a sale of encumbered property asymmetrically, by including the proceeds of the nonrecourse obligation in basis but not accounting for the proceeds upon transfer of the encumbered property. . . .

IV

When a taxpayer sells or disposes of property encumbered by a nonrecourse obligation, the Commissioner properly requires him to include among the assets realized the outstanding amount of the obligation. The fair market value of the property is irrelevant to this calculation. We find this interpretation to be consistent with Crane v. Commissioner, 331 U.S. 1 (1947), and to implement the statutory mandate in a reasonable manner.

The judgment of the Court of Appeals is therefore reversed.

It is so ordered.

JUSTICE O'CONNOR, concurring.

I concur in the opinion of the Court, accepting the view of the Commissioner. I do not, however, endorse the Commissioner's view. Indeed, were we writing on a slate clean except for the decision in Crane v. Commissioner, 331 U.S. 1 (1947), I would take quite a different approach — that urged upon us by Professor Barnett as amicus.

Crane established that a taxpayer could treat property as entirely his own, in spite of the "coinvestment" provided by his mortgagee in the form of a nonrecourse loan. That is, the full basis of the property, with all its tax consequences, belongs to the mortgagor. That rule alone, though, does not in any way tie nonrecourse debt to the cost of property or to the proceeds upon disposition. I see no reason to treat the purchase, ownership, and eventual disposition of property differently because the taxpayer also takes out a mortgage, an independent transaction. In this case, the taxpayer purchased property, using nonrecourse financing, and sold it after it declined in value to a buyer who assumed the mortgage. There is no economic difference between the events in this case and a case in which the taxpayer buys property with cash; later obtains a nonrecourse loan by pledging the property as security; still later, using cash on hand, buys off the mortgage for the market value of the devalued property; and finally sells the property to a third party for its market value.

The logical way to treat both this case and the hypothesized case is to separate the two aspects of these events and to consider, first, the ownership and sale of the property, and, second, the arrangement and retirement of the loan. Under *Crane*, the fair market value of the property on the date of acquisition — the purchase price — represents the taxpayer's basis in the property, and the fair market value on the date of disposition represents the proceeds on sale. The benefit received by the taxpayer in return for the property is the cancellation of a mortgage that is worth no more than the fair market value of the property, for that is all the mortgagee can expect to collect on the mortgage. His gain or loss on the disposition of the property equals the difference between the proceeds and the cost of acquisition. Thus, the taxation of the transaction *in property* reflects the economic fate of the *property*. If the property has declined in value, as was the case here, the taxpayer recognizes a loss on the disposition of the property. The new purchaser then takes as his basis the fair market value as of the date of the sale.

In the separate borrowing transaction, the taxpayer acquires cash from the mortgagee. He need not recognize income at that time, of course, because he also incurs an obligation to repay the money. Later, though, when he is able to satisfy the debt by surrendering property that is worth less than the face amount of the debt, we have a classic situation of cancellation of indebtedness, requiring the taxpayer to recognize income in the amount of the difference between the proceeds of the loan and the amount for which he is able to satisfy his creditor. The taxation of the financing transaction then reflects the economic fate of the loan.

The reason that separation of the two aspects of the events in this case is important is, of course, that the Code treats different sorts of income differently. A gain on the sale of the property may qualify for capital gains treatment, §§1202, 1221, while the cancellation of indebtedness is ordinary income, but income that the taxpayer may be able to defer. §§108, 1017. Not only does Professor Barnett's theory permit us to accord appropriate treatment to each of the two types of income or loss present in these sorts of transactions, it also restores continuity to the system by making the taxpayer-seller's proceeds on the disposition of property equal to the purchaser's basis in the property. Further, and most important, it allows us to tax the events in this case in the same way that we tax the economically identical hypothesized transaction.

Persuaded though I am by the logical coherence and internal consistency of this approach, I agree with the Court's decision not to adopt it judicially. We do not write on a slate marked only by *Crane*. The Commissioner's long-standing position, Rev. Rul. 76-111, 1976-1 Cum. Bull. 214, is now reflected in the regulations. Treas. Reg. §1.1001-2. In the light of the numerous cases in the lower courts including the amount of the unrepaid proceeds of the mortgage in the proceeds on sale or disposition, it is difficult to conclude that the Commissioner's interpretation of the statute exceeds the bounds of his discretion. As the Court's opinion demonstrates, his interpretation is defensible. One can reasonably read §1001(b)'s reference to "the amount realized *from* the sale or other disposition of property" (emphasis added) to permit the Commissioner to collapse the two aspects of the transaction. As long as his view is a reasonable reading of §1001(b), we should defer to the regulations promulgated by the agency charged with intepretation of the statute. Accordingly, I concur.

b.   Recourse Indebtedness

In Revenue Ruling 90-16, which follows, the Service held that §61(a)(3) income from dealings in property *and* §61(a)(12) income from debt cancellation arose in a transfer of property to a bank in satisfaction of a debt. Can the Revenue Ruling be reconciled with the *Tufts* decision? If so, how?

REV. RUL. 90-16
1990-1 C.B. 12

ISSUE

A taxpayer transfers to a creditor a residential subdivision that has a fair market value in excess of the taxpayer's basis in satisfaction of a debt for which the taxpayer was personally liable. Is the transfer a sale or disposition resulting in the realization and recognition of gain by the taxpayer under sections 1001(c) and 61(a)(3) of the Internal Revenue Code?

FACTS

X was the owner and developer of a residential subdivision. To finance the development of the subdivision, X obtained a loan from an unrelated bank. X was unconditionally liable for repayment of the debt. The debt was secured by a mortgage on the subdivision.

X . . . defaulted on the debt. X negotiated an agreement with the bank whereby the subdivision was transferred to the bank and the bank released X from all liability for the amounts due on the debt. When the subdivision was transferred pursuant to the agreement, its fair market value was 10,000*x* dollars, *X*'s adjusted basis in the subdivision was 8,000*x* dollars, and the amount due on the debt was 12,000*x* dollars which did not represent any accrued but unpaid interest. . . .

LAW AND ANALYSIS

Section 61(a)(3) and 61(a)(12) of the Code provide that, except as otherwise provided, gross income means all income from whatever source derived, including (but not limited to) gains from dealings in property and income from discharge of indebtedness. . . .

Section 1.61-6(a) of the Income Tax Regulations provides that the specific rules for computing the amount of gain or loss from dealings in property under section 61(a)(3) are contained in section 1001 and the regulations thereunder.

Section 1001(a) of the Code provides that gain from the sale or other disposition of property shall be the excess of the amount realized therefrom over the adjusted basis provided in section 1011 for determining gain.

Section 1001(b) of the Code provides that the amount realized from the sale or other disposition of property shall be the sum of any money received plus the fair market value of the property (other than money) received.

Section 1001(c) of the Code provides that, except as otherwise provided in subtitle A, the entire amount of the gain or loss, determined under section 1001, on the sale or exchange of property shall be recognized.

Section 1.1001-2(a)(1) of the regulations provides that, except as provided in section 1.1001-2(a)(2) and (3), the amount realized from a sale or other disposition of property includes the amount of liabilities from which the transferor is discharged as a result of the sale or disposition. Section 1.1001-2(a)(2) provides that the amount realized on a sale or other disposition of property that secures a recourse liability does not include amounts that are (or would be if realized and recognized) income from the discharge of indebtedness under section 61(a)(12). *Example (8)* under section 1.1001-2(c) illustrates these rules as follows:

> *Example (8).* In 1980, *F* transfers to a creditor an asset with a fair market value of $6,000 and the creditor discharges $7,500 of indebtedness for which *F* is personally liable. The amount realized on the disposition of the asset is its fair market value ($6,000). In addition, *F* has income from the discharge of indebtedness of $1,500 ($7,500 −$6,000).

In the present situation, *X* transferred the subdivision to the bank in satisfaction of the 12,000*x* dollar debt. To the extent of the fair market value of the property transferred to the creditor, the transfer of the subdivision is treated as a sale or disposition upon which gain is recognized under section 1001(c) of the Code. To the extent the fair market value of the subdivision, 10,000*x* dollars, exceeds its adjusted basis, 8,000*x* dollars, *X* realizes and recognizes gain on the transfer. *X* thus recognizes 2,000*x* dollars of gain.

To the extent the amount of debt, 12,000*x* dollars, exceeds the fair market value of the subdivision, 10,000*x* dollars, *X* realizes income from the discharge of indebtedness. . . .

If the subdivision had been transferred to the bank as a result of a foreclosure proceeding in which the outstanding balance of the debt was discharged (rather than having been transferred pursuant to the settlement agreement), the result would be the same. A mortgage foreclosure, like a voluntary sale, is a "disposition" within the scope of the gain or loss provisions of section 1001 of the Code.

HOLDING

The transfer of the subdivision by X to the bank in satisfaction of a debt on which X was personally liable is a sale or disposition upon which gain is realized and recognized by X under sections 1001(c) and 61(a)(3) of the Code to the extent the fair market value of the subdivision transferred exceeds X's adjusted basis. . . .

Problems

2-27. On January 15, Carla Jones purchased a used car in exchange for $10,000 cash and her $20,000 promissory note.

    a. What result if Jones sold the car to Michael Adams in return for $22,000 in cash, and in addition, Adams agreed to acquire the property subject to the $20,000 obligation?

    b. What result if Jones sold the car (still subject to a $20,000 debt) to Virginia Smith in return for Smith's agreement to cancel Jones's pre-existing $22,000 obligation to Smith?

    c. What result if Jones sold the car (still subject to a $20,000 debt) to Kathy Johnson in exchange for Johnson's unencumbered truck worth $22,000?

2-28. On January 1, year 1, Thomas Wyatt purchased an office computer from Computo-Tech, Inc. for $10,000. Wyatt gave the seller $1,000 cash and his nonrecourse note for $9,000.

For the taxable year ending December 31, year 1, Wyatt claimed the appropriate $1,000 depreciation deduction. On December 15, year 2, Wyatt received an offer from Smith to purchase the computer for $15,000, its market value at the time. Smith's offer, which was accompanied by a $2,000 check, was not subject to any conditions other than the transfer of clear title. Wyatt refused the offer and returned the check, although he orally agreed with Smith that the property was worth $15,000. On December 30, year 2, Wyatt borrowed $4,000 from National Bank, securing the loan by giving the bank a second nonrecourse mortgage on the property. For the taxable year ending December 31, year 2, Wyatt claimed $1,000 of depreciation. On January 2, year 2, Wyatt used the $4,000 loan proceeds from the second mortgage to reduce the balance of the principal amount of his Computo-Tech, Inc. loan from $9,000 to $5,000.

During year 3, the value of Wyatt's computer decreased from $15,000 to $8,000. For the taxable year ending December 31, year 3, Wyatt claimed $1,000 of depreciation. Wyatt, realizing that the computer was subject to more debt than its current value, abandoned the property at the main headquarters of Computo-Tech, Inc. on January 1, year 4.

   a. What was Wyatt's adjusted basis in the computer on January 1, year 1?

   b. What was Wyatt's adjusted basis in the computer on January 1, year 2?

   c. What was the tax effect of Smith's offer on December 15, year 2?

   d. What was the tax effect of the agreement executed between National Bank and Wyatt on December 30, year 2?

   e. What was the tax effect of Wyatt's repayment, on January 2, year 3, of $4,000 of the $9,000 loan from Computo-Tech, Inc.?

   f. What was the tax effect of Wyatt's abandonment of the computer on January 1, year 4?

   g. What result if, instead of abandoning the computer, Wyatt found someone to purchase it for $10,000 on January 1, year 4, with the purchaser paying Wyatt $1,000 and acquiring the property subject to the $9,000 debt ($5,000 to Computo-Tech and $4,000 to National Bank)?

2-29. On January 1, year 1, Jon Rose purchased a parcel of undeveloped land from Dick Morgan in exchange for $100,000 cash and Rose's $900,000 promissory note. Rose was unconditionally liable for repayment of the note, which was secured by the parcel of land. On January 15, year 3, after making a total of $25,000 principal payments on the note, Rose informed Morgan that because the property had declined in value to $850,000, Rose would not make any additional payments. What result to Rose if:

   a. Morgan foreclosed on the property and received $850,000 at a foreclosure sale. Rose had a $25,000 deficiency judgment assessed against him.

   b. Rose deeded the property to Morgan in lieu of foreclosure. Morgan accepted the property in cancellation of only $850,000 of Rose's $875,000 personal obligation.

   c. Rose deeded the property to Morgan in lieu of foreclosure. Morgan accepted the property in cancellation of the entire $875,000 obligation.

5. Discharge of Indebtedness Redux: Reconciling Tufts and Zarin

Recall the disputed debt and unenforceable debt issues discussed in *Zarin* and *Rood*. In both cases, the courts considered whether the debt was in dispute at the time it arose and whether it was enforceable against the obligor at the time of discharge. *Tufts* considered the same issue with respect to nonrecourse debt. More specifically, the taxpayer in *Tufts* contended that because the debt was nonrecourse it was unenforceable against the taxpayer to the extent it exceeded the value of the property securing the debt, and thus the excess was not "real" debt and should not be included in amount realized. The Supreme Court rejected this theory because not to do so would permit taxpayers the benefit of full basis for nonrecourse debt under *Crane* without the corresponding gain when relieved of such debt. Does this conclusion in *Tufts* fundamentally alter the contested liability doctrine? Is there really a difference between the liability contested in *Zarin* and a nonrecourse debt? The following case considers these issues.

PRESLAR v. COMMISSIONER
167 F.3d 1323 (10th Cir. 1999)

BRISCOE, CIRCUIT JUDGE.

The Commissioner of Internal Revenue appeals the United States Tax Court's decision to redetermine the tax deficiency assessed against Layne and Sue Preslar for underpayment of 1989 federal income taxes. The Tax Court held the Preslars' settlement of a loan obligation for less than the face amount of the loan did not create taxable income because the contested liability/disputed debt exception to the general discharge-of-indebtedness income rule rendered the write-off nontaxable. We . . . reverse and remand.

On July 12, 1983, after six months of talks, Layne and Sue Preslar agreed to purchase the ranch for $1 million, with the sale to be financed by Moncor Bank. The agreement expressly referred to the fact that Moncor Bank was financing the purchase, but only the Preslars and the president of High Nogal signed the contract on September 1, 1983. The Preslars executed a $1 million promissory note in favor of Moncor Bank, secured by a mortgage on the ranch. The Preslars were to pay fourteen annual installments of $66,667, with interest at 12 percent per annum, with final payment due September 1, 1998.

Moncor Bank used $760,000 of the loan proceeds to satisfy the mortgages of Citizens State Bank and Security Bank and Trust. The Preslars thus received title to the ranch free and clear of all of High Nogal's prior mortgages.

The Preslars intended to develop the ranch as a sportsman's resort by subdividing 160 acres and selling one-to-two acre lots for cabins or vacation homes, and permitting lot owners to hunt and engage in other outdoor recreational activities on the remaining 2,340 acres. The goal was to sell each cabin lot for approximately $16,500, with total gross revenues exceeding $1.5 million. The Preslars' 1989 joint tax return indicates several lots sold for substantially higher amounts.

Moncor Bank permitted the Preslars to repay their loan by assigning the installment sales contracts of purchasers of cabin lots to Moncor Bank at a discount. There is no reference to this unique repayment arrangement in the loan documents. . . . Between September 1983 and August 1985, the Preslars sold nineteen cabin lots and had assigned most of the contracts to Moncor Bank prior to its declared insolvency. . . .

In August 1985, Moncor Bank was declared insolvent and the Federal Deposit Insurance Corporation (FDIC) was appointed as receiver. The FDIC notified the Preslars of the insolvency and advised them to make all future payments on their loan to the FDIC. The FDIC refused to accept further assignments of sale contracts as repayment and ordered the Preslars to suspend sales of cabin lots. The Preslars complied with the suspension directive, but made no further payments on the loan.

The Preslars filed an action against the FDIC for breach of contract in September 1985, seeking an order requiring the FDIC to accept assignment of sales contracts as loan repayment. The parties settled the action in December 1988 after the FDIC agreed to accept $350,000 in full satisfaction of the Preslars' indebtedness. The Preslars borrowed the $350,000 from another bank and, after the funds were remitted to the FDIC, the original $1 million promissory note was marked "paid."

At the time of the settlement, the unpaid balance on the Preslars' loan was $799,463. The Preslars paid a total of $550,537 on the loan ($350,000 settlement plus $200,537 credited for assignment of sales contracts). Therefore, as a result of the settlement, the Preslars' outstanding debt obligation was reduced by $449,463 ($1 million less $550,537). . . .

DISCHARGE-OF-INDEBTEDNESS INCOME

Section 61(a) of the Internal Revenue Code broadly defines "gross income" as "all income from whatever source derived" except as expressly provided otherwise. . . . The phrase is intended to capture all "accessions to wealth, clearly realized, and over which the taxpayers have complete dominion." Commissioner v. Glenshaw Glass Co., 348 U.S. 426 (1955). From its enactment, the "sweeping scope" of this provision and its statutory predecessors has been consistently emphasized by the Supreme Court.

This case centers around the Commissioner's determination of the Preslars' discharge-of-indebtedness income after they settled their loan obligation with the FDIC in December 1988. The concept of discharge-of-indebtedness income, first articulated in United States v. Kirby Lumber Co., 284 U.S. 1 (1931), and later codified in §61(a)(12), requires taxpayers who have incurred a financial obligation that is later discharged in whole or in part, to recognize as taxable income the extent of the reduction in the obligation. Two rationales have been identified for this rule:

> This rule is based on the premise that the taxpayer has an increase in wealth due to the reduction in valid claims against the taxpayer's assets. In the alternative it has been suggested that taxation is appropriate because the consideration received by a taxpayer in exchange for [his] indebtedness is not included in income when received because of the obligation to repay and the cancellation of that obligation removes the reason for the original exclusion. . . .

. . . Loans ordinarily are not taxable because the borrower has assumed an obligation to repay the debt in full at some future date. See Commissioner v. Tufts, 461 U.S. 300 (1983). Discharge-of-indebtedness principles come into play, however, if that assumption of repayment proves erroneous. Otherwise, taxpayers could secure income with no resulting tax liability.

It is undisputed that the Preslars financed their purchase of the ranch in 1983 by executing a $1 million promissory note in favor of Moncor Bank. It is similarly uncontested that when the Preslars settled their lawsuit with the FDIC in 1988, thereby extinguishing all obligations arising from the 1983 loan, only $550,537 had been paid on the loan principal. Nevertheless, the Tax Court ruled the Preslars' underlying debt was disputed and fell within the judicially-created "contested liability" exception to discharge-of-indebtedness income.

CONTESTED LIABILITY/DISPUTED DEBT EXCEPTION

The "contested liability" or, as it is occasionally known, "disputed debt" doctrine rests on the premise that if a taxpayer disputes the original amount of a debt in good faith, a subsequent settlement of that dispute is "treated as the amount of debt cognizable for tax purposes." Zarin v. Commissioner, 916 F.2d 110, 115 (3d Cir.1990). In other words, the "excess of the original debt over the amount determined to have been due" may be disregarded in calculating gross income. The few decisions that have interpreted this doctrine have generated considerable controversy.

The origins of the contested liability doctrine can be traced to N. Sobel, Inc. v. Commissioner, 40 B.T.A. 1263 (1939). . . . In *Zarin*, the court embraced the reasoning of *N. Sobel* while reversing the Commissioner's recognition of discharge-of-indebtedness income. . . . Citing no authority, the majority reasoned that "[w]hen a debt is unenforceable, it follows that the amount of the debt, and not just the liability thereon, is in dispute." Therefore, the $500,000 settlement "fixed the amount of loss and the amount of debt cognizable for tax purposes."

The problem with the Third Circuit's holding is it treats liquidated and unliquidated debts alike. The whole theory behind requiring that the amount of a debt be disputed before the contested liability exception can be triggered is that only in the context of disputed debts is the Internal Revenue Service (IRS) unaware of the exact consideration initially exchanged in a transaction. . . . The mere fact that a taxpayer challenges the enforceability of a debt in good faith does not necessarily mean he or she is shielded from discharge-of-indebtedness income upon resolution of the dispute. To implicate the contested liability doctrine, the original amount of the debt must be unliquidated. . . .

A holding to the contrary would strain IRS treatment of unenforceable debts and, in large part, disavow the Supreme Court's mandate that the phrase "gross income" be interpreted as broadly as the Constitution permits.

This conclusion is underscored by the Supreme Court's holding in *Tufts* that a nonrecourse mortgage (i.e., taxpayer has no personal liability upon default) must be treated as an enforceable loan both when it is made and when it is discharged. The Court reasoned that because the indebtedness is treated as a true debt when it is incurred, it must be treated as a true debt when it is discharged, with all the attendant tax consequences. It seems evident from this ruling that if the distinction between the recourse and nonrecourse nature of a loan has no bearing on calculation of gross income, the enforceability of a debt should be of equally minimal importance.

The Tax Court in this case and the court in *Zarin* cited United States v. Hall, 307 F.2d 238 (10th Cir.1962), in support of their contested liability holdings. . . .

Whether *Hall* has continued viability is questionable in light of the Supreme Court's holding in *Tufts*. The emphasis on a taxpayer's lack of legal obligation to pay a gambling debt in *Hall* is difficult to reconcile with *Tuft*'s disregard of the nonrecourse nature of a loan in calculating gross income. Even if parts of *Hall* remain viable, however, the opinion would offer little refuge to the Preslars. The debt in *Hall* was unliquidated. The taxpayer's underlying obligation, therefore, could not be assessed prior to settlement with the club owner. Such a scenario is not present here.

. . . The dispute with the FDIC focused only on the terms of repayment; it did not touch upon the amount or validity of the Preslars' debt. . . . This conclusion is highlighted by the relief sought from the FDIC. As an alternative to accepting assignment of contracts, the Preslars requested that the FDIC "substantially discount the remaining amount due on their loan." Such a position "evidences the Preslars' recognition that they had a fixed and certain liability at the time the FDIC took control of their loan from Moncor Bank." In fact, Layne Preslar conceded he understood he was personally liable for the full amount of the $1 million note in the event he could not sell a sufficient number of lots. In sum, the Preslars' underlying indebtedness remained liquidated at all times.

. . . Finally, the Preslars contend their transaction with Moncor Bank made little economic sense and was done only to accommodate Moncor Bank in its attempts to pacify bank regulators. This argument has little merit. It is highly doubtful that an experienced real estate agent like Layne Preslar would spend six months negotiating the price of the ranch only to then agree to a grossly over-stated figure. Even more incredible is the notion that the Preslars would have exposed themselves to $1 million of personal liability out of pure benevolence for the bank. As the Commissioner points out, if the Preslars had sold all ninety-six lots for $16,500 as they claimed they could during loan negotiations with Moncor Bank, they would have netted a gross profit of more than $300,000. Moncor Bank fully expected the Preslars to be successful in their sales of lots and anticipated profits. The deal that the Preslars brokered with Moncor Bank made total economic sense. The Tax Court's invocation of the contested liability doctrine in the face of the record presented was unwarranted.

. . . We REVERSE the Tax Court's vacatur of the Commissioner's determination of tax deficiency and imposition of untimely filing penalties and REMAND the case with instructions to enter judgment in favor of the Commissioner.

EBEL, CIRCUIT JUDGE, dissenting.

I respectfully dissent. . . .

Under the contested liability doctrine or disputed debt exception, when "there is a legitimate dispute between a creditor and a debtor concerning the existence of a liability, and a compromise between the parties is reached, no discharge of indebtedness income will arise as to the contested and unpaid portion of the original liability." . . . Thus, contrary to the majority's view, the contested liability doctrine is not limited to instances where the taxpayer specifically disputes only the amount of the debt and the original amount was unliquidated.

. . . Given *N. Sobel*, I believe that the majority's view that the contested liability doctrine applies only when the original amount of a debt is disputed and unliquidated is mistakenly narrow. This view ignores the fact that the original amount of a debt is necessarily disputed and may be unliquidated under a good faith dispute over liability "that can be traced to the circumstances in existence at the time of the debt's creation." . . . Only upon resolution of the dispute over the existence of liability traceable to the origin of the debt does the "question as to [the taxpayer's] liability and the amount thereof" become "actual and present by any practical purpose," including taxation. Thus, settlement of a dispute over the enforceability of a debt traceable to its origin, such as the settlements in *N. Sobel* and *Zarin*, does not result in a windfall. Such settlements merely establish the original amount of liability, as opposed to discharging any amount of the original liability.

[T]he Tax Court accepted the Preslars' contention that the $1 million purchase price for the Ranch had been inflated and that the Preslars and Moncor Bank had agreed to a correspondingly inflated method of repayment involving the assignment of installment sales contracts. . . . According to the Tax Court, "[w]hen the FDIC refused to honor this payment arrangement with regard to the Bank loan, a legitimate dispute arose regarding the nature and amount of [the Preslars'] liability on the Bank loan." Thus, given the proper scope of the contested liability doctrine, I believe that the Preslars' settlement with the FDIC would not result in discharge of indebtedness income if the Tax Court's finding is correct.

. . . [T]he majority relies on *Tufts*, which held that cancellation of a nonrecourse loan realizes discharge of indebtedness income. The majority believes that this "underscore[s]" its own holding that cancellation of an unenforceable debt realizes discharge of indebtedness income, stating that "if the distinction between the recourse and nonrecourse nature of a loan has no bearing on calculation of gross income, the enforceability of a debt should be of equally minimal importance." Although unstated, the only way *Tufts'* holding "underscores" the majority's holding is if a nonrecourse loan is treated as the functional equivalent of an unenforceable debt.

To the extent the majority relies on this premise, I disagree. Nonrecourse loans and unenforceable debts are not functional equivalents. Nonrecourse loans are enforceable, unenforceable debts are not. A party may sue to collect on a nonrecourse loan, but cannot sue to collect on an unenforceable debt. While a taxpayer has no personal liability upon default of a nonrecourse loan, the taxpayer nonetheless is always liable for the loan. That liability merely is capped by the value of the underlying security interest. . . . Given an unenforceable debt, the taxpayer has no liability. This distinction can make all the difference for tax purposes.

. . . From *Tufts'* reasoning, it is apparent that the lack of distinction between a nonrecourse and a recourse debt for discharge of indebtedness purposes does not negate but rather reinforces the applicability of the contested liability doctrine in this case. Because a nonrecourse debt is an enforceable obligation to repay, the cancellation of that debt would result in discharge of indebtedness income. Although the mortgagee's only remedy upon default is acquisition of the secured property, that limited remedy does not affect the mortgagor's gain upon cancellation of the mortgage. That gain is the difference between the original amount of the debt which the mortgagor was obligated to repay and the canceled balance. In contrast, the borrower realizes no economic gain in the settlement of disputed debt which is unenforceable for reasons relating back to the origin of the debt. The settlement determines the original amount of liability. On the other hand, cancellation of an enforceable debt would realize income to the extent of the discharge. Thus, contrary to the majority's reasoning, I believe an unenforceable debt is not the functional equivalent of a nonrecourse loan either in concept or in consequence, and the enforceability of a debt is of critical importance for purposes of the contested liability doctrine. Indeed, although cancellation of a nonrecourse loan ordinarily would result in discharge of indebtedness income, cancellation of a nonrecourse loan which is unenforceable for a reason relating back to the origin of the loan might have no tax consequences.

CHAPTER 3

ITEMS EXCLUDED
FROM GROSS INCOME

A. OVERVIEW

For various policy considerations, Congress explicitly permits certain "accessions to wealth" which would otherwise be includable in gross income under §61(a) to bypass taxation through specific statutory provisions that will be introduced in this chapter. A related topic, the deferral of recognition of certain accessions to wealth, will be discussed in Chapter 5.

The exclusions from gross income presented in this chapter are divided into three general categories: (1) donative transfers, (2) employee fringe benefits, and (3) other specific exclusions that reflect public policy concerns. The first category, the one most familiar, includes certain donative transfers such as gifts, bequests, and scholarships. Such receipts are characterized generally by an absence of an employment or business relationship.

The second category of exclusions includes benefits received pursuant to an employment relationship, which are excludable from gross income for specific policy reasons. The excludable items include certain employer-provided meals and lodging and a broad category of statutorily enumerated employer-provided fringe benefits for employees. But perhaps the most familiar and most controversial of these involves employer-provided health and life insurance. A variety of rationales underlie such exclusions, including the involuntary nature of certain employment-related benefits that deprive the recipient of freedom of choice, the valuation difficulties regarding in-kind receipts, and the interest in fostering socially preferred behavior.

The final and broadest category of exclusions includes diverse receipts excluded for various public policy reasons. This category includes such items as discharge of an insolvent taxpayer's indebtedness, social security benefits, and interest derived from state and municipal obligations. The governmental goals of assisting those experiencing personal and financial hardships, or of providing financial support to state and local governments, undergird many of these exclusions.

In studying the scope and application of the statutory exclusions, it is important to remember that each provision was adopted to further a specific congressional policy. Thus, an understanding of the underlying social, economic, and political policies supporting the enactment of a particular Code section may prove invaluable in its interpretation and application. Often, the most effective arguments are those that rely on the legislative intent of the applicable provision.

B. GIFTS AND BEQUESTS

Code: §§102, 1014(a)(1), 1015(a)
Regulations: §§1.102-1(a), (b), (c); Prop. Reg. §1.102-1(f)(2)

1. Introduction

Section 102(a) excludes from gross income the receipt of gifts, bequests, devises, and inheritances. Bequests, devises, and inheritances are usually easily identified, but characterization of a transfer as a gift is often less clear. Neither the Code nor the Regulations define the term "gift," and the courts have had dubious success in formulating a definition. In Commissioner v. Duberstein, 363 U.S. 278 (1960), the landmark decision in this area, the Supreme Court attempted to define the term gift for purposes of the §102(a) exclusion. In *Duberstein*, the taxpayer received a Cadillac from a person to whom he had given the names of potential customers. The Supreme Court upheld the trial court's finding that the Cadillac was not a gift but was compensation for past services or an inducement to perform future services.

According to *Duberstein*, some of the factors to take into consideration in determining whether a payment or transfer is a gift include whether it was

1. made out of a detached and disinterested generosity;
2. made out of affection, respect, admiration, charity, or like impulses;
3. not made primarily from the constraining force of any moral or legal duty;
4. not made from the incentive of anticipated benefit of an economic nature; and
5. not made in return for services rendered.

Under this standard, whether a payment is an excludable gift or includable income is determined by the donor's actual intent or motive in transferring the property to the recipient. A resolution of the issue, therefore, is dependent on all the relevant facts and circumstances.

What factors should be considered in an actual intent analysis? Gift-giving occurs in a wide variety of relationships from family and friends to acquaintances and coworkers. In the family context should generosity be assumed as a motive? Is it possible that family members might not like each other? Would a transfer to a sibling made out of a sense of moral obligation be a gift? What about caring for a young child? What if the law required parents to care for minor children? Would it matter if the child also worked for the family business?

While it is often difficult enough to discern a gift in the familial context, as seen in *Duberstein* it becomes particularly difficult to identify gifts in a commercial setting. The main concern is that an alleged gift, excludable from gross income, may actually be disguised compensation, that is, the payment results from an exchange relationship rather than from a true gift motivation. While §102(c) safeguards against this abuse in the employer-employee relationship, other settings in which the relationship between the parties cannot be so classified apparently are outside its purview.

In *Duberstein*, the Supreme Court also addressed the role of the finders of fact in making this inherently factual determination, and thus the issue of appellate review in determining whether a transfer was an excludable gift or taxable compensation as well, dictating a limited role for the appellate courts:

> One consequence of this is that the appellate review of determinations in this field must be quite restricted. Where a jury has tried the matter upon correct instructions, the only inquiry is whether it cannot be said that reasonable men could reach differing conclusions on the issue. . . . Where the trial has been by a judge without jury, the judge's findings must stand unless "clearly erroneous."

Id. at 290-91.

Gifts, bequests, devises, and inheritances are, like treasure trove and prizes, windfalls to the recipient. Yet treasure trove and prizes are included in gross income, and gifts and bequests are not. Perhaps Congress perceived gifts and bequests as merely the shifting of property among a unit, rather than the exchange of income, and thus not properly in the tax base; perhaps Congress simply wanted gifts to be covered under the separate and independent system of estate and gift tax laws. On the other hand, Congress may have concluded that it is unfair to impose an income tax on the receipt of an item that may have been unexpected and beyond the recipient's control. Treasure trove, however, also falls within the ambit of this rationale. Is the receipt of a gift truly beyond the recipient's control?

The true policy justification may be a practical one. If every birthday, Christmas, and Valentine's Day gift were required to be included in gross income, the administrative burden would increase exponentially. Each gift would have to be recorded, and its fair market value determined. Although there are similar valuation difficulties for treasure trove, actual instances of finding treasure trove are rare compared with intra-family gift giving. The gift exclusion also avoids hardships that could arise when a donee or heir receives valuable property — perhaps a family heirloom — and would otherwise be required to sell it to pay the resulting income tax liability.

Pursuant to §102(b), even if the gift is excludable, the gift exclusion does not apply to income subsequently earned from the gift or devised property. Thus, for example, if one were to receive Microsoft stock as a gift, §102(a) would exclude the fair market value of the stock from income. Under §102(b), however, any future Microsoft dividends paid to the recipient would be included in the gross income of the recipient. This is true notwithstanding that, at a minimum, a substantial amount of the fair market value of the Microsoft stock itself represents nothing more than the discounted present value of its future dividend streams.

On the other hand, a purported gift may in fact be treated as a partial gift and a partial sale. For example, a transfer of property worth $10,000 in exchange for $1,000 in cash may be considered a part sale and a part gift, if "detached and disinterested generosity" on behalf of the transferor was the motivation for selling the property for less than its fair market value.

There is some support for the revocation of the statutory provisions granting an exclusion from gross income for gifts and bequests. Proponents argue that this reform would increase the equity of the Code; if income is taxed because it roughly measures each person's "ability to pay," gifts should be included in gross income and taxed to the donee because they clearly represent an increased ability to pay.

A second, more practical argument for the elimination of the gift exclusion is simplicity. If the concept of gross income were to encompass gifts, the courts would be spared the difficult litigation of the type found in Olk v. United States, which follows. Moreover, Congress could eliminate the dual rate system created by the current coexistence of the income tax and the estate and gift taxes. On the other hand, as discussed above, other practical problems would emerge, such as the possible unfairness in demanding taxes from a taxpayer who has received a large, in-kind gift but has no cash or other liquid assets with which to pay those taxes.

OLK v. UNITED STATES
536 F.2d 876 (9th Cir. 1976)

SNEED, J.

. . . The issue is whether monies, called "tokes" in the relevant trade, received by the taxpayer, a craps dealer employed by Las Vegas casinos, constitute taxable income or gifts within the meaning of section 102(a). . . .

I. THE FACTS

. . . The district court's finding with respect to such facts which we accept are, in part, as follows:

> In 1971 plaintiff was employed as a craps dealer in two Las Vegas gambling casinos. . . . There are four persons involved in the operation of the game, a boxman and three dealers. One of the three dealers, the stickman, calls the roll of the dice and then collects them for the next shooter. The other two dealers collect losing bets and pay off winning bets under the supervision of the boxman. The boxman is the casino employee charged with direct supervision of the dealers and the play at one particular table. He in turn is supervised by the pit boss who is responsible for several tables. The dealers also make change, advise the boxman when a player would like a drink and answer basic questions about the game for the players.
>
> Dealers are forbidden to fraternize or engage in unnecessary conversation with the casino patrons, and must remain in separate areas while on their breaks. Dealers must treat all patrons equally, and any attempt to provide special service to a patron is grounds for termination.

At times, players will give money to the dealers or place bets for them. The witnesses testified that most casinos do not allow boxmen to receive money from patrons because of their supervisory positions, although some do permit this. The pit bosses are not permitted to receive anything from patrons because they are in a position in which they can insure that a patron receives some special service or treatment.

The money or tokes are combined by the four dealers and split equally at the end of each shift so that a dealer will get his share of the toke received even while he is taking his break. Uncontradicted testimony indicated that a dealer would be terminated if he kept a toke rather than placed it in the common fund.

Casino management either required the dealers to pool and divide tokes or encouraged them to do so. Although the practice is tolerated by management, it is not encouraged since tokes represent money that players are not wagering and thus cannot be won by the casino. . . .

Additional findings of fact by the district court are that the taxpayer worked as a stickman and dealer and at all times was under the supervision of the boxman who in turn was supervised by the pit boss. Also the district court found that patrons sometimes give money to dealers, other players or mere spectators at the game, but that between 90-95 percent of the patrons give nothing to a dealer. No obligation on the part of the patron exists to give to a dealer and "dealers perform no service for patrons which a patron would normally find compensable." Another finding is that there exists "no direct relation between services performed for management by a dealer and benefit or detriment to the patron."

There then follows two final "findings of fact" which taken together constitute the heart of the controversy before us. These are as follows:

> 17. The tokes are given to dealers as a result of impulsive generosity or superstition on the part of players, and not as a form of compensation for services.
> 18. Tokes are the result of a detached and disinterested generosity on the part of a small number of patrons.

These two findings, together with the others set out above, bear the unmistakable imprint of Commissioner v. Duberstein, 363 U.S. 278 (1959), particularly that portion of the opinion which reads as follows:

> The course of decision here makes it plain that the statute does not use the term "gift" in the common-law sense, but in a more colloquial sense. This Court has indicated that a voluntary executed transfer of his property by one to another, without any consideration or compensation therefor, though a common-law gift, is not necessarily a "gift" within the meaning of the statute. For the Court has shown that the mere absence of a legal or moral obligation to make such a payment does not establish that it is a gift. . . . [I]mportantly, if the payment proceeds primarily from "the constraining force of any moral or legal duty," or from "the incentive of anticipated benefit" of an economic nature, Bogardus v. Commissioner, 302 U.S. 34, 41, it is not a gift. And, conversely, "[w]here the payment is in return for services rendered, it is irrelevant that the donor derives no economic benefit from it." Robertson v. United States, 343 U.S. 711, 714. A gift in the statutory sense, on the other hand, proceeds from a "detached and disinterested generosity," Commissioner v. Lo Rue,

351 U.S. 243, 246, "out of affection, respect, admiration, charity or like impulses."[343 U.S. at 1240]. And in this regard, the most critical consideration . . . is the transferor's "intention." "What controls is the intention with which payment, however voluntary, has been made."[302 U.S. at 45.][1]

II.   Finding Number 18 Is a Conclusion of Law

The position of the taxpayer is simple. The above findings conform to the meaning of gifts as used in section 102 of the Code. *Duberstein* further teaches, the taxpayer asserts, that whether a receipt qualified as a non-taxable gift is "basically one of fact," and appellate review of such findings is restricted to determining whether they are clearly erroneous. Because none of the recited findings are clearly erroneous, concludes the taxpayer, the judgment of the trial court must be affirmed.

We could not escape this logic were we prepared to accept as a "finding of fact" the trial court's finding number 18. We reject the trial court's characterization. The conclusion that tokes "are the result of detached and disinterested generosity" on the part of those patrons who engage in the practice of toking is a conclusion of law, not a finding of fact. Finding number 17, on the other hand, which establishes that tokes are given as the result of impulsive generosity or superstition on the part of the players is a finding of fact to which we are bound unless it is "clearly erroneous" which it is not.

The distinction is between a finding of the dominant reason that explains the player's action in making the transfer and the determination that such dominant reason requires treatment of the receipt as a gift. Finding number 17 is addressed to the former while number 18 the latter. A finding regarding the basic facts, i.e., the circumstances and setting within which tokes are paid, and the dominant reason for such payments are findings of fact, our review of which is restricted by the clearly erroneous standard. Whether the dominant reason justifies exclusion from gross income under section 102 as interpreted by *Duberstein* is a matter of law. Finding number 18 is a determination that the dominant reason for the player's action, as found in number 17, justifies exclusion. This constitutes an application of the statute to the facts. Whether the application is proper is, of course, a question of law. . . .

. . . Otherwise an appellate court's inescapable duty of appellate review in this type of case would be all but foreclosed by a finding, such as in number 18, in which the resolution of the ultimate legal issue was disguised as a finding of fact. The error in insisting that findings numbers 17 and 18 are both findings of fact with respect to the "dominant reason" is revealed when the language of finding number 18 is compared with *Duberstein*'s statement, "A gift in the statutory sense, on the other hand, proceeds from a 'detached and disinterested generosity,'[351 U.S. at 246] 'out of affection, respect, admiration, charity or like impulses.'" 363 U.S. at 285. Their similarity is not coincidental and demonstrates that finding number 18 is but an application of the statutory definition of a gift to all previous findings of fact including finding number 17. Number 18 merely characterizes all previous findings in a manner that makes classification of the receipt as a gift inevitable. . . .

---

1. The court substantially quoted Duberstein, 363 U.S. at 285-86. Eds.

III. Finding Number 18 and Other Conclusions of Law Based Thereon Are Erroneous

Freed of the restraint of the "clearly erroneous" standard, we are convinced that finding number 18 and all derivative conclusions of law are wrong. "Impulsive generosity or superstition on the part of the players" we accept as the dominant motive. In the context of gambling in casinos open to the public such a motive is quite understandable. However, our understanding also requires us to acknowledge that payments so motivated are not acts of "detached or disinterested generosity." Quite the opposite is true. Tribute to the gods of fortune which it is hoped will be returned bounteously soon can only be described as an "involved and intensely interested" act.

Moreover, in applying the statute to the findings of fact, we are not permitted to ignore those findings which strongly suggest that tokes in the hands of the ultimate recipients are viewed as a receipt indistinguishable, except for erroneously anticipated tax differences, from wages. The regularity of the flow, the equal division of the receipts, and the daily amount received indicate that a dealer acting reasonably would come to regard such receipts as a form of compensation for his services. The manner in which a dealer may regard tokes is, of course, not the touchstone for determining whether the receipt is excludable from gross income. It is, however, a reasonable and relevant inference well grounded in the findings of fact.

. . . Generalizations are treacherous but not without utility. One such is that receipts by taxpayers engaged in rendering services contributed by those with whom the taxpayers have some personal or functional contact in the course of the performance of the services are taxable income when in conformity with the practices of the area and easily valued. Tokes, like tips, meet these conditions. That is enough.

The taxpayer is not entitled to the refund he seeks.

Reversed.

Note on Gift versus Compensation

In *Olk*, the Ninth Circuit neatly avoided the *Duberstein* restriction on appellate review by holding that Finding of Fact 18 was not a finding of fact but a conclusion of law that the court was free to overturn. Because "detached and disinterested generosity" were the operative words of the *Duberstein* definition of a gift, the court held that a finding that the patrons paid the tokes out of a detached and disinterested generosity was merely a disguised conclusion that the tokes were gifts.

As discussed previously, it is generally easier to identify a gift in the family context than in a commercial setting. Nevertheless, exceptions to this generality do occur. For example, in Altman v. Commissioner, 475 F.2d 876 (2d Cir. 1973), a mother who gave her son checks and securities totaling over $122,000 lacked the requisite detached and disinterested generosity. The transfer was motivated by information from a business associate who told the mother that her son had threatened to drive the family business into bankruptcy and to report his mother to the Service for alleged tax violations. Because the transfer of property was in response to the son's threat and not the result of the mother's generosity, the son was required to include the checks and securities in his gross income.

Similarly, in Wolder v. Commissioner, 493 F.2d 608 (2d Cir. 1974), there was no gift or bequest where, pursuant to a contract to perform lifetime legal services for a client, a taxpayer/attorney received stock and cash as a bequest in his client's will. The stock and the cash, although a bequest for state property law purposes, were compensation for tax purposes and thus includable in gross income.

Does the analysis differ if the purported gift came from the state rather than from a person or entity? This issue was faced in the case of Greisen by and through Greisen v. United States, 831 F.2d 916 (9th Cir. 1987). In *Greisen*, the taxpayer had received a payment under an Alaskan law dividing the royalties from the sale of oil among all Alaskan residents based on the amount of total oil revenues generated in each year. The taxpayers contended that the payment was an excludable gift from the state under §102(a). The court disagreed, concluding that, although a state could make a gift if the payment was intended as a gift, this payment was adopted under a sense of moral or legal duty rather than as a gift. The IRS has used similar reasoning in other contexts, stating in an internal memorandum that payments by a state could not be gifts if the payments were made out of a "moral obligation" rather than detached and disinterested generosity as required by *Duberstein*. How can one distinguish between a moral obligation and detached and disinterested generosity? Although the effect of this position may seem harsh to the recipients of such largesse, especially in the case of disaster relief or other hardship payments made by a state, recall from Chapter 2 that payments by a state or the federal government may be excluded from income under the "general welfare" doctrine. In light of the general welfare doctrine, should any government payments ever qualify as gifts for purposes of §102?

Problems

3-1. Ronald Hart's series of civic lectures were extremely popular, and in appreciation of his efforts one of the patrons of the lecture club sent his wife, Jennifer Hart, several items of jewelry. The retail value of these items was $3000.
   a.   How much, if any, gross income arises as a result of the jewelry transfer?
   b.   What result in *a* if the jewelry was sent to Hart as an inducement to lecture again the next year?

3-2. Jessalyn Chase's employer, Mike Gurney, had two racing bicycles delivered to her, with a note that read, "To Jessalyn, with many thanks." Does Chase have gross income?

3-3. Mary Moss, the daughter of Jennifer Moss, was seriously injured in a car accident. Jennifer's employer sent Jennifer a check for $500 expressing his concern over Mary's injury. Does Jennifer Moss have gross income?

3-4.   Bob Thomas approached his two sons, Ronald and Donald, and offered to pay $500 to the one who earned the highest grade point average by the end of the academic year. As a result of the offer, both spent extra time and effort studying during the semester; however, Donald finished the year with a 3.75 G.P.A. while Ronald could muster only a 3.6 G.P.A. What result to Donald on the receipt of the $500?

3-5.   Assume in problem 3-4 that instead of transferring cash Thomas transferred to Donald an interest-bearing bond worth $500.

   a.   Does Donald have gross income?

   b.   If in the next year Donald receives $50 of interest payable on the bond, does he have gross income resulting from the receipt of the interest?

2. Section 1015 — Basis for Property Received as a Gift

Code: §§1015(a), (d)(1), (2), (4), (6)
Regulations: §§1.1015-1(a), (c), (d)

Once it is determined that the transferee has received a gift, another issue arises if the gift is one of property other than cash: what is the transferee's basis in the acquired property? Under §1012, property has a basis equal to its cost, except as otherwise provided by the Code. But recipients of gifts typically pay nothing for the property. Does this mean they have a zero basis? Fortunately for the donee/transferee, who would have a zero basis if §1012 applied, gifts are "otherwise provided" for in §1015.

Pursuant to §1015, a taxpayer who receives a gift acquires a "carryover" basis in the gift property — that is, the donee's basis is generally the donor's basis in the property at the time of the transfer; this is referred to as "transferred basis" property. See §7701(a)(43). One effect of the carryover basis is that the appreciation in value that accrued while the property was held by the donor is not taxed to the donor but is taxed to the donee on a subsequent taxable disposition of that property. As previously discussed, in Taft v. Bowers, 278 U.S. 470 (1929), the Supreme Court held that taxation of the inherent appreciation in such property to the donee does not violate the Sixteenth Amendment of the Constitution. In that case, the donees of stocks sought to avoid recognizing income on the appreciation in the market value of the stock that arose while it was owned by the donor. The Court rejected their arguments and stressed that to hold otherwise would defeat Congress's purpose to tax all gain derived from capital investments.

As is evident from the *Taft* decision and §1015, the appreciation in value of property transferred by gift is not permanently excluded from the income tax base but rather is taken into account by the donee if and when he or she subsequently sells the property for a gain. Nevertheless, this means that gifts can permit taxpayers to shift gain through the use of a gift. For example, if a taxpayer wants to finance his sibling's college expenses by selling appreciated stock, the taxpayer could reduce the resulting tax liability by transferring the stock to his sibling who in turn sells the stock, thus shifting the gain from his marginal rate of tax (assume 40 percent) to his sibling's (assume 10 percent). In this case, under the following hypothetical, the transfer would reduce the family's tax liability by $1,800:

Fair market value	$10,000
Basis in stock	4,000
Gain from sale	$ 6,000
Tax liability on $6,000 at 40%	$ 2,400
Tax liability on $6,000 at 10%	600
Tax savings	$ 1,800

If the intent of the taxpayer in making the gift is to reduce tax liability, does that undermine the likelihood that it would be treated as a gift under *Duberstein*? Should it?

Because the inherent gain generally is not realized at the time of the gift, potential advantages exist for transferring appreciated property. However, Congress has chosen not to allow a similar transfer of tax losses. As a result, the rule for computing the basis of property received by gift is dependent on whether the *donee's* subsequent disposition results in gain, in loss, or in neither gain nor loss. Section 1015 sets forth the rules for determining the basis of property acquired by gift.

The first step in calculating a donee's basis is to determine whether the fair market value of the property at the time of the gift is greater or less than the donor's adjusted basis in the property. If the fair market value is greater than or equal to the donor's adjusted basis, the donee's basis will be the donor's adjusted basis increased (but not above the property's fair market value) by the gift tax paid, if any, which is attributable to the net appreciation in the property. See §1015(a), (d). These carry-over basis rules preserve any inherent gain in the property until a subsequent realization event.

If the value of the property at the time of the gift is less than the donor's adjusted basis (that is, if there is a "built-in" loss), however, the rules become more complex. In such cases, the donee will have *two* bases in the property: a basis for determining gain and a basis for determining loss. The basis for gain is, as described above, the donor's adjusted basis. The basis for loss, however, is the fair market value of the property at the time of the gift. If the donee sells the property for more than the gain basis, the excess is a realized gain. If the property is sold for less than the loss basis, the excess is a realized loss.

Thus, if *A* gives property with a $3,000 fair market value and a $5,000 adjusted basis to *B*, who subsequently sells the property for $6,000, *B*'s basis for computing gain is $5,000. *B* will realize a $1,000 gain. If *A* gives the same property to *B*, who sells it for $2,000, *B*'s basis for computing loss is $3,000—the property's fair market value at the time of the gift. *B* therefore realizes only a $1,000 loss, and $2,000 of the loss inherent in the property at the time of transfer disappears. What should happen, however, if the donee sells the property for an amount greater than the loss basis (fair market value at the time of the gift), but less than the gain basis (donor's basis)? There appears to be no way to solve the problem: if *B* subsequently sells the property for $4,000, the amount realized is less than the gain basis

($5,000) and more than the loss basis ($3,000), so neither can be used. The regulations concede this point, concluding that *B* will realize neither gain nor loss on the disposition in such a case. Reg. §1.1015-1(a)(2).

A final component of the calculation of a donee's basis is the adjustment, referred to above, for the amount of federal gift tax paid with respect to the gift. The increase in the donee's basis for gift tax paid is limited to the portion of the gift tax attributable to the net appreciation in value of the gift property — that is, the amount by which the fair market value of the property at the time of the gift exceeds the donor's adjusted basis. §1015(d). This concept is relatively straightforward, but the calculations can at times become complex. See Reg. §1.1015-5.

Problem

3-6. William Lazarini purchased two properties in year 1 for the following amounts: property *A*, $10,000, and property *B*, $14,000. In year 5, the properties were valued at $15,000 and $9,000, respectively.

    a.   In year 5, Lazarini gave property *A* to his daughter, Monica Sanderson, incurring a $1,000 gift tax liability as a result of the transfer. Sanderson sold the property one month later for $17,000. What was Sanderson's gain or loss from the sale?

    b.   In year 5, Lazarini gave property *B* to his younger daughter, Pearl. Pearl sold the property one month later for $8,000. What was Pearl's gain or loss from the sale?

    c.   What result in *b* if Pearl had sold property *B* for $12,000?

    d.   What result in *b* if Lazarini had incurred a $750 gift tax liability as a result of the transfer?

3. Basis of Property Acquired by Bequest, Inheritance, or Devise

Code: §§1014(a); 1014(b)(1), (2); 1014(e)
Regulations: §§1.1014-1(a); 1.1014-2(b)(1)

Unlike the §1015 rules for the basis of property acquired by gift, §1014(a) provides the general rule that the basis of property received from a decedent is the fair market value of the property on the date of death. When the fair market value of the property at the date of death is greater than its adjusted basis, the devisee receives a "stepped-up" basis. In such cases, the difference between the decedent's basis and the stepped-up basis effectively escapes income taxation. If, however, the property had a basis in excess of its fair market value on the date of death, there is a step-down in basis, and neither the decedent nor the person receiving the property can realize the inherent tax loss. Thus, tax planners generally recommend that economically depreciated property be sold prior to death to recognize the tax loss, whereas appreciated property should be held until death so that the beneficiary receives a §1014 step-up in basis and pre-death appreciation escapes income taxation.

As an illustration of the dramatic effects of §1014, consider the following hypothetical. Two taxpayers, X and Y, own identical assets, each having a $1,000,000 value and a $400,000 adjusted basis. Each begins negotiations for a sale to a common purchaser for $1,000,000. X's sale is completed at noon on April 13, while Y's sale is still in the process of negotiations. On their way to dinner on the evening of April 13, both are killed in an auto accident. Y's nephew inherits Y's asset and sells the asset several months later, on the above terms.

X's sale, completed during his life, results in a $600,000 gain realized ($1,000,000 amount realized, less $400,000 adjusted basis). Y's heir, however, realizes no gain on his disposition of the inherited property. On inheriting the asset, the nephew received a step-up in basis to the $1,000,000 fair market value at the time of Y's death. The amount realized on the sale therefore does not exceed the nephew's adjusted basis.

Carryover basis, however, is required for one limited situation set forth in §1014(e) and described by the following statement from that section's legislative history:

> Because an heir receives property from a decedent with a stepped-up basis, an heir can transfer appreciated property to a decedent immediately prior to death in the hope of receiving the property back at the decedent's death with a higher basis. The donor-heir might pay gift taxes on the fair market value of the gift . . . but will pay no income tax on the appreciation. Then, upon the death of the donee-decedent, the donor-heir could receive back the property with a stepped-up basis equal to its fair market value. The stepped-up basis would permanently exempt the appreciation from income tax. . . .
>
> Because the committee believes that allowing a stepped-up basis in this situation permits unintended and inappropriate tax benefits, the committee provides that the stepped-up basis rules should not apply with respect to appreciated property acquired by the decedent through gift within [one year] of death where such property passes from the decedent to the original donor or the donor's spouse. . . .
>
> [T]he stepped-up basis rules contained in section 1014 will not apply with respect to appreciated property acquired by the decedent through gift within [one year] of death (including the gift element of a bargain sale), if such property passes, directly or indirectly, from the donee-decedent to the original donor or the donor's spouse. The denial of a stepped-up basis applies where the donor receives the benefit of the appreciated property regardless of whether the bequest by the decedent to the donor is a specific bequest, a general bequest, a pecuniary bequest, or a residuary bequest. . . .
>
> For example, assume that A transfers appreciated property with a basis of $10 and a fair market value of $100 to D within [one year] of D's death and that D's date of death basis was $20 and the date of death fair market value of the property was $200. If A is entitled to receive the property from the decedent, A's basis in the property will be $20. If A subsequently sells the property for its fair market value of $200, he will recognize gain of $180.

H.R. Rep. No. 201, 97th Cong., 1st Sess., 188 (1981).

At one point, Congress adopted a provision which would have replaced §1014 with a modified version of the §1015 carryover basis rules as part of a broader repeal of the estate tax regime. This provision was never fully implemented, and was effectively repealed in 2010. Although the final contours of estate tax reform remain to be finalized, it appears that §1014 will remain in some form for purposes of calculating the basis of property received by bequest, devise or inheritance going forward.

Problem

3-7.   a.   William Levanthol purchased property for $10,000. Five years later, when the property was valued at $40,000, Levanthol died, leaving the property to Veronica Wessels. One month later, Wessels sold the property for $40,000. Did Wessels have gross income on receipt of the bequest? What was Wessels's gain or loss from the sale? What if she had sold the property for $15,000?

   b.   Assume that, prior to death, Levanthol purchased other business property for $25,000. Three years after the purchase, when the property was valued at $10,000, he was on his deathbed. Should he allow this property to pass to his heirs through his estate, or should he sell it prior to his death?

   c.   Tom Levanthol gave his father, William, property with an adjusted basis of $5,000 and a fair market value of $50,000, incurring a gift tax liability of $10,000 as a result of the transfer. One month later, William died and bequeathed the property to Tom. Three months later, Tom sold the property for $80,000. What was Tom's gain or loss from the sale?

   d.   What result in *c* if William had bequeathed the property to Tom's son (William's grandson)?

4.   *Part Sale/Part Gift Transactions*

Code: §§1015(a), 1011(b)
Regulations: §§1.1015-4; 1.1001-1(e); 1.1001-2(a)(1), (4)(iii)

A part sale/part gift arises when property is transferred in return for consideration totaling less than the property's fair market value and the intent of the seller in selling at less than the fair market value was to make a gift to the buyer of the difference. To the extent consideration is received, the transaction is treated as a sale. To the extent the fair market value of the property exceeds the consideration, the transaction is generally treated as a gift. In effect, the tax law treats a part sale/part gift as two separate transactions. However, since the donee receives only one gift, the basis rules must provide a method by which to calculate a single basis for the gifted property. As a result, the rules for determining the basis of property acquired in a part sale/part gift transaction are, as one might expect, a hybrid of the cost basis and gift basis rules. These rules are set forth in Regulation §1.1015-4.

Generally, in a sale the transferee takes a "cost" basis in the acquired property pursuant to §1012, whereas in a gift transaction the transferee takes the donor's basis (carryover basis) pursuant to §1015. Where the transaction is a part sale/part gift, however, the transferor is deemed to have sold the property for the amount of consideration received. Reg. §1.1015-4(a). In such cases, the transferee takes a basis in the property received equal to the amount paid or the transferor's adjusted basis, whichever is greater, increased by the gift tax attributable to the net appreciation on the gift.

By selling property to a family member for an amount below fair market value, the taxpayer can recoup his or her original investment. For example, assume that a taxpayer sells property, with a $100,000 fair market value and $40,000 adjusted basis, to a third party for $100,000. The taxpayer realizes a gain of $60,000. If, on the other hand, she sells the property to her child for $35,000, she realizes no gain on the transaction because her amount realized does not exceed her adjusted basis. Yet she recoups $35,000 of her original investment. Although it might initially appear that the taxpayer suffers an economic loss of $5,000 on the part sale and thus could have deducted $5,000 as a result of the transaction, no loss deduction is permitted to the transferor on a part sale/part gift. Reg. §1.1001-1(e).

Under Regulation §1.1015-4(a), the child in the previous example has a basis of $40,000 — the *greater* of (1) the amount the child paid ($35,000) or (2) the parent's adjusted basis at the time of the transfer ($40,000). The $60,000 of potential gain not taxed to the parent will be realized by the child, if she later sells the property for $100,000 or more.

In determining whether a loss is realized on the transferee's subsequent sale of property acquired in a part sale/part gift, the calculation of basis differs from the computation of basis for gain purposes. Regulation §1.1015-4(a) provides that the basis in such situations is the *lesser* of (1) the transferee's basis (the greater of cost or the transferor's adjusted basis) or (2) the fair market value of the property at the time of the transfer.

A part sale/part gift can also arise when the property transferred is subject to an encumbrance assumed by the transferee or where, as in the case that follows, the donor's gift tax liability arising from the transfer is paid by the donee. As discussed in Chapter 2, upon a sale or exchange of encumbered property a taxpayer includes in his or her amount realized an amount equal to the amount of the obligation from which the taxpayer is relieved of liability, in part because the initial loan proceeds were excluded from income when borrowed due to the offsetting liability. For example, under *Tufts*, if a taxpayer sells property with an adjusted basis of $10,000 and a fair market value of $30,000 in exchange for $25,000 in cash plus the assumption of a $5,000 mortgage, the taxpayer has an amount realized of $30,000 (the $25,000 cash plus the $5,000 liability relief) and gain of $20,000. What would happen if instead the taxpayer gifts the property subject to the $5,000 mortgage? The taxpayer clearly intended to make a gift within the meaning of *Duberstein*, but also clearly received a benefit in the form of relief of liability under *Tufts*. Consider the following case, in which the Supreme Court struggled with a similar issue.

DIEDRICH v. COMMISSIONER
457 U.S. 191 (1982)

CHIEF JUSTICE BURGER delivered the opinion of the Court. . . .

I . . .

In 1972 petitioners Victor and Frances Diedrich made gifts of approximately 85,000 shares of stock to their three children, using both a direct transfer and a trust arrangement. The gifts were subject to a condition that the donees pay the resulting federal and state gift taxes. There is no dispute concerning the amount of the gift tax paid by the donees. The donors' basis in the transferred stock was

$51,073; the gift tax paid in 1972 by the donees was $62,992. Petitioners did not include as income on their 1972 federal income tax returns any portion of the gift tax paid by the donees. After an audit the Commissioner of Internal Revenue determined that petitioners had realized income to the extent that the gift tax owed by petitioners but paid by the donees exceeded the donors' basis in the property. Accordingly, petitioners' taxable income for 1972 was increased by $5,959.[2] . . .

II

A

Pursuant to its constitutional authority, Congress has defined "gross income" as income "from whatever source derived," including "[i]ncome from discharge of indebtedness." This Court has recognized that "income" may be realized by a variety of indirect means. In Old Colony Trust Co. v. Commissioner, 279 U.S. 716 (1929), the Court held that payment of an employee's income taxes by an employer constituted income to the employee. Speaking for the Court, Chief Justice Taft concluded that "[t]he payment of the tax by the employe[r] was in consideration of the services rendered by the employee and was a gain derived by the employee from his labor." The Court made clear that the substance, not the form, of the agreed transaction controls. "The discharge by a third person of an obligation to him is equivalent to receipt by the person taxed." The employee, in other words, was placed in a better position as a result of the employer's discharge of the employee's legal obligation to pay the income taxes; the employee thus received a gain subject to income tax.

The holding in *Old Colony* was reaffirmed in Crane v. Commissioner, 331 U.S. 1 (1947). In *Crane* the Court concluded that relief from the obligation of a nonrecourse mortgage in which the value of the property exceeded the value of the mortgage constituted income to the taxpayer. The taxpayer in *Crane* acquired depreciable property, an apartment building, subject to an unassumed mortgage. The taxpayer later sold the apartment building, which was still subject to the nonrecourse mortgage, for cash plus the buyer's assumption of the mortgage. This Court held that the amount of the mortgage was properly included in the amount realized on the sale, noting that if the taxpayer transfers subject to the mortgage, "the benefit to him is as real and substantial as if the mortgage were discharged, or as if a personal debt in an equal amount had been assumed by another." Id. at 14. Again, it was the "reality," not the form, of the transaction that governed. The Court found it immaterial whether the seller received money prior to the sale in order to discharge the mortgage, or whether the seller merely transferred the property subject to the mortgage. In either case the taxpayer realized an economic benefit.

---

2. Subtracting the stock basis of $51,073 from the gift tax paid by the donees of $62,992 the Commissioner found that petitioners had realized a long-term capital gain of $11,919. After a 50 percent reduction in long-term capital gain, 26 U.S.C. §1202, the Diedrichs' taxable income increased by $5,959.

B

The principles of *Old Colony* and *Crane* control. A common method of structuring gift transactions is for the donor to make the gift subject to the condition that the donee pay the resulting gift tax, as was done in each of the cases now before us. When a gift is made, the gift tax liability falls on the donor. When a donor makes a gift to a donee, a "debt" to the United States for the amount of the gift tax is incurred by the donor. Those taxes are as much the legal obligation of the donor as the donor's income taxes; for these purposes they are the same kind of debt obligation as the income taxes of the employee in *Old Colony*. Similarly, when a donee agrees to discharge an indebtedness in consideration of the gift, the person relieved of the tax liability realizes an economic benefit. In short, the donor realizes an immediate economic benefit by the donee's assumption of the donor's legal obligation to pay the gift tax.

An examination of the donor's intent does not change the character of this benefit. Although intent is relevant in determining whether a gift has been made, subjective intent has not characteristically been a factor in determining whether an individual has realized income. Even if intent were a factor, the donor's intent with respect to the condition shifting gift tax obligation from the donor to the donee was plainly to relieve the donor of a debt owed to the United States; the choice was made because the donor would receive a benefit in relief from the obligation to pay the gift tax.

Finally, the benefit realized by the taxpayer is not diminished by the fact that the liability attaches during the course of a donative transfer. It cannot be doubted that the donors were aware that the gift tax obligation would arise immediately upon the transfer of the property; the economic benefit to the donors in the discharge of the gift tax liability is indistinguishable from the benefit arising from discharge of a preexisting obligation. Nor is there any doubt that had the donors sold a portion of the stock immediately before the gift transfer in order to raise funds to pay the expected gift tax, a taxable gain would have been realized. The fact that the gift tax obligation was discharged by way of a conditional gift rather than from funds derived from a pregift sale does not alter the underlying benefit to the donors.

C

Consistent with the economic reality, the Commissioner has treated these conditional gifts as a discharge of indebtedness through a part gift and part sale of the gift property transferred. The transfer is treated as if the donor sells the property to the donee for less than the fair market value. The "sale" price is the amount necessary to discharge the gift tax indebtedness; the balance of the value of the transferred property is treated as a gift. The gain thus derived by the donor is the amount of the gift tax liability less the donor's adjusted basis in the entire property. Accordingly, income is realized to the extent that the gift tax exceeds the donor's adjusted basis in the property. This treatment is consistent with §1001 of the Internal Revenue Code, which provides that the gain from the disposition of property is the excess of the amount realized over the transferor's adjusted basis in the property.

III

We recognize that Congress has structured gift transactions to encourage transfer of property by limiting the tax consequences of a transfer. Congress may obviously provide a similar exclusion for the conditional gift. Should Congress wish to encourage "net gifts," changes in the income tax consequences of such gifts lie within the legislative responsibility. Until such time, we are bound by Congress' mandate that gross income includes income "from whatever source derived." We therefore hold that a donor who makes a gift of property on condition that the donee pay the resulting gift taxes realizes taxable income to the extent that the gift taxes paid by the donee exceed the donor's adjusted basis in the property. . . .

JUSTICE REHNQUIST, dissenting.

It is a well-settled principle today that a taxpayer realizes income when another person relieves the taxpayer of a legal obligation in connection with an otherwise taxable transaction. See Crane v. Commissioner, 331 U.S. 1 (1947) (sale of real property); Old Colony Trust Co. v. Commissioner, 279 U.S. 716 (1929) (employment compensation). In neither *Old Colony* nor *Crane* was there any question as to the existence of a taxable transaction; the only question concerned the amount of income realized by the taxpayer as a result of the taxable transaction. The Court in this case, however, begs the question of whether a taxable transaction has taken place at all when it concludes that "[t]he principles of *Old Colony* and *Crane* control" this case.

In *Old Colony*, the employer agreed to pay the employee's federal tax liability as part of his compensation. The employee provided his services to the employer in exchange for compensation. The exchange of compensation for services was undeniably a taxable transaction. The only question was whether the employee's taxable income included the employer's assumption of the employee's income tax liability.

In *Crane*, the taxpayer sold real property for cash plus the buyer's assumption of a mortgage. Clearly a sale had occurred, and the only question was whether the amount of the mortgage assumed by the buyer should be included in the amount realized by the taxpayer. The Court rejected the taxpayer's contention that what she sold was not the property itself, but her equity in that property.

Unlike *Old Colony* or *Crane*, the question in this case is not the amount of income the taxpayer has realized as a result of a concededly taxable transaction, but whether a taxable transaction has taken place at all. Only *after* one concludes that a partial sale occurs when the donee agrees to pay the gift tax do *Old Colony* and *Crane* become relevant in ascertaining the amount of income realized by the donor as a result of the transaction. Nowhere does the Court explain why a gift becomes a partial sale merely because the donor and donee structure the gift so that the gift tax imposed by Congress on the transaction is paid by the donee rather than the donor.

In my view, the resolution of this case turns upon congressional intent: whether Congress intended to characterize a gift as a partial sale whenever the donee agrees to pay the gift tax. Congress has determined that a gift should not be considered income to the donee. Instead, gift transactions are to be subject to a tax system wholly separate and distinct from the income tax. Both the donor and the donee may be held liable for the gift tax. Although the primary liability for the gift tax is on the donor, the donee is liable to the extent of the value of the gift should the donor fail to pay the tax. I see no evidence in the tax statutes that Congress forbade the parties to agree among themselves as to who would pay the gift tax upon pain of such an agreement being considered a taxable event for the purposes of the income tax. Although Congress could certainly determine that the payment of the gift tax by the donee constitutes income to the donor, the relevant statutes do not affirmatively indicate that Congress has made such a determination.

I dissent.

Problem

3-8.   Shaun O'Collins transferred property with an adjusted basis of $30,000 and a fair market value of $90,000 to his son, Michael, in return for $60,000. One year later, Michael sold the property for $100,000.

    a.   Ignoring gift tax implications, what was Michael's gain or loss from the sale?

    b.   What result in *a* if Michael sold the property for $25,000?

    c.   Assume that Shaun transferred other property to Michael having an adjusted basis of $60,000 and a fair market value of $90,000, in return for $30,000. One year later, Michael sold the property for $100,000. Ignoring gift tax implications, what was Michael's gain or loss from the sale?

    d.   What result in *c* if Michael sold the property for $25,000?

    e.   Assume that Shaun transferred to Michael other property with an adjusted basis of $90,000 and a fair market value of $60,000, in return for $30,000. Two years later, Michael sold the property for $100,000. Ignoring gift tax implications, what was Michael's gain or loss from the sale?

    f.   What result in *e* if Michael sold the property for $25,000?

C.   EMPLOYEE BENEFITS

1.   Introduction

The relationship between employer and employee is one of the most common in our society. Many exchanges, which would undeniably be "accessions to wealth" if they resulted from arm's-length transactions between strangers, create interesting problems when they occur between employers and employees.

The Regulations provide that all compensation for personal services, regardless of the form of payment, is gross income unless otherwise excluded by the Code. Reg. §§1.61-1, 1.61-2. This general rule, however, leaves many questions unanswered. Should an employee be deemed to have received income when presented with something of value from an employer, even if the employee does not place a similar value on it? Must the benefit conferred on the employee be in exchange for services? Does it matter whether the benefit is provided primarily for the convenience of the employer?

The Code affords preferential treatment to many benefits conferred by employers on employees. Items excluded from gross income include certain meals and lodging (§119) and employer-provided life and health insurance (§§79, 106). Prior to 1984, other fringe benefits that fell outside the statutory exclusions were traditionally excluded for administrative reasons. For example, merchandise discounts to a department store employee or a free pass given to an airline employee were not included in the recipient's income because such benefits were considered too difficult to value. Congress replaced this regime with a detailed statutory regime in which all fringe benefits are included in gross income absent meeting a specific statutory exclusion. Fortunately, the Code provides for the exclusion from gross income of any fringe benefit that qualifies as an employee benefit at no additional cost to the employer, an employee discount, a working condition fringe, a de minimis fringe, a transportation fringe, or a moving expense reimbursement. §132.

2. Meals and Lodging

Code: §§107; 119(a), (b), (d)
Regulations: §1.119-1(a), (b), (c), (f)

Employer-provided meals and lodging are the first of several employee benefits considered in this section. Employees clearly benefit economically from employer-provided meals and lodging, especially since those are typically the first things people purchase with their salary. Nevertheless, §119 permits employees to exclude the value of meals and lodging furnished by an employer when those benefits satisfy two conditions: They must be provided (1) for the convenience of the employer and (2) on the employer's business premises. Lodging is subject to the additional requirement that it be accepted as a condition of employment.

Regulation §1.119-1(a)(2) states that "[m]eals furnished by an employer without charge to the employee will be regarded as furnished for the convenience of the employer if such meals are furnished for a *substantial noncompensatory business reason* of the employer" (emphasis added). The condition of employment requirement, applicable to lodging only, is also addressed by the Regulations. To meet this requirement, the taxpayer must be "required to accept the lodging in order to enable him properly to perform the duties of his employment." Reg. §1.119-1(b). Moreover, if the employee's living quarters qualify for the §119 exclusion, the value of any meals furnished without charge to the employee on such premises is also excludable.

Unlike §119, §107, which applies to lodging provided to clergymen, permits the exclusion of cash housing allowances as well as the rental value of housing furnished in-kind. Although the Code refers to "minister[s] of the gospel," the exclusion also applies to persons who are the equivalent of ministers in other religions. See, for example, Salkov v. Commissioner, 46 T.C. 190 (1966).

From a policy standpoint, why should any expense for basic necessities, such as meals and lodging, be excludable from income? As will be seen in subsequent chapters, personal living expenses are generally nondeductible. §262. Arguably, horizontal equity requires that when an employee is relieved by the employer of personal expenses such as meals and lodging, their value should be included in gross income. The key policy supporting the §119 exclusion appears to be that meals and lodging, when provided for the convenience of the employer rather than for the benefit of the employee, are not compensation and thus not gross income. In addition, Congress, when it enacted §119, envisioned an employee who, because of the nature of the job, was compelled to eat meals and/or sleep on the employer's premises, as for example, a firefighter, a worker on the Alaskan pipeline, or a hospital intern on call. Were taxpayers able to choose their own meals or lodging, they might select something more modest, prefer to live elsewhere, or eat different foods. Each taxpayer's choice, however, is constrained by the employer's requirements.

As a result, §§119 and 107 have been interpreted narrowly, excluding meals and lodging from gross income only if they meet the specific statutory terms. This raises some difficult questions. For example, if the employer furnishes the employee with *groceries*, is there a sufficient constraint on the employee's freedom of choice that such a receipt should be excluded from gross income? If the employee is able to designate what groceries are provided, the element of compulsion is lacking. However, the courts have been inconsistent in the application of the underlying rationale of §119 to similar, if not identical, settings. In Tougher v. Commissioner, 51 T.C. 737 (1969), aff'd per curiam, 441 F.2d 1148 (9th Cir. 1971), the court construed §119 narrowly and held that "meals" did not include groceries. But in Jacob v. United States, 493 F.2d 1294 (3d Cir. 1974), the court permitted the exclusion of the value of groceries where the taxpayer was required to live on the employer's premises and the groceries were cooked and consumed on the premises. Consider the following cases in which the courts struggle with the contours of the exclusion provided for in §119.

COMMISSIONER v. KOWALSKI
434 U.S. 77 (1977)

Mr. Justice Brennan delivered the opinion of the Court.

This case presents the question whether cash payments to state police troopers, designated as meal allowances, are included in gross income under §61(a) and, if so, are otherwise excludable under §119.

I

. . . Respondent is a state police trooper employed by the Division of State Police of the Department of Law and Public Safety of the State of New Jersey. During 1970, . . . he received a base salary of $8,739.38 and an additional $1,697.54 designated as an allowance for meals.

The State instituted the cash meal allowance for its state police officers in July 1949. Prior to that time, all troopers were provided with midshift meals in kind at various meal stations located throughout the State. A trooper unable to eat at an official meal station could, however, eat at a restaurant and obtain reimbursement.

The meal-station system proved unsatisfactory to the State because it required troopers to leave their assigned areas of patrol unguarded for extended periods of time. As a result, the State closed its meal stations and instituted a cash-allowance system. Under this system, troopers remain on call in their assigned patrol areas during their midshift break. Otherwise, troopers are not restricted in any way with respect to where they may eat in the patrol area and, indeed, may eat at home if it is located within that area. Troopers may also bring their midshift meal to the job and eat it in or near their patrol cars.

The meal allowance is paid biweekly in advance and is included, although separately stated, with the trooper's salary. The meal-allowance money is also separately accounted for in the State's accounting system. Funds are never commingled between the salary and meal-allowance accounts. Because of these characteristics of the meal-allowance system, the Tax Court concluded that the "meal allowance was not intended to represent additional compensation."

Notwithstanding this conclusion, it is not disputed that the meal allowance has many features inconsistent with its characterization as a simple reimbursement for meals that would otherwise have been taken at a meal station. For example, troopers are not required to spend their meal allowances on their midshift meals, nor are they required to account for the manner in which the money is spent. [N]o reduction in the meal allowance is made for periods when a trooper is not on patrol because, for example, he is assigned to a headquarters building or is away from active duty on vacation, leave, or sick leave. In addition, the cash allowance for meals is described on a state police recruitment brochure as an item of salary to be received in addition to an officer's base salary and the amount of the meal allowance is a subject of negotiations between the State and the police troopers' union. Finally, the amount of an officer's cash meal allowance varies with his rank and is included in his gross pay for purposes of calculating pension benefits. . . .

Respondent . . . argu[es] that the cash allowance was not compensatory but was furnished for the convenience of the employer and hence was not "income" within the meaning of §61(a) and that, in any case, the allowance could be excluded under §119. . . .

II

A

The starting point in the determination of the scope of "gross income" is the cardinal principle that Congress in creating the income tax intended "to use the full measure of its taxing power." . . . In the absence of a specific exemption, therefore, respondent's meal-allowance payments are income within the meaning of §61 since, like the payments involved in *Glenshaw Glass Co.*, the payments are "undeniabl[y] accessions to wealth, clearly realized, and over which the [respondent has] complete dominion."

Respondent contends, however, that §119 can be construed to be a specific exemption covering the meal-allowance payments to New Jersey troopers. Alternatively, respondent argues that notwithstanding §119 a specific exemption may be found in a line of lower-court cases and administrative rulings which recognize that benefits conferred by an employer on an employee "for the convenience of the employer" — at least when such benefits are not "compensatory" — are not income within the meaning of the Internal Revenue Code. . . .

B

. . . By its terms, §119 covers *meals* furnished by the employer and not *cash* reimbursements for meals. This is not a mere oversight. As we shall explain at greater length below, the form of §119 which Congress enacted originated in the Senate and the Report accompanying the Senate bill is very clear: "Section 119 applies only to meals or lodging furnished in kind." Accordingly, respondent's meal-allowance payments are not subject to exclusion under §119.

C

The convenience-of-the-employer doctrine is not a tidy one. . . .

The rationale . . . appears to have been that benefits conferred by an employer on an employee in the designated circumstances were not compensation for services and hence not income. Subsequent rulings equivocate on whether the non-compensatory character of a benefit could be inferred merely from its characterization by the employer or whether there must be additional evidence that employees are granted a benefit solely because the employer's business could not function properly unless an employee was furnished that benefit on the employer's premises. . . .

D

Even if we assume that respondent's meal-allowance payments could have been excluded from income under the 1939 Code pursuant to the doctrine we have just sketched, we must nonetheless inquire whether such an implied exclusion survives the 1954 recodification of the Internal Revenue Code. . . .

In enacting §119, the Congress was determined to "end the confusion as to the tax status of meals and lodging furnished an employee by his employer." However, the House and Senate initially differed on the significance that should be given the convenience-of-the-employer doctrine for the purposes of §119. . . .

After conference, the House acquiesced in the Senate's version of §119. Because of this, respondent urges that §119 as passed did not discard the convenience-of-the-employer doctrine, but indeed endorsed the doctrine. . . . We disagree.

. . . [C]learly the Senate refused completely to abandon the convenience-of-the-employer doctrine as the House wished to do. On the other hand, the Senate did not propose to leave undisturbed the convenience-of-the-employer doctrine as it had evolved. . . . The language of §119 quite plainly rejects the reasoning . . . which rest[s] on the employer's characterization of the nature of a payment. . . . [Case law] expressly rejected the theory of "convenience of the employer" . . . and adopted as the exclusive rationale the business-necessity theory. . . .

. . . Thus §119 comprehensively modified the prior law, both expanding and contracting the exclusion for meals and lodging previously provided, and it must therefore be construed as its draftsmen obviously intended it to be — as a replacement for the prior law, designed to "end [its] confusion."

Because §119 replaces prior law, respondent's further argument — that . . . the existence under §61 of an exclusion for a class of noncompensatory cash payments — is without merit. If cash meal allowances could be excluded on the mere showing that such payments served the convenience of the employer, as respondent suggests, then cash would be more widely excluded from income than meals in kind, an extraordinary result given the presumptively compensatory nature of cash payments and the obvious intent of §119 to narrow the circumstances in which meals could be excluded.

. . . [T]o avoid the completely unwarranted result of creating a larger exclusion for cash than kind, the meal allowances here would have to be demonstrated to be necessary to allow respondent "properly to perform his duties." There is not even a suggestion on this record of any such necessity. . . .

Judgment for Petitioner.

ADAMS v. UNITED STATES
585 F.2d 1060 (Ct. Cl. 1978)

Per Curiam.

The issue in this tax refund suit is whether the fair rental value of a Japanese residence furnished the plaintiffs by the employer of plaintiff Faneuil Adams, Jr., is excludable from their gross income under Section 119.

. . . In 1970 and 1971, Faneuil Adams [hereinafter "plaintiff"] was president of Mobil Sekiyu Kabushiki Kaisha ("Sekiyu"), a Tokyo-based Japanese corporation which was wholly owned by Mobil Oil Corporation ("Mobil"). . . .

In order to attract qualified employees for foreign service and to maintain an equitable relationship between its domestic and American foreign-based employees, thereby preventing any employee from gaining a benefit or suffering a hardship from serving overseas, Mobil maintained a compensation policy for its American employees assigned outside the United States. One of the components of the policy involved the procurement by Mobil of housing for such employees, regardless of their position or duties. Mobil first calculated a "U.S. Housing Element" for each American foreign-based employee, based on a survey of the Bureau of Labor Statistics, which reflected the approximate average housing costs in the United States at various family sizes and income levels. Mobil then subtracted from that employee's salary the amount of his particular U.S. Housing Element. If Mobil provided housing to the employee, the employee would include in his gross income for federal tax purposes the U.S. Housing Element amount. If the employee instead obtained his own housing abroad, Mobil reimbursed him for the full amount, subject to certain predetermined limitations based upon reasonableness, and the employee would then include the full amount reimbursed in his gross income.

Pursuant to the above policy, Mobil provided plaintiff with a residence for the years in question. The three-level house, which was built and owned by Sekiyu, was 3 miles from headquarters and consisted of a large living room, dining room, pantry and kitchen, three bedrooms, a den, two bathrooms, two maid's rooms, two garage areas, and a garden and veranda. . . . Sekiyu felt that it was important to house its chief executive officer in prestigious surroundings because, particularly in Japan, there is less of a distinction than in the United States between business activities and social activities. The effectiveness of a president of a company in Japan is influenced by the social standing and regard accorded to him by the Japanese business community. If the president of Sekiyu had not resided in a residence equivalent to the type provided the plaintiff, it would appear that he would have been unofficially downgraded and slighted by the business community and his effectiveness for Sekiyu correspondingly impaired. Sekiyu, therefore, provided such a house to plaintiff and required him to reside there as a matter of company policy.

The house was also designed so that it could accommodate the business activities of the plaintiff. The den was built specifically for the conduct of business, and the kitchen and living room were sufficiently large for either business meetings or receptions. Plaintiff worked in the house in the evenings and on weekends and held small meetings there for mixed business and social purposes. He regularly used the telephone for business purposes from his home after regular working hours, both for business emergencies and also for communicating with persons in the United States because of the time difference. In addition, he regularly discharged his business entertainment responsibilities in his residence, generally averaging about 35-40 such occasions in a normal year. In 1970 his entertaining declined considerably because of the absence of his wife from Japan for 10 months, but it resumed again in 1971. Plaintiff was provided with two maids, only one of whom was needed for his family's personal requirements.

Plaintiff included in his gross income for federal tax purposes, as the value of the housing furnished him by his employer, the U.S. Housing Element amounts which had been subtracted from his gross salary. Those amounts which were designed to approximate the average housing costs of a similarly situated person in the United States during 1970 and 1971, totalled $4,439 for 1970 and $4,824 for 1971. However, because the cost of housing in Tokyo in those years was considerably higher than that in the United States, it is agreed by the parties that the fair rental value of the residence furnished plaintiff by Sekiyu was $20,000 in 1970 and $20,599.09 in 1971. . . .

Plaintiff contends that the fair rental value of the residence supplied to him by Sekiyu in 1970 and 1971 is excludable from his gross income because of Section 119 of the 1954 Code. . . .

[I]n order to qualify for the exclusion of Section 119, each of three tests must be met:

(1) the employee must be required to accept the lodging as a condition of his employment;
(2) the lodging must be furnished for the convenience of the employer; and
(3) the lodging must be on the business premises of the employer. [Treas. Reg. §1.119-1(b) (1956).]

The Regulations further provide that the first test is met where the employee is "required to accept the lodging in order to enable him properly to perform the duties of his employment." Id.

It is clear that the first requirement of the statute has been met because the plaintiff was explicitly required to accept the residence provided by Sekiyu as a condition of his employment as president of the company. Sekiyu's goal was twofold: first, it wanted to insure that its president resided in housing of sufficiently dignified surroundings to promote his effectiveness within the Japanese business community. Secondly, Sekiyu wished to provide its president with facilities which were sufficient for the conduct of certain necessary business activities at home. Since at least 1954 Sekiyu had required that its chief executive officer reside in the residence provided to plaintiff, as a condition to appointment as president.

With respect to this first test of Section 119, then, this case is as compelling as United States Junior Chamber of Commerce v. United States, 334 F.2d 660 ([Ct. Cl.] 1964). In that case, the court found that it was not *necessary* for the taxpayer-president to reside in the Chamber's "White House" during his term of office so long as he lived in the Tulsa area. But, as a practical matter, for the convenience of his employer and as a condition of his tenure, the president was *required* to live there. Therefore, it was held that the "condition of employment" test was met. The court noted that the "condition of employment" test is met if

> due to the nature of the employer's business, a certain type of residence for the employee is required and that it would not be reasonable to suppose that the employee would normally have available such lodging for the use of his employer.

Here, because the size and style of one's residence had an important effect upon the Japanese business community, a certain type of residence was both required by Mobil and Sekiyu for the plaintiff and necessary for the proper discharge of his duties in Sekiyu's best interests.

In contrast, the Tax Court in James H. McDonald, 66 T.C. 223 (1976), found that the taxpayer was not expressly required to accept his accommodations as a condition of his employment in Tokyo. Moreover, the court noted that the apartment provided to the taxpayer was not integrally related to the various facets of the employee's position. In the present case, plaintiff was required to accept the housing, and the residence was directly related to plaintiff's position as president, both in terms of physical facilities and psychic significance. It is held, therefore, that plaintiff was required to accept the lodging in order to enable him properly to perform the duties of his employment.

As to the "for the convenience of the employer" test, in United States Junior Chamber of Commerce v. United States, the court stated,

> There does not appear to be any substantial difference between the . . . "convenience of the employer" test and the "required as a condition of his employment" test.

Since it has already been determined that the condition of employment test has been satisfied, on that basis alone it could be held that the convenience of the employer test has also been met.

In *McDonald*, the court stated that the convenience of the employer test is satisfied where there is a direct nexus between the housing furnished the employee and the business interests of the employer served thereby. In *McDonald*, the taxpayer was a principal officer of Gulf who was furnished an apartment by his employer which totalled only about 1,500 square feet of living space. The taxpayer was not required to live in the apartment, and it was found that the only benefit Gulf received in maintaining the apartment was the flexibility it afforded Gulf in personnel transfers. There was no prestige consideration. The court held that there was an insufficient nexus between the apartment and the employer's business interests to meet the convenience of the employer test requirements. Moreover, the court further noted that:

> While its practice of maintaining various leasehold interests for assignment to expatriate employees may have accorded Gulf a benefit in terms of flexibility in personnel transfers, that is not to conclude that the assignments of these lodgings to petitioners at a discount similarly served the interests of Gulf; that is, although convenience may have dictated the form in which the leasehold arrangements were structured, the convenience of Gulf did not require it to subsidize the assignments.

Here there was a sufficiently direct relationship between the housing furnished the plaintiff by Sekiyu and Sekiyu's business interests to meet the convenience of the employer test. The lodging had been built and was owned by Sekiyu. It was specially identified with the business of Sekiyu, for the house had served as the home of its presidents since at least 1954. If Sekiyu's president had not resided in housing comparable to that supplied plaintiff, Sekiyu's business would have been adversely affected. The house had been designed for this purpose to accommodate substantial business activities, and therefore further served Sekiyu's business interests.

Moreover, the fact that Sekiyu subsidized plaintiff's use of the house was also in its best business interests. Sekiyu was interested in attracting a qualified person as its chief executive officer. Because of the unusual housing situation in Tokyo during the years in question, a person would have had to pay up to four times his U.S. housing costs to obtain comparable housing in Tokyo. Certainly, such a factor would have been a strong deterrent to any qualified person's interest in Sekiyu's presidency, absent a housing subsidy from Sekiyu. Furthermore, it was clearly in Mobil-Sekiyu's best business interests to maintain an equitable compensation relationship between its domestic employees and its American foreign-based ones. The housing subsidy was designed to accomplish that.

That the plaintiff also incurred a benefit from this residence and that it was, in part, a convenience to him, does not disturb the conclusion. As noted in William I. Olkjer, 32 T.C. 464, 469 (1959):

> No doubt the facilities furnished benefited the employee also. The test which the statute provides, however, is that of convenience to the employer. There is no provision to the effect that the employee is to be deprived of his right to exclude from gross income the value of food and lodging otherwise excludable because he, too, is convenienced.

The third and final test is whether the lodging was on the business premises of the employer. Observe first that "[t]he operative framework of [the clause 'on the business premises'] is at best elusive and admittedly incapable of generating any hard and fast line." Jack B. Lindeman, 60 T.C. 609, 617 (1973) (Tannenwald, J., concurring). This question is largely a factual one requiring a commonsense approach. The statute should not be read literally. As noted by the Tax Court in *Lindeman*, supra, 60 T.C. at 614:

> [T]he statutory language ordinarily would not permit any exclusion for lodging furnished a domestic servant, since a servant's lodging is rarely furnished on "the business premises of his employer"; yet the committee report shows a clear intention to allow the exclusion where the servant's lodging is furnished in the employer's home.

In the original version of the 1954 Code, as enacted in the House, the term that was used in Section 119 was "place of employment." The Senate changed the wording to "business premises," which was accepted by the House. However, the change was without substance, for the House Conference Report stated that "[t]he term 'business premises of the employer' is intended, in general, to have the same effect as the term 'place of employment' in the House bill." H. Conf. Rep. No. 2543, 83d Cong., 2d Sess. 27, reprinted in [1954] U.S. Code Cong. & Admin. News, pp. 5280, 5286. The pertinent Treasury regulation similarly provides that "business premises" generally refers to the place of employment of the employee. Treas. Reg. Sec. 1.119-1(c)(1) (1956). The phrase, then, is not to be limited to the business compound or headquarters of the employer. Rather, the emphasis must be upon the place where the employee's duties are to be performed. In United States Junior Chamber of Commerce v. United States, the court stated, "We think that the business premises of Section 119 means premises of the employer on which the duties of the employee are to be performed." The phrase has also been construed to mean either (1) living quarters that constitute an integral part of the business property, or (2) premises on which the company carries on some substantial segment of its business activities.

In *United States Junior Chamber of Commerce*, the taxpayer-president had an office in the employer-owned "White House" which he used at night for the conduct of business meetings. In addition, he used his residence for business entertainment purposes. The court held that, because of these two factors, the White House constituted a part of the business premises of the employer, though not physically contiguous to headquarters. In this case plaintiff, although he had an office at the employer's headquarters, worked in his residence in the evenings and on weekends, had business meetings and performed required business telephone calls from there which could not be made during normal business hours, and conducted regular business entertaining in the residence. In this sense plaintiff's residence was a part of the business premises of his employer, for it was a "premises on which the duties of the employee are to be performed," and a "premises on which the company carries on some of its business activities."

Interpretations of the phrase which are limited to the geographic contiguity of the premises or to questions of the quantum of business activities on the premises are too restrictive. Rather, the statutory language "on the business premises of the employer"[implies] a functional rather than a spatial unity. In Rev. Rul. 75-540, 1975-2 Cum. Bull. 53, it was determined that the fair rental value of the official residence furnished a governor by the state is excludable from the governor's gross income under Section 119 of the Code. The Ruling noted that the business premises test was met because the residence provided by the state enabled the governor to carry out efficiently the administrative, ceremonial, and social duties required by his office. The governor's mansion, thus, served an important business function in that it was clearly identified with the business interests of the state. It was, in short, an inseparable adjunct. Similarly, in *United States Junior Chamber of Commerce*, one of the main objectives of the employer was to promote and foster the growth of civic organizations in the United States. The White House, as official residence of the president of the organization, served a significant public relations function in furtherance of the organization's goals. In the present case, even apart from the strictly business activities which took place in plaintiff's residence, the house was a symbol to the Japanese business community of the status of Sekiyu's chief executive officer and a place where he officially entertained for business purposes. As such, it influenced plaintiff's effectiveness in the business community and directly served a business function for Sekiyu.

The situation, thus, is not the same as in *James H. McDonald*. In that case, the court found the quantum of business activities performed by the taxpayer in his home to be insignificant. There was no suggestion of prestige value to the employer or of its use for significant business entertainment. . . .

The three statutory requisites for exclusion are met. Accordingly, . . . the fair rental value of the residence is excludable from plaintiff's gross income.

Problems

3-9. Elaine Okuma, a law firm associate, was required to attend the afternoon luncheons of her employer on every Monday and Thursday except for holidays, sick days, and vacation days. Her employer, wishing to encourage social interaction among its employees, had arranged for all key personnel to eat at a restaurant located across the street from the office. The employer felt that the luncheons, at $20 a plate, were a good investment.
   a.   Does Okuma have gross income?
   b.   If so, how is the amount determined?

3-10. Rob Pinter, a waiter at a fashionable restaurant, is on duty from 10 A.M. to 6 P.M. daily. Under the terms of his employment agreement, he is to eat lunch at 2 P.M. and dinner at 7 P.M. and may select any item on the menu at no charge.
   a.   Does Pinter have gross income?
   b.   If so, how is the amount determined?

3-11. The state of Illinois contracted with several restaurants, located at strategic spots on state roads and highways, to reimburse those restaurants for the cost of any meals eaten by on-duty policemen. The state police were told that they could eat at the "approved restaurants" within their assigned area of duty whenever they were entitled to a midshift meal. Do the state troopers have gross income?

3-12. Julie Doans, a graduate student, is the resident head of a college dormitory. Resident heads are provided, at no charge, spacious suites. In addition, they have the option of receiving free meals in the dormitory cafeteria, but because of the poor quality of the food, Doans prepared most of her meals in the suite and ate with the students only at Sunday dinner. As resident head, Doans also received a cash stipend of $1,000 per month.

Although a resident head is not required to do anything but live in the dormitory, there is a general expectation by the college administration that resident heads will have social functions for the dormitory residents and offer advice if asked. The university offers the position of resident head only to those whom it feels are temperamentally qualified for the job.

a. What are the includable and excludable items of gross income?

b. What would be the result in *a* if, instead of a dormitory room, Doans requested and received rent-free use of a university-owned home located off campus but directly across the street from the dormitory? What if the home was five blocks from campus?

3-13. Julie Arias's fine work at Cartographers, Inc., led competing firms to vie for her services. The attractive offers she received forced her employer to make an equally attractive proposal: It would increase her responsibilities, raise her salary by $8,000, and provide her with a large, lavishly furnished house if she would agree to remain with Cartographers for three years and consent to using the house for entertaining clients and for conducting business. Arias accepted, and Cartographers purchased a $400,000 house, equipping it with a large office, kitchen, ballroom, tennis court, housekeeper, and cook. At the outer gate, a sign read: "The Cartographers' House." Arias and her family moved into the house and began entertaining prospective and current clients on a weekly basis. Does Arias have any gross income as a result of these arrangements?

3. *Reimbursed Employee Expenses*

Code: §62(a)(2)(A)
Regulations: Reg. §1.62-2

Recall in Chapter 2 the discussion of *Gotcher*. In that case, a taxpayer did not have gross income from a business trip because the trip was solely for business reasons and had no personal component to it. But what if an employee incurs expenses for a business trip and then the employer reimburses the employee with cash? On its face, it is difficult to distinguish a cash reimbursement from any other cash compensation, and there is no guarantee that the employee would not use the cash for other unrelated consumption. Does that mean the employee has gross income equal to the amount of the cash reimbursement, even if the sole purpose of the trip was for the employer's business? The general answer to the question is yes. It seems clear, however, that a reimbursement from an employer for expenses incurred on a business trip is different from salary since the money is simply meant to make the employee whole. Excluding such payments from gross income could open a huge potential for abuse, however, as it would allow employers to pay a form of compensation in the form of free trips, such as in *McCann*, to employees tax-free.

The regulations recognize this dilemma and address it through so-called "accountable plan" programs. Pursuant to an accountable plan, the cash reimbursement is essentially disregarded; so long as the employee maintains records of the expenses, such as detailed receipts, and submits them to the employer, who then reimburses the employee for that amount and no more, the regulations provide that the reimbursement is disregarded and the employee is treated as if they received no gross income and incurred no expenses. Conversely, since the employer is not treated as having paid salary to the employee under an accountable plan, the employer is not entitled to a wage deduction. As will be discussed in Chapter 6, the employer might be entitled to a deduction for the actual business expenses, but only if the trip was ordinary and necessary to the conduct of the employer's business.

Accountable plans resolve a number of theoretical and administrative problems by providing a way to reach the same result as in *Gotcher* without needing to prove that the employee had no personal consumption at all from the trip. Rather, so long as the employer sends the employee on the trip and willingly pays for it, the regulations effectively assume the trip is primarily for business reasons. Conceptually, however, it would be possible for an employee to have a similar result if the reimbursement was treated as gross income and the underlying expenses were treated as deductions, thus completely offsetting the amount of the income. But what if those deductions were limited or disallowed in some manner? Clearly if the deductions were limited or disallowed the exclusion approach would be superior for the employee. But even if the deductions would offset all the gross income, there are still two significant advantages to an accountable plan: (1) the employee would not be required to report the income on their tax return and maintain the paperwork to deduct the expenses, and (2) the employer would not withhold any payroll taxes with respect to the reimbursement. Reg. §1.62-2(c)(4).

4.   Employee Fringe Benefits

Code: §132(a) to (f), (h), (j)(1)
Regulations: §§1.132-1(a), 1.132-2, 1.132-3(a) and (b), 1.132-5(a), 1.132-6; 1.61-21(a), (b)(1), (2), (3)

a.   Introduction

An employer furnishes coffee and soft drinks free of charge to employees; a trucking company allows an employee to ship a personal package on its trucks when there is space available; a lawyer utilizes firm-provided computer and e-mail account for personal correspondence—in each instance the employee has received a work-related "fringe benefit."

There is no doubt that an employee enjoys "an accession to wealth" that is "clearly realized" in accepting a fringe benefit. The mere fact that the employee accepted or used the fringe benefit establishes as much. Prior to 1984, however, employer-provided fringe benefits were largely ignored by the IRS in computing gross income. The primary justifications for not taxing such benefits were that they were too difficult to value and that keeping track of such items presented insurmountable record keeping problems. For example, even if the amount of coffee and soda consumed by an employee could be ascertained with reasonable accuracy and the cost per serving determined from the employer's records, the employer's cost might not be the true measure of the value to the employee. Perhaps the employee would have purchased a less expensive brand of soda or perhaps would not have consumed any at all had it not been offered for free or at a reduced cost by the employer. Thus, the value the employee placed on the benefit might be less (or more) than the employer's cost.

As discussed in Chapter 2, receipts are not generally excluded from gross income merely because they are difficult to value. This is especially true in the employment context where a compensatory motive can be presumed. Thus, the fact that fringe benefits were not being included in gross income by the IRS drew a significant amount of attention, particularly considering that fringe benefits necessarily arise in the employment context. Faced with relentlessly mounting budget deficits, Congress moved to curtail the noncash forms of compensation that had escaped taxation. In 1984, it specifically addressed the taxation of fringe benefits and provided specific rules governing the exclusion of fringe benefits from gross income. In general, §132 provides that gross income does not include any fringe benefit that qualifies as a (1) no-additional-cost service, (2) qualified employee discount, (3) working condition fringe, (4) de minimis fringe, (5) qualified transportation fringe, (6) qualified moving expense reimbursement, (7) on-premises athletic facility, or (8) qualified retirement planning services. By specifying a limited number of excludable fringe benefits, Congress also provided that any noncash forms of compensation that do not fall within one of the statutory categories *must* be included in the employee's gross income. Consequently, numerous previously untaxed fringe benefits have been brought within the ambit of gross income.

The legislative history of §132 elucidates the objective of the legislation.

In providing statutory rules for exclusion of certain fringe benefits for income and payroll tax purposes, the committee has attempted to strike a balance between two competing objectives.

First, the committee is aware that in many industries, employees may receive, either free or at a discount, goods and services which the employer sells to the general public. In many cases, these practices are long established, and have been treated by employers, employees, and the IRS as not giving rise to taxable income. Although employees may receive an economic benefit from the availability of these free or discounted goods or services, employers often have valid business reasons, other than simply providing compensation, for encouraging employees to avail themselves of the products which they sell to the public. For example, a retail clothing business will want its salespersons to wear, when they deal with customers, the clothing which it seeks to sell to the public. . . . The committee believes, therefore, that many present practices under which employers may provide to a broad group of employees, either free or at a discount, the products and services which the employer sells or provides to the public do not serve merely to replace cash compensation.

The second objective of the committee's bill is to set forth clear boundaries for the provision of tax-free benefits. . . .

In addition, the committee is concerned that without any well-defined limits on the ability of employers to compensate their employees tax-free by using a medium other than cash, new practices will emerge that could shrink the income tax base significantly, and further shift a disproportionate tax burden to those individuals whose compensation is in the form of cash.

H.R. Rep. No. 432, 98th Cong., 2d Sess. 1591 (1984).

b.   Section 132 — Statutory Criteria for Excludable Fringe Benefits

No-additional-cost service fringe benefits. No-additional-cost service fringe benefits include the value of any service provided by an employer to an employee for the use of that employee, for which the employer incurs no additional cost. The exclusion applies whether the service is provided directly at no charge, at a reduced price, or through a cash rebate.

The no-additional-cost fringe benefit exclusion is subject to two conditions — a nondiscrimination requirement and a line of business limitation. The exclusion for no-additional-cost fringe benefits is available to officers, directors, owners, and highly compensated employees of an employer only if the benefits are available to all employees on a nondiscriminatory basis. Failure to satisfy the non-discrimination requirement results in the taxation of the benefits received by favored employees. The line of business limitation requires that to be excludable as a no-additional-cost fringe benefit, a service must be the same type of service as that sold to the public in the ordinary course of the employer's line of business in which the employee works. If an employee provides services that directly benefit more than one line of business of the employer, such as a payroll department employee, that employee is treated as performing services for all of the employer's lines of business. In addition, reciprocal arrangements are permitted allowing the employees of one employer to qualify for the no-additional-cost exclusion for benefits provided by an unrelated employer, as long as (1) both employers are in the same line of business, (2) both employers are parties to a written reciprocity agreement, and (3) neither employer incurs any substantial additional cost.

The House Committee Report provided the following examples of excludable no-additional-cost service fringe benefits.

[A]ssume that a corporation which operates an airline as its only line of business provides all of its employees . . . free travel, on the same terms to all employees, as stand-by passengers on the employer airline if the space taken on the flight has not been sold to the public shortly before departure time. In such a case, the entire fair market value of the free travel is excluded under the no-additional-cost service rule in the bill. This conclusion follows because the service provided by the employer to its employees who work in the employer's airline line of business is the same as that sold to the general public (airline flights), the service is provided at no substantial additional cost to the employer (the seat would have been unsold to nonemployees if the employee had not taken the trip), and the eligibility terms satisfy the nondiscrimination rules of the bill since all employees are eligible for the benefit on the same terms.

The House Report noted that the exclusion would not be available

> to employees in the hotel line of business of a corporation for receipt of free stand-by travel on an airline operated by the same corporation, or to employees of a consumer goods manufacturer who travel for personal purposes on a company plane (even if the plane is otherwise making a trip on company business). In each of these cases, even assuming that there were no substantial additional cost to the employer in providing the service on a space-available basis, the service is not the same type generally provided to the general public in the specific line of business of the employer in which the employee recipient works.

H.R. Rep. No. 432 at 1596.

Qualified employee discounts. An employee discount is defined as "the amount by which — (A) the price at which the property or services are provided by the employer to an employee for use by such employee is less than (B) the price at which such property or services are being offered by the employer to customers." §132(c)(3). Employee discounts are allowed from the selling price of qualified goods or services if the discounts are available to employees on a nondiscriminatory basis.

As with the no-additional-cost fringe benefit, the employee discount exclusion is also subject to a line of business limitation — the discounted goods or services must be offered for sale to nonemployee customers in the ordinary course of the employer's line of business in which the employee works. Thus, if an employee works for a company that conducts more than one line of business, the employee is eligible for the discount exclusion only for merchandise or services offered to customers in the ordinary course of the particular line of business in which the employee works.

It is relatively easy to understand why Congress would permit employers to provide excludable discounts to employees for goods sold to the public in the ordinary course of business. For example, it could be beneficial to a car dealership for a salesperson to drive the model of a car sold at the lot, or it may be important to a fashion retailer that its employees dress in the fashions sold at the store. In effect, providing discounts to employees encourages employees to act as a form of low-cost advertising, or "moving billboards," for the business.

Without any limitations, however, it would be quite simple for employers to use employee discounts as a way to provide tax-exempt compensation to their employees. For example, the owner of a consumer electronics store that sells a new video game console for $600 could offer to sell the video game console to employees for $100, knowing that there are customers in the store willing to pay $600 cash to the employee immediately for the console. In effect, the employee is guaranteed to receive $500 cash indirectly from the employer. This scheme would effectively serve as a means to provide additional compensation to the employee of $500 per console, while providing no benefit to the employer other than serving as a means to compensate the employee.

To prevent this perceived abuse of using employee discounts to provide a tax-free form of compensation to employees that would not otherwise serve the convenience of the employer, an employee discount is excludable as a "qualified employee discount" only if it is with respect to qualified property or services and falls within a specified percentage requirement. Further, the exclusion is not available for discounts on property that is highly liquid or otherwise similar to cash, such as personal property of the kind which is usually held for investment, including securities and gold coins or real property. §132(c)(4). A discount for services may not exceed 20 percent of the price offered to the employer's customers. §132(c)(1)(B). The discount percentage on goods may not exceed the employer's "gross profit percentage," determined by reference to the sales price to customers compared with the employer's cost for the merchandise. §132(c)(2).

> For example, if total sales of such merchandise during a year were $1,000,000 and the employer's cost for the merchandise was $600,000, then gross profit percentage for the year is 40 percent ($1,000,000 minus $600,000 equals 40 percent of $1,000,000). Thus, an employee discount with respect to such merchandise is excluded from income to the extent it does not exceed 40 percent of the selling price of the merchandise to nonemployee customers. If in this case the discount allowed to the employee exceeds 40 percent (for example, 50 percent), the excess discount on a purchase (10 percent in the example) is included in the employee's gross income.

H.R. Rep. No. 432 at 1599.

Working condition fringe benefits. Section 132(d) defines a working condition fringe as "any property or services provided to an employee of the employer to the extent that, if the employee paid for such property or services, such payment would be allowable as a deduction under §162 or §167." In effect, §132(d) excludes from income those fringe benefits for which the expense to incur the benefit, had the employee purchased the fringe benefit directly, would have been deductible by the employee. For example, if an employee was paid $100 in salary and used the salary to purchase office supplies in connection with his or her employment, the employee would likely be entitled to deduct the $100 cost of the office supplies from his or her income under §162. Under §132(d), if the employer provides the office supplies directly to the employee, the $100 value of the office supplies would be excluded from the employee's gross income. At first glance, it might appear that the employee is, and should be, indifferent between the two, because in the first case the employee would have $100 of income and $100 of deduction (netting to zero) while in the second the employee would have no income and no deduction (also netting to zero). This is not always the case, however; at times, an exclusion can be much more valuable than a deduction. The distinction between exclusions and deductions, and why a taxpayer would prefer one over the other, will be explored in more detail in Chapter 8.

The House Committee Report provided the following illustrations of working condition fringe benefits.

[T]he value of use by an employee of a company car or airplane for business purposes is excluded as a working condition fringe. (However, use of a company car or plane for personal purposes is not excludable. Merely incidental personal use of a company car, such as a small detour for personal errands, might qualify for exclusion as a de minimis fringe.) As another example, assume the employer subscribes to business periodicals for an employee (e.g., a brokerage house buys a financial publication for its brokers). In that case, the fair market value of the subscriptions is an excluded working condition fringe, since the expense could have been deducted as a business expense if the employee had directly paid for the subscription.

Examples of other benefits excluded as working condition fringes are those provided by an employer primarily for the safety of its employees, if such safety precautions are considered ordinary and necessary business expenses. . . .

In contrast, assume that an employer agrees to pay the real estate broker's commission on the sale of an employee's house to assist the employee in moving to another job site for the employer. The payment of the commission by the employer is not excludable as a working condition fringe, because direct payment of the commission expense by the employee would not be deductible by the employee as a section 162 business expense.

H.R. Rep. No. 432 at 1601.

De minimis fringe benefits. Section 132(e) defines a de minimis fringe benefit as any property or service the value of which is so small that accounting for it is made unreasonable or administratively impracticable. The exemption includes employer-operated eating facilities that offer meals to employees at below fair market value prices, provided the employer charges enough to recover its direct operating costs. §132(e)(2)(B). Eating facility fringe benefits must be available on a nondiscriminatory basis. Other de minimis fringe benefits may, however, be bestowed discriminatorily.

The House Report suggests a variety of benefits that may be de minimis, including

[t]he typing of personal letters by a company secretary, occasional personal use of the company copying machine, monthly transit passes provided at a discount not exceeding $21, occasional company cocktail parties or picnics for employees, occasional supper money or taxi fare because of overtime work, traditional holiday gifts of property with a low fair market value, occasional theatre or sporting event tickets, and coffee and doughnuts furnished to employees.

H.R. Rep. No. 432 at 1603.

A fringe benefit is not de minimis if the employer grants it to a particular employee so regularly that it, in effect, serves as a means of disguised compensation. For example, if an employer grants one employee coffee and meals every day and does not provide anything to the other employees, the fringe benefit is not de minimis notwithstanding that the total value of the coffee and meals to the employer is small. An interesting aspect of de minimis fringe benefits, however, is that there is no statutory or regulatory limit on the benefit any particular employee may receive so long as the employer's overall fringe benefit program is de minimis. Thus, for example, if an employer permits personal photocopies for all employees, but restricts total personal use of the photocopier to less than 15 percent of the total use of the photocopier, all employees could exclude the value of the free photocopies from gross income regardless whether one employee makes one photocopy a year and another makes 400. Similarly, meals at employer-provided cafeterias are excluded as de minimis (assuming the employer meets the other requirements described above) regardless whether an employee eats at the cafeteria once a year or three times a day. Does this distinction make sense in light of the purported policy behind the de minimis exception, or even §132 as a whole?

Qualified transportation fringe. Section 132(f) defines this category as including employer-provided commuter transportation, transit pass, qualified parking, or qualified bicycle commuting reimbursement. Ceilings are imposed on the amounts that will qualify for exclusion, which, for years after 1999, are annually adjusted for inflation under §132(f)(6). For example, in 2011, the limit for commuter transportation was $120 per month, and the limit for parking was $230 per month.

Qualified moving expense reimbursement. Section 132(g) excludes from gross income the amount of moving expenses paid by the taxpayer's employer, which would have been deductible if directly paid or incurred by the taxpayer. The exclusion applies if the taxpayer is reimbursed or if the employer pays the expenses directly. Moving expenses are defined as (1) the reasonable costs of moving household goods and personal effects from the former residence to the new residence and (2) the reasonable costs of traveling (including lodging) from the former residence to the new residence. Moving expenses do not include expenses for meals.

On-premises athletic facilities. Section 132(j)(4) specifically excludes from gross income the fair market value of on-premises athletic facilities for employees if substantially all of the use of the facility is by employees and their spouses and children. The exclusion does not apply to country clubs or athletic facility memberships, unless the facility is owned and operated by the employer and satisfies the other requirements for exclusion. The nondiscrimination requirement does not apply to the athletic facilities exemption.

Qualified retirement planning services. Section 132(m) excludes from gross income any retirement planning advice provided to an employee and spouse by an employer maintaining a qualified plan, contract, pension, or account. This exemption is also subject to the nondiscrimination requirement.

Family members. Most fringe benefits, such as de minimis fringe benefits and working condition fringe benefits, inure directly to the benefit of the employee in the conduct of the employee's business. Other fringe benefits, however, are intended for the benefit of the employee and the employee's family. For example, an airline may permit its employees and their family members to fly for free or at a discounted rate. Absent a specific provision, these types of fringe benefits to family members would be included in the employee's gross income. Section 132(h)(2) addresses this by treating either a no-additional-cost fringe benefit or a qualified employee discount fringe benefit used by the employee's spouse or dependent children as if it had been received by the employee. Why was such treatment limited only to these two types of fringe benefits and not others, such as de minimis fringe benefits? If an employee's dependent child visits the employee's office and drinks an employer-provided beverage, do the administrative difficulties of accounting for the beverage become smaller solely because a family member consumed it rather than the employee?

Interestingly, §132(h)(2) is limited in scope only to *spouses* and *dependent children* of the employee. Thus, for example, non-married partners, former spouses, siblings, children over the age of 25, and close friends are not eligible to receive such benefits without including the value of the benefit in the employee's gross income. Why do you think that §132(h)(2) was limited in this manner? Further, §132(h)(3) permits the employee's *parents* to receive a fringe benefit without including the value of the transportation in gross income, but *only* if the fringe benefit is in the form of air transportation. Is there something unique about either parents or air transportation that justifies such a special rule?

NOTICE 2011-72
2011-38 I.R.B. 407

Tax Treatment of Employer-Provided Cell Phones

PURPOSE

This notice provides guidance on the tax treatment of cellular telephones or other similar telecommunications equipment (hereinafter collectively "cell phones") that employers provide to their employees primarily for noncompensatory business purposes.

BACKGROUND

. . . Since enactment of the [Small Business Jobs Act of 2010, Pub. L. No. 111-240], the IRS has received questions about the proper tax treatment of employer-provided cell phones. Accordingly, this notice addresses the treatment of employer-provided cell phones as an excludible fringe benefit.

Gross Income

Section 61 of the Internal Revenue Code (Code) defines gross income as all income, from whatever source derived. Section 61(a)(1) provides that gross income includes compensation for services, including fees, commissions, fringe benefits, and similar items. A fringe benefit provided by an employer to an employee is presumed to be income to the employee unless it is specifically excluded from gross income by another section of the Code. See Income Tax Regulations §1.61-21(a).

Working Condition Fringe Benefits

Section 132(a)(3) of the Code provides that gross income does not include any fringe benefit which qualifies as a working condition fringe. Section 132(d) provides that "working condition fringe" means any property or services provided to an employee of the employer to the extent that, if the employee paid for such property or services, such payment would be allowable as a deduction under §§162 or 167.

. . . Section 162(a) of the Code provides that a deduction is allowed for all the ordinary and necessary expenses paid or incurred during the taxable year in carrying on any trade or business. However, section 262(a) of the Code provides that, except as otherwise expressly provided, no deduction shall be allowed for personal, living, or family expenses. . . .

De Minimis Fringe Benefits

Section 132(a)(4) of the Code provides that gross income does not include any fringe benefit which qualifies as a de minimis fringe. Section 132(e) defines a de minimis fringe as any property or service the value of which is (after taking into account the frequency with which similar fringes are provided by the employer to the employer's employees) so small as to make accounting for it unreasonable or administratively impracticable. Except as specifically provided (i.e., occasional meal money or local transportation fare and reimbursements for public transit passes), a cash fringe benefit is not excludable as a de minimis fringe. See Regulations §1.132-6(c).

Guidance Regarding Employer-Provided Cell Phones

Many employers provide their employees with cell phones primarily for noncompensatory business reasons. The value of the business use of an employer-provided cell phone is excludable from an employee's income as a working condition fringe to the extent that, if the employee paid for the use of the cell phone themselves, such payment would be allowable as a deduction under section 162 for the employee.

An employer will be considered to have provided an employee with a cell phone primarily for noncompensatory business purposes if there are substantial reasons relating to the employer's business, other than providing compensation to the employee, for providing the employee with a cell phone. For example, the employer's need to contact the employee at all times for work-related emergencies, the employer's requirement that the employee be available to speak with clients at times when the employee is away from the office, and the employee's need to speak with clients located in other time zones at times outside of the employee's normal work day are possible substantial noncompensatory business reasons. A cell phone provided to promote the morale or good will of an employee, to attract a prospective employee or as a means of furnishing additional compensation to an employee is not provided primarily for noncompensatory business purposes.

This notice provides that, when an employer provides an employee with a cell phone primarily for noncompensatory business reasons, the IRS will treat the employee's use of the cell phone for reasons related to the employer's trade or business as a working condition fringe benefit, the value of which is excludable from the employee's income. . . . In addition, the IRS will treat the value of any personal use of a cell phone provided by the employer primarily for noncompensatory business purposes as excludable from the employee's income as a de minimis fringe benefit. . . . The application of the working condition and de minimis fringe benefit exclusions under this notice apply solely to employer-provided cell phones and should not be interpreted as applying to other fringe benefits.

REV. RUL. 2006-57
2006-47 I.R.B. 911

ISSUE

Whether, under the facts described, employer-provided transportation benefits provided through smartcards, debit or credit cards, or other electronic media are excluded from gross income under §§132(a)(5) and 132(f) of the Internal Revenue Code. . . .

FACTS

Situation 1. For 2006, Employer *A* provides to its employees transportation benefits. . . . Transit system *X* provides smartcards that may be used by employers in the metropolitan area served by *X* as a mechanism to provide fare media for transit system *X* to employees. . . . The amount stored as fare media on the smartcard is not authorized to be used to purchase anything other than fare media for *X*. . . . *A* makes monthly payments to *X* on behalf of its employees who participate in the transportation benefit program, which *X* then electronically allocates to each employee's smartcard as instructed by *A*. . . .

Situation 2. For 2006, Employer *B* provides to its employees transportation benefits. . . . Debit card provider *P* provides debit cards that may be used by employers to provide transportation benefits to their employees. The debit cards are restricted for use only at merchant terminals at points of sale at which only fare media for transit system *Y* is sold. *B* uses the terminal-restricted debit cards provided by *P* as a mechanism to provide transportation benefits to its employees. *B* makes monthly payments to *P* on behalf of its employees who participate in the transportation benefit program, which *P* then electronically allocates to each employee's terminal-restricted debit card as instructed by *B*. . . .

Situation 3. For 2006, Employer *C* provides to its employees transportation benefits. . . . Debit card provider *Q* provides debit cards that may be used by employers as a mechanism to provide transportation benefits to their employees. . . . The cards are restricted for use at merchants that have been assigned [codes] indicating the merchant sells fare media for some or all of the following categories: local and suburban commuter passenger transport; passenger railway; bus lines, excluding charters and tours; and transportation service (not elsewhere classified). The merchant may or may not sell other merchandise. . . . *C* uses the [code]-restricted debit cards provided by *Q* as a mechanism to provide transportation benefits to its employees. A voucher or similar item exchangeable only for a transit pass is not otherwise readily available for purchase by *C* for direct distribution to *C*'s employees within the meaning of §132(f)(3). . . .

Situation 4. The facts are the same as in Situation 3, except in the following respects. Employer *C* provides employees with [code]-restricted debit cards as soon as they begin work. Prior to using the [code]-restricted debit cards, *C*'s employees certify that the card will be used only to purchase transit passes. In addition, written on each debit card is the statement that the card is to be used only for transit passes, and, by using the card, the employee certifies that the card is being used only to purchase transit passes. At no time do *C*'s employees substantiate to *C* the amount of fare media expenses that have been incurred. . . .

ANALYSIS

In Situation 1, the fare media value stored on the smartcards is useable only as fare media for transit system X. . . . Accordingly, the value of the fare media provided by A to its employees through the use of the smartcards is excluded from the employees' gross income as a qualified transportation fringe benefit . . . without requiring the employees to substantiate their use of the smartcards.

In Situation 2, the terminal-restricted debit card provided by B to its employees qualifies as a transit system voucher . . . because it can be used only at merchant terminals at points of sale at which only fare media for transit system Y can be purchased. In addition, the amount allocated to each employee's debit card each month is within the amount specified by §132(f)(2)(A). Therefore, the value of the fare media provided by B to its employees through the use of the terminal-restricted debit cards is excluded from its employees' gross income as a qualified transportation fringe benefit . . . without requiring the employees to substantiate their use of the debit cards.

In Situation 3, the debit card provided by C to its employees does not qualify as a transit system voucher . . . because it is possible that a [code]-restricted debit card may be used to purchase items other than transit passes. A merchant properly classified to accept the debit card as payment may sell merchandise other than transit passes, and there is nothing in the debit card technology which prevents its use to purchase things other than transit passes. . . .

In Situation 4, as discussed above, the [code]-restricted debit card does not qualify as a transit system voucher. . . . Because a voucher or similar item is not otherwise readily available to C, C may provide qualified transportation fringe benefits in the form of cash reimbursements for transit passes under a bona fide reimbursement arrangement. C provides the debit cards in advance, requiring its employees to certify that they will use the cards exclusively to purchase transit passes. This arrangement does not constitute a bona fide reimbursement arrangement . . . because it provides for advances rather than reimbursements and because it relies solely on employee certifications provided before the expense is incurred. Those certifications, standing alone, do not provide the substantiation of expenses incurred necessary for there to be a bona fide reimbursement arrangement. Because C is providing restricted-use debit cards that are not transit system vouchers, and because C is not reimbursing its employees for fare media expenses under a bona fide reimbursement arrangement, the amounts C provides to its employees through the use of the [code]-restricted debit cards are included in its employees' gross income and wages.

HOLDINGS

Situation 1. The value of the transit pass benefits provided by A to its employees through the use of the smartcards is excluded from gross income under §132(a)(5). . . .

Situation 2. The value of the transit pass benefits provided by B to its employees through the use of the terminal-restricted debit card is excluded from gross income under §132(a)(5). . . .

Situation 3. The value of the transit pass benefits provided by *C* to its employees through the use of the [code]-restricted debit card is excluded from gross income under §132(a)(5). . . .

Situation 4. The amounts provided by *C* to its employees through the use of the [code]-restricted debit cards are not excluded from gross income under §132(a)(5). . . .

Problems

3-14. Elizabeth Hacker is an attorney working full-time in the legal department of United Airlines. During the current year she received and used the following benefits at no charge pursuant to her negotiated employment agreement with United. What tax consequences attend the following receipts?

  a. One round-trip, first-class standby ticket for United flights between New York and Paris for herself and her spouse.

  b. What result in *a* if the tickets were reserved seats, not standby?

  c. What result in *a* if the tickets were on Air France?

  d. What result in *a* if her daughter and brother used the tickets?

  e. Household items worth $1,000 listed in United's in-flight sales brochure purchased at a 30-percent discount. (United's legal department and management staff receive a 30-percent discount, while all other employees receive a discount of 20 percent.)

  f. What result in *e* if all employees received a 30-percent discount, despite the fact that United's profit for those items was only 25 percent?

  g. Ten nights' lodging at the Hilton Hotel in Paris at a 50-percent discount price of $70 per night.

  h. Ten nights' lodging at an Inter-Continental Hotel, owned and operated by United, at a 50-percent discount price of $70 per night.

  i. Would the result in *h* change if Hacker were a United flight attendant, not a lawyer with United? What if it was only one night's lodging? What if she was a self-employed travel agent?

  j. Unlimited international phone calls on the United business VOIP line. (Hacker's personal calls on that line during the year would have totaled $500 had they been paid for by the minute.)

  k. Cash reimbursement of $750 by United for the cost of dinners she purchased on the twenty-five evenings that she worked late during the year.

  l. Approximately 100 hours spent during the year by her secretary working on Hacker's personal activities, such as calling and writing hotels and arranging her family's vacation itinerary and typing letters to friends.

  m. Approximately 1,000 copies of her mother's campaign brochures made during the year on the office copying machine.

  n. A free parking space in the garage below her office building. Because she walks to work, she rents the space to a third party for $100 per month.

  o. Yearly dues of $600 paid by United at the health club in the basement of her office building. Assume the health club is owned and operated by United and is open to the public.

3-15. Joe Johnson, a Mercedes Benz sales representative, purchased a new Mercedes from the dealer for whom he worked. Although the typical sales price for the car was $60,000, Johnson only paid $48,000 because he received a customary 20-percent employee discount. Assume that the dealer profit ratio is 30 percent.

    a.   How much, if any, gross income does Johnson have as a result of the purchase?

    b.   What result if Johnson sells the car for $53,000 one week after he receives it?

D. CAFETERIA PLANS

Code: §125

As discussed earlier, statutory exclusions are generally interpreted narrowly. Thus, for example, under *Kowalski*, lodging that is not located on the premises of the employer is not eligible for exclusion under §119 notwithstanding that it was provided for the convenience of the employer; similarly, under Revenue Ruling 2006-57, debit cards were not eligible for exclusion under §132(a)(5) where there was a possibility the cards might be used on non-transportation expenses. As a result, it becomes important (if an employer desires to provide benefits that will be excluded from the income of the employee) for the employer to tailor the terms of any noncash benefit carefully to comply specifically with a particular statutory exclusion.

Realistically, however, employers tend not to provide employees with every possible benefit that could be excluded from gross income under one of these statutory provisions. Conversely, not all employees prefer to receive the identical set of fringe benefits or to receive fringe benefits instead of cash. A solution available to such businesses is the "cafeteria plan," one in which employees are permitted to select among a choice of alternative noncash benefits or choose cash. For example, under a cafeteria plan, one employee may choose retirement benefits and health insurance while another may choose health insurance and increased salary while foregoing retirement benefits. In effect, a cafeteria plan gives employees control over their package of salary and benefits by choosing from a "menu" of options.

The problem that arises, however, is that accessions to wealth over which a taxpayer exercises dominion and control, such as cafeteria plans, are generally included in income absent a statutory provision to the contrary, as discussed in Chapter 2. In other words, because the employee exercises dominion and control over which benefits to receive, the employee would be treated as having gross income even if the employee received a benefit that would otherwise have been excluded had the employee received it outside a cafeteria plan. For example, if an employee could receive $1,000 cash or $1,000 worth of life insurance, there would be no economic difference between the employee electing to receive the cash and purchasing life insurance or electing to receive the insurance directly from the employer. Thus, absent a specific statutory exclusion, the employee would be treated as receiving $1,000 of gross income regardless which choice the employee made.

This is true notwithstanding that under §79(a) the cost of such insurance would be excluded from the gross income of the employee if the employer had offered only the life insurance.

Section 125 was enacted to address this problem. Under §125, certain employee benefits that would otherwise be excluded under certain provisions of the Internal Revenue Code are excluded from the employee's gross income notwithstanding the employee's ability to choose cash or other taxable benefits instead; in other words, the employee can exclude from income nontaxable benefits even if they are received in a cafeteria plan.

The benefits of §125 are not unlimited, however. Certain benefits that are inherently related to the business (or "convenience") of the employer, such as fringe benefits excluded by §132, are not within the scope of §125. In addition, the benefits offered under a cafeteria plan must satisfy any nondiscrimination or other qualification rules applicable to such benefits.

As with fringe benefits under §132, one concern under §125 is the ability to use cafeteria plans to pay an employee disguised deferred compensation. To prevent this, a cafeteria plan will not qualify under §125 unless all of the payments under the plan are required to be made by the end of the year; this is often referred to as the "use-it-or-lose-it" rule. The use-it-or-lose-it rule makes sense to the extent the focus is to prevent disguised compensation, but it also imposes hardships on legitimate cafeteria plans where certain payments at the end of the year may not be processed or paid in the ordinary course of business until the beginning of the next year. For example, assuming a calendar year plan, under a strict interpretation of the use-it-or-lose-it rule, a reimbursement of even $1 on January 1, year 2, for benefits used by the employee on December 30, year 1, would disqualify the entire cafeteria plan for year 1. Consider the following notice, in which the IRS struggles with this dichotomy of policy concerns.

NOTICE 2005-42
2005-1 C.B. 1204

Purpose

The purpose of this notice is to modify the application of the rule prohibiting deferred compensation under a §125 cafeteria plan. This notice permits a grace period immediately following the end of each plan year during which unused benefits or contributions remaining at the end of the plan year may be paid or reimbursed to plan participants for qualified benefit expenses incurred during the grace period.

Background

In general, no amount is included in the gross income of a participant in a cafeteria plan solely because, under the plan, the participants may choose among the benefits of the plan. §125(a). A cafeteria plan is defined in §125(d)(1) as a written plan maintained by an employer under which all participants are employees, and the participants may choose among two or more benefits consisting of cash and qualified benefits. Section 125(f) defines a "qualified benefit" as any benefit which, with the application of §125(a), is not includable in the gross income of the employee by reason of an express provision of Chapter I of the Internal Revenue Code (other than §§106(b), 117, 127 or 132). Qualified benefits include employer-provided accident and health plans excludable from gross income under §§106 and 105(b), group-term life insurance excludable under §79, dependent care assistance programs excludable under §129, and adoption assistance programs excludable under §137. Elections under a cafeteria plan, once made, can be changed or revoked only as provided in [the regulations]. A cafeteria plan must have a plan year specified in the written plan document.

Section 125(d)(2)(A) states that the term "cafeteria plan" does not include any plan which provides for deferred compensation. The statutory prohibition on deferred compensation in a cafeteria plan is addressed in [proposed regulations, which state]:

> A cafeteria plan may not include any plan that offers a benefit that defers the receipt of compensation. In addition, a cafeteria plan may not operate in a manner that enables employees to defer compensation. For example, a plan that permits employees to carry over unused elective contributions or plan benefits (e.g., accident or health plan coverage) from one plan year to another operates to defer compensation. This is the case regardless of how the contributions or benefits are used by the employee in the subsequent plan year (e.g., whether they are automatically or electively converted into another taxable or nontaxable benefit in the subsequent plan year or used to provide additional benefits of the same type). Similarly, a cafeteria plan operates to permit the deferral of compensation if the plan permits participants to use contributions for one plan year to purchase a benefit that will be provided in a subsequent plan year. . . .

Thus, a cafeteria plan does not include any plan that defers the receipt of compensation or operates in a manner that enables participants to defer compensation by, for example, permitting participants to use contributions for one plan year to purchase a benefit that will be provided in a subsequent plan year. This rule is commonly referred to as the "use-it-or-lose-it" rule, requiring that unused contributions or benefits remaining at the end of the plan year be "forfeited."

However, other areas of tax law provide that for a short, limited period, compensation for services paid in the year following the year in which the services that are being compensated were performed is not treated as "deferred compensation." . . . Consistent with these other areas of tax law, Treasury and the IRS believe it is appropriate to modify the current prohibition on deferred compensation in the proposed regulations under §125 to permit a grace period after the end of the plan year during which unused benefits or contributions may be used.

. . . The rule that a cafeteria plan may not defer the receipt of compensation . . . is modified as follows: A cafeteria plan document may, at the employer's option, be amended to provide for a grace period immediately following the end of each plan year. The grace period must apply to all participants in the cafeteria plan. Expenses for qualified benefits incurred during the grace period may be paid or reimbursed from benefits or contributions remaining unused at the end of the immediately preceding plan year. The grace period must not extend beyond the fifteenth day of the third calendar month after the end of the immediately preceding plan year to which it relates (i.e., "the 2 and month rule"). If a cafeteria plan document is amended to include a grace period, a participant who has unused benefits or contributions relating to a particular qualified benefit from the immediately preceding plan year, and who incurs expenses for that same qualified benefit during the grace period, may be paid or reimbursed for those expenses from the unused benefits or contributions as if the expenses had been incurred in the immediately preceding plan year. The effect of the grace period is that the participant may have as long as 14 months and 15 days (the 12 months in the current cafeteria plan year plus the grace period) to use the benefits or contributions for a plan year before those amounts are "forfeited" under the "use-it-or-lose-it" rule.

During the grace period, a cafeteria plan may not permit unused benefits or contributions to be cashed-out or converted to any other taxable or nontaxable benefit. Unused benefits or contributions relating to a particular qualified benefit may only be used to pay or reimburse expenses incurred with respect to that particular qualified benefit. . . . To the extent any unused benefits or contributions from the immediately preceding plan year exceed the expenses for the qualified benefit incurred during the grace period, those remaining unused benefits or contributions may not be carried forward to any subsequent period (including any subsequent plan year) and are "forfeited" under the "use-it-or-lose-it" rule. . . .

E. LIFE INSURANCE

Code: §§79(a), (c), (d)(1) to (2), 101(a), (c), (d), (g)
Regulations: §§1.79-1(a), 1.79-3(a) to (d), 1.101-1(a)(1), (b)(1), (2); 1.101-3; 1.101-4(a)

To encourage employers to purchase life insurance for their employees, Congress has excluded from gross income amounts paid by the employer for such insurance. Section 79(a) excludes the cost of up to $50,000 of group term life insurance from an employee's gross income; the cost of any additional term life insurance is includable. For example, if an employer pays the premiums for $75,000 of group term life insurance for an employee, the premiums for the first $50,000 are excludable, but the cost of the remaining $25,000 of coverage determined under §79(c) must be included in the employee's gross income. Because §79 only applies to group term life insurance, any premiums that the employer pays for endowment or whole life policies are includable in the employee's gross income.

In recent years, restrictions have been added to §79 to discourage employers from providing insurance benefits that discriminate among employees. To qualify for the exclusion, the life insurance plan must meet the nondiscrimination requirements of §79(d). In general, if an employer's life insurance plan does not cover all employees, or if it offers more substantial benefits to key employees than those offered to other employees, the nondiscrimination rules require that the cost of coverage be included in the key employees' gross income. §79(d).

Section 101 excludes from gross income death benefits received as life insurance proceeds. Under a typical life insurance policy, an insured may pay, for example, $60,000 in premiums during his lifetime in order to provide his beneficiaries with $100,000 on his death. Although it would be consistent with accepted tax policy to exclude the first $60,000 from the beneficiaries' gross income as a "return of capital," the policy supporting the exclusion of the entire $100,000 face amount is less clear. The exclusion probably rests on notions of public policy and the tragic consequences of death—family bereavement and financial hardship. It may be that Congress wanted to encourage taxpayers to provide for their families in case of death and that Congress concluded it would be inappropriate to tax insurance proceeds needed by a family that had lost a bread winner. Additionally, the exclusion is consistent with §102, which excludes *bequests* from gross income, and with §1014, which provides a step-up in basis for appreciated property acquired from a decedent.

Life insurance policies can be divided into three basic categories: term, endowment, and whole life. Term policies only provide insurance coverage for a stated period; the insured acquires no cash value while the policy is in force. Thus, the premium purchases only insurance coverage. Endowment policies, on the other hand, provide two types of coverage. Endowment policies generally provide that if the insured lives for a specified number of years, he or she will receive a predetermined sum at the end of that period. If, however, the insured dies before becoming entitled to receive the policy benefit, a beneficiary will receive a predetermined death benefit. Whole life policies have characteristics of both term and endowment insurance. Like endowment policies, whole life policies acquire a cash value; however, more of the premium goes toward purchasing a death benefit than does the endowment policy premium.

Despite these differences, the §101(a) exclusion applies to death benefits received from all three policies. If, however, the policyholder lives to see the endowment policy mature, or if he or she cashes in a whole life policy, the tax consequences are substantially different and may be governed by §72.

If certain requirements are satisfied, a terminally ill or chronically ill individual may exclude the proceeds of a life insurance contract, even though they are not paid by reason of death as otherwise required by §101. §101(g)(1). Similarly, the exclusion applies to amounts received for the sale or assignment of any portion of a life insurance contract to a viatical settlement provider. §101(g)(2). For both of the exclusions, an amount received by a chronically ill individual is excludable only if it is received under a rider or other provision of a contract that is treated as a qualified long-term insurance contract. §101(g)(3). A "terminally ill individual" is a person who, by physician certification, has an illness or physical condition that is expected to result in death within twenty-four months. A "chronically ill individual" has diminished activity capacities or severe cognitive impairments, as defined by statute. §7702B(c)(2).

Problem

3-16. Ramon Salazar's uncle died, and Ramon received $20,000 from a whole life insurance policy that his uncle had purchased several years earlier. The relevant figures in regard to the insurance policy were:

1.	Death benefit	$20,000
2.	Total premiums paid by uncle	9,600
3.	Actuarial cost of insurance	4,000
4.	Cash value of policy at time of uncle's death	14,100
5.	Term insurance benefits ((1) minus (4))	5,900
6.	Net mortality gain ((1) minus (2))	10,400

a. Does Salazar have gross income?
b. Would the result be altered if, instead of receiving a $20,000 lump sum payment, the proceeds had been paid to Salazar over ten years in annual installments of $2,300?
c. What result in *a* if Salazar had purchased the policy from his uncle for $14,100?

F. HEALTH INSURANCE AND OTHER COMPENSATION FOR PERSONAL INJURIES AND SICKNESS

Code: §§104(a)(1) to (3), 105(a), (b), (e), (h)(1), (2), and (7), 106(a)
Regulations: §§1.104-1(a) to (d); 1.105-2; 1.61-14(a)

a. Employer-provided Health Insurance

Historically, the tax law has been very friendly to, if not downright encouraging of, employer provided health care. There have been myriad justifications for this. One justification was similar to that of employee fringe benefits under §132, i.e., that employees have no choice in the health care offered by employers. Another justification was similar to the exclusion for meals and lodging under §119, i.e., that health insurance is in the interest of the employer since it keeps employees healthy and at work and thus should not be gross income. Another justification was unique to health insurance, however: employers could buy health insurance more cheaply than employees because they are buying in bulk, and society should encourage this type of efficient purchases of health insurance through the tax law. That such a major and significant policy decision such as how to subsidize and provide health insurance arose in such an indirect and haphazard way was often criticized as a fundamental flaw in the national health insurance scheme.

In 2010, Congress enacted the Patient Protection and Affordable Care Act (the "ACA") which provided, among other things, that all residents of the United States would be required to purchase health insurance and in exchange would receive certain tax subsidies to offset the cost. Although revolutionary from a national health policy standpoint, from a tax standpoint the ACA was built upon the existing framework applicable to employer-provided health insurance. Thus, notwithstanding the vast changes made by the ACA and the debate over its other controversial aspects, the tax rules regarding employer-provided health insurance remained substantially unchanged, with only some minor exceptions. The Supreme Court recognized as much in *NFIB*, finding the health insurance purchase mandate Constitutional under the Congressional taxing power of Article I, Section 8.

Sections 104, 105, and 106 interact to prescribe the tax effects of compensation received in the form of health insurance benefits. When an employer pays a portion of the premium for an employee's health insurance, it is economically identical to the employer paying the premium to the employee in cash and the employee paying the premium. Thus, such amounts would be gross income to the employee under §61. Generally, however, employer contributions to health or accident plans are excluded from the employee's gross income under §106.

Sections 104 and 105 work together to exclude from gross income amounts received by an employee on account of personal injury or illness, regardless of whether they are received through workers' compensation, accident or health insurance. The mechanism chosen to do so, however, can prove complicated.

Sections 104 and 105(a) deny an exclusion from gross income for amounts received through accident or health insurance to the extent that (1) the amounts are paid by the taxpayer's employer or (2) the amounts are attributable to contributions by the employer that were not includable in the employee's gross income. Notwithstanding this denial of an exclusion for benefits received from an employer-provided health and accident plan, §105(b) provides an exception to the exception, thereby excluding many such payments from the scope of §105(a). Under §105(b), payments for personal injuries or illness may be excluded if they are paid, directly or indirectly, to the employee as reimbursement for expenses incurred for the medical care of the employee or the employee's spouse or dependents. Section 105(c) also excludes amounts that (1) "constitute payment for the permanent loss or loss of use of a member or function of the body, or permanent disfigurement, of the taxpayer, his spouse, or a dependent" *and* (2) "are computed with reference to the nature of the injury without regard to the period the employee is absent from work."

To illustrate the, at times, convoluted interrelationship of §§104, 105, and 106, consider the following example. Over a period of several years, an employer makes aggregate payments of $20,000 for a particular employee to an insurance company health plan covering its employees. These contributions are excluded from the employee's gross income under §106. In the current year, the employee loses his left leg in an auto accident. The employee receives payments totaling $100,000 from the insurance company — $40,000 representing reimbursement for medical expenses and $60,000 representing compensation for the loss of his leg. Under §104 and the general rule of §105(a), the employee would have to include the entire $100,000 in gross income. However, pursuant to §105(b) the employee is allowed to exclude the $40,000 medical expense reimbursement and, pursuant to §105(c), the $60,000 compensation for loss of a limb is also excludable.

The privileged treatment of such benefits is curtailed if a self-insured plan is utilized by the employer and discriminates in favor of highly compensated individuals. §105(h).

The tax treatment of benefits received from employer-provided health or accident insurance or coverage should be contrasted with the tax treatment of similar insurance benefits for which the taxpayer may have personally contracted with an insurance company. Unlike benefits received under employer-provided insurance, *all* payments received from self-provided insurance coverage are excludable from gross income. §104(a)(3).

In some instances a taxpayer may have medical insurance coverage under two plans, one furnished by the employer and the other purchased individually by the taxpayer. In such cases, the taxpayer may receive medical reimbursements in excess of actual expenses. Revenue Ruling 69-154, 1969-1 C.B. 46, indicates that the amount of incurred medical expense deemed to have been paid by each policy is based on the proportion of the reimbursement from each policy to the total benefits received from both policies. For example, assume the taxpayer had total medical expenses of $20,000, with the employer-provided policy paying $15,000 and the taxpayer's policy paying $10,000. The employee has therefore received $25,000 in insurance proceeds. Sixty percent ($15,000 ÷ $25,000) of the taxpayer's $20,000 medical expenses is deemed to have been paid by the employer's policy and excludable under §105(b). Thus, the taxpayer will exclude $12,000 (60 percent of $20,000) and report the remaining $3,000 received under the employer's policy as income. The entire $10,000 received under the taxpayer's individual policy is excludable under §104(a)(3).

If the taxpayer contributes to a health insurance policy furnished by the employer and also obtains a personal policy, an additional step will be required to allocate the proceeds for purposes of the §105 exclusion. First, the taxpayer-employee allocates the proceeds between the two policies as discussed above. Then, it is necessary to allocate the excess indemnification attributable to the employer's policy, based on the employer's contribution. Consequently, if the employer paid 75 percent of the premiums and the total premium was $1,000, the employer's contribution is $750. The ratio of the employer's contribution to the total premium determines the portion of the excess indemnification ($3,000 in the above example) attributable to the employer's contribution and therefore included in gross income — that is, $750 ÷ $1,000 × $3,000 = $2,250.

Note on Insurance Mandates and Tax Penalties

The most controversial aspect of the ACA has been the so-called "individual mandate" — or the requirement that all individuals acquire health insurance or face a penalty. As discussed above, the Supreme Court upheld the Constitutionality of the individual mandate in *NFIB*. Regardless, from a tax policy standpoint it is interesting to note that there is little substantive difference between an individual mandate and the long-standing treatment of health insurance under the Internal Revenue Code.

Consider the following hypothetical: Erica Chang works for an employer that provides the option to receive $10,000 per year in additional cash compensation or to pay $10,000 in premiums toward health insurance. Section 106 would generally exclude the payment of premiums by the employer from gross income, while the cash would clearly be included in gross income. The power to choose between insurance and cash would typically render the provisions of §106 inapplicable, but §125 permits employees to make the choice between health care and cash without endangering the §106 exclusion. Consequently, if Erica chooses the health insurance, she receives $10,000 in compensation tax free, while if she chooses the $10,000 in cash she has gross income. Assume Erica chooses the cash and pays $3,000 in tax, and then purchases health insurance for $7,000. During the year, Erica needs surgery which costs $15,000. Under either scenario, the health insurance pays the $15,000 and Erica would have no gross income under §104. By contrast, assume she chooses to receive the $10,000 in cash, pay $3,000 in tax, and then invest $7,000 in stocks rather than purchase health insurance. During the year the stocks appreciate to $15,000, at which time she needs the surgery. Erica sells the stocks to pay for the surgery, resulting in $8,000 of gross income and a tax liability of $1,250.

Notice the consequences. If Erica chooses employer-provided health insurance, she has no tax liability, while if she chooses privately purchased health insurance, she pays a tax "penalty" of $3,000, and if she chooses not to carry health insurance at all she incurs a tax "penalty" of $3,000 plus an additional "penalty" of $1,250 when she does in fact get sick. This is functionally equivalent to an individual mandate to purchase health insurance backed by a tax penalty for failure to do so, calculated in reference to the taxpayer's income. Thus, §§104, 105, and 106 work to substantially replicate the mandate, although in a more implicit manner, for anyone who earns enough to pay income taxes. Regardless of the litigation over the ACA's individual mandate, it seems like a waste of time and energy to endlessly fight over a provision as if it were unprecedented when the basic premise has served as the basis for U.S. tax policy toward health insurance for over fifty years.

b.   Damages for Physical Injuries and Sickness

Of course, health insurance is not the only way the sick or injured receive compensation. In addition, an injured person may sue a tortfeasor for damages. If these damages are for medical expenses or compensation for the injury, they are similar to a form of health insurance. Accordingly, §104 also addresses the compensation for physical injuries or sickness caused by the tortious conduct of another. Given the financial hardship and personal trauma resulting from such physical injuries (such as car accident caused by another), §104 provides for the exclusion from gross income of payments received as damages for the injuries, partially subsidizing the receipt of such damage awards. These payments may be in the form of a settlement of a tort claim or monies received on a judgment.

Historically, there had been substantial debate over the excludability of damage awards. Prior to 1997, the statute excluded "damages received . . . on account of *personal* injuries or sickness." Courts disagreed on the interpretation of §104, finding the statute ambiguous and the legislative history unclear. In 1992, the Supreme Court agreed that all damages received on account of personal, but nonphysical, injuries and sickness, such as gender discrimination and injury to reputation, are nontaxable so long as the action was brought under a tort or tort-like claim that has a broad range of compensatory damages available under it. See United States v. Burke, 504 U.S. 229 (1992), holding that damages received for sex discrimination were not excludable because the statute under which the action was brought did not provide for compensatory damages for personal injuries. Most observers interpreted *Burke* to mean that no allocation was required between economic interests (lost wages, injury to business reputation) and noneconomic (personal) interests (pain, suffering, medical expenses, mental anguish). The Supreme Court corrected this interpretation in 1995, when it held that, to be excludable, damages must be received "on account of personal injuries or sickness" in addition to requiring the action to arise out of a tort or tort-like claim. See United States v. Schleier, 515 U.S. 323 (1995), holding that damages received based on a claim under the Age Discrimination in Employment Act are not excludable. In light of *Schleier*, only damages awarded to compensate for personal, but nonphysical, injuries, including such intangible injuries as emotional pain, suffering and distress, were excludable.

The Service and the courts disagreed about whether §104(a)(2) applied to exclude punitive damages. The Supreme Court agreed with the majority of the courts and held that, because punitive damages are designed to punish and deter rather than compensate, punitive damages were not excludable because they were not received "on account of" personal injuries. See O'Gilvie v. United States, 519 U.S. 79 (1996) (involving 1988 award of punitive damages related to physical injury). Congress amended §104 to clarify that the exclusion should not be available for punitive damages. The restriction does not apply to punitive damages awarded in a wrongful death action if applicable state law provides (or has been construed to provide on or before that date) that *only* punitive damages may be awarded in a wrongful death action. A punitive damage award in that case is excludable to the extent it was received on account of a *personal*, not necessarily *physical*, injury or sickness.

The exclusion from gross income only applies to damages (other than punitive damages) received on account of a personal *physical* injury or *physical* sickness. §104(a)(2). Therefore, if an action has its origin in a physical injury or physical sickness, all damages (other than punitive damages) related to that injury or sickness are excludable regardless whether the recipient is the injured party. For example, damages (other than punitive damages) received by an individual on account of a claim for loss of consortium due to the physical injury of the individual's spouse are excludable from gross income. Damages received on account of a wrongful death claim continue to be excludable. Emotional distress, including the physical symptoms of emotional distress, is not considered a physical injury or sickness, however, meaning damages for emotional distress and other nonphysical injuries or sickness are excludable only to the extent they are attributable to a physical injury or sickness. The provisions also allow an exclusion for emotional distress damages not attributable to a physical injury or physical sickness to the extent of the amount paid for actual medical care attributable to the emotional distress. §104(a). Amounts received on account of nonphysical injuries or sickness, such as employment discrimination or injury to reputation, are not excludable from gross income.

SMALL BUSINESS JOB PROTECTION ACT OF 1996
H.R. Conf. Rep. No. 737, 104th Cong., 2d Sess. (1996)

MODIFY EXCLUSION OF DAMAGES RECEIVED ON ACCOUNT OF PERSONAL INJURY OR SICKNESS

PRESENT LAW

Under present law, gross income does not include any damages received (whether by suit or agreement and whether as lump sums or as periodic payments) on account of personal injury or sickness (§104(a)(2)).

The exclusion from gross income of damages received on account of personal injury or sickness specifically does not apply to punitive damages received in connection with a case not involving physical injury or sickness. Courts presently differ as to whether the exclusion applies to punitive damages received in connection with a case involving a physical injury or physical sickness. Certain states provide that, in the case of claims under a wrongful death statute, only punitive damages may be awarded.

Courts have interpreted the exclusion from gross income of damages received on account of personal injury or sickness broadly in some cases to cover awards for personal injury that do not relate to a physical injury or sickness. For example, some courts have held that the exclusion applies to damages in cases involving certain forms of employment discrimination and injury to reputation where there is no physical injury or sickness. The damages received in these cases generally consist of back pay and other awards intended to compensate the claimant for lost wages or lost profits. The Supreme Court recently held that damages received based on a claim under the Age Discrimination in Employment Act could not be excluded from income. In light of the Supreme Court decision, the Internal Revenue Service has suspended existing guidance on the tax treatment of damages received on account of other forms of employment discrimination.

INCLUDE IN INCOME ALL PUNITIVE DAMAGES

The House bill provides that the exclusion from gross income does not apply to any punitive damages received on account of personal injury or sickness whether or not related to a physical injury or physical sickness. Under the House bill, present law continues to apply to punitive damages received in a wrongful death action if the applicable state law (as in effect on September 13, 1995 without regard to subsequent modification) provides, or has been construed to provide by a court decision issued on or before such date, that only punitive damages may be awarded in a wrongful death action. No inference is intended as to the application of the exclusion to punitive damages prior to the effective date of the House bill in connection with a case involving a physical injury or physical sickness.

INCLUDE IN INCOME DAMAGE RECOVERIES FOR NONPHYSICAL INJURIES

The House bill provides that the exclusion from gross income only applies to damages received on account of a personal physical injury or physical sickness. If an action has its origin in a physical injury or physical sickness, then all damages (other than punitive damages) that flow therefrom are treated as payments received on account of physical injury or physical sickness whether or not the recipient of the damages is the injured party. For example, damages (other than punitive damages) received by an individual on account of a claim for loss of consortium due to the physical injury or physical sickness of such individual's spouse are excludable from gross income. In addition, damages (other than punitive damages) received on account of a claim of wrongful death continue to be excludable from taxable income as under present law.

The House bill also specifically provides that emotional distress is not considered a physical injury or physical sickness. Thus, the exclusion from gross income does not apply to any damages received (other than for medical expenses as discussed below) based on a claim of employment discrimination or injury to reputation accompanied by a claim of emotional distress. Because all damages received on account of physical injury or physical sickness are excludable from gross income, the exclusion from gross income applies to any damages received based on a claim of emotional distress that is attributable to a physical injury or physical sickness. In addition, the exclusion from gross income specifically applies to the amount of damages received that is not in excess of the amount paid for medical care attributable to emotional distress.

Problems

3-17. Gail Michaud sued and recovered against the owner of a truck that struck her car and injured her. The jury returned a special verdict for $53,000, categorized as follows:

1.	Past medical expenses	$ 8,000
2.	Future medical expenses	4,000
3.	Pain and suffering	16,000
4.	Loss of earnings	20,000
5.	Attorney's fees	5,000

Michaud deducted the $8,000 in past medical expenses on her prior year's tax return. Which payments, if any, constitute gross income?

3-18. Roger Jackson sued Basil Valentine for slander. Jackson won $5,000 for emotional distress. How much, if any, of this recovery must Jackson include in his gross income?

a. Assume Valentine had slandered Jackson because Jackson broke his leg at Valentine's place of business. Jackson's subsequent recovery of $5,000 was 25 percent compensation for his injury and 75 percent for the slanderous comment. How much of the $5,000 recovery does Jackson include in his gross income?

     b.   Assume that Jackson was also awarded $2,000 in punitive damages. How much of the punitive damage award would Jackson include in his gross income? Would it make a difference if the punitive damages were awarded based on Jackson's injuries?

3-19.   Florence Jackson's daughter broke her arm during the year. Her medical expenses totaled $1,765 and were promptly reimbursed through a self-insured health plan provided by her employer. Does Jackson have gross income?

G. DISCHARGE OF INDEBTEDNESS

    Code: §§108(a), (b)(1) and (2), (d)(1) to (3), and (e)(5); 1017(a)

Although the discharge of indebtedness generally creates income for the debtor whose debt is discharged (see discussion at Chapter 2), the debtor may, in certain circumstances, be able to exclude that debt relief from gross income. For example, if a lender forgives a debt as a gift, the income is excluded under §102. When a debtor is experiencing substantial financial difficulties, two legislative policies concerning debt relief conflict: first, the Code seeks to tax all accessions to wealth, and second, Congress, through bankruptcy proceedings, attempts to give debtors a "fresh start." Section 108, which provides an exclusion from gross income for certain cancellations of indebtedness income, represents a compromise between these policies.

To qualify for the §108 exclusion, the debt relief must be pure cancellation of indebtedness income. Section 108 does not apply when the debt forgiveness is merely the method by which a creditor makes payment to a debtor. For example, debt relief may be received as compensation for services or as a constructive dividend, or a debtor may be relieved from liability on a debt as payment for property. In these circumstances, the debt relief is not "pure" because it does not arise solely from the creditor-debtor relationship. Therefore, the circumstances surrounding debt relief must be analyzed "to determine whether the discharge of indebtedness results in 'pure' income therefrom or whether the debt is discharged as a means of making an indirect payment for services, property, or other purposes." O.K.C. Corp. v. Commissioner, 82 T.C. 638 (1984).

Income that qualifies as "pure" cancellation of indebtedness income may be excluded by §108. If the discharge occurred under the federal bankruptcy laws, 11 U.S.C. §§101 et seq., the entire amount of the discharged debt is excluded from gross income. Debt relief also is excluded to the extent the debtor is insolvent, defined in §108(d)(3) as total liabilities in excess of the fair market value of all assets. Thus, unlike debtors in bankruptcy, insolvent debtors may only be entitled to exclude part of their cancellation of debt from gross income. For example, assume that *T* has debts of $18,000 and assets of $10,000. The extent of his insolvency is $8,000. If *T* receives a discharge of indebtedness of $11,000, he will be solvent after the discharge — that is, his assets will exceed his debts. Because *T* was insolvent by $8,000, only $8,000 is treated as debt relief received by an insolvent debtor; $3,000 must be treated as debt relief of a solvent debtor. If both of these §108 exclusions apply, the bankruptcy exclusion takes precedence over the insolvency exclusion.

Unlike many other exclusions from gross income, however, the §108 exclusion is not free. As a condition of the §108 exclusion, the debtor must, under §108(b), make adjustments to certain "tax attributes." If the bankruptcy or insolvency exclusion applies, the taxpayer reduces by the amount of the discharge the amount of (1) any net operating loss, passive loss, and capital loss carryovers, (2) any carryover of certain tax credits, and (3) the basis of his or her property. The reductions are made in a specified order and are dollar-for-dollar except for tax credits, which are reduced by one-third of the amount of the exclusion.

Section 108 also simplifies the tax treatment of a commonly encountered situation that would otherwise give rise to debt relief income. Where the taxpayer purchases property from a seller on credit or for a promissory note, and a dispute subsequently arises as to the quality or performance of that property, the seller may agree to reduce the amount of the debt. If so, the purchaser technically has realized debt relief income. Section 108(e)(5), however, considers the substance of the transaction and treats the debt relief as a reduction in the purchase price. The debt reduction thus results in a lower cost basis and the purchaser has no gross income.

BANKRUPTCY TAX ACT OF 1980
S. Rep. No. 1035, 96th Cong., 2d Sess. 8 (1980)

EXPLANATION OF THE BILL

A. TAX TREATMENT OF DISCHARGE OF INDEBTEDNESS

Present Law

In General

Under present law, income is realized when indebtedness is forgiven or in other ways cancelled. For example, if a corporation has issued a $1,000 bond at par which it later repurchases for only $900, thereby increasing its net worth by $100, the corporation realizes $100 of income in the year of repurchase (United States v. Kirby Lumber Co., 284 U.S. 1 (1931)).

There are several exceptions to the general rule of income realization. Under a judicially developed "insolvency exception," no income arises from discharge of indebtedness if the debtor is insolvent both before and after the transaction; and if the transaction leaves the debtor with assets whose value exceeds remaining liabilities, income is realized only to the extent of the excess. Treasury regulations provide that the gratuitous cancellation of a corporation's indebtedness by a shareholder-creditor does not give rise to debt discharge income to the extent of the principal of the debt, since the cancellation amounts to a contribution to capital of the corporation. Some courts have applied this exception even if the corporation had previously deducted the amount owed to the shareholder-creditor. Under a related exception, cases have held that no income arises from discharge of indebtedness if stock is issued to a creditor in satisfaction of the debt, even if the creditor was previously a shareholder, and even if the stock is worth less than the face amount of the obligation satisfied. Further, cancellation of a previously accrued and deducted expense does not give rise to income if the deduction did not result in a reduction of tax (Code sec. 111). A debt cancellation which constitutes a gift or bequest is not treated as income to the donee debtor (Code sec. 102).

Reasons for Change

Overview

In P.L. 95-598, Congress repealed provisions of the Bankruptcy Act governing Federal income tax treatment of debt discharge in bankruptcy, effective for cases instituted on or after October 1, 1979. The committee's bill provides tax rules in the Internal Revenue Code applicable to debt discharge in the case of bankrupt or insolvent debtors. . . .

The rules of the bill concerning income tax treatment of debt discharge in bankruptcy are intended to accommodate bankruptcy policy and tax policy. To preserve the debtor's "fresh start" after bankruptcy, the bill provides that no income is recognized by reason of debt discharge in bankruptcy, so that a debtor coming out of bankruptcy (or an insolvent debtor outside bankruptcy) is not burdened with an immediate tax liability. The bill provides that the debt discharge amount thus excluded from income is applied to reduce the taxpayer's net operating losses and certain other tax attributes, unless the taxpayer elects to apply the debt discharge amount first to reduce basis in depreciable assets. . . .

Debtors Given Flexibility

The committee believes that these attribute-reduction provisions of the bill give flexibility to the debtor to account for a debt discharge amount in a manner most favorable to the debtor's tax situation. For example, a bankrupt or insolvent debtor which wishes to retain net operating losses and other carryovers will be able to elect to reduce asset basis in depreciable property. . . . On the other hand, a debtor having an expiring net operating loss which otherwise would be "wasted" will be able (by not making the election) to apply the debt discharge amount first against the net operating loss.

At the same time, in developing the rules of the bill, the committee recognized that the basis-reduction mechanism of present law fails to effectuate the Congressional intent of deferring, but eventually collecting tax on, ordinary income realized from debt discharge.

Thus present law permits both solvent and insolvent taxpayers to apply the amount of their discharged debts to reduce the basis of nondepreciable assets which may never be sold, such as stock in a subsidiary corporation or the land on which the company operates its business, thereby avoiding completely, rather than deferring, the tax consequences of debt discharge. Also under present law, a related party (such as the parent corporation of a debtor) can acquire the taxpayer's debt at a discount and effectively eliminate it as a real liability to outside interests, but the debtor thereby avoids the tax treatment which would apply if the debtor had directly retired the debt by repurchasing it. In other cases, the debtor may be able to convert ordinary income from discharge of indebtedness into capital gain, as where the debtor reduces basis in a nondepreciable capital asset.

Deferral of Ordinary Income on Debt Discharge

Accordingly, the rules of the bill are intended to carry out the Congressional intent of deferring, but eventually collecting within a reasonable period, tax on ordinary income realized from debt discharge. Thus in the case of a bankrupt or insolvent debtor, the debt discharge amount is applied to reduce the taxpayer's net operating losses and certain other tax attributes, unless the taxpayer elects to apply the amount first to reduce basis in depreciable assets.

To insure that the debt discharge amount eventually will result in ordinary income . . . , the bill provides that any gain on a subsequent disposition of the reduced-basis property will be subject to a "recapture" under rules similar to those now applicable with respect to depreciation recapture. Also, the bill contains rules relating to discharge of indebtedness as a capital contribution, acquisition of debt by a related party, discharge of partnership debt, and other income tax aspects of discharge of indebtedness. . . .

REV. RUL. 92-53
1992-2 C.B. 48

ISSUE

Is the amount by which a nonrecourse debt exceeds the fair market value of the property securing the debt taken into account in determining whether, and to what extent, a taxpayer is insolvent within the meaning of section 108(d)(3) of the Internal Revenue Code?

FACTS

Situation 1. In 1988, individual *A* borrowed $1,000,000 from *C* and signed a note payable to *C* for $1,000,000 that bore interest at a fixed market rate payable annually. The note was secured by an office building valued in excess of $1,000,000 that *A* acquired from *B* with the proceeds of the note. *A* was not personally liable on the note. In 1989, when the value of the office building was $800,000 and the outstanding principal on the note was $1,000,000, *C* agreed to modify the terms of the note by reducing the note's principal amount to $825,000. The modified note bore adequate stated interest within the meaning of section 1274(c)(2) of the Code. At the time of the modification, *A*'s only other assets had an aggregate fair market value of $100,000, and *A* was personally liable to *D* on other indebtedness in the amount of $50,000.

Situation 2. The facts are the same as *Situation 1*, except that *D* agreed to accept assets from *A* with a fair market value (and basis to *A*) of $40,000 in settlement of *A*'s recourse indebtedness of $50,000, and *C* did not reduce *A*'s nonrecourse note.

Situation 3. The facts are the same as *Situation 1*, except that pursuant to a prearranged work-out plan *D* agreed to accept assets from *A* with a fair market value (and basis to *A*) of $40,000 in settlement of *A*'s recourse indebtedness of $50,000, and shortly thereafter *C* reduced the principal amount of *A*'s nonrecourse note to $825,000. . . .

LAW AND ANALYSIS

Section 61(a)(12) of the Code provides that gross income includes income from the discharge of indebtedness. Section 1.61-12(a) of the Income Tax Regulations provides that the discharge of indebtedness, in whole or in part, may result in the realization of income.

Section 108(a)(1)(B) of the Code generally excludes discharged indebtedness from a taxpayer's gross income if the discharge occurs when the taxpayer is insolvent. Section 108(a)(3) limits the amount of income excluded by reason of section 108(a)(1)(B) to the amount by which the taxpayer is insolvent.

Section 108(d)(3) of the Code defines "insolvent" as the excess of liabilities over the fair market value of assets. That section further provides that whether a taxpayer is insolvent, and the amount by which the taxpayer is insolvent is determined on the basis of the taxpayer's assets and liabilities immediately before the discharge.

Section 108 of the Code does not define the term "liabilities" as used in the section 108(d)(3) definition of insolvency. However, the legislative history underlying the section 108 insolvency exclusion provides, as a rationale for the insolvency exclusion, that an insolvent taxpayer should not be burdened with current taxation on the discharge of indebtedness to preserve the taxpayer's "fresh start" resulting from that discharge. That is, discharging a taxpayer from liability gives the taxpayer a fresh start that should not be impeded by imposing a tax liability on the taxpayer when the taxpayer is unable to pay either the indebtedness or the tax. But, to the extent a discharge of indebtedness removes a taxpayer from insolvency, the taxpayer is treated as having the ability to pay tax, and thus must pay a current tax on that portion of the discharge.

To provide tax relief that will preserve a fresh start, the amount by which a nonrecourse debt exceeds the fair market value of the property securing the debt ("excess nonrecourse debt") should be treated as a liability in determining insolvency for purposes of section 108 of the Code to the extent that the excess nonrecourse debt is discharged. Otherwise, the discharge could give rise to a current tax when the taxpayer lacks the ability to pay that tax. Nonrecourse debt should also be treated as a liability in determining insolvency under section 108 to the extent of the fair market value of the property securing the debt.

However, excess nonrecourse debt that is not discharged does not have a similar effect on a taxpayer's ability to pay a current tax resulting from the discharge of another debt (whether recourse or nonrecourse). Thus, that excess nonrecourse debt should not be treated as a liability in determining insolvency for purposes of section 108 of the Code.

Situation 1. In this situation, $175,000 of *A*'s $200,000 excess nonrecourse debt is discharged and, therefore, that portion of the excess nonrecourse debt is taken into account in determining whether, and to what extent, *A* is insolvent within the meaning of section 108(d)(3) of the Code. Thus, *A* has liabilities of $1,025,000, consisting of the full $50,000 amount for which *A* is personally liable, plus the portion of the nonrecourse debt equal to the sum of the $800,000 fair market value of the property securing the nonrecourse debt and the $175,000 of excess nonrecourse debt that is discharged. Because *A*'s $1,025,000 of liabilities exceed the $900,000 fair market value of *A*'s assets ($800,000 + $100,000) by $125,000 immediately before the indebtedness is discharged, *A* is insolvent to the extent of $125,000. Accordingly, pursuant to section 108(a)(1)(B) and (a)(3), *A* must include only $50,000 of the $175,000 of discharged indebtedness ($175,000 − $125,000) in income under section 61(a)(12).

Situation 2. In this situation no portion of the excess nonrecourse debt is discharged. Instead, $10,000 of *A*'s recourse debt is discharged. Therefore, the excess nonrecourse debt is not taken into account in determining whether, and to what extent, *A* is insolvent within the meaning of section 108(d)(3) of the Code. As a result, *A* is solvent immediately before the discharge because its $850,000 of liabilities ($800,000 + $50,000) do not exceed the $900,000 fair market value of its assets ($800,000 + $100,000). Accordingly, *A* must include the entire $10,000 of discharged indebtedness in income under section 61(a)(12).

Situation 3. In this situation, pursuant to the prearranged work-out plan, $10,000 of *A*'s recourse debt is discharged, and shortly thereafter $175,000 of *A*'s nonrecourse debt is discharged. Because of the prearranged plan, the discharges are viewed as occurring simultaneously, but solely for purposes of determining whether, and to what extent, *A* is insolvent within the meaning of section 108(d)(3) of the Code. As a result, *A* must include only $60,000 of the total of $185,000 of discharged indebtedness in income under section 61(a)(12). The $60,000 is comprised of (1) the $50,000 discharge of indebtedness income as determined with respect to the nonrecourse debt in *Situation 1*, and (2) the $10,000 discharge of indebtedness income as determined with respect to the recourse debt in *Situation 2*.

HOLDING

The amount by which a nonrecourse debt exceeds the fair market value of the property securing the debt is taken into account in determining whether, and to what extent, a taxpayer is insolvent within the meaning of section 108(d)(3) of the Code, but only to the extent that the excess nonrecourse debt is discharged.

Problems

3-20. Harriet Simmons incurred unreimbursed living expenses with her creditors of $160,000. At that time, she had a $35,000 mortgage on her home, an outstanding personal loan of $15,000, and the fair market value of all her assets was $185,000. Realizing that Simmons was in dire financial straits, the creditors agreed to reduce her obligations from $160,000 to $120,000.

a. Did Simmons realize income from the discharge of indebtedness? If so, how much?

b. What if, instead of reaching an agreement with the creditors, she had filed for bankruptcy and, after having paid her creditors $75,000, had been completely discharged from all of the remaining debts?

3-21. Harry Pelton bought a new car for $5,000, with the dealer agreeing to finance the purchase. The following week, Pelton returned to the dealer's showroom, claiming that the car was a defective "lemon." Rather than exchange cars, the dealer agreed to reduce Pelton's debt from $5,000 to $4,500. What are the tax consequences to Pelton?

H. GAINS FROM THE SALE OF A PRIMARY RESIDENCE

Code: §§121(a) to (c)

When a taxpayer sells their personal home for more than they paid for it, it would seem on its face that the taxpayer has enjoyed an accession to wealth and thus would have gross income. Congress has decided, however, that up to $250,000 of gain from the sale of a primary residence ($500,000 for married couples) should be excluded from gross income. Why do you think this would be the case? Do people use gains from the sale of their primary residence to fund consumption, or is there something different about housing? Should Congress encourage home buying in this manner? What does this do to the price of homes, especially if taxpayers begin to think of houses as merely another type of investment just like stocks or bonds?

JOINT COMMITTEE ON TAXATION, GENERAL EXPLANATION OF TAX LEGISLATION ENACTED IN 1997 JCS-23-97
54 (1997)

Under prior law, no gain was recognized on the sale of a principal residence if a new residence at least equal in cost to the sales price of the old residence was purchased and used by the taxpayer as his or her principal residence within a specified period of time. This replacement period generally began two years before and ended two years after the date of sale of the old residence. The basis of the replacement residence was reduced by the amount of any gain not recognized on the sale of the old residence by reason of this gain rollover rule.

Also, under prior law, in general, an individual, on a one-time basis, could exclude from gross income up to $125,000 of gain from the sale or exchange of a principal residence if the taxpayer (1) had attained age 55 before the sale and (2) had owned the property and used it as a principal residence for three or more of the five years preceding the sale. . . .

Calculating [taxable] gain from the sale of a principal residence was among the most complex tasks faced by a typical taxpayer. Many taxpayers buy and sell a number of homes over the course of a lifetime and are generally not certain of how much housing appreciation they can expect. Thus, even though most homeowners never paid any income tax on the . . . gain of their principal residences, as a result of the rollover provisions and the $125,000 one-time exclusion under prior law detailed records of transactions and expenditures on home improvements still had to be kept, in most cases, for decades. To claim the exclusion, many taxpayers had to determine the basis of each home they owned and appropriately adjust the basis of their current home to reflect any untaxed gains from previous housing transactions. This determination could involve augmenting the original cost basis of each home by expenditures on improvements. In addition to the record-keeping burden this created, taxpayers faced the difficult task of drawing a distinction between improvements that add to basis, and repairs that do not. The failure to account accurately for all improvements could lead to errors in the calculation of . . . gains, and hence to an under- or over-payment of the capital gains on principal residences. By excluding from taxation . . . gains on principal residences below a relatively high threshold, few taxpayers will have to refer to records in determining income tax consequences of transactions related to their house.

To have postponed the entire . . . gain from the sale of a principal residence under prior law, the purchase price of a new home must have been greater than the sales price of the old home. This provision of prior law encouraged some taxpayers to purchase larger and more expensive houses than they otherwise would in order to avoid a tax liability, particularly those who move from areas where housing costs are high to lower-cost areas. This promoted an inefficient use of taxpayer's financial resources.

Prior law also may have discouraged some older taxpayers from selling their homes. Taxpayers who would have realized a . . . gain in excess of $125,000 if they sold their home and taxpayers who had already used the exclusion may have chosen to stay in their homes even though the home no longer suited their needs. By raising the $125,000 limit and by allowing multiple exclusions, this constraint to the mobility of the elderly was removed. . . .

While most homeowners do not pay tax when selling their homes, prior law created certain tax traps for the unwary that resulted in significant . . . taxes or loss of the benefits of the prior-law exclusion. For example, an individual was not eligible for the one-time . . . gains exclusion if the exclusion was previously utilized by the individual's spouse. This restriction had the unintended effect of penalizing individuals who married someone who had already taken the exclusion. Households that moved from a high housing-cost area to a low housing-cost area may have incurred an unexpected . . . tax liability. Divorcing couples may have incurred substantial . . . taxes if they did not carefully plan their house ownership and sale decisions. . . .

Under the [new law], a taxpayer generally is able to exclude up to $250,000 ($500,000 if married and file a joint return) of gain realized on the sale or exchange of a principal residence. The exclusion is allowed each time a taxpayer selling or exchanging a principal residence meets the eligibility requirements, but generally no more frequently than once every two years. . . .

To be eligible for the exclusion, a taxpayer must have owned the residence and occupied it as a principal residence for at least two of the five years prior to the sale or exchange. A taxpayer who fails to meet these requirements by reason of a change of place of employment, health, or other unforeseen circumstances is able to exclude the fraction of the $250,000 ($500,000 if married filing a joint return) equal to the fraction of two years that these requirements are met.

In the case of joint filers not sharing a principal residence, an exclusion of $250,000 is available on a qualifying sale or exchange of the principal residence of one of the spouses. Similarly, if a single taxpayer who is otherwise eligible for an exclusion marries someone who has used the exclusion within the two years prior to the marriage, the [new law] would allow the newly married taxpayer a maximum exclusion of $250,000. Once both spouses satisfy the eligibility rules and two years have passed since the last exclusion was allowed to either of them, the taxpayers may exclude up to $500,000 of gain on their joint return. . . .

The provision limiting the exclusion to only one sale every two years by the taxpayer does not prevent a husband and wife filing a joint return from each excluding up to $250,000 of gain from the sale or exchange of each spouse's principal residence provided that each spouse would be permitted to exclude up to $250,000 of gain if they filed separate returns. . . .

Problem

3-22. Tom Smith, a single individual, sold his principal residence for $500,000. The residence, which he purchased 36 months earlier for $200,000, was the first principal residence he owned.

    a.   How much gross income does Smith recognize on the sale of the residence?

    b.   What result in *a* if, three months after the sale, Smith purchased a second principal residence for $525,000?

    c.   What is his basis in the second residence?

    d.   What result in *a* if Smith moved out of, and rented, the residence one year prior to the sale?

    e.   What result in *a* if Smith was a contractor who personally constructed the house?

    f.   What result in *a* if Smith resided in the house for a total of only one year and sold it solely to make a profit?

    g.   What result in *f* if he sold the house because of poor health?

    h.   What result in *a* if Smith owned the house as a joint tenant with his spouse and filed a joint return?

    i.   What result in *a* if, instead of joint ownership with his wife, Smith was the sole owner of the property and both he and his wife resided in the house for three years and filed a joint return?

    j.   What result in *a* if, one year before the sale, Smith married? Assume his wife resided in his house with him for one year.

    k.   What result in *a* if Smith's house was a duplex and he resided in one of the two units (assume both units are identical)?

I. OTHER MISCELLANEOUS EXCLUSIONS

Code: §§103, 86(a) to (c), 121(a) to (c)

1. Tax-exempt Interest

State and local government bonds are a popular investment for high-bracket taxpayers because the interest is generally excluded from gross income by §103(a). The tax-exempt interest on government obligations creates a tax-favored invest-ment, an incentive for taxpayers to engage in what Congress has deemed to be a preferred activity. The exclusion operates as an indirect form of federal assistance to states and municipalities because they can raise funds at lower interest rates than would be possible if the lenders were taxed on their interest income.

Consider, for example, a taxpayer in the 40-percent tax bracket with $100,000 to invest. The taxpayer is weighing two alternative investments: municipal bonds with a 7-percent rate of interest or bank certificates of deposit (CDs) with a 9-percent rate of interest. The lower rate of interest on the municipal bonds reflects the tax benefits derived from such investments. If the taxpayer invests in the CDs, at the end of year one he will realize $9,000 in interest income and incur a $3,600 tax liability, leaving him with a net after-tax return of $5,400. On the other hand, if he invests in municipal bonds, he will realize $7,000 in interest income, none of which will be taxed. Consequently, in the first case he has a 5.4-percent after-tax return, while in the second case his after-tax return is 7 percent.

This example highlights a controversial issue: The value of the tax preference increases as the taxpayer's income tax bracket rises. For example, had the taxpayer been in the 10-percent, rather than the 40-percent, bracket, he would have paid only $900 in taxes on the certificate of deposit interest income and would have been better off investing in the certificate of deposit (8.1-percent after-tax return) rather than the municipal bonds.

This income tax exclusion has led to perceived abuses, resulting in the enact-ment of a series of exceptions to the general exclusionary rule. A mere glance at §103 and §§141 through 150 reveals that the taxation of interest from government obligations is complex and interest from a bond will not always be tax exempt merely because the bond was issued by a state or local government. For example, §103(b), an exception to the general exclusionary rule of §103(a), revokes the exemptions for a private activity bond, which is not a qualified bond, an arbitrage bond, or a bond not in registered form. Section 103(b) attempts to prevent the use of the interest exclusion to benefit private industry.

2. Social Security

Section 86 reflects another policy-based exclusion. Because of the financial hardships experienced by many recipients of social security, Congress has histor-ically refrained from taxing such amounts. However, given the revenue needs of the government and the fact that the policy, as applied, afforded blanket exclusions even to wealthy taxpayers, Congress, through §86, sought to limit the exclusion. That provision limits the blanket exclusion for social security, among other things, in cases where the recipient's income exceeds a statutorily designated amount.

GOLDIN v. BAKER
809 F.2d 187 (2d Cir. 1987)

FEINBERG, C.J.

This case requires us to examine the scope of the intergovernmental tax immunity doctrine. Plaintiffs Harrison J. Goldin, Comptroller of the City of New York, and the City (collectively referred to herein as the City) appeal from a judgment of the United States District Court, . . . denying the City's motion for summary judgment and granting the motion of defendant Secretary of the Treasury to dismiss the City's complaint for failure to state a claim upon which relief can be granted. The City challenges the constitutionality of section 86 of the Internal Revenue Code. . . . The City contends that section 86 effectively places a tax on municipal bond interest and therefore violates the intergovernmental immunity doctrine and the Tenth Amendment of the United States Constitution. Because we think section 86 is constitutionally sound, we affirm.

In 1983, Congress enacted section 86 in order to tax a portion of the social security benefits received by persons who have substantial income from other sources. Section 86 requires that, if a taxpayer's "modified adjusted gross income" plus one-half of his social security benefits exceeds a certain "base amount," a portion of the taxpayer's social security benefits shall be included in his taxable income. The amount included in taxable income is either (i) one-half of the social security benefits received or (ii) one-half of the amount by which his modified adjusted gross income plus one-half of his social security benefits exceeds his base amount, whichever is less. The base amount is $32,000 for taxpayers filing joint returns and $25,000 for most other taxpayers. In determining a taxpayer's modified adjusted gross income, section 86 includes "interest received or accrued by the taxpayer during the taxable year which is exempt from tax." It is this last proviso that gives rise to the controversy before us.

The Secretary's excellent brief offers two examples to illustrate the operation of section 86.

> Taxpayer A, who files a joint return, has an adjusted gross income . . . of $29,000. He received $2,000 in tax-exempt interest income and $5,000 in Social Security benefits. To compute A's "modified adjusted gross income," add his tax-exempt interest income ($2,000) to his adjusted gross income ($29,000). Thus, his "modified adjusted gross income" is $31,000. Section 86 applies to A only if this sum plus one-half of his Social Security benefits exceeds the base amount of $32,000. In this example, A's "modified adjusted gross income" ($31,000) plus one-half of his Social Security benefits ($2,500) totals $33,500, and exceeds his base amount by $1,500. Some portion of his Social Security benefits is thus taxable. Because one-half of the excess ($750) is less than one-half of the total Social Security benefits received, the taxpayer would be required to include $750 from his Social Security benefits in his gross income for purposes of computing his taxable income.

Taxpayer B, who files a joint return, has an adjusted gross income of . . . $35,000. He also received $2,000 in tax-exempt interest income and $5,000 in Social Security benefits. B's "modified adjusted gross income" is thus $37,000; when added to one-half of his Social Security benefits, the total is $39,500, which exceeds his base amount by $7,500. Some portion of his Social Security benefits is thus taxable. Because one-half of his Social Security benefits ($2,500) is less than one-half of the excess, only one-half of his Social Security benefits is included in gross income for purposes of computing taxable income.

Thus, for certain taxpayers (like taxpayer A), the effect of section 86 can be as follows: If they have interest income from tax-exempt municipal securities, a portion of their social security benefits will be taxed. On the other hand, if that tax-exempt income did not exist, their social security benefits would be taxed to a lesser degree or not at all. This effect of section 86 operates on a fairly narrow group of taxpayers. Nonetheless, it could make municipal securities marginally less attractive to investors and thereby increase the interest rate the City has to pay to attract lenders. The City contends that section 86 is a tax on interest income from municipal securities and that it threatens the City's ability to provide essential services by impairing the City's ability to borrow money.

In support of its claim that section 86 violates the intergovernmental immunity doctrine, the City relies on Pollock v. Farmers' Loan & Trust Co., 157 U.S. 429, modified on rehearing, 158 U.S. 601 (1895). In *Pollock*, the Supreme Court held a federal statute imposing a tax on income from municipal bonds to be unconstitutional, see 157 U.S. at 583-86. Whether the rule of *Pollock* has survived the ninety years since it was announced is questionable, see South Carolina v. Regan, 465 U.S. 367, 404-15 (1984) (Stevens, J., dissenting). The passage of the Sixteenth Amendment to the Constitution in 1913 and numerous Supreme Court decisions since that time have cast doubt on the vitality of *Pollock*. We need not face this question, however, since we find that section 86 is not a tax on interest paid by the City.

By its terms, section 86 is part of a tax on social security income . . . the tax is intended to strengthen the social security system by requiring "taxpayers who have a comfortable flow of income" to pay a tax on part of their social security benefits. . . . Admittedly, tax-exempt municipal bond income will, in certain cases, affect this new tax on social security benefits. However, that by itself does not make section 86 a direct tax on municipal bond income.

Indeed, in United States v. Atlas Life Ins. Co., 381 U.S. 233 (1965), the Supreme Court upheld a statute that, like section 86, required certain recipients of tax-exempt income to pay a larger tax than they would have paid had they not received the tax-exempt income. In *Atlas*, the Court was presented with a statute that required life insurance companies to allocate a pro rata share of all their income, tax-exempt or otherwise, to their reserves. The reserves were required in order to guarantee payment to policyholders. Income placed in the reserves was not taxed. Rather than include a pro rata share of its tax-exempt income in its reserves, the insurance company naturally preferred to attribute none of its tax-exempt income to the mandatory reserve deposits: using regular income for this purpose would reduce its tax bill by decreasing the amount of taxable income remaining after it took its reserve deduction. In an argument similar to that advanced by the City here, the company contended that the statute, as applied, was unconstitutional because an insurance company that received tax-exempt income from "investing its 'idle' assets in municipal bonds" would be subject to a greater tax than an insurance company that did not make "the additional investment at all." . . . The Supreme Court firmly rejected this view, adopting instead "the principle of charging exempt income with a fair share of the burdens properly allocable to it." . . . The Court concluded that an added burden on tax-exempt income did not constitute a tax on that income.

Furthermore, *Pollock* has not been a barrier to taxes on the profits from the sale of municipal bonds, Willcuts v. Bunn, 282 U.S. 216 (1931), or to estate taxes on their transfer at death, Greiner v. Lewellyn, 258 U.S. 284 (1922). Section 86 is merely another example of a federal tax that makes a municipal security marginally less attractive — here, to some persons who also receive social security benefits. A taxpayer who does not receive such benefits is affected only remotely, if at all, by section 86, even if the taxpayer owns municipal bonds. In short, section 86 is not a tax on income from that type of security.

The City argues that even if the narrow rule of *Pollock* does not cover this case, the broader principles of intergovernmental immunity underlying *Pollock* require us to invalidate the statute. We disagree. The origins of intergovernmental tax immunity lie as far back as McCulloch v. Maryland, 4 Wheat. 316 (1819), and Collector v. Day, 11 Wall. 113 (1871). The policy behind the doctrine is restricted to insuring that a federal tax does not destroy the state's ability to function:

> [T]he Court was concerned with the continued existence of the states as governmental entities, and their preservation from destruction by the national taxing power. The immunity which it implied was sustained only because it was one deemed necessary to protect the states from destruction by the federal taxation of those governmental functions which they were exercising when the Constitution was adopted and which were essential to their continued existence.

Helvering v. Gerhardt, 304 U.S. 405, 414 (1938).

Because federal taxes that place indirect burdens on states and municipalities have not generally implicated this policy, the intergovernmental immunity doctrine has not been a bar to a broad array of taxes at least as burdensome on states and municipalities as section 86, e.g., Willcuts v. Bunn, 282 U.S. 216 (tax on profits from sale of municipal bonds); Grenier v. Lewellyn, 258 U.S. 384 (tax on transfer of municipal securities after death); Metcalf & Eddy v. Mitchell, 269 U.S. 514 (1926) (tax on income of independent contractor earned from contracts with a state); Helvering v. Gerhardt, 304 U.S. 405 (tax on salaries of employees of state-controlled corporations). Simply put, "an economic burden on traditional state functions without more is not a sufficient basis for sustaining a claim of immunity." Massachusetts v. United States, 435 U.S. 444, 461 (1978).

The Court stated as long ago as Willcuts v. Bunn, 282 U.S. at 225:

> The power to tax is no less essential than the power to borrow money, and, in preserving the latter, it is not necessary to cripple the former by extending the constitutional exemption from taxation to those subjects which fall within the general application of nondiscriminatory laws, and where no direct burden is laid upon the governmental instrumentality, and there is only a remote, if any, influence upon the exercise of the functions of government.

Section 86, which is a tax on social security benefits, imposes just this kind of indirect burden. See Shapiro v. Baker, No. 84-2492, slip op. (D.N.J. Nov. 5, 1986). The intergovernmental immunity doctrine does not apply.

The City's argument that section 86 violates the Tenth Amendment of the United States Constitution merits little discussion. The Tenth Amendment provides:

> The powers not delegated to the United States by the Constitution, nor prohibited by it to the States, are reserved to the States respectively, or to the people.

The City claims that section 86 impairs its "ability to function effectively in a federal system," citing Fry v. United States, 421 U.S. 542, 547 n.7 (1975). Such a drastic view of section 86 is totally unsupportable. Moreover, "[b]ecause the power to tax private income has been expressly delegated to Congress, the Tenth Amendment has no application to this case." South Carolina v. Regan, 465 U.S. at 418 (Stevens, J., dissenting).

Accordingly, the judgment of the district court is affirmed.

Problem

3-23.   On November 30 of the current year, Robert Stillwater retired from his job. During the year, he received salary of $28,000, $600 of interest income from a bank savings account, $500 of social security payments, and $1,500 of interest from his State of Michigan bonds. What items, if any, will Stillwater have to include as gross income?

J.   POLICY CONSIDERATIONS

1.   *Temporary versus Permanent Exclusions: The Relationship of Debt, Gross Income, and Basis*

Whenever analyzing an exclusion from gross income, it is important to consider its long-term impact. Some exclusions are permanent — that is, the excluded income will never be subject to tax. Others are temporary in that the exclusion acts only as a form of deferral of tax liability. Consider for example the exclusion for qualified employee discounts under §132. If a salesman at a car dealership pays $12,000 for a car worth $20,000, what should be the basis of the car in the hands of the salesman? Does it matter?

Similar problems are confronted in analyzing the exclusion from gross income for return of capital discussed in Chapter 2. For example, if a taxpayer purchases stock for $100 and sells it one year later for $100, none of the $100 received upon the sale is gross income because it is a return of capital. In other words, the §1012 cost basis was $100 and, because the stock was sold for $100, there was no gain under §1001. In effect, the basis of property serves as an account of invested capital that can be returned to a taxpayer without realizing gross income. But what if the taxpayer had borrowed the $100 to purchase the stock? The initial borrowing would not be gross income. Because the taxpayer receives a $100 basis in the stock, the taxpayer also will not have any gross income upon the sale of the stock for $100. What would be the consequences, however, if the law provided that taxpayers did not receive basis for borrowed proceeds? In this scenario, the taxpayer would have $100 gross income upon the sale of the stock. Which is the appropriate answer?

This precise question arises in the context of exclusions from gross income: Are proceeds that a taxpayer receives that are excluded from gross income under an administrative, public policy, or statutory exclusion meant to be permanently or temporarily excluded from gross income? If the former, and the taxpayer acquires property with the proceeds, granting basis in the property effectively results in such proceeds being permanently excluded from the tax base; if the latter, not granting basis in the property simply results in taxation of such proceeds being deferred until the property is sold. In other words, whether to grant basis for such proceeds effectively determines whether the exclusion will be permanent. In the following case, the court considers this precise issue in analyzing the exclusion of proceeds from gross income under the general welfare doctrine. Does the court reach the proper conclusion?

BAILEY v. COMMISSIONER
88 T.C. 1293 (1987), *acq.*, 1989-2 C.B. 1

NIMS, J.

. . . Respondent takes the position that the $63,121 facade grant to rehabilitate petitioner's property was income to petitioner. The parties have agreed that if the facade grant was income to petitioner, it is includable in petitioner's income in the years in which the contractor received payments, i.e., $19,256, $38,865, and $5,000 in 1978, 1979, and 1980, respectively. Respondent concedes that to the extent that petitioner must include the amount of the facade grant in income, his basis in the property should be increased for depreciation purposes. . . .

Relying on positions taken by the Internal Revenue Service (IRS) as exemplified by Rev. Rul. 76-395, 1976-2 C.B. 16, petitioner argues that the facade grant payments are excludable from gross income because the project under which the payments were made was a social benefit program for the promotion of general welfare. Alternatively, petitioner argues that since he did not have "complete dominion" over the facade portion of his premises, the facade grant falls outside the concept of gross income as defined in Commissioner v. Glenshaw Glass Co., 348 U.S. 426, 431 (1955). . . .

INCLUDABILITY OF THE FACADE GRANT

"Except as otherwise provided . . . , gross income means all income from whatever source derived." Section 61(a). Because neither the Internal Revenue Code nor the legislation authorizing the facade grant contains a provision exempting the facade grant from income, respondent argues that the facade grant is includable in petitioner's gross income.

Petitioner argues that because the facade grant program was established to promote the general welfare of the community, the grant he received is tax exempt under the general welfare doctrine. He notes that the IRS itself has stated that "The Internal Revenue Service has consistently held that payments made under legislatively provided social benefit programs for the promotion of general welfare are not includable in an individual's gross income."

In each of respondent's Revenue Rulings in which the general welfare doctrine has been applied, the grant was received under a program requiring the individual recipient to establish need. See, e.g., Rev. Rul. 76-395, 1976-2 C.B. 16 (Home Rehabilitation Housing and Community Act; grants to low income recipients primarily for correction of critical code violations); Rev. Rul. 78-170, 1978-1 C.B. 24 (Ohio payments to reduce energy costs for low income elderly or disabled heads of households); Rev. Rul. 76-144, 1976-1 C.B. 17 (Disaster Relief Act; grants to persons who as a result of a major disaster are unable to meet necessary expenses and needs). Grants received under social welfare programs that did not require recipients to establish individual need have not qualified under respondent's rulings for tax exempt status under the general welfare doctrine. See, e.g., Rev. Rul. 76-75, 1976-1 C.B. 14 (section 236 of the National Housing Act; interest reduction payments to a mortgagee on behalf of a limited profit corporation formed to acquire and leave apartments in a lower income rental housing project were includable in the corporation's gross income); Rev. Rul. 76-131, 1976-1 C.B. 16 (payments made by the State of Alaska to long term residents distinguished from general welfare payments because they were based on the recipient's age and residency requirements regardless of financial status, health, educational background or employment status).

At least one court has validated respondent's general welfare exclusion. In *Graff*, the Circuit Court stated (referring to the National Housing Act):

> Section 236 payments are substitutes for rentals, permitting the sponsor to operate profitably at lower rates at such returns. Rentals, however, are gross income, where Section 235 payments are not rental substitutes but rather direct general welfare benefits not taxable.

The facade grants in this case were awarded without regard to any need of the recipients. The only requirements for participation in the facade grant program were ownership of the property and compliance with the building code. Accordingly, facade grants awarded under the program are not tax exempt under the general welfare doctrine.

Nevertheless, the facade grant awarded to petitioner is not includable in petitioner's gross income. In Commissioner v. Glenshaw Glass Co., 348 U.S. 426, 431 (1955), the Supreme Court held that the term "gross income" as used in the Internal Revenue Code, includes all "accessions to wealth, clearly realized, and over which the taxpayers have complete dominion."

Respondent maintains that petitioner realized an accession to wealth when the URA paid the contractor to renovate the facade on his property. The grant in this case was not income to petitioner, however, because petitioner lacked complete dominion over the new facade.

To receive the facade grant, petitioner was required to grant an easement to the URA permitting the URA or its agents to enter the property, at first to perform the initial rehabilitation work on the facade and at any time in the future to repair the facade at petitioner's expense should petitioner fail to maintain it in accordance with the terms of the indenture agreement. Petitioner was also required to maintain the interior of the structure on his property and was restricted from altering the exterior without written consent of the URA.

Petitioner had no control over the rehabilitation work performed on the facade of his property. No payments for the rehabilitation of the facade were made directly to petitioner. The URA was the party that selected the contractor, negotiated the terms of the contract and paid for the work that was performed on the facade. The amount of the facade grant was not even made known to petitioner at the time he signed the facade rehabilitation agreement. Therefore, the facade grant is not includable in petitioner's gross income.

Unquestionably, in many contexts courts have held that payments made by the government to reimburse a taxpayer for expenditures to construct or purchase property or to make repairs were income to the recipient. However, in each of these cases, unlike the instant case, the taxpayer received funds over which he had complete dominion and control. In *Baboquivari Cattle Co.* and *Lykes Bros. S.S. Co.*, the taxpayer's unfettered use of the funds received was an important factor in determining that they were includable in income.

Respondent's reliance on Helvering v. Bruun, 309 U.S. 461 (1940), is misplaced. In Helvering v. Bruun, the Supreme Court held that the fortuitous gain accruing to a lessor by reason of the forfeiture of a lessee's improvements on the rental property was a taxable windfall in the year of forfeiture. We note that the value of lessee's improvement on the property was not includable in the lessor's income until the year of forfeiture when the lessor gained complete dominion over the property. In this case petitioner lacked complete dominion over the rehabilitation, maintenance and alteration of the facade. To the extent that he has benefited from the facade grant, petitioner will have to include in income any gain that he receives from the increased value of his property attributable to the new facade when he sells or otherwise disposes of the property.

The regulations provide that "In general, the basis of property is the cost thereof. The cost is the amount paid for such property in cash or other property." Section 1.1012-1, Income Tax Regs. Respondent concedes that if petitioner is required to include the facade grant in gross income, the amount of the facade grant should be included in petitioner's basis in the property.

We have concluded, however, that the amount of the facade grant is not includable in petitioner's gross income. By receiving the facade grant free of tax liability, petitioner has incurred no cost attributable to the improvements made to the facade on his property. Accordingly, the amount of the facade grant is not includable in petitioner's basis in the property.

Because petitioner may not include the amount of the facade grant in his basis in the property, petitioner will recognize a greater gain when he sells or disposes of the property. Section 1001; section 1001-1(a), Income Tax Regs. At that time he can use the proceeds to pay the tax on the benefit he received as a result of the facade grant. . . .

2. *Protecting the Tax Base*

As evidenced by the preceding sections, Congress, for various policy reasons, has excluded a number of accessions to wealth that arguably could be includable in gross income. Various reformers have chastised the system for its liberal hodge-podge of exclusions and advocated an adoption of a comprehensive tax base with few, if any, exclusions. In 1967, prior to the enactment of §86 discussed above, Professor Bittker, in the excerpt that follows, responded to the zealous advocacy of the reformers. Is his prose equally responsive today, given the recent effort to eliminate many of the exclusions encountered in this chapter?

BITTKER, A "COMPREHENSIVE TAX BASE" AS A GOAL OF INCOME TAX REFORM
80 Harv. L. Rev. 925 (1967)

Since World War II, our ablest commentators on federal income taxation have repeatedly attacked the "exceptions," "preferences," "loopholes," and "leakages" in the income tax provisions of the Internal Revenue Code and have called upon Congress to reverse the "erosion of the income tax base" caused by these "special provisions." It is no exaggeration to say that a "comprehensive tax base" (hereafter CTB) has come to be the major organizing concept in most serious discussions of our federal income tax structure.

Some of this discontent with "preferences" and "leakages" has focused on the economic or social shortcomings of the particular provision under discussion but increasingly a different line of argument has become popular. This approach accepts the rationale advanced in defense of the "preference," at least arguendo, but goes on to assert that equally persuasive arguments may be offered in support of virtually all other "preferences," including many that are still embryonic. More-over, it is argued, a tax concession is a poor way to distribute a government bounty or to encourage activities that are in the public interest; the value of the concession varies with the beneficiary's tax status, the impact of the program may be erratic and unpredictable, its cost cannot be accurately estimated or budgeted in advance, and its operation is covert rather than open to public inspection and criticism. The only road to a simplified and improved tax structure, it is contended, is to eliminate "preferences" ruthlessly, no matter how persuasive or seductive their individual appeals may be, and to impose the tax on the resulting CTB. The broader base will permit rates to be reduced, and with lower rates the benefit to be reaped by the restoration of any one "preference" will be lessened; this will let some of the steam out of efforts to renew the process of "eroding" the base. Alternatively, Congress could tax the augmented base at rates that will produce additional revenue, using the surplus to finance directly the programs that are now covertly financed by tax concessions. In either event, Congress will be willing and able (it is argued) to resist attempts to "erode" the new tax base since it will be armed with an argument—"one exception inevitably breeds another"—that now lacks persuasive force because today's Code is already riddled with "preferences" and "exceptions."

The aim, in short, is a reformed Internal Revenue Code with a "correct" tax base, to which all men of good will can and will rally when it is threatened by "exceptions," "special provisions," "preferences," "loopholes," and "leakages."

In trying to come to grips with the CTB approach to income taxation, I have encountered a distressing vagueness in the use of terms like "preference." Sometimes we are offered a goal no more precise than an income-tax system which refuses special benefits to some taxpayers because their income comes from particular sources, and which taxes alike all dollars of income. . . . Thus, the concept of "erosion" embraces deductions (percentage depletion), . . . rules relating to timing (postponement by qualified pension plans), and other provisions, regardless of the technical form in which they appear in the Code.

So far as I know, however, no one has attempted to list all the sources of "erosion" to be found in existing law, although the philosophy of "treating all income alike" in order to achieve a CTB, with no seeds from which new "exceptions" can grow is premised on our ability to identify the provisions to be eliminated. For this task we need more than a compilation of everyone's favorite complaints.

From the rhetoric of the broad base approach to tax reform, one might get the impression that its advocates (or at least the lawyers among them) would compute the taxpayer's gross income by using section 61(a) as a starting point, discarding as a "preference" any provision which alters the result that would be reached if section 61(a) stood alone, whether it does so by excluding an item from gross income, by assigning it to a different year or to a different person, or otherwise. Having computed gross income by looking solely to section 61(a), we would then convert it into taxable income by deducting the expenses, losses, bad debts, and depreciation incurred in the taxpayer's business or profit-motivated transactions — but nothing else. A rigorous application of the "comprehensive base" approach, then, seems to imply that sections 61(a), 162, 165, 166, 167, and 212 are the only operative provisions needed for an ideal computation of taxable income.

Another answer to the same question — how can we arrive at a comprehensive base, devoid of all "preferences"? — that is suggested or implied by the commentators, especially the economists, is use of the Haig-Simons definition of income as the touchstone. Haig defined personal income as "the money value of the net accretion to one's economic power between two points of time," a formulation that was intended to include the taxpayer's consumption, and that was thought by Simons to be interchangeable with his own: "Personal income may be defined as the algebraic sum of (1) the market value of rights exercised in consumption and (2) the change in the value of the store of property rights between the beginning and end of the period in question." At times, the "broad base" commentators seem to imply that a "true" or rigorous CTB would be achieved if Congress enacted the Haig-Simons formulation. It is always admitted, to be sure, that valuation difficulties or administrative problems require some departures from the ideal (for example, with respect to unrealized appreciation, imputed income from assets, and domestic services by the taxpayer or his wife); but I take it that these concessions assume that the departure is a preference, albeit an unavoidable one. Such concessions, in other words, are adjustments to practicality, rather than an integral part of the definition. . . .

For reasons that will be set out in more detail hereafter, I have concluded that a systematic and rigorous application of the "no preference" or CTB approach would require many more sweeping changes in the existing tax structure than have been acknowledged. I also believe that many of these changes would be quite unacceptable, despite their conformity to the Haig-Simons definition, to many of those who are attracted, in the abstract, by the idea of a CTB. At the same time, there are in my view many more ambiguities in the concept than have been acknowledged, and at these points it sheds less light than some of its supporters seem to claim. Some alleged "preferences," in other words, are as compatible with the Haig-Simons definition as their elimination would be. Finally, those who continue, in defiance of all experience, to hope for a simplified tax structure in a complex society are doubly deluded, in my view, if they believe that a CTB will make a significant contribution to simplification. Most of our troublesome complexities concern issues that are either independent of the definitional criteria or unavoidable once we accept the departures that even the most committed believers in a CTB accept as desirable or necessary.

I. Exclusions from Gross Income

Because tax differentials among taxpayers based on the source of their income are inconsistent with the Haig-Simons emphasis on consumption and net accretions to wealth as the proper measures of income, lists of "preferences" almost invariably begin with items that are now excluded from gross income, such as interest on tax-exempt bonds and social security payments. Indeed, although the concept of "erosion" takes in such tax concessions as deductions, credits, . . . it has at its very core the idea that many items properly belonging in the income tax base have been excluded from it by statutory or administrative fiat. It is appropriate, therefore, to begin with the statutory and other exclusions from gross income in analyzing the implications of a CTB.

A. Social Security, Welfare, and Other Public Transfer Payments

An important theme in the literature of "erosion" is that social security payments are earned by the taxpayer's personal services and increase his wealth just as much as receipts from traditionally taxable sources. Since these payments are not geared to the taxpayer's financial needs, it is argued that their exclusion from gross income is a poor way to protect a minimum subsistence level and that direct public aid to the poor would insure that any given amount of governmental assistance would reach those who deserve it, rather than being wasted on less needy claimants. Including social security payments in gross income (with an adjustment to permit the taxpayer to recover his contributions) along with analogous benefits like railroad retirement and veterans' pensions, therefore, has been a favorite way of "restoring" the tax base.

Social security, railroad retirement, and veterans' benefits are nominated for inclusion in the proposed CTB because they increase the taxpayer's net worth in the Haig-Simons sense and because if excluded they will have a differential value depending on his tax bracket and will not be openly reflected in the federal budget-making process. These characteristics are shared, however, by many other federal, state, and local government benefits, such as soil conservation and reforestation grants, subsidies to attract industrial plants, scholarships and fellowships, aid to the blind and other disabled persons, meals, clothing, and shelter supplied to patients and inmates of hospitals, prisons, and other public institutions, veterans' readjustment allowances, Medicare protection. . . . Some advocates of a CTB are prepared to tax these benefits (and those who eschew this responsibility impair their credentials as consistent enemies of "preferences"); but it must be noted that this route soon brings one face to face with the fact that every modern nation — even if it does not call itself a welfare state or a Great Society — provides its citizens with a variety of benefits through programs that involve no transfer of cash or identifiable "property." This means that the "comprehensive tax base" must either measure the benefit derived by the taxpayer from all governmental services, or grant a "preference" to those who benefit from indirect government programs.

Thus, to tax the student who receives a federal or state scholarship, while exempting the one who can attend a public institution without charge, is a "preference" — as that term is used by the advocates of a CTB — to the latter; and the same can be said of an exemption for the businessman whose plant is made more accessible and valuable by public improvements while his competitor is taxed on a grant of land which was given him to induce a change of location; of an exemption for the farmer who benefits from a flood control project while his neighbor is taxed when a public agency plants trees on his land to check erosion; and of rental allowances vis-à-vis public or subsidized housing. Other troublesome areas are the services of welfare workers, county agricultural agents, and the like; the net deficit of the postal service; and government guarantees of loans to homeowners and businessmen. Even if we look only to public programs providing benefits that are susceptible to valuation and can be accepted or refused at the recipient's option, a policy of rigorously taxing direct grants would inevitably discriminate in favor of indirect benefits.

To be sure, a decision to tax all direct grants while exempting indirect benefits in order to avoid a valuation quagmire is not unreasonable; but it would require an admission that the aim of "taxing all income alike" and extirpating all "preferences" had been compromised. And once this is acknowledged, it is only a short step to the conclusion that public policy is not necessarily served by a single-minded effort to tax all grants that can be measured, and that it might be better to decide, program by program, which should be taxed and which should be exempt. . . .

For a fully committed enemy of "preferences," governmental benefits belong in the CTB even if the recipient must pass a means test to qualify; thus, the exclusion allowed by existing law for public assistance is a hidden subsidy to local welfare programs, and it creates geographical disparities since it is worth more to the residents of a city that is generous in its welfare allowances or lenient in disregarding outside earnings than to those whose city is more strict in these respects. Pechman, for example, would include such payments in the tax base, relying on the personal exemptions (raised above the existing level, if necessary) and on increases in the welfare payments themselves to prevent the income tax from encroaching on the taxpayer's ability to feed, clothe, and house himself. Even if every welfare recipient received a federal subvention precisely equal to the tax burden resulting from including his welfare payments in his gross income, I presume that this reform would be viewed as an improvement over existing law by a thorough-going enemy of "preferences" because it would bring the federal grant into the open and compel it to pass through the budgetary process. Some advocates of the CTB may falter at this point, opening themselves to the charge of being "soft on preferences": but even they, presumably, would favor including welfare payments in gross income if, as with social security payments, the recipient is not subjected to a means test. If so, they may reach the same practical result as Pechman (despite their rejection of his logical rigor) as the means test comes increasingly to be rejected as degrading and self-defeating in the administration of welfare programs.

In the foregoing discussion, I have accepted arguendo the theory that public assistance, veterans' benefits, scholarships and free tuition at public educational institutions, and the like are "subsidies" in their entirety and that social security payments are "subsidies" to the extent that they exceed the recipient's . . . payments. This premise is not unassailable, however; its validity depends upon the kind of cost accounting one chooses to use. If we take account of all taxes paid by the recipients of these public programs over their lifetime, it may be that they pay in full for what they get. Another possibility is that the price they pay cannot be estimated with reasonable accuracy; and that the case for excluding the benefits from income in order to make sure that the recipients are not taxed on a return of their contributions is as good as the case for treating the benefits as "subsidies." The CTB is to take no account of police, fire, and military protection, I assume, because there is no feasible way of comparing the taxpayer's benefits with his payments. In the case of public assistance and social security, the cash receipts can be measured, but it takes an act of faith to come to a firm conclusion about the amount paid by the recipient for these benefits. Perhaps the exclusion of these items does not "erode" the base after all. . . .

Both Haig and Simons, who might be regarded as the spiritual forefathers of the CTB, believed that gifts and bequests constituted "income" as they defined the term. The theory that these items should be excluded from gross income because we have separate transfer taxes on gifts and bequests—which take no account of the recipient's other income—was characterized by Simons as "one of the most spurious and naive types of argument in the literature." To his rebuttal at the theoretical level one might add that only about one-eighth of inherited property finds its way into the taxable estates of decedents subject to the federal estate tax. Most amounts received by bequest, in other words, bear no federal estate tax burden; and for those that do, the death tax burden is often less than the income tax that would be imposed on the recipient if this "leakage" were eliminated. As to gifts, the existence of a federal gift tax is an even weaker reason for excluding them from a CTB. The statistics on inter vivos transfers are fragmentary, but experience tells us that the donor who pays a gift tax is a rara avis.

Although advocates of a CTB sometimes call attention to this issue, the dominant mood is acquiescence in existing law. I do not know whether they have steered clear of section 102 (excluding gifts and bequests from gross income) because they think it is a "good" preference or out of political realism. Bunching of income would be a problem, of course, if section 102 were repealed; but the advocates of a CTB almost always favor income averaging rather than an exclusion as the appropriate remedy for this phenomenon, and sometimes they promise rates so low that timing will be unimportant. There are other reasons for excluding gifts and bequests from the income tax base, such as the distortions in family transfer patterns that would result from efforts to bypass as many generations or intermediate donees as possible, and the difficulties in taxing the beneficiaries of discretionary trusts. These, however, are no more self-evident or compelling — to me, at any rate — than the reasons that led Congress to enact many of the other "preferences" of existing law. Nor can gifts and bequests be excluded from gross income without inviting the exclusion of many other items that share some of their characteristics — scholarships and fellowships, . . . some employee death benefits, life insurance proceeds, public assistance, social security payments, . . . and so on. . . .

The exclusion from gross income, as presently defined, of the net rental value of owner-occupied residences has been a common target of commentators, and some have also criticized the failure to tax imputed income from other assets, for example, the net rental value of household furnishings and the value of bank services provided in lieu of interest on idle balances in checking accounts. Acknowledging that it would not be easy to value these economic advantages or to enforce compliance, most advocates of a CTB would evidently be satisfied with taxing the imputed rent of owner-occupied residences and willing to exempt imputed income from other assets. I presume that they would agree, however, that this tolerance, even if impelled by the pain and suffering that consistency would require, would "erode" the tax base. I do not know the order of magnitude of the "special exception" that is thus to be granted to the owners of personal property, but it must be at least as substantial as many "preferences" that we are asked to nullify. . . .

Appreciation in the value of the taxpayer's assets is not included in gross income under existing law until it has been "realized" by sale or other disposition. None of the proponents of a CTB, so far as I know, wants to substitute an annual net worth computation to take account each year of the taxpayer's increase or decrease in wealth. I do not quarrel with this exemption of unrealized appreciation, but it unquestionably tolerates a "preference" and is inconsistent with the hope of achieving a tax base unsullied by human compromises. Although Henry Simons acknowledged that a yearly computation of the taxpayer's net worth was implied by his definition of income, and called the realization concept a "professional conspiracy against truth," he thought that no "workable scheme" could be devised to reach the theoretically correct result. He was not explicit about his reason for this conclusion, however, except for the statement that income taxation "simply must follow, in the main, the established procedures of accounting practice."

Perhaps this source of "erosion" in the CTB is to be tolerated because of the difficulty of valuing the taxpayer's assets each year. In point of fact, of course, we somehow manage to value assets of almost every description in computing the gain or loss on taxable in-kind exchanges and in applying gift and death taxes; and Simons, like many other advocates of a CTB, wanted transfers by gift and at death to be treated as taxable realizations of gain, thus accepting the responsibility of valuing the assets at that time. Moreover, once the giant step of taxing unrealized appreciation was taken for the first year, it would produce a grand list of values, and later changes in value might be satisfactorily approximated by index figures based on economic trends (subject to rebuttal evidence at the taxpayer's option). The first year, in other words, would be the hardest. At the very least, before accepting the "special exception" or "loophole" that is created by the exclusion of unrealized appreciation from gross income, the advocates of a CTB might be expected to examine the possibility of applying to this area the principle used elsewhere in the tax field: value those assets that do have an ascertainable market value, and hold the others in abeyance until valuation becomes feasible. This is what the proposed taxation of life insurance savings by requiring the annual increase in the policy's terminal reserve or cash surrender value to be reported would amount to. If the exclusion of this type of unrealized appreciation erodes the tax base, what is the rationale for excluding other readily measurable appreciation?

Perhaps unrealized appreciation is to be excluded from the proposed CTB not because of anticipated difficulty in valuing assets but because "paper profits" produce no cash to pay the tax and may be wiped out in a later year. These are not untenable grounds for exempting unrealized appreciation, but they furnish equally persuasive support for other exclusions as well. One example: employees get no ready cash when their employer contributes on their behalf to a qualified pension or profit-sharing plan, and they will be involuntarily at the risk of the market until the benefits are paid in cash. Why not then, preserve the employee's right under existing law to exclude the employer's contribution from gross income; it is a "preference," to be sure, but so is the exclusion of unrealized appreciation. Indeed, if lack of cash and continued risk of the market are legitimate grounds for taking appreciation into income when it is realized, why should we not amend existing law to allow employees to deduct or exclude from gross income their contributions to pension plans and their social security taxes? The employee's claim is not properly answered by the assertion that he wants a "preference" while the investor is getting only what natural law requires. The employee, in fact, is in the usual case asking only for postponement; under existing law, the investor's unrealized appreciation will be excluded from income permanently if he holds the property until death. . . .

VII. CONCLUSION

This attempt to work out the implications of the "no preference, comprehensive base" approach in a systematic way, and thus to ascertain where it would take us if it were converted from a slogan into a program for action, has led me to these conclusions:

(1) The systematic elimination of "preferences" in order to achieve a truly "comprehensive" base would require many more fundamental changes in existing law than are usually acknowledged. Among the areas that would be drastically affected by a whole-hearted use of the Haig-Simons definition are: mortality gains on life insurance; governmental benefits furnished in kind or in services; recoveries in suits for personal injury or death. . . . Some of these areas seem to have been disregarded by the proponents of the CTB, and others have not received the attention their importance deserves.

(2) At many points, the most enthusiastic proponents of a CTB have drawn back from its implications: they almost always advocate the exclusion from gross income of unrealized annual net worth increases, gifts and bequests, and imputed income from personal services. . . . Their reasons for departing from the Haig-Simons definition are, in my opinion, no different from the reasons that are offered in support of all of the "preferences" of existing law: the necessity or desirability of avoiding difficulties in valuation or enforcement, of stimulating economic growth,

of encouraging behavior thought to be socially useful, of alleviating economic hardship, or retaining the freedom of choice that results from use of tax concessions rather than some other governmental mechanics, or of pursuing other social policies. I dare to say that they would give similar reasons for favoring perpetuation of many other preferences of existing law if they were required to express an opinion on all of those mentioned in this article. In short, they harbor, in my opinion, the same attitude toward the Haig-Simons definition of income that Congress is said to exhibit toward our progressive rate schedule: a declaration of faith, combined with advocacy or tolerance of numerous exceptions, each of which inures to the benefit of a "special" group of taxpayers.

(3) If I am right in asserting that most professed supporters of the CTB concept favor a host of important departures from the Haig-Simons standard, there ought to be equally drastic revision of their rhetoric, including a renunciation of the claim that we can or should eliminate all, or even most, "preferences" and "special provisions" from the Internal Revenue Code. This means not that all provisions of existing law are equally good, but rather that we cannot avoid an examination of each one on its merits in a discouragingly inconclusive process that can derive no significant assistance from a "no preference" presumption that would at best be applied only on a wholly selective basis. Put another way, there are "preferences" and "preferences"; some are objectionable, some are tolerable, some are unavoidable, and some are indispensable. A truly "comprehensive" base, in short, would be a disaster.

It may be argued that the rhetoric of the CTB approach does not matter; we are used to political slogans and exhortations that contain a kernel of truth and do no harm though they promise more than they can deliver. What concerns me is that the rhetoric will foster changes in the tax structure not because they are desirable in themselves, but merely because they will broaden the base. Since I am convinced that a full-fledged CTB will, and should, remain miles away, I see no automatic advantage in moving a few feet in its direction. . . .

(4) To the extent that a departure from the Haig-Simons definition is compelled by administrative difficulties (valuation, enforcement, and the like) rather than by its contribution to a social or economic goal, the advocates of the CTB have given too little attention to the paradox of the "second best." I take it that one of the virtues they see in the Haig-Simons definition is that its rigorous application would lead to an "ideal" distribution of the tax burden, by measuring the ability to pay that arises from "income" in the most accurate way. If this is their view, it would be appropriate to quantify the tax burden distribution that would result from a rigorous application of the definition by taking into account, at the best estimates available, such difficult items as annual increases in net worth, imputed income from personal assets, housewives' services, and gifts and bequests. Even if the valuation problems are too formidable to justify inclusion of these items in the tax structure itself on a taxpayer-by-taxpayer basis, a rough and ready estimate would be better than nothing for the kind of macroeconomic model that I am suggesting. Having worked out in this way an approximation of the "ideal" distribution of the tax burden, it would be possible to test alternative reform programs to see which comes closest to the "ideal." The "best" practical program, on this theory, would not be the one that eliminated the most "preferences," but the one whose tax burden distribution was closest to the ideal.

This method of judging the proximity of a proposal to the professed ideal would recognize that unavoidable preferences (those compelled by limitations in valuation techniques, anticipated problems in compliance, and similar factors) might be offset by deliberately preserving (or even creating) other preferences. It has often been pointed out that the elimination of an exclusion would serve no purpose if it is so equally distributed that the tax burden would be unaffected by the tidier system resulting from the change. I am suggesting nothing more than a generalized application of this well-known principle. If the tax base is to continue to exclude gifts and bequests, annual net worth increases, and imputed income from personal property, for example, the continued exclusion of . . . social security payments, and similar items may distribute the tax burden more equitably (using the Haig-Simons definition as the touchstone) than a reform program that adds the latter category of items to the base.

(5) There are many problem areas in which the search for "preferences" is doomed to fail because we cannot confidently say which provisions are "rules" and which are "exceptions." In these areas, we cannot comply with . . . advice to "lean over backward" to avoid "preferences" because, in the absence of a generally acceptable or scientifically determinable vertical, we cannot know whether we are leaning forward or backward. The central source of difficulty is the fact that the income tax structure cannot be discovered, but must be constructed; it is the final result of a multitude of debatable judgments.

If we were dealing not with an income tax but with a tax whose label described its reach with greater precision, an "exception" would be easier to identify. For example, in constructing a poll tax we would have at the outset a consensus on what constitutes a natural person whose "head" is to be taxed. To be sure, even here there would be marginal cases — conceived but unborn children, persons who have been legally declared dead but who reappear, Siamese twins, and so on. These peripheral cases aside, a consensus on the base to which the tax is to be applied would be feasible, and it would warrant the use of terms like "exception" and "preference" to describe proposals to exempt soldiers on combat duty, Boy Scout leaders, or persons over the age of sixty-five or blind that, however merito- rious such "preferences" might be when considered individually, there would be no satisfactory criteria for exempting one group of meritorious persons while refusing to exempt other persons such as Peace Corps workers, nurses, or the unemployed. Under these circumstances, it could be persuasively argued that a "pure" tax base would be a fortress that could be effectively defended against all comers, no matter how appealing their claims. When we turn to the field of income taxation, however, we do not begin with a consensus on the meaning of income, but with a myriad of arguments about what should be taxed, when and to whom. The CTB concept is simply irrelevant to many of these issues . . . hence, notwithstanding the contrary assumption of some commentators, it can make no contribution to the elimination of "preferences" from these areas.

C H A P T E R   4

CHOOSING THE
PROPER TAXPAYER

The United States system of income taxation treats individuals, rather than families or same other group, as the primary unit of taxation. In other words, income earned by each individual is treated as that individual's income alone. The United States uses a "strict" form of the individual as the taxable unit, which means that all individuals are treated as separate taxpayers regardless of their costs, abilities, relationships, or other considerations. For example, as would be expected, two adult individuals who are unrelated, live in separate apartments, have never met, and have no interactions are treated as separate "taxpayers" for federal income tax purposes, but perhaps more surprisingly a parent and his or her 1-year-old child are also treated as two separate taxpayers, notwithstanding that the 1-year-old child lives with the parent, relies on the parent for all of its needs, does not work in the market economy, and has all of its economic decisions made by the parent.

This strict application of the individual as the taxable unit can lead to several difficult income tax issues, including issues of fairness in the calculation and alloca-tion of the total tax burden, as well as attempts by related taxpayers to exploit differences between the two, such as different marginal tax rates, to minimize their overall tax liability. This chapter focuses on the latter—that is, attempts to exploit the strict form of the individual as the taxable unit to reduce income tax liability—and certain common law, administrative, regulatory, and statutory responses. Issues of fairness, and the tax burden arising as a result of treating related individuals as separate taxpayers, are discussed in more detail in Chapter 10.

A. ASSIGNMENT OF INCOME—SERVICES

Code: §§61, 73

1. *The Concept of Income Splitting*

As discussed in detail in Chapter 10, the federal system of income taxation employs a progressive rate structure—up to a certain point, the greater the taxable income, the greater the rate of tax. Therefore, if an individual is able to transfer or shift a portion of his or her income to others in a lower marginal tax bracket, the tax liability for the transferred income will be reduced. For instance, assume that a 40-percent bracket taxpayer has gross income from dividends of $10,000. Her income tax liability attributable to the dividends is $4,000. If the taxpayer were able to shift all $10,000 of dividend income to her 15-year-old child, who is in the 10-percent marginal tax bracket, the resulting tax liability would be reduced. The taxpayer would pay no income tax on that income and her child would pay $1,000 in tax on that income, a savings of $3,000 compared to if the parent was taxed on the $10,000.

The problem with this strategy is that the taxpayer would somehow have to give the $10,000 of income to the child. But why would a taxpayer give $10,000 to a 15-year-old child? If $10,000 suddenly appeared in the pocket of a 15-year-old, what do you think that 15-year-old would do? Presumably, no parent would permit his or her child to have unfettered access to such a large amount of money solely for tax savings. But what if, because the child was a minor, the parent could transfer nominal ownership of the money to the child but retain actual control over the use of the money, such as depositing the money in a guardianship account for the benefit of the child. In this case, what does "shifting" the income to the child mean? If the parent retains effective control over the money and would have spent it on the child's health and well-being anyway, is there any difference (other than tax savings) in saying the income is "earned" by the parent or "earned" by the child?

The assignment of income doctrine arose to address this issue — that is, to ensure that taxpayers do not circumvent the congressional policy underlying progressive taxation by "shifting" income to a low-bracket taxpayer while still effectively controlling the use and enjoyment of it. In other words, if income is taxed to the person whose services or property created it, the taxpayer will pay tax at the rate that Congress has decided reflects the proper social burden for a particular level of income.

In Lucas v. Earl, 281 U.S. 111 (1930), the first major case to apply the assignment of income doctrine to income from services, the Supreme Court held:

> [The case] turns on the import and reasonable construction of the taxing act. There is no doubt that the statute [§61] could tax salaries to those who earned them and provide that tax could not be escaped by anticipatory arrangements and contracts however skillfully devised to prevent the salary when paid from vesting even for a second in the man who earned it.

Id. at 114.

In *Lucas*, the taxpayer-husband entered into a contract with his wife in 1901 which provided that "any property either of us now has or may hereinafter acquire . . . in any way, either by earnings (including salaries, fees, etc.), or any rights by contract or otherwise, during the existence of our marriage . . . shall be . . . owned by us as joint tenants." The taxpayers contended that, as a result, half of any salary earned by Earl should be treated as income of Earl's spouse and not Earl for income tax purposes, since the spouse was entitled to the income under the agreement.

The court held that, in spite of this agreement, Earl's salary was taxable in its entirety to him. The opinion formulated the infamous — and often overworked — fruit and tree metaphor: fruit is the equivalent of income, and the tree is the equivalent of the persons or property generating that income. In the opinion, Justice Holmes opined that Earl (the tree) could not assign to his wife by contract the income tax liability attributable to income earned by him (the fruit), to wit: "[T]he tax could not be escaped by anticipatory arrangements and contracts however skilfully devised to prevent the salary when paid from vesting even for a second in the man who earned it. That seems to us the import of the statute before us and we think that no distinction can be taken according to the motives leading to the arrangement by which the fruits are attributed to a different tree from that on which they grew." Id. at 115.

Lucas stands for the proposition that those who earn income cannot voluntarily determine who should be taxed on such income. This doctrine has grown beyond the mere contractual assignment of income, however. Fifty years after *Lucas* was decided, for example, one of the many variations on its theme was considered in Vnuk v. Commissioner, 621 F.2d 1318 (8th Cir. 1980). In *Vnuk*, a doctor and his wife established an inter vivos trust and transferred to the trust all of their property, exclusive use of their future services, and any income derived from their services. Vnuk, his wife, and their son served as trustees. The trust paid all family expenses including housing, food, clothing, vacations, and education. Vnuk did not report the income from his services on his tax return; instead, the income was reported by the trust. Vnuk argued that the conveyance of lifetime services to the trust shifted income from him to the trust, and contended that when an individual performs services as an agent or "leased employee" of a trust, it is the trust, rather than the individual, that is taxed on the income derived from the services.

The court considered the principles established in *Lucas* and applied a refinement of the assignment of income doctrine that had developed over the years. Under this test, the properly taxed party is the one who *controls* the earning of the income, rather than the one who merely receives it. The court noted that it is well established that income is taxed to the person who earns it, and that attempts to avoid taxation through the deflection of income to another person or entity who is not the true earner do not, in and of themselves, shift the incidence of taxation. The determination of the proper taxpayer requires an analysis of which person or entity controls the earning of the income.

In deciding that Vnuk, and not the trust, earned and controlled the income, the court stated:

> Where the taxpayer simply assigns his lifetime services and income earned from the performance of those services, and the taxpayer rather than the trust has the "ultimate direction and control over the earning of the compensation," the conveyance is ineffective to shift the tax burden from the taxpayer to the trust.
>
> Here, it is clear that the "ultimate direction and control" rested in the taxpayer and not in the Trust. While the taxpayer may have conveyed, at least in form, his services to the Trust, he was not in substance a bona fide servant of the Trust. The Trust had no right to supervise the taxpayer's employment or determine his

remuneration, and the taxpayer had no legal duty to earn money or perform services for the Trust. In such circumstances, the conveyance merely constituted an anticipatory assignment of income and was insufficient to shift the incidence of taxation from the petitioners to the Trust.

Id. at 1320.

The general rule of *Lucas* — income is taxed to the one who earns it — is easy to state but not always easy to apply. For example, assume that a first-year associate in a 100-person law firm performs 1,000 hours of legal services for a client during the current year at a billable rate of $100 per hour. On December 15, the client remits a $100,000 payment to the law firm for the associate's services performed during the year. Is the $100,000 included in the gross income of the associate or the law firm? Although the associate "earned" the payment, the law firm had "ultimate direction and control" because it controlled both the money received and the associate's services. In this case, of course, the law firm, not the associate, should have $100,000 of gross income. In the real world, however, the issue quickly becomes more complicated. For example, would it matter if the lawyer was of counsel rather than an associate? Would it matter if the lawyer had been the client's personal lawyer before joining the firm?

In determining which party has "ultimate direction and control," it is important to consider who has the authority to dictate (1) the nature and extent of the individual's services and (2) to whom those services should be rendered. This precise issue often arises in corporate employee loan-out cases. In those cases, a corporation directs its employee to provide services to a third party with the corporation maintaining the right to direct the employee's activities and to control the amount of income the employee receives for those activities. Because the corporation, not the employee, had ultimate direction and control, it was the corporation which was taxable on income that the employee earned on its behalf notwithstanding that the employee was providing the services to the third party. See, e.g., Foglesong v. Comm, 621 F.2d 865 (7th Cit. 1980). The courts have struggled with this doctrine, however, especially with respect to professional athletes. For example, one court held that when a professional athlete formed a corporation in which he owned 100 percent of the stock and then had the corporation contract with a professional team for the player's services, the corporation and not the player was the proper taxpayer, see Sargent v. Commissioner, 929 F.2d 1252 (8th Cir. 1991), while another court facing nearly identical facts found the player to be the proper taxpayer, see Leavell v. Commissioner, 104 T.C. 140 (1995).

2. Shifting Income within the Family by Gratuitous Transfer

In the case that follows, the taxpayer had "ultimate direction and control" over his own services but participated in an activity the benefits for which he could not receive. Although he was not permitted to receive the benefits, he was permitted to designate the recipient.

TESCHNER v. COMMISSIONER
38 T.C. 1003 (1962)

TRAIN, J. . . .

Petitioners Paul A. and Barbara M. Teschner are husband and wife. . . . Sometime prior to October 2, 1957, Johnson & Johnson, Inc., in cooperation with the Mutual Benefit Life Insurance Company of Newark, New Jersey, announced a contest called the "Annual Youth Scholarship Contest." An entrant was required to complete in fifty additional words or less the statement "A good education is important because . . ." . . . The prizes consisted of annuity policies in the face amount of the respective prizes. Rule 4 of the contest stated that:

> Only persons under age 17 years and 1 month (as of May 14, 1957) are eligible to receive the policies for education. A contestant over that age must designate a person below the age of 17 years and 1 month to receive the policy for education. In naming somebody else, name, address and age of both contestant and designee *must* be filled in on entry blank.

As of May 14, 1957, both petitioners were over the age of 17 years and 1 month.

The preclusion of Paul from eligibility to receive any of the policies was neither directly nor indirectly attributable to any action taken by him. He had not suggested such a contest to anyone; had never discussed such a contest with representatives of either Johnson & Johnson or Mutual; and had no knowledge of the contest until the official announcement of it was first brought to his attention. Neither at the time Paul prepared and submitted the entry nor at any other time has there been any arrangement or agreement between petitioners and their daughter to divide or share in anything of value she might receive.

Paul, an attorney, entered the contest, submitting two statements on the form supplied by Johnson & Johnson. At that time, he designated his daughter, Karen Janette Teschner, age 7, as the recipient should either of the entries be selected.

One of the statements submitted by Paul was selected, [and] petitioners' daughter received from Mutual, during 1957, a fully paid-up annuity policy, having a face value of $1,500. This policy contained no limitation whatsoever on the manner in which Karen would be entitled to use the proceeds or any other benefits available under the policy. Specifically, the use of these proceeds or benefits was not limited to educational or similar purposes.

Petitioners did not include any amount in their 1957 income tax return with regard to the foregoing annuity policy. Respondent determined that the policy constituted gross income to petitioners, and assigned a value thereto of $1,287.12, the consideration paid by Johnson & Johnson. . . .

. . . The sole question in this case is whether the prize (annuity policy) is taxable to petitioners.

Respondent, relying on Lucas v. Earl, 281 U.S. 111 (1930), and Rev. Rul. 58-127, 1958-1 C.B. 42, contends that the annuity policy which Karen received is includible in petitioners' gross income. Respondent states on brief that the issue here "is whether a prize attributable to a taxpayer's contest efforts, which, if received by him, would constitute taxable income in the nature of compensation for services rendered, may be excluded by him because paid to his designee."

Respondent declares his theory of the case to be "that whenever *A* receives something of value attributable to services performed by *B*, *B*, the earner, is the proper taxpayer."

Petitioners contend that the value of the annuity policy should not be included in their gross income because they did not receive anything either actually or constructively and never had a right, at anytime, to receive anything that could have been the subject of an anticipatory assignment or similar arrangement.

We agree with the petitioners.

. . . Certainly, it was Paul's effort that generated the income, to whomever it is to be attributed. However, as we have found, he could not under any circumstances whatsoever receive the income so generated, himself. He had no right to either its receipt or its enjoyment. He could only designate another individual to be the beneficiary of that right. Moreover, under the facts of this case, the payment to the daughter was not in discharge of an obligation of petitioners. At age 18, Karen will be entitled to $1,500. She can use that money, in her uncontrolled and unfettered discretion, for any purpose she chooses. Nor does respondent here contend that petitioners received income by virtue of a satisfaction of an obligation to support. Finally, there is no evidence whatsoever that the arrangement here involved was a sham or the product of connivance.

As pointed out above, respondent relies, in part, on Rev. Rul. 58-127, supra, and a consideration of that ruling is useful because it reveals the error into which the respondent has here fallen. Under the circumstances stated by that ruling, the taxpayer prepared and submitted a winning entry in an essay contest. Pursuant to the terms of that contest, the taxpayer received a check payable to his child, the use of which was entirely without restriction imposed by the sponsors of the contest. The respondent ruled that, under such circumstances, the amount of the prize was includible in the gross income of the taxpayer. While the facts set out in that ruling do not disclose whether the taxpayer could himself have received the prize, it would seem that in all salient respects the facts therein are identical to those before us.

In his ruling, the respondent declared, "The basic rule in determining to whom an item of income is taxable is that income is taxable to the one who earns it." If by this statement the respondent means that income is in all events includible in the gross income of whomsoever generates or creates the income by virtue of his own effort, the respondent is wrong. If this were the law, agents, conduits, fiduciaries, and others in a similar capacity would be personally taxable on the proceeds of their efforts. The charity fund-raiser would be taxable on sums contributed as the result of his efforts. The employee would be taxable on income generated for his employer by his efforts. Such results, completely at variance with every accepted concept of Federal income taxation, demonstrate the fallacy of the premise.

If, on the other hand, the respondent used the term "earn," not in such a broad sense, but in the commonly accepted usage of "to acquire by labor, service, or performance; to deserve and receive compensation" (Webster's New International Dictionary), then the rule is intelligible but does not support the conclusion reached by the respondent either in the ruling in question or in the case before us. The taxpayer there, as here, acquired nothing himself; he received nothing nor did he have a right to receive anything.

In Rev. Rul. 58-127, supra, respondent relied heavily, as he does here, on Helvering v. Horst, 311 U.S. 112 (1940), especially the language of the opinion to the effect that — "The power to dispose of income is the equivalent of ownership of it. The exercise of that power to procure the payment of income to another is the enjoyment, and hence the realization, of the income by him who exercises it." The respondent's reliance on this language is misplaced. The power of disposition assumes possession or the right of possession. To dispose is to part with. Where there is neither possession nor the right to possession, there can be no disposition. . . .

In Lucas v. Earl, 281 U.S. 111 (1930), upon which respondent heavily relies, the Supreme Court refused to allow a husband to escape taxes on his income by way of salaries and attorney fees through a contractual arrangement by which he and his wife were to receive, hold, and own such earnings as joint tenants. The Court declared that tax on a salary could not be avoided by the person earning the salary by anticipatory arrangements and contracts. Shortly thereafter, in Poe v. Seaborn, 282 U.S. 101, 117 (1930), the Supreme Court stated:

> In the *Earl* case . . . the husband's professional fees, earned in years subsequent to the date of contract, were his individual income. . . . The very assignment in that case was bottomed on the fact that the earnings would be the husband's property, else there would have been nothing on which it could operate. That case presents quite a different question from this, because here, by law, the earnings are never the property of the husband, . . .

In Harrison v. Schaffner, 312 U.S. 579, 580, 582 (1941), the Supreme Court stated that the rule applicable to an anticipatory assignment of income applies when the assignor is *entitled* at the time of the assignment to receive the income at a future date and is vested with such a right. In the instant case, petitioners themselves received nothing and were *never entitled* to anything. What was said in the early case of Marion Stone Burt Lansill, 17 B.T.A. 413, 423 (1929), affd. 58 F.2d 512 (C.A.D.C. 1932), seems appropriate here:

> The right in the taxpayer to receive the income at the time it is attributed and taxed to him is likewise not essential, where . . . the taxpayer has by his own volition chosen to dispose of the right to receive income while retaining that from which the income is derived. The volition in disposing of the right is important, *for while all will agree that one who never received or had a right to receive or who has involuntarily lost it should not be taxed*, it is also plain that his voluntary exercise of the right to dispose of the income before receipt may be just as valuable and important practically as its exercise after receipt. . . . [Emphasis supplied.]

It cannot be argued that Paul voluntarily gave up *his* right to get the annuity policy and designated his daughter to receive it in his place. There was no discretion on his part; the choice was to accept the terms of the contest or reject them.

In the case before us, the taxpayer, while he had no power to *dispose* of income, had a power to appoint or designate its recipient. Does the existence or exercise of such a power alone give rise to taxable income in his hands? We think clearly not. In Nicholas A. Stavroudes, 27 T.C. 583, 590 (1956), we found it to be settled doctrine that a power to direct the distribution of trust income to others is not alone sufficient to justify the taxation of that income to the possessor of such a power.

Granted that an individual cannot escape taxation on income to which he is entitled by "turning his back" upon that income, the fact remains that he must have received the income or had a right to do so before he is taxable thereon. As stated by the court in United States v. Pierce, 137 F.2d 428, 431 (C.A. 8, 1943):

> The sum of the holdings of all cases is that for purposes of taxation income is attributable to the person entitled to receive it, although he assigns his right in advance of realization, and although, in the case of income derived from the ownership of property, he transfers the property producing the income to another as trustee or agent, in either case retaining all the practical benefits of ownership.

Section 1(a) of the Code imposes a tax on the "income of every individual." Where an individual neither receives nor has the right to receive income, he is not the taxable individual within the contemplation of the statute. There is no basis in the statute or in the decided cases for a construction at variance with this fundamental rule. . . .

Decision will be entered for the petitioners.

DAWSON, J., concurring.

Harrison v. Shaffner, 312 U.S. 579 (1941), settled the proposition that there can be no anticipatory assignment of income unless the assignor is entitled at the time of assignment to receive the income at a future date and is vested with such a right. Paul Teschner was at no time "vested with the right to receive income" under the rules of the contest and, therefore, could not possibly "escape the tax by any kind of anticipatory arrangement." Consequently, the cases cited by the dissent, Lucas v. Earl, 281 U.S. 111 (1930), Helvering v. Horst, 311 U.S. 112 (1940), and Helvering v. Eubank, 311 U.S. 122 (1940), all of which held that "one *vested with the right to receive income* [does] not escape the tax by any kind of anticipatory arrangement, however skillfully devised." Harrison v. Shaffner, supra at 582 (emphasis supplied), are inapposite here.

It is true that a taxpayer having the right to dispose of income would be taxable on the exercise of such a right where the disposition results in an economic benefit to him. However, in the instant case Paul Teschner had no *right of disposition*, but only a *duty* under the contest rules to designate a person under the age of 17 years, 1 month. Compliance with this duty was a *condition precedent* for entry of persons over that age into the contest. While it might be said concomitantly that there was a right to designate to *whom* the prize would go if it *were* won, no economic benefit could be conferred upon anyone when this right was exercised since there was no income upon which such a right of designation could operate at the time the designation was made. If those who disagree with this result fear the prize (annuity policy) will escape taxation, there is no problem because it would appear to be taxable to the daughter under the provisions of section 74. . . .

ATKINS, J., dissenting.

It is a well-settled principle of our income tax law that personal earnings are taxable to the earner, and that cases involving the taxation of personal earnings are not to be decided by attenuated subtleties. Lucas v. Earl, 281 U.S. 111, in which the Supreme Court held an anticipatory assignment of future personal earnings to be ineffective to relieve the earner of tax. The Court stated:

A very forcible argument is presented to the effect that the statute seeks to tax only income beneficially received, and that taking the question more technically the salary and fees became the joint property of Earl and his wife on the very first instant on which they were received. We well might hesitate upon the latter proposition, because however the matter might stand between husband and wife he was the only party to the contracts by which the salary and fees were earned, and it is somewhat hard to say that the last step in the performance of those contracts could be taken by anyone but himself alone. But this case is not to be decided by attenuated subtleties. It turns on the import and reasonable construction of the taxing act. There is no doubt that the statute could tax salaries to those who earned them and provide that the tax could not be escaped by anticipatory arrangements and contracts however skillfully devised to prevent the salary when paid from vesting even for a second in the man who earned it. That seems to us the import of the statute before us and we think that no distinction can be taken according to the motives leading to the arrangement by which the fruits are attributed to a different tree from that on which they grew.

The annuity policy which Paul won resulted from his personal efforts. The fruit of his labor consisted of the payment of the award to his designee, his daughter. His efforts alone generated the income in question; and it is a matter of no consequence that, under the rules of the contest, such income could not be paid to him, for he had the power to control its disposition. He in fact exercised that power when he entered the contest, by designating the natural object of his bounty, his daughter, as the recipient of any prize which he might win. The exercise of such power, with resultant payment to the daughter, constituted the enjoyment and hence the realization of the income by Paul. In the circumstances he should be fully charged with the income. Cf. Helvering v. Horst, 311 U.S. 112, and Helvering v. Eubank, 311 U.S. 122. There is no more basis here for narrowing the broad scope of the holding in Lucas v. Earl than there was in the *Horst* and *Eubank* cases. The decision of the majority herein rests upon "attenuated subtleties" similar to those disapproved, first in Lucas v. Earl and then again in Burnet v. Leininger, 285 U.S. 136, Helvering v. Horst, Helvering v. Eubank, Harrison v. Schaffner, 312 U.S. 579, and Commissioner v. P. G. Lake, Inc., 356 U.S. 260. . . .

3. *Shifting Income within the Family by Compensatory Arrangement*

FRITSCHLE v. COMMISSIONER
79 T.C. 152 (1982)

Fay, J. . . .

Findings of Fact . . .

Petitioners have 11 children. The 8 youngest children lived at home with their parents during the years in issue.

Since 1956, petitioner Robert T. Fritschle (Robert) has been employed by American Gold Label Co. (AGL), a sole proprietorship owned by Elsie Walsh Fabel and engaged in the printing business. . . .

Prior to 1970, AGL was engaged in a printing business generally limited to letterheads and stationery. Beginning in 1970, the business expanded to include more specialized types of printing which included printing on metals and cloth. Specifically, new items printed included ribbons and rosettes, much like the ribbons seen at horse and dog shows or the ribbon awarded the prize bull at the county fair. Even though AGL employed 15 people, outside help was needed to assemble the ribbons when the printing was completed. Petitioner Helen R. Fritschle (Helen) agreed with Elsie Walsh Fabel, the owner of AGL, to assemble the ribbons at home. Accordingly, in 1970, Helen, with the help of their children then living at home, began assembling ribbons and rosettes for AGL. . . .

All materials were furnished by AGL at no cost to Helen. When the work was completed, Helen submitted a bill and received payment accordingly. During the years in issue, Helen was paid 3 cents per ribbon and 15 cents to 25 cents per rosette. Total payments received during 1975, 1976, and 1977 were $9,429.74, $11,136.41, and $8,262, respectively.

The children performed approximately 70 percent of all the work. Robert, the father, did not participate. The children were not employees of either Helen or AGL, nor was there any other arrangement for them to share directly in the compensation paid to Helen by AGL. . . .

OPINION . . .

Helen and the children assembled the ribbons and rosettes in the basement of their home. There is no question that payments received for this work are income under section 61. The issue is who is taxable on those payments. Since a portion of the compensation was attributable to work performed by their children, petitioners argue that a proportionate amount of the payments should be included in the income of the children. Respondent contends Helen was responsible for, and retained total control over, the earnings, and, therefore, the income is properly includable in her income. We find for respondent.

It is axiomatic that income must be taxed to him who earns it. Moreover, it is the command of the taxpayer over the income which is the concern of the tax laws. Recognizing that the true earner cannot always be identified simply by pointing "to the one actually turning the spade or dribbling the ball," this Court has applied a more refined test — that of who controls the earnings of the income. Applying this test, it is clear that, for purposes of taxation, Helen, and not the children, was the true earner of the income attributable to the work performed on the ribbons and rosettes.

Helen was solely responsible for the performance of all services. AGL contracted only with Helen, and no contract or agreement existed between AGL and any of the children. All checks were made payable to Helen, and the children received no direct payments or compensation for their work. Clearly, the compensation was made in payment purely for the services of Helen. Although the company knew the children were performing part of the work, that does not change the fact that AGL looked exclusively to Helen for performance of the services. In short, Helen managed, supervised, and otherwise exercised total control over the entire operation. It was she who controlled the capacity to earn the income, and it was she who in fact received the income. It does not necessarily follow that income is taxable to the one whose personal efforts produced it. Thus, despite the fact that a portion of the amounts received can be traced to work actually performed by their children, Helen is treated as the true earner of all such income for tax purposes. . . .

Nevertheless, petitioners argue section 73 mandates a result in their favor. Section 73(a) provides:

> Sec. 73(a). Treatment of amounts received. — Amounts received in respect of the services of a child shall be included in his gross income and not in the gross income of the parent, even though such amounts are not received by the child.

Petitioners argue the language and meaning of section 73 are clear, and that the amounts received by Helen with respect to the services performed by the children clearly are included in the gross income of the children. However, when viewed in light of the origin and purpose of section 73, it is apparent that section was enacted in response to a different situation and, under these facts, does not purport to tax the children on a portion of the income at issue herein.

The purpose of section 73 is to provide, for Federal tax purposes, consistent treatment of compensation paid for the services of a minor child regardless of different rights conferred by State laws on parents' entitlement to such compensation. . . . Since [prior to 1944] parents in all States were not entitled to the earnings of their minor children and since even in those States following the common law doctrine of the parents' right to those earnings, a parent could lose such rights if the child had been emancipated, different tax results obtained depending on State law. To eliminate this discrepancy in the tax treatment of the earnings of minor children, Congress, in 1944, enacted the predecessor to section 73 to provide a uniform rule that all amounts received "in respect of the services of a child" shall be included in the income of that child regardless of the fact that, under State law, the parent may be entitled to those amounts. Thus, section 73 operates to tax a minor child on income he is deemed, in the tax sense, to have earned. Section 73 does not purport to alter the broad principle of taxation that income is taxed to the earner. . . .

If, on the other hand, we made a finding that it was the services of the children that were being contracted for and that the children were the true earners of the income, then section 73 would tax the children on that income.

. . . However, section 73 simply does not tax a child on income until and unless he is recognized as the earner thereof. Petitioners' argument that these amounts must be included in the children's gross income because the income can be traced to services performed by the children must be rejected. Carrying this argument to its logical extreme, any parent could exclude a portion of the income received for services if his children helped him in the performance of those services. Congress surely did not intend such a result.[11] . . .

[Judgment for respondent.]

---

11. The Committee reports state: "Thus, even though the contract of employment is made directly by the parent and the parent receives the compensation for the services, for the purposes of the Federal income tax, the amounts would be considered to be taxable to the child because earned by him." H. Rept. 1365, 1944 C.B. 821, 838; S. Rept. 885, 1944 C.B. 858, 876. Citing these reports, petitioners argue it could not be clearer that the children are taxable on the amounts in issue. This language, however, merely recognizes parents must be the contracting party when, due to their legal incapacity, minor children cannot enter into valid contracts. It must still be shown that the services of the child were being contracted for and that the children controlled the earning of the income therefrom.

Problems

4-1. Gordon Peabody entered an employment contract with the Greensleeves Mattress Co. that required him to work a forty-hour week in return for $1,000 per week.

   a.   What result if Peabody requests, and Greensleeves agrees, that the contract is to provide $800 per week, payable to Peabody, and $200 per week, payable to Peabody's 15-year-old son, Joseph?

   b.   What result in *a* if both Gordon and Joseph Peabody sign the employment agreement?

   c.   What result if the contractual provision referred to in *a* does not result from Peabody's request but is a standard and required part of every contract that Greensleeves has with its employees (that is, if employees have children, 80 percent of the employee's compensation is payable to the employee, with the remaining 20 percent payable to employee's children)?

   d.   Disregarding *a, b,* and *c,* what result if, after working for Greensleeves for one year, Peabody directs Greensleeves to pay Joseph $100 per week for his services and to reduce Peabody's salary by a corresponding amount? Joseph will assist his father by updating his appointment calendar and performing other secretarial tasks.

   e.   Would the result in *d* change if Joseph signed an employment contract with Greensleeves?

4-2. Tracey Sams, an 8-year-old third grade student, won a city sponsored 100-yard dash for her age category. As a prize for winning, she received a free trip to Disneyland for herself and any other four children whom she designated.

   a.   Who is taxed on the value of the five trips?

   b.   What result if Tracey does not designate anyone and goes alone?

   c.   What result if Tracey designates each child in return for a $250 payment from each?

4-3. Maria Theresa, a clinical psychologist, is a devout follower of a religious order which requires all members to take a vow of poverty and transfer all worldly possessions to the order. Maria does so by signing a contract stipulating that the order will be entitled to all income she earns in her psychology practice for the remainder of her life. Maria continues to work as a psychologist seeing private patients four days a week, but she also agrees to spend one day a week counseling patients at the offices of the order.

   a.   After Maria signs the contract, Andre Thompson, a long-time client of Maria's, agrees to pay $5,000 in professional consulting fees he owed her from previously rendered services directly to the order instead of Maria. To whom are the payments gross income?

   b.   After Maria signs the contract, Jorge Valladares is referred to Maria as a new patient by Andre. Before Jorge begins therapy, he signs a contract with Maria agreeing that, in exchange for her services, he would pay her fee directly to the order. He subsequently pays $3,000 to the order for her services. To whom are the payments gross income?

   c.   During her day working at the offices of the order, Maria begins seeing a new patient, Debra Kim. Debra had a traumatic experience in her childhood and is seeking treatment but is also considering joining the order and is seeking advice on that decision. Maria counsels Debra with respect to the trauma and separately recommends that Debra join the order. Debra decides Maria is right and subsequently pays the order a fee of $1,000 for Maria's counseling services, and then also transfers her total wealth of $50,000 to the order to join as a full member. To whom, if any, are the payments gross income?

4-4.   George Mast, a management consultant, established Shallot, Inc., a Delaware corporation, of which Mast was the sole shareholder. After inviting his wife and brother-in-law to serve on the board of directors and after granting Shallot, Inc., the exclusive right to his services for the next ten years (in return for a monthly salary of $2,000), Mast contacted three clients for whom he consulted on a regular basis and requested a modification of their employment contracts.

a.   One client refused to agree to a modification but agreed to pay Mast's salary directly to Shallot, Inc., pursuant to a valid assignment of the earnings Mast had made to Shallot. To whom are the payments gross income?

b.   Two of his clients released Mast from his existing employment contracts and signed new contracts with Shallot, Inc. The new contracts required Shallot, Inc., to perform the services previously rendered by Mast on whatever terms Mast and his clients negotiated. In return, amounts payable to Mast under the old agreements were payable directly to Shallot, Inc., as compensation for services rendered. To whom are the payments gross income?

B.   ASSIGNMENT OF INCOME — PROPERTY

Code: §§102, 1015(a)
Regulations: §§1.102-1, 1.61-9(c)

1.   *Appreciated Property Transferred by Gift*

As discussed in Chapter 3, §102(a) excludes the value of a gift from the recipient's gross income, while §102(b) includes future revenue that the gift may produce (such as interest or dividends) in the recipient's gross income. Consider this provision in light of the assignment of income doctrine. If a parent in a high tax bracket were to transfer a corporate bond to a child in a low tax bracket as a gift, under §102(b) the future interest payments received by the child would be taxed at the child's lower tax bracket. What if instead the parent kept the bond and received the interest payments, but then made a gift of the interest to the child? How would this be analyzed under the assignment of income doctrine?

Consider the same issue with respect to appreciation in the gifted property accruing prior to its transfer. What happens to taxable gain on the eventual sale or exchange of an asset when it is gifted to a recipient?

Section 1015, which sets forth the rules for determining the basis for property acquired by gift, effectively embodies a legislative exception to the assignment of income doctrine for gifts of appreciated property. Under §1015 a donee assumes the donor's basis, and pursuant to §102 the donee recognizes no income on the receipt of the property. The donor has enjoyed an economic benefit by transferring appreciated property to the donee of his or her choice. Is this benefit fundamentally different from the economic benefit realized by assigning salary rights to a family member?

Because the transfer of appreciated property by gift is not a realization event to the donor, the gift of such property from a high-bracket donor to a low-bracket donee may result in a lower tax liability when the appreciation is finally realized. Thus, the taxpayer is permitted to choose the tax rate for the appreciated value: a direct contradiction of the policy of progressive taxation generally enforced by assignment of income principles.

Consider two taxpayers: X is an employee who began work on October 1 for a salary of $1,000 a month, and Y is an investor who purchased 100 shares of stock on October 1 for $1 per share, with the stock appreciating to $11 per share by October 31. What would the tax results be if, on October 31, X transferred the rights to his salary and Y transferred the stock to their respective 15-year-old children? Under the assignment of income principles governing personal service income, X has $1,000 of gross income on October 31 because he earned and controlled the income. Y, however, is not taxed on the $1,000 gain on the stock because the gain is transferred to the child by way of the §1015 carryover basis. This is true even though the stock appreciated in value while it was owned by Y. Thus, property transfers have been granted a substantial measure of statutory and judicial immunity in being excepted from the general assignment of income principles.

Numerous problems arise from the interaction of the statutory rules governing gifts of property and the nonstatutory assignment of income principles. A typical question that arises can be stated in one of two ways: (1) will an otherwise legally effective transfer of property be regarded as such for tax purposes; or (2) has there been merely the transfer of a right to receive income, thus requiring application of assignment of income principles? In answering these questions, the issue becomes whether there has been a transfer of property and the income it produces; if so, the application of assignment of income principles will be avoided. If, however, there has merely been a transfer of the income from property, the assignment of income principles will apply. Like wages, which are taxable to the person whose services are being compensated, payments for the use of property, money, or other capital are attributable to the owner of the property. Determining the owner of property for these purposes can raise a number of unique and difficult considerations, however.

2. Transfers of Income from Property

HELVERING v. HORST
311 U.S. 112 (1940)

Mr. Justice Stone delivered the opinion of the Court.

The sole question for decision is whether the gift, during the donor's taxable year, of interest coupons detached from the bonds, delivered to the donee and later in the year paid at maturity, is the realization of income taxable to the donor. . . .

The court below thought that as the consideration for the coupons had passed to the obligor, the donor had, by the gift, parted with all control over them and their payment, and for that reason the case was distinguishable from Lucas v. Earl, [281 U.S. 111,] and Burnet v. Leininger, 285 U.S. 136, where the assignment of compensation for services had preceded the rendition of the services, and where the income was held taxable to the donor.

The holder of a coupon bond is the owner of two independent and separable kinds of right. One is the right to demand and receive at maturity the principal amount of the bond representing capital investment. The other is the right to demand and receive interim payments of interest on the investment in the amounts and on the dates specified by the coupons. Together they are an obligation to pay principal and interest given in exchange for money or property which was presumably the consideration for the obligation of the bond. Here respondent, as owner of the bonds, had acquired the legal right to demand payment at maturity of the interest specified by the coupons and the power to command its payment to others, which constituted an economic gain to him. . . .

. . . The question here is whether, because one who in fact receives payment for services or interest payments is taxable only on his receipt of the payments, he can escape all tax by giving away his right to income in advance of payment. If the taxpayer procures payment directly to his creditors of the items of interest or earnings due him, he does not escape taxation because he did not actually receive the money.

Underlying [this] reasoning . . . is the thought that income is "realized" by the assignor because he, who owns or controls the source of the income, also controls the disposition of that which he could have received himself and diverts the payment from himself to others as the means of procuring the satisfaction of his wants. The taxpayer has equally enjoyed the fruits of his labor or investment and obtained the satisfaction of his desires whether he collects and uses the income to procure those satisfactions, or whether he disposes of his right to collect it as the means of procuring them.

Although the donor here, by the transfer of the coupons, has precluded any possibility of his collecting them himself, he has nevertheless, by his act, procured payment of the interest as a valuable gift to a member of his family. Such a use of his economic gain, the right to receive income, to procure a satisfaction which can be obtained only by the expenditure of money or property, would seem to be the enjoyment of the income whether the satisfaction is the purchase of goods at the corner grocery, the payment of his debt there, or such non-material satisfactions as may result from the payment of a campaign or community chest contribution, or a gift to his favorite son. Even though he never receives the money, he derives money's worth from the disposition of the coupons which he has used as money or money's worth in the procuring of a satisfaction which is procurable only by the expenditure of money or money's worth. The enjoyment of the economic benefit accruing to him by virtue of his acquisition of the coupons is realized as completely as it would have been if he had collected the interest in dollars and expended them for any of the purposes named.

In a real sense he has enjoyed compensation for money loaned or services rendered, and not any the less so because it is his only reward for them. To say that one who has made a gift thus derived from interest or earnings paid to his donee has never enjoyed or realized the fruits of his investment or labor, because he has assigned them instead of collecting them himself and then paying them over to the donee, is to affront common understanding and to deny the facts of common experience. Common understanding and experience are the touchstones for the interpretation of the revenue laws.

The power to dispose of income is the equivalent of ownership of it. The exercise of that power to procure the payment of income to another is the enjoyment, and hence the realization, of the income by him who exercises it. We have had no difficulty in applying that proposition where the assignment preceded the rendition of the services, for it was recognized in the *Leininger* case that in such a case the rendition of the service by the assignor was the means by which the income was controlled by the donor and of making his assignment effective. But it is the assignment by which the disposition of income is controlled when the service precedes the assignment, and in both cases it is the exercise of the power of disposition of the interest or compensation, with the resulting payment to the donee, which is the enjoyment by the donor of income derived from them.

. . . The dominant purpose of the revenue laws is the taxation of income to those who earn or otherwise create the right to receive it and enjoy the benefit of it when paid. The tax laid by the 1934 Revenue Act upon income "derived from . . . wages, or compensation for personal service, of whatever kind and in whatever form paid, . . . ; also from interest . . ." therefore cannot fairly be interpreted as not applying to income derived from interest or compensation when he who is entitled to receive it makes use of his power to dispose of it in procuring satisfactions which he would otherwise procure only by the use of the money when received.

It is the statute which taxes the income to the donor although paid to his donee. True, in those cases the service which created the right to income followed the assignment, and it was arguable that in point of legal theory the right to the compensation vested instantaneously in the assignor when paid, although he never received it; while here the right of the assignor to receive the income antedated the assignment which transferred the right and thus precluded such an instantaneous vesting. But the statute affords no basis for such "attenuated subtleties." The distinction was explicitly rejected as the basis of decision in Lucas v. Earl. It should be rejected here; for no more than in *Lucas* can the purpose of the statute to tax the income to him who earns, or creates and enjoys it be escaped by "anticipatory arrangements however skillfully devised" to prevent the income from vesting even for a second in the donor.

Nor is it perceived that there is any adequate basis for distinguishing between the gift of interest coupons here and a gift of salary or commissions. The owner of a negotiable bond and of the investment which it represents, if not the lender, stands in the place of the lender. When, by the gift of the coupons, he has separated his right to interest payments from his investment and procured the payment of the interest to his donee, he has enjoyed the economic benefits of the income in the same manner and to the same extent as though the transfer were of earnings, and in both cases the import of the statute is that the fruit is not to be attributed to a different tree from that on which it grew.

Reversed. . . .

3. *Property and Income Transfers Compared*

As the cases above demonstrate, the assignment of income analysis can differ significantly depending on whether a taxpayer is considered to have transferred the right to *receive* income as opposed to the *ownership* of income producing property. In some cases, however, the distinction between the two can prove difficult. For example, if a university professor writes a textbook and then transfers the right to collect future royalties to his children, has he transferred an interest in the intellectual property or merely assigned the right to collect income from the book? See Moore v. Commissioner, T.C. Memo 1968-110 (holding that assignment of income applies and the income is taxable to the professor). Would the result differ if the taxpayer had retained the copyright to his textbook and transferred the copyright to the children along with the right to future royalties? See Rev. Rul. 71-33, 1971-1 C.B. 30 (holding taxpayer was not required to include royalties in gross income because the entire property was transferred). Consider the following cases, one of which required the Supreme Court to resolve a long-standing and messy conflict among the circuits on precisely this issue.

MEISNER v. UNITED STATES
133 F.3d 654 (8th Cir. 1998)

HANSEN, CIRCUIT JUDGE.

Jennifer Meisner was married to Randall Meisner from 1963 to 1981. Randall held certain pieces of intellectual property, consisting of licenses and copyrights related to songs performed by the Eagles, a singing group to which he at one time belonged. In 1978, Randall entered into a termination agreement with the Eagles. In this agreement, Randall ceded all of this intellectual property to the Eagles in return for a royalties contract entitling him to a portion of proceeds from the sales of certain of the Eagles' recordings. He has not been a shareholder, director, or member of the Eagles since that time.

In 1981, the Meisners divorced. At divorce, the couple entered into a property settlement agreement (PSA), pursuant to which Jennifer acquired an undivided forty percent interest in the royalty contract . . .

. . . [T]he PSA clarifies that the rights ceded to Jennifer include royalties, and provides, inter alia, that Jennifer's rights to an undivided forty percent interest in the royalty contract was not subject to any reversionary or contingent interests, but would survive her own death as well as that of her ex-husband. It also provides that Jennifer's 40 percent would be paid directly from the Eagles to Jennifer . . .

Jennifer has received royalties consistent with her forty percent interest every year since 1982. In 1994, she requested a refund of the federal income taxes she had paid on these royalties, claiming that the royalties were properly taxable to her ex-husband rather than to her. A jury trial was held regarding her claims for 1987, 1988, 1990, and 1993. . . . The jury found that Randall had not exerted power or control over Jennifer's rights — a verdict for the government. Jennifer appeals . . .

When a taxpayer is firmly entitled to receive income but anticipatorily assigns this income to another, the donor will be taxed on it just as though he had actually received it. See Harrison v. Schaffner, 312 U.S. 579, 580 (1941) (taxing assignor on assigned income); see also Greene v. United States, 13 F.3d 577, 581–82 (2d Cir.1994) (discussion). This is true even if the income will not accrue until some future date. See Helvering v. Horst, 311 U.S. 112 (1940) (assignment of bond coupons constituted anticipatory assignment). However, if the taxpayer instead assigns an income-producing asset, the result is different. All income that is thereafter produced by the asset is taxed to the assignee. This distinction between income and income-producing assets is generally discussed in terms of "fruits" and "trees," and the rule is that fruits may not, for tax purposes, be attributed "to a different tree from that on which they grew." Lucas v. Earl, 281 U.S. 111, 115 (1930).

The district court rightly determined that this case . . . turns on the amount of "power and control" retained by Randall after the transfer.

Our review of the record reveals no evidence of retained control by Randall. Randall unconditionally assigned Jennifer an undivided forty percent interest. He carved out no reversionary interest for either himself or his estate and retained no direct or indirect ability to affect the value of the rights transferred. Nor did he retain power over Jennifer's receipt of royalty payments — the checks did not come through him, but went directly to Jennifer. In short, the relevant facts here are much more similar to those at issue in Reece, 233 F.2d at 34–35 (finding no anticipatory assignment where taxpayer unconditionally assigned royalty rights to wife), and Greene, 13 F.3d at 582 (finding no anticipatory assignment where donor retained no control over the donated asset's ability to produce income), than they are to the facts in . . . Caruth, 865 F.2d at 648–49 (5th Cir.1989) (finding anticipatory assignment because donor carved out only a short-term interest for donee and retained a reversionary interest) . . .

Accordingly, we affirm the judgment of the district court.

COMMISSIONER v BANKS
543 U.S. 426 (2005)

Justice Kennedy delivered the opinion of the Court.

The question in these consolidated cases is whether the portion of a money judgment or settlement paid to a plaintiff's attorney under a contingent-fee agreement is income to the plaintiff under the Internal Revenue Code. The issue divides the courts of appeals. In one of the instant cases . . . the Court of Appeals for the Sixth Circuit held the contingent-fee portion of a litigation recovery is not included in the plaintiff's gross income. The Courts of Appeals for the Fifth and Eleventh Circuits also adhere to this view. . . . In the other case under review . . . the Court of Appeals for the Ninth Circuit held that the portion of the recovery paid to the attorney as a contingent fee is excluded from the plaintiff's gross income if state law gives the plaintiff's attorney a special property interest in the fee, but not otherwise. Six Courts of Appeals have held the entire litigation recovery, including the portion paid to an attorney as a contingent fee, is income to the plaintiff. Some of these Courts of Appeals discuss state law, but little of their analysis appears to turn on this factor. Other Courts of Appeals have been explicit that the fee portion of the recovery is always income to the plaintiff regardless of the nuances of state law.

We hold that, as a general rule, when a litigant's recovery constitutes income, the litigant's income includes the portion of the recovery paid to the attorney as a contingent fee. We reverse the decisions of the Courts of Appeals for the Sixth and Ninth Circuits.

I

* * *

B.   COMMISSIONER V. BANAITIS[1]

After leaving his job as a vice president and loan officer at the Bank of California in 1987, Sigitas J. Banaitis retained an attorney on a contingent-fee basis and brought suit in Oregon state court against the Bank of California and its successor in ownership, the Mitsubishi Bank. . . . After resolution of all appeals and post-trial motions, the parties settled. The defendants paid $4,864,547 to Banaitis; and, following the formula set forth in the contingent-fee contract, the defendants paid an additional $3,864,012 directly to Banaitis' attorney.

Banaitis did not include the amount paid to his attorney in gross income on his federal income tax return, and the Commissioner issued a notice of deficiency. The Tax Court upheld the Commissioner's determination, but the Court of Appeals for the Ninth Circuit reversed. In contrast to the Court of Appeals for the Sixth Circuit, the Banaitis court viewed state law as pivotal. Where state law confers on the attorney no special property rights in his fee, the court said, the whole amount of the judgment or settlement ordinarily is included in the plaintiff's gross income. Oregon state law, however, like the law of some other States, grants attorneys a superior lien in the contingent-fee portion of any recovery. As a result, the court held, contingent-fee agreements under Oregon law operate not as an anticipatory assignment of the client's income but as a partial transfer to the attorney of some of the client's property in the lawsuit.

* * *

III

The Internal Revenue Code defines "gross income" for federal tax purposes as "all income from whatever source derived." 26 U.S.C. §61(a). The definition extends broadly to all economic gains not otherwise exempted. Commissioner v. Glenshaw Glass Co., 348 U.S. 426, 429-430 (1955). . . . A taxpayer cannot exclude an economic gain from gross income by assigning the gain in advance to another party. Lucas v. Earl, 281 U.S. 111, (1930). . . . The rationale for the so-called anticipatory assignment of income doctrine is the principle that gains should be taxed "to those who earned them,". . . a maxim we have called "the first principle of

---

1. The Supreme Court consolidated two cases, Commissioner v. Banks and Commissioner v. Banaitis, under the case heading Commissioner v. Banks. The specific issue in Banks partially turned on a Title VII statutory fee-shifting rule and the resolution to that issue did not impact the assignment of income analysis. Accordingly, the facts and analysis specific to Banks have been removed. Eds.

income taxation[.]" The anticipatory assignment doctrine is meant to prevent tax-payers from avoiding taxation through "arrangements and contracts however skill-fully devised to prevent [income] when paid from vesting even for a second in the man who earned it." Lucas, 281 U.S., at 115. The rule is preventative and motivated by administrative as well as substantive concerns, so we do not inquire whether any particular assignment has a discernible tax avoidance purpose. As Lucas explained, "no distinction can be taken according to the motives leading to the arrangement by which the fruits are attributed to a different tree from that on which they grew." Ibid.

Respondents argue that the anticipatory assignment doctrine is a judge-made antifraud rule with no relevance to contingent-fee contracts of the sort at issue here. The Commissioner maintains that a contingent-fee agreement should be viewed as an anticipatory assignment to the attorney of a portion of the client's income from any litigation recovery. We agree with the Commissioner.

In an ordinary case attribution of income is resolved by asking whether a tax-payer exercises complete dominion over the income in question. In the context of anticipatory assignments, however, the assignor often does not have dominion over the income at the moment of receipt. In that instance the question becomes whether the assignor retains dominion over the income-generating asset, because the tax-payer "who owns or controls the source of the income, also controls the disposition of that which he could have received himself and diverts the payment from himself to others as the means of procuring the satisfaction of his wants." Looking to control over the income-generating asset, then, preserves the principle that income should be taxed to the party who earns the income and enjoys the consequent benefits.

In the case of a litigation recovery the income-generating asset is the cause of action that derives from the plaintiff's legal injury. The plaintiff retains dominion over this asset throughout the litigation. We do not understand respondents to argue otherwise. Rather, respondents advance two counterarguments. First, they say that . . . the value of a legal claim is speculative at the moment of assignment, and may be worth nothing at all. Second, respondents insist that the claimant's legal injury is not the only source of the ultimate recovery. The attorney, according to respondents, also contributes income-generating assets-effort and expertise-without which the claimant likely could not prevail. On these premises respondents urge us to treat a contingent-fee agreement as establishing, for tax purposes, some-thing like a joint venture or partnership in which the client and attorney combine their respective assets — the client's claim and the attorney's skill — and apportion any resulting profits.

We reject respondents' arguments. Though the value of the plaintiff's claim may be speculative at the moment the fee agreement is signed, the anticipatory assignment doctrine is not limited to instances when the precise dollar value of the assigned income is known in advance. . . . That the amount of income the asset would produce was uncertain at the moment of assignment is of no consequence.

We further reject the suggestion to treat the attorney-client relationship as a sort of business partnership or joint venture for tax purposes. The relationship between client and attorney, regardless of the variations in particular compensa-tion agreements or the amount of skill and effort the attorney contributes, is a quintessential principal-agent relationship. The client may rely on the attorney's expertise and special skills to achieve a result the client could not achieve alone.

That, however, is true of most principal-agent relationships, and it does not alter the fact that the client retains ultimate dominion and control over the underlying claim. The control is evident when it is noted that, although the attorney can make tactical decisions without consulting the client, the plaintiff still must determine whether to settle or proceed to judgment and make, as well, other critical decisions. Even where the attorney exercises independent judgment without supervision by, or consultation with, the client, the attorney, as an agent, is obligated to act solely on behalf of, and for the exclusive benefit of, the client-principal, rather than for the benefit of the attorney or any other party.

The attorney is an agent who is dutybound to act only in the interests of the principal, and so it is appropriate to treat the full amount of the recovery as income to the principal. . . . The portion paid to the agent may be deductible, but absent some other provision of law it is not excludable from the principal's gross income.

This rule applies whether or not the attorney-client contract or state law confers any special rights or protections on the attorney, so long as these protections do not alter the fundamental principal-agent character of the relationship. . . .

For the reasons stated, the judgments of the Courts of Appeals for the Sixth and Ninth Circuits are reversed, and the cases are remanded for further proceedings consistent with this opinion.

4.   *Substance versus Form Analysis*

At times, it can be difficult to determine what happened in a particular case, let alone what its tax treatment should be. Often, this is particularly apparent in assignment of income cases. The courts have developed a doctrine of "substance over form" to attempt to address these situations. Pursuant to this doctrine, courts look to the true economic substance of the transactions rather than the nominal events themselves. For example, what results if a taxpayer owns the right to collect future income and then sells that right to a third party? The courts addressing this issue have generally held that if the taxpayer sold all rights to the income before it was collected, the taxpayer is not taxable on the income collected subsequently. See, e.g., Schering-Plough Corp. v. United States, 651 F.Supp.2d 219 (D.N.J. 2009); Estate of Stranahan v. Commissioner, 472 F.2d 867 (6th Cir. 1973).

By contrast, when a taxpayer has agreed to sell property and then attempts to transfer the property prior to the closing of the sale solely to avoid being taxed on the gain, courts have been less sympathetic. For example, in Salvatore v. Commissioner, T.C. Memo 1970-30, after contracting to sell property but before the sale was completed, the taxpayer conveyed a one-half interest in the property to her children. The court held that, although the taxpayer's transfer to her children was in form a gift of property, in substance it constituted an anticipatory assignment of one-half of the *income* from the sale of the property and not a transfer of property.

If the transfer to the children in *Salvatore* had occurred *prior* to the execution of the contract, would the result have differed? In assessing questions of this nature, courts consider the substance, not the form, of control over the property by the transferee and other indicia that the ownership of the property has, in fact, been transferred. The following case considers these issues.

FERGUSON v. COMMISSIONER
174 F.3d 997 (9th Cir. 1999)

CHOY, CIRCUIT JUDGE

. . . The primary issue before us is whether the Tax Court correctly held that by the date that the transfer was completed, the stock already had ripened from an interest in a viable corporation into a fixed right to receive cash via an ongoing tender offer or a pending merger agreement such that despite the transfer of the stock, the gain in the appreciated stock was taxable to the Fergusons under the anticipatory assignment of income doctrine. For the following reasons, we affirm the decision of the Tax Court.

FACTUAL AND PROCEDURAL BACKGROUND

On April 1, 1985, American Health Companies, Inc. ("AHC"), a Delaware corporation, acquired Diet Center, Inc. ("DC"), an Idaho corporation, which was wholly owned and managed by petitioners Roger and Sybil Ferguson and their five children, including petitioner Michael Ferguson, who files tax returns jointly with his wife, petitioner Valene Ferguson. Through franchises still operating under the name of DC, AHC marketed weight loss and diet counseling services and a variety of vitamins, minerals, and food products. . . .

In late 1987 and early 1988, Goldman, Sachs & Co. was contacted and eventually was authorized by the board of directors to find a purchaser of AHC and to assist in the negotiations. By July 22, 1988, Goldman, Sachs & Co. had found four prospective purchasers.

On July 28, 1988, AHC entered into a merger agreement with CDI Holding, Inc. ("CDI"). . . . The merger agreement provided that: (1) [CDI] would purchase the majority of the AHC stock through a tender offer at $22.50 per share; (2) [a subsidiary of CDI] would merge into AHC, leaving AHC as a wholly owned subsidiary of CDI; and (3) as permitted under Delaware corporate law, concurrently with the merger, each still-outstanding share of AHC stock would be converted into a fixed right to receive $22.50 in cash. As stated in the terms of the tender offer, one of the purposes of the tender offer was to acquire, prior to the merger itself, 90% or more of the outstanding AHC stock.

. . . Importantly, the tender offer, and hence the merger agreement, was conditioned on the acquisition by [CDI] of at least 85% of the outstanding shares of AHC by the expiration date of the tender offer, which originally was set at August 30, 1988. However, this minimum tender condition was waivable at the sole discretion of [CDI]. . . .

. . . On August 3, 1988, the tender offer was started. . . . Importantly, the expiration date for the tender offer, originally set for August 30, 1988, was extended to September 9, 1988, as a result of a fire that completely destroyed AHC's product manufacturing plant on August 25, 1988.

On the final day of the tender offer, the Fergusons exchanged a significant amount of their AHC stock for CDI common and preferred stock, and they tendered the remainder of their AHC stock pursuant to the tender offer.

On September 12, 1988, [CDI] announced its acceptance of all tendered or guaranteed AHC shares. The next day, [CDI] purchased all of the shares in accordance with the stated terms of the tender offer.

2. THE TRANSFER OF THE AHC STOCK FROM THE FERGUSONS TO THE CHARITIES

While the aforementioned events were occurring, the Fergusons transferred some of their AHC stock to three charitable organizations ("Charities"). . . .

To obtain assistance in making their intended donations, the Fergusons contacted [a stock broker]. On August 15, 1988, with the [broker's] assistance, Michael Ferguson executed a donation-in-kind record with respect to his intention to donate 30,000 shares of AHC. . . . Then, on August 16, 1988, Roger and Sybil Ferguson executed a donation-in-kind record with respect to 31,111 shares of AHC that they intended to donate. . . . These documents were not signed by all of the Fergusons because they were intended merely to be notification . . . of the Fergusons' intention to donate their shares rather than any sort of legally binding document.

Of particular significance, the original handwritten date in a printed box entitled "date of donation" in the [donation] documents, had been completely scratched out, and the date "9-9-88" had been written next to the scratched-out date. . . . The "date of donation" date was supposed to be the date when the Charities finally had instructed [the Fergusons] to do something with the AHC stock rather than the date when the Fergusons actually had donated the stock to the Charities.

On August 15, 1988, and on August 21, 1988, respectively, [the stock broker] allegedly assisted Michael Ferguson, and then Roger and Sybil Ferguson, with executing signed letters of authorization. . . . According to [the stock broker's] testimony before the Tax Court, these original letters were destroyed by him after they had been replaced by a final set of letters because he had made handwritten notes on the original letters and because changes had been made to the amount of stock that the Fergusons would be exchanging with CDI. . . . At this point, if, as alleged, the letters of authorization actually had been signed and finally executed, then [the stock broker] would have considered the AHC stock to be the property of the Charities.

. . . On September 9, 1988, the Fergusons executed final letters of authorization that permitted the transfers [to the Charities]. . . . AHC then forwarded to the Securities and Exchange Commission, a disclosure form dated October 5, 1988, which indicated that a change in the beneficial ownership of the AHC stock had occurred on September 9, 1988. . . .

DISCUSSION AND ANALYSIS

1. COMPLETION OF THE CONTRIBUTIONS . . .

. . . The key issue here is whether the Fergusons had completed their contributions of the appreciated AHC stock before it had ripened from an interest in a viable corporation into a fixed right to receive cash. If the Fergusons had done so, then they cannot be taxed on the gain realized when the stock ripened; if they had not, then they can. Because the evidence in the record and the applicable law support the conclusion that the Fergusons' contributions were not completed until after the appreciated AHC stock had ripened, we affirm the Tax Court's decision.

. . . The Fergusons make two contentions. . . . First, they contend that the date of delivery directly to the Charities . . . was the date that [the stock broker] made the in-house journal entries on [their] computers: September 8, 1988. Second, they contend alternatively (and preferably for them) that [the stock broker] was acting as the Charities' agent . . . and that the dates of delivery to the Charities' agent therefore were the dates that the Fergusons purportedly executed the alleged original letters of authorization: August 15, 1988 . . . [and] August 21, 1988. . . .

However, the evidence in the record does not support any of the Fergusons' contentions but instead supports a finding that the Fergusons' contributions were not completed until September 9, 1988, the date that they executed their final letters of authorization.

2.   THE RIPENING OF THE AHC STOCK

Under the anticipatory assignment of income doctrine, once a right to receive income has "ripened" for tax purposes, the taxpayer who earned or otherwise created that right will be taxed on any gain realized from it, notwithstanding the fact that the taxpayer has transferred the right before actually receiving the income.

While the Ninth Circuit has not addressed the issue of "ripening" yet, several other courts (both tax and appellate) have considered the issue. . . . In light of the soundness of their reasoning and that of the Tax Court in the present case, we now adopt the doctrine as followed by those courts.

To determine whether a right has "ripened" for tax purposes, a court must consider the realities and substance of events to determine whether the receipt of income was practically certain to occur (i.e., whether the right basically had become a fixed right). While the finding of a mere anticipation or expectation of the receipt of income has been deemed insufficient to conclude that a fixed right to income existed, courts also have made it quite clear that the overall determination must not be based on a consideration of mere formalities and remote hypothetical possibilities.

In the present case, the Tax Court determined that the realities and substance of the ongoing tender offer and the pending merger agreement indicated that the AHC stock already had ripened from an interest in a viable corporation into a fixed right to receive cash, by August 31, 1988 — the first date by which over 50% of the AHC share had been tendered. To wit, the Tax Court determined that by August 31, 1988, it was practically certain that the tender offer and the merger would be completed successfully and that all AHC stock, even un-tendered stock, either already had been converted into cash (via the tender offer) or imminently would be converted into cash (via the merger).

The Fergusons contend that until September 12, 1988, the date when [CDI] formally announced its acceptance of over 95% of the outstanding AHC shares, the tender offer and the merger still could have been derailed and their AHC stock thus had not ripened. However, in support of their many contentions, the Fergusons raise only possibilities that the Tax Court correctly considered to be remote and hypothetical and therefore irrelevant.

Turning to the Fergusons' individual contentions, we find them to be unpersuasive. First, the Fergusons correctly point out that in the majority of the anticipatory assignment of income cases, some kind of formal shareholder vote (approving a merger, liquidation, or distribution) already had occurred by the time that the stock was deemed to have ripened. However, the language of these cases does not suggest that such formalities are a prerequisite of finding that a ripening has occurred. Indeed, the language of these cases only indicates that such formalities are sufficient, not that they are necessary.

Second, the Fergusons contend that prior to [CDI's] acceptance of the tendered stock on September 12, 1988, either of two occurrences might have blocked the successful completion of the tender offer and the merger: (1) the Fergusons, the Charities, or the other shareholders might have withdrawn their tendered shares or simply not tendered their shares; or (2) [CDI] might have decided not to accept the tendered stock because the minimum tender condition had not been met yet and because the material change condition had not been waived yet. However, by August 31, 1988, the surrounding circumstances indicate that it was quite unlikely that any of the relevant parties would back out of the tender offer or the merger, and it also was quite unlikely that the requisite number of shares would not be tendered by the close of the tender offer window. As discussed previously, by August 31, 1988, the tender offer already had gained a great deal of momentum. Moreover, all of the relevant parties seemed to be getting what they wanted. The Fergusons were receiving a fair amount of cash, generous stock incentives, and assurances that they would continue to play major active roles in the management of their business. CDI . . . was receiving a very successful business. . . . Therefore, since the clearly stated intentions and expectations of all of the relevant parties, and the surrounding circumstances as of August 31, 1988, suggest that the receipt of cash (as either tender offer or merger proceeds) was practically certain to occur, the Fergusons' AHC stock had ripened by that date. . . .

On a final note, the Fergusons raise two policy considerations, but these considerations do not support their contentions. First, the Fergusons rightly point out that there is a distinction between tax evasion (i.e., choosing an impermissible path) and tax avoidance (i.e., choosing the least costly permissible path) and that so long as they are acting in accordance with the existing tax laws, the motives for their actions should not dictate the consequences of their actions. However, simply because the Fergusons have the right to choose the least costly path (from a tax perspective) upon which to walk, they do not have the right to be free from taxation if they decide to walk the line between what is and what is not permissible, and happen to stray across it, as they have here. Second, the Fergusons note that the logic of the Tax Court's decision implies that their AHC stock already might have ripened by some date even earlier than August 31, 1988. In essence, they note that there is no clear line demarcating the first date upon which a taxpayer's appreciated stock has ripened into a fixed right to receive cash pursuant to a pending merger. However, from the perspective of taxpayers, walking the line between tax evasion and tax avoidance seems to be a patently dangerous business. Any tax lawyer worth his fees would not have recommended that a donor make a gift of appreciated stock this close to an ongoing tender offer and a pending merger, especially when they were negotiated and planned by the donor. Therefore, we will not go out of our way to make this dangerous business any easier for taxpayers who knowingly assume its risks. Moreover, from the perspective of judging such cases, there is no special reason that we should curtail the application of this doctrine simply because it requires "engaging in an exercise in line drawing, a difficult task which nevertheless is part of the daily grist of judicial life."

Conclusion

Thus, because the Fergusons' contributions of their AHC stock were not completed until September 9, 1988 — at least nine days after the stock had ripened — we affirm the Tax Court's decision holding the Fergusons taxable on the gain in the appreciated stock.

5. Dividends on Stock

The *Salvatore* and *Ferguson* decisions consider whether the right to receive future income that is accruing on transferred property has matured prior to the transfer of that property. In *Salvatore*, the property transfer was too late to shift the income since the transferor's right to the payment from the sale of property had matured at the time that she entered into the contract to sell. Similarly, *Ferguson* considered whether the fruit "had ripened" before the donation to the charities — that is, whether the right to income produced by the transferred property had matured prior to the transfer of the property. Conversely, if the right to payment for a sale of stock has not ripened prior to the making of a gift of such stock, evidence of the mere intent of the donor to sell the stock prior to making the gift (such as a tender offer or a nonbinding sales agreement) will not necessarily cause the assignment of income doctrine to apply. See Rauenhorst v. Commissioner, 119 T.C. 157 (2002).

The concept of ripeness is particularly relevant in the sale or gift of stock. As explained in Regulation §1.61-9(c), the issue of who is taxed on dividend income received after the transfer of stock is a matter of timing. The Regulation focuses on three dates: (1) the date of the declaration of the dividend; (2) the record date, the date that determines which shareholders are eligible to receive the dividend; and (3) the date of the transfer of the stock. The interaction of these dates determines to whom the dividends on transferred stock will be taxed. If stock is transferred prior to the date on which a dividend is declared, any dividend payable after the date of transfer is taxed to the transferee. If stock is transferred after declaration of a dividend but before the record date, then the dividend is the transferee's income. If, however, the stock is transferred after the record date, the dividend income has matured (ripened) prior to the transfer, and the dividend income is taxable to the transferor, regardless of who receives it.

As illustrated by the following example, a stockholder can shift dividend income by properly timing the stock transfer. Assume that ABC, Inc. declares a dividend on June 1 to shareholders of record on July 1. The dividend is payable on

August 1. Jerry Roberts, a holder of stock in ABC, Inc., transfers his stock to his 15-year-old daughter, Mary, on June 15. Because the transfer occurs prior to the record date, Jerry has shifted the dividend income to Mary. If, however, the transfer does not take place until July 15, the dividend is too ripe to transfer, and Jerry must include it in his gross income.

6. Statutory Response: The "Kiddie" Tax

Notwithstanding complexities at the margins, the common law assignment of income doctrine permits well-advised taxpayers to use properly structured gifts as a means to shift future interest, dividend, and similar income to their children in lower tax brackets. This tactic has become increasingly popular, especially as parents continue to save for the college and higher education costs of their children at an earlier age. For example, rather than investing in stocks or bonds with the intent to use the income from such investment to pay for a child's college tuition, parents could purchase the same stocks or bonds and then give them to the child as a gift at an early age. As a result, the future interest and dividend income would be subject to the child's lower tax rates. From an economic standpoint, however, the parents would be indifferent because the money was intended for the use of the child's education under either approach. The enactment of §1(g) in 1986 severely curtailed the ability of taxpayers to use the low tax brackets of their children to reduce the family's overall tax liability. The Senate Finance Committee Report documents that Congress believed that prior law created an inappropriate tax reduction opportunity:

> The committee believes that the present law rules governing the taxation of minor children provide inappropriate tax incentives to shift income-producing assets among family members. In particular, the committee is aware that the treatment of a child as a separate taxpayer encourages parents whose income would otherwise be taxed at a high marginal rate bracket to transfer income-producing property to a child to ensure that the income is taxed at the child's lower marginal rates. In order to reduce the opportunities for tax avoidance through intrafamily transfers of income producing property, the committee concluded that it is generally appropriate to tax the income on property transferred from a parent to a minor child at the parent's marginal rates.

S. Rep. No. 313, 99th Cong., 2d Sess. 862 (1986).

The act significantly limits the effectiveness of income splitting among family members. The "kiddie tax" (as §1(g) has become generally known) is aimed at the shifting of certain passive income, such as interest and dividends, to children through the use of gifts of income-producing property. For this reason, the kiddie tax applies only to the "net unearned income" of a child — generally types of passive income such as interest, dividends, rents, and similar income — above a statutory threshold amount.

Although enacted to address a type of assignment of income problem, the mechanics of the kiddie tax depart from those under general assignment of income principles. Rather than treating the child's unearned income (the fruit) as income of the parent (the tree), as would be the case under the assignment of income doctrine, the kiddie tax treats such unearned income as the child's income but applies a tax rate equal to the *greater* of the child's marginal tax rate or the parent's marginal tax rate. Other income of the child (for example, income earned through a part-time job) is unaffected by the kiddie tax and thus is subject to tax at the child's marginal tax rate.

The scope of the kiddie tax is both incredibly broad and surprisingly narrow. For example, because the kiddie tax applies to all of a child's unearned income, and not just that income generated from assets gifted by the child's parents, a child may be subject to the kiddie tax if, for example, the child received substantial gifts of income-producing property from people other than his parents (such as grandparents), or if he earned his own money (such as from a part-time job) and then invested it in income-producing assets. As a result, the kiddie tax has the ignominy of simultaneously failing to eliminate the types of transactions it was enacted to prevent while adversely affecting many more taxpayers than originally intended.

The kiddie tax generally applies to children under the age of 18, and, since it is intended to prevent the shifting of income from a parent to a child, at least one of the child's parents must still be living. As originally enacted, however, the kiddie tax applied only to children under the age of 14, under the assumption that such children generally owned few investment assets purchased with their own earned income. Congress raised the threshold age from 14 to 18 in 2006, and in 2007 Congress further expanded the kiddie tax by applying it, in certain circumstances, to full-time students older than 18 but younger than 24. With these increases in the applicable age, the reach of the kiddie tax has grown substantially. As a result, it has become increasingly relevant to taxpayers as more children work and save during high school or college to pay for their own higher education.

Problems

4-5. Martin Lake owns 100 shares of IBM stock with a market value of $100 per share. The stock was purchased by Lake three years ago for $20 per share. On November 1, IBM declared a $5 per share dividend payable on December 20 to shareholders of record on November 15.

  a. What result to Lake if, on October 1, Lake retained the stock and transferred to Karla, his 15-year-old daughter, the right to receive the current year's dividend? What if instead Karla received the right to the dividend for as long as Lake owns the stock?

  b. What result to Karla in *a* when Karla receives the $500 dividend on December 20?

  c. What result to Lake if, on October 1, Lake gave to Karla all 100 shares, including the right to all future dividends of the 100 shares?

  d. What result to Karla in *c* when Karla receives the $500 dividend on December 20?

  e. What result if the transfer to Karla in *c* took place on November 20?

  f. What result if, on October 1, Lake gave to Karla ten shares, and the right to all future dividends on his remaining ninety shares?

  g. What result if, on October 1, Lake gave to Karla 100 shares as a gift for a period of five years, at the end of which the shares are to be returned to Lake?

    h.   What result if, on October 1, Lake gave all 100 shares of stock to Karla, and Karla sold the stock on October 2 for $100 per share?

    i.   Assume the same facts as *h* except that on September 30 Lake had signed a contract with the buyer for Karla's sale of October 2. What if Lake had not signed a contract but had negotiated the ultimate terms of the October 2 sale?

    j.   What result if, on October 1, Lake sold to Karla the right to two years' dividends (totaling $10,000), in return for $8,000?

    k.   What result in *j* if Karla paid $500 for the right to the dividends?

4-6. Theodore Armstrong has recently completed and copyrighted a book on federal income taxation.

    a.   Assume that Armstrong transferred his rights in the book, including the copyright, to a publisher in return for annual royalties of 20 percent of net sales. What result if Armstrong then assigns his right to those royalties to his 15-year-old child?

    b.   Assume that Armstrong transferred to the publisher the right to print and sell the book in return for stated royalties but Armstrong retained the copyright. What result if Armstrong then assigns his copyright and the right to royalties to his child?

    c.   What result in *b* if Armstrong's transfer of the copyright to his child took place near the end of the first year of the agreement, one month before the first year's royalties were to be calculated and paid?

    d.   Assume the same facts as *b* except that Armstrong retained the copyright and only transferred the right to the royalties to his child. What result? What result if he transferred the copyright to his wife and transferred the right to royalties to his children?

    e.   Assume that, prior to negotiations with the publisher, Armstrong assigned all of his rights in the book, including the copyright, to his child. What result if Armstrong and his child then enter into a contract with the publisher specifying that the child receive the royalties in exchange for the copyright to the book?

    f.   Assume that Armstrong transferred his copyright to the publisher but retained the exclusive right to prepare supplements when and if he deems it appropriate, plus the right to terminate the agreement with the publisher at the end of five years if he does not wish to write a second edition. What result if Armstrong then transfers his royalty and contractual rights to his child?

    g.   What result in *a* if instead of giving the right to royalties to his child, Armstrong sold those rights to his child for $1? What if he sold the right to royalties to his child for $1,000?

C. BELOW-MARKET AND INTEREST-FREE LOANS

1. Interest-free Loans as an Income-shifting Device

Notwithstanding the detailed and repeated application of the assignment of income doctrine by courts, there was one area where taxpayers were able to assign income among related parties with relative ease and the courts consistently respected the form, rather than the substance, of the transaction: below-market loans. For instance, assume a parent desired to make a gift to a child from the income generated by a $100,000 corporate bond paying simple interest of 10 percent (meaning the bond would pay $10,000 a year in interest to the parent). If the parent were in the 40-percent marginal tax bracket, the parent would owe $4,000 in tax on the interest income, leaving $6,000 to give to the child as a gift. Instead, assume that the parent loans all $100,000 to the child interest-free, and the child invests the $100,000 in the same corporate bond. The child would receive $10,000 per year in interest and, assuming the child were in the 10-percent marginal tax bracket, the child would owe $1,000 in taxes on the interest, leaving $9,000 for the child. Thus, the family would save $3,000 in after-tax dollars. Despite the similarity with the assignment of income doctrine's application to property (where a property owner who assigns the income from his or her property to another must continue to pay tax on that income unless the owner's interest in the property is also conveyed), the interest income on the loaned funds was not deemed to have been earned by the parent.

In addition to using interest-free loans to shift interest income to lower-bracket family members, interest-free loans were also employed as a means of using untaxed interest income to satisfy pecuniary obligations. If an employer owed an employee $10,000 for past services, the employer could pay the amount owed to the employee by means of an interest-free loan to the employee. For example, the employer could make an interest-free, one-year loan of $100,000 to the employee. The employee would invest the principal at, for instance, a 10-percent rate of interest. The employee would retain the $10,000 interest earned on the invested loan funds as payment for his or her services and repay the $100,000 loan principal to the employer. Thus, the employer would appear to have avoided tax on the $10,000 interest earned by the loaned funds.

The argument that the employer/employee variation of the interest-free loan scheme did not violate tax policy rested on the notion that the employer's overall tax effect was a wash. Had the employer kept the $100,000 principal, earned the $10,000 of interest income, and then paid $10,000 to the employee, the employer would have $10,000 of interest income and an offsetting $10,000 business expense deduction for the payment of compensation. It is important to note, however, that the wash transaction rationale would not apply if payment for the compensated services was not a deductible expense. See §262. For example, if the interest-free borrower rendering the services were the lender's personal gardener, then the interest-free loan clearly shifted income from the lender to the gardener and allowed the lender to satisfy a nondeductible obligation with untaxed income. Thus, despite the employer/employee relationship, a circumvention of the assignment of income principles occurred.

This form-driven tax treatment of below-market interest rate loans is usually traced to J. Simpson Dean v. Commissioner, 35 T.C. 1083 (1961). In *Dean*, the court held that the amount that the borrowers would have had to pay in interest had they not received an interest-free loan was not income to the borrowers. The court refused to impute interest on the loan, reasoning that if the borrowers had been required to make an interest payment, it would have been fully deductible, thus resulting in a tax wash. The court did not consider whether the borrower might have invested the interest-free loan and generated interest income or to whom to attribute such interest income if there were such an investment. Furthermore, after the enactment of §163(h), personal interest is no longer deductible.

Because the treatment of below-market interest rate loans was often inconsistent with the assignment of income principles, Congress enacted §7872 to prevent assignment of income through such devices. The following legislative history describes the reasons for the enactment of these provisions as well as their intended application.

JOINT COMMITTEE ON TAXATION, EXPLANATION OF THE TAX REFORM ACT OF 1984
524-538 (1985)

BELOW-MARKET AND INTEREST-FREE LOANS

PRIOR LAW

Transfers of Income Other than by Interest-free or Below-market Interest Rate Loans

Direct assignments of income. —Investment income is generally taxed to the owner of the income producing property, even if the owner of the property makes a gift of the right to receive the income prior to its receipt. The rationale for this rule is that the owner of the property realizes the income upon the exercise of control over its disposition. Helvering v. Horst, 311 U.S. 112 (1940). Further, an assignment of the right to receive income is a taxable gift by the assignor to the assignee which occurs at the time of the assignment. In such case, the amount of the gift is the value of the right received by the donee.

For example, if a cash method taxpayer detaches coupons from a bond and gives them to his or her son, without receiving fair value in exchange, and the son receives the interest represented by the coupons, the interest income would be included in income by the parent donor under the principles of *Horst*. . . .

Demand or Term Loans to Family Members

Under prior law, an interest-free or below-market interest rate loan (each of which is referred to herein as a "below-market loan") without consideration resulted in a gift from the lender to the borrower for Federal tax purposes. Dickman v. Commissioner, 465 U.S. 330 (1984). In the case of a demand loan, the amount of the gift was the value of the right to the use of the money for "such portion of the year as the [lender] in fact allows the [borrower] the use of the money." Rev. Rul. 73-61, 1973-2 C.B. 408. Under this approach, the amount of the gift was calculable as of the last day of each calendar year during which the loan was outstanding.

In the case of a term loan, the amount of the gift was the excess, at the time of the exchange of the money and the note, of the amount of money borrowed over the present value of the principal and interest payments required to be made under the terms of the loan.

Under prior law, the Federal income tax consequences of these below-market loans were not clear. Prior to enactment of the provision, the courts had addressed only the gift tax consequences of the transactions.

Loans to Employees or Shareholders

Demand loans. —Under prior law, the Internal Revenue Service consistently asserted that, in the case of a below-market demand loan to an employee or shareholder (other than a loan to which section 482 applied), the borrower derived an economic benefit that should be included in income for Federal income tax purposes. Under the Service's position, the amount of the income was the excess of the interest that would have been charged by an independent lender over the interest, if any, that was actually charged under the terms of the loan.

Notwithstanding the Internal Revenue Service's position, the Tax Court consistently held that non-family below-market demand loans did not result in taxable income. In J. Simpson Dean v. Commissioner, 35 T.C. 1083 (1961), for example, the controlling shareholder of Nemours Corporation borrowed substantial sums of money from the corporation on a non-interest bearing basis. The Internal Revenue Service sought to impute interest income to the borrowers. The Tax Court, however, held that the transactions did not result in income to the borrowers on the grounds that had they "borrowed the funds in question on interest bearing notes, their payment of interest would have been fully deductible by them under section 163." . . .

REASONS FOR CHANGE

A below-market loan is the economic equivalent of a loan bearing a market rate of interest, and a payment by the lender to the borrower to fund the payment of interest by the borrower. The Congress believed that, in many instances, the failure of the tax laws to treat these transactions in accordance with their economic substance provided taxpayers with opportunities to circumvent well-established tax rules.

Under prior law, loans between family members (and other similar loans) were being used to avoid the assignment of income rules. . . . A below-market loan to a family member, for example, generally involves a gratuitous transfer of the right to use the proceeds of the borrowing until repayment is demanded (in the case of a demand loan) or until the end of the term of the loan (in the case of a term loan). If the lender had assigned the income from the proceeds to the borrower instead of lending the proceeds to the borrower, the assignment of income doctrine would have taxed the lender (and not the borrower) on the income. . . .

Finally, loans to persons providing services were being used to avoid rules requiring the payment of employment taxes and rules restricting the deductibility of interest in certain situations by the person providing the services. A below-market loan to a person providing services is the economic equivalent of a loan requiring the payment of interest at a market rate, and a payment in the nature of compensation equal to the amount of interest required to be paid under the terms of the loan. Under prior law, a transaction structured as a loan and a payment in the nature of compensation often did not result in any tax consequences for either the lender or the borrower because each would have offsetting income and deductions.

However, there were a number of situations in which the payment of compensation and a loan requiring the payment of interest at a market rate did not offset. For example, if a taxpayer used the proceeds of an arm's-length loan to invest in tax-exempt obligations, the deduction for interest paid on the loan would be disallowed under section 265. Similarly, if a term loan extended beyond the taxable year in which it was made, income and deductions did not offset because the compensation income was includible in the year the loan was made. In such circumstances, substantial tax advantages could have been derived by structuring the transaction as a below-market loan.

EXPLANATION OF PROVISION

Overview

The Act adds to the Code new section 7872 (relating to the tax treatment of loans that, in substance, result in a gift, payment of compensation . . . or other similar payment from the lender to the borrower). Loans that are subject to the provision and that do not require payment of interest, or require payment at a rate below the statutory rate (referred to as the "applicable Federal rate"), are recharacterized as an arm's-length transaction in which the lender made a loan to the borrower in exchange for a note requiring the payment of interest at the applicable Federal rate. This rule results in the parties being treated as if:

(1) The borrower paid interest to the lender that may be deductible to the borrower and is included in income by the lender; and

(2) The lender made a gift . . . (in the case of a gratuitous transaction), or . . . paid compensation (in the case of a loan to a person providing services), or made some other payment characterized in accordance with the substance of the transaction.

The Congress intended that, in general, in the case of a loan subject to this provision, the amount of the deemed payment from the lender to the borrower is to be determined solely under this provision. . . . Further, in the case of a loan from an employer to an employee, the amount of the compensation is to be determined under section 7872, and not under section 83, even if the applicable Federal rate is less than a fair market interest rate.

Payments deemed made under this provision are, in general, treated as actually made for all purposes of the Code. . . .

Loans Subject to the Provision

The provision applies to term or demand loans that are gift loans, compensation-related loans . . . and tax avoidance loans. In addition, the Congress intended that, under regulations to be prescribed by the Treasury, the provision is to apply to other similar transactions (i.e., loan transactions that in substance affect a transfer from the lender to the borrower other than the transfer of the principal amount of the loan) if the interest arrangements have a significant effect on the tax liability of either the borrower or the lender.

Generally, it was intended that the term "loan" be interpreted broadly in light of the purposes of the provision. Thus, any transfer of money that provides the transferor with a right to repayment is a loan. For example, advances and deposits of all kinds are treated as loans.

Demand loans and term loans. —A demand loan is any loan which is payable in full at any time upon the demand of the lender. A term loan is any loan which is not a demand loan.

Gift loans. —A gift loan is any below-market loan where the forgone interest is in the nature of a gift. In general, there is a gift if property (including forgone interest) is transferred for less than full and adequate consideration under circumstances where the transfer is a gift for gift tax purposes. A sale, exchange, or other transfer made in the ordinary course of business (i.e., a transaction which is bona fide, at arm's length and free from any donative intent) generally is considered as made for full and adequate consideration. A loan between unrelated persons can qualify as a gift loan. . . .

Compensation-related loans. —A compensation-related loan is any below-market loan made in connection with the performance of services directly or indirectly between (1) an employer and an employee, or (2) an independent contractor and a person for whom such independent contractor provides services.

The Congress intended that an arrangement be treated as a compensation-related loan if, in substance, there is a compensatory element arising from the transaction. Thus, for example, a below-market loan by an employer to a child of an employee generally will be recharacterized under the provision as a compensation-related loan by the employer to the employee and a gift loan by the employee to the child.

The Congress intended that if an employer makes a payment to an unrelated third-party lender to buy-down a mortgage loan for an employee and, taking into account all the facts and circumstances, the transaction is in substance (1) a loan at a market rate by a third-party lender to the employee, and (2) a payment by the employer to secure a valuable benefit for the employee, the payment by the employer to the lender is to be treated as compensation under generally applicable principles of tax law. To that extent, the below-market loan rules do not apply. However, if the transaction is in substance a loan by the employer made with the aid of services provided by the third-party lender acting as an agent of the employer, there is a compensation-related loan subject to this provision.

Also, if an employee receives payment from a customer for services rendered on behalf of an employer, and is permitted to retain the money for a period without paying interest at a rate equal to or greater than the applicable Federal rate, there is generally a compensation-related loan. For example, if an investment banker is permitted by an issuer to retain the proceeds from a public offering of stock or debt for a period without paying interest, there is a below-market loan from the issuer to the banker. To the extent the benefit is in lieu of a fee for services, the loan is a compensation-related loan.

In the case of a compensation-related loan, the deemed payment by the lender to the borrower is treated as wages. . . . Further, unless otherwise provided in regulations, a payment must be included in gross income by the borrower, even if the borrower is likely to be entitled to an offsetting deduction. . . .

Tax avoidance loans. — A below-market loan is a tax-avoidance loan if one of the principal purposes of the interest arrangement is the avoidance of any Federal tax by either the borrower or the lender. Tax avoidance is a principal purpose of the interest arrangement if it is a principal factor in the decision to structure the transaction as a below-market loan, rather than a loan requiring the payment of interest at a rate that equals or exceeds the applicable Federal rate and a payment by the lender to the borrower.

Other below-market loans. — A loan that is not a gift loan, compensation-related loan, corporation-shareholder loan or tax avoidance loan may be subject to these provisions under Treasury regulations if the interest arrangement has a significant effect on the tax liability of the borrower or the lender.

The interest arrangement of a below-market loan has an effect on the tax liability of the borrower or the lender if, among other things, it results in the conversion of a nondeductible expense into the equivalent of a deductible expense. Generally, there is such a conversion when a taxpayer makes a non-interest bearing refundable deposit in partial or total payment of the cost of a nondeductible item or expense. For example, if a member of a club makes a non-interest bearing refundable deposit to the club in lieu of part or all of his or her membership fee, the member is paying the fee with money that has not been included in his income (i.e., the investment income from the proceeds of the deposit), and has, in effect, converted the fee into the equivalent of a deductible expense. . . .

The Congress anticipated that in determining whether an effect is significant, the Treasury will consider all the facts and circumstances, including (1) whether items of income and deduction generated by the loan offset each other, (2) the amount of such items, (3) the cost to the taxpayer of complying with the provision, and (4) any non-tax reasons for deciding to structure the transaction as a below-market loan rather than a loan with interest at a rate equal to or greater than the applicable Federal rate and a payment by the lender to the borrower.

In general, the Congress did not intend that the provision apply to below-market loans in the form of interest-bearing or other accounts in a financial institution in the ordinary course of its trade or business, loans by a financial institution in the ordinary course of its trade or business, loans by an insurance company to a policyholder of the cash value of such policyholder's insurance policy, or to most loans subsidized by the government (such as government insured or guaranteed student loans or residential mortgages). . . .

Timing and Amount of Transfers . . .

Demand loans and term gift loans. — Generally, in the case of a demand loan, the lender is treated as transferring to the borrower, and the borrower is treated as receiving from the lender, an amount equal to the forgone interest on an annual basis. The Congress believed that this rule is appropriate for demand loans because the borrower's right to the use of the funds is always subject to a substantial risk of forfeiture and no avoidance of the rules of section 83 is possible. . . .

In addition, in the case of a demand loan or a term gift loan, the borrower is treated as transferring to the lender, and the lender is treated as receiving from the borrower, an amount equal to the forgone interest on an annual basis. This forgone interest is included in income by the lender and deductible by the borrower to the same extent as interest actually due on the loan from the borrower. The Congress believed it is appropriate to apply this rule to term loans that are gift loans, because, in light of the familial or other personal relationship that is likely to exist between the borrower and the lender, the technical provisions of the loan, such as the maturity of the loan, may not be viewed as being binding by the parties. . . .

Compensation-related deemed demand loans. —The Act provides that, for purposes of determining the timing and amount of the transfers deemed made under the provision, a compensation-related term loan is treated as a demand loan if it is (1) non-transferable and (2) conditioned on the future performance of substantial services by the employee. . . .

Applicable Federal Rate

Under the Act, the adequacy of any stated interest, and the amount of any deemed payments are determined by reference to an applicable Federal rate as determined under section 1274(d). For any period beginning on or after January 1, 1985, there will be three such rates: a short-term rate; a mid-term rate; and a long-term rate. In the case of a demand loan, the relevant rate generally is the short-term rate. In the case of a term loan the relevant rate is determined by reference to the term of the loan, as set forth below:

Term	*Rate*
3 years or less	The Federal short-term rate
Over 3 years but not over 9 years	The Federal mid-term rate
Over 9 years	The Federal long-term rate

These rates are to be determined by the Treasury within 15 days after the close of 6-month periods ending September 30 and March 31, respectively, and are to reflect the average market yield during such 6-month periods on outstanding marketable obligations of the United States with comparable maturities. . . .

Under the Act, in the case of a term loan, the applicable Federal rate is the rate for the day on which the loan is made. In the case of a demand loan, amounts are treated as transferred and retransferred on a daily basis, and the applicable Federal rate for any day is the relevant rate for the 6-month period in which such day falls. Further, in the case of a demand loan, the relevant applicable Federal rate is always the Federal short-term rate. . . .

De Minimis Exceptions

The Act provides specific de minimis rules. For purposes of applying these rules, all loans between the same parties are aggregated.

De minimis exception for gift loans between individuals. —As a general rule, no amount is treated as transferred by the lender to the borrower, or retransferred by the borrower to the lender, for any day during which the aggregate outstanding amount of loans does not exceed $10,000. . . . For this purpose, the aggregate outstanding amount of loans includes all loans between the lender and the borrower regardless of the rate of interest.

This de minimis rule does not apply if the loan is directly attributable to the purchase or carrying of income-producing assets. Although a "directly attributable" test requires that there be some direct link between the loan and the borrower's purchase or continued ownership of income-producing assets, this is an anti-abuse provision, and the Congress anticipated that it will be interpreted in light of its purpose of preventing the avoidance of the assignment of income rules. . . .

Because a term gift loan is treated as a demand loan for purposes of determining the timing and amount of the deemed transfers by the borrower to the lender, generally no amount is deemed transferred by the borrower to the lender for any day on which the aggregate amount owed is $10,000 or less. Thus, if the balance of a term gift loan fluctuates, there may be income tax consequences for some days but not for other days. . . .

Special rules for gift loans. — The amount treated as retransferred by the borrower to the lender for any day on which the aggregate outstanding amount of loans between the lender and the borrower does not exceed [$100,000] is limited to the borrower's net investment income for the year. If the borrower has outstanding two or more gift loans, net investment income is allocated among such loans in proportion to the respective amounts that would be treated as retransferred by the borrower without regard to this limitation.

The term net investment income has the same meaning as it does for purposes of section 163(d)(3). Thus, the term generally means the excess of investment income over investment expense. . . .

In addition, if a borrower has less than $1,000 of net investment income for the year, such borrower's net investment income for the year is deemed to be zero. Thus, if the aggregate outstanding amount of loans from the lender to the borrower does not exceed $100,000 on any day during a year, and the borrower has less than $1,000 of net investment income for the year, no amount is treated as retransferred by the borrower to the lender for such year. . . .

2. The Mechanics of §7872

Code: §§7872(a) to (f)
Regulations: Prop. Reg. §§1.7872-1, 1.7872-2, 1.7872-4

Section 7872 was enacted to equalize the tax treatment of transactions using interest-free or below-market loans with other economically similar transactions. Section 7872 accomplishes this goal by creating a set of fictional transactions such that, after applying these fictional transactions, a lender and borrower undertaking an interest-free loan are generally treated the same as if the lender had charged interest and then repaid the money on an after-tax basis. The following examples demonstrate one of the problems that §7872 was intended to address.

Example 1. A deposits $100,000 in a bank and earns $5,000 per year interest. Assume A is in the 40-percent marginal tax bracket and thus pays $2,000 in tax on the $5,000 interest, leaving $3,000 after taxes. A then makes a gift of the $3,000 to B. Under these facts, making a $3,000 gift to B would cost a total $5,000 to A. In order to make a gift of $5,000 to B, A would have to incur a total cost of $7,000 (the $5,000 gift plus the $2,000 in taxes).

Example 2. A makes an interest-free loan of $100,000 to *B* for one year. By not depositing the $100,000 in the bank, *A* forfeits $5,000 in interest, and thus the loan costs *A* $5,000. *B* deposits the $100,000 in the bank, earning $5,000 in interest. If *B* were in the 40-percent marginal tax bracket, then *B* would pay $2,000 in tax on the interest, resulting in the same after-tax amount — that is, $3,000, as before. If, however, *B* were in the 20-percent marginal tax bracket, then *B* would pay only $1,000 in tax on the interest, resulting in a total of $4,000 after taxes. In other words, *B* would be $1,000 better off due solely to the tax savings.

Example 3. B needs money independent of *A*'s gift to pay for college. If *B* borrowed $100,000 from the bank, *B* would owe $5,000 in interest on the debt (none of which would be deductible under §163). Instead, *B* borrows $100,000 from *A* as an interest-free loan. As before, not depositing the $100,000 in the bank costs *A* $5,000 in foregone interest. *B*, however, saves $5,000 per year that *B* would have had to pay to the bank as interest. In effect, *A* has made an after-tax gift to *B* of $5,000 rather than $3,000.

Under all three examples, *A* incurs an out-of-pocket cost of $5,000. Under Examples 2 and 3, however, *B* receives a greater after-tax gift than in Example 1. Prior to the enactment of §7872, therefore, *A* and *B* would always structure their gift as an interest-free loan to *B* rather than have *A* deposit money in the bank and make a gift of the after-tax proceeds.

To equalize the tax treatment of these transactions, §7872 constructs a series of "deemed," or fictional, transactions. Under §7872, *A* is first deemed to receive a $5,000 interest payment from *B*, and then *A* is subsequently deemed to make a gift to *B* of $5,000. As a result, *A* would have $5,000 of interest income for tax purposes and, assuming a 40-percent marginal tax rate, would owe $2,000 in taxes. Thus, after the application of these fictional transactions, *A* pays $7,000 out of pocket — precisely the same result as if *A* had invested the $100,000 in the bank, earned $5,000 in interest, incurred a $2,000 tax liability, and then made a gift of $5,000 to *B*. This is the intention of the mechanics of §7872 — to equalize the tax treatment of below-market loans with economically similar transactions.

Section 7872 does not automatically apply to all below-market loans, however. As the foregoing materials illustrate, §7872 is a complex and technical provision. The first step in the statutory analysis is to determine whether the transaction is a loan. The Proposed Regulations define a "loan" as an extension of credit in any transaction where one person transfers money to another for any period of time after which it is to be retransferred to the owner or applied according to an express or implied agreement with the owner. See Prop. Reg. §1.7872-2(a)(1). Each extension of credit or other transfer of money is treated as a separate loan. See Prop. Reg. §1.7872-2(a)(3).

If it is a loan, the second step is to determine whether the loan is a "below-market" loan to which §7872 applies. The definition of a below-market loan focuses on whether the loan is a term loan or a demand loan. Gift loans, regardless of their terms, are treated as demand loans. A demand loan is a below-market loan if the interest rate payable on the loan is less than the applicable federal rate. The applicable federal rate for demand loans is the federal short-term rate compounded semiannually in effect under §1274(d) for the period during which the forgone interest is being computed.

Once it has been determined that a loan is below the market rate, §7872(c) determines whether it is the type of below-market loan to which §7872 applies (i.e., (1) gifts, (2) compensation-related loans, (3) corporation-shareholder loans, or (4) tax avoidance loans).

If the loan is one to which §7872 applies, the next step is to consider whether an applicable de minimis exception exempts the loan from §7872. There are two de minimis exceptions to §7872, one for gift loans and the other for compensation-related and corporation-shareholder loans. Gift loans are exempted if (1) the aggregate outstanding amount of the loans between the lender and the borrower does not exceed $10,000 and (2) the loan proceeds were not used by the borrower to purchase or to carry income-producing assets. Compensation-related and corporation-shareholder loans are exempted (1) for any day on which the aggregate outstanding amount of loans between lender and borrower does not exceed $10,000 and (2) if the principal purpose of the loan was not tax avoidance.

If the de minimis exception does not apply to the below-market loan, then §7872(a) and (b) govern its tax consequences. For example, if the loan is a gift loan or a demand loan:

1. The forgone interest is computed as follows: Interest determined under §7872(e)(2)(A) less interest payable, allocable to that period.
2. The forgone interest is treated, on the last day of the calendar year to which it is attributable, as
   a. transferred from the lender to the borrower and characterized by the underlying transaction — that is, gift, compensation, and so forth, and then as
   b. retransferred by the borrower to the lender as the payment of interest.
3. The amount of forgone interest treated as retransferred from the borrower to the lender in a gift transaction is limited to the borrower's net investment income (generally defined as investment income less investment expenses) for the year, if:
   a. the aggregate amount of loans by the lender to the borrower does not exceed $100,000; and
   b. there is no principal purpose of tax avoidance.

Assume, for example, that taxpayer B borrowed $20,000 from his parent, P, at a below-market rate. The loan is a "gift loan" and, because B's aggregate loans from P exceed $10,000, the §7872(c)(2) de minimis exception does not apply. However, assuming that B is a law student who used the proceeds of the loan to pay tuition and other expenses and B had no investment income, the limitation of §7872(d) intervenes and the amount of interest otherwise deemed to be paid to P is zero. Thus, P will include only the interest, if any, he actually received in income.

Notwithstanding its complex and technical nature, §7872 does not specify the tax consequences of the deemed transactions it creates. Rather, §7872 provides that foregone interest is deemed to be transferred from the lender to the borrower, but the attendant tax treatment depends on whether the transfer was properly treated as a gift (in which case it would be exempt from gross income to the borrower under §102) or salary (in which case it would be gross income to the borrower and would likely result in a deduction to the employer under §162). The retransfer of the foregone interest from the borrower to the lender is generally treated as interest income to the lender and as an interest payment to the borrower, which may or may not be deductible under §163.

KTA-TATOR, INC. V. COMMISSIONER
108 T.C. 100 (1997)

Opinion

Foley, J. . . .

The issue for decision is whether petitioner, pursuant to section 7872, has interest income from loans it made to its shareholders. We hold that it does.

BACKGROUND

. . . During the years in issue, petitioner provided various services within the coatings industry, including consulting, engineering, inspection, and lab analysis. Kenneth B. Tator is the president of petitioner, and he and his wife (the Tators) are its sole shareholders.

In 1991, the Tators began two construction projects. The first project involved the expansion of petitioner's Pittsburgh headquarters, which the Tators owned and leased to petitioner. The second project involved the construction of a new office building in Houston, Texas, which the Tators would own and lease to petitioner. Petitioner was authorized by its board of directors to loan funds to the Tators for construction, the purchase of land, and other business purposes. During the construction phase of the two projects, petitioner made over 100 advances of funds to the Tators. Each advance was executed by issuing a separate corporate check, and the Tators used the advances to pay contractors and meet other expenses. The advances were not subject to written repayment terms. . . .

Upon the completion of each project, the Tators prepared an amortization schedule and began repaying the advances. The amortization schedule for each project delineated monthly payments over 20 years at an interest rate of eight percent. The amortization schedule for the Houston project had a beginning principal balance of $400,218, while the amortization schedule for the Pittsburgh project had a beginning principal balance of $225,777.60.

On its 1992 and 1993 Federal income tax returns, petitioner did not report interest income from the advances. . . .

DISCUSSION

. . . Section 7872 sets forth the income and gift tax treatment for certain categories of "below-market" loans (i.e., loans subject to a below-market interest rate). Section 7872 recharacterizes a below-market loan as an arm's-length transaction in which the lender made a loan to the borrower in exchange for a note requiring the payment of interest at a statutory rate. As a result, the parties are treated as if the lender made a transfer of funds to the borrower, and the borrower used these funds to pay interest to the lender. The transfer to the borrower is treated as a gift, dividend, contribution of capital, payment of compensation, or other payment depending on the substance of the transaction. The interest payment is included in the lender's income and generally may be deducted by the borrower.

Section 7872 applies to a transaction that is: (1) A loan; (2) subject to a "below-market" interest rate; and (3) described in one of several enumerated categories. The parties agree that the third requirement has been met. We discuss the remaining requirements in turn.

I. Loan Requirement

Respondent contends that each advance petitioner made to the Tators should be treated as a separate loan. Petitioner contends that the corporation was authorized to fund both projects with a single loan and that the advances were analogous to "draw downs" on an open line of credit. Petitioner further contends that, for purposes of §7872, a loan did not exist until petitioner advanced all the funds necessary to complete the Pittsburgh and Houston projects. . . .

Section 1.7872-2(a)(3), Proposed Income Tax Reg., supra, provides that "each extension or [sic] credit or transfer of money by a lender to a borrower is treated as a separate loan." Thus, the proposed regulations upon which petitioner relies provide that each advance should be treated as a separate loan. Indeed, petitioner reported, on its corporate balance sheets, each advance as a separate loan. . . .

Accordingly, we conclude that the loan requirement is satisfied and that each advance is a separate loan for purposes of §7872.

II. Below-market Loan Requirement

To determine if the below-market loan requirement is satisfied, we must ascertain whether the loan is (1) a demand or term loan and (2) subject to a below-market interest rate. See §7872(e)(1).

A. Demand or Term Loan

Below-market loans fit into one of two categories: demand loans and term loans. A demand loan includes "any loan which is payable in full at any time on the demand of the lender." A term loan is "any loan which is not a demand loan."

The determination of whether a loan is payable in full at any time on the demand of the lender is a factual one. Loans between closely held corporations and their controlling shareholders are to be examined with special scrutiny. Petitioner made loans, without written repayment terms, to its only shareholders and had unfettered discretion to determine when the loans would be repaid. Therefore, the loans are demand loans. . . .

Petitioner's loans, payable on demand and having indefinite maturities, are demand, rather than term loans. Next, we must determine whether petitioner's loans are subject to a below-market interest rate.

B. Below-market Interest Rate

A demand loan is a below-market loan if it is interest free or if interest is provided at a rate that is lower than the applicable Federal rate (AFR) as determined under §1274(d). If a demand loan is classified as a below-market loan, the lender has interest income (foregone interest) equal to the difference between

(1) the interest that would have accrued on the loan using the AFR as the interest rate and (2) any actual interest payable on the loan. The parties are treated as though, on the last day of each calendar year, the lender transferred an amount equal to the foregone interest to the borrower and the borrower repaid this amount as interest to the lender.

During the construction phase of each project, petitioner made loans to the Tators. Prior to the completion of construction and the preparation of the amortization schedules, the Tators did not pay interest on these loans. Therefore, we conclude that the loans are below-market demand loans.

Petitioner contends that even if the requirements of §7872 are met, a temporary regulation provides that §7872 is not applicable, because the loans' interest arrangements have no significant effect on any Federal tax liability of the lender or the borrower. To determine whether a loan lacks a significant tax effect, all facts and circumstances should be considered including the following factors: (1) Whether the items of income and deduction generated by the loan offset each other; (2) the amount of such items; (3) the cost to the taxpayer of complying with the provisions of §7872 if such section were applied; and (4) any nontax reasons for deciding to structure the transaction as a below-market loan rather than a loan with interest at a rate equal to or greater than the applicable Federal rate and a payment by the lender to the borrower.

Petitioner contends that if §7872 applies, the Tators would be entitled to claim an interest expense deduction equal to the interest they are deemed to have paid petitioner, and as a result, the items of income and deduction offset each other. Implicit in this contention is the assumption that the temporary regulation permits the borrower's reduction in tax from the interest deduction to offset the lender's increase in tax from the interest income. Petitioner has misinterpreted the scope of the exception. Because §7872(h)(1)(C) and the temporary regulation refer to the tax liability of the "lender or the borrower," the factors must be applied separately to each taxpayer.

The following example illustrates this point. In the case of a below-market demand loan from a corporation to a shareholder, the corporation is treated as transferring to the shareholder, and the shareholder is treated as paying to the corporation, an amount equal to the foregone interest. The deemed transfer from the corporation to the shareholder is treated as a distribution, which generally is taxed as a dividend to the shareholder. The shareholder generally may deduct the deemed interest payment to the corporation. The shareholder's income from the deemed dividend and the shareholder's deduction for the deemed payment of interest may offset each other within the meaning of the temporary regulation. The corporation, on the other hand, is subject to tax on the foregone interest but is not entitled to a deduction for the deemed distribution it made to the shareholder. Therefore, it has no deduction to offset the interest income from the loan. Similarly, petitioner has interest income but is not entitled to a deduction for the deemed distribution it made to the Tators. As a result, petitioner's reliance on the exception is misplaced.

Accordingly, we hold that petitioner, pursuant to §7872, has interest income from below-market loans it made to its shareholders.

To reflect the foregoing,

Decision will be entered for respondent.

Problems

For problems 4-7 and 4-8 assume that the federal short-term rate, compounded semiannually, is an annual figure of 10 percent and is in effect throughout year 1 and year 2.

4-7. What result to John Jefferson and his 18-year-old son, Bob, if on January 1, year 1, John made an interest-free loan to Bob under the following alternatives?

    a. $5,000 to Bob in return for a $5,000 demand note. Bob spends all $5,000 on a summer vacation. Bob works during the fall to save enough money to repay the loan and does so on January 1, year 2.

    b. $5,000 to Bob in return for a $5,000 demand note. Bob deposits the money in a bank account that earns $450 interest during year 1. On January 1, year 2, Bob repays the loan.

    c. $20,000 to Bob in return for a $20,000 demand note. Bob spends all $20,000 for college tuition and room and board. Bob has no income for year 1.

    d. $50,000 to Bob in return for a $50,000 demand note. Bob spends $20,000 on college tuition and room and board and deposits the remainder in a new bank account that earns $4,000 interest in year 1. Bob does not repay the loan in year 1, and he has no other income in year 1.

    e. $120,000 to Bob in return for a $120,000 demand note. Bob spends $20,000 for college tuition and room and board and deposits the remainder in a new bank account that earns $9,000 interest in year 1.

    f. What result in *e* in year 1 and year 2 if Bob's note was a two-year term loan and not a demand note? Repayment is made on schedule on January 1, year 3.

    g. What result in *f* if John's loan to Bob requires interest payments of 5-percent simple interest per year?

4-8. What result to Jim Smith and his employee, Steve Jones, if Smith made an interest-free loan to Jones on the following terms?

    a. On January 1, year 1, $5,000 in return for a demand note. The loan, which was intended to help Jones pay his wife's hospital expenses of $6,000, was repaid on January 1, year 2.

    b. On January 1, year 1, $5,000 in return for a demand note. The loan was intended as additional compensation and was repaid on January 1, year 2.

    c. What result in *b* if the loan was for $50,000?

4-9. How, if at all, does §7872 apply to the following situations?

    a. Employer makes an interest-free loan to a 14-year-old child of an employee.

    b. Employee receives a $5,000 payment for services rendered from employer's customer, and employer permits employee to keep the money interest free for one year.

    c. Taxpayer makes a $20,000 interest-free loan (refundable deposit) to a country club in lieu of the customary membership fees.

D. DIVORCE AND ALIMONY

Code: §§71, 215, 1041(a) to (c)
Regulations: §§1.71-1T, 1.1041-1T

1. *Alimony versus Property Settlements*

A divorce or separation may entail significant tax ramifications for the parties. Because the tax laws afford numerous income-shifting alternatives, awareness by both parties of the tax issues and a willingness to negotiate a mutually satisfactory agreement are essential to a successful resolution of the dispute.

Prior to 1942, alimony or separate maintenance payments made to a former spouse were neither income to the recipient nor deductible by the payor. With the commencement of World War II, tax rates increased dramatically. As a result, alimony payments combined with the payor's income tax liability could exceed the entire income of the divorced payor spouse. In response to that potential hardship, Congress enacted a provision requiring alimony to be included in the gross income of the recipient (§71) and permitting a corresponding deduction by the payor to the extent that the amount was included in gross income by the recipient (§215). Thus, Congress specifically sanctioned income splitting between former spouses.

For payments to be deductible by the payor and includable by the payee, the payments had to be in the nature of "alimony or separate maintenance." Payments were characterized as such if they were (1) in discharge of a legal obligation arising out of the family or marital relationship; (2) periodic; (3) attributable to the payee's maintenance or support rather than to marital property rights; and (4) made pursuant to (a) a decree of divorce or separate maintenance or written instrument incident to divorce or separation, (b) a written separation agreement, or (c) a decree of support. All four elements had to be present for the payments to be classified as "alimony."

Congress in 1984 and 1986 substantially changed the rules governing the definition and treatment of alimony payments. The underlying reasons for the changes are enumerated in the attendant legislative history.

> A principal purpose for the present tax treatment of alimony is to relieve the payor of the burden of paying tax on the income which is transferred to the payee spouse as alimony and to impose that burden on the spouse receiving the alimony. . . .
>
> [T]he present law definition of alimony is not sufficiently objective. Differences in State laws create differences in Federal tax consequences and administrative difficulties. . . . The committee believes that a uniform Federal standard should be set forth to determine what constitutes alimony for Federal tax purposes. This will make it easier for the Internal Revenue Service, the parties to a divorce, and the courts to apply the rules to the facts in any particular case and should lead to less litigation. The . . . bill attempts to define alimony in a way that would conform to general notions of what type of payments constitute alimony as distinguished from property settlements and to prevent the deduction of large, one-time lump-sum property settlements.

H.R. Rep. No. 432, 98th Cong., 2d Sess. 1495 (1984).

2. *Statutory Requirements*

The revisions made to the divorce and alimony provisions of the Code were extensive. To qualify as an alimony or separate maintenance payment, the payment must be (1) in cash; (2) made pursuant to a divorce or separation instrument that does not specifically provide that such payment is not includable in gross income to the payee and is not allowable as a deduction to the payor; (3) between spouses who are not members of the same household at the time payment is made; and (4) subject to discontinuance on the death of the payee spouse. Moreover, annual payments are subject to restrictions against the front loading of payments in early years.

Cash payment. Section 71(b)(1) provides that, to qualify as alimony, the payment received by the payee must be in cash. Payments may be made on behalf of the payee spouse — that is, to creditors — and still qualify as alimony. In addition, payments do not have to be made directly by the payor spouse but can be paid, for example, by a trustee or insurance company on his or her behalf.

Divorce or separation instrument. Section 71(b)(2) defines a divorce or separation instrument as (1) a decree of divorce or separate maintenance or a written instrument incident to such a decree, (2) a written separation agreement, or (3) a decree, other than a decree of divorce or separate maintenance, requiring a spouse to make payments for the support or maintenance of the other spouse. Absent a required written instrument, payments from one spouse to another will not qualify as alimony or separate maintenance.

Section 71(b)(1)(B) allows the parties to designate in the divorce or separation instrument that a payment by one spouse to another, which would otherwise be classified as alimony, is not to be treated as alimony. This provision allows the parties to structure the tax aspects of the alimony or separate maintenance payments. Thus, the payee spouse might agree to accept a lesser amount if the payor spouse agrees that the payments are not to be treated as alimony. However, this statutory option must be properly exercised. The written agreement must include the statutory formula — the payment is not includable in gross income under §71(a) and is not allowable as a deduction under §215.

Prohibition against payor and payee membership in same household. Section 71(b)(1)(C) provides that for a payment to qualify as alimony, the payor and payee spouses must not live together. The §71(b)(1)(C) requirement of separate households applies only if the parties are legally separated under a decree of divorce or of separate maintenance. Thus, if no final decree has been entered and payments are being made under a written separation agreement between the parties (§71(b)(2)(B)), the payments may be alimony, despite the fact that the parties are part of the same household.

Payor cannot be required to make payments after payee's death. Section 71(b)(1)(D) provides another requirement designed to discourage attempts to disguise property settlements as alimony. If the payor is required to make payments after the death of the payee, those payments appear less like alimony (support) and more like an agreement to pay a fixed sum, such as a property settlement, in installments.

Therefore, when the payor spouse is obligated to make payments after the death of the payee spouse, none of the payments, made either before or after the payee's death, will be considered alimony.

In addition to the four strict definitional requirements for alimony discussed above, §71(f) was added to the Code as another means of preventing an installment property settlement from being disguised as alimony. This prohibition, designed to prevent "excess front loading," is discussed in the following excerpt.

> Under the new recapture rule, alimony or separate maintenance payments made in the *second* post-separation year will be "recaptured" (i.e., included in the taxable income of the payor and deducted from the taxable income of the payee) if such payments exceed the payments made in the third post-separation year by more than $15,000. Alimony or separate maintenance payments made in the *first* post-separation year will be recaptured if such payments exceed the average alimony or separate maintenance payments made in the second post-separation year (not including the payments recaptured as described above) and the third post-separation year by more than $15,000. The excess amounts with respect to both the first and second post-separation years will be recaptured only in the third post-separation year.
>
> The new recapture rule is illustrated by the following example. Assume that a payor makes alimony payments of $50,000 during the first post-separation year, $20,000 during the second post-separation year, and zero during the third post-separation year. All of the payments made during the first and second years are deductible by the payor and includible in the income of the payee; no recapture calculation is made until the third post-separation year. In the third year, the recapture amount with respect to the payments made in the second year is $5,000. This is the amount by which the payments in the second year ($20,000) exceed the payments in the third year (zero) by more than $15,000. The recapture amount with respect to the payments made in the first year is $27,500. This is the amount by which the payments in the first year ($50,000) exceed the average of the payments in the second year (and not recaptured) and the third year ($7,500, the average of $15,000 and zero) by more than $15,000. Note that in calculating the recapture amount with respect to the first year, only $15,000, rather than $20,000, is treated as paid in the second year. This is because the average of payments made in the second and third years does not include the $5,000 payment made in the second year that is recaptured in the third year.

Notice 87-9, 1987-3 1 C.B. 421.

Child support. Child support, unlike alimony, is not deductible to the payor and is not income to the payee. This distinction between alimony and child support arises from the purpose of the payments. A spouse who pays alimony to a former spouse is dividing income with that spouse. However, payments of child support are not treated as divisions of income. A noncustodial spouse might be required by law to make child support payments, and the custodial spouse is theoretically only the conduit through which these payments are funneled for the benefit of the child. Thus, no income splitting occurs through the payment of child support.

An agreement between former spouses to reduce monthly payments by, for example, $300 as of the date of the child's twenty-first birthday is specific enough to fix payments of that amount as child support. A reduction in payments tied to an event in the child's life is sufficient specificity to have that monthly amount characterized as child support. §71(c).

3.   *Property Transfers between Spouses*

As explained in the previous discussion, Congress wanted to create a single federal regime for the treatment of alimony and support payments. But what happens if there is a transfer of appreciated property from one spouse in exchange for a release of the other spouse's marital property rights? Prior to 1984, the Supreme Court's decision in United States v. Davis, 370 U.S. 65 (1962), provided the controlling rule that the transferor spouse must recognize gain on the exchange as if there had been a sale of the property to a third party. As discussed in the House Ways and Means Committee Report, however, Congress believed that, as a matter of policy, transfers of property within the marital community, effectively a single economic unit although technically two separate taxpayers, should not be taxed. As a result, Congress enacted §1041, which provides for nonrecognition of gain or loss and a carryover of basis to the transferee on transfers of property between spouses or pursuant to divorce.

REV. RUL. 2002-22
2002-1 C.B. 849

Issues

. . . Is the taxpayer or the former spouse required to include an amount in gross income when the former spouse exercises the stock options . . . made available to the former spouse?

Facts

Prior to their divorce in 2002, *A* and *B* were married individuals residing in State *X* who used the cash receipts and disbursements method of accounting.

A is employed by Corporation *Y*. Prior to the divorce, *Y* issued nonstatutory stock options to *A* as part of *A*'s compensation. . . . [N]o amount was included in *A*'s gross income with respect to those options at the time of grant.

. . . Under the law of State *X*, stock options . . . earned by a spouse during the period of marriage are marital property subject to equitable division between the spouses in the event of divorce. Pursuant to the property settlement incorporated into their judgment of divorce, *A* transferred to *B* . . . one-third of the nonstatutory stock options issued to *A* by *Y*. . . .

In 2006, *B* exercises all of the stock options and receives *Y* stock with a fair market value in excess of the exercise price of the options. . . .

Law and Analysis

Section 1041(a) provides that no gain or loss is recognized on a transfer of property from an individual to or for the benefit of a spouse or, if the transfer is incident to divorce, a former spouse. Section 1041(b) provides that the property transferred is generally treated as acquired by the transferee by gift and that the transferee's basis in the property is the adjusted basis of the transferor.

Section 1041 was enacted in part to reverse the effect of the Supreme Court's decision in United States v. Davis, 370 U.S. 65 (1962), which held that the transfer of appreciated property to a spouse (or former spouse) in exchange for the release of marital claims was a taxable event resulting in the recognition of gain or loss to the transferor. Section 1041 was intended to "make the tax laws as un-intrusive as possible with respect to relations between spouses" and to provide "uniform Federal income tax consequences" for transfers of property between spouses incident to divorce, "notwithstanding that the property may be subject to differing state property laws." Congress thus intended that §1041 would eliminate differing federal tax treatment of property transfers and divisions between divorcing taxpayers who reside in community property states and those who reside in non-community property states.

The term "property" is not defined in §1041. However, there is no indication that Congress intended "property" to have a restricted meaning under §1041. To the contrary, Congress indicated that §1041 should apply broadly to transfers of many types of property, including those that involve a right to receive ordinary income that has accrued in an economic sense (such as interests in trusts and annuities). Accordingly, stock options . . . may constitute property within the meaning of §1041.

Although §1041 provides non-recognition treatment to transfers between spouses and former spouses, whether income derived from the transferred property and paid to the transferee is taxed to the transferor or the transferee depends upon the applicability of the assignment of income doctrine. As first enunciated in Lucas v. Earl, 281 U.S. 111 (1930), the assignment of income doctrine provides that income is ordinarily taxed to the person who earns it, and that the incidence of income taxation may not be shifted by anticipatory assignments. However, the courts and the Service have long recognized that the assignment of income doctrine does not apply to every transfer of future income rights.

. . . [A]pplying the assignment of income doctrine in divorce cases to tax the transferor spouse when the transferee spouse ultimately receives income from the property transferred in the divorce would frustrate the purpose of §1041 with respect to divorcing spouses. That tax treatment would impose substantial burdens on marital property settlements involving such property and thwart the purpose of allowing divorcing spouses to sever their ownership interests in property with as little tax intrusion as possible. Further, there is no indication that Congress intended §1041 to alter the principle established in the pre-1041 cases . . . that the application of the assignment of income doctrine generally is inappropriate in the context of divorce. . . .

CONCLUSION

Under the present facts, the interests in nonstatutory stock options . . . that A transfers to B are property within the meaning of §1041. Section 1041 confers non-recognition treatment on any gain that A might otherwise realize when A transfers these interests to B in 2002. Further, the assignment of income doctrine does not apply to these transfers. Therefore, *A* is not required to include in gross income any income resulting from *B*'s exercise of the stock options in 2006. . . .

Holdings

(1) A taxpayer who transfers interests in nonstatutory stock options . . . to the taxpayer's former spouse incident to divorce is not required to include an amount in gross income upon the transfer.

(2) The former spouse, and not the taxpayer, is required to include an amount in gross income when the former spouse exercises the stock options.

Problem

4-10. Harold and Maude Johnson received their final divorce decree. What result to each party if the decree requires the following?
   a. Harold is to pay Maude $9,000 per year for five years.
   b. Harold is to pay Maude $9,000 per year for five years, but the payments terminate at the time of her death if she dies within five years.
   c. Same as *b* except that if payments to Maude terminate as a result of her death, then payments during the remainder of the five-year period are payable to Maude's sister.
   d. Harold is to pay Maude $11,000 per year for five years, with the payments to terminate during that five-year period at the time of Maude's remarriage.
   e. Harold is to pay $5,000 per year for three years (or until the date of her death if she dies within those three years) to the bank holding the mortgage on Maude's home.
   f. Harold is to transfer to Maude 100 shares of AT&T stock in each of the first four post-divorce years. At the time of the transfers the 100 shares of stock have a $5,000 value and a $2,000 adjusted basis to Harold.
   g. Harold is to pay Maude $15,000 per year for ten years or until Maude's death if she dies within ten years. The decree provides that $5,000 of the $15,000 payment is for child support.
   h. Harold is to pay Maude $15,000 per year for ten years, or until Maude's death if she dies within ten years, with the amount of the payment to decrease by $5,000 during that period on the date their child dies, marries, or reaches majority.
   i. Harold is to pay Maude $70,000 in year 1, $40,000 in year 2, and $10,000 in year 3. Payments cease at the time of her death if she dies before the end of the third year.
   j. Harold is to sell his car to Maude for $5,000 cash. The car has a $10,000 value and a $3,000 adjusted basis to Harold.
   k. What result in *j* if the car was also subject to a $2,000 bank loan, which Maude assumed?

l. Maude is permitted to reside, rent free, in a home owned by Harold for seven years or until her death if she dies before seven years have passed. The fair market rental value of the home is $9,000 per year.

m. What result in *l* if Harold is required to spend $300 per month for maintenance of the house he provides Maude?

n. What result in *m* if Maude has a one-half interest in the house?

C H A P T E R 5
TIMING OF GROSS INCOME

A. GENERAL PRINCIPLES

Code: §§441(a) to (e), (g); 446(a) to (d); 448(a); 451(a)
Regulations: §§1.446-1(a)(1) to (3), (c), (d)

Once it is determined that an item is includable in gross income and to whom the income is properly attributable, the issue of *when* that item should be included must be addressed. The issue of when gross income arises is a question of timing — that is, in which taxable year should all, or a portion, of an item actually be included in gross income? Determining when gross income arises may be as important in defining tax liability as determining the amount of gross income. For instance, the tax liability attributable to a particular item of income in a given year may be affected by a statutory increase or decrease in the overall tax rates, fluctuations in the taxpayer's other income, changes in the taxpayer's filing status, or substantive changes in the tax laws.

Sections 441(c) and 451(a) are central to the timing of gross income. These provisions constitute two of the three pillars of tax accounting: (1) the annual accounting period (generally a twelve-month period) and (2) the permissible methods of tax accounting. The third pillar, consisting of relief provisions, ameliorates inequities resulting from the interaction of the rigid annual accounting concept and the progressive rate structure of federal income tax. These relief provisions include statutory and judicial rules, such as installment sale reporting, net operating loss carryovers, and nonrecognition provisions.

1. Annual Accounting Period

The annual accounting period is defined in §441(c) as the annual period in which a taxpayer regularly computes income in keeping his records. This annual period becomes the taxpayer's taxable year and may be either a calendar year or a fiscal year. A calendar year, commonly used by individual taxpayers, is the twelve-month period ending on December 31, while a fiscal year, more often used by businesses, is generally the twelve-month period ending on the last day of any month other than December. Occasionally, a period of less than twelve months is used as the taxable year. Such short period returns, however, arise only in exceptional circumstances, such as the death of a taxpayer or the initial formation or liquidation of a corporation or a partnership or certain corporate-level transactions.

The federal income tax is computed on an annual basis primarily to produce determinable government revenues at regular intervals. In addition to producing a regular flow of income, the annual accounting concept dovetails with economic life in the United States, which is traditionally measured in monthly, quarterly, semi-annual, or annual periods.

The annual nature of the income tax may, however, create inequities because each taxable year stands on its own. Each year is generally a separate taxable period in which income and deductions from transactions of previous and subsequent years do not affect the current taxable year. As illustrated in Burnet v. Sanford & Brooks Co., 282 U.S. 359 (1931), the annual accounting concept is a fundamental and rigid element in income taxation, notwithstanding that many transactions have economic repercussions in two or more years. In *Burnet*, the taxpayer incurred $176,000 of expenses in excess of profits on a dredging project in 1913 and 1915 and brought suit to recover these costs. In 1920, a court awarded the taxpayer $176,000, plus $16,000 of interest. The taxpayer viewed the project, including litigation and award, as a single transaction resulting in neither a loss nor a profit. Thus, for the taxable year of 1920, the taxpayer reported only the $16,000 of interest income from the lawsuit recovery.

The Supreme Court did not, however, permit the taxpayer to net the recovery with the earlier loss. Instead, the Court required the taxpayer to report the entire $192,000 recovery as income in 1920. Although financial accounting principles, as well as common sense, might indicate that the project did not yield $192,000 of income, the Court relied on public policy and the Sixteenth Amendment to hold that each tax accounting period must be treated separately, currently taxing the income from all transactions during that particular period. In support of this interpretation, the Court cited the necessity of a systematic, regular assessment of taxes to allow the tax-supported federal government to function. Consequently, the Court held that the taxpayer's transactional tax accounting violated the annual accounting principle.

The Code and Regulations recognize inequities resulting from the annual accounting period and permit transactional accounting in limited circumstances. For instance, in a long-term construction contract, income and expenses may be reported under either the completed contract method or the percentage-of-completion method. §460. In addition, Congress has attempted to mitigate the burdensome effect of annual accounting by enacting provisions that allow a net operating loss incurred in one taxable year to be carried over to another. Section 172 permits business losses (net operating loss) to be carried back two years and forward twenty years, permitting current losses to be deducted from income arising in the earlier or later period.

Another transactional problem arises when a taxpayer reports an item of income in one year and, in a subsequent year, discovers that he or she has no right to the payments and is required to repay the amount previously included. The claim-of-right doctrine, analyzed by the Supreme Court in United States v. Lewis, 340 U.S. 590 (1951), and discussed in Chapter 2, addresses this problem. In *Lewis*, the Court strictly applied the annual accounting concept to payments received without restriction under a claim of right, even though there was a chance the taxpayer was not entitled to the payment and would have to repay it in the future. In such cases, the claim-of-right doctrine requires that the initial income inclusion remain undisturbed, with the taxpayer's only remedy being some form of a deduction or credit at the time of repayment in the subsequent year. (See the discussion in Chapter 9 and the relief-oriented provisions of §1341.)

Problems

5-1. What is the taxable period for a taxpayer who selects a January 23 through January 22 year?

5-2. What is the taxable period for a calendar-year taxpayer who dies on October 1?

2. Tax Accounting Method

The second pillar of tax accounting, the permissible methods of tax accounting, is conceptually more difficult than the annual accounting concept. Section 446(a) allows taxpayers to compute taxable income by the method of accounting they regularly use in keeping their books, with the §446(b) qualification that the method must clearly reflect income. Section 446(c) enumerates the permissible methods of accounting: cash method, accrual method, or other methods permitted by the Code (such as installment reporting and long-term contracts).

In general, cash method taxpayers report income in the taxable year in which they *actually* or *constructively* receive an item of income in the form of cash (or its equivalent), property, or services. Actual receipt poses few interpretive problems; it requires the physical acquisition and unrestricted use of the item. Constructive receipt is, however, more complex because it does not require physical acquisition. In general, income is constructively received in the year in which an item is credited, set apart, or otherwise made available to the taxpayer. Thus, the constructive receipt doctrine prevents taxpayers from turning their backs on items of income earned and available to them solely in an attempt to defer inclusion and taxation.

Another doctrine developed in conjunction with the cash receipts and disbursements method of accounting is the cash equivalency doctrine. This doctrine requires that promissory notes or other contractual obligations actually received as consideration by cash method taxpayers must be analyzed to determine whether they are receipts of income or merely the receipt of a promise to pay in the future. This analysis generally turns on whether the promise to pay has a readily ascertainable fair market value. Obligations having a readily ascertainable fair market value are included in a cash method taxpayer's gross income (or treated as an amount realized in the case of a sale of property) at their fair market value; obligations in respect of services that do not have a readily ascertainable fair market value are generally not included in gross income in the year of their receipt.

Although the constructive receipt and cash equivalency doctrines are theoretically different, they share a common element: each doctrine determines the precise time, or taxable year, in which a receipt should be included in gross income. Where the constructive receipt doctrine applies, an amount may be deemed to have been received, and therefore included in gross income, in a taxable year preceding actual receipt. Similarly, under the cash equivalency doctrine, an obligation may be included in gross income at its fair market value in the year of its receipt rather than a later taxable year in which the cash payment is actually received.

In contrast to the rules governing a cash method taxpayer, which look to actual or constructive receipt, accrual method accounting requires that income be reported in the year in which (1) all events have occurred that fix the right to receive the income and (2) the amount of such income can be determined with reasonable accuracy.

3.   *Relief Provisions*

Progressive tax rates, annually fluctuating income levels, the bunching of income, and the annual accounting concept may interact to produce an inequitably high tax liability in a particular taxable year. For instance, because of the progressive tax rates, a given amount of income may result in a greater tax liability when the entire amount is included in one taxable year than when it is spread over two or more taxable years. Onerous taxation resulting from graduated tax rates, bunching, and fluctuating income led to the adoption of exceptions to the general rules for annual accounting and tax accounting methods. These exceptions, generally known as relief provisions, have been created both congressionally and judicially.

Section 453 installment reporting (probably the most important and widely used relief provision) is, like the cash and accrual accounting methods, another statutorily permissible method of accounting. Installment reporting may be used in deferred payment sales of property in lieu of either the cash or accrual methods. The operative feature of the installment method is embodied in §453(c), which permits a taxpayer to defer income by prorating payments as they are received in order to recover a portion as basis and to report the remainder as income. Thus, under installment reporting, the receipt of the purchaser's obligation is generally not considered a payment in the year of sale, regardless of whether the note is a cash equivalent or the seller is a cash or accrual method taxpayer.

A second exception to the general rules of tax accounting is the judicially created open transaction reporting method. Open transaction reporting applies only in those rare cases in which the consideration received has *no* readily ascertainable fair market value — for example, contracts and claims to receive indefinite amounts of income such as a percentage of future earnings. Burnet v. Logan, 283 U.S. 404 (1931). This alternative method of reporting income has always had limited application. When applicable, the transaction is held "open" until the taxpayer first recovers his or her basis in the property sold and then reports income when and if receipts exceed the basis. Thus, open transaction reporting permits the deferral of income until basis has been completely recovered. In contrast, installment reporting permits the deferral of income and the pro rata recovery of basis as payments are received.

B.   CASH METHOD OF ACCOUNTING

The cash receipts and disbursements method of accounting possesses the virtue of simplicity. Cash method accounting generally requires income to be reported in the year in which money (or its equivalent), property, or services are received. Although this method is often easy to apply and administer, the concepts of constructive receipt and cash equivalency can produce unexpected results. Legislation precludes the use of the cash method of accounting by certain taxpayers. §448.

1. Cash Equivalency

Code: §§446(c); 451(a)
Regulations: §§1.446-1(c)(1)(i), (d); 1.451-1(a)

Cash method taxpayers are required to include in gross income the receipt of cash and items other than cash, such as tangible and intangible property and services. See Reg. §1.446-1(c)(1). Specifically, Regulation §1.446-1(a)(3) provides that items "of gross income . . . need not be in the form of cash. It is sufficient that such items can be valued in terms of money." Thus, the actual receipt of cash or *its equivalent* must be included in income if the item can be valued in terms of money. For this reason, the cash equivalency doctrine addresses the problem of determining which items should be included in gross income for the cash method taxpayer — that is, when is there gross income?

In general, in the case of tangible property, gross income arises when the property is received, in an amount equal to the property's fair market value. Thus, for example, as discussed in Chapter 2, taxpayers have gross income in the year they actually receive food or housing in exchange for services (absent the application of a specific statutory exception).

Issues regarding the application of the cash equivalency doctrine most often relate to the receipt of intangible property, which represents the right to receive something in the future, such as contract rights, evidences of indebtedness, and promissory obligations. In addition to raising substantial valuation problems, questions often arise as to whether these intangible items should be characterized as mere promises to pay in the future or, alternatively, as current payments that are substantively the equivalent of cash. In characterizing an item as either a promise to pay in the future or a receipt of present payment, it is important to consider the equitable notion that it is unfair to tax the taxpayer before something of value is received. Therefore, promissory notes and contractual obligations received by cash method taxpayers are scrutinized under the cash-equivalency doctrine to determine whether they have a readily ascertainable fair market value, and thus that it is the appropriate time to require inclusion in gross income.

a. Negotiable Instruments as Payment for Services

KAHLER v. COMMISSIONER
18 T.C. 31 (1952)

RICE, J.
The sole issue is when did the petitioner realize the income represented by the commission check delivered December 31, 1946. Was it in 1946, as determined by respondent, or in 1947, as claimed by petitioner? This, in turn, is based on the

question whether the receipt of a check by a cash basis taxpayer after banking hours on the last day of the taxable period constitutes a realization of income. . . .

In his brief, petitioner argues that "the mere receipt of a check does not give rise to income within the taxable year of receipt unless the check is received in sufficient time before the end of the taxable year so the check may be converted into cash within the taxable year." In support of such result, petitioner relies upon L. M. Fischer, 14 T.C. 792 (1950); Urban A. Lavery, 5 T.C. 1283 (1945), affd. (C.A. 7, 1946) 158 F.2d 859; and Harvey H. Ostenberg, 17 B.T.A. 738 (1929).

In the *Fischer* case, we held that a check delivered to the taxpayer on December 31, 1942, which was not deposited until 1943, was not income in 1942 but in 1943, since the check was subject to a substantial restriction. At the time of delivery of such check, there was an oral agreement made between the drawer and the taxpayer that the latter would hold the check for a few days before he cashed it since the drawer was short of money in the bank. Such a situation is completely distinguishable from that in the instant case.

The *Lavery* and *Ostenberg* cases both decided that checks delivered to the taxpayers were income in the year of delivery. In the *Lavery* case delivery was on December 30, and in the *Ostenberg* case delivery was on December 31. Petitioner relies on the dicta appearing in these cases to the effect that the result might have been different had the petitioner in either case been able to show that he could not have cashed the check in the year drawn. We fail to see where there should be any difference in result just because it might be impossible to cash a check in the year in which drawn, where delivery actually took place in such year. Respondent's regulations provide that all items of gross income shall be included in the taxable year in which received by the taxpayer, and that where services are paid for other than by money, the amount to be included as income is the fair market value of the thing taken in payment.

Analogous cases to the instant case are those which were concerned with the proper year in which deductions might be taken where a check was drawn and delivered in one year and cashed in a subsequent year. Under the negotiable instruments law, payment by check is a conditional payment subject to the condition that it will be honored upon presentation; and once such presentation is made and the check is honored, the date of payment relates back to the time of delivery. See Estate of Modie J. Spiegel, 12 T.C. 524 (1949); and cases cited therein. In the *Spiegel* case we said, at page 529:

> It would seem to us unfortunate for the Tax Court to fail to recognize what has so frequently been suggested, that as a practical matter, in everyday personal and commercial usage, the transfer of funds by check is an accepted procedure. The parties almost without exception think and deal in terms of payment except in the unusual circumstance, not involved here, that the check is dishonored upon presentation, or that it was delivered in the first place subject to some condition or infirmity which intervenes between delivery and presentation.

Under such circumstances, we feel that it is immaterial that delivery of a check is made too late in the taxable year for the check to be cashed in that year. The petitioner realized income upon receipt of the commission check on December 31, 1946. . . .

Decision will be entered for the respondent.

Murdock, J., concurring.

I agree with the result reached that the receipt of a check is regarded as payment and income unless it is subject to some restriction but feel that the petitioner's case is weaker in some respects than the majority opinion might indicate. A finding is made that the check in question was received by the petitioner "sometime after 5 P.M. on December 31, 1946." There is also evidence that he could not have obtained cash for the check at the drawee bank but he could have deposited the check in that bank, later on December 31, 1946. There was another bank in the town and the evidence does not show whether or not he could have cashed the check in that bank after regular banking hours. Furthermore he might have made some other use of the check during 1946. For example, he might have cashed it at some place other than at a bank or he might have used it to discharge some obligation, within the year 1946.

b. Other Obligations as Payment for Services

COWDEN v. COMMISSIONER
289 F.2d 20 (5th Cir. 1961)

Jones, J.

. . . In April 1951, Frank Cowden, Sr. and his wife made an oil, gas and mineral lease for themselves and their children upon described lands in Texas to Stanolind Oil and Gas Company. By related supplemental agreements, Stanolind agreed to make "bonus" or "advance royalty" payments in an aggregate amount of $511,192.50. On execution of the instruments $10,223.85 was payable, the sum of $250,484.31 was due "no earlier than" January 5 "nor later than" January 10, 1952, and $250,484.34 was stipulated to be paid "no earlier than" January 5 "nor later than" January 10, 1953. One-half of the amounts was to be paid to Frank Cowden, Sr. and his wife, and one-sixth was payable to each of their children. In the deferred payments agreements it was provided that:

> This contract evidences the obligation of Stanolind Oil and Gas Company to make the deferred payments referred to in subparagraphs (b) and (c) of the preceding paragraph hereof, and it is understood and agreed that the obligation of Stanolind Oil and Gas Company to make such payments is a firm and absolute personal obligation of said Company, which is not in any manner conditioned upon development or production from the demised premises, nor upon the continued ownership of the leasehold interest in such premises by Stanolind Oil and Gas Company, but that such payments shall be made in all events.

On November 30, 1951, the taxpayer assigned the payments due from Stanolind in 1952 to the First National Bank of Midland, of which Frank Cowden, Sr. was a director. Assignments of the payments due in 1953 were made to the bank on November 20, 1952. . . . The Commissioner computed the fair market value of the Stanolind obligations, which were not interest bearing, by the deduction of a discount of four percent on the deferred payments from the date of the agreements until the respective maturities. Such computation fixed a 1951 equivalent of cash value of $487,647.46 for the bonus payments, paid in 1951 and agreed to be paid thereafter, aggregating $511,192.50. The Commissioner determined that the tax-payers should be taxed in 1951 on $487,647.46, as ordinary income. . . .

. . . While it is true that the parties may enter into any legal arrangement they see fit even though the particular form in which it was cast was selected with the hope of a reduction in taxes, it is also true that if a consideration for which one of the parties bargains is the equivalent of cash it will be subjected to taxation to the extent of its fair market value. Whether the undertaking of the lessee to make future bonus payments was, when made, the equivalent of cash and, as such, taxable as current income is the issue in this case. In a somewhat similar case, decided in 1941, the Board of Tax Appeals stated that "where no notes, bonds, or other evidences of indebtedness other than the contract were given, such contract had no fair market value." Kleberg v. Commissioner, 43 B.T.A. 277. In 1959 the Tax Court held that where the deferred bonus payments were evidenced by promissory notes the equivalent of cash doctrine might be applicable. Barnsley v. Commissioner, 31 T.C. 1260. . . .

The test announced in *Kleberg*, from which *Barnsley* does not depart, seems to be whether the obligation to make the deferred payments is represented by "notes, bonds, or other evidences of indebtedness other than the contract." In this case, the literal test of *Kleberg* is met as the obligation of Stanolind to the Cowdens was evidenced by an instrument other than the contract of lease. This instrument is not, however, one of the kind which fall into the classification of notes or bonds. The taxpayers urge that there can be no "equivalent of cash" obligation unless it is a negotiable instrument. Such a test, to be determined by the form of the obligation, is as unrealistic as it is formalistic. The income tax law deals in economic realities, not legal abstractions, and the reach of the income tax law is not to be delimited by technical refinements or mere formalism.

A promissory note, negotiable in form, is not necessarily the equivalent of cash. Such an instrument may have been issued by a maker of doubtful solvency or for other reasons such paper might be denied a ready acceptance in the market place. We think the converse of this principle ought to be applicable. We are convinced that if a promise to pay of a solvent obligor is unconditional and assignable, not subject to set-offs, and is of a kind that is frequently transferred to lenders or investors at a discount not substantially greater than the generally prevailing premium for the use of money, such promise is the equivalent of cash and taxable in like manner as cash would have been taxable had it been received by the taxpayer rather than the obligation. . . .

Reversed and remanded.

c. Distinguishing Negotiable Instruments and Other Promises to Pay

BRIGHT v. UNITED STATES
926 F.2d 383 (5th Cir. 1991)

PER CURIAM:

. . . The district court held that for income tax purposes the check that [the taxpayer] received on December 27, 1985, constituted the receipt of cash or a cash equivalent . . . on that date. We affirm.

OPERABLE FACTS

In 1970 Ms. Cornell entered into a trust agreement whereby the Elizabeth R. Cornell Trust was created for her benefit. . . . Both Cornell and the trust used a calendar year as their taxable year, and both used the cash basis method of accounting.

The trust owned 188,848 shares of stock of the Southland Royalty Company. Southland had agreed to merge with Burlington Northern, Inc. and M-R Holdings, Inc. (Holdings), a Burlington subsidiary . . .

On Friday, December 27, 1985, an employee of Cornell's received the Holdings check . . . at her office in Fort Worth. Neither Holdings, as maker of the check, nor [the] payor bank, placed any restrictions on the check's negotiability. . . . Cornell's employee endorsed and mailed the check . . . for deposit in the trust's account. [The bank] posted the check to the trust's account on Monday, December 30, 1985. On the 30th of December, Cornell's employee placed an order . . . to buy government securities with the funds from the Holdings check. [The bank], however, informed the employee that it would restrict the availability of the funds to the trust until [it] had collected the funds from [the payor bank]. Because of this restriction, [the bank] did not execute the purchase order until January 3, 1986.

[The taxpayer] contended that because [the bank] restricted the use of the funds until January 1986, [the taxpayer] neither actually nor constructively received in 1985 the funds from the sale of the stocks. The government maintained that the Holdings check was a "cash equivalent" that [the taxpayer] had actually received in 1985 and, in the alternative, that as the check's negotiability had no substantial restrictions placed on it, the income was constructively received in 1985. In either case, the income was, the government argued, includable in 1985 . . .

DISCUSSION

In declaring receipt of the Holdings check to be receipt of a cash equivalent, the district court relied solely upon Kahler, 18 T.C. 31 (1952). . . . Even if cashing the check in the year in which drawn "might be impossible," stated the tax court, the check was still income in the year in which drawn if actual delivery occurred in that year. Kahler, 18 T.C. at 34.

The Kahler court recognized as "completely distinguishable" a situation in which a check was "subject to a substantial restriction" which the drawer had imposed on the check. . . . The third circuit has also agreed that when the payor imposes a restriction upon the payee's use of a check, an exception exists to the general rule that ordinarily a check constitutes taxable income to a cash-basis taxpayer when he receives it. Estate of Kamm v. Commissioner, 349 F.2d 953, 955 (3rd Cir.1965). The court in Kamm refused, however, to admit the exception when the payee is responsible for the restrictions. . . .

In Kamm the taxpayer's attorney received two checks on Friday December 30th after banking hours and deposited them in his trustee account that afternoon. On December 31st, the attorney drew checks on his account payable to the taxpayer and dated January 3rd, on which date the checks were deposited in the taxpayer's account in accordance with her instructions. The court acknowledged that "the time of receipt made it impracticable . . . to convert the check into cash before the end of the taxable year." Id. The court, nevertheless, reasoned that because a certified check "has value and commercial utility so much like money, and its acceptance and convertibility into money are so routine," it is income upon receipt. Id. at 955-56 (citing Kahler, 18 T.C. 31).

The situation confronting the court in this appeal favors the cash-equivalent-upon-receipt rule even more than do the situations in Kahler and Kamm. As [the taxpayer] received the Holdings check . . . during business hours on Friday, December 27, 1985, [the taxpayer] had five calendar days and at least two business days before the end of the year in which to acquire access to the funds.

Furthermore . . . the payor bank did not impose any restrictions on the nego-tiability of the check. . . . Had [the taxpayer] opened an account at [the payor bank], she would have had immediate access to her funds. . . .

Neither Cornell nor the remaining trustee chose to exercise the alternative option of immediate access to the funds. . . . Instead, the taxpayer . . . chose to deposit the check in [the taxpayer's bank], which limited access to the funds. In doing so, [the taxpayer] "voluntarily subjected [her]self to a routine which delayed somewhat [her] personal receipt" of the funds. See Kamm, 349 F.2d at 956 (reject-ing argument that taxpayer did not receive proceeds until January because attor-ney required to deposit check in trust account and not obliged to remit to taxpayer until checks had cleared).

The executor also claims that as the Holdings check was drawn for such a large amount, it is not a cash equivalent because it fails the readily marketable and immediately convertible test which this circuit established in Cowden v. Commis-sioner, 289 F.2d 20, 24 (5th Cir.1961). Because the funds were available as "same day funds" to the taxpayer through [the payor bank], this is a bootless argument. The large amount for which the check was drawn did not ultimately affect its ready marketability.

. . . Consequently, the judgment of the district court is AFFIRMED.

Problem

5-3.   Patricia Ann Howett, the proprietor of a beauty salon, is a cash method taxpayer. Howett performed hairdressing and cosmetic services from June to December, year 1, for Linda Blakely, a prominent engineering executive. Under the following facts, in what year should Howett include income from the payment for such services.

   a.   On December 31, year 1, Linda writes a personal check for $5,000 to Howett in payment for the services.

   b.   Assume in *a* that Linda is waiting for her year-end bonus and conse-quently will not have enough money in her account to cover the check until the bonus is paid on January 3, year 2.

   c.   Assume instead that Blakely pays Howett $1,000 cash plus a $4,000 personal promissory note, with principal due on February 14, year 2, and stated interest of 5 percent per year. The note is assignable but unsecured.

   d.   Assume in *c* that the promissory note was unassignable and had a fair market value of only $1,200.

2. *Actual versus Constructive Receipt*

Code: §§446, 451(a)
Regulations: §§1.446-1(c)(1)(i), 1.451-1(a), 1.451-2

For cash method taxpayers, actual receipt of income items is the primary factor governing the year of inclusion. If taxation turned solely on actual receipt, however, cash method taxpayers could easily defer the year in which an item is included in gross income simply by choosing not to collect the item when due. It is not surprising, therefore, that the Regulations incorporate "constructive receipt" in the definition of cash method accounting by providing that all items of gross income are included in income in the year in which they are actually or constructively received. See Reg. §1.446-1(c)(1)(i).

In Ross v. Commissioner, 169 F.2d 483 (1st Cir. 1948), the court explained the purpose for the development of the doctrine of constructive receipt as follows:

> [T]he doctrine of constructive receipt was . . . conceived by the Treasury in order to prevent a taxpayer from choosing the year in which to return income merely by choosing the year in which to reduce it to possession. Thereby the Treasury may subject income to taxation when the only thing preventing its reduction to possession is the volition of the taxpayer.

Id. at 491.

The Regulations provide a framework for the application of the constructive receipt doctrine. Pursuant to Regulation §1.451-2(a), constructive receipt occurs when income is credited without restriction, set apart, or otherwise made available to the taxpayer. Thus, the Regulation establishes that taxpayers are not permitted to avoid the inclusion in income of items over which they have sufficient *control* to compel payment even though they may not yet have actually received payment. Regulation §1.451-2(a) also provides that there is constructive receipt only if there are no substantial limitations or conditions on the taxpayer's right to bring the funds within his or her *control*. For example, if the terms of a sales contract provide that the seller's right to receive sale proceeds is contingent on the buyer's approval of the seller's title, there is a substantial restriction barring constructive receipt until that condition is satisfied.

An interesting application of the doctrine of constructive receipt occurred in Hornung v. Commissioner, 47 T.C. 428 (1967). In *Hornung*, the taxpayer was selected by Sport Magazine as the outstanding player in the 1961 National Football League championship game. The announcement and acceptance of the award occurred following the football game, at approximately 4:30 P.M., on the afternoon of December 31, 1961. The award included a new Chevrolet Corvette, to which the taxpayer was entitled on December 31, 1961, although the taxpayer did not actually receive the car until January 3, 1962. The taxpayer argued that, based on the doctrine of constructive receipt, the value of the car should be included in his gross income for 1961. The court held, however, that the taxpayer did not exercise "unfettered control" over the car until its actual receipt on January 3. The court stated:

> At the time the award was announced in Green Bay, . . . Sport had neither the title nor keys to the car, and nothing was given or presented to petitioner to evidence his ownership or right to possession of the car at that time.
> Moreover, since December 31, 1961 was a Sunday, it is doubtful whether the car could have been transferred to petitioner before Monday. . . . The New York dealership at which the car was located was closed. The car had not been set aside for petitioner's use and delivery was not dependent solely upon the volition of petitioner.

Id. at 434. The doctrine of constructive receipt was, therefore, inapplicable, and the value of the car was included in income in the later year.

MIELE v. COMMISSIONER
72 T.C. 284 (1979)

WILES, J. . . .

Petitioners maintained their books and filed their Federal income tax returns under the calendar year cash receipts and disbursements method of accounting. The law firm maintained its . . . books and filed its Federal . . . income tax returns under the calendar year cash receipts and disbursements method of accounting, except that it included in gross income only that portion of client advances held in a special bank account which were actually transferred to its general partnership account.

In compliance with Pennsylvania's Code of Professional Responsibility, the law firm preserved the identity of their client's funds and property through segregation and accounting measures. First, the law firm transferred all client advances, including advances for both future client costs and future legal services, to the Fierro and Miele Trustee Account (hereinafter trustee account). Second, the law firm provided an accounting of each client's funds by maintaining a ledger card reflecting all client transactions. When a case was closed, the firm would transfer the earned portion of the prepaid legal fees held in the trustee account to the general partnership account; the unearned portion was refunded to the client.

The law firm, operating under a cash receipts and disbursements method of accounting, would include the prepaid legal fees in income only when the funds were transferred to its general account. For administrative purposes, the firm would transfer funds from the trustee account only about four times a year, and it generally never made any transfers in November or December. Consequently, fees were not always included in income in the year earned and therefore otherwise available to the firm. . . .

OPINION . . .

We must first decide how petitioners' law firm must account for client advances which, in turn, requires us to determine in what year they are taxable. . . .

Petitioners argue, in essence, that their law firm utilizes the cash method of accounting for income and expenses. As such, they argue that the law firm is not taxable on client advances until received, which is when the funds are transferred from the trustee account to the general partnership account. Respondent argues that the client advances are merely prepaid legal fees and are taxable in full when received by the firm regardless of whether they are subsequently transferred to the trustee account. We cannot entirely agree with either party.

Respondent's argument with regard to the first and third portions of his adjustment is that the firm must include in income all prepaid fees actually received in 1972, $44,627 on deposit in the trustee account and $2,337 on hand. He cites Schlude v. Commissioner, 372 U.S. 128 (1963); American Automobile Association v. United States, 367 U.S. 687 (1961); and Automobile Club of Michigan v. Commissioner, 353 U.S. 180 (1957), for the proposition that prepaid service income is taxable in the year received even though the services are to be performed in the future. We do not question the vitality of the cases cited by respondent, only their applicability to the facts of this case.

In each of the three cases cited, the Supreme Court treated the accrual method taxpayers as taxable on prepaid income when received. The effect of the holding was to treat an accrual method taxpayer as a cash method taxpayer with regard to prepaid income — taxable on receipt. But the law firm in this case is already a cash method taxpayer and admittedly taxable on income when received. The narrow issue presented here is whether the law firm was in receipt of income when the prepaid legal fees were received by it. This in turn depends upon whether the firm received the fees under a claim of right and without restriction as to their disposition. North American Oil Consolidated v. Burnet, 286 U.S. 417, 424 (1932).

DR 9-102(A) of the Pennsylvania Code of Professional Responsibility requires the law firm to transfer all client advances received to a special segregated bank account. Moreover, the funds so deposited and segregated may not be commingled with funds belonging to the lawyer or law firm; the firm must maintain records and account to the client for all transactions concerning the funds; and the firm may withdraw only the undisputed amount from the fund when actually due. Violation of the minimum standards set forth in the Disciplinary Rule subjects the firm and its members to disciplinary action. These facts clearly indicate that the prepaid legal fees received by the firm are to be treated as owned by the client until an undisputed amount is due the firm. Under these circumstances, we view the law firm as a mere conduit for passing the client advances to the trustee account. Moreover, the prohibition against commingling these funds with the law firm's and restrictions upon use until an undisputed amount is due clearly indicate the firm did not receive these funds under a claim of right and without substantial restriction as to disposition. Accordingly, we hold that the law firm is not in receipt of income when the payments were actually received. But this is not the end of the matter. Even though the law firm is not taxable on receipt of the payments from the clients, it may be in constructive receipt of amounts held in the trustee account at the end of the year.

The doctrine of constructive receipt requires taxation of income which is subject to the taxpayer's unfettered command and which he is free to enjoy at his own option even though he chooses not to. Income is not constructively received, however, if the taxpayer's control of its receipt is subject to substantial limitations or restrictions. Thus, we must decide whether the funds held in the trustee account are subject to substantial limitations or restrictions which bar the application of constructive receipt doctrine. This, in turn, depends upon when the funds are earned.

DR 9-102(A)(2) provides that client advances belonging solely to the client must be deposited in a segregated bank account, but when the amount becomes due, the law firm may withdraw it. Client advances should be kept separate from the law firm's funds until such time that the firm has an undisputed right to those funds, when the funds are earned. Until the funds are earned, the firm's control of their receipt is subject to a substantial limitation; the firm cannot commingle them with its own funds and use them for its own personal purposes. Consequently, the firm is not free to enjoy the use of the funds until earned.

Fierro testified that $35,623.75 of the 1972 ending balance in the trustee account was earned in 1972 but not included in income until 1973, the year transferred to the law firm's general account. We find the law firm constructively received this amount in 1972. Clearly, all the events defining the firm's right to this amount transpired in 1972 even though, for administrative purposes, it chose not to exercise the right until 1973. Further, respondent determined that $2,337 of client advances on hand at the end of 1972 but not yet deposited to the trustee account was income in 1972. Since petitioners failed to present any evidence that this entire portion was not earned in 1972, we find that they constructively received this amount in 1972. Accordingly . . . we find the law firm's 1972 taxable income is increased by $37,960.75 . . . the amount earned and constructively received in 1972.

3. Contractual Agreements Postponing Receipt

Miele involved an attempt by attorneys to defer income by manipulating their billing practices. A more common method employed by taxpayers to defer income is to contractually postpone the receipt of payments. A leading case construing arrangements to postpone income is Amend v. Commissioner, 13 T.C. 178 (1949). For seven years, Amend, a wheat farmer, sold his wheat in August or December of the year in which the wheat was harvested, but the oral contract with the purchaser required delivery and payment in January of the succeeding year. Even though the buyer was ready, willing, and able to pay in the year of production, the taxpayer postponed the purchaser's payment to produce more uniform income. The Service argued that the taxpayer had the unqualified right to receive payment for the wheat in the production year because all he had to do to receive the money was ask for it (or more specifically, stop asking the buyer *not* to pay until a future date).

In holding against the Commissioner, the court stated that the constructive receipt doctrine does not apply where a bona fide, arm's-length agreement prevents the taxpayer from demanding payment before the date specified in the contract. The court noted that if the taxpayer had started selling wheat in the year in question, in which there had been a bumper crop, then under his delayed payment method "there might be reason to doubt the bona fides of the contract."

In Reed v. Commissioner, which follows, the First Circuit extended the reasoning of *Amend* to the use of an escrow account as an income deferral device.

REED v. COMMISSIONER

723 F.2d 138 (1st Cir. 1983)

GIBSON, J. . . .

I. BACKGROUND

. . . Reed acquired stock in Reed Electromech Corporation (Electromech) in 1963. . . . In 1967, Reed and several of his fellow Electromech shareholders (the selling stockholders) entered into an agreement with Joseph Cvengros, also an Electromech shareholder, granting Cvengros an option to purchase the selling stockholder's stock, or to cause the selling shareholders to purchase Cvengros' stock. The agreement, as amended on October 16, 1973, set a $3,300 per share price, for an aggregate price of $808,500.00, and provided that if Cvengros failed to exercise his purchase option by November 27, 1973, the selling shareholders could purchase all of Cvengros' stock at the set per share price. The amended agreement further provided that whether Cvengros purchased the selling stockholder's stock, or vice versa, the closing would be on December 27, 1973, at which time the stock and purchase price were to be delivered.

On November 23, 1973, Cvengros exercised his option to purchase the Electromech stock held by the selling shareholders. Shortly thereafter, Reed and his fellow selling shareholders became concerned about the federal income tax implications of a sale in 1973. Reed, in particular, wanted to defer closing until 1974 so that he would have time to make an orderly sale of certain securities ("loss securities"), the capital loss from which he desired to write-off against the capital gain on the Electromech sale. Reed was understandably reluctant to sell the loss securities prior to the December 27 closing, fearing that Cvengros' outside financing might fall through before the closing, thus preventing the Electromech stock sale. On the other hand, Reed believed that after the December 27 closing there would not be enough time remaining in 1973 to properly identify and sell these loss securities in that year. Hence, Reed wanted to postpone closing until January of 1974.

Nevertheless, Cvengros and his financial backer insisted on the December 27, 1973 closing, apparently because the financial backer wanted the stock transaction reflected on his 1973 books. In early December 1973, Reed[3] and Cvengros, desiring to accommodate all involved, orally agreed to modify the purchase-sale agreement to provide that: (1) Reed and the other selling shareholders would not be entitled to receive payment for their stocks until January 3, 1974; and (2) Reed would remain on Electromech's Board of Directors after the stock sale. Both Reed and Cvengros considered the deferred payment provision to be part of the purchase-sale agreement and legally binding. Reed, in fact, indicated that he would not have gone through with the sales transaction if Cvengros had not agreed to the deferred payment provision.

This oral modification was memorialized in a written escrow agreement, executed by Reed and Cvengros immediately prior to the closing on December 27,

---

3. Reed was acting as the agent and attorney in fact for the rest of the selling shareholders in connection with their sale of Electromech stock to Cvengros.

1973. Under the terms of the escrow agreement, the stock sales proceeds were to be paid by Cvengros to the escrowee (the American National Bank and Trust Company) at the December 27, 1973 closing and the escrowee was then to make disbursements of the sales proceeds to a number of selling shareholders, including Reed, on January 3, 1974. Under the agreement, these selling shareholders were not entitled to receive interest, investment income or any other incidental benefits (e.g., bank letter of credit) on the sales proceeds while they were in escrow. The agreement provided for no conditions precedent, other than the passage of time, to the January 3, 1974 payment.

At the closing on December 27, 1973, the following events occurred: (1) Cvengros' financial backer loaned and delivered to Cvengros a cashier's check in the amount of $808,500 payable to the order of Cvengros; (2) Cvengros endorsed and delivered the $808,500 check to the escrowee; and (3) the selling shareholders delivered their Electromech stock to Cvengros. The escrowee subsequently disbursed the sales proceeds pursuant to the escrow agreement instructions; hence Reed did not actually receive his share of the proceeds until January 3, 1974. Reed realized a long-term capital gain of $256,000 on the sale of his Electromech stock. This gain was reported on his 1974 Federal Income Tax Return.

In the Tax Court, the Commissioner argued that Reed recognized a taxable gain from the sale in 1973 rather than in 1974 because: (1) he constructively received the income from the stock sale in 1973; (2) he received an economic benefit (or cash equivalent) in 1973; and (3) the escrow arrangement lacked economic reality, other than as a tax deferral device. Reed, a cash basis taxpayer, claimed the gain was taxable in 1974 because he did not actually or constructively receive payment in 1973. He urged then, as he does now, that the escrow arrangement was a valid income deferral device because it was part of a bona fide modification of the purchase-sale agreement with Cvengros. Under that modification, Reed was not entitled to receive any payment until January 3, 1974.

The Tax Court, while recognizing that a cash basis taxpayer such as Reed could postpone income recognition by a bona fide agreement providing for deferred payment, nevertheless held that "when, upon receipt of the [purchased stocks], the buyer deposits the full purchase price in an escrow account to be paid to the seller at a later date and no condition other than the passage of time is placed on the seller's right to receive the escrow funds, courts have held that the seller recognizes income when the buyer deposits funds with the escrowee." The court emphasized that because nothing could have prevented Reed's receipt of the funds once they were deposited with the escrowee, Reed recognized income when Cvengros deposited the funds in escrow in 1973.

II. Discussion . . .

A. CONSTRUCTIVE RECEIPT

The Commissioner contends Reed constructively received the stock sales proceeds when they were deposited in the escrow account on December 27, 1973. A cash basis taxpayer such as Reed is required to recognize income from the sale of property in the taxable year in which he actually or constructively receives payment for the property. §451(a); Treas. Reg. §1.451-1(a). Treasury Regulation §1.451-2(a) explains the constructive receipt doctrine as follows:

> Income although not actually reduced to a taxpayer's possession is constructively received by him in the taxable year during which it is credited to his account, *set apart for him, or otherwise made available so that he may draw upon it at any time*, or so that he could have drawn upon it during the taxable year if notice of intention to withdraw had been given. *However, income is not constructively received if the taxpayer's control of its receipt is subject to substantial limitations or restrictions.*

(Emphasis added.)

Thus, under the constructive receipt doctrine, a taxpayer recognizes taxable income when he has an unqualified, vested right to receive immediate payment. However, a taxpayer-seller has the right to enter into an agreement with the buyer that he, the seller, will not be paid until the following year. As long as the deferred payment agreement is binding between the parties and is made prior to the time when the taxpayer-seller has acquired an absolute and unconditional right to receive payment, then the cash basis taxpayer is not required to report the sales proceeds as income until he actually receives them.

Applying the language of Regulation §1.451-2(a), if the deferred payment agreement provides that the taxpayer-seller has no right to payment until the taxable year following the sale, then the income received from the sale is not "set apart for him, or otherwise made available so that he may draw upon it" in the year of the sale. Alternatively stated, such a deferred payment agreement restricts the time of payment and therefore serves as a "substantial limitation" on the taxpayer control of the proceeds in the taxable year of the sale.

Hence, as the parties agree and the Tax Court stated, courts have generally recognized that a cash basis taxpayer-seller may effectively postpone income recognition through the use of a bona fide arms-length agreement between the buyer and seller calling for deferred payment of the sales proceeds.

Similarly, an existing agreement which has been amended or modified to provide for deferred payment of an amount not yet due serves to postpone income recognition. This is true even though: (1) the purchaser was initially willing to contract for immediate payment; and (2) the taxpayer's primary objective in entering into the deferred payment agreement was to minimize taxes. A deferred payment agreement is considered bona fide and hence given its full legal effect, if the parties intended to be bound by the agreement and were, in fact, legally bound.

While recognizing these principles, the Commissioner claims the escrow modification providing for disbursement of the sales proceeds to Reed in 1974 was not a bona fide arms-length agreement between the Cvengros and Reed and, hence, did not "substantially limit" Reed's access to the sales proceeds deposited in escrow after the December 27, 1973 closing. Instead, the purported escrow modification was nothing more than Reed's self-imposed limitation, designed to defer income recognition on proceeds he already had an unqualified, vested right to receive on December 27, 1973. . . .

We agree with the Commissioner that a deferred escrow arrangement that is not part of a bona fide agreement between the buyer and the seller-taxpayer, but rather is a "self-imposed limitation" created by the seller-taxpayer, is legally ineffective to shift taxability on escrowed funds from one year to the next. However, in this case the escrow arrangement was the product of an arms-length, bona fide modification to the purchase-sale agreement between Reed and Cvengros; it was not Reed's self-imposed limitation on the receipt of sales proceeds he had an unqualified, vested right to receive in 1973.

The modification setting up the escrow arrangement was orally agreed upon by the parties in early December, 1973, and, as the Tax Court found, was memorialized in the escrow agreement instruction letter executed prior to closing on December 27, 1973. Thus, the modification became effective prior to the time when Reed had an unqualified right to demand immediate payment under the then existing purchase agreement. As discussed above, an existing purchase-sale agreement can be modified to provide for deferred payment of an amount not already due under the existing agreement, provided the modification is considered by the parties to be legally binding. Both Cvengros and Reed testified that they considered the deferred payment provision to be a legally binding modification, defining their rights and obligations under the purchase-sale agreement. Nothing in the Tax Court's opinion indicates that we should discredit this testimony. In fact, the record reveals that the provision was the product of some arms-length negotiations between Cvengros and Reed. Cvengros, at his financial backer's insistence, was initially unwilling to make the deferred payment but agreed to the escrow device after Reed promised to remain on the Electromech Board of Directors following the sale to insure a smooth ownership transaction. And, despite the government's suggestion, on the record here we are unable to say that the deferred payment agreement was any less bona fide or any less a part of the purchase-sale agreement merely because it was not memorialized until just prior to closing.

The Commissioner relies heavily upon Williams v. United States, 219 F.2d 523 (5th Cir. 1955), in support of its claim that the escrow arrangement here amounted to a "self-imposed," rather than "substantial," limitation on the taxpayer's access to the sales proceeds in 1973. However, the *Williams* case is clearly distinguishable and does not control here. In *Williams*, the seller-taxpayer entered into an agreement to sell timber to a lumber company for a cash price. After the sale contract was executed, the taxpayer-seller decided, for tax reasons, that he wanted to receive part of the purchase payment in four installments in later years. The taxpayer himself prepared an escrow agreement naming the bank as the escrow agent and the taxpayer personally secured the bank's approval of the arrangement. The *Williams* court, emphasizing that the escrow arrangement was unilaterally set up by the seller-taxpayer, concluded that under the terms of the purchase agreement, the entire purchase price became available to the taxpayer upon completion of the sale.

Unlike in *Williams*, the escrow arrangement here was not unilaterally imposed by Reed, but rather was part of a bona fide modification to the purchase-sale agreement between Reed and Cvengros. Under that agreement, as modified, the purchase price did not become available to Reed until the taxable year following the year of the sale.

The instant case is thus much closer to another Fifth Circuit case, Busby v. United States, 679 F.2d 48 (5th Cir. 1982), involving a cotton farmer's use of an escrow device to defer income from the sale of a cotton crop until the year after it was harvested and delivered to the buyer. In *Busby*, the taxpayer-farmer emphasized the importance of a deferred payment and conditioned the sale upon it.

Accordingly, the cotton gin, the buyer's purchasing agent, agreed to establish an irrevocable escrow account in a bank. Under the terms of purchase agreement, the buyer was to deposit the proceeds of the sale into the escrow account following the delivery of the cotton in 1973. The escrowee was to then pay the purchase price to the farmer in 1974. Once the purchase price had been deposited with the escrowee in 1973, there was no condition on the farmer's receipt of the funds other than the passage of time. The 5th Circuit in *Busby* concluded that there was an arms-length agreement to defer payment which was effective to shift the farmer's tax on the proceeds until the year following the sale.

The only notable distinction between *Busby* and this case is that the deferred payment arrangement in this case was part of a modification of the original purchase-sale agreement. However, as we discussed above, this distinction is not controlling where, as here, the modification was bona fide and became binding prior to the time when the taxpayer's right to immediate payment had vested. . . .

[I]n the instant case, and in *Busby*, the taxpayer's right to demand payment of the escrowed purchase proceeds in the year of the sale was restricted by a binding agreement with the purchaser requiring that payments to the taxpayer be made the following year. Under Treasury Regulation §1.451-2(a), such an agreement, even though it restricts only the time of payment, serves as a "substantial limitation" on the taxpayer's right to demand payment of the escrowed purchase proceeds in the year of the sale. See McDonald, Deferred Compensation: Conceptual Astigmatism, 24 Tax L. Rev. 201, 204 (1969) ("[Section 1.451-2(a)] does not say that income is constructively received merely because its eventual payment is not subject to conditions of restrictions; the central consideration is whether the taxpayer's control of the time of its payment is subject to restrictions or limitations").

Furthermore, Treasury Regulation §1.451-2(a) also provides that income is recognized by a cash basis taxpayer "in the taxable year during which it is credited to his account, set apart for him, *or otherwise made available so that he may draw upon it at any time.*" (Emphasis added.) Here, as in *Busby* . . . , the binding deferred payment agreement between the purchaser and seller prevented the taxpayer from "drawing" upon the escrowed funds in the year of the sale.

B.   ECONOMIC BENEFIT

The Commissioner next contends that in 1973 Reed received a taxable economic benefit by virtue of Cvengros' deposit of the sales proceeds into the escrow account. The Commissioner argues that upon the December 27, 1973 closing, there were no open transactions remaining and Reed's right to future payment from the escrow account was irrevocable, being conditioned only upon the passage of time; hence, Reed received the "cash equivalent" of the sales proceeds deposited in the escrow account. The Commissioner points out that Reed could have assigned his irrevocable right to receive future payment of the escrow funds.

This argument, which was largely embraced by the Tax Court, is predicated upon a misapplication of various cases the Commissioner says espouse the economic benefit doctrine. These cases held that escrow arrangements were ineffective to defer income tax because of the existence of one of two factors, not present in the instant case: (1) the taxpayer received some present, beneficial interest from the escrow account; (2) the escrow arrangement was the product of the taxpayer's self-imposed limitation on funds the taxpayer had an unqualified, vested right to control.

Specifically, Kuehner [v. Commissioner, 214 F.2d 437 (1954)], the First Circuit case upon which the Commissioner principally relies, held that a taxpayer recognized income when the purchase price was deposited with the escrowee because the taxpayer's interest in the escrowed funds constituted a property interest equivalent to cash. The taxpayer's interest in the escrow fund was so viewed because the taxpayer was entitled to investment income earned while the funds were in escrow and hence enjoyed a complete and present economic interest in the funds. As the court stated:

> Under the terms of the 1947 agreement the interest from the invested [escrow fund] was payable to the petitioner. The Trustee's duties were ministerial and the economic benefits of the [escrow] fund held by it belonged to the [taxpayer].

214 F.2d at 440.

By contrast, in this case Reed was not entitled to receive the income earned from the investment of funds held by the escrowee, but merely obtained an unconditional promise that he would ultimately be paid on January 3, 1974 in accordance with the deferred payment provision.

The Commissioner, however, seizes upon broad language in *Kuehner* as support for the proposition that one who has an unconditional right to future payment from an irrevocable escrow account receives taxable income in the year the escrow account was created. There are three reasons why we do not interpret *Kuehner* as supporting this proposition. First, as the *Kuehner* court apparently recognized, the deposited escrow funds could be characterized as "the equivalent of cash" only if the taxpayer received a present beneficial interest in such funds — e.g., investment income. The *Kuehner* court's discussion of the taxpayer's present, beneficial interest in the escrow funds would have been superfluous if it were holding that the taxpayer's unconditional right to future payment of such funds was the equivalent of cash. Hence, we believe it is reasonable to interpret the *Kuehner* court's discussion of the unconditional nature of a right to future payment as relating to the court's determination of the appropriate value of the economic benefit conferred, the court having determined that the taxpayer had received a present economic benefit.

Second, to apply the Commissioner's interpretation of *Kuehner* to this case would be at odds with the well established principle that a deferred payment arrangement is effective to defer income recognition to a cash basis taxpayer, provided it is part of an arms-length agreement between the purchaser and seller. That the cash basis taxpayer's right to receive future payment of the escrowed proceeds may be characterized as unconditional or irrevocable does not render the contractually binding restriction on the time of payment any less substantial.

Third, to apply the Commissioner's interpretation of *Kuehner* here would require an extension of the economic benefit doctrine that would significantly erode the distinction between cash and accrual methods of accounting. The economic benefit doctrine, a nonstatutory doctrine emerging from and primarily related to the area of the employee deferred compensation, is based on the idea that an individual should be taxed on any economic benefit conferred upon him, to the extent that the benefit has an ascertainable fair market value.[6] However, in applying the economic benefit doctrine to a cash basis taxpayer's contractual right to receive future payment, as we must do here, courts generally go beyond an inquiry into the fair market value of the contract right to ask the separate question of whether the contract right is the equivalent of cash. Without this separate inquiry, the economic benefit doctrine, as applied to a cash basis taxpayer, could be broadly construed to cover all deferred compensation and deferred payment contracts.

In order to meet the cash equivalency requirement for income recognition, a cash basis taxpayer's contractual right to future payment must be reflected in a negotiable note, bond, or other evidence of indebtedness which, like money, commonly and readily changes hands in commerce. . . . And, in addition to being readily transferable, the evidence of indebtedness received by the taxpayer must be intended as present payment of the amount owed, rather than merely as evidence that payment will be forthcoming in the future.

In this case, it is difficult to conceive Reed's contractual right to future payment, even though unconditional and evidenced by an escrow account, as a right which commonly and readily changes hands in commerce. However, even assuming Reed's right to future payment of the escrowed proceeds was readily transferable in commerce, the escrow account was not intended by the parties as present payment of the purchase price, but rather was intended to serve as an added assurance that payment would be made in the next year. As such, the escrow account cannot be characterized fairly as the equivalent of cash to Reed in 1973. We would have to ignore the distinction between cash and accrual methods of accounting to adopt a rule requiring immediate recognition of income by a cash basis taxpayer who has a contractual right to future payment from an escrow account, but who has received no present beneficial interest from that account.

The Commissioner alternatively suggests that Reed received a present beneficial interest in the escrow funds in the sense that he could have assigned his right to receive payment under the agreement. This argument proves either too much or too little. It proves too much because any promisee under a contract for deferred payment could conceivably assign his right to receive future payment, provided the contract does not specifically include a non-assignment clause. Hence, to base the economic benefit rule on whether a taxpayer could have assigned his contractual right to future payment would eviscerate the well recognized rule that a taxpayer can defer income recognition pursuant to a bona fide deferred payment agreement. Furthermore, it proves too little in this case because Reed never attempted to make any assignment of his right to receive the escrow funds and thus did nothing to charge himself with any economic benefit to be derived from the funds.

C.   RECEIPT OF PROCEEDS BY TAXPAYER'S AGENT

The Commissioner's last argument, neither raised nor addressed in the Tax Court, is that the escrowee bank served as Reed's agent in receiving and holding the

---

6. "[U]nlike constructive receipt, economic benefit requires the actual receipt of property or the actual receipt of a right to receive property in the future, at which point, the doctrine asks whether the property or the right confers a present economic benefit with an ascertainable fair market value." Metzer, Constructive Receipt, Economic Benefit, and Assignment of Income, 29 Tax L. Rev. at 551.

sales proceeds in 1973. The Commissioner cites cases recognizing the principle that receipt of proceeds by the seller's agent is tantamount to receipt by the principal. The Commissioner essentially contends that the escrowee bank must have been Reed's agent because the escrow device served only the benefit of the taxpayer, and the buyer Cvengros was essentially indifferent to the deferral device; hence, the escrow arrangement really amounted to a self-imposed limitation. The Commissioner accordingly heavily relies upon [Warren v. United States, 613 F.2d 591 (5th Cir. 1980)], where that court states: "a self-imposed limitation, not part of the sales transaction between the buyer and seller . . . does not serve to change the general rule that receipt by an agent is receipt by the principal."

The Commissioner's argument here is closely tied to its constructive receipt argument and fails for the same reason. In all of the cases the Commissioner cites as holding that the escrowee served as the taxpayer's agent, the courts found dispositive that the deferral arrangement was unilaterally set up by the taxpayer-seller and was not part of any bona fide agreement with the buyer.

By contrast, the escrow arrangement here was a product of a bona fide modification to the purchase-sale agreement between the seller, Reed, and the buyer, Cvengros. The escrow agreement was in fact signed by both Reed and Cvengros. Hence, the purchaser . . . not only knew about but actively participated in the escrow agreement giving the escrowee the authority to hold the purchase proceeds until 1974. Further, the escrow agreement itself provided that the escrowee bank was acting on the behalf of both Reed and Cvengros.

Courts have generally recognized that an escrowee does not serve as a taxpayer's agent for income recognition purposes where, as in this case, the escrow arrangement is a valid one, under which the escrowee represents both the taxpayer-seller and the other party to the escrow agreement, i.e., the buyer.

Furthermore, we cannot accept the Commissioner's argument that an agency relationship for income recognition purposes is established by the mere fact that the escrowed funds would eventually inure to the benefit of Reed. All escrow accounts set up under a deferred payment agreement ultimately inure to the benefit of the receiving party. Hence, if the Commissioner's argument were accepted, no bona fide agreement between the purchaser and seller calling for deferred payment through the use of an escrow arrangement would be legally effective to postpone income recognition.

Thus, to establish an agency relationship between the escrowee and taxpayer, the Commissioner must show that the escrow device was set up unilaterally by the taxpayer or that the escrowee was functioning under the exclusive authority of the taxpayer. The Commissioner has failed to make such a showing here. . . .

Judgment reversed.

Problems

5-4. On the morning of December 31, employer has a check for employee's December salary delivered to employee's office mailbox.

a. What result if employee takes the check from the mailbox at 10 A.M. but because of a busy work schedule does not have time to go to the bank and cash it during that day?

b. What result if the employee does not go to the office and pick up the check from his mailbox until 6:35 P.M., which is after all of the local banks have closed?

c. What result to employee if he intentionally refrains from going to his office on December 31 in an attempt to avoid receipt of the check?

d. What result in *c* if the check were written on an account in which there were no funds until Monday, January 3?

e. What result if employee does not go to his office on December 31 because he was ill and at home in bed?

f. What result if December 31 was a Sunday, and all banks were closed?

g. What result if, instead of delivering the check to the employee's mailbox, the employer mailed it to the employee's home on December 31, and it was received by the employee on January 2?

h. What result if the mailing in *g* was not customary but was done at the employee's request?

5-5. On December 1, year 1, Jim Hughes executed a one-year lease to rent a dance studio to Lyndsey Morris, a professional dance instructor, for $12,000 per year with rent payable in monthly installments on the last day of each month ($1,000 per month). Hughes usually required commercial tenants to pay six months' rent in advance, but because year 1 had been a financially good year, Hughes did not require Morris to pay the six-month advance. In further pursuit of the goal of income deferral, on December 29 Hughes requested that Morris not pay rent for December of year 1 until January 10, year 2. Morris agreed and paid the December rent on the latter date. Hughes and Morris used the cash receipts and disbursements method of accounting and were calendar year taxpayers.

a. Was Hughes in constructive receipt of one year's rent as of December 1, year 1?

b. Was Hughes in constructive receipt of rent for six months as of December 1, year 1?

c. Was Hughes in constructive receipt of the December, year 1 rent as of December 31, year 1?

d. What result in *c* if Morris's dance studio had been a new enterprise and, as a result, did not have customers or receipts in the first month of business?

Assume that the Lyndsey Morris dance studio was a financial success and that she wished to purchase the property she had been renting from Jim Hughes. On December 2, year 2, the parties agreed to a purchase price of $90,000 cash. On December 3, year 2, Morris deposited the $90,000 in an escrow account. The escrow instructions provided that on Morris's approval of title, to occur within thirty days of the opening of the escrow, title was to be transferred to Morris and the cash in escrow transferred to Hughes.

e. Was Hughes in constructive receipt of $90,000 on December 3, year 2?

f. If Morris approved title on December 29, year 2 and on January 3, year 3 Hughes received a $90,000 check from the escrow agent, what was the proper year for Hughes to report gain on the sale? Assume the check was mailed to Hughes on December 29, year 2.

g. Would it have made any difference in *f* if Morris had approved title on January 1, year 3, instead of December 29, year 2?

h. Assume that in addition to Morris's approval of title, the completion of the transaction required that Hughes remove certain property from the premises. Morris approved title on December 29, year 2, and Hughes removed the property on January 1, year 3.

i. Would it have made a difference in *h* if Hughes had waited to remove the property until January 1, year 3, because that was the earliest that a moving company could be hired?

4. Promises to Pay in the Future: Deferred Compensation

The preceding sections considered taxpayer attempts to defer income for one-time payments, such as the taxpayer in *Cowden* seeking to defer payment for advance royalties and the law firm in *Miele* seeking to defer income by waiting to bill for services rendered. What if a taxpayer agrees to payment for services that span multiple years? If an employer hires an employee for a fixed number of years, at a fixed annual salary, and guarantees the salary even if the taxpayer cannot perform, should all the future salary be included in the taxpayer's income immediately? This unusual set of facts tends to arise in some particular arenas; for example, it is not uncommon in the entertainment industry (such as a guarantee to pay an actor a share of the profits after a movie is released) and in professional sports (such as a guaranteed contract for a baseball player). Is a guaranteed contract for future salary payments more similar to the check in *Kahler* or the placement of proceeds in escrow in *Reed*? As in prior cases, taxpayers sought to defer the income until it was actually paid. Although the Service argued for many years that contractually deferring the receipt of compensation did not defer its inclusion in income, the Service in Revenue Ruling 60-31, which follows, ultimately affixed its stamp of approval on certain deferral techniques.

REV. RUL. 60-31
1960-1 C.B. 174

Advice has been requested regarding the taxable year of inclusion in gross income of a taxpayer, using the cash receipts and disbursements method of accounting, of compensation for services received under the circumstances described below.

(1) On January 1, 1958, the taxpayer and corporation X executed an employment contract under which the taxpayer is to be employed by the corporation in an executive capacity for a period of five years. Under the contract, the taxpayer is entitled to a stated annual salary and to additional compensation of 10*x* dollars for each year. The additional compensation will be credited to a bookkeeping reserve account and will be deferred, accumulated, and paid in annual installments equal to one-fifth of the amount in the reserve as of the close of the year immediately preceding the year of first payment. The payments are to begin only upon (a) termination of the taxpayer's employment by the corporation; (b) the taxpayer's becoming a part-time employee of the corporation; or (c) the taxpayer's becoming partially or totally incapacitated. Under the terms of the agreement, corporation X

is under a merely contractual obligation to make the payments when due, and the parties did not intend that the amounts in the reserve be held by the corporation in trust for the taxpayer.

The contract further provides that if the taxpayer should fail or refuse to perform his duties, the corporation will be relieved of any obligation to make further credits to the reserve (but not of the obligation to distribute amounts previously contributed); but, if the taxpayer should become incapacitated from performing his duties, then credits to the reserve will continue for one year from the date of the incapacity, but not beyond the expiration of the five-year term of the contract. There is no specific provision in the contract for forfeiture by the taxpayer of his right to distribution from the reserve; and, in the event he should die prior to his receipt in full of the balance in the account, the remaining balance is distributable to his personal representative at the rate of one-fifth per year for five years, beginning three months after his death. . . .

(3) On October 1, 1957, the taxpayer, an author, and corporation Y, a publisher, executed an agreement under which the taxpayer granted to the publisher the exclusive right to print, publish and sell a book he had written. This agreement provides that the publisher will (1) pay the author specified royalties based on the actual cash received from the sale of the published work, (2) render semiannual statements of the sales, and (3) at the time of rendering each statement make settlement for the amount due. On the same day, another agreement was signed by the same parties, mutually agreeing that, in consideration of, and notwithstanding any contrary provisions contained in the first contract, the publisher shall not pay the taxpayer more than $100x$ dollars in any one calendar year. Under this supplemental contract, sums in excess of $100x$ dollars accruing in any one calendar year are to be carried over by the publisher into succeeding accounting periods; and the publisher shall not be required either to pay interest to the taxpayer on any such excess sums or to segregate any such sums in any manner.

(4) In June 1957, the taxpayer, a football player, entered into a two-year standard player's contract with a football club in which he agreed to play football and engage in activities related to football during the two-year term only for the club. In addition to a specified salary for the two-year term, it was mutually agreed that as an inducement for signing the contract the taxpayer would be paid a bonus of $150x$ dollars. The taxpayer could have demanded and received payment of this bonus at the time of signing the contract, but at his suggestion there was added to the standard contract form a paragraph providing substantially as follows:

> The player shall receive the sum of $150x$ dollars upon signing of this contract, contingent upon the payment of this $150x$ dollars to an escrow agent designated by him. The escrow agreement shall be subject to approval by the legal representatives of the player, the Club, and the escrow agent.

Pursuant to this added provision, an escrow agreement was executed on June 25, 1957, in which the club agreed to pay $150x$ dollars on that date to the Y bank, as escrow agent; and the escrow agent agreed to pay this amount, plus interest, to the taxpayer in installments over a period of five years. The escrow agreement also provides that the account established by the escrow agent is to bear the taxpayer's name; that payments from such account may be made only in accordance with the terms of the agreement; that the agreement is binding upon the parties thereto and their successors or assigns; and that in the event of the taxpayer's death during the escrow period the balance due will become part of his estate. . . .

[T]he individual concerned in each of the situations described above, employs the cash receipts and disbursements method of accounting. Under that method, he is required to include the compensation concerned in gross income only for the taxable year in which it is actually or constructively received. Consequently, the question for resolution is whether in each of the situations described the income in question was constructively received in a taxable year prior to the taxable year of actual receipt.

A mere promise to pay, not represented by notes or secured in any way, is not regarded as a receipt of income within the intendment of the cash receipts and disbursements method. . . . Also C. Florian Zittel v. Commissioner, 12 B.T.A. 675, in which, holding a salary to be taxable when received, the Board said: "Taxpayers on a receipts and disbursements basis are required to report only income actually received no matter how binding any contracts they may have to receive more."

This should not be construed to mean that under the cash receipts and disbursements method income may be taxed only when realized in cash. For, under that method a taxpayer is required to include in income that which is received in cash or cash equivalent. And, as stated in the above-quoted provisions of the regulations, the "receipt" contemplated by the cash method may be actual or constructive. . . .

[U]nder the doctrine of constructive receipt, a taxpayer may not deliberately turn his back upon income and thereby select the year for which he will report it. Nor may a taxpayer, by a private agreement, postpone receipt of income from one taxable year to another.

However, the statute cannot be administered by speculating whether the payor would have been willing to agree to an earlier payment. See, for example, J. D. Amend, et ux., v. Commissioner, 13 T.C. 178, acquiescence, C.B. 1950-1, 1; and C. E. Gullett, et al. v. Commissioner, 31 B.T.A. 1067, in which the court, citing a number of authorities for its holding, stated:

> It is clear that the doctrine of constructive receipt is to be sparingly used; that amounts due from a corporation but unpaid, are not to be included in the income of an individual reporting his income on a cash receipts basis unless it appears that the money was available to him, that the corporation was able and ready to pay him, that his right to receive was not restricted, and that his failure to receive resulted from exercise of his own choice.

Consequently, it seems clear that in each case involving a deferral of compensation a determination of whether the doctrine of constructive receipt is applicable must be made upon the basis of the specific factual situation involved.

Applying the foregoing criteria to the situations described above, the following conclusions have been reached:

(1) The additional compensation to be received by the taxpayer under the employment contract concerned will be includible in his gross income only in the taxable years in which the taxpayer actually receives installment payments in cash or other property previously credited to his account. To hold otherwise would be contrary to the provisions of the regulations and the court decisions mentioned above. . . .

(3) Here the principal agreement provided that the royalties were payable substantially as earned, and this agreement was supplemented by a further concurrent agreement which made the royalties payable over a period of years. This supplemental agreement, however, was made before the royalties were earned; in fact, it was made on the same day as the principal agreement and the two agreements were a part of the same transaction. Thus, for all practical purposes, the arrangement from the beginning is similar to that in (1) above. Therefore, it is also held that the author concerned will be required to include the royalties in his gross income only in the taxable years in which they are actually received in cash or other property.

(4) In arriving at a determination as to the includibility of the 150x dollars concerned in the gross income of the football player, under the circumstances described, in addition to the authorities cited above, consideration also has been given to Revenue Ruling 55-727, C.B. 1955-2, 25, and to the decision in E. T. Sproull v. Commissioner, 16 T.C. 244.

In Revenue Ruling 55-727, the taxpayer, a professional baseball player, entered into a contract in 1953 in which he agreed to render services for a baseball club and to refrain from playing baseball for any other club during the term of the contract. In addition to specified compensation, the contract provided for a bonus to the player or his estate, payable one-half in January 1954 and one-half in January 1955, whether or not he was able to render services. The primary question was whether the bonus was capital gain or ordinary income; and, in holding that the bonus payments constituted ordinary income, it was stated that they were taxable for the year in which received by the player. However, under the facts set forth in Revenue Ruling 55-727 there was no arrangement, as here, for placing the amount of the bonus in escrow. Consequently, the instant situation is distinguishable from that considered in Revenue Ruling 55-727.

In E. T. Sproull v. Commissioner, 16 T.C. 244, affirmed, 194 Fed. (2d) 541, the petitioner's employer in 1945 transferred in trust for the petitioner the amount of $10,500. The trustee was directed to pay out of principal to the petitioner the sum of $5,250 in 1946 and the balance, including income, in 1947. In the event of the petitioner's prior death, the amounts were to be paid to his administrator, executor, or heirs. The petitioner contended that the Commissioner erred in including the sum of $10,500 in his taxable income for 1945. In this connection, the court stated:

> it is undoubtedly true that the amount which the Commissioner has included in petitioner's income for 1945 was used in that year for his benefit . . . in setting up the trust of which petitioner, or, in the event of his death then his estate, was the sole beneficiary. . . .
>
> The question then becomes . . . was "any economic or financial benefit conferred on the employee as compensation" in the taxable year. If so, it was taxable to him in that year. This question we must answer in the affirmative. The employer's part of the transaction terminated in 1945. It was then that the amount of the compensation was fixed at $10,500 and irrevocably paid out for petitioner's sole benefit. . . .

Applying the principles stated in the *Sproull* decision to the facts here, it is concluded that the 150x-dollar bonus is includible in the gross income of the football player concerned in 1957, the year in which the club unconditionally paid such amount to the escrow agent. . . .

Note on Indefinite Deferred Compensation

Due to the ability of well-advised taxpayers to defer income from compensation for services under the law described above, in 2004 Congress enacted §409A, limiting the ability of most service providers to defer compensation income for more than a fixed period of time. Although §409A was intended to prevent taxpayers from deferring compensation income indefinitely, it did so by adopting a highly detailed and complex regime that can prove quite daunting in its application. In general, under §409A an employee may defer income from compensation for services only for a single fixed period of time, but only if the employer elects to do so in the preceding taxable year. Further, once the election is made, the deferred compensation may not be paid earlier than the elected date except in a few limited circumstances. To the extent deferred compensation does not comply with these rules, not only is the compensation included in the employee's income immediately, but the employee also is subject to a 20-percent penalty on the deferred income and interest on the tax deferred.

5.   Treatment of Nonqualified Deferred Compensation Plans

Joint Committee on Taxation General Explanation of Tax Legislation Enacted in the 108th Congress
JCS-5-05 at 467 (2005)

PRESENT AND PRIOR LAW

IN GENERAL

Under present and prior law, the determination of when amounts deferred under a nonqualified deferred compensation arrangement are includible in the gross income of the individual earning the compensation depends on the facts and circumstances of the arrangement. A variety of tax principles and Code provisions may be relevant in making this determination, including the doctrine of constructive receipt, [and] the economic benefit doctrine. . . . Under prior law, the Code did not include rules specifically governing nonqualified deferred compensation.

In general, the time for income inclusion of nonqualified deferred compensation depends on whether the arrangement is unfunded or funded. If the arrangement is unfunded, then the compensation is generally includible in income when it is actually or constructively received. If the arrangement is funded, then income is includible for the year in which the individual's rights are transferable or not subject to a substantial risk of forfeiture . . .

. . . Income is constructively received when it is credited to an individual's account, set apart, or otherwise made available so that it may be drawn on at any time. Income is not constructively received if the taxpayer's control of its receipt is subject to substantial limitations or restrictions . . .

Rabbi Trusts

Arrangements have developed in an effort to provide employees with security for nonqualified deferred compensation, while still allowing deferral of income inclusion. A "rabbi trust" is a trust or other fund established by the employer to hold assets from which nonqualified deferred compensation payments will be made. The trust or fund is generally irrevocable and does not permit the employer to use the assets for purposes other than to provide nonqualified deferred compensation, except that the terms of the trust or fund provide that the assets are subject to the claims of the employer's creditors in the case of insolvency or bankruptcy.

. . . In the case of a rabbi trust, terms providing that the assets are subject to the claims of creditors of the employer in the case of insolvency or bankruptcy have been the basis for the conclusion that the creation of a rabbi trust does not cause the related nonqualified deferred compensation arrangement to be funded for income tax purposes. As a result, no amount is included in income by reason of the rabbi trust; generally income inclusion occurs as payments are made from the trust . . .

Since the concept of rabbi trusts was developed, arrangements have developed which attempt to protect the assets from creditors despite the terms of the trust. Arrangements also have developed which attempt to allow deferred amounts to be available to individuals, while still purporting to meet the safe harbor requirements set forth by the IRS.

Reasons for Change

The Congress was aware of the popular use of deferred compensation arrangements by executives to defer current taxation of substantial amounts of income. Many nonqualified deferred compensation arrangements had developed which allowed improper deferral of income. Executives often used arrangements that allowed deferral of income, but also provided security of future payment and control over amounts deferred. . . .

The Congress believed that certain arrangements that allow participants inappropriate levels of control or access to amounts deferred should not result in deferral of income inclusion. The Congress also believed that certain arrangements, such as offshore trusts, which effectively protect assets from creditors, should be treated as funded and not result in deferral of income inclusion.

Explanation of Provision

In General

Under the Act, all amounts deferred under a nonqualified deferred compensation plan for all taxable years are currently includible in gross income to the extent not subject to a substantial risk of forfeiture and not previously included in gross income, unless certain requirements are satisfied. If the requirements of the Act are not satisfied, in addition to current income inclusion, interest at the underpayment rate plus one percentage point is imposed on the underpayments that would have occurred had the compensation been includible in income when first deferred, or if later, when not subject to a substantial risk of forfeiture. The amount required to be included in income is also subject to a 20-percent additional tax.

PERMISSIBLE DISTRIBUTIONS

In General

Under the Act, distributions from a nonqualified deferred compensation plan may be allowed only upon separation from service . . . death, a specified time (or pursuant to a fixed schedule), change in control of a corporation . . . occurrence of an unforeseeable emergency, or if the participant becomes disabled. A nonqualified deferred compensation plan may not allow distributions other than upon the permissible distribution events and, except as provided in regulations by the Secretary, may not permit acceleration of a distribution. . . .

Prohibition on Acceleration of Distributions

As mentioned above, except as provided in regulations by the Secretary, no accelerations of distributions may be allowed. In general, changes in the form of distribution that accelerate payments are subject to the rule prohibiting acceleration of distributions. . . .

It is intended that the Secretary will provide other, limited, exceptions to the prohibition on accelerated distributions, such as when the accelerated distribution is required for reasons beyond the control of the participant and the distribution is not elective. For example, it is anticipated that an exception could be provided if a distribution is needed in order to comply with Federal conflict of interest requirements or a court-approved settlement incident to divorce . . . .

REQUIREMENTS WITH RESPECT TO ELECTIONS

The Act requires that a plan must provide that compensation for services performed during a taxable year may be deferred at the participant's election only if the election to defer is made no later than the close of the preceding taxable year, or at such other time as provided in Treasury regulations. In the case of any performance-based compensation based on services performed over a period of at least 12 months, such election may be made no later than six months before the end of the service period. It is not intended that the Act override the constructive receipt doctrine, as constructive receipt rules continue to apply.

Problem

5-6. Harry Smith and his employer, Acme Machine Tool Company, have entered into a deferred compensation agreement providing that Acme will credit $1,000 of Smith's compensation to a deferred compensation account on the first day of each month for as long as Acme employs Smith. The terms of the agreement permit Acme to invest the funds in the account at its discretion. Any gains or losses realized on the investment will be credited or debited to the account. On Smith's retirement from or termination by Acme, the funds in the account are to be paid to him in monthly installments over the succeeding fifteen years. If Smith dies before he becomes eligible to receive the funds, his estate will receive the deferred compensation payments.

a. Assuming that the deferred compensation benefits cannot be anticipated, assigned, or sold by Smith, has he successfully deferred the gross income resulting from this compensation?

b. Will deferral be successful if Acme invests the funds in an annuity contract with Smith as beneficiary? What result if Acme is the beneficiary of the contract?

c. What effect on deferral if the agreement gave Acme the power to invest the funds and Smith is permitted to recommend investments?

d. What if Smith could veto Acme's proposed investments?

e. Assume that under Smith's agreement with Acme, the deferral amounts are to be invested in an interest-bearing account and Smith is permitted to borrow against the account. Will this thwart Smith's attempt to defer compensation? If so, when will he be required to recognize income?

6. *Section 83: Property Received for Services Performed*

Code: §83(a) to (c)
Regulations: §§1.83-1(a)(1), 1.83-2, 1.83-3(c)(1) to (3)

In addition to contractual arrangements between an employer and an employee like those described in Revenue Ruling 60-31, Congress has statutorily provided for deferral of compensation. For example, pursuant to §401, income may be deferred when an employer contributes to a "qualified" pension, profit-sharing, or stock bonus plan on behalf of an employee. These plans provide several tax benefits. First, the employee is not taxed on the employer's contribution to the plan; rather, employees are taxed only when they actually receive payments during retirement. Second, the employer receives a current business expense deduction for the amount contributed. Third, earnings on the funds are not currently taxed.

Statutorily authorized qualified plans do not govern attempts to defer income by compensating an employee with shares of a corporate employer's stock. Section 83 was enacted to govern the taxation of stock or other property that is received in connection with the performance of services.

Generally, §83 provides that one who receives property in connection with the performance of services must include in gross income the excess of the fair market value of the property received over the amount paid by the transferee at the earlier of (1) the time the property is no longer subject to a substantial risk of forfeiture or (2) the time at which the transferee has the right to transfer the property. For purposes of computing the amount includable in gross income, fair market value is determined as of the time the substantial risk of forfeiture lapses or the property becomes transferable.

A substantial risk of forfeiture exists if the taxpayer's right to full enjoyment of the property is conditioned on the performance of substantial services by any individual. §83(c). Transferability of property is limited only if there is a substantial risk of forfeiture. Thus, if a taxpayer receives property such as stock in connection with services but must return the property if she does not remain with the company for a stated period, she has received property subject to a substantial risk of forfeiture.

The effect of §83(a) is to defer gain recognition on property received in connection with the performance of services if that property is subject to a substantial risk of forfeiture or a limitation on transferability. On the other hand, when the property received is subject to forfeiture, §83(b) permits the taxpayer to elect to recognize the income, represented by the property's value, in the taxable year in which the taxpayer received the property. To be effective, the §83(b) election must be made not more than thirty days after the date of the transfer.

The effect of the §83(b) election is to enable the taxpayer to defer income realization, a point best illustrated by example. Assume that taxpayer T receives property worth $1,000 in year 1 subject to a substantial risk of forfeiture that lapses in year 4. By year 4, the value of the property has increased to $3,500. Under the general rule of §83(a), T must recognize $3,500 as ordinary income in year 4. If, however, T had made a timely §83(b) election, she would have accelerated her income recognition on $1,000 to year 1 but deferred realization of the $2,500 of appreciation until the ultimate disposition of the property. If T subsequently sells the property for $5,000, she will realize additional income of $4,000 if she elected §83(b) or $1,500 if §83(a) triggered income recognition in year 4. When T disposes of the property, the total income realized will be the same, §83 having affected only the timing of the realization of incremental portions of that income. Thus, if a taxpayer expects property that he or she has received subject to §83 to increase substantially in value before the risk of forfeiture lapses, the taxpayer may want to elect to recognize income in the year the property is received. If, however, the property is unlikely to appreciate, the taxpayer may choose to postpone income recognition until the substantial risk of forfeiture lapses.

One crucial aspect of §83(b) is that it includes the full fair market value of the property in income on the date of receipt of restricted property as if the restrictions did not apply, less any amount paid by the taxpayer. At one time, taxpayers contended that Congress did not have the power to tax this full unrestricted value of property because the property was in fact subject to restrictions and property with restrictions is worth less than property without restrictions. Pursuant to this analysis, taxpayers contended that their "accession to wealth" was only the restricted value of the property less any amount paid. Courts have consistently rejected this argument. See Pledger v. Comm., 641 F.2d 287 (5th Cir.), cert. denied, 454 U.S. 964 (1981); Sakol v. Comm., 574 F.2d 694 (2nd Cir.), cert. denied, 439 U.S. 859 (1978).

A collateral effect of §83 will be explored in Chapter 7, which addresses the characterization of gains and losses as ordinary or capital. Income recognized pursuant to either §83(a) or (b) is ordinary in character. If, however, the taxpayer holds the property received as a capital asset, he or she will generally recognize capital gain, which may be treated preferentially, on the sale of the asset. Consequently, §83(a) may reduce the amount of capital gain that is realized. For example, assume that in year 1 taxpayer P received stock worth $750. However, by the time the substantial risk of forfeiture lapses in year 4, the stock was worth $2,000. Under

§83(a), *P* must recognize $2,000 of ordinary income in year 4. Thus, $1,250 of unrealized appreciation was taxed as ordinary income. If, however, *P* had elected §83(b), he would recognize only $750 of ordinary income in year 1 and taxation of all appreciation in the value of the property would be deferred until the taxpayer sold the property, at which time $1,250 would be characterized as capital gain.

The preceding examples illustrate the need for a taxpayer, attempting to defer income under §83, to consider all the tax ramifications of the proposed transaction.

REV. RUL. 2007-49
2007-31 I.R.B. 237

ISSUES

(1) Is there a transfer of substantially nonvested stock subject to §83 of the Internal Revenue Code where restrictions imposed on substantially vested stock cause the substantially vested stock to become substantially nonvested? . . .

(3) Is there a transfer of substantially nonvested stock subject to §83 where a service provider exchanges substantially vested stock for substantially nonvested stock in a taxable stock acquisition?

FACTS

Investors form Corporation X in 2004, by contributing $1,000 each to Corporation X in exchange for 100 shares of Corporation X stock. In exchange for Individual A's agreement to perform services for Corporation X, Corporation X issues 100 shares of its stock to A. The fair market value of the Corporation X stock on that date is $10 per share. The shares of Corporation X stock transferred to A are "substantially vested" within the meaning of §1.83-3(b) of the Income Tax Regulations.

For the 2004 taxable year, the amount included in A's income under §83(a) is $1,000 (the fair market value of the stock ($10 × 100 shares) less the amount paid ($0)). A's basis in the stock is $1,000.

Situation 1. In connection with its plan to start a new business venture, Corporation X seeks financing from Investor M on July 9, 2007. Investor M agrees to invest funds in Corporation X in exchange for a specified number of shares and the further requirement that A agree to subject A's shares to a restriction that will cause the stock to be "substantially nonvested" within the meaning of §1.83-3(b). . . . A remains employed with Corporation X, and on July 9, 2009, the fair market value of Corporation X stock is $250 per share.

Situation [3]. Corporation Y, a corporation unrelated to Corporation X, agrees to acquire all of the stock of Corporation X. . . . The fair market value of the Corporation X stock on August 9, 2010, is $310 per share.

In the merger, A's 100 shares of substantially vested Corporation X stock are exchanged for 100 shares of Corporation Y stock [in a taxable transction] subject to a restriction that will cause the stock to be "substantially nonvested" within the meaning of §1.83-3(b). . . .

A timely files an election under §83(b) with respect to the substantially non-vested Corporation Y stock A receives in the merger.

A continues to be employed by Corporation X until August 9, 2013 at which time the fair market value of the stock is $500. A sells the stock on October 31, 2014 when the fair market value of the stock is $550 per share.

LAW

Section 83, provides that if, in connection with the performance of services, property is transferred to any person other than the service recipient, the excess of the fair market value of the property (determined without regard to any restriction other than a restriction which by its terms will never lapse), on the first day that the rights to the property are either transferable or not subject to a substantial risk of forfeiture, over the amount paid for the property is included in the service provider's gross income for the first taxable year in which the rights to the property are either transferable or not subject to a substantial risk of forfeiture.

Section 1.83-3(f) provides that property transferred to an employee or independent contractor (or beneficiary thereof) in recognition of the performance of, or the refraining from performance of, services is considered transferred in connection with the performance of services within the meaning of §83. . . .

Subjecting stock to a restriction that will cause it to be "substantially nonvested" (within the meaning of §1.83-3(b)) indicates that the property is transferred in connection with the performance of services even if the employee pays fair value for the stock. See Alves v. Commissioner, 734 F.2d 478 (9th Cir. 1984), aff'g 79 T.C. 864 (1982).

Section 1.83-1(a)(1) provides that property transferred in connection with the performance of services is not taxable under §83(a) until it has been transferred (as defined in §1.83-3(a)) to an employee or independent contractor and becomes substantially vested (as defined in §1.83-3(b)) in such person. Until such property becomes substantially vested, the transferor is regarded as the owner of the property, and any income from such property received by the employee or independent contractor (or beneficiary thereof) or the right to the use of such property by the employee or independent contractor constitutes additional compensation and must be included in the gross income of such employee or independent contractor for the taxable year in which such income is received or such use is made available.

Section 83(b) provides that any person who has performed services in connection with which property is transferred to any person may elect to include in gross income, for the taxable year in which such property is transferred, the excess of the fair market value of such property at the time of transfer (determined without regard to any restriction other than a restriction which by its terms will never lapse) over the amount paid for such property.

Section 1.83-2(a) provides, in part, that the fact that the transferee has paid full value for the property transferred, realizing no bargain element in the transaction, does not preclude the use of the election under §83(b). If this election is made, the substantial vesting rules of §83(a) and the regulations thereunder do not apply with respect to such property. Thus, with respect to such property, the excess (if any) of the fair market value of the property at the time of transfer (determined without regard to any restriction other than a restriction which by its terms will never lapse) over the amount (if any) paid for such property is includible in gross income as compensation at the time of transfer, and no compensation will be includible in gross income when such property becomes substantially vested. An employee who makes an election under §83(b) is considered to be the owner of the property. . . .

Section 1.83-3(g) provides that for purposes of §83 and its regulations, the term "amount paid" refers to the value of any money or property paid for the transfer of property to which §83 applies.

ANALYSIS—SITUATION 1

In Situation 1, in connection with the new investment, the substantially vested shares of Corporation X stock owned by A are subjected to a restriction causing them to be "substantially nonvested." Because the substantially vested shares of Corporation X stock are already owned by A for purposes of §83, there is no "transfer" under §83. Thus, the imposition of new restrictions on the substantially vested shares has no effect for purposes of §83.

When the substantially nonvested Corporation X stock becomes substantially vested on July 9, 2009, A does not recognize compensation income under §83(a). A's basis in the stock continues to be $1,000. . . .

ANALYSIS—SITUATION 3

In Situation 3, A holds substantially vested Corporation X stock with a basis of $1,000 at the time of the merger. A exchanges that substantially vested Corporation X stock for substantially nonvested Corporation Y stock with a fair market value of $310 per share in a taxable transaction. . . . A recognizes . . . gain on the disposition of the Corporation X stock in the amount of $30,000 ($31,000 fair market value of substantially non-vested Corporation Y stock ($310 per share × 100 shares) less $1,000 basis in the Corporation X stock). A's basis in the Corporation Y stock is $31,000.

Because the substantially vested Corporation X stock is exchanged for Corporation Y stock that is subjected to a restriction causing the shares to be "substantially nonvested," the substantially non-vested shares are treated as having been transferred in connection with the performance of services, and thus, are subject to §83.

. . . [T]he "amount paid" for the stock under §83 is $31,000. When A makes an election under §83(b) with respect to the Corporation Y stock, A does not report any additional amount of income for the 2010 taxable year as a result of such election because the fair market value of the stock less the amount paid for the stock is $0. A does not include any amount in compensation income in the 2013 taxable year when the stock becomes substantially vested because of the prior §83(b) election. A's basis in the Corporation Y stock continues to be $31,000. On the sale of the 100 shares in 2014, A will recognize capital gain of $24,000, the amount by which $55,000 ($550, the sale price, × 100 shares) exceeds A's $31,000 basis in the shares.

If A had not made an election under §83(b) with respect to the Corporation Y stock, when the stock becomes substantially vested on August 9, 2013, A would include $19,000 in gross income as compensation under §83(a). This is the amount by which the fair market value of 100 Corporation Y shares ($50,000 or $500 per share) exceeds the amount paid for those shares ($31,000). Consequently, A's basis in the Corporation Y stock would be increased by $19,000 to $50,000. On the sale of the 100 shares, A would recognize capital gain of $5,000, the amount by which $55,000 ($550, the sale price, × 100 shares) exceeds A's basis of $50,000 in the shares.

Holdings

(1) There is not a transfer of substantially nonvested stock subject to §83 where restrictions imposed on substantially vested stock cause the substantially vested stock to become substantially nonvested. . . .

(3) There is a transfer of substantially nonvested stock subject to §83 where a service provider exchanges substantially vested stock for substantially nonvested stock in a taxable stock acquisition.

Problem

5-7. Cornelia Swift had worked for Land Ho Corporation for twenty years as a salesperson. On her twentieth anniversary with the company, she was given fifty shares of stock with a fair market value of $1,500. Fifteen of the shares were in recognition of her past services. The balance of the shares were part of an incentive plan that had been recently initiated by Land Ho and contained a requirement that if Cornelia left the company within five years, she forfeited seven shares for every year of that period in which she did not continue her employment. Cornelia plans to take early retirement at the end of her twenty-first year of employment and start her own business.

   a.   What tax result to Swift on receipt of the fifteen shares received for past services?

   b.   What tax advice should be given to Swift regarding the thirty-five shares that she received under the incentive program?

C.   ACCRUAL METHOD OF ACCOUNTING

Code: §§446(c)(2), 451(a)
Regulations: §§1.446-1(c)(1)(ii), 1.451-1(a)

1.   All Events Test

Unlike cash method taxpayers, who include items in gross income when they are actually or constructively received, accrual method taxpayers generally do not focus upon receipt, but instead include items in gross income on the basis of an "all events" test. The all events test requires amounts to be included in gross income when "all the events have occurred which fix the right to receive such income and the amount thereof can be determined with reasonable accuracy." Reg. §1.451-1(a); see also Reg. §1.446-1(c)(1)(ii). Although the all events test is easy to state, it is often difficult to establish precisely when a right to receive income becomes "fixed." Moreover, pursuant to this test, accrual method taxpayers may be required to report income once it has been earned, even though the contract requires payment to be received in a subsequent taxable period.

The Service provides some general guidance by stating "that all the events that fix the right to receive income under an accrual method of accounting occur when (1) the required performance occurs, (2) payment therefor is due, or (3) payment therefor is made, whichever happens first." Rev. Rul. 79-292, 1979-2 C.B. 287. Contrary to the literal language of the all events test, Revenue Ruling 79-292 requires that advance payments be included in income when received, not at a later date when services are actually performed or title transferred.

2. Fixed Rights to Receipt

The primary focus of the all events test is the determination of when the taxpayer's right to receive income becomes fixed. This concept was examined by the Ninth Circuit in Flamingo Resort v. United States, which follows. In *Flamingo Resort*, the court addressed the question of whether gambling-debt markers represent a right to income that has become "fixed" for accrual purposes.

FLAMINGO RESORT v. UNITED STATES
664 F.2d 1387 (9th Cir. 1982)

Sneed, J.

The taxpayer, Flamingo Resort, Inc. (Flamingo), appeals from summary judgment by the district court in favor of the government.

I

FACTS

. . . Flamingo is a legal, licensed, gambling casino operating in the State of Nevada. The casino, an accrual basis taxpayer, excluded $676,432.00 of casino receivables in its 1967 tax return. . . .

The receivables in dispute arose from uncollected loans extended by Flamingo in the course of its business. In order to facilitate its gambling operations, Flamingo extended credit to some of its customers. That line of credit was proffered only after an extensive credit check of the patron was conducted by the casino. The customer would sign a "marker" signifying his liability for the sum loaned. Approximately sixty percent of the casino's total play resulted from such credit extensions.

Extensive collection efforts were undertaken on behalf of Flamingo to receive payment of those outstanding casino receivables not repaid prior to the patron's departure. Flamingo's estimates of collectibility of those receivables ranged as high as ninety-six percent. The extension of credit and high incidence of payment occurred despite the fact that Nevada does not recognize the legal enforceability of gambling debts.

II

ANALYSIS

The time of reporting of income of accrual basis taxpayers is governed by the "all events" test. The origins of this test can be traced to United States v. Anderson, 269 U.S. 422 (1926). There the Supreme Court held a tax payment for sale of munitions was *deductible* only in the year the sale occurred and not the following year in which the tax was paid. The taxpayer had contended the tax could not be accrued as an expense prior to its assessment and due date. The Court, in rejecting that argument, found "that in advance of the assessment of a tax, all the events may occur which fix the amount of the tax and determine the liability of the taxpayer to pay it." This approach was subsequently adopted by the Treasury Department with respect to the accrual of income. "Under an accrual method of accounting, income is includable in gross income when all the events have occurred which fix the right to receive such income and the amount thereof can be determined with reasonable accuracy." Treas. Reg. §1.451-1(a). See also Treas. Reg. §1.446-1(c)(1)(ii).

This case does not involve the question of "reasonable accuracy." Rather the issue is when does the right to receive the income which the "markers" represent become "fixed" for accrual purposes. Commentators and the courts have generally stated that the existence of a definite liability is a prerequisite to the accrual of any obligation. . . . Flamingo, relying on these authorities, contends that because the persons who gave the "markers" for gambling purposes had no legal obligation to repay the casino, the "markers" being void as a matter of law under Evans v. Cook, 11 Nev. 69, 75 (1876), the "liability" they represent was not "fixed." Rather discharge of the "liability" was contingent on the customer's volition. Therefore, Flamingo should not be required to accrue the "markers."

Flamingo also relies on H. Liebes & Co. v. Commissioner, 90 F.2d 932 (9th Cir. 1937). There the issue was when should a debt due an accrual basis taxpayer by the government be accrued. The debt was owed by the government as the result of litigation. This court stated:

> We may conclude that income has not accrued to a taxpayer until there arises to him a fixed or unconditional right to receive it. . . .
>   The complete definition would therefore seem to be that income accrues to a taxpayer, when there arises to him a fixed or unconditional right to receive it, if there is a reasonable expectancy that the right will be converted into money or its equivalent.

The court held that the right was fixed immediately upon expiration of the time for appeal by the government from the judgment in favor of the taxpayer. At that point there was a reasonable expectancy that the claim would be converted into money even if the funds to satisfy the judgment had not been appropriated. Although *Liebes* clearly establishes that an obligation must be "fixed" and that there be a "reasonable expectancy" of the obligation being converted into cash or its equivalent, it did not hold that in *all* situations the existence of a legal liability to pay is a prerequisite to the existence of a "fixed or unconditional right" to receive payment.

Nor do we believe that this prerequisite universally exists. Support for this position is provided by the line of authority that originates in Barker v. Magruder, 95 F.2d 122 (D.C. Cir. 1938), a case involving a taxpayer-lender who charged a rate of interest that violated the usury statute of the District of Columbia. The court held that, despite the fact the statute prohibited the taxpayer from legally enforcing the recovery of any interest, the uncollected usurious interest was properly accruable. It stated, "[t]he correct answer, as we think, depends not so much, as appellants urge, upon the legal right to enforce collection as upon the existing probability of its being received."

The taxpayer's course of dealing with its debtor was considered determinative in fashioning the definition of "fixed." In doing so the *Barker* court can be seen as properly avoiding a rigid definition of the term "fixed" in order to be responsive to unique facts and practical considerations.

Barker addresses a problem analogous to that presented in this case. Both involve a taxpayer attempting, as the district court below aptly phrased it, to "shield its *unsanctioned* operations from the normal incidents of the United States tax laws." Flamingo attacks this characterization as both astonishing and wrong and argues that the casino's operations are sanctioned by law. This is not the point the district court was addressing. Its comments were directed at the unsanctioned activity of gambling debt *enforcement*, not the day-to-day legally authorized gambling operations of the appellant. Gambling debt enforcement in Nevada in 1967 and usurious interest enforcement in the District of Columbia at the time of *Barker* were each confronted by a bar to the use of the courts. In neither case would the courts have been available to aid enforcement.

Flamingo here, as did the taxpayer in *Barker*, points to certain speculative and potential legal objections to payment available to its debtors. The practical answer emerges from the facts. Few, if any, debtors raise these objections and usually they pay up. Gambling is big business in Nevada. Flamingo and others lawfully engaged in gambling in Nevada who employ the accrual basis in tax accounting should not be permitted to distort that method of accounting merely because the State of Nevada chooses not to permit the use of its courts to collect gambling debts. . . .

. . . Flamingo, as noted earlier, conducted approximately sixty percent of its business through extensions of credit, and its own estimates of collectibility on outstanding casino receivables ranged as high as *ninety-six* percent. The lack of legal liability did not interfere with Flamingo's operation and it is doubtful that legal enforceability of the "markers" would or could increase its recovery rate. Under these circumstances, the obligations of Flamingo's patrons are as "fixed" as it is possible to be and, in fact, no less so than those of other businesses. Flamingo should not be heard to argue that it should be taxed differently from other legitimate businesses. Its inability to enforce its "markers" in court is not a sufficient burden to justify such a differential. The debts which the "markers" represent are, therefore, fixed; there is a reasonable expectancy of collection; and no contention has been made that the amounts cannot be determined with reasonable accuracy. . . .

3.   Timing of Inclusion of Various Forms of Income

The following discussion examines various forms of income and the timing of inclusion in gross income by accrual method taxpayers—focusing on the determinative issue of when "all events" have occurred.

a.   Interest Income

Generally, interest income is taxable as it is earned over the life of the interest-bearing obligation. Where, however, interest is paid in advance of the date on which it is actually earned, differing standards govern the reporting of interest income, depending on the circumstances. The Service has ruled that interest collected in advance is generally taxable income in the year of receipt even if the lender uses the accrual method of accounting. Rev. Rul. 58-225, 1958-1 C.B. 258. To reach this result, the Service applied the claim-of-right doctrine, which requires an item to be included in gross income when it is received under a claim of right without restriction as to its disposition. North American Oil Consolidated v. Burnet, 286 U.S. 417 (1932).

The Tax Court, on the other hand, has held that finance charges that are part of an installment sale should be included in income over the life of the contract, if a portion of the finance charges is abated in the event that the purchaser prepays any of the principal. Gunderson Bros. Engineering Corp. v. Commissioner, 42 T.C. 419 (1964) acq. 1967-2 C.B. 1. In *Gunderson Bros.*, the court reasoned that the event fixing the right to the interest did not occur until the interest became due. Until then, the buyer may have a right to a refund under state law, contract, or custom.

Where interest due becomes uncollectible, neither the judiciary nor the Service requires accrual. Clifton Manufacturing Co. v. Commissioner, 137 F.2d 290 (4th Cir. 1943); Rev. Rul. 80-361, 1980-2 C.B. 164. The proper method for reporting interest that is earned but cannot be collected is to include in gross income the amounts that accrued up to the date of default; amounts accruing after the date of default are not included. Rev. Rul. 80-361, 1980-2 C.B. 164. Amounts that are included in gross income prior to the date of default, but that were never received, entitle the taxpayer to a bad debt deduction. Accrual of interest recommences only when the interest can once again be collected.

b.   Dividend Income

Both accrual and cash method taxpayers report dividend income in the taxable year in which dividend checks are received. Tar Products Corp. v. Commissioner, 130 F.2d 866 (3d Cir. 1942); Reg. §1.301-1(b).

c. Sales in the Course of a Trade or Business

The all events test is satisfied for sales in the course of a trade or business in the year in which the goods are shipped, delivered, or accepted, or when title passes, provided the taxpayer's method is consistent from year to year. Reg. §1.446-1(c)(1)(ii). Moreover, the sale of goods on credit does not bar accrual of the sales price; instead, accrual method taxpayers report all accounts receivable in gross income, regardless of the buyer's ability to pay. Spring City Foundry Co. v. Commissioner, 292 U.S. 182 (1934). In fashioning this rule, the Supreme Court dismissed the taxpayer's argument that an uncollectible debt was not gross income by stating:

> Keeping accounts and making returns on the accrual basis, as distinguished from the cash basis, import that it is the *right* to receive and not the actual receipt that determines the inclusion of the amount in gross income. When the right to receive an amount becomes fixed, the right accrues.

Id. at 184-85 (emphasis added). An accrual method taxpayer's remedy for an account that becomes uncollectible, in whole or in part, is to claim a tax deduction in the year in which the unrecoverable amount is ascertained. The lesson of *Spring City Foundry* is that accrual method taxpayers who harbor doubts about the collection of the sales price should not sell goods on credit. This broad doctrine is not unlimited. If a taxpayer has no right to collect income from an insolvent buyer until the buyer satisfies the other creditors, at least one court has held that accrual can be deferred. *See* Commercial Solvents Corp. v. Commissioner, 42 T.C. 455 (1964), acq. 1965-2 C.B. 3 (payment not required to be included in income when taxpayer waives right to collect until payor becomes solvent). The sale of goods on consignment is an exception to the general rule of Regulation §1.446-1(c)(1)(ii). In such cases, income is not reported until the actual sale of the goods. Goods on consignment therefore are included in the consignor's ending inventory unless sold by the consignee. Reg. §1.471-1.

Reg. §1.451-5 provides an exception to the general rule for sales of inventory by permitting deferral for sales of gift certificates and gift cards redeemable for inventory in the future. Under the regulation, income from the purchase of gift cards can be deferred until the earlier of (1) the year in which the gift card is redeemed, (2) the year in which the income is included for financial accounting purposes, or (3) the second subsequent year to the sale of the gift card. At least with respect to one taxpayer, however, the Service has concluded that this rule is not available for retailers that sell gift cards redeemable at *other* retailers, for example gift cards sold by Walgreens for use at iTunes or Barnes & Noble. *See* Tech. Advice Mem. 200849015.

d. Prepayment for Services

At the center of the rule requiring taxation of income from services on receipt of payment is the statutory command of §446(b) that the taxpayer's method of accounting "clearly reflect income." The clear reflection of income doctrine gives the Commissioner broad discretion to require taxpayers to compute taxable income under any method that clearly reflects the amount of income received.

Prior to the Supreme Court's decision in Automobile Club of Michigan v. Commissioner, 353 U.S. 180 (1957), commentators and courts disputed whether accrual method taxpayers were permitted to defer taxation of prepaid income (that is, advance receipts for services to be performed in the future) until the tax years in which the services were performed. Despite the Court's holding in *Automobile Club of Michigan* that prepaid service income is taxable in the year of *receipt*, a minority of courts attempted to fashion exceptions. See, e.g., Bressner Radio v. Commissioner, 267 F.2d 520 (2d Cir. 1959), nonacq. Rev. Rul. 60-85, 1960-1 C.B. 181. The Supreme Court subsequently considered two additional cases, American Automobile Association v. United States, 367 U.S. 687 (1961), and Schlude v. Commissioner, 372 U.S. 128 (1963). This line of cases, often referred to as the "trilogy" of prepayment cases, was intended to resolve the issue — prepayments are to be included in income of accrual method taxpayers when received. Difficult questions continued to arise, however, as evidenced by the disparate analyses from the district court and circuit court in the *RCA* case below.

RCA v. UNITED STATES
499 F. Supp. 507 (S.D.N.Y. 1980)

LASKER, J. . . .

At issue is the extent to which a taxpayer may properly rely on the accrual method of accounting in computing its income for tax purposes. The case involves service contracts made in 1958 and 1959 between RCA and purchasers of new television sets. Under those contracts, the purchaser generally paid RCA a lump sum at the time of purchase, and, in return, RCA agreed to service the television any time trouble developed over a specified period of from three to twenty-four months. . . .

RCA kept [its] books on an accrual basis. The amounts received from the sale of service contracts were initially divided between that portion to be treated as revenue immediately, which covered the costs of selling and processing the contract, plus a profit, and that portion to be treated as unearned revenue, which was credited to a reserve account. Each month throughout the life of the contract a portion of this reserve was credited to revenue, based on statistically derived schedules designed to take into account as revenue each month that portion of prepaid service contract receipts attributable to the services performed that month under such contracts. This scheme was intended to ensure that such receipts were treated as revenue from month to month only in proportion to related expenses incurred, and thus that RCA's income — the difference between its revenues and expenses — was accurately reflected in its books.

In computing its 1958 and 1959 income for tax purposes, RCA employed the same method of accounting that it used in keeping its own books. . . .

In auditing RCA's returns for 1958 and 1959, the Commissioner concluded that RCA's method of spreading the recognition as revenue of prepaid service contract receipts over the life of the contracts did not "clearly reflect income," as required under I.R.C. §446(a). Invoking his authority under §446(b), the Commissioner treated RCA's prepaid receipts as revenue in the year received. . . .

. . . Briefly stated, RCA treated all contracts of a particular length entered into during a particular month as a single category. Drawing on its past experience, RCA developed statistical estimates of the percentage of all the service calls expected to be made under contracts of a particular category that would be made during each month of those contracts' term. These estimates were aggregate figures: RCA did not purport to predict when individual televisions covered by contract within a given category would require service, but only the incidence of service calls under such contracts. RCA continuously refined these estimates in light of its continuing experience.

These estimates of relative monthly service call volume provided the basis for RCA's monthly allocation to revenue of a portion of its receipts from the sale of contracts in each category, and ultimately for the recognition of those receipts as revenue in tax years other than that in which they were received. For instance, RCA's projections indicated that 4.33 percent of all service calls that would be required under all one-year service contracts entered into in September, 1959, would be made in September of that year, 9.08 percent in October, 7.87 percent in November, and 8.71 percent in December. The remaining service calls would all occur during the first nine months of 1960. Consequently, for tax purposes RCA treated as revenue in 1959 (in addition to the amounts treated as immediate revenue attributable to the costs of selling and processing contracts) only 29.96 percent of the amounts it received in September, 1959 from the sale of one year service contracts. The remainder would have been treated as revenue in 1960, had the Commissioner not intervened and insisted that RCA treat all amounts received in 1959 as revenue in 1959. . . .

Prior to 1916, the Revenue Acts recognized only the "cash receipts and disbursements" method of accounting. However, in the Revenue Act of 1916 Congress provided that a corporate taxpayer that kept its books on some basis other than actual receipts and disbursements could report its income on the same basis, "unless such other basis does not clearly reflect its income." The purpose of the new provision

> was to enable taxpayers to keep their books and make their returns according to scientific accounting principles, by charging against income earned during the taxable period, the expenses incurred in and properly attributable to the process of earning income during that period.

United States v. Anderson, 269 U.S. 422, 440 (1926). This provision of the 1916 Act is reflected today in section 446 of the Code. . . . The first and principal question to be resolved here is whether the accrual method of accounting, as implemented by RCA, "clearly reflects income" within the meaning of section 446(a).

A

The Government relies principally on a trilogy of decisions of the United States Supreme Court: Automobile Club of Michigan v. Commissioner, 353 U.S.

180 (1957), American Automobile Association v. United States, 367 U.S. 687 (1961), and Schlude v. Commissioner, 372 U.S. 128 (1963). In each of these cases the Court upheld the Commissioner's determination that the accrual method of accounting used by the taxpayer did not clearly reflect income; the Government argues here that together they establish that the Commissioner may reject the use, for tax purposes, of any accounting method which defers until subsequent tax years the inclusion in gross income of payments received for services to be rendered at unspecified dates in the future.

In the first case in the trilogy, Automobile Club of Michigan v. Commissioner, 353 U.S. 180 (1957) ("*Michigan*"), the automobile club provided a variety of services to its members, at their request, such as road maps and highway repairs. Membership dues were collected annually, in advance. On its books, the club recorded one-twelfth of each dues payment as revenue each month of the membership year. For tax purposes, it reported its gross income as recorded on its books. Thus, it did not include the full amount of each dues payment in its gross income for the tax year in which it was received. Instead dues payments were split, one portion included in gross income for the tax year of receipt, the remainder in gross income for the following tax year, in proportion to the number of months of the membership year which fell within each tax year. The Court, holding that this method of accounting did not clearly reflect income, expressed its rationale in a single sentence: "The pro rata allocation of the membership dues in monthly amounts is purely artificial and bears no relation to the services which petitioner may in fact be called upon to render for the member." Id. at 189. In a footnote, the Court distinguished Beacon Publishing Co. v. Commissioner, 218 F.2d 697 (10th Cir. 1955), in which it was held that the Commissioner exceeded his authority in requiring the taxpayer to treat sums received for prepaid newspaper subscriptions as revenue during the year they were received, rather than over the life of the subscriptions, and Schuessler v. Commissioner, 230 F.2d 722 (5th Cir. 1956), in which the court rejected the Commissioner's attempt to require the taxpayer to treat as revenue during the year received that portion of receipts from the sale of gas furnaces which was properly attributable to the taxpayer's contractual obligation to turn the furnaces on and off each year for five years:

> In *Beacon*, performance of the subscription, in most instances, was, in part, necessarily deferred until the publication dates after the tax year. In *Schuessler*, performance of the service agreement required the taxpayer to furnish services at specified times in years subsequent to the tax year. In this case, substantially all services are performed only upon a member's demand and the taxpayer's performance was not related to fixed dates after the tax year.

353 U.S. at 189 n.20. . . . RCA, relying on the statement quoted from the text of the decision, contends that the teachings of this decision and the subsequent decisions in the trilogy is simply that an accounting method that is "purely artificial" is not acceptable, but that a method which can be shown to accurately record related revenues and expenses in the proper accounting period is not. The Government, relying on the quotation from the footnote, argues that the Commissioner may reject any method for deferring recognition of receipts as revenue, no matter how accurately it matches revenues and expenses, if "the contract revenues in question

are tied to future services to be performed without relation to fixed dates in the future." We conclude that RCA's position is the correct one. In our view, the subsequent decisions of the Supreme Court establish that the fact that the services paid for are not to be performed on fixed dates is not in and of itself determinative, but is significant only insofar as it throws light on the question whether the challenged accounting method is "artificial" because it fails adequately to ensure that receipts are included in gross income in any tax year only in proportion to related expenses incurred during that year.

Two years after the Supreme Court's decision in *Michigan*, the Second Circuit, in Bressner Radio, Inc. v. Commissioner, 267 F.2d 520 (2d Cir. 1959), nonacq., Rev. Rul. 60-85, 1960-1 C.B. 181 (1960), adopted the interpretation of *Michigan* which RCA urges here. The facts in *Bressner* were virtually identical to those of the case at hand. . . .

Distinguishing the Supreme Court's decision in *Michigan*, the Second Circuit stated:

> It is apparent from the decision of the majority that at least for purposes of the decision of the case it assumed that a realistic deferral would have been permissible, and found only that no realistic deferral was made. . . . The majority appears to have proceeded from an assumption that accrual accounting would be acceptable tax practice.

Id. at 526-527. The court found that unlike the taxpayer in *Michigan*, Bressner had proven that its deferral method was "realistic":

> There is nothing apparently artificial about the petitioner's method of deferral here. Drawing on its experience with thousands of contracts it has demonstrated that it was subjected to a reasonably uniform demand for services, so that it could and did anticipate that the expenses incident to the performance which alone would entitle it to regard the sum received as earned would be distributed across the life of the contract. It therefore deferred revenues until they were earned, and thus matched them with foreseeably related expenses, which is the essential purpose of accrual accounting.

Id. at 528. It is clear that if *Bressner* were the last word on the issue, RCA would prevail here. The question, however, is whether subsequent decisions of the Supreme Court have limited or overruled *Bressner*, and if so to what extent.

The second decision in the trilogy is American Automobile Association v. United States, 367 U.S. 687 (1961) ("*AAA*"). There the taxpayer, also an automobile club, had accounted for membership dues using the same method as the taxpayer in *Michigan* — that is, it had recorded dues as revenue on its books ratably over the twelve month membership period, thereby including dues payments in its gross income each tax year only to the extent that that tax year coincided with the membership period. However, in *AAA* the taxpayer presented

> expert accounting testimony indicating that the system used was in accord with generally accepted accounting principles; that its proof of cost of member service was detailed; and that the correlation between that cost and the period of time over which the dues were credited as income was shown and justified by proof of experience.

Id. at 691. Relying on this testimony, the taxpayer argued that it had demonstrated that its method of deferring the recognition of revenue ratably was not "artificial."

The Court of Claims rejected this argument. . . .

In affirming the Court of Claims' decision on remand, the [Supreme] Court relied on its earlier decision in *Michigan*, stating that its earlier holding

> that the system of accounting was "purely artificial" was based upon the finding that "substantially all services are performed only upon a member's demand and the tax-payer's performance was not related to fixed dates after the tax year."

Id. Responding to the taxpayer's argument that the proof at trial established that in the aggregate it provided services to its members evenly throughout the year (despite the fact that it was impossible to know beforehand when any *individual* member would seek services), and therefore that it was justified in recognizing membership dues as revenue ratably over the membership year, the Court remarked:

> [O]ther findings merely reflecting statistical computations of average monthly cost per member on a group or pool basis are without determinate significance to our decision that the federal revenue cannot, without legislative consent and over objection of the Commissioner, be made to depend upon average experience in rendering perfor-mance and turning a profit. Indeed, such tabulations themselves demonstrate the inadequacy from an income tax standpoint of the *pro rata* method of allocating each year's membership dues in equal monthly installments not in fact related to the expenses incurred. Not only did individually incurred expenses actually vary from month to month, but even the average expenses varied — recognition of income nonetheless remaining ratably constant.

It would be less than candid to say that we do not find this passage to be cryptic. While it appears to reject out of hand the use of "statistical computations" made on a "group or pool basis" in computing income for tax purposes, it provides as a rationale for doing so only the observation that the taxpayer's pro rata deferral method did not in fact accurately match revenues and expenses. If read broadly as a blanket proscription of the use of statistical computations of average cost "on a group or pool basis," it presents a formidable hurdle to RCA's recovery in this case. We believe, however, that in view of its opacity, and in the light of subsequent decisions, the passage should be more narrowly construed. . . .

This brings us to the third decision of the trilogy, Schlude v. Commissioner, 372 U.S. 128 (1963). . . . Though the Court did affirm the Court of Appeals' deter-mination that the accrual method employed by the taxpayers did not "clearly reflect income," this does not, in view of the facts in *Schlude*, necessarily indicate that the Court endorsed a broad reading of *AAA*. To the contrary, we believe that *Schlude*, by implication, narrowed the scope of *AAA*.

The taxpayers in *Schlude*, who operated dance studios, sold contracts for spec-ified numbers of hours of dance lessons, ranging from five to 1,200. The contracts specified the period during which the lessons had to be taken, but the actual dates of lessons were arranged from time to time as they were taken. Under the contracts, the student was obliged to pay the full contract price whether or not any or all of the lessons were actually taken. The Court summarized the taxpayers' method of accounting for the amounts received under these contracts as follows:

> When a contract was entered into, a "deferred income" account was credited for the total contract price. At the close of each fiscal period, the student record cards were analysed and the total number of taught hours was multiplied by the designated rate per hour of each contract. The resulting sum was deducted from the deferred income account and reported as earned income on the financial statements and the income tax return. In addition, if there had been no activity in a contract for over a year, or if a course were reduced in amount, an entry would be made canceling the untaught portion of the contract, removing that amount from the deferred income account, and recognizing gain to the extent that the deferred income exceeded the balance due on the contract, i.e., the amounts received in advance. . . . The balance of the deferred income account would be carried forward into the next fiscal year to be increased or decreased in accordance with the number of new contracts, lessons taught and cancellations recognized.

Id. at 131-132. The Court held that it was proper for the Commissioner to reject this method of accounting as not clearly reflecting income, finding the question "squarely controlled" by *AAA*. The Court concluded that the system employed by the taxpayers suffered from the same vice as the systems disallowed in *Michigan* and *AAA*, "since the advance payments related to services which were to be performed only upon customers' demands without relation to fixed dates in the future." The Court's analysis, however, establishes that this fact was significant only because it ensured that the accounting method the taxpayers employed could not accurately match revenues and related expenses:

> [T]he studio sought to defer its cash receipts on the basis of contracts which did not provide for lessons on fixed dates after the taxable year, but left such dates to be arranged from time to time by the instructor and his student. Under the contracts, the student could arrange for some or all of the additional lessons or could simply allow their rights under the contracts to lapse. But even though the student did not demand the remaining lessons, the contracts permitted the studio to insist upon payment in accordance with the obligations undertaken and to retain whatever prepayments were made without restriction as to use and without obligation of refund. *At the end of each period, while the number of lessons taught had been meticulously reflected, the studio was uncertain whether none, some or all of the remaining lessons would be rendered.*

Id. at 135-136 (emphasis added). . . . [I]t appears that what the Court found "artificial," and therefore impermissible, about the taxpayers' method of accounting for advance payments related to services to be performed "only upon customers' demand without relation to fixed dates in the future" was not that the *time* of performance was not specified, but rather that the *extent* of performance was not specified, and consequently there was no assurance that including receipts in gross income to the extent of *actual* expenses incurred each year was equivalent to including receipts in gross income in proportion to that year's share of total expenses to be incurred over the life of the contract. As the dissent in *Schlude* points out, this inadequacy could be remedied only through the use of statistical projections of anticipated expenses not unlike those employed by RCA here. And, as the dissenting opinion further indicates, the majority's reference to the use of "estimated cancellations" as the cure for the defect dispels any suggestion that the broad but cryptic language used by the Court in *AAA* was intended to bar the use of such projections, provided they are adequately supported. . . .

In our view, the teachings of the trilogy can be briefly summarized as follows: *Michigan* and *AAA* establish that a taxpayer may not simply prorate recognition of receipts as revenue over the period in which the service covered by those receipts is to be rendered, because there is no assurance that those services will be rendered ratably over that period. *Schlude*, on the other hand, established that a taxpayer may not, automatically each year, recognize revenue to the extent of *actual* expenses incurred that year, because there is no assurance that this amount will accurately reflect the portion of the total expenses to be incurred under the contract attributable to that year. In each of these cases the Court found the taxpayers' method of accounting for prepaid receipts "artificial" not, as the Government contends here, because those receipts related to services to be performed at unspecified times in tax years subsequent to that of their receipt, but rather, as RCA argues, because in each case the taxpayers' accounting method failed to account properly for that fact through the use of adequately supported statistical projections.

As *Schlude* makes clear, the use of such projections is essential to any system of accounting on an accrual basis for prepaid revenues covering services to be performed at unspecified times. The Government argues, however, that such projections may not be used in computing income for tax purposes. . . .

We find the Government's position unpersuasive. As indicated above, the language the Court used in *AAA* is far from clear, and must be read in light of the Court's subsequent statements in *Schlude*. . . . A taxpayer's method of accounting must be justified by hard evidence, *including statistical evidence*, rather than assumptions based on "general business experience," or "well-educated guesses." In our view, a taxpayer is entitled to rely on reliable statistical projections of anticipated expenses in determining the extent to which prepaid amounts should be included in gross income in tax years other than that of their receipt, in accordance with the principles of accrual accounting.

Accordingly, we conclude that the Commissioner is not authorized to reject a deferral method of accounting *simply* because the deferred revenues relate to services to be performed at unspecified times in tax years subsequent to that of receipt. Through the use of statistical projections, a taxpayer using a deferral method may achieve a reasonably precise matching of revenues and expenses despite the fact that the actual time services will have to be performed is not known, thereby computing income "according to scientific accounting principles, by charging against income earned during the taxable period, the expenses incurred in and properly attributable to the process of earning income during that period." RCA contends that the method of accounting it used in 1958 and 1959, which was based, unlike those employed by the taxpayers in *Michigan*, *AAA*, and *Schlude*, on hard statistical data rather than informed hunches, did just that. Assuming that RCA's statistical projections were reliable and properly used, we believe the Commissioner could not require RCA to use a different method of accounting simply because RCA could not know, in advance, when it would be required to provide service under *individual* service contracts.

B

The Government, however, argues more broadly, in the alternative, that the Commissioner may reject any method of accounting that defers the inclusion of payments for future services until later tax years, unless that method is expressly authorized by statute. The short answer to this argument is that the accrual method of accounting is expressly authorized by statute. The longer answer is that the authorities on which the Government relies do not establish that the Commissioner enjoys the unbridled discretion that the Government's argument would vest in him; the ultimate question remains whether a taxpayer's method of accounting "clearly reflects income."

. . . The proper test, under the statute, remains whether the accounting method in question "clearly reflects income" — that is, in our view, whether it ensures, with reasonable precision, that deferred revenues are included in gross income in tax years subsequent to that in which they are received only in proportion to the related services performed, and expenses incurred, during those tax years.

C

. . . [W]e conclude that as a matter of law RCA was entitled to use a deferral method of accounting based on reliable statistical projections in computing its income for tax purposes, so long as that method did "clearly reflect income," and we [also] conclude that RCA has adequately demonstrated that the method it used in 1958 and 1959 matched revenues and related expenses with such precision that it was beyond the Commissioner's discretion to conclude that that method did not "clearly reflect income." . . .

RCA v. UNITED STATES
664 F.2d 881 (2d Cir. 1981)

KEARSE, J.

This case well illustrates the fundamental tension between the purposes of financial accounting and those of tax accounting. As the Supreme Court has recognized, these two systems of accounting have "vastly different objectives":

> The primary goal of financial accounting is to provide useful information to management, shareholders, creditors, and others properly interested; the major responsibility of the accountant is to protect these parties from being misled. The primary goal of the income tax system, in contrast, is the equitable collection of revenue; the major responsibility of the Internal Revenue Service is to protect the public fisc. Consistently with its goals and responsibilities, financial accounting has as its foundation the principle of conservatism, with its corollary that "possible errors in measurement [should] be in the direction of understatement rather than overstatement of net income and net assets." In view of the Treasury's markedly different goals and responsibilities, understatement of income is not destined to be its guiding light.

Thor Power Tool Co. v. Commissioner, 439 U.S. 522, 542 (1979). The case also highlights the fundamentally different perspective that courts must adopt when reviewing the propriety of an exercise of administrative discretion rather than deciding a naked question of substantive law. We conclude that the district court gave too little weight to the objectives of tax accounting and to the Commissioner's wide discretion in implementing those objectives.

. . . It is well established that the Commissioner enjoys "broad discretion" to determine whether, "in [his] opinion,'" a taxpayer's accounting methods clearly reflect income, and the Commissioner's exercise of his discretion must be upheld unless it is clearly unlawful. . . . The task of a reviewing court, therefore, is not to determine whether in its own opinion RCA's method of accounting for prepaid service contract income "clearly reflect[ed] income," but to determine whether there is an adequate basis in law for the Commissioner's conclusion that it did not. Our review of the relevant decisions persuades us that the law adequately supports the Commissioner's action. . . .

The policy considerations that underlie *Michigan, AAA*, and *Schlude* are quite clear. When a taxpayer receives income in the form of prepayments in respect of services to be performed in the future upon demand, it is impossible for the taxpayer to know, at the outset of the contract term, the amount of service that his customer will ultimately require, and, consequently, it is impossible for the taxpayer to predict *with certainty* the amount of net income, i.e., the amount of the excess of revenues over expenses of performance, that he will ultimately earn from the contract. For purposes of financial accounting, this uncertainty is tolerable; the financial accountant merely estimates future demands for performance and defers recognition of income accordingly. Tax accounting, however, "can give no quarter to uncertainty." The entire process of government depends on the expeditious collection of tax revenues. Tax accounting therefore tends to compute taxable income on the basis of the taxpayer's present ability to pay the tax, as manifested by his current cash flow, without regard to deductions that may later accrue. By the same token, tax accounting is necessarily hostile to accounting practices that defer recognition of income, and thus payment of the tax on it, on the basis of estimates and projections that may ultimately prove unsound.

In view of the relevant Supreme Court decisions and the policies they reflect, we cannot say that the Commissioner abused his discretion in rejecting RCA's method of accounting for service contract income. Like the service agreements at issue in *Michigan, AAA*, and *Schlude*, RCA's service contracts obligated it to perform services only upon the customer's demand. Thus, at the beginning of the contract term, RCA could not know the extent of the performance that the customer might ultimately require, and it could not be certain of the amount of income that it would ultimately earn from the contract. The Commissioner was not required to subject the federal revenues to the vicissitudes of RCA customers' future demands for services. Accordingly, he acted within his discretion in requiring RCA to report its prepaid service contract income upon receipt.

RCA's arguments against the Commissioner's exercise of his discretion are unpersuasive. RCA contends principally that its accounting method must be upheld on the basis of our decision in *Bressner Radio*, which upheld an accounting system that was based on reasonably accurate predictions of the demand for services. We think, however, that the Supreme Court's post-*Bressner* decisions in *AAA* and *Schlude* have deprived *Bressner* of controlling force. First, the *AAA* Court seems to have believed that it was overruling *Bressner*, for the Court stated that it had granted certiorari to review the lower court's decision in *AAA* because it perceived "a conflict between" that decision, which the Court affirmed, and our contrary ruling in *Bressner*. Second, the holdings of *AAA* and *Schlude* are sufficiently contrary to that of *Bressner* that we must regard *Bressner* as invalid even if *AAA* did not expressly overrule it. As *AAA* and *Schlude* make plain, it is not simply the "artificiality" of a taxpayer's method of deferring recognition of income from services performable on demand that offends the clear reflection principle of §446(b), but rather the uncertainty inherent in any method that relies on prognostications and assumptions about the future demand for services. The method upheld by us in *Bressner* relied on such prognostications as much as did the methods rejected in *AAA* and *Schlude*. Because the latter cases underscore the Commissioner's discretion to disallow accounting methods that subject the federal revenues to such uncertainty, we cannot invoke *Bressner* to invalidate the Commissioner's exercise of his discretion here.

Equally unpersuasive are RCA's efforts to distinguish *AAA* and *Schlude*. [T]he vice of the systems treated in *AAA* and *Schlude* was their tendency to subject government revenues to the uncertainties inherent in prognostications about the rate at which customers would demand services in the future. RCA's system shared this vice. Although RCA's predictions may have been more accurate than those of the taxpayers in *AAA* and *Schlude*, they were predictions nonetheless, and the Commissioner was not required to accept them as determinants of the federal revenue.

. . . In addition, although the district court found that RCA's accounting practices did "clearly reflect income," we are not bound by that finding under the "clearly erroneous" standard of Fed. R. Civ. P. 52. The issue before the district court was not whether RCA's accounting method adequately reflected income, but whether the Commissioner abused his discretion in determining that it did not. The latter question is one of law, and for the reasons stated above we conclude that the Commissioner did not abuse his discretion. . . .

. . . [W]e reverse the judgment of the district court and remand the matter with instructions to dismiss the complaint.

Note

RCA demonstrates the general rule requiring prepayment for services to be included in income in the year of receipt if the taxpayer either (1) prorates recognition of receipts as revenue over the period in which the service covered by those receipts is to be rendered (because there is no assurance that those services will be rendered ratably over that period) or (2) automatically recognizes revenue each year, to the extent of actual expenses incurred during the year, because there is no assurance that this amount accurately reflects the portion of the total expenses incurred under the contract for that twelve-month period. The common thread in the accrual accounting cases that prohibits postponement of prepaid receipts is the use of statistical projections, regardless of accuracy, to match income to the performance of services on unspecified dates.

As becomes quickly apparent from the *RCA* cases, the application of the "all events" test to prepayments for services can often result in seemingly unfair results, such as in *RCA*, in which the circuit court required the company to include all prepayments in income immediately even though the company would not perform the services to earn the income until the future. This potential unfairness has only grown in relevance given the rise of modern technology companies, which sell both software and the promise of future services. For example, for every copy of Windows that Microsoft sells, Microsoft knows it will have to provide future updates and security patches; similarly, paid versions of apps, such as Angry Birds, entitle the owner to future updates with additional levels or other enhancements. Clearly, a portion of the initial purchase price for these items must be for future services. Under the *AAA/Auto Club/Schlude* trilogy, however, these companies would be required to include the entire payment in income in the year of sale, notwithstanding that the payment relates, in part, to future services.

In response to this perceived unfairness, several exceptions to the prepayment rule have emerged. One judicially created exception applies to future services to be performed on a specific date only rather than an expected date. In Tampa Bay Devil Rays v. Commissioner, T.C. Memo 2002-248, and Artnell Co. v. Commissioner, 400 F.2d 981 (7th Cir. 1968), prepayments to baseball teams for games to be played on specific dates did not have to be taken into account as income until the date of the game played. These cases are relatively rare, however. In Revenue Procedure 2004-34, 2004-1 C.B. 991, the Service issued an additional administrative exception permitting accrual method taxpayers to defer income from prepayments for services for one year. The benefits of Revenue Procedure 2004-34 are available only if the taxpayer also defers the income until the following year for financial accounting purposes. As a result, this represents a narrow exception to the general rule for prepayments, although it is much larger than previous incarnations. In 2011 the Service extended the scope of Revenue Procedure 2004-34 to apply to sales of gift cards redeemable for future services well. Revenue Procedure 2011-17, 2011-5 I.R.B. 441.

Problems

Assume, in the following questions, that the parties are calendar year, accrual method taxpayers.

5-8.   David Johnson rendered architectural services to Anne Jones in year 1, with his services on the project extending into January year 2. In year 1, Johnson sent Jones a bill for $10,000 for all services performed or to be performed on the project.
   a.   Assuming that Johnson was not paid until year 2, in which year should Johnson report the $10,000 as income?
   b.   What if Johnson received the entire $10,000 payment in year 1?
   c.   What if Jones never paid the bill?

    d. What if Jones was insolvent in year 1 but became solvent in year 2?

    e. What if Jones paid $5,000 in year 1 and $5,000 in year 2?

    f. What would be the tax consequences if, in year 1, Jones telephoned Johnson, disputed the amount of the bill, and refused to pay?

    g. How would your answer change if Johnson was a cash-method taxpayer?

5-9. In November, Joe Case agreed to sell an option to Clifford Burger to purchase a parcel of Case's land for $120,000. The option to purchase was for a two-month period. In late December, Burger notified Case that he planned to exercise the option, and, as a result, the closing was scheduled for December 31. On December 31, the title commitment policy was not yet prepared, and Burger was unable to finalize his loan. Finally, in January of the next year, the closing was held, and Case transferred title in exchange for $120,000.

    a. In which year should Case include the $120,000 in his income?

    b. What effect, if any, would there be on Case's year of inclusion if the closing had been held in year 1 instead of year 2?

    c. Same as *b*, except the title and the purchase money were held in escrow until a certain condition was met in year 2?

    d. What if, instead of paying with cash only, Burger bought the property in year 2 for $50,000 cash and a promissory note with a market rate of interest in the amount of $70,000?

5-10. On January 1, year 1, Fidelity Bank loaned $100,000 to Miguel Bustamonte. Interest accrued on that loan at the rate of $8,000 per annum, payable December 31, over a period of five years.

    a. What result to Fidelity if the December 31, year 1, payment was received late, on January 15, year 2?

    b. What would be the tax consequences to Fidelity Bank if, in year 1, Bustamonte had prepaid two years of interest?

    c. What if Bustamonte failed to make any interest payments until year 5?

5-11. Pierce Corporation declared a $1,000 dividend in year 1 but did not make payment until year 2.

    a. When should Harold Samuelson, a shareholder, include the dividend as income?

    b. What if Pierce Corporation had cash flow problems and was unable to pay the dividend until year 3?

5-12. Mary Martin made and sold decorative iPad covers. In year 1, she sold 100 covers to Specialty Shop, Inc. for $25 each; in year 2, Specialty Shop returned all 100 covers to Martin, having found them to be defective.

    a. What were the tax consequences to Martin in year 1?

    b. What were the tax consequences to Martin in year 2?

    c. What result if Martin had sold the slings to Specialty on credit for $20 each, plus a percentage of the profit made on each sale to a maximum of $10?

    d. Assume that Martin delivered the covers to Specialty Shop to sell on consignment. Specialty Shop sold 50 in year 1 for $30 each. In year 2, it sold 25 more at $40 each and returned the other 25 to Martin. What were the tax consequences to Martin in year 1? In year 2?

4. Security Deposits

The single largest (and perhaps most confusing) exception to the prepayment rules relates to "deposits" as distinguished from "prepayments." The rationale for holding security deposits in abeyance is that, at the time of receipt, it is unknown whether the deposit will be retained by the taxpayer (and treated as gross income) or returned to the depositor (and treated as a nontaxable loan). Clinton Hotel Realty Corp. v. Commissioner, 128 F.2d 968 (5th Cir. 1942); Gilken Corp. v. Commissioner, 10 T.C. 445 (1948). True security deposits, which may offset the lessee's damages to the lessor's property or be returned in the event that all covenants are fulfilled, are not included in the lessor's income in the year of receipt. However, security deposits can assume many forms, and, not surprisingly, the label security deposit does not necessarily dictate the actual substance of the transaction or tax treatment. For instance, a security deposit by name may be, in substance, an advance payment of rent.

In Clinton Hotel Realty Corp. v. Commissioner, 128 F.2d 968 (5th Cir. 1942), both the Commissioner and the Board of Tax Appeals characterized a payment received by the lessor as income when received because the lease provided for that amount to be credited toward the last rental payment. The Court of Appeals reversed, however, finding that the payment, which was always referred to as a security or a deposit, might be used as a payment for items other than rent. For example, the payment was made to protect the lessor against damages, to secure the inventory of equipment and supplies, and to secure maintenance of the lessor's property as agreed. The court also found that the lessor's obligation to pay $1,000 per year as interest on the payment (to be credited against rents) emphasized the character of the deposit as security rather than rent, likening the transaction to borrowing by the lessor. Most important, the court noted that the lessor was obligated to return the deposit to the lessee in the event that the premises were destroyed before the beginning of the last year of the lease. Thus, the lessor was actually accountable to the lessee for principal as well as interest. Accordingly, the payment was characterized as a security deposit, not prepaid rental income.

On the other hand, if a lease agreement provides that a deposit is held primarily for the payment of rent, the amount may constitute prepaid rent, taxable in the year of receipt, even though the deposit secures performance of the lease agreement. In Gilken Corp. v. Commissioner, 10 T.C. 445 (1948), the agreement (including subsequent amendments) provided for deposits received at the beginning of the lease to be applied to rents due for the final period and also to secure the performance of the lessee's obligation. (To complicate matters further, the agreement also provided for the application of the deposit to the payment of an agreed purchase price if the option granted in the lease agreement was exercised. See discussion at section 5D, infra.) The lessor contended that the money received was merely a security deposit, not rental income, because the money was to be applied to rents due in the final period only if the lessee had not defaulted. The Tax Court found, however, that the primary purpose of the deposit was the payment of rents for the closing period of the lease. Unlike Clinton, no interest was required to be paid on the money. Thus, the arrangement lacked the "characteristic of a loan." Furthermore, application of the deposit to rents due in the final period of the lease was subject to the lessor's "unrestrained control" under the terms of the lease, with no obligation to return the deposit to the lessee if the premises were destroyed. The Tax Court concluded therefore that the rental payment element controlled and rejected any finding that the payments were "mere deposits for security of lessee's performance" as contended by the lessor. The court looked through the form to the substance of the transaction in order to determine that the "primary purpose" intended by the parties was the prepayment of rent.

In characterizing a security deposit, it is important to determine the nature of the taxpayer's protected interest. A security deposit protects the taxpayer's interest in the property, while prepaid rent protects the taxpayer's income from the property.

COMMISSIONER v. INDIANAPOLIS
POWER & LIGHT CO.
493 U.S. 203 (1990)

JUSTICE BLACKMUN delivered the opinion of the Court.

Respondent Indianapolis Power & Light Company (IPL) requires certain customers to make deposits with it to assure payment of future bills for electric service. Petitioner Commissioner of Internal Revenue contends that these deposits are advance payments for electricity and therefore constitute taxable income to IPL upon receipt. IPL contends otherwise. . . .

In March 1976, IPL amended its rules governing the deposit program. Under the amended rules, the residential customers from whom deposits were required were selected on the basis of a fixed formula. The interest rate was raised to 6 percent but was payable only on deposits held for 12 months or more. A deposit was refunded when the customer made timely payments for either nine consecutive months, or for ten out of 12 consecutive months so long as the two delinquent months were not themselves consecutive. A customer could obtain a refund prior to that time by satisfying the credit test. As under the previous rules, the refund would be made in cash or by check, or, at the customer's option, applied against future bills. Any deposit unclaimed after seven years was to escheat to the State.

IPL did not treat these deposits as income at the time of receipt. Rather, as required by state administrative regulations, the deposits were carried on its books as current liabilities. Under its accounting system, IPL recognized income when it mailed a monthly bill. If the deposit was used to offset a customer's bill, the utility made the necessary accounting adjustments. Customer deposits were not physically segregated in any way from the company's general funds. They were commingled with other receipts and at all times were subject to IPL's unfettered use and control. It is undisputed that IPL's treatment of the deposits was consistent with accepted accounting practice and applicable state regulations.

Upon audit of respondent's returns for the calendar years 1974 through 1977, the Commissioner asserted deficiencies. . . . The Commissioner took the position that the deposits were advance payments for electricity and therefore were taxable to IPL in the year of receipt. He contended that the increase or decrease in customer deposits outstanding at the end of each year represented an increase or decrease in IPL's income for the year. . . .

In a reviewed decision, with one judge not participating, a unanimous Tax Court ruled in favor of IPL. The court followed the approach it had adopted in City Gas Co. of Florida v. Commissioner of Internal Revenue, 74 T.C. 386 (1980), revd., 689 F.2d 943 (C.A.11 1982). It found it necessary to "continue to examine all of the circumstances," and relied on several factors in concluding that the deposits in question were properly excluded from gross income. It noted, among other things, that only 5 percent of IPL's customers were required to make deposits; that the customer rather than the utility controlled the ultimate disposition of a deposit; and that IPL consistently treated the deposits as belonging to the customers, both by listing them as current liabilities for accounting purposes and by paying interest.

The United States Court of Appeals for the Seventh Circuit affirmed the Tax Court's decision. The court stated that "the proper approach to determining the appropriate tax treatment of a customer deposit is to look at the primary purpose of the deposit based on all the facts and circumstances. . . ." The court appeared to place primary reliance, however, on IPL's obligation to pay interest on the deposits. It asserted that "as the interest rate paid on a deposit to secure income begins to approximate the return that the recipient would be expected to make from 'the use' of the deposit amount, the deposit begins to serve purposes that comport more squarely with a security deposit." Noting that IPL had paid interest on the customer deposits throughout the period in question, the court upheld, as not clearly erroneous, the Tax Court's determination that the principal purpose of these deposits was to serve as security rather than as prepayment of income.

Because the Seventh Circuit was in specific disagreement with the Eleventh Circuit's ruling in *City Gas Co. of Florida*, supra, we granted certiorari to resolve the conflict.

We begin with the common ground. IPL acknowledges that these customer deposits are taxable as income upon receipt if they constitute *advance payments* for electricity to be supplied.[3] The Commissioner, on his part, concedes that customer deposits that secure the performance of nonincome-producing covenants — such as a utility customer's obligation to ensure that meters will not be damaged — are not taxable income. And it is settled that receipt of a loan is not income to the borrower. IPL, stressing its obligation to refund the deposits with interest, asserts that the payments are similar to loans. The Commissioner, however, contends that a deposit which serves to secure the payment of future income is properly analogized to an advance payment for goods or services.

In economic terms, to be sure, the distinction between a loan and an advance payment is one of degree rather than of kind. A commercial loan, like an advance payment, confers an economic benefit on the recipient: a business presumably does not borrow money unless it believes that the income it can earn from its use of the borrowed funds will be greater than its interest obligation. Even though receipt of the money is subject to a duty to repay, the borrower must regard itself as better off

---

3. This Court has held that an accrual-basis taxpayer is required to treat advance payments as income in the year of receipt. These cases concerned payments — nonrefundable fees for services — that indisputably constituted income; the issue was *when* that income was taxable. Here, in contrast, the issue is whether these deposits, as such, are income at all.

after the loan than it was before. The economic benefit of a loan, however, consists entirely of the opportunity to earn income on the use of the money prior to the time the loan must be repaid. And in that context our system is content to tax these earnings as they are realized. The recipient of an advance payment, in contrast, gains both immediate use of the money (with the chance to realize earnings thereon) *and* the opportunity to make a profit by providing goods or services at a cost lower than the amount of the payment.

The question, therefore, cannot be resolved simply by noting that respondent derives some economic benefit from receipt of these deposits. Rather, the issue turns upon the nature of the rights and obligations that IPL assumed when the deposits were made. In determining what sort of economic benefits qualify as income, this Court has invoked various formulations. It has referred, for example, to "undeniable accessions to wealth, clearly realized, and over which the taxpayers have complete dominion." It also has stated: "When a taxpayer acquires earnings, lawfully or unlawfully, without the consensual recognition, express or implied, of an obligation to repay and without restriction as to their disposition, 'he has received income. . . . '" IPL hardly enjoyed "complete dominion" over the customer deposits entrusted to it. Rather, these deposits were acquired subject to an express "obligation to repay," either at the time service was terminated or at the time a customer established good credit. So long as the customer fulfills his legal obligation to make timely payments, his deposit ultimately is to be refunded, and both the timing and method of that refund are largely within the control of the customer.

The Commissioner stresses the fact that these deposits were not placed in escrow or segregated from IPL's other funds, and that IPL therefore enjoyed unrestricted use of the money. That circumstance, however, cannot be dispositive. After all, the same might be said of a commercial loan; yet the Commissioner does not suggest that a loan is taxable upon receipt simply because the borrower is free to use the funds in whatever fashion he chooses until the time of repayment. In determining whether a taxpayer enjoys "complete dominion" over a given sum, the crucial point is not whether his use of the funds is unconstrained during some interim period. The key is whether the taxpayer has some guarantee that he will be allowed to keep the money. IPL's receipt of these deposits was accompanied by no such guarantee.

Nor is it especially significant that these deposits could be expected to generate income greater than the modest interest IPL was required to pay. Again, the same could be said of a commercial loan, since, as has been noted, a business is unlikely to borrow unless it believes that it can realize benefits that exceed the cost of servicing the debt. A bank could hardly operate profitably if its earnings on deposits did not surpass its interest obligations; but the deposits themselves are not treated as income. Any income that the utility may earn through use of the deposit money of course is taxable, but the prospect that income will be generated provides no ground for taxing the principal.

The Commissioner's advance payment analogy seems to us to rest upon a misconception of the value of an advance payment to its recipient. An advance payment, like the deposits at issue here, concededly protects the seller against the risk that it would be unable to collect money owed it after it has furnished goods or services. But an advance payment does much more: it protects against the risk that the purchaser will back out of the deal before the seller performs. From the moment an advance payment is made, the seller is assured that, so long as it fulfills its contractual obligation, the money is its to keep. Here, in contrast, a customer submitting a deposit made no commitment to purchase a specified quantity of electricity, or indeed to purchase any electricity at all. IPL's right to keep the money depends upon the customer's purchase of electricity, and upon his later decision to have the deposit applied to future bills, not merely upon the utility's adherence to its contractual duties. Under these circumstances, IPL's dominion over the fund is far less complete than is ordinarily the case in an advance-payment situation.

The Commissioner emphasizes that these deposits frequently will be used to pay for electricity, either because the customer defaults on his obligation or because the customer, having established credit, chooses to apply the deposit to future bills rather than to accept a refund. When this occurs, the Commissioner argues, the transaction, from a cash-flow standpoint, is equivalent to an advance payment. In his view this economic equivalence mandates identical tax treatment.

Whether these payments constitute income when received, however, depends upon the parties' rights and obligations *at the time the payments are made.* The problem with petitioner's argument perhaps can best be understood if we imagine a loan between parties involved in an ongoing commercial relationship. At the time the loan falls due, the lender may decide to apply the money owed him to the purchase of goods or services rather than to accept repayment in cash. But this decision does not mean that the loan, when made, was an advance payment after all. The lender in effect has taken repayment of his money (as was his contractual right) and has chosen to use the proceeds for the purchase of goods or services from the borrower. Although, for the sake of convenience, the parties may combine the two steps, that decision does not blind us to the fact that in substance two transactions are involved. It is this element of choice that distinguishes an advance payment from a loan. Whether these customer deposits are the economic equivalents of advance payments, and therefore taxable upon receipt, must be determined by examining the relationship between the parties at the time of the deposit. The individual who makes an advance payment retains no right to insist upon the return of the funds; so long as the recipient fulfills the terms of the bargain, the money is its to keep. The customer who submits a deposit to the utility, like the lender in the previous hypothetical, retains the right to insist upon repayment in cash; he may *choose* to apply the money to the purchase of electricity, but he assumes no obligation to do so, and the utility therefore acquires no unfettered "dominion" over the money at the time of receipt.

When the Commissioner examines privately structured transactions, the true understanding of the parties, of course, may not be apparent. It may be that a transfer of funds, though nominally a loan, may conceal an unstated agreement that the money is to be applied to the purchase of goods or services. We need not, and do not, attempt to devise a test for addressing those situations where the nature of the parties' bargain is legitimately in dispute. This particular respondent, however, conducts its business in a heavily regulated environment; its rights and obligations vis-à-vis its customers are largely determined by law and regulation rather than by private negotiation. That the utility's customers, when they qualify for refunds of deposits, frequently choose to apply those refunds to future bills rather than taking repayment in cash does not mean that any customer has made an unspoken commitment to do so.

Our decision is also consistent with the Tax Court's long-standing treatment of lease deposits — perhaps the closest analogy to the present situation. The Tax Court traditionally has distinguished between a sum designated as a prepayment of rent — which is taxable upon receipt — and a sum deposited to secure the tenant's performance of a lease agreement. In fact, the customer deposits at issue here are less plausibly regarded as income than lease deposits would be. The typical lease deposit secures the tenant's fulfillment of a contractual obligation to pay a specified rent throughout the term of the lease. The utility customer, however, makes no commitment to purchase any services at all at the time he tenders the deposit.

We recognize that IPL derives an economic benefit from these deposits. But a taxpayer does not realize taxable income from every event that improves his economic condition. A customer who makes this deposit reflects no commitment to purchase services, and IPL's right to retain the money is contingent upon events outside its control. We hold that such dominion as IPL has over these customer deposits is insufficient for the deposits to qualify as taxable income at the time they are made.

The judgment of the Court of Appeals is affirmed.

Note on Prepayments vs. Deposits: The Problem of Volume Discounts

A recurring issue causing a split among the courts has involved volume discount loans. In a typical volume discount loan, a franchisee agrees to buy products from a franchisor for a fixed period of years. The franchisor lends money to the franchisee to start the business and make the initial purchase. If the franchisee purchases the product from the franchisor over the course of those years, the loan is forgiven, while if the franchisee buys from someone else the loan becomes immediately due and payable. Are the loan proceeds includible in income? If so, when?

The Ninth Circuit has held that the loan in such a situation was not included in income when received because it might be repaid and thus was not a prepayment under *Indianapolis Power*. See Westpac Pacific Food v. Commissioner, 451 F.3d 970 (9th Cir. 2006). The Third Circuit, in a sharply split opinion, held that the amount was a prepayment for services since the recipient had unfettered control over it and thus the full amount had to be included in income in the year of receipt under the *Auto Club/AAA/Schlude* trilogy. See Karns Prime & Fancy Food, Ltd., v. Commissioner, 494 F.3d 404 (3rd Cir. 2007). A concurrence in *Karns* used the following hypothetical to explain the difficulty of the issue:

II. The Ninth Circuit Tax Shelter, or How to Make Money By Buying Things

Consider a hypothetical involving Hal Homeowner, who would like to open a grocery distribution center out of his garage. Hal goes to the supermarket and, like Harry, is short on cash. Also consider what happens when Hal Homeowner files his taxes, which makes any simple hypothetical more complex. We will suppose that Hal makes a 100 percent profit on the value of each carton, meaning that for every $2,000 worth of food he buys he resells for $4,000. We will also assume a typical corporate tax rate of 34 percent (which the Government applied to Karns) applies here.

Scenario 1. Hal Homeowner walks into a supermarket and eyes cartons of food for $400 each that would be ideal for his garage mini-mart. The store owner sees what Hal Homeowner has in mind, and when it becomes clear that Hal has no money but a lot of potential, the owner puts this offer on the table: "I will give you 20 percent off now if you agree to buy five cartons ($2,000 worth of food) each year for the next six years." Under this scheme, Hal pays each year just $1,600 for five cartons. This is an example of a "volume supply discount" similar to the one that Harry Homeowner negotiated; Hal has gotten a 20-percent-off deal, except there is no cash advance involved here, which makes the tax calculation straightforward. Each year, Hal simply pays $1,600 for $2,000 worth of goods. He deducts that $1,600 in business expenses and reports $4,000 in resale to yield a taxable income of $2,400, which carries a tax liability of $816 per year . . .

Scenario 2. Suppose the store owner proposes this: "I'll give you $400 now if you agree to buy five cartons ($2,000 worth of food) each year for the next six years. If you can manage that, you don't have to worry about paying me back at the end of the year." This seems like quite a deal to Hal, who readily agrees. At the end of the first year, Hal deducts on his tax returns $1,600 in business expenses ($2,000 for the food minus $400 "cash back" off the full purchase price given in exchange for the purchase commitment) and reports $4,000 in resale proceeds to yield a gross income of $2,400, which carries a tax liability of $816. This is the same as the tax liability in Scenario 1, for Hal has made the same amount. In subsequent years, Hal deducts $2,000 in business expenses and reports $4,000 in resale proceeds to yield a gross income of $2,000 each year, which carries an annual tax liability of $680 . . .

Scenario 4. The facts are the same as Scenario 2, but Hal does his tax reporting differently. Instead of deducting $1,600 in the first year, Hal deducts $2,000 in business expenses and reports resale proceeds of $4,000 to yield a gross income of $2,000 in the first year, which carries a $680 tax liability. Hal plans on waiting until the end of his six-year term to pay tax on the $400 as "other income" (i.e., "loan" forgiveness). He has realized a $136 tax savings (the difference between $816 due on $2,400 in Scenario 3 and $680 due on $2,000 in this scenario).

By deferring the taxes due on the $400, Hal is able to take advantage now of $2,400 (the up-front cash plus the $2,000 he makes in profits) without paying taxes on that full amount. Put differently, this means that he is able to take advantage of a $136 tax savings in the first year. If he pays taxes on the $400 as income in the year of receipt (as in Scenario 3), the present value of his tax liability over the course of the six-year deal is $3,368.35. But if Hal defers payment of taxes on the $400 until the end of Year 6 (as in Scenario 4), the present value of his tax liability will be only

$3,331.87 over this same period. The present value of his total tax savings is a difference of $36.48 ($3,368.35 in Scenario 3 minus $3,331.87 in Scenario 4), which is negligible when dealing in amounts so small. But the amount grows when dealing in millions. *Karns*, 494 F.3d at 414-16.

Subsequent to the holding in *Karns*, the Service announced that it would follow the Ninth Circuit's holding in *Westpac*, but only if taxpayers did not claim a deduction for the amount representing the volume discount and treated the discounts consistently for financial accounting purposes. Rev. Proc. 2007-53, 2007-30 I.R.B. 233. Why would the Service fight against *Westpac* in the *Karns* case and then agree to follow *Westpac* almost immediately thereafter?

Problem

5-13. In year 1, Michael Joseph leased his property to Vickie Frissell for one year. Joseph and Frissell were calendar year taxpayers who reported income on the cash receipts and disbursements method of accounting. The terms of the lease required Frissell to pay a $2,000 "security deposit" to secure her performance under the agreement. The deposit could be applied to the last two months' rent or be refunded at the end of the one-year lease, provided that Frissell performed all covenants to pay rent and provided maintenance and insurance. In the event that Frissell failed to perform the covenants, the $2,000 was to be retained by Joseph as liquidated damages. Joseph was required to hold the deposit in an account that did not permit him to use the funds unless Frissell breached a material term of the lease.

    a. Should Joseph report the $2,000 as income for year 1?

    b. What tax consequences to Joseph in year 2 if Frissell breached a material term of the lease and Joseph retained the funds as liquidated damages?

    c. Would the answer to *a* change if Joseph held the deposit in a general account—that is, one that entitled him to unrestricted use of the $2,000 deposit?

5-14. In year 1, Hal Homeowner decides to start his own small business by opening a gas station. Hal has two choices: (1) start an independent station and buy gasoline on the market at its spot price, or (2) work with a major oil producer and agree to buy gasoline exclusively from that producer. Hal would prefer to do (1) but cannot find a bank to make a loan to start the business. American Petroleum ("AP") approaches Hal and offers to lend him $100,000 if he agrees to buy gasoline exclusively from AP for five years, and in addition for each year in which Hal buys at least $80,000 of gasoline during the first five years AP will forgive $20,000 of the loan. Hal agrees, and in December, year 1, he borrows $100,000 from AP and in January, year 2, he opens the station.

    a. In year 1, how much, if any, gross income must Hal report?

    b. Assume in year 2, Hal purchases $90,000 of gasoline from AP and AP forgives $20,000 of the loan. Does this change your answer to *a*?

    c. Assume in year 3 Hal purchases $100,000 of gasoline from AP but in year 4 Hal purchases only $50,000 of gasoline from AP. What results?

5. *Mandatory Accrual Method: Original Issue Discount*

Code: §§1272 to 1274
Regulations: §§1.1272-1(a), 1.1272-1(b)(1), 1.1273-2, 1.1274-2, 1.1275-
1(b), 1.1001-1(g)

a. Introduction

In most cases, the timing of income is determined by the taxpayer's method of accounting for tax purposes. In certain circumstances, however, the tax laws require a taxpayer to use a specific method of accounting regardless of their regular method of tax accounting. The most common of these are the rules applicable to "original issue discount" (OID).

Money has an inherent time value — that is, some amount of money is worth more today than that same amount of money tomorrow. For this reason, lenders generally will not lend money without charging interest. The interest comprises three components: (1) time value of money, (2) expected inflation, and (3) credit risk. In a traditional loan, interest is charged as a stated amount and compounds if it is not paid. For example:

Loan 1. John loans $1,000 to Mary, and the loan bears 10-percent interest per year compounded semiannually. At the end of the first 6 months, $50 of interest (i.e., 5 percent of $1,000) compounds, resulting in a total principal of $1,050. At the end of the second 6 months, interest of $52.50 (i.e., 5 percent of $1,050) compounds. At the end of the year, the total amount due would be the principal of $1,000 plus interest of $102.50 for a total of $1,102.50.

From an economic standpoint, however, the following loan would be identical to Loan 1:

Loan 2. John loans $1,000 to Mary, and the loan bears no stated interest. However, at the end of the year, Mary must repay $1,102.50.

This type of loan is described as being issued with "original issue discount" or OID. It is called OID because the "original" amount loaned (i.e., $1,000) is less than (or at a "discount" to) the amount due to be repaid in the future (i.e., $1,102.50). Thus, even though there is no stated interest, the OID serves as an economic replacement for interest, which is why the two loans are economically identical.

Although Loan 1 and Loan 2 are economically identical, prior to the enactment of the OID rules they could be treated differently for tax purposes. Thus, if John made Loan 1 to Mary and John was a cash method taxpayer, John would likely be required to include the $50 interest in income when the first interest payment accrued, under the constructive receipt doctrine, the cash-equivalency doctrine, or the economic benefit doctrine (since accruing the interest is the same as John being paid the interest and relending it back to Mary). Similarly, if John were an accrual method taxpayer, he would have to accrue the $50 interest income when the first interest payment accrued because all events fixing his right to the $50 would have occurred at the end of six months. However, prior to the OID rules, if John made

Loan 2 to Mary, then John would not have to include any amount in income from the loan at the end of the first six months, since no payments were "due" or accrued until the end of the loan.

b. The OID Rules

The OID rules, located in §§1271 to 1275 of the Code and the Regulations promulgated thereunder, were enacted to cure this different treatment for economically identical loans. These rules can be complicated, although for most purposes it is necessary to understand only their basic mechanics and principles.

The basic OID rules provide that a holder of a debt instrument must accrue (i.e., take into account for tax purposes as if it were paid) the OID of a debt instrument in the same manner as if it were interest paid on a regular basis. OID is defined by statute as the difference between the "stated redemption price at maturity" (SRPM) and the "issue price." As a result, these two concepts are fundamental to understanding the OID rules.

i. Issue Price

The issue price of a debt instrument differs depending on whether the debt instrument is issued for money or for property. Under §§1273(b)(1) to (2), the issue price of a debt instrument issued for money is the price paid by the first buyer or buyers of the debt instrument. Thus, under Loan 2, the issue price would be $1,000 because John "purchased" the debt instrument from Mary for $1,000.

The issue price of a debt instrument issued in exchange for property is more complicated. If a debt instrument is issued in exchange for publicly traded property, the issue price is the fair market value of the property; similarly, if the debt instrument itself is publicly traded, the issue price of the debt instrument is its fair market value on its issue date.

If, however, the debt instrument is issued for property and neither the debt instrument nor the property is publicly traded, the issue price is calculated by determining the present value of the debt instrument, as calculated under the rules of §1274. These rules provide that, if the debt instrument bears stated interest equal to at least the "applicable federal rate" (AFR),* the issue price of the debt instrument will be considered the stated principal amount of the debt instrument. If, however, the instrument bears stated interest less than the AFR, the present value of the debt instrument is calculated by discounting the total payments (other than certain interest paid at least annually) to be made on the debt instrument using the AFR.

Example 1. Mary sells Blackacre to John for $1,000,000, to be payable without interest 5 years after the sale. If the AFR is 6 percent compounded semiannually,

---

*Under §1274(d), the AFR applicable to a loan is generally the interest rate at which the United States could borrow under the circumstances. Because the United States is considered to have no credit risk, the AFR is intended to reflect solely the time value and inflation value of money. As a result, the AFR will always be lower than a person's actual borrowing rate.

the issue price is $744,093 (the present value of $1,000,000 discounted at 6 percent compounded semiannually for five years).

The present value of a debt instrument issued for property is discounted on a compounded basis, which can easily be calculated on a financial calculator or on a computer spreadsheet (present value discounted on a compound basis can prove difficult to estimate otherwise).

ii.   Stated Redemption Price at Maturity

Under §1273(a)(2), the SRPM is equal to the sum of all payments to be made under a debt instrument that are not required to be made at least annually.* For debt instruments that do not charge interest, this amount will be the same as the stated amount required to be repaid at maturity. Thus, under Loan 2, the SRPM is $1,102.50, and in the sale of Blackacre in Example 1 it is $1,000,000.

iii.   Accrual of Daily Portions

After a loan's issue price and SRPM are determined, the lender must take into income on a daily basis the "daily portion" of OID during an accrual period regardless of the lender's regular method of accounting for interest. The OID attributable to an accrual period is the product of the adjusted issue price and the yield to maturity under §§1272(a)(3) to (4). The accrued OID is added to the adjusted issue price for purposes of calculating the next OID accrual.

Determining the yield to maturity is relatively straightforward: the yield to maturity is whatever yield is necessary to cause the issue price to grow to the SRPM over the life of the loan.† Thus, in Loan 2, the yield to maturity would be 10 percent because 10 percent compounded semiannually for one year would result in $1,102.50, and in the sale of Blackacre in Example 1, the yield to maturity would be 6 percent for the same reason. As with present value, this calculation can be done quickly on a financial calculator or on a computer spreadsheet.

Example 2. Assume a 5-year, $1,000, zero-coupon bond (a bond bearing no stated interest) is sold for $675.56. The issue price is $675.56, and the stated redemption price at maturity (SRPM) is $1,000. Thus, the bond's yield to maturity, based on semiannual compounding, is 8 percent (i.e., if $675.56 is invested at 8 percent compounded semiannually, the amount grows to $1,000 in five years). For the first 6 months of the bond's term, the OID accrual is one-half of the product of 8 percent and $675.56: $675.56 × 0.08 ÷ 2 = $27.02. This amount is spread ratably over the days within these six months. For the second 6 months of the bond's term, the first accrual of $27.02 is added to the original issue price of $675.56 to result in an adjusted issue price of $702.58, which is used to compute the OID accrual for the second six months, as follows: $702.58 × 0.08 ÷ 2 = $28.10.

---

*Payments required to be made at least annually are referred to as "qualified stated interest" and are treated as normal interest payments in accordance with a taxpayer's regular method of accounting. Reg. §§1.1272-1(a) (1), 1.1273-1(c).

† Specifically, the Regulations provide that "the yield to maturity of a debt instrument is the discount rate that, when used in computing the present value of all principal and interest payments to be made under the debt instrument, produces an amount equal to the issue price of the debt instrument." Reg. §1.1272-1(b) (1) (i).

Problem

5-15. In year 1, John (who is a cash method taxpayer) lends Mary $100,000. In exchange, Mary agrees to repay $121,550 to John in year 3. Mary would have to pay 10-percent interest, compounded semiannually, for a bank to loan her $100,000. The AFR for Mary's loan is 6 percent, and the present value of the loan on the date the loan is made using the AFR is $108,000.

    a.   What is the issue price of the loan?

    b.   What is the stated redemption price at maturity for the loan?

    c.   Is John required to accrue original issue discount on the loan?

    d.   Do your answers to *a* through *c* change if instead the loan required Mary to repay $100,000 in year 3 plus accrued interest (payable at Mary's option) in an amount equal to 10-percent interest, compounded semiannually?

D. JUDICIAL EXCEPTIONS POSTPONING INCLUSION

Judicially created exceptions to both cash and accrual tax accounting principles postpone the inclusion of amounts received for security deposits or for the sale of an option. The payment received for the sale of an option to purchase property is also held in abeyance because generally it is not known at the time of receipt whether the option will be exercised (and included as part of the seller's amount realized on the sale of property) or will not be exercised (and treated as ordinary income to the seller). Virginia Iron Coal & Coke Co. v. Commissioner, 99 F.2d 919 (4th Cir. 1938); Commissioner v. Dill Co., 294 F.2d 291 (3d Cir. 1961).

A distinguishing characteristic of option purchase contracts is that neither the option grantor (the one who receives the payment) nor the option holder (the one who makes the payment) realizes tax consequences at the time the option is purchased. The grantor generally defers income until either the option holder exercises the option or allows it to lapse, whichever comes first.

The Fourth Circuit in Virginia Iron Coal & Coke Co. v. Commissioner, 99 F.2d 919 (4th Cir. 1938), explicated the rationale underlying the unusual treatment afforded to options and enumerated the distinguishing characteristics of an option. In that case, an option agreement provided for a payment of $300,000 the first year and a payment of $125,000 in each subsequent year of a five-year period in order to keep the option open. In the event that the option was exercised, all funds received were to be applied to the purchase price. Otherwise, the grantor was permitted to use the payments received without restriction.

After the first year, the optionee notified the grantor that it did not intend to exercise the option and thus permitted the option to expire. At issue was whether the payments made in the first year were to be included in the grantor's income in that year or held in abeyance until the year the option expired. In reaching its decision, the court reasoned that

> [A]t the time the payments were made it was impossible to determine whether they were taxable or not. In the event the sale should be completed, the payments became return of capital, taxable only if a profit should be realized on the sale. Should the option be surrendered it would then become certain, for the first time, that the payments constituted taxable income. Thus it will be readily seen that it was impossible to tax these payments in the year in which they were made.

Id. at 921. Thus, the court established the rule that option payments are taxable in the year the optionee surrenders (or exercises) all rights under the option contract and not in the year the option payment is actually received. The option holder similarly delays realizing tax consequences until the option is exercised, lapses, or is resold.

Several economic and tax benefits flow from the use of options. For instance, the grantor enjoys the tax-free use of the option payment for the period that the proceeds are held in abeyance. The option holder, meanwhile, may participate in unpredictable markets with a relatively small amount at risk — the option payment. If the underlying property appreciates, the holder may either resell the option contract for more than its cost or exercise the option. If the underlying property depreciates in value, the option holder may minimize the loss by reselling the option at a discounted price. In either event, however, the option holder can wait and see if the initial investment becomes profitable without purchasing the asset.

Although straight options — the purchase of a right to buy property at a future time for a fixed price — are common, many other transactions, such as lease-options, use the option arrangement. If straight-option principles apply to the lease-option, the grantor-lessor may receive the deferral benefits of options and, at the same time, receive business deduction advantages such as depreciation (discussed in Chapter 6). In analyzing the lease-option, the principal issue is whether payments should be characterized as rental payments taxed in the years received or as sales proceeds held in abeyance until the option is acted on.

KITCHIN v. COMMISSIONER
353 F.2d 13 (4th Cir. 1965)

BELL, J.

The principal question in this appeal is whether payments made under a lease-option contract should be prospectively characterized as either rental payments or sales proceeds and taxed accordingly in the years in which they are made or held in abeyance until the option is acted upon. In our former opinion, we held that the incidence of the tax could be postponed until the classification was fixed by the decision of the lessee/buyer in exercising or declining to exercise the option. We have granted the petitions for rehearing. . . . [T]he contracts covered the use of machinery for a relatively short term construction project which was to be completed in a period of 24 months. Thus the maximum term during which the machinery was to be used could be no more than two years and in most cases considerably less. At most then the delay in recognizing income in this case would be to the third tax year. Furthermore, the contracts involved in this case were exceptions to the petitioner's regular practice of straight leases without option to buy. The government, however, insists that this factual situation is far from typical; that there is a tremendous volume of business done under lease-option contracts and that many of these contracts run for a much longer period of time with consequent delays in tax treatment which would be detrimental and disruptive to both the taxpayer and the government if the decision were to prevail. While a short delay may not be upsetting either to the taxpayer or to the government's administration of the tax laws in exceptional cases, in general our tax laws are based upon the principle that only a system of annual accounting will produce a regular flow of income to the treasury and permit the application of methods of accounting, assessment and collection capable of practical application by both the government and the taxpayer.

Our former decision was based upon the rationale of Virginia Iron Coal & Coke Co. v. C.I.R., 99 F.2d 919 (4 Cir. 1938), cert. denied, 307 U.S. 630. That case involved the so-called "straight" option. The taxpayer had entered into an option to sell mining lands at an agreed price. The option was to remain open for a period of years upon payment of an annual amount which was to be credited on the purchase price or forfeited if the option was not exercised. The seller reported the payments as "option income" in the year that the holder notified the taxpayer in writing that the option would not be exercised. While it is true as a matter of logic that the same difficulty arises in prospectively categorizing the payments in the case before us as existed in the *Virginia Coal* case, nevertheless, we are convinced that there are differences in the underlying economic consequences to the parties in such a "straight" option and in the average lease-option contract involving the concurrent use of the property by the lessee/buyer which justify a distinction for purposes of taxation. In a sense, the straight option exists in an economic vacuum. Its creation does not normally cause any appreciable change in the ownership or possession of the property. At its inception there are no tax consequences for the purchaser of the option. If the option is exercised, the consideration paid for the option is likely to represent only a minor fraction of the consideration received for the entire transaction, but in any event there is no tax-necessity of differentiating between the amount paid for the privilege of the option and that paid as consideration for the thing optioned. Further the issuance of straight options are likely to be isolated transactions. Because straight options are thus insulated from other tax occurrences, they present substantially different problems with regard to tax administration than do the periodic payments involved in the normal lease-option agreement which is so common in modern business.

Since the lease-option contemplates possession by the lessee (optionee) the periodic payments are likely to represent a much larger portion of the total transaction. In many cases these payments will represent the total consideration. Thus if the lease runs until the option price is paid in "rent," half the total consideration will have been paid at points in time closer to the inception than the termination of the transaction. Failure to exercise the option in long term lease-contracts would result in bunching of income in the year the option expires and may result in a heavy tax burden on the lessor.

Failure to characterize the transaction in the beginning would not only interfere with the recognition of income but also with the allowance of a deduction for depreciation. Only the "owner" may take the depreciation deduction. If ownership is left in doubt until exercise or forfeiture of the option, then depreciation must also be held in suspense. This would involve a change in the practice of allowing the depreciation deduction only in the year in which the wear and tear occurred. The principle behind this yearly deduction for depreciation is that the deduction roughly corresponds to the income produced in the process of that wear and tear. If characterization is delayed and the option is forfeited no violence is done to this principle. Depreciation could be applied against the rental income. If the option is exercised, however, there is a totally different situation. The lessee has no deferred income; depreciation would be charged against current income which is unrelated to the wear and tear.

Finally, we think it clear in this case that the periodic payments represented a fair return for the use of the equipment and that the contracts were exactly what they purported to be; i.e., leases with options to purchase and not disguised sales. . . .

Accordingly we conclude that the Tax Court correctly categorized the payments here involved as rental income. . . .

Affirmed.

Note

The decision in *Kitchin* focuses on the economic features of a lease coupled with an option-to-purchase as compared to a straight option in determining whether the lease-option should be afforded special tax treatment. Referring to its decision in *Virginia Iron*, the court noted that the straight option "does not normally cause any appreciable change in the ownership or possession of the property." 353 F.2d at 15. In contrast, the lease-option not only secures the purchase opportunity but also contemplates possession by the lessee-optionee. In addition, lease-option payments may represent a much larger portion or even the entire amount of the purchase price (due on exercise of the option), whereas the consideration paid for a straight option is likely to represent only a small portion of the value of the underlying property.

Equally important, the decision in *Kitchin* points to the practical difficulties of the administration of tax laws if a lease option were treated in the same manner as a straight option. If the two were treated similarly, the periodic payments held in abeyance until the option terminates or is exercised would result in "bunching" the grantor-lessor's income in one tax year. Correspondingly, deductions for depreciation would also have to be suspended. Because the annual depreciation deduction is normally allowed in the year in which wear and tear occurs and the leasing arrangement contemplates such use, treating the lease option as a sale held open for tax purposes becomes impractical. Thus, the court concluded that rental payments received under a lease option must be treated as income in the year received, with depreciation taken that roughly corresponds to the wear and tear incurred, in order to preserve the principles of tax accounting and to ensure the orderly administration of the tax laws.

Problem

5-16. Mary Fuller, a calendar year, cash method taxpayer, wished to sell her prize-winning dog, Jacob, to a reputable owner. Mary purchased Jacob for $500. Tom Baskin, a calendar year, cash method taxpayer and renowned dog breeder, wanted to acquire Jacob to crossbreed with his dog, but Baskin was uncertain whether their offspring would possess the temperament and agility that distinguished Jacob. On December 1, Baskin paid Fuller $1,000 for an eighteen-month option to purchase Jacob. The stated option purchase price was $5,000; if Baskin exercised the option, the $1,000 option payment was to be credited toward the purchase price.

    a.   What were the tax consequences to Fuller on receipt of the $1,000?

    b.   What would be the amount of income to Fuller if the option was exercised eighteen months later?

    c.   What would be the tax consequences to Fuller if Baskin permitted the option to lapse?

    d.   Assume that, instead of the above facts, Baskin was to pay Fuller $3,000 for the right to breed Jacob and keep him with Baskin's dogs for a two-year period. At the expiration of two years, Baskin had the option to purchase Jacob for $2,000. What were the tax consequences to both Fuller and Baskin?

E. DEFERRED PAYMENT SALES OF PROPERTY

Deferred payment sales arise whenever property is sold and all or a portion of the sales proceeds are to be received at a future date. When future payments are to be received after the close of the taxable year of sale, tax accounting problems surface. Should all payments, even those to be received in future years, be included in gross income for the year of sale or should only the payments received in any one year be included in gross income at annual intervals?

To illustrate this problem, assume that a seller transfers property with a $20,000 adjusted basis and a $100,000 fair market value, in return for $10,000 cash and the purchaser's promise to pay $30,000 in each of the three succeeding years. If payment is made as promised, the seller's income from the transaction will be $80,000 ($100,000 amount realized less $20,000 adjusted basis). If the entire $100,000 is "realized" in the year of the sale, the seller will have $80,000 of gross income in year 1. If, on the other hand, the payments are to be "realized" annually as they are received, how should the seller report the $80,000 of income: in one year or prorated over three years?

There are three ways to report deferred payment sales: (1) closed transaction reporting; (2) open transaction reporting; and (3) installment reporting. Closed transaction and installment reporting are based on §§1001 and 453, respectively, while open transaction reporting (that is, *cost recovery*) is a judicial creation of limited application.

1. *Closed Transaction Reporting*

Code: §1001(a) to (d)
Regulations: §1.1001-1(a), (g)

As a general rule, gross income includes all income derived from any source, including gains from dealings in property. Thus, under §1001(c), unless a nonrecognition provision applies, the entire gain or loss realized on the sale or exchange of property is to be recognized. If all gain realized in a deferred payment sale is recognized in the year of sale, the transaction is referred to as a "closed transaction" because the tax consequences are established at the time of the sale. In this case, a taxpayer generally recognizes gain to the extent the amount realized exceeds the adjusted basis of the property sold.

For the taxpayer using the cash receipts and disbursements method of accounting, items are included in gross income when cash or its equivalent, services, or property is actually or constructively received. If a purchaser's promissory note is considered property received, then the taxpayer must determine the fair market value of the note and include that value in the amount realized. See §1001(b). Thus, a cash method seller who closes a transaction and recognizes gain in the year of sale may have a tax liability in excess of cash received in the year of sale.

For the taxpayer using the accrual method for reporting a closed transaction, "income is includable in gross income when all the events have occurred which fix the right to receive such income and the amount thereof can be determined with reasonable accuracy." Reg. §1.451-1(a). Thus, in general, an accrual method seller who receives a purchaser's note theoretically must include the *face* amount of the note as an amount realized at the time of sale because the obligation to pay that amount is fixed.

This approach is problematic because not all promises to pay in the future are created equal. Thus, if Warren Buffett promised to pay $100 million in five years, that promise probably would be worth more than the same promise made by a law professor. Similarly, a note issued by a publicly traded corporation and traded on a public exchange would be worth far more than a non-tradable note issued by an individual.

For years, the tax law struggled with this problem, trying to determine the proper amount to include in income in a "closed transaction" in which the purchase price was a note or a promise to pay in the future. For example, in Warren Jones Co. v. Commissioner, 524 F.2d 788 (9th Cir. 1975), the court faced a situation in which a taxpayer sold an apartment building to two individuals for $20,000 plus the promise to pay $1,000 per month (plus interest) for the next fifteen years.

The taxpayer contended that only the $20,000 payment plus $4,000 of monthly payments had to be included in income in the year of sale, because the promise to pay future amounts was uncertain and the taxpayer could not "sell" the right to receive future payments. The Service countered that the contractual right had a current value that could be determined based on the interest rate and the likelihood that the buyers would actually pay.

The Tax Court, in an unusual opinion, held that the right did have an ascertainable fair market value of $76,980, but that it would be unfair to include it in income in the year of sale since the taxpayer would not have the cash for fifteen years, and the discount reflected a high risk that the buyers might not pay in full. The circuit court reversed, holding that anytime there was an ascertainable fair market value, the fair market value had to be included in amount realized in the year of sale.

The struggle reflected in *Warren Jones* reflects the concern that not all promises to pay are the same. The Tax Court concluded that, because the fair market value of the promise to pay was so much less than the future payments, it would be unfair to force the taxpayer to include the fair market value in income in the year of sale. Would the Tax Court have reached the same conclusion if Bill Gates or Warren Buffett had made the same promise? Given the circuit court's conclusion that income must be recognized, however, the issue turned to placing a value on promises to pay in the future. Thus, taxpayers, the Service, and courts were continuously embroiled in valuation fights whenever a sale or exchange of property involved a promise to pay in the future.

This unsustainable case-by-case valuation fight was finally resolved when the OID rules were promulgated. Regulation §1.1001-1(g) provides that the amount realized in a sale of property for a debt instrument is equal to the "issue price" of the debt instrument determined for OID purposes. As discussed above, the issue price of debt issued for property depends on whether the property or the debt instrument is publicly traded: If so, the fair market value is used as the issue price; if not, the Regulations assume that the issue price is equal to the present value of all future payments discounted at the AFR. This rule resolved the factual difficulties of valuing debt instruments by assuming a value based on a straightforward formula. For a taxpayer like the one in *Warren Jones*, however, this means that the amount realized is not discounted for the risk that the future payments might not be made. Is this a more equitable result than the one adopted by the circuit court in *Warren Jones*?

2. Open Transaction Reporting

Code: §1001(a) to (c)
Regulations: §1.1001-1(a)

Occasionally a purchaser's obligation may not have a specific face amount *and* may be incapable of valuation. In such "rare and extraordinary" cases, if it is virtually impossible to determine the amount to be realized under §1001(b), open transaction reporting may be permitted. In those limited situations, the seller is permitted to *hold the transaction open*, treating payments received as a tax-free recovery of basis to the extent of the basis of the property sold and thereafter treating any payments received in excess of basis as taxable gain in the year received. Consequently, open reporting permits *total* deferral of gain until basis has been completely recovered.

Under Burnet v. Logan, which follows, the touchstone for open transaction reporting was the inability to value the consideration received with reasonable certainty. The Supreme Court found that the value of the taxpayer's right to receive future payments, based on the recovery of iron ore, would become apparent only with time and that tax assessment should therefore be deferred until basis was fully recovered. In considering the timing of taxation, the Court was concerned not only with the practical difficulties associated with valuing the consideration received but also with the fairness to the seller. At the time of sale, the seller was not assured that the total payments to be received would actually exceed her basis in the property. Accordingly, the Court ruled that the taxpayer would be allowed to hold the transaction open and report the income received on the cost recovery method.

BURNET v. LOGAN
283 U.S. 404 (1931)

Mr. Justice McReynolds delivered the opinion of the Court. . . .

Prior to March, 1913, and until March 11, 1916, respondent, Mrs. Logan, owned 250 of the 4,000 capital shares issued by the Andrews & Hitchcock Iron Company. It held 12 percent of the stock of the Mahoning Ore & Steel Company, an operating concern. In 1895 the latter corporation procured a lease for 97 years upon the "Mahoning" mine and since then has regularly taken therefrom large, but varying, quantities of iron ore. . . . Through an agreement of stockholders (steel manufacturers) the Mahoning Company is obligated to apportion extracted ore among them according to their holdings.

On March 11, 1916, the owners of all the shares in Andrews & Hitchcock Company sold them to Youngstown Sheet & Tube Company, which thus acquired, among other things, 12 percent of the Mahoning Company's stock and the right to receive the same percentage of ore thereafter taken from the leased mine.

For the shares so acquired the Youngstown Company paid the holders $2,200,000 in money and agreed to pay annually thereafter for distribution among them 60 cents for each ton of ore apportioned to it. Of this cash Mrs. Logan received 250/4000ths — $137,500; and she became entitled to the same fraction of any annual payment thereafter made by the purchaser under the terms of sale. . . .

During 1917, 1918, 1919 and 1920 the Youngstown Company paid large sums under the agreement. . . .

Reports of income for 1918, 1919 and 1920 were made by Mrs. Logan upon the basis of cash receipts and disbursements. They included no part of what she had obtained from annual payments by the Youngstown Company. She maintains that until the total amount actually received by her from the sale of her shares equals their [basis], no taxable income will arise from the transaction. . . .

The Commissioner ruled that the obligation of the Youngstown Company to pay 60 cents per ton had a fair market value of $1,942,111.46 on March 11, 1916; that this value should be treated as so much cash and the sale of the stock regarded as a closed transaction with no profit in 1916. He also used this valuation as the basis for apportioning subsequent annual receipts between income and return of capital. . . .

The 1916 transaction was a sale of stock — not an exchange of property. We are not dealing with royalties or deductions from gross income because of depletion of mining property. Nor does the situation demand that an effort be made to place according to the best available data some approximate value upon the contract for future payments. . . . As annual payments on account of extracted ore come in they can be readily apportioned first as return of capital and later as profit. The liability for income tax ultimately can be fairly determined without resort to mere estimates, assumptions and speculation. When the profit, if any, is actually realized, the taxpayer will be required to respond. The consideration for the sale was $2,200,000.00 in cash and the promise of future money payments wholly contingent upon facts and circumstances not possible to foretell with anything like fair certainty. The promise was in no proper sense equivalent to cash. It had no ascertainable fair market value. The transaction was not a closed one. Respondent might never recoup her capital investment from payments only conditionally promised. Prior to 1921 all receipts from the sale of her shares amounted to less than their [basis]. She properly demanded the return of her capital investment before assessment of any taxable profit based on conjecture.

"In order to determine whether there has been gain or loss, and the amount of the gain, if any, we must withdraw from the gross proceeds an amount sufficient to restore the capital value that existed at the commencement of the period under consideration." Doyle v. Mitchell Bros. Co., 247 U.S. 179, 184, 185. Ordinarily, at least, a taxpayer may not deduct from gross receipts a supposed loss which in fact is represented by his outstanding note. And, conversely, a promise to pay indeterminate sums of money is not necessarily taxable income. "Generally speaking, the income tax law is concerned only with realized losses, as with realized gains." Lucas v. American Code Co., 280 U.S. 445, 449. . . .

The judgments above are affirmed.

Problem

5-17. In year 1, Frances Grandi uses the cash method of accounting. Grandi sold a tractor for $10,000 in which she had an adjusted basis of $2,000. The purchaser, Harry Houlihan, paid Grandi $1,000 cash plus a promissory note for $11,388 to be paid in year 4. The fair market value of the note is $9,000, and the present value of the note using the AFR is $9,537.

   a.   What is Grandi's amount realized on the sale of the tractor?
   b.   What is the total OID on Houlihan's promissory note?
   c.   Do your answers to *a* or *b* change if the fair market value of the note was $7,500?

3. *Installment Reporting*

   Code: §§453(a) to (g), (i); 453B(a), (b); 1001(c), (d); 1041(a)
   Regulations: §§15A.453-1(a), (b)(1) to (3)(i), (c)(1) to (2)(i), (3), (4), (d)(1) to (2), (e)(1)

The most widely used deferred payment reporting method is §453 installment reporting. Since 1918, when installment reporting was first recognized in a

Treasury Regulation, there has been some form of relief for the tax consequences of closed transaction reporting. As discussed earlier, when a sale of property for a deferred payment obligation is considered "closed,"§1001(c) requires all gain realized to be recognized and reported as income in the year of sale, despite the fact that some payments are deferred to future years, and thus the cash received in that year might be less than the tax liability arising from the sale.

In 1926, Congress first provided relief for closed transaction reporting by permitting the installment seller to "return as income . . . in any taxable year that proportion of the installment payments actually received in that year which the total profit realized or to be realized . . . bears to the total contract price." Revenue Act of 1926 §212(d). Although the statute has undergone substantial revisions, its purpose remains clear: installment sale reporting is designed (1) to relieve taxpayers from having to pay an income tax in the year of sale based on anticipated profits when they have, in fact, received only a portion of the sales price and (2) to avoid the difficult task of appraising the value of the purchaser's promissory obligations in uncertain markets. Thus, §453 installment reporting, which automatically applies unless the taxpayer "elects out," eliminates the hardship often created by the general tax accounting methods. This is accomplished by placing the seller on a hybrid tax reporting method. As payments are collected, the seller treats a portion of each payment as a return of basis and a portion as income. After the total sales proceeds have been collected, the entire gain will have been taxed, with the seller generally incurring tax liability at the time cash or other payments are received.

Thus, by using §453 installment reporting, the seller may discharge the resulting tax liability from the proceeds collected each year, spread the tax liability over the payment period, and maintain a positive after-tax cash position.

This treatment alleviates the hardship often associated with closed transaction reporting, which may require the seller to recognize an amount of realized gain in the year of sale in excess of cash received. For example, assume a seller sells property with a $100,000 fair market value and a $30,000 adjusted basis. In return, the purchaser agrees to pay the seller $10,000 in the year of sale, plus $30,000 a year for the next three years (plus interest). Assume the seller's gain is taxed at an effective rate of 20 percent (for ease of calculation). The following equation illustrates the seller's year of sale tax consequences if closed transaction reporting were applied to the example given above (assuming the purchaser's note has a value equal to its face amount):

	Year of sale
Amount realized	$100,000
−Adjusted basis	− 30,000
Realized gain	$70,000
Recognized gain	$70,000
Tax due	14,000
−Payments received	− 10,000
Cash deficiency	$4,000

In this example of closed transaction reporting, collections in the year of sale are insufficient to discharge the resulting tax liability. The seller incurs a $4,000 after-tax cash deficiency.

Assuming that the seller in the above example qualifies for open transaction reporting, the result is illustrated in Table 5-1.

TABLE 5-1

	Year of sale	Year 2	Year 3	Year 4	Total
Total basis	$30,000	$0	$0	$0	$30,000
Unrecovered basis	30,000	20,000	0	0	0
Payment received	10,000	30,000	30,000	30,000	100,000
Remaining basis	20,000	0	0	0	0
Gain recognized	0	10,000	30,000	30,000	70,000
Tax	0	2,000	6,000	6,000	14,000
Surplus cash	10,000	28,000	24,000	24,000	86,000

The open transaction reporting example illustrates that when open reporting applies, the taxable gain and associated tax liability is concentrated in later years, thereby providing a postponement of gain recognition and a significantly increased after-tax cash flow in earlier years. For the seller, these results are preferable to those of Table 5-2 where installment reporting was utilized. Nevertheless, open transaction reporting is available only in "rare and extraordinary" cases.

The mechanics of §453(c) divide each payment received by a seller of property between income and return of basis based on the "gross profit percentage." For each taxable year, the seller's taxable gain equals the payment received in that year multiplied by the gross profit percentage. The gross profit percentage is calculated by dividing the gross profit of the sale by the total contract price. Under §453, gross profit equals the "selling price" minus the adjusted basis of the property sold. This amount generally is equal to the total taxable gain on the sale if it were a closed transaction because the selling price is equal to the total amount of future principal payments.

As a result, calculating the gain recognized requires the identification of three items: (1) payments received in a taxable year, (2) gross profit, and (3) total contract price. Represented as a formula, the installment sale taxable income for any particular year is computed as follows:

$$\text{Gain recognized} = \text{Payment} \times \frac{\text{Gross profit}}{\text{Total contract price}}$$

Applying the §453 formula to the example above, the gross profit percentage is 70 percent, computed as follows:

$$\text{Gross profit percentage} = \frac{\text{Gross profit}}{\text{Total contract price}} = \frac{\$100,000 - \$30,000}{\$100,000} = 70$$

Thus, in the year of sale, the seller's taxable gain under §453 would be $7,000 (70 percent of the payment of $10,000). The untaxed $3,000 payment received in the year of sale would be treated as a nontaxable return of basis. Similarly, the same 70 percent gross profit percentage will be applied as the remaining $90,000 of payments are received, producing an additional $63,000 (70%×$90,000) of gross income.

It is important to note that §453 is a timing provision only. The seller's total amount realized remains unchanged regardless of whether §453 applies. Thus, in the above example, the seller realizes $70,000 of gain on the sale ($100,000 amount realized −$30,000 adjusted basis), and thus at the end of the §453 payment schedule the seller will recognize $70,000 of gain and pay $14,000 in tax. For example, after all payments have been received, the entire $70,000 will have been taxed as illustrated in Table 5-2.

TABLE 5-2

	Year of sale	Year 2	Year 3	Year 4	Total
Payments received	$10,000	$30,000	$30,000	$30,000	$100,000
Gross profit %	70%	70%	70%	70%	70%
Recognized gain	7,000	21,000	21,000	21,000	70,000
Return of basis	3,000	9,000	9,000	9,000	30,000
Tax due	1,400	4,200	4,200	4,200	14,000
Surplus cash	8,600	25,800	25,800	25,800	86,000

Under §453, the receipt of a debt instrument generally is not treated as a payment (unless the debt instrument is payable on demand or is readily tradable) but rather as a promise to make payments in the future. The amount of such future payments to be made is included in the selling price for purposes of calculating the gross profit under §453. Subsequent to the finalization of the OID rules, the issue price of a debt instrument as calculated under the OID rules should be the amount included in the selling price for purposes of §453. The difference between the issue price and the SRPM (if any) is treated as the equivalent of interest, and thus not included in selling price.

Although §453 addresses some of the fairness, liquidity, and other problems arising from the "cash equivalency" and "constructive receipt" doctrines, disputes continue to arise as to when an evidence of indebtedness should be treated as a promise to pay in the future or as cash equivalent or constructive receipt. This is relevant both in the context of §453, since only sales of property where at least one payment will be made in the future qualify, but also where taxpayers elect out of §453 and need to determine whether they are subject to "open transaction" or "closed transaction" treatment. Did the enactment of §453, which substantially mitigated some of the fairness concerns around closed transaction treatment faced by the Tax Court in *Warren Jones*, change this analysis?

ESTATE OF SILVERMAN v. COMMISSIONER
98 T.C. 54 (1992)

RUWE, JUDGE:

. . . The issue for decision is whether petitioners are entitled to use the installment method to report the gain on exchange of their shares of stock in a savings and loan association for savings accounts of another savings and loan association.

FINDINGS OF FACT

... In 1982, Mr. and Mrs. Silverman owned 29,162 shares of stock in Olympic Savings and Loan Association (Olympic). On October 21, 1982, Coast Federal Savings and Loan Association (Coast), a federally chartered mutual savings and loan association, offered to acquire all outstanding shares of stock of Olympic in exchange for Coast savings accounts in the principal amount of $28.5487 per share.

The Exchange Offer provided that:

> In accepting the Exchange Offer, an Olympic Savings stockholder will receive savings accounts in Coast Federal as follows:
>   (1) 30% of the Exchange Price paid to each stockholder will be in a withdrawable statement savings account of Coast Federal, bearing interest, commencing on the effective date of the transaction, at a rate of 5-1/2% per annum, compounded daily, with an effective yield of 5.65%, (the "Statement Savings Account");
>   (2) 70% of the Exchange Price paid to each stockholder will be in a NONWITH-DRAWABLE fixed-rate six-year statement savings account of Coast Federal, bearing interest, commencing on the effective date of the transaction, at the rate of 6-1/2% per annum, compounded daily, with an effective yield of 6.72%, and payable semi-annually commencing six months from the effective date of the transaction (the "Term Account").

Mr. and Mrs. Silverman accepted the Coast offer and received $249,761 principal amount of statement savings accounts, and $582,776 principal amount of term accounts in exchange for their Olympic stock. The term accounts were certificates of deposit.

... Mr. and Mrs. Silverman received a passbook for each account issued. These passbooks were basically identical to those evidencing any other account at Coast. If a passbook represented a certificate of deposit, the passbook stated that it was a "certificate of deposit." All Coast's passbooks stated on the first page that they were "Not transferable except on the books of the Association." The only situation in which title to one of Coast's certificates of deposit could be changed was if the owner or one of the joint owners died. In such a case, title would be vested in the executor or administrator of the decedent's estate.

... The passbooks evidencing the term accounts received in the exchange, in addition to stating they were certificates of deposit, contained the following language: "Per Stock Exchange Offer." This language indicated that, in addition to the usual restrictions on certificates of deposit, the account was subject to the terms of the exchange offer. Pursuant to the exchange offer, no part of the principal amount of the term accounts could be withdrawn for 6 years from the effective date of the exchange. Interest, payable semi-annually, could be withdrawn during the term of the account. ... The term accounts were not readily tradable in an established securities market. ...

OPINION

Respondent contends that Mr. and Mrs. Silverman were required to include the entire gain on disposition of their Olympic stock in their 1982 income.

Petitioners . . . argue . . . that the gain on the exchange may be reported on the installment method. We must decide whether the Silvermans were entitled to report the exchange under the installment method.

Section 1001(a) provides that the gain from the sale of property shall be the excess of the amount realized therefrom over the adjusted basis. Amount realized is defined as the sum of any money received plus the fair market value of property (other than money) received. All gain realized under §1001 must be recognized absent a statutory exception.

Section 453 provides such an exception. It allows income from an installment sale to be reported in the year "payment" is received. The amount of income to be recognized for any taxable year is the "proportion of the payments received in that year which the gross profit (realized or to be realized when payment is completed) bears to the total contract price."

An "installment sale" is defined as "a disposition of property where at least 1 payment is to be received after the close of the taxable year in which the disposition occurs." Generally, and for purposes of this case, the term 'payment' does not include the receipt of evidences of indebtedness of the person acquiring the property."

Mr. and Mrs. Silverman disposed of property (Olympic stock) to Coast. Coast was thus "the person acquiring the property." In return, the Silvermans received withdrawable statement savings accounts and term accounts that could not be withdrawn for 6 years. If the Coast term accounts which Mr. and Mrs. Silverman received in the exchange are "evidences of indebtedness of the person acquiring the property," then Mr. and Mrs. Silverman's receipt of the term accounts would not constitute "payment" for purposes of §453, and they would therefore be entitled to report the disposition of their Olympic stock on the installment method.

Whether certificates of deposit are "evidences of indebtedness" of the issuing savings and loan association was answered by the Supreme Court in Paulsen v. Commissioner, 469 U.S. 131 (1985). In that case, . . . the Court recognized that the certificates of deposit had both "equity and debt characteristics" . . . but found that the debt characteristics predominated, and that the equity characteristics were insubstantial.

. . . We perceive no meaningful distinction between the certificates of deposit in *Paulsen* and those involved here. The certificates of deposit received by Mr. and Mrs. Silverman represent "evidences of indebtedness" of the person acquiring their property. Petitioners meet all of the literal statutory requirements of §453 so as to entitle them to report income from the disposition of Olympic stock using the installment method.

Respondent argues that the term accounts are "cash equivalents" and therefore must be included in income in the year of sale. . . .

We have previously held that a finding that a taxpayer is entitled to installment sale reporting makes it unnecessary for us to address issues involving the application of the cash equivalence doctrine. However, since respondent relies heavily upon the cash equivalence argument and application of that doctrine is far from clear . . . we will examine respondent's position.

. . . In Warren Jones Co. v. Commissioner, 524 F.2d 788 (9th Cir. 1975), revg. 60 T.C. 663 (1973), the Circuit Court to which the instant case would be appealable, reversed this Court's holding that the fair market value of a contract was not includable in the amount realized from a sale. We had held that the contract was not a cash equivalent because it could not have been transferred to a lender or investor at a discount which was not substantially greater than the generally prevailing premium for the use of money. (The discount factor was found to be approximately 42 percent.) After an analysis of the evolution of the language of §1001, the accompanying legislative history, and the case law of that circuit, the Ninth Circuit held that if the fair market value of a contract can be ascertained, the ascertainable fair market value must be included as an amount realized under §1001(b). Consequently, under *Warren Jones Co.*, whether gain is or is not realized under §1001 upon receipt of purchaser's debt obligation depends on whether the obligation has an ascertainable fair market value, regardless of the size of the discount.

The result of satisfying either the cash equivalence or the ascertainable fair market value tests is that gain is realized under §1001(b). Petitioners do not dispute that gain was realized in 1982. Such realized gain under §1001 must be recognized absent a statutory exception, but, as previously pointed out, §453 provides such an exception. A finding that a transaction may be reported under §453 assumes there has been a realization event and makes any further consideration of the cash equivalence doctrine redundant. Thus, despite the inclusion of the value of the buyer's obligation in the amount realized under §1001(b), a taxpayer is entitled to report gain from the transaction under the installment method.

The legislative history of §453 indicates that Congress believed that the cash equivalence characteristics of certain types of debt instruments made it inappropriate to allow them to be reported under the installment method. As a result, it enacted specific provisions to preclude certain debt instruments from being reported under the installment method. . . . The Senate Finance Committee report stated:

> Debentures, however, in most cases can be readily traded on the market and therefore are a close approximation of cash. Thus, the problem of the seller not having the cash with which to pay the tax due would not appear to be present where he receives debentures or other readily marketable securities. [S. Rept. 91-552 (1969), 1969-3 C.B. 423, 515.]

However, the report goes on to state that:

> The committee amendments also provide that bonds in registered form which the taxpayer establishes will not be readily tradeable [sic] in an established securities market are not to be treated as payments received in the year of sale, since because of their lack of ready marketability they do not possess the characteristics which would render them essentially similar to cash. [S. Rept. 91-552 at 516.]

Therefore, while Congress has created an exception to installment reporting based on the cash equivalence characteristics of certain obligations, it specifically enumerated the type of debt obligations which fell within the exception. We conclude that cash equivalence is not an exception to the installment method except as specifically provided in the statute. The term accounts in issue in this case were not readily tradable in an established securities market, and, thus, were not within the aforementioned statutory exception.

Respondent contends, in the alternative, that the Silvermans received the present economic benefit of full payment when they received the term accounts, and, therefore, must recognize the gain realized in the year of sale. . . . [A] taxpayer certainly may not receive the benefits of the installment sales provisions if, through his machinations, he achieves in reality the same result as if he had immediately collected the full sales price. . . . [I]n order to receive the installment sale benefits the seller may not directly or indirectly have control over the proceeds or possess the economic benefit therefrom.

During 1982, the Silvermans never possessed the right to receive payment of the amounts represented by the term accounts. The term accounts were not withdrawable until 1988, were not readily tradable in an established securities market, and were not assignable except upon the death of a joint owner, in which case title could only be vested in the decedent's personal representative or the surviving joint owner. The passbooks evidencing the accounts stated on their face that transferability was limited. In short, it is difficult to see how the Silvermans received the economic benefits of payment when the term accounts could not be withdrawn, sold, or borrowed against during the year in issue.

Respondent relies on Pozzi v. Commissioner, 49 T.C. 119 (1967), in support of his argument that the economic benefit associated with receipt of "payments," such as the term accounts, has been uniformly held to disqualify a transaction from installment sale treatment. Respondent's reliance is misplaced. *Pozzi* is one of a series of cases in which installment sale treatment was denied where factual analysis led to the conclusion that the sellers were no longer looking to the purchaser for payment, but, instead, expected to collect from funds which the purchasers had placed in escrow with a third party. . . . The instant case is clearly distinguishable from the facts of these cases.

. . . Unlike the instant case, in each of the above cases the transaction involved a party other than the buyer and the seller. The purchasers parted with the full amount of the purchase price in the year of sale, either by furnishing certificates of deposit or cash. Thus, in those cases, the purchaser had fully extinguished its payment obligation in the year of sale. In reality, the seller was not looking to or relying on the "indebtedness of the person acquiring the property" in order to receive payment. Instead, the seller-taxpayer had received the obligation of a third party to whom he was looking to collect. Evidence of the obligation of a third party is not excluded from the definition of the term "payment" for purposes of §453.

. . . Unlike the aforementioned cases, the Silvermans never looked to anyone or anything other than the Coast term accounts for payment of Coast's obligation. The fact that the obligor here is a savings and loan association, and the obligation is a certificate of deposit, does not affect our analysis. It is the substance of the transaction that governs its tax consequences[,] not the labels applied to the obligations by the parties . . . and it is clear that the term accounts represented a debt of the purchaser.

The relevant inquiry is whether, in substance . . . [t]he purchaser sheds his obligation by irrevocably placing in escrow sufficient cash or its equivalent to pay the full amount of his debt to the seller. At that point, the transaction is essentially complete for the purchaser, who has no further interest in it. The escrow agent becomes a substitute obligor if, at the time of sale, the seller is able to look to the escrowed funds for unconditional periodic payment of the purchase price.

. . . Finally, the fact that the accounts were insured does not bring them within the definition of "payment." Section 453(f)(3) provides that unless readily tradable or payable on demand, payment does not include purchaser evidences of indebtedness "(whether or not payment of such indebtedness is guaranteed by another person.)"

. . . We find that the Silvermans did not receive the economic benefit of payment of the sales price of their stock in 1982 when they received the term accounts. We hold that petitioners were entitled to report the transaction using the installment method. This result is consistent with the Congressional objective in enacting §453 which was to relieve taxpayers from having to pay tax in the year of sale based on the full amount of anticipated profits when they had received in cash only a portion of the sales price. Decision will be entered for petitioners.

Note

While the use of the installment method will provide for the deferral of the attendant tax liability until actual sales proceeds are received, Congress concluded that "too much of a good thing" should not be permitted. Thus, under §453A(a)(1), in certain cases if the face amount of all installment obligations exceeds $5,000,000, an interest charge is imposed on the deferred tax liability. In addition to the interest charge on installment sales for amounts in excess of $5,000,000, Congress placed other limitations on installment reporting. An example of such a limitation is §453(e) where the buyer and seller are related and the buyer subsequently disposes of the property.

Problems

5-18. In year 1 Erica purchases Blackacre, a parcel of undeveloped land, for $20,000 in cash. In year 3, Justin approaches Erica and offers to purchase Blackacre for $20,000 cash plus a note with a face amount of $80,000, bearing adequate stated interest and with scheduled payments of $20,000 per year for each of years 4 through 7. The note has a current fair market value of $70,000. Erica accepts the offer and at the end of year 3 Justin pays Erica the initial $20,000 cash payment plus the $80,000 note.

    a. If Erica is a cash method taxpayer and does not make the election under §453(d), what are Erica's tax consequences from the sale of Blackacre in years 3 through 7 (ignoring interest)?

    b. If Erica is an accrual method taxpayer and does not make the election under §453(d), what are Erica's tax consequences from the sale of Blackacre in years 3 through 7 (ignoring interest)?

    c. If Erica is a cash method taxpayer and does make the election under §453(d), what are Erica's tax consequences from the sale of Blackacre in years 3 through 7 (ignoring interest)?

5-19. Same facts as above, except that in year 1 Erica paid $10,000 cash and borrowed $10,000 on a nonrecourse basis to acquire Blackacre. Between year 1 and year 3, Erica timely paid interest but not principal on the debt. In year 3, Justin purchases Blackacre for the $80,000 note, $10,000 in cash, and assumption of Erica's $10,000 nonrecourse debt.

    a. If Erica is a cash method taxpayer and does not make the election under §453(d), what are Erica's tax consequences from the sale of Blackacre in years 3 through 7 (ignoring interest)?

    b. If Erica is an accrual method taxpayer and does not make the election under §453(d), what are Erica's tax consequences from the sale of Blackacre in years 3 through 7 (ignoring interest)?

    c. If Erica is a cash method taxpayer and does make the election under §453(d), what are Erica's tax consequences from the sale of Blackacre in years 3 through 7 (ignoring interest)?

5-20. Walter and his daughter, Jenny Todd, were calendar-year, cash method taxpayers. In year 1, Walter sold a 1990 Mercedes to Jenny for its $16,000 fair market value. Jenny made a $1,000 down payment. She also executed a fifteen-year negotiable promissory note, bearing a face amount of $15,000, payable $1,000 per year commencing in year 2, plus interest at the market rate of 10 percent per annum. Walter, who had used the car only for weekend outings, had purchased it for $4,000. In year 2, before making any payments on the note to Walter, Jenny sold the car to Kevin Gage for $17,000 in cash.

    a. What were the tax consequences to Walter in year 1 as a result of the sale of the car to Jenny?

    b. What were the tax consequences to Walter and Jenny in year 2 when Jenny sold the car to Gage for $17,000 cash?

    c. Would it make a difference in *b* if Jenny had sold the car to Gage in year 4? What result to Walter?

    d. Would it make a difference in *a* and *b* if Walter sold the car to his brother instead of Jenny?

    e. Assume that Jenny sold the car to Gage in year 2, for a $7,000 down payment, plus a five-year balloon payment note having a $9,000 face amount, bearing interest at the market rate of 10 percent per annum and a $6,000 fair market value, and that she did not "elect out" of §453. What result? What result if she elected out of §453?

    f. What result in *e* if Gage paid no cash and gave her a $16,000 note due in twenty years instead of five years?

Note on Disposition of Installment Obligations

The first statutory provision governing dispositions of installment obligations was enacted in 1928. According to the committee reports, it was designed to prevent tax evasion in connection with (1) the transfer of installment obligations on death, (2) the distribution of installment obligations in corporate liquidations or as dividends, (3) the making of a gift of such obligations, and (4) the transfer of obligations in similar situations. In most of these settings, gain was not recognized upon the transfer of the obligation, yet the transferee received a stepped-up basis in the property. As a consequence, the transferree would avoid any gain recognition on the subsequent collection on the instrument. Section 453B is intended to act as a safeguard against such abuse.

Upon the disposition of an installment obligation, gain or loss is recognized to the extent of the difference between the basis in the obligation and *either* (1) the amount realized in the case of satisfaction at other than face value or a sale or exchange, or (2) the fair market value of the obligation at the time of any other distribution, transmission, or disposition.

Under §453B, a taxpayer's basis in an installment note is the face value of the note minus the amount that would be taxable if the note was satisfied in full. For example, assume that S sells real property to P for $20,000, receiving $5,000 cash and P's note for $15,000 payable in subsequent years. S acquired the property for $8,000. In year 2, before P makes payment on the note, S sells the note for $13,000. In the year of disposition, S calculates gain as follows:

Amount Realized		
Proceeds on sale of the note		$13,000
Less Basis		
Sales price of property	$20,000	
Cost (basis in property)	(8,000)	
Total profit	$12,000	
Total contract price	$20,000	
Gross profit percentage		
(profit/total contract price)	60%	
Face value of note	15,000	
Income returnable had notes		
been satisfied in full		
($15,000 × 60%)	(9,000)	
Basis in note		6,000
Taxable income on disposition		$7,000

This example demonstrates the calculation of gain or loss as well as the procedure for calculating the seller's basis in the installment obligation. If, instead of a sale, S had given the note to his daughter, D, and at the time of the gift the fair market value of the notes was $14,000, gain or loss is computed as follows:

Fair market value of note at time of disposition	$14,000
Less basis in note	6,000
Taxable income on disposition	$8,000

UNITED SURGICAL STEEL CO. v. COMMISSIONER
54 T.C. 1215 (1970)

QUEALEY, J. . . . .
The [issue] for decision [is]: . . .

Whether petitioner "disposed of" installment obligations during its taxable years ended November 30, 1965 and 1966, so as to preclude its reporting income on the installment method under section 453. . . .

The petitioner was incorporated on April 1, 1962. At all times from that date until November 30, 1966, Mr. John O. Hope owned over 96 percent of petitioner's outstanding common stock.

During the taxable years involved in this case, petitioner was engaged in the business of selling cookware, china, and related items to consumers. Most of petitioner's sales were made on conditional sales contracts with installment notes where a 10-percent down payment was made by the customer and the balance of the contract was secured by a note payable in monthly installments over a period of 12, 15, 18, or 24 months. . . .

On May 31, 1965, a loan agreement was entered into by and between petitioner as the borrower, Modern China & Table Institute, Inc., and United Discount Co., Inc., as the guarantors, and the First National Bank of Montgomery, Montgomery, Ala. (the bank). The agreement provided, in part, that:

> 1. Subject to all the terms of this agreement and concurrently with assignment to the Bank by the Borrower of collateral acceptable to the Bank and during the life of this agreement, Bank shall lend to the Borrower from time to time, such amounts as the Borrower may request. . . .
>
> 5. This loan agreement and the financing arrangement contemplated hereunder is based on the following method of operation:
>
> a. Notes and conditional sales contracts or chattel mortgages securing said notes will be transferred, assigned and delivered to the Bank. Said transfers and assignment shall be in form and substance satisfactory to bank and shall be with full recourse.
>
> b. There will be attached to each contract evidence showing delivery of merchandise, and a credit statement on the individual buyer.
>
> c. The Bank will advance 88 percent of the unpaid balance on the note and assigned collateral and place 12 percent of the unpaid balance in a dealer reserve account. The advance of 88 percent of the unpaid balance shall be considered "money in use" as mentioned herein.
>
> d. The dealer reserve account will be built up to and then shall be maintained at 35 percent of aggregate unpaid balance of assigned collateral; any excess shall be paid to Borrower. . . .
>
> f. Collections on assigned collateral shall be deposited daily in kind to a collection account subject to withdrawal by Bank only, which account shall be the property of the Bank. Borrower shall maintain an impounded balance of $1,000.00 in said account. On Monday of each week borrower will send bank a recapitulation of payments deposited to the Collection Account the previous week. From this recapitulation, bank will withdraw the collected funds and apply as a credit to borrower's loan account. Returned checks shall be charged back to this account.
>
> g. Any account represented by collateral which is three payments past due is to be bought back in cash by Borrower for the full unpaid balance. This repurchase is to take place no later than five days before the fourth payment falls due. . . .

With respect to the transaction with the First National Bank of Montgomery, the respondent argues, first, that the agreement with the bank "amounted to much more than a mere pledge" of the installment obligations and, secondly, even assuming that the transaction was a "pledge," that there was a disposition of the installment obligations within the meaning of section 453[B] on the authority of Rev. Rul. 65-185. . . .

The respondent does not contend that the installment obligations were "satisfied," "distributed," "transmitted," or "sold." Rather the respondent argues that the transactions were "otherwise disposed of." The respondent recognizes, however, and this Court has held, that the pledge of an installment obligation as collateral security for a loan is not *generally* a "disposition" of that obligation within the meaning of section 453[B].

The respondent contends, nevertheless, that where the amount borrowed on the collateral is "substantially equal" to the obligation, there is a disposition of the obligation. . . . [T]here is no basis in law upon which to conclude that merely because the amount borrowed is substantially equal to the face amount of the collateral, the taxpayer has thereby disposed of the collateral. This might follow under the facts of a particular case, such as where the transaction was found not to be a loan, but cannot be advanced as a rule of law.

In Town & Country Food Co., [51 T.C. 1049 (1969)], this Court had under consideration a financing plan somewhat similar to that in the case before us. The Court said:

> Section 453[B] predicates its application upon a sale or exchange or other disposition of installment obligations. We think it is obvious that a disposition involves the relinquishment of the substantial incidents of ownership of the obligations. It may well be that in some instances involving claimed borrowing arrangements the taxpayer parts with such a substantial portion of his ownership rights in the obligations as to require the conclusion that he has, in effect, sold or otherwise disposed of the obligations. On the other hand, if it is clear that the taxpayer has merely subjected the obligations to a lien for the payment of indebtedness, he does not lose the privilege of reporting the income from the installment method. As stated in Elmer v. Commissioner (C.A.2) 65 F.2d 568, affirming 22 B.T.A. 224:
>
> If a merchant discounts his customer's note at a bank, endorsing it, but getting immediate credit for its discount value, it would be a most unnatural thing to consider it a loan from the bank. He remains liable if the customer defaults, but the collection is in the bank's hands, and the transaction is closed in the absence of a default. If on the other hand, a merchant pledges his accounts to a "finance" company and collects them himself, paying the loan out of his collections, it is clearly a loan, and has always been so considered.

The facts here clearly establish that the transaction between the petitioner and the bank was *in form*, as well as substance, a loan and not a sale of the collateral. The petitioner and its guarantors entered into an agreement with the bank pursuant to which the bank agreed to extend a line of credit up to a maximum of $650,000, subsequently increased to $850,000. The petitioner executed a note payable to the bank for the full amount of its authorized borrowings, or the sum of $850,000. The note was described as a "draw" note by the lender which meant that the note itself did not represent the amount owing but was intended, along with the collateral, to secure loans by the bank to the petitioner.

Pursuant to the terms of the loan agreement, the petitioner assigned its installment obligations to the bank and became entitled to borrow up to 88 percent of the face amount of such obligations. The petitioner continued to make all collections on the obligations, which were deposited daily in a special bank account. The funds thus deposited could not be withdrawn by the petitioner but the total amount on deposit would be credited to the petitioner's revolving account on a weekly basis. In the case of a default on any installment obligation, the petitioner was required to reduce its account with the bank by an equal amount and the obligation was released from escrow.

While the procedures, pursuant to which the petitioner financed its installment obligations, may not have differed in some respects from the procedures which are followed where a taxpayer discounts or sells its trade obligations to a bank subject to recourse, other duties and restrictions imposed on the petitioner served to distinguish the transaction from a sale or disposition of the installment obligations.

The bank did not realize any income from the installment obligations but only realized interest charges measured by the actual balance owing by the petitioner. Thus, while the bank assumed no risk, other than as a lender of money to the petitioner, the bank could realize no gain except as interest on that loan.

The petitioner continued to handle all collections and otherwise to service its customers. In fact, there was no contact between the customer and the bank. As far as the customer knew, the petitioner was the person to whom he was indebted.

The bank did not look to the debtors under the installment obligation for payment. The obligation to pay the bank remained at all times an obligation of the petitioner and its guarantors. The loan agreement makes this clear.

The loan agreement imposed restrictions on the operations of petitioner which are wholly inconsistent with the view that the transaction was not a loan by the bank to the petitioner. For example, the petitioner was required to keep its records in a manner satisfactory to the bank; the bank had the right to audit the books of petitioner; the petitioner had to furnish the bank periodically with financial statements of its operations; the petitioner had to pay all its taxes as such taxes came due; the petitioner had to keep its property insured; the petitioner could not purchase any additional fixed assets other than automobiles and individual purchases of less than $1,000 without prior approval of the bank; and, the petitioner was restricted in the payment of compensation, the creation of other indebtedness, and the payment of dividends.

[I]t is our opinion that the petitioner did not dispose of its installment obligations within the meaning of section 453[B]. Accordingly, the petitioner is entitled to use the installment basis in reporting the gain on the sales represented by such obligations. . . .

Note on Pledges of Installment Obligations

In response to perceived abuses, Congress enacted §453A, which provides that certain pledges of installment notes will result in gain recognition even though the pledge is not a §453B taxable disposition. Pursuant to §453A, if an installment obligation arises from the disposition of business or investment property and the sales price for such property exceeds $150,000, the proceeds from the pledge will be treated as a deemed payment on the installment obligation. For example, assume taxpayer sells investment property with a $200,000 fair market value and a $20,000 adjusted basis in return for a $200,000 note and subsequently "pledges" the note as collateral for a $190,000 loan. If the loan constitutes a sale of an installment obligation (a §453B taxable disposition), the taxpayer's recognized gain equals $170,000, the $190,000 amount realized from the proceeds minus the $20,000 adjusted basis of the note. If, however, the loan is a true "pledge," and §453A applies, the $190,000 loan proceeds will be treated as a deemed payment on the installment obligation. The taxpayer will, therefore, recognize a $171,000 gain, the $190,000 deemed payment times the 90-percent gross profit percentage. Section 453A(d)(2) limits the amount of deemed payments to an amount equal to the total contract price minus previous payments. Section 453A(d)(3) provides that the subsequent actual payments on the installment obligation are not taken into account unless they exceed previous deemed payments.

Problem

5-21. Carl Wallace sold an apartment building in return for a $300,000 cash down payment and the purchaser's $500,000 promissory note. Later in the year, Wallace borrowed $350,000 from a bank, pledging the $500,000 note as collateral for the loan. What factors are relevant in determining whether there has been a taxable disposition of the note?

Note on Installment Sales of Encumbered Property

If encumbered property is sold on the installment method and the purchaser assumes the debt or acquires the property subject to the debt, application of the general mechanics of §453 does not result in taxation of all the seller's inherent gain. For instance, if property with a $100,000 fair market value, a $50,000 adjusted basis, and subject to a $30,000 mortgage is sold for $100,000, the inherent gain is $50,000 ($100,000 value − $50,000 basis). If the purchaser assumes the mortgage, pays $10,000 cash, and executes a $60,000 note payable in three equal installments, the gross profit percentage under general §453 principles equals 50 percent.

$$\frac{\text{Gross profit}}{\text{Total contract price}} = \frac{\begin{array}{c}\text{Selling price}\\ -\text{Adjusted basis}\end{array}}{\text{Total contract price}} = \frac{\$100,000 - \$50,000}{\$100,000} = 50\%$$

Because the purchaser has assumed the $30,000 mortgage, the seller will receive cash payments from the purchaser totaling only $70,000 ($10,000 down payment plus $60,000 pursuant to the note), of which $35,000 is taxable gain. The total amount taxed ($35,000) would, however, be $15,000 less than the $50,000 inherent gain.

Regulation §1.453-4(c) and Temporary Regulation §15A.453-1(b)(3) prevent this potential underreporting of gain through two adjustments, one to the contract price and one to year of sale payments, based on the relationship between the seller's adjusted basis and the mortgage. Two situations may occur: (1) the debt assumed does not exceed the adjusted basis, or (2) the debt assumed exceeds the adjusted basis. In the first situation, one adjustment is necessary: the total contract price is reduced by the amount of qualifying indebtedness assumed.

In the above example, the debt assumed does not exceed the seller's adjusted basis. Thus, in computing the gross profit percentage the total contract price is reduced by the $30,000 mortgage. The gross profit percentage is thereby increased to 71.4 percent.

$$\frac{\text{Gross profit}}{\text{Total contract price} -} = \frac{\$50,000}{\$100,000 - \$30,000} = \frac{\$50,000}{\$70,000} = 71.4\%$$
$$\qquad \text{Qualifying}$$
$$\qquad \text{indebtedness}$$

Applying the 71.4-percent gross profit percentage to the total payments to be received ($70,000) results in all $50,000 of inherent gain being taxed.

In the second situation, where the debt relief exceeds the adjusted basis, two adjustments are required: (1) the total contract price is reduced by the amount of qualifying indebtedness not in excess of the adjusted basis; and (2) qualifying indebtedness exceeding the adjusted basis is treated as a constructive payment in the year of sale.

Temporary Regulation §15A.453-1(b)(2)(iv) defines "qualifying indebtedness" as a mortgage or other indebtedness encumbering the disposed property and other indebtedness not secured by the property but incurred or assumed by the purchaser incident to the purchaser's acquisition or operation of the property in the ordinary course of business or investment. Excluded from the definition of qualifying indebtedness are any obligations of the seller functionally unrelated to the acquisition, holding, or operation of the property (e.g., the taxpayer's medical bill) and any obligations related to the disposition of the property (e.g., the taxpayer's legal fees). The following example illustrates the application of, and the need for, the two adjustments.

Assume that *A* owns property worth $120,000, which has a $30,000 adjusted basis and is encumbered by a $40,000 mortgage. *A* agrees to sell the property to *B* in return for $20,000 cash, *B*'s assumption of the $40,000 mortgage, and *B*'s note for $60,000, payable in three equal installments. *A*'s total inherent gain is $90,000 and the selling price is $120,000. Because the property is encumbered, an adjustment to the contract price must be made. In this case, the total contract price will be reduced by $30,000, which is the amount of the mortgage not in excess of the property's adjusted basis. This will produce a gross profit percentage of 100 percent.

Gross profit = $90,000 ($120,000 selling
price − $30,000 adjusted
basis)

Total contract price = $90,000 ($120,000 selling
price − $30,000 mortgage
not in excess of basis)

If no further adjustments were made, this gross profit percentage would be applied to the $20,000 down payment and the three $20,000 note payments to yield a total taxable gain of $80,000 (100%×$80,000). Because the inherent gain was $90,000, $10,000 of the seller's profit would escape taxation. Thus, if a second adjustment were not made, the gross profit percentage would have to be in excess of 100 percent in order to properly tax all of A's gain. (In this example, the gross profit percentage would have to be 112.5 percent. This percentage times the $80,000 payments would yield the correct $90,000 taxable gain.)

Because a gross profit percentage in excess of 100 percent was not deemed to be the appropriate adjustment, a second adjustment has been adopted by the Regulations. Pursuant to this second adjustment, a constructive payment is deemed to have been received by A to the extent the mortgage relief exceeds the adjusted basis. In the above example, the excess is $10,000, which, like the $80,000 of actual payments, is taxed according to the gross profit percentage of 100 percent. Through these two adjustments the proper inherent gain in the transaction is subject to tax: $100\% \times \$90,000$ ($80,000 + $10,000) = $90,000 of taxable gain.

Problems

5-22. In year 1, Frances Grandi accepted Harry Houlihan's offer to purchase her 100-unit apartment building for $1,000,000. The building, which had a $500,000 adjusted basis, was encumbered by a $300,000 first mortgage. Grandi agreed to pay John Major, a local realtor, his normal 5-percent ($50,000) sales commission. The terms of the sale provided that Houlihan would pay $200,000 cash, assume the $300,000 first mortgage, and give Grandi his interest-bearing promissory note for the remaining $500,000. The note provided for 8-percent market interest and a $100,000 principal payment to be made to Grandi on December 31, year 2, and each December 31 for four years thereafter.

    a. How much gross income did Grandi have in year 1 as a result of the sale to Houlihan?

    b. How much gross income did Grandi have when she collected the $100,000 payment from Houlihan on December 31, year 2?

    c. What would be the result if on January 1, year 3, Grandi sold Houlihan's note (now requiring four $100,000 payments) to the First National Bank of Hemet for $350,000?

    d. What would be the result if, instead of selling Houlihan's note on January 1, year 3 (when it was worth $350,000), Grandi had given the note to her son, Carlo?

5-23. On December 15, year 1, John Major presented Frances Grandi with Bob Westfall's offer to purchase her 120-unit retirement home located in Hemet, California. Although Grandi had not considered selling the home, she accepted the offer the next day. Grandi had a $400,000 adjusted basis in the property, which was encumbered by a $350,000 first mortgage and a $200,000 second mortgage. The second mortgage, placed on the property on December 10 of the preceding year, was incurred so that she could obtain $200,000 cash, which she had intended to, but never did, use to repair faulty plumbing, wiring, and structural damage to the retirement home. Westfall offered to purchase the property in return for his assumption of both mortgages and a $450,000 promissory note payable to Grandi. The balloon payment note provided for interest at the market rate of 8 percent per year and a $450,000 lump sum principal payment due on January 1, year 6. Once again, Grandi agreed to pay Major a 5-percent sales commission.

    a. How much gross income, if any, did Grandi recognize in year 1 as a result of the retirement home sale?

    b. How much gross income, if any, did Grandi recognize when she sold Westfall's $450,000 note for $300,000?

    c. What result in *a* if the second mortgage were incurred on December 10, year 1, so that Grandi would receive $200,000 cash, which she intended to use to purchase a vacation home?

5-24. In year 1, Frances Grandi sold 100,000 shares of Radar, Inc. stock, which had a $300,000 adjusted basis and a $1,000,000 market value. The purchaser, Bill Goode, who knew that her ownership and management of Radar, Inc. was burdensome to her, offered Grandi $1,000,000 for her controlling interest. The offer provided that Goode would pay her $200,000 in cash plus his $800,000 promissory note, which bore interest at the market rate of 8 percent per year. Grandi insisted that Goode secure the $800,000 note with something in addition to a security interest in the acquired Radar, Inc. stock. Goode agreed. The First National Bank of Hemet guaranteed payment of his obligation to Grandi. In addition, Grandi insisted that, as part of the sales agreement, Goode be required to pay her $25,000 in legal fees arising from the sale and her $5,000 bill for dental work. Goode agreed but in turn required that the face amount of his promissory note be reduced by this $30,000 additional expense. Grandi consented.

    a. What result to Grandi if the sale to Goode is executed as proposed?

    b. Are there other options for Grandi that might produce a more favorable tax result?

F. NONRECOGNITION OF GROSS INCOME

    Although tax principles typically require gain to be recognized whenever there is a realization event, taxation of such realized gain may be deferred under various statutory nonrecognition provisions. With these provisions, Congress has extended nonrecognition status to a number of transactions that would otherwise produce taxable gain or allowable loss. Thus, not all realized gains and losses will have an immediate impact for tax purposes. Nonrecognition provisions do not permanently exclude gains and losses from taxation; they merely defer the timing of their inclusion by requiring that the basis of the property acquired be adjusted to reflect the taxpayer's unrecognized gain or loss on the property disposition. This assures that the unrecognized gain will be included at a later date, presumably on disposition of the newly acquired property. Thus, the term "nonrecognition" is somewhat deceptive because, in reality, it is primarily a timing or deferral device.

Nonrecognition treatment is based on the premise that a taxpayer who has retained an investment in property that is essentially similar to the original investment property has not terminated the investment. Because the taxpayer has not "cashed out" on his original investment, it is considered equitable to defer taxation of realized gains and losses. This is true even if the investment has changed in form or identity so long as the investment has not changed in substance.

1. Like-kind Exchanges

Code: §§1031(a) to (d), 453(f)(6)
Regulations: §§1.1031(a)-1; 1.1031(b)-1; 1.1031(b)-2; 1.1031(d)-1; 1.1031(d)-2

Section 1001(c) provides a general rule requiring *recognition* of any gain or loss *realized* on the disposition of *property*. Section 1031 provides an exception to this rule by permitting the exchange of qualifying, like-kind property without the immediate recognition of realized gain or loss. In effect, §1031 temporarily defers taxable gain from gross income and defers the recognition of losses that might otherwise reduce taxable income with regard to a specific type of property disposition.

There are two important policies underlying §1031: First, a taxpayer who continues an investment in newly acquired property that is of a like-kind to the property the taxpayer transferred has not changed the economic substance of ownership; second, because the taxpayer who has received like-kind property has not cashed in his investment, it is equitable to defer recognition and the accompanying tax consequences until there is a taxable disposition of the newly acquired property.

Three strict requirements must be met to qualify for §1031 nonrecognition. First, both the property given and the property received must be held for "productive use in trade or business or for investment." Thus, the exchange of one's personal automobile will not qualify for §1031 nonrecognition. Second, the transaction must qualify as an exchange as distinguished from a sale and purchase. In an exchange, property is transferred in return for other property. Thus, if the taxpayer sells qualifying property and immediately reinvests the proceeds in other qualifying property, the exchange requirement is not met and §1031 does not apply. Third, the properties exchanged must be of like kind. The Regulations state that the term "like kind" refers to "the nature or character of property and not to its grade or quality." Reg. §1.1031(a)-1(b). For example, real property may not be exchanged for personal property because the nature and character of the exchanged properties are not of like kind. On the other hand, in an exchange of two parcels of real estate, it is immaterial that one is improved and the other is not because the improvement relates only to the "grade or quality" of the property, not to its "nature or character." Concerning personal property, Regulation §1.1031(a)-2(b)(1) establishes detailed rules for compliance with the like-kind standard as regards depreciable tangible property held for productive use in business and intangible property.

Section 1031 nonrecognition need not apply to all parties to a transaction. Whether a particular taxpayer meets the three requirements of §1031 is determined solely with regard to that taxpayer. Thus, one party to an exchange may qualify for §1031 nonrecognition even if the other does not. For example, assume that *A* transfers a parcel of real estate, which *A* uses exclusively as rental property, in exchange for *B*'s personal residence. If *A* does not use *B*'s home as her personal residence but instead holds it as a rental property, *A* satisfies both the like-kind and qualifying property requirements of §1031. *A* thus receives nonrecognition treatment; *B*'s nonqualifying use of the property received by *A* is not relevant to *A*'s tax treatment. *B*, however, does not receive §1031 nonrecognition even if *B* continues the rental use of the property received from *A* and selects other property as a residence.

If the §1031 requirements are met, even unintentionally, nonrecognition is *mandatory;* it may not be elected or waived. Because §1031 applies to losses as well as gains, this mandatory application may be detrimental to a taxpayer who wishes to recognize a loss when trading in depreciated or obsolete property. For example, assume *A* has office equipment with a $2,000 adjusted basis and a $500 fair market value. *A* wishes to sell this equipment to *B*, recognize the $1,500 inherent loss, and then purchase new equipment from *B* for $9,000. Thus, *A* wants to recognize a $1,500 loss on the sale of the old equipment and to receive a $9,000 cost basis in the new equipment.

The Service takes the position that the two steps of such a transaction could be collapsed into one §1031 exchange in order to disallow recognition of the realized loss on the disposition of the old equipment. In Revenue Ruling 61-119, 1961-1 C.B. 395, the taxpayer's old equipment had a $500 adjusted basis and a $1,000 fair market value, so the taxpayer had a potential gain on the disposition of the old equipment. The Ruling held that, even though the taxpayer effectuated the sale of the old equipment and purchase of the new equipment through two separately executed contracts, the two steps were in fact reciprocal and mutually dependent. Consequently, the steps in these two transactions were collapsed and characterized as an exchange within the meaning of §1031. Although the actual facts in the Ruling were slightly different from those in the example, the same approach can be used to apply §1031 to disallow losses.

MOORE v. COMMISSIONER
T.C. Memo 2007-134

HALPERN, JUDGE . . .

FINDINGS OF FACT

BACKGROUND

On April 15, 1988, petitioners purchased two contiguous parcels of lakefront real property, along with a mobile home located on one of those parcels, on Clark Hill Lake in Lincoln County, Georgia (the Clark Hill property). On December 3,

1999, petitioners entered into a purchase and sale agreement wherein they agreed to purchase improved lakefront property in Forsyth County, Georgia (the Lake Lanier property). Thereafter, during 2000, petitioners were involved in a series of transactions whereby they purported to . . . through an intermediary, exchange the Clark Hill property for the escrow agent's 25-percent interest in the Lake Lanier property in a transaction intended to qualify as a . . . like-kind exchange satisfying the requirements of [§1031]. . . .

. . . In order for petitioners to prevail on the §1031 issue, the evidence must show that (1) the Clark Hill and Lake Lanier properties were of like kind (a matter not in dispute), [and] (2) petitioners held both properties for investment. . . . Because we find that petitioners held neither property for investment, we make no findings of fact relating to the sufficiency of petitioners' attempt to satisfy the other requirements for a deferred like-kind exchange.

. . . Petitioners' decision to purchase the Clark Hill property was motivated, in part, by their familiarity with the area, both having grown up in the vicinity of Clark Hill Lake. In addition, both their families owned property on or near Clark Hill, and Mr. Moore's father advised them that property on Clark Hill Lake had appreciated and would continue to appreciate. Petitioners' decision to invest in real estate rather than in intangibles, such as stocks or bonds, was influenced by a prior bad experience with a financial adviser who had stolen their money.

. . . Beginning in late March of each year during which they owned the Clark Hill property, Mr. Moore would spend a couple of weekends there getting it ready for the summer months. Then, beginning in mid to late April, petitioners' family would visit the property two and, sometimes, three weekends a month until Labor Day, when Mr. Moore closed the property for the winter. Between Labor Day and the following March, Mr. Moore would occasionally visit the property to rake leaves and perform other caretaker functions.

. . . Until they decided to acquire the Lake Lanier property in late 1999, petitioners had never advertised the Clark Hill property for sale although they had been offered money for it. Also, petitioners never rented or attempted to rent the property to others.

. . . After petitioners changed their principal residence from Norcross to Marietta, Georgia, the length of the drive to the Clark Hill property coupled with their children's increased weekend activities (in particular, their son's participation in weekend sports) made it inconvenient for the family to spend weekends at the property. As a result, they used that property less frequently and, during the two years before their disposition of it, they may have visited the property a total of three times. During that period, it became a chore for Mr. Moore just to maintain the property, with the result that it became rundown and had to be either renovated or disposed of.

. . . Beginning in late 1997 or early 1998, the foregoing problems associated with the Clark Hill property caused petitioners to investigate properties on Lake Lanier, which is much closer to what was at the time petitioners' Marietta, Georgia, residence. Petitioners felt that a house on Lake Lanier would be of more use to them than the Clark Hill property. Petitioners also believed that property on Lake Lanier would appreciate more rapidly than the Clark Hill property because it was closer to the metropolitan Atlanta area. Petitioners acquired the Lake Lanier property in January 2000.

. . . Petitioners and their children engaged in essentially the same activities at the Lake Lanier property as they had at the Clark Hill property. They visited the property two weekends per month beginning in mid-March (depending on the weather) and ending around Labor Day. In addition, the family might visit the property once or twice each winter, and Mr. Moore and his son would fish off the dock one Saturday night each month during the fall.

OPINION

. . . [T]he issue before us is whether petitioners held the Clark Hill and Lake Lanier properties "for investment." That depends on their intent or purpose in holding the properties, determined as of the time of the exchange.

Petitioners point to their interest in the appreciation potential of the Clark Hill and Lake Lanier properties, both before and after acquisition. . . . Petitioners' argument, if carried to its logical extreme, is that the existence of any investment motive in holding a personal residence, no matter how minor a factor in the overall decision to acquire and hold (or simply to hold) the property before its inclusion in an exchange of properties, will render it "property held for investment" with any gain on the exchange eligible for nonrecognition treatment under §1031. Petitioners are mistaken. . . .

. . . As a preliminary matter, we accept as a fact that petitioners hoped that both the Clark Hill and Lake Lanier properties would appreciate. However, the mere hope or expectation that property may be sold at a gain cannot establish an investment intent if the taxpayer uses the property as a residence. Moreover, a taxpayer cannot escape the residential status of property merely by moving out. . . . [T]he holding of a primary or secondary (e.g., vacation) residence motivated in part by an expectation that the property will appreciate in value is insufficient to justify the classification of that property as property "held for investment" under §212(2) and, by analogy, §1031.

. . . [P]utting aside petitioners' expectations that both the Clark Hill and Lake Lanier properties would appreciate in value, there is no convincing evidence that the properties were held for the production of income, and there is convincing evidence that petitioners and their families used the properties as vacation retreats. Petitioners made neither the Clark Hill nor Lake Lanier property available for rent. Nor is there any evidence that petitioners held either property primarily for sale at a profit. They did not offer the Clark Hill property for sale until late 1999 when they decided to acquire the more accessible Lake Lanier property. . . . While it is true that Mr. Moore spent considerable time fixing up and maintaining both properties and petitioners made substantial improvements at the Clark Hill property, those actions are consistent with enjoying the properties as vacation homes. Petitioners did not hold the Clark Hill property out for rent or sale, yet they added a deck and screened-in porch, installed a satellite television receiver, and purchased a television, a VHS recorder, and a new washer and dryer for their use at the property. They replaced furniture and kept a boat on the lake, which they used for boating and fishing. Petitioners added similar electronic equipment to the Lake Lanier house. . . .

In short, the evidence overwhelmingly demonstrates that petitioners' primary purpose in acquiring and holding both the Clark Hill and Lake Lanier properties was to enjoy the use of those properties as vacation homes; i.e., as secondary, personal residences. That conclusion is buttressed by Mr. Moore's testimony that, after petitioners' regular weekend use of the Clark Hill property ceased during the last two years of their ownership, they allowed it to become "run down" so that it "needed to be looked after or . . . [disposed of]." That lack of upkeep is inconsistent with a professed intention to protect their investment in and maximize their profit on the sale of the property but consistent with an attitude that continued upkeep and maintenance were warranted only in connection with petitioners' regular, personal use of the property. . . .

Neither the Clark Hill nor Lake Lanier property constituted property held for investment for purposes of §1031(a). Therefore, petitioners' disposition of the former and acquisition of the latter did not qualify as a tax-free "like-kind" exchange of properties under §1031.

Note on Mixed Investment / Personal Properties

Following *Moore*, the Internal Revenue Service decided to provide guidance to rental vacation home owners by announcing when it would consider rental vacation homes eligible for like-kind exchange treatment. See Rev. Proc. 2008-16, 2008-10 I.R.B. 547. In that Revenue Procedure, the Service announced it would consider a rental home eligible for like-kind treatment if the home was rented to third parties for at least 14 days per year and the owners did not occupy it for more than 14 days or 10 percent of the days rented to third parties per year, whichever was greater. In effect, the Service conceded that a rental house in which the owners stay for less than two weeks is held for the production of income rather than for personal use, notwithstanding the actual personal use.

Note on Deferred Multiparty Exchanges

Because §1031 is limited to an actual exchange of properties, a sale of property followed by an immediate reinvestment in like-kind property can never qualify. Thus, two taxpayers wishing to engage in a §1031 exchange must first identify the property and then agree to exchange them to qualify. In reality, however, it is often difficult for two taxpayers with suitable property to find one another and directly exchange their property in a manner that literally complies with §1031. Out of necessity, therefore, the scope of §1031 has been expanded to include transactions where the parties are unable to exchange properties directly, either because one wishes to sell for cash and thus is unwilling to participate in an exchange, or because the two parties are unable to agree upon exchange terms. Such exchanges are referred to as "multiparty" exchanges, and those which involve cash temporarily held through intermediaries "deferred multiparty" exchanges.

In 1984 Congress enacted §1031(a)(3), which permits deferred multiparty exchanges in certain limited circumstances. Section 1031(a)(3) provides that property received in such a deferred exchange will not qualify for §1031 unless two specific time requirements are satisfied. First, the replacement property must be identified "on or before the day which is 45 days after the date on which the taxpayer transfers the property relinquished in the exchange." Second, the property must be received before the earlier of (1) "the day which is 180 days after the date on which the taxpayer transfers the property relinquished in the exchange" or (2) the due date of the transferor's return for the taxable year in which the transfer of the relinquished property occurs.

REV. RUL. 90-34
1990-1 C.B. 154

ISSUE

If X transfers property to Y in exchange for property of a like kind, may the exchange as to X qualify for nonrecognition of gain or loss under §1031 of the Internal Revenue Code even though legal title to the property received by X is never held by Y?

FACTS

X and Y are unrelated persons. X files its U.S. income tax return on a calendar year basis. On May 14, 1989, X and Y enter into a contract that requires X to transfer Blackacre to Y and Y to transfer to X property of a like kind with the same fair market value. Blackacre, unencumbered real property, has been held by X for productive use in its trade or business and has a fair market value of $1,000,000. Under the contract, X is required to locate and identify property with a fair market value of $1,000,000 that is of a like kind to Blackacre within 45 days of X's transfer of Blackacre to Y (the "identification period"), and Y is required to purchase and transfer the identified property to X before the earlier of 180 days from the transfer of Blackacre or the due date (including extensions) for X's U.S. income tax return for the taxable year in which X's transfer of Blackacre to Y occurs (the "exchange period"). If X fails to identify the property to be received in the transaction before the end of the identification period or Y fails to purchase and transfer such property to X before the end of the exchange period, Y is required to pay $1,000,000 to X. Neither X nor Y contracts to exchange Blackacre with any other party.

On May 23, 1989, X transfers Blackacre to Y. On June 1, 1989, X properly identifies Whiteacre as the property to be received. Whiteacre, owned by Z, a person unrelated to X, is unencumbered real property that has a fair market value of $1,000,000 and is of a like kind to Blackacre. On July 10, 1989, Y purchases Whiteacre from Z, and at Y's direction, Z transfers legal title to Whiteacre directly to X before the end of the exchange period. X, thereafter holds Whiteacre for productive use in its trade or business.

Under §1031(a)(1) of the Code, no gain or loss is recognized on the exchange of property held for productive use in a trade or business or for investment if such property is exchanged solely for property of like kind that is to be held either for productive use in a trade or business or for investment.

Section 1031(a)(3) of the Code provides that any property received by a taxpayer will be treated as property which is not like-kind property if (A) such property is not identified as property to be received in the exchange on or before the day which is 45 days after the date on which the taxpayer transfers the property relinquished in the exchange or (B) such property is received after the earlier of (i) the day which is 180 days after the date on which the taxpayer transfers the property relinquished in the exchange, or (ii) the due date (including extensions) for the taxpayer's federal income tax return for the taxable year in which the transfer of the relinquished property occurs.

If Z had actually transferred legal title to Whiteacre to Y and Y had then transferred legal title to Whiteacre to X, the exchange of Whiteacre for Blackacre, as to X, would clearly qualify for nonrecognition of gain or loss under §1031(a) of the Code. However, §1031(a) does not require that Y hold legal title to Whiteacre, but merely that X receive solely property of a like kind to the property transferred in order for the exchange to qualify for nonrecognition of gain or loss. Therefore, the failure of Y to acquire legal title to Whiteacre does not disqualify X from nonrecognition of gain or loss under §1031(a) on the transfer of Blackacre to Y in exchange for Whiteacre.

HOLDING

X's transfer of property to Y, in exchange for property of a like kind, qualifies as to X for nonrecognition of gain or loss on the exchange under §1031 of the Code even though legal title to the property received by X is never held by Y.

Note on the Basis of Acquired Property

As previously discussed, §1031 defers, rather than excludes, recognition of realized gains and losses. If §1031 applies to an exchange, the taxpayer's basis in the newly acquired property is determined by reference to the basis of the property he or she exchanged. §1031(d). As a result of the §1031(d) basis mechanism, recognition of the inherent gain or loss in the property transferred is deferred until a subsequent taxable disposition of the acquired property.

For example, assume that A and B each have investment land worth $50,000, but A's basis in the land is $20,000 while B's is $70,000. If the two taxpayers exchange these parcels, A will have a $30,000 realized gain and B a $20,000 realized loss. If this transaction qualifies for §1031 nonrecognition, neither A's realized gain nor B's realized loss will be recognized. Instead, A and B will receive a §1031(d) carryover basis in their newly acquired property, $20,000 and $70,000, respectively. On a later taxable disposition for the property's current fair market value of $50,000, *A* would recognize the previously deferred $30,000 gain and *B* would recognize the previously deferred $20,000 loss.

A different situation arises when, in addition to receiving qualifying like-kind property, the taxpayer also receives money or other property. If nonqualifying property (called *boot*) is received in addition to qualifying like-kind property, §1031 may still apply, but the exchange results in partial gain recognition to the extent that boot is received. This is a logical result because there has been a partial change in the substance of the taxpayer's ownership as well as a cashing-in of his or her investment.

For example, assume *A* exchanges property with a $20,000 adjusted basis and a $50,000 fair market value for *B*'s like-kind property, which has a $70,000 adjusted basis and a $40,000 fair market value, and $10,000 cash. *A* realizes a $30,000 ($50,000 −$20,000) gain on the exchange, none of which would be recognized under the §1031(a) general rule. But because of the §1031(b) boot provision, *A* *recognizes* $10,000 of that realized gain. Had *A* received $40,000 in boot and $10,000 in like-kind property, *A* would have recognized a $30,000 gain because §1031(b) only recognizes gain to the extent of realized gain. As to *B*, no gain or loss will be recognized because *B* received only like-kind property. Also, because the §1031(b) boot provision only triggers partial *gain* recognition (but not *loss* recognition) with respect to the like-kind property, *B* would not recognize any loss even if B had received boot in the exchange.

When boot is received, the §1031(d) substituted basis in the acquired property is decreased by the amount of any money received by the taxpayer and increased by the gain recognized in the exchange. Thus, in the above example, *A*'s basis in the property received will be $20,000, determined under §1031(d) by taking *A*'s $20,000 basis in the property transferred, reducing it by the $10,000 cash received, and increasing it by the $10,000 gain recognized. Should *A* thereafter sell the newly acquired property for $40,000 in a taxable disposition, *A* would recognize another $20,000 gain. The amount of gain recognized in these two transactions would then correctly total $30,000 — *A*'s inherent gain in the property before the exchange. *B* would receive a basis in the newly acquired property of $80,000, which is equal to the basis *B* had in the property, plus the cash *B* transferred. Assuming *B* has a taxable disposition of the newly acquired property when its fair market value is $50,000, *B* will recognize a loss of $30,000, which is equal to the inherent loss *B* had in the property before the exchange.

If both like-kind and nonlike-kind property (other than money) are received in a tax-free exchange, the taxpayer must allocate the §1031(d) aggregate basis between those properties. The allocation is made, first, to nonqualifying property (other than money) received to the extent of its fair market value, and then, to the extent any basis remains, to the qualifying property received.

For example, assume in the above scenario that *B* had transferred to *A* stock with an adjusted basis of $5,000 and a fair market value of $10,000. *A*'s basis in the land and stock equals the old basis ($20,000) plus the gain recognized ($10,000) — that is, $30,000. The basis is allocated to the stock to the extent of its fair market value. Thus, *A* would have a $10,000 basis in the stock. The remaining $20,000 is *A*'s basis in the property received. *B* must recognize his $5,000 gain on the stock transferred because it is not like-kind property. Thus, *B*'s basis in the like-kind property he receives is $80,000 (old basis from land and stock + gain recognized). When *B* sells the property, he still has the $30,000 inherent loss.

Exchange of encumbered property. When exchanging encumbered property, the taxpayer continues to use the same formula for determining his new basis. Debt incurred in the exchange is treated as cash paid, while debt relieved in the exchange is treated as cash received. Assume *A* exchanges property with a $50,000 fair market value, a $20,000 adjusted basis, and encumbered by a $10,000 mortgage, in return for *B*'s property worth $40,000, with a $30,000 adjusted basis to *B*. By transferring encumbered property, *A* will have been relieved of his mortgage liability. This debt relief is treated as money received by *A*, regardless of whether *A* was personally liable. Therefore, *A* receives boot of $10,000 and recognizes any realized gain to the extent of this amount — that is, $10,000, because *A*'s *realized* gain is $30,000 ($50,000 − $20,000). *A* has a basis in the acquired property of $20,000 (original basis of $20,000 decreased by the $10,000 mortgage relief treated as money received and increased by the $10,000 gain recognized).

B is not affected by the §1031 boot provision because *B* did not receive boot. By taking *A*'s property subject to a mortgage, *B* has in effect transferred boot to *A*, and boot *transferred* is subject to neither the §1031(a) nonrecognition rule nor the §1031(b) partial nonrecognition rule. Therefore, *B* does not recognize gain on this exchange, and *B* receives a basis in the acquired property of $40,000 ($30,000 basis in the property surrendered, plus $10,000 in additional consideration in the form of property acquired subject to the liability).

In the above example, *A* recognizes a $10,000 gain. Had *A* assumed a liability or acquired property subject to a liability, then the amount of boot received through debt relief could have been reduced. This result arises because when both parties assume or take property subject to a liability, the mortgages (or other liabilities) are *netted* to determine the amount of each party's net mortgage relief or net mortgage acquired.

For example, assume *A* exchanges property with a $60,000 fair market value, a $20,000 adjusted basis, and encumbered by a $15,000 mortgage, in return for property of *B* worth $55,000, with a $30,000 adjusted basis, and encumbered by a $10,000 mortgage. Although *A* has $15,000 of mortgage relief on the transfer, *A* acquires property subject to a $10,000 mortgage on the same exchange. The net effect to *A* is a $5,000 reduction in liabilities (net debt relief), and only this amount will be treated as boot. Thus, *A* recognizes a $5,000 gain, and *A*'s basis in the acquired property is $20,000 ($20,000 basis in property surrendered less $15,000 mortgage relief, plus $10,000 mortgage taken subject to, and $5,000 gain recognized). *B*'s realized gain is recognized to the extent of net mortgage relief, or zero. *B*'s basis is $35,000 ($30,000 basis in property surrendered, less $10,000 mortgage relief, plus $15,000 mortgage taken subject to).

In addition to netting mortgage liabilities exchanged, the taxpayer may offset net mortgage relief by transferring money. For example, assume *A* exchanges property with a $75,000 fair market value, a $45,000 adjusted basis, and encumbered by a $25,000 mortgage, in return for $10,000 cash, *B*'s property worth $95,000, with a $60,000 adjusted basis, and encumbered by a $55,000 mortgage. The amount of gain that *A* will recognize depends on how much "other property or money" *A* has received in the exchange. Because mortgage relief received by *A*

($25,000) is fully offset by the $55,000 liability encumbering the acquired property, only the $10,000 cash received is treated as "other property or money" under §1031(b). Although A has net mortgage acquired (net increase in indebtedness) of $30,000, the netting rules do not permit A to offset that amount against the $10,000 cash boot received. Thus, A must recognize a $10,000 gain. A's basis in the acquired property is $75,000 ($45,000 carryover basis, less $25,000 mortgage transferred and $10,000 cash received, plus $55,000 mortgage taken subject to and $10,000 gain recognized).

Under the netting rules, B has received $20,000 of "other property or money." B transferred $10,000 cash, acquired property subject to a $25,000 mortgage, and received $55,000 of debt relief. Therefore, a $20,000 gain is recognized by B. B's basis in the acquired property is $60,000 ($60,000 carryover basis, less $55,000 mortgage relief, plus $25,000 mortgage taken subject to, $20,000 gain recognized, and $10,000 cash paid).

In summary, the ability to reduce the amount of boot received by mortgage netting is limited to cases in which boot may arise as a result of mortgage relief. In contrast, when the boot received is "other property" or money, the taxpayer is generally not permitted to net or reduce this amount, either by transferring cash or nonlike-kind property or by assuming or taking property subject to a mortgage.

REV. RUL. 79-44
1979-1 C.B. 265

ISSUES

Is the transfer of interests in real property held by tenants in common that results in the conversion of two jointly owned parcels into two individually owned parcels a nontaxable partition or an exchange under section 1001(a) of the Internal Revenue Code of 1954?

If the transfer is an exchange, does it qualify for treatment as a like-kind exchange under section 1031 of the Code?

FACTS

Two unrelated individuals, A and B, neither of whom are dealers in real estate, respectively owned undivided one-half interests in two separate parcels of land as tenants in common. Both parcels were used in the taxpayers' business of farming. One parcel was subject to a mortgage for which A and B were each personally liable in the face amount of 1,000x dollars.

A and B rearranged their interests so that each owned 100 percent of a separate parcel. At the time of the transaction, each parcel had a fair market value of 2,000x dollars and an adjusted basis of 100x dollars. A received the parcel subject to the mortgage and B received the remaining parcel, which was free of debt. B also executed a promissory note to A in the amount of, and with a fair market value of, 500x dollars to compensate A for taking the property subject to the mortgage. A and B continued to use the parcels in their respective businesses of farming.

Law and Analysis . . .

Section 1.1031(d)-2 of the Income Tax Regulations provides that the amount of any liabilities of a taxpayer assumed by the other party to an exchange is treated as money received by the taxpayer upon the exchange. Example (2)(c) of this regulation illustrates that the amount of a taxpayer's liabilities assumed by the other party to an exchange is offset by the amount of money paid by the taxpayer and the amount of the other party's liabilities assumed by the taxpayer as a result of the exchange. However, the amount of cash or other property received by a taxpayer in an exchange is not offset by the taxpayer's assumption of the liabilities of the other party in the exchange.

Rev. Rul. 73-476, 1973-2 C.B. 300, holds that any gain or loss realized by three taxpayers who each exchanged an undivided interest in three separate parcels of real estate that were not subject to mortgages for a 100 percent ownership of one parcel is not recognized pursuant to section 1031(a) of the Code.

In this case, the transfer of interests in real property held by tenants in common that resulted in the conversion of two jointly owned parcels into two individually owned parcels is an exchange. The provisions of section 1001(a) of the Code apply to the exchange for purposes of determining the amount of gain realized. However, because the property interests exchanged are like-kind property that were being used in the taxpayers' business of farming and have continued to be so used after the exchange, the provisions of section 1031 apply to determine to what extent, if any, the gain is to be recognized.

As a result of the exchange, A owns 100 percent of one parcel of real estate, with a fair market value of $2,000x$ dollars and subject to a mortgage of $1,000x$ dollars. The value of the one-half interest received by A was $1,000x$ dollars, one-half of the fair market value of the real estate. The value of the mortgage liability assumed by A as a result of the exchange was $500x$ dollars. A also received a note from B for $500x$ dollars. The note received by A is other property for purposes of section 1031(b) of the Code. A realized a gain of $950x$ dollars computed as follows:

Value of property received	$1,000x$	dollars
Other property received (note)	$\underline{500x}$	
Total consideration received	$1,500x$	
Less:		
Adjusted basis of property transferred (one-half of $100x$ dollars)	$50x$	
Liabilities to which new property is subject	$500x$	
	$\underline{550x}$	
Gain realized	$950x$	dollars

For purposes of section 1031(b) of the Code the amount of "other property or money" received by A is $500x$ dollars. Consideration received by A in the form of money or other property is not offset by consideration given in the form of an assumption of liabilities or receipt of property subject to a liability. Accordingly, under section 1031(b), 500x dollars of the 950x dollar gain will be recognized. See section 1.1031(d)-2 of the regulations.

B received 100 percent ownership of the parcel of real estate that was not subject to a mortgage. The value of the one-half interest received by B is 1,000x dollars, one-half of the fair market value of the real estate. B realized a gain of 950x dollars computed as follows:

Value of property received		1,000x dollars
Liabilities subject to which old property was transferred		500x
Total consideration received		1,500x
Less:		
Adjusted basis of property transferred (one-half of 100x dollars)	50x	
Other property paid (note)	500x	
		550x
Gain realized		950x dollars

For purposes of section 1031(b) of the Code, the amount of "other property or money" received by B is zero. Consideration received by B in the form of a transfer subject to a liability of 500x dollars is offset by consideration given in the form of other property. Accordingly, under section 1031(b), B will not recognize any of the gain to be realized from the exchange. See section 1.1031(d)-2 of the regulations.

HOLDING

The transfer of interests in real property held by tenants in common that resulted in the conversion of two jointly owned parcels into two individually owned parcels is an exchange under section 1001(a).

Because the property interests that were exchanged are like-kind property that were being used in the taxpayers' business of farming and have continued to be so used after the exchange, the provisions of section 1031 of the Code apply. Under section 1031, A will recognize the gain realized from the exchange, but not in excess of the fair market value of the note received from B. B will not recognize any of the gain realized from the exchange.

Note

In Revenue Ruling 79-44, A recognized gain because the note received is other property. A's gain recognized was $500x. A's basis in the property was $600x (old basis + gain recognized). Because B did not recognize any gain, his basis remained $100x.

INSTALLMENT SALES REVISION ACT OF 1980
S. Rep. No. 1000, 96th Cong., 2d Sess. 19 (1980)

H. RECEIPT OF LIKE KIND PROPERTY

PRESENT LAW

Under present law, the transfer of property for cash payments and like-kind property may qualify both for installment method reporting and, with respect to the gain attributable to the like-kind exchange, nonrecognition treatment (Code sec. 1031 and Rev. Rul. 65-155, 1965-1 C.B. 356). In this case, the gain to be recognized under installment method reporting is the total gain realized on the transaction less the gain eligible for nonrecognition under the like-kind exchange provision. However, the value of the like-kind property received by the seller is taken into account in determining the amount of the selling price, the contract price, and payments received for purposes of the installment sale provision. [Thus, the value of the like-kind property received is taxed in the taxable year in which the sale or exchange is made.]

REASONS FOR CHANGE

The committee believes that, when like-kind property and an installment obligation are received, the like-kind property should not be treated as payment in order to achieve the basic purpose of installment sale reporting, i.e., gain should be recognized as cash (and other property with respect to which gain is recognized) is received.

EXPLANATION OF PROVISION

Under the bill, property permitted to be received without recognition of gain in an exchange described in Code section 1031(b) will not be treated as payment for purposes of reporting income under the installment method.

Thus, in reporting the gain on the exchange under the installment method where an installment obligation is received in addition to the like-kind property, the gross profit will be the amount of gain which will be recognized on the exchange if the installment obligation were satisfied in full at its face amount. Also, the total contract price will not include the value of the like-kind property but instead will consist solely of the sum of the money and fair market value of other property received plus the face amount of the installment obligation.

The basis of the like-kind property received (determined under section 1031(d)) will be determined as if the obligation had been satisfied at its face amount. Thus, the taxpayer's basis in the property transferred will first be allocated to the like kind property received (but not in excess of its fair market value) and any remaining basis will be used to determine the gross profit ratio.

These provisions may be illustrated by the following example. Assume that the taxpayer exchanges property with a basis of $400,000 for like-kind property worth $200,000, and an installment obligation for $800,000 with $100,000 payable in the taxable year of the sale and the balance payable in the succeeding taxable year. The example compares present law, which takes like kind property into account as payment, with the bill which reverses this rule. . . .

	Rev. Rul. 65-155— Like Kind Property Taken into Account	Like Kind Property not Taken into Account
Contract price	$1,000,000	$800,000
Gross profit	600,000	600,000
Gross profit ratio (percent)	(60)	(75)

Gain to be reported for:
1. Taxable year of sale:

(a) 60% of $300,000 (payments "received" of $100,000 cash and $200,000 value of like property)	180,000	
(b) 75% of $100,000 (cash payments)		75,000

2. Succeeding taxable year:

(a) 60% of $700,000 (cash received)	420,000	
(b) 75% of $700,000 (cash received)		525,000
Total gain recognized	$600,000	$600,000
3. Basis of like kind property received	$200,000	$200,000

Problems

5-25. Francesca Grant exchanged an unimproved fifty-acre parcel of land, having a $100,000 adjusted basis, for Roscoe Jones's four-unit apartment building, worth $200,000, plus $50,000 in cash.
  a. How much gain did Grant realize on the exchange?
  b. How much gain did she recognize on the exchange?
  c. What was her basis in the apartment building?
Grant exchanged a 100-acre parcel of undeveloped land and 1,000 shares of Radar, Inc. stock (a privately held company) for ten acres of income-producing Napa Valley vineyards, worth $500,000, plus $100,000 in cash. The 100-acre parcel had a value of $500,000 and a $200,000 adjusted basis, and the Radar, Inc. stock had a $100,000 fair market value and an adjusted basis of $5,000.
  d. How much gain did Grant realize on the exchange?
  e. How much gain did she recognize as a result of the exchange?
5-26. Dr. William Dudley wished to cash in one of his primary investments, a ninety-unit apartment building in Reno, Nevada. The building, which was subject to a $300,000 first mortgage, had a $1,500,000 market value

and a $500,000 adjusted basis. Although Dudley wished to sell the property for cash, he realized that if he did he would be required to recognize a substantial taxable gain. He therefore sought a lawyer's advice in order to maximize cash received and minimize gain recognition on the disposition of the building as well as other investments that he owned.

a. George Little offered to exchange his unencumbered office building, with a $1,200,000 fair market value and a $1,500,000 adjusted basis, in return for Dudley's apartment building. What result to Dudley?

b. What result in *a* to Little?

c. Tammy Jo Green offered to exchange farmland, currently worth $1,500,000 and encumbered by a $400,000 mortgage, plus $100,000 in cash, in return for Dudley's apartment building. What result to Dudley?

d. What result to Green in *c* if her basis in the farm was $600,000?

e. Was there a better way for Dudley to structure the exchange in *c* above?

   1. What if, prior to the exchange, Dudley increased the mortgage encumbering his property from $300,000 to $400,000? What would the Internal Revenue Service have argued? What would Dudley have contended?

   2. What result if, instead of transferring $100,000 in cash, Green transferred IBM stock having a $100,000 fair market value and a $120,000 basis? What would have been the resulting basis to Dudley? What result to Green?

   3. What result to Green if, instead of transferring $100,000 in cash, she gave Dudley her $100,000 promissory note?

   4. What result if, prior to the transaction, Green used $100,000 in cash to reduce her mortgage?

Dudley also wanted to rid himself of investment property that he purchased in Everglades City, Florida. The property, which rested under four feet of water, had been purchased for $100,000 from Helen Richardson, a persuasive local developer. It was worth $20,000 solely because of its potential use as an alligator spawning enclave.

f. What result to Dudley if he had exchanged the swampland for like-kind investment property worth $5,000, plus $15,000 in cash? Was there another way to accomplish the exchange which would have yielded a more favorable tax result to Dudley?

Another item Dudley wished to transfer was an almost new, long wheel-base Cadillac, which had an adjusted basis of $30,000 but was currently worth only $10,000. Dudley had purchased the car solely as an investment; it had never been driven.

g. Dudley wanted to exchange his Cadillac for a Lincoln of comparable worth. What result? Assume, alternatively, that his car had not been purchased as an investment but instead had been used exclusively in Dudley's business — that is, making house-calls. What result to Dudley if he had exchanged the Cadillac for the Lincoln? Was there a way in which to structure this transaction that would have allowed Dudley to recognize his inherent loss in the Cadillac?

5-27.   Francesca Grandi agreed to sell 100 acres of orange groves, having a
$300,000 adjusted basis, in return for Steve Smith's $250,000 promissory
note, $100,000 in cash, and Smith's avocado farm, worth $150,000.
   a.   How much gross income, if any, did Grandi recognize as a result of the
        orange grove sale if she elected out of §453?
   b.   What result in *a* if she did not elect out of §453?
   c.   How much gross income, if any, would Grandi have recognized in *b* if
        she sold the avocado farm for $150,000? What if she sold Smith's
        $250,000 note for $225,000?
   d.   How much income would be recognized by Grandi if the avocado farm
        were worth $350,000, the note's face amount were $50,000, and
        $100,000 in cash was received?

2. *Involuntary Conversions*

Code: §1033(a)(2), (b)(2), (g)(1)
Regulations: §1.1033(a)-1(a), 1.1033(a)-2(a) to (c)(2)

Without the nonrecognition protection of §1033, gain realized as a result of
the involuntary conversion of property would be recognized, despite the involuntary nature of the event. To relieve the owner from having to recognize a forced
or involuntary gain, Congress enacted rules to provide nonrecognition for gains
realized from certain involuntary conversions. Those rules, found in §1033, permit
deferral of gain recognition if qualified replacement property is acquired within a
time period prescribed by statute. When the cost of the replacement property is less
than the amount realized from the conversion, the taxpayer must recognize gain to
the extent of the excess. Losses from involuntary conversions are not deferred.

Section 1033(a) defines involuntary conversion of property to include destruction, in whole or in part, by theft, seizure, the requisition or condemnation of
property, or the sale of property under threat or imminence of requisition or
condemnation. There may be either a direct conversion into other property (for
instance, an exchange of real estate threatened with condemnation for property at
another location or the transfer of condemned property to the condemning
authority for other property) or an indirect conversion into other property through
reinvestment of the conversion proceeds.

In a direct conversion, nonrecognition of gain is mandatory; but in an indirect
conversion, nonrecognition of gain is elective. The election required in an indirect
conversion can be made in the year of the conversion or in the year of replacement,
with failure to elect resulting in the recognition of realized gain. Reg. §1.1033(a)-
2(c)(2), (3). An indirect conversion into qualified property must be by purchase.
Section 1033(a)(2)(A)(ii) provides that a taxpayer is considered to have purchased
the property if, but for §1033(b), the unadjusted basis of the property would be its
cost. Thus, the acquisition of replacement property by gift, or by another transaction resulting in a basis other than cost, would not qualify under §1033.

Sections 1033(a)(1) and (a)(2)(A) require that the replacement property be
"similar or related in service or use" to the converted property. Section
1033(g)(1) provides a more liberal like-kind replacement rule, however, for certain

types of condemned property. If business or investment real property is involuntarily converted because of seizure, requisition, or condemnation or threat thereof into property of a like-kind also held for productive use in trade or business or investment, the replacement property is deemed to satisfy the "similar or related in service or use" requirement of §1033. In applying the like-kind rule to involuntary conversions, Regulation §1.1033(g)-1 provides that the principles relating to §1031 like-kind exchanges are also applicable.

Section 1033(a)(2)(B) requires generally that the replacement property be purchased by the taxpayer-owner within a period: (1) beginning with the date of the disposition of the converted property by destruction, theft, condemnation, etc., or the date on which condemnation or requisition was first threatened or became imminent, whichever is earlier; and (2) ending two years after the close of the first taxable year in which any part of the gain on the conversion is realized. In the case of an involuntary conversion of real property into like-kind property that qualifies under §1033(g), the replacement period is extended to three years by §1033(g)(4).

The following example illustrates the replacement period rules. A calendar year taxpayer received official notice on February 15, year 1, that his vacation home might be condemned. The property was in fact condemned, and, on August 15, year 1, the taxpayer received a condemnation award of $85,000. The adjusted basis of the property at the time of the condemnation was $70,000. The taxpayer's replacement period started on February 15, year 1, the date on which the condemnation was first threatened, and ended on December 31, year 3, two years after the close of the taxable year in which gain on the property was realized. Had the residence been held by the taxpayer for investment purposes, the replacement period would have ended on December 31, year 4, three years after the close of the taxable year in which the gain was realized. See §1033(g)(4).

The basis of replacement property received in a qualified §1033 transaction is determined under §1033(b). Section 1033(b)(1) provides that if property is converted directly into qualified replacement property, the basis of the property received is the same as that of the property converted, decreased by the amount of any money received that was not expended in acquiring the replacement property, and increased by the amount of any gain recognized or decreased by the amount of loss recognized. Under §1033(b)(2), the basis of the property acquired by purchase, following a §1033(a) conversion into cash or other property, equals the cost of the new replacement property, decreased by the amount of realized gain not recognized. If two or more replacement properties are purchased, the total basis must be allocated among the properties in proportion to their respective replacement costs. In the previous example, the taxpayer received an $85,000 condemnation award for his vacation home, which had an adjusted basis of $70,000. Because the taxpayer received cash, the transaction is an indirect conversion. If the taxpayer purchases a qualifying replacement property for $90,000, the basis of that property will be $75,000 — its $90,000 cost minus the $15,000 realized gain that was not recognized. Thus, if the taxpayer subsequently sells the replacement property for $90,000, the $15,000 inherent gain in the involuntarily converted property will be taxed.

LIANT RECORD v. COMMISSIONER
303 F.2d 326 (2d Cir. 1962)

LUMBARD, J. . . .

The taxpayers and Norman Einstein owned a 25-story, steel-frame office building located at 1819 Broadway, Manhattan, New York. The building, which had been erected about 1913 was, on November 17, 1953, rented to 82 commercial tenants, including accountants, attorneys, real estate firms, a doctor, a dentist, and a bank, all of whom used it exclusively to conduct business. On November 17, 1953 the City of New York instituted condemnation proceedings against the taxpayers' office building and acquired title on the same date. Each of the taxpayers received payments in settlement for the condemned property during 1954 and 1955 which substantially exceeded their respective tax bases in the property.

Between July 12, 1955 and November 1, 1956 the taxpayers acquired three pieces of real estate each containing an apartment building. Each taxpayer's contribution to the total purchase prices of the three parcels exceeded his share of the proceeds from the condemnation. The nine-story building located at 55 West 11th Street, New York City, contained 77 apartments used for residential purposes and six commercial tenants. The six-story brick building at 400 East 80th Street, New York City, contained 47 residential apartments and four stores. The 11-story, steel-frame building located at 35 East 84th Street, New York City, contained 40 residential apartments and six commercial tenants. The taxpayers held the properties for rental income and did not occupy any of the properties.

The taxpayers, contending that their gain on the involuntary conversion was nontaxable under §1033 of the Internal Revenue Code of 1954, did not report any income from the disposition of the condemned office building. . . .

When a taxpayer's property is involuntarily converted into cash which the taxpayer immediately expends in replacing the converted property, Congress thought it fair to postpone any tax on the gain. However, the fortuity of an involuntary conversion should not afford the taxpayer an opportunity to alter the nature of his investment tax-free. Therefore, under §1033 tax postponement turns on whether the replacement property is "similar or related in service or use" to the converted property.

Most of the early cases interpreting this phrase involved owners of property who themselves used the property in their businesses. In these cases the Tax Court adopted a so-called "functional test" to determine whether the replacement property was similar or related in service or use to the converted property, i.e., the Tax Court compared the actual physical uses of both properties. In those cases where an owner of property, instead of being a user, held the property for rental to others and replaced it with rental property, the Commissioner, the Third Circuit and the Tax Court literally applied this "functional test" by holding that the tenants' actual physical use of the converted and replacement properties must be similar or related. Some courts, however, refusing to apply the "functional test" so strictly, have held that if the owner of rental property replaces it with rental property of "the same general class," he has maintained sufficient continuity of interest to deserve tax postponement.

Since in enacting this section Congress intended the taxpayer-owner to maintain continuity of interest and not to alter the nature of his investment tax-free, it is the service or use which the properties have to the taxpayer-owner that is relevant. Thus when the taxpayer-owner himself uses the converted property, the Tax Court is correct in comparing the actual physical service or use which the end user makes of the converted and the replacement properties. However, if the taxpayer-owner is an investor rather than a user, it is not the lessees' actual physical use but the nature of the lessor's relation to the land which must be examined. For example, if the taxpayer-owner himself operated a retail grocery business on the original land and operated an automobile sales room on the replacement land, it would be obvious that by changing his own end use he had so changed the nature of his relationship to the property as to be outside the nonrecognition provision. However, where the taxpayer is a lessor, renting the original land and building for a retail grocery store and renting the replacement land and building for an automobile sales room, the nature of the taxpayer-owner's service or use of the property remains similar although that of the end user changes. There is, therefore, a single test to be applied to both users and investors, i.e., a comparison of the services or uses of the original and replacement properties *to the taxpayer-owner*. In applying such a test to a lessor, a court must compare, inter alia, the extent and type of the lessor's management activity, the amount and kind of services rendered by him to the tenants, and the nature of his business risks connected with the properties.

Section 1031 has many similarities to §1033, the provision here in question. . . . [Section] 1031 postpones the taxation of gain when a narrower category, "property held for productive use in trade or business or for investment," is voluntarily exchanged directly for other property "of a like kind." "Like kind" has been interpreted as being much broader than "similar or related in service or use." In 1958 Congress, disapproving of the narrow manner in which the §1033 standard had been applied amended §1033 and made the "like kind" standard applicable to the condemnation of real estate "held for productive use in trade or business or for investment." The government argues that because this amendment is specifically made prospective only, Congress meant to tax the gain on condemnations of real estate held for investment in transactions which antedated the amendment such as in the present case. However, the mere fact office buildings and apartment buildings are clearly of "like kind" does not mean that they are not also "similar or related in service or use."

Since the Tax Court examined only the actual physical end use of the properties in this case rather than comparing the properties' service or use to the taxpayer-lessor, we reverse and remand for further consideration in light of this opinion.

REV. RUL. 76-319
1976-2 C.B. 242

Advice has been requested whether, under the circumstances described below, property qualifies as replacement property for purposes of section 1033 of the Internal Revenue Code.

The taxpayer, a domestic corporation, was engaged in the operation of a recreational bowling center prior to the center's complete destruction by fire on

June 30, 1974. The bowling center had consisted of bowling alleys, together with a lounge area and a bar. The center was fully insured against loss by fire. As a result of such insurance coverage the taxpayer received insurance proceeds in compensation for the destruction of the bowling center in an amount that exceeded the taxpayer's basis in the property. On its Federal income tax return for 1974, the taxpayer elected to defer recognition of the gain under the provisions of section 1033 of the Code.

Within the period specified in section 1033(a)(3)(B) of the Code, the taxpayer invested the insurance proceeds in a new recreational billiard center. In addition to billiard tables, this center includes a lounge area, and a bar. . . .

The specific question is whether the recreational billiard center (replacement property) is "similar or related in service or use" to the recreational bowling center (involuntarily converted property) within the meaning of section 1033(a) of the Code.

Rev. Rul. 64-237 states that, with respect to an owner-user, property is not considered similar or related in service or use to the converted property unless the physical characteristics and end uses of the converted and replacement properties are closely similar.

. . . The physical characteristics of the replacement property are not closely similar to those of the converted property since bowling alleys and bowling equipment are not closely similar to billiard tables and billiard equipment.

Accordingly, in the instant case, the billiard center is not similar or related in service or use to the bowling center within the meaning of section 1033(a)(3)(A) of the Code. Therefore the billiard center does not qualify as replacement property for purposes of section 1033.

Problem

5-28. On June 1, Florence Garber's office building was destroyed by fire. Garber, who had a $200,000 adjusted basis in the building, received a $500,000 insurance settlement on September 1. Determine the tax consequences (including gain recognition and adjusted basis) for each of the following mutually exclusive alternatives, assuming each occurred on September 15.

  a. Garber acquired a new office building, worth $550,000, in exchange for undeveloped land she then owned.

  b. Garber purchased an apartment building for $400,000 in cash.

  c. Garber purchased an office building for $100,000 in cash and her $400,000 promissory note, secured by a mortgage on the property.

  d. Garber purchased a fifty-acre parcel of undeveloped land for $600,000.

  e. What would be the answer to *d* if Garber's office building had been condemned instead of having been destroyed by fire?

CHAPTER 6
DEDUCTIONS FOR TRADE OR BUSINESS EXPENSES

A. DEDUCTIONS—IN GENERAL

Chapter 6 shifts the focus from income inclusion to deductions—expenditures that may be subtracted from gross income in arriving at taxable income. Although the Sixteenth Amendment does not expressly mandate deductions, the current weight of authority and commentary indicates that the authorization to tax *income* means net income or gain, not gross income or gross receipts. To fulfill this less than definitive constitutional mandate and to determine which expenditures should be deductible, lawmakers look to several guiding policies such as fairness, revenue generation, and economic stimulation. Governing their efforts is a basic dichotomy: business expenses are deductible (§162), while personal expenses are not (§262).

Although it is easy to state the theory and the general rules regarding business and personal expenses, it is often difficult to determine into which category certain expenditures fall. Essentially, this confrontation raises the question of which expenditures may be deductible. Congress has had to decide which taxpayer expenditures should be recognized and subsidized in the form of tax deductions. This tension between the taxpayer's business expenses and personal, living, or family expenses is a recurrent theme in determining deductibility. In practice, determining which expenses are deductible is largely a matter of matching them to deduction-granting sections in the Code, but in interpreting those sections one must also understand the source and the general policies underlying the congressional decision to grant each specific deduction. Courts view congressional decisions to treat an expenditure as deductible as a matter of legislative grace. Therefore, deductions are narrowly construed and only those items that qualify as one of the specific, statutorily authorized deductions may be deducted. The legislative specificity and narrow statutory construction endemic to deductions stand in bold contrast to the broad statutory language defining gross income under §61 ("income from whatever source derived").

The tax imposed by §1 is a function of the taxable, or net, income during a specific taxable period. Reduction of gross income to taxable income results in imposing an income tax only on annual accretions in wealth. This approach represents a middle ground between taxation of gross receipts and taxation of savings alone (that is, income less all current expenses). For instance, assume that during the taxable year a sole proprietor receives $50,000 for services rendered. Her net income, however, is not determined solely by the gross receipts; the costs incurred in producing the income during that year must be taken into account. Such expenses as employee salaries, office rental, advertising, employee health insurance, business-related travel expenses (including meals and lodging), interest on business loans, and business-related entertainment for clients are all costs that may be necessary and reasonable in her business. Thus, if these expenses total $55,000, the taxpayer has not made a profit and does not have net or taxable income. On the other hand, if the expenses total $10,000, the taxpayer has net business income of $40,000. In the latter case, the taxpayer will have income subject to the income tax, but in the former case she will not.

Deduction issues include questions, similar to those encountered with regard to income, of which expenses are deductible and by whom (Chapters 6, 7, and 8), whether a deduction is available for property transactions (Chapter 7), where in the taxing formula a deduction is allowed (Chapters 6, 7, and 8), and in which taxable year a deduction may be taken (Chapter 9). The following chapters divide the treatment of deductions into two categories: (1) deductions generally available in arriving at adjusted gross income (Chapters 6 and 7); and (2) deductions generally subtracted from adjusted gross income in arriving at taxable income (Chapter 8). The timing of available deductions is considered thereafter (Chapter 9).

B. ADJUSTED GROSS INCOME

Code: §§62(a); 63 (skim)
Regulations: §§1.62-1T(a) to (d); 1.162-17(a) to (c)

Not all deductions are created equal. Some deductions are granted to accurately reflect a taxpayer's true accession to wealth, while other out of a sense of equity or fairness, and still others to subsidize specific behavior. The Internal Revenue Code has a mechanism to distinguish among these different types of deductions: the concept of adjusted gross income (AGI). Deductions that directly reduce gross income (to reach AGI) are commonly referred to as "above-the-line" deductions, while those subtracted from AGI are commonly referred to as "below-the-line" deductions. In effect, AGI is the "line," and deductions fall either below or above the line. Thus, for individuals, deductions are subtracted from gross income to produce taxable income in a two-step process. First, above-the-line deductions (primarily business deductions) are deducted from gross income to determine AGI. Second, either the standard deduction or itemized deductions (the subject of Chapter 8) are deducted from AGI to determine taxable income.

Adjusted gross income is defined as gross income minus the deductions specified by §62. AGI deductions are primarily, but not exclusively, business-related or profit-related deductions that are intended to yield the net amount available to a taxpayer to pay for food, housing, and other costs of living (that is, disposable income). Section 62 does not create deductions; it merely describes where in the taxing formula certain deductions permitted by other Code sections may be taken.

One of the purposes of AGI is to arrive at disposable income. The AGI concept also attempts to equalize the tax treatment of self-employed taxpayers and the treatment of employees. For example, compare an employee, who is paid a salary of $40,000 and has no business expenses, to a sole proprietor, who has gross business receipts of $70,000 and business expenses of $30,000. Because both parties have the same net business income and their pretax economic positions are the same, they should be taxed similarly. In general, the Code attempts to reach this equitable result by granting business deductions from gross income to produce AGI. Thus, according to the statute, both of these taxpayers have an AGI of $40,000.

The mechanism used to equalize the tax treatment between employee and nonemployee taxpayers is the categories of deductions assigned to each class by §62. Under §62(a)(1), nonemployees may deduct all business expenses other than those arising under §211 through §219. Section 62(a)(2), on the other hand, restricts employees to business deductions that have been reimbursed by their employer. Consequently, if an employee business expense is deductible but is not reimbursed, its tax utility is determined under the potentially less favorable rules for itemized deductions. (A broader rule under §62(a)(2)(B) applies to performing artists who may deduct any §162 business expense in arriving at adjusted gross income.)

As discussed in Chapter 8, AGI also serves a computational purpose ancillary to its role in assessing disposable income. For below-the-line deductions such as medical expenses (§213), casualty losses (§165), miscellaneous itemized deductions (§67), and overall itemized deductions (§68), AGI is the base on which the deductible amount is computed. Thus, for example, only medical expenses exceeding 10 percent of AGI casualty losses exceeding 10 percent of AGI, miscellaneous itemized deductions exceeding 2 percent of AGI, and overall itemized deductions exceeding 3 percent of AGI are deductible. By restricting medical, casualty loss, miscellaneous, and overall itemized deductions, Congress permits only those taxpayers burdened with abnormally large expenses or losses to deduct a portion of these amounts. Because they are considered personal or de minimis in nature, average medical expenses, casualty losses, miscellaneous itemized deductions, and overall itemized deductions are generally nondeductible. See §262.

In practice, above-the-line deductions may be more useful than itemized deductions, because of these limitations and the impact of the standard deduction. The standard deduction is a deduction available to all individual taxpayers, regardless of any particular expenses. The amount of the standard deduction depends on the filing status of the taxpayer (single, married, and so forth). Further, in certain policy settings (such as for older people and those who are blind), an additional deduction is available. The standard deduction furthers the policies of administrative convenience and tax simplification in that it entitles every taxpayer to deduct a fixed amount regardless the taxpayer's individualized expenses, without requiring the cumbersome reporting of itemized deductions. Taxpayers whose itemized deductions exceed their standard deduction are entitled to deduct the full amount of their itemized deductions. Only the excess of their itemized deductions over their standard deduction amount will alter their tax liability, however, since they would have been entitled to the standard deduction regardless. For example, if the standard deduction was $2,000, an itemized deduction of $1,000 would be of no benefit to the taxpayer, while itemized deductions of $2,500 would result in only an additional $500 deduction. By contrast, every dollar of an above-the-line deduction reduces gross income — and, accordingly, taxable income — by the full dollar. As a result, taxpayers generally prefer deductions to be treated as business deductions rather than as itemized deductions.

C.   STATUTORY REQUIREMENTS FOR BUSINESS DEDUCTIONS

Code: §§162(a); 212; 262; 263(a); 263A(a) to (c), (h)
Regulations: §§1.162-1(a); 1.162-4; 1.262-1(a), (b); 1.263(a)-1(a), (b); 1.263(a)-2

Section 162 authorizes the deduction of "all the ordinary and necessary expenses paid or incurred during the taxable year in carrying on any trade or business." Section 162 is the most broadly written of the deduction-granting provisions (§161 through §220) and encompasses most expenditures encountered in operating a business. The generous language of §162 focuses on the distinction between deductible business expenses and nondeductible personal or cost of living expenses. The deductibility of business expenditures conforms with the notion of a tax on net business income or profit, and Congress has generally allowed deductions dictated by reasonable business practice.

Although broad in language and scope, the business expense provision is not without limits. Section 162 specifies three criteria for deductibility: (1) the item must be ordinary and necessary, (2) the item must be incurred in a trade or business, and (3) the item must be an expense rather than a capital expenditure.

1. Ordinary and Necessary

For an expense to be deductible under §162(a), it must be an expense that is *ordinary and necessary* in the taxpayer's particular trade or business. It is therefore important to define the two terms. In Deputy v. Du Pont, 308 U.S. 488, 495 (1940), the Supreme Court provided the following definition of "ordinary":

> *Ordinary has the connotation of normal, usual or customary.* To be sure, an expense may be ordinary though it happens but once in the taxpayer's lifetime. . . . Yet the transaction which gives use to it must be of common or frequent occurrence in the type of business involved. (Emphasis added.)

"Necessary" merely requires that the expense be appropriate and helpful in the taxpayer's business. Commissioner v. Tellier, 383 U.S. 687 (1966).

Although, at first glance, the necessary requirement appears more difficult to apply because it is dependent on subjective factors such as appropriateness and helpfulness while ordinary appears to be a more objective, clear-cut requirement, this is not the way that the courts have approached the problem. Most courts have focused on the ordinary half of the test because the ordinary requirement is more difficult to define and thus to establish. Attempts to deduct business expenses that are avoidable or otherwise not customary or unusual have led the courts to look for a workable definition of ordinary in an attempt to outline the parameters of allowable deductions. In reading the following cases, consider the adequacy of a frequency test for this purpose.

MASON AND DIXON LINES, INC. v. UNITED STATES
708 F.2d 1043 (6th Cir. 1983)

LIVELY, Circuit Judge.

. . . The question in this case is whether a trucker convicted of weight violations may deduct the "liquidated damages" paid to Virginia as ordinary and necessary business expenses in computing its federal income tax.

. . . The district court found that the payments of liquidated damages to Virginia were not deductible because they were not "necessary." Section 162(a) of the Internal Revenue Code, 26 U.S.C. §162(a), provides a deduction for "all ordinary and necessary expenses paid or incurred during the taxable year in carrying on any trade or business. . . . " The district court reasoned that the payments in question were not necessary because they could have been "easily averted." . . .

. . . A number of reported cases provide examples of easily averted expenses being allowed as necessary business deductions. This court approved the deductibility under a predecessor statute to §162(a) of settlement payments and legal expenses of a taxpayer found guilty of civil fraud. Obviously the taxpayer could easily have averted these expenses by merely refraining from defrauding the victims. Even more compelling is the holding in *Tellier* where a securities dealer was permitted to deduct as ordinary and necessary business expenses the cost of unsuccessfully defending criminal charges of securities fraud, mail fraud and conspiracy. All of these expenses could have been easily averted by refraining from the illegal activities which led to the expenditures . . .

. . . A court should determine first whether the expenditures come within the literal requirements of §162(a). This test is satisfied if the expenses are incurred in connection with a business and if they are ordinary and necessary. The significance of "ordinary" is to distinguish between capital expenditures which must be amortized if deductible at all and expenditures for current operations of the business. The "necessary" limitation imposes "only the minimal requirement that the expense be 'appropriate and helpful' for the development of the [taxpayer's] business." . . .

It is clear that the liquidated damages paid by M-D satisfy the general requirements of §162(a). They were incurred in carrying on M-D's business. They were current rather than capital expenditures and they were "appropriate and helpful" for the development of M-D's business. In fact, failure to pay the damages could have led to the banning of M-D's trucks from all Virginia highways. . . .

The judgment of the district court is reversed, and the case is remanded for entry of an appropriate judgment for the plaintiff.

TREBILCOCK v. COMMISSIONER
64 T.C. 852 (1975), aff'd per curiam, 557 F.2d 1226
(6th Cir. 1977)

During 1969 and 1970, petitioner was sole proprietor of Litco Products (hereinafter Litco), which engaged in the brokerage of wood products. He employed five people: his father, his brother, a secretary, a traveling salesman, and the Rev. James Wardrop (hereinafter Wardrop).

Petitioner met Wardrop, an ordained minister, in the early 1950's. Before 1968, he sought Wardrop's advice but paid him no fee except reimbursement for expenses. In early 1968, however, petitioner began paying Wardrop $585 per month. In 1969 and 1970, petitioner continued paying Wardrop $585 per month, or $7,020 per year, primarily to minister spiritually to petitioner and his employees. Wardrop conducted prayer meetings, at which he tried to raise the level of spiritual awareness of the participants, and counseled petitioner and individual employees concerning their business and personal problems. When he offered advice about business problems it was not based upon his knowledge of the brokerage business for he had no such knowledge. Rather, he would receive a problem, turn to God in prayer, and then propose an answer resulting from that prayer. Wardrop was not assigned specific secular or nonreligious duties in 1969 and 1970, but he did perform certain business-related tasks. For example, he visited sawmills with petitioner, ran errands, and mailed materials for Litco.

Petitioner and his wife deducted the $7,020 paid to Wardrop in both 1969 and 1970 as an ordinary and necessary business expense under section 162(a). . . .

OPINION

The issue is whether petitioner may deduct $7,020 paid in both 1969 and 1970 to Wardrop, who conducted prayer meetings, ministered to petitioner and his employees, and performed various business-related tasks.

The case of Fred W. Amend Co., 55 T.C. 320 (1970), affd., 454 F.2d 399 (7th Cir. 1971), is applicable here. Fred W. Amend (hereinafter Amend) was treasurer and chairman of the board of the Fred W. Amend Co. (hereinafter company), an Illinois corporation manufacturing jellied candies. R. M. Halverstadt . . . was a Christian Science practitioner and teacher. Amend sought the assistance of Halverstadt in both business and personal matters. Halverstadt did not offer concrete solutions to Amend's problems but tried instead to induce new spiritual awareness in Amend so that he could approach problems with detachment and understanding. . . . The company paid Halverstadt directly; it put him on retainer so that he would be available whenever a business problem arose. Amend continued to pay Halverstadt for consultations relating to personal problems. . . . After the company put Halverstadt on retainer, his assistance was available to various members of the company's supervisory staff, but Amend alone consulted him. The company deducted the fee paid to Halverstadt as "professional services" under section 162.

This Court conceded that Halverstadt's consultations promoted Amend's spiritual balance and thus allowed him to cope more easily with the strain of running a large business. But we noted that Halverstadt's aid did not sharpen his business skills; instead, it gave him heightened spiritual awareness. We concluded that Halverstadt's services were no different from those regularly provided by ministers, that all benefits derived from such services are inherently personal in nature, and that the proscription of section 262 against deduction of personal expenses prohibited deduction under section 162.

Turning to the facts of this case, Wardrop performed four types of services; we will treat each of them in turn. When he conducted prayer meetings, this Court's opinion in *Amend* must control and therefore a portion of the deduction must be disallowed. Halverstadt tried to induce a new spiritual awareness in Amend, and Wardrop did essentially the same for petitioner and his employees. The benefits that petitioner and his employees received are personal in nature and so the proscription of section 262 must be invoked.

When Wardrop counseled petitioner and his employees about personal problems, *Amend* does not strictly apply for it did not concern personal problems. But section 262 must be invoked since the benefits derived from Wardrop's consultations were personal in nature.

When Wardrop counseled petitioner and his employees about business problems the weight of *Amend* is uncertain for in *Amend* Halverstadt offered no specific solutions to given problems while in this case Wardrop did. However, we need not decide the applicability of *Amend* since the deduction for this particular task is otherwise disallowed. The solutions Wardrop offered were not based upon his expertise in the brokerage of wood products; he admits he had no such expertise. Rather, his solutions came through prayer from God. A deduction under section 162(a) is allowed for all ordinary and necessary expenses paid or incurred during the taxable year in carrying on a trade or business. "Ordinary," as used in section 162(a), refers to items which arise from "transactions . . . of common or frequent occurrence in the type of business involved." Lilly v. Commissioner, 343 U.S. 90, 93 (1952). . . . Petitioner has offered no proof that his payments to Wardrop for solutions to business problems, considering the method Wardrop used, were "ordinary" in his type of business. We hold that petitioner has failed to carry his burden of proof.

Although petitioner did not assign Wardrop specific secular duties, there is no dispute that Wardrop visited sawmills, ran errands, mailed materials, and performed various other business related tasks. A deduction under section 162 is allowable for payments made to Wardrop for performing such tasks. The record provides no specific allocation between these deductible payments and those which have been disallowed. We thus apply the rule in Cohan v. Commissioner, 39 F.2d 540, 543-544 (2d Cir. 1930), which is essentially that certainty in determining expenses is usually impossible but that as close an approximation as possible should be made if the taxpayer had genuinely allowable expenses. Looking at the record as a whole, we think $1,000 in each year was payment for services related to business activities.

We accordingly hold that $1,000 is deductible in both 1969 and 1970 under section 162 and that the remaining $6,020 for each year is nondeductible under section 262.

Note

The courts have struggled with what should be considered "ordinary" since the inception of the modern Internal Revenue Code. For example, Justice Cardozo in the first Supreme Court case to confront the issue described it as follows:

> We try to classify this act as ordinary or the opposite, and the norms of conduct fail us. No longer can we have recourse to any fund of business experience, to any known business practice. . . . Here, indeed, as so often in other branches of the law, the decisive distinctions are those of degree and not of kind. One struggles in vain for any verbal formula that will supply a ready touchstone. The standard set up by the statute is not a rule of law; it is rather a way of life. Life in all its fullness must supply the answer to the riddle.

Welch v. Helvering, 290 U.S. 111, 114-115 (1933). The court in *Trebilcock* attempted to overcome this problem by adhering to a literal definition of ordinary emphasizing frequency of the business expense. The court seems to imply that the imaginative business person will be denied a deduction for innovative practices, while those who later adopt those techniques (thus making them "frequent") will be rewarded for their cautious approach. Although this approach may have made sense in the unusual context of *Trebilcock*, it leads to a strange result: innovators in a business could be disallowed a deduction for the cost of their innovation, while competitors copying the innovation would be permitted a deduction. For example, the first law firm to use portable e-mail devices (such as BlackBerry devices) for their associate attorneys could be denied a deduction while all subsequent law firms adopting them would be permitted to claim a deduction. Would this deter businesses (such as law firms) from adopting new technology in the first place?

Notwithstanding *Trebilcock*, courts generally are hesitant to question whether a particular expense is in fact sufficiently related to the business to permit a deduction under §162, because to do so would require the courts to substitute their business judgment for that of the proprietor of the business.

Problems

6-1. Jay Johnson hired a doctor to administer monthly physical examinations to his employees, directed particularly toward the detection of job-related ailments such as those caused by stress, and to treat any other employee complaints. Johnson deducted the payments to the doctor as a business expense. Are the expenses deductible?

6-2. Beth Smith hired a psychiatrist to meet with her employees once a month to help them cope with job-related stress. The psychiatrist is an M.D., and the employees consult him for any health complaint, which he diagnoses and, if need be, refers them to specialists. Smith deducts the payments to the doctor as a business expense. Are the expenses deductible?

6-3. Warren Cox hired an analyst to meet with his employees as frequently as the analyst deems necessary. The employees are required to attend the sessions. Cox believes it is beneficial for employees and for the organization to be "more in touch with themselves." Cox deducts the payments to the analyst as a business expense. Are the expenses deductible?

6-4. In August, Marjorie van der Neff, a professional author, was sued by Guido Settembrini on the grounds that she had plagiarized his work in her book. In December, a jury found van der Neff guilty of plagiarism and awarded Settembrini $40,000 in damages, which van der Neff promptly paid. Are the damages deductible?

2. *Defining a Trade or Business*

The second explicit statutory requirement of §162 is that the expenditure arise in the taxpayer's "trade or business." In general, two problem areas arise under the trade or business requirement: (1) the taxpayer's activities must constitute a trade or business, not merely personal activity; and (2) to be deductible, the expense must be incurred pursuant to that trade or business and not pursuant to some personal activity. In the absence of a statutory or regulatory definition of a trade or business, the courts have formulated various interpretations of the phrase.

In Deputy v. Du Pont, 308 U.S. 488, 499 (1940), Justice Frankfurter in his concurring opinion stated that carrying on any trade or business "involves holding one's self out to others as engaged in the selling of goods or services." In *Du Pont*, the taxpayer, who held 16 percent of a corporation's shares, incurred interest expenses and other costs in accommodating the corporation in its plan to sell stock to nine employees appointed to a new executive committee. The Court held that the shareholder's expenses were not incurred in connection with his trade or business, even though they may have been related to the corporation's business interests.

The *Du Pont* goods and services concept was developed at a time when courts were struggling to decide whether certain activities, not traditionally business in nature, were included within the phrase "trade or business." The recurring focus was on investors' activities in managing their own securities. In 1941, the Supreme Court settled the issue when it held that managing one's stock investments, even as continuous activity, did not constitute the carrying on of a trade or business. Thus, expenses related thereto were nondeductible. Higgins v. Commissioner, 312 U.S. 212 (1941).

One year after the Supreme Court's decision in *Higgins*, Congress responded by enacting the predecessor of current §212 (considered in detail in Chapter 8), which allows the deduction of expenses arising from the production or collection of income or the management, conservation, or maintenance of property held for the production of income. Thus, for many nonbusiness investment activities, including securities investments, expenses are now deductible under §212. Although the allowance of §212 expenses is significant, the issue of where in the taxing formula such expenses are deducted is equally important. With the sole exception of §62(a)(4) expenses, expenses incurred in the production of income are itemized deductions.

In addition to its preoccupation with distinguishing business activities from investor activities, the Supreme Court struggled to provide a workable definition of "carrying on any trade or business." Although the *Du Pont* goods and services concept was often noted, some courts developed their own definitions. For example, the Ninth Circuit interpreted the standard as an activity "entered into, in good faith, with the dominant hope and intent of realizing a profit." Hirsch v. Commissioner, 315 F.2d 731, 736 (9th Cir. 1963).

COMMISSIONER v. GROETZINGER
480 U.S. 23 (1987)

JUSTICE BLACKMUN delivered the opinion of the Court.

The issue in this case is whether a full-time gambler who makes wagers solely for his own account is engaged in a "trade or business," within the meaning of §§162(a) and 62(1) of the Internal Revenue Code. . . . The tax year with which we here are concerned is the calendar year 1978; technically, then, we look to the Code as it read at that time.

I

There is no dispute as to the facts. The critical ones are stipulated. Respondent Robert P. Groetzinger had worked for 20 years in sales and market research for an Illinois manufacturer when his position was terminated in February 1978. During the remainder of that year, respondent busied himself with parimutuel wagering, primarily on greyhound races. He gambled at tracks in Florida and Colorado. He went to the track 6 days a week for 48 weeks in 1978. He spent a substantial amount of time studying racing forms, programs, and other materials. He devoted from 60 to 80 hours each week to these gambling-related endeavors. He never placed bets on behalf of any other person, or sold tips, or collected commissions for placing bets, or functioned as a bookmaker. He gambled solely for his own account. He had no other profession or type of employment.

Respondent kept a detailed accounting of his wagers and every day noted his winnings and losses in a record book. In 1978, he had gross winnings of $70,000, but he bet $72,032; he thus realized a net gambling loss for the year of $2,032.

Respondent received $6,498 in income from other sources in 1978. This came from interest, dividends, capital gains, and salary earned before his job was terminated.

On the federal income tax return he filed for the calendar year 1978 respondent reported as income only the $6,498 realized from nongambling sources. He did not report any gambling winnings or deduct any gambling losses. He did not itemize deductions. Instead, he computed his tax liability from the tax tables.

Upon audit, the Commissioner of Internal Revenue determined that respondent's $70,000 in gambling winnings were to be included in his gross income and that, pursuant to §165(d) of the Code, a deduction was to be allowed for his gambling losses to the extent of these gambling gains. But the Commissioner further determined that, under the law as it was in 1978, a portion of the respondent's $70,000 gambling-loss deduction was an item of tax preference and operated to subject him to the minimum tax under §56(a) of the Code. At that time, under statutory provisions in effect from 1976 until 1982, "items of tax preference" were lessened by certain deductions, but not by deductions not "attributable to a trade or business carried on by the taxpayer."§§57(a)(1) and (b)(1)(A), and §62(1).

These determinations by the Commissioner produced a §56(a) minimum tax of $2,142 and, with certain other adjustments not now in dispute, resulted in a total asserted tax deficiency of $2,522 for respondent for 1978.

Respondent sought redetermination of the deficiency in the United States Tax Court. That court, in a reviewed decision, with only two judges dissenting, held that respondent was in the trade or business of gambling. . . .

The United States Court of Appeals for the Seventh Circuit affirmed. Because of a conflict on the issue among Courts of Appeals, we granted certiorari.

II

The phrase "trade or business" has been in §162(a) and in that section's predecessors for many years. Indeed, the phrase is common in the Code, for it appears in over 50 sections and 800 subsections and in hundreds of places in proposed and final income tax regulations. The slightly longer phrases, "carrying on a trade or business" and "engaging in a trade or business," themselves are used no less than 60 times in the Code. The concept thus has a well-known and almost constant presence on our tax-law terrain. Despite this, the Code has never contained a definition of the words "trade or business" for general application, and no regulation has been issued expounding its meaning for all purposes. Neither has a broadly applicable authoritative judicial definition emerged. Our task in this case is to ascertain the meaning of the phrase as it appears in the sections of the Code with which we are here concerned.

In one of its early tax cases, Flint v. Stone Tracy Co., 220 U.S. 107 (1911), the Court was concerned with the Corporation Tax imposed by the Tariff Act of 1909, 36 Stat., ch. 6, 11, 112-117, and the status of being engaged in business. It said: "'Business' is a very comprehensive term and embraces everything about which a person can be employed." 220 U.S., at 171. It embraced the Bouvier Dictionary definition: "That which occupies the time, attention and labor of men for the purpose of a livelihood or profit." Ibid. And Justice Frankfurter has observed that "we assume that Congress uses common words in their popular meaning, as used in the common speech of men."

With these general comments as significant background, we turn to pertinent cases decided here. Snyder v. Commissioner, 295 U.S. 134 (1935), had to do with margin trading and capital gains, and held, in that context, that an investor, seeking merely to increase his holdings, was not engaged in a trade or business. Justice Brandeis, in his opinion for the Court, noted that the Board of Tax Appeals theretofore had ruled that a taxpayer who devoted the major portion of his time to transactions on the stock exchange for the purpose of making a livelihood could treat losses incurred as having been sustained in the course of a trade or business. He went on to observe that no facts were adduced in *Snyder* to show that the taxpayer "might properly be characterized as a 'trader on an exchange who makes a living in buying and selling securities.'" Id., at 139. These observations, thus, are dicta, but, by their use, the Court appears to have drawn a distinction between an active trader and an investor.

In Deputy v. Du Pont, 308 U.S. 488 (1940), the Court was concerned with what were "ordinary and necessary" expenses of a taxpayer's trade or business. . . . In ascertaining whether carrying charges on short sales of stock were deductible as ordinary and necessary expenses of the taxpayer's business, the Court *assumed* that the activities of the taxpayer in conserving and enhancing his estate constituted a trade or business, but nevertheless disallowed the claimed deductions because they were not "ordinary" or "necessary." Justice Frankfurter, in a concurring opinion joined by Justice Reed, did not join the majority. He took the position that whether the taxpayer's activities constituted a trade or business was "open for determination," id. at 499, and observed:

> . . . "carrying on any trade or business," within the contemplation of §23(a), involves holding one's self out to others as engaged in the selling of goods or services. This the taxpayer did not do. . . . Without elaborating the reasons for this construction and not unmindful of opposing considerations, including appropriate regard for administrative practice, I prefer to make the conclusion explicit instead of making the hypothetical litigation-breeding assumption that this taxpayer's activities, for which expenses were sought to be deducted, did constitute a "trade or business." Ibid.

Next came Higgins v. Commissioner, 312 U.S. 212 (1941). There the Court, in a bare and brief unanimous opinion, ruled that salaries and other expenses incident to looking after one's own investments in bonds and stocks were not deductible . . . as expenses paid or incurred in carrying on a trade or business. While surely cutting back on *Flint*'s broad approach, the Court seemed to do little more than announce that since 1918 "the present form [of the statute] was fixed and has so continued"; that "[n]o regulation has ever been promulgated which interprets the meaning of 'carrying on a business'"; that the comprehensive definition of "business" in *Flint* was "not controlling in this dissimilar inquiry"; that the facts in each case must be examined; that not all expenses of every business transaction are deductible; and that "[n]o matter how large the estate or how continuous or extended the work required may be, such facts are not sufficient as a matter of law to permit the courts to reverse the decision of the Board." 312 U.S., at 215-218. The opinion, therefore — although devoid of analysis and not setting forth what elements, if any, in addition to profit motive and regularity, were required to render an activity a trade or business — must stand for the propositions that full-time market activity in managing and preserving one's own estate is not embraced within the phrase "carrying on a business," and that salaries and other expenses incident to the operation are not deductible as having been paid or incurred in a trade or business. It is of interest to note that, although Justice Frankfurter was on the *Higgins* Court and this time did not write separately, and although Justice Reed, who had joined the concurring opinion in *Du Pont*, was the author of the *Higgins* opinion, the Court in that case did not even cite *Du Pont* and thus paid no heed whatsoever to the content of Justice Frankfurter's pronouncement in his concurring opinion. Adoption of the Frankfurter gloss obviously would have disposed of the case in the Commissioner's favor handily and automatically, but that easy route was not followed.

Less than three months later, the Court considered the issue of the deduct-ibility, as business expenses, of estate and trust fees. In unanimous opinions issued the same day and written by Justice Black, the Court ruled that the efforts of an estate or trust in asset conservation and maintenance did not constitute a trade or business. City Bank Farmers Trust Co. v. Helvering, 312 U.S. 121 (1941); United States v. Pyne, 313 U.S. 127 (1941). The *Higgins* case was deemed to be relevant and controlling. Again, no mention was made of the Frankfurter concurrence in *Du Pont*. Yet Justices Reed and Frankfurter were on the Court.

Snow v. Commissioner, 416 U.S. 500 (1974), concerned a taxpayer who had advanced capital to a partnership formed to develop an invention. On audit of his 1966 return, a claimed deduction under §174(a)(1) of the 1954 Code for his pro rata share of the partnership's operating loss was disallowed. The Tax Court and the Sixth Circuit upheld that disallowance. This Court reversed. Justice Douglas, writing for the eight Justices who participated, observed: "Section 174 was enacted in 1954 to dilute some of the conception of 'ordinary and necessary' business expenses under §162(a) (then §23(a)(1) of the Internal Revenue Code of 1939) adumbrated by Mr. Justice Frankfurter in a concurring opinion in Deputy v. Du Pont . . . where he said that the section in question . . . 'involves holding one's self out to others as engaged in the selling of goods or services.'" 416 U.S., at 502-503. He went on to state, id., at 503, that §162(a) "is more narrowly written than is §174."

From these observations and decisions, we conclude (1) that, to be sure, the statutory words are broad and comprehensive (*Flint*); (2) that, however, expenses incident to caring for one's own investments, even though that endeavor is full-time, are not deductible as paid or incurred in carrying on a trade or business (*Higgins, City Bank, Pyne*); (3) that the opposite conclusion may follow for an active trader (*Snyder*); (4) that Justice Frankfurter's attempted gloss upon the decision in *Du Pont* was not adopted by the Court in that case; (5) that the Court, indeed, later characterized it as an "adumbration" (*Snow*); and (6) that the Frankfurter observa-tion, specifically or by implication, never has been accepted as law by a majority opinion of the Court, and more than once has been totally ignored. We must regard the Frankfurter gloss merely as a two-Justice pronouncement in a passing moment and, while entitled to respect, as never having achieved the status of a Court ruling. One also must acknowledge that *Higgins*, with its stress on examining the facts in each case, affords no readily helpful standard, in the usual sense, with which to decide the present case and others similar to it. The Court's cases, thus, give us results, but little general guidance.

III . . .

The issue this case presents has "been around" for a long time and, as indicated above, has not met with consistent treatment in the Tax Court itself or in the Federal Courts of Appeals. The Seventh Circuit, in the present case, said the issue "has proven to be most difficult and troublesome over the years." 771 F.2d, at 271. The difficulty has not been ameliorated by the persistent absence of an all-purpose definition, by statute or regulation, of the phrase "trade or busi-ness" which so frequently appears in the Code. Of course, this very frequency well may be the explanation for legislative and administrative reluctance to take a position as to one use that might affect, with confusion, so many others.

Be that as it may, this taxpayer's case must be decided and, from what we have outlined above, must be decided in the face of a decisional history that is not positive or even fairly indicative, as we read the cases, of what the result should be. There are, however, some helpful indicators.

If a taxpayer, as Groetzinger is stipulated to have done in 1978, devotes his full-time activity to gambling, and it is his intended livelihood source, it would seem that basic concepts of fairness (if there be much of that in the income tax law) demand that his activity be regarded as a trade or business just as any other readily accepted activity, such as being a retail store proprietor or, to come closer categorically, as being a casino operator or as being an active trader on the exchanges.

It is argued, however, that a full-time gambler is not offering goods or his services, within the line of demarcation that Justice Frankfurter would have drawn in *Du Pont*. Respondent replies that he indeed is supplying goods and services, not only to himself but, as well, to the gambling market; thus, he says, he comes within the Frankfurter test even if that were to be imposed as the proper measure. "It takes two to gamble." Brief for Respondent 3. Surely, one who clearly satisfies the Frankfurter adumbration usually is in a trade or business. But does it necessarily follow that one who does not satisfy the Frankfurter adumbration is not in a trade or business? One might well feel that a full-time gambler ought to qualify as much as a full-time trader, as Justice Brandeis in *Snyder* implied and as courts have held. The Commissioner, indeed, accepts the trader result. Tr. of Oral Arg. 17. In any event, while the offering of goods and services usually would qualify the activity as a trade or business, this factor, it seems to us, is not an absolute prerequisite.

We are not satisfied that the Frankfurter gloss would add any helpful dimension to the resolution of cases such as this one, or that it provides a "sensible test," as the Commissioner urges. See Brief for Petitioner 36. It might assist now and then, when the answer is obvious and positive, but it surely is capable of breeding litigation over the meaning of "goods," the meaning of "services," or the meaning of "holding one's self out." And we suspect that — apart from gambling — almost every activity would satisfy the gloss. A test that everyone passes is not a test at all. We therefore now formally reject the Frankfurter gloss which the Court has never adopted anyway.

Of course, not every income-producing and profit-making endeavor constitutes a trade or business. The income tax law, almost from the beginning, has distinguished between a business or trade, on the one hand, and "transactions entered into for profit but not connected with . . . business or trade," on the other. Congress "distinguished the broad range of income or profit producing activities from those satisfying the narrow category of trade or business." Whipple v. Commissioner, 373 U.S. 193, 197 (1963). We accept the fact that to be engaged in a trade or business, the taxpayer must be involved in the activity with continuity and regularity and that the taxpayer's primary purpose for engaging in the activity must be for income or profit. A sporadic activity, a hobby, or an amusement diversion does not qualify.

It is suggested that we should defer to the position taken by the Commissioner and by the Solicitor General, but, in the absence of guidance, for over several decades now, through the medium of definitive statutes or regulations, we see little reason to do so. We would defer, instead, to the Code's normal focus on what we regard as a common-sense concept of what is a trade or business. Otherwise, as here, in the context of a minimum tax, it is not too extreme to say that the taxpayer is being taxed on his gambling losses, a result distinctly out of line with the Code's focus on income.

We do not overrule or cut back on the Court's holding in *Higgins* when we conclude that if one's gambling activity is pursued full time, in good faith, and with regularity, to the production of income for a livelihood, and is not a mere hobby, it is a trade or business within the meaning of the statutes with which we are here concerned. Respondent Groetzinger satisfied that test in 1978. Constant and large-scale effort on his part was made. Skill was required and was applied. He did what he did for a livelihood, though with a less than successful result. This was not a hobby or a passing fancy or an occasional bet for amusement.

We therefore adhere to the general position of the *Higgins* Court, taken 45 years ago, that resolution of this issue "requires an examination of the facts in each case." 312 U.S. at 217. This may be thought by some to be a less-than-satisfactory solution, for facts vary. But the difficulty rests in the Code's wide utilization in various contexts of the term "trade or business," in the absence of an all-purpose definition by statute or regulation, and in our concern that an attempt judicially to formulate and impose a test for all situations would be counterproductive, unhelpful, and even somewhat precarious for the overall integrity of the Code. We leave repair or revision, if any be needed, which we doubt, to the Congress where we feel, at this late date, the ultimate responsibility rests.

The judgment of the Court of Appeals is affirmed.

Note

Subsequent to *Groetzinger*, many taxpayers claimed activities such as gambling to be a trade or business so as to be able to deduct their costs, to mixed success. One particularly interesting case involved a taxpayer who was a devout believer in Feng shui and who gambled substantial amounts of money on "lucky days" as determined under Feng shui principles. The Service contended that relying on Feng shui and lucky days was un-businesslike and irrational, and thus not a trade or business. The Tax Court disagreed, holding that the profit objective was "honest and actual" and the taxpayer worked numerous hours testing the approach, thus satisfying *Groetzinger*. Le v. Commissioner, T.C. Summ.Op. 2010-94.

Another area where the line between business and personal often arises is that of the deductibility of expenses incurred by a job seeker, i.e., someone who is required to travel to a distant city for a job interview or to compensate an employment agency for its efforts in securing him a job. Such expenses are business-related, but do they meet the §162 requirement that they be "incurred in carrying on a trade or business"? Does it make a difference whether the taxpayer is seeking his first job, changing careers, or looking for a better opportunity in his present field? What if the expenses are incurred in an unsuccessful job search?

A critical factor in answering these questions is whether the job seeker has an existing trade or business. Thus, a student seeking his first position cannot deduct expenses that he incurs for resume preparation or travel. On the other hand, a computer engineer, employed by a company that manufactures computer software, may be permitted to deduct expenses incurred in seeking a new job with a personal computer manufacturer. In fact, even if the computer engineer's job search is unsuccessful, he may nevertheless be entitled to a deduction. The Service has sanctioned the deduction of fees paid to an employment agency for seeking employment in the same trade or business even if no job is secured. See Rev. Rul. 75-120, 1975-1 C.B. 55. Conversely, the Service has ruled that employment agency fees are not deductible if the taxpayer is seeking initial employment or employment in a new trade or business. See Rev. Rul. 77-16, 1977-1 C.B. 37 clarifying Rev. Rul. 75-120.

Consider the following examples of taxpayers who may incur job-seeking expenses: the teacher who returns to school and becomes a lawyer, the factory worker in a depressed market whose factory closes its doors and therefore seeks work in a new field, or the clerical worker who seeks a more lucrative position selling office equipment. Can any of these job changers successfully argue that they have not entered a new trade or business? Should public policy permit a deduction to displaced workers who, because of changes in technology or the economy, must seek a job in a new trade or business?

Although there is little guidance in this area, Evans v. Commissioner, 42 T.C.M. 602 (1981), provides some insight. Evans retired from the Air Force and sought employment in the private sector. He claimed that he was entitled to deduct his job-seeking expenses, arguing that he was seeking employment closely related to the public relations duties he performed in the last four years of his military career. The Tax Court rejected Evans' arguments, reasoning that he was seeking employment in a new trade or business and was therefore not entitled to a §162(a) deduction. The court stated that while "petitioner undoubtedly sought employment that would utilize the skills he acquired during his military career, he has failed to show us that there would not be substantial differences between the employment he sought to obtain in the private sector and his service as an Air Force officer." Id. at 605. Thus, in analyzing whether a taxpayer has incurred job-seeking expenses in the same trade or business, the focus appears to be on whether the new employment will differ substantially from the taxpayer's previous position.

Problem

6-5. Julian Hall is a third-year law student interviewing with law firms for a permanent position in law. In preparation for these interviews, Hall spent $500 for a new suit and paid a resume service $200 to print his resume. In addition, Hall spent $1,800 traveling by car or plane to various law and corporate offices for interviews. One off-campus interviewer gave Hall a $150 reimbursement for the cost of meals and transportation.

a. Was Hall entitled to any §162 deductions for the costs of seeking employment?

b. Should he have included any reimbursements in gross income?

> c. What result in *a* if Hall were a first-year law associate, not a third-year law student?
>
> d. What result in *c* if Hall was a first-year law associate interviewing for a job as a corporate executive?

3. *Expenses Incurred in a Trade or Business*

Section 262 disallows deductions for personal, living, or family expenses, and the few exceptions to the §262 rule generally arise from specific statutory authorization. The problem is that many personal expenses are necessary to engage in work. For example, there is no doubt that a person needs to eat to find or maintain employment, but grocery bills would appear to be the ultimate in personal expenses. Perhaps no single issue calls the business-personal distinction into play at a more refined level than clothing. Although no specific Code section authorizes a deduction for clothing expenses, in certain instances such expenses may fall within the boundaries of §162. Clearly, clothes worn by a taxpayer solely while away from work are not related to a trade or business, while unique safety equipment with no use other than in the context of a job site, such as a hard hat for construction workers, seem to clearly fit within the trade or business rule. So how to tell when expenses for clothing should be deductible? See Tilman v. Commissioner, 644 F.Supp.2d 391 (S.D.N.Y 2009) (haircuts and manicures for concert performer not deductible); Drake v. Commissioner, 52 T.C. 842 (1969) (haircuts every two weeks to comply with military rules not deductible).

The question is whether an expense can be both personal in nature and also help a taxpayer's business such that it is "ordinary and necessary" for purposes of §162. The Tax Court faced this issue in the case of Hymel v. Commissioner, T.C. Memo 1985-198, in which the taxpayer deducted the costs of membership dues to the Bacchus Mardi Gras krewe. The taxpayer argued that membership in the krewe, although a social club, directly increased tourism to New Orleans which benefited his insurance business. The Tax Court held that the dues would have to primarily benefit the taxpayer's business to be "ordinary and necessary" under §162, and that in this case the primary purpose of the dues was personal in nature. Under this rationale, the Tax Court disallowed the deduction.

On appeal, the United States Court of Appeals for the Fifth Circuit held in a per curiam opinion that the ruling of the Tax Court impermissibly failed to take into account a factual stipulation of the parties, that "one of the purposes of Bacchus is to improve tourism, namely the food and entertainment and hotel industries in New Orleans. Mr. Hymel has earned substantial insurance commissions through sales of insurance to members of these industries (who are members of Bacchus). . . . Mr. Hymel's income is directly impacted by tourism in New Orleans." Taking into account this stipulated fact, the court held that the membership dues were deductible under §162 because they "directly impacted" Mr. Hymel's income.

Subsequent to the holding in in *Hymel*, Congress enacted §274(a)(3), which disallows a deduction for membership dues paid to clubs organized for business, pleasure, recreation, or other social purpose even if such dues would be "ordinary and necessary" under §162. Thus, the particular expense at issue in *Hymel* would no longer be deductible. Regardless, the analysis of the Tax Court and the Fifth Circuit in *Hymel* indicates just how difficult it can be to determine whether expenses that have both a personal and business component are deductible under §162. The case that follows exemplifies one taxpayer's attempted reliance on §162 to avoid the prohibition of §262.

PEVSNER v. COMMISSIONER
628 F.2d 467 (5th Cir. 1980)

Johnson, J. . . .

Since June 1973 Sandra J. Pevsner, taxpayer, has been employed as the manager of the Sakowitz Yves St. Laurent Rive Gauche Boutique located in Dallas, Texas. The boutique sells only women's clothes and accessories designed by Yves St. Laurent (YSL), one of the leading designers of women's apparel. Although the clothing is ready to wear, it is highly fashionable and expensively priced. Some customers of the boutique purchase and wear the YSL apparel for their daily activities and spend as much as $20,000 per year for such apparel.

As manager of the boutique, the taxpayer is expected by her employer to wear YSL clothes while at work. In her appearance, she is expected to project the image of an exclusive lifestyle and to demonstrate to her customers that she is aware of the YSL current fashion trends as well as trends generally. Because the boutique sells YSL clothes exclusively, taxpayer must be able, when a customer compliments her on her clothes, to say that they are designed by YSL. In addition to wearing YSL apparel while at the boutique, she wears them while commuting to and from work, to fashion shows sponsored by the boutique, and to business luncheons at which she represents the boutique. During 1975, the taxpayer bought, at an employee's discount, the following items: four blouses, three skirts, one pair of slacks, one trench coat, two sweaters, one jacket, one tunic, five scarves, six belts, two pairs of shoes, and four necklaces. The total cost of this apparel was $1,381.91. In addition, the sum of $240 was expended for maintenance of these items.

Although the clothing and accessories purchased by the taxpayer were the type used for general purposes by the regular customers of the boutique, the taxpayer is not a normal purchaser of these clothes. The taxpayer and her husband, who is partially disabled because of a severe heart attack suffered in 1971, lead a simple life and their social activities are very limited and informal. Although taxpayer's employer has no objection to her wearing the apparel away from work, taxpayer stated that she did not wear the clothes during off-work hours because she felt that they were too expensive for her simple everyday lifestyle. Another reason why she did not wear the YSL clothes apart from work was to make them last longer. Taxpayer did admit at trial, however, that a number of the articles were things she could have worn off the job and in which she would have looked "nice." . . .

The principal issue on appeal is whether the taxpayer is entitled to deduct as an ordinary and necessary business expense the cost of purchasing and maintaining the YSL clothes and accessories worn by the taxpayer in her employment as the manager of the boutique. This determination requires an examination of the relationship between Section 162(a) of the Internal Revenue Code . . . which allows a deduction for ordinary and necessary expenses incurred in the conduct of a trade or business, and Section 262 of the Code, which bars a deduction for all "personal, living, or family expenses." Although many expenses are helpful or essential to one's business activities — such as commuting expenses and the cost of meals while at work — these expenditures are considered inherently personal and are disallowed under Section 262.

The generally accepted rule governing the deductibility of clothing expenses is that the cost of clothing is deductible as a business expense only if: (1) the clothing is of a type specifically required as a condition of employment, (2) it is not adaptable to general usage as ordinary clothing, and (3) it is not so worn.

In the present case, the Commissioner stipulated that the taxpayer was required by her employer to wear YSL clothing and that she did not wear such apparel apart from work. The Commissioner maintained, however, that a deduction should be denied because the YSL clothes and accessories purchased by the taxpayer were adaptable for general usage as ordinary clothing and she was not prohibited from using them as such. The tax court, in rejecting the Commissioner's argument for the application of an objective test, recognized that the test for deductibility was whether the clothing was "suitable for general or personal wear" but determined that the matter of suitability was to be judged subjectively, in light of the taxpayer's lifestyle. Although the court recognized that the YSL apparel "might be used by some members of society for general purposes," it felt that because the "wearing of YSL apparel outside work would be inconsistent with . . . [taxpayer's] lifestyle," sufficient reason was shown for allowing a deduction for the clothing expenditures.

In reaching its decision, the tax court relied heavily upon Yeomans v. Commissioner, 30 T.C. 757 (1958). In *Yeomans*, the taxpayer was employed as fashion coordinator for a shoe manufacturing company. Her employment necessitated her attendance at meetings of fashion experts and at fashion shows sponsored by her employer. On these occasions, she was expected to wear clothing that was new, highly styled, and such as "might be sought after and worn for personal use by women who make it a practice to dress according to the most advanced or extreme fashions." However, for her personal wear, Ms. Yeomans preferred a plainer and more conservative style of dress. As a consequence, some of the items she purchased were not suitable for her private and personal wear and were not so worn. The tax court allowed a deduction for the cost of the items that were not suitable for her personal wear. Although the basis for the decision in *Yeomans* is not clearly stated, the tax court in the case *sub judice* determined that

> [a] careful reading of *Yeomans* shows that, without a doubt, the Court based its decision on a determination of Ms. Yeomans' lifestyle and that the clothes were not suitable for her use in such lifestyle. Furthermore, the Court recognized that the clothes Ms. Yeomans purchased were suitable for wear by women who customarily wore such highly styled apparel, but such fact did not cause the court to decide the issue against her. Thus, *Yeomans* clearly decides the issue before us in favor of the petitioner.

T.C. Memo 1979-311 at 9-10.

Notwithstanding the tax court's decision in *Yeomans*, the Circuits that have addressed the issue have taken an objective, rather than subjective, approach. An objective approach was taken by the tax court in Drill v. Commissioner, 8 T.C. 902 (1947). Under an objective test, no reference is made to the individual taxpayer's lifestyle or personal taste. Instead, adaptability for personal or general use depends upon what is generally accepted for ordinary street wear.

The principal argument in support of an objective test is, of course, administrative necessity. The Commissioner argues that, as a practical matter, it is virtually impossible to determine at what point either price or style makes clothing inconsistent with or inappropriate to a taxpayer's lifestyle. Moreover, the Commissioner argues that the price one pays and the styles one selects are inherently personal choices governed by taste, fashion, and other unmeasurable values. Indeed, the tax court has rejected the argument that a taxpayer's personal taste can dictate whether clothing is appropriate for general use. An objective test, although not perfect, provides a practical administrative approach that allows a taxpayer or revenue agent to look only to objective facts in determining whether clothing required as a condition of employment is adaptable to general use as ordinary street wear. Conversely, the tax court's reliance on subjective factors provides no concrete guidelines in determining the deductibility of clothing purchased as a condition of employment.

In addition to achieving a practical administrative result, an objective test also tends to promote substantial fairness among the greatest number of taxpayers. It apparently would be the tax court's position that two similarly situated YSL boutique managers with identical wardrobes would be subject to disparate tax consequences depending upon the particular manager's lifestyle and "socio-economic level." This result, however, is not consonant with a reasonable interpretation of Sections 162 and 262.

For the reasons stated above, the decision of the tax court upholding the deduction for taxpayer's purchase of YSL clothing is reversed. Consequently, the portion of the tax court's decision upholding the deduction for maintenance costs for the clothing is also reversed.

Problems

6-6.   Ensign Pulver, United States Navy, serves full time and spends $2,750 annually for uniforms and their care. Ensign Ramirez is a reservist and spends $500 a year on uniforms.

   a.   Can Pulver deduct his clothing expenses?

   b.   Can Ramirez deduct his clothing expenses?

6-7.   Raphael Bowa, a farmer, paid $1,400 for overalls, boots, and flannel shirts that he loathed but found necessary to wear when farming. What amounts, if any, are deductible?

4.   Current Expense versus Capital Expenditure

Section 162 requires that to be currently deductible an item must be an *expense* as opposed to a *capital expenditure*. Thus, expenses may be currently deductible under §162, whereas deductions for capital expenditures must be postponed at least partially to future taxable years. Two Code sections work together to produce these results. Section 162 authorizes deductions for ordinary and necessary expenses;

§§263 and 263A prohibit a current deduction for capital expenditures even if they are ordinary and necessary and incurred in the taxpayer's trade or business. Sections 263(a)(1) and 263(a)(2) provides that capital expenditures include "any amount paid out for new buildings or for permanent improvements or betterments made to increase the value of any property or estate" and amounts "expended in restoring property or in making good the exhaustion thereof for which an allowance is or has been made." Capital expenditures are not limited to costs incurred in the acquisition of buildings but also encompass the acquisition of "machinery and equipment, furniture and fixtures, and similar property having a useful life substantially beyond the taxable year." Reg. §1.263(a)-2(a). Section 263A provides that capital expenditures include the costs of real or tangible property produced by the taxpayer.

In Woodward v. Commissioner, 397 U.S. 572 (1970), and United States v. Hilton Hotels Corp., 397 U.S. 580 (1970), the Supreme Court considered the deductibility of appraisal and litigation costs incurred in determining a price for stock to be acquired. The Commissioner disallowed the deductions in both cases, characterizing the costs as capital expenditures incurred in connection with the acquisition of stock. The taxpayers maintained that the costs had been incurred in fixing the price of the property rather than in the actual acquisition of the property. Commenting that "where property is acquired by purchase, nothing is more clearly part of the process of acquisition than the establishment of a purchase price," 397 U.S. at 579, the Court held that these costs were capital expenditures and were therefore not currently deductible business expenses.

In Indopco v. Commissioner, 503 U.S. 79 (1992), the Supreme Court held that an expenditure may require capital treatment even if it does not lead to a separate and distinct asset. Therein, legal and professional fees incurred by a target corporation to facilitate its acquisition were classified as capital expenditures. The Supreme Court stated that "a taxpayer's realization of benefits beyond the taxable year in which the expenditure is incurred is undeniably important in determining whether the appropriate tax treatment is immediate deduction or capitalization." Id. at 87.

REV. RUL. 92-80
1992-2 C.B. 57

ISSUE

Does the Supreme Court's decision in Indopco, Inc. v. Commissioner, 503 U.S. 79 (1992), affect the treatment of advertising costs as business expenses which are generally deductible under section 162 of the Internal Revenue Code?

LAW AND ANALYSIS

Section 162(a) of the Code allows a deduction for all the ordinary and necessary expenses paid or incurred during the taxable year in carrying on any trade or business.

Section 1.162-1(a) of the Income Tax Regulations expressly provides that "advertising and other selling expenses" are among the items included in deductible business expenses under section 162 of the Code.

Section 1.162-20(a)(2) of the regulations provides, in part, that expenditures for institutional or goodwill advertising which keeps the taxpayer's name before the public are generally deductible as ordinary and necessary business expenses provided the expenditures are related to the patronage the taxpayer might reasonably expect in the future.

Section 263(a) of the Code provides that no deduction is allowed for any amount paid out for permanent improvements or betterments made to increase the value of any property.

In Indopco, Inc. v. Commissioner, 503 U.S. 79, 112 S. Ct. 1039 (1992), the Supreme Court concluded that certain legal and professional fees incurred by a target corporation to facilitate a friendly acquisition were capital expenditures. The Court stated that the acquisition costs created significant long-term benefits for the taxpayer. In reaching this decision, the Court specifically rejected the argument that its decision in Commissioner v. Lincoln Savings & Loan Association, 403 U.S. 345 (1971), should be read as holding "that *only* expenditures that create or enhance separate and distinct assets are to be capitalized under §263."

The *Indopco* decision does not affect the treatment of advertising costs under section 162(a) of the Code. These costs are generally deductible under that section even though advertising may have some future effect on business activities, as in the case of institutional or goodwill advertising. Only in the unusual circumstance where advertising is directed towards obtaining future benefits significantly beyond those traditionally associated with ordinary product advertising or with institutional or goodwill advertising, must the costs of that advertising be capitalized.

HOLDING

The *Indopco* decision does not affect the treatment of advertising costs as business expenses which are generally deductible under section 162 of the Code.

Note on Repairs versus Improvements

Complex expense versus capital expenditure issues often arise in characterizing costs incurred with regard to assets the taxpayer already owns. For example, is the replacement of a warehouse roof a repair (deductible as a current expense) or a capital improvement (which must be capitalized and deducted over the life of the asset)? The Regulations attempt to answer this question by permitting a current deduction for

> the cost of incidental repairs which neither materially add to the value of the property nor appreciably prolong its life, but keep it in an ordinarily efficient operating condition . . . provided the . . . basis of the . . . property . . . is not increased by the amount of such expenditure.

Reg. §1.162-4. See also Reg. §1.263(a)-l(b). Thus, the cost of a new roof would be a capital expenditure if it either materially added to the value or substantially prolonged the useful life of the building.

In an attempt to distinguish incidental repairs from capital improvements, the Tenth Circuit in United States v. Wehrli, 400 F.2d 686 (1968), adopted the *general plan* test. In *Wehrli*, the taxpayer deducted "repair" costs incurred in preparing an office building for new tenants. The government challenged the deduction, alleging that the work had been part of a general plan of rehabilitation, modernization, and improvement and thus was a capital expenditure that was not currently deductible as a business expense. Under this test, any expenditure that is part of such a "general plan" must be capitalized, even if that expenditure, standing alone, would have been classified as a repair expense. The case provides a list of factors to be considered in ascertaining the existence of a general plan:

> [W]hether the plan exists, and whether a particular item is part of it, are usually questions of fact to be determined by the fact finder based upon a realistic appraisal of all the surrounding facts and circumstances, including, but not limited to, the purpose, nature, extent, and value of the work done, e.g., whether the work was done to suit the needs of an incoming tenant, or to adapt the property to a different use, or in any event, whether what was done resulted in an appreciable enhancement of the property's value.

Id. at 690.

The *acquisition* of property also raises interesting issues concerning whether a cost is an expense or a capital expenditure. Costs characterized as capital expenditures include the "cost of acquisition, construction or erection of buildings, machinery and equipment, furniture and fixtures, and similar property having a useful life substantially beyond the taxable year." Reg. §1.263(a)-2(a). On its face, this Regulation appears to draw a clear distinction between business expenses and capital expenditures. For example, assume that a company purchases a dozen wooden pencils and a word processor, both for use by company secretaries. The cost of the pencils is an expense, but the cost of the word processor is a capital expenditure because it has a useful life that extends beyond the taxable year.

Usually, however, the issues under this Regulation do not involve the nature of the property acquired. Rather, the interesting questions arise in determining what constitutes a cost of acquisition. The cases tend to broadly interpret this phrase, encompassing such costs as fees paid to consultants, attorneys, appraisers, and other professionals whose services are rendered in connection with the acquisition of an asset. Thus, a cost otherwise constituting a business expense may be disallowed because it is an acquisition cost to be treated as a capital expenditure. If the cost is so characterized, it is added to the basis of the acquired asset and is recoverable through depreciation deductions, if the asset is depreciable, or, if it is not depreciable, through reduced gain or increased loss realized on disposition of the asset.

COMMISSIONER v. IDAHO POWER CO.
418 U.S. 1 (1974)

MR. JUSTICE BLACKMUN delivered the opinion of the Court.

This case presents the sole issue whether, for federal income tax purposes, a taxpayer is entitled to a deduction from gross income, under §167(a) of the Code, for depreciation on equipment the taxpayer owns and uses in the construction of its own capital facilities, or whether the capitalization provision of §263(a) bars the deduction.

The taxpayer claimed the deduction, but the Commissioner of Internal Revenue disallowed it. . . .

I

Nearly all the relevant facts are stipulated. The taxpayer-respondent, Idaho Power Company, is a Maine corporation organized in 1915, with its principal place of business at Boise, Idaho. It is a public utility engaged in the production, transmission, distribution, and sale of electric energy. The taxpayer keeps its books and files its federal income tax returns on the calendar year accrual basis. The tax years at issue are 1962 and 1963.

For many years, the taxpayer has used its own equipment and employees in the construction of improvements and additions to its capital facilities. The major work has consisted of transmission lines, transmission switching stations, distribution lines, distribution stations, and connecting facilities.

During 1962 and 1963, the tax years in question, taxpayer owned and used in its business a wide variety of automotive transportation equipment, including passenger cars, trucks of all descriptions, power operated equipment, and trailers. Radio communication devices were affixed to the equipment and were used in its daily operations. The transportation equipment was used in part for the construction of capital facilities having a useful life of more than one year.

On its books, the taxpayer used various methods of charging costs incurred in connection with its transportation equipment either to current expense or to capital accounts. To the extent the equipment was used in construction, the taxpayer charged depreciation of the equipment, as well as all operating and maintenance costs (other than pension contributions, social security and motor vehicle taxes) to the capital assets so constructed. This was done either directly or through clearing accounts in accordance with procedures prescribed by the Federal Power Commission and adopted by the Idaho Public Utilities Commission.

For federal income tax purposes, however, the taxpayer treated the depreciation on transportation equipment differently. It claimed as a deduction from gross income *all* the year's depreciation on such equipment, including that portion attributable to its use in constructing capital facilities. The depreciation was computed on a composite life of 10 years and under straight-line and declining balance methods. The other operating and maintenance costs the taxpayer had charged on its books to capital were not claimed as current expenses and were not deducted.

To summarize: On its books, in accordance with Federal Power Commission-Idaho Public Utilities Commission prescribed methods, the taxpayer capitalized the construction-related depreciation, but for income tax purposes that depreciation increment was claimed as a deduction under §167(a).

Upon audit, the Commissioner disallowed the deduction for the construction-related depreciation. He ruled that depreciation was a nondeductible capital expenditure to which §263(a) had application. He added the amount of the depreciation so disallowed to the taxpayer's adjusted basis in its capital facilities, and then allowed a deduction for an appropriate amount of depreciation on the addition, computed over the useful life (30 years or more) of the property constructed. A deduction for depreciation of the transportation equipment to the extent of its use in day-to-day operation and maintenance was also allowed. . . .

The taxpayer asserts that its transportation equipment is used in its "trade or business" and that depreciation thereon is therefore deductible under §167(a)(1) of the Code. The Commissioner concedes that §167 may be said to have a literal application to depreciation on equipment used in capital construction, Brief for Petitioner 16, but contends that the provision must be read in the light of §263(a)(1) which specifically disallows any deduction for an amount "paid out for new buildings or for permanent improvements or betterments." He argues that §263 takes precedence over §167 by virtue of what he calls the "priority-ordering" terms (and what the taxpayer describes as "housekeeping" provisions) of §161 of the Code, and that sound principles of accounting and taxation mandate the capitalization of this depreciation.

It is worth noting the various items that are not at issue here. The mathematics, as such, is not in dispute. The taxpayer has capitalized, as part of its cost of acquisition of capital assets, the operating and maintenance costs (other than depreciation, pension contribution, and social security and motor vehicle taxes) of the transportation equipment attributable to construction. This is not contested. The Commissioner does not dispute that the portion of the transportation equipment's depreciation allocable to operation and maintenance of facilities, in contrast with construction thereof, qualifies as a deduction from gross income. There is no disagreement as to the allocation of depreciation between construction and maintenance. The issue, thus comes down primarily to a question of timing, . . . that is, whether the construction-related depreciation is to be amortized and deducted over the *shorter* life of the equipment or, instead, is to be amortized and deducted over the *longer* life of the capital facilities constructed.

II

Our primary concern is with the necessity to treat construction-related depreciation in a manner that comports with accounting and taxation realities. Over a period of time a capital asset is consumed and, correspondingly over that period, its theoretical value and utility are thereby reduced. Depreciation is an accounting device which recognizes that the physical consumption of a capital asset is a true cost, since the asset is being depleted. As the process of consumption continues, and depreciation is claimed and allowed, the asset's adjusted income tax basis is reduced to reflect the distribution of its cost over the accounting periods affected. The Court stated in Hertz Corp. v. United States, 364 U.S. 122, 126 (1960), "[T]he purpose of depreciation accounting is to allocate the expense of using an asset to the various periods which are benefited by that asset." When the asset is used to further the taxpayer's day-to-day business operations, the periods of benefit usually correlate to the production of income. Thus, to the extent that equipment is used in such operations, a current depreciation deduction is an appropriate offset to gross income currently produced. It is clear, however, that different principles are implicated when the consumption of the asset takes place in the construction of other assets that, in the future, will produce income themselves. In this latter situation, the cost represented by depreciation does not correlate with production of current income. Rather, the cost, although certainly presently incurred, is related to the future and is appropriately allocated as part of the cost of acquiring an income-producing capital asset.

The Court of Appeals opined that the purpose of the depreciation allowance under the Code was to provide a means of cost recovery, and that this Court's decisions, e.g., Detroit Edison Co. v. Commissioner of Internal Revenue, 319 U.S. 98, 101 (1943), endorse a theory of replacement through "a fund to restore the property." Although tax-free replacement of a depreciating investment is one purpose of depreciation accounting, it alone does not require the result claimed by the taxpayer here. Only last Term, in United States v. Chicago, Burlington & Quincy R. Co., 412 U.S. 401 (1973), we rejected replacement as the strict and sole purpose of depreciation:

> Whatever may be the desirability of creating a depreciation reserve under these circumstances, as a matter of good business and accounting practice, the answer is . . . "Depreciation reflects the cost of an existing capital asset, not the cost of a potential replacement."

Id. at 415. Even were we to look to replacement, it is the replacement of the constructed facilities, not the equipment used to build them, with which we would be concerned. If the taxpayer now were to decide not to construct any more capital facilities with its own equipment and employees, it, in theory, would have no occasion to replace its equipment to the extent that it was consumed in prior construction.

Accepted accounting practice and established tax principles require the capitalization of the cost of acquiring a capital asset. In Woodward v. Commissioner of Internal Revenue, 397 U.S. 572, 575 (1970), the Court observed, "It has long been recognized, as a general matter, that costs incurred in the acquisition . . . of a capital asset are to be treated as capital expenditures." This principle has obvious application to the acquisition of a capital asset by purchase, but it has been applied, as well, to the costs incurred in a taxpayer's construction of capital facilities.

There can be little question that other construction-related expense items, such as tools, materials, and wages paid construction workers, are to be treated as part of the cost of acquisition of a capital asset. The taxpayer does not dispute this. Of course, reasonable wages paid in the carrying on of a trade or business qualify as a deduction from gross income. §162(a)(1). But when wages are paid in connection with the construction or acquisition of a capital asset, they must be capitalized and are then entitled to be amortized over the life of the capital asset so acquired. See Treas. Reg. §1.266-1(e).

Construction-related depreciation is not unlike expenditures for wages for construction workers. The significant fact is that the exhaustion of construction equipment does not represent the final disposition of the taxpayer's investment in that equipment; rather, the investment in the equipment is assimilated into the cost of the capital asset constructed. Construction-related depreciation on the equipment is not an expense to the taxpayer of its day-to-day business. It is, however, appropriately recognized as a part of the taxpayer's cost or investment in the capital asset. The taxpayer's own accounting procedure reflects this treatment, for on its books the construction-related depreciation was capitalized by a credit to the equipment account and a debit to the capital facility account. By the same token, this capitalization prevents the distortion of income that would otherwise occur if depreciation properly allocable to asset acquisition were deducted from gross income currently realized.

An additional pertinent factor is that capitalization of construction-related depreciation by the taxpayer who does its own construction work maintains tax parity with the taxpayer who has its construction work done by an independent contractor. The depreciation on the contractor's equipment incurred during the performance of the job will be an element of cost charged by the contractor for his construction services, and the entire cost, of course, must be capitalized by the taxpayer holding the construction work performed. The Court of Appeals holding would lead to disparate treatment among taxpayers because it would allow the firm with sufficient resources to construct its own facilities and to obtain a current deduction, whereas another firm without such resources would be required to capitalize its entire cost including depreciation charged to it by the contractor. . . .

The presence of §263(a) in the Code is of significance. Its literal language denies a deduction for "[a]ny amount paid out" for construction of permanent improvement of facilities. The taxpayer contends, and the Court of Appeals held, that depreciation of construction equipment represents merely a decrease in value and is not an amount "paid out," within the meaning of §263(a). We disagree.

The purpose of §263 is to reflect the basic principle that a capital expenditure may not be deducted from current income. It serves to prevent a taxpayer from utilizing currently a deduction properly attributable, through amortization, to later tax years when the capital asset becomes income producing. The regulations state that the capital expenditures to which §263(a) extends include the "cost of acquisition, construction, or erection of buildings." Treas. Reg. §1.263(a)-2(a). This manifests an administrative understanding that for purposes of §263(a), "amount paid out" equates with "cost incurred." The Internal Revenue Service for some time has taken the position that construction-related depreciation is to be capitalized. Rev. Rul. 59-380, 1952-2 C.B. 87; Rev. Rul. 55-252, 1955-1 C.B. 319.

There is no question that the cost of the transportation equipment was "paid out" in the same manner as the cost of supplies, materials, and other equipment and the wages of construction workers. The taxpayer does not question the capitalization of these other items as elements of cost of acquiring a capital asset. We see no reason to treat construction-related depreciation differently. In acquiring the transportation equipment, taxpayer "paid out" the equipment's purchase price; depreciation is simply the means of allocating the payment over the various accounting periods affected. As the Tax Court stated in Brooks v. Commissioner,

50 T.C., at 935, "depreciation — inasmuch as it represents a using up of capital — is as much an 'expenditure' as the using up of labor or other items of direct cost."

Finally, the priority-ordering directive of §161 — or, for that matter, §261 of the Code — requires that the capitalization provision of §263(a) take precedence, on the facts here, over §167(a). Section 161 provides that deductions specified in Part VI of Subchapter B of the Income Tax Subtitle of the Code are "subject to the exceptions provided in part IX." Part VI includes §167 and Part IX includes §263. The clear import of §161 is that, with stated exceptions set forth either in §263 itself or provided for elsewhere (as, for example, in §404 relating to pension contributions), none of which is applicable here, an expenditure incurred in acquiring capital assets must be capitalized even when the expenditure otherwise might be deemed deductible under Part VI.

The Court of Appeals concluded, without reference to §161, that §263 did not apply to a deduction, such as that for depreciation of property used in a trade or business, allowed by the Code even though incurred in the construction of capital assets. We think that the court erred in espousing so absolute a rule, and it obviously overlooked the contrary direction of §161. To the extent that reliance was placed on the congressional intent, in the evolvement of the 1954 Code, to provide "liberalization of depreciation," H.R. Rep. No. 1337, 83d Cong., 2d Sess., 22 (1954), that reliance is misplaced. The House Report also states that the depreciation provisions would "give the economy added stimulus and resilience without departing from realistic standards of depreciation accounting." Id., at 24. To be sure, the 1954 Code provided for new and accelerated methods for depreciation, resulting in greater depreciation deductions currently available. These changes, however, relate primarily to computation of depreciation. Congress certainly did not intend that provisions for accelerated depreciation should be construed as enlarging the class of depreciable assets to which §167(a) has application or as lessening the reach of §263(a).

We hold that the equipment depreciation allocable to taxpayer's construction of capital facilities is to be capitalized.

Note on Capitalization of Inventory

In response to growing concerns that businesses were manipulating the capitalization rules with respect to inventories, Congress enacted §263A in 1986 to provide a uniform method of capitalization for inventory. According to the Senate Finance Committee, "in order to more accurately reflect income and make the income tax system more neutral, a single, comprehensive set of rules should govern the capitalization of costs of producing, acquiring, and holding property, including interest expense, subject to appropriate exceptions. . . ." S. Rep. No. 99-313, at 140 (1986). Under §263A, all direct and indirect costs attributable to the acquisition or production of inventory items, including general and administrative and overhead costs, must be capitalized into the basis of the inventory and not deducted currently. Thus, for retailers and wholesalers, the basis of inventory includes not only the cost of purchasing the inventory but also the costs incident to purchasing it (including the salaries of employees purchasing inventory). Similarly, interest on debt must be capitalized if such debt is incurred to finance inventory with a production period greater than two years, such as wine, which can age for several years before sale.

Problems

6-8. Tom Smith spent $8,000 for a new roof on his house. Harry Jones, Smith's neighbor, who owns a lumber yard, spent $15,000 for a new roof on his warehouse.

    a. Does Smith have a currently deductible expense? If not, how should the cost incurred for Smith's new roof be treated for tax purposes?

    b. Is Jones entitled to a current deduction? If not, how should Jones treat the costs for his new roof for tax purposes?

6-9. Professor Tim Matheson entered a contract to publish a book on income taxation. During January, he collected supplies and materials, spent $1,000 purchasing relevant books, $500 photocopying relevant information, $200 on paper and pencils, and $5,000 on a new word processor.

    Matheson convinced university officials to provide the funds to hire two research assistants. Because research assistants were normally paid $900 and the university was able to provide Matheson with only $1,500, Matheson contributed $300 toward their salaries. The manuscript was completed and ready for publication by December.

    a. Which, if any, of the costs incurred are currently deductible?

    b. Are the deductions, if any, taken in arriving at AGI?

D. STATUTORY DEDUCTIONS FOR MIXED BUSINESS-PERSONAL EXPENSES

Because of the strict policy precluding the deductibility of personal expenses, certain business expenses of a quasi-personal nature are subject to statutory, administrative, and judicial requirements in addition to the three prerequisites of §162(a). Clear-cut distinctions between deductible business and nondeductible personal expenses are often elusive because of overlap between the two categories. For example, an argument can be made that all business-related costs for travel to and from work, meals purchased during the workday, and clothing worn to work should be deducted as an ordinary and necessary business expense. Equally persuasive, however, is the notion that because such expenditures are merely personal costs of living, they should remain nondeductible despite the fact that they arise in a business setting.

The ease with which taxpayers were able initially to satisfy the broad requirements of §162(a) has influenced the shape of subsequent statutory enactments and regulatory pronouncements. As a result, the requirements for deductibility have become technical and involve significant administrative and compliance costs. The following sections of this chapter consider the requirements applicable to specific types of business expense deductions.

1. Business-related Travel

Code: §§62(a)(1), (2); 162(a)(2); 262; 274(c), (m)(3), (n)
Regulations: §§1.162-2, 1.262-1(b)(5)

Section 162(a)(2) permits a deduction for travel and travel-related expenses. In order to qualify for a §162 travel deduction, an expense must have three characteristics. The expense must be (1) for travel or be travel related (including meals and lodging), (2) incurred in pursuit of the taxpayer's trade or business, and (3) incurred while away from home. Conversely, §262 expressly precludes a deduction for expenses (including travel) that are personal in nature.

Numerous characterization issues have arisen because neither §162 nor §262 provides guidance for distinguishing between business travel expenses and personal travel expenses. Moreover, the drafters of §162 neglected to provide criteria for determining the situs of the taxpayer's home for purposes of the §162 "away from home" requirement. For example, are expenses incurred in commuting between a taxpayer's home and place of business deductible business travel expenses or are they personal? Is it possible to have no tax home for purposes of §162? Is a taxpayer's tax home his residence, business office, or general area of employment? Does travel away from home for mixed motives (part-business and part-personal) qualify for deduction under §162?

a. Commuting Expenses

Commissioner v. Flowers, 326 U.S. 465 (1946), is the landmark case regarding the deduction of commuting expenses. Flowers, a lawyer residing in Jackson, Mississippi, was offered the position of general solicitor with a company that had its main office in Mobile, Alabama. Flowers accepted the position conditioned on his ability to continue residing in Jackson. Although Flowers's principal post of duty was ostensibly at the company's main office in Mobile, he spent most of his time in Jackson. During the tax years in question, however, Flowers was required to make frequent trips to Mobile. The arrangement with the employer did not provide for company reimbursement for Flowers's living expenses in either city, nor for expenses incurred in traveling between them. Flowers claimed §162 deductions for the travel expenses incurred in traveling to Mobile and for his meals and lodging while there.

In denying Flowers's §162(a)(2) travel expense deductions, the Supreme Court articulated three requirements necessary for a travel expense to be an allowable deduction: the expense must be (1) ordinary and necessary; (2) incurred "while away from home"; and (3) "incurred in pursuit of business." The Court held that the third part of the *Flowers* test required a direct connection between the expenditure and the carrying on of the taxpayer's (or his employer's) trade or business. Furthermore, the expenditure must have been necessary and appropriate to the development and pursuit of that trade or business. The Court held that, since Flowers's job did not require him to maintain homes in two cities, the commuting expenses were a result of Flowers's *personal* choice of where to live. Because the exigencies of business were not the principal factor causing Flowers to incur the expenses, the third part of the Supreme Court's test was not met and no deduction was allowed.

The *Flowers* prohibition against deducting commuting expenses has been applied even in cases where housing was not available within the proximity of the taxpayer's job site and, thus, the commute was *not* based on the taxpayer's "personal choice." For example, in White v. Commissioner, 31 T.C.M. 273 (1972), traveling expenses incurred by an engineer working at the White Sands Missile Range in New Mexico were not deductible. The taxpayer claimed that, due to the remote location of the missile range, there was no habitable housing within 45 miles and that his job frequently required him to work into the night, when public transportation was unavailable. The court sympathized with the taxpayer's plight but denied the travel expense deduction. See also Coombs v. Commissioner, 608 F.2d 1269 (9th Cir. 1979) (taxpayers denied deduction for costs incurred in commuting at least 65 miles from their homes in Las Vegas, the nearest habitable community, to their jobs at a nuclear testing facility).

Despite the courts' strong stance against allowing deductions for commuting expenses, there are certain narrow exceptions to the general rule. For instance, in Fausner v. Commissioner, 413 U.S. 838 (1973), the Supreme Court carved out an exception for commuting expenses incurred in transporting job-required tools to and from the workplace. Fausner, a commercial airline pilot, sought to deduct the entire cost of commuting by private automobile because he was required to carry his flight bag and overnight bag to and from work. Although the Court denied the deduction for Fausner's commuting expenses, it indicated by a per curiam opinion that in proper circumstances some deduction could be allowed. The allowable deduction would be calculated by separating nondeductible commuting expenses from deductible expenses incurred in transporting "incidentals of [the taxpayer's] occupation" when the latter represent ordinary and necessary business expenses. See also Rev. Rul. 75-380, 1975-2 C.B. 59 (providing a method of allocating non-deductible commuting expenses and deductible costs of transporting work-related tools). Unlike many exceptions in the law, which ultimately swallow the rule from which they were drawn, the *Fausner* exception for expenses incurred in transporting a taxpayer's tools has been applied narrowly.

Another exception to the *Flowers* rule arises when the taxpayer incurs expenses traveling between two or more places of employment. In Revenue Ruling 55-109, 1955-1 C.B. 261, the Commissioner ruled that a member of a reserve unit of the Armed Forces was permitted to deduct expenses incurred in traveling from his civilian job to a site for Reserve training drills. Although the taxpayer's expenses of traveling were not incurred in discharging the duties of either job, the Commissioner reasoned that "since both such positions constitute part of the [taxpayer's] trade or business, local transportation expenses in getting from one place of employment to another constitute ordinary and necessary expenses incurred in carrying on his combined trade or business and in discharging his duties at both locations during that same day." Id. at 263.

Buccino v. United States, 83-2 U.S.T.C. ¶9697 (Ct. Cl. 1983), further illustrates the limited scope of commuting expenses that may be deducted. The taxpayer in *Buccino* was a physician who practiced principally at a clinic four and one-half miles from his residence. The doctor's practice involved frequent rounds at a hospital located between his residence and the clinic. Occasionally, the taxpayer would travel from his residence to the hospital and return without stopping at the clinic. The issue in *Buccino* concerned the taxpayer's deduction of the expenses incurred in traveling from his residence to the hospital and back. The court initially noted that all commuting expenses are in a sense ordinary and necessary business expenses, incurred in the pursuit of a trade or business. Nonetheless, the court stated that, based on the interests of "fairness, equity, and practicality," the personal nature of commuting expenses outweighs any business characteristics they may have. Thus, because the hospital rounds were a part of the taxpayer's business, expenses incurred in traveling between his residence and the hospital were nondeductible. The fact that most of the taxpayer's after-hour trips were in response to emergency calls did not move the court. The court viewed those trips, including after-hours emergency calls, as a regular and recurrent part of the taxpayer's profession.

Problems

6-10. Margaret Hastings works as a civilian scientist for the Defense Department at a nuclear testing facility in New Mexico. The military base on which her laboratory is located is off-limits to all persons except authorized employees during working hours. No base housing exists and the government owns all land within a thirty-mile radius of the base, which is equally devoid of housing. Hastings purchased the nearest house she could find to her job; nevertheless, she drives thirty miles to and from her laboratory. Is she entitled to deduct her travel costs?

6-11. Dorothy Samuelson, an editor at Randolph Publishing, has a steady routine. Each workday at 8 A.M., she drives one mile to her office. She stays in her office until 3 P.M., at which time she drives to her second job as a part-time legal secretary in a small town thirty miles from her home. At 8 P.M. she leaves the law offices, stops by Randolph Publishing to check her messages, and then drives home. Is she permitted to deduct these expenses?

6-12. Jennifer Sorensen, a carpenter, initially commuted to and from work on public transportation at a cost of $2 per day. When it became necessary to carry her tools to and from work she began driving to work. It cost $3 per day to drive her car and $5 per day to rent a trailer for carrying the tools. How much, if any, of her daily transportation expenses are deductible?

b. The Tax Home Doctrine

As demonstrated in *Flowers*, whether travel is for "commuting"—which is a nondeductible personal expense—or "business travel"—which is deductible—turns on whether the taxpayer is "home" for tax purposes. But how should the tax law decide where is a taxpayer's home? How large is the taxpayer's tax home—a neighborhood, a district, a city, a metropolitan area? Even assuming these questions can be answered, under what circumstances does a taxpayer travel away from home for a sufficient period of time that the taxpayer *changes* their tax home? Is it possible to have *no* tax home?

1. Business vs. Personal

A particular complication arises in determining whether a taxpayer's abode or principal place of business is his or her home for tax purposes. When the taxpayer's regular place of abode and principal place of business are in different locales, it becomes difficult to establish the location of the taxpayer's tax home. Does the concept of "home" for tax purposes mean something different than "home" for other purposes? Hantzis v. Commissioner, which follows, illustrates the elusiveness of this issue.

HANTZIS v. COMMISSIONER
638 F.2d 248 (1st Cir. 1981)

CAMPBELL, J. . . .

In the fall of 1973 Catharine Hantzis (taxpayer) . . . entered Harvard Law School in Cambridge, Massachusetts, as a full-time student. During her second year of law school she sought unsuccessfully to obtain employment for the summer of 1975 with a Boston law firm. She did, however, find a job as a legal assistant with a law firm in New York City, where she worked for ten weeks beginning in June 1975. Her husband, then a member of the faculty of Northeastern University with a teaching schedule for that summer, remained in Boston and lived at the couple's home there. At the time of the Tax Court's decision in this case, Mr. and Mrs. Hantzis still resided in Boston.

On their joint income tax return for 1975, Mr. and Mrs. Hantzis reported the earnings from taxpayer's summer employment ($3,750) and deducted the cost of transportation between Boston and New York, the cost of a small apartment rented by Mrs. Hantzis in New York and the cost of her meals in New York ($3,204). The deductions were taken under section 162(a)(2). . . .

The Commissioner disallowed the deduction on the ground that taxpayer's home for purposes of section 162(a)(2) was her place of employment and the cost of traveling to and living in New York was therefore not "incurred . . . while away from home." The Commissioner also argued that the expenses were not incurred "in the pursuit of a trade or business." Both positions were rejected by the Tax Court, which found . . . the expenses to be deductible under section 162(a)(2). . . .

The Commissioner has directed his argument at the meaning of "in pursuit of a trade or business." He interprets this phrase as requiring that a deductible traveling expense be incurred under the demands of a trade or business which predates the expense, i.e., an "already existing" trade or business. Under this theory, section 162(a)(2) would invalidate the deduction taken by the taxpayer because she was a full-time student before commencing her summer work at a New York law firm in 1975 and so was not continuing in a trade or business when she incurred the expenses of traveling to New York and living there while her job lasted. The

Commissioner's proposed interpretation erects at the threshold of deductibility under section 162(a)(2) the requirement that a taxpayer be engaged in a trade or business *before* incurring a travel expense. Only if that requirement is satisfied would an inquiry into the deductibility of an expense proceed to ask whether the expense was a result of business exigencies, incurred while away from home, and reasonable and necessary.

Such a reading of the statute is semantically possible and would perhaps expedite the disposition of certain cases. Nevertheless, we reject it as unsupported by case law and inappropriate to the policies behind section 162(a)(2). . . .

Nor would the Commissioner's theory mesh with the policy behind section 162(a)(2). As discussed, the travel expense deduction is intended to exclude from taxable income a necessary cost of producing that income. Yet the recency of entry into a trade or business does not indicate that travel expenses are not a cost of producing income. To be sure, the costs incurred by a taxpayer who leaves his usual residence to begin a trade or business at another location may not be truly *travel* expenses, i.e., expenses incurred while "away from home," see infra, but practically, they are as much incurred "in the pursuit of a trade or business" when the occupation is new as when it is old.

An example drawn from the Commissioner's argument illustrates the point. The Commissioner notes that "if a construction worker, who normally works in Boston for Corp. *A*, travels to New York to work for Corp. *B* for six months, he is traveling . . . in the pursuit of his own trade as a construction worker." Accordingly, the requirement that travel expenses be a result of business exigencies is satisfied. Had a construction worker just entering the labor market followed the same course his expenses under the Commissioner's reasoning would not satisfy the business exigencies requirement. Yet in each case, the taxpayer's travel expenses would be costs of earning an income and not merely incidents of personal lifestyle. Requiring that the finding of business exigency necessary to deductibility under section 162(a)(2) be predicated upon the prior existence of a trade or business would thus captiously restrict the meaning of "in pursuit of a trade or business."

In other contexts the phrase "in the pursuit of a trade or business" may permit the interpretation urged upon us by the Commissioner,[9] but to require under section 162(a)(2) that a travel expense be incurred in connection with a preexisting trade or business is neither necessary nor appropriate to effectuating the purpose behind the use of that phrase in the provision. Accordingly, we turn to the question whether, in the absence of the Commissioner's proposed threshold limit on deductibility, the expenses at issue here satisfy the requirements of section 162(a)(2) as interpreted in Flowers v. Commissioner. . . .

. . . *Flowers* construed section 162(a)(2) to mean that a traveling expense is deductible only if it is (1) reasonable and necessary, (2) incurred while away from home, and (3) necessitated by the exigencies of business. . . .

The meaning of the term "home" in the travel expense provision is far from clear. When Congress enacted the travel expense deduction, it apparently was unsure

---

9. Under the general provision of section 162(a), no deduction is allowed for expenses incurred in preparing to enter a new business and the phrase "in the pursuit of a trade or business" has in cases concerned with such expenses been read to "presuppose [] an existing business with which [the taxpayer] is connected." Frank v. Commissioner, 20 T.C. 511, 513-514 (1953). See, e.g., Weinstein v. United States, 420 F.2d 700 (Ct. Cl. 1970).

whether, to be deductible, an expense must be incurred away from a person's residence or away from his principal place of business.[10] It has been suggested that these conflicting definitions are due to the enormous factual variety in the cases. We find this observation instructive, for if the cases that discuss the meaning of the term "home" in section 162(a)(2) are interpreted on the basis of their unique facts as well as the fundamental purposes of the travel expense provision, and not simply pinioned to one of two competing definitions of home, much of the seeming confusion and contradiction on this issue disappears and a functional definition of the term emerges.

We think the critical step in defining "home" in these situations is to recognize that the "while away from home" requirement has to be construed in light of the further requirement that the expense be the result of business exigencies. The traveling expense deduction obviously is not intended to exclude from taxation every expense incurred by a taxpayer who, in the course of business, maintains two homes. Section 162(a)(2) seeks rather "to mitigate the burden of the taxpayer who, *because of the exigencies of his trade or business, must* maintain two places of abode and thereby incur additional and duplicate living expenses." Consciously or unconsciously, courts have effectuated this policy in part through their interpretation of the term "home" in section 162(a)(2). Whether it is held in a particular decision that a taxpayer's home is his residence or his principal place of business, the ultimate allowance or disallowance of a deduction is a function of the court's assessment of the reason for a taxpayer's maintenance of two homes. If the reason is perceived to be personal, the taxpayer's home will generally be held to be his place of employment rather than his residence and the deduction will be denied. If the reason is felt to be business exigencies, the person's home will usually be held to be his residence and the deduction will be allowed. We understand the concern of the concurrence that such an operational interpretation of the term "home" is somewhat technical and perhaps untidy, in that it will not always afford bright line answers, but we doubt the ability of either the Commissioner or the courts to invent an unyielding formula that will make sense in all cases. . . .

Construing in the manner just described the requirement that an expense be incurred "while away from home," we do not believe this requirement was satisfied in this case. Mrs. Hantzis' *trade or business* did not require that she maintain a home in Boston as well as one in New York. Though she returned to Boston at various times during the period of her employment in New York, her visits were all for personal reasons. It is not contended that she had a business connection in Boston that necessitated her keeping a home there; no professional interest was served by maintenance of the Boston home—as would have been the case, for example, if Mrs. Hantzis had been a lawyer based in Boston with a New York client whom she was temporarily serving. The home in Boston was kept up for reasons involving Mr. Hantzis, but those reasons cannot substitute for a showing by *Mrs.* Hantzis that the exigencies of *her* trade or business required *her* to maintain two homes.[11] Mrs. Hantzis' decision to keep two homes must be seen as a choice dictated by

10. The Tax Court has, with a notable exception, consistently held that a taxpayer's home is his place of business. See Daly v. Commissioner, 72 T.C. 190 (1979). The exception, of course, is the present case.

11. In this respect, Mr. and Mrs. Hantzis' situation is analogous to cases involving spouses with careers in different locations. Each must independently satisfy the requirement that deductions taken for travel expenses incurred in the pursuit of a trade or business arise while he or she is away from home.

personal, albeit wholly reasonable, considerations and not a business or occupational necessity. We therefore hold that her home for purposes of section 162(a)(2) was New York and that the expenses at issue in this case were not incurred "while away from home."[12]

We are not dissuaded from this conclusion by the temporary nature of Mrs. Hantzis' employment in New York. Mrs. Hantzis argues that the brevity of her stay in New York excepts her from the business exigencies requirement of section 162(a)(2) under a doctrine supposedly enunciated by the Supreme Court in Peurifoy v. Commissioner, 358 U.S. 59 (1958) (per curiam).[13] The Tax Court here held that Boston was the taxpayer's home because it would have been unreasonable for her to move her residence to New York for only ten weeks. At first glance these contentions may seem to find support in the court decisions holding that, when a taxpayer works for a limited time away from his usual home, section 162(a)(2) allows a deduction for the expense of maintaining a second home so long as the employment is "temporary" and not "indefinite" or "permanent." This test is an elaboration of the requirements under section 162(a)(2) that an expense be incurred due to business exigencies and while away from home. . . .

The temporary employment doctrine does not, however, purport to eliminate any requirement that continued maintenance of a first home have a business justification. We think the rule has no application where the taxpayer has no business connection with his usual place of residence. If no business exigency dictates the location of the taxpayer's usual residence, then the mere fact of his taking temporary employment elsewhere cannot supply a compelling business reason for continuing to maintain that residence. Only a taxpayer who lives one place, works another and has business ties to *both* is in the ambiguous situation that the temporary employment doctrine is designed to resolve. In such circumstances, unless his employment away from his usual home is temporary, a court can reasonably assume that the taxpayer has abandoned his business ties to that location and is left with only personal reasons for maintaining a residence there. Where only personal needs require that a travel expense be incurred, however, a taxpayer's home is defined so as to leave the expense subject to taxation. Thus, a taxpayer who

12. The concurrence reaches the same result on essentially the same reasoning, but under what we take to be an interpretation of the "in pursuit of business" requirement. We differ from our colleague, it would seem, only on the question of which precondition to deductibility best accommodates the statutory concern for "'the taxpayer who, because of the exigencies of his trade or business, must maintain two places of abode and thereby incur additional and duplicate living expenses.'" Neither the phrase "away from home" nor "in pursuit of business" effectuates this concern without interpretation that to some degree removes it from "the ordinary meaning of the term." However, of the two approaches, we find that of the concurrence more problematic than that adopted here.

13. In *Peurifoy*, the Court stated that the Tax Court had "engrafted an exception" onto the requirement that travel expenses be dictated by business exigencies, allowing "a deduction for expenditures . . . when the taxpayer's employment is 'temporary' as contrasted with 'indefinite' or 'indeterminate.'" Because the Commissioner did not challenge this exception, the Court did not rule on its validity. It instead upheld the circuit court's reversal of the Tax Court and disallowance of the deduction on the basis of the adequacy of the appellate court's review. The Supreme Court agreed that the Tax Court's finding as to the temporary nature of taxpayer's employment was clearly erroneous. Despite its inauspicious beginning, the exception has come to be generally accepted. Some uncertainty lingers, however, over whether the exception properly applies to the "business exigencies" or the "away from home" requirement. In fact, it is probably relevant to both.

Because we treat these requirements as inextricably intertwined, we find it unnecessary to address this question: applied to either requirement, the temporary employment doctrine affects the meaning of both.

pursues temporary employment away from the location of his usual residence, but has no business connection with that location, is not "away from home" for purposes of section 162(a)(2).

On this reasoning, the temporary nature of Mrs. Hantzis' employment in New York does not affect the outcome of her case. She had no business ties to Boston that would bring her within the temporary employment doctrine. By this holding, we do not adopt a rule that "home" in section 162(a)(2) is the equivalent of a taxpayer's place of business. Nor do we mean to imply that a taxpayer has a "home" for tax purposes only if he is already engaged in a trade or business at a particular location. Though both rules are alluringly determinate, we have already discussed why they offer inadequate expressions of the purposes behind the travel expense deduction. We hold merely that for a taxpayer in Mrs. Hantzis' circumstances to be "away from home in the pursuit of a trade or business," she must establish the existence of some sort of business relation both to the location she claims as "home" and to the location of her temporary employment sufficient to support a finding that her duplicative expenses are necessitated by business exigencies. . . .

Reversed.

KEETON, J., concurring in the result. . . .

. . . Thus, on the facts in this case, I am in agreement with the court that the taxpayer's deductions must be disallowed because she was not required by her trade or business to maintain both places of residence. However rather than resting its conclusion on an interpretation of the language of section 162(a)(2) taken as a whole, which allows a deduction for ordinary and necessary expenses incurred "while away from home in the pursuit of trade or business," the court reaches the same result by incorporating the concept of business-related residence into the definition of "home," thereby producing sometimes, but not always, a meaning of "home" quite different from ordinary usage. . . .

. . . I read the opinion as indicating that in a dual residence case, the Commissioner must determine whether the exigencies of the taxpayer's trade or business require her to maintain both residences. If so, the Commissioner must decide that the taxpayer's *principal residence* is her "home" and must conclude that expenses associated with the secondary residence were incurred "while away from home," and are deductible. If not, as in the instant case, the Commissioner must find that the taxpayer's *principal place of business* is her "home" and must conclude that the expenses in question were not incurred "while away from home." The conclusory nature of these determinations as to which residence is her "home" reveals the potentially confusing effect of adopting an extraordinary definition of "home." . . .

The result reached by the court can easily be expressed while also giving home its ordinary meaning, and neither Congress nor the Supreme Court has directed that "home" be given an extraordinary meaning in the present context. In Rosenspan v. United States, [438 F.2d 905 (2d Cir. 1971)], Judge Friendly, writing for the court, rejected the Commissioner's proposed definition of home as the taxpayer's business headquarters, concluding that in section 162(a)(2) "'home' means 'home.'"

> When Congress uses a non-technical word in a tax statute, presumably it wants administrators and courts to read it in the way that ordinary people would understand, and not "to draw on some unexpressed spirit outside the bounds of the normal meaning of words."

In analyzing dual residence cases, the court's opinion advances compelling reasons that the first step must be to determine whether the taxpayer has business as opposed to purely personal reasons for maintaining both residences. This must be done in order to determine whether the expenses of maintaining a second residence were, "necessitated by business, as opposed to personal, demands," and were in this sense incurred by the taxpayer "while away from home in pursuit of trade or business." Necessarily implicit in this proposition is a more limited corollary that is sufficient to decide the present case: When the taxpayer has a business relationship to only one location, no traveling expenses the taxpayer incurs are "necessitated by business, as opposed to personal demands," regardless of how many residences the taxpayer has, where they are located, or which one is "home."

In the present case, although the taxpayer argues that her employment required her to reside in New York, that contention is insufficient to compel a determination that it was the nature of her trade or business that required her to incur the additional expense of maintaining a second residence, the burden that section 162(a)(2) was intended to mitigate. Her expenses associated with maintaining her New York residence arose from personal interests that led her to maintain two residences rather than a single residence close to her work. While traveling from her principal residence to a second place of residence closer to her business, even though "away from home," she was not "away from home in pursuit of business." Thus, the expenses at issue in this case were not incurred by the taxpayer "while away from home in pursuit of trade or business."

Note

Unlike in *Hantzis*, where the court specifically rejected a bright-line test, the Tax Court has at times applied a strict version of the rule that a taxpayer's tax home is the taxpayer's principal place of business. Daly v. Commissioner, 72 T.C. 190 (1979) rev'd, 631 F.2d 351 (4th Cir. 1980), aff'd on reh'g en banc, 662 F.2d 253 (1981); Foote v. Commissioner, 67 T.C. 1 (1976); Kroll v. Commissioner, 49 T.C. 557 (1968). In *Daly*, the taxpayer maintained an abode in McLean, Virginia, with his wife, who worked in nearby Washington, D.C. The taxpayer was employed as a regional sales manager, which necessitated personal calls on customers in his sales territory. The taxpayer's territory encompassed parts of Delaware, New Jersey, and Pennsylvania, although 80 percent of his sales calls were in the Philadelphia area. Only 6 percent of the taxpayer's sales calls were in the vicinity of McLean, but he maintained an office in his home for job-related paper work. The taxpayer deducted the travel expenses incurred in traveling from McLean to the Philadelphia area. The Tax Court found that the taxpayer's home for tax purposes was Philadelphia, his principal place of business, and disallowed the deductions as personal expenses. The court found that the taxpayer resided in McLean to enable his wife to work in Washington, and thus any work at his residence was incidental and not the taxpayer's principal place of business.

In Paolini v. Commissioner, 43 T.C.M. 513 (1982), the taxpayer attempted to rely on an exception to the rule that a person's tax home is his or her principal place of business. In *Paolini*, the taxpayer was in the construction business and performed a substantial amount of his work in New Jersey. The taxpayer resided in Pennsylvania, but because his job required him to be in New Jersey, he also maintained an apartment there. The nature of the taxpayer's business required him to be at any one construction site for only a short time. The taxpayer argued that he should be allowed to deduct the costs of maintaining the New Jersey apartment because he only temporarily left his Pennsylvania abode to work on a given job. Not surprisingly, the court disallowed the deduction for the living expenses incurred in New Jersey. Although the precise locations of the taxpayers's job sites were constantly changing, almost all were in New Jersey. The court ruled, therefore, that Paolini was permanently employed in the New Jersey area and that New Jersey would be treated as his tax home. See also Lamb v. Commissioner, T.C. Summ.Op. 2008-153 (2008).

In more extreme circumstances, under this rationale the Tax Court has disallowed expenses for travel on the theory that the taxpayer had *no* tax home. For example, if a traveling salesperson is always traveling and staying in hotels, and maintains no permanent abode, there is no tax home to be away from while traveling and no travel expenses are deductible pursuant to §162(a)(2). Rosenspan v. United States, 438 F.2d 905 (2d Cir. 1971). Similarly, in McNeil v. Commissioner, T.C. Memo. 2003-65, the taxpayer was a long-haul truck driver who maintained a mobile home in Missouri in which he spent approximately twenty days a year and for which the taxpayer incurred $1,000 a year in expenses. For the substantial remainder of the year, the taxpayer was traveling in the truck. The taxpayer claimed deductions for travel expenses incurred while on the road. The Tax Court ruled that the taxpayer did not spend sufficient time in Missouri to consider it a tax home, and thus, because he had no other fixed place of business, he had no tax home. Without a tax home, the taxpayer was not entitled to claim any deductions for travel away from home.

Problems

6-13. John Collins, an assistant professor at Michigan State University (MSU) who is married and has a 4-year-old child, accepted a visiting professorship at the University of Michigan for the fall semester. During the four-month semester, Collins rented a two-bedroom apartment for his family for $1,600 per month; other monthly expenses included $800 for groceries, $300 for food eaten in restaurants, $225 for gas used commuting to work, and $100 for wine.

    a. What tax deductions would be available to Collins if he returned to MSU on December 31?

    b. What would be the tax consequences if Collins's visiting professorship had been for three semesters and he returned to MSU on December 31 of the following year?

Assume that on November 30, the University of Michigan offered Collins a permanent, tenured appointment, which he accepted on December 1, to begin with the fall semester of the following year. Collins then returned to MSU for the spring because he was contractually obligated to do so.

    c. What are the tax consequences of this changed situation?

    d. Would the answer in *c* change if, instead of returning to MSU, Collins stayed at the University of Michigan?

2.   *Temporary vs. indefinite travel*

The travel-expense deduction assumes that the taxpayer is away from home for only a short or temporary period of time, because if a taxpayer travels away for an indefinite period of time it becomes reasonable to consider the taxpayer to have moved his or her tax home to the new place of employment. This rule, labeled the "temporary or indefinite" rule, is explained in Kroll v. Commissioner, 49 T.C. 557 (1968):

> The purpose of the "away from home" provision is to mitigate the burden of the taxpayer who, because of the exigencies of his trade or business, must maintain two places of abode and thereby incur additional and duplicate living expenses. . . . The "tax home" doctrine is directed toward accomplishing this purpose. In effect, it asks the question whether in a particular case it is reasonable to expect the taxpayer to maintain a residence near his trade or business and thereby incur only one set of living expenses, which are of course nondeductible under section 262. If it is reasonable so to expect, as where a taxpayer has only one post of duty, which is permanent, then if he in fact chooses to maintain his residence elsewhere and incur living expenses near his trade or business as well, the duplication of expenses thereby resulting arises not from the needs of his business but from the taxpayer's personal choice. When, then, a taxpayer moves to a new permanent post of employment, it is generally reasonable to expect him to move his residence as well, and if he does not do so, and thereby incurs living expenses at his new post of employment while maintaining his old residence, the duplication again does not arise from business needs, but from personal considerations. If, however, the taxpayer's stay at the new post of business is to be temporary — "the sort of employment in which termination within a short period could be foreseen" — it is not reasonable to expect him to move his residence; so if he incurs living expenses at the temporary post, these are traveling expenses required by the trade or business rather than by personal choice, and they are therefore deductible.

Id. at 562-63.

The period of time the taxpayer is stationed at the remote duty post affects the temporary or indefinite status of his travel. Under §162(a), in any case where employment away from home lasts more than one year, the employment will be treated as indefinite regardless of any other factors, and related travel expenses will be nondeductible.

REV. RUL. 93-86
1993–2 C.B. 71

Issue

What effect does the one-year limitation on temporary travel . . . have on the deductibility of away from home travel expenses under section 162(a)(2) of the Internal Revenue Code?

FACTS

Situation 1. Taypayer A is regularly employed in city CI-1. In 1993, *A* accepted work in city CI-2, which is 250 miles from CI-1. *A* realistically expected the work in CI-2 to be completed in 6 months and planned to return to CI-1 at that time. In fact, the employment lasted 10 months, after which time *A* returned to CI-1.

Situation 2. The facts are the same as in Situation 1, except that Taxpayer *B* realistically expected the work in CI-2 to be completed in 18 months, but in fact it was completed in 10 months.

Situation 3. The facts are the same as in Situation 1, except that Taxpayer *C* realistically expected the work in CI-2 to be completed in nine months. After 8 months, however, *C* was asked to remain for 7 more months (for a total actual stay of 15 months).

LAW AND ANALYSIS

Section 162(a)(2) of the Code allows a deduction for all the ordinary and necessary expenses paid or incurred during the taxable year in carrying on a trade or business, including travel expenses (including amounts of expended for meals and lodging other than amounts that are lavish or extravagant under the circumstances) while away from home in the pursuit of a trade or business. Under section 262(a), no deduction is allowed for personal, living, or family expenses, unless expressly provided by law.

For travel expenses to be deductible under section 162(a)(2) of the Code, they must satisfy the following three conditions: (1) they must be ordinary and necessary, (2) they must be incurred while away from home, and (3) they must be incurred in pursuit of a trade or business.

A taxpayer's "home" for purposes of section 162(a)(2) of the Code is generally considered to be located at (1) the taxpayer's regular or principal (if more than one regular) place of business, or (2) if the taxpayer has no regular or principal place of business, then at the taxpayer's regular place of abode in a real and substantial sense. If a taxpayer comes within neither category (1) nor category (2), the taxpayer is considered to be an itinerant whose "home" is wherever the taxpayer happens to work.

Travel expenses paid or incurred in connection with an indefinite or permanent work assignment are generally nondeductible. Travel expenses paid or incurred in connection with a temporary work assignment away from home are deductible under section 162(a)(2) of the Code. The courts and the Service have held that employment is temporary for this purpose only if its termination can be foreseen within a reasonably short period of time.

Employment that is initially temporary may become indefinite due to changed circumstances. In Rev. Rul. 73-578, a citizen of a foreign country comes to the United States under a 6-month nonimmigrant visa to work for a United States employer, intending to resume regular employment in the foreign country after this period. After 4 months, however, the individual agrees to continue the employment for an additional 14 months. Rev. Rul. 73-578 holds that the individual may deduct ordinary and necessary travel expenses paid or incurred during the first four months of the employment. However, the individual may not deduct travel expenses paid or incurred thereafter, unless the expenses are paid or incurred in connection with temporary employment away from the location of the individual's regular employment with the United States employer. . . .

Accordingly, if employment away from home in a single location is realistically expected to last (and does in fact last) for one year or less, the employment will be treated as temporary in the absence of facts and circumstances indicating otherwise. If employment away from home in a single location is realistically expected to last for more than one year or there is no realistic expectation that the employment will last for one year or less, the employment will be treated as indefinite, regardless of whether it actually exceeds one year. If employment away from home in a single location initially is realistically expected to last for one year or less, but at some later date the employment is realistically expected to exceed one year, that employment will be treated as temporary (in the absence of facts and circumstances indicating otherwise) until the date that the taxpayer's realistic expectation changes.

In Situation 1, *A* realistically expected that the work in CI-2 would last only six months, and it did in fact last less than one year. Because *A* had always intended to return to CI-1 at the end of *A*'s employment in CI-2, CI-2 employment is temporary. Thus, *A*'s travel expenses paid or incurred in CI-2 are deductible.

In Situation 2, *B*'s employment in CI-2 is indefinite because *B* realistically expected that the work in CI-2 would last longer than one year, even though it actually lasted less than one year. Thus, *B*'s travel expenses paid or incurred in CI-2 are nondeductible.

In Situation 3, *C* at first realistically expected that the work in CI-2 would last only nine months. However, due to changed circumstances occurring after eight months, it was no longer realistic for *C* to expect that the employment in CI-2 would last for one year or less. Therefore, *C*'s employment in CI-2 is temporary for eight months, and indefinite for the remaining seven months. Thus, *C*'s travel expenses paid or incurred in CI-2 during the first eight months are deductible, but *C*'s travel expenses paid or incurred thereafter are nondeductible.

HOLDING

Under section 162(a)(2) of the Code, if employment away from home in a single location is realistically expected to last (and does in fact last) for one year or less, the employment is temporary in the absence of facts and circumstances indicating otherwise. If employment away from home in a single location is realistically expected to last for more than one year or there is no realistic expectation that the employment will last for one year or less, the employment is indefinite, regardless of whether it actually exceeds one year. If employment away from home in a single location initially is realistically expected to last for one year or less, but at some later date the employment is realistically expected to exceed one year, that employment will be treated as temporary (in the absence of facts and circumstances indicating otherwise) until the date that the taypayer's realistic expectation changes.

c. Travel Away from Home

Once a taxpayer's tax home has been identified, §162(a)(2) requires that the taxpayer must travel "away from home" for an expense to be deductible. In an attempt to define when a taxpayer is away from home, the Service has adopted the so-called "sleep or rest" rule. Of course, requiring taxpayers to be away from home for a long enough period of time to claim a deduction potentially conflicts with the "temporary or indefinite" rule which denies a deduction if the taxpayer is away from home for too long. The Supreme Court has ruled that it will defer to the Service in adopting this rule notwithstanding that, as will readily become apparent, "[a]ny rule in this area must make some rather arbitrary distinctions." United States v. Correll, 389 U.S. 299, 303 (1967).

BISSONNETTE v. COMMISSIONER
127 T.C. 124 (2006)

HAINES, JUDGE.

. . . [T]he issues for decision are . . . [w]hether Marc G. Bissonnette (petitioner) was "away from home" within the meaning of §162(a)(2) by virtue of his duties as a passenger ferryboat captain on turnaround voyages completed within twenty-four hours. . . .

FINDINGS OF FACT

. . . After petitioner graduated from high school in 1976, he was nominated to attend the Merchant Marine Academy by Senator Claiborne Pell. Petitioner graduated from the Academy in 1980 with a bachelor of science degree. For the next four to five years, petitioner operated deep sea vessels. He then returned to school to earn a master's degree in marine transportation at the University of Rhode Island in 1985. Petitioner has two oceans licenses. One permits him to be master of a ship up to 1,600 tons, the other to be a third mate on a ship without limitations as to the ship's tonnage.

. . . During the years at issue, petitioner was employed as the director of marine operations and senior captain for Clipper Navigation, Inc. (the company). The company owned and operated ferryboats that carried travelers on sea voyages throughout Puget Sound. The company's main office, terminal, and home port are in Seattle, Washington. The company paid petitioner an hourly rate. His duties included captaining the ferryboats named Victoria Clipper (Clipper), Victoria Clipper III (Clipper III), and the Lewis and Clark to Victoria, B.C., Canada (Victoria), and/or Friday Harbor, Washington, in the San Juan Islands (Friday Harbor). On all voyages, each ferryboat was maintained by a crew and a first mate. Each ferryboat carried up to 1,200 passengers, and as captain petitioner was responsible for the safety of all passengers. This responsibility required his full attention at all times. Any trouble or incident on the ferryboat during a voyage was his responsibility.

The voyages petitioner captained began and ended within the same twenty-four hour period at the company's home port in Seattle, Washington. He generally worked 15 to 17 hours a day for seven consecutive days with the following seven consecutive days off. . . . At the end of a workday, petitioner usually did not have time to return to his personal residence for dinner. On account of his early starting time and long commute to and from his residence, he remained in Seattle and slept on a cot stored aboard one of the company's vessels. The company did not require him to stay overnight, pay him during this time, nor provide him an allowance for meals or incidental expenses. Regardless, during overnight periods he helped out with maintenance problems and kept watch for bad weather. On one occasion, severe weather forced petitioner to move a ferryboat in the middle of the night. Usually half of the captains employed by the company stay overnight on the ferryboats.

. . . During each off-peak season petitioner typically captained the Clipper from Seattle to Victoria and back. The Clipper generally departed Seattle between 7:30 and 8:30 A.M., arrived in Victoria between 10:30 and 11 A.M., departed Victoria between 5:00 and 6:30 P.M., and arrived back in Seattle between 8:30 P.M. and 9:30 P.M. During the six to seven-hour layover the passengers would explore the city of Victoria.

The company provided a four-bedroom condominium in Victoria where the Clipper's crew rested during the layover. Because most of the crew were young and noisy, petitioner did not go to the condominium. Instead, he had lunch, swam for 30 minutes, and returned to the Clipper to sleep or rest for approximately four hours on a cot he stored on board. If the sleeping accommodations on the ferryboat had not been available, petitioner would have rented a room at a hotel.

Opinion

Petitioner argues his [expenses] are deductible because they were incurred while he was traveling away from home on business trips requiring sleep or rest. Section 262 provides that a taxpayer generally cannot deduct personal, living, or family expenses. However, §162(a)(2) allows taxpayers to deduct traveling expenses paid or incurred while away from home in the pursuit of a trade or business. Traveling expenses include travel fares, meals, lodging, and other expenses incident to travel. For purposes of §162, the term "home" generally means the taxpayer's principal place of employment and not where his or her personal residence is located.

A. Section 162(a)(2) Sleep or Rest Rule

The standard used to determine whether a taxpayer is "away from home" . . . is:

> If the nature of the taxpayer's employment is such that when away from home, during released time, it is reasonable for him to need and to obtain sleep or rest in order to meet the exigencies of his employment or the business demands of his employment, his expenditures (including incidental expenses, such as tips) for the purpose of obtaining sleep or rest are deductible traveling expenses under §162(a)(2). . . .

This standard is commonly referred to as the "sleep or rest rule."

. . . [T]he rest period contemplated by the sleep or rest rule . . . normally involves a rest of sufficient duration to cause an increase in expenses. A brief rest period which "anyone can, at any time, without special arrangement and without special expense, take in his own automobile or office" does not qualify. The Court [has] disallowed expenses for meals claimed by a taxpayer on one-day business trips that lasted between 16 and 19 hours during which the taxpayer rested briefly once or twice in his automobile.

If the nature of petitioner's employment was such that when away from home, during released time, it was reasonable for him to need and to obtain sleep or rest in order to meet the exigencies or business demands of his employment, his expenses for this purpose would be traveling expenses. However, the released time must be of a sufficient duration that it would ordinarily be related to a significant increase in expenses.

B. PEAK TRAVEL SEASON

. . . In 2001 and 2002, during peak-season, petitioner's layovers in Victoria and Friday Harbor never exceeded an hour, and he did not produce evidence showing he rested during that time. Petitioner also did not show he rested during the five-hour layover in Friday Harbor during peak-season in 2003. Instead, petitioner testified that during this layover he was operating the ferryboat. Even though petitioner testified he did sleep or rest while another captain took command of the ferryboat, he did not produce evidence showing the rest period was part of a layover (released time) or was of sufficient duration that it caused him to incur a significant increase in expenses. . . . Therefore, the Court finds petitioner was not away from home during peak-season Victoria/Friday Harbor runs in 2001 and 2002 and the Friday Harbor runs in 2003.

C. OFF-PEAK TRAVEL SEASON

Respondent . . . argues that petitioner is not entitled to a deduction for the expenses incurred during the off-peak-season six to seven-hour layovers in Victoria because the layovers were solely the result of scheduling rather than petitioner's need for sleep or rest.

However, the proper inquiry is into the nature of petitioner's employment and his need for sleep or rest, not whether a layover was the result of scheduling. The factors to consider in determining whether petitioner needed sleep or rest include his age, his physical condition, the length of his workday, and the importance of being alert so that he could carry out his job's responsibilities without fear of injury to others. These factors are applied against the background of petitioner's experience in his employment and the practices and customs of similarly situated individuals.

Petitioner's background is impressive. After attending the Merchant Marine Academy, he earned a master's degree in marine transportation, and he has been employed in this field for over 25 years. In the years at issue, petitioner was the director of marine operations and senior captain for the company. His workday lasted on average 15 to 17 hours including a six to seven-hour layover in Victoria during off-peak season. He was responsible for his crew and the safety of up to

1,200 passengers during all voyages. Because of possible extreme weather conditions, high sea levels, log tows, and other obstacles in the ocean, petitioner as captain had to give his full attention at all times, and any trouble or incident on the ferryboat was his responsibility. Petitioner also needed to consider that his workday could be significantly lengthened on account of any of the above situations. As a result, petitioner's job was very demanding.

Considering the facts, this Court finds it was reasonable for petitioner to obtain sleep or rest in order to meet the exigencies and business demands of his employment. Further, the released time of six to seven hours during the Victoria voyage was sufficient in duration that it would normally be related to an increase in expenses. Accordingly, petitioner was "away from home" for purposes of section 162(a)(2).

d. Multiple Homes

As noted above, it is not only possible to have a tax home separate from one's personal home if business needs do not require the maintaining of two homes, it is also possible to have no tax home if business needs do not necessitate maintaining a single home. What if a taxpayer's job requires maintaining two homes in different locations? Similarly, what if a taxpayer engages in more than one unrelated business, but in different locations and each requires a home? If a taxpayer had only one tax home, travel to the other job would presumably be fully deductible as "away from home" notwithstanding that travel was not necessitated by the first job but rather to engage in the second, unrelated, job. Conversely, how could a taxpayer have more than one tax home if the policy of the tax home doctrine is, according to the Supreme Court, to make arbitrary bright line distinctions so as to ease the administration of the tax laws? See *Corell*, 389 U.S. at 303.

The courts were forced to confront this issue in a series of related cases involving Northwest Airlines mechanics. The mechanics for Northwest Airlines, based in Minneapolis, were laid off, but certain senior mechanics could elect to work temporarily at other airports, as needed. The electing senior mechanics spent significant time away from Minneapolis at other airports, including those in Washington, New York, and Detroit, while their families remained in Minneapolis. Further complicating the issue, many of these employees took other part-time jobs in Minneapolis. Do these mechanics have none, one, two, or more tax homes?

WILBERT v. COMMISSIONER
553 F.3d 544 (7th Cir. 2009)

Posner, Circuit Judge.

The question presented by this appeal is whether an employee who uses "bumping" rights to avoid or postpone losing his job can deduct the living expenses that he incurs when he finds himself working far from home as a result of exercising those rights. The Tax Court ruled against the taxpayer, This is one of a number of largely identical cases in the Tax Court . . . all brought by mechanics formerly employed by Northwest Airlines, like Wilbert, and all resolved against the taxpayer. But this seems the first case to be appealed.

Hired by Northwest in 1996, Wilbert worked for the airline at the Minneapolis airport for some years. He lived with his wife in Hudson, Wisconsin, across the Mississippi River from Minneapolis. Hudson is a suburb of Minneapolis, roughly 25 miles from the airport.

Facing financial pressures and a decline in airline traffic in the wake of the terrorist attacks of September 11, 2001, Northwest laid off many employees, including, in April 2003, Wilbert. But Northwest's mechanics each had a right to bump a more junior mechanic employed by the airline, that is, to take his job. Wilbert was able to bump a mechanic who worked for the airline in Chicago, but he worked there for only a few days before being bumped by a more senior mechanic. A few days later he was able to bump a mechanic in Anchorage, Alaska, and he worked there for three weeks before being himself bumped. He was soon able to bump a mechanic who worked in New York, at LaGuardia Airport, but he worked there for only a week before he was bumped again. At this point, he had exhausted his bumping rights. But for reasons that the parties have not explained, three weeks later the airline hired him back, outside the bumping system, to fill an interim position (maximum nine months) in Anchorage. He occupied that position for several months before being laid off again, this time for good. At no point in his hegira did he have realistic prospects of resuming work for Northwest in Minneapolis. He now lives in a Chicago suburb and works for Federal Express at O'Hare Airport. He sells real estate on the side (self-employed), as he did when he lived in Minneapolis, but his income from his real estate business there was only $2,000 in 2003, the relevant tax year, and he did not actually receive the money (a commission) until the following year.

He did not sell or rent his home in Hudson, where his wife continued to live, while working intermittently in 2003. Because he was working too far from home to be able to live there, he incurred living expenses (amounting to almost $20,000) that he would not have incurred had he remained working in Minneapolis, and those are the expenses he deducted from the taxable income shown on his 2003 return.

The Internal Revenue Code allows the deduction, as part of "the ordinary and necessary expenses . . . incurred during the taxable year in carrying on any trade or business," of "traveling expenses . . . *while [the taxpayer is] away from home* in the pursuit of a trade or business." 26 U.S.C. §162(a)(2) (emphasis added). There is an exception for "personal, living, or family expenses." §262(a). The phrase we have italicized is critical. It is by an interpretation of that phrase that commuting expenses are disallowed because of "a natural reluctance . . . to lighten the tax burden of people who have the good fortune to interweave work with consumption. To allow a deduction for commuting would confer a windfall on people who live in the suburbs and commute to work in the cities." Moss v. Commissioner, 758 F.2d 211, 212 (7th Cir.1985). The length of the commute is thus irrelevant. If Wilbert had had a permanent job in Anchorage but decided to retain his home in Minneapolis and return there on weekends and during the week live in a truck stop in Wasilla, Alaska, he could not have deducted from his taxable income the expense of traveling to and fro between Minnesota and Alaska or his room and board in

Wasilla. (We ignore for the moment the possibility that Mrs. Wilbert had a job in Minneapolis, and if so its relevance.)

Similarly, he could not have deducted his traveling expenses if he had had no home separate from the places he traveled to — if he had been, in the language of the cases, an "itinerant" worker, for then he would never have been "away from home" on his travels. He would have been like someone whose only residence is a recreational vehicle, or a truck driver who lives in the cab of his truck, or an itinerant professional musician, [who] traveled from city to city performing, solo, in various hotel dining rooms and cocktail lounges. These engagements varied in duration from three to four weeks, or as long as seven or eight months. His wife and child traveled and lived with taxpayer wherever he was situated.

With our hypothetical Wilbert the long-distance commuter, compare a lawyer whose home and office are both in Minneapolis but who has an international practice and as a result spends more time on the road than he does at home. Nevertheless he can deduct his traveling expenses. His work requires him to maintain a home within normal commuting distance of Minneapolis because that is where his office is, but his work also requires him to travel, and the expenses he incurs in traveling are necessary to his work and he cannot offset them by relocating his residence to the places to which he travels because he has to maintain a home near his office. And likewise if, as in Andrews v. Commissioner, 931 F.2d 132 (1st Cir.1991), the taxpayer has to make such frequent trips to a particular site that it is more economical for him to rent or buy a second residence, at that site, than to live there in a hotel.

Wilbert's case falls in between our two hypothetical cases. Unlike the lawyer, he did not have to live near Minneapolis after the initial layoff because he had no work there (ignoring for the moment his real estate business). But unlike the imaginary Wilbert who has a permanent job in Alaska and so could readily relocate his home there, the real Wilbert had jobs of indefinite, unpredictable duration in Alaska (and Chicago, and New York). It would hardly have been realistic to expect him to pull up stakes and move to Anchorage and then to Chicago and then to New York and then back to Anchorage. Remember that his first stint after the initial layoff lasted only days, his second only weeks, and the third only one week. His situation was unlike that of the employee of a New York firm who, if he chooses to live in Scarsdale rather than on Fifth Avenue, is forbidden to deduct from his taxable income the commuting expense that he incurs by virtue of his choice; it is a personal choice — suburban over urban living — rather than anything necessitated by his job.

The Tax Court, with some judicial support, has tried to resolve cases such as this by asking whether the taxpayer's work away from home is "temporary" or "indefinite," and allowing the deduction of traveling expenses only if it is the former. The Internal Revenue Code does not explicitly adopt the distinction . . .

The problem with the Tax Court's distinction is that work can be, and usually is, both temporary and indefinite, as in our lawyer example. A lawsuit he is trying in London might settle on the second day, or last a month; his sojourn away from his office will therefore be both temporary and indefinite. Indeed all work is indefinite and much "permanent" work is really temporary. An academic lawyer might accept a five-year appointment as an assistant professor with every expectation of obtaining tenure at the end of that period at that or another law school; yet one would not describe him as a "temporary" employee even if he left after six months and thus was not barred from claiming temporary status by the one-year rule. Our imaginary Wilbert who has a permanent job in Anchorage but is reluctant to move there from Minneapolis might argue (at least until he had worked a year, the statutory cutoff for "temporary" work) that no job is "permanent" — he might be fired, or he might harbor realistic hopes of getting a better job back in Minneapolis. That possibility would not permit him to deduct the expense of commuting from Minnesota to Alaska.

So "temporary versus indefinite" does not work well as a test of deductibility and neither does "personal choice versus reasonable response to the employment situation," tempting as the latter formula is because of its realism. If no reasonable person would relocate to his new place of work because of uncertainty about the duration of the new job, his choice to stay where he is, unlike a choice to commute from a suburb to the city in which one's office is located rather than live in the city, is not an optional personal choice like deciding to stay at a Four Seasons or a Ritz Carlton, but a choice forced by circumstances. Wilbert when first notified that he was being laid off could foresee a series of temporary jobs all across the country and not even limited, as we know, to the lower 48 states, and the costs of moving his home to the location of each temporary job would have been prohibitive. It would have meant moving four times in one year on a mechanic's salary to cities hundreds or (in the case of Anchorage versus Minneapolis, Chicago, or New York) thousands of miles apart.

The problem with a test that focuses on the reasonableness of the taxpayer's decision not to move is that it is bound to prove nebulous in application. For it just asks the taxpayer to give a good reason for not moving his home when he gets a job in a different place, and if he gave a good reason then his traveling expenses would be deductible as the product of a reasonable balancing of personal and business considerations. In the oft-cited case of Hantzis v. Commissioner, 638 F.2d 248 (1st Cir.1981), the question was whether a law student who lived in Boston with her husband during the school year could deduct her traveling expenses when she took a summer job in New York. Given the temporary nature of the job, it made perfectly good sense for her to retain her home in Boston and just camp out, as it were, in New York. What persuaded the court to reject the deduction was that she had no business reason to retain the house in Boston. Stated differently, she had no business reason to be living in two places at once, unlike the lawyer in our example. And so the expenses she incurred living in New York could not be thought "ordinary and necessary expenses . . . incurred . . . in carrying on any trade or business."

If this seems rather a mechanical reading of the statute, it has the support not only of the influential precedent of Hantzis but also of the even more influential precedent of Commissioner v. Flowers, 326 U.S. 465, 474, (1946), where the Supreme Court said that "the exigencies of business rather than the personal conveniences and necessities of the traveler must be the motivating factors" in the decision to travel. The "business exigencies" rule, though harsh, is supported by compelling considerations of administrability. To apply a test of reasonableness the Internal Revenue Service would first have to decide whether the taxpayer should have moved to his new place of work. This might require answering such questions as whether the schools in the area of his new job were far worse than those his children currently attend, whether his elderly parents live near his existing home and require his attention, and whether his children have psychological problems that make it difficult for them to find new friends. Were it decided that it was reasonable for the taxpayer to stay put, it would then become necessary to determine whether the expenses he incurred in traveling to and from his various places of work for home visits had been reasonable—whether in other words such commutes, in point of frequency, were "ordinary and necessary" business expenses. The Internal Revenue Service would have to establish norms of reasonable home visits that presumably would vary with such things as distance and how many of the taxpayer's children were living at home and how old they were.

We are sympathetic to Wilbert's plight and recognize the artificiality of supposing that, as the government argues, he made merely a personal choice to "commute" from Minneapolis to Anchorage, and Chicago, and New York, as if Minneapolis were a suburb of those cities. But the statutory language, the precedents, and the considerations of administrability that we have emphasized persuade us to reject the test of reasonableness. The "temporary versus indefinite" test is no better, so we fall back on the rule of *Flowers* and *Hantzis* that unless the taxpayer has a business rather than a personal reason to be living in two places he cannot deduct his traveling expenses if he decides not to move. Indeed, Wilbert's situation is really no different from the common case of the construction worker who works at different sites throughout the country, never certain how long each stint will last and reluctant therefore to relocate his home. The construction worker loses, as must Wilbert.

We might well have a different case if Wilbert had had a firm, justified expectation of being restored to his job at the Minneapolis airport within a short time of his initial layoff. Suppose the airline had said to him, "We must lay you off, but you will be able to bump a less senior employee in Anchorage for a few weeks, and we are confident that by then, given your seniority, you will be able to return to Minneapolis." His situation would then be comparable to that of a Minneapolis lawyer ordered by his senior partner to spend the next month trying a case in Anchorage. But that is not this case.

Wilbert has another string to his bow, however, arguing that he had two businesses, not one, the other being the sale of real estate, and that because that business was centered in Minneapolis he had a business reason to live near there. This would be a good argument if selling real estate were his main business. But obviously it is not, or at least was not in 2003, when his total income (and in an accrual rather than a cash sense) from selling real estate was only $2,000.

As explained in *Andrews*, "The guiding policy must be that the taxpayer is reasonably expected to locate his 'home,' for tax purposes, at his 'major post of duty' so as to minimize the amount of business travel away from home that is required; a decision to do otherwise is motivated not by business necessity but by personal considerations, and should not give rise to greater business travel deductions." 931 F.2d at 138. If Wilbert had had to travel back to Minneapolis from his new tax "homes" from time to time in order to attend to his real estate business, the travel expense (if the business was really the reason for the travel home), and conceivably even some of his living expenses at his home (his "secondary" home, in a tax sense, since his primary home for tax purposes would follow his work), might have been deductible, just as his expenses for the office equipment that he purchased in his real estate business were. But he does not argue for such a deduction.

For completeness we note that if Wilbert's wife had a business in Minneapolis, this would make it all the more reasonable for Wilbert not to move away from Minneapolis. But it would not permit him to deduct his traveling expenses, because his decision to live with his wife (if only on occasional weekends) would (setting aside any considerations relating to his real estate sideline) be a personal rather than a business decision. Hantzis v. Commissioner, supra, 638 F.2d at 254 and n. 11 ("in this respect, Mr. and Mrs. Hantzis' situation is analogous to cases involving spouses with careers in different locations. Each must independently satisfy the requirement that deductions taken for travel expenses incurred in the pursuit of a trade or business arise while he or she is away from home"). . . .

Affirmed.

Problem

6-14. Sue and Stanley Summers live in Houston, Texas. Stanley, a graduate student in chemical engineering, drives a cab on weekends to supplement Sue's salary as a computer programmer. Stanley accepted a summer job with a petroleum company located in Dallas. Sue remained in Houston and Stanley commuted on weekends, renting an apartment in Dallas for the summer.

    a. Can Stanley deduct either his apartment rental or commuting expenses?

    b. What result in *a* if he drives one shift for the cab company each weekend he returns to Houston?

    c. Assume that the petroleum company has offices in both Dallas and Houston. If Stanley was hired to work in Dallas because the Houston operation did not have a chemical engineering department, is he entitled to a travel expense deduction?

    d. What result in *c* if both facilities chemical engineering students during the summer and the company placed Stanley in its Dallas office because it was short-staffed?

    e. What result in *c* if Stanley brings work home with him every weekend? What if he frequently attends weekend meetings at the Houston office?

    f. What result if Sue took a leave of absence from her job and obtained a programming position in Dallas for the summer?

e. Exceptions for Specific Mixed Business/Pleasure Travel

The deductibility of travel expenses incurred for business trips motivated by both personal and business purposes is a recurring problem. The §162 Regulations provide that on trips in which the taxpayer engages in both business and personal activities, transportation costs to and from the destination will be deductible only if the *primary purpose* of the trip is business. Thus, if the purpose for the taxpayer's trip is primarily personal, no deduction will be allowed for transportation costs, even though the taxpayer engages in business activities at the destination. In either case, however, a deduction may be allowed for travel expenses other than transportation costs (such as food, subject to the 50-percent limitation of §274(n), and lodging) on days devoted to business. Reg. §1.162-2(b)(1).

To illustrate, assume a taxpayer travels from her home in Dallas to a business meeting in Phoenix on Monday. The taxpayer spends all day Monday, Tuesday, and Wednesday in business meetings directly related to the taxpayer's trade or business. Instead of returning home on Wednesday evening after the conclusion of business, the taxpayer remains in Phoenix until Friday to swim and play golf. In this case, if the taxpayer's primary purpose for the trip is business, the taxpayer is permitted to deduct transportation expenses for travel between Dallas and Phoenix and those food, lodging, and other expenses that are properly allocable to Monday, Tuesday, and Wednesday.

On the other hand, if the taxpayer decided to extend her stay through the weekend and return home on Sunday and the primary purpose of the trip is pleasure, the taxpayer is not permitted a deduction for transportation costs. Nevertheless, she is still entitled to deduct expenses for meals and lodging incurred on Monday through Wednesday, subject to the limitations of §274(n). The Regulations state that the amount of time spent on business versus pleasure is an important factor in determining the primary purpose of the trip, but the relative-time test is not always dispositive of the issue. The determination of the primary purpose of travel is to be made on the basis of all the facts and circumstances. Reg. §1.162-2(b)(2).

Foreign travel. Where mixed business and personal travel takes place outside the United States, the additional requirements of §274(c) may apply to further restrict the §162(a)(2) travel expense deductions. Under §274(c), transportation costs incurred for foreign business travel are to be allocated by reference to the number of days devoted to business and personal activities. For example, assume that the taxpayer paid $1,000 for airfare to travel to Paris for ten days. If three days were spent on personal sightseeing, with seven days devoted to business activities, then $700 of the $1,000 plane fare is deductible. For purposes of §274, a day is devoted to business if the taxpayer's principal activity during the hours normally appropriate for business activity is, in fact, related to the taxpayer's trade or business. In addition, travel days are considered to be business days if the taxpayer can establish that he was traveling in pursuit of trade or business. Reg. §1.274-4(d)(2)(i).

Before the §274 limitation applies, the travel expenses must first meet the requirements of §162 (the primary purpose of the trip must be business). If §162 is not satisfied, then none of the transportation costs are deductible. As a practical matter, the restriction of §274(c) applies only to limit the deduction of transportation costs because, even if §274(c) applies, the taxpayer may deduct the meals, subject to the 50-percent limitation of §274(n) and lodging expenses allocable to days devoted to business. Moreover, there are two primary exceptions to the application of §274(c) to foreign travel: first, §274(c) applies only if the trip outside the United States exceeds one week (the first day of travel will not be counted, but the day on which travel ends will be considered, Reg. §1.274-4(c); and second, §274(c) applies only if 25 percent or more of the time outside the United States is devoted to nonbusiness activity.

Spousal travel on business trips. Taxpayers often have their spouses accompany them on business trips and attempt to deduct the spouses' traveling expenses as a business deduction. Regulation §1.162-2(c) provides that for a deduction to be permitted for a spouse's traveling expenses, the taxpayer must show that the spouse's presence on the trip served a bona fide business purpose. In general, the performance of incidental services by the accompanying spouse will not satisfy the bona fide business purpose requirement.

Despite the Service's obvious concern, taxpayers have successfully established valid business purposes for the spouse's travel with the taxpayer on business. For example, in United States v. Disney, 413 F.2d 783 (9th Cir. 1969), the taxpayer, Roy Disney, successfully argued that his wife fulfilled a valid business purpose by accompanying him on several overseas trips. Disney was president and chairman of the board of Walt Disney Productions, a publicly held company engaged in producing "family-type" entertainment. Disney's position required him to travel in pursuit of new business and to inspect the operations of the company's fifty-eight foreign subsidiaries, representatives, and licensees.

Although Mrs. Disney did not perform any duties of a "business office nature" while on these trips, she did accompany her husband to many social events that her husband felt obligated to attend for business reasons. Disney argued, and the trial court found, that the "company . . . virtually insisted on the [wife's] presence on trips taken by executives where it is believed their presence would enhance the company's 'image' or would otherwise promote its interest." Id. at 785. In allowing the deduction, the appellate court found that Disney was conforming with established company policy and that Mrs. Disney's travel met the bona fide business purpose requirement. Recognizing that a different factual setting might require a different result, the court formulated the following test for determining whether a deduction should be allowed for a spouse's traveling expenses: "The critical inquiries are whether the *dominant* purpose of the trip was to serve her husband's business purpose in making the trip and whether she actually spent a *substantial* amount of her time in assisting her husband in fulfilling that purpose." Id. at 788 (emphasis added).

In 1993, Congress amended §274(m) in an attempt to end much of the controversy concerning such travel expenses. Section 274(m)(3) provides that no deduction is allowed for travel expenses of a spouse, dependent, or other individual who accompanies the taxpayer on business travel unless a three-part test is satisfied. He or she must be an employee of the taxpayer, the travel must be for a bona fide business purpose, *and* the expenses must be otherwise deductible.

If a spouse's presence does not satisfy the requirements of §274(m)(3), the additional expenses attributable to the spouse are nondeductible personal expenses. In such cases, in computing deductible lodging expenses, the amount by which the total lodging expenses is increased by the spouse's presence is not deductible. Rev. Rul. 56-168, 1956-1 C.B. 93. For example, assume that a taxpayer is traveling on business and that the rate for a hotel room is $125 per night single occupancy and $175 per night for double occupancy. If the taxpayer is traveling alone, the full cost of the single lodging, $125 per night, is deductible. If, however, the taxpayer's spouse also goes on the trip for nonbusiness, personal reasons, $125 per night would still be allowed as a deduction, and the $50 per night increment above the single occupancy rate would be nondeductible. Moreover, no part of the spouse's meals would be deductible.

Problem

6-15. Arthur Ames is president and general manager of Silk, Inc., a California corporation that manufactures designer clothing for women. Ames frequently travels to fashion centers such as New York, London, Paris, and Rome, where he promotes Silk's line among exclusive boutiques. In the current year, Ames made the following business-related trips.

a. Ames flew from California to Phoenix at 8 A.M. and returned home that evening at 9 P.M. Is he entitled to deduct any portion of his $500 first-class airfare? Can he deduct the $10 he spent for lunch and the $30 he spent for dinner in Phoenix?

b. Ames flew from California to New York on the evening of Monday, February 1, and returned home on the morning of Wednesday, February 10. The first-class ticket cost $2,000, and he spent $50 per day for meals and $150 per day for lodging.

    1. What are the tax consequences to Ames if he spent six days in all-day business meetings and two days sightseeing while in New York?

    2. What result in *1* if the days spent sightseeing were Saturday and Sunday, days during which his customers do not conduct business?

    3. What result if he had spent six days sightseeing and two days in business meetings?

    4. What result in *2* if the trip had been to Paris instead of New York?

    5. What result in *3* if the trip had been to Paris?

c. Ames's wife, a former model, frequently accompanies him on business trips. She acts as his hostess at business functions and wears Silk's clothing at these functions.

    1. Is Ames entitled to a deduction for his wife's travel expenses for a trip to New York during which they entertained nightly, taking prospective distributors and their spouses to dinner?

    2. What if Ames had paid his wife a fee for such activity?

    3. What if they were in New York for ten days but entertained only once?

    4. If Ames's deduction of his wife's travel expenses is disallowed, how will his lodging expense deduction be affected if the cost of a double room is $120 per night, contrasted with the rate of $95 for a single room?

2. Education Expenses

Code: §§162; 274(h), (m)(2), (n)
Regulations: §§1.162-2(d); 1.162-5

Although the general requirements of §162(a) control the deduction of business-related educational expenses, such expenses must also satisfy additional requirements listed in the Regulations. Pursuant to Regulation §1.162-5(a), educational expenses are deductible as ordinary and necessary business expenses only if the education either (1) maintains or improves skills required by the taxpayer's employment or other trade or business or (2) meets requirements imposed by the employer, or applicable law or regulations, as a condition of retaining the taxpayer's established employment relationship, status, or rate of compensation. Even if an expense meets one of these requirements, a deduction will be disallowed if the expense is incurred to (1) meet the minimum educational requirements of the taxpayer's employment or other trade or business or (2) is part of a program of study qualifying the taxpayer for a new trade or business. Reg. §1.162-5(b).

a. Education versus Personal Expenses

Taxpayers sometimes attempt to deduct personal expenses under the guise of business-related educational expenses. These schemes often arise in the context of seminars and conventions and in attempts to convert vacations into deductible business trips.

Conventions are specifically addressed by the Regulations, which dictate a facts and circumstances test focusing on whether a "sufficient relationship" exists between the convention attended and the taxpayer's trade or business. Reg. §1.162-2(d). Two standards have been suggested for determining deductibility of these convention costs under the Regulations' sufficient relationship test: the "referral standard" and the "agenda standard." Under the referral standard, the taxpayer claims deductibility for activities that generate business (future clients, business connections, and so forth). The agenda standard focuses on the relationship of the agenda for the seminar or conference to the taxpayer's trade or business, both as to subject matter and time allotted to actual business. The Service uses the agenda standard, arguably the sounder of the two from a policy standpoint, given its objectivity.

Even if convention expenses qualify for deduction, travel expenses should still be tested separately under the primarily related test. Reg. §1.162-2(b)(2). The Regulation qualifies as deductions only expenses for meals, lodging, registration, and materials — expenses that can be characterized as education expenses under Regulation §1.162-5. With regard to otherwise deductible expenditures for meals, the limitations of §274(k) and (n) must be confronted. In the international context, stricter rules for deductibility are established by §274(h).

Recall *McCann* from Chapter 2, which involved taxpayers who attended an employer-financed insurance seminar held at a Las Vegas resort. After unsuccessfully arguing that the trip did not constitute income, the McCanns attempted to claim the travel and other expenses associated with their attendance at the seminar as educational expenses deductible as ordinary and necessary business expenses. The court found that because the employer's promotion of the seminar emphasized the pleasure aspects of the trip and because Mrs. McCann, the insurance agent, attended only one two-hour business session that was of any educational value to her, "the element of a business purpose . . . was de minimis." Id.

Two methods apparently are accepted for reporting reimbursement for business expenses. Under one method, the taxpayer is required to include in gross income the full amount of the reimbursement but is then permitted to offset this income by deducting expenses, only if the activity was deductible under §162. By contrast, the Regulations (§1.162-17) provide for netting reimbursement and authorized expenses together. Thus, it appears that a taxpayer can choose between either method for reporting such business expenses. Of course, the pitfall in this area is that the reimbursement may be offset or netted only to the extent that the reimbursed expense is deductible under §162.

Prior to 1986, the deduction of "travel as education" expenses in the context of a family vacation was litigated regularly. See Hilt v. Commissioner, T.C. Memo 1981-672 (taxpayers failed to provide evidence proving a direct relationship between travel to Hawaii and the enhancement of their skills as elementary school teachers) and Reg. §1.162-5(d). Notwithstanding the fact that the Service and the courts frequently intervened to preclude the deduction of such expenditures, Congress enacted §274(m)(2) to disallow any deduction for travel as a form of education.

> Under the bill, no deduction is allowed for travel as a form of education. This rule applies when a travel deduction would otherwise be allowable only on the ground that the travel itself serves educational purposes (for example, in the case of a teacher of French who travels to France in order to maintain general familiarity with the French language and culture). This disallowance rule does not apply when a deduction is claimed with respect to travel that is a necessary adjunct to engaging in an activity that gives rise to a business deduction relating to education (for example, where a scholar of French literature travels to Paris in order to do specific library research that cannot be done elsewhere, or to take courses that are offered only at the Sorbonne, in circumstances such that the nontravel research or course costs are deductible).

S. Rep. No. 313, 99th Cong., 2d Sess. 75 (1986).

Problems

6-16. Thomas Moots, a personal injury lawyer in Cincinnati, Ohio, experiencing a decline in business, attended three conventions during the year. In March, he attended the Ohio Home Economics Teachers Convention in Columbus, spending $200 on transportation, $30 on meals, $120 on lodging, and $50 on the convention registration fee. In June, he attended the three-day State Bar convention in Cleveland and after its conclusion stayed for another four days to experience the cultural highlights of Cleveland. Transportation expenses totaled $300, room was $125 a day, meals were $50 a day, and the convention registration fee was $80. Finally, in August, Moots attended the four-day American Bar Association (ABA) annual meeting in London, England, spending $800 for transportation, $175 a day for lodging, $75 a day for meals, and $110 on convention registration.
> a. What expenses, if any, are deductible for the Home Economics convention?
> b. What expenses, if any, are deductible for the State Bar convention?
> c. What expenses, if any, are deductible for the ABA convention?

6-17. Dolores Matheson, a certified public accountant practicing in Iowa City, Iowa, has religiously attended the annual meeting of Iowa CPAs, which has been held in various communities throughout Iowa. This year, the governing board decided to hold the annual meeting (scheduled for December 11 through 15) in Honolulu, Hawaii. What costs, if any, for transportation, meals, lodging, convention registration, and miscellaneous items qualify for deductions? What should Matheson do in order to maximize any available deductions arising from her attendance?

6-18. Pamela Ryan is a high school anthropology teacher. In the summer, she and her husband went to Africa for a month. They avoided major cities and tourist areas and remained exclusively in the provinces where Ryan could observe anthropological discoveries. What costs, if any, are deductible?

b. Minimum Education Requirements

The Regulations do not allow deductions for educational expenses that enable the taxpayer to meet the "minimum educational requirements for qualification" in a trade or business. Reg. §1.162-5(b).

An example of the scope of this limitation is found in Sharon v. Commissioner, 591 F.2d 1273 (9th Cir. 1978). In *Sharon*, the taxpayer was a California tax lawyer who had worked for the Service. His claim was in the alternative: that the costs of his college education, legal education, bar review courses, bar exam fees, and court-admittance fees should be deductible as business expenses or that he should be permitted to amortize them as costs of obtaining a capital asset — that is, his license to practice law. The court held that his education and bar review expenses fulfilled minimum educational requirements and thus were neither deductible nor amortizable. However, the court did allow the amortization of the taxpayer's bar and court-admittance fees, apparently agreeing that his license to practice law was a capital asset (though the court did not discuss the useful life of the asset).

In the case that follows, also involving a tax lawyer, the Tax Court considered the deductibility of expenses incurred in obtaining a master of law degree in taxation.

WASSENAAR v. COMMISSIONER
72 T.C. 1195 (1980)

Simpson, J.

... The [issue] for decision [is]: Whether the petitioner may deduct as an ordinary and necessary business expense the cost of his master of law degree in taxation. ...

The petitioner graduated from Wayne State University Law School (Wayne State) in Detroit, Mich., in June 1972. He served on law review while at Wayne State in both 1971 and 1972, and although he was a member of the board of editors, his services were no different from those of any other law review member. His duties included editing legal material, checking sources of legal articles, and writing legal articles. He received compensation for such services from Wayne State in the amounts of $845 in 1971 and $1,314 in 1972.

From June to September 1971, the petitioner worked for the law firm of Warner, Norcross & Judd (Warner firm). He prepared legal memorandums, drafted legal documents, and consulted with clients in the presence of an attorney from the firm. He received $2,920 from the Warner firm as compensation for his services that summer.

The petitioner was not employed during the summer following his graduation from law school; instead, he prepared for the Michigan bar, which he took in July 1972. However, he continued to search for employment with a law firm during such period. In October 1972, he passed the bar exam, but he was not formally admitted to the Michigan bar until May of 1973.

In September 1972, the petitioner began courses in the graduate law program in taxation at New York University (NYU), and he graduated with a masters degree in taxation in May 1973. During 1973, he incurred the following expenses in connection with his studies at NYU:

Travel	$ 96
Meals and lodging	1,075
Auto expenses	64
Tuition and books	1,450
Miscellaneous expenses	96
Total	$2,781

. . . Following his graduation from NYU, the petitioner returned to Detroit to commence employment with the law firm of Miller, Canfield, Paddock & Stone (Miller firm). . . .

The first issue for decision is whether the petitioner may deduct as an ordinary and necessary expense incurred in his trade or business the expense for tuition, books, meals, lodging, and other miscellaneous items paid by him while he obtained his masters degree in taxation. . . .

Section 162(a) allows a deduction for all the ordinary and necessary expenses of carrying on a trade or business, including amounts expended for education. Deductible educational expenses under section 162(a) may include expenditures for tuition and books as well as amounts for travel and meals and lodging while the taxpayer is away from home. (Sec. 1.162-5(e)(1), Income Tax Regs.) Section 1.162-5(a)(1), Income Tax Regs., expressly allows a deduction for those educational expenditures which maintain or improve skills "required by the individual in his employment or other trade or business." . . .

The petitioner artfully attempts to characterize his trade or business as "analyzing and solving legal problems for compensation," and he received compensation for the performance of such services. Nevertheless, it is clear that the petitioner's intended trade or business at the time he attended NYU was that of an attorney, with an emphasis on the law of taxation. We observe that he enrolled in the masters in taxation program at NYU directly from law school, and there was thus an uninterrupted continuity in his legal education. Although the work the petitioner performed before his graduation from law school and NYU was admittedly of a legal nature, such work in no way constituted his being engaged in the practice of law. Before his admission to the bar in May of 1973, he was not authorized to practice law as an attorney. Therefore, his expenses at NYU were not incident to the trade or business of practicing law, and thus, he was not maintaining or improving the skills of that profession within the purview of section 1.162-5(a)(1).

Moreover, although the petitioner completed the requirements for admission to the bar in 1972, he was not formally admitted until May of 1973, and until that time, he could not engage in the practice of law. It is a well-established principle that being a member in good standing of a profession is not tantamount to *carrying on* that profession for the purpose of section 162(a).

Because the petitioner had not practiced law as an attorney before his attendance at NYU, his situation is not analogous to that of other professionals who have been allowed educational expense deductions under section 162(a). In such cases, the taxpayer was already firmly established in his profession and was truly taking courses or attending a seminar for the purpose of maintaining or improving the skills of his profession. See Coughlin v. Commissioner, 203 F.2d 307 (2d Cir. 1953), revg. and remanding 18 T.C. 528 (1952) (attorney allowed business deduction for expenses incurred in attending NYU Tax Institute seminar); Bistline v. United States, 145 F. Supp. 802 (E.D. Idaho 1956), affd. per curiam on another issue 260 F.2d 80 (9th Cir. 1958) (attorney allowed a business deduction for expenses incurred in attending 2-week course in Federal taxation at the Practising Law Institute); Watson v. Commissioner, 31 T.C. 1014 (1959) (doctor specializing in internal medicine allowed deduction under earlier regulations for courses in psychiatry since such courses helped him to better understand psychosomatic illnesses); Furner v. Commissioner, 393 F.2d 292 (7th Cir. 1968), revg. 47 T.C. 165 (1966) (teacher who took year off to secure masters degree was still carrying on a trade or business and allowed to deduct educational expenses); see also sec. 1.162-5(c), Income Tax Regs.

In addition, the petitioner is also denied a deduction for his expenses at NYU by section 1.162-5(b)(3), Income Tax Regs., which provides that educational expenses are not deductible if the education "is part of a program of study being pursued by him which will lead to qualifying him in a new trade or business." The petitioner's attendance at NYU was part of his "program of study" of becoming a lawyer, a trade or business in which he was not previously engaged before his attendance there. After his admission to the bar in May of 1973 and his completion of the program at NYU, he was authorized to and began the practice of law, a wholly different trade or business from any in which he had been previously engaged.

The petitioner is also not entitled to an educational expense deduction on the theory that he was engaged in the trade or business of "rendering his services to employers for compensation." It is a well-established principle that educational expenses must bear a direct and proximate relation to the taxpayer's trade or business. In Carroll v. Commissioner, 51 T.C. at 215, this Court stated that it is not sufficient that "the petitioner's education is helpful to him in the performance of his employment." The education must be more than tenuously related to the skills required in the taxpayer's occupation; it must be proximately related to such skills. We cannot accept the petitioner's argument that courses in the more advanced fields of tax law have any proximate relation to his past employment with the Sunday School Guide Publishing Co., Fleetwood Furniture, or the Capital Park Motel — some of his employers as many as seven years before his attendance at NYU.

In support of his position, the petitioner cites the case of Primuth v. Commissioner, 54 T.C. 374, 377 (1970), in which this Court recognized "that a taxpayer may be in the trade or business of being an employee." However, *Primuth* simply held that a fee expended to secure employment is deductible as a business expense under section 162. The case did not involve a claim for an educational expense deduction, and thus, it offers no support for the petitioner's position. Accordingly, we hold that the petitioner's expenses in obtaining a masters of law degree in taxation are not deductible as an ordinary and necessary business expense since he was not engaged in the trade or business of being an attorney at the time such expenses were incurred and since, therefore, he was not maintaining or improving the skills of such trade or business. Such expenses are nondeductible personal expenses. . . .

Note

Although the Tax Court decided in *Wassenaar* that costs incurred in obtaining a master of law degree did not qualify as deductible business expenses where the taxpayer was not previously engaged in the trade or business of being an attorney, in Ruehmann v. Commissioner, T.C. Memo 1971-157, the court reached a different conclusion. In *Ruehmann*, a University of Georgia law student, who secured permanent employment during the first semester of his third year of law school, sought to claim as deductions $808 of costs incurred completing his LL.B. degree the following spring semester. The student arranged with his employer to defer full-time employment at the firm until he completed an LL.M. degree at Harvard Law School during the following academic year. He did, however, work at the firm during the interim summer after obtaining his LL.B. degree, prior to entering Harvard. The student also deducted his $1,257 fall educational expenses at Harvard.

The court disallowed the expenses incurred to complete the LL.B. degree, finding that the degree constituted a nondeductible minimum educational requirement for the type of employment secured by the student. On the other hand, because the student had practiced law during the summer before attending Harvard, the court allowed the $1,257 educational expense deduction explaining that, because the taxpayer was engaged in law practice prior to entering Harvard, the purpose of the advanced study was to improve his legal skills, not to qualify the student in a new trade or business.

The holding in *Ruehmann* has been applied narrowly, however. For example, in Weyts v. Commissioner, T.C. Memo 2003-68, the taxpayer was a Belgian citizen who earned a law degree in Europe and then subsequently enrolled in an LL.M. program at Columbia Law School. After completing the LL.M., the taxpayer decided to enter the J.D./M.B.A. program at Columbia and was granted one year of credit for having completed the LL.M. During the summers between the LL.M. and the J.D./M.B.A. program, the taxpayer worked at different law firms in

New York as a summer associate. Citing *Ruehmann*, the taxpayer claimed that the educational expenses for the J.D./M.B.A. were deductible. The Tax Court disagreed, concluding that employment as a summer associate was more like a law clerk (which is not a trade or business) than an associate attorney (which was held to be a trade or business in *Ruehmann*).

c. New Trade or Business Limitation

In addition to disallowing a deduction for costs of minimum educational requirements, the Regulations prohibit deduction of "expenditures made by an individual for education . . . which would lead to qualifying him in a new trade or business." Reg. §1.162-5(b)(3)(i). The examples in the Regulations provide some guidance for defining the parameters of the new trade or business limitation, but the cases present facts and results that are less clear.

The *Sharon* case, discussed in the preceding section in the context of the minimum education requirements limitation, also involved a new trade or business question. The taxpayer in *Sharon* was a practicing attorney with the Service. His job did not require that he be admitted to the bar, but he was encouraged to seek admission, which he did, after taking a bar review course. The taxpayer deducted the cost of the bar review course as a business expense, but the court held that the expense was not deductible because the course "qualified Sharon to perform significantly different tasks and activities than he could have performed prior to the course." 591 F.2d at 1275. The court apparently based its holding on the ground that the expenses incurred for the bar review course allowed the taxpayer to pursue private practice rather than to continue practice as a Service attorney. The court thus determined that private law practice and Service tax practice were not the same trade or business.

In Vetrick v. Commissioner, 628 F.2d 885 (5th Cir. 1980), the court applied a similarly narrow definition of what constitutes a new trade or business. In *Vetrick*, the taxpayer was an attorney who was qualified to practice only in federal courts. Because the court found that completion of law school enabled the taxpayer to perform substantially different legal tasks than he was previously able to perform, the travel and educational expenses incurred by Vetrick in obtaining a law degree were held to be nondeductible. In so ruling, the court rejected the taxpayer's argument that the additional legal education served only to improve his skills as a practicing attorney. The *Vetrick* and *Sharon* decisions are examples of courts finding a narrow ground on which to base the decision to disallow a deduction, particularly in light of the Regulations that seem to postulate a change in profession or field of business as the criterion for denying a deduction. See, e.g., Reg. §1.162-5(b)(3)(i).

The distinctions drawn in *Sharon* and *Vetrick* are particularly strict when contrasted with the extremely liberal treatment afforded the taxpayer in Toner v. Commissioner, 623 F.2d 315 (3d Cir. 1980). The taxpayer in *Toner* was a teacher. The court allowed a deduction for the cost of obtaining a bachelor's degree when the taxpayer's job required only a high school diploma. This liberal treatment of the teaching profession, which is supported by the Regulations, may be viewed from a policy standpoint as encouraging further education for teachers, while discouraging such attempts at self-improvement for attorneys and perhaps other professionals. Do the Regulations intend these anomalous results and, if so, are they desirable?

Regardless, the Tax Court has continued to apply *Vetrick* and *Sharon* to lawyers strictly, even holding that a law student who claimed such deductions (ironically, again a former IRS employee) was subject to a penalty for taking a frivolous tax position on the basis that the taxpayer should have been aware of the "litany" of cases disallowing such deductions. See Goldenberg v. Commissioner, T.C. Memo 1993-150 ("By the time petitioner prepared his 1987 tax return, he had taken six Federal tax law courses and was able to discern that the deduction he was claiming had been repeatedly disallowed by the Court . . . therefore, he is liable for the additions to tax in 1987.").

Problems

6-19. Gail Sunberg is a paralegal with a law firm. The firm suggests that she attend law school and agrees to reimburse her expenses while providing her part-time employment. Sunberg agrees.

   a.   What tax consequences ensue?

   b.   What if Sunberg was a practicing accountant who attended law school at her own expense?

6-20. Ralph McCarthy graduated from law school in June. He accepted a job with a law firm in Fresno, California, and practiced law until January of the next year when he enrolled in a Los Angeles graduate tax program. In June, he returned to Fresno and practiced law for the summer. During the fall semester of the next year, he completed his studies in Los Angeles and was awarded his LL.M. Can McCarthy deduct his living, traveling, and tuition expenses for the time spent going to school in Los Angeles?

6-21. What result in problem 6-20 if McCarthy did not work after completing law school but instead studied for the bar until September and went to school in Los Angeles from September to June of the following year?

3.   Entertainment Expenses

   Code: §§162(a); 274(a), (d), (l), (n)
   Regulations: §§1.274-2(a) to (d); 1.274-5T(a) to (c)

Prior to 1962, when §274 was enacted, deductions for business-related entertainment expenses were easily obtained, even for unnecessarily lavish items. For example, in Cleveland-Sandusky Brewing Corp. v. Commissioner, 30 T.C. 539 (1958), the taxpayer was permitted to deduct expenses incurred to operate its yacht. The Tax Court allowed the deduction because the yacht was used for business purposes, including sales meetings and customer entertainment, and because the taxpayer claimed that there was a "constant need to generate goodwill in the business of distributing beer." Id. at 546.

The legislative intent in enacting §274 can be gleaned from the following excerpt from its legislative history:

> Much of the abuse . . . can be traced to the broad judicial and administrative inter-pretation given to the term "ordinary and necessary" which has resulted in many entertainment expenses being allowed as deductions where their connection with a trade or business is quite remote. Under present law, where a business purpose, however slight, exists, then the entertainment expenses generally are fully deductible if they are "ordinary and necessary" business expenses.
>
> [D]eductions for entertainment and traveling expenses and business gifts should be restricted to prevent abuses. [T]his abuse of the tax law should not be condoned, but on the other hand . . . complete disallowance . . . is [not] the proper solution to the problem. Rather, . . . expenses incurred for valid business purposes should not be discouraged since such expenses serve to increase business income, which in turn produces additional tax revenues for the Treasury.

S. Rep. No. 1881, 87th Cong., 2d Sess. 25 (1962). Thus, the carte blanche previ-ously afforded business-related entertainment costs has been substantially restricted. To be deductible, entertainment expenses must meet certain require-ments in addition to those of §162 and be adequately substantiated. For those expenditures meeting these standards, additional limitations are imposed by §274(n), which creates a 50-percent ceiling on the amount of the deduction.

a. General Requirements for the Deduction

To be deductible, entertainment expenses must not only be ordinary and necessary as required by §162, but must also meet additional §274 tests. In general, to meet the §274(a) standard, entertainment expenditures must be either "directly related to" or "associated with" the active conduct of the taxpayer's business.

In meeting the directly related-to test, the taxpayer must satisfy three require-ments. Reg. §1.274-2(c)(3). First, at the time of the expenditure, the taxpayer must have a reasonable expectation of deriving income or some other *specific* business benefit, other than goodwill, from the business discussion and entertainment. The taxpayer, however, is not required to show that the intended benefit actually resulted. Second, the taxpayer must actively engage in a business discussion, nego-tiation, or some other bona fide business transaction *during* the entertainment. Third, the business meeting or transaction must be the *principal* reason for the entertainment. This does not require that more time be spent on business than entertainment. On the other hand, unless the taxpayer clearly shows otherwise, it is presumed that business is not the principal reason for hunting or fishing trips or meetings held on yachts or pleasure boats. If deduction of the entertainment expenditure is permitted, only amounts allocable to the taxpayer (and persons closely connected with the taxpayer) and the person(s) with whom the taxpayer conducted business during the entertainment may be deducted.

In general, an entertainment expenditure may be deemed directly related to the active conduct of the taxpayer's business only if the entertainment occurred in a business setting. Reg. §1.274-2(c)(4). If entertainment expenses are incurred in surroundings in which there is little or no possibility of engaging in business discussions, the expenses will not qualify as directly related to the taxpayer's business. Reg. §1.274-2(c)(7). For example, when the taxpayer is not present or the expenses are incurred in surroundings with substantial distractions, the entertainment expenses are generally deemed to have occurred in circumstances where there was little or no possibility of the taxpayer's engaging in business. Substantial distractions are presumed, for example, when business meetings or discussions take place at nightclubs, theaters, or sporting events or during cocktail parties.

Entertainment expenses arising from an activity associated with business are deductible, subject to the limitation of §274(n), provided they precede or follow a substantial, bona fide business discussion. Reg. §1.274-2(d). This requirement is satisfied if business was the principal aspect of the combined activity, but this does not require that more time be spent on business than entertainment. Reg. §1.274-2(d)(3)(i). The purpose of the business discussion must be to obtain income or some other specific business benefit. Unlike the directly related-to requirement, associated-with business entertainment can be for the purpose of maintaining customer goodwill. There is no requirement that any business discussion actually take place *during* the entertainment. Entertainment occurring on the same day as the business meeting will generally satisfy the directly preceding or following requirement. If the two do not occur on the same day, the facts and circumstances of the situation are examined to determine whether the requirement is met. Reg. §1.274-2(d)(3)(ii). Relevant factors include place, date, duration of business discussion, whether the taxpayer or the business associate is from out of town (and, if so, date of arrival and departure), and reasons that the business meeting and entertainment did not occur on the same day.

In the following case, Walliser v. Commissioner, note that §274(a) may supplant the authority of §162(a) and disallow deductions otherwise allowable under §162.

WALLISER v. COMMISSIONER
72 T.C. 433 (1979)

TANNENWALD, J. . . .

At issue is whether amounts expended by petitioners for foreign travel are deductible as ordinary and necessary business expenses under section 162 and, if so, whether the requirements of section 274 have been satisfied.

FINDINGS OF FACT . . .

James B. Walliser (James) and Carol Sue Walliser (Carol), husband and wife, filed joint individual income tax returns for the taxable years 1973 and 1974. . . .

During the taxable years 1973 and 1974, James was vice president and branch manager of the First Federal Savings & Loan Association (First Federal) of Dallas, Tex., Richardson branch office. . . .

During the taxable years at issue, petitioners traveled abroad in tour groups organized primarily for people involved in the building industry. In 1973, petitioners took two such trips. The first was to Rio de Janeiro and was sponsored by General Electric Co. (General Electric). Their second trip, to London and Copenhagen, was sponsored by Fedders Co. (Fedders). . . .

In 1974, petitioners went to Santo Domingo on a tour organized by Fedders. . . .

The basic price of each of the builders' tours covered transportation, lodging, and meals. Petitioners paid the basic prices. . . .

On their 1973 and 1974 tax returns, petitioners deducted, as employee business expenses, one-half of the price of each of the tours (the portion attributable to James' travel). . . .

OPINION . . .

Section 162(a)(2) allows a deduction for all ordinary and necessary expenses paid or incurred during the taxable year in carrying on any trade or business, including traveling expenses incurred while away from home in the pursuit of a trade or business. The question is essentially one of fact. Petitioners must show that the expenses were incurred primarily for business rather than social reasons and that there was a proximate relation between the cost of the builders' tours and James' business as an officer of First Federal.

James' primary responsibility as an officer of First Federal was marketing loans. He was assigned loan production quotas and considered yearly increases in his salary to be contingent upon meeting those quotas. The participants in the General Electric and Fedders tours were not a random group of Texas vacationers. On the contrary, they were largely builders and developers from Texas, the area in which First Federal operated. Thus, the tours were a useful means of maintaining relations with existing customers of First Federal and reaching prospective customers. Indeed, the record indicated that some of the participants considered the social relationships with James, including their association with him on the tours, as an influencing factor in their decisions to seek loans from First Federal.

The fact that, during the years at issue, First Federal did not reimburse James for the costs of his travel does not render his expenses nondeductible. Where a corporate officer personally incurs expenditures which enable him to better perform his duties to the corporation and which have a direct bearing on the amount of his compensation or his chances for advancement, unreimbursed expenses may be deductible under section 162.

First Federal expected its officers in charge of marketing activities to participate in public or social functions without reimbursement and examined their performance in this regard when evaluating their compensation and overall value to the company. James met his loan quotas in 1973 and 1974 and received raises in his salary at the end of those years. In a later year, he became head of First Federal's interim loan department.

Moreover, the evidence tends to show that First Federal considered the trips valuable in generating goodwill. . . .

Finally, the testimony of petitioners, and particularly of Carol, which we found straightforward and credible, tended to show that the tours were strenuous, and not particularly enjoyable, experiences because of the amount of time expended in cultivating business and, therefore, that petitioners did not under-take the tours for primarily personal reasons.

We conclude that, under the circumstances of this case, the requisite proxi-mate relation has been shown to constitute James' travel expenses as "ordinary and necessary" business expenses within the meaning of section 162(a)(2).

We now turn our attention to the applicability of section 274, the issue on which respondent has concentrated most of his fire. That section disallows a deduc-tion in certain instances for expenses which would otherwise be deductible under section 162. Respondent argues that the requirements of section 274 are applicable here and have not been satisfied in that petitioners have failed: (1) To show that James' trips were "directly related" to the active conduct of his business (sec. 274(a)); (2) to substantiate the business purpose of his expenditures (sec. 274(d)); and (3) to allocate his time spent in foreign travel between personal and business activities (sec. 274(c)). . . .

Petitioners urge that the "directly related" test of section 274(a) is not appli-cable because the expenditures at issue were incurred for travel, not entertainment. We disagree.

Section 274(a) relates to activities of a type generally considered to constitute "entertainment, amusement, or recreation." Section 1.274-2(b) defines "entertain-ment, amusement, or recreation" as follows:

> (b) *Definitions* — (1) *Entertainment defined* — (i) *In general.* For purposes of this section, the term *"entertainment" means any activity which is of a type generally considered to constitute entertainment, amusement, or recreation, such as* entertaining at night clubs, cocktail lounges, theaters, country clubs, golf and athletic clubs, sporting events, and on hunt-ing, fishing, *vacation and similar trips, including such activity relating solely to the taxpayer* or the taxpayer's family. . . .
>
> (ii) *Objective test. An objective test shall be used to determine whether an activity is of a type generally considered to constitute entertainment.* . . . [Emphasis added.]

This regulation is squarely based on the language of the legislative history of section 274 and we find it to be valid as it relates to the issue herein.

This regulation and the Congressional committee reports from which it is derived leave no doubt that the deductibility of an expenditure for travel, on what would objectively be considered a vacation trip, is subject to the limitations of sub-section 274(a), even where the expenditure relates solely to the taxpayer himself. Furthermore, section 1.274-2(b)(1)(iii) provides that "any expenditure which might generally be considered . . . either for travel or entertainment, shall be considered an expenditure for entertainment rather than for . . . travel." This regulation too has a solid foundation in the statute, which provides, in section 274[(o)], authority for the promulgation of regulations necessary to carry out the purpose of section 274 and in the committee reports, which provide that rules be prescribed for determining whether section 274(a) should govern where another section is also applicable.

Although the participants in the tours that petitioners took were drawn, for the most part, from the building industry, their activities — sightseeing, shopping, dining — were the same as those of other tourists. Fedders . . . did not conduct any business meetings. Nor is there any evidence that any business meetings were conducted on the 1973 General Electric tour. . . . Under the objective test set forth in the regulations, it is irrelevant that petitioners did not regard the trips as vacations or did not find them relaxing. Clearly, the tours were of a type generally considered vacation trips and, thus, under the objective test, constituted entertainment for the purposes of section 274(a). Therefore, the requirements of that section must be satisfied.

For a deduction to be allowed for any item under section 274(a)(1)(A), the taxpayer must establish that the item was directly related to the active conduct of the taxpayer's trade or business or, in the case of an item directly preceding or following a substantial and bona fide business discussion, that such item was associated with the active conduct of the taxpayer's trade or business.

The "directly related" test requires that a taxpayer show a greater degree of proximate relationship between an expenditure and the taxpayer's trade or business than that required by section 162. Section 1.274-2(c)(3) provides that, for an expenditure to be directly related to the active conduct of the taxpayer's trade or business, it must be shown that the taxpayer had more than a general expectation of deriving some income or business benefit from the expenditure, *other than the goodwill* of the person or persons entertained. While the language of this regulation is awkward and not completely apt in a situation where the entertainment expenditure relates to the taxpayer alone, it is clear, nevertheless, that more than a general expectation of deriving some income at some indefinite future time is necessary for an expenditure to be deductible under section 274(a).

The record shows that petitioners participated in the builders' tours because they provided an opportunity for James to meet new people who might be interested in the services he, and First Federal, had to offer and to maintain good personal relations with people already using those services. While James discussed business continually during the tours, his wife testified that this was typical of his behavior during all social activities. He engaged in general discussions about business conditions and the services he could provide to a builder but did not engage in business meetings or negotiations on the tours. James could not directly connect particular business transactions with specific discussions which occurred during the trips. In short, petitioners' purpose in taking the trips was to create or maintain goodwill for James and First Federal, his employer, in order to generate some future business. Although the evidence tends to indicate that the trips did, in fact, enhance goodwill and contribute to James' success in loan production and otherwise constituted ordinary and necessary business expenses deductible under section 162, we hold, nevertheless, that Congress intended, by means of the more stringent standard of the "directly related" test in section 274(a), to disallow deductions for this type of activity, which involves merely the promotion of goodwill in a social setting.

We also hold that the petitioners' trips do not qualify as entertainment "associated with" the active conduct of a trade or business. To be deductible, entertainment "associated with" the active conduct of a trade or business must directly precede or follow a substantial business discussion. In St. Petersburg Bank & Trust Co. v. United States, [362 F. Supp. 674 (M.D. Fla. 1973), affd. in an unpublished order, 503 F.2d 1402 (5th Cir. 1974),] a decision affirmed by the Fifth Circuit, the District Court concluded that the phrase "directly preceding or following" in section 274(a)(1)(A) should be read restrictively in cases in which entertainment expenditures are related to the taxpayer's trade or business only in that they promote goodwill. In view of the legislative history, which reveals that the "associated with" test is an exception to the general rule intended to limit deductions for entertainment which has as its sole business purpose the promotion of goodwill, we agree with the District Court's conclusion. Accordingly, we do not consider the costs of the vacation trips to be deductible under section 274(a)(1)(A) as entertainment directly preceded or followed by a substantial and bona fide business discussion merely because James had general discussions of a business nature intended to promote goodwill during the course of the trips.

We conclude that section 274(a) bars a deduction for the costs of James' trips. . . .

The *Walliser* doctrine has consistently been cited by the courts where taxpayers claim business-related entertainment-type expenses. For example, in Beck v. Commissioner, T.C. Memo. 2001-270, the taxpayer operated a liquor business near the Canadian border and often earned substantial income in Canadian dollars. The taxpayer took several trips per year to Las Vegas to spend the Canadian dollars and deducted the costs of such trips. The taxpayer claimed that he traveled to Las Vegas to obtain a better exchange rate to convert Canadian dollars into U.S. dollars than was available in his hometown. The court, citing *Walliser*, disagreed, finding that "[a]lthough Mr. Beck was able to get a better exchange rate for the Canadian currency, we are convinced that the trips to Las Vegas were primarily to allow Mr. Beck to gamble."

A more difficult case arose in the context of officers and directors of a corporation flying on a corporate jet for personal reasons. Under §61, the fair market value of a flight for personal reasons constitutes a fringe benefit, and thus gross income, to the officer or director. Conversely, the cost of the fringe benefit would be deductible to the corporation as compensation under §162. The issue that arose was whether the other costs of owning and operating a corporate jet were similarly deductible. For example, assume that the fair market value of a flight on a private jet is $5,000, and thus the president has $5,000 of compensation income each time the president flies for free on the jet for personal reasons. However, it costs the corporation an additional $10,000 for fuel, maintenance, pilots, and other costs to operate the jet for the day. Can the corporation deduct the additional $10,000?

This question arose in Sutherland Lumber-Southwest, Inc. v. Commissioner, 114 T.C. 197 (2000), aff'd per curiam, 255 F.3d 495 (8th Cir. 2001), in which both the Tax Court and the circuit court, after an extensive review of the statute and legislative history, permitted the corporation to deduct the full costs of operating the aircraft. In response to *Sutherland*, Congress enacted §274(e)(2)(B), which provides that, with respect to corporate officers and directors, the corporation may deduct only an amount equal to the amount the officer or director includes in his or her gross income.

b. Entertainment Facilities

Additional rules exist under §274 concerning the deductibility of costs incurred for entertainment facilities. Entertainment facilities are defined as "any item of personal or real property owned, rented, or used by a taxpayer . . . for, or in connection with, an activity normally considered to be of an entertainment nature." S. Rep. No. 498, 96th Cong., 1st Sess. 60 n.1 (1979); S. Rep. No. 1036, 96th Cong., 2d Sess. 24 n.1 (1980). Regulation §1.274-2(e)(2) provides examples of entertainment facilities, including "yachts, hunting lodges, fishing camps, . . . and homes in vacation resorts." The following excerpt from the legislative history of the act illustrates the manner in which Congress viewed prior law and why it felt a modification was necessary.

> The [pre-1978] law's treatment of expenses relating to entertainment facilities may encourage some taxpayers to attempt to deduct, as business expenses, items that essentially represent nondeductible personal expenses. Moreover, in some instances these expenses may be incurred largely as a method of providing additional compensation for highly paid employees and executives. The complexity of the provisions of [pre-1978] law make its effective administration and uniform application extremely difficult and provide significant opportunities for abuse. Consequently, and notwithstanding the fact that . . . some legitimate business expenses may be incurred with respect to entertainment facilities, . . . such expenses should be disallowed as business deductions.

S. Rep. No. 1263, 95th Cong., 2d Sess. 174 (1978).

As a result of the amendment, no deduction is permitted for expenses relating to most entertainment facilities. In addition, dues or fees to social, athletic, or sporting clubs or organizations are not deductible. §274(a)(3).

c.   Substantiation Requirements and the 50-Percent Limitation

Prior to 1962, if taxpayers could prove that they incurred deductible travel or entertainment expenses but could not produce any evidence to substantiate the *amount* claimed, the courts would approximate the amount of the expenses and allow that amount as a deduction. This practice, referred to as the *Cohan* rule, was based on the holding in Cohan v. Commissioner, 39 F.2d 540 (2d Cir. 1930). Cohan was a theatrical manager, producer, and writer. As a producer, Cohan was "free-handed" in his entertainment of actors, employees, and drama critics. He incurred substantial entertainment expenses but kept no record of the amount expended. Because Cohan had proven that he incurred deductible travel and entertainment expenses, the Second Circuit held that his claimed deduction should not be totally disallowed; rather, it should be limited to "as close an approximation as [the trial court can make], bearing heavily if it chooses upon the taxpayer whose inexactitude is of his own making." Id. at 544. Section 274(d) was added to overrule the application of the *Cohan* decision to travel and entertainment expenses.

Since the enactment of §274(d), if the taxpayer does not adequately substantiate travel, entertainment, and business gift expenses, the entire claimed deduction will be disallowed. To meet the substantiation requirement, the taxpayer must produce adequate records or sufficient corroborative evidence showing (1) the amount of the expense; (2) the time and place of the event giving rise to the expense; (3) the business purpose of the expense; and (4) the business relationship between the taxpayer and the person benefited by the expense. See Reg. §1.274-5T.

In Mann v. Commissioner, T.C. Memo 1981-684, the taxpayer attempted to use credit card statements to substantiate claimed business expenses. Because the statements were not specific concerning the business purpose of the expense or the business relationship with the guest entertained, the court disallowed the entertainment expense deduction. A taxpayer can, however, meet the adequate records requirement by maintaining an account book, diary, statement of expense, or similar record and documentary evidence (receipts), which together are sufficient to establish the amount, time and place, business purpose, and business relationship between the taxpayer and beneficiary of the expenditure. Reg. §1.274-5T(c)(2).

Congress responded to the rampant abuse of the business entertainment deduction by providing additional limitations on the amount of allowable deductions. In enacting §274(n), which imposes a 50-percent ceiling on otherwise allowable entertainment and meal deductions, Congress attempted to recognize the personal consumption benefits otherwise available through the deduction.

> Since the 1960's, the Congress has sought to address various aspects of deductions for meals, entertainment, and travel expenses that the Congress and the public have viewed as unfairly benefiting those taxpayers who are able to take advantage of the tax benefit of deductibility. In his 1961 Tax Message, President Kennedy reported that "too many firms and individuals have devised means of deducting too many personal living expenses as business expenses, thereby charging a large part of their cost to the Federal Government." He stated: "This is a matter of national concern, affecting not only our public revenues, our sense of fairness, and our respect for the tax system, but our moral and business practices as well."
>
> The committee shares these concerns, and believes that these concerns are not addressed adequately by present law. In general, present law requires some heightened showing of a business purpose for travel and entertainment costs, as well as stricter substantiation requirements than those applying generally to all business deductions. However, the present-law approach fails to address a basic issue inherent in allowing deductions for many travel and entertainment expenditures—the fact that, even if reported accurately and having some connection with the taxpayer's business, such expenditures also convey substantial personal benefits to the recipients.
>
> The committee believes that present law, by not focusing sufficiently on the personal-consumption element of deductible meal and entertainment expenses, unfairly permits taxpayers who can arrange business settings for personal consumption to receive, in effect, a Federal tax subsidy for such consumption that is not available to other taxpayers. The taxpayers who benefit from deductibility under present law tend to have relatively high incomes, and in some cases the consumption may bear only a loose relationship to business necessity. For example, when executives have dinner at an expensive restaurant following business discussions and then deduct the cost of the meal, the fact that there may be some bona fide business connection does not alter the imbalance between the treatment of those persons, who have effectively transferred a portion of the cost of their meal to the Federal Government, and other individuals, who cannot deduct the cost of their meals.
>
> The significance of this imbalance is heightened by the fact that business travel and entertainment often may be more lavish than comparable activities in a

nonbusiness setting. For example, meals at expensive restaurants and season tickets at sporting events are purchased to a significant degree by taxpayers who claim business deductions for these expenses. This disparity is highly visible, and contributes to public perceptions that the tax system is unfair. Polls indicate that the public identifies the deductibility of normal personal expenses such as meals to be one of the most significant elements of disrespect for and dissatisfaction with the present tax system.

In light of these considerations, the committee bill generally reduces by [50] percent the amount of otherwise allowable deductions for business meals and entertainment. This reduction rule reflects the fact that meals and entertainment inherently involve an element of personal living expenses, but still allows [a 50] percent deduction where such expenses also have an identifiable business relationship. The bill also tightens the requirements for establishing a bona fide business reason for claiming meal and entertainment expenses as deductions.

S. Rep. No. 313, 99th Cong., 2d Sess. 67 (1986).

Problems

6-22. Laura Vandegrift is an editor of travel guides, which rate hotels, motels, and restaurants. Whenever she and her family travel on personal vacations, they stay in hotels and eat in restaurants listed in the guides. On their return, she writes reports on those hotels and restaurants, appraising the quality of the food and service. She then sends the reports to the appropriate editors, who make adjustments in their descriptions or ratings of these establishments where they feel that it is appropriate. What expenses may the Vandegrifts deduct and under what circumstances?

6-23. For which of the following expenses is Joe Johnson, a personal injury lawyer, entitled to a business expense deduction?
    a. $500 spent for cocktails purchased for patrons in local taverns. Johnson discussed his work with these people and hoped that they would remember him if they needed a personal injury lawyer.
    b. $1,000 spent on dinners with clients, during which Johnson discussed their cases.
    c. $700 on dinners with a major client at which no business was discussed but that took place after lengthy meetings with the client.
    d. $200 for dinners with a waitress who sustained a neck injury in a car accident. Johnson saw her wearing a neck brace and immediately began taking her to dinner while describing how he would handle her prospective lawsuit. On the day following the last dinner, the waitress hired Johnson to act as her attorney.

6-24. On January 1 of the current year, Tom Johnson, the president of Bama, Inc., paid $20,000 to join a golf and country club. The monthly dues for the year were $2,400 ($200 per month). Johnson joined the club in order to network with potential and established business clients and to discuss business issues with associates in a relaxed setting. He used the club exclusively for business purposes — that is, at no time did he use the club for his own personal purposes. As a result of the time spent at the club, Johnson was able to develop twenty new business customers as well as maintain his established clients.

a. How much, if any, of the $20,000 initiation fee is deductible?

b. How much, if any, of the $2,400 spent for monthly dues is deductible?

d. Business Meals

Code: §§119(a), 162(a), 262, 274(n)
Regulations: §1.162-17(a)

Business meal expenses fall into two general categories: (1) those incurred while the taxpayer is traveling away from home (see section D1b of this chapter, which discusses travel expenses) and (2) those incurred while the taxpayer is not away from home. The potential for abuse in the second category has made the business lunch deduction the target of serious criticism. In fact, the business lunch has become a symbol of the need to reform the tax law generally. Much of this concern springs from public misconception of the issues and interests involved as well as from political rhetoric.

1. Requirements for the Deduction

The deduction for business lunches may not be as easy to attain as many taxpayers believe. Meal costs straddle that all-important fence between personal and nonpersonal expenses, and thus the courts have developed tests for determining on which side a claimed deduction should fall. In Sutter v. Commissioner, 21 T.C. 170 (1953), the Tax Court established the "different from or in excess of the taxpayer's personal expenses" standard, which appears to prevail currently. In *Sutter*, a doctor attempted to deduct as business expenses the cost of luncheons at the local chamber of commerce and the local hospital council. Although the luncheons were related to the taxpayer's business as a doctor, the court disallowed the deductions because there was no evidence that the expenditures were greater than those that the taxpayer would have incurred for his own personal purposes. Had the luncheon expenditures been "in excess of" his normal lunch expenditures, the court would have allowed the entire cost of the luncheons, not merely the excess, as a deduction. Therefore, the court's holding implied that expenditures for business meals that are "different from" or "in excess of" the taxpayer's normal expenses should be treated similarly, allowing the expenditure to be deducted.

In another case, involving a Chicago attorney, the Tax Court held that expenses for the taxpayer's luncheon meetings to discuss Chicago Bar Association (CBA) business were not deductible. Caldwell v. Commissioner, T.C. Memo 1982-241. The taxpayer was treasurer of the CBA, and his attendance at the meetings, which were held on CBA premises, was required as part of the duties of his office. However, the court held that

> [s]ince petitioner did not offer any evidence indicating that the amount he allegedly expended on meals at the luncheons exceeded that which he would have spent on personal meals in any event, such expenditures would be considered personal and nondeductible pursuant to Section 262.

Id. at 1038.

The policy expressed in *Sutter, Caldwell*, and Moss v. Commissioner, which follows, is questioned by some because it causes taxpayers to be treated differently based on their personal eating habits. Thus, someone who eats an expensive lunch daily might never be able to deduct a business lunch expense, while another individual who normally eats a "brown bag" lunch could deduct a business lunch expense. Similarly, permitting a taxpayer to deduct meals eaten on business trips away from home seems inconsistent with the limited deductibility of business lunch expenses. Would it not be more consistent to allow a deduction for the difference between what one would normally spend for meals and what one spends for them on a business trip? Do both the business lunch deduction and the travel expense deduction encourage unwarranted consumption?

MOSS v. COMMISSIONER
758 F.2d 211 (7th Cir. 1985)

POSNER, J.

The taxpayers, a lawyer named Moss and his wife, appeal from a decision of the Tax Court disallowing federal income tax deductions of a little more than $1,000 in each of two years, representing Moss's share of his law firm's lunch expense at the Cafe Angelo in Chicago. The Tax Court's decision in this case has attracted some attention in tax circles because of its implications for the general problem of the deductibility of business meals.

Moss was a partner in a small trial firm specializing in defense work, mostly for one insurance company. Each of the firm's lawyers carried a tremendous litigation caseload, averaging more than 300 cases, and spent most of every working day in courts in Chicago and its suburbs. The members of the firm met for lunch daily at the Cafe Angelo near their office. At lunch the lawyers would discuss their cases with the head of the firm, whose approval was required for most settlements, and they would decide which lawyer would meet which court call that afternoon or the next morning. Lunchtime was chosen for the daily meeting because the courts were in recess then. The alternatives were to meet at 7:00 A.M. or 6:00 P.M., and these were less convenient times. There is no suggestion that the lawyers dawdled over lunch, or that the Cafe Angelo is luxurious.

The framework of statutes and regulations for deciding this case is simple, but not clear. Section 262 of the Internal Revenue Code disallows, "except as otherwise expressly provided in this chapter," the deduction of "personal, family, or living expenses." Section 119 excludes from income the value of meals provided by an employer to his employees for his convenience, but only if they are provided on the employer's premises; and section 162(a) allows the deduction of "all the ordinary and necessary expenses paid or incurred during the taxable year in carrying on any trade or business, including— . . . (2) traveling expenses (including amounts expended for meals . . .) while away from home. . . ." Since Moss was not an employee but a partner in a partnership not taxed as an entity, since the meals were not served on the employer's premises, and since he was not away from home (that is, on an overnight trip away from his place of work, see United States v. Correll, 389 U.S. 299 (1967)), neither section 119 nor section 162(a)(2) applies to this case. The Internal Revenue Service concedes, however, that meals are deductible under section 162(a) when they are ordinary and necessary business expenses (provided the expense is substantiated with adequate records, see section 274(d)) even if they are not within the express permission of any other provision and even though the expense of commuting to and from work, a traveling expense but not one incurred away from home, is not deductible. Treasury Regulations on Income Tax §1.262-1(b)(5); Fausner v. Commissioner, 413 U.S. 838 (1973) (per curiam).

The problem is that many expenses are simultaneously business expenses in the sense that they conduce to the production of business income and personal expenses in the sense that they raise personal welfare. This is plain enough with regard to lunch; most people would eat lunch even if they didn't work. Commuting may seem a pure business expense, but is not; it reflects the choice of where to live, as well as where to work. Read literally, section 262 would make irrelevant whether a business expense is also a personal expense; so long as it is ordinary and necessary in the taxpayer's business, thus bringing section 162(a) into play, an expense is (the statute seems to say) deductible from his income tax. But the statute has not been read literally. There is a natural reluctance, most clearly manifested in the regulation disallowing deduction of the expense of commuting, to lighten the tax burden of people who have the good fortune to interweave work with consumption. To allow a deduction for commuting would confer a windfall on people who live in the suburbs and commute to work in the cities; to allow a deduction for all business-related meals would confer a windfall on people who can arrange their work schedules so they do some of their work at lunch.

Although an argument can thus be made for disallowing *any* deduction for business meals, on the theory that people have to eat whether they work or not, the result would be excessive taxation of people who spend more money on business meals because they are business meals than they would spend on their meals if they were not working. Suppose a theatrical agent takes his clients out to lunch at the expensive restaurants that the clients demand. Of course he can deduct the expense of their meals, from which he derives no pleasure or sustenance, but can he also deduct the expense of his own? He can, because he cannot eat more cheaply; he cannot munch surreptitiously on a peanut butter and jelly sandwich brought from home while his client is wolfing down tournedos Rossini followed by soufflé au grand marnier. No doubt our theatrical agent, unless concerned for his longevity, derives personal utility from his fancy meal, but probably less than the price of the meal. He would not pay for it if it were not for the business benefit; he would get more value from using the same money to buy something else; hence the meal confers on him less utility than the cash equivalent would. The law could require him to pay tax on the fair value of the meal to him; this would be (were it not for costs of administration) the economically correct solution. But the government does not attempt this difficult measurement; it once did, but gave up the attempt as not worth the cost, see United States v. Correll, supra, 389 U.S. at 301 n.6. The taxpayer is permitted to deduct [his meal], provided the expense is "different from or in excess of that which would have been made for the taxpayer's personal purposes." Sutter v. Commissioner, 21 T.C. 170, 173 (1953).

Because the law allows this generous deduction, which tempts people to have more (and costlier) business meals than are necessary, the Internal Revenue Service has every right to insist that the meal be shown to be a real business necessity. This condition is most easily satisfied when a client or customer or supplier or other outsider to the business is a guest. Even if Sydney Smith was wrong that "soup and fish explain half the emotions of life," it is undeniable that eating together fosters camaraderie and makes business dealings friendlier and easier. It thus reduces the costs of transacting business, for these costs include the frictions and the failures of communication that are produced by suspicion and mutual misunderstanding, by differences in tastes and manners, and by lack of rapport. A meeting with a client or customer in an office is therefore not a perfect substitute for a lunch with him in a restaurant. But it is different when all the participants in the meal are coworkers, as essentially was the case here (clients occasionally were invited to the firm's daily luncheon, but Moss has made no attempt to identify the occasions). They know each other well already; they don't need the social lubrication that a meal with an outsider provides — at least don't need it daily. If a large firm had a monthly lunch to allow partners to get to know associates, the expense of the meal might well be necessary, and would be allowed by the Internal Revenue Service. See Wells v. Commissioner, 36 T.C.M. 1698, 1699 (1977), affd. without opinion, 626 F.2d 868 (9th Cir. 1980). But Moss's firm never had more than eight lawyers (partners and associates), and did not need a daily lunch to cement relationships among them.

It is all a matter of degree and circumstance (the expense of a testimonial dinner, for example, would be deductible on a morale-building rationale); and particularly of frequency. Daily — for a full year — is too often, perhaps even for entertainment of clients, as implied by Hankenson v. Commissioner, 47 T.C.M. 1567, 1569 (1984), where the Tax Court held nondeductible the cost of lunches consumed three or four days a week, 52 weeks a year, by a doctor who entertained other doctors who he hoped would refer patients to him, and other medical personnel.

We may assume it was necessary for Moss's firm to meet daily to coordinate the work of the firm, and also, as the Tax Court found, that lunch was the most convenient time. But it does not follow that the expense of the lunch was a necessary business expense. The members of the firm had to eat somewhere, and the Cafe Angelo was both convenient and not too expensive. They do not claim to have incurred a greater daily lunch expense than they would have incurred if there had been no lunch meetings. Although it saved time to combine lunch with work, the meal itself was not an organic part of the meeting, as in the examples we gave earlier where the business objective, to be fully achieved, required sharing a meal.

The case might be different if the location of the courts required the firm's members to eat each day either in a disagreeable restaurant, so that they derived less value from the meal than it cost them to buy it, cf. Sibla v. Commissioner, 611 F.2d 1260, 1262 (9th Cir. 1980); or in a restaurant too expensive for their personal tastes, so that, again, they would have gotten less value than the cash equivalent. But so far as appears, they picked the restaurant they liked most. Although it must be pretty monotonous to eat lunch the same place every working day of the year, not all the lawyers attended all the lunch meetings and there was nothing to stop the firm from meeting occasionally at another restaurant proximate to their office in downtown Chicago; there are hundreds.

An argument can be made that the price of lunch at the Cafe Angelo included rental of the space that the lawyers used for what was a meeting as well as a meal. There was evidence that the firm's conference room was otherwise occupied throughout the working day, so as a matter of logic Moss might be able to claim a part of the price of lunch as an ordinary and necessary expense for work space. But this is cutting things awfully fine; in any event Moss made no effort to apportion his lunch expense in this way.

Affirmed.

2. Amount of the Deduction

As discussed at section D2c regarding the deductibility of entertainment expenses, a ceiling exists on the amount of otherwise permissible meal deductions. Under §274(n), the deduction is limited to 50 percent of the amount of the expense. As evidenced by the subsection's legislative history, Congress was concerned that the deduction encouraged unwarranted personal consumption. See also §274(k), hinting at the perceived abuse in the area, which reiterates the §162(a)(2) prohibition on deductions for lavish or extravagant meals.

Problem

6-25. Karen Maysfield is requested, but not required, to eat lunch with her fellow employees every Friday.
   a. Can she deduct the costs of the lunches if she generally does not eat lunch?
   b. Can she deduct the cost of the lunches if she generally does eat lunch? What factors are relevant?
   c. What result in *a* and *b* if her employer requires her to lunch with her fellow employees on Fridays?

---

4. Legal Expenses

Code: §§162(a); 212; 262; 263(a); 280E
Regulations: §1.263(a)-2

The deduction of legal fees raises two familiar questions: (1) whether the costs are business related or are personal in nature and (2) whether the costs are currently deductible expenses or capital expenditures.

To qualify legal expenses as a current deduction, the business nature of the expense must be established. For example, legal expenses incurred by a business for collection of past due accounts are business related and deductible. Likewise, legal expenses incurred by an employee in litigating a salary dispute may also be treated as business related. On the other hand, legal expenses incurred in purchasing a personal residence or in a child custody battle pursuant to a divorce are purely personal. Many cases, however, are not as clear as the foregoing examples. What if one spouse seeks to be awarded a portion of the other spouse's business as part of a divorce settlement? In analyzing such cases, the courts have developed the origin of claim doctrine: If the origin of the claim from which the legal expenses arose is personal, there is no deduction; if it is business related, the cost may qualify for a §162 deduction.

Not all business related legal expenses that satisfy the origin of claim requirement give rise to current deductions. For example, legal expenses incurred in the acquisition of property that has a useful life beyond the taxable year are generally treated as capital expenditures. Reg. §1.263(a)-2(a); Woodward v. Commissioner, 397 U.S. 572 (1970). Similarly, legal expenses incurred in defending or perfecting title to property are usually considered capital expenditures. Reg. §1.263(a)-2(c). The scope of Regulation §1.263(a)-2(c) has, however, been judicially limited through the application of the primary purpose test. Under the test, legal expenses are capitalized only if the primary purpose in incurring the expenses was to defend or perfect title. Thus, if the taxpayer had more than one reason for incurring the expense, the taxpayer will be required to capitalize the expense only if the intent to defend or perfect title was paramount, not secondary or incidental.

UNITED STATES v. GILMORE
372 U.S. 39 (1963)

MR. JUSTICE HARLAN delivered the opinion of the Court.

In 1955 the California Supreme Court confirmed the award to the respondent taxpayer of a decree of absolute divorce, without alimony, against his wife Dixie Gilmore. The case before us involves the deductibility for federal income tax purposes of that part of the husband's legal expense incurred in such proceedings as is attributable to his successful resistance of his wife's claims to certain of his assets asserted by her to be community property under California law. . . .

At the time of the divorce proceedings, instituted by the wife but in which the husband also cross-claimed for divorce, respondent's property consisted primarily of controlling stock interests in three corporations, each of which was a franchised General Motors automobile dealer. As president and principal managing officer of the three corporations, he received salaries from them aggregating about $66,800 annually, and in recent years his total annual dividends had averaged about $83,000. His total annual income derived from the corporations was thus approximately $150,000. His income from other sources was negligible.

[T]he husband's overriding concern in the divorce litigation was to protect these assets against the claims of his wife. . . .

The respondent wished to defeat those claims for two important reasons. *First*, the loss of his controlling stock interests, particularly in the event of their transfer in substantial part to his hostile wife, might well cost him the loss of his corporate positions, his principal means of livelihood. *Second*, there was also danger that if he were found guilty of his wife's sensational and reputation-damaging charges of marital infidelity, General Motors Corporation might find it expedient to exercise its right to cancel these dealer franchises.

The end result of this bitterly fought divorce case was a complete victory for the husband. He, not the wife, was granted a divorce on his cross-claim; the wife's community property claims were denied in their entirety; and she was held entitled to no alimony.

Respondent's legal expenses in connection with this litigation amounted to $32,537.15 in 1953 and $8,074.21 in 1954 — a total of $40,611.36 for the two taxable years in question. The Commissioner of Internal Revenue found all of these expenditures "personal" or "family" expenses and as such none of them deductible. In the ensuing refund suit, however, the Court of Claims held that 80 percent of such expense (some $32,500) was attributable to respondent's defense against his wife's community property claims respecting his stockholdings and hence deductible as an expense "incurred . . . for the . . . conservation . . . of property held for the production of income." In so holding the Court of Claims stated:

> Of course it is true that in every divorce case a certain amount of the legal expenses are incurred for the purpose of obtaining the divorce and a certain amount are incurred in an effort to conserve the estate and are not necessarily deductible . . . but when the facts of a particular case clearly indicate [as here] that the property, around which the controversy evolves, is held for the production of income and without this property the litigant might be denied not only the property itself but the means of earning a livelihood, then it must [be deductible].

290 F.2d, at 947.

The Government does not question the amount or formula for the expense allocation made by the Court of Claims. Its sole contention here is that the court below misconceived the test governing deductions, in that the deductibility of these expenses turns, so it is argued, not upon the *consequences* to respondent of a failure to defeat his wife's community property claims but upon the *origin* and *nature* of the claims themselves. So viewing Dixie Gilmore's claims, whether relating to the existence or division of community property, it is contended that the expense of resisting them must be deemed nondeductible "personal" or "family" expense. For reasons given hereafter we think the Government's position is sound and that it must be sustained.

I

For income tax purposes Congress has seen fit to regard an individual as having two personalities: "one is [as] a seeker after profit who can deduct the expenses incurred in that search; the other is [as] a creature satisfying his needs as a human and those of his family but who cannot deduct such consumption and related expenditures." . . .

A basic restriction upon the availability of a deduction is that the expense item involved must be one that has a business origin. . . . The pivotal issue in this case then becomes: was this part of respondent's litigation costs a "business" rather than a "personal" or "family" expense?

The answer to this question has already been indicated in prior cases. In Lykes v. United States, 343 U.S. 118, the Court rejected the contention that legal expenses incurred in contesting the assessment of a gift tax liability were deductible. The taxpayer argued that if he had been required to pay the original deficiency he would have been forced to liquidate his stockholdings, which were his main source of income, and that his legal expenses were therefore incurred in the "conservation" of income-producing property and hence deductible. The Court first noted that the "deductibility [of the expenses] turns wholly upon the nature of the activities to which they relate" (343 U.S., at 123), and then stated:

> Legal expenses do not become deductible merely because they are paid for services which relieve a taxpayer of liability. That argument would carry us too far. It would mean that the expense of defending almost any claim would be deductible by a tax-payer on the ground that such defense was made to help him keep clear of liens whatever income-producing property he might have. For example, it suggests that the expense of defending an action based upon personal injuries caused by a tax-payer's negligence while driving an automobile for pleasure should be deductible. . . .

In Kornhauser v. United States, 276 U.S. 145, this Court considered the deductibility of legal expenses incurred by a taxpayer in defending against a claim by a former business partner that fees paid to the taxpayer were for services rendered during the existence of the partnership. In holding that these expenses were deductible even though the taxpayer was no longer a partner at the time of suit, the Court formulated the rule that "where a suit or action against a taxpayer is directly connected with, or . . . proximately resulted from, his business, the expense incurred is a business expense. . . ." 276 U.S., at 153. Similarly, in a case involving an expense incurred in satisfying an obligation (though not a litigation expense), it was said that "it is the origin of the liability out of which the expense accrues" or "the kind of transaction out of which the obligation arose . . . which [is] crucial and controlling." Deputy v. Du Pont, 308 U.S. 488, 494, 496.

The principle we derive from these cases is that the characterization, as "business" or "personal," of the litigation costs of resisting a claim depends on whether or not the claim *arises in connection with* the taxpayer's profit-seeking activities. It does not depend on the *consequences* that might result to a taxpayer's income-producing property from a failure to defeat the claim. . . .

For these reasons, we resolve the conflict among the lower courts on the question before us in favor of the view that the origin and character of the claim with respect to which an expense was incurred, rather than its potential consequences upon the fortunes of the taxpayer, is the controlling basic test of whether the expense was "business" or "personal" and hence whether it is deductible or not. . . .

We turn then to the determinative question in this case: did the wife's claims respecting respondent's stockholdings arise in connection with his profit-seeking activities?

II

. . . [T]he wife's claims stemmed entirely from the marital relationship, and not, under any tenable view of things, from income-producing activity. This is obviously so as regards the claim to more than an equal division of any community property found to exist. For any such right depended entirely on the wife's making good her charges of marital infidelity on the part of the husband. The same conclusion is no less true respecting the claim relating to the existence of community property. For no such property could have existed but for the marriage relationship. Thus none of respondent's expenditures in resisting these claims can be deemed "business" expenses, and they are therefore not deductible.

In view of this conclusion it is unnecessary to consider the further question suggested by the Government: whether that portion of respondent's payments attributable to litigating the issue of the existence of community property was a capital expenditure or a personal expense. In neither event would these payments be deductible from gross income.

The judgment of the Court of Claims is reversed and the case is remanded to that court for further proceedings consistent with this opinion.

Note

Three years after the *Gilmore* case, the Supreme Court was again asked to decide whether legal expenses were sufficiently business related to be allowed as a deduction. The case, Commissioner v. Tellier, 383 U.S. 687 (1966), involved a stockbroker convicted on thirty-six counts of securities and mail fraud. In his unsuccessful defense of the indictments, the broker incurred approximately $23,000 in legal expenses, which he claimed as a deduction.

Although the Commissioner conceded that the legal expenses were ordinary and necessary within the meaning of §162(a) and were incurred in carrying on respondent's business as required by *Gilmore*, he argued that the deduction should be disallowed as a matter of public policy. The Court, however, rejected the public policy argument, stating that only deductions that "frustrate sharply defined national or state policies proscribing particular types of conduct" would be disallowed. 383 U.S. at 694. In addition, the Court stated that these policies must be "evidenced by some *governmental* declaration of them" and that the case fell outside this sharply limited and defined category. Id. (emphasis in original). The Court held that

> [n]o public policy is offended when a man faced with serious criminal charges employs a lawyer to help in his defense. That is not "proscribed conduct." It is his constitutional right. . . . [W]e can find no warrant for attaching to a criminal punishment an additional financial burden that Congress had neither expressly nor implicitly directed.

Id. at 694. Thus, the Court concluded that disallowance of such legal expenses would result in a distortion of the income tax laws that Congress neither intended nor desired.

Problems

6-26.   Motley Chemical Co. has been charged with a violation of the Environmental Protection Act. The government alleges that Motley is releasing excessive levels of itchy peely propylene (IPP) into the air. IPP, while not highly toxic, causes respiratory irritation. Motley is contesting the charge, claiming that the Regulation setting the standards for IPP emission was improperly adopted. Are Motley's legal expenses deductible?

6-27.   Henry Modiker wrote an unflattering book about Richmond Motors. Thereafter, the company embarked on a campaign to destroy Modiker's reputation and credibility. They hired detectives to investigate his background, had him followed, hired prostitutes to try to lure him into compromising situations, and so forth. Modiker discovered Richmond Motors' clandestine activities and sued for invasion of privacy. Richmond Motors incurred legal expenses in fighting the suit and eventually settled with Modiker out of court. Which, if any, of Richmond Motors' expenses are deductible under §162?

6-28.   John Stevenson was accused of trafficking cocaine and brought to trial. The government alleged that his participation was attributable to his need for research and development funds to invest in his slumping business. Are his legal fees deductible

a.   if he is found innocent?

b.   if he is found guilty? See §280E.

E.   STATUTORY LIMITATIONS ON BUSINESS EXPENSES

Business expense deductions are not without limitations. Certain categories of expenditures are limited by express provisions even though they otherwise meet the general statutory standards for deductibility. The categories discussed below include expenditures for the business use of one's home and for certain illegal activities.

1.   Illegality and Public Policy

Code: §§162(c), (f); 280E
Regulations: §§1.162-18(b)(1) to (4); 1.162-21

As a matter of public policy, the Code disallows deductions for certain illegal payments, such as bribes or kickbacks. §162(c). Similarly, the Code disallows deductions for "any fine or similar penalty paid to a government for the violation of any law,"§162(f). The policy behind this provision is that, if deductions were allowed for fines or penalties, the "sting" of the penalty would be lessened by the tax savings. See Rev. Rul. 80-334, 1980-2 C.B. 61.

Along the same lines, other deductions are disallowed under the Code for expenditures in connection with the illegal sale of drugs. §280E. Such provisions are necessary because under *Groetzinger* illegal activities such as selling drugs can clearly meet the definition of a trade or business. Congress reasoned that to allow taxpayers to deduct expenses in incurred in the conduct of such a trade or business would constitute an endorsement of the illegal activity.

An interesting constitutional issue arises in this area since the federal income tax is a tax on *net income*. In Commissioner v. Tellier, 383 U.S. 687 (1966), the Supreme Court stated:

> We start with the proposition that the federal income tax is a tax on net income, not a sanction against wrongdoing. That principle has been firmly imbedded in the tax statute from the beginning.

Id. at 691. If deductions from gross income are disallowed because the claimed expenses result from illegal payments, the tax may look more like a penalty itself since it would be imposed on the higher gross income rather than net income. This tax versus penalty distinction served as the basis for one of the most controversial aspects of the Supreme Court decision in *NFIB* upholding the ACA individual mandate. According to the opinion of Chief Justice Roberts, a tax may rise to the level of a penalty, and thus be outside the scope of Congressional taxing power, depending on the circumstances. It is unclear how, or whether, this portion of the opinion could affect these provisions.

Nevertheless, constitutional challenges to the disallowance of illegal payments as *deductions* have generally proven unsuccessful. This result reinforces the oft-quoted maxim that deductions are a matter of "legislative grace." See Commissioner v. Sullivan, 356 U.S. 27, 28 (1958) ("Deductions are a matter of grace and Congress can, of course, disallow them as it chooses."); New Colonial Ice Co. v. Helvering, 292 U.S. 435, 440 (1934) ("Whether and to what extent deductions shall be allowed depends upon legislative grace; and only as there is clear provision therefor can any particular deduction be allowed.").

A distinction must be made, however, between deductions subtracted from gross income to determine taxable income and adjustments made to calculate the amount of gross income, such as the basis of property in calculating gain on sale. In Revenue Ruling 82-149, 1982-2 C.B. 56, the Service ruled that §162(c) was intended to disallow only deductions from gross income and could not be used to prevent adjustments in the computation of gross income itself, citing Pittsburgh Milk Co. v. Commissioner, 26 T.C. 707 (1956) and Max Sobel Wholesale Liquors v. Commissioner, 69 T.C. 477 (1977), affd., 630 F.2d 670 (9th Cir. 1980). Similarly, the Senate Finance Committee report on §280E specifies that adjustments to gross receipts for costs of goods sold in determining gross income are not disallowed by §280E.

CALIFORNIANS HELPING TO ALLEVIATE MEDICAL PROBLEMS, INC., v. COMMISSIONER
128 T.C. 173 (2007)

Laro, Judge.

. . . [W]e decide whether section 280E precludes petitioner from deducting the ordinary and necessary expenses attributable to its provision of medical marijuana pursuant to the California Compassionate Use Act of 1996. We hold that those deductions are precluded. We also decide whether section 280E precludes petitioner from deducting the ordinary and necessary expenses attributable to its provision of counseling and other caregiving services (collectively, caregiving services). We hold that those deductions are not precluded.

FINDINGS OF FACT

. . . Petitioner['s] . . . articles of incorporation stated that it "is organized and operated exclusively for charitable, educational and scientific purposes" and "The property of this corporation is irrevocably dedicated to charitable purposes." Petitioner did not have Federal tax-exempt status, and it operated as an approximately break-even (i.e., the amount of its income approximated the amount of its expenses) community center for members with debilitating diseases. Approximately 47 percent of petitioner's members suffered from Acquired Immune Deficiency Syndrome (AIDS); the remainder suffered from cancer, multiple sclerosis, and other serious illnesses. Before joining petitioner, petitioner's executive director had 13 years of experience in health services as a coordinator of a statewide program that trained outreach workers in AIDS prevention work.

Petitioner operated with a dual purpose. Its primary purpose was to provide caregiving services to its members. Its secondary purpose was to provide its members with medical marijuana pursuant to the California Compassionate Use Act of 1996 and to instruct those individuals on how to use medical marijuana to benefit their health.

Petitioner required that each member have a doctor's letter recommending marijuana as part of his or her therapy and an unexpired photo identification card from the California Department of Public Health verifying the authenticity of the doctor's letter. Petitioner required that its members not resell or redistribute the medical marijuana received from petitioner, and petitioner considered any violation of this requirement to be grounds to expel the violator from membership in petitioner's organization.

Each of petitioner's members paid petitioner a membership fee in consideration for the right to receive caregiving services and medical marijuana from petitioner. Petitioner's caregiving services were extensive. . . .

Petitioner furnished its services at its main facility in San Francisco, California, and at an office in a community church in San Francisco. . . . This location also was the site where petitioner's members received their distribution of medical marijuana; the medical marijuana was dispensed at a counter of the main room of the facility, taking up approximately 10 percent of the main facility. The peer group meetings and yoga classes were usually held at the church, where petitioner rented space. Pursuant to the rules of the church, petitioner's members were prohibited from bringing any marijuana into the church. Petitioner also maintained a storage unit at a third location in San Francisco. Petitioner used the storage unit to store confidential medical records; no medical marijuana was distributed or used there.

Petitioner paid for the services it provided to its members by charging a membership fee that covered, and in the judgment of petitioner's management approximated, both the cost of petitioner's caregiving services and the cost of the medical marijuana that petitioner supplied to its members. Petitioner notified its members that the membership fee covered both of these costs, and petitioner charged its members no additional fee. Members received from petitioner a set amount of medical marijuana; they were not entitled to unlimited supplies.

. . . In a notice of deficiency . . . respondent disallowed all of petitioner's deductions and costs of goods sold, determining that those items were "Expenditures in Connection with the Illegal Sale of Drugs" within the meaning of section 280E . . .

Opinion

The parties agree that during the subject year petitioner had at least one trade or business for purposes of section 280E. According to respondent, petitioner had a single trade or business of trafficking in medical marijuana. Petitioner argues that it engaged in two trades or businesses. Petitioner asserts that its primary trade or business was the provision of caregiving services. Petitioner asserts that its secondary trade or business was the supplying of medical marijuana to its members. As to its trades or businesses, petitioner argues, the deductions for those trades or businesses are not precluded by section 280E in that the trades or businesses did not involve "trafficking" in a controlled substance. Respondent argues that section 280E precludes petitioner from benefiting from any of its deductions.

. . . [T]axpayers such as petitioner may generally deduct the ordinary and necessary expenses incurred in carrying on a trade or business. See sec. 162(a). Items specified in section 162(a) are allowed as deductions, subject to exceptions listed in section 261. See sec. 161. Section 261 provides that "no deduction shall in any case be allowed in respect of the items specified in this part." The phrase "this part" refers to part IX of subchapter B of chapter 1, entitled "Items Not Deductible." "Expenditures in Connection With the Illegal Sale of Drugs" is an item specified in part IX. Section 280E provides:

> No deduction or credit shall be allowed for any amount paid or incurred during the taxable year in carrying on any trade or business if such trade or business (or the activities which comprise such trade or business) consists of trafficking in controlled substances (within the meaning of schedule I and II of the Controlled Substances Act) which is prohibited by Federal law or the law of any State in which such trade or business is conducted.

In the context of section 280E, marijuana is a schedule I controlled substance. Such is so even when the marijuana is medical marijuana recommended by a physician as appropriate to benefit the health of the user. See United States v. Oakland Cannabis Buyers' Coop., 532 U.S. 483 (2001).

Respondent argues that petitioner, because it trafficked in a controlled substance, is not permitted by section 280E to deduct any of its expenses. We disagree. . . .

Congress enacted section 280E as a direct reaction to the outcome of a case in which this Court allowed a taxpayer to deduct expenses incurred in an illegal drug trade. In that case, Edmondson v. Commissioner, T.C. Memo.1981–623, the Court found that the taxpayer was self-employed in a trade or business of selling amphetamines, cocaine, and marijuana. The Court allowed the taxpayer to deduct his business expenses because they "were made in connection with . . . [the taxpayer's] trade or business and were both ordinary and necessary." Id. In discussing the case in the context of the then-current law, the Senate Finance Committee stated in its report:

> Ordinary and necessary trade or business expenses are generally deductible in computing taxable income. A recent U.S. Tax Court case allowed deductions for telephone, auto, and rental expense incurred in the illegal drug trade. In that case, the Internal Revenue Service challenged the amount of the taxpayer's deduction for cost of goods (illegal drugs) sold, but did not challenge the principle that such amounts were deductible.
>
> On public policy grounds, the Code makes certain otherwise ordinary and necessary expenses incurred in a trade or business nondeductible in computing taxable income. These nondeductible expenses include fines, illegal bribes and kickbacks, and certain other illegal payments.

The report then expressed the following reasons the committee intended to change the law:

> There is a sharply defined public policy against drug dealing. To allow drug dealers the benefit of business expense deductions at the same time that the U.S. and its citizens are losing billions of dollars per year to such persons is not compelled by the fact that such deductions are allowed to other, legal, enterprises. Such deductions must be disallowed on public policy grounds.

. . . Section 280E and its legislative history express a congressional intent to disallow deductions attributable to a trade or business of trafficking in controlled substances. They do not express an intent to deny the deduction of all of a taxpayer's business expenses simply because the taxpayer was involved in trafficking in a controlled substance. We hold that section 280E does not preclude petitioner from deducting expenses attributable to a trade or business other than that of illegal trafficking in controlled substances simply because petitioner also is involved in the trafficking in a controlled substance.

Petitioner argues that its supplying of medical marijuana to its members was not "trafficking" within the meaning of section 280E. We disagree. We define and apply the gerund "trafficking" by reference to the verb "traffic," which as relevant herein denotes "to engage in commercial activity: buy and sell regularly." Webster's Third New International Dictionary 2423 (2002). Petitioner's supplying of medical marijuana to its members is within that definition in that petitioner regularly bought and sold the marijuana, such sales occurring when petitioner distributed the medical marijuana to its members in exchange for part of their membership fees.

We now turn to analyze whether petitioner's furnishing of its caregiving services is a trade or business that is separate from its trade or business of providing medical marijuana. Taxpayers may be involved in more than one trade or business, and whether an activity is a trade or business separate from another trade or business is a question of fact that depends on (among other things) the degree of economic interrelationship between the two undertakings. The Commissioner generally accepts a taxpayer's characterization of two or more undertakings as separate activities unless the characterization is artificial or unreasonable.

We do not believe it to have been artificial or unreasonable for petitioner to have characterized as separate activities its provision of caregiving services and its provision of medical marijuana. Petitioner was regularly and extensively involved in the provision of caregiving services, and those services are substantially different from petitioner's provision of medical marijuana. By conducting its recurring discussion groups, regularly distributing food and hygiene supplies, advertising and making available the services of personal counselors, coordinating social events and field trips, hosting educational classes, and providing other social services, petitioner's caregiving business stood on its own, separate and apart from petitioner's provision of medical marijuana. On the basis of all of the facts and circumstances of this case, we hold that petitioner's provision of caregiving services was a trade or business separate and apart from its provision of medical marijuana. . . .

Respondent relies heavily on his assertion that "Petitioner's only income was from marijuana-related matters, except for a couple of small donations." The record does not support that assertion, and we decline to find it as a fact. Indeed, the record leads us to make the contrary finding that petitioner's caregiving services generated income attributable to those services. . . . As the record reveals, and as we find as a fact, petitioner's management set the total amount of the membership fees as the amount that management consciously and reasonably judged equaled petitioner's costs of the caregiving services and the costs of the medical marijuana.

Given petitioner's separate trades or businesses, we are required to apportion its overall expenses accordingly. . . . Accordingly . . . we allocate to petitioner's caregiving services 18/25 of the expenses for salaries, wages, payroll taxes, employee benefits, employee development training, meals and entertainment, and parking and tolls (18 of petitioner's 25 employees did not work directly in petitioner's provision of medical marijuana), all expenses incurred in renting facilities at the church (petitioner did not use the church to any extent to provide medical marijuana), all expenses incurred for "truck and auto" and "laundry and cleaning" (those expenses did not relate to any extent to petitioner's provision of medical marijuana), and 9/10 of the remaining expenses (90 percent of the square footage of petitioner's main facility was not used in petitioner's provision of medical marijuana). . . .

TUCKER v. COMMISSIONER
69 T.C. 675 (1978)

OPINION

WILBUR, J. . . .

The two issues presented for our determination are: (1) Whether $1,509, which was withheld from petitioner Carol Tucker's salary under State law for her participation in a teacher's strike, is includable in petitioner's gross income for Federal income tax purposes during taxable year 1973, and if so, (2) whether petitioners are denied a deduction for this amount under section 162(f). . . .

Petitioners are Albert Tucker and Carol Tucker (hereinafter referred to as Carol), husband and wife. . . .

During 1973, while she was employed as a teacher for the Harrison Central School District (hereinafter referred to as school district), Carol engaged in a 21-day strike. The strike in which Carol engaged was illegal under New York's Taylor Law which states, in part, that:

> No public employee or employee organization shall engage in a strike, and no public employee or employee organization shall cause, instigate, encourage, or condone a strike. [N.Y. Civ. Serv. Law sec. 210(1) (McKinney 1973).]

The principal sanction imposed upon those employees determined to have violated this law is provided by N.Y. Civil Service Law section 210(2)(g) (McKinney 1973):

> Payroll deductions. Not earlier than thirty nor later than ninety days following the date of such determination, the chief fiscal officer of the government involved shall deduct from the compensation of each such [striking] public employee an amount equal to twice his daily rate of pay for each day or part thereof that it was determined that he had violated this subdivision; such rate of pay to be computed as of the time of such violation. In computing such deduction, credit shall be allowed for amounts already withheld from such employee's compensation on account of his absence from work or other withholding of services on such day or days. . . .

While she was on strike, Carol was, of course, not paid the $1,509 she would have earned had she not been on strike. Additionally, in accordance with this State law the school district deducted from Carol's gross pay for subsequent periods in 1973 after she had returned to work a total of $1,509. These deductions from her pay were shown on the "Statement of Earnings and Deductions" sent to Carol by the school district, and this amount was included in "wages, tips and other compensation." . . . Petitioners reported this $1,509 as income on their 1973 Federal income tax return, and deducted it on the return as an employee business expense. Respondent determined a deficiency based on the conclusion that this $1,509 represented taxable income during 1973, and that section 162(f) prohibited its deduction.

Respondent's position with respect to the first issue is summarized in Rev. Rul. 76-130, 1976-1 C.B. 16. Basically respondent contends that Carol incurred a penalty as a result of the strike, and that the obligation to pay the penalty was discharged out of her normal salary when she returned to work, thus producing taxable income. We agree with this conclusion.

Section 61(a) defines "gross income" broadly, and specifically includes both "compensation for services" and "income from discharge of indebtedness" within its meaning. It is clear that when Carol engaged in an illegal strike she incurred an indebtedness because of the penalty specified by the Taylor Law. This debt was satisfied when, upon her return to work, the school district withheld a portion of her normal salary corresponding to the amount of her indebtedness. This procedure is analogous to a garnishment of wages commonly used by creditors as a collection mechanism. . . . The fact that the fine was deducted directly from Carol's salary rather than collected from her after payment of her salary is irrelevant.

Respondent's position with respect to the second issue is also summarized in Rev. Rul. 76-130, 1976-1 C.B. 16. Basically respondent contends that the $1,509 in issue constitutes the payment of a fine and hence is nondeductible under section 162(f). . . .

The sanction imposed herein on Carol has been termed a "civil penalty" by the New York courts. It reflects a deeply and consistently held policy of the State with respect to the proper relationship between the State and local governments on one hand and their employees on the other. To allow a deduction herein would frustrate that policy. An individual whose income (either alone or when combined with his spouse's on a joint return) is taxed at a marginal rate of 25 percent, would incur a net after tax penalty equal to three days at the statutory rate for being on strike for four days. Certainly teachers are sophisticated enough, particularly when informed by their unions and teachers' associations, to be aware of these basic economic facts. Section 162(f) codifies a long history of disallowing penalties under circumstances in principle analogous to those herein, and petitioners' deduction must therefore be disallowed.

We have considered several arguments that might have been advanced on petitioners' behalf. It could be suggested that the New York statute simply requires a day's service without pay for each day of the strike before compensatory service begins again, much as it requires a year's service without tenure prior to regaining tenured status. . . .

However, we do not believe this was the intent of the New York State law. A careful reading of the statute makes it clear that any raises during the strike period (due to annually scheduled increments, graduate credits, or cost of living increases) will be included in Carol's subsequent compensation, and the amount of the fine withheld will be based on the old rate of pay applicable during the strike period. For example, if a penalty is withheld in September for a strike occurring the previous June, the penalty is based on the rate of compensation for the prior school year and is withheld from Carol's total compensation, including any increases applicable in the new year. Additionally, it appears that any benefits, apparently including retirement and medical benefits that a teacher may be entitled to, continue to accrue during the pay periods from which the fine is deducted.

It also appears that the only statutory mechanism for collecting the fine is through withholding from a teacher's future compensation. . . . The State apparently felt that imposing the penalty in this context was more than sufficient to achieve the strong public policy objectives of the Taylor Act. . . .

Decision will be entered for the respondent.

Problem

6-29. Bill Malone was hired by Jonathan Murdock to drive Murdock's van, which contained illegally unregistered handguns, from a warehouse to Murdock's office. A drunk driver hit the van and in the resulting fire the entire load of guns was destroyed.

    a. Can Murdock deduct the cost of the guns or the salary payments to Malone?

    b. Assume that the guns are not totally destroyed, and the police charge Murdock with possession of illegal goods. If Murdock pleads nolo contendere and is fined, can he deduct the fine?

    c. If Murdock pays his "friend" at the police department to misplace the evidence, can he deduct the payment?

    d. Assume Murdock is tried on criminal charges. Can he deduct the cost of his defense?

    e. What if possession of the guns was legal under state law because Malone was in a state which did not require registration of guns but illegal under federal law for failure to comply with federal registration requirements?

2. *Business Use of Personal Residence — Home Offices*

Code: §280A(a) to (c)(1)

As previously discussed, the Code limits the ability of taxpayers to deduct expenses incurred for mixed business and personal purposes. Thus, the deductibility of travel expenses is circumscribed if the purpose of the trip is both business and personal. Similarly, the deductibility of expenses incurred in connection with assets used for both business and personal purposes is substantially curtailed. Even more stringent limitations restrict the deduction of expenses arising from the business use of one's personal residence or vacation home.

Section 280A disallows deductions by individuals with respect to the business use of a personal residence. Four exceptions to the general disallowance rule of §280A permit deduction of business expenses incurred for certain home offices, inventory storage, rental, and day care. The following discussion focuses on the home office exception; rental of vacation homes is discussed in Chapter 8.

Prior to 1976, principles governing deduction of expenses attributable to a taxpayer's use of property both as a personal residence and for business purposes were unsettled. A number of court decisions were conflicting and uncertain as some refused to apply a "condition of employment" test in the application of the ordinary and necessary standard. Consequently, enterprising taxpayers attempted to take advantage of the §162 business expense deduction by characterizing expenses related to their personal residence as deductible business expenses arising from the use of all or part of that property in a business activity. A popular tactic was to establish an office in the home. Congress therefore enacted §280A to stop taxpayer abuses in this area.

Section 280A(a), the general rule governing business use of a home, states that "[e]xcept as otherwise provided in this section, . . . no deduction otherwise allowable under this chapter shall be allowed with respect to the use of a dwelling unit which is used by the taxpayer during the taxable year as a residence." Thus, this section does not create any deductions. Instead, §280A serves only to limit §162 trade or business expense deductions that are incurred in connection with a dwelling unit used by the taxpayer as a personal residence. However, §280A does not limit those deductions that are allowable without reference to §162, such as interest expenses (§163) or taxes (§164).

To qualify for home office deductions, the taxpayer must satisfy two tests. First, the taxpayer must use the office exclusively for business purposes on a regular basis. Second, the office must be either the principal place of the taxpayer's business (§280A(c)(1)(A)) or a place of business where the taxpayer meets patients, clients, or customers in the normal course of business (§280A(c)(1)(B)). (Section 280A(c)(1)(C), which deals with separate structures not attached to the dwelling unit, suggests a more relaxed, "in connection with taxpayer's business" test.)

GENERAL EXPLANATION OF TAX LEGISLATION ENACTED IN 1997
128 (1997)

HOME OFFICE DEDUCTION: CLARIFICATION OF DEFINITION OF PRINCIPAL PLACE OF BUSINESS

A taxpayer's business use of his or her home may give rise to a deduction for the business portion of expenses related to operating the home (e.g., a portion of rent or depreciation and repairs). Code section 280A(c)(1) provides, however, that business deductions generally are allowed only with respect to a portion of a home that is used exclusively and regularly in one of the following ways: (1) as the principal place of business for a trade or business; (2) as a place of business used to meet with patients, clients, or customers in the normal course of the taxpayer's trade or business; or (3) in connection with the taxpayer's trade or business, if the portion so used constitutes a separate structure not attached to the dwelling unit. In the case of an employee, the Code further requires that the business use of the home must be for the convenience of the employer (sec. 280A(c)(1)). These rules apply to houses, apartments, condominiums, mobile homes, boats, and other similar property used as the taxpayer's home (sec. 280A(f)(1)). Under Internal Revenue Service (IRS) rulings, the deductibility of expenses incurred for local transportation between a taxpayer's home and a work location sometimes depends on whether the taxpayer's home office qualifies under section 280A(c)(1) as a principal place of business (see Rev. Rul. 94-47).

Prior to 1976, expenses attributable to the business use of a residence were deductible whenever they were "appropriate and helpful" to the taxpayer's business. In 1976, Congress adopted section 280A, in order to provide a narrower scope for the home office deduction, but did not define the term "principal place of business." In Commissioner v. Soliman, the Supreme Court reversed lower court rulings and upheld an IRS interpretation of section 280A that disallowed a home office deduction for a self-employed anesthesiologist who practiced at several hospitals but was not provided office space at the hospitals. Although the anesthesiologist used a room in his home exclusively to perform administrative and management activities for his profession (i.e., he spent two or three hours a day in his home office on bookkeeping, correspondence, reading medical journals, and communicating with surgeons, patients, and insurance companies), the Supreme Court upheld the IRS position that the "principal place of business" for the taxpayer was not the home office, because the taxpayer performed the "essence of the professional service" at the hospitals. Because the taxpayer did not meet with patients at his home office and the room was not a separate structure, a deduction was not available under the second or third exception under section 280A(c)(1).

Section 280A(c)(2) contains a special rule that allows a home office deduction for business expenses related to a space within a home that is used on a regular (even if not exclusive) basis as a storage unit for the inventory or product samples of the taxpayer's trade or business of selling products at retail or wholesale, but only if the home is the sole fixed location of such trade or business.

Home office deductions may not be claimed if they create (or increase) a net loss from a business activity, although such deductions may be carried over to subsequent taxable years (sec. 280A(c)(5)).

The Congress believed that the Supreme Court's decision in *Soliman* unfairly denied a home office deduction to a growing number of taxpayers who manage their business activities from their homes. Thus, the statutory modification adopted by the Congress will reduce the prior-law bias in favor of taxpayers who manage their business activities from outside their homes, thereby enabling more taxpayers to work efficiently at home, save commuting time and expenses, and spend additional time with their families. Moreover, the statutory modification is an appropriate response to the computer and information revolution, which has made it more practical for taxpayers to manage trade or business activities from a home office.

Section 280A is amended to specifically provide that a home office qualifies as the "principal place of business" if (1) the office is used by the taxpayer to conduct administrative or management activities of a trade or business and (2) there is no other fixed location of the trade or business where the taxpayer conducts substantial administrative or management activities of the trade or business. As under present law, deductions will be allowed for a home office meeting the above two-part test only if the office is exclusively used on a regular basis as a place of business by the taxpayer and, in the case of an employee, only if such exclusive use is for the convenience of the employer.

Thus, under the provision, a home office deduction is allowed (subject to the present-law "convenience of the employer" rule governing employees), if a portion of a taxpayer's home is exclusively and regularly used to conduct administrative, or management activities for a trade or business of the taxpayer, who does not conduct substantial administrative or management activities at any other fixed location of the trade or business, regardless of whether administrative or management activities connected with his trade or business (e.g., billing activities) are performed by others at other locations. The fact that a taxpayer also carries out administrative or management activities at sites that are not fixed locations of the business, such as car or hotel room, will not affect the taxpayer's ability to claim a home office deduction under the provision. Moreover, if a taxpayer conducts some administrative or management activities at a fixed location of the business outside the home, the taxpayer still is eligible to claim a deduction so long as the administrative or management activities conducted at any fixed location of the business outside the home are not substantial (e.g., the taxpayer occasionally does minimal paperwork at another fixed location of the business). In addition, a taxpayer's eligibility to claim a home office deduction under the provision will not be affected by the fact that the taxpayer conducts substantial *non-administrative* or *non-management* business activities at a fixed location of the business outside the home (e.g., meeting with, or providing services to, customers, clients, or patients at a fixed location of the business away from home).

If a taxpayer in fact does not perform substantial administrative or management activities at any fixed location of the business away from home, then the second part of the test will be satisfied, regardless of whether or not the taxpayer opted not to use an office away from home that was available for the conduct of such activities. However, in the case of an employee, the question whether an employee chose not to use suitable space made available by the employer for administrative activities is relevant to determining whether the present-law "convenience of the employer" test is satisfied. In cases where a taxpayer's use of a home office does not satisfy the provision's two-part test, the taxpayer nonetheless may be able to claim a home office deduction under the present-law "principal place of business" exception or any other provision of section 280A.

Problems

6-30. Mary Carson works at home in her basement where she knits sweaters for a business that distributes home craft items. Carson is paid by a manufacturer on a per piece basis and receives a fixed amount for each sweater she produces. Is Carson entitled to a §162 deduction for the use of her basement in her business?

6-31. Joanna James, a CPA, often takes work home from the office and works during the evenings in the study in her house. She uses the study only when she is working on files that she brought home from work. She does not bring work home every evening; however, during tax season she not only works during the evenings but also works long hours at home on the weekends.
   a. Is she entitled to a home office deduction for her business-related expenses?
   b. What planning techniques, if any, might enhance her position?

6-32. How would one determine how much a taxpayer, successful under §280A, should be allowed to deduct? Does one use the number of rooms devoted to business use? Amount of square footage? Should the relative amount of time spent in the rooms devoted to business use affect the determination?

F. DEPRECIATION AND COST RECOVERY

Code: §§167(a), (c)(1); 168(a) to (e)(3); 179; 197(a) to (d); 263(a); 280F(a) to (b)
Regulations: §§1.167(a)-1, (a)-3, (a)-10, (b)-1, (b)-2, (g)-1; 1.168(d)-1(a) to (b); 1.197-2(a) to (b)

To stimulate economic growth, encourage investment in technological innovations, and permit a recoupment of business-oriented or profit-oriented expenditures, Congress has provided a means by which taxpayers can recover capital invested in certain assets that have a finite physical or technological life. The depreciation provisions, §§167 and 168, allow a deduction over a period of time for the costs of most business-related capital expenditures. Section 167 was the predecessor of §168, which incorporated many of the concepts and provisions of §167. Expenditures for tangible or intangible property that will be used for more than one year and incurred in producing income are classified as capital expenditures. Examples of capital expenditures include the acquisition of a typewriter, delivery van, or office furnishings.

1. The Concept of Depreciation

The underlying rationale for the §167 depreciation allowance is similar to that for the §162 business expense deduction. Both sections permit deductions in an attempt to reflect the costs that a business incurs in producing income, thereby ensuring that net income rather than gross income is taxed. For ordinary business expenses, this can be accomplished by deducting the cost in the current year from the gross receipts of the business. For investments in assets that will generate income for multiple years, the issue becomes more complicated. How much of such an investment is "used up" generating income for any particular year?

A tenet of general financial accounting and of tax accounting requires the matching of expenses with the income they generate. The only way to match a capital expenditure properly to the annual income it generates is to capitalize and amortize the cost of the asset over its useful life. Thus, the entire cost of a capital expenditure is not expensed or deducted in the year in which it is incurred. Instead, a portion of the cost is matched with a particular accounting period and then recovered as a depreciation deduction. Depreciation deductions are taken over the property's useful life — that is, the years in which the property is expected to be used in the business. Thus, the useful life of the asset must be finite or ascertainable. Consequently, assets such as land, which have an infinite useful life, are not depreciable.

In addition to matching income and expenses, depreciation deductions also help taxpayers replace wasting assets by reducing taxable income. If taxable income is reduced, the taxpayer reduces tax liability and retains more income that can be used to purchase a new asset when the old one wears out or becomes obsolete. It may be possible, however, to recoup the total cost of the asset in depreciation deductions, thereby leaving the asset with a zero basis even though the asset retains a positive fair market value. This phenomenon occurs because the depreciation allocated to various accounting periods usually do not equal declines or fluctuations in the value of an asset. Thus, depreciation is a process designed to allocate the cost of an asset, not to reflect its decline in value. For example, when one says a car depreciates $1,000 as soon as it is driven off the lot, the term "depreciation" is being used in a valuation, not in a tax accounting, sense.

Even if the depreciation deductions coincide with the decline in value of the asset, the depreciation deductions cannot completely fund the purchase of a replacement asset. A single dollar of a depreciation deduction does not save a dollar in tax liability because the marginal tax rates do not rise to 100 percent.

The mechanics of §167. The Supreme Court in United States v. Ludey, 274 U.S. 295 (1927), articulated the following definition of depreciation:

> The depreciation charge permitted as a deduction from the gross income in determining the taxable income of a business for any year represents the reduction, during the year, of the capital assets through wear and tear. . . . The amount of the allowance for depreciation is the sum which should be set aside for the taxable year, in order that, at the end of the [asset's] useful life . . . in the business, the aggregate of the sums set aside will (with the salvage value) suffice to provide an amount equal to the original cost. The theory underlying this allowance for depreciation is that by using up the [asset], a gradual sale is made of it. The depreciation charged is the measure of the cost of the part which has been sold. When the [asset] is disposed of after years of use, the thing then sold is not the whole thing originally acquired. The amount of the depreciation must be deducted from the original cost of the whole in order to determine the cost of that disposed of in the final sale of properties.

Id. at 300.

The percentage of an asset's cost allocable to a particular year can be determined by several methods. The method chosen depends in part on whether cost is being allocated for financial accounting purposes or for tax purposes. The differences in methods of cost allocation arise because accountants and legislators have different objectives in providing for depreciation. Accountants allocate the cost of the asset so that the financial records of a business accurately state its financial condition. Legislators, in structuring the tax laws, provide depreciation deductions to accomplish two objectives: (1) to give the taxpayer a deduction for the reasonable business-related costs denied a current deduction by the §§263 and 263A capital expenditure limitation and (2) to implement a national economic policy that encourages capital investment and adjusts tax revenues accordingly. Accounting and tax practice may therefore require two separate depreciation calculations, resulting in the taxes actually due being less than those calculated using the accounting figures if the tax law permits a faster write-off than accounting practice.

The following example illustrates the depreciation concept. Assume that a calendar-year taxpayer, John Harry, starts a new business selling legal outlines to fellow law students. Harry purchases new business equipment for $20,000. Harry assumes that the equipment will be obsolete in this particular business in four years (its useful life), after which time its estimated salvage value will be $5,000. Because Harry plans to dispose of the equipment at the end of four years, before it has lost all value, only $15,000 of its cost will have been used to help produce income. This $15,000 represents the *depreciable cost* of the asset.

How is the depreciable cost to be allocated to the four accounting periods in which the equipment is used? One alternative would be to allocate the entire cost to the first year as a current deduction. Section 263 prevents this result, which would have the effect of understating the first year's income and overstating the income in years 2, 3, and 4. If Harry were permitted a current deduction for the entire cost of the equipment, year 1 would reflect a deduction for the total cost of an expense that was not depleted in that year, and in years 2, 3, and 4, the business would receive the benefit of a working asset without bearing any of its cost.

Because the new business equipment has a useful life of more than one year, the cost of acquiring the equipment is a capital expenditure and not currently deductible. Section 167(b), before amendment, listed the methods by which a "reasonable allowance" for depreciation could be computed. Harry could, for example, have elected the straight-line method of depreciation, which had the effect of evenly allocating the expense over the useful life of the asset. The annual allowable straight-line depreciation deduction was computed by dividing the depreciable cost of the asset by its useful life according to the following formula:

$$\frac{\text{Annual straight-line}}{\text{depreciation}} = \frac{\text{Adjusted basis of asset} - \text{Salvage value}}{\text{Useful life}}$$

Thus, Harry would have been entitled to an annual deduction of \$3,750:

$$\frac{\$20,000 - \$5,000}{4} = \$3,750$$

Section 167(b) also provided accelerated methods of depreciation: the declining balance method and the sum of the years-digits method. These methods allowed the taxpayer to deduct more of the cost in the year of purchase. Additionally, §167(b)(4) permitted the taxpayer to elect any other consistent method of computing depreciation that did not result in deductions during the first two-thirds of an asset's life that were in excess of the deductions allowable under the declining balance method. None of these methods was available for assets having a useful life of less than three years. Additionally, neither the sum of the years-digits nor §167(b)(4) methods could be used to depreciate property acquired secondhand.

If Harry elected a declining balance method, his rate of deduction was determined by the nature of the asset being depreciated and the rate of allowable straight-line depreciation. Under that method, the depreciation rate was calculated by multiplying the applicable percentage, depending on whether the property was new or used, by the straight-line rate. If Harry acquired used property, he was limited to a rate of 150 percent or less of allowable straight-line depreciation. The rate permitted for new tangible property with a useful life of three years or more was 200 percent or double declining balance. In the above hypothetical, Harry's equipment had a four-year useful life. Harry therefore was entitled to elect the double declining balance method. Under that method, depreciation for a given year was determined by applying twice the straight-line rate to the adjusted basis (original cost less depreciation taken in prior years) as of the beginning of that year. Harry's straight-line rate of depreciation was 25 percent per year. His rate of depreciation under the double declining balance method, therefore, was 50 percent (2 × 25%). The declining balance methods did not deduct the salvage value from the adjusted basis of the asset. However, the salvage value limited the total amount of deductions that could be taken with regard to the depreciable asset. Harry's deductions over the useful life of the new business equipment therefore was computed as follows.

In the year of purchase, Harry deducted 50 percent of his $20,000 purchase price ($10,000). His declining balance (adjusted basis) thereafter was $10,000. In year 2, his deduction was $5,000 (50% × $10,000) and his balance declined to $5,000. Thus, in year 3, Harry reached the salvage value limitation and could take no further depreciation deductions.

2.   *The Accelerated Cost Recovery System*

Because capital investment may be stimulated or curtailed through various depreciation rates, depreciation is one area to which Congress continually turns in its efforts to affect national economic policy. The accelerated cost recovery system (ACRS), enacted in 1981, illustrates congressional efforts to manipulate the depreciation rules in order to achieve economic goals by permitting taxpayers to depreciate assets at a more rapid rate than existed under pre-1981 law. See S. Rep. No. 144, 97th Cong., 1st Sess. 48 (1981).

In addition to focusing on economic goals, the ACRS eliminated two areas of controversy that existed under §167: the determinations of useful life and of salvage value. Previously, a taxpayer would contend that the salvage value was low in order to maximize deductions. In response, the Service would, of course, argue for a higher salvage value. Section 168 disregards salvage value in computing cost recovery, removing it as a potential issue for litigation. See §168(b)(4). A similar area of controversy existed with regard to the useful life of an asset. Taxpayers favored short useful lives (to accelerate deductions to earlier years), while the Service argued for long ones (to defer deductions). ACRS eliminates this conflict by providing statutory periods over which allowable deductions may be taken. See §168(c).

TAX REFORM ACT OF 1986
H.R. Rep. No. 841, 99th Cong., 2d Sess. II-38 (1986)

CAPITAL COST PROVISIONS

A.   COST RECOVERY: DEPRECIATION . . .

1.   ACCELERATED DEPRECIATION

a.   Cost Recovery Classes . . .

Conference Agreement

In General

The conference agreement modifies the Accelerated Cost Recovery System (ACRS) for property placed in service after December 31, 1986. . . .

The conference agreement provides more accelerated depreciation for the revised three-year, five-year and ten-year classes, reclassifies certain assets according to their present class life (or "ADR * midpoints," Rev. Proc. 83-35, 1983-1 C.B. 745), and creates a seven-year class, a 20-year class, a 27.5-year class, and a [39]-year class. The conference agreement prescribes depreciation methods for each ACRS class. . . . Eligible personal property and certain real property are assigned among a three-year class, a five-year class, a seven-year class, a ten-year class, a 15-year class, or a 20-year class.

The depreciation method applicable to property included in the three-year, five-year, seven-year, and ten-year classes is the double declining balance method, switching to the straight-line method at a time to maximize the depreciation allowance. For property in the 15-year and 20-year class, the conference agreement applies the 150-percent declining balance method, switching to the straight-line method at a time to maximize the depreciation allowance. The cost of section 1250 real property generally is recovered over 27.5 years for residential rental property and [39] years for nonresidential property, using the straight-line method.

Classes of Property

Property is classified as follows:

Three-year class. — ADR midpoints of four years or less, except automobiles and light trucks, and adding horses which are assigned to the three-year class under present law.

Five-year class. — ADR midpoints of more than four years and less than ten years, and adding automobiles, light trucks, qualified technological equipment, computer-based telephone central office switching equipment, research and experimentation property, and geothermal, ocean thermal, solar, and wind energy properties, and biomass properties that constitute qualifying small power production facilities (within the meaning of section 3(17)(C) of the Federal Power Act).

Seven-year class. — ADR midpoints of ten years and less than 16 years, and adding single-purpose agricultural or horticultural structures and property with no ADR midpoint that is not classified elsewhere.

Ten-year class. — ADR midpoints of 16 years and less than 20 years.

15-year class. — ADR midpoints of 20 years and less than 25 years, and adding municipal wastewater treatment plants, and telephone distribution plant and comparable equipment used for the two-way exchange of voice and data communications.

20-year class. — ADR midpoints of 25 years and more, other than section 1250 real property with an ADR midpoint of 27.5 years and more, and adding municipal sewers.

27.5-year class. — Residential rental property (including manufactured homes that are residential rental property and elevators and escalators).

[39]-year class. — Nonresidential real property (section 1250 real property that is not residential rental property and that either does not have an ADR

---

* The generally employed depreciation method prior to the enactment of §168. — Eds.

midpoint or whose ADR midpoint is 27.5 years or more, including elevators and escalators). . . .

c.   Changes in Classification . . .

Under the conference agreement, the Treasury Department has the authority to adjust class lives of most assets (other than residential rental property and non-residential real property) based on actual experience. Any new class life will be used for determining the classification of such property and in applying an alternative depreciation system.

Any class life prescribed under the Secretary's authority must reflect the anticipated useful life, and the anticipated decline in value over time, of an asset to the industry or other group. Useful life means the economic life span of property over all users combined and not, as under prior law, the typical period over which a taxpayer holds the property. Evidence indicative of the useful life of property which the Secretary is expected to take into account in prescribing a class life includes the depreciation practices followed by taxpayers for book purposes with respect to the property. It also includes useful lives experienced by taxpayers, according to their reports. It further includes independent evidence of minimal useful life—the terms for which new property is leased, used under a service contract, or financed—and independent evidence of the decline in value of an asset over time, such as is afforded by resale price data. If resale price data is used to prescribe class lives, such resale price data should be adjusted downward to remove the effects of historical inflation. This adjustment provides a larger measure of depreciation than in the absence of such an adjustment. Class lives using this data should be determined such that the present value of straight-line depreciation deductions over the class life, discounted at an appropriate real rate of interest, is equal to the present value of what the estimated decline in value of the asset would be in the absence of inflation.

Initial studies are expected to concentrate on property that now has no ADR midpoint. . . .

4.   ACCOUNTING CONVENTIONS

a.   Half-Year Convention

Conference Agreement

. . . All property placed in service or disposed of during a taxable year is treated as placed in service or disposed of at the midpoint of such year. In the case of a taxable year less than 12 months, property is treated as being in service for half the number of months in such taxable Year. . . .

7.   EXPENSING . . .

The Senate amendment provides a [$19,000 for 1999 . . . , $20,000 for 2000 . . . , $25,000 for 2003 and thereafter] ceiling for expensing for taxpayers whose total investment in tangible personal property is $200,000 or less. For other taxpayers, for every dollar of investment in excess of $200,000, the ceiling is reduced by one dollar. The amount eligible to be expensed is limited to the taxable income derived from the active trade or business in which the property is used. The difference between expensing and ACRS deductions is recaptured if property is converted to nonbusiness use at any time before the end of the property's recovery period. . . .

The conference agreement generally follows the Senate amendment, but provides that the amount eligible to be expensed is limited to the taxable income derived from any trade or business. Married individuals filing separate returns are treated as one taxpayer for purposes of determining the amount which may be expensed and the total amount of investment in tangible personal property.

Note

The following example demonstrates the application of the §168 ACRS method. On May 1, year 1, Jane Smith purchased a light truck for use in her construction business. Jane paid $5,000 for the truck in year 1. The class life of a light truck is six years, and thus it is "5-year property" for purposes of §168(c), and it is subject to the mid-year convention. Assuming Jane elects under §168(b)(3)(D) to calculate her depreciation using the straight-line method, she would be permitted to deduct one-fifth, or 20 percent, of her initial investment for each full year, but in the first year she would be eligible to claim only one-half of a year's depreciation. Thus, her depreciation deductions would be calculated as shown in Table 6-1.

T A B L E   6-1

Year	Start of Year Adjusted Basis	Depreciation Deduction	End of Year Adjusted Basis
Year 1	$5,000	$ 500	$4,500
Year 2	4,500	1,000	3,500
Year 3	3,500	1,000	2,500
Year 4	2,500	1,000	1,500
Year 5	1,500	1,000	500
Year 6	500	500	0

Because of the combination of the five-year class life and the mid-year convention, Jane actually claims deductions through year 6.

Compare this example to one where the truck is subject to the §168(b)(1) double declining balance method of depreciation. In such a case, Jane would be entitled to a deduction in each full year equal to the *greater of* (1) the product of the adjusted basis of the truck at the beginning of the year and 40 percent (200% times a straight-line 5-year recovery), or (2) the depreciation applying the straight-line method using the adjusted basis of the truck at the beginning of the year and assuming that only the remaining class life was available. As with the straight-line example, owing to the mid-year convention, only half of the depreciation deduction is available in year 1 and year 6. Thus, Jane's depreciation deductions would be calculated as shown in Table 6-2.

TABLE 6-2

Year	Start of Year Adjusted Basis	Double Declining Balance Deduction	Straight-line Basis Deduction	Depreciation Deduction Claimed	End of Year Adjusted Basis
Year 1	$5,000	$1,000 (half of 40% × $5,000)	$500 (half of $5,000 ÷ 5)	$1,000	$4,000
Year 2	$4,000	$1,600 (40% × $4,000)	$888.89 ($4,000 ÷ 4.5)	$1,600	$2,400
Year 3	$2,400	$960 (40% × $2,400)	$685.71 ($2,400 ÷ 3.5)	$960	$1,440
Year 4	$1,440	$576 (40% × $1,440)	$576 ($1,440 ÷ 2.5)	$576	$864
Year 5	$864	$345.60 (40% × $864)	$576 (straight line from year 4)	$576	$288
Year 6	$288	$115.20 (40% × $288)	$288 (half of $576)	$288	$0

In year 4, the double declining balance method and the straight-line method deductions are the same. Before that point, the double declining balance method deductions are greater than the straight-line method, while after that point, the straight-line method deductions exceed the double declining balance (as demonstrated in years 5 and 6 in Table 6-2). Thus, in year 4, the switch is made to the straight-line method.

3. Depreciable Assets

The enactment of §168 successfully eliminated factual disputes regarding the actual useful life of assets, the actual date placed in service, and the actual salvage value of assets; it did so by replacing them with statutorily defined class lives, conventions on when assets are placed into service, and an assumption that salvage value is zero. As a result, §168 led to a substantial decrease in litigation over factual issues relating to depreciation of business assets. One threshold factual issue not addressed by §168, however, is whether an asset is in fact depreciable — that is, an asset of the type that is "used up" over time and thus permitted a depreciation deduction to offset income it generates. At first blush, this question appears relatively straightforward — machines break, factories require maintenance, trucks need new tires, and thus such assets must be used up as they are used by the business. At times the issue becomes more complicated, however. Consider the following case, in which the government, the taxpayer, the majority, and the dissent all appear to have very different opinions as to what constitutes depreciable property.

SIMON v. COMMISSIONER
68 F.3d 41 (2nd Cir. 1995)

WINTER, C.J.

This appeal from the Tax Court raises the question whether professional musicians may take a depreciation deduction for wear and tear on antique violin bows under the Accelerated Cost Recovery System ("ACRS") although the taxpayers cannot demonstrate that the bows have a "determinable useful life."

The parties agree that under the pre-ERTA Internal Revenue Code . . . and the Treasury Department regulations interpreting that Code, the bows would be considered depreciable property only if the taxpayers could demonstrate a determinable useful life. The issue here is to what extent, if any, the ACRS modified the determinable useful life requirement.

BACKGROUND

The facts are essentially undisputed. Richard and Fiona Simon are highly skilled professional violinists. . . . Mr. Simon was a full-time performer with the [New York] Philharmonic throughout the relevant tax year. . . . Ms. Simon was a full-time performer with the Philharmonic throughout the pertinent tax year.

The business property at issue consists of two violin bows ("the Tourte bows") made in the nineteenth century by Francois Tourte, a bowmaker renowned for technical improvements in bow design. These bows were purchased by the Simons in 1985 and were in a largely unused condition at the time. The Tax Court found that "[o]ld violins played with old bows produce exceptional sounds that are superior to sounds produced by newer violins played with newer bows." The Tax Court also found that violin bows suffer wear and tear when used regularly by performing musicians. With use, a violin bow will eventually become "played out," producing an inferior sound. However, a "played out" Tourte bow retains value as a collector's item notwithstanding its diminished utility. The Simons' Tourte bows, for example, were appraised in 1990 at $45,000 and $35,000, even though they had physically deteriorated since their purchase by the Simons in 1985 for $30,000 and $21,500, respectively.

The Simons use the Tourte bows regularly in their trade. In 1989, the tax year in question, the Simons performed in four concerts per week as well as numerous rehearsals with the Philharmonic. Their use of the Tourte bows during the tax year at issue subjected the bows to substantial wear and tear. Believing that they were entitled to depreciate the bows under the ACRS, the Simons claimed depreciation deductions for the two bows in the amount of $6,300 and $4,515.

The Tax Court agreed with the Simons and allowed the depreciation deductions. The Commissioner brought the present appeal.

DISCUSSION

This appeal turns on the interpretation of the ACRS provisions of §168, which provide a depreciation deduction for "recovery property" placed into service after

1980. Recovery property is defined by that section as "tangible property of a character subject to the allowance for depreciation" when "used in a trade or business, or . . . held for the production of income." The record establishes that the Simons' Tourte bows were tangible property placed in service after 1980 and used in the taxpayers' trade or business. The Commissioner contends, however, that the bows are not "property of a character subject to the allowance for depreciation."

The parties agree that section 168's phrase "of a character subject to depreciation" must be interpreted in light of the §167(a) allowances for "exhaustion, wear and tear, and . . . obsolescence." The Simons and the Tax Court maintain that, when read in conjunction with the plain language of section 167, section 168 requires only that the Tourte bows suffer wear and tear in the Simons' trade to qualify as "recovery property." The Commissioner, on the other hand, argues that because all property used in a trade or business is necessarily subject to wear and tear, the Simons' construction of section 168 would effectively render section 168's phase "of a character subject to the allowance for depreciation" superfluous, a result that Congress presumably could not have intended. Therefore, section 168's requirement that the property be "of a character subject to the allowance for depreciation" must include an element beyond wear and tear, namely the "determinable useful life" requirement embodied in §1.167(a)-1, a Treasury regulation of pre-ERTA vintage.

We do not agree with the Commissioner's premise because some tangible assets used in business are not exhausted, do not suffer wear and tear, or become obsolete. For example, paintings that hang on the wall of a law firm merely to be looked at — to please connoisseur clients or to give the appearance of dignity to combative professionals — do not generally suffer wear or tear. More to the point, the Simons' Tourte bows were playable for a time precisely because they had been kept in a private collection and were relatively unused since their manufacture. Indeed, it appears that one had never been played at all. Had that collection been displayed at a for-profit museum, the museum could not have depreciated the bows under ERTA because, although the bows were being used in a trade or business, they were not subject to wear and tear. The Tourte bows are not unlike numerous kinds of museum pieces or collectors' items. The Commissioner's textual argument thus fails because there are tangible items not subject to wear and tear.

The Commissioner next argues that Congressional intent and the notion of depreciation itself require that section 168's statutory language be supplemented by reading into the word "character" a requirement that tangible property have a demonstrable useful life. To address that issue, we must briefly examine the history of the depreciation allowance.

The tax laws have long permitted deductions for depreciation on certain income-producing assets used in a trade or business. The original rationale for the depreciation deduction was to allow taxpayers to match accurately, for tax accounting purposes, the cost of an asset to the income stream that the asset produced. In its traditional incarnation, therefore, the pace of depreciation deductions was determined by the period of time that the asset would produce income in the taxpayer's business. As the Supreme Court noted, "Congress intended by the depreciation allowance not to make taxpayers a profit thereby, but merely to protect them from a loss. . . . Accuracy in accounting requires that correct tabulations, not artificial ones, be used."

To implement this accurate tax accounting, the concept of a determinable useful life was necessary because, without such a determination, one could not calculate the proper annual allowance — "the sum which should be set aside for the taxable year, in order that, at the end of the useful life of the plant in the business, the aggregate of the sums set aside will (with the salvage value) suffice to provide an amount equal to the original cost." The regulation that the Commissioner now relies upon was promulgated under the 1954 Internal Revenue Code and reflects the rationale underlying the accounting scheme in effect just prior to ERTA.

ERTA, however, altered the depreciation scheme for two reasons other than sound accounting practice that are not consistent with the Commissioner's argument. First, the ACRS introduced accelerated depreciation periods as a stimulus for economic growth. Under ACRS, the cost of an asset is recovered over a predetermined period unrelated to — and usually shorter than — the useful life of the asset. Moreover, the depreciation deductions do not assume consistent use throughout the asset's life, instead assigning inflated deductions to the earlier years of use. Therefore, the purpose served by the determinable useful life requirement of the pre-ERTA scheme — allowing taxpayers to depreciate property over its actual use in the business — no longer exists under the ACRS. Because the ACRS is different by design, there is no logic in the Commissioner's suggestion that depreciation practice under the old section 167 calls for the imposition of a determinable useful life requirement after ERTA.

A second Congressional purpose embodied in ERTA also militates against reading a determinable useful life prerequisite into section 168. In addition to stimulating investment, Congress sought to simplify the depreciation rules by eliminating the need to adjudicate matters such as useful life and salvage value, which are inherently uncertain and result in unproductive disagreements between taxpayers and the Internal Revenue Service. Indeed, the legislation specifically sought to "deemphasize" the concept of useful life. On this point, we agree with the Tax Court that:

> [The Commissioner's] argument that a taxpayer must first prove the useful life of personal property before he or she may depreciate it over the 3-year or 5-year period would bring the Court back to pre-ERTA law and reintroduce the disagreements that the Congress intended to eliminate by its enactment of ERTA.

We also cannot accept the Commissioner's suggestion that her proposed interpretation de-emphasizes useful life by requiring establishment of a demonstrable useful life for only a "narrow category" of property. Insofar as the Commissioner seeks to do this by singling out usable antiques and other business property likely to appreciate in real economic value, she relies on a concept that has nothing whatsoever to do with the useful life of the asset in the business. As the Supreme Court noted, "useful life is measured by the use in a taxpayer's business, not by the full abstract economic life of the asset in any business." Nor, *a fortiori*, does the concept of useful life bear on the asset's eligibility under the ACRS. Indeed, the Commissioner's position that deductions for depreciation may not be taken for property that retains value after use in a business seems designed to avoid the consequences of ERTA's explicit rejection of "salvage value."[5]

---

5. We accept the Tax Court's finding that the bows have no "determinable useful life." That finding is based on the assumption that there is no distinction between the value of the bows to professional violinists and their value as antiques after they are no longer functional.

The Commissioner's strongest support for her claim that Congress intended to maintain section 1.167(a)-1's determinable useful life requirement comes from the House Conference Report, which noted that

> Under present law, assets used in a trade or business or for the production of income are depreciable if they are subject to wear and tear, decay or decline from natural causes or obsolescence. Assets that do not decline in value on a predictable basis or that do not have a determinable useful life, such as land, goodwill, and stock, are not depreciable.

The Simons unsuccessfully attempt to recharacterize this statement as an inartful catalogue of assets that are not subject to exhaustion, wear and tear, or obsolescence. The House report means what it says but gives us slight pause. In light of the overriding legislative intent to abandon the unnecessarily complicated rules on useful life, we cannot employ two sentences in a legislative report to trump statutory language and a clearly stated legislative purpose. Continued reliance on §1.167(a)-1 is in sharp conflict with the overall legislative history of ERTA, which definitively repudiates the scheme of complex depreciation rules, including "current regulations." We are thus not persuaded by the Commissioner's call for us to interpret a statute that abrogates a current regulatory regime as in fact incorporating the details of that scheme. In particular, we reject the argument that we should retain regulatory provisions now divorced from their functional purpose.

When a coherent regulatory system has been repudiated by statute — as this one has — it is inappropriate to use a judicial shoehorn to retain an isolated element of the now-dismembered regulation. We thus hold that, for the purposes of the "recovery property" provisions of section 168, "property subject to the allowance for depreciation" means property that is subject to exhaustion, wear and tear, or obsolescence. . . .

We acknowledge that the result of our holding may give favorable treatment to past investment decisions that some regard as wasteful, such as a law firm's purchase of expensive antique desks, the cost of which could have been quickly depreciated under our current ruling. However, Congress wanted to stimulate investment in business property generally, and it is not our function to draw subjective lines between the wasteful and the productive. Moreover, courts should take care that the Commissioner's role as revenue maximizer does not vitiate Congress's intent to sacrifice revenue to generate economic activity. If taxpayers cannot trust that such tax measures will be fully honored, some or all of the hoped-for activity will not occur. Id.

ERTA's abandonment of the concept of salvage value may be the rub that causes the Commissioner to take the position that the Tourte bows have no determinable useful life and are not depreciable. If salvage value could be used to offset depreciation, the Commissioner could, without loss to the Treasury, concede that the bows could be used to play the violin for only so long and simply offset the depreciation deduction by their continued value as antiques. The bows had been sparingly used, or not used at all, before they were purchased by the Simons and, having been used extensively, now have much less value as business property while retaining substantial value as antiques. The Commissioner may thus lean upon the thin reed of a supposed continuing determinable useful life requirement because Congress's intent to do away with the concept of salvage value is indisputable. In doing so, however, she fails to distinguish between a useful life as property used in a particular business — playing the violin as a professional — and value as non-functioning antiques.

One should not exaggerate the extent to which our holding is a license to hoard and depreciate valuable property that a taxpayer expects to appreciate in real economic value. The test is whether property will suffer exhaustion, wear and tear, or obsolescence in its use by a business. Even without a determinable useful life requirement, a business that displayed antique automobiles, for example, and kept them under near-ideal, humidity-controlled conditions, would still have difficulty demonstrating the requisite exhaustion, wear and tear, or obsolescence necessary to depreciate the automobiles as recovery property. Nor is valuable artwork purchased as office ornamentation apt to suffer anything more damaging than occasional criticism from the tutored or untutored, and it too would probably fail to qualify as recovery property. Indeed, even a noted artwork that serves as a day-to-day model for another artist's work cannot be depreciated as recovery property if it does not face exhaustion, wear and tear, or obsolescence in the pertinent business.

For the foregoing reasons, we affirm.

OAKES, S.C.J., dissenting:

I cannot believe that Congress, in changing the depreciation deduction from the Asset Depreciation Range System ("ADRS") for recovery of assets placed in service after December 31, 1980, to the Accelerated Cost Recovery System ("ACRS") whereby the cost of an asset is recovered over a predetermined period shorter than the useful life of the asset or the period the asset is used to produce income, intended to abandon the concept underlying depreciation, namely, that to permit the deduction the property must have a useful life capable of being estimated. I find no indication in either the changes of statutory language or the well-documented legislative history that Congress intended such a radical change. . . . Indeed, it seems to me that the statutory language and the legislative history — consistent with the dual congressional purpose of simplification and stimulating economic growth by permitting accelerated depreciation periods — retained the fundamental principle that, in order to depreciate, the asset involved must have a determinable useful life.

First, with respect to the statutory language, the question before us is whether antique violin bows constitute depreciable "recovery property" under section 168(c)(1) of the Internal Revenue Code effective during 1989, the year in issue. I.R.C. §168(c)(1) defined "recovery property" by saying:

> except as provided in subsection (e) the term "recovery property" means *tangible property of a character subject to the allowance for depreciation* — (A) used in a trade or business, or (B) held for the production of income.

Moreover, section 168(c)(2) assigned "recovery property" into four classes or tiers, and defined "recovery property" (other than real property) as "section 1245 property." Section 1245(a)(3) defined "section 1245 property" as "any property which is or has been property of a character subject to the allowance for depreciation provided in section 167. . . . "How section 168(c)(2), section 1245(a)(3), and section 167 could all be read out of the statute as they have been by the majority of this panel, seems to me incomprehensible. Needless to say, the cases are legion that under section 167, taxpayers must establish that the property being depreciated has a determinable useful life.

Under the majority's interpretation, however, the only criterion necessary to obtain a deduction under section 168(c) is that the property be subject to wear and tear. Thus, a car buff in the trade or business of buying, collecting, and selling antique automobiles, who drives his autos to auto shows may obtain a depreciation deduction, or the law office that buys fine Sheraton or Chippendale desks or chairs for office use can take a deduction, though in each case the auto or furniture is actually appreciating in value and has no determinable useful life.

As for legislative history, the majority candidly admits that House Conference Report 97-215, which states that "assets that do not decline in value on a predictable basis or that do not have a determinable useful life, such as land, goodwill, and stock, are not depreciable," "means what it says." The majority then adds that the Report "gives us slight pause."[1]

The majority of this court joins the Tax Court majority and the Third Circuit in holding that section 168(c)(1) applies to all tangible property that is subject to "wear and tear." I agree with the Commissioner that such an interpretation renders meaningless the phrase in section 168(c)(1) "of a character subject to the allowance for depreciation," since all tangible property used in a trade of business is necessarily subject to wear and tear. This point is confirmed by the General Explanation of the Economic Recovery Tax Act of 1981 which states that section 168 "does not change the determination under prior law as to whether property is depreciable or non-depreciable."

Nor can reliance be placed, as it is by the majority, upon the fact that section 168(f)(9) changed prior law by removing "salvage value" from the depreciation calculus. The fact that Congress eliminated salvage value while simultaneously defining the term "recovery property" as "tangible property of a character subject to the allowance for depreciation," cannot support the conclusion that section 168 eliminated the threshold requirement that taxpayers establish a determinable useful life for their property. Had Congress intended otherwise, the statute simply would have defined "recovery property" as "tangible property used in a trade or business" rather than as "tangible property of a character subject to the allowance for depreciation," and not specified that the recovery property be "section 1245 property," which, as stated, refers us back to section 167.

---

1. The majority, after first calling it the House Conference Report, then goes on to call it "the House Report." The majority then opposes "the House Report," which is a misnomer, to the Senate Report which the majority says "repudiates the scheme of complex depreciation rules, including 'current regulations.'" See Maj. Op. at 11 (citing S. Rep. No. 144 at 47). In fact, what the majority calls the House Report is the Joint Explanatory Statement of the Committee of Conference, and is "an explanation of the effect of the action agreed upon by the managers [on the part of the House and Senate at conference] and recommended in the accompanying report." See H.R. Conf. Rep. No. 215 at 195, reprinted in 1981 U.S.C.C.A.N. 285. The Conference Committee report surely "trumps" the Senate Report if the Senate Report did indeed "repudiate[] the scheme of complex depreciation rules, including 'current regulations.'"

But my reading of the Senate Report is that it did not repudiate "current regulations" in the sense that the majority opinion would have us believe. The Senate Report only mentions "[c]urrent regulations" in a reference to the congressional purpose of simplification, which reads "Current regulations provide numerous elections and exceptions which taxpayers — especially, small businesses — find difficult to master and expensive to apply." S. Rep. No. 144 at 47. All that the Senate committee believed was that a "new capital cost recovery system should be structured which de-emphasizes the concept of useful life, minimizes the number of elections and exceptions, and so is easier to comply with and to administer." Id. De-emphasis, I submit, is quite different from de-struction.

Since, concededly, taxpayers Richard and Fiona Simon have not established that the bows in question have determinable useful lives, the bows do not qualify for the depreciation deduction. It is a long way from the dual purpose of section 168 (to shorten the depreciation periods for property that would have been depreciable under section 167 in order to stimulate investment and to simplify the complex series of rules and regulations pertaining to useful lives by substituting a four-tier system of 3-year, 5-year, 10-year, and 15-year property), to abandonment of the underlying concept of depreciable property altogether. In my view, the decision of the Tax Court should be reversed and accordingly I hereby dissent.

4. Mixed-use Assets — §280F

A particularly difficult issue regarding depreciation concerns the deductions allowable for a mixed-use asset. Mixed-use asset issues arise when an asset, such as a car or a computer, is purchased and used for both business and personal purposes. In such cases, interesting issues arise as to the correct depreciation method and the amount of depreciation. In response to increasing taxpayer abuses, Congress issued specific directives concerning permissible methods for determining depreciation deductions for mixed-use assets and imposed limitations on the amounts of depreciation that may be deducted. Generally, the amendments apply to automobiles and other means of transportation (such as aircraft), computers, property used for entertainment, as well as any other types of property specified in Regulations issued by the Service. Mixed-use property must be predominantly used in a qualified business to be entitled to accelerated depreciation — that is, its business use percentage must be more than 50 percent. (If the business use in the first year is not more than 50 percent, it must be depreciated under the straight-line method of §168(g).) If the business use declines to 50 percent or below, depreciation taken in earlier years in excess of that allowable for those years under a specified straight-line method is recaptured. Further, due to particular congressional concerns, special rules were enacted strictly limiting depreciation deductions for the use of passenger automobiles.

Do the rules and underlying assumptions for mixed-use assets make sense for electronics such as computers or cell phones in a world where most employers (and most law schools) require or assume that employees (or students) have access to a personal computer or a cell phone? Seeing the Service and Courts struggle with this issue in the context of mobile phones, in 2009 Congress removed mobile phones from the definition of "listed property" for purposes of §280F. Small Business Jobs Act of 2010, Pub. L. No. 111-240, §2043. But what about more recent innovations such as tablet computers or iPads? Are they more like cell phones or more like personal computers? Consider the following case, where the Tax Court faced a similar issue.

BRYANT v. COMMISSIONER
T.C. Memo 1993-597

GUSSIS, SPECIAL TRIAL JUDGE:

. . . Robert and Ellen Bryant filed a joint Federal tax return for 1990. In 1990, Ellen Bryant (hereafter petitioner-wife) was employed as a third grade teacher in the lower school of the Tower Hill School. During the 1989-1990 school year Tower Hill decided to switch from written report cards and evaluations to a computerized format. Beginning in January 1991, lower school teachers had to prepare student report cards and evaluations on a disk compatible with Macintosh computers. From January, 1990, through August, 1990, there were eight Macintosh computers at Tower Hill available for faculty and student use. From September, 1990, through December, 1990, there were 15 Macintosh computers available for faculty and student use. In February of 1990, petitioners purchased a $3,233 Macintosh computer for the use of petitioner wife. Petitioners received an interest-free loan from Tower Hill to purchase the computer. . . .

. . . Section 280F(d), however, provides that an employee may not claim a [depreciation] deduction for listed property unless the employee's use of the listed property is for the convenience of the employer and required as a condition of employment. Listed property includes any computer or peripheral equipment. Respondent determined that the computer purchased by petitioner wife was not acquired for the convenience of Tower Hill and was not required as a condition of her employment, and consequently disallowed the claimed . . . deduction. . . .

. . . In order to satisfy the condition of employment requirement, the use of the property must be required in order for the employee to perform the duties of his or her employment properly. Whether the use of property is so required depends on all the facts and circumstances. The standard is an objective one. The employer need not explicitly require the employee to use the property. Similarly, a mere statement by the employer that the use of the property is a condition of employment is not sufficient. . . .

To show that her personal computer was required as a condition of her employment, petitioner wife argues that due to the insufficient number of computers available at Tower Hill for lower school faculty to use in preparing their reports, and the confidentiality and security problems which existed at the school, it was necessary for her to purchase a Macintosh computer in order to properly perform the duties of her employment. Petitioner wife argues that without her own computer she would be unable to timely prepare her reports and evaluations. She therefore contends the computer was required as a condition of employment. . . . Petitioner wife testified that the school is located across from an area of drug activity and that within the past year an unauthorized individual was found on the school premises. . . .

We are, however, unpersuaded that petitioner wife's purchase of the computer was required as a condition of her employment. Although a computer was needed for petitioner wife to file her reports and evaluations, the school had computers which could be used for this purpose. Furthermore, we note that during 1990, there were several lower school teachers who did not own personal computers and, nonetheless, they were able to file timely reports and evaluations. . . . In short, it is amply clear on this record that a personal computer was not required for the proper performance by lower school teachers of their employment duties. Although it may have been more convenient for petitioner wife to use her own personal computer, we must, as the statute requires, focus on the convenience of the employer and not the convenience of the employee. Moreover, the record shows that, beginning in 1990, the school continually purchased additional Macintosh computers available for faculty and student use. Consequently, it is evident that the "convenience of employer" requirement is not satisfied since petitioner wife's purchase of a personal Macintosh computer early in 1990 did not spare her employer the cost of providing her with suitable equipment with which to engage in her job responsibilities. . . .

5. Amortization of Intangible Assets

It had long been recognized that the cost of an intangible asset may be amortized over its useful life. Reg §1.167(a)-3. Historically, the problem was proving the useful life of an intangible asset: assets incapable of precise measurement did not qualify for a recoupment of costs under the Regulations, while purchased assets susceptible of precise valuation and an accurate determination of useful life (such as a three-year covenant not to compete) qualified for straight-line amortization. As a result, taxpayers had a strong incentive to make all intangibles appear to be short-lived assets. Further complicating the valuation issue was the fact that many intangible assets were purchased as part of an overall business rather than as a separate independent asset, meaning that determining the purchase price attributable to the specific intangible asset was often difficult if not impossible.

In response to many of these problems, Congress enacted §197 to permit the amortization of many intangible assets, including goodwill, over a statutorily stipulated fifteen-year useful life. This change eliminated or reduced several burdensome aspects of the prior law, including establishing the useful life of assets, the incentive to make goodwill appear like short-lived assets and, in conjunction with §1060, determining the portion of the purchase price allocable to the amortizable intangible.

While helpful in clarifying amortization procedure for intangible assets, §197 presented various new advantages and disadvantages. For instance, an intangible asset such as a three-year covenant not to compete, which may have previously been amortized over a useful life of three years, is now required to be amortized over the considerably longer fifteen-year period. On the other hand, an intangible asset such as a patent, which was typically amortized over a useful life of seventeen years, can now be amortized over fifteen years, while goodwill, previously non-amortizable, can also be amortized over fifteen years.

It is important to note that §197 is not applicable to self-created assets. §197(c)(2). Consequently, even after the enactment of §197, not all intangible assets qualify for amortization.

Even after the enactment of §197, however, there were disputes as to whether an intangible asset was "acquired" and thus had a basis to be amortized over fifteen years or whether it was either a short-lived asset (such as a covenant not to compete) entered into in the ordinary course of business or another ordinary and necessary business expense that could be deducted immediately. Of course, taxpayers regularly contended that specific acquisitions of short-lived intangible assets were not intended by Congress to be included under §197 and thus could be amortized over their shorter class life. In the following case, the court considered the intent and scope of §197 as applied to a covenant not to compete.

FRONTIER CHEVROLET COMPANY v. COMMISSIONER
329 F.3d 1131 (9th Cir. 2003)

Trot, Circuit Judge

Frontier Chevrolet Company ("Frontier") appeals the tax court's decision that §197 applied to a covenant not to compete entered into in connection with Frontier's redemption of 75% of its stock. We agree with the tax court that . . . Frontier had to amortize the covenant under §197.

Background

. . . Frontier engaged in the trade or business of selling and servicing new and used vehicles. Roundtree Automotive Group, Inc. ("Roundtree") was a corporation engaged in the trade or business of purchasing and operating automobile dealerships and providing consulting services to those dealerships. Frank Stinson ("Stinson") was the President of Roundtree and participated in Frontier's management from 1987 to 1994.

In 1987, Roundtree purchased all of Frontier's stock. Consistent with Roundtree and Stinson's policy of management, Frontier filled the position of its executive manager with one of Stinson's long-term employees, Dennis Menholt ("Menholt"). From 1987 to 1994, Roundtree allowed Menholt to purchase 25% of Frontier's stock as part of his employment by Frontier. Before August 1, 1994, Roundtree owned 75% and Menholt owned 25% of Frontier's stock.

Frontier entered into a "Stock Sale Agreement" with Roundtree effective August 1, 1994. Pursuant to the Stock Sale Agreement, Frontier redeemed its stock owned by Roundtree using funds borrowed from General Motors Acceptance Corporation ("GMAC"). Menholt became the sole shareholder of Frontier because of the redemption.

Roundtree, Stinson, and Frontier also entered into a "Non-Competition Agreement" ("covenant") in connection with the redemption. The covenant was effective August 1, 1994, and stated in part:

> To induce [Frontier] to enter into and consummate the Stock Sale Agreement and to protect the value of the shares of stock being purchased, Roundtree and Stinson covenant, to the extent provided in Section 1 hereof, that Roundtree and Stinson shall not compete with the automobile dealership, stock of which was sold to Frontier pursuant to the Stock Sale Agreement.

Section 1 provided that Roundtree and Stinson would not compete with Frontier in the car dealership business for five years. . . . Frontier agreed to pay Roundtree and Stinson $22,000 per month for five years as consideration for the non-compete restrictions.

. . . Frontier amortized the covenant payments under §197 on its 1994 through 1996 federal income tax returns. In 1999, Frontier filed a claim for refund for the 1995 and 1996 taxable years, asserting that the covenant should be amortized over the life of the agreement and not under §197. Frontier and the Internal Revenue Service stipulated that the only issue for the tax court was whether Frontier must amortize the covenant not to compete under §197. . . .

As a matter of first impression, the tax court held that the covenant was a §197 intangible because Frontier entered into the covenant in connection with the indirect acquisition of a trade or business. The tax court . . . concluded that Frontier's redemption was an acquisition within the meaning of §197 because Frontier regained possession and control over 75% of its stock.

The tax court also noted that §197's legislative history stated that an acquisition of stock of a corporation engaged in a trade or business is an indirect acquisition of an interest in a trade or business. . . .

DISCUSSION

We agree with the tax court that Frontier's redemption was an indirect acquisition of an interest in a trade or business under §197. . . .

The parties do not dispute that they entered into the covenant after the effective date of §197, or that Frontier held the covenant in connection with the conduct of a trade or business. Accordingly, the only issue we address is whether a redemption of 75% of a taxpayer's stock constitutes an indirect acquisition of an interest in a trade or business for purposes of §197. We need not and do not decide whether all stock redemptions made in connection with an execution of a covenant not to compete constitute an acquisition of an interest in a trade or business within the meaning of §197. . . .

[B]efore enactment of §197, taxpayers could amortize covenants not to compete over the life of the agreement. [In] 1993, however, Congress enacted §197 to govern the amortization of intangibles. Congress passed §197 to simplify amortization of intangibles by grouping certain intangibles and providing one period of amortization:

> The Federal income tax treatment of the costs of acquiring intangible assets is a source of considerable controversy between taxpayers and the Internal Revenue Service. . . . It is believed that much of the controversy that arises under present law with respect to acquired intangible assets could be eliminated by specifying a single method and period for recovering the cost of most acquired intangible assets. . . .

H.R. Rep. No. 103-111, at 760. Thus, Congress' intent to simplify the treatment of intangibles indicates that §197 treats stock acquisitions and redemptions similarly — both stock acquisitions and redemptions involve acquiring an interest in a trade or business by acquiring stock of a corporation engaged in a trade or business.

CONCLUSION

Because Frontier entered into the covenant in connection with the redemption of 75% of its stock, the covenant was a §197 intangible and Frontier must amortize it over fifteen years under §197. Accordingly, we AFFIRM the tax court.

Problems

6-33. On January 1, Ken Worth paid $12,500 for an asset to be used in his trade or business. Assuming the asset has a useful life of four years and a salvage value of $2,500, compute Worth's annual depreciation deduction and accumulated depreciation at the end of each of the four years under the following methods.

    a. Accelerated cost recovery assuming the asset is three-year class property. See §168.

    b. Same as *a* but Worth elects a three-year straight-line approach.

    c. Same as *a* but Worth elects to apply §179.

    d. In *a* through *c*, what basis adjustments are required? See §1016(a)(2).

6-34. Sammy's Chocolate Company, a sole proprietorship, purchased an airplane on January 1. The airplane is used to deliver Sammy's chocolate to specialty shops in several nearby cities. Sammy also uses the plane to fly to Las Vegas for weekend jaunts. If the plane originally cost $96,000, how should Sammy's Chocolate Company compute depreciation under the following circumstances?

    a. The plane is used for business purposes 70 percent of the time and the plane is five-year class property.

    b. The plane is used for business purposes 35 percent of the time.

CHAPTER 7
CAPITAL GAINS AND LOSSES

A. INTRODUCTION

Not all items of taxable gains and deductible losses are created equal. In fact, almost since the inception of the modern Internal Revenue Code following the ratification of the Sixteenth Amendment, there have generally been two types of gains and losses for tax purposes: "ordinary" and "capital." As a general matter, capital gains have received preferential tax treatment, while ordinary losses have been treated more favorably than capital losses. As a result, taxpayers prefer *gains* to be classified as capital gains rather than ordinary income, while they prefer *losses* to be characterized as ordinary losses. These goals are not easily met, however, because the characterization of gains and losses is determined by the interaction of ever changing Code sections, case law, and administrative Rulings.

The current tax treatment of capital gains is the product of years of congressional indecision and manipulation. Prior to 1921, all recognized gains on the sale of property were treated the same as any other income. The Revenue Act of 1921 included the first provisions for preferential tax treatment of capital gains and introduced the term "capital asset." The preference accorded to capital gains was in the form of an election to have gain from investment property held more than two years taxed either at a flat rate of 12.5 percent or at the taxpayer's normal tax rates.

The preferential treatment of capital gains was modified and revised over the years. In 1978, in an attempt to encourage investment activity, the Code effectively taxed only 40 percent of long-term capital gains.

> [T]he present level of taxes applicable to capital gains has contributed both to a slower rate of economic growth than that which otherwise might have been anticipated, and also to some taxpayers realizing fewer potential gains than they would have realized if the tax rates had been lower. In some instances, the taxes applicable to capital gains effectively may have locked some taxpayers into their existing investments. Moreover, . . . the present level of capital gains taxes has contributed to the shortage of investment funds needed for capital formation purposes generally, and especially for new and small businesses. . . .

In addition, . . . an increased capital gains deduction would tend to offset the effect of inflation by reducing the amount of gain which is subject to tax. . . . However, since the deduction is constant, unlike the adjustments generally provided for in various indexation proposals, it should not tend to exacerbate inflationary increases.

S. Rep. No. 1263, 95th Cong., 2d Sess. 192 (1978).

In 1986, Congress significantly reduced income tax rates for individuals and therefore no longer deemed it necessary to provide a reduced tax rate for capital gains. In addition, it was recognized that eliminating the requirement that the taxpayer hold capital assets for an extended period of time to obtain favorable tax treatment would encourage investment in freely traded assets (such as stocks). As a result, the 60 percent net capital gain deduction of §1202 for individuals was repealed, but at the same time the highest tax rate imposed on net capital gains was capped at 28 percent. Thus, capital gain was of no practical significance because the highest individual rate on any income was 28 percent.

This respite did not last long, however. In 1990, Congress increased the rate on ordinary income from 28 to 31 percent, while leaving the rate on capital gains at 28 percent. In 1993, Congress further tinkered with the rate structure for individuals by increasing the maximum rate on ordinary income to 39.6 percent while still holding the maximum rate on capital gains to 28 percent. In 1997, Congress reduced the maximum rate for most capital gains to 20 percent, resulting in a disparity of almost 20 percent in the rate applicable to ordinary income and that applicable to capital gain. From 2001 to 2003, Congress reduced the top marginal rate on ordinary income from 39.6 percent to 35 percent, while at the same time reducing the marginal rate on capital gains from 20 percent to 15 percent, maintaining the 20-percent differential between ordinary income and capital gain.

As is evident from its history, Congress has continually found ways to grant preferential treatment to capital gains. The more difficult question is why Congress chooses one particular form of income for such largesse. This sometimes thorny problem has been confronted by Congress, the courts, and commentators for decades, without any satisfying conclusion. Regardless, the capital gains preference not only remains, but flourishes.

In one of the first cases to confront this issue directly, the Supreme Court in Burnet v. Harmel, 287 U.S. 103, 106 (1932), cited two policies justifying the preferential tax treatment afforded capital gains: "to relieve the taxpayer from [the] excessive tax burdens on gains resulting from a conversion of capital investments, and to remove the deterrent effect of those burdens on such conversions [that is, realization]."

The first policy concern is commonly known as the *bunching* problem, and the second policy concern is often referred to as the *lock-in* effect. The bunching problem refers to gain that has accrued over several years, whether because of economic appreciation or inflation, but which is taxed entirely in the year of disposition. As a result, the accrued income, when recognized in a single transaction, may push the taxpayer into a higher tax bracket. The lock-in effect also is attributable to the principle that annual appreciation in the value of property is taxed only if and when a realization event occurs. Thus, it is argued, investors are locked in to profitable investments, and the mobility of capital is thereby impaired, because selling would result in a tax bill while merely holding the asset would not.

Bunching and lock-in, in one form or another, have been driving forces behind the capital gains preference since the early days of the Internal Revenue Code. Take, for example, the following excerpts from legislative history from 1938:

> There is no tax under existing law if a taxpayer transfers his money from one bank to another, but there may be a very heavy tax if he wishes to transfer his investment from a bond in one company to a bond in another company. Thus an excessive tax on capital gains freezes transactions and prevents the free flow of capital into productive investments. The effect of the present system of taxing capital gains is to prevent any individual with substantial capital from investing in new enterprises. This is most unfortunate, because it adversely affects the employment situation.

S. Rep. No. 1567, 75th Cong., 3d Sess. 6 (1938).

Although it is clear that bunching and lock-in have been of particular concern in the justification of the capital gains preference, they have been far from universally endorsed. Consider that more than seventy-five years after the first capital gains preference was introduced and the Supreme Court identified bunching and lock-in as the primary underlying policies, the Joint Committee on Taxation issued the following report, once again struggling with the issues of bunching and lock-in for capital gains.

JOINT COMMITTEE ON TAXATION, TAX TREATMENT OF CAPITAL GAINS AND LOSSES
30-36 (1997)

B. ISSUES RELATING TO A REDUCED RATE ON CAPITAL GAINS

ARGUMENTS FOR REDUCED RATES ON CAPITAL GAINS

Lock-in

Many argue that higher income tax rates discourage sales of assets. . . . The legislative history suggests that this lock-in effect was an important consideration in Congress' decision to lower capital gains taxes in 1978. As an example of what is meant by the lock-in effect, suppose a taxpayer paid $500 for a stock that is now worth $1,000, and that the stock's value will grow by an additional 10 percent over the next year with no prospect of further gain thereafter. Assuming a 28 percent rate, if the taxpayer sells the stock one year or more from now, he or she will net $932 after payment of $168 tax on the gain of $600. If the taxpayer sold this stock today, he or she would have, after tax of $140 on the gain of $500, $860 available to reinvest. The taxpayer would not find it profitable to switch to an alternative investment unless that alternative would earn a total pre-tax return in excess of 11.6 percent. Thus, the taxpayer is said to be "locked-in" to the existing, lower-earning investment. Preferential tax rates on capital gains impose a smaller tax on redirecting monies from older investments to projects with better prospects, which contributes to a more efficient allocation of capital. . . .

Incentives for Equity Investment and Risk-Taking

A second argument for preferential capital gains tax rates is that they encourage investors to buy corporate stock, and especially encourage investors to provide venture capital for new companies, thereby stimulating investment in productive business activities. This argument was important in the 1978 debate over capital gains taxes, and a large growth in the availability of venture capital occurred after 1978. . . .

Savings Incentive

The United States has a relatively low rate of household saving, currently less than 5 percent of disposable income. . . . At the aggregate level, a low savings rate is a concern because saving provides the wherewithal for investment in productivity-enhancing equipment and technology. At the household level, a low saving rate may imply households are accumulating insufficient assets for retirement, emergencies or other uses. By reducing tax on realized capital gains, the after-tax return to household saving is increased. . . .

Competitiveness

Related to the argument that preferential capital gains tax rates encourage savings and investment is the argument that a lower capital gains tax rate will improve the international competitive position of the United States. Proponents of a reduction in capital gains tax rates observe that many of our major trading partners have lower marginal tax rates on the realization of capital gains than does the United States. For example, the highest tax rate on capital gains in Canada is less than 25 percent. Japan imposes a tax at the taxpayer's discretion of either one percent of the gross proceeds or 20 percent of the gain. . . . In Germany, all long-term gains are exempt from income tax. . . .

Bunching

Because capital gain is generally not taxed until a disposition of an asset, taxpayers can face large jumps in taxable income when a gain is realized. With graduated tax rates, such bunching could lead to a higher tax burden than if the gain were taxed as it accrued. If the benefit of deferral is not enough to compensate for the extra tax in some of those cases, then the additional benefit of a preferential tax rate helps to achieve parity. . . .

Inflation

. . . [A]nother argument for preferential tax treatment of capital gain is that part of the gain represents the effect of inflation and does not constitute real income. This argument was also an important factor in the 1978 capital gains rate reduction. Proponents observe that a preferential capital gains tax rate may provide to taxpayers some rough compensation for inflation. . . .

ARGUMENTS AGAINST A REDUCED TAX ON CAPITAL GAINS

Measurement of Income

Opponents of a reduced tax on capital gains argue that appreciating assets already enjoy a tax benefit from the deferral of tax on accrued appreciation until

the asset is sold, which benefit reduces in whole or in part any bunching or inflationary effects. As a result, the effective rate of taxation on realized capital gains is
less than the rate of taxation applicable to assets that pay current income. The
following example illustrates the benefits of deferral. Assume a taxpayer in the
28-percent tax bracket has $1,000 to invest and may choose between two
investment alternatives, each of which generates a return of 10 percent annually.
Assume the one investment is a certificate of deposit that pays the 10-percent
return out annually as interest on which the taxpayer must pay tax. After paying
the tax, the taxpayer reinvests the principal and net proceeds in a new certificate of
deposit. The other investment, stock in a company that pays no dividends, accrues
the 10-percent return untaxed until a capital gain is realized. After eight years, the
after-tax value of the taxpayer's certificate of deposit would be $1,744. After selling
the stock and paying the tax on the realized gain, the taxpayer would have $1,823.
In this particular example, the effective rate of taxation on the realized capital gain
is 22 percent, rather than the statutory tax rate of 28 percent. . . .

Neutrality

To the extent that preferential rates may encourage investment in stock, opponents have argued that the preference tilts investment decisions toward assets that
offer a return in the form of asset appreciation rather than current income such as
dividends or interest. On the other hand, it is argued that asset neutrality is not an
appropriate goal because risky investments that produce a high proportion of their
income in the form of capital gains may provide a social benefit not adequately
recognized by investors in the marketplace.

Reduction of Conversion Opportunities

Opponents of the preferential capital gains rate contend that it also
encourages taxpayers to enter transactions designed to convert ordinary income
into capital gains. Conversion can also occur through debt-financing the cost of
assets eligible for capital gains rates. For example, if a taxpayer borrows $100 at
10-percent annual interest to acquire a capital asset that is sold for $110 a year later,
and repays the borrowing with the sales proceeds, the taxpayer has an interest
deduction of $10 that can reduce ordinary income and a capital gain of $10 subject
to preferential rates. The taxpayer thus has a net after-tax positive cash flow even
though on a pre-tax basis the transaction was not profitable. . . .

Simplification and Consistent Treatment of Taxpayers

Opponents of a preferential capital gains rate point out that the application of
different tax rates to different sources of income inevitably creates disputes over
which assets are entitled to the preferential rate and encourages taxpayers to mis-
characterize their income as derived from the preferred source. . . . A significant
body of law . . . has developed in response to conflicting taxpayer and Internal
Revenue Service positions in particular cases. Its principles are complicated in
concept and application, typically requiring careful scrutiny of the facts in each
case and leaving opportunities for some taxpayers to take aggressive . . . positions.
It has been argued that the results derived in particular cases lack even rough
consistency, notwithstanding the substantial resources consumed in the process
by taxpayers and the Internal Revenue Service. . . .

B. MECHANICS OF CAPITAL GAIN AND LOSS

Code: §§61(a)(3); 62(a)(3); 165(a), (b), (c), (f); 1202(a) to (d); 1211(b); 1212(b); 1222

1. Background

In general, all recognized gains, capital or otherwise, are included in gross income under §61. Similarly, capital losses are above-the-line deductions under §62(a)(3). The *character* of gains or losses, by comparison, primarily impacts two considerations: the rate of tax applicable to "net capital gain" and the ability to deduct capital losses. To determine these two, the amount of capital gains and losses must be computed and compared. This process is called *netting*. The rules found in §1222, the primary definitional section for capital gains and losses, dictate which gains and losses are to be netted together in determining if, and to what extent, there is either a net capital gain or a net capital loss. These netting processes may produce (1) a net capital gain or (2) a net capital loss that is deductible subject to limitations prescribed by §1211(b), and, in some cases, (3) a net capital loss that is not currently deductible as a result of the §1211(b) limitations but that may be carried forward by §1212 to later years.

Sections 1211, 1212(b), and 1222 do not independently include capital gains in gross income, nor do they deduct a portion of net capital losses from gross income. Other Code provisions control these determinations. Section 61(a)(3) includes in gross income all gains recognized from dealings in property, regardless of whether they are capital, short-term or long-term, or ordinary.

Section 62(a)(3), which provides that a deduction from gross income for losses from the sale or exchange of property will be "above the line," cross-references to §165, the provision substantively granting a deduction for losses from the sale or exchange of assets. Section 165 provides certain requirements to capital loss deductibility not present for capital gain inclusion. Gains require realization and recognition before characterization; losses, in addition to these two conditions, require *allowability* under §165(c). Section 165(c) allows losses for individuals only if they arise in a trade or business, a production of income activity, or from a casualty loss. As a result, losses from the sale of personal use property, such as a principal residence or automobile, are generally nondeductible capital losses. After the allowance of the loss has been established under §165(c), §165(f) applies and refers to §§1211 and 1212, which govern, by limitation, the amount and method for computing a capital loss deduction. Thus, although §§165(c) and 165(f) perform different functions, both subsections' requirements must be met before an above-the-line deduction for capital losses may be claimed under §62(a)(3).

2. Overview of Capital Gain and Loss Analysis

A three-step process is utilized in determining the nature of property gains and losses under the present taxing structure and helps organize the myriad rules involved. The first step is the *characterization phase*. This phase employs three important statutory concepts: (1) the definition of a *capital asset*, (2) the *sale or exchange* requirement, and (3) the taxpayer's *holding period* in the capital asset that is sold or exchanged.

The second step is the *recharacterization phase*. It considers several specific statutory exceptions that serve to prevent unduly favorable tax treatment resulting from the application of the general rules.

The third step in the treatment of gains and losses from property transactions is the *netting phase*. Rules contained in §1222 require the netting of capital gains and capital losses, which may lead to the unfavorable limitation rules reserved for capital losses (§1211).

Finally, it is important to note that the role of the §1211 capital loss limitation is to allow or disallow deductions from gross income. The deduction for capital losses is an AGI deduction under §62(a)(3). As with other AGI deductions, Code sections other than §62 must be consulted to determine the rules for their deductibility.

3. Definitions and Netting Rules

Sections 1222(1) through (4) define capital gains and losses as either short-term or long-term. A short-term asset is a capital asset held for one year or less; a long-term capital asset is one held for more than one year. Thus, long-term capital gain or capital loss is gain or loss recognized on the sale or exchange of a capital asset held for more than one year. Short-term capital gain or capital loss is defined similarly, except that the holding period is one year or less.

Sections 1222(5) through (11) provide the bulk of the netting rules. *Net short-term capital gain* or *capital loss*, and *net long-term capital gain* or *capital loss* are aggregate amounts derived from comparing gains and losses from all transactions in one particular holding period. Thus, for example, a taxpayer with a $10,000 long-term capital gain and a $4,000 long-term capital loss has a $6,000 net long-term capital gain.

4. Capital Loss Deduction

Section 1211(b) provides the rules for determining the maximum capital loss deduction permitted in a particular taxable year. In considering the §1211(b) limitation, it is helpful to divide its application into two parts. First, all capital losses can be deducted to the extent of all capital gains. If, for example, capital losses (short-term and long-term) for the taxable year total $8,000 and capital gains (short-term and long-term) for the taxable year total $10,000, the §1211(b) deduction is $8,000 regardless of the long-term or short-term composition of the $8,000 losses or the $10,000 gains. In such a case, since all capital losses are deductible, no further computation would be necessary under §1211(b). If, however, capital losses in the above example total $15,000, $10,000 of the capital losses would be deductible under the first part of the §1211(b) limitation, with the remaining $5,000 of capital losses subject to the limitation rules of §1211(b)(1) or (2).

Section 1211(b)(1) or (2) applies only to the portion of capital losses that exceed the total amount of capital gains. The applicable limitation (that is, amount deductible) is the *smaller* of (1) $3,000 ($1,500 in the case of married individuals filing separate returns) or (2) the excess of capital losses over capital gains.

5.   Carryover of Capital Losses

Section 1212(b) permits excess capital losses to be carried forward to subsequent taxable years. Losses carried forward retain their original character as either long-term or short-term and are treated as though they were sustained in the year to which they are carried. Thus, a net long-term capital loss carryover first reduces long-term capital gain recognized in the carryover year, then reduces net short-term capital gain, with the unused portion reducing ordinary income up to the $3,000 limitation. In the carryover year, short-term losses carried forward from a prior year continue to be applied against the $3,000 ordinary income limit first. If the deduction limit against ordinary income has not been reached after offsetting by the net short-term losses, the long-term losses are then applied against the limit. Consider the following examples.

Example 1. Taxpayer has taxable income of $60,000, a $1,000 net short-term capital loss, and a $6,000 net long-term capital loss. Taxpayer must first use the $1,000 net short-term capital loss against $1,000 of ordinary income, and then $2,000 of the net long-term capital loss to offset the remaining $2,000 of ordinary income ($3,000 limit). The remaining $4,000 ($6,000-$2,000) long-term capital loss is carried over to a future year, retaining its long-term character.

Example 2. Taxpayer in year 1 has $60,000 of taxable income, a $1,000 net short-term capital gain, a $100 net long-term capital gain, and a short-term capital loss carryover of $5,100 from the preceding year. Because §1212 requires that the loss carryover be treated as if incurred in the year to which it is carried, taxpayer will first offset the short-term loss carryover by the current $1,000 net short-term capital gain; next, the current $100 net long-term capital gain will offset $100 of the loss carryover. Finally, the resulting second stage deduction for year 2 would be to the extent of the $3,000 ordinary income deduction limit. The $1,000 remaining from the carryover may again be carried forward for use as a short-term capital loss in subsequent taxable years.

6.   Capital Gain Exclusion

In an attempt to stimulate the economy by encouraging investment in small businesses, Congress enacted §1202 providing for the exclusion of 50 percent of the gain from the disposition of certain small business stock. Although technically a statutory exclusion, §1202 is discussed in this chapter because, like the preferential treatment afforded net capital gain, it provides preferential treatment for long-term capital investments. Unlike the general preference afforded net capital gain which applies to all long-term capital gain, the §1202 exclusion applies only to gain recognized on the disposition of a limited and specific category of capital assets — that is, "qualified small business stock."

Section 1202 permits investors who acquire qualified small business stock from the issuer and hold that stock for at least five years to exclude 50 percent of the gain on its sale or exchange. A qualified small business is a C corporation engaged in certain specified trades or businesses and having less than $50,000,000 of aggregate capitalization. The stock may be obtained in exchange for money, property (not including stock), or as compensation for services provided to the small business.

The portion of gain excluded from gross income by §1202 is not taken into account in computing long-term capital gain or in applying §§1211 and 1212 capital loss rules. However, the remainder of the gain will be taken into account for such purposes. Thus, it may qualify under §1(h) for a maximum tax rate of 28 percent.

Problems

7-1. John Burbach has the following gains and losses: $10,000 long-term capital gain; $15,000 long-term capital gain; $5,000 short-term capital gain; $7,000 short-term capital loss; $1,000 long-term capital loss; and a $2,000 long-term capital loss.
   a. What is the amount of net short-term capital loss or capital gain?
   b. What is the amount of net long-term capital loss or capital gain?
   c. What is the net capital gain?
   d. How much capital gain is included in Burbach's gross income?
   e. Is Burbach entitled to a capital loss deduction under §§165(f) and 1211(b)?
   f. What is Burbach's adjusted gross income?
   g. Assume that Burbach did not have any short-term capital loss but that all other facts are the same. What is the net capital gain?

7-2. Betty Adams has the following capital gains and losses: long-term capital gain of $5,000; long-term capital loss of $3,000; long-term capital gain of $15,000; short-term capital loss of $2,000; short-term capital gain of $12,000; short-term capital loss of $14,000; and a long-term capital loss of $25,000. Assume that Adams' taxable income without including capital gains and losses is $40,000.
   a. What is the amount of net short-term capital loss?
   b. What is the amount of net long-term capital loss?
   c. What is Adams' capital loss deduction?
   d. What is the amount of net capital loss?
   e. What is the amount and character of Adams' capital loss carryforward?
   f. What is Adams' adjusted gross income?

7-3. Tom Johnson has taxable income of $12,000, excluding capital gains and losses, and the following capital gains and losses: long-term capital gain of $1,000; long-term capital loss of $9,000; short-term capital gain of $200; and a short-term capital loss of $1,200.

    a.   Determine the aggregate capital gains and capital losses.

    b.   What is the net long-term and net short-term capital loss?

    c.   What is the amount of the capital loss deduction?

    d.   What is the amount of net capital loss?

    e.   What is the amount and character of the capital loss carried forward?

C.   DEFINITION OF A CAPITAL ASSET

Code: §§1221(a)(1) to (4), (7); 1235(a), (b)
Regulations: §1.1221-1(a) to (d)

1.   Statutory Analysis

Capital characterization arises when a capital asset is sold or exchanged, with the resulting capital gain or capital loss being long-term or short-term depending on the asset's holding period. Thus, the threshold issue is the definition of *capital asset*.

Section 1221 broadly defines a capital asset as "property held by the taxpayer (whether or not connected with his trade or business)," except for items described in §1221(a)(1) through §1221(a)(8). Thus, the capital asset definition includes all property, with the exception of eight types. Because Congress intended capital treatment to be the exception rather than the rule and further intended to confer capital status only on specific assets, the method it chose to define a capital asset — broadly including all property and then excluding ordinary property — can seem peculiar and confusing. A more suitable definition would specifically enumerate the type of property qualifying as a capital asset. Nevertheless, as a result of defining capital asset in an exclusionary fashion, the exceptions become the focus of the initial statutory inquiry.

The first two exceptions to the broad language of §1221 list property generally found in a business. Section 1221(a)(1) excludes from the definition of capital assets: stock in trade, inventory, and property held primarily for sale to customers in the ordinary course of a trade or business. Section 1221(a)(2) excludes real or depreciable property *used* in a trade or business. For example, a taxpayer's personal use automobile is a capital asset, but a car held as *inventory* or a car that the taxpayer *uses* in a trade or business is not. (It should be noted that although §1221(a)(2) disqualifies property used in a trade or business from capital treatment, §1231(b) (discussed at section F of this chapter) may qualify such property for preferential tax treatment.)

The third exception, §1221(a)(3), excludes certain property created by the holder's personal efforts, such as copyrights, music, paintings, and so forth. In 1948, future-President Eisenhower completed a book on his World War II experiences. The tax law at that time provided that literary compositions (including copyrights) qualified as capital assets unless held for sale to customers or used in the taxpayer's business. To take advantage of this law, Eisenhower held the completed manuscript for the requisite holding period for long-term capital gain treatment and then made an outright sale of his entire interest in the work rather than enter into a customary royalty arrangement.

The Treasury ruled that the sale would qualify for capital gain treatment as long as all his interest was sold, no further control over the work or opportunity to exploit it remained, and no further income was to accrue after the sale. In 1950, in response to this and similar transactions in the entertainment business, Congress enacted the statutory predecessor of §1221(a)(3), sometimes called the Eisenhower amendment, denying capital gain treatment to literary works if held by the creator or a taxpayer with a basis carried over from the creator. In 1969, §1221(a)(3) was expanded to include letters, memoranda, and so forth. In 2006, however, Congress enacted §1221(b)(3), permitting taxpayers to elect whether to treat self-created musical compositions or copyrights in musical works as capital assets.

Treating the type of property listed in §1221(a)(3) as noncapital in the hands of its creator is consistent with taxing wages and salaries as ordinary income — gains from personal effort or services are generally taxed as ordinary income, whereas gains from capital appreciation are not. Patents, however, pose a unique problem for §1221(a)(3) self-created property because, unlike copyrights and many artworks, the creation of patentable property may entail a capital investment. In recognition, Congress has granted capital asset status to certain patent rights. §1235(a).

The fourth exception from the definition of capital assets closes a loophole otherwise available on the sale of §1221(a)(1) property (or the rendition of tax-payer's services) in exchange for notes or accounts receivable instead of cash. On receipt of a note or account receivable, a cash method taxpayer might not be required to report income. When payment is received on the note, the cash method taxpayer reports ordinary income. If, however, the note or account is sold prior to discharge, it arguably might constitute a sale of property that could qualify for capital treatment. To prevent circumvention of the purpose and intent of §1221, §1221(a)(4) classifies notes and accounts receivable received for services rendered or for the sale of §1221(a)(1) property as noncapital assets. The §1221(a)(4) exclusion, therefore, prevents conversion of ordinary income into capital gains.

The final exceptions, §1221(a)(5) through (a)(8), involve government publications, commodities and hedging transactions, and supplies.

In the landmark decisions of *Corn Products* and *Arkansas Best*, which follow, the Supreme Court addressed the definition of capital assets. Focusing on the nature of the taxpayer's business, the Court in *Corn Products* held that the purchase and sale of corn futures constituted an integral part of the taxpayer's business and, therefore, the gain was ordinary, not capital. In essence, the Court held that the exclusions from capital asset status should be broadly interpreted. Subsequent expansion of the *Corn Products* doctrine by the lower courts, however, forced the Supreme Court to confront the issue again in *Arkansas Best*. Ultimately, Congress codified *Corn Products* in §1221(a)(7). It now appears that little, if anything, remains of the judicially created business-exception to capital asset status.

CORN PRODUCTS REFINING CO. v. COMMISSIONER
350 U.S. 46 (1955)

MR. JUSTICE CLARK delivered the opinion of the Court.

This case concerns the tax treatment to be accorded certain transactions in commodity futures. . . .

Petitioner is a nationally known manufacturer of products made from grain corn. It manufactures starch, syrup, sugar, and their byproducts, feeds and oil. Its average yearly grind of raw corn during the period 1937 through 1942 varied from thirty-five to sixty million bushels. Most of its products were sold under contracts requiring shipment in thirty days at a set price or at market price on the date of delivery, whichever was lower. It permitted cancellation of such contracts, but from experience it could calculate with some accuracy future orders that would remain firm. . . .

In 1934 and again in 1936 droughts in the corn belt caused a sharp increase in the price of spot corn. With a storage capacity of only 2,300,000 bushels of corn, a bare three weeks' supply, Corn Products found itself unable to buy at a price which would permit its refined corn sugar, cerelose, to compete successfully with cane and beet sugar. To avoid a recurrence of this situation, petitioner, in 1937, began to establish a long position in corn futures "as a part of its corn buying program" and "as the most economical method of obtaining an adequate supply of raw corn" without entailing the expenditure of large sums for additional storage facilities. At harvest time each year it would buy futures when the price appeared favorable. It would take delivery on such contracts as it found necessary to its manufacturing operations and sell the remainder in early summer if no shortage was imminent. If shortages appeared, however, it sold futures only as it bought spot corn for grinding. In this manner it reached a balanced position with reference to any increase in spot corn prices. It made no effort to protect itself against a decline in prices.

In 1940 it netted a profit of $680,587.39 in corn futures, but in 1942 it suffered a loss of $109,969.38. In computing its tax liability Corn Products reported these figures as ordinary profit and loss from its manufacturing operations for the respective years. It now contends that its futures were "capital assets" and that gains and losses therefrom should have been treated as arising from the sale of a capital asset. . . .

Both the Tax Court and the Court of Appeals found petitioner's futures transactions to be an integral part of its business designed to protect its manufacturing operations against a price increase in its principal raw material and to assure a ready supply for future manufacturing requirements. Corn Products does not level a direct attack on these two-court findings but insists that its futures were "property" entitled to capital-asset treatment and as such were distinct from its manufacturing business. We cannot agree.

We find nothing in this record to support the contention that Corn Products' futures activity was separate and apart from its manufacturing operation. On the contrary, it appears that the transactions were vitally important to the company's business as a form of insurance against increases in the price of raw corn. Not only were the purchases initiated for just this reason, but the petitioner's sales policy, selling in the future at a fixed price or less, continued to leave it exceedingly vulnerable to rises in the price of corn. Further, the purchase of corn futures assured the company a source of supply which was admittedly cheaper than constructing additional storage facilities for raw corn. Under these facts it is difficult to imagine a program more closely geared to a company's manufacturing enterprise or more important to its successful operation.

Likewise the claim of Corn Products that it was dealing in the market as a "legitimate capitalist" lacks support in the record. There can be no quarrel with a manufacturer's desire to protect itself against increasing costs of raw materials. Transactions which provide such protection are considered a legitimate form of insurance. . . . However, in labeling its activity as that of a "legitimate capitalist" exercising "good judgment" in the futures market, petitioner ignores the testimony of its own officers that in entering that market the company was "trying to protect a part of [its] manufacturing costs"; that its entry was not for the purpose of "speculating and buying and selling corn futures" but to fill an actual "need for the quantity of corn [bought] . . . in order to cover . . . what [products] we expected to market over a period of fifteen or eighteen months." It matters not whether the label be that of "legitimate capitalist" or "speculator"; this is not the talk of the capital investor but of the far-sighted manufacturer. For tax purposes petitioner's purchases have been found to "constitute an integral part of its manufacturing business" by both the Tax Court and the Court of Appeals, and on essentially factual questions the findings of two courts should not ordinarily be disturbed.

Petitioner also makes much of the conclusion by both the Tax Court and the Court of Appeals that its transactions did not constitute "true hedging." It is true that Corn Products did not secure complete protection from its market operations. Under its sales policy petitioner could not guard against a fall in prices. It is clear, however, that petitioner feared the possibility of a price rise more than that of a price decline. It therefore purchased partial insurance against its principal risk, and hoped to retain sufficient flexibility to avoid serious losses on a declining market.

Nor can we find support for petitioner's contention that hedging is not within the exclusions of §[1221]. Admittedly, petitioner's corn futures do not come within the literal language of the exclusions set out in that section. They were not stock in trade, actual inventory, property held for sale to customers or depreciable property used in a trade or business. But the capital-asset provision must not be so broadly applied as to defeat rather than further the purpose of Congress. Congress intended that profits and losses arising from the everyday operation of a business be considered as ordinary income or loss rather than capital gain or loss. The preferential treatment provided applies to transactions in property which are not the normal source of business income. It was intended "to relieve the taxpayer from . . . excessive tax burdens on gains resulting from a conversion of capital investments, and to remove the deterrent effect of those burdens on such conversions." Burnet v. Harmel, 287 U.S., at 106. Since this section is an exception from the normal tax requirements of the Internal Revenue Code, the definition of a capital asset must be narrowly applied and its exclusions interpreted broadly. This is necessary to effectuate the basic congressional purpose. This Court has always construed narrowly the term "capital assets."

The problem of the appropriate tax treatment of hedging transactions first arose under the 1934 Tax Code revision. Thereafter the Treasury issued G.C.M. 17322, distinguishing speculative transactions in commodity futures from hedging transactions. It held that hedging transactions were essentially to be regarded as insurance rather than a dealing in capital assets and that gains and losses therefrom were ordinary business gains and losses. The interpretation outlined in this memorandum has been consistently followed by the courts as well as by the Commissioner. While it is true that this Court has not passed on its validity, it has been well recognized for 20 years; and Congress has made no change in it though the Code has been re-enacted on three subsequent occasions. This bespeaks congressional approval. . . .

We believe that the statute clearly refutes the contention of Corn Products. Moreover it is significant to note that practical considerations lead to the same conclusion. To hold otherwise would permit those engaged in hedging transactions to transmute ordinary income into capital gain at will. The hedger may either sell the future and purchase in the spot market or take delivery under the future contract itself. But if a sale of the future created a capital transaction while delivery of the commodity under the same future did not, a loophole in the statute would be created and the purpose of Congress frustrated. The judgment is affirmed.

ARKANSAS BEST CORP. v. COMMISSIONER
485 U.S. 212 (1988)

JUSTICE MARSHALL delivered the opinion of the Court.

The issue presented in this case is whether capital stock held by petitioner Arkansas Best Corporation (Arkansas Best) is a "capital asset" as defined in §1221 of the Internal Revenue Code regardless of whether the stock was purchased and held for a business purpose or for an investment purpose.

I

Arkansas Best is a diversified holding company. In 1968 it acquired approximately 65% of the stock of the National Bank of Commerce (Bank) in Dallas, Texas. Between 1969 and 1974, Arkansas Best more than tripled the number of shares it owned in the Bank, although its percentage interest in the Bank remained relatively stable. These acquisitions were prompted principally by the Bank's need for added capital. Until 1972, the Bank appeared to be prosperous and growing, and the added capital was necessary to accommodate this growth. As the Dallas real estate market declined, however, so too did the financial health of the Bank, which had a heavy concentration of loans in the local real estate industry. In 1972, federal examiners classified the Bank as a problem bank. The infusion of capital after 1972 was prompted by the loan portfolio problems of the bank.

Petitioner sold the bulk of its Bank stock on June 30, 1975, leaving it with only a 14.7% stake in the Bank. On its federal income tax return for 1975, petitioner claimed a deduction for an ordinary loss of $9,995,688 resulting from the sale of the stock. The Commissioner of Internal Revenue disallowed the deduction, finding that the loss from the sale of stock was a capital loss, rather than an ordinary loss, and that it therefore was subject to the capital loss limitations in the Internal Revenue Code.

Arkansas Best challenged the Commissioner's determination in the United States Tax Court. The Tax Court, relying on cases interpreting Corn Products Refining Co. v. Commissioner, 350 U.S. 46 (1955), held that stock purchased with a substantial investment purpose in a capital asset which, when sold, gives rise to a capital gain or loss, whereas stock purchased and held for a business purpose, without any substantial investment motive, is an ordinary asset whose sale gives rise to ordinary gains or losses. The court characterized Arkansas Best's acquisitions through 1972 as occurring during the Bank's "'growth' phase," and found that these acquisitions "were motivated primarily by investment purpose and only incidentally by some business purpose." The stock acquired during this period therefore constituted a capital asset, which gave rise to a capital loss when sold in 1975. The court determined, however, that the acquisitions after 1972 occurred during the Bank's "'problem' phase," and, except for certain minor exceptions, "were made exclusively for business purposes and subsequently held for the same reasons." These acquisitions, the court found, were designed to preserve petitioner's business reputation, because without the added capital the Bank probably would have failed. The loss realized on the sale of this stock was thus held to be an ordinary loss.

The Court of Appeals for the Eighth Circuit reversed the Tax Court's determination that the loss realized on stock purchased after 1972 was subject to ordinary-loss treatment, holding that all of the Bank stock sold in 1975 was subject to capital-loss treatment. The court reasoned that the Bank stock clearly fell within the general definition of "capital asset" in Internal Revenue Code §1221, and that the stock did not fall within any of the specific statutory exceptions to this definition. The court concluded that Arkansas Best's purpose in acquiring and holding the stock was irrelevant to the determination whether the stock was a capital asset. . . .

II

Section 1221 of the Internal Revenue Code defines "capital asset" broadly, as "property held by the taxpayer (whether or not connected with his trade or business)," and then excludes five specific classes of property from capital-asset status. In the statute's present form, the classes of property exempted from the broad definition are (1) "property of a kind which would properly be included in the inventory of the taxpayer"; (2) real property or other depreciable property used in the taxpayer's trade or business; (3) "a copyright, a literary, musical, or artistic composition," or similar property; (4) "accounts or notes receivable acquired in the ordinary course of trade or business for services rendered" or from the sale of inventory; and (5) publications of the Federal Government. Arkansas Best acknowledges that the Bank stock falls within the literal definition of capital asset in §1221, and is outside of the statutory exclusions. It asserts, however, that this determination does not end the inquiry. Petitioner argues that in Corn Products Refining Co. v. Commissioner, supra, this Court rejected a literal reading of §1221, and concluded that assets acquired and sold for ordinary business purposes rather than for investment purposes should be given ordinary-asset treatment. Petitioner's reading of *Corn Products* finds much support in the academic literature and in the courts. Unfortunately for petitioner, this broad reading finds no support in the language of §1221.

In essence, petitioner argues that "property held by the taxpayer (whether or not connected with his trade or business)" does not include property that is acquired and held for a business purpose. In petitioner's view an asset's status as "property" thus turns on the motivation behind its acquisition. This motive test, however, is not only nowhere mentioned in §1221, but it is also in direct conflict with the parenthetical phrase "whether or not connected with his trade or business." The broad definition of the term "capital asset" explicitly makes irrelevant any consideration of the property's connection with the taxpayer's business, whereas petitioner's rule would make this factor dispositive.

In a related argument, petitioner contends that the five exceptions listed in §1221 for certain kinds of property are illustrative, rather than exhaustive, and that courts are therefore free to fashion additional exceptions in order to further the general purposes of the capital-asset provisions. The language of the statute refutes petitioner's construction. Section 1221 provides that "capital asset" means "property held by the taxpayer[,] . . . but does not include" the five classes of property listed as exceptions. We believe this locution signifies that the listed exceptions are exclusive. The body of §1221 establishes a general definition of the term "capital asset," and the phrase "does not include" takes out of that broad definition only the classes of property that are specifically mentioned. The legislative history of the capital asset definition supports this interpretation (" [T]he definition includes all property, except as specifically excluded"), ("[A] capital asset is property held by the taxpayer with certain exceptions"), as does the applicable Treasury regulation.

Petitioner's reading of the statute is also in tension with the exceptions listed in §1221. These exclusions would be largely superfluous if assets acquired primarily or exclusively for business purposes were not capital assets. Inventory, real or depreciable property used in the taxpayer's trade or business, and accounts or notes receivable acquired in the ordinary course of business, would undoubtedly satisfy such a business-motive test. Yet these exceptions were created by Congress in separate enactments spanning 30 years. Without any express direction from Congress, we are unwilling to read §1221 in a manner that makes surplusage of these statutory exclusions.

In the end, petitioner places all reliance on its reading of Corn Products Refining Co. v. Commissioner, 350 U.S. 46 (1955) — a reading we believe is too expansive. In *Corn Products*, the Court considered whether income arising from a taxpayer's dealings in corn futures was entitled to capital-gains treatment. The taxpayer was a company that converted corn into starches, sugars, and other products. After droughts in the 1930's caused sharp increases in corn prices, the company began a program of buying corn futures to assure itself an adequate supply of corn and protect against price increases. The company "would take delivery on such contracts as it found necessary to its manufacturing operations and sell the remainder in early summer if no shortage was imminent. If shortages appeared, however, it sold futures only as it bought spot corn for grinding." The Court characterized the company's dealing in corn futures as "hedging." As explained by the Court of Appeals in *Corn Products*, "[h]edging is a method of dealing in commodity futures whereby a person or business protects itself against price fluctuations at the time of delivery of the product which it sells or buys." In evaluating the company's claim that the sales of corn futures resulted in capital gains and losses, this Court stated:

> Nor can we find support for petitioner's contention that hedging is not within the exclusions of [§1221]. Admittedly, petitioner's corn futures do not come within the literal language of the exclusions set out in that section. They were not stock in trade, actual inventory, property held for sale to customers or depreciable property used in a trade or business. But the capital-asset provision of [§1221] must not be so broadly applied as to defeat rather than further the purpose of Congress. Congress intended that profits and losses arising from the everyday operation of a business be considered as ordinary income or loss rather than capital gain or loss. . . . Since this section is an exception from the normal tax requirements of the Internal Revenue Code, the definition of a capital asset must be narrowly applied and its exclusions interpreted broadly.

The Court went on to note that the hedging transactions consistently had been considered to give rise to ordinary gains and losses, and then concluded that the corn futures were subject to ordinary-asset treatment.

The Court in *Corn Products* proffered the oft-quoted rule of construction that the definition of capital asset must be narrowly applied and its exclusions interpreted broadly, but it did not state explicitly whether the holding was based on a narrow reading of the phrase "property held by the taxpayer," or on a broad reading of the inventory exclusion of §1221. In light of the stark language of §1221, however, we believe that *Corn Products* is properly interpreted as involving an application of §1221's inventory exception. Such a reading is consistent both with the Court's reasoning in that case and with §1221. The Court stated in *Corn Products* that the company's futures transactions were "an integral part of its business designed to protect its manufacturing operations against a price increase in its principal raw material and to assure a ready supply for future manufacturing requirements." The company bought, sold, and took delivery under the futures contracts as required by the company's manufacturing needs. As Professor Bittker notes, under these circumstances, the futures can "easily be viewed as surrogates for the raw material itself." The Court of Appeals for the Second Circuit in *Corn Products* clearly took this approach. That court stated that when commodity futures are "utilized solely for the purpose of stabilizing inventory cost[,] . . . [they] cannot reasonably be separated from the inventory items," and concluded that "property used in hedging transactions properly comes within the exclusions of [§1221]." This Court indicated its acceptance of the Second Circuit's reasoning when it began the central paragraph of its opinion, "Nor can we find support for petitioner's contention that hedging is not within the exclusions of [§1221]." In the following paragraph, the Court argued that the Treasury had consistently viewed such hedging transactions as a form of insurance to stabilize the cost of inventory, and cited a Treasury ruling which concluded that the value of a manufacturer's raw-material inventory should be adjusted to take into account hedging transactions in futures contracts. This discussion, read in light of the Second Circuit's holding and the plain language of §1221, convinces us that although the corn futures were not "actual inventory," their use as an integral part of the taxpayer's inventory-purchase system led the Court to treat them as substitutes for the corn inventory such that they came within a broad reading of "property of a kind which would properly be included in the inventory of the taxpayer" in §1221.

Petitioner argues that by focusing attention on whether the asset was acquired and sold as an integral part of the taxpayer's everyday business operations, the Court in *Corn Products* intended to create a general exemption from capital-asset status for assets acquired for business purposes. We believe petitioner misunderstands the relevance of the Court's inquiry. A business connection, although irrelevant to the initial determination of whether an item is a capital asset, is relevant in determining the applicability of certain of the statutory exceptions, including the inventory exception. The close connection between the futures transactions and the taxpayer's business in *Corn Products* was crucial to whether the corn futures could be considered surrogates for the stored inventory of raw corn. For if the futures dealings were not part of the company's inventory-purchase system, and instead amounted simply to speculation in corn futures, they could not be considered substitutes for the company's corn inventory, and would fall outside even a broad reading of the inventory exclusion. We conclude that *Corn Products* is properly interpreted as standing for the narrow proposition that hedging transactions that are an integral part of a business' inventory-purchase system fall within the inventory exclusion of §1221. Arkansas Best, which is not a dealer in securities, has never suggested that the Bank stock falls within the inventory exclusion. *Corn Products* thus has no application to this case.

It is also important to note that the business-motive test advocated by petitioner is subject to the same kind of abuse that the Court condemned in *Corn Products*. The Court explained in *Corn Products* that unless hedging transactions were subject to ordinary gain and loss treatment, taxpayers engaged in such transactions could "transmute ordinary income into capital gain at will." The hedger could garner capital-asset treatment by selling the future and purchasing the commodity on the spot market, or ordinary-asset treatment by taking delivery under the future contract. In a similar vein, if capital stock purchased and held for a business purpose is an ordinary asset, whereas the same stock purchased and held with an investment motive is a capital asset, a taxpayer such as Arkansas Best could have significant influence over whether the asset would receive capital or ordinary treatment. Because stock is most naturally viewed as a capital asset, the Internal Revenue Service would be hard pressed to challenge a taxpayer's claim that stock was acquired as an investment, and that a gain arising from the sale of such stock was therefore a capital gain. Indeed, we are unaware of a single decision that has applied the business-motive test so as to require a taxpayer to report a gain from the sale of stock as an ordinary gain. If the same stock is sold at a loss, however, the taxpayer may be able to garner ordinary-loss treatment by emphasizing the business purpose behind the stock's acquisition. The potential for such abuse was evidenced in this case by the fact that as late as 1974, when Arkansas Best still hoped to sell the Bank stock at a profit, Arkansas Best apparently expected to report the gain as a capital gain.

III

We conclude that a taxpayer's motivation in purchasing an asset is irrelevant to the question whether the asset is "property held by a taxpayer (whether or not connected with his business)" and is thus within §1221's general definition of "capital asset." Because the capital stock held by petitioner falls within the broad definition of the term "capital asset" in §1221 and is outside the classes of property excluded from capital-asset status, the loss arising from the sale of the stock is a capital loss. Corn Products Refining Co. v. Commissioner, supra, which we interpret as involving a broad reading of the inventory exclusion of §1221, has no application in the present context. Accordingly, the judgment of the Court of Appeals is affirmed.

Problems

7-4.   Gus Thomas was an outdoors enthusiast and professional backcountry guide. In his spare time, Thomas wrote adventure stories and tied fishing flies. Thomas sold the copyrights to five stories to a popular outdoor magazine for $11,000 each. In his dabblings with fly-tying, he designed and patented a new dry-fly. He was able to negotiate a sales price of $23,000 for the patent. What is the character of the gain on the sale of the copyrights and patent?

7-5.   Fluff-Up Down (FUD), a major processor of goose down, has recently seen two discouraging economic events take place in the down products industry. First, goose down has fluctuated both in price and supply, making it difficult for major users, like FUD, to supply their customers. Second, the innovation of polar guard, a synthetic substitute for goose down, and its popularity with cold weather garment manufacturers have threatened to put FUD out of business.

To prevent its demise, as well as the collapse of the goose down industry, FUD expanded its operations and diversified its holdings. FUD paid $100,000 to acquire 60 percent of the stock of Goose, Inc., the third-largest goose ranch in the country. FUD was the main customer of the ranch and believed that owning a sizable portion of the ranch would help stabilize its source of down and that the ranch would eventually become a profitable, dividend-paying enterprise.

FUD had previously purchased goose down futures. After it purchased the goose ranch, however, it was unnecessary for FUD to retain the majority of the futures for use in its processing operations. It therefore sold 70 percent of its contracts and planned to pursue this practice as long as profitable trading continued.

FUD's final economic venture was to acquire a popular down garment manufacturer that was threatening to switch to polar guard. FUD purchased Boiler Works Garments (BWG) stock for $1,000,000. This takeover prevented BWG from switching to the synthetic fillings and also guaranteed FUD a future buyer for 40 percent of the down that it processed and sold.

These acquisitions coupled with the industry's recent return to down-filled garments have enabled FUD to enlarge its enterprise and sell some of its earlier acquisitions. FUD's sale of all of its stock in Goose, Inc., resulted in a loss of $50,000, and its sale of BWG resulted in a profit of $1,500,000.

FUD also sold 80 percent of the goose down futures (which it purchased a year and a half earlier) at a gain of $250,000.

a.   What is the character of the loss on the sale of Goose, Inc., stock?

b.   What is the character of the gain on the sale of goose down futures?

c.   What is the character of the gain on the sale of BWG?

2.   *Special Issues in Capital Gains: Property Held Primarily for Sale*

One of the most commonly encountered property excluded by the statutory definition of capital asset is business property. Three categories of business assets are listed in §1221(a)(1): inventory, stock in trade, and property held primarily for sale. Although the first two are relatively straightforward and can typically be easily identified through general accounting principles, the third category is a catchall with ill-defined boundaries.

Due to its uncertain scope, the phrase "property held by the taxpayer primarily for sale to customers in the ordinary course of his trade or business" has been the subject of as much litigation as any phrase in the Code. In determining the parameters of this phrase, courts initially struggled with the meaning of the word "primarily." The Supreme Court, in Malat v. Riddell, 383 U.S. 569, 572 (1966), held that "primarily" should be given its "literal" interpretation, to mean "of first importance" or "principally." Although *Malat* failed to resolve definitively which property is to be excluded from capital asset treatment because the Court addressed only the meaning of one word in the phrase, *Malat* clearly articulated the intended policy of §1221(a)(1):

> The purpose of [§1221(a)(1)] is to differentiate between the "profits and losses arising from the everyday operation of a business" on the one hand and "the realization of appreciation in value accrued over a substantial period of time" on the other.

Id. at 572 (internal citations omitted). Although the difference between everyday business profits and losses and appreciation because of the passage of time may be readily apparent in some cases, in many others it is difficult to determine which factor was the catalyst for the taxpayer's gain or loss.

Reacting to the limited application of *Malat*'s first importance or principally test, courts developed a more comprehensive analysis of §1221(a)(1). Under this analysis, property is excluded from capital asset treatment if it is (1) held primarily for sale (2) to customers (3) in the ordinary course of a trade or business.

The first element considers whether the property is held primarily for sale or primarily for investment. Numerous factual determinations, none of which is controlling, make this the most difficult of the three elements. Initially, the §1221(a)(1) limitation was applied as a one-question dealer versus investor test in order to determine whether property was a capital asset. This single question test was developed because it was reasoned that if taxpayers are classified as holding property primarily for sale rather than investment, they may be presumed to be selling the property in the ordinary course of business. As more challenging factual situations arose, however, it became apparent that this perfunctory assumption was a misconception and that the dealer versus investor inquiry supplies *only* the first of the three statutory elements.

The second element of the statutory language requires examination of the phrase "to customers." This phrase was added to §1221(a)(1) to distinguish stock investors (regardless of how active) from professional securities dealers and brokers. Thus, securities investors are not regarded as having customers, and their losses and gains are generally capital. In distinguishing a stock investor from a dealer, the Tax Court in Kemon v. Commissioner, 16 T.C. 1026 (1951), stated:

> Those who sell "to customers" are comparable to a merchant in that they purchase their stock in trade, in this case securities, with the expectation of reselling at a profit, *not because of a rise in value during the interval of time between purchase and resale*, but merely because they have or hope to find a market of buyers who will purchase from them at a price in excess of their cost. This excess or mark-up represents remuneration for their labors as a middle man bringing together buyer and seller, *and performing the usual services of retailer or wholesaler of goods*. Such sellers are known as "dealers."
>
> Contrasted to "dealers" are those sellers of securities who perform no such merchandising functions and whose status as to the source of supply is not significantly different from that of those to whom they sell. That is, the securities are as easily accessible to one as the other and the seller performs no services that need be compensated for by a mark-up of the price of the securities he sells. *The sellers depend upon such circumstances as a rise in value or an advantageous purchase to enable them to sell at a price in excess of cost.* Such sellers are known as "traders."

Id. at 1032 (emphasis added).

The third element of the statutory formula requires an analysis of the words "trade or business," as well as their impact on a taxpayer's classification as an investor or a dealer. For instance, if property is held primarily for sale, but not in a trade or business, the asset should not be excluded by §1221(a)(1). On the other hand, even when property is not held primarily for sale, if it is *used* in a trade or business the asset is excluded from the definition of a capital asset by §1221(a)(2).

In determining whether sales or exchanges are in the ordinary course of a trade or business, the resolution turns on whether the sale or exchange was a routine transaction in the course of the taxpayer's everyday affairs of business. For example, a used car dealer who sells a used car to a customer has made a sale in the ordinary course of business, but a used car dealer who sells his or her used office equipment to a neighbor has not.

UNITED STATES v. WINTHROP
417 F.2d 905 (5th Cir. 1969)

GOLDBERG, J.

We must emerge with a solution to the "old, familiar, recurring, vexing and ofttimes elusive" problem concerning capital gains versus ordinary income arising out of the sale of subdivided real estate. Finding ourselves engulfed in a fog of decisions with gossamer like distinctions, and a quagmire of unworkable, unreliable, and often irrelevant tests, we take the route of ad hoc exploration to find ordinary income.

I

The taxpayer, Guy L. Winthrop, was the owner of certain property in the environs of Tallahassee, Florida, known as Betton Hills. The property had been in his family since 1836. Winthrop first received a share of the property in 1932 upon the death of his mother. Additional portions of the property were received by him in 1946, 1948, and 1960 through inheritance and partition. As the city of Tallahassee expanded, its city limits were extended to incorporate most of the Winthrop property and the taxpayer began to sell lots for homesites. The first subdivision was undertaken in 1936, and the first sales were made in that year. Thereafter, eight other subdivisions were platted and developed by the taxpayer. Each subdivision was platted separately and the taxpayer endeavored to sell most of the lots in one subdivision before another was developed. The process was one of gradual orderly development of the property through the various subdivisions. Each was surveyed and platted. The streets were graded and paved at Winthrop's expense. Electricity and water facilities were installed; and in some subdivisions sewer lines were built, again at Winthrop's expense, although this was eventually repaid out of the utility bills incurred by homeowners who moved into the subdivisions. Moreover, the taxpayer participated in building five houses for sale in the addition in order to assist other purchasers in obtaining F.H.A. loans to finance their homes.

In selling the lots Winthrop neither advertised nor engaged brokers. The customers primarily came to his home to conduct the sale negotiations since he did not even have an office. He did however, purchase an annual occupational license as a real estate broker from the City of Tallahassee from 1948 through 1963. Despite this low pressure and selling technique, the parties stipulated that Winthrop was primarily engaged in selling the Betton Hills property and that though he was a civil engineer by profession, he did little work of this type during the period in question save that done on the Betton Hills property. Furthermore, Winthrop's technique, although unorthodox, was apparently effective. Commencing with the year 1945 and ending in December, 1963, approximately 456 lots were sold in Betton Hills. The profit and other income realized by Winthrop from the sale of these lots from 1951 through 1963 was $483,018.94 or 52.4 percent of his total income during that period. . . .

II

The government's first argument in support of its contention that the district court erred in granting capital gains treatment to the taxpayer is founded upon the proposition that capital gains treatment is available only where the appreciation in value is the result of external market changes occurring over a period of time. In other words, the government argues that where the appreciation is due to the taxpayer's efforts, all profit should be reported as ordinary income. In statutory terms the government argues that the subdivided land ceased to be a "capital asset" when the taxpayer improved the land through his own efforts by platting the lots, paving streets, and installing utilities. Although recognizing that subdivided land is not expressly removed from the "capital asset" category by the exclusionary

provisions of I.R.C. §1221 unless such land is held primarily for sale to customers in the ordinary course of business, the government, nevertheless, maintains that its taxpayer efforts rule has, in effect, been read into the statute by the courts. . . .
 . . . As this court said in *Barrios' Estate*, [265 F.2d 517 (5th Cir. 1959)]:

> The idea of selling a large tract of land in lots embraces necessarily the construction of streets for access to them, the provision of drainage and the furnishing of access to such a necessity as water. It is hardly conceivable that taxpayer could have sold a lot without doing these things. To contend that reasonable expenditures and efforts, in such necessary undertakings are not entitled to capital gains treatment is to reject entirely the established principle that a person holding lands under such circumstances may subdivide it for advantageous sale.

265 F.2d at 520. We therefore conclude that this blanket interdiction of capital gains treatment where there has been any laying on of hands is belied by the past decisions of this court.

III

While we are in disagreement with the government's first argument concerning taxpayer efforts, we find its second argument, that the land in question was primarily held for sale in the ordinary course of business and, therefore, was not a capital asset under §1221, persuasive. In holding against the government on this point the court below appears to have placed particular emphasis upon the following facts: (1) the proceeds from the sales of the property were not reinvested in real estate; (2) the taxpayer had other investments, none of which involved the sale of real estate; (3) the subdivided property was acquired by inheritance, not by purchase for the purpose of resale; (4) the taxpayer's holding period was twenty-five years; (5) the taxpayer maintained no office, made most of the sales from his home, spent no time whatever promoting sales and did not advertise; and (6) the purchasers came to him and he was selective in making the sales.

In relying on these factors the court below was obviously following earlier suggestions by this court that such facts are relevant in determining the ultimate question of whether or not the land in question was held primarily for sale to customers in the ordinary course of business. In condensed form the tests mentioned most often are: (1) the nature and purpose of the acquisition of the property and the duration of the ownership; (2) the extent and nature of the taxpayer's efforts to sell the property; (3) the number, extent, continuity and substantiality of the sales; (4) the extent of subdividing, developing, and advertising to increase sales; (5) the use of a business office for the sale of the property; (6) the character and degree of supervision or control exercised by the taxpayer over any representative selling the property; and (7) the time and effort the taxpayer habitually devoted to the sales.

Despite their frequent use, this court has often declared that these seven pillars of capital gains treatment "in and of themselves . . . have no independent significance, but only form part of a situation which in the individual case must be considered in its entirety to determine whether or not the property involved was held primarily for sale in the ordinary course of business (source cited)." Cole v. Usry, 294 F.2d at 427. . . .

In the instant case the trial court found that these test facts, about which there is no disagreement, compelled a finding of the ultimate fact that the holding was not primarily for sale in the ordinary course of the taxpayer's business. In weighing the arguments on this point this court recognizes that the characterization of the taxpayer's manner of holding lands is a question of fact. . . .

We think, therefore, that even though we accept as true the fact findings of the court below, it is nevertheless incumbent upon this court to inquire into the ultimate conclusion of law reached by that court. . . .

. . . We therefore approach first the issue of whether or not Winthrop held the property "primarily for sale" as that phrase is used in §1221.

It is undisputed that Winthrop inherited the first portion of the Betton Hills land in 1932. By 1936 the first sales had been made and further subdivisions were under way. Mrs. Winthrop's testimony indicates that, except for the subdividing and selling, the land was not used by the taxpayer. . . . On the other hand, her testimony was equally clear in showing that the taxpayer's activities regarding the land, such as paving the streets and having utilities installed, were done with the express purpose of making it more saleable. She testified that he built houses on some of the lots in order to make FHA financing available to prospective purchasers of other lots. Moreover, he built some houses on the lots because "if a person built a house and there was a house nearby, somebody wanted the lot, because people like neighbors."

There were, therefore, no multiple, dual, or changes of purpose during the relevant years of Winthrop's Betton Hills sales. The taxpayer, long before the tax years in question, had as his sole motivation the sale of Betton Hills, lot by lot, year by year, transaction by transaction. The evidence is clear and uncontradicted that the lots were at all times held by Winthrop "primarily for sale" as that phrase was interpreted by the Supreme Court in Malat v. Riddell, 1966, 383 U.S. 569.

Holding primarily for sale, however, is by itself insufficient to disqualify the taxpayer from capital gains privileges. The sales must also be made in the ordinary course of the taxpayer's trade or business. The next issue, therefore, is whether the taxpayer's activities constituted a trade or business. We think that they did. The magnitude and continuity of his operations and design all point to these sales being part of a business. This was a planned program of subdividing and selling, lasting over a quarter of a century. It constituted Winthrop's principal activity and produced over one-half of his income during the years in question. This was no minuscule operation in terms of transactions or profits. . . . [T]he taxpayer here devoted a substantial amount of his time, skill and financial resources to developing and selling the property. He thereby became engaged in the business of subdividing real estate for sale. One need not be a static holder to qualify for capital gains treatment, but the flexing of commercial muscles with frequency and continuity, design and effect does result in disqualification because it indicates one has entered the business of real estate sales. Thompson v. Commissioner, 5 Cir. 1963, 322 F.2d 122.

The taxpayer has made much over the fact that no office was used, no brokers were employed, no time was spent promoting sales, and no advertising was used. While advertising, solicitation and staff are the usual components of a business, they are not a necessary element in either the concept or the pragmatics of selling. Here it is evident that the taxpayer was quite successful in selling the lots without the assistance of these usual props. It is not necessary that customers be actively and fervently and frenetically sought. Winthrop had lots to sell and not mousetraps, so they beat a way to his door to buy his lots. As the court remarked in Thompson v. Commissioner, supra, which involved a similar lack of promotional activity, "merely because business was good, indeed brisk, does not make it any less in the ordinary course of such a good business." Winthrop was in the business of selling lots in Betton Hills, even though his salesmanship was unorthodox and low pressure. The sales were out of his lots, and were made to customers, though these customers sought him out rather than having been pursued.

In addition, we think the sales were ordinary in the course of this business. The concept of normalcy requires for its application a chronology and a history to determine if the sales of lots to customers were the usual or a departure from the norm. History and chronology here combine to demonstrate that Winthrop did not sell his lots as an abnormal or unexpected event. He began selling shortly after he acquired the land; he never used the land for any other purpose; and he continued this course of conduct over a number of years. Thus, the sales were not only ordinary, they were the sole object of Winthrop's business. It is this singleness of purpose which distinguishes Winthrop's sales from those in *Barrios' Estate* . . . relied on by the taxpayer. It is true, as the taxpayer asserts, that in each of these cases there was considerable sales activity. However, in each the property had been used for some other purpose and the sales ensued only when this primary purpose was abandoned. Here there was no change of purpose.

. . . Sale was the prime purpose of the holding and the sales were made in the ordinary course of the taxpayer's business. We conclude, therefore, that the taxpayer is not entitled to capital gains treatment on the profit made from the sales of land during the years 1959 through 1963. The judgment of the district court is reversed.

Note on Liquidation of Investment Doctrine

Occasionally, the number, frequency, and continuity of sales, along with other activities, may indicate that property is being held primarily for sale to customers in a trade or business, yet gain or loss on sales of that property may receive capital treatment under the judicially developed liquidation of investment doctrine. Under this doctrine, capital treatment may result even if property is being held primarily for sale, if sales are not in the ordinary course of business but rather in the liquidation of a former investment.

In a liquidation, the investor's primary motive for selling may be a desire to terminate the business or investment for nonprofit-related reasons, such as an illness, or simply a desire to go into a different business. The liquidation theory, therefore, presupposes that the taxpayer was initially holding the property for investment purposes but that subsequent events caused the abandonment of the investment. If the taxpayer can establish that the investment motive never changed, subsequent sales make the taxpayer an investment liquidator. For example, the taxpayer who subdivides a tract of raw land held as an investment for ten years may argue that he is merely liquidating a former investment and not making sales in the course of a new trade or business.

The result under the liquidation of investment doctrine is equitable to the investor whose true goal is liquidation and not solely maximizing profits. Thus, in the liquidation setting, capital treatment is preserved as long as "the evidence . . . indicates that disposing of the property, not making money from a new type of business was the primary purpose [of the sales]." Goldberg v. Commissioner, 223 F.2d 709, 713 (5th Cir. 1955). The presence of a liquidation, as opposed to a profit, motive entitling the taxpayer to capital treatment depends on several factors analyzed in the case that follows.

SUBURBAN REALTY CO. v. UNITED STATES
615 F.2d 171 (5th Cir. 1980)

GOLDBERG, J.

We must today answer the riddle at once adumbrated and apparently foreclosed by the false dichotomy created by the United States Supreme Court in Malat v. Riddell, 383 U.S. 569, 572 (1966) (per curiam): when profits have "aris[en] from the [ordinary] operation of a business" on the one hand and are *also* "the realization of appreciation in value over a substantial period of time" on the other, are these profits treated as ordinary income or capital gain? Lacking any clear guidance but the language of the capital asset statute itself, we turn to that language for the answer. Before we can arrive at this interesting and important question, however, we must once again tramp along (but not trample on) that time- and precedent-worn path which separates capital gains from ordinary income. By the time we emerge into the light at the far edge of the forest, we will find that the *Riddell* riddle has seemingly answered itself, and all that will remain will be a brief reassessment of our answer. In our peregrinations, we of necessity wander into virgin territory. We hope that we shed new light onto this murky terrain; at the least, we think we have neither riddled the cases nor muddled the issues.

I

Suburban Realty Company was formed in November, 1937 to acquire an undivided one-fourth interest in 1,742.6 acres of land located in Harris County, Texas ("the property"). . . . Suburban's corporate charter states that it was formed to erect or repair any building or improvement, and to accumulate and lend money for such purposes, and to purchase, sell, and subdivide real property, and to accumulate and lend money for that purpose.

The five transactions whose characterization is in dispute here concern six tracts of unimproved real estate sold from the property by Suburban between 1968 and 1971. On its tax returns, Suburban originally reported profits from these sales, as well as all of its other real estate sales, as ordinary income. Later, Suburban filed a claim for refund asserting that these six tracts, as well as three similar tracts sold later, were capital assets, and that profits from these sales were entitled to capital gain treatment. The Internal Revenue Service denied Suburban's claim as to the sales here in issue. Suburban then instituted this action for a refund. . . .

The parties' legal contentions are closely bound to the facts. It is undisputed that, at the time of sale, the tracts at issue here were subject to a grass lease which apparently covered much of the property. Except for this grass lease, the six tracts, as well as much of the rest of the property, were never put to any substantial use. However, certain other portions of the property were the subject of greater activity. The parties disagree to some degree concerning the extent of, and appropriate characterization of, the activities conducted relating to these other portions of the property, and they fundamentally dispute the weight such activities carry in properly characterizing the sales at issue here. . . .

Between 1939 and 1971, Suburban made at least 244 individual sales of real estate out of the property. [See appendix to this case. — EDS.] Of these, approximately 95 sales were unplatted and unimproved property legally suitable for commercial development for any other purpose, and at least 149 sales were from platted property restricted to residential development. In each of these 33 years, Suburban concluded at least one sale; in most years, there were four or more sales. Suburban's total proceeds from real estate sales over this period were $2,353,935. Proceeds from all other sources of income amounted to $474,845. Thus, eighty-three percent of Suburban's proceeds emanated from real estate sales; only 17 percent flowed from all other sources. . . .

In 1957, the Texas Highway Department proposed that the limited access superhighway now known as the North Loop would be located from east to west across the property. In 1959 and 1960, Suburban sold at least two parcels out of the property to the Texas Highway Department for the purpose of constructing this highway. The location of the highway had a dramatic effect on the price of land in the area. Land which had been selling for between three and five thousand dollars per acre prior to announcement of the highway rose in value to between seven and twelve thousand dollars per acre. . . .

Starting not later than 1959, Suburban's officers, directors and stockholders began discussing liquidation of the corporation. Many of these discussions occurred after 1961, when Rice University became a stockholder of Suburban and the Treasurer of Rice University became a member of the board of directors. Because Rice University desired investments in income-producing assets rather than raw land, discussions concerning liquidation of Suburban's real estate holdings and the possibility of a partition of its holding among its stockholders were common. Starting in 1966, Suburban made substantial investments in stocks and bonds and began receiving substantial income from these investments. . . .

II

Our analysis of this case must begin with Biedenharn Realty Co., Inc. v. United States, 526 F.2d 409 (5th Cir. [1976]) (en banc). *Biedenharn* is this Court's latest (and only) en banc pronouncement concerning the characterization of profits of a real estate business as ordinary income or capital gain. The decision answers the characterization question by evaluating certain "factors" often present in cases of this ilk. *Biedenharn* attempts to guide the analysis in this area by assigning different levels of importance to various of the "factors." Substantiality and frequency of sales is called the most important factor. Improvements to the land, solicitation and advertising efforts, and brokerage activities also play an important part in the *Biedenharn* analysis.

The question before us today, put into the *Biedenharn* framework, can be stated as follows: when a taxpayer engages in frequent and substantial sales over a period of years, but undertakes no development activity with respect to parts of a parcel of land, and engages in no solicitation or advertising efforts or brokerage activities, under what circumstances is income derived from sales of undeveloped parts of the parcel ordinary income?

The *Biedenharn* framework allows us to ask the question, but gives us little guidance in answering it. In the principal recent cases, there has always been a conjunction of frequent and substantial sales with development activity relating to the properties in dispute. The conjunction of these two factors "will usually conclude the capital gains issue against [the] taxpayer." . . . However, substantial and frequent sales activity, standing alone, has never been held to be automatically sufficient to trigger ordinary income treatment. In fact, we have continual reminders of the fact that "specific factors, or combinations of them are not necessarily controlling," *Biedenharn*, 526 F.2d at 415. . . .

III

The jurisprudence of the "real estate capital gains-ordinary income issue" in this Circuit has at times been cast somewhat loose of its statutory mooring. The ultimate inquiry in cases of this nature is whether the property at issue was "property held by the taxpayer primarily for sale to customers in the ordinary course of his trade or business."§1221(1). In our focus on the "tests" developed to resolve this question, we have on occasion almost lost sight entirely of the statutory framework. . . .

The tendency to overemphasize the independent meaning of the "factors" has been accompanied by, perhaps even caused by, a tendency to view the statutory language as posing only one question: whether the property was held by the taxpayer "primarily for sale to customers in the ordinary course of his trade or business." This determination was correctly seen as equivalent to the question whether the gain was to be treated as ordinary or capital. However, probably because the question "is the gain ordinary" is a single question which demands an answer of yes or no, the courts have on occasion lost sight of the fact that the statutory language requires the court to make not one determination, but several separate determinations. In statutory construction cases, our most important task is to ask the proper questions. In the context of cases like the one before us, the principal inquiries demanded by the statute are:

1. Was taxpayer engaged in a trade or business, and, if so, what business?
2. Was taxpayer holding the property primarily for sale in that business?
3. Were the sales contemplated by taxpayer "ordinary" in the course of that business? . . .

. . . It will remain true that the frequency and substantiality of sales will be the most important factor. But the reason for the importance of this factor is now clear: the presence of frequent and substantial sales is highly relevant to each of the principal statutory inquiries listed above. A taxpayer who engages in frequent and substantial sales is almost inevitably engaged in the real estate business.

The frequency and substantiality of sales are highly probative on the issue of holding purpose because the presence of frequent sales ordinarily belies the contention that property is being held "for investment" rather than "for sale." And the frequency of sales may often be a key factor in determining the "ordinariness" question.

The extent of development activity and improvements is highly relevant to the question of whether taxpayer is a real estate developer. Development activity and improvements may also be relevant to the taxpayer's holding purpose, but, standing alone, some degree of development activity is not inconsistent with holding property for purposes other than sale. The extent of development activity also seems to be only peripherally relevant to the "ordinariness" question. Thus, under the statutory framework, as under *Biedenharn*, the extent of development activity and improvements, although an important factor, is less conclusive than the substantiality and frequency of sales.

Solicitation and advertising efforts are quite relevant both to the existence of a trade or business and to taxpayer's holding purpose. Thus, their presence can strengthen the case for ordinary income treatment. However, in cases like *Biedenharn*, their absence is not conclusive on either of these statutory questions for, as we noted there, "even one inarguably in the real estate business need not engage in promotional exertions in the face of a favorable market."

We need not comment individually on each of the other *Biedenharn–Winthrop* factors. It should be apparent that each factor is relevant, to a greater or lesser extent, to one or more of the questions posed by the statute along the path to the ultimate conclusion.[24]

---

24. We will here attempt to clear up some of the confusion relating to the relevance of the percentage of taxpayer's average annual income attributable to real estate sales. This percentage has often been mentioned in the real estate cases; its significance has never been clear. Rather, these decisions have referred to the percentage, often compared it to the comparable percentage in another case, and perhaps noted that the percentage in the case being decided was like or unlike the percentage in another case. Once the percentage is related to the statutory inquiries, it can easily be seen that the percentage may or may not be relevant depending on the facts of the case and the taxpayer's claims. Two examples are appropriate here.

First, a taxpayer who has made only a few sales involving fairly modest dollar amounts may argue that he is not in the real estate business. The taxpayer's claim to capital gain treatment is likely to be weaker if he can point to no other business activities; i.e., if close to 100 percent of his income is derived from sales of real estate. Conversely, if the taxpayer is also engaged in extensive activities other than real estate sales, the presence of another trade or business may make it less likely that he will be found to be in the real estate business. However, frequent real estate sales activity substantial in dollar amount will likely conclude the "trade or business" question against taxpayer. He will be held to be engaged in both the real estate business and his other business.

The taxpayer's next argument will likely be that the property is held "primarily" for use in his other business (e.g., farming) rather than "for sale." If a large percentage of his income *derived from the land in dispute* is earned other than by sale, his claim that his primary holding purpose is for use in his other business is buttressed. This would clearly be the case if a few small tracts of land were sold from a large active farm. Conversely, if most of the income derived from the land in dispute is earned from real estate sales, it is more likely that the taxpayer's primary holding purpose is "for sale." . . .

A second situation in which a percentage is relevant involves a taxpayer attempting to demonstrate that certain parcels of land were held for purposes other than for sale. This taxpayer could concede that he was in the real estate development business, but would argue that certain specific parcels of land were not held "primarily for sale." These specific properties, he would argue, were held for other purposes. In this situation, a relevant percentage would be profits from (or number of) sales from property held primarily for sale as compared to profits from (or number of) all sales. If many of taxpayer's sales, or much of his profit, emanated from properties he claimed to hold for purposes other than "for sale," the

IV

Having laid the framework for the requisite analysis, we must now apply that framework to the facts here. We must decide whether Suburban was engaged in a trade or business, and, if so, what business; whether Suburban was holding the properties at issue here primarily for sale; and whether Suburban's contemplated sales were "ordinary" in the course of Suburban's business. . . .

A.   WAS SUBURBAN IN THE REAL ESTATE BUSINESS?

. . . It is clear to us that Suburban engaged in a sufficient quantity of activity to be in the business of selling real estate. Suburban's sales were continuous and substantial. . . .

Suburban does not claim to have been engaged in any business other than real estate; rather, it claims that during the periods at issue it simply "did not carry on a trade or business." Were additional support necessary for our conclusion, we would point to Suburban's own statements on its tax returns over the years that its principal business activity was "development and sales of real estate." These statements are by no means conclusive of the issue. However, we believe they show at least that if Suburban is engaged in a trade or business, that business is real estate. And Suburban's activities over the years were sufficient to convince us that it cannot sustain its contention that it was never engaged in any "trade or business" at all.

Suburban relies heavily on the insignificance of its subdivision and development activity and the total absence of any advertising or sales solicitation activity on its part. However, the first two absences do not concern us at all. We need not decide whether its subdivision and development activities were sufficient to compel the conclusion that Suburban was in the real estate development business. We rely solely on Suburban's real estate sales business.

The presence of any sales solicitation or advertising activity would certainly be relevant to the issue of whether Suburban was in the business of selling real estate. Strenuous, but largely unsuccessful, attempts to sell might compel the conclusion that a taxpayer with very few sales transactions was nonetheless in the business of selling. But the absence of such activity does not compel the opposite conclusion.

Suburban also seeks solace from the fact that it never purchased any additional real estate to replenish acreage it sold. As is the case with the presence of sales activity, the presence of such purchases tends to demonstrate that a taxpayer is engaged in a real estate business, but their absence is not conclusive. . . .

Additionally, Suburban points to its commencement of an investment program in securities in 1966. By itself, this cannot affect our conclusion that Suburban was in the real estate business. It merely demonstrates that, commencing in 1966, Suburban was also engaged in investing in securities. As stated earlier, the presence of other types of activities does not prevent taxpayer's real estate activities from being considered a business.

---

taxpayer would be highly unlikely to establish capital gain treatment. Conversely, if a taxpayer who engaged in a high volume subdivision business sold one clearly segregated tract in bulk, he might well prevail in his claim to capital gain treatment on the segregated tract.

Suburban also contends that, if it was ever in the real estate business, it had exited that business long before 1968, the time of the first transaction here at issue. Even if this is true, it cannot affect our ultimate conclusion. The statutory language does not demand that property actually be sold while a taxpayer is still actively engaged in its trade or business for ordinary income treatment to be required. Rather, it demands that the property have been held primarily for sale in that business. To that inquiry we now turn.

B. WHAT WAS SUBURBAN'S PRIMARY PURPOSE FOR HOLDING THE PROPERTIES WHOSE CHARACTERIZATION IS HERE IN DISPUTE?

Put into the framework being used here, Suburban's contention concerning holding purpose is two-fold. Principally, it argues that, at the time of the sales in dispute, the properties were not being held for sale. Alternatively, it contends that it "originally acquired its property as an investment . . . , and it continued to hold it for investment purposes."

We reject Suburban's statement of the legal principle upon which its first argument is premised. It simply cannot be true that "the decisive question is the purpose for which [the property] 'primarily' was held when sold." At the very moment of sale, the property is certainly being held "for sale." The appropriate question certainly must be the taxpayer's primary holding purpose at some point before he decided to make the sale in dispute. . . .

The "holding purpose" inquiry may appropriately be conducted by attempting to trace the taxpayer's primary holding purpose over the entire course of his ownership of the property. Thus, the inquiry should start at the time the property is acquired. We seek to divine the taxpayer's primary purpose for acquiring the property. In this case, we are willing to assume, as Suburban argues, that the property was acquired principally as an investment. We then seek evidence of a change in taxpayer's primary holding purpose. Here, such evidence is plentiful and convincing.

The property was acquired in December, 1937. . . . Sales commenced by 1939, and sales were transacted in each year thereafter. From 1946 through 1956, approximately 17 sales per year occurred. . . . Also during this period, the development activity pertaining to Homestead Addition Two was occurring. This development activity clearly contemplated, and was accompanied by, sales.

All of these factors convince us that, by the mid-1940's at the latest, and probably much earlier, Suburban's primary holding purpose was "for sale." . . .

With its primary holding purpose through the 1940's and 1950's fixed at "for sale," Suburban is then entitled to show that its primary purpose changed to, or back to, "for investment." Suburban claims that this shift occurred either in 1959, when its officers and directors discussed liquidation; in 1961, when Rice University became a stockholder of Suburban, further liquidation discussions were held, and the plats were withdrawn; or, at the latest, in 1966, when further liquidation discussions were held and Suburban began investing in securities.

We view this determination to be a closer call than any of the others in this case. The frequency of sales did drop off after the late 1950's. Suburban had discontinued its development activities. Also, 1961 was the year the plats for Homestead Additions Three and Four were withdrawn.

This withdrawal of plats could be quite significant. Unlike liquidation discussions, which were apparently a dime a dozen for Suburban, withdrawal of the plats was an action taken by Suburban which may evince a different relationship to its land. The critical question is whether this withdrawal indicated that henceforth the land was being held principally as an investment or simply showed that Suburban was attempting to maximize sales profits by selling to commercial users.

The continuing sales activity is strong evidence that the latter interpretation is the correct one. Moreover, the trial court found that the withdrawal evinced "an attempt to maximize profits from the sale of real estate and to capitalize on the new North Loop Freeway which would cross [Suburban's] property." Thus, we conclude that Suburban's primary purpose for holding the property remained "for sale" at the time of the transactions here disputed.[42] Suburban does not explicitly contend that its primary purpose for holding the specific parcels at issue here was different from its purpose for holding the property as a whole. However, it does attempt to rely to some degree on the lack of development activity relating to the parcels here at issue. Although in some circumstances a taxpayer in the real estate business may be able to establish that certain parcels were held primarily for investment, see n.24, supra, the burden is on the taxpayer to establish that the parcels held primarily for investment were segregated from other properties held primarily for sale. The mere lack of development activity with respect to parts of a large property does not sufficiently separate those parts from the whole to meet the taxpayer's burden. The lack of development activity with respect to the parts of the property here at issue is at least equally consistent with a primary motivation to maximize immediate sales profits as it is with a primary motivation to hold for investment.

C.   WERE THE SALES CONTEMPLATED BY SUBURBAN "ORDINARY" IN THE COURSE OF SUBURBAN'S BUSINESS?

We need say no more on this question than quote from the discussion of this issue in *Winthrop*, supra:

> The concept of normalcy requires for its application a chronology and a history to determine if the sales of lots to customers were the usual or a departure from the norm. History and chronology here combine to demonstrate that [taxpayer] did not sell his lots as an abnormal or unexpected event. [Taxpayer] began selling shortly after he acquired the land; he never used the land for any other purpose; and he continued this course of conduct over a number of years. Thus, the sales were . . . ordinary.

417 F.2d at 912. The same is true here.

---

42. Some of our skepticism over Suburban's claim to have changed its holding purpose stems from the fact that it points to so many separate times when its purpose may have changed. This leads us to believe that Suburban was merely gradually shifting its strategies as market conditions changed in an effort to maximize sales profits. We do not reject outright the possibility that a sequence of events separate in time may indicate a gradual change in holding purpose from "for sale" to "for investment." However, we would be more likely to find a "change of purpose" argument convincing if a discrete event were followed by a string of zeros in the annual sales column figures, especially if this were followed by a sale of the remainder of taxpayer's property in a small number of transactions.

V

Having relied on the language of §1221 itself to determine that the assets here at issue were not capital assets, we must return for a moment to the query posed at the outset. In this case, as we have demonstrated, sales of the type here in dispute were precisely what Suburban's business was directed towards. In other words, the profits garnered from these sales arose from the ordinary operation of Suburban's business.

At the same time, however, these profits did not arise principally from the efforts of Suburban. Rather, they arose from the same historical, demographic, and market forces that have caused the City of Houston to grow enormously during the years Suburban held the land. Shrewdly, Suburban held on to much of its land. It only sold relatively small portions year by year. Thus, by 1968, market forces and the location of the North Loop Freeway had driven up the value of Suburban's land. We must decide whether the policies motivating [preferential treatment for] capital gains and the controlling precedents expressing those policies require that we ignore the plain language of §1221 and hold for Suburban.

The key cases we must explore here number three. First is Malat v. Riddell, 389 U.S. 569 (1966). It lends us no aid. As we have previously stated, it suggests that profits cannot arise from both "the [ordinary] operation of a business" and "appreciation in value accrued over a substantial period of time." Yet here we have profits which fall squarely into both categories.

We thus turn to the two cases from which the *Malat* court quotations are taken, Commissioner v. Gillette Motor Transport, Inc., 364 U.S. 130 (1960), and Corn Products Refining Company v. Commissioner, 350 U.S. 46 (1955). In *Gillette*, the Supreme Court said:

> This Court has long held that the term "capital asset" is to be construed narrowly in accordance with the purpose of Congress to afford capital-gains treatment only in situations typically involving the realization of appreciation in value accrued over a substantial period of time, and thus to ameliorate the hardship of taxation and the entire gain in one year.

364 U.S. at 134. We note that the quoted language does not state that all gains emanating from appreciation in value over a substantial period of time are to be treated as capital gains. Rather, it states the logical converse of that proposition; i.e., that capital gain treatment will be proper only if the gain emanates from appreciation in value. Instances of gain emanating from appreciation being treated as ordinary income are not inconsistent with this proposition.

We also note the Supreme Court's recognition of the attempt by Congress to avoid taxing income earned over a period of years in one year. In Suburban's case, although it is true that with respect to each individual parcel of land there is a "bunching" effect, taxation of the overall gains from the property as a whole has been spread over a long period of years. Thus, the "bunching" effect has been minimized. Last, we note the Supreme Court's admonition to construe the term "capital asset" narrowly.

Further support for a narrow construction of the term "capital asset" and a broad interpretation of its exclusions comes from *Corn Products*, the third key case in this area. More importantly, the Supreme Court in *Corn Products* squarely stated:

> Congress intended that profits and losses arising from the everyday operation of a business be considered as ordinary income or loss rather than capital gain or loss.

It is this type of profit that is before us today.

We thus conclude that §1221(1) should be construed in accord with its plain meaning, and that, if the other requirements of §1221(1) are met, when the ordinary business of a business is to make profits from appreciation in value caused by market forces, those profits are to be treated as ordinary income. Such is the case here.

VI

Our journey over, we have nothing more to add. The decision of the district court dismissing Suburban's complaint is affirmed.

APPENDIX

Date	Number Commercial Sales	Number Residential Sales	Total Number Sales
1939	4	0	4
1940	3	?	3+
1941	1	?	1+
1942	2	?	2+
1943	1	?	1+
1944	3	?	3+
1945	5	?	5+
1946	11	6	17
1947	3	12	15
1948	0	21	21
1949	3	6	9
1950	6	46	52
1951	1	6	7
1952	4	14	18
1953	2	6	8
1954	0	5	5
1955	1	16	17
1956	1	6	7
1957	1	1	2
1958	1	3	4
1959	3	1	4
1960	1	0	2
1961	2	0	2
1962	1	0	1
1963	4	0	3
1964	6	0	4
1965	4	0	6
1966	7	0	5

1967	4	0	4
1968	1	0	3
1969	4	0	3
1970	1	0	1
1971	4	0	4
TOTAL	95	149+	244+

Problem

7-6. Maryanne Jason, a retired lawyer and ardent wine taster, collected rare wines for her personal consumption. Jason had her wine collection appraised, and much to her astonishment, the value of many of the bottles had appreciated significantly. This revelation prompted Jason to stop drinking many of the wines and, instead, to begin holding the collection for investment.

Jason continued her investment in wine for the next four years, occasionally selling less valuable wines and replacing them with more precious vintages. Jason hired a winebroker and began advertising the wine collection in a trade publication, and Jason sold 25 percent of her collection and reported the resulting profits as long-term capital gain. In the next year, she sold another 55 percent of her total collection for an aggregate gain of $100,000.

a. Should Jason report the profit as ordinary gain? Briefly explain the Commissioner's and the taxpayer's arguments. May she report a *portion* of these profits as capital gain?

b. What effect if, instead of individual sales, Jason sold her entire wine collection to one purchaser in one transaction?

c. Assume that Jason developed cirrhosis of the liver and sold her wine pursuant to her doctor's orders.

d. Are there any arguments that either Jason or the Commissioner may make to distinguish the wine sales of the two years?

D. SALE OR EXCHANGE REQUIREMENT

Code: §§1001(a), (b), (c); 1222; 1234(a)
Regulations: §§1.1001-2(a), (b); 1.1002-1

The sale or exchange requirement for capital gain or loss characterization is statutorily embodied in §1222. Section 1001(a) contains similar language, requiring a "sale or other disposition" before a gain or loss may be realized. An equitable notion underlies the §1001(a) realization requirement: The proper time to impose an income tax is when property is converted into cash or when the taxpayer's interest is sufficiently altered so that the investment is not merely continued in substantially similar property — that is, when the investor has "cashed out." The rationale for the §1222 sale or exchange requirement, however, is less certain. It may be that the different statutory phrases are creatures of accident rather than legislative purpose. What is certain, however, is that §§1001(a) and 1222 have different functions. Section 1001(a) determines those circumstances in which gain or loss, whether ordinary or capital, must be computed ("sale or other disposition"). The sale or exchange language in §1222, on the other hand, establishes a requirement that must be satisfied before a realized gain or loss may be entitled to capital treatment.

Not all transactions can easily be classified as a sale or exchange. For instance, in Helvering v. William Flaccus Oak Leather Co., 313 U.S. 247 (1941), the Supreme Court held that insurance compensation received for the loss of a building destroyed by fire did not constitute a §1222 sale or exchange. The Court reasoned that

> [g]enerally speaking, the language in the Revenue Act, just as in any statute, is to be given its ordinary meaning, and the words "sale" and "exchange" are not to be read any differently. Neither term is appropriate to characterize the demolition of property and subsequent compensation for its loss by an insurance company. Plainly that pair of events was not a sale. Nor can they be regarded as an exchange, for "exchange" . . . implies reciprocal transfers of capital assets, not a single transfer to compensate for the destruction of the transferee's asset.

Id. at 249 (internal citations omitted). By contrast, the Supreme Court has held that foreclosures of property in satisfaction of a mortgage are a sale or exchange for these purposes. See Helvering v. Hammel, 311 U.S. 504 (1941).

Other transactions may not neatly comport with the ordinary meaning of the phrase "sale or exchange," however, including abandonments, deeds in lieu of foreclosure, and the granting or lapsing of options. The difficulty arises in determining whether the taxpayer "exchanged" the property for something of value, such as relief from debt, or merely walked away and received nothing in exchange. The former would generally be treated as a sale or exchange while the latter would not.

For example, in Freeland v. Commissioner, 74 T.C. 970 (1980), the taxpayer reconveyed encumbered property to the vendor-mortgagee by a quitclaim deed. At the time of reconveyance, the nonrecourse debt on the property ($41,000) exceeded the fair market value of the property ($27,000) and the taxpayer (vendee-mortgagor) received no consideration on reconveyance. The taxpayer argued that the reconveyance by deed in lieu of foreclosure was equivalent to an abandonment, which may not constitute a sale or exchange. The Service agreed that an abandonment of property is not a sale or exchange but argued that the reconveyance was equivalent to a foreclosure sale, which is a sale or exchange. In an opinion reviewed by the entire Tax Court, the court held that "voluntary reconveyance of the property to the mortgagee for no monetary consideration . . . was a sale within the meaning of sections 1211 and 1212, . . . even though petitioner had no personal obligation on the mortgage debt. . . ." Id. at 982.

Since Freeland, courts have consistently held that transfers of property made in exchange for the relief of debt constitute a sale or exchange for these purposes, even if it takes the form of an abandonment. See Yarbro v. Commissioner, 737 F.2d 479 (5th Cir. 1984), Middleton v. Commissioner, 77 T.C. 310 (1981) aff'd per curiam 693 F.2d 124 (11th Cir. 1982). By contrast, however, abandonments of property in which there was no debt involved have been found not to constitute a sale or exchange for these purposes. *See* Echols v. Commissioner, 935 F.2d 703 (5th Cir. 1991).

Even more complex scenarios arise in the context of stock held by brokers on behalf of clients. The complication arises because often times the broker is granted certain rights over the stock, such as the ability to lend it to other customers, while the client maintains ownership over the economic appreciation. *See* Anschutz Co. v. Commissioner, 664 F.3d 313 (10th Cir. 2011). What happens when a broker sells or otherwise disposes of stock against the wishes of the client? Has the client "sold" the stock for these purposes, thus realizing a capital gain, or has the client abandoned the stock to the broker or, even worse, has the broker stolen the stock?

RENDALL v. COMMISSIONER
535 F.3d 1221 (10th Cir. 2008)

TACHA, CIRCUIT JUDGE.

John S. Rendall and his wife, Christobel D. Rendall, appeal from a decision of the United States Tax Court . . . [t]he decision was based on the Tax Court's determination that gains from the sale of stock pledged as collateral for a loan are taxable to the Rendalls . . . We . . . AFFIRM.

I. BACKGROUND

The parties have stipulated to the following facts.

A. SOLV–EX'S FORMATION AND OPERATIONS THROUGH MARCH 1997

Mr. Rendall was one of two founding shareholders of Solv–Ex Corporation and was the chief executive officer and chairman of the board from its inception until his resignation in November 2000. Mr. Rendall purchased 2,700,000 shares of Solv–Ex common stock for $.01 per share at the corporation's initial public offering in July 1980. Between 1981 and 1996, Mr. Rendall purchased 677,860 additional shares at prices ranging from $.01 to $19 per share. During 1996 and early 1997, Solv–Ex's stock traded at prices ranging from $6.25 to $38 per share.

Solv–Ex's business activity consisted of researching and developing a process to extract bitumen from oil sands and convert it to synthetic crude oil. Solv–Ex claimed to have developed a cost-effective method for extracting and processing oil and industrial minerals from oil sands. It also claimed to have developed a patented process to recover raw aluminum and other marketable mineral products from the fine clays contained in oil sands or in the waste tailings that remain after the oil sands are processed.

During 1995, Solv–Ex acquired a 90% interest in oil-shale leases in Alberta, Canada. It then sought to raise the estimated $125 million required to construct an oil extraction and upgrading plant in Alberta. After funding promised in a hand-shake deal fell through, Solv–Ex proceeded to build only an initial-stage plant in Alberta with plans to build the remaining facilities when financing could be obtained. Construction of the initial-stage plant was completed in March 1997, and Solv–Ex demonstrated the viability of its oil extraction process through test operations. At that time, however, the plant was not yet able to run continuously.

B.   1997 EFFORTS TO COMPLETE THE INITIAL–STAGE PLANT

In 1997, Mr. Rendall sought alternative funds to complete the Alberta plant. In March 1997, he loaned $2 million to Solv–Ex from funds obtained through a margin account with Merrill Lynch, Pierce, Fenner & Smith ("Merrill Lynch"). Mr. Rendall already had outstanding debts to Merrill Lynch, and the loan to Solv–Ex increased his total indebtedness to Merrill Lynch to $4 million. Solv–Ex used the $2 million received from Mr. Rendall and $10 million from outside lenders to continue work on the Alberta plant.

C.   MR. RENDALL'S PLEDGE OF SOLV–EX COMMON STOCK TO MERRILL LYNCH

To obtain the line of credit through his Merrill Lynch margin account, Mr. Rendall pledged 2,660,000 shares of his Solv–Ex common stock as security. Pursuant to the pledge agreement, Mr. Rendall delivered the stock certificates for the pledged shares to Merrill Lynch . . .

D.   MERRILL LYNCH'S SALE OF THE PLEDGED STOCK

The pledge agreement between Mr. Rendall and Merrill Lynch specified that the loans were payable on demand. On May 2, 1997, Merrill Lynch demanded repayment . . . Merrill Lynch informed Mr. Rendall that if payment was not received by that date, it would liquidate the pledged shares of Solv–Ex stock to pay the debt. Mr. Rendall did not repay the loan. Instead, the parties exchanged correspondence disputing Merrill Lynch's right to sell the pledged shares. Merrill Lynch then sent a letter to Solv–Ex and its transfer agent requesting that the transfer agent register 1,100,000 shares of the pledged stock in Merrill Lynch's name. Solv–Ex opposed the action, but the transfer agent proceeded with the transfer nonetheless. Thereafter, Merrill Lynch sold 634,100 shares of Mr. Rendall's Solv–Ex common stock at prices ranging from $6 to $7.625 per share. The total proceeds from the sales of these shares were $4,229,479 . . .

II.   DISCUSSION

. . . B.   TAXABILITY ON SALE OF SOLV–EX SHARES

The Tax Court concluded that, as the owner of the shares pledged to Merrill Lynch, Mr. Rendall was taxable on any gains resulting from their sale. On appeal, the Rendalls do not take issue with this statement of the law. Instead, they contend that the sale constituted an unlawful conversion of the stock and, accordingly, that Merrill Lynch should be taxed on the gain resulting from such theft. In support of this argument, the Rendalls claim that Merrill Lynch needed Mr. Rendall's approval before it could sell the shares and was not authorized to have the shares reissued in its name in order to sell them.

Contrary to the Rendalls' contention, the terms of the pledge agreement clearly gave Merrill Lynch an unrestricted right to demand payment at any time. We agree with the Tax Court that there is no evidence in the record to indicate that the agreement was fraudulently induced or that Merrill Lynch sold the Solv–Ex shares for any reason other than to satisfy Mr. Rendall's debt. There is no dispute that Mr. Rendall refused to repay the loan upon demand, and Merrill Lynch subsequently sold only enough shares to satisfy his indebtedness. Additionally, we are not persuaded by — and the Rendalls offer no support for — the contention that it was unlawful for Merrill Lynch to ask the transfer agent to issue new certificates in Merrill Lynch's name. We agree that any action taken by Merrill Lynch was for the sole purpose of facilitating the sale of the collateral, which it unquestionably had the right to do under the pledge agreement. Accordingly, the Tax Court did not err in holding that the Rendalls are taxable on the gain realized when Merrill Lynch sold the Solv–Ex shares. . . .

III. CONCLUSION

For the foregoing reasons, we AFFIRM the Tax Court's decision.

Problem

7-7. Tim Ball purchased two parcels of land as an investment: (1) the Alaska parcel, acquired for $100,000 cash, and (2) the Delaware parcel, purchased for $200,000, with Ball paying $50,000 cash and executing a $150,000 purchase money note and nonrecourse mortgage.

Ball had paid all property taxes and made all mortgage payments, which reduced the obligations on the Delaware parcel to $100,000. However, both parcels plunged in value. The type of timber on the Alaskan land was shunned by the consuming public, and its fair market value dropped to $20,000. The Delaware parcel was rezoned, its value dropping to $75,000.

Ball contacted the County Recorder's Office in Alaska and informed it that he would not pay any future taxes and that he would never return to, or invest in, Alaska. The mortgage and taxes on the Delaware parcel were also unpaid, and Ball notified the mortgagee of his intent not to occupy the property. Ball also offered the mortgagee a deed in lieu of foreclosure, but the mortgagee refused and elected instead to sell the property by foreclosure. The foreclosure sale netted $75,000 with Ball receiving none of the proceeds.

a. What is the character of the loss on the Alaska parcel?

b. What is the character of the loss on the Delaware parcel?

E.   HOLDING PERIOD

Code: §§1015(a); 1222(1) to (4); 1223(1), (2), (5), (6), (7), (11); 7701(a)(42) to (44)
Regulations: §§1.1012-1(c)(1); 1.1222-1(a); 1.1223-1(a), (b), (f), (g), (i)

The third factor in characterizing gains and losses is the asset's holding period. The holding period serves a different function than the capital asset and sale or exchange requirements. The two latter requirements are essential to labeling an asset as capital or ordinary. The holding period is relevant, however, only if the asset (1) receives capital status under §1221 or (2) does not attain capital asset status because of §1221(a)(2). In the first instance, the asset's holding period determines whether the gain or loss is short term or long term; in the second, the holding period determines whether the asset qualifies as a §1231 asset.

1.   Computing the Holding Period

Generally, the two relevant dates in computing an asset's holding period are the date of acquisition and the date of disposition. The day of acquisition is excluded from the calculation while the day of disposition is included. Thus, if a capital asset is purchased February 1 and sold on February 1 of the next year, it cannot qualify for long-term treatment. But if the asset is sold on or after February 2 of the next year, it has been held for more than one year and is classified as long-term.

Crucial to ascertaining the holding period is the determination of when the sale or exchange was consummated. The Supreme Court addressed this issue in McFeely v. Commissioner, 296 U.S. 102, 107 (1935), stating: "In common understanding, to hold property is to own it. In order to own or hold one must acquire. The date of acquisition is, then, that from which to compute the duration of ownership or the length of holding."

For example, the mere execution of a contract to sell on a specified date in the future is generally not a conveyance requiring the realization of gain or loss, even if a nominal payment was made, because a sale or exchange has not yet occurred. Thus, realization of gain or loss occurs on the delivery of a deed *or* on the transfer, from a practical standpoint, of the benefits and burdens of ownership to the buyer, not by virtue of the execution of a sales contract. See Rev. Rul. 69-93, 1969-1 C.B. 139. Similarly, the holding period for an asset does not commence until the requisite transfer of the incidences of ownership.

In Merrill v. Commissioner, 40 T.C. 66 (1963), affd. per curiam, 336 F.2d 771 (9th Cir. 1964), the Tax Court applied a "benefits and burdens of ownership" analysis to determine the time of sale. In *Merrill*, real estate was purchased in accordance with an escrow agreement. One issue considered was whether the taxpayer's holding period ended with the bare transfer of title on satisfaction of the numerous conditions set forth in the escrow agreement or at some earlier time.

Noting that the use of an escrow can alter the general rule that the time of sale is determined by passage of title, the court stated:

> Normally, ownership of real estate would be considered transferred on the date of delivery of the deed. But where delivery of the deed is delayed to secure payment of the purchase price or for some other reason such as the escrow arrangement here involved, we believe that the intent of the parties as to when the benefits and burdens of ownership of the property are to be transferred, as evidenced by factors other than passage of bare legal title, must control for purposes of this statute.

Id. at 74.

In examining the intent of the parties, the court noted that

1. the buyers had exercised an option to purchase the property and the parties had signed written escrow instructions consummating the sale;
2. the sellers had executed a deed that was deposited with the escrow agent;
3. the buyers paid a significant part of the purchase price; and
4. the buyers took possession and began making repairs to the property.

These events occurred prior to the transfer of title, which, in accordance with the terms of the escrow agreement, was predicated on tender of the final payment and issuance of title insurance. The court concluded that these remaining escrow conditions were insignificant in light of the benefits and burdens of ownership previously transferred. Thus, the escrow did not serve to postpone the sale date or to prolong the seller's holding period.

2. *Tacked and Split Holding Periods*

Tacking. Although the holding period requirements are inflexible, the Code does provide for specific situations in which a taxpayer may nevertheless qualify for long-term treatment for an asset owned for less than one year. A deemed holding period may be added ("tacked on") to the taxpayer's actual holding period of an asset. Section 1223 prescribes situations, most often where an exchanged (§1223(1)) or transferred (§1223(2)) basis applies to the property, in which either the taxpayer's holding period in a prior asset or the prior owner's holding period is tacked on to the taxpayer's actual holding period of the newly acquired asset. See §7701(a)(42) through (44). Exchanged basis refers to a transferor's basis in a new asset determined by reference to the basis of property transferred (such as §1031 like-kind exchange), whereas transferred basis refers to property with a basis in a transferee's hands that is determined by reference to the basis the transferor had in the property (such as §1015 gift basis).

Sale or exchange of multiple assets. When more than one asset is sold or exchanged in one transaction, the holding period for each asset must be determined. The holding period for improved real property was once the subject of debate. At common law, buildings erected on land merged into or became part of the land. Taxpayers, therefore, argued that the holding period of the land should apply to any improvements constructed thereon. This reasoning was rejected in Dunigan v. Burnet, 66 F.2d 201 (D.C. Cir. 1933), which held that an improvement may have a different holding period than the land on which it is constructed. Therefore, if a building is constructed in May on land purchased in a prior year, and the building and land are sold for a gain on December 31, gain allocable to the land is long-term capital gain while gain attributable to the building is short-term. Thus, what appears to be one asset—improved real property—actually has two holding periods.

Sales of securities. Where securities of one company are bought on different dates, a first-in, first-out (FIFO) rule may apply to determine the length of the holding period. For example, assume an investor buys 100 shares of stock on January 1, and an additional 100 shares of the same stock on February 1. On January 15 of the next year, the investor sells 100 shares of the stock at a gain but is unable to identify whether the shares sold were purchased on the earlier or later date. Regulation §§1.1223-1(i) and 1.1012-1(c)(1) apply a FIFO rule to determine the holding period and basis where the stock sold cannot be specifically identified. Thus, the investor's gain for the 100 shares of stock sold on January 15 would be entitled to a long-term holding period because the lot purchased January 1 is deemed to be sold before the lot purchased February 1.

CITIZEN'S NATIONAL BANK OF WACO
v. UNITED STATES
417 F.2d 675 (5th Cir. 1969)

GOLDBERG, J.

. . . The issue presented is whether for the purpose of determining the holding periods of several trusts, the taxpayer-trustee is entitled to tack the settlors' holding periods to those of the trusts.

The settlors acquired all of the capital stock of Bosque Investment Company in 1950. Several years later, they borrowed $500,000, pledging this stock as collateral for the loan. Shortly afterwards they created trusts for each of their children and transferred to the trusts all of the capital stock of Bosque. At the time of the transfer to the trusts, the assets of Bosque as well as its capital stock had a fair market value of $714,601. The stock was encumbered by the liens securing the settlors' indebtedness of $500,000. This debt was assumed by the trusts. The cost basis of the stock in the hands of the settlors was $498,468.

The settlors reported the transfer of the stock to the trusts on their 1961 income tax returns and treated the difference between the indebtedness assumed by the trusts ($500,000) and their basis ($498,468) as long term capital gain, and paid the tax due thereon. The settlors also filed gift tax returns, reporting as gifts the excess of the total value of the property over the amount of the indebtedness transferred ($214,601).

[A]fter the settlors transferred the Bosque stock to the trusts, Bosque was liquidated, and its assets were distributed to the trusts. On the 1961 tax return, each trust reported its share of the fair market value of the assets received in exchange for the stock, deducted its basis, and reported the gain as long term capital gain. In each trust's return the Bosque stock was shown to have been acquired by the trust on the date the stock was acquired by the settlors.

The Commissioner, however, treated the trusts' capital gain as short term on the theory that the trustee could not tack the settlors' holding periods to those of the trusts. . . .

The tacking statute, I.R.C. §1223(2), provides that if the transferee's basis is determined in whole or in part by reference to the basis of the prior holder, the holding period of the prior holder may be added to the holding period of the transferee. I.R.C. §1015 governs the determination of basis for property acquired by gift or a transfer in trust. Subsection (a) provides that if property is acquired by gift, the basis shall be the same as it would be in the hands of the donor. Subsection (b) provides that if property is acquired by a transfer in trust, not by gift, the basis shall be the same as it would be in the hands of the grantor increased in the amount of gain or decreased in the amount of loss recognized to the grantor on such transfer. Thus, under both subsections the basis of the acquired property is in part determined by reference to the basis in the hands of the prior holder and would meet the requirement of §1223 permitting tacking of holding periods.

The Commissioner, however, determined that here the transaction was in part a sale and in part a gift because the trusts assumed the $500,000 indebtedness of the settlors. He therefore applied Treas. Reg. §1.1015-4 governing transactions in part a sale and in part a gift. This regulation provides that the transferee's basis in property acquired in a part gift part sale transaction shall be the greater of (1) the amount paid by the transferee or (2) the transferor's adjusted basis. In the instant case the $500,000 debt assumed by the trust was the amount paid by the trust for the property. Since this figure is greater than the settlors' $498,468 basis, the trust under Treas. Reg. §1.1015-4 is required to determine its basis by the amount it paid for the property. This amount has no reference to the transferor's basis as required under §1223 for tacking; the Commissioner, therefore, refused to allow the trustee to tack the transferor's holding period to its own. In light of the §1223 requirement for tacking, the Commissioner's determination was clearly correct if Treas. Reg. §1.1015-4 is a valid interpretation of the provisions of I.R.C. §1015.

The general rule regarding Treasury regulations is that they must be sustained unless unreasonable and plainly inconsistent with the revenue statute. United States v. Correll, 1967, 389 U.S. 299. It is equally clear, however, that "[t]he regulations must, by their terms and in their application, be in harmony with the statute. A Regulation which is in conflict with or restrictive of the statute is, to the extent of the conflict or restriction, invalid." Scofield v. Lewis, 5 Cir. 1958, 251 F.2d 128, 132. Applying these rules to Treas. Reg. §1.1015-4, we find that insofar as it would prevent tacking of holding periods in the instant case, it is an inconsistent and unreasonable interpretation of the code provisions it purports to enforce and to that extent is invalid.

The primary purpose of §1015 is to provide the method by which a transferee must determine the dollar amount of his basis in the transferred property. As an incidental result, this section also determines whether the transferee is permitted to tack his transferor's holding period because that right under §1223 depends upon the method used to calculate basis. It is this secondary function which is the subject of this appeal, the issue being whether Reg. §1.1015-4 is a valid interpretation of §1015 insofar as that section determines a transferee's right to tack.

We note that §1015(a) dealing with gifts provides that the transferee's basis for determining gain "shall be the same as it would be in the hands of the donor." Subsection (b) dealing with sales to trusts provides that the transferee's basis "shall be the same as it would be in the hands of the grantor increased in the amount of gain or decreased in the amount of loss recognized to the grantor on such transfer." Thus both subsections (a) and (b) *require* the transferee to determine his basis at least in part by reference to the transferor's basis. Nevertheless, regulation §1.1015-4 provides that if the transfer is part a gift and part a sale, then the transferee must determine his basis by the price paid if that amount is greater than his transferor's basis. On its face, the regulation seems to be introducing a concept, price paid, not found in either subsection of the Code. However, upon closer examination it appears that "price paid" is not really at total variance with the Code. Indeed, the "price paid" method will always produce the same dollar amount as will "the grantor's basis increased in the amount of gain or decreased in the amount of loss recognized to the grantor," the method prescribed in subsection (b) of the Code. The two phrases express identical amounts in different words. Therefore, insofar as the primary function of §1015 is concerned, the change in terminology makes no change in result. The transferee's actual basis will be the same, regardless of which method is used to make the computation. However, the change in terminology is quite significant insofar as it affects the incidental function of §1015, which is the determination of whether or not the transferee is eligible to tack his transferor's holding period. As this case illustrates, by the mere change in words, the regulation cuts off the transferee's right to tack whenever, as here, the price paid is greater than the transferor's basis.

The Commissioner admits that the two concepts, "price paid" and "grantor's basis increased or decreased by the amount of gain or loss recognized to the grantor," produce identical results as far as the actual amount of the transferee's basis is concerned. He seems to justify the change in terminology with the resulting loss of tacking rights by reference to the general theory of tacking. He states:

> It should be noted that the theory of Section 1223(2) militates against tacking even if a transaction is a Section 1015(b) transfer in trust. When there is a "sale or other disposition" to a trust, the basis of the transferee is measured by its cost, not by the transferor's basis — as is the case when the transfer is by gift.
>
> Although Congress chose to phrare (sic) subsection 1015(b) in terms of the transferor's basis plus the gain which he recognized on the transfer, the conceptual and practical effect would be the same if the trustee's basis was determined under Section 1012, which defines basis as the transferee's cost. For example, if the transferor holds property with a basis of 10 and a value of 20 and sells it to a transferee for 20, the transferee's basis under Section 1012 would be 20, its cost. Under Section 1015(b), the basis to a transferee who is a trustee would be the transferor's basis, 10, plus the gain recognized to the transferor, 10, for a total of 20. To allow tacking of the transferor's holding period by the transferee simply because it is a trustee would violate the basic theory which underpins tacking succession by the transferee to the transferor's basis.

The short answer to the Commissioner's complaint is that though he may consider Congress to have made an unfortunate choice of words, Congress nevertheless chose them. As Justice Harlan remarked in United States v. Calamaro,

1957, 354 U.S. 351, "Neither we nor the Commissioner may rewrite the statute simply because we may feel that the scheme it creates could be improved upon."

Since both the gift and the sale subsections of §1015 employ words which would permit tacking, and since neither subsection makes any distinction in this regard between a transferee who pays more than his grantor's basis and one who does not, we think that such a distinction in the regulation pertaining to a part gift part sale transaction is unreasonable and inconsistent with the statute. We therefore hold that the trustee in the instant case is entitled to tack the settlors' holding periods to that of the trusts and that to the extent Treas. Reg. §1.1015-4 would prevent such it is invalid. . . .

The Commissioner apparently did not contest the actual basis used by the trustee in computing the gain realized by the trusts in the instant case. As a result, we do not have before us on this appeal the question of whether or not Treas. Reg. §1.1015-4 properly implements the principal function of the statute, i.e., to provide a method for computing the basis accorded a transferee in a part gift part sale transaction. Our decision is therefore limited to the effect of the regulation on I.R.C. §1223 tacking rights. However, we would be less than candid if we did not indicate at this point that after our brief trip into the labyrinth of the Treasury Regulations we emerged with grave doubts concerning the validity of the basis determination method prescribed by §1.1015-4.

The judgment of the trial court is affirmed.

Problems

7-8. Ken Bick owned Desert Wind radio and television station. Bick, a cash method, calendar-year taxpayer, was involved in the following transactions during the year. On August 28, Bick purchased 100 shares of TV, Inc., stock for $40,000. On each of five consecutive days in the next year — August 28, 29, 30, 31, and September 1 — he sold 20 shares of TV, Inc., for $25,000.
   a. Should the gain on the sale of TV, Inc., stock be reported as short-term or long-term capital or both?
   b. What is the amount of the gain?

7-9. On June 3, Bick paid $100,000 for a small photographic studio to be used in the production of television commercials. The cost of producing commercials proved to be too high in relation to the number of customers; thus Bick decided to sell the studio. On June 2 of the next year, a buyer agreed to pay $200,000 for the property. The terms of the June 2 agreement provided that the escrow was to close on August 2. The buyer paid $20,000 directly to the seller on June 2, $80,000 to the escrow on June 2, and agreed to pay $100,000 into escrow on August 2. The seller was to deposit title to the studio in escrow on June 2 and deliver title insurance on the premises in the buyer's name on August 2. On August 2, seller's title was to be exchanged for the $180,000 in the escrow. On June 2, buyer took possession of the studio and was fully responsible for maintenance, insurance, and risk of loss. All the events detailed in the escrow agreement occurred as scheduled, including delivery of title insurance to the escrow on August 2, and Bick received the

$180,000 deposited in escrow on that date. What is the amount and character of the gain on the sale of the photographic studio?

7-10. On January 1, Bick paid $5,000 for an option to buy fifty shares of Warner Communications stock for $30,000. Bick exercised this option on January 31 paying $25,000 cash. On January 31 of the next year, he sold twenty-five of the fifty shares for $20,000, and the next day he sold the remaining twenty-five shares for $20,000.

    a. What is the amount and character of the gain on the sale of the Warner Communications stock?

    b. What if Bick acquired the stock on the exercise of stock rights received when he purchased the stock? (See §1223(6).)

7-11. Bick received a piano from his parents on April 11. His parents had purchased the piano on February 16 for $1,500. On March 10 of the next year, Bick sold the piano for $5,000. What is the amount and character of the gain on the sale of the piano?

7-12. On April 1, Bick paid $50,000 for an undeveloped parcel of land, on which he planned to build a vacation home. Construction of the home began April 2 and was completed September 1 at a total cost of $50,000. After his first vacation in the home, Bick decided that the home was too far away. He offered the home for sale on September 15. On June 1 of the next year, Bick sold the home for $175,000, with the contract allocating $75,000 to the building and $100,000 to the land. May Bick report long-term capital gain on the sale of the vacation home and land? What arguments are available for reporting either the entire amount, a portion of, or none of the gain realized from the sale of the home as long-term capital gain? In answering the above question, assume that 50 percent of the vacation home was completed by June 1 of the year of construction.

7-13. One of Bick's friends died April 14 and left him a stamp collection valued at $3,000. His friend's basis in the collection, which had been purchased four months earlier, was $2,500. Bick sold the entire stamp collection on June 1 for $3,700. How should Bick report the gain from the sale of the stamp collection? Assume that Bick's basis in the property is determined under §1014(a).

F.   SECTION 1231 — PROPERTY USED IN A TRADE OR BUSINESS

Code: §§165(c); 1221(a)(2); 1231
Regulations: §§1.1221-1(b); 1.1231-1

Definitions and mechanics. The first step in taxing gains and losses arising on the disposition of property requires their characterization. The initial inquiry in the characterization phase concerns whether the property falls within the §1221 definition of capital asset. Section 1221(a)(2) excludes real or depreciable property used in a trade or business from the definition of a capital asset. However, the characterization of property meeting the §1221(a)(2) disqualification is not complete until the effect of §1231 has been assessed. Section 1231(b) modifies §1221(a)(2) by effectively permitting capital treatment on the disposition of certain §1221(a)(2) property. In addition, §1231 can apply to other capital assets and affect the character of their gain or loss.

To some extent, §1231 provides the best of both worlds: It may provide long-term capital treatment for gains or ordinary treatment for losses. This favorable treatment results from the two-tier consolidation, or netting, of recognized gains and losses from the sale of §1231 property. In general, if the netting process results in gains exceeding losses, *each* item of gain or loss is treated as though derived from the sale or exchange of a long-term capital asset. If, however, losses exceed gains, *each* gain and loss item is treated as ordinary income and loss. Consequently, long-term capital gain benefits are generally available when there is a net gain, and ordinary loss benefits are available when there is a net loss. It is important to understand that §1231 netting determines only the characterization of each item of §1231 property as either ordinary or capital; the net figure derived by §1231 netting has no independent significance with regard to the amount included in gross income. Finally, because it is easy to become lost in the §1231 maze, it may be helpful to remember that §1231 involves a series of interrelationships between three basic concepts: (1) §1231 property, (2) §1231 events, and (3) the two-tier netting process.

The categories of gains and losses subject to §1231 netting are (1) any recognized gain or loss from the sale or exchange of property used in trade or business (that is, §1231(b) property), and (2) any recognized gain or loss from the compulsory or involuntary conversion of property used in trade or business or of any capital asset that is held for more than one year and held in connection with a trade or business or a transaction entered into for profit. §1231(a)(3).

Section 1231(b) defines property used in a trade or business. Section 1231(b) assets are strictly limited to property, used in a trade or business and held for more than one year, that is not inventory or property held primarily for sale to customers. Thus, real property and depreciable property used in a trade or business may receive the benefits of long-term capital treatment even though they are not capital assets.

The second category of property subject to §1231 netting, long-term capital assets held in connection with a trade or business or a transaction entered into for profit, receives §1231 treatment only if it is the object of condemnation or involuntary conversion (such as theft, fire, storm, shipwreck, or other casualty). If property held for personal use, such as a home, clothing, or automobile, is subject to condemnation or involuntary conversion, it is *not* included in the §1231 netting process. Furthermore, if a long-term capital asset held in connection with a trade or business or for profit is disposed of by sale or exchange, those gains or losses are not netted in §1231 because §1231 only includes gains and losses from sales or exchanges of §1231(b) property.

There are three types of transactions or events to which §1231 may apply — involuntary conversions, sales or exchanges, and condemnations. Characterization of the gain or loss from these transactions involves a two-tier process (see Figure 7-1).

FIGURE 7-1
Two-Tier §1231 Netting

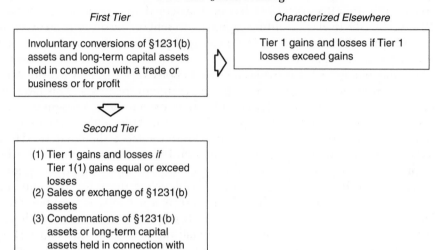

First Tier

| Involuntary conversions of §1231(b) assets and long-term capital assets held in connection with a trade or business or for profit |

Characterized Elsewhere

| Tier 1 gains and losses if Tier 1 losses exceed gains |

Second Tier

| (1) Tier 1 gains and losses *if* Tier 1(1) gains equal or exceed losses
(2) Sales or exchange of §1231(b) assets
(3) Condemnations of §1231(b) assets or long-term capital assets held in connection with a trade or business or for profit |

Involuntary conversions due to fire, theft, storm, shipwreck, or other casualty are first netted in tier 1. Both §1231(b) assets and long-term capital assets held in connection with a trade or business or a transaction entered into for profit are included in tier 1. Tier 1 losses receive two opportunities within the framework of the two-tier netting process to have losses treated as ordinary. First, if the tier 1 losses exceed the tier 1 gains, *none* of the tier 1 assets will be subject to characterization under §1231. Thus, the characterization of such gains and losses will retain their original, non-§1231 status and will be governed by the normal rules, which should yield ordinary gain or loss because there has not been a sale or exchange of the asset. The second chance for an ordinary loss arises if the tier 1 gains equal or exceed the losses, in which case all tier 1 gains and losses are renetted in tier 2.

Tier 2 netting includes sales or exchanges of §1231(b) property, gains and losses arising from condemnations, and, if required, tier 1 involuntary conversions. All gains and losses included in the second tier are netted together. If the total gains exceed total losses, all tier 2 gains and losses are individually characterized as either long-term capital gains or long-term capital losses. If tier 2 losses equal or exceed gains, all of the tier 2 assets will receive ordinary gain or loss treatment.

The rules described above apply only if the taxpayer had no §1231 netting transactions in which losses exceeded gains in the prior five years. To preclude manipulation of §1231, particularly with regard to the sale of property used in a trade or business, Congress amended §1231 to provide that net §1231 gains will be treated as ordinary income to the extent of "unrecaptured net section 1231 losses" for the preceding five years. Thus, if in any of the preceding five years §1231 losses exceeded gains resulting in ordinary characterization, and if for the current year §1231 gains exceed losses, then §1231(c) requires characterization of all or part of the gain as ordinary. If the net gain for the year exceeds the nonrecaptured §1231 losses, the excess will receive capital characterization.

The following statement of the Joint Committee explains the reason for §1231(c)'s enactment and its operation.

PRIOR LAW

Under prior law, gains and losses on the sale, exchange, or involuntary conversion of property used in a trade or business, held for more than one year, were generally treated as long-term capital gains and losses if the total gains from all such transactions during the year exceed the total losses from such transactions during the year. If the losses for the year exceed the gains, the gains and losses were treated as ordinary gains and losses. . . .

Thus, if a taxpayer had a net gain from the specified types of transactions during a taxable year, the taxpayer could treat the gain as capital gain, generally paying tax at a lower tax rate, but if the taxpayer had a net loss, the full net loss would be allowed as a deduction from ordinary income.

REASONS FOR CHANGE

The prior law rules relating to the treatment of gains and losses from sales and exchanges of trade or business property created distortions in taxable income in certain situations because they ignored transactions in prior and subsequent taxable years. The rules were subject to manipulation by taxpayers, who could bunch sales of appreciated trade or business assets in one year and sales of depreciated property in a different year to maximize their capital gains and ordinary losses.

EXPLANATION OF PROVISION

Under the Act, net section 1231 gains are treated as ordinary income to the extent of unrecaptured net section 1231 losses of the years beginning after December 31, 1981. In determining the amount of unrecaptured net section 1231 losses for the five-year period, net gains for any year will be taken into account only to the extent they were previously recaptured as ordinary income. Losses are deemed recaptured in the chronological order they arose.

Joint Committee on Taxation, General Explanation of the Revenue Provisions of the Deficit Reduction Act of 1984, p. 547 (1985).

INTERNATIONAL SHOE MACHINE CORP.
v. UNITED STATES
491 F.2d 157 (1st Cir. 1974)

COFFIN, C.J.

Appellant taxpayer contends that the Commissioner of Internal Revenue erroneously treated income realized from the appellant's sales of certain shoe machines as "property held by the taxpayer primarily for sale to customers in the ordinary course of his trade or business," §1231(b)(1)(B), thereby taxing it as ordinary income instead of treating it under the capital gains provisions of the Code. . . .

It is undisputed that during the years in question, 1964 through 1966, appellant's main source of income derived from the leases of its shoe machinery equipment, rather than from their sales. The revenue from sales of the leased machinery comprised, respectively, only seven percent, two percent, and two percent of appellant's gross revenues. In fact, because the appellant preferred the more profitable route of leasing its machines, it never developed a sales force, never solicited purchases, set prices high to make purchasing unattractive, and even attempted to dissuade customers from purchasing them.

Yet the district court found that, beginning in 1964, when the investment tax credit made it more attractive for shoe manufacturers to buy shoe machinery rather than to lease it, the selling of machinery became an accepted and predictable, albeit small, part of appellant's business. Since appellant's chief competitor was selling leased shoe machines, it was necessary for appellant to offer its customers the same option. During the years in issue, appellant never declined to quote a price, nor did it ever decline to make a sale if the customer was persistent. Unlike previous years, purchase inquiries were referred to the appellant's vice president for sales, normally charged with selling new, nonleased machines, whereupon a price was negotiated. A schedule was prepared, indicating the sales price of leased machines, based upon the number of years that the machines had been leased. In total, 271 machines were sold to customers who, at the time of the sales, had been leasing the machines for at least six months.

The case raises what has become a repeating source of difficulty in applying §1231(b)(1)(B), which denies . . . capital gains tax treatment to "property held . . . primarily for sale to customers in the ordinary course of his trade or business." In particular, does the word "primarily" invoke a contrast between sales and leases, as the appellant contends, or between sales made in the ordinary course of business and non-routine sales made as a liquidation of inventory? And, if the latter, how can sales made in the ordinary course of business be distinguished from a liquidation of inventory?

In support of its contention that "primarily" refers to a contrast between sales and leases, appellant relies upon Malat v. Riddell, 383 U.S. 569 (1966). There, the taxpayer purchased a parcel of land, with the alleged intention of developing an apartment project. When the taxpayer confronted zoning restrictions, he decided to terminate the venture, and sold his interest in the property, claiming a capital gain. The lower courts found, however, that the taxpayer had had a "dual purpose" in acquiring the land, a "substantial" one of which was to sell if that were to prove more profitable than development. Therefore, since the taxpayer had failed to establish that the property was not held primarily for sale to customers in the ordinary course of his business, his gain was treated as ordinary income. The Supreme Court vacated and remanded the case, stating that the lower courts had applied an incorrect legal standard when they defined "primarily" as merely "substantially" rather than using it in its ordinary, everyday sense of "first importance" or "principally." Although the Court in *Malat* was dealing with §1221, rather than §1231, the same clause appears in both sections. Appellant argues that the present case is analogous, since the "first" and "principal" reason for holding the shoe machinery was clearly for lease rather than for sale.

We cannot agree that *Malat* is dispositive. Even if "primarily" is defined as "of first importance" or "principally," the word may still invoke a contrast between sales made in the "ordinary course of . . . business" and those made as liquidations of inventory, rather than between leases and sales. *Malat* itself concerned the dual purposes of developing an apartment complex on the land and selling the land.

Although these two possible sources of income might be characterized as income from "lease" or "sale," a more meaningful distinction could be made between on-going income generated in the ordinary course of business and income from the termination and sale of the venture. . . .

[T]o rest the word "primarily" on the distinction between lease and sale income would lead to the absurd result that whenever lease income exceeded sale income on the same item, the sale income could be treated as capital gain.

The real question, therefore, concerns whether or not the income from the sales of appellant's shoe machinery should have been characterized as having been generated in the "ordinary course of . . . business." Appellant contests the conclusion of the district court that selling was "an accepted and predictable part of the business" by pointing out that sales were made only as a last resort, after attempts to dissuade the customer from purchasing had failed. We think that the district court was correct in its finding. While sales were made only as a last resort, it seems clear that after 1964 such sales were expected to occur, on an occasional basis, and policies and procedures were developed for handling them. Purchase inquiries were referred to the vice president for sales, a price schedule was drawn up, and discounts were offered to good customers. Appellant may not have desired such sales. It is likely that appellant would never have developed a sales policy for its leased machines had it not been forced to do so by the pressure of competition. But it was justifiable to find that such occasional sales were indeed "accepted and predictable."

Even "accepted and predictable" sales might not, however, occur in the "ordinary course of . . . business." For example, a final liquidation of inventory, although accepted and predictable, would normally be eligible for capital gains treatment. Appellant's final contention, therefore, is that the sales in question represented the liquidation of an investment. Appellant points out that the machines were leased for an average of eight and one half years before they were sold, during which time depreciation was taken on them and repairs were made. Thus, appellant seeks to bring itself within the scope of the "rental-obsolescence" decisions, which hold that the sale of rental equipment, no longer useful for renting, is taxable at capital gains rates. . . .

In the "rental obsolescence" decisions, however, equipment was sold only after its rental income-producing potential had ended and "such sales were . . . the natural conclusion of a vehicle rental business cycle." Moreover, the equipment was specifically manufactured to fit the requirements of lessees; it was sold only when lessees no longer found the equipment useful. In the present case, however, the shoe manufacturing equipment was sold, not as a final disposition of property that had ceased to produce rental income for the appellant, but, rather, as property that still retained a rental income producing potential for the appellant. Had appellant chosen not to sell the shoe machinery, the machinery would have continued to generate ordinary income in the form of lease revenue. Thus, the sale of such machinery, for a price which included the present value of that future ordinary income, cannot be considered the liquidation of an investment outside the scope of the "ordinary course of . . . business."

Affirmed.

Problems

7-14. Connie Moe, the owner of a medical laboratory, was involved in the following events during the year: A $500 loss resulted from the theft of depreciable business property held for more than one year. A tornado destroyed depreciable business property that had been held for more than one year, but because of an insurance recovery on the property there was a gain of $2,000. Moe also sold, at a loss of $1,000, laboratory equipment that had been held for more than one year. What are the tax consequences of these events?

7-15. Violet Lee is the owner of a secretarial counseling and management firm. The following occurred during the year: Machine *A*, which had been used in Lee's business for more than one year, was sold for a gain of $13,000; an automobile held for more than one year and used in her business was destroyed by a flood, resulting in a loss of $6,000; business machine *B* held for more than one year was sold for a loss of $1,000; Lee's business typewriter, purchased in the Orient two years before, was stolen, but insurance proceeds resulted in a gain of $5,000; her business tape recorder, held for three months, was also stolen, resulting in a loss of $500; business machine *C* was held for less than one year and sold at a gain of $4,000; IBM stock, held for more than one year and having no connection to Lee's firm, was sold at a loss of $2,000; Lee's yacht, acquired two years before and used for personal purposes, was sold, resulting in a loss of $15,000; business machine *D* was abandoned after three years of use, resulting in a loss of $10,000; raw land, acquired sixteen months before and held for profit, was sold under the threat of condemnation at a loss of $3,000.
   a.   Which events are subject to §1231 netting?
   b.   Which of the §1231 events fall into either tier 1 or tier 2 for netting purposes?
   c.   What is the character of each item of gain or loss?

7-16. Diane Shralow conducted a bakery business and during year 1 had a $40,000 loss from the sale of a delivery truck. In year 2, Shralow sold a delivery truck for a total gain of $50,000. All the trucks were held for more than one year.
   a.   What is the character of the loss for year 1?
   b.   What is the character of the gain for year 2?
   c.   What result in *b* if the year 2 gain had been $30,000?
   d.   What result if the year 2 gain was $30,000 and Shralow had a $25,000 gain from the sale of a truck in year 3?

G.   ASSIGNMENT OF INCOME

The *assignment of income* doctrine considers the characterization of gain arising on the sale of a right to receive future payments that would be treated as ordinary income. This concept is a variation of the basic assignment of income problems posed in Chapter 4, the twist being that a reduction in tax liability is sought by recharacterizing gain rather than by splitting or shifting income. Rights to receive ordinary income in the future are a species of property not specifically mentioned in the §1221 exclusions. Taxpayers, therefore, contend that this form of property right is a §1221 capital asset, with gain realized on its sale or exchange entitled to capital gain treatment.

For example, assume that *A* leases property to *B* for a ten-year term, with the lease providing for rent of $10,000 per year. If *A* subsequently sells his rights in the rental contract to *C* for $70,000, should *A*'s gain be treated as ordinary income or as gain from the sale or exchange of a capital asset (the lease contract)? Is *A* selling only the right to future rental payments, or is *A* selling property? The Service might argue that to permit capital gain treatment for these transactions would create too much potential for abuse. This potential is heightened when the consideration received equals the present value of the stream of ordinary income ultimately payable under the transferred right. Clearly, Congress did not intend preferential treatment merely because a taxpayer is able to assign a right to future ordinary income in return for a payment of the assigned income's present value. Permitting capital gain would allow ordinary income conversion by a transaction that in substance is nothing more than an accelerated receipt of ordinary income.

The taxpayer might argue that, in most sales of property, a portion of the consideration received is a present substitute for the future income the property would have produced for the seller. For example, the sales price for real estate or stock often reflects both the market demand for the particular asset and its future stream of income. Without adequate compensation for the future income potential, the owner might not sell. Thus, in receiving the sales price the seller effectively accelerates future income. Similarly, the sales price of an asset that will generate future income reflects the particular asset's market demand and *its* future income potential.

The Supreme Court first addressed this issue in Commissioner v. P. G. Lake, Inc., 356 U.S. 260 (1958). P. G. Lake transferred a right to receive an oil payment to its president in return for his cancellation of $600,000 in debts owed to him by the corporation. The transferred oil payment right was a bona fide property interest, giving a right to a specified portion of the income actually produced from the underlying leases, but was not an interest in the underlying leases themselves. In effect, P. G. Lake "carved out" an income right from the total bundle of rights it held under the original oil leases and transferred this "carved out" right to its president. The oil payment transferred exactly equaled the face value of the debt to be paid out in slightly more than three years. The interest was to terminate after the president had received his $600,000 plus an amount equal to three percent interest on the unpaid balance; thus, the sales price was almost the exact equivalent of the income to be produced in the future. P. G. Lake claimed that the $600,000 debt relief received for the transferred right was gain from the sale or exchange of a capital asset. This characterization was rejected by the Commissioner but was later upheld by the lower courts.

Adopting the Commissioner's reasoning, the Supreme Court reversed the lower courts and denied capital gain characterization. First, notwithstanding that the oil payment was a property interest, the Court held that it was not property within the intent of the capital asset definition:

> The purpose of [capital gain treatment] was "to relieve the taxpayer from . . . excessive tax burdens on gains resulting from a conversion of capital investments, and to remove the deterrent effect of those burdens on such conversions." . . .
>
> We do not see here any conversion of a capital investment. . . . The *substance* of what was assigned was the right to receive future income. The *substance* of what was received was the present value of income which the recipient would otherwise obtain in the future. In short, consideration was paid for the right to receive future income, not for an increase in the value of income-producing property.
>
> These arrangements seem to us transparent devices. Their forms do not control.

Id. at 265-66 (emphasis added).

Second, the Court, stating that "artful devices" should not be permitted to avoid ordinary gain, analogized income acceleration to income assignment:

> We have held that if one, entitled to receive at a future date interest on a bond . . . makes a grant of it by anticipatory assignment, he realizes taxable income as if he had collected the interest . . . and then paid it over. . . . Here, even more clearly than there, the taxpayer is converting future income into present income.

Id. at 267.

P. G. Lake did not, however, end all controversy in this area. Property interests come in as many forms as the human mind can devise, and the "substance over form" rationale on which *P. G. Lake* ultimately relied provided few guidelines. Further, at times when the tax rates applicable to ordinary income and those applicable to capital gain differ, taxpayers have an incentive to attempt to make payments that would otherwise be treated as ordinary income appear to be capital gains. Thus, in addition to the lack of firm guidance under *P. G. Lake*, the continuance of significant disparities between the capital gains and ordinary income tax rate has led to a number of disputes in this area.

For example, after *P. G. Lake* was decided, the Second Circuit confronted the issue in the case of Commissioner v. Ferrer, 304 F.2d 125 (2d Cir. 1962). In *Ferrer*, the taxpayer was an actor who agreed to produce and star in the play *Moulin Rouge* about the life of Henri de Toulouse-Lautrec. The agreement provided that Ferrer had the right to produce the play, to prevent the sale of movie and television rights of the play for a period of years, and to receive 40 percent of the proceeds generated by any movie version if he produced the play. Ferrer was approached by a movie studio and offered a starring role in a film version of the play. Ferrer agreed, waiving his rights to prevent the sale of the play and his 40-percent interest in the movie proceeds, and was paid by the studio for these rights. Ferrer contended that the rights in the play were property and thus that the sale of these rights to the movie studio resulted in capital gain. The court agreed in part and disagreed in part—with respect to the right to produce the play and prevent the sale of the movie rights, the court agreed that these were in the nature of "property" rights, the sale of which gave rise to capital gain. With respect to the 40-percent interest, however, the court determined that if Ferrer had been paid these amounts they would have constituted ordinary income, and thus the sale of this right generated ordinary income.

Ferrer established three important propositions that helped fill the void left by *P. G. Lake:* (1) whether something is a capital asset turns on the nature of the right (and remedy) involved rather than the form of the transaction, (2) gain is not characterized on an all or nothing basis but rather on a right-by-right basis, and (3) the sale or exchange requirements may apply differently in the context of sales of rights in intellectual property, depending on the nature of the rights involved. Although this ruling went a long way toward establishing a principled rule, it did nothing to prevent taxpayers from continuing to contend that such proceeds (or, post-*Ferrer*, at least a portion of them) were properly treated as capital gain.

For example, one year after *Ferrer* was decided, these issues arose again in United States v. Dresser Industries, 324 F.2d 56 (5th Cir. 1963). *Dresser* involved the sale of the right to the exclusive use of a patented process back to its grantor. The government argued that the consideration received was not for the sale of property but was a substitute for the future ordinary income the seller would have earned by retaining the exclusive patent. Thus, under *P. G. Lake*, that portion of the consideration representing the value of the future ordinary income that the right would have generated could not be characterized as capital gain.

Conceding that a literal reading of *P. G. Lake* would justify the result urged by the Commissioner because the consideration was in fact partially a present payment for future ordinary income, the court concluded, however, that such a reading was neither justified by the thrust of *P. G. Lake* nor by economic reality. The court, agreeing with *Ferrer*, held that *P. G. Lake* was properly limited to transactions involving the future right to earned income and did not reach rights to earn income in the future. Thus, the fact that the income that *could* be earned would be ordinary income was immaterial; such would be true of the sale of all income-producing property.

Examining whether economic reality dictated ruling against the Commissioner, *Dresser* noted that part of the purchase price in every commercial transaction reflects the present value of an asset's future earnings potential. The court therefore reversed an earlier decision that had accepted a literal reading of *P. G. Lake* as meaning that any money paid in exchange for a right to the present value of future income was always to be taxed as ordinary gain. Judge Brown's concurrence in *Dresser* addressed this point:

> Running through several of our prior opinions is the asserted concept that capital gains versus ordinary income is to be determined by the status of current earnings were the asset to have remained in the hands of the transferor. On this approach it is reasoned that if the current income would have been taxable ordinary income, then the sales price which represents the substitute for such future earnings is likewise taxable ordinary income.
>
> I think this is both bad economics and faulty law. A person acquires property for one of two, or both reasons. The first is to receive earnings, i.e., income. The other is to hold the property for appreciation resulting from long or short range economic conditions, inflation or the like. Normally, of course, the predominant reason is to acquire the earning capacity represented by the earnings which the property will generate.

Hence it is that among those who trade in corporate securities on established national exchanges or over-the-counter markets, there are recognized rules of thumb by which the present value, hence market price, is determined for a given stock. The same is true in the contemporary, frequent practice of large-scale corporate acquisitions by one corporation of the stock or assets of another corporation. Value — market or sales price — is determined by capitalizing earnings. [W]hat the buyer offers is his estimate of the present, discounted value of the future earnings of the assets or enterprise.

But although this sales price is determined by future earnings, and to the seller it takes the place of what he would have received had he continued his ownership, under no stretch of the imagination is it "ordinary income" either in the business world or in the sometimes more weird, tax world. Were this so, then every such sale for a price in excess of cost would entail this analysis and this tax consequence. There would first have to be ascertained what portion of the excess represented the present value of future earnings and what portion represented merely capital appreciation, from enhancement in value caused by inflation, scarcity or the like. Then as a second step, that portion or the excess of sales price representing future earnings would be taxed as ordinary income, the remainder as capital gains.

Conceding that Congress might compel this, that the ubiquitous and voracious tax gatherer might demand it, or that courts might ultimately sustain it, the fact is that as yet none has gone so fast so far. And that is so because of the practical economic realities which are, after all, of dominant significance in tax affairs. Income is one thing. When income, and income alone is sold or transferred, it keeps this status. But when the thing which generates the income is transferred, what is paid and received is not vicarious income, whether viewed from an economic or a tax standpoint. It is, as the economist and the businessman views it, the present, discounted value of its future earnings. If the "thing" generating such future earnings is "property" of a kind which the tax law recognizes as one entitled to capital gains or losses when used in the tax law sense, that present, discounted value is a capital gain, not ordinary income notwithstanding the economic fact that without such capacity to earn "ordinary income" in the hands of its owner the asset would be valueless.

Tax law, by the hand of man, the Acts of Congress, and the doubtful clarification by Judges is complex enough without making it more so through the importation of bad economics. For before we realize it, economics which knows no law of stare decisis, is infected by poor or bad law to set in train tax consequences because of what Courts have said, not because of what the actualities really are.

Id. at 61-62.

Regardless of the guidance provided by *Ferrer* and *Dresser*, issues of assignment of income in the capital gains context continue to be litigated. Although courts addressed assignment of income issues in cases involving the sale of stock, provision of services, and licenses of patents and copyrights, the treatment of the sale of the right to future lottery winnings generally had not been addressed by the turn of the century. As a result, by 2004, numerous taxpayers contended that the sale of the right to future lottery winnings generated capital gain. During this time, there was an explosion of litigation on the issue, with the Tax Court and multiple circuit courts providing different rationales and theories. Consider the following case, where the Third Circuit attempted to create a comprehensive rule. Does the court finally articulate a comprehensive and administrable solution to the assignment of income issue?

LATTERA v. COMMISSIONER
437 F.3d 399 (3d Cir. 2006)

AMBRO, CIRCUIT JUDGE.

I. FACTUAL BACKGROUND AND PROCEDURAL HISTORY

In June 1991 George and Angeline Lattera turned a one-dollar lottery ticket into $9,595,326 in the Pennsylvania Lottery. They did not then have the option to take the prize in a single lump-sum payment, so they were entitled to 26 annual installments of $369,051.

In September 1999 the Latteras sold their rights to the 17 remaining lottery payments to Singer Asset Finance Co., LLC for $3,372,342. Under Pennsylvania law, the Latteras had to obtain court approval before they could transfer their rights to future lottery payments, and they did so in August 1999.

On their joint tax return, the Latteras reported this sale as the sale of a capital asset held for more than one year. They reported a sale price of $3,372,342, a cost or other basis of zero, and a long-term capital gain of the full sale price. The Commissioner determined that this sale price was ordinary income. In December 2002 the Latteras were sent a notice of deficiency of $660,784. . . .

III. DISCUSSION

The lottery payments the Latteras had a right to receive were gambling winnings, and the parties agree that the annual payments were ordinary income. But the Latteras argue that when they sold the right to their remaining lottery payments, that sale gave rise to a long-term capital gain.

Whether the sale of a right to lottery payments by a lottery winner can be treated as a capital gain under the Internal Revenue Code is one of first impression in our Circuit. . . .

A. DEFINITION OF A CAPITAL ASSET

A long-term capital gain (or loss) is created by the "sale or exchange of a capital asset held for more than 1 year." I.R.C. §1222(3). Section 1221 of the Internal Revenue Code defines a capital asset as "property held by the taxpayer (whether or not connected with his trade or business)." This provision excludes from the definition certain property categories, none of which is applicable here. . . .

B. THE SUBSTITUTE-FOR-ORDINARY-INCOME DOCTRINE

The problem with an overly broad definition for capital assets is that it could "encompass some things Congress did not intend to be taxed as capital gains." An overly broad definition, linked with favorable capital-gains tax treatment, would encourage transactions designed to convert ordinary income into capital gains. For example, a salary is taxed as ordinary income, and the right to be paid for work is a person's property. But it is hard to conceive that Congress intends for taxpayers to get capital-gains treatment if they were to sell their rights (i.e., "property held by the taxpayer") to their future paychecks.

To get around this problem, courts have created the substitute-for-ordinary-income doctrine. This doctrine says, in effect, that "lump sum consideration [that] seems essentially a substitute for what would otherwise be received at a future time as ordinary income may not be taxed as a capital gain." . . .

The Supreme Court bolstered the doctrine in [*P.G. Lake*]. P.G. Lake, Inc. was an oil- and gas-producing company with a working interest in two oil and gas leases. It assigned an oil payment right "payable out of 25 percent of the oil attributable to [Lake's] working interest in the two leases." Lake reported this assignment as a sale of property taxable as capital gain. But the Court disagreed, holding that the consideration received was taxable as ordinary income. The Court's reasoning gave full voice to the substitute-for-ordinary-income doctrine: "The lump sum consideration seems essentially a substitute for what would otherwise be received at a future time as ordinary income." . . .

But there is a tension in the doctrine: in theory, all capital assets are substitutes for ordinary income. . . . For example, a stock's value is the present discounted value of the company's future profits. . . . Also, an "overbroad 'substitute for ordinary income' doctrine, besides being analytically unsatisfactory, would create the potential for the abuse of treating capital losses as ordinary." . . .

D. SUBSTITUTE-FOR-ORDINARY-INCOME ANALYSIS

. . . Several types of assets we know to be capital: stocks, bonds, options, and currency contracts, for example. . . . We could also include in this category physical assets like land and automobiles.

Similarly, there are several types of rights that we know to be ordinary income, e.g., rental income and interest income. . . .

[W]e can set those two categories at the opposite poles of our analysis. For example, we presume that stock, and things that look and act like stock, will receive capital-gains treatment. For the in-between transactions that do not bear a family resemblance to the items in either category, like contracts and payment rights, we use two factors to assist in our analysis: (1) type of "carve-out" and (2) character of asset.

1. Type of Carve-out

. . . There are two ways of carving out interests from property: horizontally and vertically. A horizontal carve-out is one in which "temporal divisions [are made] in a property interest in which the person owning the interest disposes of part of his interest but also retains a portion of it." . . .

A vertical carve-out is one in which "a complete disposition of a person's interest in property" is made. . . .

Horizontal carve-outs typically lead to ordinary-income treatment. . . . Vertical carve-outs are different. In *Dresser Industries*, for example, the Fifth Circuit distinguished *Lake* because the taxpayer in *Dresser* had "cut[] off a 'vertical slice' of its rights, rather than carv[ed] out an interest from the totality of its rights." But . . . a vertical carve-out does not necessarily mean that the transaction receives capital-gains treatment. . . . Because a vertical carve-out could signal either capital-gains or ordinary-income treatment, we must make another determination to conclude with certainty which treatment should apply. Therefore, when we see a vertical carve-out, we proceed to the second factor — character of the asset — to determine whether the sale proceeds should be taxed as ordinary income or capital gain.

2. *Character of the Asset*

The Fifth Circuit in *Dresser Industries* noted that "[t]here is, in law and fact, a vast difference between the present sale of the future right to earn income and the present sale of the future right to earned income." The taxpayer in *Dresser Industries* had assigned its right to an exclusive patent license back to the patent holder in exchange for a share of the licensing fees from third-party licensees. The court used this "right to earn income"/"right to earned income" distinction to hold that capital-gains treatment was applicable. It noted that the asset sold was not a "right to earned income, to be paid in the future," but was "a property which would produce income." Further, it disregarded the ordinary nature of the income generated by the asset; because "all income-producing property" produces ordinary income, the sale of such property does not result in ordinary-income treatment. (This can be seen in the sale of stocks or bonds, both of which produce ordinary income, but the sale of which is treated as capital gain.)

. . . Assets that constitute a right to earn income merit capital-gains treatment, while those that are a right to earned income merit ordinary-income treatment. . . .

[W]hen an erstwhile employee is paid a termination fee for a personal-services contract, that employee still possesses the asset (the right to provide certain personal services) and the money (the termination fee) has already been "earned" and will simply be paid. The employee no longer has to perform any more services in exchange for the fee, so this is not like *Dresser Industries*'s "right to earn income." These termination fees are therefore rights to earned income and should be treated as ordinary income.

The factor also explains, for example, the Second Circuit's complex decision in Commissioner v. Ferrer, 304 F.2d 125 (2d Cir.1962). The actor José Ferrer had contracted for the rights to mount a stage production based on the novel *Moulin Rouge*. In the contract, Ferrer obtained two rights relevant here: (1) the exclusive right to "produce and present" a stage production of the book and, if the play was produced, (2) a share in the proceeds from any motion-picture rights that stemmed from the book. After a movie studio planned to make *Moulin Rouge* into a movie — and agreed that it would feature Ferrer — he sold these, along with other, rights. Right (1) would have required Ferrer to have produced and presented the play to get income, so it was a right to earn income — thus, capital-gains treatment was indicated. Right (2), once it matured (i.e., once Ferrer had produced the play), would have continued to pay income simply by virtue of Ferrer's holding the right, so it would have become a right to earned income — thus, ordinary-income treatment was indicated. The Second Circuit held as such, dictating capital-gains treatment for right (1) and ordinary-income treatment for right (2).

. . . Applied to this case, the . . . test draws out as follows. First, we try to determine whether an asset is like either the "capital asset" category of assets (e.g., stocks, bonds, or land) or like the "income items" category (e.g., rental income or interest income). If the asset does not bear a . . . resemblance to items in either of those categories, we move to the following factors.

We look at the nature of the sale. If the sale or assignment constitutes a horizontal carve-out, then ordinary-income treatment presumably applies. If, on the other hand, it constitutes a vertical carve-out, then we look to the character-of-the-asset factor. There, if the sale is a lump-sum payment for a future right to earned income, we apply ordinary-income treatment, but if it is a lump-sum payment for a future right to earn income, we apply capital-gains treatment.

Turning back to the Latteras, the right to receive annual lottery payments does not bear a strong family resemblance to either the "capital assets" or the "income items" listed at the polar ends of the analytical spectrum. The Latteras sold their right to all their remaining lottery payments, so this is a vertical carve-out, which could indicate either capital-gains or ordinary-income treatment. But because a right to lottery payments is a right to earned income (i.e., the payments will keep arriving due simply to ownership of the asset), the lump-sum payment received by the Latteras should receive ordinary-income treatment.

This result . . . ensures that the Latteras do not "receive a tax advantage as compared to those taxpayers who would simply choose originally to accept their lottery winning in the form of a lump sum payment." . . .

IV. CONCLUSION

The lump-sum consideration paid to the Latteras in exchange for the right to their future lottery payments is ordinary income.

Problem

7-17. In year 1, Joe Popley's book was a stunning artistic and financial success. Unsure of his negotiating ability, Popley sold to his cousin Patricia Patrick all rights in the book for $10,000. Myron Martin, a film producer, contacted Patrick and offered to buy the book's screen rights. Rebecca Johnson, also excited about the book's potential, asked Patrick to consider selling her the rights to produce a musical based on the book.

In year 2, the following transactions were closed. First, in return for $50,000, Patrick sold to Martin the exclusive motion picture and television rights and agreed to produce the television version for Martin. Incident to this provision, Patrick was granted the right to prevent any film broadcast prior to the television showing. Finally, the contract provided that all rights would revert to Patrick if film production did not begin within two years.

Patrick's deals with Johnson were slightly different. In return for an immediate payment of $5,000, with an additional $55,000 payable on the first performance, Johnson was granted a lifetime, nonexclusive stage right. One year after the negotiations were completed, Patrick sold her contract rights with Johnson to Maggie Taggart for $10,000 cash.

Incident to his exclusive motion picture rights, Martin entered into a personal appearance contract with Popley. In return for $1,000 and an additional $500 per appearance, Popley agreed to tour the country and promote the movie. The contract provided that, subject to Martin's approval, Popley could assign his rights and duties under the contract. One year later Popley, with Martin's approval, assigned his personal appearance contract to Liz Abbott for $3,000.

a. Did Popley's sale to Patrick result in capital gain? If so, why?
b. Did Patrick have capital gain on her deal with Martin? Did she derive exclusively capital gain? If not, which portions of the sale gave rise to capital gain?
c. What was the significance, if any, for Patrick of the two-year reversion provision in Martin's contract?
d. How could Patrick's deal with Johnson be structured to give Patrick better tax treatment?
e. Was Patrick eligible for capital gain on her transaction with Taggart?
f. Was Popley eligible for capital gain on the sale of his exclusive personal appearance contract? If so, why?
g. Would Martin receive capital gain treatment if he sold his film rights to Larry Lawson, a first-time investor? If so, why?
h. Assuming Lawson bought the film rights from Martin, could he have capital gain if Patrick repurchased them? If Popley repurchased them? Was Popley eligible for capital gain treatment if he purchased the movie rights from Martin and sold them to Lawson?
i. Would Patrick receive capital gain treatment if she sold her right to prevent movie broadcasts?

H.   RECAPTURE OF DEPRECIATION

Code: §§1245(a)(1) to (3), (b)(1) to (4), (c), (d)
Regulations: §§1.1245-1(a) to (d); 1.1245-2(a)(1) to (4); 1.1245-3; 1.1245-4(a)(1)

1. General Principles

Tax avoidance schemes may evolve from unintended statutory consequences inherent in the taxation of property transactions. To prevent abuse, Congress has enacted exceptions to the general rules discussed in preceding sections of this chapter. In general, these exceptions create a statutory mechanism by which one Code section supersedes another.

For example, on the sale of a capital asset, §1245 (a depreciation recapture provision) may override the capital gain provisions and recharacterize as ordinary income all or a portion of the gain recognized on the sale or disposition of certain depreciable property that otherwise would have been capital gain. In addition, §1245 may also require *recognition* of gain on dispositions that would otherwise be nontaxable under other provisions of the Code. Furthermore, even if the property is not depreciable in the hands of the taxpayer who sells or exchanges it, it may be subject to depreciation recapture if it has a substituted basis (such as a gift) and was depreciable in the hands of the seller's transferor.

The recapture provisions are integrally related to the depreciation provisions of §§167, 168, and 197, which allow an annual deduction over the useful life of an asset or over a statutorily prescribed period representing the recovery of the capital investment in the asset. By permitting these deductions, Congress has provided an economic incentive for business and industry to modernize plants and other facilities. Conversely, however, permitting such deductions opened the door to two potential abuses. First, taxpayers could *recharacterize* income by claiming depreciation deductions against ordinary income but then recognizing capital gain on the sale or disposition of the asset. Second, taxpayers could exploit the *timing* benefit by taking advantage of accelerating deductions through depreciation which otherwise would not be recognized until the asset was sold. The recapture provisions were enacted to prevent both of these abuses by requiring that any depreciation deductions taken by a taxpayer with respect to depreciable property be "recaptured" at the time of the sale of such property.

Over the years, Congress has experimented with various depreciation and amortization schedules. The most recent choice is the modified accelerated cost recovery system ("MACRS") of §168. Like its predecessors, it contains an element of artificiality because the entire capital investment in the asset may be recovered before the actual useful life of the asset has expired. The amount realized on the disposition of depreciable assets may thus exceed the basis in the asset because the projected decline in value estimated by §§167, 168, or 197 was excessive. Although the mandatory §1016 basis adjustment ensures the taxation of the proper amount of excessive depreciation, characterization of the resulting gain under §§1221 or 1231 may nevertheless be unduly favorable to the taxpayer. If the entire gain receives capital treatment, the Treasury may not be made whole because the benefit to the taxpayer from depreciation deductions (that is, less ordinary income) might not be offset by the recoupment of that amount as long-term capital gain. Congress, therefore, enacted §1245 to remedy this deficiency. Gain attributable to depreciation recapture will be characterized as ordinary income. Any gain in excess of the recaptured depreciation is unaffected by §1245.

Real property, however, is generally immune from the recapture of depreciation upon its sale. See §§1250, 168. This occurs because §1250 typically recaptures only excess depreciation, that taken in excess of the straight-line amount, and under §168 most real property *must* be depreciated on a straight-line basis. However, Congress in 1997 introduced a "mini-version" of recapture for §1250 property in the rate tables restricting "unrecaptured section 1250 gain" to a special rate of tax between those applicable to ordinary income and capital gain. See discussion at Chapter 10.

The following examples demonstrate the operation of the recapture rules of §1245.

1. On January 1, year 1, Abel purchased machinery, §1245 recovery property, for use in his manufacturing business. His basis for depreciation was $10,000. After

properly claiming depreciation deductions totaling $4,000, Abel sold the asset on January 2, year 2, for its fair market value of $7,500. Abel, therefore, realized a gain of $1,500 ($7,500 amount realized — $6,000 adjusted basis). Section 1245 requires Abel to recapture that gain as ordinary income to the extent of his depreciation deductions. Thus, the entire $1,500 gain is treated as ordinary income under §1245(a)(1) and not as gain from the sale or exchange of §1231 property.

2. If Abel sold the property in example 1 for $10,500, his gain would be $4,500. Section 1245 would require recharacterization of $4,000 of the gain as ordinary income. The remaining $500 would, however, be treated as the gain from the sale or exchange of a §1231 asset.

3. In year 2, Carl, a farmer, gave his son, Don, a rototiller that he no longer needed. The rototiller, purchased in year 1 for $1,500, had been totally depreciated. Don used the rototiller once to prepare his front yard for reseeding and then sold it for $450 in year 3. Because the rototiller was a gift from Carl to Don, Don took a substituted basis in the machine. Thus, under §1015, Don's basis was zero, and he realized a $450 gain on his sale. Because Don had a substituted basis, the recapture taint that attached to the asset in Carl's hands carried over to Don and the $450 gain is recaptured as ordinary income, despite the fact that Don held the rototiller as personal, nondepreciable property.

LEGISLATIVE HISTORY OF §1245
(GAIN FROM THE DISPOSITION OF CERTAIN
DEPRECIABLE PROPERTY)
S. Rep. No. 1881, 87th Cong., 2d Sess. 95 (1962)

Under present law, in the case of depreciable property the taxpayer may write off the cost or other basis of the property over the period of the useful life of the asset in his hands. This cost or other basis can be written off evenly (i.e., in a "straight line" over the asset's life), under the declining balance method, under the sum-of-the-years digits method, or under any other consistent method which does not during the first two thirds of the useful life of the property exceed the allowances which would have been allowed under the declining balance method. The depreciation deduction is a deduction against ordinary income. If either the useful life of the asset is too short, or the particular method of depreciation allows too much depreciation in the early years, the decline in value of the asset resulting from these depreciation deductions may exceed the actual decline. Wherever the depreciation deductions reduce the basis of the property faster than the actual decline in its value, then when it is sold there will be a gain. Under present law this gain is taxed as a capital gain, even though the depreciation deductions reduced ordinary income. The taxpayer who has taken excessive depreciation deductions and then sells an asset, therefore, has in effect converted ordinary income into a capital gain.

The President stated that our capital gains concept should not encompass this kind of income. He indicated that this inequity should be eliminated. . . . He states that we should not encourage the further acquisition of such property through tax incentives as long as the loophole remains.

This problem also is of major significance in connection with the recent depreciation liberalization announced by the Treasury Department. Under this new approach, many taxpayers will be permitted to depreciate assets faster for tax purposes than has previously been the case. Therefore, additional ordinary income would be converted into capital gain if this were not dealt with in the provision. . . .*

The general rule (in sec. 1245) provides that ordinary income is to be recognized in the case of sales or exchanges to the extent the so-called recomputed basis, or the amount realized in the sale or exchange, whichever is lesser, exceeds the basis of the property in the hands of the person making the sale or exchange. "Recomputed basis" is defined generally as equaling the adjusted basis plus the depreciation deductions previously taken. The excess of the amount realized over the adjusted basis is, of course, the amount presently recognized as capital gain. Since the rule requires that the smaller of these two amounts be treated as ordinary income, this in effect means that the ordinary income in the usual case is to be the gain realized or the sum of the depreciation deductions taken, whichever is smaller. Where there is a disposition of an asset without a sale or exchange, gain is determined by reference to the fair market value of the asset.

2.   *Installment Sales*

Recapture of depreciation is also triggered by the installment sale of §1245 property. Section 453(i) requires the recapture of depreciation as ordinary income in the year of sale. The relevant legislative history provides:

> In an installment sale, the buyer gives the seller a note which is to be paid in subsequent years. The buyer immediately obtains depreciation deductions on the property based on its cost, but, under prior law, the seller recognized income only as installments were received. The Congress was concerned that this mismatch of income and deductions had been exploited to lower the overall effective rate of tax.
>
> The Congress was also concerned about the ability of the recapture rules to curb the incentives to "churn" property, i.e., to replace property as soon as its cost had been recovered through depreciation deductions. The installment sale rules permitted the deferral of recapture and capital gains tax and thus circumvented the barrier to churning. Taxpayers using the installment method were able to multiply tax benefits by selling property after the associated tax benefits were exhausted, which often occurred well before the expiration of the property's economic useful life, and acquiring replacement property.
>
> It was argued that gain on property, whether from appreciation in value or prior depreciation deductions, should be deferred until installment payments are made, i.e., until the seller gets cash to pay tax. However, with respect to section 1245 . . . recapture income, the seller has already obtained the benefits of depreciation deductions taken on the property prior to the sale. The Congress believed that deferral of gain attributable to prior depreciation deductions could not be justified on the grounds that the seller lacked the means to pay tax.
>
> Therefore, the Congress decided that tightening the prior-law installment sale rules was necessary to reduce the tax revenue cost associated with certain churning,

---

* It should be noted that this principle is particularly applicable to the accelerated cost recovery system. — Eds.

sale-leaseback, and other tax shelter transactions, narrow the tax advantage of investors who churn property compared to those investors who hold property for substantially all of its economic life, and make it more difficult for investors to multiply the tax benefits of the ACRS system to achieve negative effective tax rates (i.e., subsidies) by engaging in churning transactions.

Under the Act, in any installment sale of . . . personal property, all depreciation recapture income under [section] 1245 . . . is recognized in the taxable year of the disposition, even if no principal payments are received in that year. Any gain in excess of the depreciation recapture income is taken into account under the installment method. In determining how much of any principal payment constitutes a recovery of basis or gain, under the installment method, the seller's adjusted basis is to be increased by the amount of the depreciation recapture income. In applying these provisions, principal amounts are to be determined under general Code rules.

Joint Committee on Taxation, General Explanation of the Revenue Provisions of the Deficit Reduction Act of 1984.

The following example illustrates the application of §453(i).

[A]ssume that a taxpayer sold an item of . . . property with a $20 basis for a note with a principal amount of $100. Assume further that $20 in principal was paid in the taxable year immediately following the taxable year of the sale and in each of the 4 taxable years thereafter and that, of the $80 gain, $10 was . . . recapture income. . . . $10 would be includible as . . . recapture income in the taxable year of the sale even though no principal payments are received in that year. In each of the 5 taxable years thereafter, $14 ($20×($80 − $10)/$100) would be includible as gain, none of it as recapture income, and $6 ($20×($20 + $10)/$100) would be a recovery of basis. If, in the example above, $20 of principal payments were received in the taxable year of the sale and in each of the 4 taxable years thereafter, $14 would be includible in income in the year of the sale, $10 of it as recapture income, and $6 of basis would be treated as recovered in that year. In each of the 4 succeeding taxable years, $14 would be includible as gain, none as recapture income, and $6 would be a recovery of basis. In this latter example, if for $80 the taxpayer disposed of the installment obligation under section 453B(a) at the beginning of its second taxable year after the sale, $56 would be includible. None of the $56 would be recapture income.

Id. at 335.

Problems

7-18. Roger Boyles is a salesman who travels throughout the country by automobile. On January 1, year 1, he purchased a Volare station wagon for $10,000 to be used exclusively for business purposes. The total depreciation taken to the date of sale was $10,000. On January 2, year 4, Boyles sold the car for $7,000.

On January 1, year 1, Boyles received a Ford van as a gift from his father. His father had purchased the van for $15,000 one year earlier and used it as a delivery vehicle in his restaurant supply business. His father claimed one year of depreciation totaling $1,500 on the van. Boyles used the van in his sales business for three years, during which time he did not claim any depreciation deductions. The amount of depreciation properly allowable on the straight-line method for the three-year period was $9,000. He sold the van on January 2, year 4, for $11,000.

    a.   What is Boyles's adjusted basis in the station wagon on the date of sale?

    b.   What is Boyles's recomputed basis in the station wagon?

    c.   What is the amount realized on the sale of the station wagon?

    d.   How much depreciation recapture must Boyles recognize on the sale of the station wagon and what is the amount of the §1231 gain?

    e.   Assume that Boyles sold the station wagon for $12,000. What is the answer to *d?*

    f.   What is his father's adjusted basis in the van on January 1, year 1?

    g.   Does the father recognize §1245 recapture on the date of the gift?

    h.   What is Boyles's basis in the van on January 1, year 1?

    i.   What is Boyles's adjusted basis on January 2, year 4?

    j.   What is Boyles's recomputed basis in the van?

    k.   What is the amount and character of any gain that Boyles must recognize on the sale of the van?

7-19. In year 1, William Smith purchased an IBM Selectric typewriter for $900. On January 1, year 3, Smith entered into an installment sales agreement to sell the typewriter for $725. The agreement called for an initial payment in year 3 of $125 with the balance due on August 1, year 4. Smith had taken allowable depreciation deductions totaling $567 in year 1 and year 2.

    a.   Compute the amount and character of Smith's taxable gain in year 3.

    b.   Compute the amount and character of his taxable gain in year 4.

    c.   Compute the amount and character of Smith's taxable gain in year 4 and year 5, if the installment sales contract provided for payment of the $600 balance due in two equal installments.

I.   SALE OF BUSINESS

Code: §§1221(a)(1); 1060(a) to (c)

A business or proprietorship consists of diverse elements including, but not limited to, goodwill, real property, fixtures, machinery, and inventory. When a business is sold, there are at least two possibilities as to how the transaction will be treated for tax purposes. The entire business entity could be viewed as a capital asset of its owners, similar to a shareholder's interest in a corporation. If this were the case, the entire gain or loss on the sale would often be capital, regardless of the character of the business's underlying assets.

On the other hand, the Service views the sale of a business differently; it treats the transaction as a sale of its underlying assets and not as the sale of a single piece of property. The Service's position was adopted by the court in the following case, which analyzed the sale of a business and enunciated the generally accepted rule — that a sale of a business is to be treated as a sale of the component parts of the business.

WILLIAMS v. McGOWAN
152 F.2d 570 (2d Cir. 1945)

L. HAND, J. . . .

Williams, the taxpayer, and one, Reynolds, had for many years been engaged in the hardware business in the City of Corning, New York. On the 20th of January, 1926, they formed a partnership, of which Williams was entitled to two-thirds of the profits, and Reynolds, one-third. They agreed that on February 1, 1925, the capital invested in the business had been $118,082.05, of which Reynolds had a credit of $29,029.03, and Williams, the balance — $89,053.02. At the end of every business year, on February 1st, Reynolds was to pay to Williams, interest upon the amount of the difference between his share of the capital and one-third of the total as shown by the inventory; and upon withdrawal of one party the other was to have the privilege of buying the other's interest as it appeared on the books. The business was carried on through the firm's fiscal year, ending January 31, 1940, in accordance with this agreement, and thereafter until Reynolds' death on July 18th of that year. Williams settled with Reynolds' executrix on September 6th in an agreement by which he promised to pay her $12,187.90, and to assume all liabilities of the business; and he did pay her $2,187.98 in cash at once, and $10,000 on the 10th of the following October. On September 17th of the same year, Williams sold the business as a whole to the Corning Building Company for $63,926.28 — its agreed value as of February 1, 1940 — "plus an amount to be computed by multiplying the gross sales of the business from the first day of February, 1940 to the 28th day of September, 1940," by an agreed fraction. This value was made up of cash of about $8,100, receivables of about $7,000, fixtures of about $800, and a merchandise inventory of about $49,000, less some $1,000 for bills payable. To this was added about $6,000 credited to Williams for profits under the language just quoted, making a total of nearly $70,000. Upon this sale Williams suffered a loss upon his original two-thirds of the business, but he made a small gain upon the one-third which he had bought from Reynolds' executrix; and in his income tax return he entered both as items of "ordinary income," and not as transactions in "capital assets." This the Commissioner disallowed and recomputed the tax accordingly. . . . The only question is whether the business was "capital assets."

It has been held that a partner's interest in a going firm is for tax purposes to be regarded as a "capital asset." . . . If a partner's interest in a going firm is "capital assets" perhaps a dead partner's interest is the same. We need not say. When Williams bought out Reynolds' interest, he became the sole owner of the business, the firm had ended upon any theory, and the situation for tax purposes was no other than if Reynolds had never been a partner at all, except that to the extent of one-third of the "amount realized" on Williams' sale to the Corning Company, his "basis" was different. The judge thought that, because upon that sale both parties fixed the price at the liquidation value of the business while Reynolds was alive, "plus" its estimated earnings thereafter, it was as though Williams had sold his interest in the firm during its existence. But the method by which the parties agreed upon the price was irrelevant to the computation of Williams' income. . . . We have to decide only whether upon the sale of a going business it is to be comminuted into its fragments, . . . or whether the whole business is to be treated as if it were a single piece of property.

Our law has been sparing in the creation of juristic entities; it has never, for example, taken over the Roman "universitas facti";* and indeed for many years it fumbled uncertainly with the concept of a corporation. One might have supposed that partnership would have been an especially promising field in which to raise up an entity, particularly since merchants have always kept their accounts upon that basis. Yet there too our law resisted at the price of great and continuing confusion; and, even when it might be thought that a statute admitted, if it did not demand, recognition of the firm as an entity, the old concepts prevailed. And so, even though we might agree that under the influence of the Uniform Partnership Act a partner's interest in the firm should be treated as indivisible, and for that reason a "capital asset" we should be chary about extending further so exotic a jural concept. Be that as it may, in this instance the section itself furnishes the answer. It starts in the broadest way by declaring that all "property" is "capital assets," and then makes three exceptions. The first is "stock in trade . . . or other property of a kind which would properly be included in the inventory"; next comes "property held . . . primarily for sale to customers"; and finally, property "used in the trade or business of a character which is subject to . . . allowance for depreciation." In the face of this language, although it may be true that a "stock in trade," taken by itself, should be treated as a "universitas facti," by no possibility can a whole business be so treated; and the same is true as to any property within the other exceptions. Congress plainly did mean to comminute the elements of a business; plainly it did not regard the whole as "capital assets."

As has already appeared, Williams transferred to the Corning Company "cash," "receivables," "fixtures" and a "merchandise inventory." "Fixtures" are not capital because they are subject to a depreciation allowance; the inventory, as we have just seen, is expressly excluded. So far as appears, no allowance was made for "good will." . . . There can of course be no gain or loss in the transfer of cash; and, although Williams does appear to have made a gain of $1,072.71 upon the "receivables," the point has not been argued that they are not subject to a depreciation allowance. That we leave open for decision by the district court, if the parties cannot agree. The gain or loss upon every other item should be computed as an item in ordinary income.

Judgment reversed.

FRANK, J. (dissenting in part).

I agree that it is irrelevant that the business was once owned by a partnership. For when the sale to the Corning Company occurred, the partnership was dead, had become merely a memory, a ghost. To say that the sale was of the partnership's assets would, then, be to indulge in animism.

But I do not agree that we should ignore what the parties to the sale, Williams and the Corning Company, actually did. They did not arrange for a transfer to the buyer, as if in separate bundles, of the several ingredients of the business. They contracted for the sale of the entire business as a going concern. Here is what they said in their agreement: "The party of the first part agrees to sell and the party of the second part agrees to buy, *all of the right, title and interest* of the said party of the first part *in and to the hardware business* now being conducted by the said party of the first part, including cash on hand and on deposit in the First National Bank & Trust

---

* "By universitas facti is meant a number of things of the same kind which are regarded as a whole; e.g., a herd, a stock of wares." Mackeldey, Roman Law §162.

Company of Corning in the A. F. Williams Hardware Store account, in accounts receivable, bills receivable, notes receivable, merchandise and fixtures, including two G.M. trucks, good will and all other assets of every kind and description used in and about said business. . . . Said party of the first part agrees not to engage in the hardware business within a radius of twenty-five miles from the City of Corning, New York, for a period of ten years from the 1st day of October 1940."

To carve up this transaction into distinct sales—of cash, receivables, fixtures, trucks, merchandise, and good will—is to do violence to the realities. I do not think Congress intended any such artificial result. In the Senate Committee Report it was said: "It is believed that this Senate amendment will be of material benefit to businesses which, due to depressed conditions, have been compelled to dispose of their plant or equipment at a loss. The bill defines property used in a trade or business as property used in the trade or business of a character which is subject to the allowance for depreciation, and real property held for more than six months which is not properly includable in the inventory of the taxpayer if on hand at the close of the taxable year or property held by the taxpayer primarily for sale to customers in the ordinary course of his trade or business. If a newspaper purchased the plant and equipment of a rival newspaper and later sold such plant and equipment at a loss, such plant and equipment, being subject to depreciation, would constitute property used in the trade or business within the meaning of this section." These remarks show that what Congress contemplated was not the sale of a going business but of its dismembered parts. Where a business is sold as a unit, the whole is greater than its parts. Businessmen so recognize; so, too, I think, did Congress. Interpretation of our complicated tax statutes is seldom aided by saying that taxation is an eminently practical matter (or the like). But this is one instance where, it seems to me, the practical aspects of the matter should guide our guess as to what Congress meant. I believe Congress had those aspects in mind and was not thinking of the nice distinctions between Roman and Anglo-American legal theories about legal entities.

Problem

7-20. Sheldon Zuckerman wishes to sell his successful retail clothing business. The assets that will be sold include goodwill, the seller's covenant not to compete, building, land, and inventory.
  a. How might Zuckerman wish to allocate the sales proceeds?
  b. Assuming the same facts, how might a potential purchaser wish to allocate the purchase price?

J. SECTION 1237—STATUTORY IMMUNITY FOR SUBDIVIDED REAL PROPERTY

Code: §§1221(a)(1); 1237

In addition to the basic statutory requirements for characterizing gains or losses, other Code sections and judicial doctrines may override those basic requirements. Section 1237, unlike §1245 which prevents abuse of the general characterization rules, is a provision that affords taxpayer relief.

When selling a tract of land previously held as an investment, it is sometimes necessary to subdivide the property, develop it, and sell portions over a period of time. The major tax obstacle for such sellers is that substantial subdivision and sale activities may cause the resulting gain to be characterized as ordinary income, because the nature and extent of development and volume of sales activities may cause the taxpayer to be treated as entering the business of selling land. If this occurs, the land would be excluded from the definition of capital asset by §1221(a)(1). Section 1237 was, therefore, enacted to assure individuals capital gain treatment where subdivision activities are minimal. If applicable, §1237 may permit capital gain on the sale of parcels of real estate from a single tract.

In order to obtain the benefits of §1237, the following requirements must be satisfied: (1) the taxpayer must have owned the property for at least five years or must have acquired the property by inheritance or devise; (2) the taxpayer cannot previously have held any part of the tract primarily for sale in the ordinary course of trade or business, nor can the taxpayer hold in the year of sale any other real property for that purpose; and (3) the taxpayer cannot make improvements on the tract that substantially increase the value of the lot sold (see §1237(a)(1) to (3)). If these requirements are met, the gain from the first five lots sold may be treated as capital gain provided, however, that no more than five lots are sold in one year. In the year in which the sixth lot is sold, and every year thereafter, gain from all lots is treated as ordinary income to the extent of 5 percent of the sales price of each lot. See §1237(b)(1).

POINTER v. COMMISSIONER
48 T.C. 906 (1967), affd., 419 F.2d 213 (9th Cir. 1969)

DAWSON, J. . . .

Basically, the issue raised in this case is whether the proceeds from the sale of certain lots should be taxed as ordinary income or as capital gains. The definition of a capital asset in section 1221 excludes those assets held primarily for sale to customers in the ordinary course of a taxpayer's trade or business. If the land in question was so held, the gains realized from the sales of lots are taxable to petitioners as ordinary income. In this connection, we look first at section 1237, a special capital gains provision applying only to limited real estate transactions, which may be determinative. However, if we conclude that the petitioners fail to qualify under section 1237, it will still be necessary to consider the applicability of section 1221(1). See sec. 1.1237-1(a)(4)(i).

A taxpayer qualifying under section 1237 may sell lots from a single tract held for investment without the gain therefrom being taxed as ordinary income solely because the tract was subdivided or because he actively participated in the sales. Sec. 1.1237-1(a)(1). The requisites to qualification under section 1237 are:

1. The taxpayer must have held the property for at least five years unless it was acquired by inheritance or devise.

2. The taxpayer may not previously have held any part of the tract primarily for sale in the ordinary course of his trade or business, nor may he hold in the year of sale any other real property for that purpose.
3. The taxpayer cannot make on the tract any substantial improvement that substantially enhances the value of lots or parcels sold.

The first two conditions are met in this case. The tract was originally purchased in 1953 and 1954; the first lot was sold in 1959, at least five years after purchase. Subdivision activities within five years of the purchase are, despite respondent's argument, irrelevant to the issue of whether the land was *held* for the requisite length of time. Since the sale of each lot was only part of an overall plan for disposing of the tract, a determination that the land sold during the years in issue was or was not held primarily for sale in the ordinary course of petitioners' trade or business will be dispositive as to all other sales. Thus, if the petitioners held the lots sold in 1961, 1962, and 1963 as capital assets, the lots sold in 1959 and 1960 were similarly held, satisfying the second requirement.

Although Pointer-Willamette was actively involved in several land transactions during the years in issue, the facts demonstrate persuasively that the land was acquired solely for the business needs of the corporation and not for sale in its ordinary course of business. This land was leased and sold by the corporation, and by the petitioner individually after the corporation was dissolved, as the most expedient way to dispose of assets which had ceased to be of value in the manufacturing and construction business. Pointer-Willamette had not donned the cloak of a "dealer" in real estate. Assuming a contrary conclusion, there would be little justification for attributing the corporation's conduct to the petitioner since he had ceased all active management of the corporate affairs by 1950.

In applying the final requisite for section 1237 coverage, the nature and extent of improvements made on the undeveloped tract are critical. Improvements will not deprive petitioners the benefit of section 1237 unless they are (1) substantial in nature and (2) substantially increase the value of the lots sold.

Consistent with the legislative intent of permitting minor or minimal improvements, the surveying, leveling and clearing, and the construction of minimum all-weather access roads, including gravel roads where required by the climate, are not considered substantial. On the other hand, hard surface roads or utilities such as sewers, water, gas, or electric lines are specifically declared substantial. Sec. 1.1237-1(c)(4).

Even though the petitioners acknowledge that utilities and a paved street were installed in West Point Park, they claim an inconsistency between the regulations and section 1237(b)(3) as to the substantiality of hard surface roads. We see no inconsistency. Among other conditions, the application of the special rules of subsection (b)(3) relating to "necessary" improvements is conditioned upon the holding of the land by the taxpayer for ten years. Since the lots in question were sold within ten years of purchase, there is no occasion for referring to subsection (b)(3). Petitioners expended over $24,000, approximately equal to the original purchase price, in clearing, grading, and installing curbs, culverts, a paved street, and a waterline on the 10.63-acre tract. Under the regulations, which are reasonable and supported by the legislative history, these improvements must be viewed as substantial.

Next we must consider whether the improvements "substantially enhanced the value" of the lots sold. . . . West Point Park lots were advertised for $5,000, $5,500, and $6,000 per lot in 1959 and were sold at those figures during the years in issue. The same lots unimproved would have sold in 1959 for $2,500 to $3,000 per lot. It is undisputed that this represents approximately a 100-percent increase in the value of the lots due solely to the improvements. The regulations further provide that if the value of a lot is increased by more than ten percent all relevant factors must be considered to determine whether the increase is substantial.

"Substantial" is an illusive word. It refers to that which is large, valuable, or noteworthy, or in a negative sense, to that which is not trivial, nominal, or incomplete. Any general definition is necessarily vague because the concept is relative to the circumstances in which it is used. It would serve no useful purpose here to compare percentages and draw lines. Suffice it to say that the regulations deem it permissible to find any increase in value over ten percent to be substantial, depending upon the particular facts. In this case the added value of $2,500 to $3,000 per lot, which is equal to the value of the unimproved lot and attributable solely to improvements, is substantial. Therefore, we hold that the petitioners have failed to qualify under the provisions of section 1237.* . . .

Problem

7-21.   In year 1, Jeff Bowers, a Las Vegas restaurateur, paid $20,000 for a twenty-acre parcel of undeveloped land outside the Las Vegas city limits. He bought it with the intent of building a new and larger restaurant on the site. To his dismay, zoning enacted in year 3 restricted the area to residential use. In year 6, the twenty-acre parcel had a fair market value of $30,000. Bowers's real estate consultant advised him that if he subdivided the twenty acres and sold it in one-acre lots, the fair market value of each lot would increase. In year 6, he followed that advice and surveyed the land and filed a subdivision plat increasing the value to $33,000. In addition, he advertised the lots for sale and hired a real estate broker to help sell the property. Bowers also installed one primary water line and one sewer line and constructed one main paved road and several smaller gravel roads. Finally, he constructed one small A-frame model home that doubled as a temporary sales office. The cost of these additional improvements, $1,000, increased the total value of the twenty acres to $40,000.

In year 7, Bowers sold three one-acre lots to three different buyers for $2,000 each, and in year 8 he sold eight more lots to eight different individuals for $2,000 each.

a.   What is Bowers's basis in the twenty acres?

b.   What is his taxable gain in year 7?

c.   May he report the gain from the sale of the three lots in year 7 as long-term capital gain and, if so, why?

---

* The court also decided against the petitioners on the §1221 issue. — EDS.

    d.   Assuming that §1237 applies, determine the amount of long-term capital gain and ordinary income that Bowers reports in year 8 from the sale of the eight lots.

    e.   How would the answer to *c* change if Bowers held the property for eleven years?

K. ORIGINAL ISSUE DISCOUNT AND IMPUTED INTEREST

Code: §§483; 1272(a)(1), (3), (4); 1273(a); 1274; 1274A

As discussed in Chapters 2 and 5, the tax laws historically ignored the concept that money has time value (i.e., that future and present values of a fixed sum are not equal). Such indifference permitted the parties in deferred payment sales to manipulate both the character and timing of income and expenses to avoid or defer tax liability. Congress first attempted to curb those practices through the imputed interest rules of §483.

Before 1984, sales of property involving deferred payments and unstated interest were subject to §483. Under §483, any unstated interest was imputed so that the buyer's interest expense deduction and the seller's interest income were increased. If, for example, the seller sold property with a basis of $1 million for a payment of $6 million in five years without interest, the seller argued that he or she was entitled to a $5 million long-term capital gain. If, however, the transaction was subject to §483, the transaction was recast with a portion of the $6 million principal payment treated as interest. As a consequence, the seller was treated as having a lesser amount of preferentially treated capital gain and as also receiving interest income in the amount of the remainder taxed at ordinary rates.

Unstated interest was present when the stated interest, if any, on the deferred purchase price was less than the mandated rate of interest specified by §483. The amount of unstated interest was measured and a portion of the principal amount was recharacterized as interest by using the imputed rate. However, astute tax planners devised strategies that complied with the mechanical provisions of §483 while providing uncontemplated tax savings. Three problem areas evolved:

1. *Timing and mismatching of income.* The first problem with §483 was the mismatching of the seller's interest income and the purchaser's interest expense. For example, assume an accrual method purchaser gives a cash method seller a purchase money obligation accruing interest over the term of the obligation but deferring payment of interest until maturity. The purchaser was permitted an interest deduction in each taxable year that the interest accrued, regardless of when it was paid. On the other hand, the seller did not recognize interest income until the taxable year in which he or she actually received payment from the purchaser. Thus, the purchaser could receive interest deductions as interest accrued over the life of the obligation without paying any of the interest until maturity, while the seller could forgo recognition of accrued interest income until the purchaser's payment at maturity.

2. *Inadequate interest rates.* A second problem was the inadequacy of the §483 test rate. Although the Secretary had statutory authority to adjust the test rate, it historically lagged behind market interest rates. Additionally, the test rate, unlike market rates, was a simple rate with no compounding so that it actually required less interest on debt obligations than market rates at identical percentages. In addition, the applicable test rate did not increase as the debt's term increased even though market rates frequently did. As a result, the purchaser and seller could structure the transaction to require interest at the simple interest test rate, yielding interest payments substantially below market rates. Such understated interest caused over-stated principal payments and inflated the basis for property purchased, allowing the purchaser to take excessive depreciation deductions.

3. *Conversion of interest into principal.* A third problem was the conversion of interest into principal so that the seller recognized less interest income and more capital gain. Conversion was possible because former §483 did not adequately account for the time value of money. In exchange for below-market interest rates on deferred payment sales of capital assets, sellers could require correspond-ingly higher purchase prices, thereby increasing the portion of each deferred pay-ment allocable to the amount realized and decreasing the interest income received on the sale. The portion of deferred payments thus converted would be preferen-tially taxed as capital gain rather than as ordinary interest income. Although such sellers were in the same pretax economic position as sellers who charged market interest rates and lower purchase prices, sellers in the former group reduced their tax liability simply by recharacterizing their sales.

For example, assume that A and B each own identical capital assets with fair market values of $80,000 that were purchased for $40,000 ten years ago. A sells his asset to C for $100,000, payable in ten annual installments of $10,000 with no interest. A expects to recognize $60,000 ($100,000 selling price less $40,000 adjusted basis) of capital gain spread over the next ten years. C expects a basis in the asset of $100,000 and to depreciate the asset over its useful life.

Meanwhile, B sells her asset to D for $80,000 payable in equal installments over the next ten years, but the parties agree that D will pay an additional $20,000 in interest to compensate B for accepting the $80,000 in ten annual payments. B expects to recognize a $40,000 capital gain ($80,000 selling price less $40,000 adjusted basis) and $20,000 of interest income over the ten-year period. D will take an $80,000 basis in the asset and deduct the interest as it is paid.

As evidenced by the comparison, by ignoring interest A will convert interest income to capital gain. B, however, will receive interest income in addition to capital gain despite selling the same asset at the same price.

Alarmed by these deficiencies in former §483, Congress enacted the Original Issue Discount (OID) rules of §§1271 through 1275 and amended §483. Although §483 still exists, its importance has waned.

1.   Statutory Framework

Recall from Chapter 5 that the OID rules impose a mandatory accrual method of accounting on both the buyer and the seller of property who are using a deferred purchase price. The OID rules accomplish this by first calculating the difference between the "issue price" and the "stated redemption price at maturity." This amount, the "original issue discount," must then be accrued over the life of the deferred payment by using a constant yield to maturity. By adopting this approach, the OID rules address the timing and mismatching problems of former §483 — both the seller and the buyer must follow the same accrual methodology, and the rate must reflect the presumed cost of capital inherent in the deferred payment.

The OID rules also address the character and conversion problems inherent in former §483 by ensuring that the accrued interest is treated exactly the same as if the parties made actual interest payments. For example, under §163(e) the buyer is permitted to take interest deductions as they accrue for accruals of OID (if they are otherwise deductible) regardless of their regular method of tax accounting. Similarly, under Regulation §1.1001-1(g) the "issue price" of the deferred payment obligation is considered the "amount realized" for purposes of calculating the capital gain or loss on the sale, and the "issue price" is the amount used as the sales price for purposes of applying the installment sale rules of §453. In this manner, the OID rules integrated the numerous disparate tax rules for the sale of property using deferred purchase price, by adopting a single value (i.e., the "issue price") to calculate the timing and character consequences of such a sale. This meant that taxpayers could no longer manipulate the rules to result in a mismatch of timing or to convert interest into principal. As a result, the tax law finally incorporated a time-value-of-money concept into the rules regulating the timing and character of deferred sales of property.

JOINT COMMITTEE ON TAXATION, STAFF PAMPHLET DESCRIBING TAX TREATMENT OF IMPUTED INTEREST ON DEFERRED PAYMENT SALES OF PROPERTY
16 (1985)

ANALYSIS AND ISSUES

A.   DETERMINING THE PROPER AMOUNT OF IMPUTED INTEREST

Tax Consequences of Understatement of Interest

Understatement of interest in a seller-financed sale of depreciable property results in an overstatement of both the buyer's depreciation deductions . . . and the seller's capital gain, and an understatement of both the buyer's interest deductions and the seller's interest income. The net tax effect of understatement of interest depends on a variety of factors including: (1) the relative tax rates of the buyer and seller; (2) the amount by which basis is overstated; (3) the depreciation method used, and the number of years the property is held, by the buyer; and (4) the term of the seller-financed mortgage where capital gains are reported on the installment method. In general, the overstatement of basis (attributable to below-market seller financing) is advantageous for tax purposes to the extent that it results in a magnification of the tax benefits of rapid depreciation, capital gains treatment, and installment reporting.

The consequences of overstating basis are demonstrated below in two examples involving the seller-financed sale of an office building with (1) a third-party market interest rate mortgage, and (2) a mortgage at a below-market rate.

The first example involves the sale of a fully depreciated office building for a $100 million note with interest payable at 13.5 percent (assumed market rate) and a balloon payment of principal in 18 years. The buyer and seller are both taxable at a 50-percent rate. In this case, the seller will recognize a capital gain of $100 million in the eighteenth year, giving rise to a tax liability of $20 million (assuming there is no depreciation recapture). Over the 18-year term of the note, the buyer will depreciate the full purchase price of the property, resulting in deductions of $100 million, and giving rise to a tax reduction of $50 million. Thus, the net effect of the sale is a reduction in tax revenues of $30 million ($50 million minus $20 million) over the 18-year period. This example shows that the sale of depreciable property on the installment method can result in a reduction in tax revenues even if interest is stated at the market rate. However, the tax benefit arising from the installment sale rules and the preferential treatment of capital gains can, in many cases, be magnified as a result of understating interest.

In the second example, the parties to the sale of the office building, described above, agree to reduce the interest rate to 9.7 percent and, as an offset, to raise the purchase price to $133.4 million. Thus, the principal amount of the note is overstated, relative to a third-party mortgage, by one-third ($133.4 [million] vs. $100 million). In this case, the seller will recognize a capital gain of $133.4 million in the eighteenth year, giving rise to a tax liability of $26.7 million. Over the 18-year term of the note, the buyer will depreciate the full purchase price of the property, resulting in deductions of $133.4 million, and giving rise to a tax reduction of $66.7 million. Thus, the net effect of the sale is a reduction in tax revenues of $40 million ($66.7 million minus $26.7 million) over the 18-year period. This revenue loss is one-third greater than the $30 million revenue loss arising in the case where interest on the seller-financed mortgage was set at the market rate (see Table [7-1]). Under the facts of this example, it can be concluded that the revenue loss arising from an installment sale of depreciable property increases in proportion to the overstatement of principal. Thus, the overstatement of principal in an installment sale of depreciable property can have significant tax consequences.

TABLE 7-1
Tax Consequences of Understatement of Interest
[dollar amounts in millions]

Item	Market Rate Mortgage	Below-Market Mortgage
Stated interest rate (percent)	13.5	9.7
Stated principal amount	$100.0	$133.4
Maturity (years)	18	18
Total depreciation deductions	$100.0	$133.4
Taxable capital gains income	$40.0	$53.4
Net reduction in taxable income[1]	$60.0	$80.0
Revenue loss over 18-year period[2]	$30.0	$40.0

1. Total depreciation deductions less capital gains income.
2. Revenue loss computed assuming buyer and seller are both in the 50-percent income tax bracket.

Factors Relevant to Establishing the Proper Imputed Interest Rate. As demonstrated in the example above, distortions in the taxation of the parties to an installment sale can occur if the parties had unfettered discretion to characterize deferred payments as principal or interest for tax purposes. The role of the imputed interest rules is to establish parameters for allocating payments between principal and interest. The imputed interest provisions do not affect the total amount of payments flowing from the buyer of the property to the seller. They merely provide that, for tax purposes, a certain minimum amount of interest will be assumed to be inherent in the transaction. If the parties fail to state interest at, or above, a specified minimum rate, then the statute imputes interest at [that] rate.

The most difficult issue posed by this statutory scheme is how this minimum interest rate should be fixed. Prior to 1984, the rate was set on an ad hoc basis by the Treasury Department. This system, however, produced unsatisfactory results, for the reasons discussed above. The 1984 Act introduced a self-adjusting, statutory mechanism for determining the test rate, designed to keep the rate reasonably consistent with current rates in the financial markets. Assuming that a self-adjusting mechanism is preferable to ad hoc regulatory determinations, the next issue becomes which "market" should provide the standard for comparison. Considerable controversy has arisen over this issue since the enactment of the 1984 Act.

In designing the statutory mechanism for determining the section 483 and 1274 test rates in the 1984 Act, Congress sought to produce a system that yielded a reasonable, conservative approximation of the rate at which a good credit risk with adequate security could borrow. Although this focus on the buyer-borrower's borrowing rate was consistent with the original legislative intent behind the enactment of section 483, it has been suggested by some that the appropriate focus of the imputed interest rules is the seller's reinvestment rate (i.e., what rate of return the seller could have realized had he received cash from the buyer and invested in a security of comparable risk and maturity).

In this regard, it has also been suggested that the appropriate standard may be a rate somewhat lower than the rate at which the seller could have invested cash proceeds. It is argued that sellers of property may be willing to accept less than the rate of return they could realize on alternative investments for reasons wholly unrelated to taxes. For example, the seller may accept a below-market rate of interest in order to facilitate the sale of the property. Furthermore, a below-market rate on seller financing may reflect the seller's ability to defer gain on the sale by using the installment method. Had he received the entire purchase price in cash, the seller would have been required to pay taxes on the entire gain in the year of the sale and would have had less after-tax proceeds to invest than if installment treatment were available. He can afford to charge the buyer less interest because he (the seller) is investing with before-tax, rather than after-tax, dollars.

Even if one accepts the premise that nontax factors influence the determination of rates in the seller-financing "market," there are inherent difficulties in allowing this market to establish the minimum acceptable rate for tax purposes. First, there is no readily ascertainable market rate for seller financing as there is for third-party financing. More importantly, the fact that the rates may be distorted by noneconomic factors, whether tax-related or not, makes them of questionable relevance in a tax system that, in theory, taxes transactions based on their true economic substance.

Finally, using a seller-financing rate as the test rate would result in a minimum rate that is below the prevailing market rate at which a buyer could borrow from a third-party lender. The tax consequences for both the seller and the buyer would vary, under some circumstances dramatically, depending on whether the transaction is seller-financed or financed with a third-party loan. A buyer who finances a purchase with a third-party loan at the full market rate will presumably be willing (and perhaps able) to pay less for the property than if below-market seller financing were available, resulting in a lower tax basis for the buyer and less capital gain for the seller. . . .

2.   *Applying the New Regime*

Subsequent to the enactment of the OID rules, the focus with respect to deferred payments for sales of property shifted from the valuation of the deferred payment obligation (taking into account interest rates, credit risk, and other variables) to the statutory formula used to calculate the "issue price" of the deferred payment. As discussed in Chapter 5, §1274 controls the determination of the "issue price" of a deferred payment obligation issued in exchange for non-publicly traded property (such as real estate). Under §1274, the issue price is generally equal to the stated redemption price at maturity discounted to its present value using the "applicable federal rate" (AFR). Recall that the AFR represents the lowest cost of capital because it generally reflects the price at which the federal government could borrow. Thus, the issue price using the AFR generally is higher than the issue price would have been using the taxpayer's (higher) actual cost of capital. This means that taxpayers using deferred payments for a sale of property will have higher capital gains and less interest income than they would have had if the higher discount rate had been used. For a seller eligible for the beneficial capital gains rates, this can be an advantageous rule, but for a buyer who can use ordinary deductions, this can be a detrimental rule. Is this a proper policy choice for the income tax laws? Consider the following example.

Example. John sells real property with an adjusted basis equal to $1 million to Erica for $5 million, to be paid in two years with no interest. The AFR is 5 percent compounded annually and Erica's cost of capital is 10 percent compounded annually. Under the OID rules, the issue price of the deferred payment obligation is approximately $4,535,000, while the present value of the deferred payment under Erica's cost of capital would be approximately $4,132,000. Under the OID rules, John would realize $3,535,000 of capital gain and $465,000 of ordinary income, while using Erica's cost of capital John would realize $3,132,000 of capital gain and $868,000 of ordinary income. Conversely, under the OID rules, Erica may deduct only $465,000 of interest deductions while she could deduct $868,000 if she used her cost of capital. Since Erica in reality pays $5 million to John under either case, the only difference is the tax treatment of the payment.

Problems

Assumed Present Value Factors for Semiannual Compounding
Converted to an Annual Rate

Year	13%	10%	9%	6%
1	.88496	.90909	.91573	.94259
2	.78315	.82645	.83856	.88849
3	.69305	.75131	.76789	.83748
4	.61332	.68301	.70318	.78941
5	.54276	.62092	.64392	.74409

7-22. On January 1, year 1, X sells new equipment to Y in exchange for a note with a face amount of $500,000. The note provides that interest only is to be paid annually at the rate of 12 percent, with all principal due at the end of five years. Assume that the governing AFR (compounded semiannually) in January for a midterm debt instrument is equal to a 10-percent annual rate.
   a. If X and Y are accrual method taxpayers, what result to each?
   b. What result in a if the AFR is equal to a 13-percent annual rate?

7-23. On January 1, year 1, Z sells industrial equipment it manufactured to Y in exchange for a $500,000 note due December 31, year 5. There is no stated interest, and the governing AFR (compounded semiannually) in January for a midterm debt instrument is equal to a 10-percent annual rate. If Z and Y are accrual method taxpayers, what result to each?

7-24. On January 1, year 1, C sells an apartment building to D in exchange for a note with a face amount of $2,500,000. D is to pay interest, at a rate of 8 percent, of $200,000 at the end of each of the next five years. There is no principal due until the end of five years, at which time the note is due in full. Assume that the governing AFR (compounded semiannually) for a midterm debt instrument is equal to a 10-percent annual rate.
   a. If C and D are accrual method taxpayers, what result to each?
   b. What result in a if C had sold his personal residence instead of an apartment building?

7-25. On January 1, year 1, GP sells vacant land to his grandson, GS, in exchange for a $400,000 note, payable at the end of four years. There is no stated interest, and the governing AFR (compounded semiannually) in January for a midterm debt instrument is equal to a 10-percent annual rate.
   a. What result to GP and GS if they are cash method taxpayers?
   b. What result to GP and GS if they are accrual method taxpayers?
   c. What result in a if the note has a stated principal amount of $800,000?

L. POLICY CONSIDERATIONS

Prior to 1986, several approaches were being considered to reform the tax treatment of capital gain. At that time, a deduction under §1202 was available for 60 percent of the net long-term capital gain. In 1986, Congress eliminated the

§1202 deduction and thereby the preferential treatment of capital gain because, as discussed in Chapter 10, Congress limited the maximum tax rate on net capital gain to 28 percent, because the same as the highest individual tax rate. Since that time, however, the rate differential between most capital gain income (15 percent) and ordinary income (35 percent) has increased, and a limited §1202 exclusion has been reenacted.

As the debate over preferential rates for capital gains increases, attention continues to return to alternative proposals to address the bunching and lock-in concerns. One proposal in particular has received continued attention: indexing capital gains for inflation. By indexing for inflation, capital gains would no longer include an inflationary gains component, mitigating the bunching and lock-in problems. Instead, capital gains would include only the "real" economic gains such that capital gains may not need a preferential rate as compared to ordinary income. The Treasury Department issued a report in 1984 analyzing the benefits and problems of an indexing approach. Since that time, the government, commentators, and academics have proposed alternative versions of indexing to address some of the problems identified in 1984. In 1997, the Joint Committee on Taxation issued another detailed report on indexing capital gains for inflation, considering some of these alternatives and detailing some of the complexities of adopting an indexing system. Why have these issues proven so difficult to overcome? Would an indexed system be more complicated than the current system? Can anything be more complicated than the current system?

JOINT COMMITTEE ON TAXATION, TAX TREATMENT OF CAPITAL GAINS AND LOSSES
36-43 (1997)

C. ISSUES RELATING TO INDEXING

IN GENERAL

Proponents of indexing contend that indexing would accomplish the goals of reduced capital gains taxation while producing a more accurate measurement of economic income with greater neutrality. Opponents contend that indexing is complex and that it would not be necessary if efforts to control inflation are successful.

Inflation and Effective Real Tax Rates

Under present law, even modest annual inflation can significantly increase the effective real tax rate on income from realized capital gains. For example, assume an investor purchases stock for $100 and the stock appreciates in value at 10 percent per year. After five years the stock will be worth $161. If sold, and the investor is in the 28-percent tax bracket, the investor will incur a tax liability of $17. If over that five-year period inflation had averaged 3 percent per year, the investor would have needed to realize $116 from the sale of the asset to maintain his or her real purchasing power. Consequently, the investor's real gain is $45. A $17 tax on a $45 real gain implies an effective tax rate of 37.8 percent on real gains as compared to the statutory rate of 28 percent.

Table 1 reports transactions by a sample of individuals who realized nominal long-term capital gains on corporate stock in 1994. . . . [O]f assets acquired in 1992 and sold at a nominal gain in 1994, 20.6 percent of the gain was the inflation component on average. This implies the effective tax rate on real capital gains was increased, on average, by 25 percent by inflation. . . .

T A B L E 1
Inflationary Component of Nominal
Long-Term Gains Realized on Corporate Stock, 1994

Holding period in years	Number of transactions	Dollar value of nominal gains ($ millions)	Dollar value of real gains ($ millions)	Inflation component as a percentage of nominal gain
1	64,428	486.4	407.6	16.2
2	29,945	359.2	285.3	20.6
3	15,421	249.9	170.6	31.7
4	9,345	153.4	75.0	51.1
5	6,089	123.9	60.0	51.5
6	4,818	147.5	80.3	45.6
7	3,084	181.3	122.8	32.3
8	2,357	88.1	44.1	49.9
9	2,844	129.5	59.5	54.1
10	2,154	89.9	41.4	54.0
11	1,021	39.4	21.6	45.2
12	740	33.9	19.1	43.7
13	623	39.2	25.0	36.2
14	595	45.5	30.5	33.1
15	291	15.7	4.8	69.2
16	270	29.1	-3.6	112.2
17	251	22.0	11.2	48.9
18	261	34.0	20.9	38.5
19	239	10.8	2.5	77.3

Note. — Sample from Schedule D may not be representative of all gain recognition.
Source: Joint Committee on Taxation staff calculations from Internal Revenue Service SOI data.

While . . . the benefit of deferral can reduce the effective tax rate, proponents of indexing observe that because inflation is not predictable, non-indexed taxation implies an uncertain effective rate of taxation. This added uncertainty may discourage saving generally and, in particular, saving in assets that produce their returns in the form of accruing capital gains.

Non-Indexed Taxation of Gain and Saving and Investment

. . . It is possible that indexing might not relieve "lock-in" problems, because a taxpayer whose after-tax economic gain is protected against future inflation may decide to continue to hold an asset to obtain the benefits of tax deferral, or the benefits of tax exemption if the asset is held until death. Others contend that indexing alleviates "lock-in" by removing the burden of taxing nominal gains arising from inflation. Some critics question the value of indexing as a policy to promote risk taking. They observe that much of the basis of entrepreneurial effort, so-called "sweat equity," has a nominal basis of zero, and that indexing a zero basis provides no benefit. . . .

ISSUES RELATED TO PARTIAL INDEXING

. . . Defining Indexed Assets

If some but not all assets are indexed, additional consideration would have to be given to provisions designed to accomplish the desired results in certain special situations. For example, if stock but not debt is indexed (or if debt is indexed in a different manner than stock — for example, by interest adjustments rather than basis adjustments), the question arises whether some types of assets . . . should be classified as stock or as debt for this purpose.

. . . In the case of depreciable assets, rules are necessary to prevent the churning of assets in order for the buyer to obtain a higher basis for depreciation than the seller's basis, where the seller's gain is not taxed as a result of indexing.

Complexity. Indexing would involve a significant amount of recordkeeping. Records of the cost of property and improvements are generally maintained under present law. However, records of the dates the costs are incurred are not relevant to the determination of tax liability once the asset has been held for one year.

Indexing would substantially increase the number of calculations necessary to calculate taxable gain for many common transactions. For example, consider an individual who sells stock in a regular corporation or in a mutual fund that was purchased 10 years before the sale and who reinvested the quarterly dividends in additional stock during the entire period. Under present law, the individual can add the original cost and the dollar amounts of each of the 40 reinvested dividend payments in order to obtain the stock's basis, which is subtracted from the sales proceeds in order to determine taxable gain. Assuming qualified assets must be held for three years before the benefits of indexing can be claimed, each of the first 29 of the 41 components of basis (the original purchase plus the 40 dividend payments) would be multiplied separately by indexing factors based on the period elapsed between the calendar quarter the stock was purchased and it was sold, in order to determine the indexed basis of the stock for purposes of determining long-term indexed gain. The nominal basis of each of the next eight purchases would be added together, as under present law, to determine the basis of non-indexed long-term gain. As under present law, the nominal basis of each of the last four purchases would be added together to determine the basis of non-indexed short-term gain. Further, if the corporation or mutual fund had ever paid a return of capital distribution, adjustments would be needed to the basis of each separate block of stock. Similarly, if capital improvements were made to qualified property, records of the dates of improvements would have to be maintained in order to compute the basis of property.

. . . Further, with preferential capital gains treatment for some types of assets, depending upon the rate of inflation, taxpayers will have an incentive to engage in transactions designed to convert ordinary income to capital gains income. Thus, the complex provisions of present law dealing with situations in which capital gains treatment is available . . . will continue to be necessary.

Choice of Price Index

The rationale for indexing capital gains, and for the present-law indexing of various provisions of the Code, is to better measure the real income available to taxpayers. One price index that could be used to adjust basis for the purpose of computing gain is . . . the Labor Department's . . . Consumer Price Index (CPI). The [Internal Revenue] Code generally uses the CPI to index provisions related to individual taxpayers.* Use of the CPI would provide consistency in the measurement of real income.

Recently, some economists have criticized the CPI as an accurate measure of consumer cost of living. The CPI is a fixed-basket price index. Given an identified basket of "consumer" goods, the CPI is estimated by comparing estimated prices for the "same" goods in one year compared to another year. Generally speaking, the CPI requires estimates of prices only. The purpose of measuring consumer purchases is to approximate consumer well-being. The primary drawback of a fixed-basket price index is that, through time, the basket may fail to represent consumer purchases. For example, if gas prices move higher, consumers may substitute public transportation for consumption of gasoline. An additional problem is identifying the "same" goods in different years, that is adjusting for quality changes. For example, one should not compare the average personal computer of 1997 with the average personal computer of 1990 as the average 1990 computer was much less powerful than the average 1997 computer.

. . . An additional consideration may be the need to maintain some constancy of the index, as taxpayers may hold assets for 20 years or more before selling the asset. The CPI is never revised, save for identification of new base year baskets. . . .

---

* Indexing of rate tables and other similar considerations are discussed in more detail in Chapter 10. — Eds.

CHAPTER 8
INVESTMENT AND PERSONAL DEDUCTIONS

A. INTRODUCTION

As discussed in Chapter 6, expenses incurred in a trade or business frequently are deductible in arriving at adjusted gross income (AGI), while personal expenses generally are not. Chapter 8 discusses deductions *from* AGI, commonly referred to as "below-the-line deductions." These deductions primarily include two types of expenses: (1) business and profit-related expenses that are not deductible in computing AGI under §62, and (2) certain specific categories of personal expenses.

Commonly encountered business expenses classified as itemized deductions include most employment-related expenses incurred by employees. Section 62(a)(2) permits deductions of only *reimbursed* trade or business expenses of an employee, other than a performing artist and certain other enumerated employees as defined at §62(b), in computing AGI. All other business expenses incurred by an employee (such as legal expenses, educational expenses, travel expenses incurred away from home, and other expenses discussed in Chapter 6) are treated as itemized deductions. For this reason, many of these expenses will be subject to limitations, either within the deduction-granting provision itself or pursuant to a catch-all floor amount (2 percent of AGI) under §67 and, in some cases, a cap (3 percent of AGI) under §68.

Profit-related expenses for which individuals are granted itemized deductions include expenses incurred in the production or collection of income or in the management of property held for investment purposes. Additionally, individuals are allowed itemized deductions for tax return preparation fees and for legal or other expenses incurred in the determination, collection, or refund of any tax.

The most significant and controversial itemized deductions are those taken for purely personal expenses. These deductions result from public policies judged by Congress as sufficiently important to override the general rule prohibiting personal expense deductions. See §262. For instance, an itemized deduction for personal expenses may be enacted to create incentives to engage in conduct considered useful to society (such as the charitable contribution deduction), or it may be intended to provide greater equity in the tax system by adjusting taxable income to reflect one's ability to pay (such as medical expense and personal casualty loss deductions). Other policy considerations are suggested for the following itemized deductions discussed later in this chapter: state and local income taxes, personal property taxes, and interest expense on home mortgages.

The fact that a taxpayer has incurred expenses that qualify as itemized deductions does not guarantee a further reduction in taxable income, however. This is because most taxpayers are entitled to a set amount of deductions (the standard deduction, or SD), regardless of any actual expenses incurred, the amount of which is calculated with reference to filing status, age, vision, and dependency status. See §63(c). Therefore, each taxpayer must make two calculations to determine whether he or she can benefit from itemized deductions. First, the taxpayer must total their permissible itemized deductions. Second, the taxpayer must determine the SD pursuant to §63(c). Only if, and to the extent that, itemized deductions exceed the SD will the taxpayer benefit by a reduction in taxable income.

The SD, therefore, significantly affects the tax-reducing utility of itemized deductions, at least as compared with §62 deductions. AGI (§62) deductions (*above-the-line*) are thus more beneficial in reducing taxes than itemized (§63) deductions (*below-the-line*) precisely because AGI deductions are not limited by the SD while itemized deductions reduce AGI only to the extent they exceed the SD.

The following examples illustrate the distinction between AGI deductions and itemized deductions. Assume that *A*, *B*, and *C* are single taxpayers with a SD of $3,000:

—*A* has gross income of $30,000, $2,500 of AGI deductions, and zero itemized deductions.
—*B* has gross income of $30,000, zero AGI deductions, and $2,500 of itemized deductions.
—*C* has gross income of $30,000, zero AGI deductions, and $3,500 of itemized deductions.

The taxable income of each taxpayer, ignoring the personal exemption, is computed as in Table [8-1]. Taxpayers *A* and *B* present the most striking comparison. Both stand in similar pretax economic situations — each has gross income of $30,000 and deductible expenses totaling $2,500. *A*, however, has a smaller taxable income than *B* because *A* may deduct the full amount ($2,500) of the AGI deductions while also deducting the SD. *B*, on the other hand, may not reduce adjusted gross income by any portion of the $2,500 expenses because *B* has only itemized deductions. Further, since the itemized deductions do not exceed the SD, they do not reduce taxable income either. *C*, on the other hand, has $3,500 of itemized deductions and thus will deduct that amount, but only the amount in excess of the standard deduction ($3,500 of itemized deductions less the SD of $3,000) actually produces a tax benefit.

TABLE [8 - 1]

Taxpayer	A	B	C
Gross income	$30,000	$30,000	$30,000
Less: AGI deductions	2,500	0	0
Adjusted gross income	$27,500	$30,000	$30,000
Less: greater of standard deduction or itemized deductions	3,000	3,000	3,500
Taxable income	$24,500	$27,000	$26,500

The business-personal continuum presented in Chapter 6 provides a useful framework within which to analyze the concepts of the SD, itemized deductions, and AGI deductions. In Chapter 6, the continuum primarily served to illustrate the overall structure of the Code concerning deductible and nondeductible items. In general, expenses incurred in a trade or business are deductible, while personal expenses are not. In the present context, the continuum is more refined and serves to illustrate the decreasing degree of tax-reducing utility as one moves from business to personal expenses. Although the continuum presented in Table [8-2] is an oversimplification, it illustrates the foundations of the deduction system and the role of itemized deductions therein.

TABLE [8 - 2]

Category of Activity	Code Section	Deductible vs. Nondeductible	Utility in Reducing Tax Liability
Business	§162	Most items deductible	AGI above-the-line deductions for employers; few AGI deductions for employees
Profit oriented (e.g., investment)	§212	Most items deductible	Only rental and royalty producing activities are AGI deductions; other §212 expenses are itemized below-the-line deductions
Hobby activities	§183	Items deductible only to the extent of income from the activity	Generally itemized below-the-line deductions
Personal	§262	Items not deductible except as otherwise provided in the Code	When a deduction is permitted, most itemized below-the-line deductions. But see §62(a)(10), (15), (17), and (18)

B.   INVESTMENT ACTIVITY

1.   *Production of Income Expenses*

Code: §212
Regulations: §1.212-1

Subsections 212(1) and (2) permit individuals to deduct ordinary and necessary expenses incurred during the taxable year for the production or collection of income or for the management, conservation, or maintenance of property held for the production of income. Subsections 212(1) and (2), which serve as a bridge between deductible business expenses and generally nondeductible personal expenses, grant a deduction for expenses that do not arise in a §162 trade or business but that do arise in the "production of income." In addition, §212(3) permits a deduction for all ordinary and necessary expenses paid or incurred during the taxable year in connection with the determination, collection, or refund of any tax. Subsection (3) differs from §212(1) and (2) because a profit-oriented activity is not required.

Historically, the need for §212 arose after the Supreme Court's decision in Higgins v. Commissioner, 312 U.S. 212 (1941). In *Higgins*, the taxpayer was denied a deduction for the expenses, including salaries and rent, incurred in managing and trading investment securities. The Supreme Court concluded that the investment activity did not rise to the level of a trade or business, and given the absence of that essential prerequisite to §162, a deduction for the investment-related expenses was denied. In response to *Higgins*, Congress enacted the precursor to §212, thereby establishing an element of parity between ordinary and necessary expenses incurred in the production of income and expenses incurred in the conduct of a trade or business. Consequently, individuals in a trade or business and individuals in nonbusiness but profit-related activities generally receive similar tax treatment—their income tax liability is based on net, rather than gross, income.

The statutory analysis of §212 parallels that of §162. Indeed, as one court has stated, to "qualify as a deduction under section 212 . . . [the taxpayer] must satisfy the same requirements that apply to a trade or business expense under section 162 except that the person claiming the deduction need not be in the trade or business." Snyder v. United States, 674 F.2d 1359, 1364 (10th Cir. 1982). In *Snyder*, the taxpayer, a practicing attorney, committed time, effort, and money to the preparation of a book of photographs of the Colorado high country. His photographic efforts, as well as his efforts to find a publisher, resulted in substantial expenses, which he claimed as deductions. By stating that "the same requirements . . . apply," the *Snyder* court alluded to the ordinary and necessary phrase used in both §§212 and 162 and to the requirement that the deduction be an "expense" as opposed to a nondeductible capital expenditure. Both §§162 and 212 also require expenses to be nonpersonal and reasonable in amount. Thus, the primary distinction between §212(1) and (2) deductions and §162 deductions relates to the meaning of "for the production or collection of income" and "for the management, conservation, or maintenance of property held for the production of income."

Mechanically, §212 differs from §162 in that §212 expenses generally are itemized deductions, while §162 expenses generally are AGI deductions. Section 212 expenses attributable to property held for the production of rents and royalties represent the sole exception. See §62(a)(4). In Skoglund v. United States, 230 Ct. Cl. 833 (Ct. Cl. 1982), the taxpayer challenged the general rule that §212 expenses are itemized deductions by arguing that it was "discriminatory to allow businesses, but not individuals, to adjust gross income by deducting interest expenses." The court summarily dismissed the argument, focusing instead on the literal provisions of the Code and noting their failure to remedy the plaintiff's plight.

2. Personal versus Investment Expense

The primary issue confronted in determining the deductibility of an expense under §212(1) and (2) is whether the expense is personal or investment related. Many taxpayers attempt to deduct personal expenses by tying them to investment-related activities. The following Revenue Ruling (although codified in 1986, as discussed below) is instructive because it analyzes the relationships between §§162, 212, and 262 and states the Service's position regarding personal expenses incurred in an investment setting.

REV. RUL. 84-113
1984-2 C.B. 60

ISSUE

Are travel expenses incurred by an investor in attending an investment seminar deductible under section 212 of the Internal Revenue Code under the circumstances described below?

FACTS

A, an individual, owns corporate stocks and bonds valued at $50,000. During the taxable year, *A* traveled to a resort area in the United States for seven days. The object of the trip was to combine travel to the resort area with a two-hour investment seminar on the second and third day of the trip conducted by investment specialists employed by a national brokerage firm. The seminars pertained to many of the stocks and bonds which the taxpayers held for investment. *A* signed attendance forms at each seminar.

A made arrangements for the trip through a travel agency and paid a single fee that covered transportation, hotel and meals. No part of the cost of the package was specifically allocated to the seminars.

LAW AND ANALYSIS

Section 212 of the Code allows an individual a deduction for all the ordinary and necessary expenses paid or incurred during the taxable year for the production or collection of income or for the management, conservation, or maintenance of property held for the production of income.

Section 1.212-1(d) of the Income Tax Regulations states that expenses that are deductible under section 212 of the Code must be "ordinary and necessary." Thus, they must be reasonable in amount and must bear a reasonable and proximate relation to the production or collection of taxable income or to the management, conservation, or maintenance of property held for the production of income.

Section 1.212-1(g) of the regulations states that fees for services of investment counsel, custodial fees, clerical help, office rent, and similar expenses paid or incurred by a taxpayer in connection with investments held by the taxpayer are deductible under section 212 of the Code only if (1) they are paid or incurred by the taxpayer for the production or collection of income or for the management, conservation, or maintenance of investments held by the taxpayer for the production of income; and (2) they are ordinary and necessary under all the circumstances, having regard to the type of investment and to the relation of the taxpayer to the investment.

Section 262 of the Code provides that no deduction will be allowed for personal, living, or family expenses unless otherwise expressly provided.

The regulations under section 212 of the Code do not address the issue of deductibility of travel expenses. However, the regulations under section 162, an analogous Code section, provide guidelines for the deduction of travel expenses incurred in carrying on a trade or business. The principles enunciated in these regulations are equally applicable to section 212, except that the production of income requirement is substituted for the business requirement.

Section 1.162-2(a) of the regulations provides that only the traveling expenses that are reasonable and necessary in the conduct of the taxpayer's business and directly attributable to it may be deducted. If the trip is undertaken for other than business purposes, the travel fares and expenses incident to travel are personal expenses and the meals and lodging are living expenses.

Under section 1.162-2(b)(1) of the regulations, if a taxpayer travels to a destination, and while at the destination engages in both business and personal activities, traveling expenses to and from the destination are deductible only if the trip is related primarily to the taxpayer's trade or business. If the trip is primarily personal in nature, the traveling expenses to and from the destination are not deductible even though the taxpayer engages in business activities while at the destination. However, expenses while at the destination that are properly allocable to the taxpayer's trade or business are deductible even though the traveling expenses to and from the destination are not deductible.

Section 1.162-2(b)(2) of the regulations provides that whether a trip is related primarily to the taxpayer's trade or business or is primarily personal in nature depends upon the facts and circumstances in each case. The amount of time during the period of the trip that is spent on personal activities compared to the amount of time spent on activities directly relating to the taxpayer's trade or business is an important factor in determining whether the trip is primarily personal.

Rev. Rul. 74-292, 1974-1 C.B. 43, holds that travel expenses incurred by a doctor on a trip that combined vacation travel abroad with attendance at brief professional seminars in each of the countries visited are not deductible business expenses under section 162 of the Code. That Revenue Ruling concludes that the taxpayer's participation in some incidental activity related to the taxpayer's trade or business will not convert what otherwise was a vacation trip into a business trip. See Rev. Rul. 84-55, 1984-1 C.B. 29, which reaches a similar conclusion regarding a taxpayer attending five brief sessions of a university sponsored, education-oriented conference in a foreign country on a trip that lasted less than one week; and Rev. Rul. 79-425, 1979-2 C.B. 81, which reaches a similar conclusion regarding a taxpayer attending six brief sessions of a ten-day annual convention of a local professional association held in a foreign country.

Here, the facts disclose that (1) the time spent on investment activities was insubstantial in comparison to the time spent for personal activities, (2) the expenses incurred for travel were not primarily related to A's investment activities, and (3) none of A's other expenses were shown to be specifically allocable to the management of A's investments. Without specifically allocating and substantiating any expenses incurred with respect to the investment seminars A attended, A's participation in such incidental investment activity, although related to A's current investments, does not result in a deduction under section 212 of the Code.

Holding

The costs of A's trip are not deductible under section 212 of the Code, but rather are nondeductible personal or living expenses under section 262.

Note

The result in Revenue Ruling 84-113 was codified in 1986 by the enactment of §274(h)(7).

The committee is concerned about deductions claimed for travel and other costs of attending conventions or other meetings that relate to financial or tax planning of investors, rather than to a trade or business of the taxpayer. For example, individuals claim deductions for attending seminars about investments in securities or tax shelters. In many cases, these seminars are held in locations (including some that are overseas) that are attractive for vacation purposes, and are structured so as to permit extensive leisure activities on the part of attendees.

Since investment purposes do not relate to the taxpayer's means of earning a livelihood (i.e., a trade or business), the committee believes that these abuses, along with the personal consumption issue that arises with respect to any deduction for personal living expenses, justify denial of any deduction for the costs of attending a nonbusiness seminar or similar meeting that does not relate to a trade or business of the taxpayer. However, this disallowance rule does not apply to expenses incurred by a taxpayer in attending a convention, seminar, sales meeting, or similar meeting relating to the trade or business of the taxpayer. . . .

Under the bill, no deduction is allowed for expenses related to attending a convention, seminar, or similar meeting unless such expenses are deductible under section 162 as ordinary and necessary expenses of carrying on a trade or business. Thus, the bill disallows deductions for expenses of attending a convention, etc. where the expenses, but for the provision in the bill, would be deductible under section 212 (relating to expenses of producing income) rather than section 162. The expenses to which the provision relates typically include such items as travel to the site of such a convention, fees for attending the convention, and personal living expenses, such as meals, lodging, and local travel, that are incurred while attending the convention or other meeting. This disallowance rule does not apply to expenses incurred by a taxpayer in attending a convention, seminar, sales meeting, or similar meeting relating to the trade or business of the taxpayer.

S. Rep. No. 313, 99th Cong., 2d Sess. 70 (1986).

Several Tax Court cases provide additional insight into the personal expense versus investment-related activity issue. In Kinney v. Commissioner, 66 T.C. 122 (1976), the taxpayer was a stock market investor who visited outlets and dealerships of the corporations whose stock he owned. Numerous trips were made throughout the United States and Europe, usually to areas in which the taxpayer's relatives resided. The taxpayer's expenses were not ordinary and necessary because the court was not "convinced that the related expenses were customary or normal for an investor in stocks and commodities." Id. at 126. Moreover, the taxpayer did not show that the trips had any "direct effect on any particular stock transaction." Id.

In Walters v. Commissioner, 28 T.C.M. 22 (1969), another stock market investor was denied travel expense deductions (for gas, meals, and so forth) for trips during his lunch hour to various stock brokerage offices to observe the ticker tape to get a "feel for the market." The court stated:

> To a degree petitioner's actions impress us as smacking of personal interest, entertainment or curiosity. Thus, . . . we conclude that the trips were neither "ordinary" in the sense that they can be treated as normal or customary, nor "necessary" in the sense that they have been shown to be appropriate and helpful to petitioner in the production of income. The linchpin between the transportation expenses and the production of income is missing. In this context we regard such expenditures as too remote or too attenuated to be classified as "ordinary and necessary" expenses within the purview of section 212.

Id. at 25. Subsequent to the enactment of §274(h)(7), the Tax Court closely policed the line between personal and investment-related activities. For example, in Connelly v. Commissioner, T.C. Memo 1994-436, the Tax Court disallowed expenses incurred by a plastic surgeon for trips to Bermuda and London, in part because the trips were, at most, general fact-finding trips rather than trips directly related to income-producing activities, and thus not deductible under *Kinney* and *Walters*.

3. *Capital Expenditure Limitation*

Although the coextensive nature of §§162 and 212 is less than certain, the §263 capital expenditure limitation appears appropriately integrated into §212, given that section's usage of the word "expense." If this were not the case, investment-related capital expenditures would be more favorably treated than business-related expenditures. To this end, Regulation §1.212-1(k) provides that expenses "paid or incurred in defending or perfecting title to property, in recovering property . . . or in developing or improving property constitute a part of the cost of the property and are not deductible expenses." At times, however, the distinction between §212 deductible expenses and §263 capitalized expenditures can be difficult to discern.

REV. RUL. 86-71
1986-1 C.B. 102

ISSUE

If a taxpayer pays a person to prepare an application for a Common Carrier Radio Station Construction Permit and License from the Federal Communications Commission (F.C.C.), is the payment deductible as an expense under section 212 of the Internal Revenue Code in the circumstances described below?

FACTS

In November 1984, taxpayer A, an individual not otherwise involved in the telecommunications industry, signed a contract with X, a corporation engaged in the business of providing engineering, economic, and financial planning in the telecommunications industry. Under the agreement, X prepared and filed a Common Carrier Radio Station Application on behalf of A in December 1984. The application is guaranteed to satisfy the filing requirements of the F.C.C., although no assurance is provided that the application will be granted. The application is for participation in the F.C.C.'s random selection program to award licenses to operate cellular radio systems. If granted, the license covers a period greater than one year. The F.C.C. procedures did not permit an award of a license in 1984 for the geographic area that A's application covers, and A's application was not, in fact, acted upon in 1984. X charged a fee of $30x$ dollars for its services. A paid the fee in cash in November 1984.

LAW AND ANALYSIS

Section 212 of the Code provides that an individual shall be allowed a deduction for all ordinary and necessary expenses paid or incurred for the production or collection of income, and for the management, conservation, or maintenance of property held for the production of income. Under section 211, these deductions are limited by exceptions provided by sections 261 through 280G. One of these exceptions, contained in section 263 and sections 1.263(a)-1 and 1.263(a)-2 of the Income Tax Regulations, provides that no deduction shall be allowed for capital expenditures. In addition, section 1.212-1(n) of the regulations provides that no deduction is allowed under section 212 for a capital expenditure.

The costs of obtaining a license to operate a cellular radio-telephone system with a useful life greater than one year are costs of obtaining a capital asset and are not currently deductible as ordinary and necessary expenses for the production of income. See Dustin v. Commissioner, 53 T.C. 491 (1969), affd., 467 F.2d 47 (9th Cir. 1972); KWTX Broadcasting Co., Inc. v. Commissioner, 31 T.C. 803 (1959). See also Rev. Rul. 56-520, 1956-2 C.B. 170.

In the present situation, the fee paid by *A* is to file an application to acquire an operating license, with a useful life greater than one year, that *A* may obtain at some indefinite future date. Accordingly, the expense is related to the cost of acquiring a capital asset, and pursuant to section 263 of the Code and sections 1.263(a)-1, 1.263(a)-2 and 1.212-1(n) of the regulations, *A* is not entitled to deduct the fee paid to *X* under section 212. See Central Texas Savings & Loan Association v. United States, 731 F.2d 1181 (5th Cir. 1984). . . .

HOLDING

The fee paid by *A* to *X* in 1984 is a capital expenditure within the scope of section 263, and thus is not deductible as expense under section 212 of the Code.

Note on Legal Expenses and Pre-opening Costs

It has generally been assumed that the start-up or pre-opening expense limitations of §162 (discussed in Chapter 6) extend to §212. This doctrine denies a deduction for any expenses incurred prior to the commencement of a trade or business because they are pre-opening expenses, which, in theory, should be capitalized. Richmond Television Corp. v. United States, 345 F.2d 901 (4th Cir. 1965), vacated on other grounds, 382 U.S. 68 (1965). In Weinstein v. United States, 420 F.2d 700 (Ct. Cl. 1970), the taxpayers traveled extensively in seeking, inspecting, and evaluating prospective investments. The Court of Claims denied deductions for the attendant expenses, concluding that §212 prohibits expenses incurred in connection "with searching for or acquiring new investments." Id. at 701. It noted that a "proprietary or possessory type interest in the income producing asset" is a prerequisite to deductibility. Id. at 702. See also §195, which requires the capitalization of pre-opening and start-up costs attributable to §212 production of income activities leading to an active trade or business.

In discussing the deductibility of legal expenses, it was noted in Chapter 6 that the courts consider whether the "origin of the claim" was business or personal in nature. For example, in the leading case, United States v. Gilmore, 372 U.S. 39 (1963), the Supreme Court held that the husband's legal expenses were not deductible as business expenses, even though the husband clearly was protecting his business interests, because the origin of the claim, a divorce proceeding, was personal in nature. Therefore, in most divorce proceedings, legal expenses have not been deductible.

Regulation §1.262-1(b)(7), however, provides a limited exception to the general rule:

> Generally, attorney's fees and other costs paid in connection with a divorce, separation, or decree for support are not deductible by either the husband or the wife. However, the part of an attorney's fee and the part of the other costs paid in

connection with a divorce, legal separation, written separation agreement, or a decree for support, which are properly attributable to the production or collection of amounts includible in gross income under section 71 are deductible . . . under section 212.

Based on this regulation, the Tax Court in Wild v. Commissioner, 42 T.C. 706 (1964), held that legal expenses in a divorce action were deductible because the expenses related to the taxpayer's claim for alimony payments, which are includable in income under §71. Both the regulation and *Wild* are consistent with the concept of allowing taxpayers to offset their total income by the expenses directly related to producing that income.

Legal fees also may be deductible under §212(3) even if the underlying claim is personal in nature. This exception to the origin of the claim rule is described in Revenue Ruling 72-545, 1972-2 C.B. 179, which considered three fact patterns relating to §212(3) and explained the deductibility of the tax and divorce-related legal fees.

The first situation addressed by Revenue Ruling 72-545 considered a taxpayer who paid a law firm, with a practice limited to tax matters, for tax advice concerning a proposed property settlement. Situation two described a taxpayer who paid a law firm for advice concerning the tax consequences of establishing a trust to discharge his support responsibilities. The firm also handled the nontax aspects of the divorce, but the tax matters were handled exclusively by the firm's tax department. The firm allocated the taxpayer's bill between tax- and nontax-related services based "upon the time required, the difficulty of the tax questions presented, and the amount of taxes involved." Situation three was similar to situation two except that one attorney handled all matters. In the third case, the billing statement allocated the fee between tax and nontax matters based on "the amount of the attorney's time attributable to each, the fee customarily charged in the locality for similar services, and the results obtained in the divorce negotiations."

The Service ruled that the expenses related to tax advice in all three situations were deductible under §212(3) and Regulation §1.212-1(*l*). The Service noted that, even though Regulation §1.262-1(b)(7) provides that attorney's fees relating to "divorce, separation, or decree for support" are not deductible; if legal expenses relate "solely to tax counsel" and are "properly allocated and substantiated," they are deductible under §212(3). Reg. §1.212-1(*l*).

Even when the taxpayer is not allowed to deduct legal fees under §212(1), (2), or (3), a tax benefit still may be derived. For example, after the husband's defeat on the deduction issue in *Gilmore*, he filed a second action in the District Court, claiming that the legal expenses were related to defending his title to property and therefore should be included in the basis of his property regardless of the origin of the claim. Gilmore v. United States, 245 F. Supp. 383 (N.D. Cal. 1965). Gilmore was rewarded for his persistence. The court held that the expenses were properly included in the basis of the property and noted that the previous Supreme Court decision never intimated "that the origin of the litigation in which attorney's fees were expended — whether 'personal' or 'business' — was relevant to a determination that the fees were a 'capital expenditure.'" Id. at 384. The court noted that

[i]t is a rule virtually as old as the federal income tax itself that costs incurred in defending or perfecting taxpayer's claim to ownership of capital assets are capital

expenditures, and not expenses deductible from ordinary income. *The rule is equally applicable to business and nonbusiness activity;* . . .

The gist of the controversy between taxpayer and the managing officers in the state court litigation was the ownership of the stock. . . . Since perfection of taxpayer's claim to ownership was the essence of the suit, the costs of the litigation were capital expenditures and, . . . were not expenses deductible from ordinary income. *Taxpayer is not denied tax credit for these disbursements: as the Tax Court held, they are added to taxpayer's basis in the stock, thus receiving the same tax treatment as the property itself.*

(Emphasis in original.) Id. at 383. Apparently, the only issue regarding the capitalization of legal expenses becomes "whether the defense of title to property was the matter for which the expenditures were made." Id. at 384. In this regard, a reasonable basis for apportioning the expenses is necessary to distinguish between capital and noncapital legal expenditures.

Problems

8-1.   Evelyn Maas, a retired widow who lived in Pensacola, Florida, owned ten shares of AT&T stock, which was trading at $40 per share during May. The annual meeting of AT&T stockholders was scheduled for June 18 in Honolulu, Hawaii. Maas attended the meeting and voted her shares on each issue considered. Her total expenses for the trip were $650 airfare, $150 hotel bill (three days, two nights), $143 for meals, and $18 for taxi fares.
   a.   What amounts, if any, are deductible?
   b.   Would it make a difference if Maas had traveled to Hawaii many times in the past, the sole purpose of this trip was to attend the stockholder meeting, and she did not leave her hotel for anything but the meetings?
   c.   What if she owned 100 shares? 1,000 shares?

8-2.   What result if Mary Jones spends $5,000 for attorney's fees in her divorce proceeding against her husband and:
   a.   She won her claim for alimony of $10,000 per year for ten years or until her death or remarriage?
   b.   She lost her claim for alimony?
   c.   She was awarded a property settlement of $50,000 but no alimony?
   d.   She won her claim for alimony of $10,000 per year for three years?

C.   HOBBY LOSSES

   Code: §183
   Regulations: §§1.183-1(a), (b)(1), (2); 1.183-2

A common ploy used to convert nondeductible personal expenses into deductions is to characterize personal hobbies as business or investment activities. If successful, this characterization would allow the taxpayer to deduct, as §162 business or §212 investment expenses, costs incurred in connection with an otherwise nondeductible personal activity. To combat this abuse, Congress enacted §183 (the hobby loss section), which limits deductions for activities that are "not engaged in for profit."

The general rule of §183(a) provides that deductions for expenses incurred in activities not engaged in for profit will be allowed only as provided for in §183(b). Section 183(b) allows deductions in two general areas: (1) deductions that would be allowable, regardless of whether the activity is engaged in for profit; and (2) deductions that would be allowable were the activity engaged in for profit, but only to the extent that gross income from the activity exceeds the deductions allowed in (1) above. Section 183 thus attempts to prohibit the taxpayer from taking deductions in excess of income from the personal activity, thereby preventing the utilization of a personal hobby as a loss-creating activity offsetting income from other sources. If the activity is engaged in for profit, then §183 will not apply.

1. Mechanics

Section 183 both grants and limits deductions. It grants deductions because expenses that do not otherwise qualify under §§162 and 212 may be deducted to the extent of income from the activity, if any, in accordance with §183(b). It limits deductions to the gross income attributable to the activity.

In order to apply the §183 deduction limitations, all expenses relating to the activity must be divided into three categories. The first category includes items that are deductible "without regard to whether the activity . . . was engaged in for profit." Reg. §1.183-1(b)(1)(i). The primary expenses in this category are interest and taxes, to the extent they are deductible under §§163 and 164. See discussion at subsections D2 and D3 of this chapter. The expenses in this category are the exceptions to the general rule that §183 limits expenses to the amount of income produced. Even if these expenses exceed the income produced, they are fully deductible.

The second category of expenses includes all expenses that do not fall into the first category and that do not "result in an adjustment to the basis of property. . . ." Reg. §1.183-1(b)(1)(ii). Such expenses include maintenance, utilities, travel expenses, and other similar expenses. The expenses in this category are allowed to the extent that gross income from the activity exceeds the deductions allowed in the first category.

The third category of expenses includes items that require "an adjustment to the basis," such as depreciation and amortization. Reg. §1.183-1(b)(1)(iii). Expenses in the third category are allowed only if the expenses in categories 1 and 2 are less than the total income produced. The expenses in each of the three categories are calculated first as if the activity giving rise to the deductions were engaged in for profit, and then they are limited by the income in the above-mentioned order.

For example, assume that a taxpayer, involved in horse-breeding as a hobby, incurs the following expenses: (1) state income taxes totaling $5,000 (category 1); (2) repair, traveling, feeding, and grooming expenses totaling $7,000 (category 2); and (3) depreciation of vehicles and stables totaling $10,000 (category 3). If the total income derived from the hobby is $3,000, only category 1 expenses are deductible ($5,000), and they are deductible in full.

If the total income is $11,000, the following expenses are allowed.

Gross income	$11,000
Category 1	5,000
	$ 6,000
Category 2	6,000
Net income	$ 0

The $1,000 of the category 2 expenses and all category 3 expenses are disallowed.

If gross income from the activity is $15,000, the following expenses are allowed.

Gross income	$15,000
Category 1	5,000
	$10,000
Category 2	7,000
	$ 3,000
Category 3	3,000
Net income	$ 0

In this example, only the category 3 expenses are limited. If the category 3 expenses relating to basis adjustments are limited, the taxpayer's basis is reduced only by the amounts actually allowed because the Code requires a taxpayer to take depreciation "allowed or allowable." See §1016(a)(2). In the above examples, a $10,000 depreciation deduction was allowable in each instance, but only the amount allowed enters into adjusted basis calculations. Finally, if there is more than one asset in category 3, the deduction allowed should be allocated among the assets on a proportionate basis to determine the adjusted basis of each item. Reg. §1.183-1(b)(2).

2. *Profit Motive Defined*

The key to the operation of §183 is the determination of whether an activity is engaged in for profit. Section 183(c) defines an activity *not* engaged in for profit as "any activity other than one with respect to which deductions are allowable . . . under §162 or . . . §212." The main issue evolving from this definition is whether the taxpayer has a profit motive. The test to determine profit motive is an "all facts and circumstances" inquiry — an attempt to ascertain by objective factors whether the taxpayer had the objective of making a profit.

Regulation §1.183-2(b) lists nine nonexclusive factors that should be considered when assessing the taxpayer's motive for carrying on an activity. Each of the factors is discussed briefly below.

The first factor is the manner in which the taxpayer carries on the activity. If the taxpayer conducts the activity in a businesslike manner or in a manner similar to other profitable activities of the same nature, there is an indication of profit motive. Maintenance of businesslike records and segregation of funds from other activities may be evidence of a profit motive. Attempts to cut costs by changing methods of operation or operating in a less than extravagant manner also may indicate a profit motive. Conversely, offering goods or services at less than fair-market value may indicate the lack of a profit motive.

The second factor is the expertise of the taxpayer or the taxpayer's advisors. The taxpayer's personal knowledge, willingness to become better informed or keep up-to-date, and willingness to procure and follow expert advice are all relevant. For example, in Cox v. Commissioner, T.C. Memo 1982-667, the taxpayer opened a business as a gunsmith, although he had no experience in the trade. His efforts to educate himself in the gun business, coupled with his keeping well organized and complete records, convinced the court that he had a profit motive.

The third factor is the time and effort expended by the taxpayer in carrying on the activity. Regulation §1.183-2(b)(3) indicates that the fact that the taxpayer devotes a substantial amount of time to the activity or employs competent persons to work in the activity evidences a profit motive.

The fourth factor is the expectation that assets used in the activity may appreciate in value. Even if the activity has operating losses for several consecutive years, an expectation that there will be an overall profit when appreciation is realized may indicate a profit motive. For example, operating and repair expenses incurred in renovating a home with the intention of selling it for a profit have been held to be deductible. The expectation of appreciation argument has not been limited to real estate. In Wagner v. Commissioner, T.C. Memo 1983-606, a songwriter, who incurred expenses in copyrighting his songs and hiring a singer to promote them, was able to deduct his expenses because the taxpayer expected to receive substantial profits from royalties when the singer in whom he had invested became successful.

The fifth factor is the success of the taxpayer in carrying on other similar or dissimilar activities. If the taxpayer has successfully operated similar activities, there is a greater likelihood that a profit motive will be found. Methods of operation, relative risks, and profit potentials between the activities will be compared.

The sixth factor is the taxpayer's history of profit or loss with respect to the activity. Although numerous consecutive loss years indicate the lack of a profit motive, it is generally understood that losses are likely to occur in the initial stages of operations. On the other hand, losses that continue beyond the period that customarily is necessary to bring the operation to profitable status strongly indicate a lack of profit motive, unless the losses are shown to be due either to circumstances beyond the taxpayer's control or to business risks.

The seventh factor is the amount of occasional profits, if any, that are earned. In this regard, the amount of any profits should be compared to the amount of losses. Courts, however, sometimes overlook the relative size of the profits and losses where any profits are earned, regardless of the amount. The Regulation also indicates that an occasional substantial profit or "an opportunity to earn a substantial ultimate profit in a highly speculative venture" may indicate that an activity is engaged in for profit, despite recurring losses or small profits.

The eighth factor considered is the financial status of the taxpayer. The Regulation provides that if the taxpayer "does not have substantial income or capital from sources other than the activity, [it] may indicate that the activity is engaged in for profit."

The ninth factor addresses the elements of personal pleasure or recreation. Although deriving personal pleasure or recreation from the activity will not indicate conclusively that the taxpayer lacks a profit motive, personal pleasure or recreation, coupled with recurring losses, indicates the lack of a profit motive. The Regulation also notes that profit motive does not have to be the "exclusive intention," nor does the intent to "maximize profit" have to be the exclusive motivation. Proof of intent to derive profit will suffice, even if personal pleasure or recreation are involved. "[S]uffering has never been made a prerequisite to deductibility." Jackson v. Commissioner, 59 T.C. 312, 317 (1973).

These nine factors are not the only factors used to determine profit motive. Other factors evidencing an honest and good-faith objective to make a profit will be considered. Additionally, the taxpayer may be entitled to a statutory presumption that a profit motive is present.

Recognizing that many profit-motivated activities have loss years, Congress provided in §183(d) that a showing of gross income in excess of deductions for three of five consecutive years of operation (two of seven for horse racing activities) creates a *presumption* that the activity is engaged in for profit. This presumption, however, is rebuttable.

As the following cases indicate, courts sometimes confuse the level of profit motive required to overcome §183(a).

DREICER v. COMMISSIONER
665 F.2d 1292 (D.C. Cir. 1981)

Robinson, C.J.

Maurice C. Dreicer appeals from a decision . . . disallowing deductions . . . for losses incurred assertedly in professional endeavors as a multimedia personality. . . .

By virtue of Section 162, a taxpayer may deduct from gross income all ordinary and necessary expenses incurred in a business, and, under Section 212, in the production or collection of income. A corollary rule, embodied in Section 165, permits deduction of losses sustained in a trade or business, or in a transaction entered into for profit. Section 183 qualifies these provisions by specifically disallowing, with limited exceptions not relevant here, deductions attributable to activities "not engaged in for profit." Thus, a taxpayer claiming a deduction under Sections 162 or 212 for an expense, or under Section 165 for a loss, must be prepared to demonstrate an associated profit motive in order to avoid the ban of Section 183. Appraising the facts salient in Dreicer's instance, which we need only summarize, the Tax Court held that he did not.

Dreicer, a citizen of the United States, maintains his residence in the Canary Islands, Spain, and engages heavily in global travel. He derives a substantial income as beneficiary of a family trust, and in the early 1950's, Dreicer began to focus his professional attention on the fields of tourism and dining. In 1955, he published The Diner's Companion, a compilation of his opinions on dining and on various restaurants throughout the world, but the book was a commercial failure.

Undaunted, Dreicer conceived the idea of some day writing another book, this one to enshrine his reminiscence on a life dedicated to epicurism and travel. In preparation for this sybaritic swan song, he spent the next twenty years traveling about the world, staying in some of the finest hotels and dining in some of the best restaurants. The material he gathered was also to be utilized in lectures before travel organizations and public appearances on radio and television. By the mid-1970s, Dreicer had completed a rough draft of the second book — parts of which originally had appeared in The Diner's Companion — and titled it My 27 Year Search for the Perfect Steak — Still Looking. Two publishing houses to which he submitted the manuscript, however, returned it, and seemingly he abandoned all hope of publishing.

When Dreicer filed his federal income tax returns for 1972 and 1973, he claimed deductible losses of $21,795.76 and $28,022.05, respectively, for travel and other related business expenses. The Commissioner of Internal Revenue thereafter issued a notice of deficiency, disallowing the deductions on the ground that the losses arose from activities not pursued for profit, and the Tax Court agreed. The court disputed Dreicer's characterization of his professional self as a multimedia personality, finding instead that he was a writer-lecturer on tourism and dining. Having so defined his activity for Section 183 analysis, the court concluded that he had not entertained a bona fide expectation of profit from writing and lecturing, and on that account denied the deductions. . . .

Dreicer also argues that even if the activity for which he claims deductions was no more than writing and lecturing, the Tax Court applied the wrong legal standard in determining whether he engaged in it for profit, as defined by Section 183, because the court predicated its result on his profit *expectation* rather than to his profit *objective*. We agree. . . .

Section 183 was adopted as part of the Tax Reform Act of 1969 to replace for taxable years beginning after December 31, 1969, the so-called "hobby loss" provision of former Section 270. . . . The Conference Committee, noting that "[i]n lieu of the test of 'a reasonable expectation of profit' the Senate amendment substitutes the test of 'not engaged in for profit,'" adopted the Senate version, and in that form the legislation ultimately passed both Houses. Section 183 thus emerged as the product of a congressional purpose to pivot its operation, not on whether the taxpayer *expected* a profit, but instead on whether the taxpayer engaged in the activity with the *objective* of making a profit.

The language of both Section 183 and the Treasury regulations implementing it is faithful to this legislative intent. The statutory text bars deductibility of losses emanating from "activities not engaged in for profit," not activities lacking an expectation of profit. The regulation provides relevantly:

> The determination whether an activity is engaged in for profit is to be made by reference to objective standards, taking into account all of the facts and circumstances of each case. Although *a reasonable expectation of profit is not required*, the facts and circumstances must indicate that the taxpayer entered into the activity or continued the activity *with the objective of making a profit*. . . .

In the case at bar, the Tax Court conceded that a taxpayer need not show an expectation of profit that could be deemed reasonable. It ruled that Dreicer could not deduct the losses in question because, it said, he did not have "a bona fide expectation" of profit from the action from which those losses arose:

> [T]he record in this case shows beyond a doubt that there was no possibility of [Dreicer] realizing sufficient profit from his writing and lecturing activities to recoup the very large losses sustained in the preceding years, and therefore, we are convinced that, during the years in issue, [Dreicer] could not have had a *bona fide expectation* of realizing a profit from such activities. . . .

By thus hinging its decision on Dreicer's profit expectations instead of his profit objectives, the Tax Court utilized the wrong test. The statute, its legislative history and the implementing Treasury regulation make explicit that the objective, not the expectation, of making a profit is to govern determinations on whether a taxpayer is engaged in a business or a hobby, and the two criteria are not the same. One may embark upon a venture for the sincere purpose of eventually reaping a profit but in the belief that the probability of financial success is small or even remote. He therefore does not really expect a profit, but nonetheless is willing to take the gamble. Under the Tax Court's test of "bona fide expectation of profit," losses incurred in the enterprise could not be deducted. Yet it cannot be gainsaid that "the activity actually is engaged in for profit" — that it was undertaken "with the objective of making a profit." We do not say that Dreicer's case is equivalent; that is for the Tax Court in the first instance, and we intimate no view on the merits. We do say that Dreicer's claims of deductibility are to be evaluated by proper legal standards.

The decision appealed from is accordingly reversed and the case is remanded to the Tax Court for further consideration in light of this opinion.

DREICER v. COMMISSIONER
78 T.C. 642 (1982)

SIMPSON, J.

In Dreicer v. Commissioner, T.C. Memo. 1979-395, we sustained the Commissioner's determination that, based on all of the facts and circumstances of that case, Mr. Dreicer's activities as a writer and lecturer were not engaged in for profit within the meaning of section 183, Internal Revenue Code of 1954. Mr. Dreicer appealed such decision to the Court of Appeals for the District of Columbia Circuit. That court, although it sustained our factual findings, reversed such decision on the ground that we had applied an erroneous legal standard in determining whether Mr. Dreicer's activities were engaged in for profit and remanded the case to us to reconsider our decision in light of what it determined was the correct legal standard under section 183. . . .

In our prior opinion, we stated that the standard for determining whether an individual is carrying on a trade or business so that his expenses are deductible under section 162 is:

> *whether the individual's primary purpose and intention in engaging in the activity is to make a profit. . . . The taxpayer's expectation of profit need not be a reasonable one; it is sufficient if the*

taxpayer has a bona fide expectation of realizing a profit, regardless of the reasonableness of such expectation. . . . The issue of whether a taxpayer engages in an activity *with the requisite intention of making a profit is* one of fact to be resolved on the basis of all the surrounding facts and circumstances of the case . . . and the burden of proving *the requisite intention* is on the petitioner. . . .

We then proceeded to apply such standard to the facts and circumstances of that case, using the relevant factors outlined in section 1.183-2(b). Such factors, which are derived principally from prior case law, include: (1) The manner in which the taxpayer carried on the activity; (2) the expertise of the taxpayer or his advisors; (3) the time and effort expended by the taxpayer in carrying on the activity; (4) the expectation that assets used in the activity may appreciate in value; (5) the success of the taxpayer in carrying on other similar or dissimilar activities; (6) the taxpayer's history of income or loss with respect to the activity; (7) the amount of occasional profit, if any, which is earned; (8) the financial status of the taxpayer; and (9) whether elements of personal pleasure or recreation are involved. Based on such analysis, we concluded that Mr. Dreicer's activities were not engaged in for profit within the meaning of section 183 "since he did not have a bona fide expectation of profit."

On appeal, Mr. Dreicer argued that we had applied an incorrect legal standard, in that we predicated our decision on his profit expectation rather than his profit objective. The Court of Appeals examined the legislative history of section 183 and determined that the proper standard was whether the taxpayer engaged in the activity with the objective of making a profit, not whether he had a reasonable expectation of making a profit. The proper standard was expressed by that court as "when profit is actually and honestly his objective though the prospect of achieving it may seem dim." The Court of Appeals found that rather than focusing our analysis on whether Mr. Dreicer had an objective of making a profit, we focused on whether he had "a bona fide expectation of profit." The court apparently feared that we were equating *a bona fide expectation of profit* with *a reasonable expectation of profit.* Thus, it held that we had applied an erroneous legal standard in determining whether Mr. Dreicer's activities were engaged in for profit.

The purpose of the standard adopted by the Court of Appeals is to allow deductions where the evidence indicates that the activity is actually engaged in for profit even though it might be argued that there is not a reasonable expectation of profit. We are in total agreement with the Court of Appeals that this is the proper legal standard under section 183. However, a taxpayer's declaration of his motive to make a profit is not controlling. His motive is the ultimate question; yet, it must be determined by a careful analysis of all the surrounding objective facts, and greater weight is given to such facts than to his mere statement of intent. Thus, although a reasonable expectation of profit is not required, the facts and circumstances must indicate that the taxpayer entered into the activity, or continued the activity, with the actual and honest objective of making a profit.

Although the courts sometimes use different language to describe the test, the courts have universally sought to ascertain the taxpayer's true intent. For example, in Blake v. Commissioner, T.C. Memo. 1981-579, we used the terms "bona fide expectation of realizing a profit," "profit motive or objective," "view toward realization of a profit," and "profit oriented venture" to refer to the same thought, namely, an *objective* of making a profit. It was in this sense that we used the term "bona fide expectation of profit" in our prior opinion, and we intended that such language have the same meaning as an actual and honest profit objective. Nevertheless, in view of the difficulties generated by our use of such language, which resulted in the remand by the Court of Appeals, we have undertaken to re-examine the record with a view to determining whether the required actual and honest profit objective was present in this case.

Mr. Dreicer would have us find that he was like the wildcat driller or the inventor, continuing his endeavors in the face of adverse results in the hope of one day reaping a large profit. However, such statement of intent is not supported by the objective facts of this case. For many years, he sustained large losses; there was no realistic possibility that he could ever earn sufficient income from his activity to offset such losses; he was able to continue to bear such losses only because of his large resources; a review of the entire record fails to convince us that Mr. Dreicer conducted his activities in a businesslike manner calculated to earn a profit. Rather, there is a strong indication that he enjoyed his life of travel. In conclusion, we find and hold that Mr. Dreicer failed to meet his burden of proving that in carrying on his activity as a writer and lecturer, he had an actual and honest objective of making a profit. . . .

[Judgment for respondent.]

Problems

8-3.   After years of saving money to see her through the initial months of her new vocation, Joanna Clark quit her job to pursue a career as a potter. First, she built an addition onto her house to serve as a workshop. The cost was $14,000. Thereafter, Clark spent $5,000 on a kiln. Finally, she purchased clay, paint, and enamel for $2,000. Clark wishes to deduct the expense of her workshop, kiln, and materials. Which sections of the Code apply—§§162, 168, 183, 212, 262, or 263—and what deductions, if any, are available?

8-4.   Alexander Hendricks is a 55-year-old retired chiropractor. Until this year, he had engaged in his practice on a full-time basis. He had always intended to retire at age 55 so that he and his wife could move to their 600-acre farm in Colorado—their lifelong dream. Hendricks had no previous farming experience but had done substantial research into the growing seasons in Colorado and the types of crops that would be most successful. He often asked advice of his two sons, who held bachelor's degrees in agronomy. Because of water supply problems in the area, Hendricks also spent time attending meetings dealing with water allocation and methods of improving the supply. He and his wife planned to live on his substantial retirement savings and whatever profits were derived from the farm.

In the first year, because of the lack of water, Hendricks planted only 20 percent of the land. As a result of the first year's operation, Hendricks reported a loss on his individual income tax return filed jointly with his wife. He claimed the following income and expenses: proceeds from sale of crops, $11,800; interest expense on mortgage, $5,000; depreciation on farm equipment, $8,000; property taxes, $1,500; seed and supplies, $900; repair and maintenance of equipment, $600; and miscellaneous expenses, $350.

a. What factors indicate whether this activity should be considered as engaged in for profit for the purposes of §183?
b. Assuming that §183 applies, how much and what portion, if any, of the expenses are deductible?
c. What result if §183 does not apply?
d. If §183 does apply, what result if interest expense totals $12,000?

3. Vacation Home Rentals

Code: §280A
Regulations: §1.165-9

Under §183, problems arose when the taxpayer attempted to deduct expenses incurred for vacation homes used for personal and rental purposes during the year. The taxpayer had the burden of proving that the rental activity was engaged in for profit or was a trade or business. In many instances, it was difficult to determine (1) whether the home was held primarily for investment (profit motive) or primarily for personal purposes and (2) how to allocate the expenses between the investment and personal use.

For example, assume that a taxpayer purchases a vacation home for three reasons: potential future appreciation, rental possibilities during the periods when the taxpayer would not be using the home, and its appeal as a personal vacation home. The taxpayer rents the vacation home at fair market value to an unrelated third party for nine months each year and uses it for personal purposes for three months each year. The taxpayer obviously has mixed motives. He is producing income from the rental during nine months of the year but also is deriving personal pleasure for three months.

Even if §183 were applied to this hypothetical taxpayer, how would the expenses be allocated between the investment and the personal use? Assuming that rental income exceeds the total expenses for the year, would all expenses for the vacation home be allowed to offset the rental income as allowed under §183? If so, the taxpayer would be, in effect, deducting personal expenses in contravention of §262. If some of the expenses were not allowed, what basis should be used for allocating the expenses? If the vacation home was used every day of the year for either personal or rental purposes, allocation of the expenses, including depreciation, between the two activities could be based on a ratio of the days used to the total days in the year. But what if there were days during which the property was not used by anyone? How should those days be treated for allocation purposes? Section 183 does not provide a method for allocating such expenses; it merely provides a method for limiting all expenses relating to a hobby or not-for-profit activity. Because of the popularity of renting vacation homes and the difficulty in applying the all-or-nothing profit motive analysis of §183, Congress enacted §280A specifically to deal with the issue.

Section 280A limits the deductibility of expenses related to the rental of a dwelling unit that is also used for personal purposes during the taxable year. Section 280A(f) defines a "dwelling unit" as a "house, condominium, mobile home, boat, or similar property. . . ." In general, three scenarios can develop under §280A, each depending on the number of days of personal use and the number of days of rental use of the vacation home.

1. If the rental unit is used for personal use but not for sufficient time to be considered a residence under §280A(d)(1), the amount of deductible rental expenses is determined by applying the §280A(e) allocation. A dwelling unit is treated as a residence if it is used by the taxpayer for personal purposes in excess of the greater of fourteen days or 10 percent of the number of days during the year that the unit was rented at fair market value. The method of expense allocation is discussed below.

2. If the dwelling unit is used for personal purposes for more than fourteen days or 10 percent of the rental days during the year, the dwelling unit is treated as a residence under §280A(d) and both the §280A(e) allocation and the §280A(c)(5) limitation apply. Section 280A(c)(5) is similar to §183, which limits deductions to the amount of income derived from the activity. This limitation is consistent with §183 because as the personal uses of a dwelling unit increase, the activity becomes more like a §183 hobby.

3. Even if the taxpayer's personal use of the dwelling unit qualifies it as a residence under §280A(d), if the number of actual rental days is less than fifteen, neither the §280A(e) allocation nor the §280A(c)(5) limitation applies. Instead, no deductions are allowed, and any income received from the rental is excluded from gross income. §280A(g).

The three categories of deductions discussed in the §183 material are relevant to an understanding of the deduction allocation and limitation provisions of §280A. The §280A rental expenses are divided into the same categories as those in §183: category 1 — expenses that are deductible regardless of profit motive or rental activity (such as taxes and interest); category 2 — other rental expenses that do not require a basis adjustment; and category 3 — expenses that do require basis adjustments. The similarity with §183 ends here, however, because the expenses in each category must be allocated between the rental and personal use days before they may be deducted from the rental income. (In §183, each category of expenses is deducted in full until all income is offset.)

Rental expenses are allocated in the following manner: category 2 and 3 expenses are allocated between personal and rental use according to the ratio of rental days to the total number of rental and personal-use days (for example, rental days ÷ (rental + personal days)).

Because §280A(e) does not state how category 1 expenses are allocated, the method used is that which the Ninth Circuit adopted in the *Bolton* case that follows. Rejecting the Proposed Regulation §1.280A-3(d)(4) example, the court held that category 1 expenses, which are deductible without regard to rental activity, are allocated between rental and personal use days by the ratio of the total number of rental days to the *total number of days in the year*. This ratio, in effect, treats days when the property is unused as personal days and is considered the more appropriate allocation of expenses such as taxes and interest that accrue each day throughout the year.

The *Bolton* method of allocating category 1 expenses affords taxpayers a benefit not present under §183. In §183, all category 1 expenses offset income derived from the related activity, leaving less income available to be offset by other expenses. Under §280A, however, when the income limitation rule of §280A(c)(5) applies, only a portion of the category 1 expenses offset rental income, leaving a larger amount of income to be offset by other expenses. The unallocated category 1 expenses are deductible outside of §280A along with other itemized deductions.

The following examples demonstrate the application of the §280A rule to each of the three scenarios. Assume that a taxpayer rents his vacation home during the year and receives rent of $3,200. Over the course of the year, the taxpayer pays interest and property taxes totaling $4,000, pays maintenance expenses of $2,500, and computes depreciation expenses of $1,000.

First, assume that the taxpayer used the unit for eight days and rented it for ninety days. Because the personal use did not exceed the greater of fourteen days or 10 percent of the rental use (nine days), the unit is not considered to be a residence, and the §280A(c)(5) limitation does not apply. The §280A(e) allocation applies, however, because the taxpayer used the property for personal use. Rental-related expenses must, therefore, be categorized and allocated. Category 1 expenses (after rounding) are allocated as follows:

$$\$4,000 \times \frac{90 \text{ rental days}}{365 \text{ days}} = \$1,000$$

The category 2 and 3 expenses are allocated on the following basis:

$$\$2,500 \times \frac{90 \text{ rental days}}{100 \text{ total use days}} = \$2,250$$

$$\$1,000 \times \frac{90 \text{ rental days}}{100 \text{ total use days}} = \$900$$

The total expenses allocated to the rental activity equals $4,150. Because the §280A(c)(5) limitation does not apply, the entire amount is deductible, and a loss of $950 ($3,200 − $4,150) should be allowed. Because the loss is attributable to a rental activity, the deductions may be taken in arriving at AGI. See §62(a)(4). The remaining $3,000 of category 1 expenses are itemized deductions.

For the second scenario, assume that the taxpayer uses the unit for thirty days and rents it for ninety days. The category 1 expenses are allocated as above. The category 2 and 3 expenses are allocated as follows:

$$\$2,500 \times \frac{90 \text{ rental days}}{120 \text{ total use days}} = \$1,875$$

$$\$1,000 \times \frac{90 \text{ rental days}}{120 \text{ total use days}} = \$750$$

The total rental-related expenses are $3,625. However, because the personal use days (thirty) exceed the greater of fourteen days or 10 percent of rental use (nine days), the unit is considered to be a residence, and the income limitation of §280A(c)(5) applies. Consequently, the following expenses are allowed:

$1,000	Category 1
1,875	Category 2
325	Category 3
$3,200	Total expenses allowed

Again, the remaining $3,000 of category 1 expenses are itemized deductions. No deductions or adjustments are necessary for the $425 of nondeductible category 3 expenses. These expenses, however, may be carried forward to future years to offset subsequent income.

Finally, assume that the taxpayer used the unit for thirty days and rented it for fourteen days. The personal use qualifies this unit as a residence under §280A(d), but §280A(g) applies because the rental is less than fifteen days. Consequently, no rental expenses are allowed, and the $3,200 of rental income is excludable from gross income. Of course, the disallowance of deductions under §280A(g) does not apply to category 1 expenses, which, again, are deductible without regard to rental activity.

The *Bolton* decision, which follows, provides a good step-by-step guide to the application of §280A.

BOLTON v. COMMISSIONER
694 F.2d 556 (9th Cir. 1982)

COPPLE, J.

This appeal from the United States Tax Court presents a question involving the interpretation of statutes governing deductibility of expenses incurred in the rental of a vacation home. Dorance and Helen Bolton (taxpayers) owned a vacation home in Palm Springs, California. In 1976, taxpayers rented the unit for 91 days, used it personally for 30 days, and left it unoccupied for 244 days. During that year, taxpayers made interest payments totalling $2,854 and paid property taxes of $621. In addition, taxpayers incurred $2,693 in maintenance expenses (excluding taxes and interest). Taxpayers received $2,700 gross rents from the unit in 1976.

I.R.C. §280A, enacted in 1976, limits a taxpayer's business deductions for expenses incurred with respect to a dwelling unit if that unit was used as a personal residence during the tax year.[1] If §280A applies, as it does in this case, a general

---

1. IRC §280A applies with respect to deductions taken for rental home expenses if the taxpayer's personal use of the property exceeds the greater of 14 days or 10 percent of the number of days the unit is rented.

This section was enacted as a response to congressional concern that rental of property used personally by the taxpayer as a residence afforded unwarranted opportunities to obtain deductions for expenses of a personal nature. With respect to vacation homes, the legislative history behind the statute expresses the view that rental activities were often undertaken merely to defray the cost of maintaining a vacation home for the taxpayer's personal use, rather than for the purpose of turning a profit. Although IRC §183 could generally have been expected to apply to such rentals of vacation homes as activities not engaged in for profit, thereby limiting deductions with respect to maintenance of a vacation home to the amount of gross income received from its rental, Congress was concerned that §183 and the related

rule is invoked that no business deductions are allowable with respect to the unit. The statute, however, provides several exceptions. Section 280A(b) provides that non-business expenditures otherwise deductible (i.e. taxes, interest, and casualty losses) are not barred by the statute. Further, §280A(c)(3) allows a deduction for "any item attributable to rental of the unit" (i.e. maintenance expenses). But this latter exception to the general rule is limited. In computing deductible maintenance expenses, the taxpayer must first comply with §280A(e) and §280A(c)(5), respectively.

Section 280A(e) requires that a preliminary computation be undertaken to determine the unit's maintenance expenses which are attributable to rental and thus can be deducted. The statute provides that the following ratio be used in making this calculation:

$$\frac{\text{Number of days the unit is actually rented}}{\text{Total number of days during the year the unit is used}}$$

The figure obtained through use of this ratio is then multiplied against the total maintenance expenses of the unit to arrive at a tentative deduction figure. This formula, as applied to the above facts, generates the following calculation:

$$\frac{91 \ (\# \ \text{days rented})}{121 \ (\# \ \text{days used})} = 75\% \times \$2,693 \ (\text{total maintenance expenses}) = \$ \ 2,020$$

The figure $2,020, then, is the tentative amount of maintenance expenses deductible as attributable to rental.

Having arrived at a tentative maintenance deduction figure, there remains §280A(c)(5) to be complied with. This section provides first that deductions allowed for expenses attributed to rental of the unit (i.e., deductions of any kind — maintenance, taxes, interest) cannot exceed an amount equal to the amount of gross rental income received from the property for that year ($2,700 on the instant facts). Second, this section requires that deductions allowable whether or not the unit was used as a rental (i.e., interest and taxes in this case) be allocated between rental and non-rental use. The amount of otherwise deductible interest and taxes allocated to rental use of the property is then to be counted toward the gross rentals maximum deduction ceiling ($2,700). The statute, however, provides no formula for allocating such "always deductible" expenses (taxes and interest) between rental and non-rental use of the unit.

The primary issue in this case concerns the method by which this latter allocation is to be achieved. Taxpayers contend, and the tax court agreed, that the allocation be based on a ratio of number days rented/number days in a year. The percentage figure derived from this ratio would be the percentage of taxes and interest paid which is allocable to rental use of the unit, and in turn applied toward

---

regulations did not provide sufficiently specific rules as to the degree of personal use of a vacation home which would result in its rental being classified as an activity not engaged in for profit. Section 280A was thus intended to provide "definitive rules . . . to specify the extent to which personal use [of a vacation home] would result in the disallowance of certain deductions in excess of gross income" from the property.

the gross rentals deduction limit. The Commissioner, on the other hand, takes the position that interest and taxes should be allocated to rental use by using the same fraction as that used for maintenance expenses under §280A(e). The ratio to use under this method would accordingly be number days rented/number days the property was *actually* used. The percentage derived from this ratio would be the percent of taxes and interest which, in the Commissioner's view, would be applied toward the rental use deduction limit.[8]

The United States Tax Court, in Bolton v. Commissioner, 77 T.C. 104 (1981), held that the deduction for interest and real estate taxes attributable to the rental unit is to be computed as per the taxpayer's method, i.e. the ratio to use for the §280A allocation for taxes and interest is number days unit rented/number days in a year. One basis for the tax court's decision was the premise that interest and property taxes, unlike maintenance-type expenses, are expenses that continue on a daily basis throughout the year. The tax court recognized that a computation based on the period the unit was *actually* used (121 days in this case) is useful in

---

8. To clarify and illustrate the impact of the competing positions in this appeal, the following calculations based on the facts in this case are presented:

Taxpayer's Position

Gross rental income		$2,700
Total interest and property taxes	$3,475	
Allocation fraction $91/365 = 25\%$		
(attributable to rental use)		868
Rental income in excess of interest and property taxes		$1,832
Total maintenance expenses	$2,693	
Allocation fraction $1/121 = 75\%$		
Maximum allowable deduction for maintenance		$2,020

Given the above, the taxpayer may deduct $1,832 of the $2,020 in potentially deductible maintenance expenses as derived from §280A(e)(1).

Commissioner's Position

Gross rental income		$2,700
Total interest and property taxes	$3,475	
Allocation fraction $1/121 = 75\%$		
(attributable to rental use)		2,606
Rental income in excess of interest and property taxes		$94
Total maintenance expenses	$2,693	
Allocation fraction $1/121 = 75\%$		
Maximum allowable deduction for maintenance		$2,020

Given the above, the taxpayer may deduct $94 of the $2,020 in potentially deductible maintenance expenses as derived from §280A(e)(1).

The Commissioner's position, by allocating a greater proportion of otherwise deductible interest and taxes to rental of the unit, leaves less room under the gross rentals ceiling for deduction of maintenance expenses of the rental. By contrast, taxpayer's position allows a greater percentage of the §280A(e) maintenance expenses to be deducted. Since interest and taxes paid on the property are deductible whether or not connected to business use of the property, it is to the taxpayer's advantage to have as small a percentage as possible of taxes and interest allocated to rental use and applied toward the gross rentals deduction limit for the unit.

determining the amount of otherwise nondeductible maintenance expenses, ordinarily associated with actual use of the property, which are to be attributed to rental use. Interest and property taxes, however, accrue ratably over the entire year. The tax court accordingly found that the annual nature of tax and interest expenses as well as the legislative intent shown both by the legislative history and the language of §280A supported the taxpayer's interpretation rather than that of the Commissioner. Despite the tax court's decision, the Commissioner's position in this matter is currently the subject of a Proposed Treasury Regulation, §1.280A-3(d).

This Court is essentially faced with deciding whether to give deference to the Commissioner's interpretation of the statutes in question or to affirm the tax court in finding the Commissioner's position unreasonable. . . .

. . . This Court must therefore consider the reasonableness of the Commissioner's interpretation of §280A as applied to taxpayers and as put forth in the Proposed Regulation. Consideration must first be made of whether the Commissioner's interpretation "harmonizes with the statutory language." The legislative history and purpose behind the statute are also to be considered in determining whether the Commissioner has acted reasonably. Should the Commissioner's as well as the taxpayer's interpretation of the statute be seen as reasonable, the rule in such a situation is that "[t]he choice among reasonable interpretations is for the Commissioner, not the courts." For the reasons outlined below, however, we conclude that the Commissioner overstepped the bounds of reasonableness in this case, and that the decision of the tax court should therefore be affirmed.

I. The Statutory Language

The Commissioner's position is to allocate interest and taxes to gross rental receipts through use of the same fraction as that used for maintenance expenses specified in §280A(e)(1): number of days rented/total number of days used. Yet subsection (e)(2) of §280A continues:

> (2) Exception for Deductions Otherwise Allowable. This subsection shall not apply with respect to deductions which would be allowable under this chapter for the taxable year whether or not such unit . . . was rented.

On the very face of the statute, then, it is apparent that the "number of days rented/total number of days used" fraction is not appropriate for allocating expenses such as interest and property taxes. The Commissioner argues, on the other hand, that the meaning of subsection (e)(2) is not plain, and that other interpretations are possible. Thus, the Commissioner argues, the IRS interpretation should be accepted.

There is a major difficulty with the Commissioner's argument, however. Even if it is accepted that this subsection is subject to some different interpretation, the one fact that is clear is that subsection (e)(2) is not, from the face of the statute, subject to an interpretation along the lines of that sought by the Commissioner. Since this Court's task in the first instance is to determine the reasonableness of the Commissioner's interpretation, the Commissioner's argument as to the existence of other possible interpretations misses the focus of the analysis. The question is whether the *Commissioner's* interpretation is reasonable in the context of the language, legislative history and purpose of the statute. When solely the language on the face of the statute is considered, the Commissioner's interpretation cannot be upheld as reasonable.

II.   THE LEGISLATIVE HISTORY

The legislative history behind the statutory provisions at issue in this appeal does not adequately address the problem of the proper way to allocate interest and tax expenses. Indeed, both parties in their briefs admit that the legislative history is unclear on this point. The Commissioner nevertheless makes several arguments based on legislative history to support his position. He first argues that certain extracts of the committee reports discussing §280A support the IRS interpretation of the statute. These extracts, however, are at best inconclusive, and do not support the Commissioner's position.[12] The Commissioner also relies on legislative history in pointing out that prior to the enactment of §280A,

---

12. To support his argument that Congress intended the amount of the deductions to be based on the actual use of the unit, the Commissioner cites the House Ways and Means Committee as stating:

> In addition, if there is any personal use of a vacation home, the portion of expenses allocable to rental activities should be limited to an amount determined on the basis of the ratio of time that the home is actually rented, to the total time the vacation home is used during the taxable year for all purposes (i.e., rental, business, and personal activities).

H.R. Rep. No. 94-658, 94th Cong., 2d Sess. at 164, reprinted in U.S. Code Cong. & Ad. News at 3058 (1976). This extract, however, is taken from a part of the committee report which speaks only in general terms of the reasons for changing the existing law through enacting §280A. After evaluation of the report's discussion of the specific details of how the new §280A provisions are to apply, it appears that this statement merely refers to the general effect the new law would have upon maintenance expenses—the context of the statement does not ascribe to it the importance the Commissioner would have it bear. Further, given the generality of the statements, taxpayer makes a valid point in arguing that the statement's parenthetical conclusion does not preclude using a concept of "use of property as an investment" as part of the allocation formula for interest and taxes, i.e., investment "use" would cover the entire year. Moreover, it should again be pointed out that acceptance of the Commissioner's interpretation of the legislative history would ignore and in effect render §280A(e)(2) meaningless.

The Commissioner also points out that the Ways and Means Committee stated that:

> If a taxpayer exceeds the personal use limitations for the vacation home for a taxable year, the deductions attributable to the rental activity are limited to the amount by which the gross income derived from the rental activity exceeds the deductions otherwise allowable with respect to such rental activities (e.g., interest and certain taxes). For this purpose deductions attributable to the rental activities are those items which are of a type allowable only as expenses incurred in connection with a trade or business or the production of income (e.g., sec. 162 or 212).
>
> If the personal use limitation applies, the allowable deductions would be determined after first determining the expenses of the vacation home which are allocable to the rental activities (in accordance with the new allocation rules). H.R. Rep. No. 94-658, supra, at 165, reprinted in U.S. Code Cong. & Ad. News at 3058-3059 (1976).

From this the Commissioner argues that the computation for both maintenance expenses and interest and taxes be made "in accordance with the new allocation rules," which, the Commissioner maintains, means that the §280A(e)(1) ratio based on actual use of the unit governs the allocation for all items. Again, the Commissioner's construction is strained. The statement could just as easily support the tax court decision which holds that more than one "new rule" exists for allocating expenses to rental activities.

deductions for vacation homes were computed under the general guidelines for the "hobby loss" provisions of §183. Thus, the Commissioner argues, §183 and its regulations should be applicable to determining the interest and tax deductions under §280A, and that these regulations support the Commissioner's method for making the §280A allocation. This argument, however, is also faulty in that it ignores the language found in §280A(f) which states that §183 is not to apply at all to a unit if §280A is applicable. Moreover, such a position ignores the fact that §280A was enacted in the first instance because §183 was not working with respect to §280A-type rental units. The §183 "hobby loss" provisions are thus inapplicable to the issues in this appeal.

The legislative history of §280A as reflected in the committee reports demonstrates, if anything, a lack of support for the Commissioner's position. Both the Senate Finance Committee and House Ways and Means Committee state that the fraction, number days rented/total number of days used, is the proper way to allocate maintenance expenses. Both reports then add:

> However, the limitation (referring to the fraction) upon allocable expenses would not apply to expenses such as interest or taxes which are allocable even if not attributable to the rental activity.

Thus, while the committee reports provide no guidance as to the specific method of allocating interest and taxes, they nevertheless show that the intent of Congress is contrary to the position taken by the Commissioner, and that use of the fraction found in subsection (e)(1) is not appropriate for allocating interest and taxes. . . .

III.   Harmony with the Legislative Purpose: Tax Court v. Commissioner

The Commissioner finally argues that the tax court's method of computing the interest and tax allocation actually rewards the taxpayer with a higher deduction the less the unit is used for any purpose. As an example, the Commissioner points out that in the instant case, the taxpayers rented the unit for 91 days, or 25 percent of the time in 1976. He then contends that under the tax court's computation, taxpayers would be allowed to deduct a higher amount of maintenance expenses than they would have been allowed if the unit were rented for 120 days, or 33 percent of the year. The Commissioner maintains that this result would be counter to the congressional purpose behind §280A that taxpayers not be allowed to convert personal expenses, such as maintenance and utilities, into deductible business items.

The Commissioner's argument, however, fails to consider the fact that if the unit were rented an additional 30 days as in his example, the gross rental figure for the unit, and likewise the ceiling on maximum deductions, would be higher. Thus, 33 percent of the interest and taxes (allocable to rental under the tax court's approach) would be taken from a *higher* gross rentals limit, not the same limit as the Commissioner's example assumes. The amount of allowed deductions for maintenance and depreciation expenses under the deduction limit would therefore increase in proportion to the increase in days the unit is rented.[15]

Accordingly, taxpayers are not, as the Commissioner contends, rewarded with higher deductions for letting their unit stand idle. The Commissioner's argument as to legislative purpose is consequently misplaced. The argument further fails to consider that maintenance and utility expenses are first allotted between deductible rental/business and nondeductible personal expenses as per the fraction in §280A(e)(1) prior to taking into account interest and taxes under the deduction limit. Any maintenance expenses deductible after allocated interest and taxes are accounted for therefore have already been deemed potentially deductible business expenses. Personal expenses are not converted into business expenses under the tax court's formula.

As pointed out earlier, neither the statute itself nor its legislative history address the issue of the proper approach to follow in making the §280A interest and tax allocation. The only clear point to be derived from these sources is the incorrectness of the Commissioner's interpretation. The tax court's approach, however, is consistent with the legislative purpose of setting up a scheme whereby personal expenses are separated from the business expenses of rental homes. Following the Commissioner's approach, the facts in this case would allow a deduction of only $94 of maintenance expenses for three months' worth of rental expenses, when the maintenance expenses on the unit for the year were $2,693. The tax court's approach more evenly makes the allocation by determining that maintenance expenses, which tend to vary with occupancy rate, be allocated in accordance with occupancy (see §280A(e)(1)) whereas those expenses which are allowable without regard to whether they are personal or not be allocated giving due regard to the method in which they accrue — in this case, taxes and interest

15. To illustrate:

	90 Days Rented		120 Days Rented	
	Tax Court	*Comm'r*	*Tax Court*	*Comm'r*
Rental Income	2700	2700	3600	3600
Interest & Taxes	(868)	(2606)	(1157)	(2780)[*]
Ded. Maint. Expenses	(1832)	(94)	(2154)[**]	(820)
Ded. Depreciation	0	0	(289)[***]	0
Net Income	0	0	0	0

 * Days rented (120) divided by total days occupied (150 times total interest and taxes ($3,475) equals $2,780.
 ** Days rented (120) divided by total days occupied (150) times total maintenance ($2,693) equals $2,154.
 *** After subtracting the allocation for taxes and interest, there remains room under the gross rentals deduction ceiling for $2,443 in deductions. Since potentially deductible maintenance expenses come to only $2,154, there is room left to deduct $289 in depreciation on the rental unit.

Using the tax court's allocation method, the amount of deductible maintenance and depreciation expenses under the deduction limit increase (from $1,831 to $2,443) in proportion to the increase in days rented. As taxpayers point out, it is also interesting to note in the above example that the Commissioner's method allows the deduction for maintenance expenses to increase lopsidedly as a result of increasing the rental days by 33.3 percent (from $94 to $820, or 772 percent).

accrue on a daily basis, regardless of property use. . . . In summary, the Commissioner's interpretation of the statute is at odds with the language, history and legislative purpose behind §280A. . . . The approach of the tax court, on the other hand, is reasonable and consistent with the purpose and history behind the statute and the language of the statute itself. . . . The decision of the tax court is therefore affirmed.

Note

An interesting timing issue arises with respect to the availability of §212 expenses on a conversion of a personal asset to income-producing status. If a taxpayer owned and lived in a residence and subsequently decided to lease the premises, an issue would arise as to when the taxpayer would be entitled to §212 expenses. Regulation §1.165-9 focuses on the *rental* date as determinative for loss purposes under §165(c)(2), which addresses transactions entered into for profit. However, the language of §165(c)(2) should be contrasted with the more lenient standards of §§167(a)(2), 168(a), and 212(2) requiring property to be "held for the production of income." In the §§167, 168, and 212 cases, a mere listing for rental is sufficient to allow deductions of expenses under §§212 and 168, subject to the limitations of §280A. Robinson v. Commissioner, 2 T.C. 305 (1943), acq. If the property is listed for sale, as opposed to being available for rent, §212 deductions are not permitted without evidence of an expectation of post-listing appreciation. Newcombe v. Commissioner, 54 T.C. 1298 (1971).

Problems

8-5. Dana Reck purchased a two-bedroom condominium in Angel Fire, New Mexico, on January 1. The condominium cost $200,000 and was financed with $150,000 cash and a $50,000 mortgage. Reck's maintenance expenses are $100 per month. Heating and air conditioning costs are $150 per month. If allowable, her depreciation is $10,000. Property taxes and interest total $4,000 annually.

   a. If Reck uses the condominium for 10 days and rents it for 150 days for $3,000, does §280A limit Reck's deductions, and if so, what amounts are deductible?

   b. How should allowable expenses be allocated?

   c. Same facts and questions as in *a* except Reck uses the condominium twenty days instead of ten.

8-6. Tom and Lois Meyer, who live in San Diego, purchased a Los Angeles bungalow for $74,000 in August. Their oldest daughter, enrolled at UCLA, agreed to rent the bungalow for the fall term (September 1 to December 31) for a total of $4,000. Interest and taxes on the home during the rental period totaled $2,500, while maintenance and utilities totaled $600. Because Los Angeles was only about three hours away from the Meyer's San Diego home, Tom and Lois visited their daughter regularly during the semester. What are the tax issues raised by this arrangement?

8-7. On January 1, year 1, Connie Mortensen purchased a personal residence for $155,000. On January 1, year 2, she placed the house on the rental market when its fair market value was $150,000. On February 1, year 2, she leased the house to a tenant when its fair market value was $151,000. On January 2, year 3, because of declining market conditions, Mortensen sold the house for $142,000.

    a. What is her basis for depreciation purposes in year 2?

    b. What is the amount of the deductible loss if the available depreciation deduction totaled $4,500?

    c. What result if she sold the house for $152,000?

D.   INVESTMENT-PERSONAL DEDUCTIONS

1.   *Bad Debts*

Code: §§165(g)(1), (2); 166
Regulations: §§1.165-5(a) to (c); 1.166-1; 1.166-2(a) to (c); 1.166-5

The ability to obtain money on credit is integral to the consumer-oriented economy of the United States. One who extends credit, either by loaning money or by selling goods on credit, assumes a risk that he will not be repaid and, as a result, will suffer an economic loss. Because most people would be unwilling to take the risk associated with the extension of credit if the effect of a possible loss were not ameliorated and because the purpose of the Code is to tax economic gains (accessions to wealth), Congress has provided a deduction for bad debt losses.

Section 166(a)(1) permits a bad debt deduction for "any debt which becomes worthless within the taxable year." To be entitled to a bad debt deduction, the taxpayer must satisfy two prerequisites: (1) there must be a bona fide debt and (2) the debt must be worthless.

Regulation §1.166-1(c) defines bona fide debt as a "debt which arises from a debtor-creditor relationship based upon a valid and enforceable obligation to pay a fixed or determinable sum of money." The Regulation provides that neither gifts nor contributions to capital give rise to debts. The question of whether the taxpayer made a loan to a corporation or purchased equity often arises, and, therefore, transactions between shareholders and corporations frequently lead to litigation.

Intra-family loans are another area of controversy. Generally, the dispute is whether the transaction gave rise to a bona fide debt or was merely a gift. For example, when a loan made by a parent to a child to attend college becomes worthless, has there been a gift or a bad debt? To prevail in such cases, the taxpayer must overcome the presumption against debtor-creditor relationships among family members. Thus, the taxpayer must establish an intent, at both the time of the transaction and at the time of the claimed deduction, to enforce the collection of the debt.

Once the taxpayer has established a bona fide debt, he must still establish that the debt has become worthless. Additionally, because §166 permits bad debt deductions for the taxable year in which the debt becomes worthless, the taxpayer must establish the date on which the debt was rendered worthless. The Regulations and the courts agree that the date on which a debt becomes worthless depends on the facts and circumstances of each case. Reg. §1.166-2(a). Consequently, an identifiable event indicating an inability to pay will help to establish worthlessness (such as bankruptcy, receivership, abandonment of business, continued refusal to pay on demand, and expiration of statute of limitations). Gratuitous forgiveness of a loan does not produce a bad debt deduction; it merely creates a nondeductible gift.

Business versus nonbusiness bad debts. Most of the complexity created by §166 stems from the different tax treatment accorded business and nonbusiness bad debts. In general, business bad debt losses create ordinary deductions, whereas nonbusiness bad debts create short-term capital losses. Moreover, §166(a)(2) permits the deduction of worthless business debts from ordinary income, even if they are only partially worthless.

Nonbusiness bad debts pose other problems in addition to their characterization as short-term capital losses. Worthless nonbusiness debts may not be deducted if they are only partially worthless. Furthermore, the debt may not be carried back to earlier years as a net operating loss. See §172(d)(4).

Because the stakes are high, depending on whether the debt is determined to be business or nonbusiness in nature, the definition of nonbusiness debt has been the subject of much litigation. Section 166(d)(2) defines nonbusiness debt, by way of exclusion, as any debt other than "(A) a debt created or acquired . . . in connection with a trade or business of the taxpayer; or (B) a debt the loss from the worthlessness of which is incurred in the taxpayer's trade or business." The use to which the debtor puts the funds is irrelevant. Congress enacted subparagraph (A) to provide business status for debts that originally arise in a business but become worthless at a time when the taxpayer is no longer active in the business. For example, a note arising in the course of business may become uncollectible after the taxpayer goes out of business. Subparagraph (B) simply sets forth the obvious case of a worthless debt incurred in a trade or business.

As suggested earlier, transactions between shareholders, employees, and corporations often raise the issue of whether debts are attributable to business or nonbusiness activities. In general, the classification of a transaction depends on whether the loan is "proximately related" to the taxpayer's trade or business. A shareholder-employee of a corporation has a dual relationship to the corporation: one as an individual engaged in business as an employee and the other as an investor in the company. If the taxpayer makes a loan to the corporation to protect his employment, the loan may be classified as one arising from the taxpayer's trade or business as an employee. Trent v. Commissioner, 291 F.2d 669 (2d Cir. 1961). In instances where mixed motives exist, the status of the loan is less clear, as evidenced by the following case.

UNITED STATES v. GENERES
405 U.S. 93 (1972)

MR. JUSTICE BLACKMUN delivered the opinion of the Court.

A debt a closely held corporation owed to an indemnifying shareholder-employee became worthless in 1962. The issue in this federal income tax refund suit is whether, for the shareholder-employee, that worthless obligation was a business or a nonbusiness bad debt within the meaning and reach of §§166(a) and (d) and of the implementing Regulations §1.166-5.

The issue's resolution is important for the taxpayer. If the obligation was a business debt, he may use it to offset ordinary income and for carryback purposes under §172. On the other hand, if the obligation is a nonbusiness debt, it is to be treated as a short-term capital loss subject to the restrictions imposed on such losses by §166(d)(1)(B) and §§1211 and 1212, and its use for carryback purposes is restricted by §172(d)(4). The debt is one or the other in its entirety, for the Code does not provide for its allocation in part to business and in part to nonbusiness.

In determining whether a bad debt is a business or a nonbusiness obligation, the Regulations focus on the relation the loss bears to the taxpayer's business. If, at the time of worthlessness, that relation is a "proximate" one, the debt qualifies as a business bad debt. . . .

The present case turns on the proper measure of the required proximate relation. Does this necessitate a "dominant" business motivation on the part of the taxpayer or is a "significant" motivation sufficient? . . .

I

The taxpayer as a young man in 1909 began work in the construction business. His son-in-law, William F. Kelly, later engaged independently in similar work. During World War II the two men formed a partnership in which their participation was equal. The enterprise proved successful. In 1954 Kelly-Generes Construction Co., Inc., was organized as the corporate successor to the partnership. It engaged in the heavy construction business, primarily on public works projects.

The taxpayer and Kelly each owned 44 percent of the corporation's outstanding capital stock. The taxpayer's original investment in his shares was $38,900. The remaining 12 percent of the stock was owned by a son of the taxpayer and by another son-in-law. Mr. Generes was president of the corporation and received from it an annual salary of $12,000. Mr. Kelly was executive vice-president and received an annual salary of $15,000.

The taxpayer and Mr. Kelly performed different services for the corporation. Kelly worked full time in the field and was in charge of the day-to-day construction operations. Generes, on the other hand, devoted no more than six to eight hours a week to the enterprise. He reviewed bids and jobs, made cost estimates, sought and obtained bank financing, and assisted in securing the bid and performance bonds that are an essential part of the public-project construction business. Mr. Generes, in addition to being president of the corporation, held a full-time position as president of a savings and loan association he had founded in 1937. He received from the association an annual salary of $19,000. The taxpayer also had other sources of income. His gross income averaged about $40,000 a year during 1959-1962.

Taxpayer Generes from time to time advanced personal funds to the corporation to enable it to complete construction jobs. He also guaranteed loans made to the corporation by banks for the purchase of construction machinery and other equipment. In addition, his presence with respect to the bid and performance bonds is of particular significance. Most of these were obtained from Maryland Casualty Co. That underwriter required the taxpayer and Kelly to sign an indemnity agreement for each bond it issued for the corporation. In 1958, however, in order to eliminate the need for individual indemnity contracts, taxpayer and Kelly signed a blanket agreement with Maryland whereby they agreed to indemnify it, up to a designated amount, for any loss it suffered as surety for the corporation. Maryland then increased its line of surety credit to $2,000,000. The corporation had over $14,000,000 gross business for the period 1954 through 1962.

In 1962 the corporation seriously underbid two projects and defaulted in its performance of the project contracts. It proved necessary for Maryland to complete the work. Maryland then sought indemnity from Generes and Kelly. The taxpayer indemnified Maryland to the extent of $162,104.57. In the same year he also loaned $158,814.49 to the corporation to assist it in its financial difficulties. The corporation subsequently went into receivership and the taxpayer was unable to obtain reimbursement from it.

In his federal income tax return for 1962 the taxpayer took his loss on his direct loans to the corporation as a nonbusiness bad debt. He claimed the indemnification loss as a business bad debt and deducted it against ordinary income. . . .

II

A. The fact responsible for the litigation is the taxpayer's dual status relative to the corporation. Generes was both a shareholder and an employee. These interests are not the same, and their differences occasion different tax consequences. In tax jargon, Generes' status as a shareholder was a nonbusiness interest. It was capital in nature and it was composed initially of tax-paid dollars. Its rewards were expectative and would flow, not from personal effort, but from investment earnings and appreciation. On the other hand, Generes' status as an employee was a business interest. Its nature centered in personal effort and labor, and salary for that endeavor would be received. The salary would consist of pre-tax dollars.

Thus, for tax purposes it becomes important and, indeed, necessary to determine the character of the debt that went bad and became uncollectible. Did the debt center on the taxpayer's business interest in the corporation or on his nonbusiness interest? If it was the former, the taxpayer deserves to prevail here.

B. Although arising in somewhat different contexts, two tax cases decided by the Court in recent years merit initial mention. In each of these cases a major shareholder paid out money to or on behalf of his corporation and then was unable to obtain reimbursement from it. In each he claimed a deduction assertable against ordinary income. In each he was unsuccessful in this quest:

1. In Putnam v. Commissioner, 352 U.S. 82 (1956), the taxpayer was a practicing lawyer who had guaranteed obligations of a labor newspaper corporation in which he owned stock. He claimed his loss as fully deductible in 1948 under §23(e)(2) of the 1939 Code. The standard prescribed by that statute was incurrence of the loss "in any transaction entered into for profit, though not connected with the trade or business." The Court rejected this approach and held that the loss was a nonbusiness bad debt subject to short-term capital loss treatment under §23(k)(4).

The loss was deductible as a bad debt or not at all. See Rev. Rul. 60-48, 1960-1 Cum. Bull. 112.

2. In Whipple v. Commissioner, 373 U.S. 193 (1963), the taxpayer had provided organizational, promotional, and managerial services to a corporation in which he owned approximately an 80 percent stock interest. He claimed that this constituted a trade or business and, hence, that debts owing him by the corporation were business bad debts when they became worthless in 1953. The Court also rejected that contention and held that Whipple's investing was not a trade or business, that is, that "[d]evoting one's time and energies to the affairs of a corporation is not of itself, and without more, a trade or business of the person so engaged." 373 U.S., at 202. The rationale was that a contrary conclusion would be inconsistent with the principle that a corporation has a personality separate from its shareholders and that its business is not necessarily their business. The Court indicated its approval of the Regulations' proximate relation test:

> Moreover, there is no proof (which might be difficult to furnish where the taxpayer is the sole or dominant stockholder) that the loan was necessary to keep his job or was otherwise proximately related to maintaining his trade or business as an employee.

The Court also carefully noted the distinction between the business and the non-business bad debt for one who is both an employee and a shareholder.

These two cases approach, but do not govern, the present one. They indicate, however, a cautious and not a free-wheeling approach to the business bad debt. Obviously, taxpayer Generes endeavored to frame his case to bring it within the area indicated in the above quotation from Whipple v. Commissioner.

III

We conclude that in determining whether a bad debt has a "proximate" relation to the taxpayer's trade or business, as the Regulations specify, and thus qualifies as a business bad debt, the proper measure is that of dominant motivation, and that only significant motivation is not sufficient. We reach this conclusion for a number of reasons:

A. The Code itself carefully distinguishes between business and nonbusiness items. It does so, for example, in §165 with respect to losses, in §166 with respect to bad debts, and in §162 with respect to expenses. It gives particular tax benefits to business losses, business bad debts, and business expenses, and gives lesser benefits, or none at all, to nonbusiness losses, nonbusiness bad debts, and nonbusiness expenses. It does this despite the fact that the latter are just as adverse in financial consequence to the taxpayer as are the former. But this distinction has been a policy of the income tax structure ever since the Revenue Act of 1916 provided differently for trade or business losses than it did for losses sustained in another transaction entered into for profit. And it has been the specific policy with respect to bad debts since the Revenue Act of 1942 incorporated the distinction between business and nonbusiness bad debts.

The point, however, is that the tax statutes have made the distinction, that the Congress therefore intended it to be a meaningful one, and that the distinction is not to be obliterated or blunted by an interpretation that tends to equate the business bad debt with the nonbusiness bad debt. We think that emphasis upon the significant rather than upon the dominant would have a tendency to do just that.

B. Application of the significant-motivation standard would also tend to undermine and circumscribe the Court's holding in *Whipple* and the emphasis there that a shareholder's mere activity in a corporation's affairs is not a trade or business. As Chief Judge Lumbard pointed out in his separate and disagreeing concurrence in *Weddle*, [325 F.2d 849 (5th Cir. 1963),] both motives—that of protecting the investment and that of protecting the salary—are inevitably involved, and an inquiry whether employee status provides a significant motivation will always produce an affirmative answer and result in a judgment for the taxpayer.

C. The dominant-motivation standard has the attribute of workability. It provides a guideline of certainty for the trier of fact. The trier then may compare the risk against the potential reward and give proper emphasis to the objective rather than to the subjective. As has just been noted, an employee-shareholder, in making or guaranteeing a loan to his corporation, usually acts with two motivations, the one to protect his investment and the other to protect his employment. By making the dominant motivation the measure, the logical tax consequence ensues and prevents the mere presence of a business motive, however small and however insignificant, from controlling the tax result at the taxpayer's convenience. This is of particular importance in a tax system that is so largely dependent on voluntary compliance.

D. The dominant-motivation test strengthens and is consistent with the mandate of §262 of the Code that "no deduction shall be allowed for personal, living, or family expenses" except as otherwise provided. It prevents personal considerations from circumventing this provision. . . .

G. The Regulations' use of the word "proximate" perhaps is not the most fortunate, for it naturally tempts one to think in tort terms. The temptation, however, is best rejected, and we reject it here. In tort law factors of duty, of foreseeability, of secondary cause, and of plural liability are under consideration, and the concept of proximate cause has been developed as an appropriate application and measure of these factors. It has little place in tax law where plural aspects are not usual, where an item either is or is not a deduction, or either is or is not a business bad debt, and where certainty is desirable. . . .

[Judgment for petitioner.]

Problems

8-8. Paul Reddick billed his client, the Hellstrom Corporation, for thirty-eight hours of legal services totaling $4,000. The Hellstrom Corporation, however, went bankrupt the next year and never paid Reddick. Is Reddick entitled to a deduction?

8-9. Christy Bay worked for a small steel purchasing company, Lewinski and Co. Lewinski had fallen on hard times due to foreign competition. Bay feared that, if Lewinski closed shop and declared bankruptcy, she would lose her job. Therefore, she loaned Lewinski $25,000, but the company folded anyway two months later. Bay never recovered the money. Is she entitled to a deduction?

8-10. Nancy Webb loaned $200 to a close friend, Janet Baker. Baker promised to repay the money within three months but never did. Is Webb entitled to a deduction?

8-11. Robert Ray invested $10,000 in a small engineering company, Spellman and Associates, which hoped to land a series of government contracts to develop specialized parts for the space shuttle program. Unfortunately, Spellman failed to procure the contracts, and over a period of sixteen months the company's stock dropped from $11 per share to $0. Is Ray entitled to a deduction?

2.   *Home Mortgage Interest*

Code: §§163(a), (h)(1) to (3)(C)
Regulations: §1.163-1

Historically, §163(a) allowed a deduction for interest expenses (regardless of whether they were business-related or investment-related), a significant exception to the general rule that personal expenses are not deductible. However, various legislative enactments narrowed the exception by returning to the prerequisite that the deduction be in connection with a business activity or investment activity. Interest expenses attributable to personal activity are nondeductible, with the exception of "qualified residence interest." Qualified residence interest generally is defined as interest on debt secured by the taxpayer's principal residence or a second residence. The amount of the debt for which deductions are allowed is limited to $1,000,000 for acquisition indebtedness and $100,000 for home equity indebtedness. §163(h)(3)(A) to (C).

Deductions for qualified residential interest generally are straightforward. As a result, there tend to be few disputes regarding §163(h)(3) deductions. At times, however, issues arise regarding whether a particular debt is "acquisition indebtedness" and, if so, how much of a particular borrowing constitutes such indebtedness, both for total deductions and for calculating the $1,000,000 cap.

REV. RUL. 2010-25
2010-44 I.R.B. 571

Section 163(a) allows as a deduction all interest paid or accrued within the taxable year on indebtedness. However, for individuals §163(h)(1) disallows a deduction for personal interest. Under §163(h)(2)(D), qualified residence interest is not personal interest. Section 163(h)(3)(A) defines qualified residence interest as interest paid or accrued during the taxable year on acquisition indebtedness or home equity indebtedness secured by any qualified residence of the taxpayer. Under §163(h)(4)(A), "qualified residence" means a taxpayer's principal residence, within the meaning of §121, and one other residence selected and used by the taxpayer as a residence.

Section 163(h)(3)(B)(i) provides that acquisition indebtedness is any indebtedness that is incurred in acquiring, constructing, or substantially improving a qualified residence and is secured by the residence. However, §163(h)(3)(B)(ii) limits the amount of indebtedness treated as acquisition indebtedness to $1,000,000 ($500,000 for a married individual filing separately). Accordingly, any indebtedness described in §163(h)(3)(B)(i) in excess of $1,000,000 is, by definition, not acquisition indebtedness for purposes of §163(h)(3).

Section 163(h)(3)(C)(i) provides that home equity indebtedness is any indebtedness secured by a qualified residence other than acquisition indebtedness, to the extent the fair market value of the qualified residence exceeds the amount of acquisition indebtedness on the residence. However, §163(h)(3)(C)(ii) limits the amount of indebtedness treated as home equity indebtedness to $100,000 ($50,000 for a married individual filing separately). Accordingly, any indebtedness described in §163(h)(3)(C)(i) in excess of $100,000 is, by definition, not home equity indebtedness for purposes of §163(h)(3).

In Pau v. Commissioner, T.C. Memo. 1997-43, the Tax Court limited the taxpayers' deduction for qualified residence interest to the interest paid on $1 million of the $1.33 million indebtedness incurred to purchase their residence. The court slated that §163(h) restricts home mortgage interest deductions to interest paid on $1 million of acquisition indebtedness and $100,000 of home equity indebtedness. Citing §163(h)(3)(B), the court stated that acquisition indebtedness is defined as indebtedness that is incurred in acquiring, constructing, or substantially improving any qualified residence of the taxpayer, and is secured by the residence. Citing §163(h)(3)(C), the court further stated that home equity indebtedness is defined as any indebtedness (other than acquisition indebtedness) secured by a qualified residence. The court concluded that the taxpayers failed to demonstrate that any of their debt was not incurred in acquiring, constructing, or substantially improving their residence and thus was not acquisition indebtedness. However, the court did not address the effect of the $1 million limitation in §163(h)(3)(B)(ii) on the definition of acquisition indebtedness for purposes of §163(h)(3). The Tax Court followed Pau in Catalano v. Commissioner, T.C. Memo. 2000-82.

ANALYSIS

Taxpayer may deduct, as interest on acquisition indebtedness under §163(h)(3)(B), interest paid in 2009 on $1,000,000 of the $1,200,000 indebtedness used to acquire the principal residence. The $1,200,000 indebtedness was incurred in acquiring a qualified residence of Taxpayer and was secured by the residence. Thus, indebtedness of $1,000,000 is treated as acquisition indebtedness under §163(h)(3)(B).

Taxpayer also may deduct, as interest on home equity indebtedness under §163(h)(3)(C), interest paid in 2009 on $100,000 of the remaining indebtedness of $200,000. The $200,000 is secured by the qualified residence, is not acquisition indebtedness under §163(h)(3)(B), and does not exceed the fair market value of the residence reduced by the acquisition indebtedness secured by the residence. Thus, $100,000 of the $200,000 is treated as home equity indebtedness under §163(h)(3)(C).

Under §163(h)(3)(A), the interest on both acquisition indebtedness and home equity indebtedness is qualified residence interest. Therefore, for 2009 Taxpayer may deduct interest paid on indebtedness of $1,100,000 as qualified residence interest. Any interest Taxpayer paid on the remaining indebtedness of $100,000 is nondeductible personal interest under §163(h).

The Internal Revenue Service will not follow the decisions in Pau v. Commissioner and Catalano v. Commissioner. The holding in Pau was based on the incorrect assertion that taxpayers must demonstrate that debt treated as home equity indebtedness "was not incurred in acquiring, constructing or substantially improving their residence." The definition of home equity indebtedness in §163(h)(3)(C) contains no such restrictions, and accordingly the Service will determine home equity indebtedness consistent with the provisions of this revenue ruling, notwithstanding the decisions in Pau and Catalano.

HOLDING

Indebtedness incurred by a taxpayer to acquire, construct, or substantially improve a qualified residence can constitute home equity indebtedness to the extent it exceeds $1 million (subject to the applicable dollar and fair market value limitations imposed on home equity indebtedness by §163(h)(3)(C)).

SOPHY v. COMMISSIONER
138 T.C. No. 8 (2012)

COHEN, JUDGE:

... BACKGROUND

... In 2002 petitioners purchased a house in Beverly Hills, California. Petitioners acquired the Beverly Hills house as joint tenants and held the property as joint tenants during the years in issue. To finance the purchase, petitioners obtained a mortgage secured by the Beverly Hills house. In 2003 petitioners refinanced the Beverly Hills house by obtaining a new mortgage loan of $2 million. The proceeds of this new mortgage loan, which was secured by the Beverly Hills house, were used to pay off the original mortgage loan. Petitioners were jointly and severally liable for the mortgage on the Beverly Hills house ...

In 2006 Sophy paid mortgage interest of $94,698 for the two residences, and Voss paid $85,962. The total average balance in 2006 for the Beverly Hills house mortgage and home equity loan and the Rancho Mirage house mortgage was $2,703,568. In 2007 Sophy paid mortgage interest of $99,901, and Voss paid $76,635. The total average balance in 2007 for the two mortgages and the home equity loan was $2,669,136.

On their individual Federal income tax returns for 2006 and 2007, petitioners each claimed deductions for qualified residence interest. The Internal Revenue Service (IRS) audited petitioners' 2006 and 2007 individual income tax returns and disallowed portions of petitioners' deductions for qualified residence interest ...

In these cases, the IRS computed the applicable limitation ratio as $1.1 million ($1 million for acquisition indebtedness plus $100,000 for home equity indebtedness) over the entire average balance of the qualifying loans . . .

<h2 style="text-align:center">DISCUSSION</h2>

. . . There is no dispute that petitioners' homes meet the definition of a qualified residence and that the mortgage interest paid by petitioners is qualified residence interest because it was paid on acquisition and home equity indebtedness secured by their homes.

Petitioners' sole contention is that the section 163(h)(3) limitations on indebtedness (indebtedness limitations) are properly applied on a per-taxpayer basis with respect to residence co-owners who are not married to each other. Petitioners argue that they should each be allowed a deduction for interest paid on up to $1.1 million of acquisition and home equity indebtedness with respect to the residences that they jointly own. Under their interpretation, because these cases involve two unmarried co-owners, together they should be able to deduct interest paid on up to $2.2 million of acquisition and home equity indebtedness.

Respondent's position, on the other hand, is that the indebtedness limitations are properly applied on a per-residence basis, regardless of the number of residence owners and whether co-owners are married to each other. Under respondent's interpretation, co-owners should collectively be limited to a deduction for interest paid on a maximum of $1.1 million of acquisition and home equity indebtedness.

We must decide whether the statutory limitations on the amount of acquisition and home equity indebtedness with respect to which interest is deductible under section 163(h)(3) are properly applied on a per-residence or per-taxpayer basis where residence co-owners are not married to each other.

When we interpret a statute, our purpose is to give effect to Congress' intent. To accomplish this we begin with the statutory language, which is the most persuasive evidence of the statutory purpose. The words of the statute should be construed in their "ordinary, everyday," and plain meaning. Usually the meaning of the statutory language is conclusive. If a statute is silent or ambiguous, we may look to the statute's legislative history in an attempt to determine congressional intent. When a statute appears clear on its face, however, there must be unequivocal evidence of legislative purpose before interpreting the statute in a way that overrides the plain meaning of the words used therein.

We begin our analysis by looking closely at the definitions of acquisition indebtedness and home equity indebtedness in section 163(h)(3)(B)(i) and (C)(i). The acquisition indebtedness definition uses the phrase "any indebtedness which is incurred" in conjunction with "acquiring, constructing, or substantially improving any qualified residence of the taxpayer and is secured by such residence." We note that the word "taxpayer" in this context is used only in relation to the qualified residence, not the indebtedness. Similarly, the operative language in the definition of home equity indebtedness is "any indebtedness" that is secured by a qualified residence (other than acquisition indebtedness). Sec. 163(h)(3)(C)(i). Once again, the phrase "any indebtedness" is not qualified by language relating to an individual taxpayer.

Qualified residence interest is defined as "any interest which is paid or accrued during the taxable year on acquisition indebtedness *with respect to any qualified residence* of the taxpayer, or home equity indebtedness *with respect to any qualified residence* of the taxpayer." Sec. 163(h)(3)(A) (emphasis added). The definition of "home equity indebtedness" also includes the phrase "reduced by the amount of acquisition indebtedness *with respect to such residence*" (referring to a qualified residence). Sec. 163(h)(3)(C)(i)(II) (emphasis added). The definitions of the terms "acquisition indebtedness" and "home equity indebtedness" in section 163(h)(3)(B)(i) and (C)(i) establish that the indebtedness must be related to a qualified residence, and the repeated use of the phrases "with respect to a qualified residence" and "with respect to such residence" in the provisions discussed above focuses on the residence rather than the taxpayer.

From Congress' use of "any indebtedness" in the definition of acquisition indebtedness, which is not qualified by language regarding an individual taxpayer, it appears that this phrase refers to the total amount of indebtedness with respect to a qualified residence and which is secured by that residence. The focus is on the entire amount of indebtedness with respect to the residence itself. Thus when the statute limits the amount that may be treated as acquisition indebtedness, it appears that what is being limited is the total amount of acquisition debt that may be claimed in relation to the qualified residence, rather than the amount of acquisition debt that may be claimed in relation to an individual taxpayer . . .

Because of references to an individual taxpayer in other provisions of section 163(h), petitioners would have us interpret the indebtedness limitations as applying on a per-taxpayer basis, rather than a per-residence basis. Such an interpretation, however, reads too much into the indebtedness limitations. While Congress references "a taxpayer" and "the taxpayer" several times in section 163(h), any reference to an individual taxpayer is conspicuously absent in the language of the indebtedness limitations. Moreover, as noted above, the "taxpayer" references in the definitions of acquisition indebtedness and home equity indebtedness are in relation to the qualified residence, rather than to the indebtedness. "When 'Congress includes particular language in one section of a statute but omits it in another section of the same Act, it is generally presumed that Congress act[ed] intentionally and purposely' in so doing."

With respect to Congress' repeated use of phrases such as "with respect to any qualified residence" and "with respect to such residence" in conjunction with terms that by their own definitions must already be in relation to a qualified residence, these phrases appear to be superfluous. However, a statute ought, upon the whole, to be so construed that, if it can be prevented, no clause, sentence, or word shall be superfluous, void, or insignificant. In addition, we must construe a provision not in isolation, but as part of the statutory scheme in which it is embedded. In the light of the language in section 163(h)(3) taken as a whole, it appears that Congress used these repeated references to emphasize the point that qualified residence interest and the related indebtedness limitations are residence focused rather than taxpayer focused.

Further support regarding application of the indebtedness limitations is found in the parenthetical language addressing married taxpayers filing separate returns. The parenthetical language in the acquisition indebtedness limitation in section 163(h)(3)(B)(ii) provides that married taxpayers who file separate returns are limited to acquisition indebtedness of $500,000 each, or one-half of the otherwise allowable amount of acquisition indebtedness. Similarly, the home equity indebtedness limitation in section 163(h)(3)(C)(ii) includes parenthetical language that provides that married taxpayers who file separate returns are limited to home equity indebtedness of $50,000 each, which is one-half of the otherwise allowable amount of home equity indebtedness. Thus the language used in these provisions suggests, without expressly stating, that co-owners who are married to each other and file a joint return are limited to a deduction of interest on $1 million of acquisition indebtedness and $100,000 on home equity indebtedness. Accordingly, in a case involving acquisition indebtedness of more than $1 million, this Court has limited a married couple's qualified residence interest deduction on a joint return to the interest paid on $1 million of acquisition indebtedness. *See Pau v. Commissioner,* T.C. Memo.1997-43. (See also Rev. Rul.2010-25, 2010-44 I.R.B. 571, with respect to the amount of acquisition indebtedness that can be treated as home equity indebtedness for purposes of the section 163(h) limitations. This ruling does not vary from the holding in Pau as to the application of the limitations to co-owners who are married to each other.)

Petitioners argue that Congress, in using this particular language in the indebtedness limitations, intended to create a special rule for married couples—a "marriage penalty"—that does not apply to co-owners who are not married to each other. However, in the light of the residence-focused language used throughout section 163(h)(3) and the absence of any reference to an individual taxpayer in the indebtedness limitations themselves, this argument is not persuasive. Rather than setting out a marriage penalty, this language simply appears to set out a specific allocation of the limitation amounts that must be used by married couples filing separate tax returns, thus implying that co-owners who are not married to one another may choose to allocate the limitation amounts among themselves in some other manner, such as according to percentage of ownership . . .

3.   Other Interest Expenses

Code: §§221(a) to (d); 265(a)(2)

Section 265(a)(2) disallows interest expense deductions for interest "incurred or continued to purchase or carry obligations the interest on which is wholly" tax-exempt. Without this limitation, a taxpayer would not only benefit from the tax-exempt income but also would, in effect, purchase a deduction. For example, assume that a taxpayer in the 40-percent bracket purchases $100,000 of tax-exempt municipal bonds carrying a 10-percent rate of interest. To finance this purchase, she borrows $100,000 at an interest rate of 10 percent. The $10,000 of tax-free income from the bonds will offset the $10,000 of interest expense on the loan. Economically, the transaction is of no consequence because the income offsets the corresponding expense. If the interest on the loan is deductible, however, the taxpayer also can reduce her tax liability on other income by $4,000 (a $10,000 deduction for a 40-percent taxpayer will reduce tax liability by $4,000). Thus, the taxpayer has acquired a deduction at no economic cost.

The §265(a)(2) limitation prevents this "double dipping" by disallowing a deduction for the interest expense thus incurred. Revenue Procedure 72-18, 1972-1 C.B. 740, in considering the difficult problems that may arise in tracing the flow of funds among investments, stipulates that there must be a showing that the taxpayer borrowed the funds for the purpose of purchasing or carrying tax-exempt securities before the deduction will be disallowed.

> Accordingly, the application of section [§265(a)(2)] . . . requires a determination, based on all the facts and circumstances, as to the taxpayer's purpose in incurring or continuing each item of indebtedness. Such purpose may, however, be established either by direct evidence or by circumstantial evidence.
>
> Direct evidence of a purpose to *purchase* tax-exempt obligations exists where the proceeds of indebtedness are used for, and are directly traceable to the purchase of tax exempt obligations. . . .
>
> Direct evidence of a purpose to *carry* tax-exempt obligations exists where tax-exempt obligations are used as collateral for indebtedness.

Id. at 740 (emphasis in original). In the absence of direct evidence of the purpose to purchase or carry tax-exempt obligations, Revenue Procedure 72-18 employs an "all the facts and circumstances" analysis.

In response to the need for greater governmental assistance in funding the cost of higher education, Congress in 1997 enacted §221 providing a deduction for interest paid on a "qualified education loan." The deduction is limited to $2,500. The deduction is phased out for higher income taxpayers and is not available for a taxpayer who is claimed as a dependent by another taxpayer. A sixty-month limitation applies to the deduction. Of particular importance, the deduction may be taken under §62(a)(17) in arriving at adjusted gross income; thereby ensuring governmental assistance for such payments regardless of whether the taxpayer itemizes deductions. See generally Notice 97-60.

To qualify for the §221 educational interest deduction, a particular debt must be a "qualified educational loan" — in other words, a loan incurred for educational, as opposed to personal, reasons. The difference between the two is often clear, but at times the line can prove somewhat difficult to discern. For instance, what level of proof should be required to establish that a loan is a qualified educational loan? Should spending the proceeds on qualified education be suffficient, or should some documentation or other legal obligation to use the loan proceeds for educational purposes be required? The Tax Court faced this issue in Weyts v. Commissioner, T.C. Memo 2003-68, in which the taxpayer contended that a loan undertaken to finance an LL.M. degree at Columbia Law School was a qualified educational loan. The Tax Court found insufficient evidence that the loan qualified, and thus denied a deduction for the interest paid, since there was no documentation establishing that the loan was undertaken exclusively for qualified educational expenses and no evidence as to the source of the funds used to pay the interest on the loan. Rather, the Tax Court focused on the fact that the loan was secured by the home of the parents of the taxpayer, making it appear more like a mortgage loan to the parents than a qualified educational loan to the taxpayer.

Problems

8-12. Jean Pierce financed the purchase of a home for $100,000 with a down payment of $20,000 and a first mortgage to the First National Bank of $80,000 with interest at 10 percent. For the year, she made interest payments of $8,000 on the mortgage, $400 on her personal-use credit cards, $750 on her educational loans, and $200 on her outstanding medical bills.

    a.   Are the interest payments on her mortgage deductible?

    b.   Are the interest payments on her credit cards deductible?

    c.   Are the interest payments on her educational loans deductible?

    d.   Are the interest payments on her medical bills deductible?

    e.   What result if in the following year Pierce borrows $10,000 at a 12-percent rate of interest from Security State Bank executing a second mortgage on the home as security for the loan and uses a portion of the loan proceeds to make the interest payments in parts *b* through *d*? Are the payments deductible? Are the interest payments of $1,200 on the second mortgage deductible? Are the interest payments of $8,000 on the first mortgage deductible?

    f.   What result if in the next year, when her home has appreciated in value to $130,000, Pierce borrows $20,000 at a 9-percent rate of interest from Rockwell Savings and Loan through the execution of a third mortgage on her home in order to finance her twin daughters' college educations? Are the interest payments of $2,800 deductible? Are the interest payments of $1,200 on the second mortgage deductible? Are the interest payments of $8,000 on the first mortgage deductible? Are the tuition payments deductible?

8-13. Dr. Bernard borrowed $150,000 from Merrill Lynch & Co., pledging $200,000 worth of municipal bonds that he had previously purchased from Merrill Lynch as collateral. Is the interest he pays on the $150,000 loan deductible if he uses those funds to build his new principal residence?

4. Taxes

Code: §164(a), (b)

Regulations: §§1.164-1(a); 1.164-3(a) to (d)

Section 164 allows a deduction for the payment of certain state and local taxes, regardless of whether they are business-related or investment-related, provided that the tax arises in one of three categories: (1) real property taxes; (2) personal property taxes; or (3) income, war profits, and excess profits taxes. Property taxes imposed on a principal residence and state income taxes are familiar examples of deductible taxes. User fees, such as sewer fees, are not taxes and therefore are not deductible under §164.

Taxes arising in a business or profit-oriented activity, which do not fall within one of the three categories of §164, may be deductible under §162 or §212. For example, state and local gasoline taxes generally are not deductible under §164, but these taxes are deductible if they arise from business (§162) or income-producing (§212) activity. Additionally, Congress integrated a capital expenditure limitation on the deduction of otherwise allowable taxes. Thus, any tax incurred on the acquisition or disposition of an asset will be treated respectively as part of its basis or as a reduction in the amount realized.

Commentators have criticized the deduction for taxes because such expenses may be deductible even though purely personal. For example, some claim that the deduction unfairly discriminates between homeowners and renters. See Rev. Rul. 79-180, which follows. By contrast, others view §164 as a federal subsidy to state and local governments or as a form of revenue sharing. Still others argue that the deduction may help prevent the negative income dilemma that might otherwise occur where high-bracket taxpayers pay combined state, federal, and local taxes exceeding their taxable income.

To be deductible under §164, an expense must be a tax imposed on the taxpayer who claims the deduction and not a fee or other expense charged for services. This distinction can be difficult to police, however. According to the IRS:

> The word "taxes" as used in the statute is nowhere defined in the Code, and, it must be "given its ordinary and commonly accepted meaning as established by the judicial decisions." Generally, the word has been defined as an exaction of the state laid by some rule of apportionment according to which the persons or property taxed share the public burden and the proceeds of which go into the state's general revenue fund.
>
> An important factor in distinguishing a fee from a tax is the purpose for the imposition of the charge. Clearly, if the only or the primary purpose is the raising of revenue, the charge is a tax, and governmental regulation arising merely as an incident will not alter the character of the exaction. On the other hand, "if the fee is exacted for the primary purposes of regulating and restraining an occupation or privilege deemed dangerous to the public or to be specially in need of public control, and compliance with certain conditions is required in addition to the payment of the prescribed sum, such fee is a license * * *. A charge imposed as a consideration for a privilege granted one by a governmental unit is not a 'tax' in the sense in which the word is ordinarily used."

Rev. Rul. 60-366, 1960-2 C.B. 63 (internal citations omitted). Under this standard, the IRS denied a deduction for a filing fee paid by a political candidate to run for political office. Some courts applying a similar standard have sometimes disagreed with this conclusion, ruling that filing fees for political candidates can be deductible taxes if the primary purpose of the fee was to raise revenue. See Campbell v. Davenport, 362 F.2d 624 (5th Cir. 1966).

Additionally, to be deductible, personal property taxes, such as the automobile license, must be annual ad valorem taxes. Ad valorem taxes are based on the value of the property, not on other criteria such as weight. If, however, automobile license fees are based in part on value and in part on some other criteria, the portion of the fee that represents value is a tax and therefore deductible. See Reg. §1.164-3(c).

Section 164(d) requires that real property taxes for the year of sale must be apportioned between the buyer and the seller. This allocation gives rise to a recurring problem — determining the real party in interest. Because the date of levy and payment of real property taxes may not correlate precisely with the date of sale, an allocation procedure is necessary to insure that the party remitting such taxes was the party on whom the burden of payment actually fell. When real property is sold, the purchaser typically insists on a reduction of his or her financial outlay by the amount of real property taxes attributable to the seller's possession. If the taxing jurisdiction subsequently collected the entire real property tax from the purchaser for the year of sale, the purchaser would derive a windfall if the full amount of the payment could be deducted. Accordingly, §164(d) and its attendant Regulations prescribe an appropriate allocation of the tax liability.

Section 164(d) requires the buyer and seller to allocate the real estate taxes (and the corresponding deduction) for the year of sale in proportion to the number of days each owned the property. This apportionment is made without regard to which party paid the taxes or any allocation of the tax burden on which the parties agreed in the sales contract. In making the apportionment, the assessment date is disregarded and the focus is generally on the transfer of title.

In addition to requiring an apportionment of the tax liability for purposes of §164, if no actual apportionment occurs, §164(d)(2) requires adjustments to the seller's amount realized on the transaction and the buyer's basis in the property. If the buyer pays the real estate tax for the entire year, §164(d)(2) mandates that the seller's amount realized from the sale be increased by an amount corresponding to the portion of the tax attributable to the seller's ownership of the property. This amount is added to the buyer's basis. Conversely, if the seller pays the entire tax for the year, the seller's amount realized is reduced by the portion of the tax attributable to the buyer's ownership, and the buyer's basis receives a corresponding reduction.

The real party in interest problem is not limited to the deduction of real estate taxes by the buyer and seller of real estate. The following material suggests other circumstances giving rise to the issue. Additionally, it illustrates the pivotal role that state law may play in determining who is entitled to a disputed §164 deduction.

REV. RUL. 79-180
1979-1 C.B. 95

ISSUE

Is the New York State renter's tax deductible by renters as a real property tax under section 164(a)(1)? . . .

FACTS

On July 6, 1978, the State of New York amended the New York Real Property Tax Law to provide that certain renters of residential property have an interest in real property, are personally liable for the real property taxes due on their interest, and are entitled to a federal itemized deduction for those taxes.

Section 304 of the New York Real Property Tax Law provides that all assessments shall be against the real property itself which shall be liable to sale pursuant to law for any unpaid taxes or special ad valorem levies.

However, where real property in whole or in part is rented for residential purposes, . . . a renter who pays $150 or more a month in rent (or less than $150, if the renter makes an election) is deemed to have an interest in the real property and is subject to state and local laws covering the levy and collection of taxes and the enforcement of collection of delinquent taxes. This provision does not, however, relieve the owner of real property from the obligation of paying all taxes due on the owner's property. . . . The owner of real property is obligated to apply the first money received each month from the renter to taxes due on the owner's real property. . . .

. . . Taxes on the property not held for rental purposes are assessed solely against the owner and are not considered in determining the assessed valuation of each rental unit. . . .

Law and Analysis

Section 164(a)(1) of the Code allows as a deduction, for the taxable year within which paid or accrued, state and local, and foreign, real property taxes.

Section 1.164-3(b) of the Income Tax Regulations provides that the term "real property taxes" means taxes imposed on interests in real property and levied for the general public welfare.

Under federal law, a tax is an enforced contribution, exacted pursuant to legislative authority in the exercise of the taxing power, and imposed and collected for the purpose of raising revenue to be used for public or governmental purposes, and not as a payment for some special privilege granted or service rendered.

Rev. Rul. 58-141, 1958-1 C.B. 101, states that the question of whether a particular contribution, charge, or burden is to be regarded as a tax depends on its real nature and, if it is not in its nature a tax, it is not material that it may have been so called.

Thus, the fact that the State of New York treats a portion of the total rental amounts paid by renters to owners of real property as real property tax payments does not establish that those payments are in fact real property tax payments, because the focus is on the nature of the transaction under federal law.

The New York renters tax does not impose on the renter any economic burden that did not exist prior to the enactment of section 304 of the New York Real Property Tax Law. Rather, the renters tax merely divides the separately determined rental amount into a so-called rental payment and a so-called real property tax payment. The lack of an economic burden on the renter is further evidenced by the fact that the owner is not relieved from the obligation of paying all taxes due on the owner's property. Under section 926-a, the owner is deemed to assume the renter's interest in the unit if the renter is delinquent in making payment to the owner. In the event of the renter's nonpayment, section 304 looks to the owner for payment and the taxing authority may enforce payment against the owner's interest in the entire property.

Holding

The New York State renters tax paid by renters pursuant to sections 304 and 926-a of the New York Real Property Tax Law is not a tax on the renter for federal income tax purposes, but rather is part of the renters' rental payments.

Because the New York renters tax is not a tax on the renter for federal income tax purposes, it is not necessary to decide whether such a tax could qualify as a real property tax deductible under section 164(a)(1) by the renter. . . .

Problems

8-14. Jocelyn Sandbury, an employee of Middlebury, Inc., incurred a number of expenditures for the year, including State of Minnesota income taxes of $7,000, property taxes of $3,500, Minnesota sales taxes of $725, and state car registration and licensing fees of $500. What deductions, if any, are available?

8-15. Roxanne Smythe conducts a photocopying operation. During the year, she incurred $1,000 in sales tax on the purchase of a $20,000 copy machine as well as $150 in sales tax on the purchase of $3,000 of paper for the machine.

   a.   What amounts, if any, are deductible if Smythe's operation is a trade or business? Where in the taxing formula are such amounts taken?

   b.   What amounts, if any, are deductible if Smythe's operation is an activity engaged in for the production of income? Where in the taxing formula are such amounts taken?

E.   PERSONAL DEDUCTIONS

1.   Casualty Losses

Code: §165(c)(3), (h)
Regulations: §§1.165-1; 1.165-7(a), (b); 1.165-8(a), (c)

Section 165(a) allows a deduction for any loss sustained during the taxable year not compensated for by insurance or otherwise. The all-inclusive language of §165(a) is limited, however, by §165(c), which embodies the business/personal dichotomy that permeates the Code. Section 165(c)(1) and (2) permits the deduction of any loss incurred in one's trade or business or other profit-seeking activity and not compensated by insurance. Section 165(c)(3), however, limits the deductibility of losses of a personal nature to those that result from casualty or theft. Casualty losses include those caused by fire, storm, shipwreck, or "other casualty."

The casualty concept. By permitting a deduction for casualty losses to property held solely for personal use, Congress created another specific exception to the general rule of nondeductibility. This exception is based on the policy that tax liability should relate to the individual's ability to pay. However, Congress restricted the deductibility of personal casualty losses by limiting the type of event that will qualify and by imposing a floor amount of allowable loss.

Under §165(c)(3), the loss must be attributable to a statutorily enumerated event, i.e., "fire, storm, shipwreck, or other casualty, or . . . theft." The term "other casualty" has proved difficult to define and to apply. When defining casualty, judicial and administrative decisions have relied on legislative intent and allowed personal deductions only for extraordinary, nonrecurring losses. As the following materials demonstrate, such a loss must be "sudden," "unexpected," and "unusual" to qualify for a deduction.

Casualty loss decisions form an odd array of conflicting rationales and theories. Perhaps this confusion stems from the courts' inability to define both the precise cause of a casualty loss (Is Dutch elm disease caused by beetles or the fungi they carry?) and the limits of human responsibility and foresight (How often should homeowners inspect their houses for termite infestation? Should a Miamian expect periodic attacks of lethal yellowing or pine beetles?).

The availability of casualty loss deductions for damage resulting from insects has tested the ingenuity of courts, the Service, and taxpayers and their counsel. Although an attack of southern pine beetles qualified as a casualty loss (see Rev. Rul. 79-174, which follows), a lethal yellowing disease arising from the infiltration of a "mycoplasma-like organism" into the food-conducting veins of a tree was not of "the same qualitative characteristics" as the events described in §165(c)(3). Maher v. Commissioner, 680 F.2d 91 (11th Cir. 1982). *Maher* attempted to distinguish the two situations by noting that the pine beetles themselves cause the damage rather than a disease that they have injected into the tree.

Revenue Ruling 79-174 and *Maher* should be contrasted with the termite cases in which casualty losses were permitted, notwithstanding the passage of substantial time before the damages were detected. See Rosenberg v. Commissioner, 198 F.2d 46 (8th Cir. 1952); Buist v. United States, 164 F. Supp. 218 (E.D.S.C. 1958); Shopmaker v. United States, 119 F. Supp. 705 (E.D. Mo. 1953). In the termite cases, the requisite suddenness was found by interpreting the term in relation to the damaged property — damage arising over a two-year period was sudden when compared to the long-term life of the property.

Justifying casualty loss deductions becomes even more difficult when underlying social and economic policy considerations are analyzed. In each case, policy considerations must be examined to determine whether the taxpayer is entitled to a governmental subsidy to counterbalance the loss. Is the loss of ornamental pine trees grave enough to justify the government's intervening to assuage the tree owner's loss? Should the availability of insurance for the most remotely conceivable types of loss affect the decision to allow casualty loss deductions? In many cases, the taxpayer stands in a better position than the government to insure against such occurrences. Should a homeowner receive a tax break for failing to insure against fire? Should a car owner receive a deduction when he or she fails to purchase collision insurance?

REV. RUL. 72-592
1972-2 C.B. 101

In view of the decision of the Tax Court of the United States in John P. White v. Commissioner, 48 T.C. 430 (1967), reconsideration has been given to the meaning of the term "casualty" for purposes of section 165(c)(3) of the Internal Revenue Code. . . . That section of the Code provides that an individual may deduct:

> (3) losses of property not connected with a trade or business, if such losses arise from fire, storm, shipwreck or other casualty. . . .

The provision allowing this deduction for losses from "other casualty" has been part of the Federal tax law since the enactment of the Revenue Act of 1916. However, there is neither statutory definition of the term "other casualty," nor legislative history expressing Congressional intent as to its meaning.

The courts have consistently upheld the Internal Revenue Service position that an "other casualty" is limited to casualties analogous to fire, storm, or shipwreck. The Service position has been that a casualty is the complete or partial destruction of property resulting from an identifiable event of a sudden, unexpected, and unusual nature.

In the *White* case, however, the Tax Court found that property that was accidentally and irretrievably lost could, under the circumstances described, be the basis for a casualty loss deduction under section 165(c)(3) of the Code. The Service has acquiesced in the decision of the Tax Court in the *White* case.

In the *White* case, the taxpayer-husband accidentally slammed the car door on his wife's hand after helping her alight from the car. Her diamond engagement ring absorbed the full impact of the blow, which broke two flanges of the setting holding the diamond in place. His wife quickly withdrew her injured hand, shaking it vigorously, and the diamond dropped or flew out of the broken setting. The uninsured diamond was never found, and the taxpayer claimed a casualty loss deduction for its value in the year it was lost.

The Tax Court, convinced that the diamond was irrevocably and irretrievably lost, sustained the taxpayer's claim, indicating that the diamond was completely removed from the enjoyment of its owner and that it had no value to the owner after the loss. The Service, in acquiescing in the decision, agreed that property that is accidentally and irretrievably lost can be the basis for a casualty loss deduction under section 165(c)(3) of the Code if it otherwise qualifies as a casualty loss.

In other words, the Service position is altered only to the extent that the accidental loss of property can now qualify as a casualty. Such losses must, of course, qualify under the same rules as must any other casualty; namely, the loss must result from some event that is (1) identifiable, (2) damaging to property, and (3) sudden, unexpected, and unusual in nature. The meaning of the terms "sudden, unexpected, and unusual," as developed in court decisions, is set forth below.

To be "sudden" the event must be one that is swift and precipitous and not gradual or progressive.

To be "unexpected" the event must be one that is ordinarily unanticipated that occurs without the intent of the one who suffers the loss.

To be "unusual" the event must be one that is extraordinary and nonrecurring, one that does not commonly occur during the activity in which the taxpayer was engaged when the destruction or damage occurred, and one that does not commonly occur in the ordinary course of day-to-day living of the taxpayer.

REV. RUL. 79-174
1979-1 C.B. 99

ISSUE

Under the circumstances described below, is a loss from the death of trees as a result of attack by insects a casualty loss within the meaning of section 165(c) of the Internal Revenue Code . . . ?

FACTS

In 1976, a taxpayer owned a residential lot on which 40 ornamental pine trees were growing. The trees were in healthy condition on July 1, 1976. By July 10, 1976, all of the trees were dead. Death was attributable to a mass attack of southern pine beetles. Beetle attacks in epidemic proportions were unknown in the vicinity of the taxpayer's residential lot prior to the attack that killed the trees.

The southern pine beetle is a flying insect that normally attacks living pine trees. The female beetle bores into a tree and enters the cambium tissue beneath the bark. It then emits an attractant that leads other beetles to the tree in a mass attack. The beetles construct tunnels in the cambium tissue and deposit their eggs. These tunnels intersect and in a short time completely girdle the tree. This cuts off the food supply to the higher parts of the tree and kills the tree. In the instant case, the cambium layer of each tree was completely girdled within 5 to 10 days after the arrival of the female beetle.

LAW AND ANALYSIS . . .

Court decisions and revenue rulings have established standards for the application of the above provisions, and have developed the overall concept that the term "casualty" as used in such provisions refers to an identifiable event of a sudden, unexpected, or unusual nature. Damage or loss resulting from progressive deterioration of property through a steadily operating cause would not be a casualty loss.

Revenue Ruling 57-599, 1957-2 C.B. 112, holds in part that a loss arising from the death of trees as a result of an attack by insects does not constitute an allowable deduction as a casualty loss within the meaning of section 165(c)(3) of the Code. The loss was denied on the grounds that the death of the trees resulted from progressive deterioration, and, therefore, the element of suddenness was lacking.

To be sudden, an event must be of a swift and precipitous nature and not gradual or progressive. Whether an event is sudden must be determined from all the surrounding facts and circumstances. In the instant case, the cambium layers of the ornamental trees were completely girdled within 5 to 10 days after the arrival of the female beetle. Once the girdling occurred the trees were dead and their value as ornamentals was lost at that point. On the basis of these facts the element of suddenness is satisfied.

In addition to being sudden in nature, the event must also be unusual or unexpected before it can qualify as a casualty within the meaning of section 165(c)(3). Since there were no known attacks in epidemic proportions of southern pine beetles in the area of the taxpayer's residence, the event was both unusual and unexpected. . . .

POPA v. COMMISSIONER
73 T.C. 130 (1980)

STERRET, J. . . .

[T]he only issue for our decision is whether or not petitioner sustained a casualty loss within the meaning of section 165(c)(3), when various of his personal possessions, located in the Republic of Vietnam, were lost when the government of that nation fell to the North Vietnamese. . . .

By contending that petitioner abandoned his property in Saigon, respondent concedes the fact that petitioner has suffered an economic loss. Further, we take it as implicit in respondent's memorandum brief that he also concedes that the loss took place when Saigon fell to enemy troops a day or two after petitioner left on a business trip to Bangkok. Nevertheless, respondent argues that petitioner's loss is nondeductible because it "does not constitute a casualty loss as is contemplated by I.R.C. section 165(c)(3)." Petitioner, on the other hand, argues that his loss in Vietnam was due to an "identifiable event of a sudden, unexpected and unusual nature" which event is ejusdem generis to the events specifically described in section 165(c)(3).

We believe that petitioner's loss of his goods is an "other casualty" within the meaning of section 165(c)(3). We think that petitioner's loss in the fall of Saigon is ejusdem generis to losses due to "fire, storm, [and] shipwreck." It was a sudden, cataclysmic, and devastating loss—just the sort of loss section 165(c)(3) was designed to address. We have previously noted that the application of the principle of ejusdem generis—

> has been consistently broadened so that wherever unexpected, accidental force is exerted on property and the taxpayer is powerless to prevent application of the force because of the suddenness thereof or some disability, the resulting direct and proximate damage causes a loss which is like or similar to losses arising from the causes specifically enumerated in section 165(c)(3). [White v. Commissioner, 48 T.C. 430, 435 (1967).]

As "the events giving rise to the undisputed loss here were sudden, unexpected, violent and not due to deliberate or willful actions by petitioner," we conclude that these losses are deductible. See White v. Commissioner, supra at 433-434.

Our review of the cases convinces us that the only circumstance which could possibly have existed that would require us to deny petitioner his casualty loss would be that the property was confiscated under color of some hastily enacted local law. All the other possibilities (fire, theft, looting, etc.) are such that entitle him to a section 165(c)(3) casualty loss.

Respondent notes in his memorandum brief that "It is extremely doubtful that petitioner knows or will ever know what became of his property, since he was precluded from returning to Vietnam after the U.S. military evacuation." We are, of course, well aware of the legion of cases that hold that the taxpayer must be put to his proof. However, in unusual circumstances such as this, we do not think it fair or reasonable to require that the taxpayer eliminate all possible noncasualty causes of his loss. We do not believe that we unduly stretch the bounds of judicial notice when we take into account the abruptness with which the United States abandoned Saigon and the stories with respect to the heavy damage to the city. A few days before the city fell, the United States Government was actively evacuating its citizens from the city. We can hardly fault petitioner for not remaining to determine whether his property was destroyed by gun fire, by looting, by fire, or some form of seizure by the remaining Saigon residents, the Vietcong, or the North Vietnamese. Certainly, petitioner's failure to return to the city was not a matter of personal choice. Nor can his inexactitude in this matter be held against him.[5]

We note here that the difficulties in South Vietnam did not arise from a revolution from within such as occurred recently in Iran and Nicaragua, thus making less likely the possibility that even a despotic law authorized the taking at issue.

Accordingly, we believe that the most reasonable conclusion, on the particular facts of this case, is that the property at issue was either destroyed or pilfered with criminal intent. . . .

We, therefore, conclude that petitioner suffered a section 165(c)(3) loss when he lost his goods in Vietnam.

However, while we hold that petitioner sustained a casualty loss within the meaning of section 165(c)(3), we are not satisfied that petitioner has adequately documented the deductible amount of this loss. For example, petitioner claimed a $1,000 loss with respect to two air conditioners. The $1,000 claim represents petitioner's estimate of the fair market value of these items as of their loss date. Petitioner testified that he had purchased the air conditioners for $800. Of course, only $800 would, therefore, be allowed as a casualty deduction with respect thereto. In the face of this, and other similar failures in petitioner's proof, we allow petitioner 75 percent of his claimed loss. . . .

FAY, J., dissenting.

While I sympathize with petitioner, I must nevertheless respectfully dissent from the majority's conclusion that he sustained a deductible loss. . . .

For example, if petitioner abandoned his property as respondent contends, petitioner is not entitled to any deduction, since there is no evidence his personal property was used in a trade or business. Indeed, the findings of fact state petitioner himself claimed "he had to abandon [his property] in Vietnam." Yet, the majority opinion does not address this possibility despite its statements that "Saigon fell to enemy troops a day or two after petitioner left"; "the United States abandoned Saigon"; and "A few days before the city fell, the United States Government was actively evacuating its citizens from the city."

---

5. To hold otherwise would be analogous to holding that a taxpayer, who was rescued from his sailboat in a hurricane, was not entitled to a casualty loss because, by not staying aboard, he cannot prove that the boat did not survive the storm.

Similarly, it is clear petitioner would not be entitled to a loss deduction in the event his property was seized by the North Vietnamese Government after entering Saigon because that would not constitute a "theft."

In the instant case, petitioner and the majority rely upon that part of section 165(c)(3) which permits an individual to deduct the loss of property arising from a "fire, storm, shipwreck, or other casualty." The relevant inquiry therefore is whether petitioner has produced sufficient evidence to "show that he comes within [the statute's] terms." I submit that he has not.

In Powers v. Commissioner, 36 T.C. 1191 (1961), the taxpayer purchased an automobile in West Berlin, Germany. Three days later, while enroute from Berlin to Hamburg, the taxpayer's automobile was seized by the East German police and never returned to him. In holding that the taxpayer was not entitled to a deduction for the clear loss he sustained, we stated:

> . . . What happened was not like a "fire, storm or shipwreck." It did not embody the requisite element of "chance, accident or contingency." The deduction was not permissible either as a theft or as a casualty. Petitioner's loss, though unfortunate, "was no more than a personal expense to petitioner, for the deduction of which the statute makes no provision."

In light of *Powers*, and cases which have followed it, it is clear that if petitioner's property was confiscated by the Communist government after the fall of Saigon, he would not be entitled to a casualty loss deduction under section 165(c)(3). However, based upon petitioner's complete lack of knowledge, the wartime circumstances, and judicially noticed "stories with respect to the heavy damage to the city," the majority infers that the property was most likely destroyed or criminally pilfered.

Admittedly, if petitioner's property were destroyed by ordinance or destroyed or pilfered before order was restored, he would be entitled to a casualty loss deduction. Unfortunately, under the circumstances, petitioner cannot prove the cause of his loss and for that reason, in my opinion, has failed to meet his burden of proof.

In Allen v. Commissioner, 16 T.C. 163 (1951), the taxpayer, Mary Allen, entered the Metropolitan Museum of Art in New York wearing a diamond brooch on the left side of her dress. Before leaving the museum less than 2 hours later, Mary discovered that her brooch was missing. After carefully retracing her steps, she was unable to find the brooch. Although she testified that she didn't know whether the brooch was lost or stolen, she nevertheless argued that since the record showed that she was present only in well-lighted rooms that were so constructed that no article could have been lost, someone must have stolen her brooch and she was therefore entitled to a theft loss deduction. . . . [I]n rejecting her claim, we stated:

> She does not, and cannot, prove that the pin was stolen. All we know is that the brooch disappeared and was never found by, or returned to, petitioner.
>
> Petitioner has the burden of proof. This includes presentation of proof which, absent positive proof, reasonably leads us to conclude that the article was stolen. If the reasonable inferences from the evidence point to theft, the proponent is entitled to prevail. If the contrary be true and reasonable inferences point to another conclusion, the proponent must fail. *If the evidence is in equipoise preponderating neither to the one nor the other conclusion, petitioner has not carried her burden.*

In the present case, the record does not show whether petitioner's property was abandoned by him, confiscated by the North Vietnamese Government, pilfered, or destroyed. In my opinion, any of the above are reasonable inferences. That being so . . . I would hold that petitioner has not met his burden of proof by a preponderance of the evidence.

The majority would, however, relieve petitioner of his burden because his inability to determine what happened to his property was not his fault. This problem was addressed in Burnet v. Houston, 283 U.S. 223 (1931), wherein the taxpayer claimed it was impossible for him to prove his 1913 basis for stock which became worthless in 1920. The Supreme Court held:

> We cannot agree that the impossibility of establishing a specific fact, made essential by the statute as a prerequisite to the allowance of a loss, justifies a decision for the taxpayer based upon a consideration only of the remaining factors which the statute contemplates. . . . The impossibility of proving a material fact upon which the right to relief depends, simply leaves the claimant upon whom the burden rests with an unenforcible claim, a misfortune to be borne by him, as it must be borne in other cases, as the result of a failure of proof.

Finally, I think it important to note that in the past, Congress has enacted special legislation to deal with cases similar to that of petitioner. For example, section 165(i) (repealed 1976) allowed a deduction for losses sustained when a Communist regime came to power in Cuba. In the absence of such legislation, on these facts, I think respondent should prevail.

Note on Other Aspects of Casualty Loss Deduction

Theft losses. The dissent in *Popa* discusses the *Allen* case, in which the taxpayer claimed a deduction for the theft loss of a diamond brooch. Theft includes, but is not limited to, larceny, embezzlement, and robbery. Reg. §1.165-8(d); see also Rev. Rul 2009-9, 2009-14 I.R.B. 735 (holding that embezzlement is a theft loss and not a casualty loss). Theft losses are subject to the general rules applicable to casualty losses for determining the amount and character of the loss. Reg. §1.165-8. Section 165(e) addresses the timing issue regarding theft losses and dictates that the year of loss is that in which it is discovered. As is obvious from the *Allen* decision, mere discovery that an item is missing may be insufficient.

Mechanics of §165(c)(3). The casualty or theft loss deduction is computed separately for each casualty or each theft sustained during the year. Unlike losses incurred in a trade or business or in a transaction entered into for profit, personal casualty losses covered by (c)(3) are deductible only to the extent that the loss exceeds $100 plus 10 percent of the taxpayer's adjusted gross income. Under §165(h), the amount that is deductible depends on the amount of the taxpayer's loss, less any reimbursements, and less $100 plus 10 percent of the taxpayer's adjusted gross income as the nondeductible floor amount. The amount of the loss is the lesser of either the decline in market value of the property (that is, the difference between market value before and after (salvage value) the casualty) or the adjusted basis of the property. In the case of total destruction of business or investment property, the loss will be the property's adjusted basis regardless of value. Regulation §1.165-1(d) details the time, or taxable year, for recording the loss. Essentially, casualty losses are deducted when they are sustained; theft losses are deducted when they are discovered.

The following example illustrates these rules. Assume that a fire destroys a television worth $6,000 and an antique bird cage worth $4,000 and also damages a chair worth $2,000. Each item is nonbusiness, personal-use property. The television cost $9,000, the bird cage $2,000, and the chair $3,000. The chair had a $200 fair market value after the fire. If the taxpayer's AGI is $50,000, the deduction is computed as follows:

		Television	Bird Cage	Chair
1.	Market value before fire	$6,000	$4,000	$2,000
	Value after fire	0	0	200
	Decrease in value	$6,000	$4,000	$1,800
2.	Adjusted basis per §1011 (cost)	9,000	2,000	3,000
3.	Taxpayer's loss (lesser of 1 or 2)	6,000	2,000	1,800
4.	Less any reimbursements	0	0	0
5.	Loss	$6,000	$2,000	$1,800
6.	Total losses from this casualty	$9,800		
7.	Less nondeductible floor ($100 + 10% AGI)	5,100		
	Casualty loss deduction	$3,700		

Had three separate casualties destroyed the items, the nondeductible $100 floor amount would be subtracted from each item because the $100 amount is attributable to each casualty event, not to each item destroyed.

Once the amount of the casualty loss has been determined, the character of the loss must be determined. Because a casualty by definition cannot constitute a sale or exchange, the loss should be characterized as an ordinary loss. However, under §165(h)(2) (using a procedure similar to the application of §1231, discussed in Chapter 7), personal casualty gains and losses for the year are compared. If gains exceed losses, all transactions are characterized as capital in nature.

Insurance coverage. Insurance coverage impacts the casualty deduction in three respects: (1) the determination of whether a deduction is available if a claim pursuant to such coverage is not made, (2) the determination of the amount of the deduction, and (3) the determination of when the deduction is available.

With regard to the first issue, the Service historically contested the deduction when a taxpayer failed to file a claim under an existing policy. Congress affirmed this position in §165(h)(4)(E), which provides that any loss covered by insurance may be taken into account only if a *timely* insurance claim is filed. Thus, failure to file a claim under an existing policy will preclude the deduction. However, if coverage exists and the taxpayer recovers under a policy, the loss determined under the

Regulations (before the §165(h) limitations) must be reduced by the amount of the insurance reimbursement.

From a timing standpoint, insurance coverage may dictate the year of deduction. Regulation §1.165-1(d)(2)(i) stipulates that if a claim for reimbursement exists for which there is a "reasonable prospect of recovery, no portion of the loss with respect to which reimbursement may be received is sustained . . . until it can be ascertained with reasonable certainty whether or not such reimbursement will be received."

Problems

8-16. Determine whether a casualty loss has occurred and the amount thereof (exclusive of the $100 and 10 percent of AGI limitations).
   a. While driving on a quiet country road, a driver encounters a horse charging at full tilt. In the ensuing collision, the car, which has a $5,000 adjusted basis and a $6,000 value, is totally destroyed.
   b. A negligent driver hits a telephone pole while driving 45 miles per hour in a 25-miles-per-hour zone. The car, which has a $4,000 adjusted basis and an $8,000 value, sustains damages totaling $2,000.
   c. A 10-year-old child in his new $100 suit runs out to play soccer after church and succeeds in ripping holes in his coat and slacks.
   d. A husband picks up a piece of tissue from his wife's dresser without realizing that her wedding ring is wrapped in it and throws the tissue away. The garbage truck arrives before the wife awakes, and the ring is lost. The ring's cost (twenty-five years ago) was $2,000, but it is now valued at $11,000.
   e. A one-week-old car is hit by a California mudslide and swept into a deep ravine. The purchase price was $7,000, but the resale value of the car at the time of loss was $6,000.

8-17. In year 1, James Bennett paid $9,000 for a Ford pickup to be used for personal purposes. On January 15, year 2, Bennett's pickup was destroyed when a tree fell on it while Bennett was cutting firewood. The fair market value of the truck on January 15 was $7,200. Bennett did not have insurance.
   a. What, if any, is Bennett's casualty loss from this occurrence?
   b. What result in *a* if Bennett uses his pickup only for business purposes?

8-18. Jolene Jacobson has $100,000 of adjusted gross income, a $50,000 casualty gain and a $40,000 casualty loss (after applying the $100 floor) for the year.
   a. What is the amount and character of the casualty gain and loss?
   b. Same as in *a* except that the casualty loss for the year is $70,000.

8-19. Roger Griffin's farm operation was in serious financial difficulty. Twice in June, hail damaged his crops, reducing his total corn yield by 32 percent. He had expected to harvest 150 bushels per acre. Although Griffin sold the corn for $3.10 per bushel (an increase of 40 cents per bushel over last year), the loss from a reduced yield of 102 bushels per acre on the 1,000 acres of corn he had planted more than offset the increased price. In addition, the exceptionally hot and dry August weather had severely damaged his one and one-half acre home garden of assorted vegetables. As a result, the garden's yield, predicted at $500, was negligible. He had invested $180 in seeds, fertilizer, and insecticide, plus 125 hours of labor in the home garden during the course of the summer. What, if any, casualty losses did Griffin sustain, and what is the amount thereof (exclusive of the $100 and 10 percent of AGI limitations)?

2. *Charitable Contributions*

Code: §170(a)(1), (c)(1) and (2), (e)(1) and (2)
Regulations: §§1.170A-1(a) to (c); 1.170A-4(b)(1), (b)(2)

Section 170 permits a deduction for "charitable contributions" made within the taxable year. The charitable contribution deduction was enacted to encourage charitable giving. However, the deduction may also serve other goals of the federal government. Were the government to directly subsidize various charities, partisan politics could dominate the decision-making process. Moreover, direct government involvement in charitable organizations might inhibit private donations and thus create greater reliance on government payments. Finally, from a budgetary viewpoint, tax revenue lost through charitable deductions partially compensates for itself by relieving the government from the responsibility of financing programs for the general welfare.

A charitable contribution is defined as a contribution or gift "to" or "for the use of" any of five types of organizations listed in §170(c): (1) a state or other political subdivision; (2) a corporation, trust, or community trust fund; (3) a post or organization of war veterans; (4) an organization involved in religious, charitable, scientific, literary, or educational endeavors; and (5) a cemetery. The distinction between contributions "to" and "for the use of" a donee basically turns on whether the donee's enjoyment of the property is subject to intervening interests, such as a trust or remainder interest. A transfer directly to the donee is encompassed by "to," while intervening interests create transfers "for the use of."

The language of §170(c) focuses on the nature of the recipient of the contribution. However, as the following materials illustrate, additional factors enter into the determination of whether a payment constitutes a charitable contribution. The taxpayer has the burden of establishing that the transfer was motivated by "disinterested generosity" in order to establish the requisite donative intent.

Starting in 1983, this aspect of the charitable deduction began to raise troubling issues, particularly in the context of fees for services from religious organizations such as religious school tuition and fees for religious training. In Rev. Rul. 83-104, 1983-2 C.B. 46, the IRS attempted to comprehensively address the issue by analyzing six separate situations when such payments could and could not be deductible. As might be expected, this did not end the controversy. Eventually the issue ended up before the Supreme Court. While the Supreme Court may have intended to have finally resolved the issue, as the following cases demonstrate it continues to be litigated.

HERNANDEZ v. COMMISSIONER
490 U.S. 680 (1989)

JUSTICE MARSHALL delivered the opinion of the Court.

Section 170 of the Internal Revenue Code . . . permits a taxpayer to deduct from gross income the amount of a "charitable contribution." The Code defines that term as a "contribution or gift" to certain eligible donees, including entities organized and operated exclusively for religious purposes. We granted certiorari to determine whether taxpayers may deduct as charitable contributions payments made to branch churches of the Church of Scientology (Church) in order to receive services known as "auditing" and "training." We hold that such payments are not deductible.

I

Scientology was founded in the 1950's by L. Ron Hubbard. It is propagated today by a "mother church" in California and by numerous branch churches around the world. The mother church instructs laity, trains and ordains ministers, and creates new congregations. Branch churches, known as "franchises" or "missions," provide Scientology services at the local level, under the supervision of the mother church.

Scientologists believe that an immortal spiritual being exists in every person. A person becomes aware of this spiritual dimension through a process known as "auditing." Auditing involves a one-to-one encounter between a participant (known as a "preclear") and a Church official (known as an "auditor"). An electronic device, the E-meter, helps the auditor identify the preclear's areas of spiritual difficulty by measuring skin responses during a question and answer session. Although auditing sessions are conducted one-on-one, the content of each session is not individually tailored. The preclear gains spiritual awareness by progressing through sequential levels of auditing, provided in short blocks of time known as "intensives."

The Church also offers members doctrinal courses known as "training." Participants in these sessions study the tenets of Scientology and seek to attain the qualifications necessary to serve as auditors. Training courses, like auditing sessions, are provided in sequential levels. Scientologists are taught that spiritual gains result from participation in such courses.

The Church charges a "fixed donation," also known as a "price" or a "fixed contribution," for participants to gain access to auditing and training sessions. These charges are set forth in schedules and prices vary with a session's length and level of sophistication. In 1972, for example, the general rates for auditing ranged from $625 for a 12 1/2-hour auditing intensive, the shortest available, to $4,250 for a 100-hour intensive, the longest available. Specialized types of auditing required higher fixed donations: a 12 1/2-hour "Integrity Processing" auditing intensive cost $750; a 12 1/2-hour "Expanded Dianetics" auditing intensive cost $950. This system of mandatory fixed charges is based on a central tenet of Scientology known as the "doctrine of exchange," according to which any time a person receives something he must pay something back. In so doing, a Scientologist maintains "inflow" and "outflow" and avoids spiritual decline.

The proceeds generated from auditing and training sessions are the Church's primary source of income. The Church promotes these sessions not only through newspaper, magazine, and radio advertisements, but also through free lectures, free personality tests, and leaflets. The Church also encourages, and indeed rewards with a five percent discount, advance payment for these sessions. The Church often refunds unused portions of prepaid auditing or training fees, less an administrative charge.

The petitioners in these consolidated cases each made payments to a branch church for auditing or training sessions. They sought to deduct these payments on their federal income tax returns as charitable contributions under §170. Respondent Commissioner of the Internal Revenue Service (Commissioner or IRS) disallowed these deductions, finding that the payments were not charitable contributions within the meaning of §170. . . .

The Tax Court held a 3-day bench trial during which the taxpayers and others testified and submitted documentary exhibits describing the terms under which the Church promotes and provides auditing and training sessions. Based on this record, the court upheld the Commissioner's decision. It observed first that the term "charitable contribution" in §170 is synonymous with the word "gift," which case law had defined "as a *voluntary transfer* of property by the owner to another *without consideration* therefor." It then determined that petitioners had received consideration for their payments, namely, "the benefit of various religious services provided by the Church of Scientology."

The Ninth Circuit also found that the taxpayers had received a "measurable, specific return . . . as a quid pro quo for the donation" they had made to the branch churches. The court reached this result by focusing on "the external features" of the auditing and training transactions, an analytic technique which "serves as an expedient for any more intrusive inquiry into the motives of the payor." Whether a particular exchange generated secular or religious benefits to the taxpayer was irrelevant, for under §170 "[i]t is the structure of the transaction, and not the type of benefit received, that controls." . . .

We granted certiorari to resolve a circuit conflict concerning the validity of charitable deductions for auditing and training payments. We now affirm.

II

For over 70 years, federal taxpayers have been allowed to deduct the amount of contributions or gifts to charitable, religious, and other eleemosynary institutions. Section 170, the present provision, was enacted in 1954; it requires a taxpayer claiming the deduction to satisfy a number of conditions. The Commissioner's stipulation in this case, however, has narrowed the statutory inquiry to one such condition: whether petitioners' payments for auditing and training sessions are "contribution[s] or gift[s]" within the meaning of §170.

The legislative history of the "contribution or gift" limitation, though sparse, reveals that Congress intended to differentiate between unrequited payments to qualified recipients and payments made to such recipients in return for goods or services. Only the former were deemed deductible. The House and Senate Reports on the 1954 tax bill, for example, both define "gifts" as payments "made with no expectation of a financial return commensurate with the amount of the gift." Using

payments to hospitals as an example, both Reports state that the gift characterization should not apply to "a payment by an individual to a hospital *in consideration of* a
binding obligation to provide medical treatment for the individual's employees. It
would apply only if there were no expectation of any quid pro quo from the
hospital."

In ascertaining whether a given payment was made with "the expectation of
any quid pro quo," the Internal Revenue Service (IRS) has customarily examined
the external features of the transaction in question. This practice has the advantage
of obviating the need for the IRS to conduct imprecise inquiries into the motivations of individual taxpayers. The lower courts have generally embraced this structural analysis. We likewise focused on external features in United States v.
American Bar Endowment to resolve the taxpayers' claims that they were entitled
to partial deductions for premiums paid to a charitable organization for insurance
coverage; the taxpayers contended that they had paid unusually high premiums in
an effort to make a contribution along with their purchase of insurance. We upheld
the Commissioner's disallowance of the partial deductions because the taxpayers
had failed to demonstrate, at a minimum, the existence of comparable insurance
policies with prices lower than those of the policy they had each purchased. In so
doing, we stressed that "[t]he *sine qua non* of a charitable contribution is a transfer of
money or property *without adequate consideration.*"

In light of this understanding of §170, it is readily apparent that petitioners'
payments to the Church do not qualify as "contribution[s] or gift[s]." As the Tax
Court found, these payments were part of a quintessential *quid pro quo* exchange: in
return for their money, petitioners received an identifiable benefit, namely, auditing and training sessions. The Church established fixed price schedules for auditing and training sessions in each branch church; it calibrated particular prices to
auditing or training sessions of particular lengths and levels of sophistication; it
returned a refund if auditing and training services went unperformed; it distributed "account cards" on which persons who had paid money to the Church could
monitor what prepaid services they had not yet claimed; and it categorically barred
provision of auditing or training sessions for free. Each of these practices reveals
the inherently reciprocal nature of the exchange.

Petitioners do not argue that such a structural analysis is inappropriate under
§170, or that the external features of the auditing and training transactions do not
strongly suggest a *quid pro quo* exchange. Indeed, the petitioners in the consolidated *Graham* case conceded at trial that they expected to receive specific amounts
of auditing and training in return for their payments. Petitioners argue instead that
they are entitled to deductions because a *quid pro quo* analysis is inappropriate
under §170 when the benefit a taxpayer receives is purely religious in nature.
Along the same lines, petitioners claim that payments made for the right to participate in a religious service should be automatically deductible under §170.

We cannot accept this statutory argument for several reasons. First, it finds no
support in the language of §170. Whether or not Congress could, consistent with
the Establishment Clause, provide for the automatic deductibility of a payment
made to a church that either generates religious benefits or guarantees access to
a religious service, that is a choice Congress has thus far declined to make. Instead,
Congress has specified that a payment to an organization operated exclusively for
religious (or other eleemosynary) purposes is deductible *only* if such a payment is a

"contribution or gift." The Code makes no special preference for payments made in the expectation of gaining religious benefits or access to a religious service. The House and Senate Reports on §170, and the other legislative history of that provision, offer no indication that Congress' failure to enact such a preference was an oversight.

Second, petitioners' deductibility proposal would expand the charitable contribution deduction far beyond what Congress has provided. Numerous forms of payments to eligible donees plausibly could be categorized as providing a religious benefit or as securing access to a religious service. For example, some taxpayers might regard their tuition payments to parochial schools as generating a religious benefit or as securing access to a religious service; such payments, however, have long been held not to be charitable contributions under §170. Taxpayers might make similar claims about payments for church-sponsored counseling sessions or for medical care at church-affiliated hospitals that otherwise might not be deductible. Given that, under the First Amendment, the IRS can reject otherwise valid claims of religious benefit only on the ground that a taxpayers' alleged beliefs are not sincerely held, but not on the ground that such beliefs are inherently irreligious, the resulting tax deductions would likely expand the charitable contribution provision far beyond its present size. We are loath to effect this result in the absence of supportive congressional intent.

Finally, the deduction petitioners seek might raise problems of entanglement between church and state. If framed as a deduction for those payments generating benefits of a religious nature for the payor, petitioners' proposal would inexorably force the IRS and reviewing courts to differentiate "religious" benefits from "secular" ones. If framed as a deduction for those payments made in connection with a religious service, petitioners' proposal would force the IRS and the judiciary into differentiating "religious" services from "secular" ones. We need pass no judgment now on the constitutionality of such hypothetical inquiries, but we do note that "pervasive monitoring" for "the subtle or overt presence of religious matter" is a central danger against which we have held the Establishment Clause guards.

Accordingly, we conclude that petitioners' payments to the Church for auditing and training sessions are not "contribution[s] or gift[s]" within the meaning of that statutory expression. . . .

V

For the reasons stated herein, the judgments of the Court of Appeals are hereby affirmed.

SKLAR v. COMMISSIONER
549 F.3d 1252 (9th Cir. 2008)

Wardlaw, Circuit Judge:

Michael and Marla Sklar ("the Sklars") appeal from a decision of the Tax Court affirming the disallowance of deductions they claimed for tuition and fees paid to their children's Orthodox Jewish day schools.

I. Factual and Procedural Background

A. Taxpayers

The Sklars are Orthodox Jews who in 1995 had five school-aged children. Rather than send their children to public school to meet California State educational requirements, the Sklars enrolled each of their children in one of two Orthodox Jewish day schools . . . In 1995, the Sklars paid a total of $27,283 to [the schools] which included $24,093 for tuition, $1300 for registration fees, $1715 for other mandatory fees, and $175 for an after school . . . program . . . Both schools . . . qualified as organizations described in I.R.C. §170(b)(1)(A), which allows donors to deduct charitable donations to qualifying institutions.

Both schools provided daily exposure to Jewish heritage and values. Their goals included educating their students in Jewish heritage and values, as well as the tenets of the Jewish faith. To this end, time was allocated in the school day for prayers and religious studies, students were required to adhere to Orthodox Jewish dress codes, and boys and girls attended classes separately.

A child's day at each school included specified hours devoted to courses in religious studies and specified hours devoted to secular studies. The length of time that each student participated in secular classes, as opposed to religious studies, and the length of the total school day varied with the gender and grade level of the particular student.

Quality secular education that fulfilled the mandatory education requirements of the State of California also was a goal of both schools . . .

During the school years in issue, the Sklars paid tuition and mandatory fees to [the schools] for their children's education. To ensure payment, the Sklars, like other parents, were required to contract with each school to pay, and to give to each school postdated checks covering, the tuition for the upcoming school year. . . . Although an Orthodox Rabbinic ruling precluded either school from expelling students from the Jewish studies program during the school year, nonpayment of tuition could result in expulsion from secular studies and the schools' refusal to allow the children to register for classes in the subsequent school year.

B. The Prior Litigation

In 1993, the Sklars learned of a confidential closing agreement the Internal Revenue Service ("IRS") had executed with the Church of Scientology that purportedly allowed deductions for certain religious educational services such as auditing and training. The Sklars subsequently amended their tax returns for 1991 and 1992, and filed a return for 1993, including new deductions for a portion of the tuition they had paid to their children's schools. The IRS allowed these deductions, apparently under the impression that the Sklars were Scientologists. The Sklars claimed similar deductions in 1994, but these were disallowed. The IRS Notice of Deficiency explained that because the costs were for personal tuition expenses, they were not deductible. The Sklars pursued an unsuccessful petition for redetermination before the Tax Court regarding their 1994 deductions, which subsequently came before us. Judge Reinhardt, writing for our Court in an opinion joined by Judge Pregerson, upheld the Tax Court's denial of the deduction. . . .

On their 1995 tax return, the Sklars claimed $15,000 in deductions for purported charitable contributions that comprised a portion of their five children's tuition. . . . The deduction was based on their estimate that 55% of the tuition payments were for purely religious education, an estimate supported by letters submitted two years later (in 1997) that were drafted by each of the schools at the Sklars' request.

The IRS disallowed the $15,000 deduction. . . . The Sklars petitioned the Tax Court for a redetermination of deficiency, asserting that (1) the tuition and fee payments to exclusively religious schools are deductible under a dual payment analysis to the extent the payments exceeded the value of the secular education their children received (a question left somewhat open in Sklar I); (2) Sections 170(f)(8) and 6115 of the Internal Revenue Code, as enacted in 1993, authorized the deduction of tuition payments for religious education made to exclusively religious schools (an issue all but foreclosed by Sklar I); and (3) that the 1993 Closing Agreement between the Commissioner and the Church of Scientology constitutionally and administratively requires the IRS to allow other taxpayers to take the same charitable deductions for tuition payments to their religious schools (a question the panel discussed at length but declined to decide in Sklar I). Before the Tax Court, the Sklars and the IRS stipulated that in 1993 the IRS had executed a confidential closing agreement with the Church of Scientology, settling several outstanding issues between the IRS and the Church of Scientology. Under this agreement, members of the Church of Scientology were authorized to deduct as charitable contributions at least 80% of the fees for qualified religious services provided by the Church of Scientology.

The Tax Court again rejected the Sklars' arguments, holding that the tuition and fee payments to the Jewish Day Schools were not deductible under any of the Sklars' theories. First, the Tax Court rejected the Sklars' effort to prove that the tuition and fee payments so exceeded the market value of the secular education their children received that they took on a "dual character," i.e. that the payments had the character of both a purchase of education and a charitable contribution. . . .

II. Discussion . . .

B. THE SKLARS' 1995 TUITION PAYMENTS ARE NOT DEDUCTIBLE AS CHARITABLE CONTRIBUTIONS UNDER THE INTERNAL REVENUE CODE

Section 170 of the Internal Revenue Code allows taxpayers to deduct "any charitable contribution," defined as "a contribution or gift to or for the use of" certain eligible entities enumerated in §170(c), including those exclusively organized for religious purposes and educational purposes. I.R.C. §170(a)(1), (c). "[T]o ensure that the payor's primary purpose is to assist the charity and not to secure some benefit," we require such contributions to be "made for detached and disinterested motives." Graham v. Comm'r, 822 F.2d 844, 848 (9th Cir.1987). Therefore, "quid pro quo" payments, where the taxpayer receives a benefit in exchange for the payment, are generally not deductible as charitable contributions. See Hernandez v. Comm'r, 490 U.S. 680, 689-91 (1989). In keeping with this framework, tuition payments to parochial schools, which are made with the expectation of a substantial benefit, or quid pro quo, "have long been held not to be charitable contributions under §170." Id. at 693, 109 S.Ct. 2136; see also DeJong v. Comm'r, 309 F.2d 373, 376 (9th Cir.1962) ("The law is well settled that tuition paid for the education of the children of a taxpayer is a family expense, not a charitable contribution to the educating institution.").

In *Hernandez*, the Supreme Court considered "whether taxpayers may deduct as charitable contributions payments made to branch churches of the Church of Scientology" in return for services known as "auditing" and "training." Both are considered forms of religious education. "Auditing" involves a form of spiritual counseling whereby a person gains spiritual awareness in one-on-one sessions with an auditor. By participating in "training," a person studies the tenets of Scientology, gains spiritually, and may seek to become an auditor. Members of the Church of Scientology sought to deduct payments for auditing and training as charitable contributions for religious services. The Court held that such payments for religious educational services "do not qualify as 'contribution[s] or gift[s].'" Rather, "[t]hese payments were part of a quintessential quid pro quo exchange: in return for their money, petitioners received an identifiable benefit, namely, auditing and training sessions." Id. The Court reasoned "'[t]he sine qua non of a charitable contribution is a transfer of money or property without adequate consideration.'"

The Court further rejected the taxpayers' argument that a quid pro quo analysis was not even appropriate, because the payments for auditing and training services resulted in receipt of a purely religious benefit. The Court first found no support in the language of §170, which makes "no special preference for payments made in the expectation of gaining religious benefits or access to a religious service." Second, the Court reasoned that accepting the taxpayers' "deductibility proposal would expand the charitable contribution deduction far beyond what Congress has provided." For example, "some taxpayers might regard their tuition payments to parochial schools as generating a religious benefit or as securing access to a religious service," which would be incorrect because "such payments . . . have long been held not to be charitable contributions under §170." Finally, the Court noted that "the deduction petitioners seek might raise problems of entanglement between church and state" because it would "inexorably force the IRS and reviewing courts to differentiate 'religious' benefits from 'secular' ones." Id. at 694, 109 S.Ct. 2136. While declining to pass on the constitutionality of such hypothetical inquiries, the Court noted that "'pervasive monitoring' for 'the subtle or overt presence of religious matter' is a central danger against which we have held the Establishment Clause guards." Thus, the *Hernandez* decision clearly forecloses the Sklars' argument that there is an exception in the Code for payments for which one receives purely religious benefits.

1.   THE 1993 AMENDMENTS TO THE TAX CODE DID NOT OVERRULE HERNANDEZ

To circumvent *Hernandez's* clear holding, the Sklars resurrect their Sklar I argument that the 1993 amendments to IRS §§170(f)(8) and 6115 overruled the Court's holding in *Hernandez* that only gifts or contributions may be deducted under §170. According to the Sklars, the 1993 amendments provide for the deduction of tuition payments for which they receive only intangible religious benefits. We agree with the Tax Court that the Sklar's interpretation of the 1993 amendments is misguided.

Amended §170(f)(8) requires the taxpayer to "substantiate[ ] the contribution by a contemporaneous written acknowledgment of the contribution by the donee organization." I.R.C. §170(f)(8)(A). This acknowledgment must include an estimate of the value of any goods or services the donor received in exchange, "or, if such goods or services consist solely of intangible religious benefits, a statement to that effect." I.R.C. §170(f)(8)(B)(iii). The amendment also defines an "intangible religious benefit" as one "which is provided by an organization organized exclusively for religious purposes and which generally is not sold in a commercial transaction outside the donative context." Id. As the Tax Court correctly held . . . this amendment creates an exception only to the new substantiation requirement. . . . Nothing in the amendment's language suggests that Congress intended to expand the types of payments that are deductible contributions. . . .

Nor does the legislative history of these amendments even mention *Hernandez*, and the House Report specifically states that, although the new requirements apply only to quid pro quo contributions for commercial benefits . . . Thus, the House Report confirms that Congress intended to preserve the status quo ante, and hardly serves as support for the Sklars' argument.

2. THE TUITION PAYMENTS WERE NOT "DUAL PAYMENT" CONTRIBUTIONS

The Tax Court correctly concluded that no part of the Sklar's tuition payments is deductible under a "dual payment" analysis. In *American Bar Endowment*, the Supreme Court considered the question of the extent to which payments to organizations that bear the "dual character" of a purchase and a contribution are deductible under §170. 477 U.S. at 116-18. IRS Revenue Ruling 67-246 had set forth a two-part test for determining the extent to which such payments are deductible:

> First, the payment is deductible only if and to the extent it exceeds the market value of the benefit received. Second, the excess payment must be "made with the intention of making a gift."

Id. at 117 (quoting Rev. Rul. 67-246). The Court held that Revenue Ruling 67-246 embodied the proper standard, reasoning: "The sine qua non of a charitable contribution is a transfer of money or property without adequate consideration. The taxpayer, therefore, must at a minimum demonstrate that he purposely contributed money or property in excess of the value of any benefit he received in return." Id. at 118. . . .

The Sklars again have failed to meet their burden of satisfying either prong of the two-part test for a dual payment, and we seriously doubt that they could ever make the showing that would support a "dual payment" deduction for tuition for combined religious and secular education. In Sklar I, the panel concluded that the Sklars failed to satisfy the requirements for partial deductibility of their tuition payments. Our analysis has not changed, despite the Sklars' effort to introduce evidence as to market value.

First, the Sklar I panel reasoned that the Sklars "failed to show that they intended to make a gift by contributing any such 'excess payment.'" In fact, the

Sklars have never even argued — not in Sklar I, not before the Tax Court and not before us — that they intended to make a gift as a portion of their tuition payment. Indeed, the record is to the contrary . . . . Because they paid for religious education out of their own deeply held religious views, and because the record demonstrates that throughout the school day — during recess, lunch and secular, as well as religious, classes — the schools inculcate their children with their religion's lifestyle, heritage, and values, the Sklars have actually demonstrated the absence of the requisite charitable intent.

Second, the Sklar I panel reasoned that "the Sklars have not shown that any dual tuition payments they may have made exceeded the market value of the secular education their children received." The panel stated that the Sklars needed to present evidence that their total payments exceeded "[t]he market value [of] the cost of a comparable secular education offered by private schools." . . . The Tax Court correctly concluded that the evidence in the record indicated . . . [that] the amount of tuition petitioners paid is unremarkable and is not excessive for the substantial benefit they received in exchange; i.e., an education for their children. Before us, the Sklars have failed to demonstrate — or even argue on appeal — that the Tax Court's factual findings as to the data set forth in their expert's report are clearly erroneous.

Thus, the Tax Court did not err by concluding that the Sklars failed to show that any part of their tuition fees was a charitable deduction, subject to a dual payment analysis. We conclude that under *Hernandez* and the Internal Revenue Code, their tuition and fee payments must be treated like any other quid pro quo transaction, even if some part of the benefit received was religious in nature. See 490 U.S. at 691-94. We therefore agree with the Tax Court that the Sklars' tuition is not deductible, in whole or in part, under §170.

c. The 1993 Closing Agreement Does Not Constitutionally and Administratively Require the IRS To Allow Charitable Deductions for the Sklars' Tuition Payments to Religious Schools

The Sklars reassert their Sklar I argument that in light of allegedly similar deductions allowed for members of the Church of Scientology under a closing agreement with the IRS, the disallowance of deductions for Orthodox Jewish religious education violates the Establishment Clause and principles of administrative consistency. They also argue that the Tax Court abused its discretion in denying discovery about the Closing Agreement, including compelling its production. Before the Tax Court, the Sklars and the Commissioner stipulated that an agreement dated October 1, 1993, between the Commissioner and the Church of Scientology settled several longstanding issues. A letter the Sklars had received from the IRS was also admitted. It established that the Closing Agreement allows individuals to claim, as charitable contributions, 80 percent of the cost of qualified religious services. The Sklars argued that because of the Closing Agreement, the Commissioner is constitutionally and administratively precluded from disallowing their deductions for school tuition and fees, which they contend are "jurisprudentially indistinguishable" from the auditing and training provided by the Church of Scientology.

The Tax Court correctly dispatched that argument by citing to Sklar I. There the panel stated that "[w]e seriously doubt that the Sklars are similarly situated to the persons who benefit from the Scientology closing agreement because the religious education of the Sklars' children does not appear to be similar to the 'auditing', 'training' or other 'qualified religious services' conducted by the Church of Scientology." We also conclude that tuition and fee payments to schools that provide secular and religious education as part of one curriculum are quite different from payments to organizations that provide exclusively religious services. Because the Sklars are situated differently than members of the Church of Scientology, the Tax Court did not abuse its discretion in determining that the Closing Agreement itself was not relevant, and therefore not discoverable in the Sklars' redetermination proceedings.

Nor did the Tax Court err in its conclusion that "the agreement reached between the [IRS] and the Church of Scientology does not affect the result in this case," . . . We cannot improve upon the original panel majority's elucidation of the principles at stake:

> Applying [Larson v. Valente, 456 U.S. at 246-47] to the policy of the IRS towards the Church of Scientology, the initial inquiry must be whether the policy facially discriminates amongst religions. Clearly it does, as this tax deduction is available only to members of the Church of Scientology.
>
> The second *Larson* inquiry is whether or not the facially discriminatory policy is justified by a compelling governmental interest. 456 U.S. at 246-47. Although the IRS does not concede that it is engaging in a denominational preference, it asserts in its brief that the terms of the settlement agreement cannot be used as a basis to find an Establishment Clause violation because "in order to settle a case, both parties are required to make compromises with respect to points on which they believe they are legally correct." This is the only interest that the IRS proffers for the alleged policy. Although it appears to be true that the IRS has engaged in this particular preference in the interest of settling a long and litigious tax dispute with the Church of Scientology, and as compelling as this interest might otherwise be, it does not rise to the level that would pass strict scrutiny. The benefits of settling a controversy with one religious organization can hardly outweigh the costs of engaging in a religious preference. Even aside from the constitutional considerations, a contrary rule would create a procedure by which any denomination seeking a denominational preference could bypass Congressional law-making and IRS rulemaking by engaging in voluminous tax litigation. Such a procedure would likely encourage the proliferation of such litigation, not reduce it. Larson, 456 U.S. at 248 (holding that even assuming arguendo that the government has a compelling governmental interest for a denominational preference, it must show that the rule is "closely fitted to further the interest that it assertedly serves"). Because the facial preference for the Church of Scientology embodied in the IRS's policy regarding its members cannot be justified by a compelling governmental interest, we would, if required to decide the case on the ground urged by the Sklars, first determine that the IRS policy constitutes an unconstitutional denominational preference under Larson, 456 U.S. at 230.

However, the Sklar I panel declined to follow the Sklars' suggestion that they, too, are entitled to an unconstitutional denominational preference for three reasons:

> First, we would be reluctant ever to presume that Congress or any agency of the government would intend that a general religious preference be adopted, by extension or otherwise, as such preferences raise the highly sensitive issue of state sponsorship of religion. In the absence of a clear expression of such intent, we would be

unlikely to consider extending a policy favoring one religion where the effect of our action would be to create a policy favoring all. Second, the Supreme Court has previously stated that a policy such as the Sklars wish us to create would be of questionable constitutional validity under *Lemon*, because the administration of the policy could require excessive government entanglement with religion. Hernandez, 490 U.S. at 694; see Lemon, 403 U.S. at 612-13. Third, the policy the Sklars seek would appear to violate section §170. See Hernandez, 490 U.S. at 692-93.

The Sklar I panel also rejected the Sklars' administrative inconsistency claim on two grounds:

> First, in order to make an administrative inconsistency claim, a party must show that it is similarly situated to the group being treated differently by the agency. United States v. Kaiser, 363 U.S. 299, 308 (1960). We seriously doubt that the Sklars are similarly situated to the persons who benefit from the Scientology closing agreement because the religious education of the Sklars' children does not appear to be similar to the "auditing", "training" or other "qualified religious services" conducted by the Church of Scientology. Second, even if they were so situated, because the treatment they seek is of questionable statutory and constitutional validity under §170 of the IRC, under *Lemon*, and under *Hernandez*, we would not hold that the unlawful policy set forth in the closing agreement must be extended to all religious organizations.

These principles are as correct today as they were six years ago. We adopt the full force of the conclusions they dictate. To conclude otherwise would be tantamount to rewriting the Tax Code, disregarding Supreme Court precedent, only to reach a conclusion directly at odds with the Establishment Clause — all in the name of the Establishment Clause. The principle the Sklars advance does not stop with them and their 1995 taxes; its logic would extend to all members of religious organizations who benefit from educational services that are in whole or part religious in nature. The Tax Court correctly held that neither the Establishment Clause nor principles of administrative consistency allow the Sklars the deductions they seek, and the Tax Court's denial of discovery regarding the Closing Agreement in proceedings involving the deductibility of the Sklars' tuition and fees was not an abuse of discretion.

Conclusion

The Tax Court correctly affirmed the IRS's disallowance of deductions the Sklars claimed for tuition and fees paid to their children's Orthodox Jewish day schools. The decision of the Tax Court is AFFIRMED.

Note on Mechanics and Limitations

In general, the charitable contribution deduction equals the amount of money contributed or the fair market value of the property donated on the date of the contribution. This led to a number of concerns, however. First, Congress was concerned that donors could "double-dip" by taking a deduction for the full fair market value of appreciated property while never paying tax on the gain as there was no sale or exchange. In response, Congress enacted §170(e)(1). With respect to any property which would have resulted in short-term capital gain if the property had been sold, §170(e)(1)(A) limits the amount of the contribution to the adjusted basis of the property. With respect to long-term capital gain property, §170(e)(1)(B) limits the deduction the adjusted basis of the property if it is either (1) tangible property used by the donee in a use unrelated to the donee's charitable purpose or (2) property donated to a private foundation.

Notwithstanding these limitations, Congress continued to be concerned about abuse of the charitable contribution deduction for contributions of property. For example, numerous taxpayers were claiming large charitable contribution deductions for contributing non-operational cars and boats to charities, which would then sell them at much lower values. Congress was concerned because there was little to no market for such vehicles, making fair market value highly debatable, and the charities were not experts in valuing vehicles. In response, Congress limited the deduction for certain cars and boats to the amount for which they are sold by the charity. §170(f)(12). Similar rules were adopted to prevent manipulation of the valuation of intellectual property, although Congress carved out exceptions for a number of particular types of intellectual property including donation of certain books or computer technology to public schools. §170(e)(1)(B)(iii), (e)(3).

Similarly, Congress was extremely concerned over certain owners of valuable works of art "donating" a term-of-years interest to a museum to permit the museum to display the art while retaining the owner right to reclaim the art after the expiration of the term of years. In this manner, taxpayers were claiming extremely large deductions for what effectively was only a loan of the art to the museum. Congress limited this by adopting §170(f)(3) which denied a charitable contribution for a contribution of less than the taxpayer's entire ownership interest in property to a charity. Numerous other restrictions applicable to specific concerns can be found in §§170(e)-(f) as well.

Problems

8-20. John Ferris, whose home was destroyed by a tornado, contributed $500 to the local chapter of the Red Cross in gratitude for its assistance in providing food and temporary shelter to himself and his family. Is the contribution deductible?

8-21. A partner in a large Wall Street law firm wants to send his daughter to the most prestigious private, religious school in New York. The school is operated by the local church, of which he is a member. The school prides itself on the incredible success of its students on the SAT and its ability to place graduates in Ivy League colleges, as well as providing training in religious theology. Would the following amounts be deductible?
   a. He pays $15,000 per year for her to attend the school.
   b. He contributes $50,000 to his Ivy League alma mater, hoping to ensure that his daughter will be admitted to its undergraduate program.

8-22. Real estate magnate Walter Karamazov contributes $5 million to a law school with the express understanding that the law school's new building will be christened Karamazov Hall. Karamazov has thereby succeeded in immortalizing himself.

   a. Is the $5 million contribution deductible?

   b. What if Karamazov donates property worth $5 million with a basis of $1 million but subject to a $2 million nonrecourse liability?

8-23. A student at a law school receives $3,000 a year in financial aid directly from the university. Each year when she accepts the grant, she signs a receipt stating that she recognizes a moral obligation to repay the money she receives. Five years later, the former student sends a check for $9,000 to the law school. Is this amount deductible?

8-24. Patricia Resnik pledged stock to the local YWCA in its annual fund-raising effort for Camp Waxahachie. On December 7, she transferred the stock, which had a value of $5,000 and a basis of only $2,300. In addition, she joined the YWCA's effort and spent forty hours contacting businesses in the area about contributing to the fund.

   a. Is the contribution of stock deductible and, if so, to what extent?

   b. Can Resnik take a deduction for the value of her services?

   c. Resnik also contributed $500 to the New Hope Lutheran Church where her son, Harvey, attended vacation Bible school. The Bible school charged no tuition but requested that parents contribute whatever they could to help defray the church's expenses. What amounts, if any, are deductible?

3. *Medical Expenses*

Code: §213
Regulations: §1.213-1(e)(1)

Medical care expenses are another category of personal expense for which the Code permits a deduction. Section 213 allows individuals to deduct expenses paid during the taxable year, not reimbursed by insurance, for medical care for the taxpayer and the taxpayer's spouse and dependents. The deduction is limited to the amount by which the total annual unreimbursed medical expenses exceed 10 percent of AGI for tax years beginning after December 31, 2012. Thus, Congress has granted a limited deduction to taxpayers with substantial medical expenses. As with casualty losses, the focus in determining a taxpayer's tax liability is on the taxpayer's ability to pay.

Medical care is defined by §213(d)(1) to include reasonable amounts paid for: (1) "the diagnosis, cure, mitigation, treatment, or prevention of disease, or for the purpose of affecting any structure or function of the body" (§213(d)(1)(A)); (2) related transportation; (3) qualified long-term care services; and (4) medical insurance premiums. Additionally, medication and drugs constitute medical care expenses if they are prescribed drugs or insulin.

The definition of medical care also includes amounts paid for lodging while away from home to obtain medical care provided by a licensed physician in a licensed hospital or administered in a medical care facility that is related to a licensed hospital or is the equivalent of one. §213(d)(2). In order to preclude potential taxpayer abuse of the lodging deduction, lodging expenses are disallowed if there is a significant element of personal pleasure, recreation, or vacation in the travel away from home. Furthermore, the travel expense deduction is limited to the lower of actual lodging expense or $50 per night per eligible person.

The following example illustrates the application of the medical expense deduction. Assume that the taxpayer has an adjusted gross income of $30,000 and spends $4,000 for qualified medical care, $1,200 for prescribed medication, and $3,000 for medical insurance. The taxpayer's §213 medical expense deduction is calculated as follows:

Medical care	$4,000
Drugs and medicine	1,200
Medical insurance premiums	3,000
Total medical care expenses	$8,200
Less: 10% of AGI	3,000
Total medical expense deduction	$5,200

Note the effect of the 10 percent floor in this case. The deduction is a form of public insurance in that the federal government pays a portion of the taxpayer's medical expenses through reduced taxes. This is only available if the expense is not otherwise reimbursed by insurance. Taken together, the 10 percent floor acts as a form of penalty on those without health insurance.

Although §213 deductions are for medical *expenses*, a deduction may also be allowed for a capital expenditure. Regulation §1.213-1(e)(1)(iii) provides that capital expenditures are not precluded from qualifying as medical expenses if they have as their primary purpose the taxpayer's medical care. Thus, a deduction may be permissible for capital expenditures such as elevators or swimming pools installed for medical purposes. However, the deduction is limited to the extent that the cost exceeds the increase in the value of the related property. For example, a medically required whirlpool that costs $15,000 and adds $10,000 in value to the house would yield a $5,000 medical expense deduction.

The opportunity to deduct capital expenditures that are primarily, but not solely, for medical care has tempted many taxpayers to take questionable deductions. This temptation was most dramatically illustrated in Ferris v. Commissioner, 582 F.2d 1112 (7th Cir. 1978). In *Ferris*, the taxpayers spent approximately $195,000 to construct a swimming pool that would be architecturally and esthetically harmonious with their home. The taxpayer's physician had recommended its construction and use twice a day to prevent the onset of permanent paralysis. The Seventh Circuit concluded that those costs attributable to "such personal motivations as architectural or esthetic compatibility with the related property" were not expenses for medical care. The court held that in such a case the appropriate standard was the "minimum reasonable cost of a functionally adequate pool and housing structure." That figure would then be compared with the enhanced value of the related property in determining the amount of the medical expense.

REV. RUL. 75-187
1975-1 C.B. 92

Advice has been requested whether, under the circumstances described below, the amounts paid for treatment for sexual inadequacy and incompatibility and for meals and lodging are deductible under section 213 of the Internal Revenue Code. . . .

The taxpayers, husband and wife, underwent treatment for sexual inadequacy and incompatibility. The treatment was conducted by psychiatrists at a hospital and was based on a program of treatment developed by researchers at a biological research foundation. In the opinion of the psychiatrists the probability of successful treatment was greater if their patients resided at a hotel in the vicinity of the hospital during the two-week duration of the treatment.

The taxpayers followed their psychiatrists' recommendation and resided at a hotel near the hospital. Each morning they attended consultation sessions conducted by their psychiatrists at the hospital. . . .

[T]he amount paid to the psychiatrists for the treatment for sexual inadequacy and incompatibility is deductible under section 213(e)(1)(A), subject to the limitations prescribed therein.

REV. RUL. 75-319
1975-2 C.B. 88

Advice has been requested concerning the deductibility, for Federal income tax purposes, of certain counseling fees under the circumstances described below.

The taxpayers, husband and wife, have been consulting with a clergyman associated with a counseling center for several months. The center is a nonprofit organization funded by several religious organizations. The taxpayers went to the center for marriage counseling. As a result of the counseling, the taxpayers feel they are healthier persons and are enjoying a more meaningful relationship. . . .

In the instant case, the counseling was not for the prevention or alleviation of a physical or mental defect or illness, but rather to help improve the taxpayers' marriage.

Accordingly, the counseling fees paid by the taxpayers are not medical expenses within the meaning of section 213 of the Code, but are personal expenses within the meaning of section 262 and, therefore, nondeductible.

REV. RUL. 97-9
1997-1 C.B. 77

ISSUE

Is an amount paid to obtain a controlled substance (such as marijuana) for medical purposes, in violation of federal law, a deductible expense for medical care under §213 of the Internal Revenue Code?

FACTS

Based on the recommendation of a physician, *A* purchased marijuana and used it to treat *A*'s disease in a state whose laws permit such purchase and use.

LAW AND ANALYSIS

Section 213(a) allows a deduction for uncompensated expenses of an individual for medical care to the extent such expenses exceed 7.5 percent of adjusted gross income. Section 213(d)(1) provides, in part, that "medical care" means amounts paid for the cure, mitigation, and treatment of disease. However, under §213(b) an amount paid for medicine or a drug is an expense for medical care under §213(a) only if the medicine or drug is a prescribed drug or insulin. Section 213(d)(3) provides that a "prescribed drug" is a drug or biological that requires a prescription of a physician for its use by an individual.

Section 1.213-1(e)(2) of the Income Tax Regulations provides, in part, that the term "medicine and drugs" includes only items that are "legally procured." Section 1.213-1(e)(1)(ii) provides that amounts expended for illegal operations or treatments are not deductible. . . .

Rev. Rul. 73-201, 1973-1 C.B. 140, holds that amounts paid for a vasectomy and an abortion are expenses for medical care that are deductible under §213. The revenue ruling states that neither procedure was illegal under state law.

A's purchase and use of marijuana were permitted under the laws of *A*'s state. However, marijuana is listed as a controlled substance on Schedule I of the Controlled Substances Act (CSA). Except as authorized by the CSA, it is unlawful for any person to manufacture, distribute, or dispense, or possess with intent to manufacture, distribute, or dispense, a controlled substance. Further, it is unlawful for any person knowingly or intentionally to possess a controlled substance except as authorized by the CSA. Generally, the CSA does not permit the possession of controlled substances listed on Schedule I, even for medical purposes, and even with a physician's prescription.

Notwithstanding state law, a controlled substance (such as marijuana), obtained in violation of the CSA, is not "legally procured" within the meaning of §1.213-1(e)(2). Further, an amount expended to obtain a controlled substance (such as marijuana) in violation of the CSA is an amount expended for an illegal treatment within the meaning of §1.213-1(e)(1)(ii). Accordingly, *A* may not deduct under §213 the amount *A* paid to purchase marijuana.

HOLDING

An amount paid to obtain a controlled substance (such as marijuana) for medical purposes, in violation of federal law, is not a deductible expense for medical care under §213. This holding applies even if the state law requires a prescription of a physician to obtain and use the controlled substance and the taxpayer obtains a prescription.

REV. RUL. 2007-72
2007-50 I.R.B. 1154

ISSUE

Are amounts paid by individuals for diagnostic and certain similar procedures and devices, not compensated by insurance or otherwise, medical care expenses deductible under §213(a) of the Internal Revenue Code?

FACTS

In the situations described below, the costs paid by the taxpayers are not compensated by insurance or otherwise, and the taxpayers are not experiencing any symptoms of illness.

Situation 1. Taxpayer A undergoes an annual physical examination, which is performed by a physician. A pays for the physician's services and laboratory tests.

Situation 2. Taxpayer B pays for a full-body electronic scan, a relatively high-cost procedure, performed by a technician at a clinic. The scan examines the condition of B's internal organs and may identify disease or other abnormalities. B has not consulted a physician before undergoing the procedure, which can be obtained without a physician's direction, or determined if less expensive alternatives are available.

Situation 3. Taxpayer C buys a test kit and uses it to determine whether she is pregnant.

LAW

Section 213(a) allows a deduction for expenses paid during the taxable year, not compensated for by insurance or otherwise, for medical care of the taxpayer, spouse, or dependent, to the extent that the expenses exceed 7.5 percent of adjusted gross income. Medical care includes amounts paid for the diagnosis, cure, mitigation, treatment, or prevention of disease, or for the purpose of affecting any structure or function of the body. Section 213(d)(1)(A).

Medical care includes X-rays and laboratory and other diagnostic services. Amounts paid for obstetrical services are deemed to be for the purpose of affecting a structure or function of the body and therefore are paid for medical care. Section 1.213-1(e)(1)(ii) of the Income Tax Regulations.

"Diagnosis" is the determination of a medical condition, such as a disease, by physical examination or study of symptoms. Black's Law Dictionary (8th ed., 2004). A diagnosis may encompass a determination that disease is absent. The determination of a medical condition may include testing for changes in the functions of the body, such as those resulting from pregnancy, that are unrelated to disease.

In determining whether an expense is for either medical or personal reasons, the recommendation of a physician is important. Havey v. Commissioner, 12 T.C. 409, 412 (1949). However, this determination is unnecessary in the case of expenses for items that are wholly medical in nature and serve no other function in everyday life. Stringham v. Commissioner, 12 T.C. 580, 584 (court reviewed), aff'd 183 F.2d 579 (6th Cir. 1950).

The amount of the deduction under §213 is not limited by a ceiling and, although additional costs for personal convenience are not allowable, §213 does not limit the deduction to amounts paid for the least expensive form of medical care available. Ferris v. Commissioner, 582 F.2d 1112, 1116 (7 th Cir. 1978).

ANALYSIS

In Situation 1, the amount A pays for the annual physical examination is for diagnosis and qualifies as an expense for medical care even though A is not experiencing any symptoms of illness.

In Situation 2, the amount B pays for the full-body scan is for diagnosis and qualifies as an expense for medical care even though B is not experiencing symptoms of illness and has not obtained a physician's recommendation before undergoing the procedure. The procedure serves no non-medical function and the expense is not disallowed because of the high cost or possible existence of less expensive alternatives.

In Situation 3, the amount C pays for the pregnancy test qualifies as an expense for medical care even though its purpose is to test the healthy functioning of the body rather than to detect disease.

Therefore, the amounts paid by Taxpayers A, B, and C for the physical examination, the full-body scan, and the pregnancy test kit are deductible under §213(a). . . .

HOLDING

Amounts paid by individuals for diagnostic and certain similar procedures and devices, not compensated by insurance or otherwise, are medical care expenses deductible under §213(a), subject to the limitations of that section.

ANNOUNCEMENT 2011-14
2011-9 I.R.B. 532

The Internal Revenue Service has concluded that breast pumps and supplies that assist lactation are medical care under §213(d) of the Internal Revenue Code because, like obstetric care, they are for the purpose of affecting a structure or function of the body of the lactating woman. Therefore, if the remaining requirements of §213(a) are met . . . expenses paid for breast pumps and supplies that assist lactation are deductible medical expenses. . . .

MAGDALIN v. COMMISSIONER
T.C. Memo. 2008-293

WHERRY, JUDGE:

FINDINGS OF FACT

Petitioner is a medical doctor licensed to practice medicine in Massachusetts. At all relevant times, his sperm count and motility were found to be within normal limits. He has twin sons from a marriage to his former spouse, Deborah Magdalin. The twins were born through natural processes and without the use of in vitro fertilization (IVF).

In July 2004 petitioner entered into an Anonymous Egg Donor Agreement under which an anonymous donor was to donate eggs to be fertilized with petitioner's sperm and transferred to a gestational carrier using the IVF process. That same month, petitioner also entered into a Gestational Carrier Agreement in which a woman (the first carrier) agreed to become impregnated through the IVF embryo transfer process with the embryo created from the anonymous donor's egg and petitioner's sperm and to bear a child for petitioner. The first carrier gave birth to a child on September 17, 2005.

On November 18, 2005, petitioner entered into a similar Gestational Carrier Agreement with another woman (the second carrier). The second carrier gave birth to a child on August 12, 2006. The donor was not the spouse or dependent of petitioner. Nor was either of the carriers. Both IVF procedures occurred at the Reproduction Science Center (IVF clinic) in Lexington, Massachusetts. . . .

OPINION

I.   DEDUCTIONS FOR MEDICAL EXPENSES

Section 213(a) allows for the deduction of paid expenses "not compensated for by insurance or otherwise, for medical care of the taxpayer, his spouse, or a dependent. . . ." While Congress has indicated an intent, once section 213 applies, to broadly define medical care . . . we have characterized section 213 as carving out "a limited exception" to the general rule in section 262 that prohibits the deduction of personal, living, or family expenses. Consequently, the medical expense deduction has been narrowly construed for many years, as the Court noted more than 40 years ago in Atkinson v. Commissioner, 44 T.C. 39, 49 (1965). The deductibility of the expenses at issue hinges on whether they were paid for petitioner's medical care. If so, they are deductible medical expenses under section 213. If not, they are nondeductible personal expenses under section 262.

The term "medical care" includes amounts paid "for the diagnosis, cure, mitigation, treatment, or prevention of disease, or for the purpose of affecting any structure or function of the body." Sec. 213(d)(1)(A). . . .

We have interpreted the statute as requiring a causal relationship in the form of a "but for" test between a medical condition and the expenditures incurred in treating that condition. The "but for" test requires petitioner to prove (1) "that the expenditures were an essential element of the treatment" and (2) "that they would not have otherwise been incurred for nonmedical reasons."

It is also noteworthy that section 213(d)(1)(A), which is not a model of clarity, is phrased disjunctively — it allows for the deduction of any expenses paid "for the diagnosis, cure, mitigation, treatment, or prevention of disease, or for the purpose of affecting any structure or function of the body". . . .

III.   THE EXPENSES AT ISSUE ARE NONDEDUCTIBLE PERSONAL EXPENSES

The expenses at issue were not paid for medical care under the first portion of section 213(d)(1)(A) because the requisite causal relationship is absent. None of the expenses at issue was "incurred primarily for the prevention or alleviation of a physical or mental defect or illness." In other words, petitioner had no medical condition or defect, such as, for example, infertility, that required treatment or mitigation through IVF procedures. We therefore need not answer lurking questions as to whether (and, if so, to what extent) expenditures for IVF procedures and associated costs (e.g., a taxpayer's legal fees and fees paid to, or on behalf of, a surrogate or gestational carrier) would be deductible in the presence of an underlying medical condition. We leave such questions for another day. Further, petitioner cannot deduct those expenses under the second portion of the statute because they did not affect a structure or function of his body.[8]

Although petitioner at times attempts to frame the deductibility of the relevant expenses as an issue of constitutional dimensions, under the facts and circumstances of his case, it does not rise to that level. Petitioner's gender, marital status, and sexual orientation do not bear on whether he can deduct the expenses at issue. He cannot deduct those expenses because he has no medical condition or defect to which those expenses relate and because they did not affect a structure or function of his body. Expenses incurred in the absence of the requisite underlying medical condition or defect and that do not affect a structure or function of the taxpayer's body are nondeductible personal expenses within the meaning of section 262. . . .

Decision will be entered for respondent.

Note on Cosmetic Surgery

Section 213(d)(9) provides that medical care does not "include cosmetic surgery or other similar procedures, unless the surgery or procedure is necessary to ameliorate a deformity arising from . . . a congenital abnormality, a personal injury resulting from an accident or trauma, or disfiguring disease." Prior to this amendment, the definition of medical care included those operations done "for the purpose of affecting any structure or function of the body." This definition was construed to include cosmetic surgery regardless of whether a "physical or mental defect or illness" was thereby prevented or alleviated. See Mattes v. Commissioner, 77 T.C. 650 (1981) (deduction allowed for cost of surgical hair transplant as remedy for baldness); Rev. Rul. 76-332, 1976-2 C.B. 81 (deduction allowed for facelift). Such deductions appear to be a thing of the past.

As a result of the enactment of §213(d)(9), the first question in determining whether costs for reconstructive or elective surgeries are deductible is whether such surgeries "meaningfully promote the proper function of the body or prevent or treat illness or disease." If so, the provision will not apply, and the costs will generally be deductible. If not, then such costs may still be deductible if "the surgery or procedure is necessary to ameliorate a deformity arising from, or directly related to, a congenital abnormality, a personal injury resulting from an accident or trauma, or disfiguring disease."

Applying this two-prong test, it remains unclear as to what extent severe psychological or emotional harm could justify a deduction for what would otherwise be nondeductible cosmetic surgery. Should costs for breast reconstruction be

---

8. Where a medical procedure affects a structure or function of the taxpayer's body, the cost of such a procedure may be a deductible medical expense unless proscribed by sec. 213(d)(9). A vasectomy is an example of a noncosmetic operation that the Commissioner has determined is deductible because it affects the structure of a taxpayer's body. See Rev. Rul. 73-201, 1973-1 C.B. 140. The dictionary defines "affect" as "to produce an effect upon" or "to produce a material influence upon or alteration in." Merriam–Webster's Collegiate Dictionary 21 (11th ed.2003). Petitioner's bodily functions and structures were not "affected" by the IVF processes — they remained the same before and after those processes.

deductible under the second prong if the surgery is a result of breast cancer, notwithstanding that it clearly seems to fail the first? If so, what if the breast reconstruction is prescribed by a physician as a treatment for psychological illness? For low self-esteem? Similarly, should costs for corrective eye surgery to replace eyeglasses be deductible if the surgery substantially improves vision? What if the sole reason for undertaking the surgery is vanity, for example, not wanting to wear corrective eyeglasses? The increased diagnosis and treatment of severe psychological illness continues to place pressure on the distinction drawn between the two prongs of the test, raising continuing difficulties in applying the provision.

The Tax Court considered this issue in a case involving an individual diagnosed with Gender Identity Disorder, or GID. At the time, GID was a recognized psychological disorder that led to intense stress and psychological pain because the patient did not personally identify with the gender they physically embodied. The primary treatment for GID was gender reassignment surgery and intense hormone therapy to change the patient's physical appearance to match their gender identity. The taxpayer, being born physically a male but identifying as a female, underwent a gender reassignment surgery, involving removal of the male genitalia and insertion of artificial breast enhancements, as well as hormone therapy, and deducted the costs for tax purposes. The Service disallowed the deduction, asserting that GID was not a disease for purposes of §213(d)(9) and that, even if it was, the surgery and hormone therapy were cosmetic and not meant to treat GID. The taxpayer contended that all the expenses involved in the gender reassignment surgery should be deductible because GID was a medically recognized disease and thus the medically recommended surgery and hormones were not cosmetic. In the alternative, the taxpayer contended that the male genitalia and lack of female breast tissue were a "deformity" arising due to a congenital abnormality. The Tax Court, in a divided and controversial opinion, held that GID was a disease for purposes of §213(d)(9) and that the gender reassignment surgery and the costs of the hormone replacements were deductible, but that the costs of the breast enhancement surgery was "cosmetic" and not for treatment of the GID, and thus not deductible. O'Donnabhain v. Commissioner, 134 T.C. 34 (2010). Over a year after the holding in this case, the Service announced that it would change its position and treat GID as a disease for purposes of §213(d)(9). AOD, 2011-47 I.R.B. 789.

REV. RUL. 2003-57
2003-1 C.B. 959

ISSUE

Are amounts paid by individuals for breast reconstruction surgery, vision correction surgery, and teeth whitening medical care expenses within the meaning of §213(d) and deductible under §213 of the Internal Revenue Code?

FACTS

Taxpayer *A* undergoes mastectomy surgery that removes a breast as part of treatment for cancer and pays a surgeon to reconstruct the breast. Taxpayer *B* wears glasses to correct myopia and pays a doctor to perform laser eye surgery to correct the myopia. Taxpayer *C*'s teeth are discolored as a result of age. *C* pays a dentist to perform a teeth-whitening procedure. *A*, *B*, and *C* are not compensated for their expenses by insurance or otherwise.

LAW AND ANALYSIS

Section 213(a) allows a deduction for expenses paid during the taxable year, not compensated for by insurance or otherwise, for medical care of the taxpayer, spouse, or dependent. . . . Under §213(d)(1)(A), medical care includes amounts paid for the diagnosis, cure, mitigation, treatment, or prevention of disease, or for the purpose of affecting any structure or function of the body.

Medical care does not include cosmetic surgery or other similar procedures, unless the surgery or procedure is necessary to ameliorate a deformity arising from, or directly related to, a congenital abnormality, a personal injury resulting from an accident or trauma, or a disfiguring disease. Section 213(d)(9)(A). Cosmetic surgery means any procedure that is directed at improving the patient's appearance and does not meaningfully promote the proper function of the body or prevent or treat illness or disease. Section 213(d)(9)(B).

A's cancer is a disfiguring disease because the treatment results in the loss of *A*'s breast. Accordingly, the breast reconstruction surgery ameliorates a deformity directly related to a disease and the cost is an expense for medical care within the meaning of §213(d). . . . The cost of *B*'s laser eye surgery is allowed under 213(d)(9) because the surgery is a procedure that meaningfully promotes the proper function of the body. . . . Eye surgery to correct defective vision, including laser procedures such as LASIK and radial keratotomy, corrects a dysfunction of the body. Accordingly, the cost of the laser eye surgery is an expenses for medical care within the meaning of 213(d)(9). . . .

In contrast, the teeth-whitening procedure does not treat a physical or mental disease or promote the proper function of the body, but is directed at improving *C*'s appearance. The discoloration is not a deformity and is not caused by a disfiguring disease or treatment. Accordingly, *C* may not deduct the cost of whitening teeth as an expense for medical care.

HOLDING

Amounts paid by individuals for breast reconstruction surgery following a mastectomy for cancer and for vision correction surgery are medical care expenses under §213(d) and are deductible under §213. . . . Amounts paid by individuals to whiten teeth discolored as a result of age are not medical care expenses under §213(d) and are not deductible.

Problems

8-25. Which of the following items are medical care expenses?
   a. Taxpayer spent $1,200 for birth control pills.
   b. Taxpayer spent $5,000 on a mastectomy and subsequently spent $3,000 purchasing breast milk and infant formula due to the inability to breast feed her infant child.
   c. At the urging of his physician, taxpayer purchased a special vacuum cleaner for $200 to rid his house of the dust and pollen that aggravated his allergies.
   d. Taxpayer launched a self-improvement binge, undergoing psychiatric counseling (at a cost of $2,000). At his psychiatrist's urging, he joined a physical fitness program at a spa (for $2,750) and bought a special high-nutrient prepared food diet (for $6,000).
   e. Taxpayer, on a doctor's recommendation, spent $7,000 for a two-week cruise aboard a ship with a group of physicians who provided certain medical services, such as reviewing participants' medical records, performing certain tests on them as directed by their personal physician or as indicated by their condition, and reporting the results of their medical progress to their personal physician. In addition, they provided seminars relative to the participants' medical conditions and supervised their dietary programs. The cruise ship was not a hospital or other medical institution, and all the medical services provided aboard ship were available in the taxpayer's hometown.
   f. Taxpayer suffers from depression due to severe insomnia. Taxpayer is diagnosed with "Circadian Rhythm Sleep Disorder," a disorder recognized by the American Psychiatric Association but not defined as a mental illness. Although the insomnia is not caused by any physical illness, to combat the depression, the taxpayer's doctor recommends "septoplasty"—a surgery to remove cartilage from the nose—in hopes that it will aid in taxpayer's sleeping. Taxpayer agrees, and requests that, since the surgery is already being conducted, the surgeon do a "nose job," which taxpayer has wanted for a number of years.

F.   FLOOR ON MISCELLANEOUS DEDUCTIONS AND OVERALL LIMITATION ON ITEMIZED DEDUCTIONS

   Code: §§67(a), (b); 68(a) to (d)

In addition to the limitations, floors, and caps applicable to specific itemized deductions (such as the AGI floor for medical expenses), Congress has enacted two general limitations on the deductibility of itemized deductions. Each limitation addresses a different specific concern; some limitations are imposed for administrative convenience, while others attempt to deny deductions for taxpayers who can afford such costs. The latter issue—that is, disallowing itemized deductions for taxpayers with higher incomes — arises in several different Code provisions. In particular, as discussed in Chapter 10, it was the impetus for the enactment of the "alternative minimum tax," which was originally enacted to limit wealthy tax-payers from using certain deductions to avoid paying income tax altogether.

In 1986, Congress imposed a 2-percent floor on "miscellaneous itemized deductions" as defined in §67. Only the amount of miscellaneous deductions that exceeds 2 percent of the taxpayer's adjusted gross income is allowable as item-ized deductions. The limitation was premised primarily on administrative convenience. As noted in the Report of the Senate Finance Committee,

> The committee believes that, as part of the approach of its bill to reduce tax rates through base-broadening, it is appropriate to repeal the miscellaneous itemized deductions and to limit deductions for certain employee expenses. The committee also concluded that allowance of these deductions under present law fosters significant complexity, and that some of these expenses have characteristics of voluntary personal expenditures.
>
> For taxpayers who anticipate claiming itemized deductions, present law effec-tively requires extensive recordkeeping with regard to what commonly are small expenditures. Moreover, the fact that small amounts typically are involved presents significant administrative and enforcement problems for the Internal Revenue Ser-vice. These problems are exacerbated by the fact that taxpayers may frequently make errors of law regarding what types of expenditures are properly allowable as miscel-laneous itemized deductions. . . . Common taxpayer errors include disregarding the restrictions on home office deductions, and on the types of education expenses that are deductible; claiming a deduction for safe deposit expenses even if used only to store personal belongings; and deducting the cost of subscriptions to widely read publications outlining business information without a sufficient business or investment purpose. . . .
>
> Moreover, some miscellaneous expenses allowable under present law are suffi-ciently personal in nature that they would have been incurred apart from any business or investment activities of the taxpayer. For example, membership dues paid to pro-fessional associations may both serve business purposes and also have voluntary and personal aspects; similarly, subscriptions to publications may help taxpayers in con-ducting a profession and also may convey personal and recreational benefits. Tax-payers presumably would rent safe deposit boxes to hold personal belongings such as jewelry even if the cost, to the extent related to investment assets such as stock certi-ficates, were not deductible. . . .
>
> The floor will contribute to simplification by relieving individuals of the burden of recordkeeping unless they expect to incur such expenditures in excess of the per-centage floor. Also, the floor will relieve the Internal Revenue Service of the burden of auditing deductions for such expenditures when not significant in aggregate amount.

S. Rep. No. 313, 99th Cong., 2d Sess. 78 (1986).

In 1992, Congress enacted §68, which imposes an overall limitation on item-ized deductions for high-income individuals. Unlike §67, which prohibits itemized deductions that do not exceed a *floor*, §68 imposes a *cap* on the total amount of allowable itemized deductions. Under §68, certain itemized deductions are reduced by an amount equal to the lesser of (1) 3 percent of the amount the taxpayer's AGI exceeds $100,000 (adjusted for inflation) or (2) 80 percent of the amount of the deductions. As a result, taxpayers with an AGI less than $100,000 (indexed for inflation) are not subject to this limitation. Certain deductions, including the medical expense deduction and the casualty loss deduction, are excluded from this limitation. Further, this limitation is imposed after applying any other limitations, floors, or caps on deductions.

The disallowance of deductions in this manner has been criticized by some as unfair because it denies the benefits of otherwise generally available deductions to certain taxpayers based solely on their income. Accordingly, §68 has faced numerous calls for its repeal. In response, Congress has changed the extent to which §68 applies in particular years. In most years since its enactment the limitations have applied in full, while in other years they have been applied only partially, and in still other years they have not applied at all. To date, however, the outright repeal of §68 has never been achieved. In fact, others have advocated strengthening §68 to increase the progressivity of the Code. As a result, the future of provisions, such as §68 and the "alternative minimum tax" (discussed in Chapter 10), that limit deductions based on income remains unclear.

Problems

8-26.   Tom Ordower, an executive of a large corporation, has adjusted gross income for the year of $50,000 and *allowable* itemized deductions of $4,000 (§163), $2,000 (§164), $3,000 (§165(c)(3)), $2,500 (§162), and $1,500 (§212). What is the amount of itemized deductions that may be taken into account in determining taxable income?

8-27.   Harry Hoffman has allowable itemized deductions of $4,500 (§163), $500 (§164), $4,000 (§162), and $2,000 (§212). What is the amount of itemized deductions that may be taken into account in determining taxable income under the following facts?
   a.   His AGI is $150,000.
   b.   His AGI is $250,000.

G.   THE STANDARD DEDUCTION

Code: §63

In determining taxable income, the taxing formula permits a reduction of adjusted gross income by the *greater* of itemized deductions or the standard deduction. Thus, the determination of taxable income requires two steps: (1) calculating the taxpayer's itemized deductions and (2) determining the taxpayer's standard deduction. §63(b).

The Code generally accords each taxpayer a standard deduction, a set amount deductible from AGI regardless of whether the taxpayer is entitled to any itemized deductions. The standard deduction serves several functions, including administrative convenience (detailed records of small expenses are avoided) and economic security (the standard deduction serves to insulate an equivalent amount of income from taxation), although the latter is more generally served by personal exemptions rather than the standard deduction.

The standard deduction amounts, as originally enacted, are $3,000 for taxpayers filing individually and $4,400 for taxpayers filing as a head of household. Under current law, the standard deduction for taxpayers filing joint returns is double the amount applicable to taxpayers filing individually. The filing status of taxpayers and the impact of the standard deduction on what has historically been known as the "marriage penalty" will be discussed in more detail in Chapter 10. The standard deduction amounts are adjusted annually according to the cost-of-living index. §§63(c)(4) and 1(f). Consequently, the standard deduction amount varies yearly with the rate of inflation. To afford additional tax relief for taxpayers encountering hardship settings—the aged and the blind—an increased standard deduction is available. Under §63(f), the standard deduction is increased by $600 ($750 if the taxpayer is neither married nor a surviving spouse) if the taxpayer is either age 65 by the end of the year or is blind. If the taxpayer is both, the amount of the standard deduction is increased by $1,200 ($1,500).

Although the goal of insulating a minimum amount of income from tax may generally be meritorious, in some instances policy reasons or potential taxpayer abuses preclude the availability of the standard deduction. For example, if a taxpayer is supported by others (such as parents) and derives passive income in the form of dividends and interest from previously received parental gifts, it seems inappropriate to permit that taxpayer to shelter from tax a sizeable amount of this passive income through the standard deduction. Thus, Congress enacted §63(c)(5) and (6), which identify those taxpayers who will be denied all or a portion of the otherwise available standard deduction. The two types of taxpayers most affected by these limitations are dependent taxpayers with passive income and married taxpayers who file separately if either spouse itemizes deductions. §63(c)(5) and (6)(A).

Problems

8-28. Teresa O'Rourke, age 17, lives with her parents and has gross income of $15,000 from cash dividends on stock that she received as a gift from her parents. She has no itemized deductions for the year.
    a.   What is her standard deduction, if any?
    b.   Assume in *a* that she has summer earnings of $1,000.
    c.   Assume in *a* that she has summer earnings of $5,000.

8-29. Jessalyn Martin, a single taxpayer, has adjusted gross income of $40,000 for the year. She has the following itemized deductions for the year: medical expenses of $4,000; state income taxes of $1,700; property taxes of $600; and interest expense of $500. Should she elect to itemize deductions?

H. POLICY ISSUES

Itemized deductions, especially those relating to personal expenses, must be specifically granted by statute. This requirement stems from the fundamental notion that income is broadly interpreted while deductions are narrowly construed. Theoretically, Congress enacts statutory deductions only when presented with significant policy justifications. The following materials discuss policies for and against the use of tax deductions. The materials should be read with the following questions in mind: (1) Do the deductions studied reflect sound public policy? (2) Should Congress use the income tax laws for social legislation as well as revenue production?

SURREY, TAX INCENTIVES AS A DEVICE FOR IMPLEMENTING GOVERNMENT POLICY: A COMPARISON WITH DIRECT GOVERNMENT EXPENDITURES
83 Harv. L. Rev. 705 (1970)

Suggestions are constantly being made that many of our pressing social problems can be solved, or partially met, through the use of income tax incentives. Moreover, the present federal income tax is replete with tax incentive provisions. Some were adopted to assist particular industries, business activities, or financial transactions. Others were adopted to encourage nonbusiness activities considered socially useful, such as contributions to charity. This article will deal with the question of whether tax incentives are as useful or efficient an implement of social policy as direct government expenditures, such as grants, loans, interest subsidies, and guarantees of loans. . . .

I. THE NATURE AND EXTENT OF EXISTING TAX INCENTIVES

The term "tax expenditure" has been used to describe those special provisions of the federal income tax system which represent government expenditures made through that system to achieve various social and economic objectives. These special provisions provide deductions, credits, exclusions, exemptions, [and] deferrals . . . and serve ends similar in nature to those served by direct government expenditures or loan programs. In any specific functional area the Government may use direct expenditures, interest subsidies, direct federal loans, and federal insurance or guarantee of private loans as alternative methods to accomplish the purposes which the special tax provision seeks to achieve or encourage. . . .

The analysis also showed the relationship of tax expenditures to direct expenditures for these budget categories. In some cases the tax expenditures exceeded or were close to budget expenditures. . . . Many of the tax expenditures were expressly adopted to induce action which the Congress considered in the national interest. . . .

Other tax expenditures whose origins are cloudy are now defended as incentives to home ownership, as in the case of the deduction for mortgage interest and property taxes, or as aids to state and local governments' tax bases, as in the case of the deduction for state and local taxes. Other tax expenditure provisions were adopted as relief provisions to ease "tax hardships," or were adopted to simplify tax computations. Some of these provisions have come to be defended on the basis of their incentive effects: for example, the intangible drilling expenses deduction, the percentage depletion allowance, . . . and the research and development expense deduction. Moreover, to the extent that such tax relief — i.e., tax treatment that is special and not required by the concept and general standards of a net income tax — is granted for an activity that is voluntary, the relief is in effect an incentive to engage in that activity, even though the provisions may not be defended on incentive grounds. For example, if meals and lodging furnished an employee on the premises of an employer are not taxed, the effect is to make employees more likely to choose such employment. . . .

The only tax expenditures that are not tax incentives, as we are using the expression, are expenditures related to involuntary activities of taxpayers. Most such provisions are designed to provide tax reduction in order to relieve misfortune or hardship — situations involving "personal hardships," as contrasted with the "tax hardships" that have brought about other special tax provisions, chiefly for business activities. The extra [deduction] for the blind is one example. The extra [deduction] for the aged is another. . . .

A.   SOME ASSORTED VIRTUES OF TAX INCENTIVES — FALSELY CLAIMED

Against this general background we can now consider some of the virtues and defects generally claimed for tax incentives and, on the other side of the coin, for direct expenditures. The first level of consideration relates to virtues claimed for tax incentives, but, in light of the above background, falsely claimed.

1. Tax incentives encourage the private sector to participate in social programs.— Frequently a tax incentive is urged on the ground that the particular problem to be met is great and that the Government must assist in its solution by enlisting the participation of the private sector — generally business. The need for Government to participate can be fulfilled by a tax incentive, and this is asserted as a virtue of tax incentives — they provide government assistance. . . .

But all this is a non-sequitur; it points not to the virtue of tax incentives but to the need for government assistance. The existence of that need has no relevance to the question whether the need should be met by an incentive or by a direct expenditure.

2. Tax incentives are simple and involve far less governmental supervision and detail.— A whole swirl of virtues claimed for tax incentives is summed up in the general observation that they keep Government — that is, the government bureaucracy — out of the picture: that they involve less negotiation of the arrangements, less supervision, less red tape, no new bureaucracy, and so on. . . .

But this merely comes down to saying: "Let's have a manpower program under which the Government pays an employer who hires a certified employee an amount calculated as a percentage of the employee's wage." There is nothing so far that indicates whether the payment should be by way of a tax credit or a direct expenditure. If the employer can obtain government funds (i.e., a reduction in tax through the tax credit) for his employment activities by filling out a schedule on a tax return, a manpower program could be devised instead under which he would receive the same monetary assistance by filling out the exact same schedule on a piece of paper that had "Department of Labor" at the top in place of "Internal Revenue Service."

A government that decides it is wise to pay out tax credit money via a simple tax schedule would be highly irrational if it also decided that it would be unwise to pay the same amount directly on the same basis. A dollar is a dollar — both for the person who receives it and the government that pays it, whether the dollar comes with a tax credit label or a direct expenditure label. . . . Nor, similarly, must there be long negotiations, complex contracts, and the like. It is not the tax route that makes the program simple — it is a substantive decision to have a simple program. In many cases, it is true, direct expenditure programs are probably overstructured and the urging of tax incentives is a reaction to, and a valid criticism of, badly designed expenditure programs. The cure lies of course in better designed expenditure programs. . . .

3. Tax incentives promote private decisionmaking rather than government-centered decisionmaking. — It is said that better progress will be made towards the solution of many social problems if individual decisionmaking is promoted, and that since tax incentives promote this they should be preferred to approaches that underscore government-centered decisionmaking.

We need not discuss the merits of private enterprise as a device for solving social problems, except to note in passing that many business groups who in urging tax incentives stress the virtues of private enterprise overlook the fact that they are really stressing private enterprise *plus* government assistance. But wise or unwise, the contention that private enterprise should be allowed free play, without government interference, tells us nothing as to the choice between tax incentives and direct expenditures, given the same substantive program. This contention is really a variant of the previous "red tape" argument. Just as we could design a direct expenditure program that provides for reduction of red tape, so we could design one that provides more flexibility for private decisionmaking and less scope for government control. . . .

B.   SOME ASSERTED DEFECTS OF TAX INCENTIVES

1. Tax incentives permit windfalls by paying taxpayers for doing what they would do anyway. — It is generally argued that tax incentives are wasteful because some of the tax benefits go to taxpayers for activities which they would have performed without the benefits. When this happens, the tax credit or other benefit is a pleasant windfall, and stimulates no additional activity. With respect to many existing and proposed incentives this criticism is well taken, and indeed it is often difficult to structure a tax credit system which avoids this problem without increasing complexity and introducing arbitrariness. But this also is a problem not unique to the tax incentive technique. A direct expenditure program similarly structured would be equally open to the charge. . . .

It may be desirable in particular programs to tolerate this inefficiency or windfall. Or it may be desirable to attempt to eliminate it, perhaps by constructing a program under which taxpayers bid for the government assistance needed and the assistance goes to the lowest bidders if otherwise qualified, just as in direct government purchasing. It may be that such a substantive program is difficult to operate through the tax technique, but other ways of reaching only the marginal decision could be built into a tax incentive. The significant question is what sort of substantive program is desired.

2. Tax incentives are inequitable; they are worth more to the high-income taxpayer than the low-income taxpayer; they do not benefit those who are outside the tax system because their incomes are low, they have losses, or they are exempt from tax. — This criticism of tax incentives in terms of their inequitable effects is properly levied against most of the existing tax incentives, and probably most of the proposed incentives. The existing incentives were never really carefully structured and in many instances just grew up, without serious thought ever having been given to the question whether they were fair in these terms. The entire process was molded by the fact that the positive tax structure was being affected, and within that structure tax benefits — deductions and exclusions — had these effects as a matter of course. The deductions and exclusions of the tax incentive provisions and their inequitable effects took on the protective coloration of the deductions and exclusions that were a part of the basic tax structure.

The fact that tax benefits for the aged and the sick provide no benefits for those aged or ill who are too poor to pay income taxes was not even thought of as a difficulty, since the focus was, as in any positive tax system, on writing the rules for *taxpayers.* The problem was sometimes thought about in the context of an individual who fell outside the tax system because of current losses, and at times a carry-forward of incentive benefits was provided. Thought was occasionally given to the fact that the deduction of mortgage interest or charitable contributions is worth more to the top-bracket taxpayer than the low-bracket taxpayer, but the disparity was generally dismissed on the grounds that all deductions had that effect. Sometimes this matter was regarded as worrisome, and a tax credit was used instead of a deduction, as in the case of the retirement income credit for the aged. . . .

It is thus clear that most tax incentives have decidedly adverse effects on equity as between taxpayers on the same income level, and also, with respect to the individual income tax, between taxpayers on different income levels. As a consequence of these inequitable effects, many tax incentives look, and are, highly irrational when phrased as direct expenditure programs structured the same way. . . .

This criticism — that tax incentives produce inequitable effects and upside-down benefits — is valid as to the general run of tax incentives. It demonstrates why tax incentives make high-income individuals still better off and result in the paradox that we achieve our social goals by increasing the number of tax millionaires. The marketplace does not work this way — for the individual who earns his profits, even high profits, by meeting a need or desire of society, finds his rewards subject to the progressive income tax. The economic system is thus functioning as it is intended it should, and the tax system, which acts as a control, is also functioning as intended. But when rewards are in the form of tax incentives, the latter control is eliminated, and tax millionaires are produced.

. . . The tax incentive thus provides both financial assistance and freedom from taxation. That freedom itself means much more to the well-to-do individual than to one in the lower brackets. The tax incentive is thus a method of reward and assistance that is just upside-down from the way the country decided—when it adopted a progressive income tax—that the rewards of the marketplace should operate in combination with the income tax. The use that has been made—and is being made—of tax incentives is thus destructive of the equity of a tax system. . . .

3. Tax incentives distort the choices of the marketplace and produce unneutralities in the allocation of resources.—This criticism is in one sense always valid, because that is what the tax incentive is designed to do. Generally, the critic is also saying or implying that the distortion introduced by the particular incentive is undesirable for various reasons. In large part this criticism is true of many existing incentives for reasons earlier described. The criticism has relevance because the distorting effects of tax incentives often pass unnoticed. But the criticism is of course equally applicable to direct expenditures, some of which certainly are unwise. . . .

It is interesting to note that even within the area sought to be benefited by the tax incentive, the design of the incentive may push or pull in unneutral directions, which may or may not be desirable. Thus, a tax credit for pollution control facilities focuses on expenditures for machinery as the method of control to the exclusion of other methods, such as a different choice of materials involved in the manufacturing processes. A tax credit for businesses located in urban slums may focus concentration on monetary assistance to the neglect of the provision of technical assistance.

4. Tax incentives keep tax rates high by constricting the tax base and thereby reducing revenues.— . . . the criticism that is made against direct expenditures—that they keep our tax rates high—is often lost sight of when tax incentives are involved. This criticism of tax incentives is thus a useful reminder that government funds are being spent, and that therefore whatever degree of scrutiny and care should be applied to direct expenditures should also be applied to tax incentives. Tax incentives are usually open-ended: they place no limit on how much tax benefit a taxpayer can earn. Hence it is difficult to foretell how much will be spent by the Government through a particular incentive. It is difficult in the nature of things to structure most tax incentives in order to provide a limit on their use. Thus, tax incentives are much like the uncontrollable direct expenditures in the budget.

. . . If we choose government provision or assistance, then dollars must be spent, and whether they are dollars foregone through lost tax revenues or dollars spent directly through direct expenditures, the effect on tax rates will be the same. So also will the effect on the economy if the government program succeeds, and the resultant effect on the revenue base and tax rates of the increased economic activity that such success may mean.

C.   SUMMARY OF ASSERTED VIRTUES AND VICES OF TAX INCENTIVES

This description of the virtues and vices of tax incentives yields these conclusions: the *asserted disadvantages*—waste, inefficiency, and inequity—are true of most tax incentives existing or proposed because of the way they are structured or grew up. The whole approach to tax incentives—one of rather careless or loose analysis, failure to recognize that dollars are being spent, or to recognize the defects inherent in working within the constraints of the positive tax system — has produced very poor programs. But *if* the problems were recognized and *if* care were taken to design tax incentive programs that one would be willing to defend in substantive terms were the programs cast as direct expenditure programs, then these disadvantages would not be involved, except to the extent that they are inherent in government assistance itself. These are large conditions, and in some cases would be hard to bring about. . . . Indeed, there is no tax incentive in existence or proposed that meets the above standards. But for purposes of comparison we are here assuming that the standards could be met under some tax incentive programs.

Similarly, the *asserted advantages* of tax incentives — greater reliance on private decisionmaking and less detailed requirements — to the extent that they are true in fact (and they are often only illusory) are really criticisms of the complications and supervision built into direct expenditure programs, or else a reflection of the structural weaknesses of the tax incentive program, depending on the amount of detail and supervision appropriate to the particular program. In a rational world, one should assume that if after careful study it is considered that certain complexities and details are not needed and can be left out of a tax incentive program, then they should and can simply be dropped from the direct expenditure program. . . .

D. WHAT IS LOST BY USING A TAX INCENTIVE RATHER THAN A DIRECT EXPENDITURE

Given, under the assumptions just made, the same substantive program, under which government assistance in the same amount is being given in ways and to persons that would be equally acceptable whether tax incentives or direct expenditures were used, what factors should determine the choice of framework for a particular program? We can approach this question by asking: what is lost if the tax incentive technique is used? There are several answers.

1. Tax incentives by dividing the consideration and administration of government programs, confuse and complicate that consideration in the congress, in administration, and in the budget process. — Let us start with the congressional consideration of tax incentive programs. By definition, such programs are designed to induce action to meet a particular social goal — manpower training of the disadvantaged, education, housing, pollution control, or business location in desired areas, to use some recent examples — and would not be a part of the tax structure were they not deliberately cast as tax incentives. Such governmental programs would normally be considered by the appropriate congressional committee charged with the legislative area involved: the House Education and Labor and Senate Labor and Public Welfare Committees. . . . Tax legislation, however, goes to the House Ways and Means Committee and the Senate Finance Committee. These committees would normally not consider the substantive areas involved in tax incentive programs. Tax incentives suddenly charge them with acting on substantive matters outside their fields of responsibility simply because the program uses the tax system. Although tax committees are highly competent in tax matters, they do not have as much insight into these programs as the legislative committees normally handling the programs. . . . The purpose of the congressional committee system is to distribute expertise among the members of Congress. To cast solutions to social problems as tax measures and exchange expertise in those problems for unfamiliarity is, to say the least, both disruptive and unproductive. Moreover, the jumbling of a number of different incentive programs in the tax committees would inevitably set in motion a "log-rolling" process, in which careful consideration would be displaced by trading for support among members. . . .

These difficulties could perhaps be overcome. Tax committees might refer incentive proposals to the appropriate legislative committees and accept their judgments, or both groups of committees could consider the matter jointly. . . . But the system is awkward and leaves unanswered questions — for example, which committee would exert continuing oversight over the program? . . .

An additional problem is the difficulty of coordinating the treatment of tax incentives with the overall handling of direct expenditures. For example, when overall expenditure limits are directed by the Congress or when the President decides to cut expenditures it is essentially impossible to apply the restrictions to tax incentives.

So far none of the various expenditure control devices, such as those voted in recent years by the Congress, have in any way affected tax expenditures. Yet had these tax programs been structured as direct expenditures, they would have had no such immunity. In substantive terms they do not merit that immunity any more than the direct expenditures, yet their tax clothing shields them. . . .

Overall, therefore, a resort to tax incentives greatly decreases the ability of the Government to maintain control over the management of its priorities. This is true both as to the substantive programs to be introduced, modified, or dropped and as to the amounts to be spent in particular programs and areas. . . .

2. Tax incentives will not improve the tax system and are likely to damage it significantly. — Certainly the tax system does not gain when expenditures are made through tax incentive programs. We have already seen that tax incentives are inimical to the equity of a tax system — indeed, in a sense that is necessary to their purpose and function. Moreover, the tax system is complex enough as it is, and to have a large number of tax incentives side by side with the provisions making up the structure of the tax itself can only cause confusion and a blurring of concepts and objectives. . . . This is especially so where the tax incentive is not identifiable as such but is merged into a provision that has a genuine relationship to the measurement of net income — as is, for example, the subsidy involved in accelerated depreciation . . . since some degree of depreciation is appropriate. . . .

E.   WHAT IS GAINED — ALLEGEDLY — BY USING A TAX INCENTIVE RATHER THAN A DIRECT EXPENDITURE

Thus, a great deal is lost when tax incentives are used. What is to be gained by that approach compared with the direct expenditure approach? Some have advanced answers, which are essentially political in nature, and, I think, rooted in illusions or irrationalities. Professor Aaron has observed that the popularity of the tax devices "derives from a peculiar alliance among conservatives, who find attractive the alleged reduction in the role of government that would follow from extensive use of tax credits, and liberals anxious to solve social and economic problems — by whatever means — before it is too late." We have already discussed the illusion that tax credits for social purposes are simple and removed from the bureaucratic hand. The second illusion in the above argument is that the Congress will vote dollars through tax incentives that it refuses to appropriate through expenditure programs. Just why a Congress that focuses on the matter should be so inconsistent is not explained. . . . But perhaps irrationality will govern; perhaps administrators and legislators will devise and accept programs structured as tax provisions which they would reject as direct expenditures, or will refuse to improve direct expenditure programs, or will spend money through tax incentives that they would not appropriate as direct expenditures. In that event, rational considerations will not change matters.

There is another answer, which also appears to be irrational or illusory. This is the claim that businessmen respond to tax credits but not to other forms of government assistance. . . . To the extent that the answer rests on the claim that business regards tax incentive dollars as "clean dollars" — just part of a tax computation — but sees direct expenditure dollars as somehow unclean because they are a subsidy, one can only answer that business probably does not respond this way, or that if it does, it is behaving irrationally. . . .

There may be an aspect of this asserted preference for tax incentive programs that is not illusion or irrationality, but more serious. It may be that legislators and the beneficiaries of tax incentive programs — businesses receiving accelerated depreciation or percentage depletion, state and local governments receiving tax exemption on their bonds — fear that once the public is fully aware of the amounts involved and can weigh expenditure costs against benefits received by the nation, the tax incentives will be found wanting in many respects. In this view, . . . the more it looks like any other technical tax provision, . . . then the more desirable the tax incentive becomes. The public must dig hard and deep to find the subsidy and evaluate it. But such an approach to government expenditures — the preference for the hidden subsidy over the open subsidy — is contrary to all experience with budgets, and to efforts to achieve a rational use of resources. If this is the argument for tax incentives, it should not be accepted.

III.   Conclusion

What, then, is the balance sheet regarding these two methods of government assistance, direct expenditures and tax incentives? I conclude from the above observations that, as a generalization, the burden of proof should rest heavily on those proposing the use of the tax incentive method. In any particular situation — certainly any new situation — the first approach should be to explore the various direct expenditure alternatives. Once the most desirable of these alternatives is determined, if one still wishes to consider the tax incentive method for the same substantive program, the question must be what clear advantages can be obtained by using the tax method. Again, as a generalization, I think it unlikely that clear advantages in the tax incentive method will be found. . . .

One question raised by this discussion especially merits more research and thought. Just why is it that in many cases legislators appear willing, with hardly any thought, to accept an expensive tax incentive program when they would just as quickly reject a similar direct expenditure program, even a much smaller one? Why do they require lengthy study and analysis of direct expenditure programs before legislative and appropriation committees while they are ready to enact tax incentives on no more than generalizations and hunches? . . . Is it that tax bills are so complicated that hardly anyone studies them unless prodded by an industry or taxpayer that is hurt, in his tax pocketbook, and that therefore provisions dispensing largesse slide by? . . . Is it that the legislators know full well what is involved, despite the complexity of tax bills, but believe the public will not perceive what is being done because of the complexity of tax bills . . . ?

We could ask similar questions about administrative agencies. Just why do administrators of direct expenditure programs allow tax incentive proposals to be pushed when the funds involved in such programs could be used, and probably much better used, as coordinated parts of the direct expenditure programs? . . .

Once we begin to recognize that the existing tax incentives represent expenditures of funds that in many cases should be dispersed directly, we must develop legislative and administrative techniques to move the funds involved — to the extent that government assistance is still considered desirable from the tax expenditure budget to the regular budget. . . .

CHAPTER 9

TIMING OF DEDUCTIONS
AND TAX SHELTERS

A. INTRODUCTION

Code: §§441(a) to (e), (g); 446(a) to (d); 461(a), (f), (g)
Regulations: §§1.461-1(a)(1), (2)

As discussed in Chapter 5, in part to insure that the federal government maintains an annual source of operating revenue, the federal income tax is assessed on taxable income earned for a particular taxable period — that is, the taxable year. Because the income tax is assessed on net income rather than gross receipts or gross income, deductions as well as income must be categorized as occurring either inside or outside a particular taxable year. The concept in which taxpayers match business and investment deductions with the business or investment revenue those items help generate is referred to as the matching principle. Theoretically, by matching income and deductions, taxpayers can correctly determine net business or net investment income for each taxable period.

A method that precisely matches expenses to the income they generate and that also ensures a source of annual income for the government has proved difficult to devise, however. Consequently, the interaction of the matching principle and the annual accounting concept gives rise to numerous practical problems in determining the year in which a specific deduction should be reported. For example, for a cash method employer who pays salary to a salesperson in year 2 for work which generated income for the employer in year 1, matching of expense with income would violate the annual accounting concept. Another example of this problem involves the purchase of business assets that are utilized in income production for more than one year. The depreciation deductions are designed to "match" a deduction equal to the amount of the business asset "used up" during the taxable year against income generated in that year. Thus, Congress has determined that, although precise application of the matching principle is impossible, taxpayers can most clearly reflect income over a period of time by consistently applying a given set of tax accounting principles.

Consequently, taxpayers frequently employ devices to affect their overall tax liability by deferring or accelerating the payment of deductible expenses to years in which the deduction will have the greatest impact on tax liability. The basic concept of accelerating and deferring allowable deductions has, therefore, witnessed the introduction of ingenious tax avoidance schemes. The use of tax sheltered investments as a method of creating and accelerating tax deductions has precipitated reform legislation and proposals in this area.

The fundamentals of tax accounting are relevant to an examination of the rules governing the determination of the correct taxable year in which to claim deductions. The taxpayer's annual accounting period is that period, either a calendar or a fiscal year, which governs the determination and encompasses all transactions occurring within that time period. After a taxpayer has adopted a calendar or a fiscal year, taxable income is computed by comparing income and allowable deductions arising within that period. §441(b), (c). Items of income and deduction are allocated to the correct taxable year in accordance with the taxpayer's method of accounting. Section 446 mandates that taxable income *shall* be computed under the method of accounting on the basis of which the taxpayer regularly computes income in keeping his or her books. As discussed in Chapter 5, the two most common accounting methods are the *cash receipts and disbursements method* and the *accrual method*.

Under the cash receipts and disbursements method of accounting, deductions offset income for the taxable year in which the deductible item is *paid*. In contrast, an accrual method taxpayer is generally allowed a deduction in the taxable year in which (1) all the events have occurred that give rise to the liability and (2) the amount of the liability can be determined with reasonable accuracy.

To illustrate these principles, consider the following example: Alex renders tax consulting services for Bob on December 30 of year 1. Alex sends a bill to Bob for $10,000 on December 31, and Bob pays the bill five days later on January 5 of year 2. If Bob is a calendar-year, cash method taxpayer, Bob is allowed a $10,000 deduction in year 2, the year in which the deductible item was *paid*. On the other hand, if Bob is a calendar-year, accrual method taxpayer, he is allowed a $10,000 deduction in year 1 because all of the events that fixed the obligation to pay occurred in year 1 and the amount of the obligation could be determined with reasonable accuracy.

This chapter addresses the general deduction timing rules of the cash method and accrual method of accounting. Tax shelter devices, along with various legislative and judicial limitations placed on taxpayer attempts to manipulate deductions, are also discussed.

B.   CASH METHOD ACCOUNTING

Code: §461(a), (g)
Regulations: §1.461-1(a)(1)

1.   *Payment versus Promise to Pay*

Cash method taxpayers are permitted to claim deductible expenses only in the taxable year in which each item is actually *paid*. Reg. §1.461-1(a)(1). Technical differences between various forms of consideration may, however, create uncertainty as to when actual payment occurs. For example, payment may be made by check, promissory note, borrowed funds, letter of credit, or credit card, requiring a determination of whether there has been a payment or merely a promise to pay a stated amount in the future.

Estate of Spiegel v. Commissioner, 12 T.C. 524 (1949), is one of the early cases to address the timing of a payment issue. In that case, a calendar-year, cash method taxpayer drafted a check payable to a charitable organization on December 30 and delivered it the next day, December 31. The Commissioner denied the charitable contribution deduction in the year of delivery because the check was not paid by the bank from the taxpayer's account until the subsequent year. The Tax Court refused to enforce the Commissioner's assessment, holding that the date of payment for a check "relates back" to the date of its delivery if the check is presented and honored in due course. In reasoning that a check is conditional payment that becomes absolute when presented and honored, the court stated:

> It would seem to us unfortunate for the Tax Court to fail to recognize what has so frequently been suggested, that as a practical matter, in everyday personal and commercial usage, the transfer of funds by check is an accepted procedure. The parties almost without exception think and deal in terms of payment except in the unusual circumstance, not involved here, that the check is dishonored upon presentation.

Id. at 529.

In Estate of Hubbell v. Commissioner, 10 T.C. 1207 (1948), the Tax Court considered the result when a check is not honored by the maker's bank. In *Estate of Hubbell*, the taxpayer, prior to his death, mailed a check for payment of state taxes. The check was presented to the taxpayer's bank for payment after the taxpayer's death. Despite the presence of sufficient funds in the account, the bank refused to honor the check because of the maker's death. The Tax Court held that delivery of the check did not constitute payment because a check is only a conditional payment. If a check is not honored, the conditional payment does not become absolute and, consequently, payment is not made.

In *Estate of Hubbell*, the dishonored check never constituted payment. However, it is not unusual for the payee of a check, which was dishonored on initial presentment, to resubmit the check to the maker's bank. When the resubmitted check is honored, payment becomes absolute. As a result of the initial dishonor of the check, the date of payment apparently will not relate back to the date of delivery because the check was not honored in due course. Consequently, the second presentment should commence a new transaction for purposes of the timing of any corresponding deduction. See Heritage Organization, LLC v. Commissioner, T.C. Memo 2011-246.

Another interesting timing issue arises when a taxpayer pays an expense with funds borrowed from a third party, a situation that arose in Granan v. Commissioner, 55 T.C. 753 (1971). In *Granan*, the taxpayer used funds borrowed from a third party to pay a deductible expense in year 1. He then claimed a deduction for the expense in the year in which he repaid the loan to the third party. The Tax Court held that a deduction for a payment made with borrowed funds is properly taken in the year in which the borrowed funds are used to make the payment, not the year in which the third-party loan is repaid. This rule was adopted to prevent a taxpayer from distorting income by electing the year in which to take the deduction.

The Supreme Court has, on more than one occasion, addressed the question of whether issuance of a promissory note by the obligor constitutes payment. For example, in Eckert v. Burnet, 283 U.S. 140 (1931), a cash method taxpayer was secondarily liable on a note. When the primary obligor defaulted on the note, the taxpayer fulfilled his obligation by issuing a new promissory note to cover the note in default. The Court denied the bad debt deduction, holding that a promissory note is merely a promise to pay. Subsequently, the Court extended the rule established in *Eckert* and held that, even if fully secured, a promissory note does not constitute payment because a promissory note is neither cash nor a cash equivalent. Helvering v. Price, 309 U.S. 409 (1940). The Court reasoned that the collateral was not intended as payment but was given to secure a promise to pay. Consequently, although the note might be income to a cash method recipient, it is merely a promise to pay and not a payment by its maker.

Two additional timing considerations for cash method taxpayers include the application of constructive receipt principles and the §263 capital expenditure rule. First, unlike inclusions in gross income by cash method taxpayers of items constructively received, no deduction is permitted for constructive payment of deductible expenses. For example, in Vander Poel, Francis & Co. v. Commissioner, 8 T.C. 407 (1947), a cash method corporate taxpayer was authorized to credit salaries of two key employees to accounts from which those employees could draw an amount equal to their salaries. Both employees were authorized to draw checks on all corporate accounts, including the special accounts. Even though both employees drew only a small portion of the salary, both properly reported their entire salary as income pursuant to the doctrine of constructive receipt. The Tax Court, however, denied the corporate taxpayer's business deduction for the portion of the salary that the employees had not drawn from the accounts; those amounts had not been "paid." A doctrine of constructive receipt is based on the broad interpretation of gross income in §61. Deductions, on the other hand, are considered a matter of legislative grace and are construed narrowly; this narrow construction does not give rise to a doctrine of "constructive payment" even in cases of constructive receipt. See Unico Sales & Marketing, Inc. v. Commissioner, T.C. Memo. 1999-242; Massachusetts Mutual Life Ins. Co. v. United States, 288 U.S. 269, 275 (1933)

CHAPMAN v. UNITED STATES
527 F. Supp. 1053 (D. Minn. 1981)

MacLaughlin, J. . . .

The only issue is whether the plaintiffs are entitled to a $15,000 deduction represented by a letter of credit. For the reasons stated herein, the defendant's motion for summary judgment will be granted. . . .

This dispute arises out of a purchase of cattle feed. The plaintiffs, cash basis taxpayers, deducted $30,000 on their joint federal income tax return for the cost of cattle feed. This amount was provided for under an agreement between Loyal Chapman and the Sun River Cattle Company (the Company) in Vaughn, Montana. Under the agreement Chapman purchased cattle and feed from the Company. The cost of the feed was $30,000. Chapman paid $15,000 in cash in 1973. The balance of the feed purchase price was due and payable when each cattle lot was sold and was deductible from the proceeds of the sale of each lot prior to disbursing the balance of the proceeds, if any, to Chapman. To insure payment in case the proceeds from the cattle sale failed to cover the cost of the feed, Chapman gave the Company a promissory note for $15,000 and a secured letter of credit from the First National Bank of Minneapolis for the same amount on November 19, 1973.

The Company never drew on the letter of credit, which expired by its own terms on May 15, 1974. However, Chapman deducted $30,000 in 1973 ($15,000 cash plus $15,000 letter of credit) and then increased his income by $15,000 in 1974 when the letter of credit expired unused. . . .

The general rule for cash basis taxpayers is that they must declare income in the taxable year in which it is actually or constructively received and that they may claim deductions for expenses in the taxable year in which they are actually paid. The central issue in this case is what constitutes payment and thus qualifies for a deduction. Taxpayers are entitled to deductions at the time of unconditional delivery of a check to the payee if the bank subsequently either pays or certifies the check upon presentment. At the time a bank certifies a check, the bank usually withdraws a corresponding amount from its customer's account. Thus, the bank receives payment at the time of certification although the payee may not present the check for payment until some time later. Under Minn. Stat. §336.3-411 the drawer and all prior endorsers are discharged when a bank certifies a check for a holder. Thus, only the drawee bank remains liable for the amount.

A taxpayer is viewed as having paid an expense and is thus entitled to a deduction if the taxpayer uses borrowed funds for the payment. The taxpayer is entitled to the deduction at the time of payment not at the time the loan is repaid. In addition, if a third party pays an expense on behalf of the taxpayer, the expense is also deductible in the year of payment, not in the year the taxpayer repays the third party. However, if the taxpayer gives a promissory note for payment, the taxpayer is entitled to a deduction at the time he or she pays the note, not at the time the note is given as payment. The taxpayer who gives a note as payment is denied a deduction even if the note is secured by collateral. A cash basis taxpayer may not deduct an expense while something remains to be done to complete payment.

The plaintiffs argue that they are entitled to the deduction because they paid for the feed with borrowed funds. The defendant argues that the plaintiffs merely gave a promissory note secured by collateral and thus are not entitled to a deduction. The Court finds that the letter of credit is analogous to a promissory note secured by collateral.

The plaintiffs merely promised to pay the expense and secured their payment with the letter of credit. Thus, they are not entitled to a deduction. The parties admit that the bank never paid on the letter of credit. The plaintiffs merely had an obligation to repay the bank if the bank paid the Company. In contrast to a case in which a bank certifies a check, the bank in this case did not withdraw funds from the plaintiffs' account although it did reduce the amount the plaintiffs could borrow on their own line of credit. The bank officer who handled the transaction stated in his deposition that if the plaintiffs had not had a line of credit they would have had "to put up $15,000 as collateral."

The critical distinction between the issuance of a letter of credit and the certification of a check is the promissory nature of the bank customer's obligation in the case of a letter of credit. When a bank certifies a check, the drawer's account is debited immediately; thus the drawer has paid at that time. In contrast, when a bank issues a letter of credit, the bank's customer merely pledges collateral but does not pay over the money. Before the customer is obligated to pay, the beneficiary of the credit must present a draft to the issuer of the letter of credit and the issuer must pay the draft. If the issuer does not pay on the letter of credit, the collateral is returned to the customer. Under Minn. Stat. §336.5-114(3) the issuer of a letter of credit is not entitled to reimbursement from its customer until the issuer honors a demand for payment. . . . Thus, a certified check is a cash equivalent but a letter of credit is similar to a consumer credit card waiting to be used.

For the reasons stated herein, it is the conclusion of the Court that the letter of credit is not a cash equivalent and that the letter of credit was never drawn against. Therefore, the Court has concluded that the plaintiffs are not entitled to a deduction in 1973. . . .

REV. RUL. 78-38
1978-1 C.B. 67

The Internal Revenue Service has given further consideration to Rev. Rul. 71-216, 1971-1 C.B. 96, which holds that a taxpayer who used a bank credit card to contribute to a qualified charity may not deduct any part of the contribution under section 170(a)(1) of the Internal Revenue Code until the year the cardholder makes payment of the amount of the contribution to the bank. . . .

In Rev. Rul. 71-216 the assumption was made that a charitable contribution made by a taxpayer by use of a credit card was tantamount to a charitable contribution made by the issuance and delivery of a debenture bond or a promissory note by the obligor to a charitable organization, as discussed in Rev. Rul. 68-174, 1968-1 C.B. 81, which holds that, under the facts presented, the issuance of a debenture bond or a promissory note represents a mere promise to pay at some future date, and delivery of the bond or note to a charitable organization is not "payment" under section 170 of the Code.

Upon further study, it has been concluded that there are major distinctions between contributions made by the use of credit cards and contributions made by debenture bonds and promissory notes. In Rev. Rul. 68-174, the charitable organization that received the debenture bond or promissory note from the obligor received no more than a mere promise to pay. Conversely, the credit card holder in Rev. Rul. 71-216, by using the credit card to make the contribution, became immediately indebted to a third party (the bank) in such a way that the cardholder could not thereafter prevent the charitable organization from receiving payment. The credit card draft received by the charitable organization from the credit card holder in Rev. Rul. 71-216 was immediately creditable by the bank to the organization's account as if it were a check.

Since the cardholder's use of the credit card creates the cardholder's own debt to a third party, the use of a bank credit card to make a charitable contribution is equivalent to the use of borrowed funds to make a contribution.

The general rule is that when a deductible payment is made with borrowed money, the deduction is not postponed until the year in which the borrowed money is repaid. Such expenses must be deducted in the year they are paid and not when the loans are repaid.

Accordingly, the taxpayer discussed in Rev. Rul. 71-216, who made a contribution to a qualified charity by a charge to the taxpayer's bank credit card, is entitled to a charitable contribution deduction under section 170(a) of the Code in the year the charge was made and the deduction may not be postponed until the taxpayer pays the indebtedness resulting from such charge. . . .

Rev. Rul. 68-174 is distinguished; Rev. Rul. 71-216 is revoked.

2. *The Capital Expenditure Limitation*

When a cash method taxpayer's payment results in the acquisition or creation of an asset that has a useful life substantially beyond the current taxable year, that payment is generally treated as a capital expenditure. Reg. §1.461-1(a)(1). In such cases, the taxpayer is not entitled to a current deduction and must either amortize the expense or depreciate the asset under §167 or §168. This situation can occur under two circumstances: (1) purchases of capital assets (such as a factory) and (2) prepayments for future expenses. The former is relatively easy to recognize. For example, when a cash-basis taxpayer purchases a factory, the purchase is clearly a capital expenditure, and the purchase price is capitalized into the basis of the factory under §263. The latter case can be more difficult to determine. When is a payment a "prepayment" for future goods or services as opposed to a current payment?

The courts have devised a three-prong test to determine the deductibility of prepayments. In Grynberg v. Commissioner, 83 T.C. 255 (1984), the Tax Court applied the following three-prong test to determine the deductibility of the prepayments:

> The first requirement is that there must have been an actual payment of the item in question. A mere refundable deposit will not support a current deduction. . . . A cash basis taxpayer must actually and irretrievably pay the expense during the taxable year in order to be entitled to a deduction under section 162(a). If the taxpayer retains the unilateral power to require a refund of the money or to redirect its use, the transfer is considered a mere deposit and a deduction is not allowed in that year.
>
> The second requirement is that there must have been a substantial business reason for making the prepayment in the year in which it was made. If the prepayment occurred simply to accelerate a tax deduction, no deduction will be allowed in the year of prepayment. . . . Unless the prepayment of an item is for a valid business purpose, and not solely for a tax reduction, it "cannot fairly be characterized as an ordinary and necessary business expense" of the year of prepayment.

The third requirement is that prepayment of the item . . . must not cause a material distortion in the taxpayer's taxable income in the year of prepayment. This requirement is based on section 446(b). . . .

Id. at 265.

The prepayment did not constitute a mere deposit, thereby satisfying the first prong of the test, because no provision of the leases entitled taxpayers to a refund of the prepaid rental. The court concluded, however, that the taxpayers did not have an obligation or business reason to prepay sixty to ninety days in advance of the due date. Consequently, the payments were not ordinary and necessary business expenses in the year of prepayment and failed to satisfy the second prong.

Additional limitations on prepayments by cash method taxpayers are discussed at section F2 of this chapter. See also §448 which prohibits the use of the cash method of accounting by a tax shelter and thereby minimizes the number of settings in which the capital expenditure limitation would be required.

Problems

9-1. Harriet Beaufort, a cash method taxpayer with a calendar-year accounting period, is a sole proprietor who owns a small boutique. On December 29, year 1, she delivered a check for $10,000 to an advertising agency as payment for services rendered six months earlier.

a. Assuming that the check is honored and paid by the bank on January 3, year 2, when may Beaufort deduct the $10,000 expense?

b. Assuming that the check was mailed on December 29, year 1, delivered to the creditor on January 2, year 2, and paid by the bank on January 10, year 2, in which year is the deduction appropriate?

c. Assume the facts in *a*, except that the check is not honored by the bank on presentment because of insufficient funds but is honored by the bank when redeposited on January 10, year 2. When would the deduction be appropriate?

d. Assume that Beaufort mailed a $10,000 check on December 29, year 1, and that the check was postdated to January 3, year 2. When is the deduction appropriate?

e. Assume that instead of paying by check, Beaufort borrowed $10,000 from a bank on December 28 in order to make a December 29, year 1, payment in cash. What effect does satisfying the $10,000 loan from the bank in a subsequent year have on the timing of the deduction?

f. Instead of delivering a check for $10,000, Beaufort delivers a promissory note for $10,000, which was accepted by the creditor on December 29, year 1. When is the deduction appropriate?

g. Assume the same facts as in *f*, except that the note was secured by property worth $50,000. When is the item deductible?

h. Assume that instead of paying any of the $10,000 fee in year 1, the parties agree that the $10,000 is payable one year later if, on December 29, year 1, Beaufort delivers a check to the agency for $1,525, representing $150 of interest accruing on the $10,000 fee as of December 31, year 1, as well as $1,375 of interest for the next eleven months. What amount is deductible in year 1?

   i. Assume the facts in *a*, except that the services were not rendered six months earlier but were to be rendered six months after the date of payment. What result?

   j. Assume the facts in *a*, except that Beaufort opened her boutique on December 31, year 1. What result?

9-2. Bob Roccaforte is a key employee of Beaufort. Beaufort takes a deduction, as a salary expense, for an amount credited to an account on which Roccaforte could write checks whenever he desired, up to the amount credited to that account. Under the doctrine of constructive receipt, Roccaforte would be deemed to have received income when his account was credited and he could draw on such amount. Is Beaufort entitled to a deduction for amounts so credited to Roccaforte's salary account? If not, why not?

9-3. During year 1, Racquel Tomlinson incurs unreimbursed deductible entertainment expenses of $500 at Hilton Hotels.

   a. If Tomlinson charges those expenses on an American Express card on December 29, year 1, and pays the resulting bill on January 31, year 2, when may she deduct the expense?

   b. Assume the same facts as in *a* except that instead of using an American Express card, Tomlinson uses a Hilton Hotel charge card. When is the deduction appropriate?

   c. What is the theoretical difference between a three-party credit transaction and a two-party credit transaction?

C. ACCRUAL METHOD ACCOUNTING

Code: §§461(a), (f)
Regulations: §§1.461-1(a)(2); 1.461-2(a) to (c), (e)

Unlike cash method taxpayers, who report deductions based on the time of payment, the timing of accrual method deductions is generally not determined by reference to when actual payment occurs. Regulation §1.461-1(a)(2) states the general rule for accrual method taxpayers: "Under an accrual method of accounting, a liability (as defined in §1.446-1(c)(1)(ii)(B)) is incurred, and generally is taken into account for Federal income tax purposes, in the taxable year in which *all the events have occurred* that establish the fact of the liability, the amount of the liability can be determined with reasonable accuracy, and economic performance has occurred with respect to the liability" (emphasis added). Thus, two hurdles must be surmounted before expenses or losses are deductible under the accrual method. The first hurdle is the *all events test*, which requires that all the events establishing the fact of the liability have occurred as of the end of the taxable year. The second hurdle is to establish that the amount of the liability can be determined with reasonable accuracy.

1.   Reasonable Accuracy Test

The accrual method does not require absolute certainty of the amount to be paid. Instead, if the amount of a liability can be estimated within reasonable limits or if all of the factors exist that allow for a determination of the amount, the expense has accrued. Moreover, if the total amount of the liability cannot be determined but part of it can be computed with reasonable accuracy, that part can be accrued within the taxable year. Reg. §1.461-1(a)(2).

An example of a liability that could not be determined with reasonable accuracy arose in Lucas v. American Code Co., 280 U.S. 445 (1930). In *Lucas*, an accrual method corporate taxpayer breached a contract during the taxable year and deducted the potential loss resulting from a damage award that year. At the time the deduction was taken, the taxpayer did not know the amount, if any, of the loss. The Supreme Court upheld the Commissioner in denying the deduction. The Court reasoned that the amount of the damages was wholly unpredictable because the aggrieved party might choose not to prosecute a lawsuit or might mitigate damages completely. Even if it is possible to determine the amount of liability with reasonable accuracy, deductibility is subject to the all events test.

2.   All Events Test

The Supreme Court established the all events test in United States v. Anderson, 269 U.S. 422 (1926). In *Anderson*, an accrual method taxpayer deducted a munitions tax in 1917, the year in which the tax was assessed and paid. The taxpayer expensed the tax for financial accounting purposes in 1916, the year for which the tax was incurred. The Supreme Court held that the deduction should have been taken in 1916. Although acknowledging that, in a strict legal sense, a tax is not "accrued" until it has been assessed and becomes due, the Court stated that the tax had accrued for tax purposes in 1916 because all the events determining the fact of the liability for the tax had occurred prior to the assessment.

The all events test is not met, however, if the liability is contingent and thus not firmly established. For example, in Ad Visor, Inc. v. Commissioner, T.C. Memo 1978-141, an accrual method taxpayer agreed to pay $40,000 on the completion of future legal services and deducted the $40,000 in the taxable year even though some of the services were not rendered until the subsequent year. The Tax Court upheld the Commissioner in denying any deduction in the taxable year, even for the expenses related to legal services rendered during the taxable year, on the basis that the completion of the services, rather than the ongoing performance of the services, fixed the fact of the liability.

The all events test usually involves a factual inquiry, focusing on whether the fact of liability is certain as of the end of the taxable year. For example, assume that a taxpayer enters into a contract on December 15, year 1, agreeing to pay for services to be performed on December 16, year 1. The services are performed on December 16, year 1, and payment is then made on January 3, year 2. If the taxpayer is a cash method taxpayer, the deduction is permitted in year 2, when payment is actually made. If the taxpayer is an accrual method taxpayer, the deduction may be taken in year 1 because in that year all the events occurred to determine the fact and the amount of the taxpayer's liability.

What event finally fixes a liability for these purposes can prove challenging to determine, however. The Supreme Court addressed two extremely similar cases, one in 1986 and one in 1987, to attempt to clarify this issue. Unfortunately, the Supreme Court reached contradictory results in these cases, leaving little definitive guidance. Consequently, courts have struggled to determine precisely what constitutes the final event fixing liability, often relying on extremely fine distinctions to resolve specific disputes. Consider the following case.

CHRYSLER CORPORATION v. COMMISSIONER
436 F.3d 644 (6th Cir. 2006)

ALAN E. NORRIS, CIRCUIT JUDGE.

Chrysler Corporation appeals from . . . adverse Tax Court rulings that granted partial summary judgment to the Commissioner. . . . These rulings present the following question . . . [u]nder the accrual accounting method used by Chrysler, was the company permitted to deduct anticipated warranty expenses in the year that it sold warranted motor vehicles to its dealers even though warranty claims had not necessarily been made?

I. DEDUCTION FOR ANTICIPATED WARRANTY EXPENSES

In its opinion, the Tax Court framed the issue in these terms:

> We must decide whether for Federal income tax purposes all events necessary to determine petitioner's liability for its warranty expenses have occurred when it sells its vehicles to its dealers; in other words, has petitioner satisfied the first prong of the all events test entitling it to deduct its estimated future warranty costs on the sale of such vehicles?

Chrysler Corp. v. Comm'r, 80 T.C.M. 334 (Aug. 31, 2000). Although discussed in more detail shortly, the "all events test" alluded to by the Tax Court provides as follows:

> Under an accrual method of accounting, a liability . . . is incurred, and generally is taken into account for Federal income tax purposes, in the taxable year in which all the events have occurred that establish the fact of the liability, the amount of the liability can be determined with reasonable accuracy, and economic performance has occurred with respect to the liability. . . .

In this appeal, only the first prong of the test—whether the "fact of the liability" has been established—is at issue.

. . . In tax years 1984 and 1985, Chrysler included deductions of $567,943,243 and $297,292,155 on its federal income tax returns on the basis that it incurred those amounts as warranty expenses for motor vehicles sold in those years to its dealers. A sale generally occurred when a vehicle was delivered to the carrier for shipment to the dealer. New vehicle warranties, which are at issue here, cover defects in material and manufacture. As Chrysler points out, state and federal laws . . . impose warranty obligations on the seller. During the period at issue, every new vehicle sold by Chrysler was covered by a warranty. When selling a new vehicle, dealers would provide buyers with a warranty manual that explained its terms and limitations.

. . . Chrysler engaged [a] consultant . . . to calculate the amount of warranty expenses the company incurred for tax years 1984 and 1985. Chrysler uses the accrual method of accounting and a tax year based upon the calendar year. It is undisputed that the expenses incurred by Chrysler to fix conditions covered by warranty constitute "ordinary and necessary" business expenses under §162. During the period at issue, Chrysler accrued the entire estimated cost of its warranties in the year that it sold the vehicles to the dealers. Chrysler included this liability on its balance sheet and took it into account in the calculation of net . . . income.

. . . Whether a business expense has been "incurred" so as to entitle an accrual-basis taxpayer to deduct it under §162(a) is governed by the "all events" test as set out in United States v. Anderson, 269 U.S. 422 (1926). In *Anderson*, the Supreme Court held that a taxpayer was entitled to deduct from its 1916 income a tax on profits from munitions sales that took place in 1916. Although the tax would not be assessed and therefore would not formally be due until 1917, all the events had occurred in 1916 to fix the amount of the tax and to determine the taxpayer's liability to pay it. . . .

[U]nder the regulations, the all events test has two prongs, each of which must be satisfied before accrual of an expense is proper. First, all the events must have occurred which establish the fact of the liability. Second, the amount must be capable of being determined "with reasonable accuracy." . . . For the purpose of the first prong of the test the Supreme Court has stated that the liability must be "final and definite in amount" . . . [and] "fixed and absolute" . . . to be deductible.

. . . [Chrysler] places reliance on United States v. Hughes Properties, Inc., 476 U.S. 593 (1986), for the proposition that statutory liabilities satisfy the first prong of the all events test. . . .

In *Hughes Properties*, the taxpayer was a Nevada casino that was required by state statute to pay as a jackpot a certain percentage of the amounts gambled in progressive slot machines. The taxpayer was required to keep a cash reserve sufficient to pay the guaranteed jackpots when won. Hughes Properties, at the conclusion of each fiscal year, entered the total of the progressive jackpot amounts (shown on the payoff indicators) as an accrued liability on its books. From that total, it subtracted the corresponding figure for the preceding year to produce the current tax year's increase in accrued liability. On its Federal income tax return this net figure was asserted to be an ordinary and necessary business expense and deductible under §162(a). The Court found that the all events test had been satisfied and the taxpayer was entitled to the deduction. The Court reasoned that the State statute made the amount shown on the payout indicators incapable of being reduced. Therefore the event creating liability was the last play of the machine before the end of the fiscal year, and that event occurred during the taxable year.

. . . [The Commissioner] relies on the analysis contained in the Supreme Court's opinion in United States v. General Dynamics Corp., 481 U.S. 239 (1987). In *General Dynamics*, the taxpayer, who self-insured its employee medical plan, deducted estimated costs of medical care under the plan. The employer's liability was determinable. The employees' medical needs had manifested themselves, employees had determined to obtain treatment, and treatment had occurred. The only events that had not occurred were the employees' filing claims for reimbursement before the end of the taxable year. The Supreme Court found that the all events test was not met until the filing of properly documented claims. The filing of the claim was the last event needed to create the liability and therefore absolutely fix the taxpayer's liability under the first prong of the all events test.

. . . [T]he central issue on appeal is precisely what a taxpayer must do in order to establish liability with sufficient certainty to satisfy the first prong of the "all events test." We would be less than candid if we did not acknowledge a degree of sympathy with Justice O'Connor's observation in *General Dynamics* that "[t]he circumstances of this case differ little from those in Hughes Properties." However, given that the Court reached the opposite result in successive terms when faced with similar sets of facts, we must do our best to distinguish the two cases. As did the Tax Court, we see no viable way of reconciling *Hughes Properties* with *General Dynamics* other than by reading the former to stand of the proposition that "[t]he first prong of the all events test may be met when a statute has the effect of irrevocably setting aside a specific amount . . . by the close of the tax year and to be paid at a future date." The Court in *General Dynamics* held that the "last link in the chain of events creating liability for purposes of the all events test" was the actual filing of a medical claim. It based its reasoning on the fact that General Dynamics was . . . liable to pay for covered medical services only if properly documented claims forms were filed.

Like General Dynamics, Chrysler faces potential liability, which in its case is based upon the express and implied warranties that accompany the sale of its motor vehicles. However, that liability does not become firmly established until a valid warranty claim is submitted. As the Court explained, "Nor may a taxpayer deduct an estimated or an anticipated expense no matter how statistically certain, if it is based on events that have not occurred by the close of the taxable year." We assume that . . . software made it easier for Chrysler to track and process warranty claims; it may also have assisted [the consultant] in calculating the cost to the company of future claims. However, even if those claims were predictable with relative accuracy, they were not actually submitted during the taxable year and therefore cannot be deducted because they remain "anticipated expenses."

In reaching this conclusion, we readily acknowledge that Chrysler has raised a number of thoughtful points. First among them is the contention that the anticipated warranty claims at issue should be analyzed with reference to the second prong of the all events test, that is, whether the amount of the liability can be determined with reasonable accuracy. Despite its surface appeal, this argument fails to recognize that it is not the imprecise amount of the claims that renders them non-deductible but their contingent nature. While Chrysler relies in part upon the existence of statutes . . . to establish the "fact" of its liability, they . . . do not necessarily fix liability. . . . [S]imply because a manufacturer has provided a warranty to a consumer, the scope of which is defined to a some degree by statute, does not mean that liability has attached; until a claim has been filed invoking the terms of a warranty, liability remains contingent and, because of that fact, non-deductible.

. . . For the reasons just outlined, we detect no material distinction between *General Dynamics* and the case before us. Consequently, we affirm the judgment of the Tax Court.

3. *Economic Performance Requirement*

Code: §461(h)
Regulations: §§1.461-4(a) to (g)

In 1984, Congress added another element to the all events test to prevent premature accruals by accrual method taxpayers. See §461(h). Premature accruals are analogous to prepayments by cash method taxpayers — the deduction is taken in the current year for liabilities (services or property use) to be paid in a subsequent tax year. Prior to 1984, under the all events test, accrual method taxpayers could deduct expenses to be paid in subsequent years, as long as all the events had occurred that determined the fact and amount of liability. Congress added an "economic performance requirement" such that satisfied deduction is not available until the underlying economic performance has occurred. For example, services must be rendered before an accrual method taxpayer can deduct their cost. Therefore, if on December 15, year 1, the taxpayer contracts for services to be performed on January 2, year 2, both the cash method and accrual method taxpayers will deduct the cost of the services in year 2. In contrast to the cash method taxpayer, however, the accrual method taxpayer need not have actually paid the expenses in year 2 to deduct the amount.

REV. RUL. 2007-3
2007-4 I.R.B. 350

Issues

(1) Under §461 of the Internal Revenue Code, when does a taxpayer using an accrual method of accounting incur a liability for services?

(2) Under §461, when does a taxpayer using an accrual method of accounting incur a liability for insurance?

Facts

X is a corporation that uses an accrual method of accounting and files its federal income tax returns on a calendar year basis.

Situation 1. On December 15, 2006, *X* executes a contract with *Y* for the provision of services. The contract provides for services to begin on January 15, 2007, and end on January 31, 2007. Under the terms of the contract, payment for the services is due to *Y* on January 15, 2007, and *X* pays *Y* for the services on January 15, 2007.

Situation 2. On December 15, 2006, *X* executes a contract with *W*, an insurance company regulated under state law, for the provision of insurance. The insurance contract covers the period from January 15, 2007, through December 31, 2007. Under the terms of the contract, payment of the insurance premium is due to *W* on January 15, 2007, and *X* pays the premium to *W* on January 15, 2007.

Law

Section 461(a) provides that the amount of any deduction or credit must be taken for the taxable year that is the proper taxable year under the method of accounting used by the taxpayer in computing taxable income.

Reg. §1.461-1(a)(2)(i) provides that, under an accrual method of accounting, a liability is incurred, and is generally taken into account for federal income tax purposes, in the taxable year in which (1) all the events have occurred that establish the fact of the liability, (2) the amount of the liability can be determined with reasonable accuracy, and (3) economic performance has occurred with respect to the liability (the "all events test").

The first prong of the all events test requires that all the events have occurred that establish the fact of the liability. Therefore, it is fundamental to the all events test that although expenses may be deductible before they become due and payable, liability first must be firmly established. United States v. General Dynamics Corp., 481 U.S. 239 (1987).

Generally, under Regulation §1.461-1(a)(2), all the events have occurred that establish the fact of the liability when (1) the event fixing the liability, whether that be the required performance or other event, occurs, or (2) payment therefore is due, whichever happens earliest. The terms of a contract are relevant in determining the events that establish the fact of a taxpayer's liability.

Section 461(h) and Regulation §1.461-4 provide that, for purposes of determining whether an accrual basis taxpayer can treat the amount of any liability as incurred, the all events test is not treated as met any earlier than the taxable year in which economic performance occurs with respect to the liability.

Regulation §1.461-4(d)(2) provides that if a liability of a taxpayer arises out of the providing of services or property to the taxpayer by another person, economic performance occurs as the services or property is provided.

Analysis

Situation 1. In Situation 1, the first event that occurs to establish the fact of *X*'s liability for services is that payment is due under the contract on January 15, 2007. Thus, for purposes of §461, the fact of the liability is established on January 15, 2007. At that time, the amount can be determined with reasonable accuracy. Economic performance with respect to the liability occurs as the services are provided, from January 15, 2007, through January 31, 2007. Therefore, *X* incurs a liability for services in 2007.

The fact of the liability is not established in 2006, even though *X* executed the service contract on December 15, 2006. It is well established that an accrual basis obligor is not permitted to deduct an expense stemming from a bilateral contractual arrangement, that is, mutual promises, prior to the performance of the contracted for services by the obligee. . . . Thus, the mere execution of the contract by *X* in 2006 is not sufficient, by itself, to establish the fact of the liability. Further, the recurring item exception does not apply because the fact of the liability is not established in 2006.

Situation 2. In Situation 2, the first event that occurs to establish the fact of *X*'s liability for insurance is that the premium is due under the contract. Thus, for purposes of §461, the fact of the liability is established on January 15, 2007. At that time, the amount can be determined with reasonable accuracy. Economic performance with respect to the liability occurs as payment is made, on January 15, 2007. Therefore, X incurs a liability for insurance in 2007.

The fact of the liability is not established in 2006, even though X executed the insurance contract on December 15, 2006. Although federal or state regulations may impose certain legal obligations on taxpayers, those obligations, without more, do not necessarily establish the fact of a taxpayer's liability under §461. See Chrysler Corp. v. Commissioner, 436 F.3d 644 (6th Cir. 2006). . . .

HOLDINGS

(1) Under §461, all the events have occurred that establish the fact of the liability for services provided to the taxpayer when (i) the event fixing the liability, whether that be the required performance or other event, occurs, or (ii) payment is due, whichever happens earliest. The mere execution of a contract, without more, does not establish the fact of a taxpayer's liability for services.

(2) Under §461, all the events have occurred that establish the fact of the liability for insurance when (i) the event fixing the liability, whether that be the required performance or other event, occurs, or (ii) payment is due, whichever happens earliest. The mere execution of a contract, without more, does not establish the fact of a taxpayer's liability for insurance.

Problem

9-4.   Elaine owns and operates an oil and gas drilling business. In year 1, Elaine enters into a contract with Jerry (who is in the business of developing oil fields) for Elaine to build and operate an oil well on one of Jerry's fields. One of the requirements of the contract is that, if she discovers oil and builds a well on Jerry's land, Elaine must remove the oil drilling equipment from Jerry's land after the well is dry at her expense. Both Elaine and Jerry agree that the total cost for removing the equipment will be $50,000. Elaine builds the oil well in year 1 and operates it in year 2 and year 3. Pursuant to the contract, Jerry pays Elaine $30,000 on April 1, year 2, for all services performed in year 2, and does the same in year 3. The well goes dry on January 1, year 4, and Elaine begins dismantling the oil well. By December 15, year 4, the oil well has been fully removed from Jerry's land. Both Elaine's business and Jerry's business are accrual method taxpayers.

a.   In what year(s) may Jerry claim a deduction for the payments made to Elaine?

b.   In what year(s) may Elaine claim a deduction for the cost of removing the oil equipment from Jerry's field?

c.   Assume instead that, in year 1, Jerry prepays Elaine $60,000 for her services to be rendered in year 2 and year 3. In what year(s) may Jerry claim a deduction for the payments made to Elaine? In what year(s) does Elaine include the payments from Jerry in her gross income?

4. Contested Liabilities

Section 461(f) and §1.461-1(a)(2)(ii) of the Regulations provide two rules for the timing of deductions related to contested liabilities. Under the general rule of Regulation §1.461-1(a)(2)(ii), if a taxpayer incurs, for example, a liability of $10,000 during the taxable year but contests $5,000 of that liability, the taxpayer may properly accrue and deduct only $5,000 as an expense in that year. Likewise, if a taxpayer contests the entire liability, no amount may be deducted.

A taxpayer who not only contests a liability but also pays it before the dispute is settled experiences an economic hardship under the general rule that forbids a current deduction. Nevertheless, the Supreme Court, in United States v. Consolidated Edison, 366 U.S. 380 (1961), strictly applied the all events test in denying a current deduction for the payment of a tax under protest. The Court reasoned that the fact of the liability could not be established until the liability was no longer disputed. Congress responded to *Consolidated Edison* by enacting §461(f), as an exception to the all events test, to afford relief to taxpayers who pay and contest a liability. Section 461(f) provides a method by which both cash method and accrual method taxpayers may currently deduct a contested liability prior to the resolution of the dispute.

There are four prerequisites to a current deduction under §461(f). First, the taxpayer must contest an asserted liability. Regulation §1.461-2(b)(2) establishes a low threshold for this requirement by finding a contest if there is a bona fide dispute as to law or fact. For instance, any act denying the existence or validity of the liability is sufficient to constitute a contest. Second, the taxpayer must transfer, beyond the taxpayer's control, money or property for satisfaction of the asserted liability. Third, the contest over the asserted liability must continue after the transfer, and fourth, but for the contested liability, a deduction must otherwise be allowable for the taxable year of transfer or an earlier year. If these prerequisites are met, §461(f) permits the contested liability to be deducted currently.

Problems

9-5. Julia Black owns a tax accounting service that bills on an hourly basis. During year 1, she performed $20,000 of services for Harold Chapin, an accrual method, calendar-year taxpayer.
   a.   What result to Chapin if Black sends a bill for $20,000 on December 26, and Chapin pays it on December 30?
   b.   What if Chapin receives the bill in year 1 but does not pay it until year 2?
   c.   What tax consequences to Chapin if the bill is lost in the mail and is not received by Chapin until January, year 2?
   d.   What result to Chapin if Black sends the bill on January 1, year 2?
   e.   What result in *a* if only part of Black's services were performed for Chapin in year 1, with the remainder to be performed in year 2?
   f.   What result in *a* if there were no services performed in year 1, but all services were to be performed in year 2?

9-6. Nate Guest, an accrual method, calendar-year taxpayer, borrowed $75,000 from Lincoln Bank in year 1 for five years, with interest of $5,000 to accrue on December 31 of each year, commencing December, year 1. Assume that the interest expense is otherwise deductible.
   a. When may Guest deduct the interest payments?
   b. What if he is unable to pay the year 1 interest payment until February, year 2?
   c. What if he is insolvent until year 5?
   d. What if Guest pays the entire $25,000 of interest on December 31, year 1? Would it make a difference if he paid it by check drawn on an account with insufficient funds until January, year 2?
   e. What if, from the $75,000 borrowed from Lincoln Bank, Guest receives $50,000 in net proceeds, the difference of $25,000 representing prepaid interest?

9-7. In year 1, Luke Houseman, an accrual method, calendar-year taxpayer, paid property taxes of $10,000 for the prior year and did not elect under §461(c). In November, year 1, he received a notice from the county treasurer that there has been a mistake in the calculation of his taxes and that he underpaid his property taxes by $15,000.
   a. What tax consequences to Houseman in year 1 if he pays the additional $15,000 in December, year 1? What if the $15,000 is not paid until year 3, after all possible appeals have proved fruitless? Would it make any difference if Houseman paid the excess under protest?
   b. What tax consequences if instead of an underpayment, the government discovered that Houseman overpaid $5,000 in year 1, and it notifies him of his overpayment in year 2?

9-8. Sanford Company, an accrual method, calendar-year taxpayer, has often incurred tort liability because its customers are frequently injured on its premises. Frustrated by high premiums and excessive claim denials, Sanford decides to act as a self-insurer and sets aside $500,000 in year 1 to cover any liabilities. In year 2, it pays $400,000 to numerous claimants for accidents that occurred in year 1. In which year is Sanford entitled to a deduction, and in what amount?

D. REPAYMENTS OF ITEMS PREVIOUSLY INCLUDED IN INCOME

Code: §1341

1. *Claim of Right Doctrine*

The claim of right doctrine, first enunciated in North American Oil Consolidated v. Burnet, 286 U.S. 417 (1932), and discussed in Chapter 2, provides that when a taxpayer receives a payment (1) subject to a contingent obligation to repay either because the sum is disputed or was mistakenly paid and (2) with no limitation on the use of the funds in the interim, those funds are included in the taxpayer's income in the year in which they are received. In *North American Oil*, the taxpayer corporation received funds in 1917 that were the subject of ongoing litigation. The dispute was resolved in 1922 in favor of the taxpayer, North American, which as a result did not have to repay the sum. The question then arose concerning which year the funds held from 1917 until 1922 should be reported as income. The Supreme Court concluded that, because North American became entitled to the funds in 1917 under a claim of right, 1917 was the proper year for their inclusion in its income. The Supreme Court reasoned that such a rule supported the annual accounting period because it afforded finality to the tax year by not holding it open until the eventual resolution of the dispute.

In *North American Oil*, the Court did not have to address the issue of what would have happened if the corporation had ultimately been required to repay the funds. The Court confronted this issue in the following case, focusing on the income issue without resolving the attendant deduction issue.

UNITED STATES v. LEWIS
340 U.S. 590 (1951)

MR. JUSTICE BLACK delivered the opinion of the Court.

Respondent Lewis brought this action in the Court of Claims seeking a refund of an alleged overpayment of his 1944 income tax. The facts found by the Court of Claims are: In his 1944 income tax return, respondent reported about $22,000 which he had received that year as an employee's bonus. As a result of subsequent litigation in a state court, however, it was decided that respondent's bonus had been improperly computed; under compulsion of the state court's judgment he returned approximately $11,000 to his employer. Until payment of the judgment in 1946, respondent had at all times claimed and used the full $22,000 unconditionally as his own, in the good faith though "mistaken" belief that he was entitled to the whole bonus.

On the foregoing facts the Government's position is that respondent's 1944 tax should not be recomputed, but that respondent should have deducted the $11,000 as a loss in his 1946 tax return. The Court of Claims, however, relying on its own case, Greenwald v. United States, 57 F. Supp. 569, held that the excess bonus received "under a mistake of fact" was not income in 1944 and ordered a refund based on a recalculation of that year's tax. . . .

In the *North American Oil* case we said: "If a taxpayer receives earnings under a claim of right and without restriction as to its disposition, he has received income which he is required to return, even though it may still be claimed that he is not entitled to retain the money, and even though he may still be adjudged liable to restore its equivalent." 286 U.S. at 424. Nothing in this language permits an exception merely because a taxpayer is "mistaken" as to the validity of his claim. . . .

Income taxes must be paid on income received (or accrued) during an annual accounting period. The "claim of right" interpretation of the tax laws has long been used to give finality to that period, and is now deeply rooted in the federal tax

system. We see no reason why the Court should depart from this well-settled interpretation merely because it results in an advantage or disadvantage to a taxpayer.

Reversed.

JUSTICE DOUGLAS, dissenting.

The question in this case is not whether the bonus had to be included in 1944
income for purposes of the tax. Plainly it should have been because the taxpayer
claimed it as of right. Some years later, however, it was judicially determined that he
had no claim to the bonus. The question is whether he may then get back the tax
which he paid on the money.

Many inequities are inherent in the income tax. We multiply them needlessly
by nice distinctions which have no place in the practical administration of the law. If
the refund were allowed, the integrity of the taxable year would not be violated. The
tax would be paid when due; but the Government would not be permitted to
maintain the unconscionable position that it can keep the tax after it is shown
that payment was made on money which was not income to the taxpayer.

2.   Application of §1341

Although far from certain, the *Lewis* decision, at best, indirectly hints at the
remedy for the taxpayer's plight. By accepting the Commissioner's position
regarding the income issue, the Court implicitly accepted his offsetting treatment
through the allowance of a deduction in the year of repayment. A deduction in the
year of repayment, as suggested by *Lewis*, might not restore the taxpayer to the
economic position that he would have enjoyed had the item never been included in
gross income. Consider, for example, a taxpayer who is in the 40-percent bracket in
the year of inclusion and in the 10-percent bracket in the year of repayment and
deduction. Assuming that he received a $10,000 payment subject to a claim of right
and included it in his income in year 1, he would have a tax liability of $4,000 on the
disputed income. If he repays the $10,000 in year 2, the effect of the deduction for
the repayment will be a tax savings of approximately $1,000. Thus, he incurred
$3,000 in tax liability in year 1 that was not offset by the deduction in the year of
repayment.

Congress has attempted to correct this inequity by providing an alternative to
merely deducting an item in the year of repayment. Section 1341 provides generally
that a taxpayer who included an item in income under the claim of right doctrine and
who was subsequently required to repay that amount may utilize the more favorable
of two alternative methods for reducing tax liability in the year of repayment—
either a deduction under §1341(a)(4) or a credit under §1341(a)(5). The mechanics
of §§1341(a)(4) and 1341(a)(5) are fairly straightforward. First, however, three statutory and one judicial prerequisites must be satisfied.

The first statutory requirement is that the repaid item must have been
included in gross income for a prior taxable year (that is, year of inclusion) because
it *appeared* that the taxpayer had an unrestricted right to the item. §1341(a)(1).
Although the exact meaning of the word *appeared* is uncertain, a taxpayer's right to
income may be conceptualized as a continuum that begins with *no right* to a receipt,

moves to the *appearance of an unrestricted right*, and ends with an *absolute right* to a receipt. A no right situation embodies a "claim of wrong" receipt (such as embezzlement). Section 1341 does not apply to amounts wrongfully received, and the only remedy in the year of repayment is therefore a deduction. An absolute right situation requires the item to be included in gross income because the taxpayer has an absolute right to its receipt. An absolute right generally requires that all facts establishing the taxpayer's right to the receipt are known at the time of receipt. See Rev. Rul. 67-48, 1967-1 C.B. 50. In order to be divested of funds received under an absolute right, a subsequent event must occur. Section 1341 does not apply to repayment of funds received under an absolute right. An appearance of an unrestricted right arises where either (1) all necessary facts are not available in the year of inclusion to determine the correct amount of the inclusion or (2) the item included is subject to regulatory fiat. Rev. Rul. 68-153, 1968-1 C.B. 371. A taxpayer in this situation may use §1341 if he satisfies the remaining requirements.

The second statutory requirement is that the lack of an unrestricted right to such item must be established after the close of the year of inclusion. §1341(a)(2). The third statutory requirement is that the amount of the deduction must exceed $3,000. §1341(a)(3). The final requirement, which was judicially created, is that the repayment of the item must be involuntary. Pike v. Commissioner, 44 T.C. 787 (1965).

A taxpayer who satisfies the four prerequisites of §1341 is entitled to the benefits of either §1341(a)(4) or §1341(a)(5). Under these subsections, the tax for the current year is the *lesser* of (1) the tax for the current year computed with a deduction for the repaid amount or (2) the tax for the current year computed without a deduction for the repayment, less the decrease that would have resulted in the prior year's tax if the item were not included as gross income. Thus, if a taxpayer received $10,000 in year 1 and in that year was taxed in the 40-percent marginal tax bracket, her tax liability would have decreased by $4,000 (40%×$10,000) if the $10,000 had not been included in year 1's income. Consequently, if the taxpayer is in the 10-percent marginal tax bracket in year 2, the year of repayment, she will apply §1341(a)(5) and reduce tax liability by $4,000 because this would provide a greater tax benefit than deducting the $10,000. If she merely deducts the $10,000 repayment in year 2, tax liability will only be reduced by a maximum of $1,000. §1341(a)(4).

3. The Arrowsmith Doctrine

A taxpayer failing to qualify for §1341 (if, for example, the repayment is less than $3,000 or the repayment is voluntary) still may deduct the repayment if it qualifies as a deduction under §162 or §212. Thus, there are two situations in which a taxpayer may claim a deduction in a later year for income included in an earlier year: (1) under §1341(a)(4), or (2) under §162 or §212, if §1341 is not available. If the most favorable way to compute tax liability in the year of repayment entails a deduction as opposed to the §1341(a)(5) credit against current tax liability, the taxpayer will be required to characterize the deduction. Applying the principles enunciated by the Supreme Court in the *Arrowsmith* case, which follows, the character of the deduction is determined by looking to the character of the original transaction. Thus, if the prior year's income was a capital gain, the repayment should be deducted as a capital loss.

ARROWSMITH v. COMMISSIONER
344 U.S. 6 (1952)

Mr. Justice Black delivered the opinion of the Court.

This is an income tax controversy growing out of the following facts as shown by findings of the Tax Court. In 1937 two taxpayers, petitioners here, decided to liquidate and divide the proceeds of a corporation in which they had equal stock ownership. Partial distributions made in 1937, 1938, and 1939 were followed by a final one in 1940. Petitioners reported the profits obtained from this transaction, classifying them as capital gains. They thereby paid less income tax than would have been required had the income been attributed to ordinary business transactions for profit. About the propriety of these 1937-1940 returns, there is no dispute. But in 1944 a judgment was rendered against the old corporation and against Frederick R. Bauer, individually. The two taxpayers were required to and did pay the judgment for the corporation, of whose assets they were transferees. Classifying the loss as an ordinary business one, each took a tax deduction for 100 percent of the amount paid. Treatment of the loss as a capital one would have allowed deduction of a much smaller amount. The Commissioner viewed the 1944 payment as part of the original liquidation transaction requiring classification as a capital loss, just as the taxpayers had treated the original dividends as capital gains. . . .

. . . The losses here fall squarely within the definition of "capital losses" contained in these sections. Taxpayers were required to pay the judgment because of liability imposed on them as transferees of liquidation distribution assets. And it is plain that their liability as transferees was not based on any ordinary business transaction of theirs apart from the liquidation proceedings. It is not even denied that had this judgment been paid after liquidation, but during the year 1940, the losses would have been properly treated as capital ones. For payment during 1940 would simply have reduced the amount of capital gains taxpayers received during that year.

It is contended, however, that this payment which would have been a capital transaction in 1940 was transformed into an ordinary business transaction in 1944 because of the well-established principle that each taxable year is a separate unit for tax accounting purposes. But this principle is not breached by considering all the 1937-1944 liquidation transaction events in order properly to classify the nature of the 1944 loss for tax purposes. Such an examination is not an attempt to reopen and readjust the 1937 to 1940 tax returns, an action that would be inconsistent with the annual tax accounting principle. . . .

Affirmed.

Mr. Justice Douglas, dissenting.

I agree with Mr. Justice Jackson that these losses should be treated as ordinary, not capital, losses. There were no capital transactions in the year in which the losses were suffered. Those transactions occurred and were accounted for in earlier years in accord with the established principle that each year is a separate unit for tax accounting purposes. I have not felt, as my dissent in the *Lewis* case indicates, that the law made that an inexorable principle. But if it is the law, we should require observance of it — not merely by taxpayers but by the Government as well. We should force each year to stand on its own footing, whoever may gain or lose from it in a particular case. We impeach that principle when we treat this year's losses as if they diminished last year's gains. . . .

Problems

9-9. In year 1, Tom Powers earned a salary of $60,000 plus a special commission of $10,000 from his employer. In year 3, the employer obtained a court-ordered repayment, which Powers contested, of the special commission. Powers eventually repaid the $10,000 in year 3.

    a.   What tax consequences to Powers as a result of the repayment?

    b.   Would it make a difference whether Powers was a cash method or accrual method taxpayer?

    c.   What if Powers had not been under a court order to repay, but rather his employer had merely asked him (without fear of reproach) to pay back some or all of the commission?

    d.   Assume the same facts as in *a* except that Powers's federal income tax for year 1 was $30,200 and his tax would have been $23,900 without the inclusion of the commission; Powers's tax for year 3 without a deduction for repayment would be $20,800 and with such deduction would be $15,300. Compute Powers's tax liability in accordance with the provisions of §1341.

9-10. Determine whether §1341 applies in the following situations.

    a.   In year 3, Sam Pinter incurs $5,000 in legal expenses successfully contesting his employer's request for repayment of a bonus he received in year 1.

    b.   TPC Corporation and John Jones have an agreement whereby Jones must repay TPC any salary or related payments he receives that are later disallowed as a deduction to the corporation. In year 3, the Commissioner disallows as excessive $10,000 in year 1 salary payments to Jones. Jones repays this amount to the corporation in year 3.

    c.   Same facts and parties as in *b* except that Jones and the corporation execute the agreement in year 3 after the IRS audit, claiming that their agreement has retroactive effect.

    d.   Maureen Plummer, an accrual method taxpayer, learns in November, year 3, that she must repay $10,000 of a commission she earned and received in year 1. Plummer is temporarily short of cash at the time and is able to repay only $2,000 in year 3, although she makes arrangements to pay the balance in January, year 4. What result in year 3?

    e.   What result in *d* if Plummer is a cash method taxpayer?

9-11.   Ken Kahn sold his interest in oil and gas leases with an adjusted basis of $50,000 for $200,000, reporting the gain as long-term capital. Two years later, he was sued by one of the purchasers for fraud and settled for $50,000. What is the status and the character of the payment?

E.   TAX SHELTERS

1.   Overview

Tax shelters have caused consternation in the equitable administration of the income tax laws since the enactment of the modern income tax:

> Perhaps no single topic in the Federal income tax laws has been as vexing and difficult to address as tax shelters. In 1934, Judge Learned Hand made the statement [in Helvering v. Gregory, 69 F.2d 809, 810 (2d Cir. 1934)], often cited since, that a taxpayer "[m]ay so arrange his affairs that his taxes shall be as low as possible; he is not bound to choose that pattern which will best pay the Treasury; there is not even a patriotic duty to increase one's taxes." Since that time, taxpayers and tax administrators have struggled in determining the line between legitimate "tax planning" and unacceptable "tax shelters." Even now, more than sixty-five years after Judge Hand's opinion, there are disagreements on fundamental questions that lie at the heart of the tax shelter debate, such as the magnitude of the problem, why the problem exists, and appropriate responses to the problem.

Joint Committee on Taxation, Background and Present Law Relating to Tax Shelters (JCX-19-02) March 19, 2002 at 2. In general, however, tax-sheltered investments may be thought of as activities that create or accelerate deductions that are used to offset unrelated income. The materials that follow provide an introduction to some of the potential abuses inherent in tax shelters and discuss congressional and judicial efforts to prevent taxpayers who enter into highly leveraged tax shelters from unfairly benefiting from this strategy.

STAFF OF JOINT COMMITTEE ON TAXATION, BACKGROUND ON TAX SHELTERS
2 (1983)

I.   OVERVIEW

Tax-shelter investments enable taxpayers to reduce their tax liabilities by use of tax benefits generated by the investments. There are three selling points that are common to most tax-shelter investments: (1) the ability to defer tax liability to a later year; (2) the opportunity to convert ordinary income to tax-favored income (such as capital gains); and (3) the use of borrowed funds to finance the investment (leverage). . . .

Beginning in 1969, Congress has enacted a series of income tax laws that are designed to reduce the use of tax shelters. . . .

Certain aspects of present law continue to provide taxpayers with opportunities to obtain possibly unintended tax benefits, providing the basis for tax-shelter investments. For example, the benefits of deferring a tax liability are attributable, in large part, to the fact that present law does not take adequate account of the present value (or cost) of a future expense or receipt. . . .

II. ELEMENTS OF A TAX-SHELTER INVESTMENT

In general, a tax shelter is an investment in which a significant portion of the investor's return is derived from the realization of tax savings on other income, as well as the receipt of tax-favored (or, effectively, tax-exempt) income from the investment itself. Tax shelters are typically characterized as abusive if they are formed primarily to obtain tax benefits, without regard to the economic viability of the investment.

In some instances, tax shelters are used to take advantage of specific incentives, such as the accelerated cost recovery system, the deduction for intangible drilling costs, or the deduction for research and experimental expenses, which Congress has legislated. Other shelters use devices in the tax law to achieve tax savings which were never specifically intended by Congress, and some shelters attempt to inflate certain deductions, credits, etc. beyond the properly allowable amount.

Although tax-shelter investments take a variety of forms, there are several elements that are common to most tax shelters. The first of these is the "deferral" of tax liability to future years, resulting, in effect, in an interest-free loan from the Federal Government. The second element of a tax shelter is the "conversion" of ordinary income . . . to tax-favored income (such as capital gains). . . . Finally, many tax shelters permit a taxpayer to leverage his investment (i.e., to use borrowed funds to pay deductible expenditures), thereby maximizing the tax benefit of deductibility. What follows is a general description of the elements of a tax shelter.

DEFERRAL

Deferral generally involves the acceleration of deductions, resulting in the reduction of a taxpayer's tax liability in the early years of an investment, instead of matching the deductions against the income that is eventually generated by the investment. Deferral also occurs when, for example, taxpayers funnel U.S. investments through a foreign corporation the earnings of which are not subject to current U.S. tax.

The effect of deferral is that the taxpayer grants himself an interest-free loan from the Federal Government, which loan is repayable when, and as, the tax-shelter investment either produces taxable income or is disposed of at a gain. For example, consider the case of a taxpayer who, at the end of year one, realizes that he or she requires a $1,000 loan for use in year two. If this taxpayer obtained a one-year loan when the prevailing rate of interest is 15 percent (compounded annually), he or she would repay $1,150 at the end of year two. If, instead of obtaining a loan, the taxpayer were to invest in a tax shelter that generated a current deduction of $2,000 in year one, and the underlying investment were not expected to generate $2,000 of income until the following year, the taxpayer would have a $1,000 tax savings [assuming a 50 percent tax rate]. In the latter case, at the end of year two, instead of repaying a lender $1,150, the taxpayer would incur a Federal income tax of $1,000 on the $2,000 of income generated by the investment. Obviously, the longer the deferral period, the greater the benefit obtained by the taxpayer. Alternatively, the taxpayer could invest the $2,000 of income in another tax shelter to provide a "rollover" or further deferral of the tax.

In some cases, deferral is obtained by the use of legislatively sanctioned tax benefits, such as, for example, the Accelerated Cost Recovery System (ACRS) or the expensing of intangible drilling costs. Other benefits associated with deferral reflect the tax law's treatment of the time value of money. . . .

CONVERSION

The second aspect of most tax-shelter investments is the "conversion" of ordinary income to tax-favored income (such as capital gains or income that is otherwise subject to a reduced rate of tax). Conversion is achieved where, for example, a taxpayer takes an accelerated deduction against ordinary income, and the income that is eventually generated by the investment is taxed [as capital gain]. Also, if the taxpayer is in a lower tax bracket in the year when the investment generates income, he or she effectively "converts" the tax rate.

In the case of certain deductions (e.g., depreciation deductions), . . . Congress has dealt with conversion by requiring a portion of the gain on disposition of an investment to be treated as ordinary income (rather than capital gains). However, the current "recapture" rules apply only to prevent the conversion of some ordinary income to capital gains, and do not apply to all tax shelters.

LEVERAGE

The use of borrowed money to fund a tax-shelter investment may result in an economic benefit, as well as a tax benefit. Generally, a taxpayer will borrow an amount of money that equals or exceeds his or her equity investment. From an economic viewpoint, to the extent that a taxpayer can use borrowed money to fund a tax-shelter investment, he or she can use his or her own money for other purposes (such as other investments), resulting in an increase in earnings if the investments are profitable. From a tax viewpoint, borrowed funds generally are treated in the same manner as a taxpayer's own money that he or she puts up as equity in the investment. Because a taxpayer is allowed deductions for expenditures paid with borrowed funds, the tax benefits of deductibility (e.g., deferral) are maximized.

Because interest payments on indebtedness are themselves deductible, a debt-financed investment provides an additional tax advantage relative to an equity-financed investment. This is so because the deductibility of interest payments lowers the effective tax rate on the income generated by the investment.

The benefits of leveraging a tax-shelter investment can be illustrated by a simple example. Assume that a 50-percent bracket taxpayer invests $10,000 of his or her own money, and borrows $90,000 to fund a $100,000 investment. If the investment generates a "tax loss" of $30,000 in the first year by reason of accelerated deductions, the taxpayer will save taxes of $15,000 on his or her investment of $10,000.

The significance of leverage increases where a taxpayer obtains a nonrecourse loan (i.e., where there is no personal liability to repay the loan). . . .

2. *Judicial Restrictions on Tax Shelters*

As the courts continued to be confronted with tax shelters, they began to develop judicial doctrines denying the tax benefits of certain transactions even if they literally complied with the statutory requirements. In the preeminent case, Gregory v. Helvering, 293 U.S. 465 (1935), the Supreme Court held that the transaction at issue "though conducted according to the terms of [the Internal Revenue Code], was in fact an elaborate and devious form of conveyance. . . . [T]he transaction upon its face lies outside the plain intent of the statute. To hold otherwise would be to exalt artifice above reality and to deprive the statutory provision in question of all serious purpose." This holding eventually came to be known as the "business purpose" doctrine. In addition, courts have applied similar doctrines — such as the "substance over form," "economic substance," "step transaction," and "sham transaction" doctrines — to disallow tax benefits in abusive tax shelters. In reading the following cases, compare and contrast the approaches taken by the various courts in addressing tax shelters, and consider whether any one approach may be superior to another in combating tax shelters going forward.

KNETSCH v. UNITED STATES
364 U.S. 361 (1960)

Mr. Justice Brennan delivered the opinion of the Court.

This case presents the question of whether deductions from gross income claimed on petitioners' 1953 and 1954 joint federal income tax returns, of $143,465 in 1953 and of $147,105 in 1954, for payments made by petitioner, Karl F. Knetsch, to Sam Houston Life Insurance Company, constituted "interest paid . . . on indebtedness" within the meaning of §163(a) of the Code. The Commissioner disallowed the deductions and determined a deficiency for each year. . . .

On December 11, 1953, the insurance company sold Knetsch ten 30-year maturity deferred annuity savings bonds, each in the face amount of $400,000 and bearing interest at 21/2 percent compounded annually. The purchase price was $4,004,000. Knetsch gave the Company his check for $4,000, and signed $4,000,000 of nonrecourse annuity loan notes for the balance. The notes bore 31/2 percent interest and were secured by the annuity bonds. The interest was payable in advance, and Knetsch on the same day prepaid the first year's interest, which was $140,000. Under the Table of Cash and Loan Values made part of the bonds, their cash or loan value at December 11, 1954, the end of the first contract year, was to be $4,100,000. The contract terms, however, permitted Knetsch to borrow any excess of this value above his indebtedness without waiting until December 11, 1954. Knetsch took advantage of this provision only five days after the purchase. On December 16, 1953, he received from the company

$99,000 of the $100,000 excess over his $4,000,000 indebtedness, for which he gave his notes bearing 31/2 percent interest. This interest was also payable in advance and on the same day he prepaid the first year's interest of $3,465. In their joint return for 1953, the petitioners deducted the sum of the two interest payments, that is $143,465, as "interest paid . . . within the taxable year on indebtedness."

The second contract year began on December 11, 1954, when interest in advance of $143,465 was payable by Knetsch on his aggregate indebtedness of $4,099,000. Knetsch paid this amount on December 27, 1954. Three days later, on December 30, he received from the company cash in the amount of $104,000, the difference less $1,000 between his then $4,099,000 indebtedness and the cash or loan value of the bonds of $4,204,000 on December 11, 1955. He gave the company appropriate notes and prepaid the interest thereon of $3,640. In their joint return for the taxable year 1954 the petitioners deducted the sum of the two interest payments, that is $147,105, as "interest paid . . . within the taxable year on indebtedness."

The tax years 1955 and 1956 are not involved in this proceeding, but a recital of the events of those years is necessary to complete the story of the transaction. On December 11, 1955, the start of the third contract year, Knetsch became obligated to pay $147,105 as prepaid interest on an indebtedness which now totalled $4,203,000. He paid this interest on December 28, 1955. On the same date he received $104,000 from the company. This was $1,000 less than the difference between his indebtedness and the cash or loan value of the bonds of $4,308,000 at December 11, 1956. Again he gave the company notes upon which he prepaid interest of $3,640. Petitioners claimed a deduction on their 1955 joint return for the aggregate of the payments, or $150,745. Knetsch did not go on with the transaction for the fourth contract year beginning December 11, 1956, but terminated it on December 27, 1956. His indebtedness at that time totalled $4,307,000. The cash or loan value of the bonds was the $4,308,000 value at December 11, 1956, which had been the basis of the "loan" of December 28, 1955. He surrendered the bonds and his indebtedness was canceled. He received the difference of $1,000 in cash.

The contract called for a monthly annuity of $90,171 at maturity (when Knetsch would be 90 years of age) or for such smaller amount as would be produced by the cash or loan value after deduction of the then existing indebtedness. It was stipulated that if Knetsch had held the bonds to maturity and continued annually to borrow the net cash value less $1,000, the sum available for the annuity at maturity would be $1,000 ($8,388,000 cash or loan value less $8,387,000 of indebtedness), enough to provide an annuity of only $43 per month.

The trial judge made findings that "[t]here was no commercial economic substance to the . . . transaction," that the parties did not intend that Knetsch "become indebted to Sam Houston," that "[n]o indebtedness of [Knetsch] was created by any of the . . . transactions," and that "[n]o economic gain could be achieved from the purchase of these bonds without regard to the tax consequences. . . ." His conclusion of law . . . was that "[w]hile in form the payments to Sam Houston were compensation for the use or forbearance of money, they were not in substance. As a payment of interest, the transaction was a sham."

We first examine the transaction between Knetsch and the insurance company to determine whether it created an "indebtedness" or whether, as the trial court found, it was a sham. We put aside a finding by the District Court that Knetsch's "only motive in purchasing these 10 bonds was to attempt to secure an interest deduction." As was said in Gregory v. Helvering, 293 U.S. 465, 469: "The legal right of a taxpayer to decrease the amount of what otherwise would be his taxes, or altogether avoid them, by means which the law permits, cannot be doubted. . . . But the question for determination is whether what was done, apart from the tax motive, was the thing which the statute intended."

When we examine "what was done" here, we see that Knetsch paid the insurance company $294,570 during the two taxable years involved and received $203,000 back in the form of "loans." What did Knetsch get for the out-of-pocket difference of $91,570? In form he had an annuity contract with a so-called guaranteed cash value at maturity of $8,388,000, which would produce monthly annuity payments of $90,171, or substantial life insurance proceeds in the event of his death before maturity. This, as we have seen, was a fiction, because each year Knetsch's annual borrowings kept the net cash value, on which any annuity or insurance payments would depend, at the relative pittance of $1,000. Plainly, therefore, Knetsch's transaction with the insurance company did not appreciably affect his beneficial interest except to reduce his tax. . . . For it is patent that there was nothing of substance to be realized by Knetsch from this transaction beyond a tax deduction. What he was ostensibly "lent" back was in reality only the rebate of a substantial part of the so-called "interest" payments. The $91,570 difference retained by the company was its fee for providing the facade of "loans" whereby the petitioners sought to reduce their 1953 and 1954 taxes in the total sum of $233,297.68. There may well be single-premium annuity arrangements with non-tax substance which create an "indebtedness" for the purposes of §163(a) . . . [b]ut this one is a sham. . . .

The judgment of the Court of Appeals is affirmed.

Mr. Justice Douglas, with whom Mr. Justice Whittaker and Mr. Justice Stewart concur, dissenting. . . .

It is true that in this transaction the taxpayer was bound to lose if the annuity contract is taken by itself. At least the taxpayer showed by his conduct that he never intended to come out ahead on that investment apart from this income tax deduction. Yet the same may be true where a taxpayer borrows money at five percent or six percent interest to purchase securities that pay only nominal interest; or where, with money in the bank earning three percent, he borrows from the selfsame bank at a higher rate. His aim there, as here, may only be to get a tax deduction for interest paid. Yet as long as the transaction itself is not hocus-pocus, the interest charges incident to completing it would seem to be deductible under the Internal Revenue Code. . . . The insurance company existed; it operated under Texas law; it was authorized to issue these policies and to make these annuity loans. While the taxpayer was obligated to pay interest at the rate of 31/2 percent per annum, the annuity bonds increased in cash value at the rate of only 21/2 percent per annum. The insurance company's profit was in that one-point spread.

Tax avoidance is a dominating motive behind scores of transactions. It is plainly present here. . . . To disallow the "interest" deduction because the annuity device was devoid of commercial substance is to draw a line which will affect a host of situations not now before us and which, with all deference, I do not think we can maintain when other cases reach here. The remedy is legislative. Evils or abuses can be particularized by Congress. We deal only with "interest" as commonly understood and as used across the board in myriad transactions. Since these transactions were real and legitimate in the insurance world and were consummated within the limits allowed by insurance policies, I would recognize them tax-wise.

ESTATE OF FRANKLIN v. COMMISSIONER
544 F.2d 1045 (9th Cir. 1976)

Sneed, Circuit Judge.

This case involves another effort on the part of the Commissioner to curb the use of real estate tax shelters. In this instance he seeks to disallow deductions for the taxpayers' distributive share of losses reported by a limited partnership with respect to its acquisition of a motel and related property. These "losses" have their origin in deductions for depreciation and interest claimed with respect to the motel and related property. These deductions were disallowed by the Commissioner on the ground[s] . . . that the acquisition was a sham. . . .

The interest and depreciation deductions were taken by Twenty-Fourth Property Associates (hereinafter referred to as Associates), a California limited partnership of which Charles T. Franklin and seven other doctors were the limited partners. The deductions flowed from the purported "purchase" by Associates of the Thunderbird Inn, an Arizona motel, from Wayne L. Romney and Joan E. Romney (hereinafter referred to as the Romneys) on November 15, 1968.

Under a document entitled "Sales Agreement," the Romneys agreed to "sell" the Thunderbird Inn to Associates for $1,224,000. The property would be paid for over a period of ten years, with interest on any unpaid balance of seven and one-half percent per annum. "Prepaid interest" in the amount of $75,000 was payable immediately; monthly principal and interest installments of $9,045.36 would be paid for approximately the first ten years, with Associates required to make a balloon payment at the end of the ten years of the difference between the remaining purchase price, forecast as $975,000, and any mortgages then outstanding against the property.

The purchase obligation of Associates to the Romneys was nonrecourse. . . . The sale was combined with a leaseback of the property by Associates to the Romneys; Associates therefore never took physical possession. The lease payments were designed to approximate closely the principal and interest payments with the consequence that with the exception of the $75,000 prepaid interest payment no cash would cross between Associates and Romneys until the balloon payment. . . . [T]he Romneys were responsible for all of the typical expenses of owning the motel property including all utility costs, taxes, assessments, rents, charges, and levies of "every name, nature and kind whatsoever." The Romneys also were to continue to be responsible for the first and second mortgages until the final purchase installment was made; the Romneys could, and indeed did, place additional mortgages on the property without the permission of Associates. Finally, the Romneys were allowed to propose new capital improvements which Associates would be required to either build themselves or allow the Romneys to construct with compensating modifications in rent or purchase price.

. . . We believe the characteristics set out above can exist in a situation in which the sale imposes upon the purchaser a genuine indebtedness within the meaning of §167(a), which will support both interest and depreciation deductions. . . . In none of these cases, however, did the taxpayer fail to demonstrate that the purchase price was at least approximately equivalent to the fair market value of the property. Just such a failure occurred here. The Tax Court explicitly found that on the basis of the facts before it the value of the property could not be estimated. In our view this defect in the taxpayer's proof is fatal.

Petitioners spent a substantial amount of time at trial attempting to establish that, whatever the actual market value of the property, Associates acted in the good faith belief that the market value of the property approximated the selling price. However, this evidence only goes to the issue of sham and does not supply substance to this transaction. "Save in those instances where the statute itself turns on intent, a matter so real as taxation must depend on objective realities, not on the varying subjective beliefs of individual taxpayers." Lynch v. Commissioner, 273 F.2d 867, 872 (2d Cir. 1959).

. . . Reason supports our perception. An acquisition such as that of Associates if at a price approximately equal to the fair market value of the property under ordinary circumstances would rather quickly yield an equity in the property which the purchaser could not prudently abandon. This is the stuff of substance. It meshes with the form of the transaction and constitutes a sale.

No such meshing occurs when the purchase price exceeds a demonstrably reasonable estimate of the fair market value. Payments on the principal of the purchase price yield no equity so long as the unpaid balance of the purchase price exceeds the then existing fair market value. Under these circumstances the purchaser by abandoning the transaction can lose no more than a mere chance to acquire an equity in the future should the value of the acquired property increase.

. . . Authority also supports our perception. It is fundamental that "depreciation is not predicated upon ownership of property but rather upon an investment in property." No such investment exists when payments of the purchase price in accordance with the design of the parties yield no equity to the purchaser. In the transaction before us and during the taxable years in question the purchase price payments by Associates have not been shown to constitute an investment in the property. Depreciation was properly disallowed. Only the Romneys had an investment in the property.

Authority also supports disallowance of the interest deductions. This is said even though it has long been recognized that the absence of personal liability for the purchase money debt secured by a mortgage on the acquired property does not deprive the debt of its character as a bona-fide debt obligation able to support an interest deduction. However, this is no longer true when it appears that the debt has economic significance only if the property substantially appreciates in value prior to the date at which a very large portion of the purchase price is to be discharged. Under these circumstances the purchaser has not secured the use or forbearance of money . . . [n]or has the seller advanced money or forborne its use. Prior to the date at which the balloon payment on the purchase price is required, and assuming no substantial increase in the fair market value of the property, the absence of personal liability on the debt reduces the transaction in economic terms to a mere chance that a genuine debt obligation may arise. This is not enough to justify an interest deduction. To justify the deduction the debt must exist; potential existence will not do. For debt to exist, the purchaser, in the absence of personal liability, must confront a situation in which it is presently reasonable from an economic point of view for him to make a capital investment in the amount of the unpaid purchase price. Associates, during the taxable years in question, confronted no such situation.

Our focus on the relationship of the fair market value of the property to the unpaid purchase price should not be read as premised upon the belief that a sale is not a sale if the purchaser pays too much. Bad bargains from the buyer's point of view . . . do not thereby cease to be sales. We intend our holding and explanation thereof to be understood as limited to transactions substantially similar to that now before us.

AFFIRMED.

RICE'S TOYOTA WORLD v. COMMISSIONER
752 F.2d 89 (4th Cir. 1985)

Phillips, J.

Rice's Toyota World (Rice) appeals the Tax Court's decision upholding the Commissioner's disallowance of interest and depreciation deductions that Rice took on income tax returns filed for 1976, 1977, and 1978 on the basis that underlying sale and leaseback transactions were, for tax purposes, a sham. We affirm disallowance of the depreciation deductions and a portion of the interest deductions; but we reverse disallowance of a portion of the interest deductions.

I

In form the transactions in issue involved the sale and leaseback of a used computer and financing of the purchase by secured recourse and nonrecourse notes payable to the seller. The principal officer of Rice, a company primarily engaged in the sale of automobiles, learned about computer purchase-and-lease-back transactions through a friend who had already entered into a similar transaction through Finalco, a corporation primarily engaged in leasing capital equipment. Rice's accountant contacted Finalco to request information, and Finalco mailed Rice literature describing potential transactions. Finalco's literature noted that the transactions generate large tax losses in early years because the purchaser could claim depreciation deductions calculated under accelerated depreciation provisions as well as interest expense deductions. The transactions produce income in later years as depreciation deductions decrease.

After meeting with a Finalco representative, Rice purchased a used computer from Finalco in 1976 for a total purchase price of $1,455,227, giving Finalco a recourse note in the amount of $250,000 payable over three years, and two nonrecourse notes in the amount of $1,205,227 payable over eight years. Finalco had recently purchased the used computer for $1,297,643.

Rice leased the computer back to Finalco for a period of eight years, beginning in 1976. Under the lease, rental payments exceeded Rice's obligations on the nonrecourse debt by $10,000 annually. Finalco's obligations to pay rent were made contingent on its receiving adequate revenues in subleasing the computer. At the time of Rice's purchase and leaseback of the computer, Finalco had arranged a five year sublease of the computer. Finalco was entitled to 30 percent of proceeds generated if it arranged re-lease or sale of the computer after expiration of the five year sublease.

Rice paid off the $250,000 recourse note in three years along with $30,000 in interest on the deferred installments. On its income tax returns for 1976, 1977, and 1978, it claimed accelerated depreciation deductions based upon its ownership of the computer, and interest deductions for its payments on the notes.

The tax court upheld the Commissioner's disallowance of all the depreciation deductions and the interest expense deductions based on both the recourse and nonrecourse notes because the court found that the sale and leaseback was a sham transaction that the Commissioner is entitled to ignore for tax purposes. Rice's Toyota World, Inc. v. Commissioner, 81 T.C. 184 (1983). The tax court found as fact that Rice was not motivated by any business purpose other than achieving tax benefits in entering this transaction, and that the transaction had no economic substance because no reasonable possibility of profit existed. The court accordingly held as a matter of law that the transaction should be treated for tax purposes as if Rice paid Finalco a fee, in the form of the cash payment of $62,500 made on the recourse note in the year of purchase, in exchange for tax benefits.

This appeal followed.

II

The tax court read Frank Lyon Co. v. United States, 435 U.S. 561 (1978), to mandate a two-pronged inquiry to determine whether a transaction is, for tax purposes, a sham. To treat a transaction as a sham, the court must find that the taxpayer was motivated by no business purposes other than obtaining tax benefits in entering the transaction, and that the transaction has no economic substance because no reasonable possibility of a profit exists. We agree that such a test properly gives effect to the mandate of the Court in *Frank Lyon* that a transaction cannot be treated as a sham unless the transaction is shaped solely by tax avoidance considerations.

Whether under this test a particular transaction is a sham is an issue of fact, and our review of the tax court's subsidiary and ultimate findings on this factual issue is therefore under the clearly erroneous standard. Applying that standard, we affirm the tax court's findings on the sham issues.

A

The business purpose inquiry simply concerns the motives of the taxpayer in entering the transaction. The record in this case contains ample evidence to support the tax court's finding that Rice's sole motivation for purchasing and leasing back the computer under the financing arrangement used was to achieve the large tax deductions that the transaction provided in the early years of the lease.

First, the record supports the court's subsidiary finding that Rice did not seriously evaluate whether the computer would have sufficient residual value at the end of the eight year lease to Finalco to enable Rice to earn a profit on its purchase and seller-financed leaseback. Under the purchase and lease agreements with Finalco, Rice was obligated to pay (and did pay) $280,000 to Finalco in the form of principal and interest on the recourse note. Finalco's rental payments provided Rice with a return on the investment of $10,000 annually after payment of Rice's principal and interest obligations under the nonrecourse notes. At the time of the lease, Rice could therefore be certain of receiving a $50,000 return since Finalco had subleased the computer for five years, but Rice could recover the additional $230,000 of its investment only if it could re-lease the computer after five years or realize a substantial amount by its sale. Profit on the transaction therefore depended upon re-lease or sale because Finalco had no obligation to pay rent under its lease unless it received adequate revenues in subleasing the computer. Moreover, the sale and leaseback agreement gave Finalco a "marketing fee" of 30 percent of re-lease or sale proceeds if Finalco arranged the subsequent deal, thereby increasing further the amount Rice had to receive on re-leasing or selling the computer to earn a profit.

Residual value of the computer (either in selling or re-leasing) should therefore have been the crucial point of inquiry for a person with a business purpose of making a profit on this transaction. However, Rice's principal officer knew virtually nothing about computers, and relied almost exclusively on the representations of a Finalco salesperson regarding expected residual value. Despite the Finalco representative's frank concession that he was not an expert in predicting residual values, Rice did not pursue the representative's offer to provide an expert appraisal of likely residual value. Rice's accountant advised that the transaction appeared to be profitable, but the record does not reveal that the accountant's opinion reflects anything more than the fact that the transaction, if successful, would generate large tax deductions. Although Rice had in its possession a report containing a chart that showed a possibility that the computer would have sufficient residual value to earn Rice a profit, the report warned of great risk in predicting residual values, and also showed a large possibility of losses on the transaction.

The record contains additional support for drawing the ultimate inference that Rice was not motivated by potential profit. First off, Finalco's literature emphasized the large tax deductions the transaction would produce, not the potential for profit. To the contrary, the literature warned of great difficulty in predicting residual values.

More critical is the evidence that Rice paid an inflated purchase price for the computer: $1,455,227 for a used computer that Finalco had recently purchased, in an already declining market, for only $1,297,643. Considering that Finalco had a right to 30 percent of re-leasing or sale proceeds after five years, Rice can more accurately be said to have purchased for this amount only 70 percent of a computer, then worth less than $1,000,000. Because Rice paid so obviously inflated a purchase price for the computer and financed the purchase mainly with nonrecourse debt, it was properly inferable by the tax court that Rice intended to abandon the transaction down the road by walking away from the nonrecourse note balance before the transaction ran its stated course. The inference is amply supportable that this intended course of conduct explains Rice's apparent lack of concern with residual value or profitability of the transaction apart from tax benefits.

Rice points to several items of evidence supporting a contrary inference in respect of profit motivation. A report prepared for trial by an expert witness demonstrated that if Rice remained in the transaction until completion without walking away from the nonrecourse debt, Rice's tax benefit from early-stage deferral of taxes would amount to less than a normal rate of return on its investment. Rice contends that since it knew that the benefit from tax deferral would not amount to a normal return, it must have intended to profit from the transaction apart from tax benefits. While that factual inference was possible, it surely was not compelled on the record before the tax court. For, as will appear, Rice's knowledge of the tax consequences of a wholly consummated transaction is at least equally compatible with the inference drawn by the tax court: that Rice did not intend that it would be fully consummated with attendant full tax consequences.

Rice's main reliance on the report is upon its warning that its tax benefits would ultimately be limited because of realization of taxable "phantom income" in later years of the overall transaction. Specifically, the report indicated that although Rice would receive artificially large depreciation deductions in early years due to accelerated depreciation provisions, it would receive artificially low deductions in later years as basis was used up, thereby resulting in "phantom income." In addition, as the balance on the nonrecourse notes was paid down, interest expense deductions would be reduced, thereby further increasing income. If Rice fully recognized the phantom income generated by the transaction, its tax benefit would be limited to a deferral of tax payments.

However, as the tax court properly found, Rice most likely intended to abandon the transaction before it earned and paid any taxes on the phantom income, assuming it would have been so realized. With the heavy early-stage tax deductions taken and the prospect of achieving equity in the computer slim due to the inflated purchased price paid by Rice, Rice would have every incentive to attempt to avoid reporting phantom income. Countering this, Rice points out that it might not be able to avoid paying taxes on phantom income generated by the transaction even by abandoning or making a gift of the computer because under recent case law, termination might trigger tax recapture provisions. However, when Rice entered this transaction in 1976, the law was unclear regarding recapture in situations where loan balances exceed basis of property. In fact, many experts were then suggesting that taxpayers could legally avoid reporting phantom income by various devices. Bittker noted in 1978 that many tax shelter investors simply "forget" to report their gain upon abandonment.

Hence, though the expert report certainly lends support to Rice's contention about its "profit motivation," it as certainly does not compel its acceptance in the face of at least equally strong support for the contrary inference drawn by the tax court.

Finally, Rice contends that the tax court's motivational finding against it is unsupportable because the real cause of unprofitability of this transaction was the introduction of revolutionary new products by the IBM after the computer's purchase, a development unforeseeable by Rice. Although the IBM developments certainly had a disastrous impact on the used computer market, Rice had reports in its possession warning it of great instability in the used computer market. By the time Rice purchased the computer, its value had already declined to approximately 50 percent of the value of comparable new computers, and the machine was clearly lagging behind newer technology.

All in all, Rice's failure seriously to evaluate the likely residual value of the computer, its willingness to pay an inflated purchase price, and its use of nonrecourse debt that would facilitate abandonment of the transaction provide ample support for the tax court's finding that Rice did not have profit motivation apart from tax benefits. We cannot declare that finding clearly erroneous.

B

The second prong of the sham inquiry, the economic substance inquiry, requires an objective determination of whether a reasonable possibility of profit from the transaction existed apart from tax benefits. As noted, the transaction carried no hope of earning Rice a profit unless the computer had residual value sufficient to recoup the $280,000 in principal and interest that Rice paid Finalco on the recourse note less the $10,000 net annual return to Rice under the lease agreement. Even assuming that Finalco paid Rice $10,000 annually for the full eight-year term, which is by no means assured, and ignoring the time value of Rice's money invested, Rice would have to realize $200,000 in residual value to earn a profit. If Finalco re-leased or sold the computer for Rice, the more likely development in view of Rice's lack of computer marketing experience, Rice would receive only 70 percent of the proceeds and would profit only if residual value exceeded approximately $286,000.

The record contains estimates of residual value made by several experts that range from a low of $18,000 to a high of $375,000. Although Rice's experts presented a range of predicted residual values with a high end sufficient to earn Rice a profit, the tax court found the Commissioner's experts to be more credible and to have used more reliable forecasting techniques. The tax court's finding that residual value was not sufficient to earn Rice a profit is amply supported by the record and is not clearly erroneous. This finding, in conjunction with the tax court finding that Rice would not find it imprudent to walk away from the transaction, abandoning the property subject to the sale and leaseback, supports the ultimate inference drawn by the tax court that the transaction lacked economic substance.

Hence, we affirm as not clearly erroneous the tax court's finding that Rice's transaction is a sham because Rice subjectively lacked a business purpose and the transaction objectively lacked economic substance.

C

We turn next to the consequences of the finding of a sham. Where a transaction is properly determined to be a sham, the Commissioner is entitled to ignore the labels applied by the parties and tax the transaction according to its substance. We find no error in the tax court's determination that after stripping away the labels, Rice did not purchase or lease a computer, but rather, paid a fee to Finalco in exchange for tax benefits.

Since Rice's nonrecourse debt was similarly without economic substance, it cannot be relied upon to support the claimed interest deductions. Rice was therefore not entitled to depreciation deductions based upon inclusion of the amounts representing the nonrecourse notes in its basis on the computer because Rice had not truly made an investment in the computer. Moreover, the amount of the recourse note was also not properly includable in basis to support depreciation deductions because, as the tax court properly held, the note did not represent an investment in property.

Therefore, we affirm the tax court in its disallowance as a matter of law of depreciation deductions reflecting inclusion of the amounts of the recourse and the nonrecourse notes in basis and in its disallowance of interest deductions based on the nonrecourse loans.

III

We disagree with the tax court, however, in its disallowance, as a matter of law, of interest deductions reflecting interest on the recourse note. The tax court denied those interest deductions because they were determined not to be based upon a genuine indebtedness. . . . The tax court relied upon Grodt & McKay Realty, Inc. v. Commissioner, 77 T.C. 1221, 1243 (1981), to support the contention that after finding a sham, the court may disregard the entire transaction, including a cash investment.

Grodt does support the determination that depreciation deductions could not be based upon the amounts of debt represented by either the recourse or nonrecourse notes, because the purchase of the depreciated property was for tax purposes a sham — a nonpurchase. Similarly, it supports the determination that the nonrecourse note did not represent "genuine debt," because of its nonrecourse nature in conjunction with the inflated purchase price in the sham purchase transaction.

But it does not follow that the sham nature of the underlying purchase transaction also supports the tax court's conclusion that the recourse note debt was not genuine. *Grodt* itself recognized that a sham transaction may contain elements whose form reflects economic substance and whose normal tax consequences may not therefore be disregarded. Here the tax court, observing that principle, properly recognized the economic substance of Rice's purchase of something of economic value from Finalco, treating the "cash payment" on the recourse note as a "fee" for purchase of expected tax benefits. But the "cash payment" was merely the first installment due on the back-dated note. The other installments were equally genuine obligations notwithstanding they were deferred, and the interest due upon their payment was equally an obligation of economic substance. Rice could no more walk away without liability from the deferred principal and interest obligation than it could walk away from the obligation to pay the first installment.

For this reason, Rice's recourse note is fundamentally different from the nonrecourse notes held not to constitute genuine debt in cases such as *Hilton*, 74 T.C. at 364. Moreover, *Knetsch*, 364 U.S. at 362-365, does not suggest that the debt represented by the note was not genuine because Rice did not borrow its own money to create interest expense as, in effect, did the taxpayer in *Knetsch*.

Under *Frank Lyon*, the court may not ignore transactions that have economic substance even if the motive for the transaction is to avoid taxes. Moreover, IRC §163 does not limit deductibility of installment interest expense depending upon the item purchased by the taxpayer. Therefore, although Rice did not for tax purposes purchase property with the recourse note and may not base depreciation deductions upon it, the note nevertheless represents genuine debt upon which Rice is entitled to deduct interest expense.

IV

In summary, we affirm the tax court's factual finding of a sham transaction, its disallowance as a matter of law of depreciation deductions based upon inclusion of the nonrecourse and recourse note amounts in basis, and its disallowance as a matter of law of interest expense deductions arising out of the nonrecourse debt. We reverse its disallowance as a matter of law of deductions arising out of the recourse debt, and remand to the tax court for recalculation of Rice's deficiency and entry of an appropriate order.

Note

In response to a number of high-profile tax shelter cases in which some courts declined to apply the economic substance doctrine to particular transactions or taxpayers, in 2010 Congress enacted §7701(o) which codified the economic substance doctrine. According to the statutory language, §7701(o) was not intended to change the common law economic substance doctrine but rather only clarify that it should be applied when relevant. See §§7701(o)(1), (5). Some commentators have expressed concern, however, that §7701(o) as written might, in fact, change the way the doctrine is applied in the future. To date, no cases have been brought under §7701(o) to resolve this uncertainty.

3. Retail Tax Shelters: Statutory Responses

In response to the explosion of individual "retail" tax shelters and the perceived inadequacy of judicial doctrines, Congress enacted statutory approaches addressing tax shelters. The material that follows describes these provisions in some detail. Although these statutory provisions can seem overwhelming, the intuitions underlying them are relatively straightforward. First, the §465 "at risk" rules deny current deductions to individual taxpayers who do not bear the economic risk of loss for the claimed deduction. Second, the §469 "passive activity" rules deny individual taxpayers current deductions from passive investments if those deductions would offset income from "active" sources such as salary. The combination of §§465 and 469 effectively ended the retail tax shelter industry for most individuals. If so, why do tax shelters remain a major concern of the income tax?

a.   "At Risk" Limitations

Code: §465(a), (b), (c)(1) to (6), (d), (e)

Congress enacted §465 as the first part of an effort to curb the use of leveraged tax shelters — investments that allowed a taxpayer to shelter unrelated income by taking large deductions for assets in which the taxpayer had made only a minimal economic investment. Section 465 attempts to remove one of the underpinnings of the classic tax shelter — the ability to deduct depreciation or other expenses attributable to investments financed by nonrecourse debt.

In general, if a taxpayer engages in an activity that results in a loss, §465(a) limits the amount of the deduction for that loss to the amount at risk in that activity. A taxpayer is at risk in an activity to the extent of (1) cash or the adjusted basis of other property contributed to the activity and (2) recourse indebtedness incurred with respect to the activity unless it was borrowed from another participant in the activity or a party related to the other participant. §465(b)(1).

> A taxpayer is not to be considered at risk with respect to the proceeds from his share of any nonrecourse loan used to finance the activity or the acquisition of property used in the activity. In addition, if the taxpayer borrows money to contribute to the activity and the lender's recourse is either the taxpayer's interest in the activity or property used in the activity, the amount of the proceeds of the borrowing are to be considered amounts financed on a nonrecourse basis and do not increase the taxpayer's amount at risk.
>
> Also, under these rules, a taxpayer's capital is not "at risk" in the business, even as to the equity capital which he has contributed to the extent he is protected against economic loss of all or part of such capital by reason of an agreement or arrangement for compensation or reimbursement to him of any loss which he may suffer. Under this concept, an investor is not "at risk" if he arranges to receive insurance or other compensation for an economic loss after the loss is sustained, or if he is entitled to reimbursement for part or all of any loss by reason of a binding agreement between himself and another person. . . .
>
> Similarly, if a taxpayer is personally liable on a mortgage but he separately obtains insurance to compensate him for any payments which he must actually make under such personal liability, the taxpayer is at risk only to the extent of the uninsured portion of the personal liability to which he is exposed. The taxpayer will be able to include in the amount which he has at risk any amount of premium which he had paid from his personal assets with respect to the insurance. However, a taxpayer who obtains casualty insurance or insurance protecting himself against tort liability will not be considered "not at risk" solely because of such insurance protection.

S. Rep. No. 938, 94th Cong., 2d Sess. 45 (1976).

Because losses are deductible against other income only to the extent of the "at risk" investment in the activity generating the loss, a crucial step in applying §465 is to determine whether two investments constitute a single or separate activities. If taxpayers were not required to compartmentalize different activities, the loss from a tax shelter could be applied against and reduce income from nonsheltered activities in contravention of the matching principle.

For example, assume that *T* purchases two oil wells, each with a fair market value of $1,000,000. Well 1 was purchased subject to a nonrecourse note, and *T* has nothing at risk. In well 2, T has $1,000,000 at risk. Each oil well generates losses of $200,000 during the year. To determine the total allowable deductions, T first must determine whether the oil wells are a single or two separate activities. If they are located on the same property, they will generally be considered a single activity, and T will be permitted to take deductions for that activity to the extent of $1,000,000, the total "at risk" investment. T would therefore be able to use all $400,000 in deductions. If, however, the wells are deemed to be separate activities, T will receive no deductions from the $200,000 loss generated by well 1 because T has nothing at risk in that activity. T can, however, deduct the full amount of his losses ($200,000) from well 2 because he is at risk to the extent of his $1,000,000 economic investment in that well. Section 465's "at risk" rules, therefore, prevent T from computing taxable income by subtracting all losses from whatever source from all gains from whatever source.

For purposes of §465, a loss is defined generally as the excess of deductions attributable or allocable to the activity over the income generated by the activity. §465(d). Losses can be deducted only to the extent that the taxpayer is at risk in the loss-generating activity for the relevant taxable year. However, any losses disallowed in a taxable year can be carried over to future years. In addition to affecting future taxable years by allowing a carryover of disallowed losses, §465 affects future taxable years by requiring the taxpayer to reduce the amount considered at risk with regard to the §465 activity in subsequent years. Additionally, §465(e) requires recapture of losses when the amount at risk is less than zero.

The operation of §465(e) is best explained by example. Assume that a taxpayer purchased a farm in year 1 for $50,000 cash and a $400,000 personal (recourse) note. The taxpayer invested an additional $50,000 annually in years 1 and 2 to pay operating expenses. However, the farm generated $80,000 of losses for each of those years. The taxpayer had no loss in year 3, but converted the $400,000 recourse note to a nonrecourse loan. The taxpayer's "at risk" computation for year 3 is as follows:

Year 1	$ 50,000	Cash invested
	400,000	Personal (recourse) note
	+ 50,000	Additional cash invested
	$500,000	At risk year 1
	− 80,000	Year 1 loss deducted
Year 2	$420,000	At risk entering year 2
	+ 50,000	Cash invested
	$470,000	At risk year 2
	− 80,000	Year 2 loss deducted
Year 3	$390,000	At risk entering year 3
		Conversion of recourse
	− 400,000	obligation to nonrecourse
	($10,000)	At risk year 3

Consequently, in year 3, the taxpayer must recapture $10,000 of previously deducted losses and increase year 3 income by that amount to eliminate the negative amount at risk.

b.   Application of §465 to Real Estate Transactions

When enacted in 1976, real estate activities were specifically excluded from the coverage of the "at risk" rules. However, in 1986, Congress revoked the blanket exclusion for real estate activities from the §465 "at risk" rules for the following reasons:

> [I]t is appropriate to apply the at-risk rules to real estate activities so as to limit the opportunity for overvaluation of property (resulting in inflated deductions), and to prevent the transfer of tax benefits arising from real estate activities to taxpayers with little or no real equity in the property.
>
> The bill therefore extends the present law at-risk rules to real estate, with an exception for certain nonrecourse financing provided by organizations in the business of lending.
>
> Nonrecourse financing by the seller of real property (or a person related to the seller) is not treated as an amount at risk under the bill, because there may be little or no incentive to limit the amount of such financing to the value of the property. In the case of commercial financing secured solely by the real property, however, the lender is much less likely to make loans which exceed the property's value or which cannot be serviced by the property; it is more likely that such financing will be repaid and that the purchaser consequently has or will have equity in the activity.
>
> The committee is aware of the practice of institutional real estate joint ventures to borrow from a commercial lender who may also have a substantial equity interest in the venture. Where the lender is not the seller or related to the seller, the committee believes that the opportunities for overvaluation may be limited to the same degree as if the lender were an unrelated third party. In the case of legitimate business ventures, the committee believes that it is appropriate to permit the financing provided by such a lender to be treated as an amount at risk.

S. Rep. No. 313, 99th Cong., 2d Sess. 748 (1986).

Because the "at risk" rules apply to real estate activities, individuals can deduct losses from such activities only to the extent of the amount at risk. The amount at risk for real estate activities includes the two basic categories of amounts at risk that also apply to other activities: the amount of money and the adjusted basis of other property contributed to the activity and certain amounts borrowed for use in the activity. §465(b)(1). In general, borrowed amounts included in the amount at risk consist of amounts for which the taxpayer is personally liable for repayment, and amounts for which the taxpayer has pledged property, other than property used in such activity, as security for the borrowed amount. However, amounts borrowed from any person having an interest in the activity or from a related person to a person (other than the taxpayer) having such an interest are not considered amounts at risk. Nor does the amount at risk include any amount protected against loss through nonrecourse financing, guarantees, stop-loss agreements, or other similar arrangements.

Certain qualified nonrecourse financing, however, is considered at risk for real estate activities. Qualified nonrecourse financing is defined in §465(b)(6)(B) as any financing (1) that is borrowed with respect to the activity of holding real property; (2) that is borrowed from a qualified person or represents a loan from any federal, state, or local government or instrumentality thereof, or one guaranteed similarly;

(3) with respect to which no person is personally liable for repayment; and (4) that is not convertible debt. The definition of qualified person includes any person actively and regularly engaged in the business of lending money, under federal, state, or local law, but does not include (1) any person from whom the taxpayer acquired the property (or a person related to such a person), (2) any person who receives a fee (such as a promoter) with respect to the taxpayer's investment in the property (or a person related to such a person), or (3) a person related to the taxpayer, unless the terms of the loan are commercially reasonable and substantially the same as loans involving unrelated persons. §465(b)(6)(D).

c. Passive Activity Limitations

Code: §469(a) to (e), (g) to (i)

Congress responded to the proliferation of tax shelters and the resulting undesirable consequences by adding a new, far-reaching statutory provision designed to limit current tax benefits resulting from passive business or investment activities. This provision, §469, provides an intricate set of rules for determining the limits on passive activity losses and credits and provides for the treatment of disallowed items on disposition of the investment.

The policy underlying the enactment of the passive activity limitations was twofold: (1) to avoid the substantial loss of revenues to the government resulting from tax shelters and (2) to restore public faith in the federal income tax system. The public's loss of confidence was due to the many opportunities afforded by the Code to offset income from one source with deductions and credits from another. Under prior law, taxpayers could structure transactions specifically to take advantage of the situations in which the simpler rules led to undermeasurement or deferral of income. Moreover, the increased use of tax shelters led to the widespread public perception that the entire tax system was unfair because only the naive and unsophisticated pay their "fair share," a belief that substantially undermined compliance with the system.

In considering solutions to the problems caused by excessive tax sheltering, Congress quickly rejected the elimination of substantially all tax preferences. This approach was deemed inappropriate because many preferences are socially or economically beneficial. It also recognized that elimination of all tax preferences in favor of a tax system that measures income more accurately would be unduly complex.

Congress concluded that tax preferences should be permitted, but only for taxpayers who actively participate in the activities to which the deductible items relate. Their rationale was that

> for tax preferences to function as intended, their benefit must be directed primarily to taxpayers with a substantial and bona fide involvement in the activities to which the preferences relate. . . . [I]t is appropriate to encourage nonparticipating investors to invest in particular activities, by permitting the use of preferences to reduce the rate of tax on income from those activities; however, such investors should not be permitted to use tax benefits to shelter unrelated income.

S. Rep. No. 313, 99th Cong., 2d Sess. 716 (1986).

Congress settled on a "material participation in the activity" test to determine who should be permitted to use the tax preferences. The test was created in response to the noneconomic factors deemed important by the typical passive investor in making investment decisions. Passive investors seek a return on capital invested, including returns in the form of reductions in the taxes owed on unrelated income, rather than an ongoing source of livelihood. The rationale underlying the test was to shift the investor's primary investment motive from tax reduction to maximization of the economic benefits resulting from the investment decision. To effect this shift, the passive-active investor dichotomy was created, based on the premise that a taxpayer who materially participates in an activity is more likely to approach the activity with a significant nontax economic profit motive and to form a sound judgment as to whether the activity has genuine economic value. The Senate Finance Committee noted that

> in the case of a nonparticipating investor . . . it is appropriate to treat losses of the activity as not realized by the investor prior to disposition of his interest in the activity. The effort to measure, on an annual basis, real economic losses from passive activities gives rise to distortions, particularly due to the nontaxation of unrealized appreciation and the mismatching of tax deductions and related economic income that may occur, especially where debt financing is used heavily. Only when a taxpayer disposes of his interest in an activity is it possible to determine whether a loss was sustained over the entire time that he held the interest.

Id.

The material participation standard, however, is not applied uniformly to all investment activities. Rental activities, for example, generally are not subject to the standard because these activities presumably involve the production of income from capital and are not generated by the investor's participation. Moreover, they are frequently used specifically to shelter income. Consequently, rental activities are presumed to be passive activities under the Code, unless the taxpayer is a real estate professional. The Senate Finance Committee Report explains the rationale for this general inclusion of rental activities as passive activities:

> [Rental] activities predominantly involve the production of income from capital. For this reason, rental income generally is not now subject to the self-employment tax, whether or not the activity constitutes a trade or business (sec. 1402(a)(1)). Rental activities generally require less on-going business management activity, in proportion to capital invested, than business activities involving the production or sale of goods and services. Thus, for example, an individual who is employed full-time as a professional could more easily provide all necessary management in his spare time with respect to a rental activity than he could with respect to another type of business activity involving the same capital investment. The extensive use of rental activities for tax shelter purposes under present law, combined with the reduced level of personal involvement necessary to conduct such activities, make clear that the effectiveness of the basic passive loss provision could be seriously compromised if material participation were sufficient to avoid the limitations in the case of rental activities.

A limited measure of relief, however, is believed appropriate in the case of certain moderate-income investors in rental real estate, who otherwise might experience cash flow difficulties with respect to investments that in many cases are designed to provide financial security, rather than to shelter a substantial amount of other income.

Id. at 718.

Similarly, limited partnerships are not subject to the material participation standard because, under state law, limited partners are generally prohibited from materially participating in the business activities of the partnership. However, if a limited partner is trying to qualify as a real estate professional, he must meet one of the standards for material participation consistent with state law.

The general approach of the passive activity limitations is to identify taxpayers subject to the limitations and then to determine the activities in which the taxpayer is engaged. After each activity is classified as either a passive or an active activity, the income or loss is determined on an activity-by-activity basis. Deductions from passive activities that exceed income from all such passive activities (excluding portfolio income) may not be deducted from other income. Portfolio income such as interest, dividends, royalties, and gains from the sale of property held for investment, and earned income, such as salary or other income for services, are excluded from the determination of income and loss for all categories and instead are accounted for as a separate category.

The income and losses from the active activities are netted. If a net loss results, the loss can be deducted against any other income. Different rules apply, however, to passive activities. Like the active activity category, the income and losses from passive activities are netted. If net income results, the passive activity limitations do not apply. On the other hand, if a net loss results, the loss cannot be deducted against income from any other source. Instead, such losses become suspended until a later year when the passive activity category has net income or until the taxpayer disposes of the passive investment that generated the loss.

The passive activity limitations apply to individuals. Although partnerships are not subject to the passive activity limitations at the entity level, their income and losses pass through to their partners and shareholders, who must segregate the items into the three categories. For example, in a general partnership that has portfolio income and also is engaged in a business activity, each partner is deemed to receive a portion of the portfolio income and a portion of the business activity income or loss. Each partner must determine whether his respective portion of the business activity is passive or nonpassive. Thus, the same activity may be passive for one partner and active for one or more other partners.

Identifying each activity is essential for several reasons. First, if two undertakings are part of the same activity, the determination of whether the activity is passive or active is made by considering the activity as a whole. If each undertaking is a separate activity, however, each must be classified as either passive or active. Second, in the case of a disposition, it is essential to determine whether the taxpayer has disposed of his entire interest in the activity. Finally, defining activities either too broadly or too narrowly can lead to evasion of the passive loss rules. For example, an overly narrow definition would permit investors to claim losses against salary, portfolio, or active business income by selectively disposing of portions of their interests in activities in which there has been depreciation, or loss, in value, while retaining any portions in which there has been appreciation. An overly broad definition would permit investors to amalgamate undertakings that, in fact, are separate and thus use material participation in one undertaking as a basis for claiming, without limitation, losses and credits from another undertaking.

Although identifying each activity is a fundamental step in applying the passive activity limitations, §469 does not include a definition of the term "activity." The legislative history provides the following guidance:

> The determination of what constitutes a separate activity is intended to be made in a realistic economic sense. The question to be answered is what undertakings consist of an integrated and interrelated economic unit, conducted in coordination with or reliance upon each other, and constituting an appropriate unit for the measurement of gain or loss.

Id. at 739. This economic interrelationship test raises two important points. First, the definition of activity is not based on legal entities. Thus, a single partnership can be involved in more than one activity. Likewise, a common management, common name, or common source of financing does not establish that the undertakings are a single activity. Second, it is necessary to examine all the relevant facts and circumstances to determine what constitutes an activity.

The legislative history provides a few general rules for applying the economic interrelationship test. In general, normal commercial practices are highly probative in determining whether two or more undertakings are, or may be, parts of a single activity. Along these lines, Regulation §1.469-4 provides a list of factors to take into consideration in determining the scope of an activity, including (1) similarities and differences in types of trades or businesses, (2) the extent of common control, (3) the extent of common ownership, (4) geographical location, and (5) interdependencies between or among the activities.

A taxpayer is engaged in more than one activity if he provides two or more substantially different products or services, unless such products or services are provided together customarily or for business reasons (such as the appliance and clothing sections of a department store). For example, operating a restaurant and a paint store are sufficiently different that each will be considered a separate activity. In addition, different and nonintegrated stages in the production and sale of a particular product are not part of the same activity. Thus, operating a lumberyard and engaging in timber cutting are not part of the same activity.

The mere fact that two undertakings provide the same products or services does not establish that they are part of the same activity, absent the requisite degree of economic interrelationship. For example, separate real estate rental projects built and managed in different locations generally will constitute separate activities, unless the taxpayer is a real estate professional who chooses to aggregate all of his or her interests in rental real estate. On the other hand, an integrated apartment project or shopping center generally will be treated as a single activity. (It also is important to identify rental real estate activities for other purposes.)

After all activities are identified, it is necessary to classify each one as either passive or active. Section 469 approaches the classification problem by specifically designating certain activities as either passive or active and then applying a material participation test to analyze the remaining activities. For example, working interests in oil and gas are deemed to be active, limited partnership interests are generally considered passive, and rental activities are generally classified as passive. Other activities are generally subject to the material participation test.

Although rental activities may be deemed to be passive, substantial issues remain, such as defining which activities are rental activities and determining the scope of rental activities. The term "rental activity" is defined in §469(j)(8) as "any activity where payments are principally for the use of tangible property." An activity is not treated as a rental activity, however, if it involves significant services. It also is not treated as a rental activity when day-to-day expenses are not insignificant in relation to rents produced by the property or in relation to depreciation and the cost of carrying the rental property.

After considering the definition of a rental activity in light of the above factors, a very narrow category of activities emerges. This category is narrowed further by limitations on the scope of a rental activity. Although other activities may immediately precede the rental activity being conducted by the same persons, or in the same general location, they are not treated as part of the rental activity. For example, the construction of a building and the subsequent renting of the building are treated as two separate activities.

Activities that the Code does not specifically designate as either passive or active are categorized by applying the definition of passive activities. A passive activity is any business or investment activity in which the taxpayer does not materially participate. §469(c)(1). Thus, the key to determining whether the activity is passive or active is whether the taxpayer materially participates in the activity.

A taxpayer is treated as materially participating only if he, or his spouse, is involved in the operations of the activity on a basis that is (1) regular, (2) continuous, and (3) substantial. §469(h)(1). Although Congress has developed this tripartite test for determining material participation, it unfortunately failed to provide a definition of the terms either in the Code or in the legislative reports.

The Treasury Department has issued temporary regulations to fill this void by providing seven alternative tests for a taxpayer to satisfy the material participation standard, only one of which must be met to qualify. The tests move from a purely quantitative standard to a facts-and-circumstances test. First, a taxpayer materially participates if he spends at least 500 hours per year on the activity. Under this test, a taxpayer can spend as little as 10 hours per week on an activity and not be subject to the passive activity limits. There is no inquiry into the nature of the activity or whether it is the primary business of the taxpayer — rather, the 500-hour standard is automatically presumed to constitute material participation. For taxpayers who spend less than 500 hours per year on an activity, material participation becomes more subjective. For example, material participation also includes a taxpayer who spends more than 100 hours on an activity and participates more than any other individual in the activity. Further, a taxpayer materially participates even when spending less than 100 hours on an activity if his or her activity constitutes substantially all of the activities of all individuals. Lastly, under the "significant participation" test (not to be confused with "material participation"), a taxpayer can materially participate in an activity if the taxpayer does not materially participate in any one activity under any of the other tests, but spends more than 100 hours on the activity.

In addition to these quantitative tests, which count hours to determine material participation, a number of other tests could apply. Two of these tests apply to taxpayers who regularly materially participate in an activity. Under one test, a taxpayer materially participates even if none of the quantitative tests are met if such tests were satisfied for any five of the previous ten years. Similarly, a taxpayer in an activity in which capital is not a material income-producing factor (generally personal services such as lawyers, accountants, doctors, or architects) materially participates if the taxpayer met any of the quantitative tests for any three previous years.

Finally, a taxpayer can be considered to materially participate even if he or she does not satisfy any of the other six tests if, under all the facts and circumstances, the taxpayer regularly, continuously, and substantially participates in the activity. Notwithstanding the potentially broad application of this facts-and-circumstances test, the Regulations provide that the test cannot be satisfied if the taxpayer spends less than 100 hours participating in the activity, which substantially limits the usefulness of this alternative.

d.   Determination of Activity Income

After each passive activity is identified, it is necessary to calculate income or loss for each one. The first step in this yearly calculation requires the exclusion of all portfolio income and earned income from the income or loss calculation.

Portfolio income includes gross income from interest, dividends, annuities, or royalties not derived in the ordinary course of business, less the expenses and interest allocable to such gross income. §469(e)(1)(A). Also included in portfolio income are gains or losses attributable to the disposition of (1) property that produces interest, dividend, or royalty income and (2) property that is held for investment (and that is not a passive activity).

Although identifying portfolio income often is straightforward, difficult cases arise because portfolio income excludes any income of a type generally regarded as portfolio income that is derived in the ordinary course of a trade or business. The legislative history provides the following examples of income not considered to be portfolio income:

> [T]he business income of a bank typically is largely interest. Similarly, a securities broker/dealer may earn a substantial portion of the income from the business in the form of dividends and gains on sales of dividend-bearing instruments. Interest income may also arise in the ordinary course of a trade or business with respect to installment sales and interest charges on accounts receivable. . . . If a taxpayer directly, or through a pass-through entity, owns an interest in an activity deriving such income, such income is treated as part of the activity, which, as a whole, may or may not be treated as passive, depending on whether the taxpayer materially participates in the activity.

S. Rep. No. 313, 99th Cong., 2d Sess. 729 (1986). If the portfolio-type income can be characterized as arising in the ordinary course of a trade or business and such trade or business is a passive activity, the potential exists for offsetting passive income with unrelated passive losses.

Like portfolio income, earned income is excluded from the determination of the income or loss from the passive activity. §469(e)(3). Earned income includes wages, salaries, professional fees, and any amount received as compensation for personal services.

After segregating and excluding the portfolio income and earned income from the other income, it is necessary to determine whether each activity has produced either a gain or a loss for the taxable year. This calculation is made by applying the general income and expense provisions, but there are a number of problems regarding the allocation of expenses among activities. Specifically, the allocation of interest expense among activities could be subject to many uncertainties.

e. Treatment of Passive Activity Losses

After the net income or loss from each activity is determined, all gains and losses generated by passive activities are netted, with the net income and loss from active activities disregarded. This step is necessary because a net loss in one passive activity may be used to offset income from another passive activity. Thus, there is no passive activity loss unless the aggregate losses from all passive activities exceed the aggregate income from all passive activities.

If there is a passive activity loss, it is not deductible in the current taxable year (subject to the real estate activity rules). Instead, that loss is carried forward to subsequent taxable years, where it may offset passive income, if any, arising in those years. These deferred losses, called suspended losses, are determined for each activity by the ratio of net losses from the activity to the total net losses from all passive activities for the year. This activity-by-activity calculation is necessary because on a taxable disposition of an activity, the suspended losses of that activity become allowable.

Rental activities generally are deemed passive regardless of whether the taxpayer materially participates in the activity. Notwithstanding this treatment, certain individuals involved in rental real estate activities may receive a limited exemption from the passive activity loss rules. The Senate Finance Committee Report explains the rationale for this exception:

> [S]ome specifically targeted relief has been provided because rental real estate is held in many instances to provide financial security to individuals with moderate incomes. In some cases, for example, an individual may hold for rental a residence that he uses part-time, or that previously was and at some future time may be his primary residence. Even absent any residential use of the property by the taxpayer, the committee believes that a rental real estate investment in which the taxpayer has significant responsibilities with respect to providing necessary services, and which serves significant nontax purposes of the taxpayer, is different in some respects from the activities that are meant to be fully subject to limitation under the passive loss provision.

Id. at 736.

For example, a rental real estate investor whose cash expenses (such as mortgage payments, condominium or management fees, and costs of upkeep) exceed cash inflow (that is, rent) may have tax losses other than those relating to depreciation but may not have any cash flow benefit. In general, §469(i) permits a deduction of up to $25,000 of passive activity losses attributable to rental real estate activities in which the taxpayer actively participates. This $25,000 allowance is phased out for taxpayers with adjusted gross incomes in excess of $100,000.

The $25,000 allowance is applied by first netting the income and loss from all rental real estate activities in which the taxpayer actively participates. If there is net income for the year, the allowance does not apply. If there is a net loss, however, any net passive income remaining from passive activities is then applied against the net loss. If after this second netting a loss remains, such loss is eligible for the $25,000 allowance.

For example, assume that a taxpayer incurs a $25,000 loss in a rental real estate activity in which he actively participates. Assume further that he also actively participates in another rental real estate activity and has a $25,000 gain, resulting in no net loss from rental real estate activities in which he actively participates. In this case, no amount is allowed under the $25,000 allowance for the year. This result arises regardless of whether there are net losses from other passive activities for the year.

The $25,000 allowance is available only to individuals who actively participate in rental real estate activities. There are two requirements for determining active participation: (1) "significant and bona fide involvement"; and (2) 10-percent or more ownership interest. In general, the difference between the active participation and material participation standards is that the former can be satisfied without regular, continuous, and substantial involvement in operations, so long as the taxpayer participates (for example, in making management decisions or arranging for others to provide services, such as repairs, in a significant and bona fide sense).

In 1993, Congress enacted §469(c)(7), which provides a limited exception to the rule that all rental activities are deemed passive for certain taxpayers involved in a real estate trade or business. Pursuant to this provision, rental real estate activities will not be treated as passive if the taxpayer (1) performs more than one-half of his or her personal services during the year in such trades or businesses and (2) performs more than 750 hours of personal services in real property trades or businesses in which he or she materially participates.

In order to meet the test for material participation, a taxpayer can aggregate his or her rental real estate activities. Rental real estate activities and other real estate activities cannot be aggregated to meet the material participation test. In making the election to aggregate rental real estate, the taxpayer is forced to take an all-or-nothing approach. Once the taxpayer makes this election, it is binding in future years unless the taxpayer has a material change in circumstances. Thus, in making the election of whether to aggregate all interests in rental real estate, the taxpayer must consider not only current gains and losses, but anticipated future gains and losses as well.

If a taxpayer chooses not to aggregate his or her interests in rental real estate, he or she may have some interests that are treated as passive and others that are not. Due to the priority of application between §§469(c)(7) and 469(i), a taxpayer can first apply §469(c)(7) to make some of his or her losses nonpassive and then apply §469(i) to receive the $25,000 deduction of passive losses against nonpassive gains if he or she actively participated in the rental real estate activity.

f. Dispositions of Passive Activities

A taxpayer who disposes of an interest in a passive activity may deduct the suspended losses if:

1. the taxpayer disposes of his entire interest in the activity,
2. the disposition is in the form of a fully taxable transaction, and
3. the person acquiring the interest is not related to the taxpayer.

§469(g). The rationale for allowing the suspended losses to be deductible at the time of disposition is as follows:

> When a taxpayer disposes of his entire interest in a passive activity, the actual economic gain or loss on his investment can be finally determined. . . .
>   [P]rior to a disposition of the taxpayer's interest, it is difficult to determine whether there has actually been gain or loss with respect to the activity. For example, allowable deductions may exceed actual economic costs, or may be exceeded by untaxed appreciation. Upon a taxable disposition, net appreciation or depreciation with respect to the activity can be finally ascertained. Since the purpose of the disposition rule is to allow real economic losses of the taxpayer to be deducted, credits, which are not related to the measurement of such loss, are not specially allowable by reason of a disposition.

S. Rep. No. 313, 99th Cong., 2d Sess 725 (1986).

Because the taxpayer must dispose of the entire interest in the passive activity to trigger the recognition of loss, disposition of less than the entire interest has no effect. Moreover, a disposition of the entire interest in the activity requires a disposition of the taxpayer's interest in all entities involved in the activity. A taxpayer who operates an activity as a sole proprietorship must dispose of all the assets created and used in the activity. If a general partnership conducts two separate activities, the entity's fully taxable disposition of all the assets used or created in one activity constitutes a disposition of the partner's or shareholder's entire interest in the activity. The requirement that the disposition be fully taxable generally includes an arm's-length sale of the property to a third person, presumably for a price equal to its fair market value.

The final requirement for loss recognition is that the person acquiring the interest not be a related party. If the parties are related, the taxpayer must recognize any gain resulting from the disposition but is not permitted to deduct any of the suspended losses. The taxpayer is deemed related to the acquiring person if they bear a relationship described in §267(b) or §707(b)(1).

Problems

9-12. Arthur Felix purchased a bakery business for $10,000 cash and a $90,000 nonrecourse note. At the end of year 1, Felix's losses were $15,000. No principal had been paid on the nonrecourse loan by the end of the year.

    a. To what extent may Felix deduct the $15,000 loss?

    b. By the end of year 2, the bakery business had suffered an additional $4,000 loss, and Felix had paid $8,000 of principal on the nonrecourse note. What amount of loss can Felix deduct in year 2?

    c. During year 3, the bakery business experienced $10,000 in losses, and Felix pledged corporate securities as security for the nonrecourse mortgage on the bakery business. The fair market value of the securities was $6,000; Felix had paid $9,000 cash for them. What is the amount of Felix's loss deduction at the end of year 3?

9-13. Arthur Felix purchased a rental duplex from Steve Smith in return for $30,000 cash and a $135,000 nonrecourse note payable to the First National Bank. By the end of year 1, Felix had incurred a total tax loss of $32,000 from ownership of the duplex and had not paid any principal on the note.

    a. To what extent may Felix deduct the $32,000 loss?

    b. How much could Felix deduct if the note were payable to the seller rather than the First National Bank?

    c. Assuming the facts in *b*, if Felix incurs an $8,000 loss from the duplex rental activity in year 2 and he has made $4,000 of principal payments on the note to the seller, to what extent may Felix deduct the loss?

9-14. Beth Martin had the following items of income and loss during the taxable year: salary as an executive of $85,000; interest income of $5,000; dividend income of $2,000; and loss from her rental duplex of $38,000.

    a. What is the amount of Martin's passive activity income for the year?

    b. What is the amount of Martin's passive activity loss for the year?

    c. What amount of Martin's passive activity loss is deductible for the year?

    d. What result in *c* if her $38,000 loss had instead been from an investment in raw land?

    e. What result in *c* if her $38,000 loss had instead been from a real estate business activity?

4. Other Statutory Provisions

a. Sales or Exchanges between Related Parties

Code: §§267(a) to (d), (g); 1041
Regulations: §1.267(a)-1, (b)-1, (c)-1, (d)-1

Section 267 was enacted to prevent taxpayers from using a sale or exchange to a related party to create a tax loss when there is no substantial break in the related group's continuity of ownership. In the absence of a provision such as §267, a sale or exchange of economically depreciated property between related parties would allow the transferor a loss deduction, without surrendering "control" of the property. For example, a taxpayer who owned investment property with a $100,000 basis and a $25,000 fair market value could sell the property to his daughter and recognize a $75,000 deductible loss, without disturbing the family's ownership.

Section 267 was designed to avoid this result by disallowing losses on certain intragroup transfers.

Two elements are required for §267(a)(1) to apply. First, there must be a sale or exchange resulting in a recognized loss to the transferor. Second, the sale or exchange must be to a related person.

The concept of disallowing losses on the sale or exchange of property between related parties was enacted as an "absolute prohibition" and not a presumption against the allowance of such losses. This concept, although now expanded to include more than mere family members, continues to operate as an absolute prohibition. For example, consider Miller v. Commissioner, 75 T.C. 182 (1980), a case involving a loss disallowed on a sale between brothers. The brothers argued that because they had a hostile relationship they were not brothers within the meaning of §267. The taxpayers further argued that §267 was based on the premise that "the relationship between family members rises to some kind of unity of interest" and therefore, because the apparent hostility had eliminated the possibility of any "unity of interest," §267 should not apply to disallow the loss. The court disagreed, finding that the loss would be disallowed "irrespective of the existence of the hostility" between the related parties. The court reasoned that "Congress obviously did not want the courts to face the difficult task of looking behind the sales. Instead, Congress made its prohibition *absolute* in reach, believing this would be fair to the great majority of taxpayers." Id. at 189 (emphasis added).

> It is true that a hardship may result in particular cases, as in this one, where the transaction is in entire good faith; and there is some indication in the history of the measure that the legislators were not unaware of that fact. However, it was the belief of the drafters that, on the whole, the measure would be fair to the great majority of taxpayers. Congress could have provided that no deduction should be allowed in respect of losses from intrafamily transactions unless they were bona fide. That it did not do. . . . We could not, without indulging in judicial legislation, graft an exception upon the broad measure adopted by Congress.

Id. at 186.

Step transaction doctrine. Section 267 applies to losses realized on direct and indirect sales or exchanges between related parties. Consider, for example, a taxpayer who sells property with a $100,000 basis and a $25,000 fair market value to an intermediary who, pursuant to a prearranged plan, thereafter sells the same property to the taxpayer's daughter. Although not a direct sale between related parties, courts have looked to the substance of the transaction and evolved the step transaction doctrine, which collapses the two steps into one. Thus, the transaction is treated as an indirect sale pursuant to §267. Hence, when the sale of property by one person and the purchase of that property by another related party are so intertwined that the seller does not suffer a true economic loss, the resulting loss may be disallowed even if the sale or exchange is bona fide and not motivated by tax avoidance.

For example, in Hassen v. Commissioner, 599 F.2d 305 (9th Cir. 1979), the taxpayer was forced into an involuntary sale of his property after a creditor instituted foreclosure proceedings on the taxpayer's defaulted note. The property was purchased by the creditor at the foreclosure sale. The creditor thereafter, pursuant to a ninety-day option granted to the taxpayer, resold the property to a corporation owned and controlled by the taxpayer and his immediate family. The taxpayer argued that §267 was inapplicable because §267(a)(1): (1) applies only to voluntary sales and this sale was involuntary and (2) applies only to direct and indirect sales — not to sales where there is no binding commitment to repurchase. The court dismissed both arguments, stating: "To claim a loss, there must be an 'economically genuine realization of loss.' . . . [Taxpayer] did not suffer such loss when the property was sold and repurchased."

Section 267 is not exclusive. See Reg. §1.267(a)-1(c). For example, losses may be disallowed in transactions that are not bona fide sales, even though §267 does not technically apply because the transfer is not between related parties. Consider, for instance, a sale of stock by T to his brother-in-law. T's brother-in-law holds the stock for ten days and, pursuant to a prearranged plan, sells the stock back to T for the original contract price. A brother-in-law is not a §267 related person, as defined by §267(b); hence, the question is whether a tax loss is permitted because this is not a sale to a related party. The answer is clear — there is no bona fide sale of the stock, but only a transaction intended to create a tax loss. Thus, as provided in Regulation §1.267(a)-1(c), no loss will be permitted.

The harshness of §267(a)(1) is offset somewhat by §267(d). Section 267(d) provides that gain realized on a subsequent disposition of the property by the related transferee is recognized only to the extent that the gain exceeds the amount of the previously disallowed loss. For example, assume T pays $70,000 to purchase property from her brother B, whose basis in the property is $100,000. Pursuant to §267(a)(1), B has a disallowed loss of $30,000. If T sells the property four years later for $120,000, the $50,000 gain realized ($120,000 amount realized − $70,000 basis) is offset by the $30,000 previously disallowed loss and is reduced to $20,000 of taxable gain.

McWILLIAMS v. COMMISSIONER
331 U.S. 694 (1947)

MR. CHIEF JUSTICE VINSON delivered the opinion of the Court.

The facts of these cases are not in dispute. John P. McWilliams had for a number of years managed the large independent estate of his wife, as well as his own. On several occasions in 1940 and 1941 he ordered his broker to sell certain stock for the account of one of the two, and to buy the same number of shares of the same stock for the other, at as nearly the same price as possible. He told the broker that his purpose was to establish tax losses. On each occasion the sale and purchase were promptly negotiated through the Stock Exchange, and the identity of the persons buying from the selling spouse and of the persons selling to the buying spouse was never known. Invariably, however, the buying spouse received stock certificates different from those which the other had sold. Petitioners filed separate income tax returns for these years, and claimed the losses which he or she sustained on the sales as deductions from gross income.

The Commissioner disallowed these deductions on the authority of [§267(a)]. . . .

Petitioners contend that Congress could not have intended to disallow losses on transactions like those described above, which, having been made through a public market, were undoubtedly bona fide sales, both in the sense that title to property was actually transferred, and also in the sense that a fair consideration was paid in exchange. They contend that the disallowance of such losses would amount, pro tanto, to treating husband and wife as a single individual for tax purposes.

In support of this contention, they call our attention to the pre-1934 rule, which applied to all sales regardless of the relationship of seller and buyer, and made the deductibility of the resultant loss turn on the "good faith" of the sale, i.e., whether the seller actually parted with title and control. They point out that in the case of the usual intra-family sale, the evidence material to this issue was peculiarly within the knowledge and even the control of the taxpayer and those amenable to his wishes, and inaccessible to the Government. They maintain that the only purpose of [§267] was to overcome these evidentiary difficulties by disallowing losses on such sales irrespective of good faith. It seems to be petitioners' belief that the evidentiary difficulties so contemplated were only those relating to proof of the parties' observance of the formalities of a sale and of the fairness of the price, and consequently that the legislative remedy applied only to sales made immediately from one member of a family to another, or mediately through a controlled intermediary.

We are not persuaded that Congress had so limited an appreciation of this type of tax avoidance problem. Even assuming that the problem was thought to arise solely out of the taxpayer's inherent advantage in a contest concerning the good or bad faith of an intra-family sale, deception could obviously be practiced by a buying spouse's agreement or tacit readiness to hold the property sold at the disposal of a selling spouse, rather more easily than by a pretense of a sale where none actually occurred, or by an unfair price. The difficulty of determining the finality of an intra-family transfer was one with which the courts wrestled under the pre-1934 law, and which Congress undoubtedly meant to overcome by enacting the provisions of [§267].

It is clear, however, that this difficulty is one which arises out of the close relationship of the parties, and would be met whenever, by prearrangement, one spouse sells and another buys the same property at a common price regardless of the mechanics of the transaction. Indeed, if the property is fungible, the possibility that a sale and purchase may be rendered nugatory by the buying spouse's agreement to hold for the benefit of the selling spouse, and the difficulty of proving that fact against the taxpayer, are equally great when the units of the property which the one buys are not the identical units which the other sells.

Securities transactions have been the most common vehicle for the creation of intra-family losses. Even if we should accept petitioners' premise that the only purpose of [§267] was to meet an evidentiary problem, we could agree that Congress did not mean to reach the transactions in this case only if we thought it completely indifferent to the effectuality of its solution.

Moreover, we think the evidentiary problem was not the only one which Congress intended to meet. Section [267] states an absolute prohibition—not a presumption — against the allowance of losses on any sales between the members of certain designated groups. The one common characteristic of these groups is that their members, although distinct legal entities, generally have a near-identity of economic interests. It is a fair inference that even legally genuine intra-group transfers were not thought to result, usually, in economically genuine realizations of loss, and accordingly that Congress did not deem them to be appropriate occasions for the allowance of deductions.

The pertinent legislative history lends support to this inference. The Congressional Committees, in reporting the provisions enacted in 1934, merely stated that "the practice of creating losses through transactions between members of a family and close corporations has been frequently utilized for avoiding the income tax," and that these provisions were proposed to "deny losses to be taken in the case of [such] sales" and "to close this loophole of tax avoidance." Similar language was used in reporting the 1937 provisions. Chairman Doughton of the Ways and Means Committee, in explaining the 1937 provisions to the House, spoke of "the artificial taking and establishment of losses where property was shuffled back and forth between various legal entities owned by the same persons or person," and stated that "these transactions seem to occur at moments remarkably opportune to the real party in interest in reducing his tax liability but, at the same time allowing him to keep substantial control of the assets being traded or exchanged."

We conclude that the purpose of [§267] was to put an end to the right of taxpayers to choose, by intra-family transfers and other designated devices, their own time for realizing tax losses on investments which, for most practical purposes, are continued uninterrupted.

We are clear as to this purpose, too, that its effectuation obviously had to be made independent of the manner in which an intra-group transfer was accomplished. Congress, with such purpose in mind, could not have intended to include within the scope of [§267] only simple transfers made directly or through a dummy, or to exclude transfers of securities effected through the medium of the Stock Exchange, unless it wanted to leave a loophole almost as large as the one it had set out to close.

Petitioners suggest that Congress, if it truly intended to disallow losses on intra-family transactions through the market, would probably have done so by an amendment to the wash sales provisions, making them applicable where the seller and buyer were members of the same family, as well as where they were one and the same individual. This extension of the wash sales provisions, however, would bar only one particular means of accomplishing the evil at which [§267] was aimed, and the necessity for a comprehensive remedy would have remained.

Nor can we agree that Congress' omission from [§267] of any prescribed time interval, comparable in function to that in the wash sales provisions, indicates that [§267] was not intended to apply to intra-family transfers through the Exchange. Petitioners' argument is predicated on the difficulty which courts may have in determining whether the elapse of certain periods of time between one spouse's sale and the other's purchase of like securities on the Exchange is of great enough importance in itself to break the continuity of the investment and make [§267] inapplicable.

Precisely the same difficulty may arise, however, in the case of an intra-family transfer through an individual intermediary, who, by prearrangement, buys from one spouse at the market price and a short time later sells the identical certificates to the other at the price prevailing at the time of sale. The omission of a prescribed time interval negates the applicability of [§267] to the former type of transfer no more than it does to the latter. But if we should hold that it negated both, we would have converted the section into a mere trap for the unwary.

Petitioners also urge that, whatever may have been Congress' intent, its designation in [§267] of sales "between" members of a family is not adequate to comprehend the transactions in this case, which consisted only of a sale of stock by one of the petitioners to an unknown stranger, and the purchase of different certificates of stock by the other petitioner, presumably from another stranger.

We can understand how this phraseology, if construed literally and out of context, might be thought to mean only direct intra-family transfers. But petitioners concede that the express statutory reference to sales made "directly or indirectly" precludes that construction. Moreover, we can discover in this language no implication whatsoever that an indirect intra-family sale of fungibles is outside the statute unless the units sold by one spouse and those bought by the other are identical. Indeed, if we accepted petitioners' construction of the statute, we think we would be reading into it a crippling exception which is not there. . . .

Note

In contrast to the §267(a)(1) loss deduction disallowance, §267(a)(2) has historically operated to disallow deductions for certain expenses and interest incurred between §267(b) related parties who use different methods of tax accounting. The deductions denied by §267(a)(2) are trade or business expenses otherwise deductible under §162, expenses for production of income otherwise deductible under §212, and interest otherwise deductible under §163. Reg. §1.267(a)-1(b). The §267(a)(2) expense deduction limitation was added to the Code to prevent an accrual method taxpayer from claiming a deduction for an accrued but unpaid expense that the related cash method taxpayer was not required to report as income until payment was received at some future date. For example, assume that T, an accrual method taxpayer, leases office space from his brother B, a cash method taxpayer, and T accrues rental expense for the taxable year but fails to pay B until year 2. If it did not apply, T would be allowed a deduction in year 1 when the expense accrued, while B would not be required to report income until payment was received in year 2.

Pursuant to the 1984 modifications to §267(a)(2), an accrual method taxpayer is placed on the cash method of accounting with respect to related party transactions involving otherwise deductible expenses and interest. Consequently, the deduction by the accrual method payor will be allowed only on the recognition of corresponding income by the related party payee. To illustrate, consider again the case in which T leases office space from his brother B. Because §267(a)(2) transforms T into a cash method taxpayer for this transaction, T is denied a rental expense deduction until his brother B reports the corresponding rental income.

b. Wash Sales of Stock

Code: §§1091(a), (d); 1223(4)
Regulations: §§1.1091-1, 1.1091-2, 1.1223-1(d)

Consider a taxpayer who owns 500 shares of ABC stock with a $10 per share value and a $20 per share cost basis and wishes to recognize her inherent $5,000 tax loss in the stock while retaining the stock as a solid investment for the future. She decides to sell her shares of ABC stock to an unrelated party on May 1 — thus realizing a tax loss of $10 per share — and on May 2 to purchase 500 shares of ABC stock in an unrelated purchase. In effect, the taxpayer will realize a tax loss without relinquishing control over her stock for any significant period of time.

The wash sale provision was enacted to prohibit this type of transaction. Section 1091 will disallow a realized loss when

1. A loss is realized on a sale or disposition of stock or securities; and
2. There is an acquisition, contract to acquire, or option to acquire "substantially identical" stock or securities within thirty days before or thirty days after the sale.

ESTATE OF ESTROFF v. COMMISSIONER
T.C. Memo 1983-666

DRENNEN, J. . . .

After concessions the sole issue is whether Maxwell J. Estroff and petitioner Naomi Estroff are entitled to deduct a capital loss resulting from their sale of First Railroad and Banking Co. of Georgia common stock to a personal friend who resold it to them 34 days later.

Petitioner Naomi (petitioner) and Dale Toporek (Toporek) are executrixes of the estate of Maxwell J. Estroff (Estroff), deceased; petitioner and Toporek both legally resided in Augusta, Ga., on the date the petition was filed herein.

Estroff and petitioner were married and filed joint Federal income tax returns for the taxable years 1974 and 1975 with the Internal Revenue Service Center, Chamblee, Ga.

In 1974, Estroff and his close personal friend and business associate, Jack E. Fink (Fink), jointly owned various corporations which manufactured and sold clothing for the Army-Air Force exchange system and for the general public. Prior to September 1974, Estroff and Fink disposed of their interests in three of their jointly owned corporations. Estroff reported $216,161 of long-term capital gain from the sale on his 1974 joint Federal income tax return.

Prior to September 1974, Estroff, petitioner, and Fink had acquired common stock of the First Railroad and Banking Company of Georgia (First Railroad). At that time, Estroff, petitioner, and Fink owned 13,601, 14,073, and 23,504 shares of First Railroad common stock, respectively.

In late September 1974, a meeting was held between Estroff and A. J. Kilpatrick (Kilpatrick) of the firm, A. J. Kilpatrick & Co., Investment Securities (Investment Securities). At the meeting, Kilpatrick suggested that Estroff sell his First

Railroad stock to Fink with the understanding that he would later repurchase it. Kilpatrick believed the transaction would create tax losses which could be used by Estroff and Fink to offset the substantial capital gains they had realized earlier in the year.

Sometime after the meeting, Estroff and Fink orally agreed that Estroff would sell 21,559 shares of First Railroad to Fink using Investment Securities as the broker. Estroff agreed to loan Fink the money to purchase the stock, and Fink agreed to sell the stock back to Estroff after a minimum of 30 days and to use the proceeds from that sale to repay the loan. The sale price for both sales was to be market price.

On Oct. 1, 1974, Estroff sold 7,486 shares of his First Railroad stock over the counter to Fink. On the same date, petitioner sold her 14,073 shares of First Railroad stock over the counter to Fink. The stock was sold through Investment Securities at its market price on that date of $6.25 per share for a total of $134,743.75, less a $750 broker's commission paid to Investment Securities. Petitioner and Estroff had a combined cost basis in the 21,559 shares of $323,943.69 on the date of sale.

Estroff loaned Fink $135,000 by check dated Oct. 8, 1974, which Fink used to purchase the 21,559 shares of First Railroad stock. No interest was charged by Estroff and Fink did not put up any collateral for the loan. The shares purchased by Fink were registered in his name and a credit entry in the amount of $133,993.75 was made in the Investment Securities ledger card in the name of Estroff to reflect the sale of 21,559 shares of First Railroad stock.

Fink held the 21,559 shares of stock for approximately 34 days. During that time, Fink received a dividend of $2,100 on the stock, which he retained. On November 4, 1974, Fink sold the 21,559 shares through Investment Securities back to Estroff for $6.25 per share. The stock was sold to Estroff at this price, even though the low bid was 63/4 and the high ask was 71/2 on the date of the sale. Estroff paid a total of $134,743.75 for the shares, of which $133,933.75 was paid over to Fink, and $750 of which was paid to Investment Securities as a broker's commission. Fink, immediately after receiving the sale proceeds from the 21,559 shares of First Railroad stock, repaid the $135,000 he had borrowed from Estroff.

Estroff and petitioner claimed a loss on the sale of the First Railroad stock in the amount of $189,949.94 on their 1974 Federal income tax return. Respondent disallowed the loss in its entirety.

The sole issue is whether Estroff and petitioner are entitled to a loss deduction on the sale of their First Railroad stock. Respondent contends that the sale of the 21,559 shares of First Railroad stock to Fink was a sham and lacked economic substance; also that the sale was a "wash sale" within the purview of section 1091(a). . . .

We agree with respondent. . . . Briefly, with regard to the first ground, the stipulated facts clearly indicate that the Estroffs' only purpose in entering into this transaction with Fink was to obtain a capital loss that could be offset against Estroff's capital gain from the sale of his business. The terms of the agreement were such that it was very unlikely that the Estroffs would realize a profit or a loss on the transaction. After reacquiring the stock from Fink they were in the same economic position they were in prior to the sale, with regard to both the stock and the cash loan. The retention by Fink of the dividend paid on the stock while it was in his name was probably just icing on the cake to make the transaction look real. While there is no evidence to prove it, we believe the circumstances warrant the assumption that Estroff was acting as agent for his wife when he dealt with her stock. The courts will not allow a taxpayer to deduct a loss from a transaction that "did not appreciably affect his beneficial interest except to reduce his tax. . . ."

Turning now to respondent's second ground, we agree with respondent that Estroff was acting for both himself and his wife when he entered into the agreement with Fink to sell Fink 21,559 shares of First Railroad stock and to repurchase those shares from Fink not less than 30 days later. The record does not disclose what arrangements Estroff had with petitioner, but Estroff did not own 21,559 shares in his own name so petitioner had to be a party to the transaction. Neither does the record disclose whether the 14,073 shares owned by petitioner were reregistered in her name after Estroff repurchased them. Absent any evidence to the contrary we assume petitioner's stock was reregistered in her name after it had served their purposes. Since petitioner and Estroff filed a joint return for 1974, the return sheds no light on the subject. But if petitioner actually sold her shares to Fink and then Estroff bought the same shares from Fink, respondent's third ground would come into play.

Section 165(c)(2) in conjunction with section 165(a) allows a deduction for losses incurred in any transaction entered into for profit, though not connected with a trade or business.[9] However, section 1091(a) prohibits the deduction of a loss on the sale of stock if substantially identical stock is acquired or if the taxpayer enters into a contract or option to acquire substantially identical stock within 30 days prior to or 30 days subsequent to the sale.

On the assumption that Estroff was acting as agent for his wife, Estroff sold 21,559 shares of First Railroad stock to Fink on October 1, 1974. Sometime between late September and the date of the sale, Estroff and Fink agreed that Fink would sell the stock back to Estroff after a minimum of 30 days. Thus, within 30 days of the time of the sale to Fink, Estroff entered into a contract to acquire substantially identical stock to that which he had sold. Accordingly, section 1091(a) by its express terms prohibits the deduction of the loss realized by Estroff on the sale of his stock to Fink.

However, petitioner maintains that under State law oral understandings or agreements to purchase stock or securities are unenforceable and, accordingly, the wash sale rules were not triggered. We disagree. Section 1091(a) requires only that the taxpayer have a contract to purchase substantially identical securities. Although under Ga. Ann. Code, section 11-8-319(a) (1982), the contract may not have been enforceable at the time it was first entered into, the parties still had a contract. This is not a case where the contract was void ab initio, and furthermore, under Ga. Ann. Code, section 11-8-319(b) (1982), to the extent delivery of the stock was accepted, or payment had been made, the contract was enforceable. Section 1091(a) requires only that the taxpayer have a contract to purchase substantially identical securities. Therefore, we hold that section 1091(a) prohibits the loss deduction on the sale of the 21,559 shares of First Railroad stock by Estroff to

---

9. Respondent does not claim that this was not a transaction entered into for profit.

Fink. If it were concluded that Estroff was not acting as petitioner's agent in dealing with her stock, as petitioners contend, so that section 1091(a) does not apply to petitioner, the above reasoning prohibits the loss deduction on the sale of Estroff's 7,486 shares of the stock to Fink. . . .

Note

The Regulations provide that where the taxpayer has several purchases and sales of the same stock or securities, §1091 is to be applied "to the losses in the order in which the stock or securities the disposition of which resulted in the respective losses were disposed of (beginning with the earliest disposition)." Reg. §1.1091-1(b).

For example, consider a taxpayer who owns 500 shares of ABC stock with a cost basis of $20 per share and who executes the following transactions:

April 15	Taxpayer sells 200 shares at $15 per share.
May 1	Taxpayer buys 300 shares at $10 per share.
May 22	Taxpayer sells 300 shares of the 500 original shares for $5 per share.

The purchase on May 1 operates to disallow the loss realized on the April 15 sale of 200 shares. With respect to the sale on May 22 of 300 shares of previously owned stock, the taxpayer realizes a loss of $15 per share on 200 of the original 500 shares of ABC stock. Despite the fact that there was a purchase of 300 "substantially identical" shares less than thirty days before the May 22 sale, the loss on only 100 of the 300 shares sold on May 22 will be disallowed. This result is logical because 200 of the 300 shares purchased on May 1 had previously been used to disallow the loss on the earlier April 15 disposition. See Reg. §1.1091-1(b).

Section 1091(d) provides rules for calculating the basis in the new stock: The new stock's basis equals the basis in the old stock less the difference between the sale price and the repurchase price if the repurchase price is lower, or plus the difference between the sale price and the repurchase price if the repurchase price is higher.

For example, assume that on May 1, T receives $2,000 in exchange for 100 shares of XYZ stock with a $5,000 ($50 per share) adjusted basis. On May 10, T purchases 100 shares of XYZ stock for $3,000 ($30 per share). Ordinarily, T would have realized and recognized a loss of $30 per share on the May 1 disposition, but §1091(a) disallows the loss because of the subsequent purchase of substantially similar stock within thirty days of the sale. Further, §1091(d) provides T with a basis in the new stock equal to the basis in the old stock ($5,000) plus the difference between the sale price and the repurchase price ($1,000). T's step-up in basis takes into account that he has paid an additional $1,000 for stock identical to that which he sold at a disallowed loss.

Problems

9-15. James Pinter sold Xerox stock to his daughter, Marjorie, for its $200 value. The stock was purchased five months earlier for $1,000. Determine the tax consequences to James and Marjorie under the following circumstances.
   a. Marjorie Pinter resells the stock three months later for $400.
   b. She resells the stock three months later for $1,300.
   c. She resells the stock three months later for $100.
   d. What result in *a, b,* and *c* if James sold the stock to his wife, who then resold the stock? What if instead he sold it to his long-term girlfriend to whom he was not married?

9-16. On March 1, Molly Ingrahm purchased 1,000 shares of stock for $10,000. By May 31, the stock had declined in value to $5,000. To deduct her accrued loss against the substantial capital gains realized that year, she sold 500 shares of stock for $2,500 on June 1. Because Ingrahm felt that there was a good chance that the stock would regain its value, she purchased 500 shares on June 30 for $3,500.
   a. What is the amount of allowable loss?
   b. What is her adjusted basis in the shares purchased on June 30?
   c. What is the holding period of the shares purchased on June 30?
   d. What result in *a* if she did not purchase the new shares on June 30 but instead acquired them on July 2 pursuant to a contract to purchase executed on May 20?
   e. Assume the same facts as *d* except that the May 20 agreement was an option, not a contract to purchase. What result?
   f. What result in *a* if Ingrahm did not reacquire the shares on June 30, but her daughter did?

c. Investment Interest Limitations

Code: §163(d)

Section 163(d) limits the amount of interest on investment indebtedness that an individual may deduct. Prior to the enactment of §163(d) in 1969, taxpayers were allowed deductions for all investment interest expenses incurred during the year, thus enabling taxpayers to use the interest expense deduction to shelter other income.

> For example, a taxpayer may borrow substantial amounts to purchase stocks which have growth potential but which return small dividends currently. Despite the fact that the receipt of the income from the investment may be postponed (and may be capital gains), the taxpayer will receive a current deduction for the interest expense even though it is substantially in excess of the income from the investment. . . .
> [A] taxpayer who borrows substantial amounts in order to make investments and who is motivated by investment considerations rather than tax considerations generally is interested in investments which will produce a profit after taking the interest expense into account. Where the taxpayer's investment, however, produces little current income, the effect of allowing a current deduction for the interest is to produce

a mismatching of the investment income and related expenses of earning that income. In addition, the excess interest, in effect, is used by the taxpayer to offset other income, such as his salary, from taxation. . . .

[It is not] appropriate to allow an individual taxpayer to currently deduct interest expense on funds borrowed for investment purposes where the interest expense is substantially in excess of the taxpayer's investment income. Since the amount of funds borrowed by a taxpayer for investment purposes generally is within the taxpayer's control, it would appear that a taxpayer who incurs interest expense for this purpose, which is substantially in excess of his investment income, is primarily interested in obtaining the resulting mismatching of income and the expense of earning that income, so as to be able to insulate other income from taxation.

H.R. Rep. No. 413, 91st Cong., 1st Sess. 72 (1969).

Investment interest is deductible in any year only to the extent of that year's net investment income. Any unused investment interest is carried forward to subsequent years and deducted in those years when there is net investment income. Section 163(d) now relies on the passive activity loss limitations for the definitions of investment interest and net investment income.

Problem

9-17. Beth Shamburg borrowed $40,000 to purchase Acme Corporation stock. During the current year, she paid $4,000 of interest on this indebtedness. In addition, she incurred interest expenses of $2,900 on her commodities margin account. Shamburg's other investment expenses included $500 for an investment newsletter and a $2,100 capital loss resulting from commodity trades. Her income for the year was composed of a $150,000 salary, $5,100 of interest income, and $1,100 of dividend income.
   a. What is the amount of Shamburg's investment interest expense for the year?
   b. What is the amount of Shamburg's investment income for the year?
   c. What is the amount of Shamburg's investment interest deduction for the year?
   d. What portion, if any, of Shamburg's investment interest expense is carried forward to the following year?

F.   ETHICAL ISSUES

The prospect of sheltering taxable income, while spawning entrepreneurial instincts, often motivates investors to seek tax counsel before investing in the shifting sands of tax shelter investments. Although counsel representing the investor may be cautious in sifting through the challenges the Service might mount, as evidenced by recent events such as the Enron scandal, counsel representing the promoter may have mixed motives that color interpretation of the Code's

requirements. See United States Senate Permanent Subcommittee on Investiga-
tions of the Committee on Homeland Security and Governmental Affairs, *The Role
of Professional Firms in the U.S. Tax Shelter Industry* (February 8, 2005); Joint Committee on Taxation, *Report of Investigation of Enron Corporation and Related Entities
Regarding Federal Tax and Compensation Issues, and Policy Recommendations* (February
2003). Legislation and ethical standards attempting to influence tax counselors'
opinions may prove to be particularly treacherous.

JOINT COMMITTEE ON TAXATION, BACKGROUND AND PRESENT LAW RELATING TO TAX SHELTERS
(March 19, 2002)

I. BACKGROUND

The Internal Revenue Code ("Code") provides specific rules regarding the
computation of taxable income, including the amount, timing, and character of
items of income, gain, loss and deduction. These rules are designed to provide for
the computation of taxable income in a manner that provides for a degree of
specificity and certainty to both taxpayers and the Government. Taxpayers generally may plan their transactions in reliance on these rules to determine the Federal
income tax consequences arising from the transactions.

Notwithstanding the presence of specific rules for determining tax liability, a
body of law has evolved in response to transactions that may comply with the literal
language of a specific tax provision yet yield tax results that are unwarranted,
unintended or inconsistent with the underlying policy of the provision. These
transactions are euphemistically referred to as tax shelters.

Perhaps no single topic in the Federal income tax laws has been as vexing and
difficult to address as tax shelters. In 1934, Judge Learned Hand made the statement, often cited since, that a taxpayer "[M]ay so arrange his affairs that his taxes
shall be as low as possible; he is not bound to choose that pattern which will best pay
the Treasury; there is not even a patriotic duty to increase one's taxes."

Since that time, taxpayers and tax administrators have struggled in determining the line between legitimate "tax planning" and unacceptable "tax shelters."
Even now, more than sixty-five years after Judge Hand's opinion, there are disagreements on fundamental questions that lie at the heart of the tax shelter debate,
such as the magnitude of the problem, why the problem exists, and appropriate
responses to the problem. . . .

B. PENALTIES AND SANCTIONS APPLICABLE TO TAX SHELTERS

1. Penalties . . .

Non-taxpayer Penalties
Understatement of taxpayer's liability by income tax preparer (sec. 6694)

Section 6694 imposes a penalty on an income tax preparer for any understatement of tax liability on a tax return due to a position for which there was not a

realistic possibility of success of being sustained on its merits, but only if (1) the return preparer knew (or reasonably should have known) of the position, and (2) the position was not adequately disclosed on the return or was frivolous.

An "income tax preparer" means any person who prepares for compensation, or who employs other people to prepare for compensation, all or a substantial portion of an income tax return or claim for refund.

The penalty is $250 with respect to each return, unless the preparer establishes that there was reasonable cause for the understatement and the preparer acted in good faith. The penalty amount is increased to $1,000 if any part of the understatement is due to the preparer's willful conduct, or reckless or intentional disregard of the rules and regulations.

Penalties with respect to the preparation of income tax returns for others (sec. 6695)

Section 6695 imposes a penalty on any income tax return preparer who, in connection with the preparation of an income tax return, fails to: (1) furnish the taxpayer with a completed copy of the tax return; (2) sign the tax return (if required to do so by regulations); (3) furnish the proper identification number with respect to the tax return; (4) retain a copy of the completed return or a list (with names and taxpayer identification numbers) of the taxpayers for whom a return was prepared; or (5) comply with certain due diligence requirements in determining a taxpayer's eligibility for the earned income credit. Section 6695 also prohibits an income tax preparer from endorsing or otherwise negotiating a refund check that is issued to the taxpayer.

In most cases, the penalty is $50 for each failure, with a maximum penalty of $25,000 per category. The failure to comply with the due diligence requirements in determining eligibility for the earned income credit carries a $100 penalty for each failure.

Promoting abusive tax shelters (sec. 6700)

Section 6700 imposes a penalty on any person who organizes, assists in the organization of, or participates in the sale of any interest in, a partnership or other entity, any investment plan or arrangement, or any other plan or arrangement, if in connection with such activity the person makes or furnishes a qualifying false or fraudulent statement or a gross valuation overstatement.

A qualified false or fraudulent statement is any statement with respect to the allowability of any deduction or credit, the excludability of any income, or the securing of any other tax benefit by reason of holding an interest in the entity or participating in the plan or arrangement which the person knows or has reason to know is false or fraudulent as to any material matter. A "gross valuation overstatement" means any statement as to the value of any property or services if the stated value exceeds 200 percent of the correct valuation, and the value is directly related to the amount of any allowable income tax deduction or credit.

The amount of the penalty equals $1,000 (or, if the person establishes that it is less, 100 percent of the gross income derived or to be derived by the person from such activity). In calculating the amount of the penalty, the organizing of an entity, plan or arrangement and the sale of each interest in an entity, plan, or arrangement constitute separate activities. A penalty attributable to a gross valuation misstatement can be waived on a showing that there was a reasonable basis for the valuation and it was made in good faith.

Aiding and abetting understatement of tax liability (sec. 6701)

Section 6701 imposes a penalty on any person who (1) aids, assists, procures, or advises with respect to the preparation or presentation of any portion of a return, affidavit, claim, or other document, (2) knows (or has reason to believe) that the document will be used in connection with any material matter arising under the internal revenue laws, and (3) knows that the document would result in an understatement of another person's tax liability. The concept of aiding or abetting requires "direct involvement" in the preparation or presentation of a tax return or other tax-related document.

Several definitions and special rules apply. The penalty applies to a person who orders (or otherwise causes) a subordinate to do an act, as well as a person who knows of, and does not attempt to prevent, participation by a subordinate in an act. A subordinate means any other person over whose activities the person subject to the penalty has direction, supervision, or control. The penalty applies whether or not the understatement is with the knowledge or consent of the persons responsible for the return or other document. A person furnishing typing, reproducing, or other mechanical assistance is not subject to the penalty.

The penalty for aiding and abetting with respect to an individual's tax liability is $1,000; the penalty is $10,000 if the aiding and abetting is with respect to a corporation's tax liability. A person can only be subject to this penalty once with respect to a particular taxpayer per period. Courts have held that there is no statute of limitations for purposes of applying this penalty. . . .

C.   STANDARDS OF TAX PRACTICE AND PROFESSIONAL CONDUCT REGARDING TAX SHELTERS

1.   *Circular 230 — Treasury Regulations that Govern Practice before IRS*

An individual who is a member in good standing of the bar of the highest court of a State may represent a person before the IRS. Similarly, an individual who is duly qualified to practice as a CPA in a State may represent a person before the IRS. Individuals not qualifying under either the attorney or the CPA rules may represent a person before the IRS if they qualify either by passing an examination or by nature of their previous employment with the IRS.

The Treasury Department is authorized to regulate the practice of representatives before the Treasury Department (which includes the IRS), and (after notice and opportunity for a proceeding) to suspend or disbar any representative from practice before the Treasury Department for a violation of such rules and regulations. In accordance with this grant of authority, the Treasury Department has issued regulations that govern the practice of attorneys, certified public accountants, enrolled agents, and other persons representing clients before the IRS. These regulations are commonly referred to as Circular 230.

Circular 230 contains rules governing the standards for certain tax shelter opinions, as well as rules governing the standards for advising a taxpayer to take a position on its return. The IRS Office of Director of Practice is responsible for the enforcement of Circular 230. . . .

2. American Bar Association Guidelines

The American Bar Association ("ABA") has promulgated a series of rules and guidelines concerning the standards of practice for lawyers. The ABA rules, in and of themselves, do not have legal effect. However, most States have adopted rules of professional conduct based on rules promulgated by the ABA (which have the force and effect of law). The two primary sets of rules that have been promulgated by the ABA are the Model Code of Professional Responsibility ("Model Code") and Model Rules of Professional Conduct ("Model Rules").

The ABA, through its Standing Committee on Ethics and Professional Responsibility, issues formal and informal opinions that interpret the Model Code and Model Rules. Of particular relevance to tax practitioners are (1) ABA Formal Opinion 346, regarding a lawyer's duties and responsibilities in rendering tax shelters, and (2) ABA Formal Opinion 85-352, regarding a lawyer's duty in advising a client on a position that can be taken on a tax return.

ABA Formal Opinion 346

Formal Opinion 346 (Revised), issued by the ABA Standing Committee on Ethics and Professional Responsibility in 1982, defines a lawyer's duties and responsibilities in connection with tax shelter opinions that are offered as part of tax shelter investment offerings. The ABA does not have the authority to discipline its members for a violation of Formal Opinion 346; its application and enforcement is left to the State licensing authorities.

Formal Opinion 346 defines a "tax shelter opinion" as advice by a lawyer regarding the Federal tax law applicable to a tax shelter if the advice is referred to either (1) in offering materials or (2) in connection with sales promotion efforts. A tax shelter opinion includes the tax aspects or tax risks portion of the offering materials prepared by the lawyer regardless of whether a separate opinion letter is prepared.

A lawyer who provides a tax shelter opinion violates the disciplinary rules of the Model Code if the lawyer gives a false opinion. A "false opinion" is one that ignores or minimizes serious legal risks or misstates the facts or the law, knowingly or through gross incompetence. A false opinion also includes (1) an opinion that is intentionally or recklessly misleading, and (2) the acceptance of facts as represented by the promoter, when the lawyer should know that a further inquiry would disclose that such facts are untrue.

Formal Opinion 346 also describes the principles and considerations that should guide lawyers in the rendering of tax shelter opinions. The lawyer should verify the facts presented to him and make further inquiries when the facts are incomplete, inconsistent, or otherwise open to question. The lawyer also should relate the law to the actual facts to the extent the facts are ascertainable when the offering materials are circulated, and not issue an opinion that disclaims responsibility for inquiring as to the accuracy of the facts, fails to analyze critical facts, or discusses purely hypothetical facts. The lawyer should satisfy himself that either he or another professional has considered all material tax issues. Moreover, the tax shelter opinion should "fully and fairly address" each material tax issue for which a reasonable possibility exists that the IRS will challenge the proposed tax effects. The lawyer should, if possible, state his or her opinion of the probable outcome on the merits of each material tax issue, as well as an overall evaluation of the extent to which the tax benefits, taken as a whole, are likely to be realized (or not realized) as contemplated by the offering materials.

ABA Formal Opinion 85-352

ABA Formal Opinion 85-352 defines the basic ethical standard governing lawyers engaged in federal tax practice. It provides that "[a] lawyer may advise reporting a position on a return even where the lawyer believes the position probably will not prevail, there is no 'substantial authority' in support of the position, and there will be no disclosure of the position on the return. However, the position to be asserted must be one which the lawyer in good faith believes is warranted in existing law or can be supported by a good faith argument for an extension, modification, or reversal of existing law. This requires that there is some realistic possibility of success if the matter is litigated."

ABA Formal Opinion 85-352 represents a higher threshold than had been contained in the previous standard, as articulated in ABA Formal Opinion 314. The standard for tax practitioners under ABA Formal Opinion 314 required only that "a lawyer could freely urge the statement of positions most favorable to the client just so long as there [was] reasonable basis for the position."

The standard in ABA Formal Opinion 85-352, which Congress adopted in 1989 as its model for income tax return preparers (§6694(a)) is a lower standard than the "substantial authority" standard of §6662(b)(2). A lawyer may advise the taxpayer to take a return position that does not meet the "reasonable possibility of success standard" provided that it is not frivolous and is either adequately disclosed or it is filed as a claim for refund. Thus, a lawyer is ethically permitted to advise the taxpayer to take a position on a tax return that subjects the taxpayer to the risk of the substantial understatement penalty.

TREASURY DEPARTMENT CIRCULAR NO. 230
31 C.F.R Subtitle A, Part 10
(Revised as of June 20, 2005)

§10.20 Information to be furnished.

(a) To the Internal Revenue Service

(1) A practitioner must, on a proper and lawful request by a duly authorized officer or employee of the Internal Revenue Service, promptly submit records or information in any matter before the Internal Revenue Service unless the practitioner believes in good faith and on reasonable grounds that the records or information are privileged.

(2) Where the requested records or information are not in the possession of, or subject to the control of, the practitioner or the practitioner's client, the practitioner must promptly notify the requesting Internal Revenue Service officer or employee and the practitioner must provide any information that the practitioner has regarding the identity of any person who the practitioner believes may have possession or control of the requested records or information. The practitioner

must make reasonable inquiry of his or her client regarding the identity of any person who may have possession or control of the requested records or information, but the practitioner is not required to make inquiry of any other person or independently verify any information provided by the practitioner's client regarding the identity of such persons. . . .

§10.21 Knowledge of client's omission.

A practitioner who, having been retained by a client with respect to a matter administered by the Internal Revenue Service, knows that the client has not complied with the revenue laws of the United States or has made an error in or omission from any return, document, affidavit, or other paper which the client submitted or executed under the revenue laws of the United States, must advise the client promptly of the fact of such noncompliance, error, or omission. The practitioner must advise the client of the consequences as provided under the Code and regulations of such noncompliance, error, or omission.

§10.22 Diligence as to accuracy.

(a) *In general.* A practitioner must exercise due diligence —

(1) In preparing or assisting in the preparation of, approving, and filing tax returns, documents, affidavits, and other papers relating to Internal Revenue Service matters;

(2) In determining the correctness of oral or written representations made by the practitioner to the Department of the Treasury; and

(3) In determining the correctness of oral or written representations made by the practitioner to clients with reference to any matter administered by the Internal Revenue Service.

(b) *Reliance on others.* Except as provided in §§10.33 and 10.34, a practitioner will be presumed to have exercised due diligence for purposes of this section if the practitioner relies on the work product of another person and the practitioner used reasonable care in engaging, supervising, training, and evaluating the person, taking proper account of the nature of the relationship between the practitioner and the person.

§10.33 Best practices for tax advisors.

(a) *Best practices.* Tax advisors should provide clients with the highest quality representation concerning Federal tax issues by adhering to best practices in providing advice and in preparing or assisting in the preparation of a submission to the Internal Revenue Service. In addition to compliance with the standards of practice provided elsewhere in this part, best practices include the following:

(1) Communicating clearly with the client regarding the terms of the engagement. For example, the advisor should determine the client's expected purpose for and use of the advice and should have a clear understanding with the client regarding the form and scope of the advice or assistance to be rendered.

(2) Establishing the facts, determining which facts are relevant, evaluating the reasonableness of any assumptions or representations, relating the applicable law (including potentially applicable judicial doctrines) to the relevant facts, and arriving at a conclusion supported by the law and the facts.

(3) Advising the client regarding the import of the conclusions reached, including, for example, whether a taxpayer may avoid accuracy-related penalties under the Internal Revenue Code if a taxpayer acts in reliance on the advice.

(4) Acting fairly and with integrity in practice before the Internal Revenue Service. . . .

§10.34 Standards for advising with respect to tax return positions and for preparing or signing returns.

(a) Realistic possibility standard. A practitioner may not sign a tax return as a preparer if the practitioner determines that the tax return contains a position that does not have a realistic possibility of being sustained on its merits . . . unless the position is not frivolous and is adequately disclosed to the Internal Revenue Service. A practitioner may not advise a client to take a position on a tax return, or prepare the portion of a tax return on which a position is taken, unless—

(1) The practitioner determines that the position satisfies the realistic possibility standard; or

(2) The position is not frivolous and the practitioner advises the client of any opportunity to avoid the accuracy-related penalty in §6662 . . . by adequately disclosing the position and of the requirements for adequate disclosure.

(b) Advising clients on potential penalties. A practitioner advising a client to take a position on a tax return, or preparing or signing a tax return as a preparer, must inform the client of the penalties reasonably likely to apply to the client with respect to the position advised, prepared, or reported. The practitioner also must inform the client of any opportunity to avoid any such penalty by disclosure, if relevant, and of the requirements for adequate disclosure. . . .

(c) Relying on information furnished by clients. A practitioner advising a client to take a position on a tax return, or preparing or signing a tax return as a preparer, generally may rely in good faith without verification upon information furnished by the client. The practitioner may not, however, ignore the implications of information furnished to, or actually known by, the practitioner, and must make reasonable inquiries if the information as furnished appears to be incorrect, inconsistent with an important fact or another factual assumption, or incomplete.

JUDISCH v. UNITED STATES
755 F.2d 823 (11th Cir. 1985)

Tjoflat, J.

Section 6694(a) of the Internal Revenue Code imposes a penalty on an income tax preparer who understates a taxpayer's liability on an income tax return by negligently or intentionally disregarding revenue rules and regulations. Section 6694(b) of the Code penalizes a tax preparer who willfully understates a taxpayer's liability on a return. The principal question presented in this appeal is whether a tax preparer can be penalized under section 6694(b) if the understatement of taxpayer liabilities is caused by the tax preparer's willful disregard of revenue rules and regulations.

I

Clara Mann Judisch, the appellee here, is a federal income tax return preparer in Sarasota, Florida. She has been preparing income tax returns since 1952, when she began practicing law in Ames, Iowa. Judisch practiced law in Ames until she moved to Sarasota in 1968. Thereafter, she limited her professional work to the preparation of income tax returns.

Most of Judisch's taxpayer clients were individuals; some were sole proprietors of small businesses. Judisch's first step in preparing a client's tax return would be to mail the client a four-page questionnaire. On receipt of the filled-out questionnaire, Judisch would prepare the return and send it to the client for his signature. The client would then mail the return to the Internal Revenue Service. Usually, Judisch would prepare a client's return without communicating with him except through the questionnaire. In a few instances, she would call the client to inquire about information disclosed in his answers to her questionnaire.

In 1976 Congress amended the Internal Revenue Code, adding section 280A to limit the type of taxpayer eligible to take a "home office" deduction; to be eligible for such a deduction, the taxpayer must use the portion of his residence employed as a "home office" exclusively, and on a regular basis, as his principal place of business or as a place of business used by patients, clients, or customers in meeting or dealing with the taxpayer in the normal course of business. The amount of the deduction is limited to the gross income derived from the use of the home office. This amendment to the Code was effective for the tax years relevant to this suit, 1976 and 1977, and Judisch had knowledge of this fact.

In mailing her questionnaire to her clients for these two tax years, Judisch did not elicit the information necessary to enable her to determine whether a given client was entitled to a home office deduction. Judisch did ask the client to indicate whether a part of his home was "used for production of income," and, if so, the percentage of the home so used, and to list expenditures the client incurred in carrying out such business activity. She did not, however, seek the critical information necessary to determine the client's eligibility for a home office deduction: whether the portion of the client's home used for the production of income was used exclusively, and on a regular basis, for that purpose; whether it was the principal place of the client's trade or business; and the gross income derived therefrom. Nevertheless, Judisch routinely claimed a home office deduction on her clients' 1976 and 1977 income tax returns. She did so even when it was clear that the client either had no earnings from a trade or business or had no home office used exclusively as his principal place of business. Moreover, Judisch claimed as business expenses, items, such as cable television, the home telephone, and the home newspaper, that could not qualify as business expense. . . . The IRS discovered Judisch's home office deduction practice while auditing some of her clients' tax returns, and, after a full investigation, assessed fifty-eight penalties against her under sections 6694(a) and (b) of the Code for understating tax liability with respect to tax returns prepared by her for the 1976 and 1977 tax years.

Judisch thereafter brought this action in the district court, as authorized by section 6694(c), seeking a determination of her liability for these penalties. She demanded a trial by jury. After the parties joined issue, they agreed, for reasons unimportant to this appeal, to limit the trial of the case to the penalties assessed in connection with five tax returns, Wotring's 1977 return, the Roates' 1976 and 1977 returns, and the Joneses' 1976 and 1977 returns. The parties also agreed that the order of proof at trial would require the government to put on its evidence first.

The government produced the only witnesses called at trial, Judisch and Priscilla A. Quina, the IRS agent who audited Judisch's clients' tax returns. Judisch called no witnesses. All that she presented to the jury was a copy of a 1980 Joint Congressional Resolution, Act of Oct. 1, 1980, Pub. L. No. 96-369, 1980 U.S. Code Cong. & Ad. News (94 Stat.) §123, which prohibited the IRS from using any funds to enforce the rules or regulations it had promulgated to implement section 280A of the Code relating to "the determination of the principal place of business of the taxpayer."

At the close of all the evidence, Judisch moved for a directed verdict as to the section 6694(b) penalties for willfully understating her clients' tax liability. She contended that a finding of "willfulness" under section 6694(b) required that the tax return preparer purposely disregard "information furnished by the taxpayer" and that the evidence failed to show that she had done so. In response, the government argued that a section 6694(b) penalty for willful understatement of liability may be based on the tax preparer's intentional disregard of applicable rules and regulations and that there was ample evidence for the jury to conclude that Judisch had intentionally disregarded such rules and regulations in preparing the five returns in question. The district court directed a verdict in Judisch's favor as to the section 6694(b) penalties, because, as Judisch contended, the evidence did not demonstrate that she had intentionally disregarded information furnished by the taxpayer. The court also concluded that the evidence was insufficient to sustain the penalties under the government's theory. The court submitted the question of Judisch's liability for the section 6694(a) penalties to the jury, and the jury found for Judisch.

The government appeals, contending that the district court erred as a matter of law in removing the section 6694(b) penalties from the jury. The government also contends that, with respect to the section 6694(a) penalties that were submitted to the jury, the jury's verdict must be set aside, and a new trial ordered, because the court committed prejudicial error in admitting into evidence the 1980 Joint Congressional Resolution concerning the IRS' enforcement of section 280A of the Code. We consider these contentions in turn.

II

A

The district court directed verdicts as to the section 6694(b) penalties, relying, in part, on the assumption that an income tax preparer's intentional disregard of the Internal Revenue Code or treasury rules and regulations cannot constitute a violation of section 6694(b). The court reasoned that Congress did not intend to proscribe the same conduct in both sections 6694(a) and (b). As to the former, the court reasoned, Congress intended to proscribe the negligent or intentional disregard of the rules and regulations; as to the latter, it intended to proscribe the willful disregard of information furnished by the taxpayer for the purpose of understating the amount of taxes owed. As an alternative holding, the court found the evidence insufficient to show that Judisch had willfully understated the tax liability on any of the returns before the court.

Section 6694(b), on its face, proscribes "a willful attempt in any manner to understate the [taxpayer's] liability." The willful disregard of rules and regulations for the purpose of understating tax liability constitutes a manner of willful attempt under the section; accordingly, Judisch violated section 6694(b) if she willfully disregarded the Code or treasury rules and regulations to understate tax liability.

A tax return preparer's willful disregard of the tax code or regulations, for the purpose of understating a client's tax liability, violates both sections 6694(a) *and* (b). The text of the latter suggests this result: "the amount of the penalty payable by any person by reason of this [section] shall be reduced by the amount of the penalty paid by such person by reason of [section 6694] (a)." The treasury regulations and the legislative history also support this position. Treas. Reg. §1.6694-l(b)(2)(iv) (1984) provides as follows:

> In certain situations, a preparer shall be subject both to a penalty under [section 6694] (a) . . . for intentional disregard of rules and regulations and to a penalty under [section 6694] (b) for willful understatement of liability. A penalty for willful understatement of liability may be based on an intentional disregard of rules and regulations. For example, a preparer who claims a personal exemption deduction for the taxpayer's mother with knowledge that the taxpayer is not entitled to the deduction will have both intentionally disregarded rules and regulations within the meaning of [section 6694] (a) . . . and willfully understated liability for tax within the meaning of [section 6694] (b).

The legislative history directly supports this regulation. H.R. Rep. No. 94-658, 94th Cong. 1st Sess., at 279 (1975) states in pertinent part:

> A willful understatement of tax liability can also include an intentional disregard of Internal Revenue Code rules and regulations. For example, an income tax return preparer who deducts all of a taxpayer's medical expenses, intentionally disregarding the percent of adjusted gross income limitation, may have both intentionally disregarded Internal Revenue Code rules and regulations and willfully understated tax liability. In such a case, the Internal Revenue Service can assess either or both penalties against the income tax return preparer.

In light of the regulations and the legislative history, we conclude that an income tax preparer's willful disregard of the Code or the rules and regulations for the purpose of understating a client's tax liability violates section 6694(b) and section 6694(a) as well.

The district court erred in concluding that Judisch could not have violated both sections 6694(a) and (b). The Congress plainly contemplated that an income tax preparer could transgress both sections simultaneously. Every violation of section (b), based on evidence that the taxpayer willfully disregarded IRS rules and regulations, is also a violation of section (a); a violation of section (a) is a violation of section (b) only where the government proves willfulness.

The district court directed a verdict for Judisch on all of the section 6694(b) willfulness penalties on the ground that there was insufficient evidence in the record from which a jury could find that Judisch had intentionally disregarded the applicable rules and regulations. The sufficiency of the evidence presents a nettlesome question on review in this case because of the government's trial strategy. Inexplicably, the government decided not to establish the information Judisch's clients provided her to enable her to prepare the tax returns under scrutiny. That is, the government neither introduced the questionnaires those clients filled out and mailed to Judisch nor called the clients to testify as to the information they provided her. In short, the government did not prove the amount of tax liability understatement that resulted from the home office deduction, and, as to the Wotring return for 1977, the government even failed to establish that Judisch prepared it. A directed verdict with respect to the Wotring return was therefore in order. A directed verdict was also in order as to the Joneses' return for 1976 and 1977. The government, after auditing those returns, allowed the Joneses' home office deduction. Under these circumstances, it could not be said that Judisch intentionally disregarded the section 280A home office deduction requirements.

The government did manage, however, to present sufficient evidence to withstand a motion for directed verdict with respect to the Roates' 1976 and 1977 tax returns. Judisch admitted that she knew of the requirements for a home office deduction at the time she prepared these returns. She knew, for example, that section 280A(c)(5) of the Code specified that a home office deduction could not exceed the portion of the gross income from the taxpayers' business attributable to business activity in the home office. The Roates had no income from a trade or business, whether conducted out of the home or elsewhere, in 1976 or 1977, and Judisch reported no such income on the Roates' tax returns for those years. Nevertheless, she had the Roates take a home office deduction in both years. These deductions were false for two reasons. First, the Roates had no income from a trade or business against which a home office deduction could be taken. Second, the Roates had no "home office" as defined in section 280A. All they had was a family room where they watched television and listened to the stereo. On these facts the jury could readily have found that Judisch intentionally disregarded section 280A for the purpose of understating the Roates' tax liability for the 1976 and 1977 tax years. The district court therefore erred in directing a verdict with respect to the section 6694(b) penalties on the Roates' returns.

B

The government's second contention in this appeal is that the district court committed reversible error by admitting into evidence the 1980 Joint Congressional Resolution concerning the IRS' enforcement of section 280A of the Code because it was irrelevant. Judisch argues, in response, that the Joint Resolution, passed three years after she prepared the returns in question, demonstrated that Congress disagreed with the IRS position on home office deductions. Judisch contends that the congressional resolution was relevant in her situation, proving her good faith and reasonableness in disregarding the statute and claiming the deductions on behalf of her clients. We are not persuaded.

An income tax preparer's "good faith" and the reasonableness of a position he takes must be judged at the time the work is done. Therefore, only the information available to and considered by the income tax preparer in preparing a tax return is relevant to this good faith issue. It was pure coincidence that the Congress passed the resolution in question two years after the events in issue here. We will not permit a litigant in these circumstances to prove his good faith or a reasonable basis for his action by subsequent developments in the law.

Judisch argued to the jury that the congressional resolution indicated that the IRS was wrong in challenging the tax returns she prepared on behalf of her clients. . . . Congress did not intend to approve home office deductions for the vast majority of individual taxpayers who do not operate a trade or business from their residence. Furthermore, several of her clients had no legitimate trade or business income which the Code required to offset the deductions. In this context, the challenged evidence was highly misleading and prejudicial to the jury. In summary, we reverse and remand for a new trial, with respect to the Roates' returns, on the section 6694(a) issue of negligent understatement of liability.

For the foregoing reasons, we reverse the district court's judgment with respect to the section 6694(a) and (b) penalties on the Roates' 1976 and 1977 returns and remand the case for a new trial. In all other respects, the court's judgment is affirmed.

Affirmed in part, reversed in part, and remanded.

C H A P T E R   1 0
COMPUTING TAX LIABILITY

A. OVERVIEW

The preceding chapters have discussed the statutorily prescribed method for computing taxable income for a given taxable year. Through the deduction of certain business, personal, and investment expenses from gross income, annual economic gains subject to taxation can be ascertained. In determining tax *liability*, however, should only relative economic gains be weighed or should other factors affecting the financial condition of individual taxpayers be incorporated into the formula? For example, a taxpayer with school-age children may incur greater expenses of a nondeductible, personal nature than a childless taxpayer. If both have the same income, should their tax liability be the same or should the taxpayer with children be afforded some relief? Similarly, should the tax liability of a married couple be the same as that of an unmarried individual with an identical amount of taxable income?

These and other policy concerns led Congress to incorporate several statutory provisions that have a direct impact on the ultimate amount of tax liability. For example, as a final step in computing taxable income, the taxpayer may subtract personal exemptions for himself, his spouse, and any qualified dependents. However, arriving at a figure for §63 taxable income does not end the task.

Once *taxable income* has been computed, the taxpayer must determine the rate of taxation by reference to the Code's rate tables (§1) to arrive at tax liability. The rate tables apply different tax rates to statutorily defined types of taxpaying units — that is, married filing jointly, head of household, single, or married filing separately. Recall from Chapter 4 that the United States uses a "strict" form of the individual of the taxable unit, which does not take into account considerations such as whether taxpayers share living expenses, support dependents, or have other differing personal or financial situations. In selecting tax rates, however, Congress did base its decision in part on its perception of the relative financial status of different units. In the following materials, consider whether a more equitable rate structure would treat all taxpaying units identically, based on net income. What tradeoffs might be required in order to implement such a system?

Once the taxpayer's gross tax liability is determined, two types of adjustments may affect the amount of tax due. These adjustments depend on whether the taxpayer's liability is affected by tax credits or is subject to a minimum tax provision. If the taxpayer qualifies for any of the tax credits that Congress allows for various policy reasons, he can reduce tax liability on a dollar for dollar basis. (In some cases, taxpayers may be forced to recapture all or a portion of a previously taken credit that may *increase* tax liability.) On the other hand, if the taxpayer has reduced or sheltered income by taking advantage of too many statutorily granted tax preferences so that he is not paying a "fair share" of the tax burden, the taxpayer may owe an additional amount of tax (the alternative minimum tax).

Although these concepts constitute the final stages in computing federal income tax liability, they also reflect social and policy goals on which congressional tax decisions are premised.

B. PERSONAL EXEMPTIONS

Code: §§63; 151; 152; 7703
Regulations: §§1.151-1(b); 1.152-1; 1.152-3; 1.152-4T

Section 151 grants a statutory deduction for each personal exemption. Personal exemptions fall into three major categories: the taxpayer exemption, the spousal exemption, and the exemption for dependents.

Unlike itemized deductions, the personal exemption is a fixed amount ($2,000, increased annually to reflect a cost of living adjustment). §151(d)(1), (4). However, different taxpayers are entitled to claim a different number of personal exemptions based on differing personal characteristics outlined in §§151 and 152. Thus, the challenge is to determine the number of personal exemptions to which a taxpayer is entitled rather than the amount.

In effect, each personal exemption entitles the taxpayer to receive a specified amount of income tax-free. The number of personal exemptions to which a taxpayer is entitled depends on compliance with the criteria for three categories of exemptions — self, spouse, and dependent. Thus, a typical married couple, filing jointly and having one dependent child, is entitled to three personal exemptions. This amount, when combined with the standard deduction, equals the income the taxpaying unit may earn without incurring any tax liability.

As with similar provisions, personal exemptions are subject to an income-based "phaseout" which has been controversial and subject to calls for repeal. To date, however, some form of phaseout remains part of the taxing formula. §151(d)(3).

1.   The Taxpayer Exemption

Section 151(b) provides that a taxpayer is entitled to one exemption. Section 7701(a)(14) defines a taxpayer as any person subject to tax under the Code.

Therefore, a married couple filing a joint return is entitled to two taxpayer exemptions as each is a taxpayer. In contrast to the spousal and dependency exemptions, which are subject to numerous conditions and qualifications, the taxpayer exemption is an entitlement based solely on one's status as a taxpayer. However, there is an exception for taxpayers who may be claimed as dependency exemptions (discussed at section B3) of another. In such a case, §152(b)(2) disallows the taxpayer exemption to avoid the double benefit of a taxpayer, who is a dependency exemption of another, claiming himself as well.

2.   The Spousal Exemption

Pursuant to §151(b), a taxpayer is entitled to an exemption for a spouse if a number of requirements are met. First, the person for whom the taxpayer is claiming a spousal exemption must be his or her spouse. Whether a taxpayer is married for purposes of the spousal exemption is governed by §7703, which generally requires that marital status is determined on the last day of the taxable year, unless the spouse died during the year, in which case the determination is made on the date of death. Legally separated spouses are not considered married even though the couple has not obtained a divorce. See also §7703(b) for marital status rules when certain married taxpayers are living apart. Further, under the Defense of Marriage Act, legally married same-sex couples are not considered married for these purposes.

Once spousal status has been established, three additional requirements must be met in order to claim the exemption: (1) the spouse must not file a joint return with the taxpayer, (2) the spouse must not have any gross income during the "calendar year in which the taxable year of the taxpayer begins," and (3) the spouse must not be a dependent of another. If these requirements are met, the taxpayer may claim a spousal exemption in addition to a taxpayer exemption.

Effectively, to satisfy the requirements of a spousal exemption the spouse must not be entitled to a taxpayer exemption. Thus, when a spousal exemption is claimed, the marital unit derives two exemptions, the same as if the marital unit filed a joint return and claimed two taxpayer exemptions. If a joint return is filed by a spouse with no gross income, the conditions of §151(b) are not circumvented because a spousal exemption is not being claimed. Instead, each taxpayer is claiming the taxpayer exemption, resulting in a total of two exemptions for the marital unit.

3.   Dependency Exemptions

Section 151(c) provides an additional personal exemption for each qualifying dependent. Simply because a taxpayer provides financial support for another person does not mean that such person automatically qualifies as the taxpayer's dependent. Contemporary living patterns are fertile ground for interesting tax questions. For example, can a dependency exemption be claimed for a taxpayer's unemployed living companion? What about parents whose adult child returns to the nest?

Entitlement to a dependency exemption requires that the party claimed as a dependent meet three criteria. The first – the relationship test – requires that the taxpayer and the claimed dependent bear one of the relationships designated by

§152(a)(1) through (9). The second, the earnings test, generally requires that the party claimed as a dependent have gross income for the year less than the exemption amount. The third, the support test, requires that the claimed dependent have received more than one-half of his support from the taxpayer during the taxable year.

The relationship test generally focuses on a relationship of affinity with the taxpayer — such as daughter, uncle, grandmother, niece, son-in-law, mother-in-law. However, §152(a)(9) broadens the relationship test to include unrelated individuals (1) who are members of the taxpayer's household and (2) whose principal place of abode is the taxpayer's home. Since the "household" and "place of abode" requirements need not be met for a related party, a dependency exemption could be allowed for a related party even if that person lived elsewhere. Additionally, even if an unrelated party meets the household and principal place of abode requirements, Congress has posed another stumbling block to an unrelated person's qualification as a dependent. Section 152(b)(5) provides that if the taxpayer's relationship with an individual is in violation of local law (such as in the case of adultery, among others), the individual is not considered a member of the taxpayer's household, and the taxpayer is foreclosed from a dependency exemption.

The application of the second test, the earnings test, may require a two-step analysis. The first issue is whether the claimed party earned less than the exemption amount of gross income for the year. If so, the earnings test is satisfied. If not, the earnings limitation may still be met if the claimed party is (1) a child of the taxpayer and (2) either has not attained age 19 or is a full-time student who has not attained age 24. Thus, if the other requirements for a personal exemption are met, a taxpayer would be entitled to an exemption for his 23-year-old daughter even though she is a full-time Ph.D. candidate earning $15,000 a year. In such a case, the daughter would be denied her taxpayer exemption under §151(d)(2).

Section 152(b)(3)(A) provides that a dependent does not include a child that is not a U.S. citizen unless that child is a U.S. resident or resident of a contiguous country. Treasury regulation section 1.152-2(a)(1) specifies that children must be U.S. citizens at some time during the taxable year at issue to qualify for the personal exemption. This regulation was recently upheld against a challenge that it exceeded the scope of the statutory rule by excluding children who became U.S. citizens in subsequent years. Carlebach v. Commissioner, 139 T.C. No. 1 (2012).

The final dependency test, the support test, is generally more difficult to apply than the other two tests. To meet the support test, the taxpayer must have supplied more than one-half of the dependent's support. Undoubtedly, Congress wished to insure that the dependency exemption was given only to the person who was the primary source of support for the claimed party. As discussed below, however, Congress has legislated the determinative support standard governing multiple support agreements (§152(c)) and children of divorced or separated parents (§152(e)).

Frequently litigated issues under the support test are the meaning of "support" and whether it is limited strictly to the necessities of food, clothing, and shelter. For example, does support include the costs of singing and drama lessons, private school tuition, and summer camp? Should the health, financial resources, and other aspects of the parent-child relationship be considered in defining the term support?

SHAPIRO v. COMMISSIONER
54 T.C. 347 (1970)

Dawson, J.

. . . The basic issue for decision in this case is whether the petitioner provided in the year 1966 more than one-half of the total support of her son, Michael, so as to qualify him as a dependent under section 152(a). . . . [T]he resolution of this issue depends on whether the cost of sending petitioner's minor son to a summer residential camp constitutes part of his "support" for dependency exemption purposes. . . .

Respondent strongly contends that the cost in sending Michael to the summer residential camp was not for the necessities of life and therefore should not be considered in determining the total cost of his support.

Since the term "support" is nowhere defined in the Internal Revenue Code, we must look to the regulations and decided cases to ascertain the meaning of "support" as used in section 152(a). Section 1.152-1(a)(2)(i), Income Tax Regs., provides: "The term 'support' *includes* food, shelter, clothing, medical and dental care, *education, and the like*." (Emphasis added.) The Internal Revenue Service has even indicated that "support" includes "expenditures for providing . . . recreation."

In our opinion the cost of sending a child to camp clearly comes within the rather expansive language of the regulations. We think such an expenditure qualifies as education, recreation, or the like. Webster's Third International Dictionary defines (1) "education" as "the act or process of providing with knowledge, skill, or competence, or . . . desirable qualities of behaviour or character" and (2) "recreation" as "a means of getting diversion or entertainment." There can be no doubt that Michael derived knowledge, skill, and competence from his experience at Camp Wildwood. And the camp was surely a means of entertainment and diversion from the humdrum tedium of urban life. The importance of camp to the physical and intellectual development of an 11-year-old boy, like Michael, living in an urban environment is patently evident. . . .

At trial, respondent's counsel made the following comments with respect to petitioner's expenditure of $916.66 [$417 in 1966 and $499.66 in 1967] in sending Michael to Camp Wildwood:

> I well agree that this might be the manner in which a child in Great Neck is supposed to be supported, but for legal sake, the sake of this case, that it is not support of a child. That is a great luxury item I feel.
>
> I can just look around the City of New York; there are children who don't even have food; they don't have housing; they don't have any of the bare necessities. It is preposterous to claim something like this.

While we commend counsel's compassion for the underprivileged children of New York City, we fail to see how their plight has any bearing on the resolution of the issue before us. Respondent's contention that "support" in this context should be limited to "necessities" is without merit. The term "necessities" is a relative one which depends on the facts of any given situation. The question of what things are to be regarded as "necessities," customarily considered to be factual, generally depends on the particular facts and circumstances of each case, such as health, financial resources, and *station in life* of the child and parent. In applying the term to the facts of this case, we conclude that the cost of sending a child to camp may well be considered a necessity.

We completely disagree with respondent that "Support has been defined by courts as necessities." We realize, however, that there is some authority for this proposition. We do not regard either of these cases as persuasive authority. The better principle of law, we think, is contained in the reported opinions of this Court which have repeatedly and consistently repudiated the rationale of . . . restricting the meaning of support to necessities. For example, in Raymond M. McKay, 34 T.C. 1080, 1084 (1960), we expressly rejected the argument "that only necessities are to be taken into consideration in determining what constitutes support furnished for a dependent," holding that the expenses incurred for singing and dramatic lessons supplied the taxpayer's minor daughter constituted part of her support. In so holding, we said: "nothing in either the precise wording of section 152(a) or its legislative history . . . [convinces] us that the term 'support' as used therein should be limited to payments which a court could require parents to make as part of their common law or statutory duty to provide for their children."

Such language makes it clear that the meaning of "support" under section 152(a) is *not* restricted to necessities. This principle stems from our opinions in Bernard C. Rivers, 33 T.C. 935 (1960), holding that the cost of tuition in a parochial school is includable as an element of support, even though public schools were available; and Martha J. Blyth, 21 T.C. 275 (1953), holding that the cost of tuition at a private school constitutes an item of support. . . .

The real gravamen of respondent's argument herein does not seem to be so much the inclusion of camp as an item of support, but rather the inclusion of the particular amount ($916.66) as being *unreasonable*. It is, however, well settled that the exemption for a dependent does not depend upon the reasonableness of the amounts expended for support, or upon a comparison of what different parents may spend for the support of a child, but whether such dependent received over one-half of his actual support from the taxpayer.

For these reasons we have included the cost petitioner incurred in sending Michael to Camp Wildwood as part of the total cost of his support in 1966. The fact that petitioner paid $499.66 of such cost in 1967 is immaterial, since "The year in which the item of support was furnished is controlling in determining the year in which the value of that support shall be included." . . . Accordingly, we conclude that petitioner provided more than one-half of Michael's total support in 1966 and is entitled to the claimed dependency exemption. . . .

[Judgment for petitioner.]

REV. RUL. 76-184
1976-1 C.B. 44

A parent made expenditures for a child's wedding apparel and accessories, the wedding reception, and for flowers for the wedding party, church, and reception. The child did not file a joint return for the year in which the child was married.

Section 152(a) of the Internal Revenue Code of 1954 defines the term 'dependent' as including a child of the taxpayer, 'over half of whose support for the calendar year in which the taxable year of the taxpayer begins, was received from the taxpayer.' The term 'support' is defined in section 1.152-1(a)(2) of the Income Tax Regulations as including food, shelter, clothing, medical and dental care, education, and the like.

Held, the expenditures made by the parent in the instant case for the child's wedding apparel and accessories, the wedding reception, and for flowers for the wedding party, church, and reception, are part of the child's support for purposes of determining whether the child is the parent's dependent for Federal income tax purposes.

Note on Support Requirements in Specified Settings

Support from government agencies. The courts have frequently considered whether support derived from sources such as welfare or Medicare benefits payments can be included when computing the amount of support provided by the taxpayer. For example, in Lutter v. Commissioner, 61 T.C. 685 (1974), aff'd per curiam, 514 F.2d 1095 (7th Cir. 1975), the taxpayer sought to include amounts received from the state and federal governments (through Aid to Families with Dependent Children (AFDC) and medical assistance welfare payments) in computing support. The Tax Court focused on the purpose of the enabling legislation for welfare benefits and concluded that the primary purpose of the statutes was "to protect dependent children by payments to the parents or relatives with whom they reside." Id. at 689. Although the Tax Court acknowledged the parents' day-to-day freedom to apply such amounts, it concluded that the state, rather than the parent, should be viewed as providing the support attributable to those payments because the parents were ultimately accountable to the state for any improper use of the funds.

However, the United States Court of Appeals in Turecamo v. Commissioner, 554 F.2d 564 (2d Cir. 1977), held that Basic Medicare hospitalization benefits paid under the Social Security Act are not considered support provided by the Medicare beneficiary for the purpose of determining whether a related taxpayer can claim the Medicare beneficiary as a dependent. The taxpayers in *Turecamo* had been denied the dependency exemption by the Commissioner because the Medicare benefits were deemed to be support received by the dependent, and the taxpayers were held not to have provided more than one-half of that dependent's support. The Second Circuit, affirming the Tax Court, held that the "random and contingent receipt of insurance benefits, whether in form of private insurance proceeds or Basic Medicare benefits . . . , interrupts but does not alter the otherwise established economic relationship" between the dependent and the taxpayers, who regularly contributed to her support. Id. at 576.

> To deny taxpayers in the position of the Turecamos the right to claim as a dependent a relative like Mrs. Kavanaugh because her hospitalization costs were covered by government-sponsored . . . Basic Medicare insurance rather than privately obtained commercial hospitalization insurance would be to ignore the economic substance of . . . Medicare in deference to formal characteristics.

Id. Thus, the taxpayers were entitled to the dependency exemption. The IRS subsequently conceded the point, agreeing that Medicare payments were not to be considered support for these purposes. Rev. Rul. 79-173, 1979-1 C.B. 86.

Multiple support agreements. Section 152(c) permits a group of related taxpayers, none of whom individually has provided more than one-half of the dependent's support, to choose which member is entitled to the exemption if the group as a whole has provided more than one-half of the support. Thus, for example, four adult children, each contributing one-fourth of the support of a parent, could decide which of the four would be entitled to the exemption. Through such a procedure, the exemption would not be lost and each year the family members providing the support could assign the exemption among themselves.

Divorced parents. As divorce became a common phenomenon, the Service frequently faced the task of determining which divorced parent was entitled to the dependency deductions for the couple's children. In order to avoid excessive administrative burdens and multiple claimants, Congress enacted §152(e), which generally treats the custodial parent as the taxpayer entitled to the dependency exemption.

Dependency disqualifications. Section 152(b)(2) denies an exemption to a taxpayer for a dependent who, even if otherwise qualified, has filed a joint return with his or her spouse for the taxable year. The reasoning is relatively straightforward, since without this rule two personal exemption could be claimed on two different tax returns with respect to the same person.

Nevertheless, the Tax Court in Martino v. Commissioner, 71 T.C. 456 (1978), held that if a dependent files a joint return with his spouse in order to claim a refund for all *withheld tax*, the return is a claim for refund rather than a return for these purposes. In Martino, the taxpayers, parents of the husband, provided more than one-half of their daughter-in-law's support during the taxable year. The daughter-in-law, who had no income, signed a joint return with her husband claiming a refund for all income tax withheld from his earnings. The Tax Court held that the return was a claim for refund, and therefore, under Revenue Ruling 65-34, 1965-1 C.B. 86, the taxpayers were entitled to a dependency exemption for their daughter-in-law.

Problems

10-1. Harry Crews married Martha Stanley on December 29, year 1. On their wedding day, Harry and Martha opened a joint savings account with cash wedding gifts, which earned a few dollars in interest for year 1. Martha had been unemployed during the year. On April 16, year 2, Harry died. The next week, Martha found a job to support herself and met Melville Fishbein. Martha and Melville were married on December 20, year 2. How many personal exemptions is each party (Harry, Martha, and Melville) entitled to:

    a.   For year 1, if Martha and Harry file jointly? If they file separately?

    b.   For year 2, if Martha and Melville file jointly? If they file separately?

10-2. Karen Elaine is single and has been divorced for four years. How many dependency exemptions are available to Elaine considering the following information?

    a. For the past several years, she has continued to provide more than one-half of the support for her ex-husband's brother, Wigmore, a struggling young writer. During the year, Wigmore sold only one short story for $875.

    b. Mary, Elaine's foster daughter, for whom Elaine had contributed more than one-half of her support, died suddenly on November 8, just two weeks before her nineteenth birthday. Mary had earned $3,600 during the year.

    c. Elaine's other child, Eunice, is 20 years old and a full-time college student at Long Beach State. Eunice is married to Justin, also a student at Long Beach, where they live in student housing. Because Eunice and Justin earned only $700 from their summer jobs, Elaine contributed more than one-half of Eunice's support. Eunice and Justin, however, filed a joint return.

    d. A down-and-out character, Jonathan Hart, served as Elaine's handyman for the year in return for room and board.

10-3. How many dependency exemptions are available to Tom Reynolds, a 58-year-old divorced ceramic engineer, considering the following information?

    a. Muffy, his daughter, was an undergraduate student and Reynolds contributed $3,000 to her support. In addition to receiving financial help from her father, Muffy received $5,000 from her Grandmother Jasmine; she used half of this to pay tuition and the other half to pay for dancing lessons.

    b. Reynolds contributed $2,500 toward the support of his nephew, Nimrod, a 23-year-old college student. During the year, Nimrod received, and applied to his support, an athletic scholarship valued at $3,000 and $600 in tax-exempt interest income. He had no other income for the year.

    c. Reynolds's father, Oliver, an unemployed widower, lived with him. Reynolds, who owned his home, estimated its fair market rental value at $6,000 a year. During the year, Reynolds paid $800 for utilities, $2,000 in mortgage interest, $700 in real estate taxes, and $800 for maintenance and insurance. Oliver did not reimburse Reynolds for any of these expenses; however, he spent $3,500 of his own money on support.

    d. Reynolds's mother-in-law, Jasmine, had fallen on hard times, and he contributed $6,000 toward her support. Reynolds's brother-in-law, Max, gave Jasmine $5,000 and Max's son, William, gave her $1,000. This cash, combined with the $2,000 Jasmine spent from her savings account and the $3,000 of social security payments, which she received during the year, constituted her total support for the year.

10-4. David Blair sent $3,000 to his ex-wife, Hilda, for the support of his children, the triplets Napoleon, Nathaniel, and Montrose. David and Hilda provided the total support for the triplets during the year. Hilda had legal custody of the children, but the court decree did not specify whether Hilda or David was entitled to claim the exemptions. Who is entitled to an exemption for Napoleon, Nathaniel, and Montrose?

C. RATES AND RETURNS

1. Introduction

Over the years, Congress has adjusted tax rates to reflect various social and economic goals. Recent adjustments to the rate structure have focused on two issues: (1) bracket creep caused by inflation and (2) perceived inequities in the rate structure as it affects various taxing units. This section examines policy issues concerning the equitable nature of the rate schedules. These questions include whether it is inequitable to tax individuals more than couples in some cases and less than couples in others and the basic question of how high the tax rate ceiling should be. These issues present some of the toughest and most volatile contemporary tax policy questions. Additionally, this section examines the problems involved in determining which of the various rate schedules are available to a taxpaying unit and the advantages and disadvantages of choosing a particular schedule.

Each of the rate tables is divided into brackets of income that are taxed at progressively higher rates. Thus, as taxable income increases, the taxpayer may confront the higher tax bracket and a higher marginal tax rate. However, the higher rate applies only to *additional* income. Thus, the notion that additional earnings subject *all* income to a higher rate of tax is incorrect, although additional earnings will increase the average tax rate. Assume, for example, that a married couple files a joint return with $50,000 of taxable income, and that the applicable rate table is as follows:

If Taxable Income Is:	*The Tax Is:*
Not over $7,300	10% of taxable income
Over $7,300 but not over $29,700	$730 plus 15% of the excess over $7,300
Over $29,700 but not over $71,950	$4,090 plus 25% of the excess over $29,700
Over $71,950 but not over $150,150	$14,652 plus 28% of the excess over $71,950

The tax liability under this table is $9,165 ($4,090 plus 25 percent of $20,300, the excess income over $29,700), not $12,500 (25% of $50,000). Assume the following year the couple's taxable income is $55,000, and the same rate table is in effect. The amount of tax liability in year 2 is $10,415 ($4,090 plus 25 percent of $25,300), or an increase of $1,250. If the increase in the couple's income was due to cost of living raises attributable to inflation, they theoretically would not have improved their economic position; nevertheless, they would be moved into a higher tax bracket. This phenomenon is called *bracket creep*.

In response to bracket creep, Congress enacted §§1(f), 63(c)(4), and 151(d)(4) mandating cost of living adjustments to the rate tables, the personal exemption, and the standard deduction. As a result, new rate tables are published annually, with the inflation adjusted rates applicable for that year, making the numbers found in the §1 rate tables little more than historical.

2. Filing Status

Code: §§1(a) to (d); 2; 6013

As discussed in Chapter 2, the landmark case of Lucas v. Earl held that a contractual assignment of income between spouses was ineffective to shift income. *Earl* relied on the theory that each spouse was a separate taxpayer, who could not avoid treatment as separate taxpaying units through anticipatory assignments of income. Because each taxpayer was entitled to a separate calculation of his or her tax liability, the concern in *Earl* was that the spouses would take advantage of the progressive rate structure.

For example, assume a taxpayer has $100,000 of taxable income in year 1 and faces the same rate table as above. The taxpayer would owe tax of $14,652 plus 28 percent of $28,050 ($7,854), or a total of $22,506. However, if the taxpayer could assign half of the income to the taxpayer's spouse (who has no other income), the taxpayer would have taxable income of only $50,000 and a tax liability of $4,090 plus 25 percent of $20,300 ($5,075), or a total of $9,165. The spouse would also have income of $50,000 and a tax liability of $9,165, resulting in a total tax liability for the couple of $18,330—a tax savings of $4,176.

This savings arises from "income splitting" which exploits the low tax brackets in a progressive rate structure twice. The assignment of income doctrine as announced in *Earl* was intended to prevent married taxpayers from accomplishing this.

Soon after the holding in *Earl*, the Supreme Court visited a similar circumstance in Poe v. Seaborn, 282 U.S. 101 (1930), but reached a significantly different conclusion. The facts in *Poe* were similar to those in *Earl*, except that in *Poe* the taxpayers lived in a community property state where, as a matter of state law (as opposed to the contract in *Earl*), all assets and income of each spouse were considered income of the "community" (that is, to be shared equally between both spouses). The Supreme Court held that each spouse was considered to have earned half of the salary of the community for federal income tax purposes, regardless which spouse earned the money or exercised dominion and control over the money. In distinguishing *Earl*, the Court stated:

> In the *Earl* case a husband and wife contracted that any property they had or might thereafter acquire in any way, either by earnings (including salaries, fees, etc.), or any rights by contract or otherwise, "shall be treated and considered, and hereby is declared to be received, held, taken, and owned by us as joint tenants. . . ." We held that assuming the validity of the contract under local law, it still remained true that the husband's professional fees, earned in years subsequent to the date of the contract, were his individual income, "derived from salaries, wages, or compensation for personal service. . . ." The very assignment in that case was bottomed on the fact that the earnings would be the husband's property, else there would have been nothing on which [it] could operate. That case presents quite a different question from this, because here, by law, the earnings are never the property of the husband, but that of the community.

Id. at 117.

After the holdings in *Earl* and *Poe*, the tax treatment of a married couple effectively turned primarily on the law of the state in which they lived. — If the couple lived in a common law state, each spouse was considered a separate taxpayer under *Earl*, thereby *prohibiting* the splitting of income between the spouses. If, however, the couple lived in a community property state, *Poe* applied, *requiring* the equal splitting of income between the spouses.

Not surprisingly, this disparity led states to adopt community property laws solely for the associated federal income tax benefits. For example, Oklahoma enacted a law allowing couples to choose either common law or a community property marital regime. In Commissioner v. Harmon, 323 U.S. 44 (1944), the Supreme Court held that a taxpayer who had elected community property status under Oklahoma law was subject to *Earl* rather than *Poe*. In so ruling, the Court distinguished *Poe* by focusing on the spouses' ability to choose affirmatively to split their earnings by electing community property treatment, stating:

> We think it immaterial, for present purposes, that the community status may or may not be altered by contract between the parties, may or may not be avoided by ante-nuptial agreements, or that certain assets of a spouse may or may not be classed as "separate" property excluded from the community. The important fact is that the community system of Oklahoma is not a system, dictated by State policy, as an incident of matrimony.

Id. at 48.

As a result of *Earl*, *Poe*, and *Harmon*, not only did the tax treatment of married couples differ depending on the state in which the couple lived, but taxpayers also began to apply political pressure on the states to adopt strict community property laws solely for the associated federal income tax benefits.

In 1948, Congress responded by applying a uniform rule for married couples. It did so by enacting the predecessor of current §6013, which permits married couples to file a joint tax return, regardless of the applicable state law. Under the original 1948 joint return provisions, a married couple would file a single tax return and calculate joint tax liability as if half of the total income of the couple had been earned by a single taxpayer, then doubling that amount of tax. In effect, Congress adopted an equal income-splitting regime for married couples, effectively permitting a married taxpayer who was the sole wage earner to assign half of his or her income to his or her spouse.

Under this income-splitting approach, most married couples received favorable tax treatment over single taxpayers because, by filing a joint return, a married taxpayer could obtain the benefit of income splitting. This benefit eventually became known as the "marriage bonus." Since the entire problem arose due to differing state laws respecting the ownership of property and income by married couples, this was only available to taxpayers who were married.

In 1951, Congress responded to complaints of unfairness from unmarried taxpayers with "head of household" responsibilities (i.e., the obligation to support dependents) by enacting a separate tax schedule intended to be roughly halfway between the schedule applicable to single taxpayers without support obligations and the schedule applicable to married taxpayers. This measure was adopted because the support costs of a head of household were considered to reduce the taxpayer's ability to pay tax as compared to a single taxpayer who was not a head of household. Although this somewhat mitigated the marriage bonus, it still remained in place as between single taxpayers who were not a head of household and married taxpayers.

In 1969, Congress adopted what would eventually become the current versions of §§1(a), 1(b), 1(c), 1(d), and 6013. Under this revised §1, separate tax schedules were created to apply to married taxpayers, single head-of-household taxpayers, and single taxpayers who were not a head of household. In response to the complaints regarding the marriage bonus, the tax rates for single taxpayers who were not a head of household were set such that in no event would the "marriage bonus" exceed 20 percent. Thus, the joint tax return no longer represented a "pure" income-splitting approach, but rather represented a compromise in which joint returns were permitted for married couples (to avoid the pre-1948 problems arising under *Earl*, *Poe*, and *Harmon*) but where the resulting marriage bonus was mitigated by adjusting the tax schedule applicable to single taxpayers who were not a head of household.

As a result of these amendments, under §6013, a married couple is permitted (but not required) to file a joint tax return for the year in which the married couple jointly reports all of the income, gains, losses, deductions, and credits of both spouses on a single tax return. If they choose not do so, both spouses prepare and file separate tax returns reporting their income, gain, deduction, loss, or credit as if each spouse were a single taxpayer. If the married couple chooses to file a joint tax return, the couple will be subject to the tax rate table of §1(a). To prevent married taxpayers from strategically choosing to file separate returns, a separate tax rate schedule under §1(d) — and not the tax rate schedule under §1(c) applicable to single taxpayers who are not a head of household — applies to the separate tax return. The tax schedules of §1(d) are set to a level such that spouses filing separate returns would generally not achieve favorable tax results solely by filing separate tax returns. In this manner, Congress attempted to remove any incentive to assign income, gain, loss, or deductions between spouses filing separate returns. For married couples filing separately, the total tax liability would remain unchanged — or under certain circumstances be greater — than if the couple had simply filed a joint return. For married couples who keep separate books and records, however, this may nonetheless remain an attractive option.

As a result of the legislative amendments to §§1 and 6013, married taxpayers are no longer able to choose whether to split their income simply by living in a common law or community property state. This does not mean that it is unheard of for taxpayers to marry, divorce, or annul a marriage solely for federal income tax purposes. Although a taxpayer's marital status generally is determined under state law for purposes of §§1 and 6031, as discussed in more detail in the next section, a marriage, divorce, or annulment may be disregarded for tax purposes if the marriage or divorce is a "sham" and has no substance. See Rev. Rul. 76-255, 1976-2 C.B. 40.

Further, in 1996, Congress enacted the Defense of Marriage Act which defined marriage for federal purposes as solely between a man and a woman. This has led to an extreme amount of confusion in applying these rules in states which recognize same-sex marriage. For example, a same-sex married couple could be subject to a community property or other joint ownership regime under the laws of the state in which they are married, yet not be eligible to file a joint return since they are not married for purposes of federal law. Does this mean that such taxpayers should split their income in accordance with *Poe*?, Did the enactment of §6013 legislatively repeal *Poe*?

Recall that the *Poe* doctrine often resulted in significant tax benefits to couples with one market-based worker and one home-based worker because such couples were essentially permitted to split their income, notwithstanding the dictates of *Earl*. In fact, preventing this result was the entire point of enacting the joint return regime in the first place. Does the Defense of Marriage Act effectively permit same-sex married couples to split income under *Poe*? Upon what basis could this benefit be denied if such couples truly are not married for federal tax purposes? As the number of states recognizing same-sex marriage increases, the number of tax-payers facing this question will only continue to grow. Further, the constitutionality of the Defense of Marriage Act itself has come under increasing scrutiny, only further complicating the analysis.

Problems

10-5. Alvin Ericson and his wife, Margaret, have three children. Alvin's salary was $36,000. During the year, he paid $1,850 in state income taxes and $1,650 in property taxes. Margaret's income for the same year was $5,000 from dividends. She paid property taxes of $100 and state income taxes of $200.
   a. What is their tax liability?
   b. Should the Ericsons file jointly or separately?

10-6. Theo Blinker, age 49 and a widower, received income totaling $47,000. After Theo's wife died, three years earlier, Theo's 21-year-old son, Fred, whom Theo supported, moved into Theo's home in Phoenix. Fred was a full-time student and earned $7,000 during the summer. In addition to his house in Phoenix, Theo owned a condominium in Florida where he lived five months out of the year. Theo's daughter, Lizzy, a legal secretary, lived in the condo year-round, free of charge.
   What is Theo's rate table for the current year?

3. The Marriage Penalty

Code: §1(a), (c)

The tax burden on a single individual, determined under §1(c), is higher than that of a married couple that earns an identical amount of income and files a joint return. The policy rationale for this disparity is that a married couple incurs extra costs that are not encountered by a single individual. Nevertheless, a married couple with the same income (for example, $40,000) as two single individuals ($20,000 each) pays more income tax than the combined tax liability of the two single people. The additional tax incurred by married couples has been known as the "marriage penalty." In other words:

> Under present law, a married couple generally is treated as one tax unit which must pay tax on its total taxable income. Although couples may elect to file separate returns, the law is structured so that filing separate returns almost always results in a higher tax than filing joint returns. In addition, different tax rate schedules apply to single persons and to single heads of households. Along with other provisions of the law, these rate schedules give rise to a "marriage penalty" when persons with relatively equal incomes marry each other and a "marriage bonus" when persons with relatively unequal incomes marry each other.

S. Rep. No. 144, 97th Cong., 1st Sess. 29 (1981).

As an example, assume the following rate schedules:

Single (not head of household):

If Taxable Income Is:	*The Tax Is:*
Not over $22,100	15% of taxable income
Over $22,100 but not over $53,500	$3,315 plus 28% of the excess over $22,100
Over $53,500 but not over $115,000	$12,107 plus 31% of the excess over $53,500

Married filing jointly:

If Taxable Income Is:	*The Tax Is:*
Not over $36,900	15% of taxable income
Over $36,900 but not over $89,150	$5,535 plus 28% of the excess over $36,900
Over $89,150 but not over $140,000	$20,165 plus 31% of the excess over $89,150

If two unmarried taxpayers (Bill and Judy) each earn $70,000 and are in a long-term committed relationship, they each calculate their tax under the single (not head-of-household) rate structure. Under that rate table, each owes $12,107 plus 31 percent of $16,500 ($5,115), or a total of $17,222. Thus, Bill and Judy's total combined tax liability would be $34,444. If they were married, however, both Bill and Judy's income would be combined and subject to the tax rates for married filing jointly. Under that rate table, Bill and Judy would owe tax of $20,165 plus 31 percent of $50,850 ($15,763), or a total of $35,928. Thus, getting married would cost Bill and Judy an additional $1,484 in tax.

As the number of families with two wage earners increases, the marriage bonus occurs less frequently and the marriage penalty occurs more frequently. These inequities have led to increased challenges to the marriage penalty, both in court and in Congress. In response, in 2001 Congress enacted §1(f)(8), providing that the 15-percent tax bracket for married taxpayers would be double that of single taxpayers who are not a head of household (Congress also amended §63(c) at the same time to provide that the standard deduction for married taxpayers would be double that of single taxpayers who are not a head of household). Although these provisions mitigated the marriage penalty to an extent, both the marriage penalty and marriage bonus will remain a part of the Internal Revenue Code to some degree as long as progressive rate tables remain and individuals continue to be treated as the primary taxable unit. Interestingly, same-sex couples legally married under state law do not have to worry about the marriage penalty since they are not married for federal tax purposes, effectively providing a second federal tax benefit to same-sex marriage over opposite-sex marriage.

Consider the following cases, in which taxpayers in two different ways attempted to use the courts to challenge the marriage penalty. See also Rinehart v. Commissioner, T.C. Memo 2003-109 (Texas state annulment disregarded for federal tax purposes due, in part, to fraud perpetrated on Texas court and intent to continue to live as married couple).

DRUKER v. COMMISSIONER
697 F.2d 46 (2d Cir. 1982)

FRIENDLY, J. . . .

The principal issue on the taxpayers' appeal is the alleged unconstitutionality of the so-called "marriage penalty." The issue relates to the 1975 and 1976 income tax returns of James O. Druker and his wife Joan. During the tax years in question James was employed as a lawyer . . . and Joan was employed as a computer programmer. For each of the two years they filed separate income tax returns, checking the status box entitled "married filing separately." In computing their respective tax liabilities, however, they applied the rates in I.R.C. §1(c) for "Unmarried individuals" rather than the higher rates prescribed by §1(d) for "Married individuals filing separate returns." Prior to undertaking this course of action, James consulted with the United States Attorney for the Eastern District and with members of the Intelligence Division of the IRS, explaining that he and his wife wanted to challenge the constitutionality of the "marriage penalty" without incurring liability for fraud or willfulness. Following these conversations they filed their returns as described, attaching to each return a letter explaining that, although married, they were applying the tax tables for single persons because they believed that the "income tax structure unfairly discriminates against working married couples" in violation of the equal protection clause of the fourteenth amendment. The Tax Court rejected this constitutional challenge, sustaining the Commissioner's determination that the Drukers were subject to tax at the rates provided in §1(d) for married persons filing separately.

Determination of the proper method for federal taxation of the incomes of married and single persons has had a long and stormy history. From the beginning of the income tax in 1913 until 1948 each individual was taxed on his or her own income regardless of marital status. Thus, as a result of the progressive nature of the tax, two married couples with the same aggregate income would often have very different tax liabilities—larger if most of the income belonged to one spouse, smaller as their incomes tended toward equality. The decision in *Poe* v. Seaborn, 282 U.S. 101 (1930), that a wife was taxable on one-half of community income even if this was earned solely by the husband, introduced a further element of geographical inequality, since it gave married couples in community property states a large tax advantage over similarly situated married couples with the same aggregate income in common law states.

After *Poe* the tax status of a married couple in a community property state differed from that of a married couple in a common law state in two significant respects. First, each community property spouse paid the same tax as an unmarried person with one-half the aggregate community income, whereas each common law spouse paid the same tax as an unmarried person with the same individual income. Consequently, marriage usually reduced a couple's tax burden if they resided in a community property state but was a neutral tax event for couples in common law states. Second, in community property states all married couples with the same aggregate income paid the same tax, whereas in common law states a married couple's tax liability depended on the amount of income each spouse earned.

The decision in *Poe* touched off something of a stampede among common law states to introduce community property regimes and thereby qualify their residents for the privilege of income splitting. The Supreme Court's subsequent decision in Commissioner v. Harmon, 323 U.S. 44 (1944), that the income-splitting privileges did not extend to couples in states whose community property systems were elective, slowed but did not halt this movement. The result was considerable confusion and much upsetting of expectations founded on long experience under the common law. Congress responded in 1948 by extending the benefits of "income splitting" to residents of common law as well as community property states. Revenue Act of 1948. Pursuant to this Act, every married couple was permitted to file a joint return and pay twice the tax that a single individual would pay on one-half of their total income. This in effect taxed a married couple as if they were two single individuals each of whom earned half of the couple's combined income. The Act not only reduced the tax burden on married couples in common law states; it also ensured that all married couples with the same aggregate income paid the same tax regardless of the state in which they lived ("geographical uniformity") and regardless of the relative income contribution of each spouse ("horizontal equity").

While the 1948 Act was good news for married couples, it placed singles at a serious disadvantage. The tax liability of a single person was now sometimes as much as 41 percent greater than that of a married couple with the same income. Although constitutional challenges to the "singles' penalty" were uniformly rejected, the single taxpayer obtained some relief from Congress. The Tax Reform Act of 1969 increased the number of tax schedules from two to four; §1(a) for marrieds filing jointly; §1(b) for unmarried heads of households; §1(c) for unmarried individuals; and §1(d) for married individuals filing separately. The schedules were set so that a single persons's tax liability under §1(c) would never be more than 120 percent that of a married couple with the same income filing jointly under §1(a).

The 1969 reform spawned a new class of aggrieved taxpayers — the two wage-earner married couple whose combined tax burden, whether they chose to file jointly under §1(a) or separately under §1(d), was now greater than it would have been if they had remained single and filed under §1(c). It is this last phenomenon which has been characterized, in somewhat loaded fashion, as the "marriage penalty" or "marriage tax." . . .

[T]he Supreme Court made explicit in Zablocki v. Redhail, 434 U.S. 374 (1978), what had been implicit in earlier decisions, that the right to marry is "fundamental." The Court, however, citing Califano v. Jobst, 434 U.S. 47 (1977), took care to explain that it did "not mean to suggest that every state regulation which relates in any way to the incidents of or prerequisites for marriage must be subjected to rigorous scrutiny. To the contrary, reasonable regulations that do not significantly interfere with decisions to enter into the marital relationship may be legitimately imposed." 434 U.S. at 386. Whereas differences in race, religion, and political affiliation are almost always irrelevant for legislative purposes, "a distinction between married persons and unmarried persons is of a different character": *Jobst,* supra, 434 U.S. at 53. "Both tradition and common experience support the conclusion that marriage is an event which normally marks an important change in economic status." Id.

We do not doubt that the "marriage penalty" has some adverse effect on marriage; indeed, James Druker stated at argument that, having failed thus far in the courts, he and his wife had solved their tax problem by divorcing but continuing to live together. The adverse effect of the "marriage penalty," however, . . . is merely "indirect"; while it may to some extent weight the choice whether to marry, it leaves the ultimate decision to the individual. The tax rate structure of I.R.C. §1 places "no direct legal obstacle in the path of persons desiring to get married." *Zablocki,* supra, 434 U.S. at n.12. Nor is anyone "absolutely prevented" by it from getting married. Id. at 387. Moreover, the "marriage penalty" is most certainly not "an attempt to interfere with the individual's freedom [to marry]." *Jobst,* supra, 434 U.S. at 54. It would be altogether absurd to suppose that Congress, in fixing the rate schedules in 1969, had any invidious intent to discourage or penalize marriage—an estate enjoyed by the vast majority of its members. Indeed, as has been shown, the sole and express purpose of the 1969 reform was to provide some relief for the single taxpayer. Given this purpose Congress had either to abandon the principal of horizontal equity between married couples, a principle which had been established by the 1948 Act and the constitutionality of which has not been challenged, or to impose a "penalty" on some two-earner married couples. It was put to this hard choice because, as Professor Bittker has shown, . . . 27 Stan. L. Rev. at 1395-1396, 1429-1431, it is simply impossible to design a progessive tax regime in which all married couples of equal aggregate income are taxed equally and in which an individual's tax liability is unaffected by changes in marital status. See also Tax Treatment of Single Persons and Married Persons Where Both Spouses Are Working: Hearings Before the House Committee on Ways and Means, 92d Cong., 2d Sess. 78-79 (1972) (Statement of Edwin S. Cohen, Assistant Secretary for Tax Policy) ("No algebraic equation, no matter how sophisticated, can solve this dilemma. Both ends of a seesaw cannot be up at the same time."). . . . Faced with this choice, Congress in 1969 decided to hold fast to horizontal equity, even at the price of imposing a "penalty" on two-earner married couples like the Drukers. There is nothing in the equal protection clause that required a different choice. Since the objectives sought by the 1969 Act—the maintenance of horizontal equity and progressivity, and the reduction of the differential between single and married taxpayers—were clearly compelling, the tax rate schedules in I.R.C. §1 can survive even the "rigorous scrutiny" reserved by *Zablocki* for measures which "significantly interfere" with the right to marry. Clearly, the alternative favored by the Drukers, that married persons be permitted to file under §1(c) if they so wish, would entail the loss of horizontal equity.

In the area of family taxation every legislative disposition is "virtually fated to be both overinclusive and underinclusive when judged from one perspective or another." The result, as Professor Bittker has well said, is that there "can be no peace in this area, only an uneasy truce." 27 Stan. L. Rev. at 1443. Congress must be accorded wide latitude in striking the terms of that truce. The history we have reviewed makes clear that Congress has worked persistently to accommodate the competing interests and accomplish fairness. . . . [W]hat the Drukers choose to call the "marriage penalty" deprived them of no constitutional right. Whether policy considerations warrant a further narrowing of the gap between the schedules applied to married and unmarried persons is for Congress to determine in light of all the relevant legislative considerations.

[Judgment for appellee.]

BOYTER v. COMMISSIONER
668 F.2d 1382 (4th Cir. 1981)

WINTER, C.J.

Taxpayers (H. David Boyter and his sometime wife, Angela M. Boyter) . . . ask us to reverse the Tax Court and to rule that for the tax years 1975 and 1976 they successfully avoided the "marriage penalty" of the Internal Revenue Code. The "marriage penalty" results from the fact that a man and woman who are husband and wife on the last day of the taxable year, each having separate income, are taxed, in the aggregate, in a greater amount if they file either joint or separate income tax returns than would be the case if they were unmarried. The Tax Court ruled that the Boyters were legally married at the end of tax years 1975 and 1976, and therefore were subject to the higher tax rate, since their purported Haitian and Dominican Republic divorces . . . were invalid under the law of Maryland, the state of the Boyters' domicile. . . . In view of this conclusion the Tax Court apparently thought it unnecessary to decide the Commissioner's alternative argument that even if the divorces would be recognized in Maryland, the taxpayers should be treated as husband and wife for federal income tax purposes under the "sham" transaction doctrine.

Without expressing a view on the correctness of what was actually decided, we remand the case to the Tax Court for further findings as to the applicability of the sham transaction doctrine. . . .

[T]axpayers came to the realization that their combined federal income tax liability would be lower if they were able to report their respective incomes as unmarried individuals. They were also aware that the Internal Revenue Code provides that the determination of whether an individual is married shall be made as of the close of the taxable year.

Taxpayers thus concluded that if they obtained a divorce decree at the end of the taxable year . . . they would be entitled to file their returns as unmarried individuals. It seems clear, as the Tax Court found, that at least through 1976 taxpayers never intended to and never did physically separate from each other prior to or subsequent to either of the divorces that they obtained. Rather, they continued to reside together through the tax years in question. . . .

Late in 1975 taxpayers traveled to Haiti. Through an attorney, whose name they had obtained from a Baltimore public library and who in correspondence had quoted them an attractive estimate of his fee and expenses, they obtained a decree of divorce. The action was instituted by Angela Boyter and the divorce decree was granted on the ground of incompatibility of character notwithstanding that the parties occupied the same hotel room prior to and immediately after the granting of the decree. Moreover, Angela Boyter testified before the Tax Court that her character was not incompatible to that of David Boyter. She testified also that the sole reason for her obtaining the divorce was "because the tax laws as currently written caused us to pay a penalty for being married." Indeed she testified that she advised her Haitian counsel "that we got along quite well and planned to continue to live together. . . ." Shortly after the Haitian court granted the divorce, taxpayers returned to their matrimonial domicile in Maryland and were remarried in Howard County, Maryland on January 9, 1976. For the calendar year 1975 taxpayers filed separate income tax returns claiming the rates applicable to unmarried individuals. . . .

In November of 1976 taxpayers traveled to the Dominican Republic where David Boyter, as the moving party, obtained a divorce decree on November 22, 1976. Again the parties traveled together to and from the Dominican Republic. Whether they occupied the same hotel room is not shown by the record. The record does show, however, that although the Dominican decree was granted on the ground of "incompatibilities of temperaments existing between [the parties] that has made life together unbearable," Angela Boyter denied that she had ever said anything which would serve as a basis for such a finding by the Dominican Republic court. David Boyter testified before the Tax Court that he would not characterize the grounds as "totally" true. As he explained it: "I understood that these were strictly legalistic terms."

The taxpayers returned to Maryland to their matrimonial domicile and they were remarried on February 10, 1977. For calendar year 1976 they filed seprate federal income tax returns claiming the rates applicable to unmarried individuals. . . .

The Commissioner determined a deficiency in income taxes for each of the taxpayers for 1975 and 1976 and taxpayers sought review in the Tax Court. The Tax Court sustained the deficiencies. Although the government argued that the divorce decrees should be disregarded for federal income tax purposes because a year-end divorce whereby the parties intend to and do in fact remarry early in the next year is a sham transaction, the Tax Court expressed no view on this argument. Rather, it undertook an elaborate analysis of Maryland law with respect to the validity of the divorce decrees and concluded that Maryland would not recognize the foreign divorces as valid to terminate the marriage. On this basis, the Tax Court entered judgment for the government. . . .

We agree with the government's argument that under the Internal Revenue Code a federal court is bound by state law rather than federal law when attempting to construe marital status. The difficulty with this approach in this case, however, is that the Maryland authorities do not establish beyond peradventure of doubt that the two divorces with which we are concerned are invalid under Maryland law. . . .

In this ambiguous state of the Maryland law, we would ordinarily be disposed to invoke the certification procedure, and ask the Maryland Court of Appeals for a definitive pronouncement on the validity of these bilateral foreign migratory divorces.

But there are other factors which must be considered. The Commissioner has made it clear to us both in his brief and in oral argument that he intends to press the contention, advanced in the Tax Court but not decided by it, that under the sham transaction doctrine taxpayers must be treated as husband and wife in computing their federal income taxes for the years 1975 and 1976 even if Maryland recognizes the validity of their migratory foreign divorces. . . .

We think that certification is inappropriate here. Considerations of comity lead us to conclude that we ought not to request the Maryland Court of Appeals to answer a question of law unless and until it appears that the answer is dispositive of the federal litigation or is a necessary and inescapable ruling in the course of the litigation. . . .

We therefore turn to the question of whether in principle the sham transaction doctrine may be dispositive in this case. Although we hold that the doctrine may be applicable, we do not decide that the divorces in question are in fact shams.

The sham transaction doctrine has its genesis in Gregory v. Helvering, 293 U.S. 465 (1935). There, a taxpayer wished to effect the distribution to herself of stock of Monitor Securities Corporation, which was owned by United Mortgage Corporation of which she was the sole stockholder, without paying the tax which would apply to a direct transfer of Monitor's stock as a dividend from United. Strictly in accordance with the letter of the law, she sought to effect a tax-free reorganization of United whereby United transferred the Monitor stock to a new corporation, owned solely by taxpayer, and promptly liquidated the new corporation, distributing the stock to her. She then sold the stock, contending that she owed taxes only for the capital gain that she had realized.

The Court conceded that the reorganization was conducted in technical compliance with applicable statutes and that taxpayers are entitled to arrange their affairs so as to decrease their tax liability. It held nonetheless that the "whole undertaking . . . was in fact an elaborate and devious form of conveyance masquerading as a corporate reorganization" and should be disregarded for income tax purposes. 293 U.S. at 470. The Court relied on the fact that the transaction had no business or corporate purpose — that it was "a mere device which put on the form of a corporate reorganization as a disguise for concealing its real character, . . . the sole object of which was the consummation of a preconceived plan, not to reorganize a business, or any part of a business, but to transfer a parcel of corporate shares to [taxpayer]." Id. at 469. The Court concluded: "The rule which excludes from consideration the motive of tax avoidance is not pertinent to this situation, because the transaction upon its face lies outside the plain intent of the statute. To hold otherwise would be to exalt artifice above reality and to deprive the statutory provision in question of all serious purpose." Id. at 470.

Gregory has been subsequently invoked by the courts to disregard the form of a variety of business transactions and to apply the tax laws on the basis of the substance or economic reality of the transactions. . . .

In evaluating the substance of a transaction, the courts take care to examine the transaction as a whole, not as the sum of its component parts. . . .

Although the sham transaction doctrine has been applied primarily with respect to the tax consequences of commercial transactions, personal tax consequences have often served as the motive for those transactions. The principles involved, moreover, are fundamental to the system of income taxation in the United States and should be applicable generally. As Judge Learned Hand, the author of the *Gregory* opinion in the Court of Appeals, noted:

> The question always is whether the transaction under scrutiny is in fact what it appears to be in form; a marriage may be a joke; a contract may be intended only to deceive others; an agreement may have a collateral defeasance. In such cases the transaction as a whole is different from its appearance. True, it is always the intent that controls; and we need not for this occasion press the difference between intent and purpose. We may assume that purpose may be the touchstone, but the purpose which counts is one which defeats or contradicts the apparent transaction, not the purpose to escape taxation which the apparent, but not the whole, transaction would realize. . . .

Chisholm v. Commissioner, 79 F.2d 14, 15 (2d Cir. 1935). . . . Revenue Ruling 76-255, [1976-2 C.B. 40] applies the sham transaction doctrine to the divorce of taxpayers who promptly remarry. The underlying purpose of the transaction, viewed as a whole, is for the taxpayers to remain effectively married while avoiding the marriage penalty in the tax laws. It is the prompt remarriage that defeats the apparent divorce when assessing the taxpayers' liability, just as the prompt reincorporation of a business enterprise in continuous operation defeats the apparent liquidation of the predecessor corporation. Thus, the sham transaction doctrine may apply in this case if, as the record suggests, the parties intended merely to procure divorce papers rather than actually to effect a real dissolution of their marriage contract.

Having decided in principle that the sham transaction doctrine may apply to the conduct of the parties, we make no finding that the conduct in fact constituted a sham. In our view, the Tax Court as the trier of fact is the only body competent to make that determination in the first instance. . . .

4. Net Capital Gain Rate Differential

Code: §1(h)

In §1(h), Congress limits the maximum rate of tax on "net capital gain" as defined in §1222 for individuals. The rate varies for different categories of capital gain income, making it crucially important before applying the rate to identify any portion of net capital gain comprised of income subject to higher rates. For example, under current law collectibles income, including most investments in precious metals such as gold and silver, is subject to a tax rate of 28 percent, as compared to 15 percent for other long-term capital gains. §§1(h)(4)-(5), 408(m). Since 1993, the highest rate of tax on ordinary income has been roughly 20 percentage points higher than that applicable to long-term capital gains, although for a short period (between 1986 and 1990) the same rate applied to ordinary income and capital gain. As a result, a premium is placed on deriving capital gain rather than ordinary income.

In 2003, Congress enacted §1(h)(11), which provides that "qualified dividend income" would be eligible for the tax rate provided in §1(h) rather than the taxpayer's ordinary income rate. Qualified dividend income is generally any income from dividends of U.S. domestic corporations and certain foreign corporations. There are certain other requirements, regarding the length of time that the taxpayer must own the stock and whether the taxpayer has entered into any hedging transactions against the stock, for dividends to qualify for this preferential rate. These preferential rates were scheduled to expire in 2010 and again in 2012, and the future of qualified dividends remains unclear.

Section 1(h) applies preferential *rates* to net capital gains and qualified dividends, but it does not affect whether such amounts are included in §61 gross income. This can be important for a number of reasons, including calculating the alternative minimum tax. Perhaps most importantly, the effect of including capital gains and qualified dividends in gross income is to include them in adjusted gross income. Thus, capital gains are taken into account as part of a taxpayer's relative "wealth" in calculating the limitations on below-the-line deductions, such as the two-percent floor on miscellaneous itemized deductions of §67 and the cap on charitable deductions in §170. In other words, the treatment of capital gains (and qualified dividends) is deeply schizophrenic in the tax law: they are treated like any other form of income for purposes of measuring the relative wealth of taxpayers (measured by AGI) but effectively segregated from ordinary income for purposes of applying rates. Thus, great care should be taken with respect to capital gains and qualified dividends.

WEISS v. COMMISSIONER
129 T.C. No. 18 (2007)

THORNTON, JUDGE.

The sole issue for decision in this case is whether petitioners properly excluded qualified dividends in calculating their 2005 alternative minimum taxable income.

The parties have stipulated all the relevant facts, which we incorporate herein by this reference. On . . . their 2005 . . . Income Tax Return petitioners reported $24,376 of qualified dividends. They did not, however, include this amount in the $265,408 which they reported as taxable income and upon which they reported tax of $68,809. Instead, they separately computed $3,656 of tax on the qualified dividends (15 percent of $24,376), which they designated by handwritten notation as a "Qualified Dividend Tax" . . . adding this amount to the $68,609 of tax that they had computed on their reported taxable income, they reported total tax of $72,266.

Respondent treated petitioners' omission of their qualified dividends from taxable income as a "math error." After taking into account this and other "math errors," respondent determined that petitioners' taxable income was $315,532 rather than the $265,408 that they had reported. . . . [R]espondent also recomputed petitioner's [*sic*] alternative minimum tax. By statutory notice of deficiency, respondent determined that petitioners had a resulting deficiency of $6,073. . . .

Petitioners contend that they correctly reported their qualified dividends . . . and correctly calculated and paid tax on those qualified dividends at the rate of 15 percent. Petitioners contend that respondent erred in determining that the qualified dividends should be included in the calculation of their alternative minimum tax.

Petitioners are mistaken that qualified dividends may be disregarded in the calculation of alternative minimum tax. Alternative minimum tax is imposed, in addition to all other taxes imposed under [the Code], upon a taxpayer's . . . "taxable income" determined with [certain] adjustments. . . . The Code generally defines "taxable income" as "gross income" less allowable deductions. Section 61 expressly defines "gross income" to include, without limitation, "dividends."

. . . Contrary to what petitioners appear to believe, however, [the] special treatment [of qualified dividends] does not mean that qualified dividends may be disregarded altogether in calculating alternative minimum tax. Petitioners erroneously omitted their qualified dividends from gross income . . . which gave rise to a deficiency as determined in the statutory notice. . . .

Decision will be entered for respondent.

Problem

10-7.   Bernice Sandovol, a single taxpayer, has net capital gain of $20,000 from the disposition of an asset held for fourteen months. What is her tax liability for the year if her taxable income (inclusive of the capital gain) is $70,000?

5. Policy Issues

As the debate over tax rates and rate tables continues to this day, the issues regarding efficiency, equity, progressivity, and others tend to remain consistent. The excerpt that follows, from a Joint Committee study, discusses social and economic policies Congress considered in the Internal Revenue Act of 1986, which significantly reduced marginal tax rates as part of a broad tax reform package.

JOINT COMMITTEE ON TAXATION, ANALYSIS OF PROPOSALS RELATING TO COMPREHENSIVE TAX REFORM
9 (1984)

B.   Lowering Marginal Tax Rates

In all of the proposals, marginal tax rates are substantially reduced. This reduction appears to be motivated by efficiency and equity considerations.

EFFICIENCY

Many economists would agree that high marginal taxes can cause considerable economic inefficiency, both by interfering with the incentives for work and saving, and by magnifying the effects caused by differences between the tax base which may be chosen purely for efficiency reasons and the base which actually is implemented in the law.

An individual's marginal tax rate is the rate applicable to the last or to the next dollar of income received. If an individual is subject to a 25-percent marginal rate, then the return to additional work effort and saving is reduced by 25 percent. For example, if this individual is considering working on an overtime assignment which pays $40, then the after-tax reward to this work effort is $30. A higher marginal tax rate would reduce the return to this work effort even further, affecting the incentive to undertake the assignment. A similar point may be made with respect to investment decisions. If the individual with a 25-percent marginal rate invests in a security with a 10-percent return, the after-tax return would be 7.5 percent. Thus, the marginal tax rate affects the incentive to save rather than use the same resources for current consumption. The same reasoning may be used to show that marginal tax rates also influence the incentives to engage in activities which are heavily taxed versus those which are lightly taxed. With high marginal rates, for example, there is more incentive to invest in lightly taxed investments or to take jobs in which a high proportion of compensation is nontaxable than would be the case with low marginal rates.

EFFECT ON LABOR SUPPLY

The effect of changes in marginal tax rates in distorting incentives is sometimes referred to as the "substitution effect." Most of the studies which have been performed on the effect of after-tax wage rates on work effort have found that the substitution effect of after-tax wage changes in hours worked is quite small for husbands but rather large for wives, especially wives with children. Since the substitution effect is measured by holding after-tax income constant, this is the proper measure of the incentive effect of a marginal rate reduction, as opposed to the "income" effect which would occur because of the income increase attributable to any tax reduction. This empirical finding is confirmed in one of the more sophisticated studies, except that a significant substitution effect is found for husbands, as well as wives. Thus, these studies indicate that if marginal tax rates were lowered, holding other factors (including after-tax income) constant, some individuals would be willing to work a larger number of hours. This could be manifested as greater willingness to work full-time instead of part-time, greater acceptance of overtime assignments, less absenteeism, and a larger number of individuals in the labor force.[3]

It should also be noted that there are several other possible impacts of marginal tax rates on work-related activities. First, it has been argued that reduction in marginal tax rates could improve compliance with the income tax, although there is little evidence which bears directly on this question. Second, it has been argued that high marginal tax rates have induced employees to demand a larger portion of their compensation in the form of tax-free fringe benefits, such as health insurance, than would be the case with lower marginal rates, and this substitution of fringe benefits for cash may reduce the efficiency with which the economy satisfies

---

3. It should be noted that a tax proposal which raised after-tax income could have offsetting "income" effects because some individuals would respond to their additional income by taking more leisure time. Thus, the evidence of a significant substitution effect does not mean that a tax cut would necessarily increase labor supply, only that a cut in marginal tax rates offset by other changes in after-tax income would do so.

employees' needs. To the extent that such effects exist, they would be lessened if marginal tax rates were lowered.

EFFECT OF MARGINAL TAX RATES ON SAVING

If an individual saves a dollar rather than spending it on current consumption, he or she generally will be able to have in excess of one dollar available for consumption in a future period. The amount of this excess depends on the return available for funds saved and on the marginal tax rate applicable to this return. The quantity of consumer goods which can be purchased in the future with a given amount of money will depend on the rate of inflation. Thus, the after-tax return (adjusted for inflation) determines the extra future consumption that a person can have by saving and sacrificing one dollar of current consumption. The lower the after-tax return, the more attractive is the option to consume now rather than save. As an important determinant of the after-tax return, the marginal tax rate is likely to affect this choice.

As in the above analysis of work effort, it is important to distinguish between the income and substitution effects of marginal tax rate changes on the choice between current and future consumption. Any tax reduction, including a reduction in marginal rates, will increase after-tax income and thus generally will lead to an increase in both current and future consumption. However, as discussed above, marginal tax rate reductions also would have incentive, or substitution effects, because they change the rate at which the taxpayer can trade off between current and future consumption. This discussion emphasizes the substitution effects, which are unique to marginal tax rate reductions and which measure the economic inefficiency created by taxes.

Three distinct sources of concern with high marginal tax rates have been cited by economists who have analyzed the effects of the income tax on current and future consumption. The first concern is the effect of the marginal tax rates on individuals' incentives to consume in current rather than future periods; the second is the effect of marginal tax rates on aggregate saving, investment, and productivity; and the third involves the effect of the tax system on the composition of saving as a result of its effect on incentives to invest in lightly taxed versus heavily taxed activities. . . .

The fact that the marginal tax rates implicit in the current income tax discourage future consumption creates a distortion (relative to a tax system with a marginal rate of zero, such as a per capita head tax). The importance of this distortion depends on the responsiveness of future consumption to a change in the after-tax rate of return on saving, holding income constant. Empirical studies of this sensitivity are much less numerous than those of labor supply response. The methodological difficulties of studying the responsiveness of consumption to the rate of return are greater because the expected real return (net of expected inflation) must be measured and because the statistical analysis must be performed using time series of observations on total U.S. income and consumption. This methodology requires the assumption that the quantitative relationships among the variables have been unchanged for a long period of time. In spite of these methodological problems, some empirical studies do indicate that individuals' plans for future consumption are sensitive to the after-tax rate of return. The marginal tax rate on capital income also may affect the choice between labor and leisure, as well as the choice between present and future consumption. For example, a greater after-tax rate of return may make it more attractive for individuals to work and save for the purpose of increasing their consumption in retirement years. (Similarly, a higher after-tax return to work effort may also have this effect, establishing a connection between saving and the marginal tax rate on labor income.) However, this sort of effect has not been firmly substantiated in empirical research.

The second major concern which has been raised concerning the effect of marginal tax rates on capital income has been their effect on aggregate savings and, thus, investment and productivity. For a variety of reasons, however, the link between aggregate investment and the marginal tax rates in the individual income tax is very uncertain. First, investment may be affected much more directly by other factors, such as the tax treatment of depreciation allowances. Second, the effect of income tax changes on private savings could be offset to the extent that there is a revenue loss, which leads to less government saving. Finally, even though it is likely that a higher after-tax return may increase future consumption, it is not clear as a theoretical matter that personal savings would increase simultaneously. This is the case because a higher return on savings actually lowers the amount which an individual needs to save in the current period in order to achieve any future consumption goal. Personal saving would increase in response to an increase in the after-tax rate of return only if desired future consumption increases sufficiently to offset this effect. Whether this is, in fact, the case can be determined only by empirical studies. Although these studies are extremely difficult to perform for the reasons discussed above, there is some indication that future consumption may be stimulated sufficiently by increasing the after-tax return that total personal saving may increase modestly in response to such a change.

The income tax also influences decisions about the particular forms in which taxpayers do their saving, which affects the allocation of capital in the economy. The first concern is that the income tax imposes heavy tax rates on some activities and low or negative tax rates on others (e.g., tax shelters, owner-occupied housing, and precious metals). This provides an incentive to shift from the heavily taxed activities, which may be more productive, to lightly taxed activities. The size of this incentive depends on the marginal tax rate. Thus, it is argued, reducing the marginal tax rate may encourage individuals to shift from less productive to more productive forms of saving. . . . Finally, it is argued that because the income from assets subject to capital gains treatment is taxed only when the assets are sold, high marginal tax rates discourage sales and prevent these assets from being employed in their most efficient uses. Thus, lower marginal income tax rates could increase efficiency by reducing this "lock-in" effect.

The proposals . . . tend to take several approaches to improving saving incentives. Most of the proposals attempt to achieve greater uniformity in the tax treatment of saving and income from capital by reducing or eliminating preferential treatment for certain types of saving relative to others. Also, the proposals reduce marginal tax rates, which reduces the adverse impact of whatever distortions remain. Some of the bills, however, go farther than this and attempt to structure a system in which the effective tax rate on the income from saving is zero.

EQUITY

From an equity perspective, reducing marginal tax rates also may be viewed as desirable. Many argue that it is unfair for a high portion of each additional dollar of income earned by an individual to be absorbed as increased tax liability. In passing the Economic Recovery Tax Act of 1981, Congress lowered the highest marginal rate in the tax schedules from 70 percent to 50 percent. Much of the discussion of this change involved the belief that a marginal tax rate as high as 70 percent caused undue interference with the incentives for efficient economic performance. However, another important source of support for this reduction was the feeling that it was unfair for the tax system to claim more than half of each additional dollar earned by taxpayers. Presumably, this indicates that one accepted equity objective of tax policy is to keep marginal tax rates below some threshold level.

C. REDUCING THE PROGRESSIVITY OF THE RATE SCHEDULES

The authors of the proposals appear to believe that it is desirable to reduce significantly the number of tax brackets in the rate schedules and to reduce the difference between the bottom and top rates of the income tax. Some of the proposals have one flat tax rate that applies to all income not exempt from taxation.

It is important to emphasize that the issue of the degree of progressivity in the rate schedules is to some extent independent of the broad vertical equity issue of the relative distribution of tax burdens by income class. That is, the distribution of tax burdens is affected not only by the degree of progressivity in the rate schedules, but by other structural elements of the income tax as well. For example, during 1981 the Ways and Means Committee considered a proposal to reduce the number of brackets in the rate schedule, to widen the first bracket so that a majority of taxpayers were subject to the same tax rate, and to increase the personal exemption and [standard deduction] to offset the rate increases imposed on the lowest income taxpayers. These revised rate schedules produced approximately the same amount of progressivity as under prior law. Thus, some flattening of the rate schedule is possible even without large changes in the distribution of the tax burden.

There are several advantages to a flat or flattened rate schedule. For example, if taxpayers are more likely to be in the same tax bracket over a period of years, tax considerations would be less likely to influence the timing of transactions. This would reduce one of the sources of inefficiency of a progressive rate schedule. If most taxpayers faced the same tax rate, there would be less incentive to shift income to low bracket family members, which may improve the perception of equity in the system. The difference in tax treatment between married couples and single individuals would be reduced, since, in a system in which married couples may pool their income and file a joint return, this difference arises from the fact that the amount of income taxed at each rate depends on marital status. Finally, a flatter schedule of tax rates could allow a closer correspondence between amounts withheld and tax liability. In a system in which the tax rate did not depend on taxpayer's income, as is the case under the present social security payroll tax, withholding could be closer to tax liability in the vast majority of cases.[4] It should be emphasized

---

4. In 1982, there was about $63 billion of overwithholding and $29 billion of underwithholding. A change that eliminated most of the overwithholding, especially if it did not reduce the underwithholding significantly, could have major effects on budget receipts in the year it first took effect unless it were phased in.

that although some flattening is compatible with a progressive distribution of tax burdens, that is, a system in which tax liability as a percentage of income increases as income rises, adopting a rate schedule with just one rate would impose strict limits on the degree of progressivity which could be obtained. Some progressivity could be attained by exempting some fixed amount of income from taxation for all individuals, but the pattern of progressivity in the present system (discussed below) probably could not be duplicated.

D. CHANGING THE DISTRIBUTION OF TAX BURDENS BY INCOME CLASS

One of the central issues in analyzing an alternative proposal is the relationship of the tax burdens of taxpayers with different levels of income. Table [10-1] presents the average tax rate projected under present law for 1986. In preparing this table, taxpayers were put into categories according to their expanded income, a concept somewhat broader than the present definition of adjusted gross income. This is not a comprehensive definition of income, since it does not take account of many additional items which might be included in the tax base under alternative proposals or other possible changes in the measurement of income. In addition, it does not reflect the income and tax liability of the corporations in which individuals own shares. However, using expanded income probably provides a good indication of how progressive the system would appear if the tax base was more comprehensive.

As shown in Table [10-1], the present individual income tax system exhibits a substantial degree of progressivity. The average tax rate rises from 2 percent to about 25 percent in the highest class. The rate in the highest income class is approximately double the average tax rate of 12 percent.

Choosing a pattern of distribution by income class depends primarily on the vertical equity considerations discussed above. As noted before, this is largely a matter of value judgment. Some argue that the present distribution pattern should be preserved in any alternative proposal while others may believe that the present distribution is either too progressive or not progressive enough. In addition, efficiency may be a consideration in the selection of the distribution of tax burdens, because the relatively high marginal tax rates on higher income taxpayers necessary to achieve the desired distribution may result in a significant increase in the inefficiency caused by the system . . .

E. ACHIEVING SPECIFIED REVENUE TARGETS

One of the key decisions which must be made in analyzing or designing a comprehensive tax proposal is the choice of a revenue target. According to the most recently published estimates of the Congressional Budget Office and the Office of Management and Budget (February 1985), budget receipts on a current services basis for fiscal year 1985 will be about $735 billion, which is more than $200 billion short of the amount needed to finance outlays projected on a current services basis. The individual income tax and the corporate income tax — the principal subjects of comprehensive tax reform proposals . . . are expected to yield, respectively, 45 percent and 9 percent of total budget receipts. (Social insurance taxes and excise taxes are expected to yield about 36 percent and 5 percent, respectively, with customs duties, estate and gift taxes, and miscellaneous receipts completing the total.)

Clearly, if there is substantial base broadening with no changes in marginal tax rates, total revenue will be increased, and if marginal tax rates are lowered without changing the tax base, total revenue will be reduced. Several of the proposals appear to be designed so that the new combination of tax rates and tax base would produce approximately the same revenue as is expected under present law for a chosen fiscal year. However if a judgment is made that this level is either too low or too high base broadening and tax rate decisions can be adjusted accordingly.

BITTKER, EFFECTIVE TAX RATES: FACT OR FANCY?*
122 U. Pa. L. Rev. 780 (1974)

I. INTRODUCTION

For at least twenty-five years, tax commentators have pointed out that the Internal Revenue Code's rate schedules . . . are misleading. One source of confusion is the difference between the marginal rate applicable to a taxpayer's final dollar of taxable income and the average rate applicable to his taxable income as a whole. A married couple with $20,000 of taxable income, for example, is subject to a rate of 14 percent on their first $1,000 and to gradually increasing rates on additional increments to their income, until a rate of 28 percent is reached on their last $4,000 of taxable income. But their actual tax liability is $4,380, or about 22 percent of their taxable income of $20,000.

This difference between marginal and average rates is not the only source of confusion. Taxable income is the statutory tax base to which the statutory rates are applied, but it is not the only measure of the taxpayer's economic well-being. The couple just described, for example, may have received $25,000 of gross income from wages and investments, from which $5,000 was deducted to reflect their personal and dependency exemptions . . . leaving taxable income of $20,000. Expressed as a fraction of gross, rather than taxable income, their average rate of tax is only about 19 percent ($4,380/$25,000). A further inquiry into their financial affairs might disclose some economic benefits that were exempt from tax and hence omitted from their tax return, such as tax-exempt interest, a bequest, or the rental value of occupying their personal residence. If these exempt items were worth $10,000, the couple could be described as enjoying $35,000 of economic income. When their actual tax liability of $4,380 is computed in relation to this amount, the average rate drops to about 12.5 percent ($4,380/$35,000).

Another calculation that is sometimes of interest is the tax that would be payable if the statutory rates were applied to either the couple's gross income of $25,000 or their economic income of $35,000, rather than to the taxable income base ($20,000) that is actually specified by the Internal Revenue Code. This hypothetical liability is $6,020 if the statutory rates are applied to the alternative tax base

* The comparisons in the article are based on 1974 rates. Professor Bittker's conclusions, however, remain on point. — EDS.

of $25,000 and $9,920 if the alternative base is $35,000, resulting in hypothetical average rates of about 24 and 28 percent of these alternative bases. Finally, the same couple's aggregate federal, state and local tax burden may be estimated and expressed as a fraction of their taxable income, gross income, or economic income, resulting in an average rate of total taxes for each of these bases.

When the taxpayer's actual income tax liability is expressed as a fraction of a base other than taxable income, the resulting percentage is usually described as the "effective rate." This label can be applied, for example, to both the 19 percent and the 12.5 percent rates in the illustration above. In computing effective tax rates, the tax theorist's objective may be merely to describe the economic impact of the tax, but often such a computation is the predicate for a criticism of existing law and a proposal for change. . . .

There are, however, many different ways to compute effective tax rates, generating — despite occasional references to the "true" or "actual" rate — as many computations as there are commentators. . . .

These divergent calculations, which are only a small sample drawn from a large literature, share a common premise, viz, that the concept of "effective tax rates" is a useful tool of analysis. The purpose of this essay is to examine the validity of this basic assumption.

II.   THE MEASUREMENT OF EFFECTIVE TAX RATES

A.   THE EFFECT OF PROGRESSION

Throughout this discussion, we will be concerned only with average tax rates, not with marginal rates. . . .

This progression-induced gap between marginal and average rates is important, because journalists often confuse marginal and average rates, nourishing the illusion that a taxpayer whose last dollar is taxed at the rate of 50 percent incurs an overall tax liability of 50 percent of his entire taxable income. But the contrast between marginal and average rates, though central to the very concept of progression, is not the source of the "gap" with which tax theorists are concerned. . . . The marginal rates prescribed by current law are merely an abbreviated way to impose the desired average rates.

. . . We will be concerned exclusively with the fact that taxable income — the base used in the discussion above — is only one of numerous bases that can be plausibly used in computing the average rate of tax on a given taxpayer's income.

B.   NOMENCLATURE

Turning now to the competing ways of computing average tax rates, the best starting point is a formula for deriving the type of average rate just described:

FORMULA A

$$\text{Rate} = \frac{\text{actual tax liability}}{\text{statutory tax base (taxable income)}}$$

When applied to the married couple described at the beginning of this article, who incurred a tax liability of $4,380 on taxable income of $20,000, Formula A yields an average rate of about 22 percent.

$$\frac{\$4,380 \text{ (actual tax liability)}}{\$20,000 \text{ (taxable income)}} = 22\%$$

As we saw, however, some economic benefits received by this couple were excluded from their taxable income. If the average rate is to reflect these items, a different formula must be used:

FORMULA B

$$\text{Rate} = \frac{\text{actual tax liability}}{\text{alternative base}}$$

Depending on whether the alternative base used in applying Formula B to the couple is their gross income ($25,000) or their "economic income" ($35,000) the rate is 17.5 percent ($4,380/$25,000) or 12.5 percent ($4,380/$35,000). These two rates, however, do not exhaust the possibilities under Formula B. The composition of the alternative base used in Formula B depends on the preferences and judgments of the commentator, and every change in the way the base is defined will cause a change in the rate yielded by the formula. The alternative bases that have been used in computations of this type include "adjusted gross income," "amended adjusted gross income," "expanded adjusted gross income," "adjusted family income," "total income," "amended taxable income," and "amended gross income." Despite this smorgasbord of possibilities, it is common practice for each commentator to describe the rate resulting from applying Formula B to his preferred alternative base as "the" effective or actual rate. Of course, the more a commentator's alternative base differs from the Internal Revenue Code's definition of taxable income, the greater the disparity between the Formula A rate, which might be called the apparent rate, and the effective rate derived from Formula B. . . .

C.   ADJUSTED GROSS INCOME

Although almost every commentator employs a different alternative base in computing effective rates, the usual starting point is adjusted gross income (AGI), an amount that the theorist then expands or contracts in accordance with judgments that will be discussed shortly. Since AGI can thus be regarded as common ground, and moreover is sometimes used without change in the computation of effective tax rates, it deserves to be examined first. . . .

Since the taxpayer's AGI is always greater than his taxable income, the effective rate of tax is lower if computed as a percentage of AGI than if based on taxable income. The items deducted from AGI, such as the taxpayer's personal exemptions, are in effect taxed at a zero rate.

Because a taxpayer's AGI is ordinarily the amount available to him for personal expenditures, it is usually regarded as a better base for effective tax rate computations than taxable income. For a taxpayer at the bottom of the income ladder, however, a computation based on taxable income — the balance after personal exemptions and the low-income allowance have been deducted — may be more illuminating. Consider an urban family of four with AGI of $5,000, whose 1972 tax liability is $100. Expressed as a fraction of AGI, this liability is only 2 percent, but it is 14 percent of the family's taxable income of $700. Since the family's income is only about $800 above the urban poverty line, and a sizeable part of this margin must be paid to the Treasury, the statement that their effective tax rate is 14 percent ($100 tax on $700 of taxable income) may convey a more accurate picture of their financial sacrifice than the statement that they are taxed at only 2 percent ($100 tax on $5,000 of AGI). The expert can readily place either rate in proper context; but if a journalist or political orator describes one as "the" effective rate, he will imply that the tax either imposes a hardship on the family ("14 percent of income") or is trivial ("2 percent of income"). . . .

The choice between taxable income and AGI as a measure of the taxpayer's effective rate is further complicated by several technical aspects of AGI, which account for some of the striking examples recently offered of millionaires who pay no tax. Although AGI ordinarily reflects the taxpayer's disposable income after allowing for his business expenses and losses, it does not always do so. One of the much-publicized 106 taxpayers with AGI of $200,000 or more who paid no taxes in 1970, for example, reported $400,000 of gambling winnings and an offsetting loss of $400,000 from the same activity, with the result that his federal income tax liability was zero. Because the $400,000 of profit was included in his AGI while the loss was deducted "below the line" (i.e., deducted from AGI in computing taxable income), he appeared as a taxpayer with $400,000 of AGI and no tax liability. . . .

This statutory separation of income from its offsetting deductions is not unique to gambling, but extends to a number of other activities and transactions as well. According to the Treasury, 75 of the 106 nontaxable returns with AGI over $200,000 claimed very large deductions for interest and other investment expenses incurred in profit-oriented transactions. These were deducted "below the line," while the gross income derived from the same transactions entered into the taxpayer's AGI. When large amounts are involved, the unexplained use of AGI as a base in computing effective tax rates is misleading. . . .

Adjusted gross income, then, sometimes overstates the taxpayer's gain by failing to take account of expenses incurred in earning income. But this is neither its only, nor ordinarily its most important, deficiency as a base for computing effective tax rates. It can err in the opposite direction, understating the taxpayer's gain by omitting items that improve his economic position. This is because AGI is . . . computed after the exclusion or deduction of such perennial candidates for tax reform as exempt interest on state and municipal bonds, . . . as well as numerous less controversial receipts, such as . . . employer contributions to qualified pension and profit-sharing plans, and meals and lodging furnished to the taxpayer for the convenience of his employer. To take items like these into account in computing effective tax rates, it is necessary to construct a new base, corresponding to the taxpayer's "economic" or "true" income.

The new base may be created by taking the information now appearing on tax returns and putting it together in a different form. . . . To achieve a broader concept of "economic income," the analyst may revise the data on the returns by replacing statutory methods of computing income with methods that he deems more accurate, such as substituting straight-line depreciation for accelerated depreciation. . . . He may go further afield, by imputing receipts that the return itself does not report or even hint at, like tax-exempt interest and unrealized appreciation, and by adjusting for assumed errors by the taxpayer, employing a combination of statistical extrapolation, educated inferences and guesswork.

. . . When the tax liabilities imposed by existing law are expressed as percentages of this broad base, denominated "expanded adjusted gross income," the effective tax rates range from 0.5 percent on income under $3,000, to 32.1 percent on income of one million dollars and above. The top rate of 32.1 percent on this base compares with a top effective rate of 49 or 67.5 percent when taxable income or AGI, respectively, is used as the base. . . .

The Pechman-Okner effective rates would be lower if their comprehensive tax base had included unrealized appreciation, gifts and bequests, employer contributions to private pension plans, and some other items that they regard as embraced by an economic concept of income but that they excluded from their comprehensive base for reasons of administrative convenience or historical precedent. On the other hand, the Pechman-Okner rates would have been higher if they had preserved some of the present law's other exclusions, such as public assistance, . . . workmen's compensation, and social security; and the extra [deductions] for aged and blind taxpayers. . . .

Thus, whenever an effective rate of tax is computed not as a mathematical curiosity, but as the foundation of a normative conclusion about the tax system, the base — whether it is taxable income, adjusted gross income, or some variety of "economic income" — embodies a myriad of value judgments. These threshold judgments, often implicit rather than explicit, amount in the aggregate to an assertion that the components included in the base are relevant to taxpaying capacity, and that those excluded are not. It follows that the process of defining the base used in computing effective tax rates is comparable to the process of criticizing the Internal Revenue Code, and that there are as many effective rates as there are "ideal" Internal Revenue Codes. . . .

III.   Are the Statutory Rates Sacrosanct?

So far, we have been concerned primarily with comparisons between the effective rate on taxable income and the effective rate on the commentator's alternative nonstatutory base, in which both calculations employ the actual tax liability under existing law (Formula A and B above). But recent discussions often entail a second comparison — between the effective rate of actual tax on the proposed alternative base (Formula B) and the rate of the hypothetical tax liability that would result from applying the statutory rate schedule to the alternative base.

This comparison unveils a disparity between the "effective" and "nominal" rates whose width depends on how far the commentator travels from existing law; the greater his dissatisfaction with the Internal Revenue Code's concept of taxable income, the wider the gap. . . .

To escape the inconvenient fact that the entire Code, not just a few sections, was enacted by Congress, it may be argued that the rate structure—the 14 to 70 percent ladder and the average rate resulting from these marginal rates—embodies the General Will, but that all provisions narrowing the tax base reflect craven surrenders to special privilege. But this is not a promising way to analyze as complex a product of the political process as the Internal Revenue Code, whose major departures from a comprehensive tax base ("preferences") are tenaciously defended by an extraordinarily wide spectrum—"coalition" would not be a misnomer—of taxpayers. Among other defects, this approach treats such major components of the tax structure as income-splitting, . . . personal deductions and exemptions, accelerated depreciation, and the realization concept as though they were protuberances stealthily grafted onto the Code in a legislative twilight.

There are, of course, innumerable statutory excrescences that confer benefits exclusively on special interests in the narrowest sense. But these provisions, however objectionable, account for only a small part of the tax gap at issue. Its real causes are provisions like those listed above, and they are as prominent and persistent a part of the tax system as the rate schedule itself. . . .

IV. The Impact of Other Taxes

So far, we have been concerned with effective income tax rates, which take account of the personal income tax. . . . Because the effect of income taxes, whether progressive, proportional or regressive, can be reinforced or counterbalanced by state, local and other federal taxes, tax scholars have sought to measure the aggregate effective rate of all taxes, using the taxpayer's income as the base. Since the taxes that are to be brought into the consolidated formula are not based on the taxpayer's income but on a wide variety of other events and transactions, they must somehow be allocated among taxpayers by reference to income, rather than according to the taxpayer's participation in the activity generating the particular tax liability. . . .

The allocation to taxpayers at each income level of taxes that are deductible in computing federal taxable income can be based either on the deductions actually taken by them or, in the case of taxpayers who [do not itemize], on inferences from the amounts deducted by itemizers. More debatable inferences are required to allocate by income classes such nondeductible taxes as federal excises and federal and state death taxes, and the process becomes even more attenuated if taxes are to be allocated to persons who do not pay the tax but who bear its economic burden. Corporate income taxes, for example, eventually fall on natural persons, but economists are not agreed on whether the burden is borne by the shareholders of the corporations paying the tax, or is shifted to consumers, employees and suppliers, or investors generally. The effective rate of federal and state corporation income taxes is very sensitive to the choice among these assumptions. According to one study, for example, the effective rate for taxpayers with adjusted family income of one million dollars and over is 40 percent if the tax is allocated to shareholders, but only 19 percent if it is allocated among all investors; and the rate would be still lower if the tax was treated as shifted to consumers.

Although these computations of effective consolidated tax rates invariably assume that some taxes are passed on by the nominal taxpayers to purchasers of their goods and services and that the latter should be viewed as the real taxpayers, the contrary assumption — that the economic burden of the tax remains on the taxpayer who is required by law to pay it — is universally employed in determining who pays the personal income tax. This assumption is based on the theory that a taxpayer cannot charge more for his goods and services than those of his competitors who pay no income tax because they are operating at the break-even point, and who therefore fix their prices without regard to income taxes. The theory that income taxes are not business expenses that can, or must, be passed on to purchasers of the taxpayer's goods and services is buttressed by the theory that the prices that will maximize a taxpayer's profits before income tax will also maximize his post-tax profits. Thus, the enactment of an income tax, or an increase in the rates of an existing tax, provides neither an incentive nor an opportunity to increase prices; if there had been any slack in the market, the taxpayer would have already increased his prices to absorb it. . . .

The computation of effective tax rates is complicated still further by the fact that income taxes alter the relationship between work and leisure for taxpayers engaged in the performance of services. The taxpayer derives a lower net yield from his work, while the pleasures of leisure are unchanged. By itself, this decrease in the relative value of work would impel him to substitute leisure for labor. This "substitution" or "price" effect of the tax, however, runs counter to its "income" effect, since to regain his pre-existing level of disposable income, he will have to work harder. The income effect of the tax may be more powerful than its substitution effect for taxpayers at some income levels, and less powerful at others; and it would be astonishing if the point where they come into equilibrium was not affected by the taxpayer's age, sex, marital status, education, religion and philosophical outlook. If these variables are not distributed on a random basis among taxpayers, but are linked with occupational choices, the work-leisure impact of income taxation may alter the prices of goods and services offered on the market, and thus affect pre-tax incomes. . . .

VII.   ALLOCATION OF GOVERNMENTAL EXPENDITURES

The fairness of a tax system cannot be judged without taking account of the governmental benefits it makes possible. From an ethical perspective a tax levied to finance welfare payments is not the same as an identical tax to build a municipal polo field. Thus, a computation of effective tax rates is ethically neutral, when viewed in isolation; what counts is *fiscal*, rather than *tax*, fairness. Recognizing this, economists and other social analysts have endeavored to allocate the benefits of public expenditures to the citizenry, classified by income class. The objective is a distribution of both benefits and burdens, permitting each income group's benefits to be compared with its taxes in a consolidated display of the global incidence of the nation's fiscal system.

But any such allocation of governmental benefits encounters a familiar problem in political economy — the absence of a free market to establish the citizen's own evaluation of benefits he derives from governmental expenditures. Without a toll gate to exclude freeloaders from public education, highways, or other social goods and services, we do not know what any citizen or group of citizens would have been willing to pay for these benefits, or how much they have consumed. . . . [A]nalysts who allocate governmental expenditures by income class must choose from a range of plausible assumptions that is unfortunately even broader than the spectrum used to allocate the tax burden. . . .

VIII. Conclusion

Judgments about equity in the tax system ultimately depend on deep-seated political and philosophical convictions, which in turn are linked in a complex fashion with economic interests. The most that can be expected of the tax analyst is a description of the way the tax burden is allocated among income or other relevant classes. The analyst's role begins with a recognition that the statutory rate schedule tells us little about the actual distribution of the tax burden. . . . As we explored the techniques used by the analyst to compare the nominal and effective tax rates, however, it became painfully clear that no table or graph is better than its footnotes, and that the footnotes are almost always replete with debatable assumptions. As a result, the existence of a gap between the nominal and effective rates is a neutral bit of information, which should lead to a value judgment only if the hypothetical base used by the analyst in computing the effective rates is regarded by the informed citizen as preferable to the statutory tax base to which the nominal rates are applied. Even then, a gap that would be offensive if judged solely by the citizen's equity criterion may be salvaged if, in his view, it advances a social or economic objective that he prizes, such as low-cost housing, pollution control or economic growth.

A careful reading of the footnotes to a table of tax burdens will do more than expose its threshold assumptions. It will also disclose other reasons why the naked statistics may be a deficient foundation for policy recommendations. First, the statistics rarely if ever reflect the troublesome fact that pre-tax income is affected in real but obscure ways by the tax system. It is misleading, for example, to portray tax-exempt interest as subject to a zero effective rate if the yield on state and municipal bonds is lower than the yield on taxable securities of comparable quality. For policy purposes, it would often be more realistic to regard the investor as subject to an implicit tax; and the fact that it is difficult to estimate the appropriate amount does not improve the quality of tax-burden computations that treat it as zero, but rather illustrates one of their deficiencies. Of more global significance, and even more difficult to assess, is the fact that the pre-tax income of all taxpayers is affected by the tax system, but that their ability to shift the burden may vary with their income level, occupation, age and other characteristics. Judgments about equity would be badly undermined if it turned out that the tax burden of substantial groups of taxpayers have been neutralized — or accentuated — by changes in their pre-tax income. This possibility may be minimized by neoclassical economic theory, but it cannot be excluded. . . .

Finally, an ethical judgment about the tax burden can hardly disregard governmental expenditures financed by the tax system in question. One wants to know who benefits before deciding who should pay. Here again, however, the analyst can supply a framework, but the statistics inserted in it depend on the premises; and the wide range of plausible alternatives can lead to widely divergent social judgments about the combined effect of taxes and governmental expenditures.

D. TAX CREDITS

1. Introduction

Congress has authorized tax credits for a variety of social and economic reasons, and, as a result, they span a wide range of activities. Tax credits covered in this casebook fall into two categories: (1) those intended to further public policy goals (such as the child care credit) and (2) those intended to fulfill income maintenance purposes (such as the earned income credit).

Although the activities covered by tax credits are similar to those covered by deductions, credits differ from deductions in their impact on tax liability and in economic value. In terms of mechanics, deductions reduce gross income to taxable income, thus only indirectly reducing tax liability. Credits, on the other hand, directly reduce tax liability - every dollar of credit reduces tax liability by one dollar. Thus, once a taxpayer has determined gross tax liability under the appropriate rate table, the taxpayer can subtract any qualifying tax credits in determining the net tax owed.

Credits, therefore, are economically more valuable than an equivalent nominal amount of deductions. This is because the economic value of deductions is based on the amount of the deduction and the marginal tax rate, whereas the value of credits is based solely on the amount of the credit. For example, if two taxpayers, one in the 10-percent marginal tax bracket and the other in the 40-percent bracket, both have $10,000 in deductible business expenses, the former will save only $1,000 in taxes, while the latter will save $4,000. For every dollar spent on the deduction, the first taxpayer would have paid only 10 cents in tax without the benefit of the deduction, while the second would have paid 40 cents. In this sense, deductions are "upside down" and thus less useful than credits for policies such as income redistribution. In contrast, the economic value of a tax credit is not dependent on the taxpayer's marginal tax bracket. Consequently, many commentators assert that tax credits are more equitable than deductions.

Conceptually, because tax credits reduce tax liability dollar-for-dollar, they are valuable only to the extent that a taxpayer incurs a tax liability that he or she otherwise would have had to pay. This limits the usefulness of the credit for income redistribution and other poverty relief policies embodied in the Internal Revenue Code, precisely because it is the poorest taxpayers who likely owe little, if any, income tax. Thus, absent some other factor, tax credits would be worthless precisely to those they are often intended to help. To address this, some tax credits are "refundable"—a form of negative income tax. Assume a taxpayer with $10,000 of taxable income in the 10-percent tax bracket, who is entitled to a $1,500 tax credit. Because the total tax liability owed before credits is $1,000, the taxpayer will use $1,000 of credit to offset the tax liability and have $500 of unused credit. If the credit was not refundable, the $500 of unused credit would be worthless. If the credit was refundable, however, not only would the taxpayer not owe any income tax, but the government would "refund" — or write a check for — $500 to the taxpayer. Refundable tax credits are potentially powerful tools for income redistribution and other social policy goals. At times, however, they have been criticized as an inappropriate part of the income tax, as opposed to direct government assistance programs, since they are unrelated to calculating federal income tax liability.

2. Dependent Care Credit

Code: §21
Regulations: §1.21-1

Prior to 1971, child care expenses, even though necessary to enable a taxpayer to be gainfully employed, were classified as nondeductible, personal expenses. Thus, no distinction was drawn between business-related and purely personal child care expenses. Swelling numbers of taxpayers living in single parent or two-earner families, and thus incurring child-care expenses just to permit parents to go to work, led Congress to formulate relief, first in the form of a deduction in 1971 and finally, in 1976, through the credit mechanism. The social and economic policies underlying the credit are reflected in the Senate Finance Committee Report:

> [F]amilies with one working adult or families with two adults where the income level is such that both must obtain employment and there is a child (or incapacitated dependent) in the home, need help not only with respect to child (and incapacitated dependent) care expenses but also for household help that they must obtain in order to be gainfully employed. . . . At the same time, the committee believes that it is desirable to provide employment opportunities for persons presently having difficulty in this respect. Still a further reason for encouraging expenses for household help in the case of an incapacitated dependent (or spouse) is that the committee believes that to the extent possible it is desirable to make provisions for the care of incapacitated dependents in the home rather than in institutions outside of the home.

S. Rep. No. 437, 92d Cong., 1st Sess. 59 (1971).

Taxpayers are eligible to claim the credit with respect to a dependent (as defined in section 152(a)(1)) who has not attained age 13, a dependent (as defined in section 152, without regard to subsections (b)(1), (b)(2), and (d)(1)(B)) who is physically or mentally incapable of caring for himself or herself and who has the same principal place of abode for more than one-half of such taxable year, or the spouse of the taxpayer, if the spouse is physically or mentally incapable of caring for himself or herself and who has the same principal place of abode as the taxpayer for more than one-half of such taxable year.

Once a taxpayer has established entitlement to the child care credit, the applicable percentage must be calculated. In general, the applicable percentage is equal to 35 percent. Like a number of other provisions, however, the applicable percentage "phases out" as the taxpayer's adjusted gross income increases, but not below 20 percent. As with other phaseouts, the amount of gross income at which to begin the phaseout and how quickly to reduce the applicable percentage changes over time as Congress revisits the issue. Regardless, some form of phaseout remains a fundamental feature of the child care credit applicable percentage.

The employment-related expenses on which the tax credit is based include costs incurred for the care of a qualifying individual and household services but are limited to a maximum of $3,000 if there is one qualifying individual and $6,000 if there are two or more.

For example, assume the phaseout begins at $15,000 of adjusted gross income and is reduced by 1 percent for each $2,000 of excess, and that a taxpayer has one qualified dependent, an adjusted gross income of $33,000, and $4,000 of qualified expenses. The applicable percentage would be equal to 26 percent (35 percent minus 9 percent), since the taxpayer's adjusted gross income exceeds $15,000 by $18,000 (or nine increments of $2,000). Further, the qualified expenses of $4,000 would be capped at $3,000 since there is only one qualified dependent. Thus, the taxpayer would be entitled to a child care credit of $780 (26 percent of $3,000).

Problem

10-8. George Edwards and his wife, Sally, are both full-time employees. During the year Sally's sister, Vanessa, took care of their children, Taylor, age 15, and Tracy, age 5. The Edwards paid Vanessa $750 a month to take care of Tracy all day, to clean house, and to look after Taylor when she returned home from school. In June, July, and August, however, Vanessa did not have to concern herself with Taylor because she was away at day camp from 8 A.M. until 5 P.M. Day camp tuition was $500 per month. Assuming that George's adjusted gross income for the year was $32,000 and Sally's was $17,000, what, if any, child care credit is available?

3.   Child Tax Credit

Code: §24

In addition to the child care credit, which requires a taxpayer to incur qualified child care expenses, Congress in 1997 enacted the child tax credit, which grants a credit for each "qualifying child" for purposes of §152(c) who has not attained age 17. The child tax credit is available in addition to, and not instead of, the dependent child personal exemption. The credit is in a fixed amount, set at $1,000 per child in the statute but which has been temporarily adjusted by Congress multiple times.

As in other instances, the amount of the credit phases out as adjusted gross income increases. Unlike the child care credit, however, the phaseouts for the child tax credit generally begin to apply at higher levels of adjusted gross income. For example, at times the credit has been reduced by $50 (but not below zero) for each $1,000 increment the AGI of married taxpayers filing jointly exceeds $110,000. The child tax credit has at times been nonrefundable and at times been partially refundable, but only as income increases. Making a portion of the child tax credit refundable is intended to address certain perceived distributional unfairness arising from phaseouts of other benefits, but of course adds another level of complexity to its calculation. Also, no credit is allowed unless the taxpayer includes the name and taxpayer identification number of the qualifying child on the tax return for the taxable year.

Problem

10-9.   Art and Betty Howe earn $60,000 each for the year, and have two daughters, Thelma and Louise, whom they support. If Art and Betty file a joint return, what is the amount of the child tax credit available to them?

4. Earned Income Credit

Code: §32

The earned income credit is a tax benefit directed at low-income taxpayers. Its overall effect is to increase the amount that can be earned tax free by those with minimal income, thus increasing the portion of the low-income taxpayer's after-tax wages that are available for the necessities of life.

Originally enacted in 1975, the earned income credit has been amended to account for the effects of inflation and to foreclose certain abuses that contravened the credit's purpose. As the following excerpt explains, Congress hoped to lessen the demand for welfare assistance by providing the credit to offset the tax burdens of low-income individuals.

> [T]he earned income credit is an effective way to provide relief from the social security and income tax burdens of low-income working families and thus to lessen the need for supporting such families through large welfare payments. . . .
>   Because the purpose of the credit has been in part to offset social security taxes, and, thus, to provide a work incentive, the Congress believed it appropriate to increase the amount of the credit to take into account increases in social security taxes. . . . Thus, the Congress decided that the rate of the credit should be increased. . . . In addition, in order to provide some compensation for inflation . . . , the Congress decided to raise the income level at which the credit begins to be phased out. . . .

Joint Committee on Taxation, General Explanation of the Revenue Provisions of the Deficit Reduction Act of 1984, pp. 1160 (1985).

Section 32 allows an eligible individual a refundable credit for earned income against federal income taxes. An eligible individual is broadly defined in §32(c)(3).

The amount of the earned income tax credit (EITC) depends on whether the taxpayer has any qualifying children, and if so how many. This is because the applicable earned income limits, phaseouts, and credit rates vary depending on whether the taxpayer has no, one, or two or more qualifying children. In general, qualifying children include the child of the taxpayer; a descendant of a child; a brother, sister, stepbrother, or stepsister of the taxpayer; or a descendant of a brother, sister, stepbrother, or stepsister, but only if they share a home with the taxpayer for more than half the taxable year and are either under 19 at the end of the year or under 24 and a full-time student at the end of the year. Regardless of the number of children and the applicable limits, the basic EITC calculations are: first, the taxpayer calculates his or her "earned income" amount; second, the taxpayer calculates his or her applicable credit percentage; and third, the taxpayer determines whether the phaseout provisions apply.

For taxpayers with two or more qualifying children, the statutory earned income amount is $8,890 and the qualifying credit is 40 percent, while for a taxpayer with one qualifying child, the statutory earned income amount is $6,330 and the qualifying credit is 34 percent. For a taxpayer with no qualifying children, the amounts are reduced substantially — the statutory earned income amount is $4,220 and the applicable percentage is 7.65 percent. The statutory earned income amount is adjusted annually for inflation, and the actual earned income amounts for each year are published by the Service. Similarly, the credit is phased out at different amounts for taxpayers with two or more qualifying children, one qualifying child, and no qualifying children. Thus, the statutory phaseout amount for taxpayers without qualifying children is $5,280 and for all others is $11,610 (although this amount has been higher in certain years for married taxpayers filing jointly as part of the marriage penalty relief provisions discussed earlier in this chapter).

Thus, for example, applying the statutory rates, a taxpayer with two qualifying children and earned income of $8,000 is entitled to an earned income tax credit of $3,200 (40 percent of the total earned income, since it is less than the earned income amount), while a taxpayer with the same earned income but only one qualifying child is entitled to an earned income tax credit of approximately $2,152 (34 percent of the maximum earned income amount of $6,330).

As becomes clear from these examples, whether a taxpayer has qualifying children can significantly affect the availability and amount of the earned income tax credit. In addition, calculating the amount of earned income can also significantly affect the analysis. Under §32(b)(2), earned income is not necessarily the same as §61 gross income. Rather, earned income can include a number of items of income that are excluded from gross income. See, e.g., Neff v. United States, 43 Fed. Cl. 659 (1999) (military housing included in earned income even though excluded from gross income). Similarly, items of income that in common parlance might not be thought of as "earned" — such as gambling winnings — are included in earned income. See Petty v. Commissioner, T.C. Memo 2004-144. Some items of income are explicitly excluded from the definition of earned income by statute, however, including pension and annuity payments and salary received by inmates in penal institutions. Thus, for example, an inmate who is paid for providing services to the institution but has no other source of income will have no earned income, and thus will not qualify for the earned income tax credit. See Rogers v. Commisioner, T.C. Memo 2004-245.

One of the primary features of the EITC is that it is refundable. This makes sense, since the EITC is intended to assist precisely those who are most likely to owe little to nothing in federal income tax since it is intended to serve as a cash sup-plement to the "working poor." The refundable nature has also raised a significant concern regarding potential abuse of the EITC, however. Among the concerns include ineligible taxpayers claiming the EITC, taxpayers falsifying the existence of qualifying children to be eligible for a greater EITC, and taxpayers attempting to claim unearned income as earned income. For these reasons, the EITC is one of the most scrutinized income tax provisions by the Service, and taxpayers claiming the EITC are subject to one of the highest audit rates in the United States.

Conversely, the overwhelming complexity of the EITC makes it difficult for taxpayers who are eligible for the EITC to claim it without retaining a tax advisor, the costs of which often absorb a substantial amount of the EITC benefit. These concerns continue to plague the EITC; for example, the National Taxpayer Advo-cate has devoted significant time and resources analyzing compliance, abuse, audit, and eligibility issues for the EITC. See National Taxpayer Advocate, 2005 Annual Report to Congress at 94 (Dec. 31, 2005).

Problem

10-10. Thelma and Bill Pippin are married with six children. Thelma earned a $9,000 salary and Bill earned $5,000. Their only deductions are $300 in state income taxes for Thelma and $100 for Bill. Three of the children held part-time jobs during the year, but none earned more than $500.
    a. Are the Pippins entitled to the earned income credit and, if so, in what amount?
    b. Should the Pippins file jointly or separately?

E. ALTERNATIVE MINIMUM TAX

Code: §§55; 56(a), (b), (d), (e); (skim §§57, 58)

By granting tax preferences, Congress seeks to encourage certain types of behavior to achieve social or economic policy goals. Although tax preferences are defended on policy grounds, critics focus on the fact that some taxpayers can combine multiple tax preferences in such a way to reduce their tax liability to zero or a negligible amount. Specifically, it often appears that many high-income taxpayers could avoid paying taxes by exploiting these various provisions, while middle-income and low-income individuals who cannot do so must pay a higher percentage of their income in tax. As illustrated in the following legislative history, the alternative minimum tax (AMT) attempts to prevent this inequity by ensuring that those with substantial gross income pay some income tax.

> The committee has amended the present minimum tax provisions applying to indi-viduals with one overriding objective: no taxpayer with substantial economic income should be able to avoid all tax liability by using exclusions, deductions and credits. Although these provisions provide incentives for worthy goals, they become

counterproductive when individuals are allowed to use them to avoid virtually all tax liability. The ability of high-income individuals to pay little or no tax undermines respect for the entire tax system and, thus, for the incentive provisions themselves. Therefore, the committee has provided an alternative minimum tax which is intended to insure that, when an individual's ability to pay taxes is measured by a broad-based concept of income, . . . tax liability is at least a minimum percentage of that broad measure.

S. Rep. No. 494, 97th Cong., 2d Sess. 108 (1982).

Although the AMT was intended to prevent a limited number of wealthy taxpayers from avoiding the income tax altogether, it adopted a complex and confusing mechanism to do so. In addition, the scope of the AMT has far exceeded its original intent. Ironically, due to the recondite operations of these rules, the number of taxpayers affected by the AMT actually grows as marginal tax rates under §1 are reduced. For these reasons, the AMT has caused much consternation among taxpayers, tax policy makers, commentators, academics, and the media.

NATIONAL TAXPAYER ADVOCATE
2006 ANNUAL REPORT TO CONGRESS
3-5

The most serious problem facing taxpayers today is the complexity of the Internal Revenue Code. In this report, we are choosing to shine our primary spotlight on the poster child for tax-law complexity — the Alternative Minimum Tax for individuals (AMT).

The AMT is a parallel and complex tax structure that is imposed on top of the regular tax structure. While the AMT was originally designed to prevent wealthy taxpayers from escaping tax liability through the use of tax-avoidance transactions, it now affects large groups of middle-class taxpayers with no tax-avoidance motives at all.

Significantly, most of the significant tax loopholes that enabled taxpayers to escape tax at the time the AMT was written have long since been closed. Today, the AMT is left to punish taxpayers for engaging in such "classic tax-avoidance behavior" as having children or living in a high-tax state. In the first instance, the AMT disallows the personal exemptions that parents are allowed to claim under the regular tax rules to reflect the additional costs they incur in raising children. In the second instance, the AMT disallows the deduction for the payment of state and local income, sales, and property taxes that taxpayers are allowed to claim under the regular tax rules to reduce "double taxation" at the federal and state levels on the same income. This, in essence, is today's AMT.

The AMT is ensnaring an ever-growing number of taxpayers because the amount of income exempt from the AMT (the AMT "exemption amount") is not indexed for inflation. When Congress first enacted a minimum tax in 1969, the exemption amount was $30,000 for all taxpayers. If that amount had been indexed, it would be equal to about $165,000 today. Instead, the exemption amount, after a temporary increase that will expire after 2006, is $45,000 for married taxpayers and $33,750 for most other taxpayers . . . Among the categories of taxpayers hardest hit, 89 percent of married couples with adjusted gross income (AGI) between $75,000 and $100,000 and with two or more children will owe AMT. . . .

Perhaps most disturbingly, it is often very difficult for taxpayers to determine in advance whether they will be hit by the AMT. As a result, many taxpayers are unaware that the AMT applies to them until they receive a notice from the IRS, and some discover they have AMT liabilities that they did not anticipate and cannot pay. To make matters worse, the difficulty of projecting AMT tax liability in advance makes it challenging for taxpayers to compute and make required estimated tax payments, which often results in these taxpayers being subject to penalties.

The following . . . example[] illustrate[s] the impact of the AMT on individual taxpayers:

> A mother of five earned $57,000 in 2005. She is seeking a legal separation from her husband and lived apart from him during the final months of the year and thus claimed "married filing separately" filing status. Because she was entitled to claim the children as her dependents and claim the child tax credit, she had no tax liability under the regular tax rules. She therefore did not have any tax withheld from her paychecks. When she prepared her tax return, however, she discovered that she had a tax liability of $2,380 due to the AMT. Because of the AMT tax liability, she also owed a penalty for failure to pay estimated tax in the amount of $95 . . .

Thus, while the concept of a minimum tax is not unreasonable, the AMT as currently structured has morphed into something that was never intended: it is hitting taxpayers it was never intended to hit because its exemption amount has not been indexed for inflation; it is penalizing taxpayers for such non-tax-driven behavior as having children or choosing to live in a state that happens to impose high taxes; it is taking large numbers of taxpayers by surprise—and subjecting them to penalties to boot; it is imposing onerous compliance burdens; it is altering the distribution of the tax burden that exists under the regular tax system; it is changing the tax incentives built into the regular tax system; and it is neutralizing the effects of changes to tax rates imposed under the regular tax system. . . .

To be viewed as fair, a tax system must be transparent. Yet the complexity of the AMT is such that many if not most taxpayers who owe the AMT do not realize it until they prepare their returns. It adds insult to injury when many of these taxpayers discover that they also owe a penalty for failure to pay sufficient estimated tax because they did not factor in the AMT when they computed their withholding exemptions or estimated tax payments. Taxpayers subjected to this treatment may wonder whether their government has dealt fairly with them. To say the least, "gotcha" taxation is not good for taxpayers or the tax system.

The National Taxpayer Advocate recommends that Congress repeal the provisions of the Internal Revenue Code that pertain to the Alternative Minimum Tax for individuals.

KLAASEN v. COMMISSIONER
T.C. Memo 1998-241

ARMEN, SPECIAL TRIAL JUDGE:

. . . Respondent determined a deficiency in petitioners' Federal income tax for the taxable year 1994 in the amount of $1,085.43. . . . The deficiency in income tax is solely attributable to the alternative minimum tax prescribed by

§55. . . . [T]he only issue for decision is whether petitioners are liable for the alternative minimum tax.

FINDINGS OF FACT

. . . Petitioners are husband and wife. Petitioners are also members of the Reformed Presbyterian Church of North America (the Church). Members of the Church are taught that the production of many offspring is a blessing. Accordingly, petitioners are opposed to birth control and abortion.

Petitioners have a large family. In 1994, the taxable year in issue, petitioners had 10 children. Shortly before trial, their 13th child was born. All of petitioners' children qualify as petitioners' dependents within the meaning of §151(c).

Petitioners timely filed a joint Federal income tax return, Form 1040, for 1994. On their return, petitioners properly claimed a total of 12 exemptions; i.e., two for themselves and 10 for their children. Petitioners reduced their income by the aggregate value of the 12 exemptions, or $29,400.

. . . Petitioners neither completed nor attached Form 6251 (Alternative Minimum Tax-Individuals) to their 1994 income tax return, nor did petitioners report any liability for the alternative minimum tax on line 48 of Form 1040.

In March 1997, respondent issued a notice of deficiency to petitioners for the taxable year 1994. In the notice of deficiency, respondent did not disallow any of the deductions or exemptions claimed by petitioners on their Form 1040 for purposes of the income tax imposed by §1(a). Rather, respondent determined that petitioners are liable for the alternative minimum tax prescribed by §55. In computing the alternative minimum tax, respondent conceded that petitioners have no items of tax preference within the meaning of §57. . . .

OPINION

Our analysis necessarily begins with §55, the section of the Internal Revenue Code that imposes the alternative minimum tax. Initially, we note that the alternative minimum tax is imposed in addition to the regular tax and that the "regular tax" is, as relevant herein, the income tax computed on taxable income by reference to the pertinent tax table. . . .

Section 55(b)(2) defines the term "alternative minimum taxable income." As relevant herein, the term "alternative minimum taxable income" means the taxpayer's taxable income for the taxable year determined with the adjustments provided in §56 and increased by the amount of items of tax preference described in §57. Petitioners had no items of tax preference in 1994. Accordingly, alternative minimum taxable income means petitioners' taxable income determined with the adjustments provided in §56.

. . . As relevant herein . . . §56(b)(1)(E) states that no personal exemptions shall be allowed in computing alternative minimum taxable income.

The effect of [§56(b)(1)(E)] is to increase petitioners' taxable income by . . . $29,400, the amount claimed on petitioners' Form 1040 for personal exemptions.

After taking into account the foregoing . . . adjustments, . . . petitioners are liable for the alternative minimum tax in the amount of . . . $6,196.43 less $5,111, or $1,085.43.

Petitioners do not challenge the mechanics of the foregoing computation. Rather, petitioners contend that they are not liable for the alternative minimum tax for two independent reasons. First, petitioners contend that the elimination of personal exemptions under the alternative minimum tax adversely affects large families and results in an application of the alternative minimum tax that is contrary to congressional intent. In this regard, petitioners argue that legislative history demonstrates that the alternative minimum tax was intended to limit items of tax preference, not personal exemptions.

Second, petitioners argue that the alternative minimum tax violates various constitutional rights, particularly the right to religious freedom.

A. CONGRESSIONAL INTENT

We begin with petitioners' contention that they are not liable for the alternative minimum tax because such tax was not intended to apply to them. In this regard, petitioners emphasize that they did not have a single item of tax preference, and they argue that they are being unfairly saddled with the alternative minimum tax simply because of the size of their family.

The clearest expression of legislative intent is found in the actual language used by Congress in enacting legislation. As the Supreme Court has stated, "There is . . . no more persuasive evidence of the purpose of a statute than the words by which the legislature undertook to give expression to its wishes." Again as the Supreme Court has stated:

> in the absence of a clearly expressed legislative intention to the contrary, the language of the statute itself must ordinarily be regarded as conclusive. Unless exceptional circumstances dictate otherwise, when we find the terms of a statute unambiguous, judicial inquiry is complete.

Burlington N. R.R. Co. v. Oklahoma Tax Commn., 481 U.S. 454 (1987).

Accordingly, where, as here, a statute appears to be clear on its face, unequivocal evidence of a contrary purpose must be demonstrable if we are to construe the statute so as to override the plain meaning of the words used therein.

The statutory scheme governing the imposition and computation of the alternative minimum tax is clear and precise, and leaves, on these facts, no room for interpretation. Thus, there is no justification, in the instant case, to ignore the plain language of the statute, particularly where, as here, we have a complex set of statutory provisions marked by a high degree of specificity.

. . . If Congress had intended to tax only tax preferences, it would have defined "alternative minimum taxable income" differently, for example, solely by reference to items of tax preference. Instead, Congress provided for a tax measured by a broader base, namely, alternative minimum taxable income, in which tax preferences are merely included as potential components.

The foregoing analysis leads to the conclusion that the alternative minimum tax is triggered by a number of factors, including the value of personal exemptions claimed on a taxpayer's return, and that respondent correctly determined such tax on the facts of this case. Accordingly, because we can understand and apply the plain meaning of unambiguous statutory text, we need not defer to legislative history.

B. CONSTITUTIONAL CONSIDERATIONS

Having thus decided that the alternative minimum tax is otherwise applicable on the facts of this case, we turn now to petitioners' contention that such tax unconstitutionally inhibits the free exercise of religion.

Cases have held that the usual presumption of constitutionality is particularly strong in the case of a revenue measure. The constitutionality of the alternative minimum tax has previously been upheld by the courts.

Absent clear evidence to the contrary, we are reluctant to hold that the alternative minimum tax infringes on a taxpayer's personal religious beliefs. "The fact that a law with a secular purpose may have the effect of making the observance of some religious beliefs more expensive does not render the statute unconstitutional under the First Amendment." Moreover, we conclude . . . that "religious beliefs have consistently been held not to furnish a basis for complaint about our tax system, at least where the statutory provision attacked is not specifically based, or cannot be shown to be based, upon a classification grounded on religion."

In the present case, the alternative minimum tax is not based upon "a classification grounded on religion." Rather, the statute demonstrates that such tax is triggered by the value of deductions and exemptions claimed, the disallowance of which is unrelated to a taxpayer's religious beliefs. Consequently, we do not agree that the alternative minimum tax unconstitutionally inhibits the free exercise of petitioners' religion.

C. CONCLUSION

In view of the foregoing, we hold that petitioners are liable for the alternative minimum tax. Accordingly, we sustain respondent's determination of the deficiency in income tax.

Absent some constitutional defect, we are constrained to apply the law as written, and we may not rewrite the law because we may deem its effects susceptible of improvement. Accordingly, petitioners' appeal for relief must, in this instance, be addressed to their elected representatives. . . .

Decision will be entered for respondent as to the deficiency in income tax. . . .

F. THE FUTURE?

After surviving a thorough study of the issues presented herein, students are entitled to congratulations, if not plaudits. At the risk of understatement, the tax laws are complex, and their study can be intense. Rest assured you are not alone; one can take refuge in the words of Learned Hand:

> In my own case the words of such an act as the Income Tax, for example, merely dance before my eyes in a meaningless procession: cross-reference to cross-reference, exception upon exception — couched in abstract terms that offer no handle to seize hold of — leave in my mind only a confused sense of some vitally important, but successfully concealed, purport, which it is my duty to extract, but which is within my power, if at all, only after the most inordinate expenditure of time. I know that these monsters are the result of fabulous industry and ingenuity, plugging up this hole and casting out that net, against all possible evasion; yet at times I cannot help recalling a saying of William James about certain passages of Hegel: that they were no doubt written with a passion of rationality; but that one cannot help wondering whether to the reader they have any significance save that the words are strung together with syntactical correctness.

Learned Hand, *Thomas Walter Swan*, 57 Yale L.J. 167, 169 (1947).

Now that an overview of the taxing formula and its constituent parts has been successfully undertaken, reflection on the tax laws as a whole is appropriate. Why are the tax laws so complex? Which provisions should be changed or removed? How would doing so impact the remainder of the Code? How would taxpayers react in light of such amendments?

Consider the following report issued by the National Taxpayer Advocate in 2011, and see if you agree with the analysis and proposals based on what you have learned. When facing income tax law issues in the future, consider the issues discussed in the report — and, if possible, reflect fondly on your days studying the intricacies of the United States federal income tax laws.

NATIONAL TAXPAYER ADVOCATE
2011 ANNUAL REPORT TO CONGRESS
Most Serious Problems, 3 -12

DEFINITION OF A PROBLEM

The most serious problem facing taxpayers is the complexity of the Internal Revenue Code.

ANALYSIS OF PROBLEM

The largest source of compliance burdens for taxpayers — and the IRS — is the overwhelming complexity of the tax code. The only meaningful way to reduce these burdens is to simplify the tax code enormously. Consider the following:

- According to a [Tax Advocate Service, or] TAS analysis of IRS data, U.S. taxpayers and businesses spend about 7.6 billion hours a year complying with the filing requirements of the Internal Revenue Code. And that figure does not even include the millions of additional hours that taxpayers must spend when they are required to respond to an IRS notice or an audit.

- If tax compliance were an industry, it would be one of the largest in the United States. To consume 7.6 billion hours, the "tax industry" requires the equivalent of 3.8 million full-time workers.
- Compliance costs are huge both in absolute terms and relative to the amount of tax revenue collected. Based on Bureau of Labor Statistics (BLS) data on the hourly cost of an employee, TAS estimates that the costs of complying with the individual and corporate income tax requirements in 2006 amounted to $193 billion — or a staggering 14 percent of aggregate income tax receipts.
- Since the beginning of 2001, there have been more than 3,250 changes to the tax code, an average of more than one a day, including more than 500 changes in 2008 alone.
- The Code has grown so long that it has become challenging even to figure out how long it is. A search of the Code conducted in the course of preparing this report turned up 3.7 million words. A 2001 study published by the Joint Committee on Taxation put the number of words in the Code at that time at 1,395,000. A 2005 report by a tax research organization put the number of words at 2.1 million, and notably, found that the number of words in the Code has more than tripled since 1975.
- Tax regulations, which are issued by the Treasury Department to provide guidance on the meaning of the Internal Revenue Code, now stand about a foot tall. The CCH Standard Federal Tax Reporter, a leading publication for tax professionals that summarizes administrative guidance and judicial decisions issued under each section of the Code, now comprises 25 volumes and takes up nine feet of shelf space. Two companies publish newsletters daily that report on new developments in the field of taxation; the print editions often run 50-100 pages and the electronic databases contain substantially more detailed information.
- The complexity of the Code leads to perverse results. On the one hand, taxpayers who honestly seek to comply with the law often make inadvertent errors, causing them either to overpay their tax or to become subject to IRS enforcement action for mistaken underpayments of tax. On the other hand, sophisticated taxpayers often find loopholes that enable them to reduce or eliminate their tax liabilities.
- Individual taxpayers find the return preparation process so overwhelming that more than 80 percent pay transaction fees to help them file their returns. About 60 percent pay preparers to do the job, and another 22 percent purchase tax software to help them perform the calculations themselves.
- The Code contains no comprehensive Taxpayer Bill of Rights that explicitly and transparently sets out taxpayer rights and obligations. Taxpayers do have rights, but they are scattered throughout the Code and the Internal Revenue Manual and are neither easily accessible nor written in plain language that most taxpayers can understand. . . .

RECOMMENDATION

The National Taxpayer Advocate recommends that Congress substantially simplify the Internal Revenue Code.

America's taxpayers deserve a simpler and less burdensome tax system that enables them to comply with their tax obligations expeditiously — not one that requires them to spend 7.6 billion hours filing their returns every year, thereby consuming the equivalent of 3.8 million full-time workers. Taxpayers deserve a tax system that enables them to prepare their returns cheaply — not one that requires them to pay practitioners for help, as nearly 61 percent of individual taxpayers and 74 percent of unincorporated business taxpayers do today. Taxpayers deserve more clarity about their rights and obligations under the tax code in the form of a Taxpayer Bill of Rights. Taxpayers deserve a tax system that enables them to make wise choices about education and retirement savings — without having to wade through the details of at least 27 tax-favored alternatives. Taxpayers deserve a tax system that enables them to compute their tax liabilities fairly and transparently — not one that effectively requires them to compute their tax liability under two sets of rules (the regular rules and the AMT rules) and often to pay more tax under the AMT regime simply because they engaged in the "tax-avoidance behavior" of having children or living in a high-tax state.

Taxpayers deserve better than a tax system so complex that honest taxpayers often overpay while sophisticated taxpayers often find loopholes, and so complex that 37 million taxpayers could fail to claim a tax credit because they did not know it was available. Taxpayers deserve better than a tax system that gives financially distressed taxpayers a tax break when they default on their mortgage or other consumer debts and the debts are cancelled — but then makes claiming the tax break so burdensome that many and probably most eligible taxpayers do not claim it. Low income taxpayers deserve a simpler set of rules by which determine EITC eligibility.

Taxpayers deserve certainty about which provisions will remain in the tax code so they can plan accordingly — without having to regularly grapple with uncertainty because more than 100 provisions sunset regularly and may or may not be renewed or modified. Taxpayers deserve to understand exactly how their tax liabilities are computed — not provisions like phase-outs, which make the computations seem impenetrable and subject lower income taxpayers to higher marginal tax rates than upper income taxpayers. Taxpayers deserve simplicity and proportionality in the penalty rules; it is not reasonable that a taxpayer who claims minimal or even no tax savings may face a mandatory, non-waivable $300,000 penalty per year for failing to file a disclosure form that he may not even know he is required to file. . . .

TABLE OF CASES

Principal cases are indicated by italics.

TABLE OF REVENUE RULINGS AND PROCEDURES

INDEX